FUNDAMENTALS OF
Third Edition DATABASE SYSTEMS

FUNDAMENTALS OF
Third Edition
DATABASE SYSTEMS

Ramez Elmasri
Department of Computer Science Engineering
University of Texas at Arlington

Shamkant B. Navathe
College of Computing
Georgia Institute of Technology

Pearson
Education
Asia

ISBN 81-7808-137-7

First Indian Reprint, 2000
Second Indian Reprint, 2000
Third Indian Reprint, 2000
Fourth Indian Reprint, 2001
Fifth Indian Reprint, 2001
Sixth Indian Reprint, 2002
Seventh Indian Reprint, 2002

*This edition is manufactured in India and is authorized for sale only in India, Bangladesh, Pakistan,
Nepal, Sri Lanka and the Maldives.*

Published by Pearson Education (Singapore) Pte. Ltd., Indian Branch, 482 F.I.E. Patparganj,
Delhi 110 092, India

Printed in India by Replika Press Pvt. Ltd.

To my wife, Amalia
and to my family.
R. E.

Dedicated to my three greatest teachers,
Father Shri. B. S. Navathe
and grandfathers
Shri. S. N. Navathe and Shri. G. R. Sardesai
and
to my wife Aruna for her infinite patience
S. B. N.

PREFACE

This book introduces the fundamental concepts necessary for designing, using, and implementing database systems and applications. Our presentation stresses the fundamentals of database modeling and design, the languages and facilities provided by database management systems, and system implementation techniques. The book is meant to be used as a textbook for a one- or two-semester course in database systems at the junior, senior, or graduate level, and as a reference book. We assume that readers are familiar with elementary programming and data-structuring concepts and that they have had some exposure to basic computer organization.

We start in Part 1 with an introduction and a presentation of the basic concepts from both ends of the database spectrum—conceptual modeling principles and physical file storage techniques. We conclude the book in Part 6 with an introduction to influential new database models, such as active, temporal, and deductive models, along with an overview of emerging technologies and applications, such as data mining, data warehousing, and Web databases. Along the way—in Parts 2 through 5—we provide an in-depth treatment of the most important aspects of database fundamentals.

The following key features are included in the third edition:
- The entire book has a self-contained, flexible organization that can be tailored to individual needs.
- Complete and updated coverage is provided on the relational model—including new material on Oracle and Microsoft Access as examples of relational systems—in Part 2.

- A comprehensive new introduction is provided on object databases and object-relational systems in Part 3, including the ODMG object model and the OQL query language, as well as an overview of object-relational features of SQL3, INFORMIX, and ORACLE 8.
- Updated coverage of EER conceptual modeling has been moved to Chapter 4 to follow the basic ER modeling in Chapter 3, and includes a new section on notation for UML class diagrams.
- Two examples running throughout the book—called COMPANY and UNIVERSITY—allow the reader to compare different approaches that use the same application.
- Coverage has been updated on database design, including conceptual design, normalization techniques, physical design, and database tuning.

The chapters on DBMS system implementation concepts, including catalog, query processing, concurrency control, recovery, and security, now include sections on how these concepts are implemented in real systems.

- New sections with examples on client-server architecture, active databases, temporal databases, and spatial databases have been added.
- There is updated coverage of recent advances in decision support applications of databases, including overviews of data warehousing/OLAP, and data mining.
- State-of-the-art coverage is provided on new database technologies, including Web, mobile, and multimedia databases.
- There is a focus on important new application areas of databases at the turn of the millennium: geographic databases, genome databases, and digital libraries.

CONTENTS OF THIS EDITION

Part 1 describes the basic concepts necessary for a good understanding of database design and implementation, as well as the conceptual modeling techniques used in database systems. Chapters 1 and 2 introduce databases, their typical users, and DBMS concepts, terminology, and architecture. In Chapter 3, the concepts of the Entity-Relationship (ER) model and ER diagrams are presented and used to illustrate conceptual database design. Chapter 4 focuses on data abstraction and semantic data modeling concepts, and extends the ER model to incorporate these ideas, leading to the enhanced-ER (EER) data model and EER diagrams. The concepts presented include subclasses, specialization, generalization, and union types (categories). The notation for the class diagrams of UML are also introduced. These are similar to EER diagrams and are used increasingly in conceptual object modeling. Part 1 concludes with a description of the physical file structures and access methods used in database systems. Chapter 5 describes the primary methods of organizing files of records on disk, including static and dynamic hashing. Chapter 6 describes indexing techniques for files, including B-tree and B+-tree data structures and grid files.

Part 2 describes the relational data model and relational DBMSs. Chapter 7 describes the basic relational model, its integrity constraints and update operations, and the operations of the relational algebra. Chapter 8 gives a detailed overview of the SQL language, covering the SQL2 standard, which is implemented in most relational systems. Chapter 9 begins with two sections that describe relational schema design, starting from a conceptual database design in an ER or EER model, and concludes with three sections introducing the formal relational calculus languages and an overview of the QBE language. Chapter 10 presents overviews of the Oracle and Microsoft Access database systems as examples of popular commercial relational database management systems.

Part 3 gives a comprehensive introduction to object databases and object-relational systems. Chapter 11 introduces object-oriented concepts and how they apply to object databases. Chapter 12 gives a detailed overview of the ODMG object model and its associated ODL and OQL languages, and gives examples of two commercial object DBMSs. Chapter 13 describes how relational databases are being extended to include object-oriented concepts and presents the features of two object-relational systems—Informix Universal Server and ORACLE 8, as well as giving an overview of some of the features of the proposed SQL3 standard, and the nested relational data model.

Part 4 covers several topics related to database design. Chapters 14 and 15 cover the formalisms, theory, and algorithms developed for relational database design by normalization. This material includes functional and other types of dependencies and normal forms for relations. Step by step intuitive normalization is presented in Chapter 14, and relational design algorithms are given in Chapter 15, which also defines other types of dependencies, such as multivalued and join dependencies. Chapter 16 presents an overview of the different phases of the database design process for medium-sized and large applications, and it also discusses physical database design issues and includes a discussion on database tuning.

Part 5 discusses the techniques used in implementing database management systems. Chapter 17 introduces DBMS system architectures, including centralized and client-server architectures, then describes the system catalog, which is a vital part of any DBMS. Chapter 18 presents the techniques used for processing and optimizing queries specified in a high-level database language—such as SQL—and discusses various algorithms for implementing relational database operations. A section on query optimization in ORACLE has been added. Chapters 19 through 21 discuss transaction processing, concurrency control, and recovery techniques—this material has been revised to include discussions of how these concepts are realized in SQL. Chapter 22 discusses database security and authorization techniques.

Part 6 covers a number of advanced topics. Chapter 23 gives detailed introductions to the concepts of active and temporal databases—which are increasingly being incorporated into database applications—and also gives an overview of spatial and multimedia database concepts. Chapter 24 discusses distributed databases, issues for design, query and transaction processing with data distribution, and the different types of client-server architectures. Chapter 25 introduces the concepts of deductive database systems and surveys a few implementations. Chapter 26 discusses the new technologies of data warehousing and data mining for decision support applications. Chapter 27 surveys the new trends in database technology including Web, mobile and multimedia databases and overviews important emerging applications of databases: geographic information systems (GIS), human genome databases, and digital libraries.

Appendix A gives a number of alternative diagrammatic notations for displaying a conceptual ER or EER schema. These may be substituted for the notation we use, if the instructor so wishes. Appendix B gives some important physical parameters of disks. Appendixes C and D cover legacy database systems, based on the network and hierarchical database models. These have been used for over 30 years as a basis for many existing commercial database applications and transaction-processing systems and will take decades to replace completely. We consider it important to expose students of database management to these long-standing approaches. Full chapters from the second edition can be found at the Website for this edition.

GUIDELINES FOR USING THIS BOOK

There are many different ways to teach a database course. The chapters in Parts 1 through 3 can be used in an introductory course on database systems in the order they are given or in the preferred order of each individual instructor. Selected chapters and sections may be left out, and the instructor can add other chapters from the rest of the book, depending on the emphasis of the course. At the end of each chapter's opening section, we list sections that are candidates for being left out whenever a less detailed discussion of the topic in a particular chapter is desired. We suggest covering up to Chapter 14 in an introductory database course and including selected parts of Chapters 11 through 13, depending on the background of the students and the desired coverage of the object model. For an emphasis on system implementation techniques, selected chapters from Part 5 can be included. For an emphasis on database design, further chapters from Part 4 can be used.

Chapters 3 and 4, which cover conceptual modeling using the ER and EER models, are important for a good conceptual understanding of databases. However, they may be partially covered, covered later in a course, or even left out if the emphasis is on DBMS implementation. Chapters 5 and 6 on file organizations and indexing may also be covered early on, later, or even left out if the emphasis is on database models and languages. For students who have already taken a course on file organization, parts of these chapters could be assigned as reading material or some exercises may be assigned to review the concepts.

Chapters 10 and 13 include material specific to commercial relational database management systems (RDBMSs)—ORACLE, Microsoft Access, and Informix. Because of the constant revision of these products, no exercises have been assigned in these chapters. Depending on local availability of RDBMSs, material from these chapters may be used in projects. A total life-cycle database design and implementation project covers conceptual design (Chapters 3 and 4), data model mapping (Chapter 9), normalization (Chapter 14), and implementation in SQL (Chapter 8). Additional documentation on the specific RDBMS would be required.

The book has been written so that it is possible to cover topics in a variety of orders. The chart included here shows the major dependencies between chapters. As the diagram illustrates, it is possible to start with several different topics following the first two introductory chapters. Although the chart may seem complex, it is important to note that if the chapters are covered in order, the dependencies are not lost. The chart can be consulted by instructors wishing to use an alternative order of presentation.

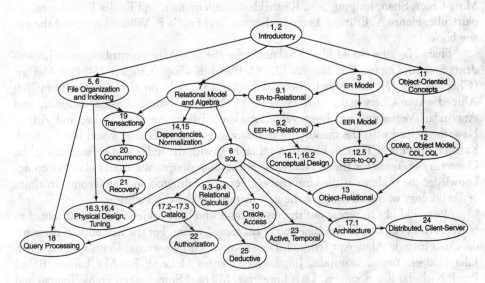

For a single-semester course based on this book, some chapters can be assigned as reading material. Chapters 5, 6, 16, 17, 26, and 27 can be considered for such an assignment. The book can also be used for a two-semester sequence. The first course, "Introduction to Database Design/Systems," at the sophomore, junior, or senior level, could cover most of Chapters 1 to 15. The second course, "Database Design and Implementation Techniques," at the senior or first-year graduate level, can cover Parts 4 through 6. Chapters from Part 6 can be used selectively in either semester, and material describing the DBMS available to the students at the local institution can be covered in addition to the material in the book. Part 6 can also serve as introductory material for advanced database courses, in conjunction with additional assigned readings.

Acknowledgments

It is a great pleasure for us to acknowledge the assistance and contributions of a large number of individuals to this effort. First, we would like to thank our editors, Maite Suarez-Rivas, Katherine Harutunian, Patricia Unubun, and Bob Woodbury. In particular we would like to acknowledge the efforts and help of Katherine Harutunian, our primary contact for the third edition. We would like to acknowledge also those persons who have contributed to the third edition and suggested various improvements to the second edition. Suzanne Dietrich wrote parts of Chapter 10 and 12, and Ed Omiecinski contributed to Chapters 17–21. We appreciated the contributions of the following reviewers: François Bançilhon, Jose Blakeley, Rick Cattell, Suzanne Dietrich, David W. Embley, Henry A. Etlinger, Leonidas Fegaras, Farshad Fotouhi, Michael Franklin, Goetz Graefe, Richard Hull, Sushil Jajodia, Ramesh K. Karne, Vijay Kumar, Tarcisio Lima, Ramon A. Mata-Toledo, Dennis McLeod, Rokia Missaoui, Ed Omiecinski, Joan Peckham, Betty Salzberg, Ming-Chien Shan, Junping Sun, Rajshekhar Sunderraman, and Emilia E. Villarreal. In particular, Henry A. Etlinger, Leonidas Fegaras, and Emilla E. Villareal reviewed the entire book.

Sham Navathe would like to acknowledge the substantial contributions of his students Sreejith Gopinath (Chapters 10, 24), Harish Kotbagi (Chapter 25), Jack McCaw (Chapters 26, 27), and Magdi Morsi (Chapter 13). Help on this revision from Rafi Ahmed, Ann Chervenak, Dan Forsyth, M. Narayanaswamy, Carlos Ordonez, and Aravindan Veerasamy has been valuable. Gwen Baker, Amol Navathe, and Aditya Nawathe helped with the manuscript in many ways. Ramez Emasri would like to thank Katrina, Riyad, and Thomas Elmasri for their help with the index and his students at the University of Texas for their comments on the manuscript. We would also like to acknowledge the students at the University of Texas at Arlington and the Georgia Institute of Technology who used drafts of the new material in the third edition.

We would like to repeat our thanks to those who have reviewed and contributed to both previous editions of *Fundamentals of Database Systems*. For the first edition these individuals include Alan Apt (editor), Don Batory, Scott Downing, Dennis Heimbigner, Julia Hodges, Yannis Ioannidis, Jim Larson, Dennis McLeod, Per-Ake Larson, Rahul Patel, Nicholas Roussopoulos, David Stemple, Michael Stonebraker, Frank Tompa, and Kyu-Young Whang; for the second edition they include Dan Joraanstad (editor), Rafi Ahmed, Antonio Albano, David Beech, Jose Blakeley, Panos Chrysanthis, Suzanne Dietrich, Vic Ghorpadey, Goetz Graefe, Eric Hanson, Junguk L. Kim, Roger King, Vram Kouramajian, Vijay Kumar, John Lowther, Sanjay Manchanda, Toshimi Minoura, Inderpal Mumick, Ed Omiecinski, Girish Pathak, Raghu Ramakrishnan, Ed Robertson, Eugene Sheng, David Stotts, Marianne Winslett, and Stan Zdonick.

Last but not least, we gratefully acknowledge the support, encouragement, and patience of our families.

R.E.
S.B.N.

ABOUT THE AUTHORS

Ramez A. Elmasri is a professor in the department of Computer Science and Engineering at the University of Texas at Arlington. Professor Elmasri previously worked for Honeywell and the University of Houston. He has been an associate editor of the *Journal of Parallel and Distributed Databases* and a member of the steering committee for the International Conference on Conceptual Modeling. He was program chair of the 1993 International Conference on Entity Relationship Approach. He has conducted research sponsored by grants from NSF, NASA, ARRI, Texas Instruments, Honeywell, Digital Equipment Corporation, and the State of Texas in many areas of database systems and in the area of integration of systems and software over the past twenty years. Professor Elmasri has received the Robert Q. Lee teaching award of the College of Engineering of the University of Texas at Arlington. He holds a Ph.D. from Stanford University and has over 70 refereed publications in journals and conference proceedings.

Shamkant Navathe is a professor and the head of the database research group in the College of Computing at the Georgia Institute of Technology. Professor Navathe has previously worked with IBM and Siemens in their research divisions and has been a consultant to various companies including Digital Equipment Corporation, Hewlett-Packard, and Equifax. He has been an associate editor of ACM *Computing Surveys* and IEEE *Transactions on Knowledge and Data Engineering*, and is currently on the editorial boards of *Information Systems* (Pergamon Press) and *Distributed and Parallel Databases* (Kluwer Academic Publishers). He is the co-author of *Conceptual Design: An Entity Relationship Approach* (Addison-Wesley, 1992) with Carlo Batini and Stefano Ceri. Professor Navathe holds a Ph.D. from the University of Michigan and has over 100 refereed publications in journals and conference proceedings.

CONTENTS

PART 1: BASIC CONCEPTS

PART 2: RELATIONAL MODEL, LANGUAGES, AND SYSTEMS   193

PART 3: OBJECT-ORIENTED AND EXTENDED RELATIONAL DATABASE TECHNOLOGY   357

PART 1

Basic Concepts

CHAPTER 1 | Databases and Database Users

Databases and database systems have become an essential component of everyday life in modern society. In the course of a day, most of us encounter several activities that involve some interaction with a database. For example, if we go to the bank to deposit or withdraw funds; if we make a hotel or airline reservation; if we access a computerized library catalog to search for a bibliographic item; or if we order a magazine subscription from a publisher, chances are that our activities will involve someone accessing a database. Even purchasing items from a supermarket nowadays in many cases involves an automatic update of the database that keeps the inventory of supermarket items.

The above interactions are examples of what we may call **traditional database applications,** where most of the information that is stored and accessed is either textual or numeric. In the past few years, advances in technology have been leading to exciting new applications of database systems. **Multimedia databases** can now store pictures, video clips, and sound messages. **Geographic information systems (GIS)** can store and analyze maps, weather data, and satellite images. **Data warehouses** and **on-line analytical processing (OLAP)** systems are used in many companies to extract and analyze useful information from very large databases for decision making. **Real-time** and **active database technology** is used in controlling industrial and manufacturing processes. And database search techniques are being applied to the World Wide Web to improve the search for information that is needed by users browsing through the Internet.

To understand the fundamentals of database technology, however, we must start from the basics of traditional database applications. So, in Section 1.1 of this chapter we define a database is, and then we give definitions of other basic terms. In Section 1.2, we provide a simple UNIVERSITY database example to illustrate our discussion. Section 1.3 describes some of the main characteristics of database systems, and Sections 1.4 and 1.5 categorize the types of personnel whose jobs involve using and interacting with database systems. Sections 1.6, 1.7, and 1.8 offer a more thorough discussion of the various capabilities provided by database systems and of the implications of using the database approach. Section 1.9 summarizes the chapter.

The reader who desires only a quick introduction to database systems can study Sections 1.1 through 1.5, then skip or browse through Sections 1.6 through 1.8 and go on to Chapter 2.

1.1 Introduction

Databases and database technology are having a major impact on the growing use of computers. It is fair to say that databases play a critical role in almost all areas where computers are used, including business, engineering, medicine, law, education, and library science, to name a few. The word *database* is in such common use that we must begin by defining a database. Our initial definition is quite general.

A **database** is a collection of related data.[1] By **data,** we mean known facts that can be recorded and that have implicit meaning. For example, consider the names, telephone numbers, and addresses of the people you know. You may have recorded this data in an indexed address book, or you may have stored it on a diskette, using a personal computer and software such as DBASE IV or V, Microsoft ACCESS, or EXCEL. This is a collection of related data with an implicit meaning and hence is a database.

The preceding definition of *database* is quite general; for example, we may consider the collection of words that make up this page of text to be related data and hence to constitute a database. However, the common use of the term *database* is usually more restricted. A database has the following implicit properties:

- A database represents some aspect of the real world, sometimes called the **miniworld** or the **Universe of Discourse (UoD).** Changes to the miniworld are reflected in the database.

- A database is a logically coherent collection of data with some inherent meaning. A random assortment of data cannot correctly be referred to as a database.

- A database is designed, built, and populated with data for a specific purpose. It has an intended group of users and some preconceived applications in which these users are interested.

In other words, a database has some source from which data are derived, some degree of interaction with events in the real world, and an audience that is actively interested in the contents of the database.

---

1. We will use the word *data* in both singular and plural, as is common in database literature; context will determine whether it is singular or plural. In standard English, *data* is used only for plural; *datum* is used for singular.

A database can be of any size and of varying complexity. For example, the list of names and addresses referred to earlier may consist of only a few hundred records, each with a simple structure. On the other hand, the card catalog of a large library may contain half a million cards stored under different categories—by primary author's last name, by subject, by book title—with each category organized in alphabetic order. A database of even greater size and complexity is maintained by the Internal Revenue Service to keep track of the tax forms filed by U.S. taxpayers. If we assume that there are 100 million taxpayers and if each taxpayer files an average of five forms with approximately 200 characters of information per form, we would get a database of $100*(10^6)*200*5$ characters (bytes) of information. If the IRS keeps the past three returns for each taxpayer in addition to the current return, we would get a database of $4*(10^{11})$ bytes (400 gigabytes). This huge amount of information must be organized and managed so that users can search for, retrieve, and update the data as needed.

A database may be generated and maintained manually or it may be computerized. The library card catalog is an example of a database that may be created and maintained manually. A computerized database may be created and maintained either by a group of application programs written specifically for that task or by a database management system.

A **database management system (DBMS)** is a collection of programs that enables users to create and maintain a database. The DBMS is hence a *general-purpose software system* that facilitates the processes of *defining, constructing,* and *manipulating* databases for various applications. **Defining** a database involves specifying the data types, structures, and constraints for the data to be stored in the database. **Constructing** the database is the process of storing the data itself on some storage medium that is controlled by the DBMS. **Manipulating** a database includes such functions as querying the database to retrieve specific data, updating the database to reflect changes in the miniworld, and generating reports from the data.

It is not necessary to use general-purpose DBMS software to implement a computerized database. We could write our own set of programs to create and maintain the database, in effect creating our own *special-purpose* DBMS software. In either case—whether we use a general-purpose DBMS or not—we usually have to employ a considerable amount of software to manipulate the database. We will call the database and DBMS software together a **database system.** Figure 1.1 illustrates these ideas.

1.2 An Example

Let us consider an example that most readers may be familiar with: a UNIVERSITY database for maintaining information concerning students, courses, and grades in a university environment. Figure 1.2 shows the database structure and a few sample data for such a database. The database is organized as five files, each of which stores data records of the same type.[2] The STUDENT file stores data on each student; the COURSE file stores data on each course; the SECTION file stores data on each section of a course; the GRADE_REPORT file stores

---

2. At a conceptual level, a *file* is a *collection* of records that may or may not be ordered.

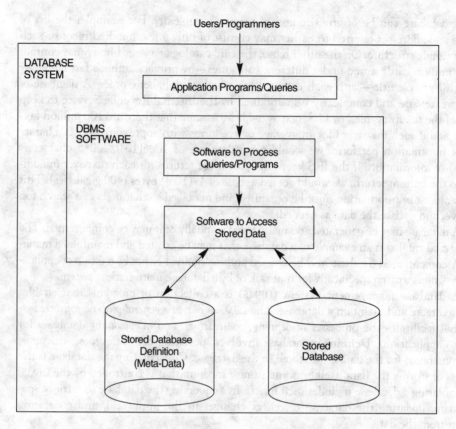

Figure 1.1   A simplified database system environment, illustrating the concepts and terminology discussed in Section 1.1.

the grades that students receive in the various sections they have completed; and the PREREQUISITE file stores the prerequisites of each course.

To *define* this database, we must specify the structure of the records of each file by specifying the different types of **data elements** to be stored in each record. In Figure 1.2, each STUDENT record includes data to represent the student's Name, StudentNumber, Class (freshman or 1, sophomore or 2, . . .), and Major (MATH, computer science or CS, . . .); each COURSE record includes data to represent the CourseName, CourseNumber, CreditHours, and Department (the department that offers the course); and so on. We must also specify a **data type** for each data element within a record. For example, we can specify that Name of STUDENT is a string of alphabetic characters, StudentNumber of STUDENT is an integer, and Grade of GRADE_REPORT is a single character from the set {A, B, C, D, F, I}. We may also use a coding scheme to represent a data item. For example, in Figure 1.2 we represent the Class of a STUDENT as 1 for freshman, 2 for sophomore, 3 for junior, 4 for senior, and 5 for graduate student.

STUDENT	Name	StudentNumber	Class	Major
	Smith	17	1	CS
	Brown	8	2	CS

COURSE	CourseName	CourseNumber	CreditHours	Department
	Intro to Computer Science	CS1310	4	CS
	Data Structures	CS3320	4	CS
	Discrete Mathematics	MATH2410	3	MATH
	Database	CS3380	3	CS

SECTION	SectionIdentifier	CourseNumber	Semester	Year	Instructor
	85	MATH2410	Fall	98	King
	92	CS1310	Fall	98	Anderson
	102	CS3320	Spring	99	Knuth
	112	MATH2410	Fall	99	Chang
	119	CS1310	Fall	99	Anderson
	135	CS3380	Fall	99	Stone

GRADE_REPORT	StudentNumber	SectionIdentifier	Grade
	17	112	B
	17	119	C
	8	85	A
	8	92	A
	8	102	B
	8	135	A

PREREQUISITE	CourseNumber	PrerequisiteNumber
	CS3380	CS3320
	CS3380	MATH2410
	CS3320	CS1310

Figure 1.2 An example of a database that stores student records and their grades.

To *construct* the UNIVERSITY database, we store data to represent each student, course, section, grade report, and prerequisite as a record in the appropriate file. Notice that records in the various files may be related. For example, the record for "Smith" in the STUDENT file is related to two records in the GRADE_REPORT file that specify Smith's grades in two sections. Similarly, each record in the PREREQUISITE file relates two course records: one representing the course and the other representing the prerequisite. Most medium-size and large databases include many types of records and have *many relationships* among the records.

Database *manipulation* involves querying and updating. Examples of queries are "retrieve the transcript—a list of all courses and grades—of Smith"; "list the names of students who took the section of the Database course offered in fall 1999 and their grades in that section"; and "what are the prerequisites of the Database course?" Examples of updates are "change the class of Smith to Sophomore"; "create a new section for the Database course for this semester"; and "enter a grade of A for Smith in the Database section of last semester." These informal queries and updates must be specified precisely in the database system language before they can be processed.

1.3 Characteristics of the Database Approach

A number of characteristics distinguish the database approach from the traditional approach of programming with files. In traditional **file processing,** each user defines and implements the files needed for a specific application as part of programming the application. For example, one user, the *grade reporting office,* may keep a file on students and their grades. Programs to print a student's transcript and to enter new grades into the file are implemented. A second user, the accounting office, may keep track of students' fees and their payments. Although both users are interested in data about students, each user maintains separate files—and programs to manipulate these files—because each requires some data not available from the other user's files. This redundancy in defining and storing data results in wasted storage space and in redundant efforts to maintain common data up-to-date.

In the database approach, a single repository of data is maintained that is defined once and then is accessed by various users. The main characteristics of the database approach versus the file-processing approach are the following.

1.3.1 Self-Describing Nature of a Database System

A fundamental characteristic of the database approach is that the database system contains not only the database itself but also a complete definition or description of the database structure and constraints. This definition is stored in the system **catalog,** which contains information such as the structure of each file, the type and storage format of each data item, and various constraints on the data. The information stored in the catalog is called **meta-data,** and it describes the structure of the primary database (Figure 1.1).

The catalog is used by the DBMS software and also by database users who need information about the database structure. A general purpose DBMS software package is not written for a specific database application, and hence it must refer to the catalog to know the structure of the files in a specific database, such as the type and format of data it will access. The DBMS software must work equally well with *any number of database applications*—for example, a university database, a banking database, or a company database—as long as the database definition is stored in the catalog.

In traditional file processing, data definition is typically part of the application programs themselves. Hence, these programs are constrained to work with only *one specific database*, whose structure is declared in the application programs. For example, a PASCAL program may have record structures declared in it; a C++ program may have "struct" or "class" declarations; and a COBOL program has Data Division statements to define its files. Whereas file-processing software can access only specific databases, DBMS software can access diverse databases by extracting the database definitions from the catalog and then using these definitions.

In the example shown in Figure 1.2, the DBMS stores in the catalog the definitions of all the files shown. Whenever a request is made to access, say, the Name of a STUDENT record, the DBMS software refers to the catalog to determine the structure of the STUDENT file and the position and size of the Name data item within a STUDENT record. By contrast, in a typical file-processing application, the file structure and, in the extreme case, the exact location of Name within a STUDENT record are already coded within each program that accesses this data item.

1.3.2 Insulation between Programs and Data, and Data Abstraction

In traditional file processing, the structure of data files is embedded in the access programs, so any changes to the structure of a file may require *changing all programs* that access this file. By contrast, DBMS access programs do not require such changes in most cases. The structure of data files is stored in the DBMS catalog separately from the access programs. We call this property **program-data independence.** For example, a file access program may be written in such a way that it can access only STUDENT records of the structure shown in Figure 1.3. If we want to add another piece of data to each STUDENT record, say the Birthdate, such a program will no longer work and must be changed. By contrast, in a DBMS environment, we just need to change the description of STUDENT records in the catalog to reflect the inclusion of the new data item Birthdate; no programs are changed. The next time a DBMS program refers to the catalog, the new structure of STUDENT records will be accessed and used.

In object-oriented and object-relational databases (see Part III), users can define operations on data as part of the database definitions. An **operation** (also called a *function*) is specified in two parts. The *interface* (or *signature*) of an operation includes the operation name and the data types of its arguments (or parameters). The *implementation*

Data Item Name	Starting Position in Record	Length in Characters (bytes)
Name	1	30
StudentNumber	31	4
Class	35	4
Major	39	4

Figure 1.3 Internal storage format for a STUDENT record.

(or *method*) of the operation is specified separately and can be changed without affecting the interface. User application programs can operate on the data by invoking these operations through their names and arguments, regardless of how the operations are implemented. This may be termed **program-operation independence.**

The characteristic that allows program-data independence and program-operation independence is called **data abstraction.** A DBMS provides users with a **conceptual representation** of data that does not include many of the details of how the data is stored or how the operations are implemented. Informally, a **data model** is a type of data abstraction that is used to provide this conceptual representation. The data model uses logical concepts, such as objects, their properties, and their interrelationships, that may be easier for most users to understand than computer storage concepts. Hence, the data model *hides* storage and implementation details that are not of interest to most database users.

For example, consider again Figure 1.2. The internal implementation of a file may be defined by its record length—the number of characters (bytes) in each record—and each data item may be specified by its starting byte within a record and its length in bytes. The STUDENT record would thus be represented as shown in Figure 1.3. But a typical database user is not concerned with the location of each data item within a record or its length; rather the concern is that, when a reference is made to Name of STUDENT, the correct value is returned. A conceptual representation of the STUDENT records is shown in Figure 1.2. Many other details of file-storage organization—such as the access paths specified on a file—can be hidden from database users by the DBMS; we will discuss storage details in Chapters 5 and 6.

In the database approach, the detailed structure and organization of each file are stored in the catalog. Database users refer to the conceptual representation of the files, and the DBMS extracts the details of file storage from the catalog when these are needed by the DBMS software. Many data models can be used to provide this data abstraction to database users. A major part of this book is devoted to presenting various data models and the concepts they use to abstract the representation of data.

With the recent trend toward object-oriented and object-relational databases, abstraction is carried one level further to include not only the data structure but also the operations on the data. These operations provide an abstraction of miniworld activities commonly understood by the users. For example, an operation CALCULATE_GPA can be applied to a student object to calculate the grade point average. Such operations can be invoked by the user queries or programs without the user knowing the details of how they are internally implemented. In that sense, an abstraction of the miniworld activity is made available to the user as an **abstract operation.**

1.3.3 Support of Multiple Views of the Data

A database typically has many users, each of whom may require a different perspective or **view** of the database. A view may be a subset of the database or it may contain **virtual data** that is derived from the database files but is not explicitly stored. Some users may not need to be aware of whether the data they refer to is stored or derived. A multiuser DBMS whose users have a variety of applications must provide facilities for defining multiple

(a)

TRANSCRIPT	StudentName	Student Transcript				
		CourseNumber	Grade	Semester	Year	SectionId
	Smith	CS1310	C	Fall	99	119
		MATH2410	B	Fall	99	112
	Brown	MATH2410	A	Fall	98	85
		CS1310	A	Fall	98	92
		CS3320	B	Spring	99	102
		CS3380	A	Fall	99	135

(b)

PREREQUISITES	CourseName	CourseNumber	Prerequisites
	Database	CS3380	CS3320
			MATH2410
	Data Structures	CS3320	CS1310

Figure 1.4 Two views derived from the example database shown in Figure 1.2. (a) The student transcript view. (b) The course prerequisite view.

views. For example, one user of the database of Figure 1.2 may be interested only in the transcript of each student; the view for this user is shown in Figure 1.4(a). A second user, who is interested only in checking that students have taken all the prerequisites of each course they register for, may require the view shown in Figure 1.4(b).

1.3.4 Sharing of Data and Multiuser Transaction Processing

A multiuser DBMS, as its name implies, must allow multiple users to access the database at the same time. This is essential if data for multiple applications is to be integrated and maintained in a single database. The DBMS must include **concurrency control** software to ensure that several users trying to update the same data do so in a controlled manner so that the result of the updates is correct. For example, when several reservation clerks try to assign a seat on an airline flight, the DBMS should ensure that each seat can be accessed by only one clerk at a time for assignment to a passenger. These types of applications are generally called **on-line transaction processing (OLTP)** applications. A fundamental role of multiuser DBMS software is to ensure that concurrent transactions operate correctly.

The preceding characteristics are most important in distinguishing a DBMS from traditional file-processing software. In Section 1.6 we discuss additional functions that characterize a DBMS. First, however, we categorize the different types of persons who work in a database environment.

1.4   Actors on the Scene

For a small personal database, such as the list of addresses discussed in Section 1.1, one person typically defines, constructs, and manipulates the database. However, many persons are involved in the design, use, and maintenance of a large database with a few hundred users. In this section we identify the people whose jobs involve the day-to-day use of a large database; we call them the "actors on the scene." In Section 1.5 we consider people who may be called "workers behind the scene"—those who work to maintain the database system environment, but who are not actively interested in the database itself.

1.4.1   Database Administrators

In any organization where many persons use the same resources, there is a need for a chief administrator to oversee and manage these resources. In a database environment, the primary resource is the database itself and the secondary resource is the DBMS and related software. Administering these resources is the responsibility of the **database administrator (DBA).** The DBA is responsible for authorizing access to the database, for coordinating and monitoring its use, and for acquiring software and hardware resources as needed. The DBA is accountable for problems such as breach of security or poor system response time. In large organizations, the DBA is assisted by a staff that helps carry out these functions.

1.4.2   Database Designers

Database designers are responsible for identifying the data to be stored in the database and for choosing appropriate structures to represent and store this data. These tasks are mostly undertaken before the database is actually implemented and populated with data. It is the responsibility of database designers to communicate with all prospective database users, in order to understand their requirements, and to come up with a design that meets these requirements. In many cases, the designers are on the staff of the DBA and may be assigned other staff responsibilities after the database design is completed. Database designers typically interact with each potential group of users and develop a **view** of the database that meets the data and processing requirements of this group. These views are then analyzed and *integrated* with the views of other user groups. The final database design must be capable of supporting the requirements of all user groups.

1.4.3   End Users

End users are the people whose jobs require access to the database for querying, updating, and generating reports; the database primarily exists for their use. There are several categories of end users:

- **Casual end users** occasionally access the database, but they may need different information each time. They use a sophisticated database query language to specify their requests and are typically middle- or high-level managers or other occasional browsers.

- **Naive** or **parametric end users** make up a sizable portion of database end users. Their main job function revolves around constantly querying and updating the database, using standard types of queries and updates—called **canned transactions**—that have been carefully programmed and tested. The tasks that such users perform are varied:

  Bank tellers check account balances and post withdrawals and deposits.

  Reservation clerks for airlines, hotels, and car rental companies check availability for a given request and make reservations.

  Clerks at receiving stations for courier mail enter package identifications via bar codes and descriptive information through buttons to update a central database of received and in-transit packages.

- **Sophisticated end users** include engineers, scientists, business analysts, and others who thoroughly familiarize themselves with the facilities of the DBMS so as to implement their applications to meet their complex requirements.

- **Stand-alone users** maintain personal databases by using ready-made program packages that provide easy-to-use menu- or graphics-based interfaces. An example is the user of a tax package that stores a variety of personal financial data for tax purposes.

A typical DBMS provides multiple facilities to access a database. Naive end users need to learn very little about the facilities provided by the DBMS; they have to understand only the types of standard transactions designed and implemented for their use. Casual users learn only a few facilities that they may use repeatedly. Sophisticated users try to learn most of the DBMS facilities in order to achieve their complex requirements. Stand-alone users typically become very proficient in using a specific software package.

1.4.4 System Analysts and Application Programmers (Software Engineers)

System analysts determine the requirements of end users, especially naive and parametric end users, and develop specifications for canned transactions that meet these requirements. **Application programmers** implement these specifications as programs; then they test, debug, document, and maintain these canned transactions. Such analysts and programmers (nowadays called **software engineers**) should be familiar with the full range of capabilities provided by the DBMS to accomplish their tasks.

1.5 Workers behind the Scene

In addition to those who design, use, and administer a database, others are associated with the design, development, and operation of the DBMS *software and system environment*. These persons are typically not interested in the database itself. We call them the "workers behind the scene," and they include the following categories.

- **DBMS system designers and implementers** are persons who design and implement the DBMS modules and interfaces as a software package. A DBMS is a complex software system that consists of many components or **modules,** including modules for implementing the catalog, query language, interface processors, data access, concurrency control, recovery, and security. The DBMS must interface with other system software, such as the operating system and compilers for various programming languages.

- **Tool developers** include persons who design and implement **tools**—the software packages that facilitate database system design and use, and help improve performance. Tools are optional packages that are often purchased separately. They include packages for database design, performance monitoring, natural language or graphical interfaces, prototyping, simulation, and test data generation. In many cases, independent software vendors develop and market these tools.

- **Operators and maintenance personnel** are the system administration personnel who are responsible for the actual running and maintenance of the hardware and software environment for the database system.

Although the above categories of workers behind the scene are instrumental in making the database system available to end users, they typically do not use the database for their own purposes.

1.6   Advantages of Using a DBMS

In this section we discuss some of the advantages of using a DBMS and the capabilities that a good DBMS should possess. The DBA must utilize these capabilities to accomplish a variety of objectives related to the design, administration, and use of a large multiuser database.

1.6.1   Controlling Redundancy

In traditional software development utilizing file processing, every user group maintains its own files for handling its data-processing applications. For example, consider the UNIVERSITY database example of Section 1.2; here, two groups of users might be the course registration personnel and the accounting office. In the traditional approach, each group independently keeps files on students. The accounting office also keeps data on registration and related billing information, whereas the registration office keeps track of student courses and grades. Much of the data is stored twice: once in the files of each user group. Additional user groups may further duplicate some or all of the same data in their own files.

This **redundancy** in storing the same data multiple times leads to several problems. First, there is the need to perform a single logical update—such as entering data on a new student—multiple times: once for each file where student data is recorded. This leads to *duplication of effort*. Second, *storage space is wasted* when the same data is stored repeatedly, and this problem may be serious for large databases. Third, files that represent the same data may become *inconsistent*. This may happen because an update is applied to some of the files but not to others. Even if an update—such as adding a new student—is applied to all the appropriate files, the data concerning the student may still be *inconsistent* since the updates are applied independently by each user group. For example, one user group may

(a)

GRADE_REPORT	StudentNumber	StudentName	SectionIdentifier	CourseNumber	Grade
	17	Smith	112	MATH2410	B
	17	Smith	119	CS1310	C
	8	Brown	85	MATH2410	A
	8	Brown	92	CS1310	A
	8	Brown	102	CS3320	B
	8	Brown	135	CS3380	A

(b)

GRADE_REPORT	StudentNumber	StudentName	SectionIdentifier	CourseNumber	Grade
	17	Brown	112	MATH2410	B

Figure 1.5   The redundant storage of data items. (a) *Controlled redundancy:* Including Student-Name and CourseNumber in the GRADE_REPORT file. (b) *Uncontrolled redundancy:* A GRADE_REPORT record that is inconsistent with the STUDENT records in Figure 1.2, because the Name of student number 17 is Smith, not Brown.

enter a student's birthdate erroneously as JAN-19-1974, whereas the other user groups may enter the correct value of JAN-29-1974.

In the database approach, the views of different user groups are integrated during database design. For consistency, we should have a database design that stores each logical data item—such as a student's name or birth date—in *only one place* in the database. This does not permit inconsistency, and it saves storage space. However, in some cases, **controlled redundancy** may be useful for improving the performance of queries. For example, we may store StudentName and CourseNumber redundantly in a GRADE_REPORT file (Figure 1.5a), because, whenever we retrieve a GRADE_REPORT record, we want to retrieve the student name and course number along with the grade, student number, and section identifier. By placing all the data together, we do not have to search multiple files to collect this data. In such cases, the DBMS should have the capability to *control* this redundancy so as to prohibit inconsistencies among the files. This may be done by automatically checking that the StudentName-StudentNumber values in any GRADE_REPORT record in Figure 1.5(a) match one of the Name-StudentNumber values of a STUDENT record (Figure 1.2). Similarly, the SectionIdentifier-CourseNumber values in GRADE_REPORT can be checked against SECTION records. Such checks can be specified to the DBMS during database design and automatically enforced by the DBMS whenever the GRADE_REPORT file is updated. Figure 1.5(b) shows a GRADE_REPORT record that is inconsistent with the STUDENT file of Figure 1.2, which may be entered erroneously if the redundancy is *not controlled*.

1.6.2 Restricting Unauthorized Access

When multiple users share a database, it is likely that some users will not be authorized to access all information in the database. For example, financial data is often considered confidential, and hence only authorized persons are allowed to access such data. In addition, some users may be permitted only to retrieve data, whereas others are allowed both to retrieve and to update. Hence, the type of access operation—retrieval or update—must also be controlled. Typically, users or user groups are given account numbers protected by passwords, which they can use to gain access to the database. A DBMS should provide a **security and authorization subsystem,** which the DBA uses to create accounts and to specify account restrictions. The DBMS should then enforce these restrictions automatically. Notice that we can apply similar controls to the DBMS software. For example, only the DBA's staff may be allowed to use certain **privileged software,** such as the software for creating new accounts. Similarly, parametric users may be allowed to access the database only through the canned transactions developed for their use.

1.6.3 Providing Persistent Storage for Program Objects and Data Structures

Databases can be used to provide **persistent storage** for program objects and data structures. This is one of the main reasons for the emergence of the **object-oriented database systems.** Programming languages typically have complex data structures, such as record types in PASCAL or class definitions in C++. The values of program variables are discarded once a program terminates, unless the programmer explicitly stores them in permanent files, which often involves converting these complex structures into a format suitable for file storage. When the need arises to read this data once more, the programmer must convert from the file format to the program variable structure. Object-oriented database systems are compatible with programming languages such as C++ and JAVA, and the DBMS software automatically performs any necessary conversions. Hence, a complex object in C++ can be stored permanently in an object-oriented DBMS, such as ObjectStore or O2 (now called Ardent, see Chapter 12). Such an object is said to be **persistent,** since it survives the termination of program execution and can later be directly retrieved by another C++ program.

The persistent storage of program objects and data structures is an important function of database systems. Traditional database systems often suffered from the so-called **impedance mismatch problem,** since the data structures provided by the DBMS were incompatible with the programming language's data structures. Object-oriented database systems typically offer data structure **compatibility** with one or more object-oriented programming languages.

1.6.4 Permitting Inferencing and Actions Using Rules

Some database systems provide capabilities for defining *deduction rules* for *inferencing* new information from the stored database facts. Such systems are called **deductive database systems.** For example, there may be complex rules in the miniworld application for determining when a student is on probation. These can be specified *declaratively* as **rules,** which when compiled and maintained by the DBMS can determine all students on probation. In a traditional DBMS, an explicit *procedural program code* would have to be written to support such applications. But if the miniworld rules change, it is generally more convenient to change the declared deduction rules than to recode procedural programs. More powerful functionality is provided by **active database systems,** which provide active rules that can automatically initiate actions.

1.6.5 Providing Multiple User Interfaces

Because many types of users with varying levels of technical knowledge use a database, a DBMS should provide a variety of user interfaces. These include query languages for casual users; programming language interfaces for application programmers; forms and command codes for parametric users; and menu-driven interfaces and natural language interfaces for stand-alone users. Both forms-style interfaces and menu-driven interfaces are commonly known as **graphical user interfaces (GUIs).** Many specialized languages and environments exist for specifying GUIs. Capabilities for providing World Wide Web access to a database—or web-enabling a database—are also becoming increasingly common.

1.6.6 Representing Complex Relationships Among Data

A database may include numerous varieties of data that are interrelated in many ways. Consider the example shown in Figure 1.2. The record for Brown in the student file is related to four records in the GRADE_REPORT file. Similarly, each section record is related to one course record as well as to a number of GRADE_REPORT records—one for each student who completed that section. A DBMS must have the capability to represent a variety of complex relationships among the data as well as to retrieve and update related data easily and efficiently.

1.6.7 Enforcing Integrity Constraints

Most database applications have certain **integrity constraints** that must hold for the data. A DBMS should provide capabilities for defining and enforcing these constraints. The simplest type of integrity constraint involves specifying a data type for each data item. For example, in Figure 1.2, we may specify that the value of the Class data item within each student record must be an integer between 1 and 5 and that the value of Name must be a string of no more than 30 alphabetic characters. A more complex type of constraint that occurs frequently involves specifying that a record in one file must be related to records in other files. For example, in Figure 1.2, we can specify that "every section record must be related to a course record." Another type of constraint specifies uniqueness on data item values, such as "every course record must have a unique value for CourseNumber." These constraints are derived from the meaning or **semantics** of the data and of the miniworld it represents. It is the database designers' responsibility to identify integrity constraints during database design. Some constraints can be specified to the DBMS and automatically enforced. Other constraints may have to be checked by update programs or at the time of data entry.

A data item may be entered erroneously and still satisfy the specified integrity constraints. For example, if a student receives a grade of A but a grade of C is entered in the database, the DBMS *cannot* discover this error automatically, because C is a valid value for the Grade data type. Such data entry errors can only be discovered manually (when the student receives the grade and complains) and corrected later by updating the database. However, a grade of Z can be rejected automatically by the DBMS, because Z is not a valid value for the Grade data type.

1.6.8   Providing Backup and Recovery

A DBMS must provide facilities for recovering from hardware or software failures. The **backup and recovery subsystem** of the DBMS is responsible for recovery. For example, if the computer system fails in the middle of a complex update program, the recovery subsystem is responsible for making sure that the database is restored to the state it was in before the program started executing. Alternatively, the recovery subsystem could ensure that the program is resumed from the point at which it was interrupted so that its full effect is recorded in the database.

1.7   Implications of the Database Approach

In addition to the issues discussed in the previous section, there are other implications of using the database approach that can benefit most organizations.

Potential for Enforcing Standards.   The database approach permits the DBA to define and enforce standards among database users in a large organization. This facilitates communication and cooperation among various departments, projects, and users within the organization. Standards can be defined for names and formats of data elements, display formats, report structures, terminology, and so on. The DBA can enforce standards in a centralized database environment more easily than in an environment where each user group has control of its own files and software.

Reduced Application Development Time.   A prime selling feature of the database approach is that developing a new application—such as the retrieval of certain data from the database for printing a new report—takes very little time. Designing and implementing a new database from scratch may take more time than writing a single specialized file application. However, once a database is up and running, substantially less time is generally required to create new applications using DBMS facilities. Development time using a DBMS is estimated to be one-sixth to one-fourth of that for a traditional file system.

Flexibility.   It may be necessary to change the structure of a database as requirements change. For example, a new user group may emerge that needs information not currently in the database. In response, it may be necessary to add a file to the database or to extend the data elements in an existing file. Modern DBMSs allow certain types of changes to the structure of the database without affecting the stored data and the existing application programs.

Availability of Up-to-Date Information.   A DBMS makes the database available to all users. As soon as one user's update is applied to the database, all other users can immediately see this update. This availability of up-to-date information is essential for many transaction-processing applications, such as reservation systems or banking databases, and it is made possible by the concurrency control and recovery subsystems of a DBMS.

Economies of Scale. The DBMS approach permits consolidation of data and applications, thus reducing the amount of wasteful overlap between activities of data-processing personnel in different projects or departments. This enables the whole organization to invest in more powerful processors, storage devices, or communication gear, rather than having each department purchase its own (weaker) equipment. This reduces overall costs of operation and management.

1.8   When Not to Use a DBMS

In spite of the advantages of using a DBMS, there are a few situations in which such a system may involve unnecessary overhead costs as that would not be incurred in traditional file processing. The overhead costs of using a DBMS are due to the following:

- High initial investment in hardware, software, and training.
- Generality that a DBMS provides for defining and processing data.
- Overhead for providing security, concurrency control, recovery, and integrity functions.

Additional problems may arise if the database designers and DBA do not properly design the database or if the database systems applications are not implemented properly. Hence, it may be more desirable to use regular files under the following circumstances:

- The database and applications are simple, well defined, and not expected to change.
- There are stringent real-time requirements for some programs that may not be met because of DBMS overhead.
- Multiple-user access to data is not required.

1.9   Summary

In this chapter we defined a database as a collection of related data, where *data* means recorded facts. A typical database represents some aspect of the real world and is used for specific purposes by one or more groups of users. A DBMS is a generalized software package for implementing and maintaining a computerized database. The database and software together form a database system. We identified several characteristics that distinguish the database approach from traditional file-processing applications:

- Existence of a catalog.
- Program-data independence and program-operation independence.
- Data abstraction.
- Support of multiple user views.
- Sharing of data among multiple transactions.

We then discussed the main categories of database users, or the "actors on the scene":

- Administrators.
- Designers.
- End users.
- System analysts and application programmers.

We noted that, in addition to database users, there are several categories of support personnel, or "workers behind the scene," in a database environment:

- DBMS system designers and implementers.
- Tool developers.
- Operators and maintenance personnel.

Then we presented a list of capabilities that should be provided by the DBMS software to the DBA, database designers, and users to help them design, administer, and use a database:

- Controlling redundancy.
- Restricting unauthorized access.
- Providing persistent storage for program objects and data structures.
- Permitting inferencing and actions by using rules.
- Providing multiple user interfaces.
- Representing complex relationships among data.
- Enforcing integrity constraints.
- Providing backup and recovery.

We listed some additional advantages of the database approach over traditional file-processing systems:

- Potential for enforcing standards.
- Reduced application development time.
- Flexibility.
- Availability of up-to-date information to all users.
- Economies of scale.

Finally, we discussed the overhead costs of using a DBMS and discussed some situations in which it may not be advantageous to use a DBMS.

Review Questions

1.1. Define the following terms: *data, database,* DBMS, *database system, database catalog, program-data independence, user view,* DBA, *end user, canned transaction, deductive database system, persistent object, meta-data, transaction processing application.*

1.2. What three main types of actions involve databases? Briefly discuss each.

1.3. Discuss the main characteristics of the database approach and how it differs from traditional file systems.

1.4. What are the responsibilities of the DBA and the database designers?

1.5. What are the different types of database end users? Discuss the main activities of each.

1.6. Discuss the capabilities that should be provided by a DBMS.

Exercises

1.7. Identify some informal queries and update operations that you would expect to apply to the database shown in Figure 1.2.

1.8. What is the difference between controlled and uncontrolled redundancy? Illustrate with examples.

1.9. Name all the relationships among the records of the database shown in Figure 1.2.

1.10. Give some additional views that may be needed by other user groups for the database shown in Figure 1.2.

1.11. Cite some examples of integrity constraints that you think should hold on the database shown in Figure 1.2.

Selected Bibliography

The October 1991 issue of *Communications of the* ACM and Kim (1995) includes several articles describing "next-generation" DBMSs; many of the database features discussed in this issue are now commercially available. The March 1976 issue of ACM *Computing Surveys* offers an early introduction to database systems and may provide a historical perspective for the interested reader.

CHAPTER 2

Database System Concepts and Architecture

The architecture of DBMS packages has evolved from the early monolithic systems, where the whole DBMS software package is one tightly integrated system, to the modern DBMS packages that are modular in design, with a client-server system architecture. This evolution mirrors the trends in computing, where the large centralized mainframe computers are being replaced by hundreds of distributed workstations and personal computers connected via communications networks. In a basic client-server architecture, the system functionality is distributed between two types of modules. A **client module** is typically designed so that it will run on a user workstation or personal computer. Typically, application programs and user interfaces that access the database run in the client module. Hence, the client module handles user interaction and provides the user-friendly interfaces such as forms or menu-based GUIs (graphical *user* interfaces). The other kind of module, called a **server module,** typically handles data storage, access, search, and other functions.

We will discuss client-server architectures in Chapters 17 and 24. First, we must study more basic concepts that will give us a better understanding of the modern database architectures when they are presented later in this book. In this chapter we thus present the terminology and basic concepts that will be used throughout the book. We start, in Section 2.1, by discussing data models and defining the concepts of schemas and instances, which are fundamental to the study of database systems. We then discuss the three-schema DBMS architecture and data independence in Section 2.2; this provides a user's perspective on what a DBMS is supposed to do. In Section 2.3, we describe the types of interfaces and languages that are typically provided by a DBMS. Section 2.4 discusses the database system software environment, and Section 2.5 presents a classification of the types of DBMS packages. Section 2.6 summarizes the chapter.

The material in Sections 2.4 and 2.5 provides more detailed concepts that may be looked upon as a supplement to the basic introductory material.

2.1 Data Models, Schemas, and Instances

One fundamental characteristic of the database approach is that it provides some level of data abstraction by hiding details of data storage that are not needed by most database users. A **data model**—a collection of concepts that can be used to describe the structure of a database—provides the necessary means to achieve this abstraction.[1] By *structure of a database* we mean the data types, relationships, and constraints that should hold on the data. Most data models also include a set of **basic operations** for specifying retrievals and updates on the database.

In addition to the basic operations provided by the data model, it is becoming more common to include concepts in the data model to specify the **dynamic aspect** or **behavior** of a database application. This allows the database designer to specify a set of valid **user-defined operations** that are allowed on the database objects.[2] An example of a user-defined operation could be COMPUTE_GPA, which can be applied to a STUDENT object. On the other hand, generic operations to insert, delete, modify, or retrieve any kind of object are often included in the *basic data model operations*. Concepts to specify behavior are fundamental to object-oriented data models (see Chapters 11 and 12) but are also being incorporated in more traditional data models by extending these models. For example, object-relational models (see Chapter 13) extend the traditional relational model to include such concepts, among others.

2.1.1 Categories of Data Models

Many data models have been proposed, and we can categorize them according to the types of concepts they use to describe the database structure. **High-level** or **conceptual data models** provide concepts that are close to the way many users perceive data, whereas **low-level** or **physical data models** provide concepts that describe the details of how data is stored in the computer. Concepts provided by low-level data models are generally meant for computer specialists, not for typical end users. Between these two extremes is a class of **representational** (or **implementation**) **data models,** which provide concepts that may be understood by end users but that are not too far removed from the way data is organized within the computer. Representational data models hide some details of data storage but can be implemented on a computer system in a direct way.

---

1. Sometimes the word *model* is used to denote a specific database description, or schema—for example, "the marketing data model." We will not use this interpretation.

2. The inclusion of concepts to describe behavior reflects a trend where database design and software design activities are increasingly being combined into a single activity. Traditionally, specifying behavior is associated with software design.

Conceptual data models use concepts such as entities, attributes, and relationships. An **entity** represents a real-world object or concept, such as an employee or a project, that is described in the database. An **attribute** represents some property of interest that further describes an entity, such as the employee's name or salary. A **relationship** among two or more entities represents an interaction among the entities; for example, a works-on relationship between an employee and a project. In Chapter 3, we will present the Entity-Relationship model—a popular high-level conceptual data model. Chapter 4 describes additional data modeling concepts, such as generalization, specialization, and categories.

Representational or implementation data models are the models used most frequently in traditional commercial DBMSs, and they include the widely-used **relational data model,** as well as the so-called legacy data models—the **network** and **hierarchical models**—that have been widely used in the past. Part II of this book is devoted to the relational data model, its operations and languages, and also includes an overview of two relational systems.[3] The SQL standard for relational databases is described in Chapter 8. Representational data models represent data by using record structures and hence are sometimes called **record-based data models.**

We can regard **object data models** as a new family of higher-level implementation data models that are closer to conceptual data models. We describe the general characteristics of object databases, together with an overview of two object DBMSs, in Part III of this book. The ODMG proposed standard for object databases is described in Chapter 12. Object data models are also frequently utilized as high-level conceptual models, particularly in the software engineering domain.

Physical data models describe how data is stored in the computer by representing information such as record formats, record orderings, and access paths. An **access path** is a structure that makes the search for particular database records efficient. We discuss physical storage techniques and access structures in Chapters 5 and 6.

2.1.2 Schemas, Instances, and Database State

In any data model it is important to distinguish between the *description* of the database and the *database itself*. The description of a database is called the **database schema,** which is specified during database design and is not expected to change frequently.[4] Most data models have certain conventions for displaying the schemas as diagrams.[5] A displayed schema is called a **schema diagram.** Figure 2.1 shows a schema diagram for the database shown in Figure 1.2; the diagram displays the structure of each record type but not the actual instances of records. We call each object in the schema—such as STUDENT or COURSE—a **schema construct.**

---

3. A summary of the network and hierarchical data models is included in Appendices C and D. The full chapters from the second edition of this book are accessible from the Internet Web site.

4. Schema changes are usually needed as the requirements of the database applications change. Newer database systems include operations for allowing schema changes, although the schema change process is more involved than simple database updates.

5. It is customary in database parlance to use *schemas* as plural for *schema*, even though *schemata* is the proper plural form. The word *scheme* is sometimes used for schema.

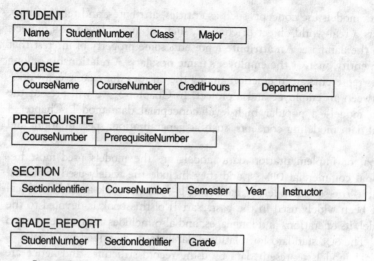

Figure 2.1   Schema diagram for the database of Figure 1.2.

A schema diagram displays only *some aspects* of a schema, such as the names of record types and data items, and some types of constraints. Other aspects are not specified in the schema diagram; for example, Figure 2.1 shows neither the data type of each data item nor the relationships among the various files. Many types of constraints are not represented in schema diagrams; for example, a constraint such as "students majoring in computer science must take CS1310 before the end of their sophomore year" is quite difficult to represent.

The actual data in a database may change quite frequently; for example, the database shown in Figure 1.2 changes every time we add a student or enter a new grade for a student. The data in the database at a particular moment in time is called a **database state** or **snapshot.** It is also called the *current* set of **occurrences** or **instances** in the database. In a given database state, each schema construct has its own *current* set of instances; for example, the STUDENT construct will contain the set of individual student entities (records) as its instances. Many database states can be constructed to correspond to a particular database schema. Every time we insert or delete a record, or change the value of a data item in a record, we change one state of the database into another state.

The distinction between database schema and database state is very important. When we **define** a new database, we specify its database schema only to the DBMS. At this point, the corresponding database state is the *empty state* with no data. We get the *initial state* of the database when the database is first **populated** or **loaded** with the initial data. From then on, every time an update operation is applied to the database, we get another database state. At any point in time, the database has a *current state*.[6] The DBMS is partly responsible for ensuring that *every* state of the database is a **valid state**—that is, a state that satisfies the structure and constraints specified in the schema. Hence, specifying a

---

6. The current state is also called the *current snapshot* of the database.

correct schema to the DBMS is extremely important, and the schema must be designed with the utmost care. The DBMS stores the descriptions of the schema constructs and constraints—also called the **meta-data**—in the DBMS catalog so that DBMS software can refer to the schema whenever it needs to. The schema is sometimes called the **intension,** and a database state an **extension** of the schema.

Although, as mentioned earlier, the schema is not supposed to change frequently, it is not uncommon that changes need to be applied to the schema once in a while as the application requirements change. For example, we may decide that another data item needs to be stored for each record in a file, such as adding the DateOfBirth to the STUDENT schema in Figure 2.1. This is known as **schema evolution.** Most modern DBMSs include some operations for schema evolution that can be applied while the database is operational.

2.2 DBMS Architecture and Data Independence

Three important characteristics of the database approach, listed in Section 1.3, are (1) insulation of programs and data (program-data and program-operation independence); (2) support of multiple user views; and (3) use of a catalog to store the database description (schema). In this section we specify an architecture for database systems, called the **three-schema architecture,**[7] which was proposed to help achieve and visualize these characteristics. We then discuss the concept of data independence.

2.2.1 The Three-Schema Architecture

The goal of the three-schema architecture, illustrated in Figure 2.2, is to separate the user applications and the physical database. In this architecture, schemas can be defined at the following three levels:

1. The **internal level** has an **internal schema,** which describes the physical storage structure of the database. The internal schema uses a physical data model and describes the complete details of data storage and access paths for the database.

2. The **conceptual level** has a **conceptual schema,** which describes the structure of the whole database for a community of users. The conceptual schema hides the details of physical storage structures and concentrates on describing entities, data types, relationships, user operations, and constraints. A high-level data model or an implementation data model can be used at this level.

3. The **external** or **view level** includes a number of **external schemas** or **user views.** Each external schema describes the part of the database that a particular user group is interested in and hides the rest of the database from that user group. A high-level data model or an implementation data model can be used at this level.

---

7. This is also known as the ANSI/SPARC architecture, after the committee that proposed it (Tsichritzis and Klug 1978).

Figure 2.2   Illustrating the three-schema architecture.

The three-schema architecture is a convenient tool for the user to visualize the schema levels in a database system. Most DBMSs do not separate the three levels completely, but support the three-schema architecture to some extent. Some DBMSs may include physical-level details in the conceptual schema. In most DBMSs that support user views, external schemas are specified in the same data model that describes the conceptual-level information. Some DBMSs allow different data models to be used at the conceptual and external levels.

Notice that the three schemas are only *descriptions* of data; the only data that *actually* exists is at the physical level. In a DBMS based on the three-schema architecture, each user group refers only to its own external schema. Hence, the DBMS must transform a request specified on an external schema into a request against the conceptual schema, and then into a request on the internal schema for processing over the stored database. If the request is a database retrieval, the data extracted from the stored database must be reformatted to match the user's external view. The processes of transforming requests and results between levels are called **mappings.** These mappings may be time-consuming, so some DBMSs—especially those that are meant to support small databases—do not support external views. Even in such systems, however, a certain amount of mapping is necessary to transform requests between the conceptual and internal levels.

2.2.2 Data Independence

The three-schema architecture can be used to explain the concept of **data independence,** which can be defined as the capacity to change the schema at one level of a database system without having to change the schema at the next higher level. We can define two types of data independence:

1. **Logical data independence** is the capacity to change the conceptual schema without having to change external schemas or application programs. We may change the conceptual schema to expand the database (by adding a record type or data item), or to reduce the database (by removing a record type or data item). In the latter case, external schemas that refer only to the remaining data should not be affected. For example, the external schema of Figure 1.4(a) should not be affected by changing the GRADE_REPORT file shown in Figure 1.2 into the one shown in Figure 1.5(a). Only the view definition and the mappings need be changed in a DBMS that supports logical data independence. Application programs that reference the external schema constructs must work as before, after the conceptual schema undergoes a logical reorganization. Changes to constraints can be applied also to the conceptual schema without affecting the external schemas or application programs.

2. **Physical data independence** is the capacity to change the internal schema without having to change the conceptual (or external) schemas. Changes to the internal schema may be needed because some physical files had to be reorganized—for example, by creating additional access structures—to improve the performance of retrieval or update. If the same data as before remains in the database, we should not have to change the conceptual schema. For example, providing an access path to improve retrieval of SECTION records (Figure 1.2) by Semester and Year should not require a query such as "list all sections offered in fall 1998" to be changed, although the query would be executed more efficiently by the DBMS by utilizing the new access path.

Whenever we have a multiple-level DBMS, its catalog must be expanded to include information on how to map requests and data among the various levels. The DBMS uses additional software to accomplish these mappings by referring to the mapping information in the catalog. Data independence is accomplished because, when the schema is changed at some level, the schema at the next higher level remains unchanged; only the *mapping* between the two levels is changed. Hence, application programs referring to the higher-level schema need not be changed.

The three-schema architecture can make it easier to achieve true data independence, both physical and logical. However, the two levels of mappings create an overhead during compilation or execution of a query or program, leading to inefficiencies in the DBMS. Because of this, few DBMSs have implemented the full three-schema architecture.

2.3 Database Languages and Interfaces

In Section 1.4 we discussed the variety of users supported by a DBMS. The DBMS must provide appropriate languages and interfaces for each category of users. In this section we discuss the types of languages and interfaces provided by a DBMS and the user categories targeted by each interface.

2.3.1 DBMS Languages

Once the design of a database is completed and a DBMS is chosen to implement the database, the first order of the day is to specify conceptual and internal schemas for the database and any mappings between the two. In many DBMSs where no strict separation of levels is maintained, one language, called the **data definition language (DDL),** is used by the DBA and by database designers to define both schemas. The DBMS will have a DDL compiler whose function is to process DDL statements in order to identify descriptions of the schema constructs and to store the schema description in the DBMS catalog.

In DBMSs where a clear separation is maintained between the conceptual and internal levels, the DDL is used to specify the conceptual schema only. Another language, the **storage definition language (SDL),** is used to specify the internal schema. The mappings between the two schemas may be specified in either one of these languages. For a true three-schema architecture, we would need a third language, the **view definition language (VDL),** to specify user views and their mappings to the conceptual schema, but in most DBMSs the DDL is used to define both conceptual and external schemas.

Once the database schemas are compiled and the database is populated with data, users must have some means to manipulate the database. Typical manipulations include retrieval, insertion, deletion, and modification of the data. The DBMS provides a **data manipulation language (DML)** for these purposes.

In current DBMSs, the preceding types of languages are usually *not considered distinct languages*; rather, a comprehensive integrated language is used that includes constructs for conceptual schema definition, view definition, and data manipulation. Storage definition is typically kept separate, since it is used for defining physical storage structures to fine-tune the performance of the database system, and it is usually utilized by the DBA staff. A typical example of a comprehensive database language is the SQL relational database language (see Chapter 8), which represents a combination of DDL, VDL, and DML, as well as statements for constraint specification and schema evolution. The SDL was a component in earlier versions of SQL but has been removed from the language to keep it at the conceptual and external levels only.

There are two main types of DMLs. A **high-level** or **nonprocedural** DML can be used on its own to specify complex database operations in a concise manner. Many DBMSs allow high-level DML statements either to be entered interactively from a terminal (or monitor) or to be embedded in a general-purpose programming language. In the latter case, DML statements must be identified within the program so that they can be extracted by a pre-compiler and processed by the DBMS. A **low-level** or **procedural** DML *must* be embedded in a general-purpose programming language. This type of DML typically retrieves individual records or objects from the database and processes each separately.

Hence, it needs to use programming language constructs, such as looping, to retrieve and process each record from a set of records. Low-level DMLs are also called **record-at-a-time DMLs** because of this property. High-level DMLs, such as SQL, can specify and retrieve many records in a single DML statement and are hence called **set-at-a-time** or **set-oriented DMLs.** A query in a high-level DML often specifies *which* data to retrieve rather than *how* to retrieve it; hence, such languages are also called **declarative.**

Whenever DML commands, whether high-level or low-level, are embedded in a general-purpose programming language, that language is called the **host language** and the DML is called the **data sublanguage.**[8] On the other hand, a high-level DML used in a stand-alone interactive manner is called a **query language.** In general, both retrieval and update commands of a high-level DML may be used interactively and are hence considered part of the query language.[9]

Casual end users typically use a high-level query language to specify their requests, whereas programmers use the DML in its embedded form. For naive and parametric users, there usually are **user-friendly interfaces** for interacting with the database; these can also be used by casual users or others who do not want to learn the details of a high-level query language. We discuss these types of interfaces next.

2.3.2 DBMS Interfaces

User-friendly interfaces provided by a DBMS may include the following.

Menu-Based Interfaces for Browsing. These interfaces present the user with lists of options, called **menus,** that lead the user through the formulation of a request. Menus do away with the need to memorize the specific commands and syntax of a query language; rather, the query is composed step by step by picking options from a menu that is displayed by the system. Pull-down menus are becoming a very popular technique in window-based user interfaces. They are often used in **browsing interfaces,** which allow a user to look through the contents of a database in an exploratory and unstructured manner.

Forms-Based Interfaces. A forms-based interface displays a **form** to each user. Users can fill out all of the form entries to insert new data, or they fill out only certain entries, in which case the DBMS will retrieve matching data for the remaining entries. Forms are usually designed and programmed for naive users as interfaces to canned transactions. Many DBMSs have **forms specification languages,** special languages that help programmers specify such forms. Some systems have utilities that define a form by letting the end user interactively construct a sample form on the screen.

---

8. In object databases, the host and data sublanguages typically form one integrated language—for example, C++ with some extensions to support database functionality. Some relational systems also provide integrated languages—for example, ORACLE's PL/SQL.

9. According to the meaning of the word *query* in English, it should really be used to describe only retrievals, not updates.

Graphical User Interfaces.   A graphical interface (GUI) typically displays a schema to the user in diagrammatic form. The user can then specify a query by manipulating the diagram. In many cases, GUIs utilize both menus and forms. Most GUIs use a **pointing device,** such as a mouse, to pick certain parts of the displayed schema diagram.

Natural Language Interfaces.   These interfaces accept requests written in English or some other language and attempt to "understand" them. A natural language interface usually has its own "schema," which is similar to the database conceptual schema. The natural language interface refers to the words in its schema, as well as to a set of standard words, to interpret the request. If the interpretation is successful, the interface generates a high-level query corresponding to the natural language request and submits it to the DBMS for processing; otherwise, a dialogue is started with the user to clarify the request.

Interfaces for Parametric Users.   Parametric users, such as bank tellers, often have a small set of operations that they must perform repeatedly. Systems analysts and programmers design and implement a special interface for a known class of naive users. Usually, a small set of abbreviated commands is included, with the goal of minimizing the number of keystrokes required for each request. For example, function keys in a terminal can be programmed to initiate the various commands. This allows the parametric user to proceed with a minimal number of keystrokes.

Interfaces for the DBA.   Most database systems contain privileged commands that can be used only by the DBA's staff. These include commands for creating accounts, setting system parameters, granting account authorization, changing a schema, and reorganizing the storage structures of a database.

2.4   The Database System Environment

A DBMS is a complex software system. In this section we discuss the types of software components that constitute a DBMS and the types of computer system software with which the DBMS interacts.

2.4.1   DBMS Component Modules

Figure 2.3 illustrates, in a simplified form, the typical DBMS components. The database and the DBMS catalog are usually stored on disk. Access to the disk is controlled primarily by the **operating system (OS),** which schedules disk input/output. A higher-level **stored data manager** module of the DBMS controls access to DBMS information that is stored on disk, whether it is part of the database or the catalog. The dotted lines and circles marked A, B, C, D, and E in Figure 2.3 illustrate accesses that are under the control of this stored data manager. The stored data manager may use basic OS services for carrying out low-level data transfer between the disk and computer main storage, but it controls other aspects of data transfer, such as handling buffers in main memory. Once the data is in main memory buffers, it can be processed by other DBMS modules, as well as by application programs.

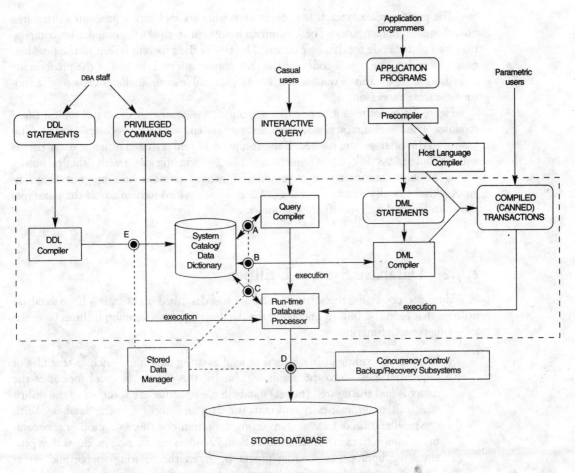

Figure 2.3 Typical component modules of a DBMS. Dotted lines show accesses that are under the control of the stored data manager.

The **DDL compiler** processes schema definitions, specified in the DDL, and stores descriptions of the schemas (meta-data) in the DBMS catalog. The catalog includes information such as the names of files, data items, storage details of each file, mapping information among schemas, and constraints, in addition to many other types of information that are needed by the DBMS modules. DBMS software modules then look up the catalog information as needed.

The **run-time database processor** handles database accesses at run time; it receives retrieval or update operations and carries them out on the database. Access to disk goes through the stored data manager. The **query compiler** handles high-level queries that are entered interactively. It parses, analyzes, and compiles or interprets a query by creating database access code, and then generates calls to the run-time processor for executing the code.

The **pre-compiler** extracts DML commands from an application program written in a host programming language. These commands are sent to the **DML compiler** for compilation into object code for database access. The rest of the program is sent to the host language compiler. The object codes for the DML commands and the rest of the program are linked, forming a canned transaction whose executable code includes calls to the run-time database processor.

Figure 2.3 is not meant to describe a specific DBMS; rather it illustrates typical DBMS modules. The DBMS interacts with the operating system when disk accesses—to the database or to the catalog—are needed. If the computer system is shared by many users, the OS will schedule DBMS disk access requests and DBMS processing along with other processes. The DBMS also interfaces with compilers for general-purpose host programming languages. User-friendly interfaces to the DBMS can be provided to help any of the user types shown in Figure 2.3 to specify their requests.

2.4.2   Database System Utilities

In addition to possessing the software modules just described, most DBMSs have **database utilities** that help the DBA in managing the database system. Common utilities have the following types of functions:

1. *Loading:* A loading utility is used to load existing data files—such as text files or sequential files—into the database. Usually, the current (source) format of the data file and the desired (target) database file structure are specified to the utility, which then automatically reformats the data and stores it in the database. With the proliferation of DBMSs, transferring data from one DBMS to another is becoming common in many organizations. Some vendors are offering products that generate the appropriate loading programs, given the existing source and target database storage descriptions (internal schemas). Such tools are also called **conversion tools.**

2. *Backup:* A backup utility creates a backup copy of the database, usually by dumping the entire database onto tape. The backup copy can be used to restore the database in case of catastrophic failure. Incremental backups are also often used, where only changes since the previous backup are recorded. Incremental backup is more complex but it saves space.

3. *File reorganization:* This utility can be used to reorganize a database file into a different file organization to improve performance.

4. *Performance monitoring:* Such a utility monitors database usage and provides statistics to the DBA. The DBA uses the statistics in making decisions such as whether or not to reorganize files to improve performance.

Other utilities may be available for sorting files, handling data compression, monitoring access by users, and performing other functions.

2.4.3 Tools, Application Environments, and Communications Facilities

Other tools are often available to database designers, users, and DBAs. **CASE tools**[10] are used in the design phase of database systems. Another tool that can be quite useful in large organizations is an expanded **data dictionary** (or **data repository) system.** In addition to storing catalog information about schemas and constraints, the data dictionary stores other information, such as design decisions, usage standards, application program descriptions, and user information. Such a system is also called an **information repository.** This information can be accessed *directly* by users or the DBA when needed. A data dictionary utility is similar to the DBMS catalog, but it includes a wider variety of information and is accessed mainly by users rather than by the DBMS software.

Application development environments, such as the PowerBuilder system, are becoming quite popular. These systems provide an environment for developing database applications and include facilities that help in many facets of database systems, including database design, GUI development, querying and updating, and application program development.

The DBMS also needs to interface with **communications software,** whose function is to allow users at locations remote from the database system site to access the database through computer terminals, workstations, or their local personal computers. These are connected to the database site through data communications hardware such as phone lines, long-haul networks, local-area networks, or satellite communication devices. Many commercial database systems have communication packages that work with the DBMS. The integrated DBMS and data communications system is called a **DB/DC** system. In addition, some distributed DBMSs are physically distributed over multiple machines. In this case, communications networks are needed to connect the machines. These are often **local area networks** (LANs) but they can also be other types of networks.

2.5 Classification of Database Management Systems

Several criteria are normally used to classify DBMSs. The first is the **data model** on which the DBMS is based. The two types of data models used in many current commercial DBMSs are the **relational data model** and the **object data model.** Many legacy applications still run on database systems based on the **hierarchical** and **network data models.** The relational DBMSs are evolving continuously, and, in particular, have been incorporating many of the concepts that were developed in object databases. This has led to a new class of DBMSs that are being called **object-relational DBMSs.** We can hence categorize DBMSs based on the data model: relational, object, object-relational, hierarchical, network, and other.

---

10. Although CASE stands for Computer Aided Software Engineering, many CASE tools are used primarily for database design.

The second criterion used to classify DBMSs is the **number of users** supported by the system. **Single-user systems** support only one user at a time and are mostly used with personal computers. **Multiuser systems,** which include the majority of DBMSs, support multiple users concurrently.

A third criterion is the **number of sites** over which the database is distributed. A DBMS is **centralized** if the data is stored at a single computer site. A centralized DBMS can support multiple users, but the DBMS and the database themselves reside totally at a single computer site. A **distributed DBMS (DDBMS)** can have the actual database and DBMS software distributed over many sites, connected by a computer network. **Homogeneous DDBMSs** use the same DBMS software at multiple sites. A recent trend is to develop software to access several autonomous preexisting databases stored under **heterogeneous DBMSs.** This leads to a **federated DBMS** (or **multidatabase system**), where the participating DBMSs are loosely coupled and have a degree of local autonomy. Many DDBMSs use a client-server architecture.

A fourth criterion is the **cost** of the DBMS. The majority of DBMS packages cost between $10,000 and $100,000. Single-user low-end systems that work with microcomputers cost between $100 and $3000. At the other end, a few elaborate packages cost more than $100,000.

We can also classify a DBMS on the basis of the **types of access path** options for storing files. One well-known family of DBMSs is based on inverted file structures. Finally, a DBMS can be **general-purpose** or **special-purpose.** When performance is a primary consideration, a special-purpose DBMS can be designed and built for a specific application; such a system cannot be used for other applications without major changes. Many airline reservations and telephone directory systems developed in the past are special-purpose DBMSs. These fall into the category of **on-line transaction processing (OLTP) systems,** which must support a large number of concurrent transactions without imposing excessive delays.

Let us briefly elaborate on the main criterion for classifying DBMSs: the data model. The basic relational data model represents a database as a collection of tables, where each table can be stored as a separate file. The database in Figure 1.2 is shown in a manner very similar to a relational representation. Most relational databases use the high-level query language called SQL and support a limited form of user views. We discuss the relational model, its languages and operations, and two sample commercial systems in Chapters 7 through 10.

The object data model defines a database in terms of objects, their properties, and their operations. Objects with the same structure and behavior belong to a **class,** and classes are organized into **hierarchies** (or **acyclic graphs**). The operations of each class are specified in terms of predefined procedures called **methods.** Relational DBMSs have been extending their models to incorporate object database concepts and other capabilities; these systems are referred to as **object-relational** or **extended-relational systems.** We discuss object databases and extended-relational systems in Chapters 11 through 13.

The **network model** represents data as record types and also represents a limited type of 1:N relationship, called a **set type.** Figure 2.4 shows a network schema diagram for the database of Figure 1.2, where record types are shown as rectangles and set types are shown

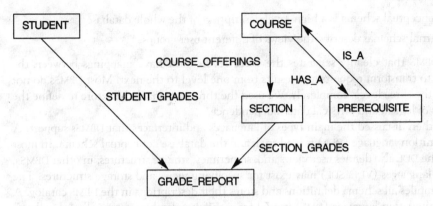

Figure 2.4 The schema of Figure 2.1 in the notation of the network data model.

as labeled directed arrows. The network model, also known as the CODASYL DBTG model,[11] has an associated record-at-a-time language that must be embedded in a host programming language. The **hierarchical model** represents data as hierarchical tree structures. Each hierarchy represents a number of related records. There is no standard language for the hierarchical model, although most hierarchical DBMSs have record-at-a-time languages. We give a brief overview of the network and hierarchical models in Appendices C and D.[12]

2.6 Summary

In this chapter we introduced the main concepts used in database systems. We defined a data model, and we distinguished three main categories of data models:

- High-level or conceptual data models (based on entities and relationships).
- Low-level or physical data models.
- Representational or implementation data models (record-based, object-oriented).

We distinguished the schema, or description of a database, from the database itself. The schema does not change very often, whereas the database state changes every time data is inserted, deleted, or modified. We then described the three-schema DBMS architecture, which allows three schema levels:

- An internal schema describes the physical storage structure of the database.

---

11. CODASYL DBTG stands for Computer Data Systems Language Data Base Task Group, which is the committee that specified the network model and its language.

12. The full chapters on the network and hierarchical models from the second edition of this book are available over the Internet from the Web site.

- A conceptual schema is a high-level description of the whole database.
- External schemas describe the views of different user groups.

A DBMS that cleanly separates the three levels must have mappings between the schemas to transform requests and results from one level to the next. Most DBMSs do not separate the three levels completely. We used the three-schema architecture to define the concepts of logical and physical data independence.

We then discussed the main types of languages and interfaces that DBMSs support. A data definition language (DDL) is used to define the database conceptual schema. In most DBMSs, the DDL also defines user views and, sometimes, storage structures; in other DBMSs, separate languages (VDL, SDL) may exist for specifying views and storage structures. The DBMS compiles all schema definitions and stores their descriptions in the DBMS catalog. A data manipulation language (DML) is used for specifying database retrievals and updates. DMLs can be high-level (set-oriented, nonprocedural) or low-level (record-oriented, procedural). A high-level DML can be embedded in a host programming language, or it can be used as a stand-alone language; in the latter case it is often called a query language.

We discussed different types of interfaces provided by DBMSs, and the types of DBMS users with which each interface is associated. We then discussed the database system environment, typical DBMS software modules, and DBMS utilities for helping users and the DBA perform their tasks.

In the final section, we classified DBMSs according to several criteria: data model, number of users, number of sites, cost, types of access paths, and generality. The main classification of DBMSs is based on the data model. We briefly discussed the main data models used in current commercial DBMSs.

Review Questions

2.1. Define the following terms: *data model, database schema, database state, internal schema, conceptual schema, external schema, data independence,* DDL, DML, SDL, VDL, *query language, host language, data sublanguage, database utility, catalog, client-server architecture.*

2.2. Discuss the main categories of data models.

2.3. What is the difference between a database schema and a database state?

2.4. Describe the three-schema architecture. Why do we need mappings between schema levels? How do different schema definition languages support this architecture?

2.5. What is the difference between logical data independence and physical data independence?

2.6. What is the difference between procedural and nonprocedural DMLs?

2.7. Discuss the different types of user-friendly interfaces and the types of users who typically use each.

2.8. With what other computer system software does a DBMS interact?

2.9. Discuss some types of database utilities and tools and their functions.

Exercises

2.10. Think of different users for the database of Figure 1.2. What types of applications would each user need? To which user category would each belong, and what type of interface would each need?

2.11. Choose a database application with which you are familiar. Design a schema and show a sample database for that application, using the notation of Figures 2.1 and 1.2. What types of additional information and constraints would you like to represent in the schema? Think of several users for your database, and design a view for each.

Selected Bibliography

Many database textbooks, including Date (1995), Silberschatz et al. (1998), Ramakrishnan (1997), Ullman (1988, 1989), and Abiteboul et al. (1995), provide a discussion of the various database concepts presented here. Tsichritzis and Lochovsky (1982) is an early textbook on data models. Tsichritzis and Klug (1978) and Jardine (1977) present the three-schema architecture, which was first suggested in the DBTG CODASYL report (1971) and later in an American National Standards Institute (ANSI) report (1975). An in-depth analysis of the relational data model and some of its possible extensions is given in Codd (1992). The proposed standard for object-oriented databases is described in Cattell (1997).

An example of database utilities is the ETI Extract Toolkit (www.eti.com) and the database administration tool DB Artisan from Embarcadero Technologies (www.embarcadero.com).

CHAPTER 3

Data Modeling Using the Entity-Relationship Model

Conceptual modeling is an important phase in designing a successful database application. Generally, the term **database application** refers to a particular database—for example, a BANK database that keeps track of customer accounts—and the associated *programs* that implement the database queries and updates—for example, programs that implement database updates corresponding to customers making deposits and withdrawals. These programs often provide user-friendly graphical user interfaces (GUIs) utilizing forms and menus. Hence, part of the database application will require the design, implementation, and testing of these **application programs.** Traditionally, the design and testing of application programs has been considered to be more in the realm of the software engineering domain than in the database domain. However, it is becoming clearer that there is some commonality between database design methodologies and software engineering design methodologies. As database design methodologies attempt to include more of the concepts for specifying operations on database objects, and as software engineering methodologies specify in more detail the structure of the databases that software programs will use and access, it is certain that this commonality will increase. We will briefly discuss some of the concepts for specifying database operations in Chapter 4, and again when we discuss object databases in Part III of this book.

In this chapter, we will follow the traditional approach of concentrating on the database structures and constraints during database design. We will present the modeling concepts of the **Entity-Relationship (ER) model,** which is a popular high-level conceptual data model. This model and its variations are frequently used for the conceptual design of database applications, and many database design tools employ its concepts. We describe the basic data-structuring concepts and constraints of the ER model and discuss their use in the design of conceptual schemas for database applications.

This chapter is organized as follows. In Section 3.1 we discuss the role of high-level conceptual data models in database design. We introduce the requirements for an example database application in Section 3.2 to illustrate the use of the ER model concepts. This example database is also used in subsequent chapters. In Section 3.3 we present the concepts of entities and attributes, and we gradually introduce the diagrammatic technique for displaying an ER schema. In Section 3.4, we introduce the concepts of binary relationships and their roles and structural constraints. Section 3.5 introduces weak entity types. Section 3.6 shows how a schema design is refined to include relationships. Section 3.7 reviews the notation for ER diagrams, summarizes the issues that arise in schema design, and discusses how to choose the names for database schema constructs. Section 3.8 summarizes the chapter.

The material in Sections 3.3 and 3.4 provides a somewhat detailed description, and some may be left out of an introductory course if desired. On the other hand, if more thorough coverage of data modeling concepts and conceptual database design is desired, the reader should continue on to the material in Chapter 4 after concluding Chapter 3. In Chapter 4, we describe extensions to the ER model that lead to the Enhanced-ER (EER) model, which includes concepts such as specialization, generalization, inheritance, and union types (categories). We also introduce object modeling and the Universal Modeling Language (UML) notation in Chapter 4, which has been proposed as a standard for object modeling.

3.1 Using High-Level Conceptual Data Models for Database Design

Figure 3.1 shows a simplified description of the database design process. The first step shown is **requirements collection and analysis.** During this step, the database designers interview prospective database users to understand and document their **data requirements.** The result of this step is a concisely written set of users' requirements. These requirements should be specified in as detailed and complete a form as possible. In parallel with specifying the data requirements, it is useful to specify the known **functional requirements** of the application. These consist of the user-defined **operations** (or **transactions**) that will be applied to the database, and they include both retrievals and updates. In software design, it is common to use *data flow diagrams, sequence diagrams, scenarios,* and other techniques for specifying functional requirements. We will not discuss any of these techniques here because they are usually part of software engineering texts.

Once all the requirements have been collected and analyzed, the next step is to create a **conceptual schema** for the database, using a high-level conceptual data model. This step is called **conceptual design.** The conceptual schema is a concise description of the data requirements of the users and includes detailed descriptions of the entity types, relationships, and constraints; these are expressed using the concepts provided by the high-level data model. Because these concepts do not include implementation details, they are

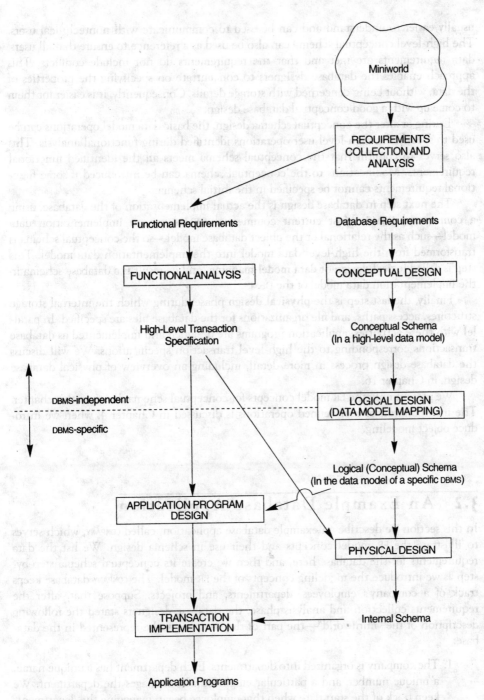

Figure 3.1   A simplified diagram to illustrate the main phases of database design.

usually easier to understand and can be used to communicate with nontechnical users. The high-level conceptual schema can also be used as a reference to ensure that all users' data requirements are met and that the requirements do not include conflicts. This approach enables the database designers to concentrate on specifying the properties of the data, without being concerned with storage details. Consequently, it is easier for them to come up with a good conceptual database design.

During or after the conceptual schema design, the basic data model operations can be used to specify the high-level user operations identified during functional analysis. This also serves to confirm that the conceptual schema meets all the identified functional requirements. Modifications to the conceptual schema can be introduced if some functional requirements cannot be specified in the initial schema.

The next step in database design is the actual implementation of the database, using a commercial DBMS. Most current commercial DBMSs use an implementation data model—such as the relational or the object database model—so the conceptual schema is transformed from the high-level data model into the implementation data model. This step is called **logical design** or **data model mapping,** and its result is a database schema in the implementation data model of the DBMS.

Finally, the last step is the **physical design** phase, during which the internal storage structures, access paths, and file organizations for the database files are specified. In parallel with these activities, application programs are designed and implemented as database transactions corresponding to the high-level transaction specifications. We will discuss the database design process in more detail, including an overview of physical database design, in Chapter 16.

We present only the ER model concepts for conceptual schema design in this chapter. The incorporation of user-defined operations is discussed in Chapter 4, when we introduce object modeling.

3.2 An Example Database Application

In this section we describe an example database application, called COMPANY, which serves to illustrate the ER model concepts and their use in schema design. We list the data requirements for the database here, and then we create its conceptual schema step-by-step as we introduce the modeling concepts of the ER model. The COMPANY database keeps track of a company's employees, departments, and projects. Suppose that, after the requirements collection and analysis phase, the database designers stated the following description of the "miniworld"—the part of the company to be represented in the database:

1. The company is organized into departments. Each department has a unique name, a unique number, and a particular employee who manages the department. We keep track of the start date when that employee began managing the department. A department may have several locations.

2. A department controls a number of projects, each of which has a unique name, a unique number, and a single location.

3. We store each employee's name, social security number,[1] address, salary, sex, and birth date. An employee is assigned to one department but may work on several projects, which are not necessarily controlled by the same department. We keep track of the number of hours per week that an employee works on each project. We also keep track of the direct supervisor of each employee.

4. We want to keep track of the dependents of each employee for insurance purposes. We keep each dependent's first name, sex, birth date, and relationship to the employee.

Figure 3.2 shows how the schema for this database application can be displayed by means of the graphical notation known as **ER diagrams.** We describe the process of deriving this schema from the stated requirements—and explain the ER diagrammatic notation—as we introduce the ER model concepts in the following section.

3.3 Entity Types, Entity Sets, Attributes, and Keys

The ER model describes data as entities, relationships, and attributes. In Section 3.3.1 we introduce the concepts of entities and their attributes. We discuss entity types and key attributes in Section 3.3.2. Then, in Section 3.3.3, we specify the initial conceptual design of the entity types for the COMPANY database. Relationships are described in Section 3.4.

3.3.1 Entities and Attributes

Entities and Their Attributes. The basic object that the ER model represents is an **entity,** which is a "thing" in the real world with an independent existence. An entity may be an object with a physical existence—a particular person, car, house, or employee—or it may be an object with a conceptual existence—a company, a job, or a university course. Each entity has **attributes**—the particular properties that describe it. For example, an employee entity may be described by the employee's name, age, address, salary, and job. A particular entity will have a **value** for each of its attributes. The attribute values that describe each entity become a major part of the data stored in the database.

Figure 3.3 shows two entities and the values of their attributes. The employee entity e_1 has four attributes: Name, Address, Age, and HomePhone; their values are "John Smith," "2311 Kirby, Houston, Texas 77001," "55," and "713-749-2630," respectively. The company entity c_1 has three attributes: Name, Headquarters, and President; their values are "Sunco Oil," "Houston," and "John Smith," respectively.

Several types of attributes occur in the ER model: *simple* versus *composite; single-valued* versus *multivalued;* and *stored* versus *derived.* We first define these attribute types and illustrate their use via examples. We then introduce the concept of a *null value* for an attribute.

---

1. The social security number, or SSN, is a unique 9-digit identifier assigned to each individual in the United States to keep track of their employment, benefits, and taxes. Other countries may have similar identification schemes, such as personal identification card numbers.

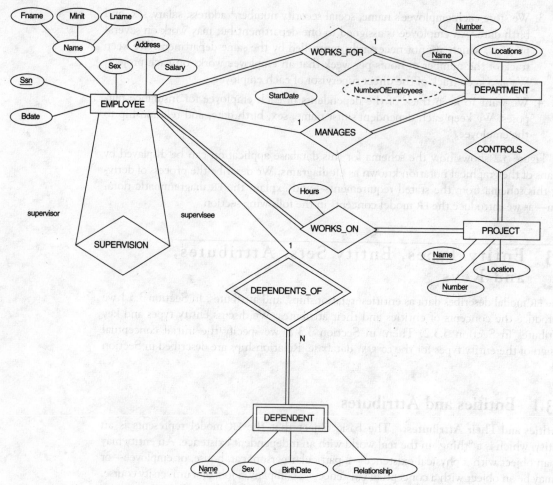

Figure 3.2   ER schema diagram for the COMPANY database.

Composite Versus Simple (Atomic) Attributes.   **Composite attributes** can be divided into smaller subparts, which represent more basic attributes with independent meanings. For example, the Address attribute of the employee entity shown in Figure 3.3 can be subdivided into StreetAddress, City, State, and Zip,[2] with the values "2311 Kirby," "Houston," "Texas," and "77001." Attributes that are not divisible are called **simple** or **atomic attributes.** Composite attributes can form a hierarchy; for example, StreetAddress can be subdivided into three simple attributes, Number, Street, and ApartmentNumber, as shown in Figure 3.4. The value of a composite attribute is the concatenation of the values of its constituent simple attributes.

---

2. The zip code is the name used in the United States for a postal code.

Figure 3.3   Two entities, an employee e_1 and a company c_1, and their attribute values.

Composite attributes are useful to model situations in which a user sometimes refers to the composite attribute as a unit but at other times refers specifically to its components. If the composite attribute is referenced only as a whole, there is no need to subdivide it into component attributes. For example, if there is no need to refer to the individual components of an address (Zip, Street, and so on), then the whole address is designated as a simple attribute.

Single-valued Versus Multivalued Attributes.   Most attributes have a single value for a particular entity; such attributes are called **single-valued.** For example, Age is a single-valued attribute of person. In some cases an attribute can have a set of values for the same entity—for example, a Colors attribute for a car, or a CollegeDegrees attribute for a person. Cars with one color have a single value, whereas two-tone cars have two values for Colors. Similarly, one person may not have a college degree, another person may have one, and a third person may have two or more degrees; so different persons can have

Figure 3.4   A hierarchy of composite attributes; the StreetAddress component of an Address is further composed of Number, Street, and Apart-mentNumber.

different *numbers of values* for the CollegeDegrees attribute. Such attributes are called **multivalued.** A multivalued attribute may have lower and upper bounds on the number of values allowed for each individual entity. For example, the Colors attribute of a car may have between one and three values, if we assume that a car can have at most three colors.

Stored Versus Derived Attributes.   In some cases two (or more) attribute values are related—for example, the Age and BirthDate attributes of a person. For a particular person entity, the value of Age can be determined from the current (today's) date and the value of that person's BirthDate. The Age attribute is hence called a **derived attribute** and is said to be **derivable from** the BirthDate attribute, which is called a **stored attribute.** Some attribute values can be derived from *related entities*; for example, an attribute NumberOfEmployees of a department entity can be derived by counting the number of employees related to (working for) that department.

Null Values.   In some cases a particular entity may not have an applicable value for an attribute. For example, the ApartmentNumber attribute of an address applies only to addresses that are in apartment buildings and not to other types of residences, such as single-family homes. Similarly, a CollegeDegrees attribute applies only to persons with college degrees. For such situations, a special value called **null** is created. An address of a single-family home would have null for its ApartmentNumber attribute, and a person with no college degree would have null for CollegeDegrees. Null can also be used if we do not know the value of an attribute for a particular entity—for example, if we do not know the home phone of "John Smith" in Figure 3.3. The meaning of the former type of null is *not applicable*, whereas the meaning of the latter is *unknown*. The unknown category of null can be further classified into two cases. The first case arises when it is known that the attribute value exists but is *missing*—for example, if the Height attribute of a person is listed as null. The second case arises when it is *not known* whether the attribute value exists—for example, if the HomePhone attribute of a person is null.

Complex Attributes.   Notice that composite and multivalued attributes can be nested in an arbitrary way. We can represent arbitrary nesting by grouping components of a composite attribute between parentheses ( ) and separating the components with commas, and by displaying multivalued attributes between braces {}. Such attributes are called **complex attributes.** For example, if a person can have more than one residence and each residence can have multiple phones, an attribute AddressPhone for a PERSON entity type can be specified as shown in Figure 3.5.

{AddressPhone({Phone(AreaCode, PhoneNumber)},
Address(StreetAddress(Number, Street, ApartmentNumber),City, State, Zip)) }

Figure 3.5   A complex attribute AddressPhone with multivalued and composite components.

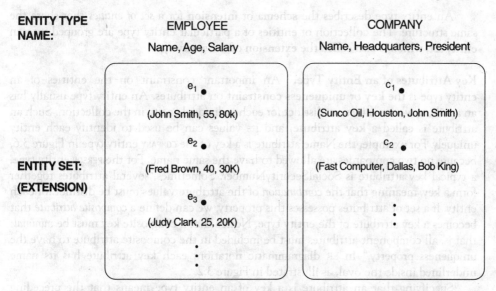

ENTITY TYPE NAME:

EMPLOYEE
Name, Age, Salary

COMPANY
Name, Headquarters, President

ENTITY SET:
(EXTENSION)

e_1 •
(John Smith, 55, 80k)

e_2 •
(Fred Brown, 40, 30K)

e_3 •
(Judy Clark, 25, 20K)

c_1 •
(Sunco Oil, Houston, John Smith)

c_2 •
(Fast Computer, Dallas, Bob King)

Figure 3.6 Two entity types named EMPLOYEE and COMPANY, and some of the member entities in the collection of entities (or entity set) of each type.

3.3.2 Entity Types, Entity Sets, Keys, and Value Sets

Entity Types and Entity Sets. A database usually contains groups of entities that are similar. For example, a company employing hundreds of employees may want to store similar information concerning each of the employees. These employee entities share the same attributes, but each entity has *its own value(s)* for each attribute. An **entity type** defines a *collection* (or *set*) of entities that have the same attributes. Each entity type in the database is described by its name and attributes. Figure 3.6 shows two entity types, named EMPLOYEE and COMPANY, and a list of attributes for each. A few individual entities of each type are also illustrated, along with the values of their attributes. The collection of all entities of a particular entity type in the database at any point in time is called an **entity set;** the entity set is usually referred to using the same name as the entity type. For example, EMPLOYEE refers to both a *type of entity* as well as the current *set of all employee entities* in the database.

An entity type is represented in ER diagrams[3] (see Figure 3.2) as a rectangular box enclosing the entity type name. Attribute names are enclosed in ovals and are attached to their entity type by straight lines. Composite attributes are attached to their component attributes by straight lines. Multivalued attributes are displayed in double ovals.

---

3. We are using a notation for ER diagrams that is close to the original proposed notation (Chen 1976). Unfortunately, many other notations are in use. We illustrate some of the other notations in Appendix A and later in this chapter.

An entity type describes the **schema** or **intension** for a *set of entities* that share the same structure. The collection of entities of a particular entity type are grouped into an entity set, which is also called the **extension** of the entity type.

Key Attributes of an Entity Type.   An important constraint on the entities of an entity type is the **key** or **uniqueness constraint** on attributes. An entity type usually has an attribute whose values are distinct for each individual entity in the collection. Such an attribute is called a **key attribute,** and its values can be used to identify each entity uniquely. For example, the Name attribute is a key of the COMPANY entity type in Figure 3.6, because no two companies are allowed to have the same name. For the PERSON entity type, a typical key attribute is SocialSecurityNumber. Sometimes, several attributes together form a key, meaning that the *combination* of the attribute values must be distinct for each entity. If a set of attributes possesses this property, we can define a *composite attribute* that becomes a key attribute of the entity type. Notice that a composite key must be *minimal*; that is, all component attributes must be included in the composite attribute to have the uniqueness property.[4] In ER diagrammatic notation, each key attribute has its name **underlined** inside the oval, as illustrated in Figure 3.2.

Specifying that an attribute is a key of an entity type means that the preceding uniqueness property must hold for *every extension* of the entity type. Hence, it is a constraint that prohibits any two entities from having the same value for the key attribute at the same time. It is not the property of a particular extension; rather, it is a constraint on *all extensions* of the entity type. This key constraint (and other constraints we discuss later) is derived from the constraints of the miniworld that the database represents.

Some entity types have *more than one* key attribute. For example, each of the VehicleID and Registration attributes of the entity type CAR (Figure 3.7) is a key in its own right. The Registration attribute is an example of a composite key formed from two simple component attributes, RegistrationNumber and State, neither of which is a key on its own. An entity type may also have *no key*, in which case it is called a *weak entity type* (see Section 3.5).

Value Sets (Domains) of Attributes.   Each simple attribute of an entity type is associated with a **value set** (or **domain** of values), which specifies the set of values that may be assigned to that attribute for each individual entity. In Figure 3.6, if the range of ages allowed for employees is between 16 and 70, we can specify the value set of the Age attribute of EMPLOYEE to be the set of integer numbers between 16 and 70. Similarly, we can specify the value set for the Name attribute as being the set of strings of alphabetic characters separated by blank characters and so on. Value sets are not displayed in ER diagrams.

Mathematically, an attribute A of entity type E whose value set is V can be defined as a **function** from E to the power set[5] $P(V)$ of V:

$$A : E \rightarrow P(V)$$

---

4. Superfluous attributes must not be included in a key; however, a **superkey** may include superfluous attributes, as we explain in Chapter 7.

5. The **power set** $P(V)$ of a set V is the set of all subsets of V.

CAR
Registration(RegistrationNumber, State), VehicleID, Make, Model, Year, {Color}

car$_1$ •

((ABC 123, TEXAS), TK629, Ford Mustang, convertible, 1998, {red, black})

car$_2$ •

((ABC 123, NEW YORK), WP9872, Nissan Maxima, 4-door, 1999, {blue})

car$_3$ •

((VSY 720, TEXAS), TD729, Chrysler LeBaron, 4-door, 1995, {white, blue})

⋮

Figure 3.7 The CAR entity type, with two key attributes Registration and VehicleID. Multivalued attributes are shown between set braces {}. Components of a composite attribute are shown between parentheses ().

We refer to the value of attribute A for entity e as $A(e)$. The previous definition covers both single-valued and multivalued attributes, as well as nulls. A null value is represented by the empty set. For single-valued attributes, $A(e)$ is restricted to being a singleton for each entity e in E whereas there is no restriction on multivalued attributes.[6] For a composite attribute A, the value set V is the Cartesian product of $P(V_1), P(V_2), \ldots, P(V_n)$, where $V_1, V_2, \ldots, V_n$ are the value sets of the simple component attributes that form A:

$$V = P(V_1) \times P(V_2) \times \ldots \times P(V_n)$$

3.3.3 Initial Conceptual Design of the COMPANY Database

We can now define the entity types for the COMPANY database, based on the requirements described in Section 3.2. After defining several entity types and their attributes here, we *refine* our design in Section 3.4 (after introducing the concept of a relationship). According to the requirements listed in Section 3.2, we can identify four entity types—one corresponding to each of the four items in the specification (see Figure 3.8):

1. An entity type DEPARTMENT with attributes Name, Number, Locations, Manager, and ManagerStartDate. Locations is the only multivalued attribute. We can specify that both Name and Number are (separate) key attributes, because each was specified to be unique.

---

6. A **singleton** is a set with only one element (value).

DEPARTMENT
Name, Number, {Locations}, Manager, ManagerStartDate

PROJECT
Name, Number, Location, ControllingDepartment

EMPLOYEE
Name (FName, MInit, LName), SSN, Sex, Address, Salary,
BirthDate, Department, Supervisor, {WorksOn (Project, Hours)}

DEPENDENT
Employee, DependentName, Sex, BirthDate, Relationship

Figure 3.8 Preliminary design of entity types for the COMPANY
database whose requirements are described in
Section 3.2.

2. An entity type PROJECT with attributes Name, Number, Location, and ControllingDepartment. Both Name and Number are (separate) key attributes.

3. An entity type EMPLOYEE with attributes Name, SSN (for social security number), Sex, Address, Salary, BirthDate, Department, and Supervisor. Both Name and Address may be composite attributes; however, this was not specified in the requirements. We must go back to the users to see if any of them will refer to the individual components of Name—FirstName, MiddleInitial, LastName—or of Address.

4. An entity type DEPENDENT with attributes Employee, DependentName, Sex, BirthDate, and Relationship (to the employee).

So far, we have not represented the fact that an employee can work on several projects, nor have we represented the number of hours per week an employee works on each project. This characteristic is listed as part of requirement 3 in Section 3.2, and it can be represented by a multivalued composite attribute of EMPLOYEE called WorksOn with simple components (Project, Hours). Alternatively, it can be represented as a multivalued composite attribute of PROJECT called Workers with simple components (Employee, Hours). We choose the first alternative in Figure 3.8, which shows each of the entity types described above. The Name attribute of EMPLOYEE is shown as a composite attribute, presumably after consultation with the users.

3.4 Relationships, Relationship Types, Roles, and Structural Constraints

In Figure 3.8 there are several *implicit relationships* among the various entity types. In fact, whenever an attribute of one entity type refers to another entity type, some relationship exists. For example, the attribute Manager of DEPARTMENT refers to an employee who manages the department; the attribute ControllingDepartment of PROJECT refers to the department that controls the project; the attribute Supervisor of EMPLOYEE refers to another employee (the one who supervises this employee); the attribute Department of EMPLOYEE refers to the department for which the employee works; and so on. In the ER model, these references should not be represented as attributes but as **relationships,** which are discussed in this section. The COMPANY database schema will be refined in Section 3.6 to represent relationships explicitly. In the initial design of entity types, relationships are typically captured in the form of attributes. As the design is refined, these attributes get converted into relationships between entity types.

This section is organized as follows. Section 3.4.1 introduces the concepts of relationship types, sets, and instances. Section 3.4.2 defines the concepts of relationship degree, role names, and recursive relationships. Section 3.4.3 discusses structural constraints on relationships, such as cardinality ratios (1:1, 1:N, M:N) and existence dependencies. Section 3.4.4 shows how relationship types can also have attributes.

3.4.1 Relationship Types, Sets and Instances

A **relationship type** R among n entity types $E_1, E_2, \ldots, E_n$ defines a set of associations—or a **relationship set**—among entities from these types. As for entity types and entity sets, a relationship type and its corresponding relationship set are customarily referred to by the *same name* R. Mathematically, the relationship set R is a set of **relationship instances** r_i, where each r_i associates n individual entities $(e_1, e_2, \ldots, e_n)$, and each entity e_j in r_i is a member of entity type E_j, $1 \leq j \leq n$. Hence, a relationship type is a mathematical relation on $E_1, E_2, \ldots, E_n$, or alternatively it can be defined as a subset of the Cartesian product $E_1 \times E_2 \times \ldots \times E_n$. Each of the entity types $E_1, E_2, \ldots, E_n$ is said to **participate** in the relationship type R, and similarly each of the individual entities $e_1, e_2, \ldots, e_n$ is said to participate in the relationship instance $r_i = (e_1, e_2, \ldots, e_n)$.

Informally, each relationship instance r_i in R is an association of entities, where the association includes exactly one entity from each participating entity type. Each such relationship instance r_i represents the fact that the entities participating in r_i are related in some way in the corresponding miniworld situation. For example, consider a relationship type WORKS_FOR between the two entity types EMPLOYEE and DEPARTMENT, which associates each employee with the department the employee works for. Each relationship instance in the relationship set WORKS_FOR associates one employee entity and one department entity. Figure 3.9 illustrates this example, where each relationship instance r_i is shown connected to the employee and department entities that participate in r_i. In the miniworld represented by Figure 3.9, employees e_1, e_3, and e_6 work for department d_1; e_2 and e_4 work for d_2; and e_5 and e_7 work for d_3.

In ER diagrams, relationship types are displayed as diamond-shaped boxes, which are connected by straight lines to the rectangular boxes representing the participating entity types. The relationship name is displayed in the diamond-shaped box (see Figure 3.2).

3.4.2 Relationship Degree, Role Names, and Recursive Relationships

Degree of a Relationship Type. The **degree** of a relationship type is the number of participating entity types. Hence, the WORKS_FOR relationship is of degree two. A relationship type of degree two is called **binary,** and one of degree three is called **ternary.**

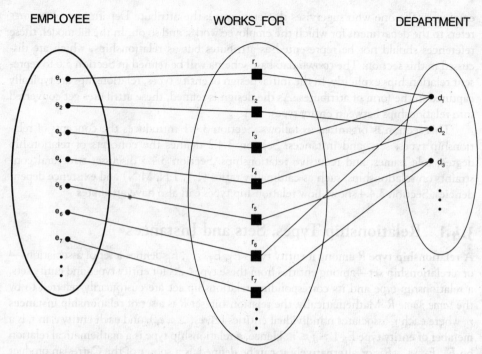

Figure 3.9   Some instances of the WORKS_FOR relationship between EMPLOYEE and
DEPARTMENT.

An example of a ternary relationship is SUPPLY, shown in Figure 3.10, where each relationship instance r_i associates three entities—a supplier s, a part p, and a project j—
whenever s supplies part p to project j. Relationships can generally be of any degree, but
the ones most common are binary relationships. Higher-degree relationships are generally more complex than binary relationships, and we shall characterize them further in
Chapter 4.

Relationships as Attributes.   It is sometimes convenient to think of a relationship type
in terms of attributes, as we discussed in Section 3.3.3. Consider the WORKS_FOR relationship
type of Figure 3.9. One can think of an attribute called Department of the EMPLOYEE entity
type whose value for each employee entity is (a reference to) the *department entity* that
the employee works for. Hence, the value set for this Department attribute is the *set of all
DEPARTMENT entities*. This is what we did in Figure 3.8 when we specified the initial design of
the entity type EMPLOYEE for the COMPANY database. However, when we think of a binary relationship as an attribute, we always have two options. In this example, the alternative is to
think of a multivalued attribute Employees of the entity type DEPARTMENT whose values for
each department entity is the *set of employee entities* who work for that department. The
value set of this Employees attribute is the EMPLOYEE entity set. Either of these two

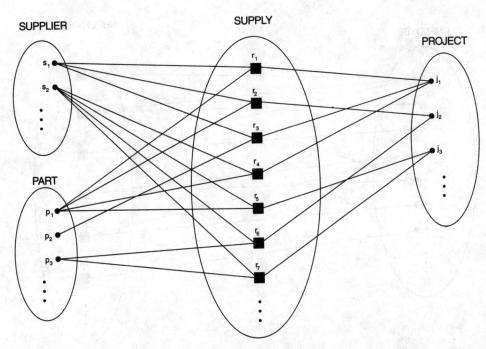

Figure 3.10   Some relationship instances of a ternary relationship SUPPLY.

attributes—Department of EMPLOYEE or Employees of DEPARTMENT—can represent the WORKS_FOR relationship type. If both are represented, they are constrained to be inverses of each other.[7]

Role Names and Recursive Relationships.   Each entity type that participates in a relationship type plays a particular **role** in the relationship. The **role name** signifies the role that a participating entity from the entity type plays in each relationship instance, and helps to explain what the relationship means. For example, in the WORKS_FOR relationship type, EMPLOYEE plays the role of *employee* or *worker* and DEPARTMENT plays the role of *department* or *employer*.

Role names are not technically necessary in relationship types where all the participating entity types are distinct, since each entity type name can be used as the role name. However, in some cases the *same* entity type participates more than once in a relationship type in *different roles*. In such cases the role name becomes essential for

---

7. This concept of representing relationship types as attributes is used in a class of data models called **functional data models.** In object databases (see Chapters 11 and 12), relationships can be represented by reference attributes, either in one direction or in both directions as inverses. In relational databases (see Chapters 7 and 8), foreign keys are a type of reference attribute used to represent relationships.

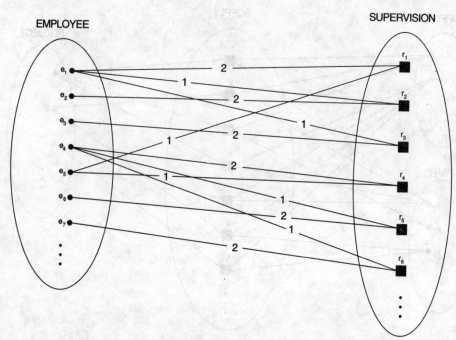

Figure 3.11   The recursive relationship SUPERVISION, where the EMPLOYEE entity type plays the two roles of supervisor (1) and supervisee (2).

distinguishing the meaning of each participation. Such relationship types are called **recursive relationships,** and Figure 3.11 shows an example. The SUPERVISION relationship type relates an employee to a supervisor, where both employee and supervisor entities are members of the same EMPLOYEE entity type. Hence, the EMPLOYEE entity type *participates twice* in SUPERVISION: once in the role of *supervisor* (or boss), and once in the role of *supervisee* (or subordinate). Each relationship instance r_i in SUPERVISION associates two employee entities e_j and e_k, one of which plays the role of supervisor and the other the role of supervisee. In Figure 3.11, the lines marked "1" represent the supervisor role, and those marked "2" represent the supervisee role; hence, e_1 supervises e_2 and e_3; e_4 supervises e_6 and e_7; and e_5 supervises e_1 and e_4.

3.4.3   Constraints on Relationship Types

Relationship types usually have certain constraints that limit the possible combinations of entities that may participate in the corresponding relationship set. These constraints are determined from the miniworld situation that the relationships represent. For example, in Figure 3.9, if the company has a rule that each employee must work for exactly one department, then we would like to describe this constraint in the schema. We can distinguish two main types of relationship constraints: *cardinality ratio* and *participation*.

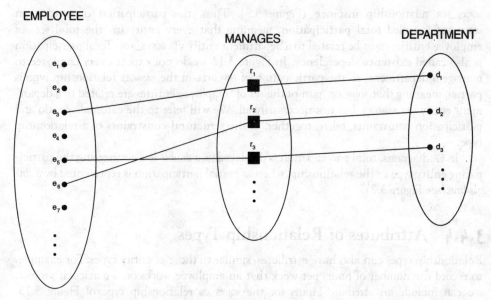

Figure 3.12   The 1:1 relationship MANAGES, with partial participation of EMPLOYEE and total participation of DEPARTMENT.

Cardinality Ratios for Binary Relationships.   The **cardinality ratio** for a binary relationship specifies the number of relationship instances that an entity can participate in. For example, in the WORKS_FOR binary relationship type, DEPARTMENT:EMPLOYEE is of cardinality ratio 1:N, meaning that each department can be related to (that is, employs) numerous employees,[8] but an employee can be related to (work for) only one department. The possible cardinality ratios for binary relationship types are 1:1, 1:N, N:1, and M:N.

An example of a 1:1 binary relationship is MANAGES (Figure 3.12), which relates a department entity to the employee who manages that department. This represents the miniworld constraints that an employee can manage only one department and that a department has only one manager. The relationship type WORKS_ON (Figure 3.13) is of cardinality ratio M:N, because the miniworld rule is that an employee can work on several projects and a project can have several employees.

Cardinality ratios for binary relationships are displayed on ER diagrams by displaying 1, M, and N on the diamonds as shown in Figure 3.2.

Participation Constraints and Existence Dependencies.   The **participation constraint** specifies whether the existence of an entity depends on its being related to another entity via the relationship type. There are two types of participation constraints—total and partial—which we illustrate by example. If a company policy states that *every* employee must work for a department, then an employee entity can exist only if it participates in a

---

8. N stands for *any number* of related entities (zero or more).

WORKS_FOR relationship instance (Figure 3.9). Thus, the participation of EMPLOYEE in WORKS_FOR is called **total participation,** meaning that every entity in "the total set" of employee entities must be related to a department entity via WORKS_FOR. Total participation is also called **existence dependency.** In Figure 3.12 we do not expect every employee to manage a department, so the participation of EMPLOYEE in the MANAGES relationship type is **partial,** meaning that *some* or "part of the set of" employee entities are related to a department entity via MANAGES, but not necessarily all. We will refer to the cardinality ratio and participation constraints, taken together, as the **structural constraints** of a relationship type.

In ER diagrams, total participation is displayed as a *double line* connecting the participating entity type to the relationship, whereas partial participation is represented by a *single line* (see Figure 3.2).

3.4.4 Attributes of Relationship Types

Relationship types can also have attributes, similar to those of entity types. For example, to record the number of hours per week that an employee works on a particular project, we can include an attribute Hours for the WORKS_ON relationship type of Figure 3.13. Another example is to include the date on which a manager started managing a department via an attribute StartDate for the MANAGES relationship type of Figure 3.12.

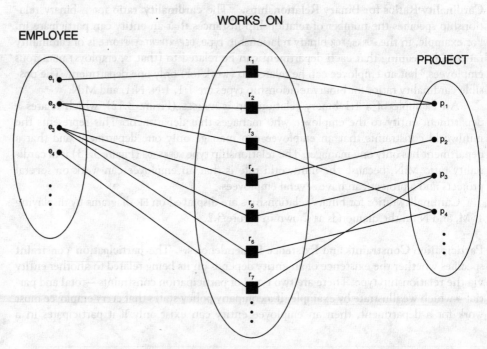

Figure 3.13   The M:N relationship WORKS_ON between EMPLOYEE and PROJECT.

Notice that attributes of 1:1 or 1:N relationship types can be migrated to one of the participating entity types. For example, the StartDate attribute for the MANAGES relationship can be an attribute of either EMPLOYEE or DEPARTMENT—although conceptually it belongs to MANAGES. This is because MANAGES is a 1:1 relationship, so every department or employee entity participates in *at most one* relationship instance. Hence, the value of the StartDate attribute can be determined separately, either by the participating department entity or by the participating employee (manager) entity.

For a 1:N relationship type, a relationship attribute can be migrated *only* to the entity type at the N-side of the relationship. For example, in Figure 3.9, if the WORKS_FOR relationship also has an attribute StartDate that indicates when an employee started working for a department, this attribute can be included as an attribute of EMPLOYEE. This is because each employee entity participates in at most one relationship instance in WORKS_FOR. In both 1:1 and 1:N relationship types, the decision as to where a relationship attribute should be placed—as a relationship type attribute or as an attribute of a participating entity type—is determined subjectively by the schema designer.

For M:N relationship types, some attributes may be determined by the *combination of participating entities* in a relationship instance, not by any single entity. Such attributes *must be specified as relationship attributes*. An example is the Hours attribute of the M:N relationship WORKS_ON (Figure 3.13); the number of hours an employee works on a project is determined by an employee-project combination and not separately by either entity.

3.5   Weak Entity Types

Entity types that do not have key attributes of their own are called **weak entity types.** In contrast, **regular entity types** that do have a key attribute are sometimes called **strong entity types.** Entities belonging to a weak entity type are identified by being related to specific entities from another entity type in combination with some of their attribute values. We call this other entity type the **identifying** or **owner entity type,**[9] and we call the relationship type that relates a weak entity type to its owner the **identifying relationship** of the weak entity type.[10] A weak entity type always has a *total participation constraint* (existence dependency) with respect to its identifying relationship, because a weak entity cannot be identified without an owner entity. However, not every existence dependency results in a weak entity type. For example, a DRIVER_LICENSE entity cannot exist unless it is related to a PERSON entity, even though it has its own key (LicenseNumber) and hence is not a weak entity.

Consider the entity type DEPENDENT, related to EMPLOYEE, which is used to keep track of the dependents of each employee via a 1:N relationship (Figure 3.2). The attributes of DEPENDENT are Name (the first name of the dependent), BirthDate, Sex, and Relationship

---

9. The identifying entity type is also sometimes called the **parent entity type** or the **dominant entity type.**

10. The weak entity type is also sometimes called the **child entity type** or the **subordinate entity type.**

(to the employee). Two dependents of *two distinct employees* may, by chance, have the same values for Name, BirthDate, Sex, and Relationship, but they are still distinct entities. They are identified as distinct entities only after determining the *particular employee entity* to which each dependent is related. Each employee entity is said to **own** the dependent entities that are related to it.

A weak entity type normally has a **partial key,** which is the set of attributes that can uniquely identify weak entities that are *related to the same owner entity.*[11] In our example, if we assume that no two dependents of the same employee ever have the same first name, the attribute Name of DEPENDENT is the partial key. In the worst case, a composite attribute of *all the weak entity's attributes* will be the partial key.

In ER diagrams, both a weak entity type and its identifying relationship are distinguished by surrounding their boxes and diamonds with *double lines* (see Figure 3.2). The partial key attribute is underlined with a dashed or dotted line.

Weak entity types can sometimes be represented as complex (composite, multivalued) attributes. In the preceding example, we could specify a multivalued attribute Dependents for EMPLOYEE, which is a composite attribute with component attributes Name, BirthDate, Sex, and Relationship. The choice of which representation to use is made by the database designer. One criterion that may be used is to choose the weak entity type representation if there are many attributes. If the weak entity participates independently in relationship types other than its identifying relationship type, then it should *not* be modeled as a complex attribute.

In general, any number of levels of weak entity types can be defined; an owner entity type may itself be a weak entity type. In addition, a weak entity type may have more than one identifying entity type and an identifying relationship type of degree higher than two, as we shall illustrate in Chapter 4.

3.6 Refining the ER Design for the COMPANY Database

We can now refine the database design of Figure 3.8 by changing the attributes that represent relationships into relationship types. The cardinality ratio and participation constraint of each relationship type are determined from the requirements listed in Section 3.2. If some cardinality ratio or dependency cannot be determined from the requirements, the users must be questioned to determine these structural constraints.

In our example, we specify the following relationship types:

1. MANAGES, a 1:1 relationship type between EMPLOYEE and DEPARTMENT. EMPLOYEE participation is partial. DEPARTMENT participation is not clear from the requirements. We question the users, who say that a department must have a manager at all times, which implies total participation.[12] The attribute StartDate is assigned to this relationship type.

---

11. The partial key is sometimes called the **discriminator.**

12. The rules in the miniworld that determine the constraints are sometimes called the *business rules*, since they are determined by the "business" or organization that will utilize the database.

2. WORKS_FOR, a 1:N relationship type between DEPARTMENT and EMPLOYEE. Both participations are total.

3. CONTROLS, a 1:N relationship type between DEPARTMENT and PROJECT. The participation of PROJECT is total, whereas that of DEPARTMENT is determined to be partial, after consultation with the users.

4. SUPERVISION, a 1:N relationship type between EMPLOYEE (in the supervisor role) and EMPLOYEE (in the supervisee role). Both participations are determined to be partial, after the users indicate that not every employee is a supervisor and not every employee has a supervisor.

5. WORKS_ON, determined to be an M:N relationship type with attribute Hours, after the users indicate that a project can have several employees working on it. Both participations are determined to be total.

6. DEPENDENTS_OF, a 1:N relationship type between EMPLOYEE and DEPENDENT, which is also the identifying relationship for the weak entity type DEPENDENT. The participation of EMPLOYEE is partial, whereas that of DEPENDENT is total.

After specifying the above six relationship types, we remove from the entity types in Figure 3.8 all attributes that have been refined into relationships. These include Manager and ManagerStartDate from DEPARTMENT; ControllingDepartment from PROJECT; Department, Supervisor, and WorksOn from EMPLOYEE; and Employee from DEPENDENT. It is important to have the least possible redundancy when we design the conceptual schema of a database. If some redundancy is desired at the storage level or at the user view level, it can be introduced later, as discussed in Section 1.6.1.

3.7   ER Diagrams, Naming Conventions, and Design Issues

3.7.1   Summary of Notation for ER Diagrams

Figures 3.9 through 3.13 illustrate the entity types and relationship types by displaying their extensions—the individual entities and relationship instances. In ER diagrams the emphasis is on representing the schemas rather than the instances. This is more useful because a database schema changes rarely, whereas the extension changes frequently. In addition, the schema is usually easier to display than the extension of a database, because it is much smaller.

Figure 3.2 displays the COMPANY ER **database schema** as an ER diagram. We now review the full ER diagrams notation. Entity types such as EMPLOYEE, DEPARTMENT, and PROJECT are shown in rectangular boxes. Relationship types such as WORKS_FOR, MANAGES, CONTROLS, and WORKS_ON are shown in diamond-shaped boxes attached to the participating entity types with straight lines. Attributes are shown in ovals, and each attribute is attached by a straight line to its entity type or relationship type. Component attributes of a composite attribute are attached to the oval representing the composite attribute, as illustrated by the Name attribute of EMPLOYEE. Multivalued attributes are shown in double ovals, as illustrated by the Locations attribute of DEPARTMENT. Key attributes have their names under-lined. Derived attributes are shown in dotted ovals, as illustrated by the NumberOfEm-ployees attribute of DEPARTMENT.

Weak entity types are distinguished by being placed in double rectangles and by having their identifying relationship placed in double diamonds, as illustrated by the DEPENDENT entity type and the DEPENDENTS_OF identifying relationship type. The partial key of the weak entity type is underlined with a dotted line.

In Figure 3.2 the cardinality ratio of each *binary* relationship type is specified by attaching a 1, M, or N on each participating edge. The cardinality ratio of DEPART-MENT : EMPLOYEE in MANAGES is 1:1, whereas it is 1:N for DEPARTMENT : EMPLOYEE in WORKS_FOR, and it is M:N for WORKS_ON. The participation constraint is specified by a single line for partial participation and by double lines for total participation (existence depen-dency).

In Figure 3.2 we show the role names for the SUPERVISION relationship type because the EMPLOYEE entity type plays both roles in that relationship. Notice that the cardinality is 1:N from supervisor to supervisee because, on the one hand, each employee in the role of supervisee has at most one direct supervisor, whereas an employee in the role of supervisor can supervise zero or more employees.

Figure 3.14 summarizes the conventions for ER diagrams.

3.7.2 Proper Naming of Schema Constructs

The choice of names for entity types, attributes, relationship types, and (particularly) roles is not always straightforward. One should choose names that convey, as much as possible, the meanings attached to the different constructs in the schema. We choose to use *singular names* for entity types, rather than plural ones, because the entity type name applies to each individual entity belonging to that entity type. In our ER diagrams, we will use the convention that entity type and relationship type names are in uppercase letters, attribute names are capitalized, and role names are in lowercase letters. We have already used this convention in Figure 3.2.

As a general practice, given a narrative description of the database requirements, the *nouns* appearing in the narrative tend to give rise to entity type names, and the *verbs* tend to indicate names of relationship types. Attribute names generally arise from additional nouns that describe the nouns corresponding to entity types.

Another naming consideration involves choosing relationship names to make the ER diagram of the schema readable from left to right and from top to bottom. We have generally followed this guideline in Figure 3.2. One exception is the DEPENDENTS_OF relationship type, which reads from bottom to top. This is because we say that the DEPENDENT entities (bottom entity type) are DEPENDENTS_OF (relationship name) an EMPLOYEE (top entity type). To change this to read from top to bottom, we could rename the relationship type to HAS_DEPENDENTS, which would then read: an EMPLOYEE entity (top entity type) HAS_DEPENDENTS (relationship name) of type DEPENDENT (bottom entity type).

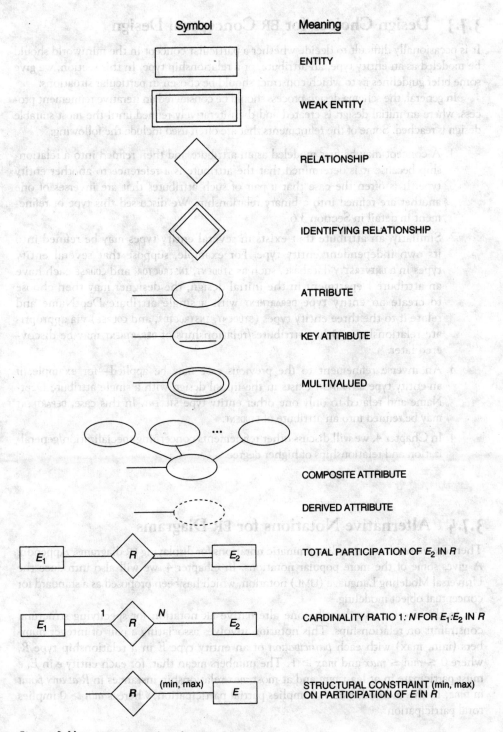

Symbol	Meaning
ENTITY	
WEAK ENTITY	
RELATIONSHIP	
IDENTIFYING RELATIONSHIP	
ATTRIBUTE	
KEY ATTRIBUTE	
MULTIVALUED	
COMPOSITE ATTRIBUTE	
DERIVED ATTRIBUTE	
TOTAL PARTICIPATION OF E_2 IN R	
CARDINALITY RATIO 1: N FOR E_1:E_2 IN R	
STRUCTURAL CONSTRAINT (min, max) ON PARTICIPATION OF E IN R	

Figure 3.14   Summary of ER diagram notation.

3.7.3 Design Choices for ER Conceptual Design

It is occasionally difficult to decide whether a particular concept in the miniworld should be modeled as an entity type, an attribute, or a relationship type. In this section, we give some brief guidelines as to which construct should be chosen in particular situations.

In general, the schema design process should be considered an iterative refinement process, where an initial design is created and then iteratively refined until the most suitable design is reached. Some of the refinements that are often used include the following:

1. A concept may be first modeled as an attribute and then refined into a relationship because it is determined that the attribute is a reference to another entity type. It is often the case that a pair of such attributes that are inverses of one another are refined into a binary relationship. We discussed this type of refinement in detail in Section 3.6.

2. Similarly, an attribute that exists in several entity types may be refined into its own independent entity type. For example, suppose that several entity types in a UNIVERSITY database, such as STUDENT, INSTRUCTOR, and COURSE each have an attribute Department in the initial design; the designer may then choose to create an entity type DEPARTMENT with a single attribute DeptName and relate it to the three entity types (STUDENT, INSTRUCTOR, and COURSE) via appropriate relationships. Other attributes/relationships of DEPARTMENT may be discovered later.

3. An inverse refinement to the previous case may be applied—for example, if an entity type DEPARTMENT exists in the initial design with a single attribute DeptName and related to only one other entity type STUDENT. In this case, DEPARTMENT may be refined into an attribute of STUDENT.

4. In Chapter 4, we will discuss other refinements concerning specialization/generalization and relationships of higher degree.

3.7.4 Alternative Notations for ER Diagrams

There are many alternative diagrammatic notations for displaying ER diagrams. Appendix A gives some of the more popular notations. In Chapter 4, we will also introduce the Universal Modeling Language (UML) notation, which has been proposed as a standard for conceptual object modeling.

In this section, we describe one alternative ER notation for specifying structural constraints on relationships. This notation involves associating a pair of integer numbers (min, max) with each *participation* of an entity type E in a relationship type R, where $0 \leq min \leq max$ and $max \geq 1$. The numbers mean that, for each entity e in E, e must participate in at least min and at most max relationship instances in R at any point in time. In this method, $min = 0$ implies partial participation, whereas $min > 0$ implies total participation.

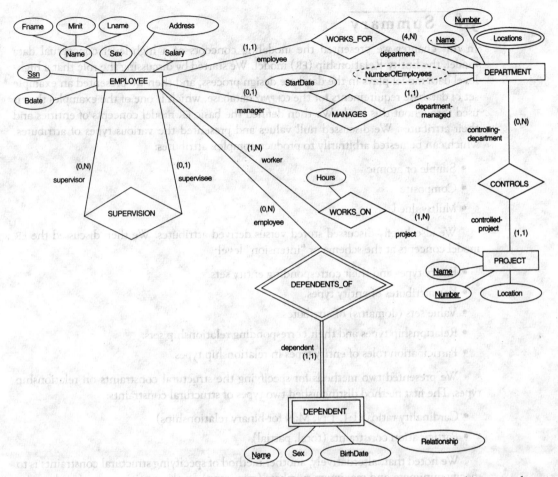

Figure 3.15 ER diagram for the COMPANY schema, with all role names included and with structural constraints on relationships specified using the alternate notation (min, max).

Figure 3.15 displays the COMPANY database schema using the (min, max) notation.[13] Usually, one uses either the cardinality ratio/single line/double line notation *or* the min/max notation. The min/max notation is more precise, and we can use it easily to specify structural constraints for relationship types of *any degree*. However, it is not sufficient for specifying some key constraints on higher degree relationships, as we shall discuss in Chapter 4.

Figure 3.15 also displays all the role names for the COMPANY database schema.

---

13. In some notations, particularly those used in object modeling, the placing of the (min, max) is on the *opposite sides* to the ones we have shown. For example, for the WORKS_FOR relationship in Figure 3.15, the (1,1) would be on the DEPARTMENT side and the (4,N) would be on the EMPLOYEE side. We used the original notation from Abrial (1974).

3.8 Summary

In this chapter we presented the modeling concepts of a high-level conceptual data model, the Entity-Relationship (ER) model. We started by discussing the role that a high-level data model plays in the database design process, and then we presented an example set of database requirements for the COMPANY database, which is one of the examples that is used throughout this book. We then defined the basic ER model concepts of entities and their attributes. We discussed null values and presented the various types of attributes, which can be nested arbitrarily to produce complex attributes:

- Simple or atomic
- Composite
- Multivalued

We also briefly discussed stored versus derived attributes. We then discussed the ER model concepts at the schema or "intension" level:

- Entity types and their corresponding entity sets.
- Key attributes of entity types.
- Value sets (domains) of attributes.
- Relationship types and their corresponding relationship sets.
- Participation roles of entity types in relationship types.

We presented two methods for specifying the structural constraints on relationship types. The first method distinguished two types of structural constraints:

- Cardinality ratios (1:1, 1:N, M:N for binary relationships)
- Participation constraints (total, partial)

We noted that, alternatively, another method of specifying structural constraints is to specify minimum and maximum numbers (min, max) on the participation of each entity type in a relationship type. We discussed weak entity types and the related concepts of owner entity types, identifying relationship types, and partial key attributes.

Entity-Relationship schemas can be represented diagrammatically as ER diagrams. We showed how to design an ER schema for the COMPANY database by first defining the entity types and their attributes and then refining the design to include relationship types. We displayed the ER diagram for the COMPANY database schema.

The ER modeling concepts we have presented thus far—entity types, relationship types, attributes, keys, and structural constraints—can model traditional business data-processing database applications. However, many newer, more complex applications—such as engineering design, medical information systems, or telecommunications—require additional concepts if we want to model them with greater accuracy. We will discuss these advanced modeling concepts in Chapter 4. We will also describe ternary and higher-degree relationship types in more detail in Chapter 4, and discuss the circumstances under which they are distinguished from binary relationships.

Review Questions

3.1. Discuss the role of a high-level data model in the database design process.

3.2. List the various cases where use of a null value would be appropriate.

3.3. Define the following terms: *entity, attribute, attribute value, relationship instance, composite attribute, multivalued attribute, derived attribute, complex attribute, key attribute, value set (domain)*.

3.4. What is an entity type? What is an entity set? Explain the differences among an entity, an entity type, and an entity set.

3.5. Explain the difference between an attribute and a value set.

3.6. What is a relationship type? Explain the differences among a relationship instance, a relationship type, and a relationship set.

3.7. What is a participation role? When is it necessary to use role names in the description of relationship types?

3.8. Describe the two alternatives for specifying structural constraints on relationship types. What are the advantages and disadvantages of each?

3.9. Under what conditions can an attribute of a binary relationship type be migrated to become an attribute of one of the participating entity types?

3.10. When we think of relationships as attributes, what are the value sets of these attributes? What class of data models is based on this concept?

3.11. What is meant by a recursive relationship type? Give some examples of recursive relationship types.

3.12. When is the concept of a weak entity used in data modeling? Define the terms *owner entity type, weak entity type, identifying relationship type*, and *partial key*.

3.13. Can an identifying relationship of a weak entity type be of a degree greater than two? Give examples to illustrate your answer.

3.14. Discuss the conventions for displaying an ER schema as an ER diagram.

3.15. Discuss the naming conventions used for ER schema diagrams.

Exercises

3.16. Consider the following set of requirements for a university database that is used to keep track of students' transcripts. This is similar but not identical to the database shown in Figure 1.2:

   a. The university keeps track of each student's name, student number, social security number, current address and phone, permanent address and phone, birthdate, sex, class (freshman, sophomore, . . ., graduate), major department, minor department (if any), and degree program (B.A., B.S., . . ., Ph.D.). Some user applications need to refer to the city, state, and zip code of the student's permanent address and to the student's last name. Both social security number and student number have unique values for each student.

   b. Each department is described by a name, department code, office number, office phone, and college. Both name and code have unique values for each department.

c. Each course has a course name, description, course number, number of semester hours, level, and offering department. The value of course number is unique for each course.

d. Each section has an instructor, semester, year, course, and section number. The section number distinguishes sections of the same course that are taught during the same semester/year; its values are 1, 2, 3, . . ., up to the number of sections taught during each semester.

e. A grade report has a student, section, letter grade, and numeric grade (0, 1, 2, 3, or 4).

Design an ER schema for this application, and draw an ER diagram for that schema. Specify key attributes of each entity type and structural constraints on each relationship type. Note any unspecified requirements, and make appropriate assumptions to make the specification complete.

3.17. Composite and multivalued attributes can be nested to any number of levels. Suppose we want to design an attribute for a STUDENT entity type to keep track of previous college education. Such an attribute will have one entry for each college previously attended, and each such entry will be composed of college name, start and end dates, degree entries (degrees awarded at that college, if any), and transcript entries (courses completed at that college, if any). Each degree entry contains the degree name and the month and year the degree was awarded, and each transcript entry contains a course name, semester, year, and grade. Design an attribute to hold this information. Use the conventions of Figure 3.5.

3.18. Show an alternative design for the attribute described in Exercise 3.17 that uses only entity types (including weak entity types, if needed) and relationship types.

3.19. Consider the ER diagram of Figure 3.16, which shows a simplified schema for an airline reservations system. Extract from the ER diagram the requirements and constraints that produced this schema. Try to be as precise as possible in your requirements and constraints specification.

3.20. In Chapters 1 and 2, we discussed the database environment and database users. We can consider many entity types to describe such an environment, such as DBMS, stored database, DBA, and catalog/data dictionary. Try to specify all the entity types that can fully describe a database system and its environment; then specify the relationship types among them, and draw an ER diagram to describe such a general database environment.

3.21. Design an ER schema for keeping track of information about votes taken in the U.S. House of Representatives during the current two-year congressional session. The database needs to keep track of each U.S. STATE's Name (e.g., Texas, New York, California) and includes the Region of the state (whose domain is {Northeast, Midwest, Southeast, Southwest, West}). Each CONGRESSPERSON in the House of Representatives is described by their Name, and includes the District represented, the StartDate when they were first elected, and the political Party they belong to (whose domain is {Republican, Democrat, Independent, Other}). The database keeps track of each BILL (i.e., proposed law), and includes the BillName, the DateOfVote on the bill, whether the bill PassedOrFailed (whose domain is {YES, NO}), and the Sponsor (the congressperson(s) who sponsored—i.e., proposed—the bill). The database keeps track of how each congressperson voted on each bill

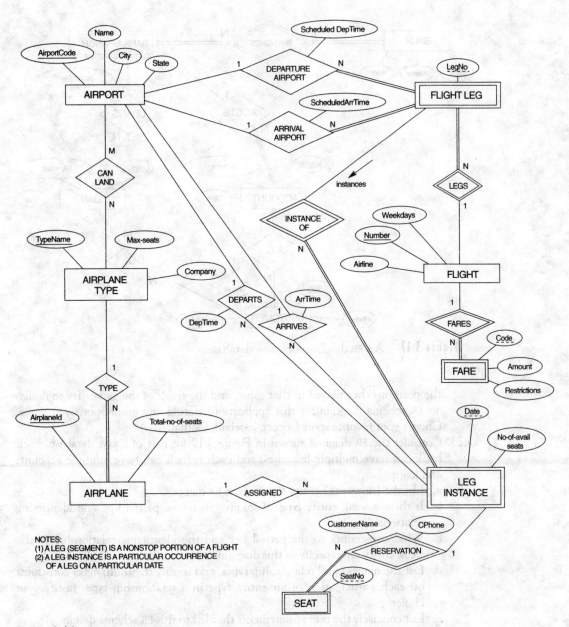

Figure 3.16 An ER diagram for an AIRLINE database.

(domain of vote attribute is {Yes, No, Abstain, Absent}). Draw an ER schema diagram for the above application. State clearly any assumptions you make.

3.22. A database is being constructed to keep track of the teams and games of a sports league. A team has a number of players, not all of whom participate in each game. It is desired to keep track of the players participating in each game for each team,

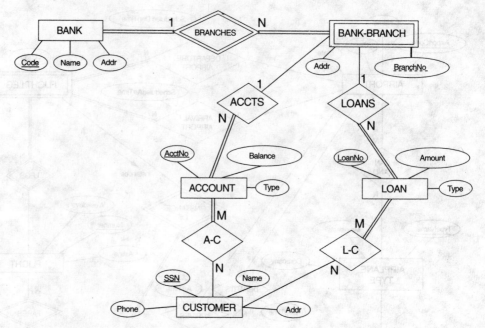

Figure 3.17   An ER diagram for a BANK database.

the positions they played in that game, and the result of the game. Try to design an ER schema diagram for this application, stating any assumptions you make. Choose your favorite sport (soccer, baseball, football, . . .).

3.23. Consider the ER diagram shown in Figure 3.17 for part of a BANK database. Each bank can have multiple branches, and each branch can have multiple accounts and loans.

a. List the (nonweak) entity types in the ER diagram.

b. Is there a weak entity type? If so, give its name, partial key, and identifying relationship.

c. What constraints do the partial key and the identifying relationship of the weak entity type specify in this diagram?

d. List the names of all relationship types, and specify the (min, max) constraint on each participation of an entity type in a relationship type. Justify your choices.

e. List concisely the user requirements that led to this ER schema design.

f. Suppose that every customer must have at least one account but is restricted to at most two loans at a time, and that a bank branch cannot have more than 1000 loans. How does this show up on the (min, max) constraints?

3.24. Consider the ER diagram in Figure 3.18. Assume that an employee may work in up to two departments, but may also not be assigned to any department. Assume that each department must have one and may have up to three phone numbers. Supply (min, max) constraints on this diagram. *State clearly any additional assumptions*

Figure 3.18   An ER diagram for a database that keeps track of company and employee phones.

you make. Under what conditions would the relationship HAS_PHONE be redundant in the above example?

3.25. Consider the ER diagram in Figure 3.19. Assume that a course may or may not use a textbook, but that a text by definition is a book that is used in some course. A course may not use more than five books. Instructors teach from two to four courses. Supply (min, max) constraints on this diagram. *State clearly any additional assumptions you make*. If we add the relationship ADOPTS between INSTRUCTOR and TEXT, what (min, max) constraints would you put on it? Why?

3.26. Consider an entity type SECTION in a UNIVERSITY database, which describes the section offerings of courses. The attributes of SECTION are: SectionNumber, Semester, Year, CourseNumber, Instructor, RoomNo (where section is taught), Building (where section is taught), Weekdays (domain is the possible combinations of weekdays in which a section can be offered {MWF, MW, TT, etc.}), and Hours

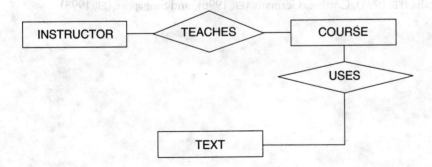

Figure 3.19   An ER diagram for a database that keeps track of textbooks used in courses.

(domain is all possible time periods during which sections are offered {9–9.50 A.M., 10–10.50 A.M., . . ., 3.30–4.50 P.M., 5.30–6.20 P.M., etc.}). Assume that SectionNumber is unique for each course within a particular semester/year combination (that is, if a course is offered multiple times during a particular semester, its section offerings are numbered 1, 2, 3, etc.). There are several composite keys for SECTION, and some attributes are components of more than one key. Identify three composite keys; and show how they can be represented in an ER schema diagram.

Selected Bibliography

The Entity-Relationship model was introduced by Chen (1976), and related work appears in Schmidt and Swenson (1975), Wiederhold and Elmasri (1979), and Senko (1975). Since then, numerous modifications to the ER model have been suggested. We have incorporated some of these in our presentation. Structural constraints on relationships are discussed in Abrial (1974), Elmasri and Wiederhold (1980), and Lenzerini and Santucci (1983). Multivalued and composite attributes are incorporated in the ER model in Elmasri et al. (1985). Although we did not discuss languages for the entity-relationship model and its extensions, there have been several proposals for such languages. Elmasri and Wiederhold (1981) propose the GORDAS query language for the ER model. Another ER query language is proposed by Markowitz and Raz (1983). Senko (1980) presents a query language for Senko's DIAM model. A formal set of operations called the ER algebra was presented by Parent and Spaccapietra (1985). Gogolla and Hohenstein (1991) present another formal language for the ER model. Campbell et al. (1985) present a set of ER operations and show that they are relationally complete. A conference for the dissemination of research results related to the ER model has been held regularly since 1979. The conference, now known as the International Conference on Conceptual Modeling, has been held in Los Angeles (ER 1979, ER 1983, ER 1997), Washington (ER 1981), Chicago (ER 1985), Dijon, France (ER 1986), New York City (ER 1987), Rome (ER 1988), Toronto (ER 1989), Lausanne, Switzerland (ER 1990), San Mateo, California (ER 1991), Karlsruhe, Germany (ER 1992), Arlington, Texas (ER 1993), Manchester, England (ER 1994), Brisbane, Australia (ER 1995), Cottbus, Germany (ER 1996), and Singapore (ER 1998).

CHAPTER 4

Enhanced Entity-Relationship and Object Modeling

The ER modeling concepts discussed in Chapter 3 are sufficient for representing many database schemas for "traditional" database applications, which mainly include data-processing applications in business and industry. Since the late 1970s, however, newer applications of database technology have become commonplace; these include databases for engineering design and manufacturing (CAD/CAM[1]), telecommunications, images and graphics, multimedia[2], data mining, data warehousing, geographic information systems (GIS), and databases for indexing the World Wide Web, among many other applications. These types of databases have more complex requirements than do the more traditional applications. To represent these requirements as accurately and clearly as possible, designers of database applications must use additional *semantic data modeling* concepts. Various semantic data models have been proposed in the literature.

In this chapter, we describe features that have been proposed for semantic data models, and show how the ER model can be enhanced to include these concepts, leading to the **enhanced-ER** or **EER** model.[3] We start in Section 4.1 by incorporating the concepts of *class/subclass relationships* and *type inheritance* into the ER model. Then, in Section 4.2, we add the concepts of *specialization* and *generalization*. Section 4.3 discusses *constraints* on

---

1. This stands for computer-aided design/computer-aided manufacturing.

2. These store multimedia data, such as pictures, voice messages, and video clips.

3. EER has also been used to stand for *extended* ER model.

specialization/generalization, and Section 4.4 shows how the UNION construct can be modeled by including the concept of *category* in the EER model. Section 4.5 gives an example UNIVERSITY database schema in the EER model, and summarizes the EER model concepts by giving formal definitions.

The object data model (see Chapters 11 and 12) includes many of the concepts proposed for semantic data models. Object modeling methodologies, such as OMT (Object Modeling Technique) and UML (Universal Modeling Language) are becoming increasingly popular in software design and engineering. These methodologies go beyond database design to specify detailed design of software modules and their interactions using various types of diagrams. An important part of these methodologies—namely, the *class diagrams*[4]—are similar in many ways to EER diagrams. However, in addition to specifying attributes and relationships in class diagrams, the *operations* on objects are also specified. Operations can be used to specify the *functional requirements* during database design, as we discussed in Section 3.1 and illustrated in Figure 3.1. We will present the UML notation and concepts for class diagrams in Section 4.6, and briefly compare these to EER notation and concepts.

Section 4.7 discusses some of the more complex issues involved in modeling of ternary and higher-degree relationships. In Section 4.8, we discuss the fundamental abstractions that are used as the basis of many semantic data models. Section 4.9 summarizes the chapter.

For a detailed introduction to conceptual modeling, Chapter 4 should be considered a continuation of Chapter 3. However, if only a basic introduction to ER modeling is desired, this chapter may be omitted. Alternatively, the reader may choose to skip some or all of the later sections of this chapter (Sections 4.3 through 4.8).

4.1 Subclasses, Superclasses, and Inheritance

The EER (Enhanced-ER) model includes all the modeling concepts of the ER model that were presented in Chapter 3. In addition, it includes the concepts of **subclass** and **superclass** and the related concepts of **specialization** and **generalization** (see Sections 4.2 and 4.3). Another concept included in the EER model is that of a **category** (see Section 4.4), which is used to represent a collection of objects that is the *union* of objects of different entity types. Associated with these concepts is the important mechanism of **attribute and relationship inheritance.** Unfortunately, no standard terminology exists for these concepts, so we use the most common terminology. Alternative terminology is given in footnotes. We also describe a diagrammatic technique for displaying these concepts when they arise in an EER schema. We call the resulting schema diagrams **enhanced-ER** or **EER diagrams.**

The first EER model concept we take up is that of a **subclass** of an entity type. As we discussed in Chapter 3, an entity type is used to represent both a *type of entity*, and the *entity set* or *collection of entities of that type* that exist in the database. For example, the

---

4. A **class** is similar to an *entity type* in many ways.

entity type EMPLOYEE describes the type (that is, the attributes and relationships) of each employee entity, and also refers to the current set of EMPLOYEE entities in the COMPANY database. In many cases an entity type has numerous subgroupings of its entities that are meaningful and need to be represented explicitly because of their significance to the database application. For example, the entities that are members of the EMPLOYEE entity type may be grouped further into SECRETARY, ENGINEER, MANAGER, TECHNICIAN, SALARIED_EMPLOYEE, HOURLY_EMPLOYEE, and so on. The set of entities in each of the latter groupings is a subset of the entities that belong to the EMPLOYEE entity set, meaning that every entity that is a member of one of these subgroupings is also an employee. We call each of these subgroupings a **subclass** of the EMPLOYEE entity type, and the EMPLOYEE entity type is called the **superclass** for each of these subclasses.

We call the relationship between a superclass and any one of its subclasses a **superclass/subclass** or simply **class/subclass relationship.**[5] In our previous example, EMPLOYEE/SECRETARY and EMPLOYEE/TECHNICIAN are two class/subclass relationships. Notice that a member entity of the subclass represents the *same real-world entity* as some member of the superclass; for example, a SECRETARY entity 'Joan Logano' is also the EMPLOYEE 'Joan Logano'. Hence, the subclass member is the same as the entity in the superclass, but in a distinct *specific role*. When we implement a superclass/subclass relationship in the database system, however, we may represent a member of the subclass as a distinct database object—say, a distinct record that is related via the key attribute to its superclass entity. In Section 9.2, we discuss various options for representing superclass/subclass relationships in relational databases.

An entity cannot exist in the database merely by being a member of a subclass; it must also be a member of the superclass. Such an entity can be included optionally as a member of any number of subclasses. For example, a salaried employee who is also an engineer belongs to the two subclasses ENGINEER and SALARIED_EMPLOYEE of the EMPLOYEE entity type. However, it is not necessary that every entity in a superclass be a member of some subclass.

An important concept associated with subclasses is that of **type inheritance.** Recall that the *type* of an entity is defined by the attributes it possesses and the relationship types in which it participates. Because an entity in the subclass represents the same real-world entity from the superclass, it should possess values for its specific attributes *as well as* values of its attributes as a member of the superclass. We say that an entity that is a member of a subclass **inherits** all the attributes of the entity as a member of the superclass. The entity also inherits all the relationships in which the superclass participates. Notice that a subclass, with its own specific (or local) attributes and relationships together with all the attributes and relationships it inherits from the superclass, can be considered an *entity type* in its own right.[6]

---

5. A class/subclass relationship is often called an **IS-A** (or **IS-AN**) **relationship** because of the way we refer to the concept. We say "a SECRETARY IS-AN EMPLOYEE," "a TECHNICIAN IS-AN EMPLOYEE," and so forth.

6. In some object-oriented programming languages, a common restriction is that an entity (or object) has *only one type*. This is generally too restrictive for conceptual database modeling.

4.2 Specialization and Generalization

Specialization is the process of defining a *set of subclasses* of an entity type; this entity type is called the **superclass** of the specialization. The set of subclasses that form a specialization is defined on the basis of some distinguishing characteristic of the entities in the superclass. For example, the set of subclasses {SECRETARY, ENGINEER, TECHNICIAN} is a specialization of the superclass EMPLOYEE that distinguishes among EMPLOYEE entities based on the *job type* of each entity. We may have several specializations of the same entity type based on different distinguishing characteristics. For example, another specialization of the EMPLOYEE entity type may yield the set of subclasses {SALARIED_EMPLOYEE, HOURLY_EMPLOYEE}; this specialization distinguishes among employees based on the *method of pay.*

Figure 4.1 shows how we represent a specialization diagrammatically in an **EER diagram.** The subclasses that define a specialization are attached by lines to a circle, which is connected to the superclass. The *subset symbol* on each line connecting a subclass to the circle indicates the direction of the superclass/subclass relationship.[7] Attributes that apply only to entities of a particular subclass—such as TypingSpeed of SECRETARY—are attached to the rectangle representing that subclass. These are called **specific attributes** (or **local attributes**) of the subclass. Similarly, a subclass can participate in **specific relationship types,** such as the HOURLY_EMPLOYEE subclass participating in the BELONGS_TO relationship in Figure 4.1. We will explain the **d** symbol in the circles of Figure 4.1 and additional EER diagram notation shortly.

Figure 4.2 shows a few entity instances that belong to subclasses of the {SECRETARY, ENGINEER, TECHNICIAN} specialization. Again, notice that an entity that belongs to a subclass represents *the same real-world entity* as the entity connected to it in the EMPLOYEE superclass, even though the same entity is shown twice; for example, e_1 is shown in both EMPLOYEE and SECRETARY in Figure 4.2. As this figure suggests, a superclass/subclass relationship such as EMPLOYEE/SECRETARY somewhat resembles a 1:1 relationship *at the instance level* (see Figure 3.12). The main difference is that in a 1:1 relationship two *distinct entities* are related, whereas in a superclass/subclass relationship the entity in the subclass is the same real-world entity as the entity in the superclass but playing a *specialized role*—for example, an EMPLOYEE specialized in the role of SECRETARY, or an EMPLOYEE specialized in the role of TECHNICIAN.

There are two main reasons for including class/subclass relationships and specializations in a data model. The first is that certain attributes may apply to some but not all entities of the superclass. A subclass is defined in order to group the entities to which these attributes apply. The members of the subclass may still share the majority of their attributes with the other members of the superclass. For example, the SECRETARY subclass may have an attribute TypingSpeed, whereas the ENGINEER subclass may have an attribute

---

7. There are many alternative notations for specialization; we present the UML notation in Section 4.6 and other proposed notations in Appendix A.

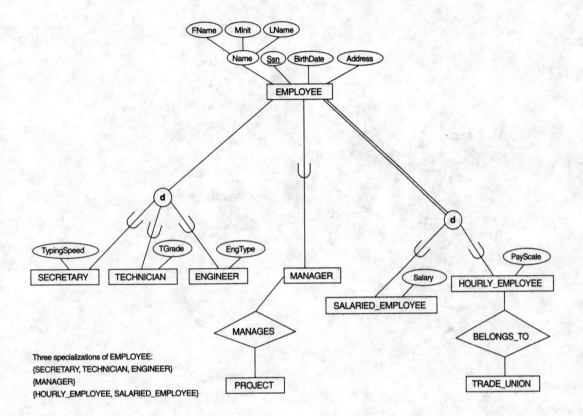

Three specializations of EMPLOYEE:
{SECRETARY, TECHNICIAN, ENGINEER}
{MANAGER}
{HOURLY_EMPLOYEE, SALARIED_EMPLOYEE}

Figure 4.1 EER diagram notation for representing specialization and subclasses.

EngineerType, but SECRETARY and ENGINEER share their other attributes as members of the EMPLOYEE entity type.

The second reason for using subclasses is that some relationship types may be participated in only by entities that are members of the subclass. For example, if only HOURLY_EMPLOYEEs can belong to a trade union, we can represent that fact by creating the subclass HOURLY_EMPLOYEE of EMPLOYEE and relating the subclass to an entity type TRADE_UNION via the BELONGS_TO relationship type, as illustrated in Figure 4.1.

In summary, the specialization process allows us to do the following:

• Define a set of subclasses of an entity type.
• Establish additional specific attributes with each subclass.
• Establish additional specific relationship types between each subclass and other entity types or other subclasses.

Generalization. We can think of a *reverse process* of abstraction in which we suppress the differences among several entity types, identify their common features, and **generalize**

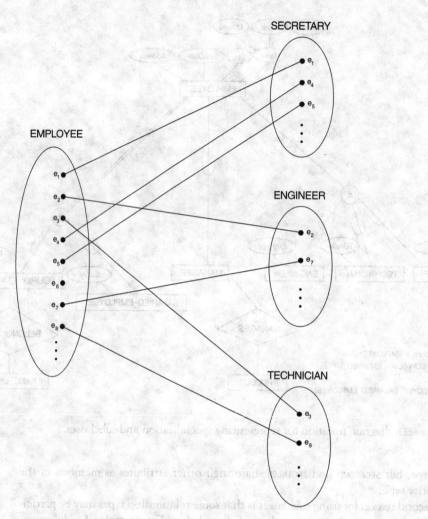

Figure 4.2   Some instances of the specialization of EMPLOYEE into the {SECRETARY, ENGINEER, TECHNICIAN} set of subclasses.

them into a single **superclass** of which the original entity types are special **subclasses.** For example, consider the entity types CAR and TRUCK shown in Figure 4.3(a); they can be generalized into the entity type VEHICLE, as shown in Figure 4.3(b). Both CAR and TRUCK are now subclasses of the **generalized superclass** VEHICLE. We use the term **generalization** to refer to the process of defining a generalized entity type from the given entity types.

Notice that the generalization process can be viewed as being functionally the inverse of the specialization process. Hence, in Figure 4.3 we can view {CAR, TRUCK} as a

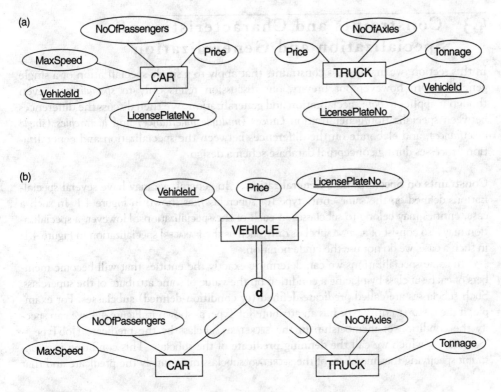

Figure 4.3   Examples of generalization. (a) Two entity types CAR and TRUCK. (b) Generalizing CAR and TRUCK into VEHICLE.

specialization of VEHICLE, rather than viewing VEHICLE as a generalization of CAR and TRUCK. Similarly, in Figure 4.1 we can view EMPLOYEE as a generalization of SECRETARY, TECHNICIAN, and ENGINEER. A diagrammatic notation to distinguish between generalization and specialization is used in some design methodologies. An arrow pointing to the generalized superclass represents a generalization, whereas arrows pointing to the specialized subclasses represent a specialization. We will *not* use this notation, because the decision as to which process is more appropriate in a particular situation is often subjective. Appendix A gives some of the suggested alternative diagrammatic notations for schema diagrams/class diagrams.

So far we have introduced the concepts of subclasses and superclass/subclass relationships, as well as the specialization and generalization processes. In general, a superclass or subclass represents a collection of entities of the same type and hence also describes an *entity type;* that is why superclasses and subclasses are shown in rectangles in EER diagrams (like entity types). We now discuss in more detail the properties of specializations and generalizations.

4.3   Constraints and Characteristics of Specialization and Generalization

In this section, we first discuss constraints that apply to a single specialization or a single generalization; however, for brevity, our discussion refers only to *specialization* even though it applies to *both* specialization and generalization. We then discuss the differences between specialization/generalization *lattices* (*multiple inheritance*) and *hierarchies* (*single inheritance*), and elaborate on the differences between the specialization and generalization processes during conceptual database schema design.

Constraints on Specialization/Generalization.   In general, we may have several specializations defined on the same entity type (or superclass), as shown in Figure 4.1. In such a case, entities may belong to subclasses in each of the specializations. However, a specialization may also consist of a *single* subclass only, such as the {MANAGER} specialization in Figure 4.1; in such a case, we do not use the circle notation.

In some specializations we can determine exactly the entities that will become members of each subclass by placing a condition on the value of some attribute of the superclass. Such subclasses are called **predicate-defined** (or **condition-defined**) **subclasses.** For example, if the EMPLOYEE entity type has an attribute JobType, as shown in Figure 4.4, we can specify the condition of membership in the SECRETARY subclass by the predicate (JobType = 'Secretary'), which we call the **defining predicate** of the subclass. This condition is a *constraint* specifying that members of the SECRETARY subclass must satisfy the predicate and that

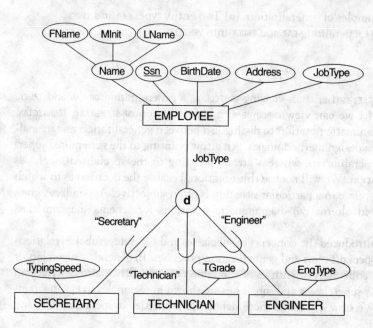

Figure 4.4   An attribute-defined specialization on the JobType attribute of EMPLOYEE.

all entities of the EMPLOYEE entity type whose attribute value for JobType is 'Secretary' must belong to the subclass. We display a predicate-defined subclass by writing the predicate condition next to the line that connects the subclass to the specialization circle.

If *all* subclasses in a specialization have the membership condition on the *same* attribute of the superclass, the specialization itself is called an **attribute-defined specialization,** and the attribute is called the **defining attribute** of the specialization.[8] We display an attribute-defined specialization, as shown in Figure 4.4, by placing the defining attribute name next to the arc from the circle to the superclass.

When we do not have a condition for determining membership in a subclass, the subclass is called **user-defined.** Membership in such a subclass is determined by the database users when they apply the operation to add an entity to the subclass; hence, membership is *specified individually for each entity by the user*, not by any condition that may be evaluated automatically.

Two other constraints may apply to a specialization. The first is the **disjointness constraint,** which specifies that the subclasses of the specialization must be disjoint. This means that an entity can be a member of *at most one* of the subclasses of the specialization. A specialization that is attribute-defined implies the disjointness constraint if the attribute used to define the membership predicate is single-valued. Figure 4.4 illustrates this case, where the **d** in the circle stands for disjoint. We also use the **d** notation to specify the constraint that user-defined subclasses of a specialization must be disjoint, as illustrated by the specialization {HOURLY_EMPLOYEE, SALARIED_EMPLOYEE} in Figure 4.1. If the subclasses are not constrained to be disjoint, their sets of entities may **overlap;** that is, the same (real-world) entity may be a member of more than one subclass of the specialization. This case, which is the default, is displayed by placing an **o** in the circle, as shown in Figure 4.5.

The second constraint on specialization is called the **completeness constraint,** which may be total or partial. A **total specialization** constraint specifies that *every* entity in the superclass must be a member of some subclass in the specialization. For example, if every EMPLOYEE must be either an HOURLY_EMPLOYEE or a SALARIED_EMPLOYEE, then the specialization {HOURLY_EMPLOYEE, SALARIED_EMPLOYEE} of Figure 4.1 is a total specialization of EMPLOYEE; this is shown in EER diagrams by using a double line to connect the superclass to the circle. A single line is used to display a **partial specialization,** which allows an entity not to belong to any of the subclasses. For example, if some EMPLOYEE entities do not belong to any of the subclasses {SECRETARY, ENGINEER, TECHNICIAN} of Figures 4.1 and 4.4, then that specialization is partial.[9] Notice that the disjointness and completeness constraints are *independent*. Hence, we have the following four possible constraints on specialization:

- Disjoint, total
- Disjoint, partial
- Overlapping, total
- Overlapping, partial

---

8. Such an attribute is called a *discriminator* in UML terminology.

9. The notation of using single/double lines is similar to that for partial/total participation of an entity type in a relationship type, as we described in Chapter 3.

Figure 4.5   Notation for specialization with overlapping (nondisjoint) subclasses.

Of course, the correct constraint is determined from the real-world meaning that applies to each specialization. However, a superclass that was identified through the *generalization* process usually is **total,** because the superclass is *derived from* the subclasses and hence contains only the entities that are in the subclasses.

Certain insertion and deletion rules apply to specialization (and generalization) as a consequence of the constraints specified earlier. Some of these rules are as follows:

- Deleting an entity from a superclass implies that it is automatically deleted from all the subclasses to which it belongs.

- Inserting an entity in a superclass implies that the entity is mandatorily inserted in all *predicate-defined* (or *attribute-defined*) subclasses for which the entity satisfies the defining predicate.

- Inserting an entity in a superclass of a *total specialization* implies that the entity is mandatorily inserted in.at least one of the subclasses of the specialization.

The reader is encouraged to make a complete list of rules for insertions and deletions for the various types of specializations.

Specialization/Generalization Hierarchies and Lattices.   A subclass itself may have further subclasses specified on it, forming a hierarchy or a lattice of specializations. For example, in Figure 4.6 ENGINEER is a subclass of EMPLOYEE and is also a superclass of ENGINEERING_MANAGER; this represents the real-world constraint that every engineering manager is required to be an engineer. A **specialization hierarchy** has the constraint that

Figure 4.6 A specialization lattice with the shared subclass ENGINEERING_MANAGER.

every subclass participates *as a subclass* in *only one* class/subclass relationship. In contrast, for a **specialization lattice** a subclass can be a subclass in *more than one* class/subclass relationship. Hence, Figure 4.6 is a lattice.

Figure 4.7 shows another specialization lattice of more than one level. This may be part of a conceptual schema for a UNIVERSITY database. Notice that this arrangement would have been a hierarchy except for the STUDENT_ASSISTANT subclass, which is a subclass in two distinct class/subclass relationships. In Figure 4.7, all person entities represented in the database are members of the PERSON entity type, which is specialized into the subclasses {EMPLOYEE, ALUMNUS, STUDENT}. This specialization is overlapping; for example, an alumnus may also be an employee and may also be a student pursuing an advanced degree. The subclass STUDENT is superclass for the specialization {GRADUATE_STUDENT, UNDERGRADUATE_STUDENT}, while EMPLOYEE is superclass for the specialization {STUDENT_ASSISTANT, FACULTY, STAFF}. Notice that STUDENT_ASSISTANT is also a subclass of STUDENT. Finally, STUDENT_ASSISTANT is superclass for the specialization into {RESEARCH_ASSISTANT, TEACHING_ASSISTANT}.

In such a specialization lattice or hierarchy, a subclass inherits the attributes not only of its direct superclass but also of all its predecessor superclasses *all the way to the root* of the hierarchy or lattice. For example, an entity in GRADUATE_STUDENT inherits all the attributes of that entity as a STUDENT *and* as a PERSON. Notice that an entity may exist in several *leaf nodes* of the hierarchy, where a **leaf node** is a class that has *no subclasses of its own*. For example, a member of GRADUATE_STUDENT may also be a member of RESEARCH_ASSISTANT.

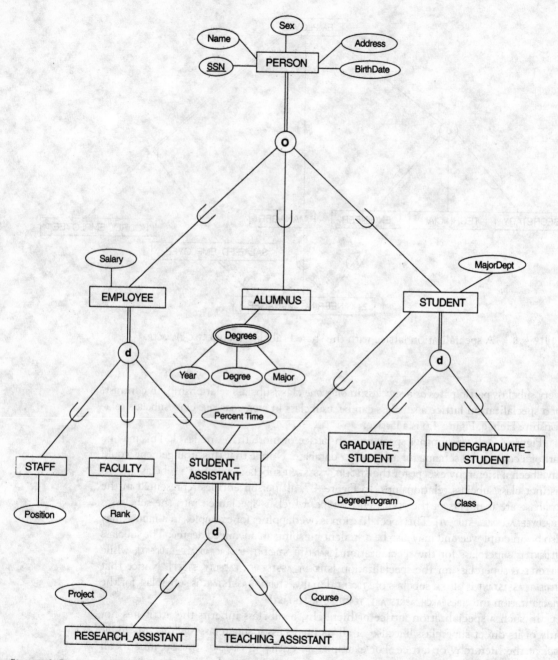

Figure 4.7   A specialization lattice (with multiple inheritance) for a UNIVERSITY database.

A subclass with *more than one* superclass is called a **shared subclass.** For example, if every ENGINEERING_MANAGER must be an ENGINEER but must also be a SALARIED_EMPLOYEE and a MANAGER, then ENGINEERING_MANAGER should be a shared subclass of all three superclasses (Figure 4.6). This leads to the concept known as **multiple inheritance,** since the shared subclass ENGINEERING_MANAGER directly inherits attributes and relationships from multiple classes. Notice that the existence of at least one shared subclass leads to a lattice (and hence to *multiple inheritance*); if no shared subclasses existed, we would have a hierarchy rather than a lattice. An important rule related to multiple inheritance can be illustrated by the example of the shared subclass STUDENT_ASSISTANT in Figure 4.7, which inherits attributes from both EMPLOYEE and STUDENT. Here, both EMPLOYEE and STUDENT inherit *the same attributes* from PERSON. The rule states that if an attribute (or relationship) originating in the *same superclass* (PERSON) is inherited more than once via different paths (EMPLOYEE and STUDENT) in the lattice, then it should be included only once in the shared subclass (STUDENT_ASSISTANT). Hence, the attributes of PERSON are inherited *only once* in the STUDENT_ASSISTANT subclass of Figure 4.7.

It is important to note here that some inheritance mechanisms *do not allow* multiple inheritance (shared subclasses). In such a model, it is necessary to create additional subclasses to cover all possible combinations of classes that may have some entity belong to all these classes simultaneously. Hence, any *overlapping* specialization would require multiple additional subclasses. For example, in the overlapping specialization of PERSON into {EMPLOYEE, ALUMNUS, STUDENT} (or {E, A, S} for short), it would be necessary to create seven subclasses of PERSON: E, A, S, E_A, E_S, A_S, and E_A_S in order to cover all possible types of entities. Obviously, this can lead to extra complexity.

It is also important to note that some inheritance mechanisms that allow multiple inheritance do not allow an entity to have multiple types, and hence an entity can be a member *of only one class*.[10] In such a model, it is also necessary to create additional shared subclasses as leaf nodes to cover all possible combinations of classes that may have some entity belong to all these classes simultaneously. Hence, we would require the same seven subclasses of PERSON.

Although we have used specialization to illustrate our discussion, similar concepts *apply equally* to generalization, as we mentioned at the beginning of this section. Hence, we can also speak of **generalization hierarchies** and **generalization lattices.**

Utilizing Specialization and Generalization in Conceptual Data Modeling.   We now elaborate on the differences between the specialization and generalization processes during conceptual database design. In the specialization process, we typically start with an entity type and then define subclasses of the entity type by successive specialization; that is, we repeatedly define more specific groupings of the entity type. For example, when designing the specialization lattice in Figure 4.7, we may first specify an entity type PERSON for a university database. Then we discover that three types of persons will be represented in the database: university employees, alumni, and students. We create the specialization {EMPLOYEE, ALUMNUS, STUDENT} for this purpose and choose the overlapping constraint because a person

---

10. In some cases, the class is further restricted to be a *leaf node* in the hierarchy or lattice.

may belong to more than one of the subclasses. We then specialize EMPLOYEE further into {STAFF, FACULTY, STUDENT_ASSISTANT}, and specialize STUDENT into {GRADUATE_STUDENT, UNDERGRADUATE_STUDENT}. Finally, we specialize STUDENT_ASSISTANT into {RESEARCH_ASSISTANT, TEACHING_ASSISTANT}. This successive specialization corresponds to a **top-down conceptual refinement process** during conceptual schema design. So far, we have a hierarchy; we then realize that STUDENT_ASSISTANT is a shared subclass, since it is also a subclass of STUDENT, leading to the lattice.

It is possible to arrive at the same hierarchy or lattice from the other direction. In such a case, the process involves generalization rather than specialization and corresponds to a **bottom-up conceptual synthesis.** In this case, designers may first discover entity types such as STAFF, FACULTY, ALUMNUS, GRADUATE_STUDENT, UNDERGRADUATE_STUDENT, RESEARCH_ASSIS-TANT, TEACHING_ASSISTANT, and so on; then they generalize {GRADUATE_STUDENT, UNDERGRADUATE_STUDENT} into STUDENT; then they generalize {RESEARCH_ASSISTANT, TEACHING_ASSISTANT} into STUDENT_ASSISTANT; then they generalize {STAFF, FACULTY, STUDENT_ASSISTANT} into EMPLOYEE; and finally they generalize {EMPLOYEE, ALUMNUS, STUDENT} into PERSON.

In structural terms, hierarchies or lattices resulting from either process may be identical; the only difference relates to the manner or order in which the schema superclasses and subclasses were specified. In practice, it is likely that neither the generalization process nor the specialization process is followed strictly, but a combination of the two processes is employed. In this case, new classes are continually incorporated into a hierarchy or lattice as they become apparent to users and designers. Notice that the notion of representing data and knowledge by using superclass/subclass hierarchies and lattices is quite common in knowledge-based systems and expert systems, which combine database technology with artificial intelligence techniques. For example, frame-based knowledge representation schemes closely resemble class hierarchies. Specialization is also common in software engineering design methodologies that are based on the object-oriented paradigm.

4.4   Modeling of UNION Types Using Categories

All of the superclass/subclass relationships we have seen thus far have a *single superclass*. A shared subclass such as ENGINEERING_MANAGER in the lattice of Figure 4.6 is the subclass in three *distinct* superclass/subclass relationships, where each of the three relationships has a *single* superclass. It is not uncommon, however, that the need arises for modeling a single superclass/subclass relationship with *more than one* superclass, where the superclasses represent different entity types. In this case, the subclass will represent a collection of objects that is (a subset of) the UNION of distinct entity types; we call such a *subclass* a **union type** or a **category**.[11]

---

11. Our use of the term *category* is based on the ECR (Entity-Category-Relationship) model (Elmasri et al. 1985).

For example, suppose that we have three entity types: PERSON, BANK, and COMPANY. In a database for vehicle registration, an owner of a vehicle can be a person, a bank (holding a lien on a vehicle), or a company. We need to create a class (collection of entities) that includes entities of all three types to play the role of *vehicle owner*. A category OWNER that is a *subclass of the UNION* of the three entity sets of COMPANY, BANK, and PERSON is created for this purpose. We display categories in an EER diagram, as shown in Figure 4.8. The superclasses COMPANY, BANK, and PERSON are connected to the circle with the ∪ symbol, which stands for the *set union operation*. An arc with the subset symbol connects the circle to the (subclass) OWNER category. If a defining predicate is needed, it is displayed next to the line from the superclass to which the predicate applies. In Figure 4.8 we have two categories: OWNER, which is a subclass of the union of PERSON, BANK, and COMPANY; and REGISTERED_VEHICLE, which is a subclass of the union of CAR and TRUCK.

A category has two or more superclasses that may represent *distinct entity types*, whereas other superclass/subclass relationships always have a single superclass. We can compare a category, such as OWNER in Figure 4.8, with the ENGINEERING_MANAGER shared subclass of Figure 4.6. The latter is a subclass of *each of* the three superclasses ENGINEER, MANAGER, and SALARIED_EMPLOYEE, so an entity that is a member of ENGINEERING_MANAGER must exist in *all three*. This represents the constraint that an engineering manager must be an ENGINEER, a MANAGER, *and* a SALARIED_EMPLOYEE; that is, ENGINEERING_MANAGER is a subset of the *intersection* of the three subclasses (sets of entities). On the other hand, a category is a subset of the *union* of its superclasses. Hence, an entity that is a member of OWNER must exist in *only one* of the superclasses. This represents the constraint that an OWNER may be a COMPANY, a BANK, *or* a PERSON in Figure 4.8.

Attribute inheritance works more selectively in the case of categories. For example, in Figure 4.8 each OWNER entity inherits the attributes of a COMPANY, a PERSON, or a BANK, depending on the superclass to which the entity belongs. On the other hand, a shared subclass such as ENGINEERING_MANAGER (Figure 4.6) inherits *all* the attributes of its superclasses SALARIED_EMPLOYEE, ENGINEER, and MANAGER.

It is interesting to note the difference between the category REGISTERED_VEHICLE (Figure 4.8) and the generalized superclass VEHICLE (Figure 4.3(b)). In Figure 4.3(b) every car and every truck is a VEHICLE; but in Figure 4.8 the REGISTERED_VEHICLE category includes some cars and some trucks but not necessarily all of them (for example, some cars or trucks may not be registered). In general, a specialization or generalization such as that in Figure 4.3(b), if it were *partial*, would not preclude VEHICLE from containing other types of entities, such as motorcycles. However, a category such as REGISTERED_VEHICLE in Figure 4.8 implies that only cars and trucks, but not other types of entities, can be members of REGISTERED_VEHICLE.

A category can be **total** or **partial.** For example, ACCOUNT_HOLDER is a predicate-defined partial category in Figure 4.9(a), where c_1 and c_2 are predicate conditions that specify which COMPANY and PERSON entities, respectively, are members of ACCOUNT_HOLDER. However, the category PROPERTY in Figure 4.9(b) is total because every building and lot must be a member of PROPERTY; this is shown by a double line connecting the category and the circle. Partial categories are indicated by a single line connecting the category and the circle, as in Figures 4.8 and 4.9(a).

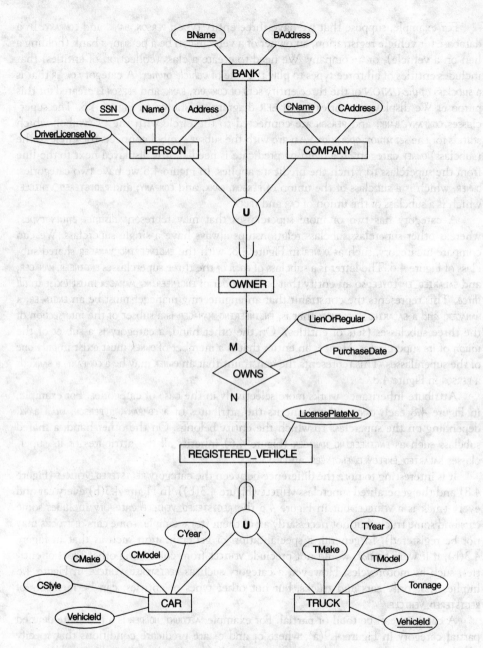

Figure 4.8 An illustration of how to represent the UNION of two or more entity types/classes using the category notation. Two categories are shown: OWNER and REGISTERED_VEHICLE.

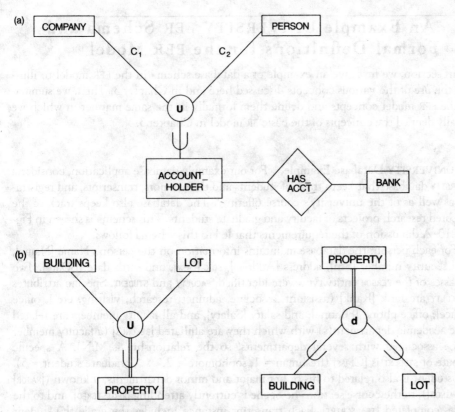

Figure 4.9   Total and partial categories. (a) Partial category ACCOUNT_HOLDER that is a subset of the union of two entity types COMPANY and PERSON. (b) Total category PROPERTY and a similar generalization.

The superclasses of a category may have different key attributes, as demonstrated by the OWNER category of Figure 4.8; or they may have the same key attribute, as demonstrated by the REGISTERED_VEHICLE category. Notice that if a category is total (not partial), it may be represented alternatively as a specialization (or a generalization), as illustrated in Figure 4.9(b). In this case the choice of which representation to use is subjective. If the two classes represent the same type of entities and share numerous attributes, including the same key attributes, specialization/generalization is preferred; otherwise, categorization (union type) is more appropriate.

4.5 An Example UNIVERSITY EER Schema and Formal Definitions for the EER Model

In this section, we first give an example of a database schema in the EER model to illustrate the use of the various concepts discussed here and in Chapter 3. Then, we summarize the EER model concepts and define them formally in the same manner in which we formally defined the concepts of the basic ER model in Chapter 3.

The UNIVERSITY Database Example.   For our example database application, consider a UNIVERSITY database that keeps track of students and their majors, transcripts, and registration as well as of the university's course offerings. The database also keeps track of the sponsored research projects of faculty and graduate students. This schema is shown in Figure 4.10. A discussion of the requirements that led to this schema follows.

For each person, the database maintains information on the person's Name [Name], social security number [Ssn], address [Address], sex [Sex], and birth date [BDate]. Two subclasses of the PERSON entity type were identified: FACULTY and STUDENT. Specific attributes of FACULTY are rank [Rank] (assistant, associate, adjunct, research, visiting, etc.), office [FOffice], office phone [FPhone], and salary [Salary], and all faculty members are related to the academic department(s) with which they are affiliated [BELONGS] (a faculty member can be associated with several departments, so the relationship is M:N). A specific attribute of STUDENT is [Class] (freshman = 1, sophomore = 2, . . . , graduate student = 5). Each student is also related to his or her major and minor departments, if known ([MAJOR] and [MINOR]), to the course sections he or she is currently attending [REGISTERED], and to the courses completed [TRANSCRIPT]. Each transcript instance includes the grade the student received [Grade] in the course section.

GRAD_STUDENT is a subclass of STUDENT, with the defining predicate Class = 5. For each graduate student, we keep a list of previous degrees in a composite, multivalued attribute [Degrees]. We also relate the graduate student to a faculty advisor [ADVISOR] and to a thesis committee [COMMITTEE] if one exists.

An academic department has the attributes name [DName], telephone [DPhone], and office number [Office] and is related to the faculty member who is its chairperson [CHAIRS] and to the college to which it belongs [CD]. Each college has attributes college name [CName], office number [COffice], and the name of its dean [Dean].

A course has attributes course number [C#], course name [Cname], and course description [CDesc]. Several sections of each course are offered, with each section having the attributes section number [Sec#] and the year and quarter in which the section was offered ([Year] and [Qtr]).[12] Section numbers uniquely identify each section. The sections being offered during the current semester are in a subclass CURRENT_SECTION of SECTION, with the defining predicate Qtr = CurrentQtr and Year = CurrentYear. Each

---

12. We assume that the *quarter* system rather than the *semester* system is used in this university.

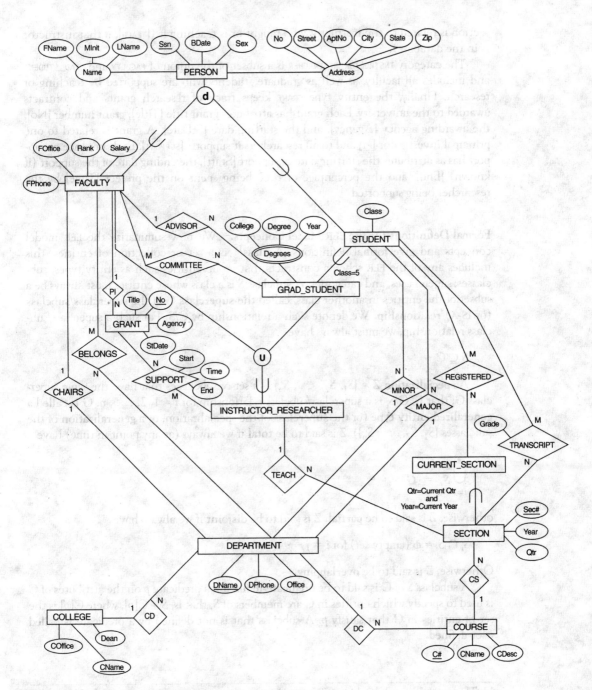

Figure 4.10 An EER conceptual schema for a UNIVERSITY database.

section is related to the instructor who taught or is teaching it ([TEACH], if that instructor is in the database).

The category INSTRUCTOR_RESEARCHER is a subset of the union of FACULTY and GRAD_STUDENT and includes all faculty, as well as graduate students who are supported by teaching or research. Finally, the entity type GRANT keeps track of research grants and contracts awarded to the university. Each grant has attributes grant title [Title], grant number [No], the awarding agency [Agency], and the starting date [StDate]. A grant is related to one principal investigator [PI] and to all researchers it supports [SUPPORT]. Each instance of support has as attributes the starting date of support [Start], the ending date of the support (if known) [End], and the percentage of time being spent on the project [Time] by the researcher being supported.

Formal Definitions for the EER Model Concepts.   We now summarize the EER model concepts and give formal definitions. A **class**[13] is a set or collection of entities; this includes any of the EER schema constructs that group entities such as entity types, subclasses, superclasses, and categories. A **subclass** S is a class whose entities must always be a subset of the entities in another class, called the **superclass** C of the **superclass/subclass** (or **IS-A**) **relationship.** We denote such a relationship by C/S. For such a superclass/subclass relationship, we must always have

$$S \subseteq C$$

A **specialization** $Z = \{S_1, S_2, \ldots, S_n\}$ is a set of subclasses that have the same superclass G; that is, G/S_i is a superclass/subclass relationship for $i = 1, 2, \ldots, n$. G is called a **generalized entity type** (or the **superclass** of the specialization, or a **generalization** of the subclasses $\{S_1, S_2, \ldots, S_n\}$). Z is said to be **total** if we always (at any point in time) have

$$\bigcup_{i=1}^{n} S_i = G$$

otherwise, Z is said to be **partial.** Z is said to be **disjoint** if we always have

$$S_i \cap S_j = \phi \text{ (empty set) for } i \neq j$$

Otherwise, Z is said to be **overlapping.**

A subclass S of C is said to be **predicate-defined** if a predicate p on the attributes of C is used to specify which entities in C are members of S; that is, $S = C[p]$, where $C[p]$ is the set of entities in C that satisfy p. A subclass that is not defined by a predicate is called **user-defined.**

---

13. The use of the word *class* here differs from its more common use in object-oriented programming languages such as C++. In C++, a class is a structured type definition along with its applicable functions (operations).

A specialization Z (or generalization G) is said to be **attribute-defined** if a predicate $(A = c_i)$, where A is an attribute of G and c_i is a constant value from the domain of A, is used to specify membership in each subclass S_i in Z. Notice that, if $c_i \neq c_j$ for $i \neq j$, and A is a single-valued attribute, then the specialization will be disjoint.

A **category** T is a class that is a subset of the union of n defining superclasses $D_1, D_2, \ldots, D_n, n > 1$, and is formally specified as follows:

$$T \subseteq (D_1 \cup D_2 \ldots \cup D_n)$$

A predicate p_i on the attributes of D_i can be used to specify the members of each D_i that are members of T. If a predicate is specified on every D_i, we get

$$T = (D_1[p_1] \cup D_2[p_2] \ldots \cup D_n[p_n])$$

We should now extend the definition of **relationship type** given in Chapter 3 by allowing any class—not only any entity type—to participate in a relationship. Hence, we should replace the words *entity type* with *class* in that definition. The graphical notation of EER is consistent with ER because all classes are represented by rectangles.

4.6 Conceptual Object Modeling Using UML Class Diagrams

Object modeling methodologies, such as UML (Universal Modeling Language) and OMT (Object Modeling Technique) are becoming increasingly popular. Although these methodologies were developed mainly for software design, a major part of software design involves designing the databases that will be accessed by the software modules. Hence, an important part of these methodologies—namely, the *class diagrams*[14]—are similar to EER diagrams in many ways. Unfortunately, the terminology often differs. In this section, we briefly review some of the notation, terminology, and concepts used in UML class diagrams, and compare them with EER terminology and notation. Figure 4.11 shows how the COMPANY ER database schema of Figure 3.15 can be displayed using UML notation. The *entity types* in Figure 3.15 are modeled as *classes* in Figure 4.11. An *entity* in ER corresponds to an *object* in UML.

In UML class diagrams, a class is displayed as a box (see Figure 4.11) that includes three sections: the top section gives the class name; the middle section includes the attributes for individual objects of the class; and the last section includes operations that can be applied to these objects. Operations are *not* specified in EER diagrams. Consider the EMPLOYEE class in Figure 4.11. Its attributes are Name, Ssn, Bdate, Sex, Address, and Salary. The designer can optionally specify the *domain* of an attribute if desired, by placing a : followed by the domain name or description (see the Name, Sex, and Bdate attributes of EMPLOYEE in Figure 4.11). A composite attribute is modeled as a *structured domain,* as illus-

---

14. A **class** is similar to an *entity type* except that it can have *operations*.

Figure 4.11   The UML conceptual schema for the COMPANY database in Figure 3.15.

trated by the Name attribute of EMPLOYEE. A multivalued attribute will generally be modeled as a separate class, as illustrated by the LOCATION class in Figure 4.11.

Relationship types are called *associations* in UML terminology, and relationship instances are called *links*. A binary association (binary relationship type) is represented as a line connecting the participating classes (entity types), and may (optional) have a name. A relationship attribute, called a *link attribute*, is placed in a box that is connected to the association's line by a dashed line. The (min, max) notation described in Section 3.7.4 is used to specify relationship constraints, which are called *multiplicities* in UML terminology. Multiplicities are specified in the form *min..max,* and an asterisk (∗) indicates no maximum limit on participation. However, the multiplicities are placed *on the opposite ends of the relationship* when compared to the notation discussed in Section 3.7.4 (compare Figures 4.11 and 3.15). In UML, a single asterisk indicates a multiplicity of 0..∗, and a single 1 indicates a multiplicity of 1..1. A recursive relationship (see Section 3.4.2) is called a *reflexive association* in UML, and the role names—like the multiplicities—are placed at the opposite ends of an association when compared to the placing of role names in Figure 3.15.

In UML, there are two types of relationships: association and aggregation. *Aggregation* is meant to represent a relationship between a whole object and its component parts, and it has a distinct diagrammatic notation. In Figure 4.11, we modeled the locations of a department and the single location of a project as aggregations. However, aggregation and association do not have different structural properties, and the choice as to which type of relationship to use is somewhat subjective. In the EER model, both are represented as relationships. UML also distinguishes between *unidirectional* associations/aggregations—which are displayed with an arrow to indicate that only one direction for accessing related objects is needed—and *bi-directional* associations/aggregations—which are the default. In addition, relationship instances may be specified to be *ordered*. Relationship (association) names are *optional* in UML, and relationship attributes are displayed in a box attached with a dashed line to the line representing the association/aggregation (see StartDate and Hours in Figure 4.11).

The operations given in each class are derived from the functional requirements of the application, as we discussed in Section 3.1. It is generally sufficient to specify the operation names initially for the logical operations that are expected to be applied to individual objects of a class, as shown in Figure 4.11. As the design is refined, more details are added, such as the exact argument types (parameters) for each operation, plus a functional description of each operation. UML has *function descriptions* and *sequence diagrams* to specify some of the operation details, but these are beyond the scope of our discussion, and are usually described in software engineering texts.

Weak entities can be modeled using the construct called *qualified association* (or *qualified aggregation*) in UML; this can represent both the identifying relationship and the partial key, which is placed in a box attached to the owner class. This is illustrated by the DEPENDENT class and its qualified aggregation to EMPLOYEE in Figure 4.11.[15]

Figure 4.12 illustrates the UML notation for generalization/specialization by giving a possible UML class diagram corresponding to the EER diagram in Figure 4.7. A blank triangle indicates a *disjoint* specialization/generalization, and a filled triangle indicates *overlapping*.

The above discussion and examples give a brief overview of UML class diagrams and terminology. There are many details that we have not discussed because they are outside the scope of this book. The bibliography at this end of the chapter gives some references to books that describe complete details of UML.

4.7 Relationship Types of a Degree Higher Than Two

In Section 3.4.2 we defined the **degree** of a relationship type as the number of participating entity types and called a relationship type of degree two *binary* and a relationship type of degree three *ternary*. In this section, we elaborate on the differences between binary and higher-degree relationships, when to choose higher-degree or binary relationships, and constraints on higher-degree relationships.

---

15. Qualified associations are not restricted to modeling weak entities, and they can be used to model other situations as well.

Figure 4.12   Specialization/generalization notation in UML shown by a class diagram corresponding to the EER diagram in Figure 4.7.

Choosing Between Binary and Ternary (or Higher-Degree) Relationships.   The ER diagram notation for a ternary relationship type is shown in Figure 4.13(a), which displays the schema for the SUPPLY relationship type that was displayed at the instance level in Figure 3.10. In general, a relationship type R of degree n will have n edges in an ER diagram, one connecting R to each participating entity type.

Figure 4.13(b) shows an ER diagram for the three binary relationship types CAN_SUPPLY, USES, and SUPPLIES. In general, a ternary relationship type represents more information than do three binary relationship types. Consider the three binary relationship types CAN_SUPPLY, USES, and SUPPLIES. Suppose that CAN_SUPPLY, between SUPPLIER and PART,

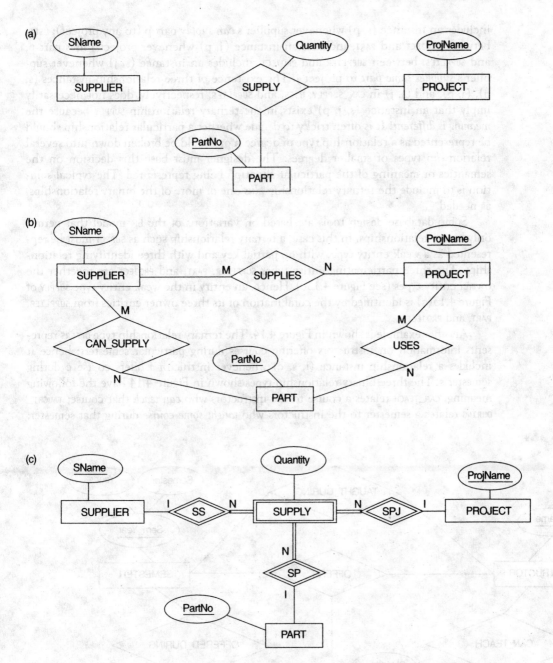

Figure 4.13   An illustration of ternary relationship types. (a) The ternary relationship type SUPPLY. (b) Three binary relationship types that are not equivalent to the ternary relationship type SUPPLY. (c) SUPPLY represented as a weak entity type.

includes an instance (s, p) whenever supplier s *can supply* part p (to any project); USES, between PROJECT and PART, includes an instance (j, p) whenever project j *uses* part p; and SUPPLIES, between SUPPLIER and PROJECT, includes an instance (s, j) whenever supplier s *supplies some part* to project j. The existence of three relationship instances (s, p), (j, p), and (s, j) in CAN_SUPPLY, USES, and SUPPLIES, respectively, does not necessarily imply that an instance (s, j, p) exists in the ternary relationship SUPPLY because the *meaning is different!* It is often tricky to decide whether a particular relationship should be represented as a relationship type of degree n or should be broken down into several relationship types of smaller degrees. The designer must base this decision on the semantics or meaning of the particular situation being represented. The typical solution is to include the ternary relationship *plus* one or more of the binary relationships, as needed.

Some database design tools are based on variations of the ER model that permit only binary relationships. In this case, a ternary relationship such as SUPPLY must be represented as a weak entity type, with no partial key and with three identifying relationships. The three participating entity types SUPPLIER, PART, and PROJECT are together the owner entity types (see Figure 4.13c). Hence, an entity in the weak entity type SUPPLY of Figure 4.13(c) is identified by the combination of its three owner entities from SUPPLIER, PART, and PROJECT.

Another example is shown in Figure 4.14. The ternary relationship type OFFERS represents information on instructors offering courses during particular semesters; hence it includes a relationship instance (i, s, c) whenever instructor i offers course c during semester s. The three binary relationship types shown in Figure 4.14 have the following meaning: CAN_TEACH relates a course to the instructors who *can teach* that course; TAUGHT_DURING relates a semester to the instructors who *taught some course* during that semester;

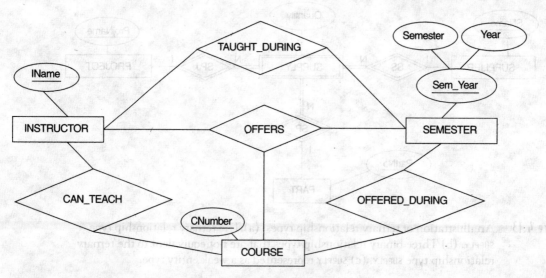

Figure 4.14   Another example of ternary versus binary relationship types.

and OFFERED_DURING relates a semester to the courses offered during that semester *by any instructor*. In general, these ternary and binary relationships represent different information, but certain constraints should hold among the relationships. For example, a relationship instance (i, s, c) should not exist in OFFERS *unless* an instance (i, s) exists in TAUGHT_DURING, an instance (s, c) exists in OFFERED_DURING, and an instance (i, c) exists in CAN_TEACH. However, the reverse is not always true; we may have instances (i, s), (s, c), and (i, c) in the three binary relationship types with no corresponding instance (i, s, c) in OFFERS. Under certain *additional constraints*, the latter may hold—for example, if the CAN_TEACH relationship is 1:1 (an instructor can teach one course, and a course can be taught by only one instructor). The schema designer must analyze each specific situation to decide which of the binary and ternary relationship types are needed.

Notice that it is possible to have a weak entity type with a ternary (or *n*-ary) identifying relationship type. In this case, the weak entity type can have *several* owner entity types. An example is shown in Figure 4.15.

Constraints on Ternary (or Higher-Degree) Relationships.   There are two notations for specifying structural constraints on n-ary relationships, and they specify different constraints. They should thus *both be used* if it is important to fully specify the structural constraints on a ternary or higher-degree relationship. The first notation is based on the cardinality ratio notation of binary relationships, displayed in Figure 3.2. Here, a 1, M, or N is specified on each participation arc. Let us illustrate this constraint using the SUPPLY relationship in Figure 4.13.

Recall that the relationship set of SUPPLY is a set of relationship instances (s, j, p), where s is a SUPPLIER, j is a PROJECT, and p is a PART. Suppose that the constraint exists that for a particular project-part combination, only one supplier will be used (only one supplier supplies a particular part to a particular project). In this case, we place 1 on the SUPPLIER participation, and M, N on the PROJECT, PART participations in Figure 4.13. This

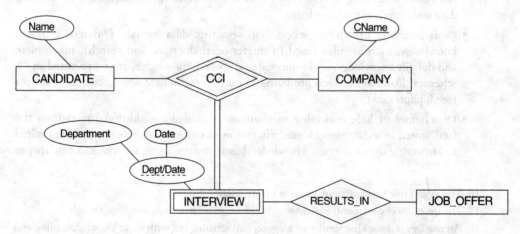

Figure 4.15   A weak entity type INTERVIEW, with a ternary identifying relationship type.

specifies the constraint that a particular (j, p) combination can appear *at most once* in the relationship set. Hence, any relationship instance (s, j, p) is *uniquely identified* in the relationship set by its (j, p) combination, which makes (j, p) a key for the relationship set. In general, the participations that have a 1 specified on them are not required to be part of the key for the relationship set.[16]

The second notation is based on the (min, max) notation displayed in Figure 3.15 for binary relationships. A (min, max) on a participation here specifies that each entity is related to at least *min* and at most *max* relationship instances in the relationship set. These constraints have no bearing on determining the key of an n-ary relationship, where $n > 2$,[17] but specify a different type of constraint that places restrictions on how many relationship instances each entity can participate in.

4.8 Data Abstraction and Knowledge Representation Concepts

In this section we discuss in abstract terms some of the modeling concepts that we described quite specifically in our presentation of the ER and EER models in Chapters 3 and 4. This terminology is used both in conceptual data modeling and in artificial intelligence literature when discussing **knowledge representation** (abbreviated as **KR**). The goal of KR techniques is to develop concepts for accurately modeling some **domain of discourse** by creating an **ontology**[18] that describes the concepts of the domain. This is then used to store and manipulate knowledge for drawing inferences, making decisions, or just answering questions. The goals of KR are similar to those of *semantic data models*, but we can summarize some important similarities and differences between the two disciplines:

- Both disciplines use an abstraction process to identify common properties and important aspects of objects in the miniworld (domain of discourse) while suppressing insignificant differences and unimportant details.

- Both disciplines provide concepts, constraints, operations, and languages for defining data and representing knowledge.

- KR is generally broader in scope than semantic data models. Different forms of knowledge, such as rules (used in inference, deduction, and search), incomplete and default knowledge, and temporal and spatial knowledge, are represented in KR schemes. Database models are being expanded to include some of these concepts (see Chapter 23).

- KR schemes include **reasoning mechanisms** that deduce additional facts from the facts stored in a database. Hence, whereas most current database systems are limited to answering direct queries, knowledge-based systems using KR schemes can answer

---

16. This is also true for cardinality ratios of binary relationships.

17. The (min, max) constraints can determine the keys for binary relationships, though.

18. An *ontology* is somewhat similar to a conceptual schema, but with more knowledge, rules, and exceptions.

queries that involve **inferences** over the stored data. Database technology is being extended with inference mechanisms (see Chapter 25).

• Whereas most data models concentrate on the representation of database schemas, or meta-knowledge, KR schemes often mix up the schemas with the instances themselves in order to provide flexibility in representing exceptions. This often results in inefficiencies when these KR schemes are implemented, especially when compared to databases and when a large amount of data (or facts) needs to be stored.

In this section we discuss four **abstraction concepts** that are used in both semantic data models, such as the EER model, and KR schemes: (1) classification and instantiation, (2) identification, (3) specialization and generalization, and (4) aggregation and association. The paired concepts of classification and instantiation are inverses of one another, as are generalization and specialization. The concepts of aggregation and association are also related. We discuss these abstract concepts and their relation to the concrete representations used in the EER model to clarify the data abstraction process and to improve our understanding of the related process of conceptual schema design.

4.8.1 Classification and Instantiation

The process of **classification** involves systematically assigning similar objects/entities to object classes/entity types. We can now describe (in DB) or reason about (in KR) the classes rather than the individual objects. Collections of objects share the same types of attributes, relationships, and constraints, and by classifying objects we simplify the process of discovering their properties. **Instantiation** is the inverse of classification and refers to the generation and specific examination of distinct objects of a class. Hence, an object instance is related to its object class by the **IS-AN-INSTANCE-OF** relationship.[19]

In general, the objects of a class should have a similar type structure. However, some objects may display properties that differ in some respects from the other objects of the class; these **exception objects** also need to be modeled, and KR schemes allow more varied exceptions than do database models. In addition, certain properties apply to the class as a whole and not to the individual objects; KR schemes allow such **class properties.**[20]

In the EER model, entities are classified into entity types according to their basic properties and structure. Entities are further classified into subclasses and categories based on additional similarities and differences (exceptions) among them. Relationship instances are classified into relationship types. Hence, entity types, subclasses, categories, and relationship types are the different types of classes in the EER model. The EER model does not provide explicitly for class properties, but it may be extended to do so. In UML, objects are classified into classes, and it is possible to display both class properties and individual objects.

---

19. UML diagrams allow a form of instantiation by permitting the display of individual objects. We *did not* describe this feature in Section 4.6.

20. UML diagrams also allow specification of class properties.

Knowledge representation models allow multiple classification schemes in which one class is an *instance* of another class (called a **meta-class**). Notice that this *cannot be* represented directly in the EER model, because we have only two levels—classes and instances. The only relationship among classes in the EER model is a superclass/subclass relationship, whereas in some KR schemes an additional class/instance relationship can be represented directly in a class hierarchy. An instance may itself be another class, allowing multiple-level classification schemes.

4.8.2   Identification

Identification is the abstraction process whereby classes and objects are made uniquely identifiable by means of some **identifier.** For example, a class name uniquely identifies a whole class. An additional mechanism is necessary for telling distinct object instances apart by means of object identifiers. Moreover, it is necessary to identify multiple manifestations in the database of the same real-world object. For example, we may have a tuple <*Matthew Clarke*, 610618, 376-9821> in a PERSON relation and another tuple <*301-54-0836*, CS, 3.8> in a STUDENT relation that happens to represent the same real-world entity. There is no way to identify the fact that these two database objects (tuples) represent the same real-world entity unless we make a provision *at design time* for appropriate cross-referencing to supply this identification. Hence, identification is needed at two levels:

- To distinguish among database objects and classes.
- To identify database objects and to relate them to their real-world counterparts.

In the EER model, identification of schema constructs is based on a system of unique names for the constructs. For example, every class in an EER schema—whether it is an entity type, a subclass, a category, or a relationship type—must have a distinct name. The names of attributes of a given class must also be distinct. Rules for unambiguously identifying attribute name references in a specialization or generalization lattice or hierarchy are needed as well.

At the object level, the values of key attributes are used to distinguish among entities of a particular entity type. For weak entity types, entities are identified by a combination of their own partial key values and the entities they are related to in the owner entity type(s). Relationship instances are identified by some combination of the entities that they relate, depending on the cardinality ratio specified.

4.8.3   Specialization and Generalization

Specialization is the process of classifying a class of objects into more specialized subclasses. Generalization is the inverse process of generalizing several classes into a higher-level abstract class that includes the objects in all these classes. Specialization is conceptual refinement, whereas generalization is conceptual synthesis. Subclasses are used in the EER model to represent specialization and generalization. We call the relationship between a subclass and its superclass an **IS-A-SUBCLASS-OF** relationship or simply an **IS-A** relationship.

4.8.4   Aggregation and Association

Aggregation is an abstraction concept for building composite objects from their component objects. There are three cases where this concept can be related to the EER model. The first case is the situation where we aggregate attribute values of an object to form the whole object. The second case is when we represent an aggregation relationship as an ordinary relationship. The third case, which the EER model does not provide for explicitly, involves the possibility of combining objects that are related by a particular relationship instance into a *higher-level aggregate object*. This is sometimes useful when the higher-level aggregate object is itself to be related to another object. We call the relationship between the primitive objects and their aggregate object IS-A-PART-OF; the inverse is called IS-A-COMPONENT-OF. UML provides for all three types of aggregation.

The abstraction of **association** is used to associate objects from several *independent classes*. Hence, it is somewhat similar to the second use of aggregation. It is represented in the EER model by relationship types and in UML by associations. This abstract relationship is called IS-ASSOCIATED-WITH.

In order to understand the different uses of aggregation better, consider the ER schema shown in Figure 4.16(a), which stores information about interviews by job applicants to various companies. The class COMPANY is an aggregation of the attributes (or component objects) CName (company name) and CAddress (company address), whereas JOB_APPLICANT is an aggregate of Ssn, Name, Address, and Phone. The relationship attributes ContactName and ContactPhone represent the name and phone number of the person in the company who is responsible for the interview. Suppose that some interviews result in job offers, while others do not. We would like to treat INTERVIEW as a class to associate it with JOB_OFFER. The schema shown in Figure 4.16(b) is *incorrect* because it requires each interview relationship instance to have a job offer. The schema shown in Figure 4.16(c) is not allowed, because the ER model does not allow relationships among relationships (although UML does).

One way to represent this situation is to create a higher-level aggregate class composed of COMPANY, JOB_APPLICANT, and INTERVIEW and to relate this class to JOB_OFFER, as shown in Figure 4.16(d). Although the EER model as described in this book does not have this facility, some semantic data models do allow it and call the resulting object a **composite** or **molecular object.** Other models treat entity types and relationship types uniformly and hence permit relationships among relationships (Figure 4.16c).

To represent this situation correctly in the ER model as described here, we need to create a new weak entity type INTERVIEW, as shown in Figure 4.16(e), and relate it to JOB_OFFER. Hence, we can always represent these situations correctly in the ER model by creating additional entity types, although it may be conceptually more desirable to allow direct representation of aggregation as in Figure 4.16(d) or to allow relationships among relationships as in Figure 4.16(c).

The main structural distinction between aggregation and association is that, when an association instance is deleted, the participating objects may continue to exist. However, if we support the notion of an aggregate object—for example, a CAR that is made up of objects ENGINE, CHASSIS, and TIRES—then deleting the aggregate CAR object amounts to deleting all its component objects.

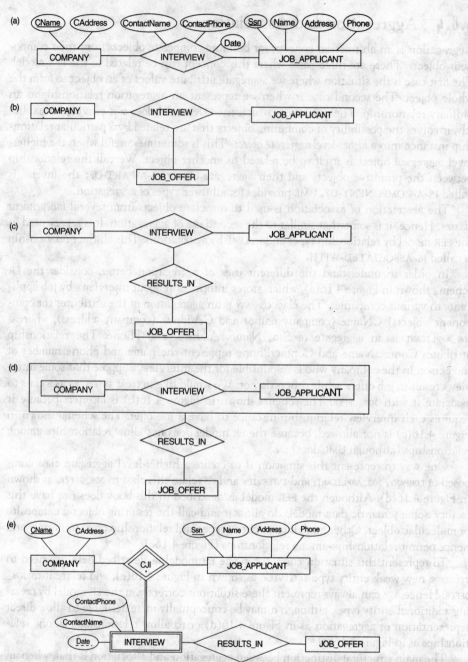

Figure 4.16   An illustration of aggregation. (a) The INTERVIEW relationship type. (b) Including JOB_OFFER in a ternary relationship type (incorrect). (c) Including JOB_OFFER by having a relationship in which another relationship participates (generally not allowed in ER). (d) Using aggregation and a composite (molecular) object (generally not allowed in ER). (e) Correct representation in ER.

4.9 Summary

In this chapter we first discussed extensions to the ER model that improve its representational capabilities. We called the resulting model the enhanced-ER or EER model. The concept of a subclass and its superclass and the related mechanism of attribute/relationship inheritance were presented. We saw how it is sometimes necessary to create additional classes of entities, either because of additional specific attributes or because of specific relationship types. We discussed two main processes for defining superclass/subclass hierarchies and lattices—specialization and generalization.

We then showed how to display these new constructs in an EER diagram. We also discussed the various types of constraints that may apply to specialization or generalization. The two main constraints are total/partial and disjoint/overlapping. In addition, a defining predicate for a subclass or a defining attribute for a specialization may be specified. We discussed the differences between user-defined and predicate-defined subclasses and between user-defined and attribute-defined specializations. Finally, we discussed the concept of a category, which is a subset of the union of two or more classes, and we gave formal definitions of all the concepts presented.

We then introduced the notation and terminology of the Universal Modeling Language (UML), which is being used increasingly in software engineering. We briefly discussed similarities and differences between the UML and EER concepts, notation, and terminology. We also discussed some of the issues concerning the difference between binary and higher-degree relationships, under which circumstances each should be used when designing a conceptual schema, and how different types of constraints on n-ary relationships may be specified. In Section 4.8 we discussed briefly the discipline of knowledge representation and how it is related to semantic data modeling. We also gave an overview and summary of the types of abstract data representation concepts: classification and instantiation, identification, specialization and generalization, aggregation and association. We saw how EER and UML concepts are related to each of these.

Review Questions

4.1. What is a subclass? When is a subclass needed in data modeling?

4.2. Define the following terms: *superclass of a subclass, superclass/subclass relationship, IS-A relationship, specialization, generalization, category, specific (local) attributes, specific relationships*.

4.3. Discuss the mechanism of attribute/relationship inheritance. Why is it useful?

4.4. Discuss user-defined and predicate-defined subclasses, and identify the differences between the two.

4.5. Discuss user-defined and attribute-defined specializations, and identify the differences between the two.

4.6. Discuss the two main types of constraints on specializations and generalizations.

4.7. What is the difference between a specialization hierarchy and a specialization lattice?

4.8. What is the difference between specialization and generalization? Why do we not display this difference in schema diagrams?

4.9. How does a category differ from a regular shared subclass? What is a category used for? Illustrate your answer with examples.

4.10. For each of the following UML terms, discuss the corresponding term in the EER model, if any: *object, class, association, aggregation, generalization, multiplicity, attributes, discriminator, link, link attribute, reflexive association, qualified association.*

4.11. Discuss the main differences between the notation for EER schema diagrams and UML class diagrams by comparing how common concepts are represented in each.

4.12. Discuss the two notations for specifying constraints on n-ary relationships, and what each can be used for.

4.13. List the various data abstraction concepts and the corresponding modeling concepts in the EER model.

4.14. What aggregation feature is missing from the EER model? How can the EER model be further enhanced to support it?

4.15. What are the main similarities and differences between conceptual database modeling techniques and knowledge representation techniques.

Exercises

4.16. Design an EER schema for a database application that you are interested in. Specify all constraints that should hold on the database. Make sure that the schema has at least five entity types, four relationship types, a weak entity type, a superclass/subclass relationship, a category, and an n-ary (n > 2) relationship type.

4.17. Consider the BANK ER schema of Figure 3.17, and suppose that it is necessary to keep track of different types of ACCOUNTS (SAVINGS_ACCTS, CHECKING_ACCTS, . . .) and LOANS (CAR_LOANS, HOME_LOANS, . . .). Suppose that it is also desirable to keep track of each account's TRANSACTIONS (deposits, withdrawals, checks, . . .) and each loan's PAYMENTS; both of these include the amount, date, and time. Modify the BANK schema, using ER and EER concepts of specialization and generalization. State any assumptions you make about the additional requirements.

4.18. The following narrative describes a simplified version of the organization of Olympic facilities planned for the 1996 Olympics in Atlanta. Draw an EER diagram that shows the entity types, attributes, relationships, and specializations for this application. State any assumptions you make. The Olympic facilities are divided into sports complexes. Sports complexes are divided into *one-sport* and *multisport* types. Multisport complexes have areas of the complex designated to each sport with a location indicator (e.g., center, NE-corner, etc.). A complex has a location, chief organizing individual, total occupied area, and so on. Each complex holds a series of events (e.g., the track stadium may hold many different races). For each event there is a planned date, duration, number of participants, number of officials, and so on. A roster of all officials will be maintained together with the list of events each official will be involved in. Different equipment is needed for the events (e.g., goal posts, poles, parallel bars) as well as for maintenance. The two types of facilities (*one-sport* and *multisport*) will have different types of information. For each type, the number of facilities needed is kept, together with an approximate budget.

4.19. Identify all the important concepts represented in the library database case study described below. In particular, identify the abstractions of classification (entity types and relationship types), aggregation, identification, and specialization/generalization. Specify (min, max) cardinality constraints, whenever possible. List details that will impact eventual design, but have no bearing on the conceptual design. List the semantic constraints separately. Draw an EER diagram of the library database.

Case Study: The Georgia Tech Library (GTL) has approximately 16,000 members, 100,000 titles, and 250,000 volumes (or an average of 2.5 copies per book). About 10 percent of the volumes are out on loan at any one time. The librarians ensure that the books that members want to borrow are available when the members want to borrow them. Also, the librarians must know how many copies of each book are in the library or out on loan at any given time. A catalog of books is available on-line that lists books by author, title, and subject area. For each title in the library, a book description is kept in the catalog that ranges from one sentence to several pages. The reference librarians want to be able to access this description when members request information about a book. Library staff is divided into chief librarian, departmental associate librarians, reference librarians, check-out staff, and library assistants. Books can be checked out for 21 days. Members are allowed to have only five books out at a time. Members usually return books within three to four weeks. Most members know that they have one week of grace before a notice is sent to them, so they try to get the book returned before the grace period ends. About 5 percent of the members have to be sent reminders to return a book. Most overdue books are returned within a month of the due date. Approximately 5 percent of the overdue books are either kept or never returned. The most active members of the library are defined as those who borrow at least ten times during the year. The top 1 percent of membership does 15 percent of the borrowing, and the top 10 percent of the membership does 40 percent of the borrowing. About 20 percent of the members are totally inactive in that they are members but do never borrow. To become a member of the library, applicants fill out a form including their SSN, campus and home mailing addresses, and phone numbers. The librarians then issue a numbered, machine-readable card with the member's photo on it. This card is good for four years. A month before a card expires, a notice is sent to a member for renewal. Professors at the institute are considered automatic members. When a new faculty member joins the institute, his or her information is pulled from the employee records and a library card is mailed to his or her campus address. Professors are allowed to check out books for three-month intervals and have a two-week grace period. Renewal notices to professors are sent to the campus address. The library does not lend some books, such as reference books, rare books, and maps. The librarians must differentiate between books that can be lent and those that cannot be lent. In addition, the librarians have a list of some books they are interested in acquiring but cannot obtain, such as rare or out-of-print books and books that were lost or destroyed but have not been replaced. The librarians must have a system that keeps track of books that cannot be lent as well as books that they are interested in acquiring. Some books may have the same title; therefore, the title cannot be used as a means of identification. Every book is identified by its International Standard Book Number (ISBN), a unique international code assigned to all books. Two books with the same title can have different ISBNs if they are in different languages or have different bindings (hard cover or soft cover). Editions of the same book have different ISBNs. The proposed database system must be designed to keep track of the members, the books, the catalog, and the borrowing activity.

4.20. Design a database to keep track of information for an art museum. Assume that the following requirements were collected:

- The museum has a collection of ART_OBJECTs. Each ART_OBJECT has a unique IdNo, an Artist (if known), a Year (when it was created, if known), a Title, and a Description. The art objects are categorized in several ways as discussed below.
- ART_OBJECTs are categorized based on their type. There are three main types: PAINTING, SCULPTURE, and STATUE, plus another type called OTHER to accommodate objects that do not fall into one of the three main types.
- A PAINTING has a PaintType (oil, watercolor, etc.), material on which it is DrawnOn (paper, canvas, wood, etc.), and Style (modern, abstract, etc.).
- A SCULPTURE has a Material from which it was created (wood, stone, etc.), Height, Weight, and Style.
- An art object in the OTHER category has a Type (print, photo, etc.) and Style.
- ART_OBJECTs are also categorized as PERMANENT_COLLECTION that are owned by the museum (which has information on the DateAcquired, whether it is OnDisplay or stored, and Cost) or BORROWED, which has information on the Collection (from which it was borrowed), DateBorrowed, and DateReturned.
- ART_OBJECTs also have information describing their country/culture using information on country/culture of Origin (Italian, Egyptian, American, Indian, etc.), Epoch (Renaissance, Modern, Ancient, etc.).
- The museum keeps track of ARTIST's information, if known: Name, Date-Born, DateDied (if not living), CountryOfOrigin, Epoch, MainStyle, Description. The Name is assumed to be unique.
- Different EXHIBITIONs occur, each having a Name, StartDate, EndDate, and is related to all the art objects that were on display during the exhibition.
- Information is kept on other COLLECTIONs with which the museum interacts, including Name (unique), Type (museum, personal, etc.), Description, Address, Phone, and current ContactPerson.

Draw an EER schema diagram for this application. Discuss any assumptions you made, and that justify your EER design choices.

4.21. Figure 4.17 shows an example of an EER diagram for a small private airport data-base that is used to keep track of airplanes, their owners, airport employees, and pilots. From the requirements for this database, the following information was collected. Each airplane has a registration number [Reg#], is of a particular plane type [OF-TYPE], and is stored in a particular hangar [STORED-IN]. Each plane type has a model number [Model], a capacity [Capacity], and a weight [Weight]. Each hangar has a number [Number], a capacity [Capacity], and a location [Location]. The

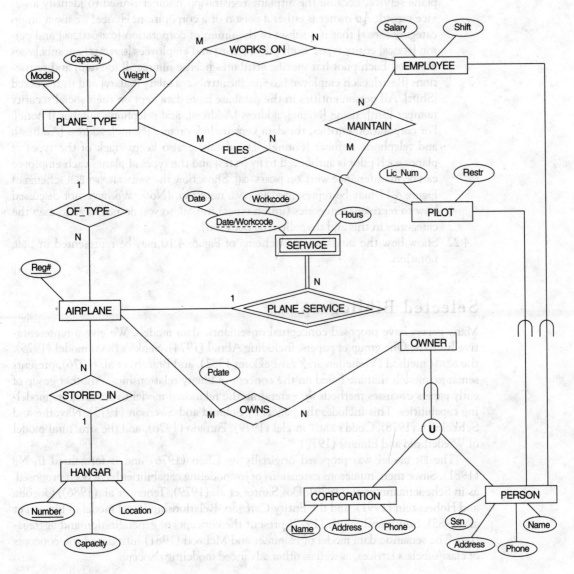

Figure 4.17   EER schema for a SMALL AIRPORT database.

database also keeps track of the owners of each plane [OWNS] and the employees who have maintained the plane [MAINTAIN]. Each relationship instance in OWNS relates an airplane to an owner and includes the purchase date [Pdate]. Each relationship instance in MAINTAIN relates an employee to a service record [SERVICE]. Each plane undergoes service many times; hence, it is related by [PLANE-SERVICE] to a number of service records. A service record includes as attributes the date of maintenance [Date], the number of hours spent on the work [Hours], and the type of work done [Workcode]. We use a weak entity type [SERVICE] to represent airplane service, because the airplane registration number is used to identify a service record. An owner is either a person or a corporation. Hence, we use a union category [OWNER] that is a subset of the union of corporation [CORPORATION] and person [PERSON] entity types. Both pilots [PILOT] and employees [EMPLOYEE] are subclasses of PERSON. Each pilot has specific attributes license number [Lic-Num] and restrictions [Restr]; each employee has specific attributes salary [Salary] and shift worked [Shift]. All person entities in the database have data kept on their social security number [Ssn], name [Name], address [Address], and telephone number [Phone]. For corporation entities, the data kept includes name [Name], address [Address], and telephone number [Phone]. The database also keeps track of the types of planes each pilot is authorized to fly [FLIES] and the types of planes each employee can do maintenance work on [WORKS-ON]. Show how the SMALL AIRPORT EER schema of Figure 4.17 may be represented in UML notation. (*Note:* We have not discussed how to represent categories (union types) in UML so you do not have to map the categories in this and the following question).

4.22. Show how the UNIVERSITY EER schema of Figure 4.10 may be represented in UML notation.

Selected Bibliography

Many papers have proposed conceptual or semantic data models. We give a representative list here. One group of papers, including Abrial (1974), Senko's DIAM model (1975), the NIAM method (Verheijen and VanBekkum 1982), and Bracchi et al. (1976), presents semantic models that are based on the concept of binary relationships. Another group of early papers discusses methods for extending the relational model to enhance its modeling capabilities. This includes the papers by Schmid and Swenson (1975), Navathe and Schkolnick (1978), Codd's RM/T model (1979), Furtado (1978), and the structural model of Wiederhold and Elmasri (1979).

The ER model was proposed originally by Chen (1976) and is formalized in Ng (1981). Since then, numerous extensions of its modeling capabilities have been proposed, as in Scheuermann et al. (1979), Dos Santos et al. (1979), Teorey et al. (1986), Gogolla and Hohenstein (1991), and the Entity-Category-Relationship (ECR) model of Elmasri et al. (1985). Smith and Smith (1977) present the concepts of generalization and aggregation. The semantic data model of Hammer and McLeod (1981) introduced the concepts of class/subclass lattices, as well as other advanced modeling concepts.

A survey of semantic data modeling appears in Hull and King (1987). Another survey of conceptual modeling is Pillalamarri et al. (1988). Eick (1991) discusses design and transformations of conceptual schemas. Analysis of constraints for n-ary relationships is given in Soutou (1998). UML is described in detail in Booch, Rumbaugh, and Jacobson (1999).

CHAPTER 5 | Record Storage and Primary File Organizations

Databases are stored physically as files of records, which are typically stored on magnetic disks. This chapter and the next deal with the organization of databases in storage and the techniques for accessing them efficiently using various algorithms, some of which require auxiliary data structures called indexes. We start in Section 5.1 by introducing the concepts of computer storage hierarchies and how they are used in database systems. Section 5.2 is devoted to a description of magnetic disk storage devices and their characteristics, and we also briefly describe magnetic tape storage devices. Section 5.3 describes a more recent data storage system alternative called RAID (Redundant Arrays of Inexpensive (or Independent) Disks), which provides better reliability and improved performance. Having discussed different storage technologies, we then turn our attention to the methods for organizing data on disks. Section 5.4 covers the technique of double buffering, which is used to speed retrieval of multiple disk blocks. In Section 5.5 we discuss various ways of formatting and storing records of a file on disk. Section 5.6 discusses the various types of operations that are typically applied to records of a file. We then present three primary methods for organizing records of a file on disk: unordered records, discussed in Section 5.7; ordered records, in Section 5.8; and hashed records, in Section 5.9.

Section 5.10 very briefly discusses files of mixed records and other primary methods for organizing records, such as B-trees. These are particularly relevant for storage of object-oriented databases, which we discuss later in Chapters 11 and 12. In Chapter 6 we discuss techniques for creating auxiliary data structures, called indexes, that speed up the search for and retrieval of records. These techniques involve storage of auxiliary data, called index files, in addition to the file records themselves.

Chapters 5 and 6 may be browsed through or even omitted by readers who have already studied file organizations. They can also be postponed and read later after going through the material on the relational model and the object-oriented models. The material covered here is necessary for understanding some of the later chapters in the book—in particular, Chapters 16 and 18.

5.1 Introduction

The collection of data that makes up a computerized database must be stored physically on some computer **storage medium.** The DBMS software can then retrieve, update, and process this data as needed. Computer storage media form a *storage hierarchy* that includes two main categories:

- **Primary storage.** This category includes storage media that can be operated on directly by the computer *central processing unit* (CPU), such as the computer main memory and smaller but faster cache memories. Primary storage usually provides fast access to data but is of limited storage capacity.

- **Secondary storage.** This category includes magnetic disks, optical disks, and tapes. These devices usually have a larger capacity, cost less, and provide slower access to data than do primary storage devices. Data in secondary storage cannot be processed directly by the CPU; it must first be copied into primary storage.

We will first give an overview of the various storage devices used for primary and secondary storage in Section 5.1.1 and will then discuss how databases are typically handled in the storage hierarchy in Section 5.1.2.

5.1.1 Memory Hierarchies and Storage Devices

In a modern computer system data resides and is transported throughout a hierarchy of storage media. The highest-speed memory is the most expensive and is therefore available with the least capacity. The lowest-speed memory is tape storage, which is essentially available in indefinite storage capacity.

At the *primary storage level,* the memory hierarchy includes at the most expensive end **cache memory,** which is a static RAM (Random Access Memory). Cache memory is typically used by the CPU to speed up execution of programs. The next level of primary storage is DRAM (Dynamic RAM), which provides the main work area for the CPU for keeping programs and data and is popularly called **main memory.** The advantage of DRAM is its low cost, which continues to decrease; the drawback is its volatility[1] and lower speed compared with static RAM. At the *secondary storage level,* the hierarchy includes magnetic

---

1. Volatile memory typically loses its contents in case of a power outage, whereas nonvolatile memory does not.

disks, as well as **mass storage** in the form of CD-ROM (Compact Disk–Read-Only Memory) devices, and finally tapes at the least expensive end of the hierarchy. The **storage capacity** is measured in kilobytes (Kbyte or 1000 bytes), megabytes (Mbyte or 1 million bytes), gigabytes (Gbyte or 1 billion bytes), and even terabytes (1000 Gbytes).

Programs reside and execute in DRAM. Generally, large permanent databases reside on secondary storage, and portions of the database are read into and written from buffers in main memory as needed. Now that personal computers and workstations have tens of megabytes of data in DRAM, it is becoming possible to load a large fraction of the database into main memory. In some cases, entire databases can be kept in main memory (with a backup copy on magnetic disk), leading to **main memory databases;** these are particularly useful in real-time applications that require extremely fast response times. An example is telephone switching applications, which store databases that contain routing and line information in main memory.

Between DRAM and magnetic disk storage, another form of memory, **flash memory,** is becoming common, particularly because it is nonvolatile. Flash memories are high-density, high-performance memories using EEPROM (Electrically Erasable Programmable Read-Only Memory) technology. The advantage of flash memory is the fast access speed; the disadvantage is that an entire block must be erased and written over at a time.[2]

CD-ROM disks store data optically and are read by a laser. CD-ROMs contain prerecorded data that cannot be overwritten. WORM (Write-Once-Read-Many) disks are a form of optical storage used for archiving data; they allow data to be written once and read any number of times without the possibility of erasing. They hold about half a gigabyte of data per disk and last much longer than magnetic disks. **Optical juke box memories** use an array of CD-ROM platters, which are loaded onto drives on demand. Although optical juke boxes have capacities in the hundreds of gigabytes, their retrieval times are in the hundreds of milliseconds, quite a bit slower than magnetic disks.[3] This type of storage has not become as popular as it was expected to be because of the rapid decrease in cost and increase in capacities of magnetic disks. The DVD (Digital Video Disk) is a recent standard for optical disks allowing four to fifteen gigabytes of storage per disk.

Finally, **magnetic tapes** are used for archiving and backup storage of data. **Tape jukeboxes**—which contain a bank of tapes that are catalogued and can be automatically loaded onto tape drives—are becoming popular as **tertiary storage** to hold terabytes of data. For example, NASA's EOS (Earth Observation Satellite) system stores archived databases in this fashion.

It is anticipated that many large organizations will find it normal to have terabyte-sized databases in a few years. The term **very large database** cannot be defined precisely any more because disk storage capacities are on the rise and costs are declining. It may very soon be reserved for databases containing tens of terabytes.

---

2. For example, the INTEL DD28F032SA is a 32-megabit capacity flash memory with 70-nanosecond access speed, and 430 KB/second write transfer rate.

3. Their rotational speeds are lower (around 400 rpm), giving higher latency delays and low transfer rates (around 100 to 200 KB per second).

5.1.2   Storage of Databases

Databases typically store large amounts of data that must *persist* over long periods of time. The data is accessed and processed repeatedly during this period. This contrasts with the notion of *transient* data structures that persist for only a limited time during program execution. Most databases are stored permanently (or *persistently*) on magnetic disk secondary storage, for the following reasons:

- Generally, databases are too large to fit entirely in main memory.
- The circumstances that cause permanent loss of stored data arise less frequently for disk secondary storage than for primary storage. Hence, we refer to disk—and other secondary storage devices—as **nonvolatile storage,** whereas main memory is often called **volatile storage.**
- The cost of storage per unit of data is an order of magnitude less for disk than for primary storage.

Some of the newer technologies—such as optical disks, DVDs, and tape jukeboxes—are likely to provide viable alternatives to the use of magnetic disks. Databases in the future may therefore reside at different levels of the memory hierarchy from those described in Section 5.1.1. For now, however, it is important to study and understand the properties and characteristics of magnetic disks and the way data files can be organized on disk in order to design effective databases with acceptable performance.

Magnetic tapes are frequently used as a storage medium for backing up the database because storage on tape costs even less than storage on disk. However, access to data on tape is quite slow. Data stored on tapes is **off-line;** that is, some intervention by an operator—or an automatic loading device—to load a tape is needed before this data becomes available. In contrast, disks are **on-line** devices that can be accessed directly at any time.

The techniques used to store large amounts of structured data on disk are important for database designers, the DBA, and implementers of a DBMS. Database designers and the DBA must know the advantages and disadvantages of each storage technique when they design, implement, and operate a database on a specific DBMS. Usually, the DBMS has several options available for organizing the data, and the process of **physical database design** involves choosing from among the options the particular data organization techniques that best suit the given application requirements. DBMS system implementers must study data organization techniques so that they can implement them efficiently and thus provide the DBA and users of the DBMS with sufficient options.

Typical database applications need only a small portion of the database at a time for processing. Whenever a certain portion of the data is needed, it must be located on disk, copied to main memory for processing, and then rewritten to the disk if the data is changed. The data stored on disk is organized as **files** of **records.** Each record is a collection of data values that can be interpreted as facts about entities, their attributes, and their relationships. Records should be stored on disk in a manner that makes it possible to locate them efficiently whenever they are needed.

There are several **primary file organizations,** which determine how the records of a file are *physically placed* on the disk, *and hence how the records can be accessed.* A *heap file* (or *unordered file*) places the records on disk in no particular order by appending new records at the end of the file, whereas a *sorted file* (or *sequential file*) keeps the records ordered by the value of a particular field (called the sort key). A *hashed file* uses a hash function applied to a particular field (called the hash key) to determine a record's placement on disk. Other primary file organizations, such as *B-trees*, use tree structures. We discuss primary file organizations in Sections 5.7 through 5.10. A **secondary organization** or **auxiliary access structure** allows efficient access to the records of a file based on *alternate fields* than those that have been used for the primary file organization. Most of these exist as indexes and will be discussed in Chapter 6.

5.2   Secondary Storage Devices

In this section we describe some characteristics of magnetic disk and magnetic tape storage devices. Readers who have studied these devices already may just browse through this section.

5.2.1   Hardware Description of Disk Devices

Magnetic disks are used for storing large amounts of data. The most basic unit of data on the disk is a single **bit** of information. By magnetizing an area on disk in certain ways, one can make it represent a bit value of either 0 (zero) or 1 (one). To code information, bits are grouped into **bytes** (or **characters**). Byte sizes are typically 4 to 8 bits, depending on the computer and the device. We assume that one character is stored in a single byte, and we use the terms *byte* and *character* interchangeably. The **capacity** of a disk is the number of bytes it can store, which is usually very large. Small floppy disks used with microcomputers typically hold from 400 Kbytes to 1.5 Mbytes; hard disks for micros typically hold from several hundred Mbytes up to a few Gbytes; and large disk packs used with minicomputers and mainframes have capacities that range up to a few tens or hundreds of Gbytes. Disk capacities continue to grow as technology improves.

Whatever their capacity, disks are all made of magnetic material shaped as a thin circular disk (Figure 5.1a) and protected by a plastic or acrylic cover. A disk is **single-sided** if it stores information on only one of its surfaces and **double-sided** if both surfaces are used. To increase storage capacity, disks are assembled into a **disk pack** (Figure 5.1b), which may include many disks and hence many surfaces. Information is stored on a disk surface in concentric circles of *small width*,[4] each having a distinct diameter. Each circle is called a **track.** For disk packs, the tracks with the same diameter on the various surfaces are called a **cylinder** because of the shape they would form if connected in space. The concept of a cylinder is important because data stored on one cylinder can be retrieved much faster than if it were distributed among different cylinders.

The number of tracks on a disk ranges from a few hundred to a few thousand, and the capacity of each track typically ranges from tens of Kbytes to 150 Kbytes. Because a track usu-

---

4. In some disks, the circles are now connected into a kind of continuous spiral.

(a)

(b)

Figure 5.1   (a) A single-sided disk with read/write hardware. (b) A disk pack with read/write hardware.

ally contains a large amount of information, it is divided into smaller blocks or sectors. The division of a track into **sectors** is hard-coded on the disk surface and cannot be changed. One type of sector organization calls a portion of a track that subtends a fixed angle at the center as a sector (Figure 5.2a). Several other sector organizations are possible, one of which is to have the sectors subtend smaller angles at the center as one moves away, thus maintaining a uniform density of recording (Figure 5.2b). Not all disks have their tracks divided into sectors.

The division of a track into equal-sized **disk blocks** (or **pages**) is set by the operating system during disk **formatting** (or **initialization**). Block size is fixed during initialization and cannot be changed dynamically. Typical disk block sizes range from 512 to 4096 bytes. A disk with hard-coded sectors often has the sectors subdivided into blocks during initialization. Blocks are separated by fixed-size **interblock gaps,** which include specially coded control information written during disk initialization. This information is used to determine which block on the track follows each interblock gap. Table 5.1 represents specifications of a typical disk.

(a)   track   sector (arc of a track)

(b)   three sectors
       two sectors
       one sector

Figure 5.2 Different sector organizations on disk. (a) Sectors subtending a fixed angle. (b) Sectors maintaining a uniform recording density.

There is a continuous improvement in the storage capacity and transfer rates associated with disks; they are also progressively getting cheaper—currently costing only a fraction of a dollar per megabyte of disk storage. Costs are going down so rapidly that costs as low as one cent per megabyte or $10K per terabyte by the year 2001 are being forecast.

A disk is a *random access* addressable device. Transfer of data between main memory and disk takes place in units of disk blocks. The **hardware address** of a block—a combination of a surface number, track number (within the surface), and block number (within the track)—is supplied to the disk input/output (I/O) hardware. The address of a **buffer**—a contiguous reserved area in main storage that holds one block—is also provided. For a **read** command, the block from disk is copied into the buffer; whereas for a **write** command, the contents of the buffer are copied into the disk block. Sometimes several contiguous blocks, called a **cluster,** may be transferred as a unit. In this case the buffer size is adjusted to match the number of bytes in the cluster.

The actual hardware mechanism that reads or writes a block is the disk **read/write head,** which is part of a system called a **disk drive.** A disk or disk pack is mounted in the disk drive, which includes a motor that rotates the disks. A read/write head includes an electronic component attached to a **mechanical arm.** Disk packs with multiple surfaces are controlled by several read/write heads—one for each surface (see Figure 5.1b). All arms are connected to an **actuator** attached to another electrical motor, which moves the read/write heads in unison and positions them precisely over the cylinder of tracks specified in a block address.

Disk drives for hard disks rotate the disk pack continuously at a constant speed (typically ranging between 3600 and 7200 rpm). For a floppy disk, the disk drive begins to rotate the disk whenever a particular read or write request is initiated and ceases rotation

Table 5.1   Specification of Typical High-end Cheetah Disks from Seagate

Description		
Model number	ST136403LC	ST318203LC
Model name	Cheetah 36	Cheetah 18LP
Form Factor (width)	3.5-inch	3.5-inch
Weight	1.04 Kg	0.59 Kg
Capacity/Interface		
Formatted capacity	36.4 Gbytes, formatted	18.2 Gbytes, formatted
Interface type	80-pin Ultra-2 SCSI	80-pin Ultra-2 SCSI
Configuration		
Number of Discs (physical)	12	6
Number of heads (physical)	24	12
Total cylinders (SCSI only)	9,772	9,801
Total tracks (SCSI only)	N/A	117,612
Bytes per sector	512	512
Track Density (TPI)	N/A tracks/inch	12,580 tracks/inch
Recording Density (BPI, max)	N/A bits/inch	258,048 bits/inch
Performance		
Transfer Rates		
Internal Transfer Rate (min)	193 Mbits/sec	193 Mbits/sec
Internal Transfer Rate (max)	308 Mbits/sec	308 Mbits/sec
Formatted Int transfer rate (min)	18 Mbits/sec	18 Mbits/sec
Formatted Int transfer rate (max)	28 Mbits/sec	28 Mbits/sec
External (I/O) Transfer Rate (max)	80 Mbits/sec	80 Mbits/sec
Seek Times		
Average seek time, read	5.7 msec typical	5.2 msec typical
Average seek time, write	6.5 msec typical	6 msec typical
Track-to-track seek, read	0.6 msec typical	0.6 msec typical
Track-to-track seek, write	0.9 msec typical	0.9 msec typical
Full disc seek, read	12 msec typical	12 msec typical
Full disc seek, write	13 msec typical	13 msec typical
Average Latency	2.99 msec	2.99 msec
Other		
Default buffer (cache) size	1,024 Kbytes	1,024 Kbytes
Spindle Speed	10,000 RPM	10,016 RPM
Nonrecoverable error rate	1 per 10^{15} bits read	1 per 10^{15} bits read
Seek errors (SCSI)	1 per 10^8 bits read	1 per 10^8 bits read

Courtesy Seagate Technology © 1999.

soon after the data transfer is completed. Once the read/write head is positioned on the right track and the block specified in the block address moves under the read/write head, the electronic component of the read/write head is activated to transfer the data. Some disk units have fixed read/write heads, with as many heads as there are tracks. These are called **fixed-head** disks, whereas disk units with an actuator are called **movable-head**

disks. For fixed-head disks, a track or cylinder is selected by electronically switching to the appropriate read/write head rather than by actual mechanical movement; consequently, it is much faster. However, the cost of the additional read/write heads is quite high, so fixed-head disks are not commonly used.

A **disk controller,** typically embedded in the disk drive, controls the disk drive and interfaces it to the computer system. One of the standard interfaces used today for disk drives on PC and workstations is called SCSI (Small Computer Storage Interface). The controller accepts high-level I/O commands and takes appropriate action to position the arm and causes the read/write action to take place. To transfer a disk block, given its address, the disk controller must first mechanically position the read/write head on the correct track. The time required to do this is called the **seek time.** Typical seek times are 12 to 14 msec on desktops and 8 or 9 msecs on servers. Following that, there is another delay—called the **rotational delay** or **latency**—while the beginning of the desired block rotates into position under the read/write head. Finally, some additional time is needed to transfer the data; this is called the **block transfer time.** Hence, the total time needed to locate and transfer an arbitrary block, given its address, is the sum of the seek time, rotational delay, and block transfer time. The seek time and rotational delay are usually much larger than the block transfer time. To make the transfer of multiple blocks more efficient, it is common to transfer several consecutive blocks on the same track or cylinder. This eliminates the seek time and rotational delay for all but the first block and can result in a substantial saving of time when numerous contiguous blocks are transferred. Usually, the disk manufacturer provides a **bulk transfer rate** for calculating the time required to transfer consecutive blocks. Appendix B contains a discussion of these and other disk parameters.

The time needed to locate and transfer a disk block is in the order of milliseconds, usually ranging from 12 to 60 msec. For contiguous blocks, locating the first block takes from 12 to 60 msec, but transferring subsequent blocks may take only 1 to 2 msec each. Many search techniques take advantage of consecutive retrieval of blocks when searching for data on disk. In any case, a transfer time in the order of milliseconds is considered quite high compared with the time required to process data in main memory by current CPUs. Hence, locating data on disk is a *major bottleneck* in database applications. The file structures we discuss here and in Chapter 6 attempt to *minimize the number of block transfers* needed to locate and transfer the required data from disk to main memory.

5.2.2 Magnetic Tape Storage Devices

Disks are **random access** secondary storage devices, because an arbitrary disk block may be accessed "at random" once we specify its address. Magnetic tapes are **sequential access** devices; to access the nth block on tape, we must first scan over the preceding $n - 1$ blocks. Data is stored on reels of high-capacity magnetic tape, somewhat similar to audio or video tapes. A **tape drive** is required to read the data from or to write the data to a **tape reel.** Usually, each group of bits that forms a byte is stored across the tape, and the bytes themselves are stored consecutively on the tape.

A read/write head is used to read or write data on tape. Data records on tape are also stored in blocks—although the blocks may be substantially larger than those for disks, and interblock gaps are also quite large. With typical tape densities of 1600 to 6250 bytes per inch, a typical interblock gap[5] of 0.6 inches corresponds to 960 to 3750 bytes of wasted storage space. For better space utilization it is customary to group many records together in one block.

The main characteristic of a tape is its requirement that we access the data blocks in **sequential order.** To get to a block in the middle of a reel of tape, the tape is mounted and then scanned until the required block gets under the read/write head. For this reason, tape access can be slow and tapes are not used to store on-line data, except for some specialized applications. However, tapes serve a very important function—that of **backing up** the database. One reason for backup is to keep copies of disk files in case the data is lost because of a disk crash, which can happen if the disk read/write head touches the disk surface because of mechanical malfunction. For this reason, disk files are copied periodically to tape. Tapes can also be used to store excessively large database files. Finally, database files that are seldom used or outdated but are required for historical record keeping can be **archived** on tape. Recently, smaller 8-mm magnetic tapes (similar to those used in camcorders) that can store up to 50 Gbytes, as well as 4-mm helical scan data cartridges and CD-ROMs (compact disks–read only memory) have become popular media for backing up data files from workstations and personal computers. They are also used for storing images and system libraries. In the next section we review the recent development in disk storage technology called RAID.

5.3 Parallelizing Disk Access Using RAID Technology

With the exponential growth in the performance and capacity of semiconductor devices and memories, faster microprocessors with larger and larger primary memories are continually becoming available. To match this growth, it is natural to expect that secondary storage technology must also take steps to keep up in performance and reliability with processor technology.

A major advance in secondary storage technology is represented by the development of **RAID,** which originally stood for **Redundant Arrays of Inexpensive Disks.** Lately, the "I" in RAID is said to stand for Independent. The RAID idea received a very positive endorsement by industry and has been developed into an elaborate set of alternative RAID architectures (RAID levels 0 through 6). We highlight the main features of the technology below.

The main goal of RAID is to even out the widely different rates of performance improvement of disks against those in memory and microprocessors.[6] While RAM capacities have quadrupled every two to three years, disk *access times* are improving at less than

---

5. Called *interrecord gaps* in tape terminology.

6. This was predicted by Gordon Bell to be about 40 percent every year between 1974 and 1984 and is now supposed to exceed 50 percent per year.

Table 5.2 Trends in Disk Technology

	1993 Parameter Values[*]	Historical Rate of Improvement per Year (%)[*]	Expected 1999 Values[**]
Areal density	50–150 Mbits/sq. inch	27	2–3 GB/sq. inch
Linear density	40,000–60,000 bits/inch	13	238 Kbits/inch
Inter-track density	1,500–3,000 tracks/inch	10	11550 tracks/inch
Capacity (3.5" form factor)	100–2000 MB	27	36 GB
Transfer rate	3–4 MB/s	22	17–28 MB/sec
Seek time	7–20 ms	8	5–7 msec

[*]*Source:* From Chen, Lee, Gibson, Katz and Patterson (1994), ACM *Computing Surveys*, Vol. 26, No. 2 (June 1994). Reprinted by permission.
[**]*Source:* IBM Ultrastar 36XP and 18ZX hard disk drives.

10 percent per year, and disk *transfer rates* are improving at roughly 20 percent per year. Disk *capacities* are indeed improving at more than 50 percent per year, but the speed and access time improvements are of a much smaller magnitude. Table 5.2 shows trends in disk technology in terms of 1993 parameter values and rates of improvement.

A second qualitative disparity exists between the ability of special microprocessors that cater to new applications involving processing of video, audio, image, and spatial data (see Chapters 23 and 27 for details of these applications), with corresponding lack of fast access to large, shared data sets.

The natural solution is a large array of small independent disks acting as a single higher-performance logical disk. A concept called **data striping** is used, which utilizes *parallelism* to improve disk performance. Data striping distributes data transparently over multiple disks to make them appear as a single large, fast disk. Figure 5.3 shows a file distributed or *striped* over four disks. Striping improves overall I/O performance by allowing multiple I/Os to be serviced in parallel, thus providing high overall transfer rates. Data striping also accomplishes load balancing among disks. Moreover, by storing redundant information on disks using parity or some other error correction code, reliability can be improved. In Sections 5.3.1 and 5.3.2, we discuss how RAID achieves the two important objectives of improved reliability and higher performance. Section 5.3.3 discusses RAID organizations.

Figure 5.3 Data striping. File A is striped across four disks.

5.3.1   Improving Reliability with RAID

For an array of n disks, the likelihood of failure is n times as much as that for one disk. Hence, if the MTTF (Mean Time To Failure) of a disk drive is assumed to be 200,000 hours or about 22.8 years (typical times range up to 1 million hours), that of a bank of 100 disk drives becomes only 2000 hours or 83.3 days. Keeping a single copy of data in such an array of disks will cause a significant loss of reliability. An obvious solution is to employ redundancy of data so that disk failures can be tolerated. The disadvantages are many: additional I/O operations for write, extra computation to maintain redundancy and to do recovery from errors, and additional disk capacity to store redundant information.

One technique for introducing redundancy is called **mirroring** or **shadowing.** Data is written redundantly to two identical physical disks that are treated as one logical disk. When data is read, it can be retrieved from the disk with shorter queuing, seek, and rotational delays. If a disk fails, the other disk is used until the first is repaired. Suppose the mean time to repair is 24 hours, then the mean time to data loss of a mirrored disk system using 100 disks with MTTF of 200,000 hours each is $(200,000)^2/(2 * 24) = 8.33 * 10^8$ hours, which is 95,028 years.[7] Disk mirroring also doubles the rate at which read requests are handled, since a read can go to either disk. The transfer rate of each read, however, remains the same as that for a single disk.

Another solution to the problem of reliability is to store extra information that is not normally needed but that can be used to reconstruct the lost information in case of disk failure. The incorporation of redundancy must consider two problems: (1) selecting a technique for computing the redundant information, and (2) selecting a method of distributing the redundant information across the disk array. The first problem is addressed by using error correcting codes involving parity bits, or specialized codes such as Hamming codes. Under the parity scheme, a redundant disk may be considered as having the sum of all the data in the other disks. When a disk fails, the missing information can be constructed by a process similar to subtraction.

For the second problem, the two major approaches are either to store the redundant information on a small number of disks or to distribute it uniformly across all disks. The latter results in better load balancing. The different levels of RAID choose a combination of these options to implement redundancy, and hence to improve reliability.

5.3.2   Improving Performance with RAID

The disk arrays employ the technique of data striping to achieve higher transfer rates. Note that data can be read or written only one block at a time, so a typical transfer contains 512 bytes. Disk striping may be applied at a finer granularity by breaking up a byte of data into bits and spreading the bits to different disks. Thus, **bit-level data striping** consists of splitting a byte of data and writing bit j to the jth disk. With 8-bit bytes, eight physical disks may be considered as one logical disk with an eightfold increase in the data transfer rate. Each disk participates in each I/O request and the total amount of data read

---

7. The formulas for MTTF calculations appear in Chen et al. (1994).

per request is eight times as much. Bit-level striping can be generalized to a number of disks that is either a multiple or a factor of eight. Thus, in a four-disk array, bit n goes to the disk which is (n mod 4).

The granularity of data interleaving can be higher than a bit; for example, blocks of a file can be striped across disks, giving rise to **block-level striping.** Figure 5.3 shows block-level data striping assuming the data file contained four blocks. With block-level striping, multiple independent requests that access single blocks (small requests) can be serviced in parallel by separate disks, thus decreasing the queuing time of I/O requests. Requests that access multiple blocks (large requests) can be parallelized, thus reducing their response time. In general, the more the number of disks in an array, the larger the potential performance benefit. However, assuming independent failures, the disk array of 100 disks collectively has a $1/100^{th}$ the reliability of a single disk. Thus, redundancy via error-correcting codes and disk mirroring is necessary to provide reliability along with high performance.

5.3.3 RAID Organizations and Levels

Different RAID organizations were defined based on different combinations of the two factors of granularity of data interleaving (striping) and pattern used to compute redundant information. In the initial proposal, levels 1 through 5 of RAID were proposed, and two additional levels—0 and 6—were added later.

RAID level 0 has no redundant data and hence has the best write performance since updates do not have to be duplicated. However, its read performance is not as good as RAID level 1, which uses mirrored disks. In the latter, performance improvement is possible by scheduling a read request to the disk with shortest expected seek and rotational delay. RAID level 2 uses memory-style redundancy by using Hamming codes, which contain parity bits for distinct overlapping subsets of components. Thus, in one particular version of this level, three redundant disks suffice for four original disks whereas, with mirroring—as in level 1—four would be required. Level 2 includes both error detection and correction, although detection is generally not required because broken disks identify themselves.

RAID level 3 uses a single parity disk relying on the disk controller to figure out which disk has failed. Levels 4 and 5 use block-level data striping, with level 5 distributing data and parity information across all disks. Finally, RAID level 6 applies the so-called $P + Q$ redundancy scheme using Reed-Soloman codes to protect against up to two disk failures by using just two redundant disks. The seven RAID levels (0 through 6) are illustrated in Figure 5.4 schematically.

Rebuilding in case of disk failure is easiest for RAID level 1. Other levels require the reconstruction of a failed disk by reading multiple disks. Level 1 is used for critical applications such as storing logs of transactions. Levels 3 and 5 are preferred for large volume storage, with level 3 providing higher transfer rates. Designers of a RAID setup for a given application mix have to confront many design decisions such as the level of RAID, the number of disks, the choice of parity schemes, and grouping of disks for block-level striping. Detailed performance studies on small reads and writes (referring to I/O requests for one striping unit) and large reads and writes (referring to I/O requests for one stripe unit from each disk in an error-correction group) have been performed.

Non-Redundant (RAID Level 0)

Mirrored (RAID Level 1)

Memory-Style ECC (RAID Level 2)

Bit-Interleaved Parity (RAID Level 3)

Block-Interleaved Parity (RAID Level 4)

Block-Interleaved Distribution-Parity (RAID Level 5)

P+Q Redundancy (RAID Level 6)

Figure 5.4   Multiple levels of RAID. From Chen, Lee, Gibson, Katz, and Patterson (1994), ACM Computing Survey, Vol. 26, No. 2 (June 1994). Reprinted with permisson.

5.4 Buffering of Blocks

When several blocks need to be transferred from disk to main memory and all the block addresses are known, several buffers can be reserved in main memory to speed up the transfer. While one buffer is being read or written, the CPU can process data in the other buffer. This is possible because an independent disk I/O processor (controller) exists that, once started, can proceed to transfer a data block between memory and disk independent of and in parallel to CPU processing.

Figure 5.5 illustrates how two processes can proceed in parallel. Processes A and B are running **concurrently** in an **interleaved** fashion, whereas processes C and D are running **concurrently** in a **parallel** fashion. When a single CPU controls multiple processes, parallel execution is not possible. However, the processes can still run concurrently in an interleaved way. Buffering is most useful when processes can run concurrently in a parallel fashion, either because a separate disk I/O processor is available or because multiple CPU processors exist.

Figure 5.6 illustrates how reading and processing can proceed in parallel when the time required to process a disk block in memory is less than the time required to read the next block and fill a buffer. The CPU can start processing a block once its transfer to main memory is completed; at the same time the disk I/O processor can be reading and transferring the next block into a different buffer. This technique is called **double buffering** and can also be used to write a continuous stream of blocks from memory to the disk. Double buffering permits continuous reading or writing of data on consecutive disk blocks, which

Figure 5.5 Interleaved concurrency versus parallel execution.

Figure 5.6   Use of two buffers, A and B, for reading from disk.

eliminates the seek time and rotational delay for all but the first block transfer. Moreover, data is kept ready for processing, thus reducing the waiting time in the programs.

5.5   Placing File Records on Disk

In this section we define the concepts of records, record types, and files. We then discuss techniques for placing file records on disk.

5.5.1   Records and Record Types

Data is usually stored in the form of **records.** Each record consists of a collection of related data **values** or **items,** where each value is formed of one or more bytes and corresponds to a particular **field** of the record. Records usually describe entities and their attributes. For example, an EMPLOYEE record represents an employee entity, and each field value in the record specifies some attribute of that employee, such as NAME, BIRTHDATE, SALARY, or SUPERVISOR. A collection of field names and their corresponding data types constitutes a **record type** or **record format** definition. A **data type,** associated with each field, specifies the type of values a field can take.

The data type of a field is usually one of the standard data types used in programming. These include numeric (integer, long integer, or floating point), string of characters (fixed-length or varying), Boolean (having 0 and 1 or TRUE and FALSE values only), and sometimes specially coded **date** and **time** data types. The number of bytes required for each data type is fixed for a given computer system. An integer may require 4 bytes, a long integer 8 bytes, a real number 4 bytes, a Boolean 1 byte, a date 10 bytes (assuming a format of YYYY-MM-DD), and a fixed-length string of k characters k bytes. Variable-length strings may require as many bytes as there are characters in each field value. For example, an EMPLOYEE record type may be defined—using the C programming language notation—as the following structure:

```
struct employee{
    char name[30];
    char ssn[9];
    int salary;
    int jobcode;
    char department[20];
};
```

In recent database applications, the need may arise for storing data items that consist of large unstructured objects, which represent images, digitized video or audio streams, or free text. These are referred to as **BLOBs** (Binary Large Objects). A BLOB data item is typically stored separately from its record in a pool of disk blocks, and a pointer to the BLOB is included in the record.

5.5.2 Files, Fixed-Length Records, and Variable-Length Records

A **file** is a *sequence* of records. In many cases, all records in a file are of the same record type. If every record in the file has exactly the same size (in bytes), the file is said to be made up of **fixed-length records.** If different records in the file have different sizes, the file is said to be made up of **variable-length records.** A file may have variable-length records for several reasons:

- The file records are of the same record type, but one or more of the fields are of varying size (**variable-length fields**). For example, the NAME field of EMPLOYEE can be a variable-length field.

- The file records are of the same record type, but one or more of the fields may have multiple values for individual records; such a field is called a **repeating field** and a group of values for the field is often called a **repeating group.**

- The file records are of the same record type, but one or more of the fields are **optional;** that is, they may have values for some but not all of the file records (**optional fields**).

- The file contains records of *different record types* and hence of varying size (**mixed file**). This would occur if related records of different types were *clustered* (placed together) on disk blocks; for example, the GRADE_REPORT records of a particular student may be placed following that STUDENT's record.

The fixed-length EMPLOYEE records in Figure 5.7(a) have a record size of 71 bytes. Every record has the same fields, and field lengths are fixed, so the system can identify the starting byte position of each field relative to the starting position of the record. This facilitates locating field values by programs that access such files. Notice that it is possible to represent a file that logically should have variable-length records as a fixed-length records file. For example, in the case of optional fields we could have *every field* included in *every*

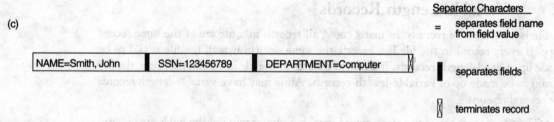

Figure 5.7   Three record storage formats. (a) A fixed-length record with six fields and size of 71 bytes. (b) A record with two variable-length fields and three fixed-length fields. (c) A variable-field record with three types of separator characters.

file record but store a special null value if no value exists for that field. For a repeating field, we could allocate as many spaces in each record as the *maximum number of values* that the field can take. In either case, space is wasted when certain records do not have values for all the physical spaces provided in each record. We now consider other options for formatting records of a file of variable-length records.

For *variable-length fields,* each record has a value for each field, but we do not know the exact length of some field values. To determine the bytes within a particular record that represent each field, we can use special **separator** characters (such as ? or % or $)— which do not appear in any field value—to terminate variable-length fields (Figure 5.7b), or we can store the length in bytes of the field in the record, preceding the field value.

A file of records with *optional fields* can be formatted in different ways. If the total number of fields for the record type is large but the number of fields that actually appear in a typical record is small, we can include in each record a sequence of <field-name, field-value> pairs rather than just the field values. Three types of separator characters are used in Figure 5.7(c), although we could use the same separator character for the first two purposes—separating the field name from the field value and separating one field from the next field. A more practical option is to assign a short **field type** code—say, an integer number—to each field and include in each record a sequence of <field-type, field-value> pairs rather than <field-name, field-value> pairs.

A *repeating field* needs one separator character to separate the repeating values of the field and another separator character to indicate termination of the field. Finally, for a file that includes *records of different types*, each record is preceded by a **record type** indicator. Understandably, programs that process files of variable-length records—which are usually part of the file system and hence hidden from the typical programmers—need to be more complex than those for fixed-length records, where the starting position and size of each field are known and fixed.[8]

5.5.3 Record Blocking and Spanned Versus Unspanned Records

The records of a file must be allocated to disk blocks because a block is the *unit of data transfer* between disk and memory. When the block size is larger than the record size, each block will contain numerous records, although some files may have unusually large records that cannot fit in one block. Suppose that the block size is B bytes. For a file of fixed-length records of size R bytes, with $B \geq R$, we can fit bfr = $\lfloor B/R \rfloor$ records per block, where the $\lfloor (x) \rfloor$ *(floor function) rounds down* the number x to an integer. The value *bfr* is called the **blocking factor** for the file. In general, R may not divide B exactly, so we have some unused space in each block equal to

$$B - (bfr * R) \text{ bytes}$$

To utilize this unused space, we can store part of a record on one block and the rest on another. A **pointer** at the end of the first block points to the block containing the remainder of the record in case it is not the next consecutive block on disk. This organization is called **spanned,** because records can span more than one block. Whenever a record is larger than a block, we *must* use a spanned organization. If records are not allowed to cross block boundaries, the organization is called **unspanned.** This is used with fixed-length records having $B > R$ because it makes each record start at a known location in the block, simplifying record processing. For variable-length records, either a spanned or an unspanned organization can be used. If the average record is large, it is advantageous to use spanning to reduce the lost space in each block. Figure 5.8 illustrates spanned versus unspanned organization.

For variable-length records using spanned organization, each block may store a different number of records. In this case, the blocking factor *bfr* represents the *average* number of records per block for the file. We can use *bfr* to calculate the number of blocks b needed for a file of r records:

$$b = \lceil (r/bfr) \rceil \text{ blocks}$$

where the $\lceil (x) \rceil$ *(ceiling function)* rounds the value x up to the next integer.

---

8. Other schemes are also possible for representing variable-length records.

Figure 5.8   Types of record organization. (a) Unspanned. (b) Spanned.

5.5.4 Allocating File Blocks on Disk

There are several standard techniques for allocating the blocks of a file on disk. In **contiguous allocation** the file blocks are allocated to consecutive disk blocks. This makes reading the whole file very fast using double buffering, but it makes expanding the file difficult. In **linked allocation** each file block contains a pointer to the next file block. This makes it easy to expand the file but makes it slow to read the whole file. A combination of the two allocates **clusters** of consecutive disk blocks, and the clusters are linked. Clusters are sometimes called **file segments** or **extents.** Another possibility is to use **indexed allocation,** where one or more **index blocks** contain pointers to the actual file blocks. It is also common to use combinations of these techniques.

5.5.5 File Headers

A **file header** or **file descriptor** contains information about a file that is needed by the system programs that access the file records. The header includes information to determine the disk addresses of the file blocks as well as to record format descriptions, which may include field lengths and order of fields within a record for fixed-length unspanned records and field type codes, separator characters, and record type codes for variable-length records.

To search for a record on disk, one or more blocks are copied into main memory buffers. Programs then search for the desired record or records within the buffers, using the information in the file header. If the address of the block that contains the desired record is not known, the search programs must do a **linear search** through the file blocks. Each file block is copied into a buffer and searched either until the record is located or all the file blocks have been searched unsuccessfully. This can be very time-consuming for a large file. The goal of a good file organization is to locate the block that contains a desired record with a minimal number of block transfers.

5.6 Operations on Files

Operations on files are usually grouped into **retrieval operations** and **update operations.** The former do not change any data in the file, but only locate certain records so that their field values can be examined and processed. The latter change the file by insertion or deletion of records or by modification of field values. In either case, we may have to **select** one or more records for retrieval, deletion, or modification based on a **selection condition** (or **filtering condition**), which specifies criteria that the desired record or records must satisfy.

Consider an EMPLOYEE file with fields NAME, SSN, SALARY, JOBCODE, and DEPARTMENT. A **simple selection condition** may involve an equality comparison on some field value—for example, (SSN = '123456789') or (DEPARTMENT = 'Research'). More complex conditions can involve other types of comparison operators, such as > or ≥; an example is (SALARY ≥ 30000). The general case is to have an arbitrary Boolean expression on the fields of the file as the selection condition.

Search operations on files are generally based on simple selection conditions. A complex condition must be decomposed by the DBMS (or the programmer) to extract a simple condition that can be used to locate the records on disk. Each located record is then checked to determine whether it satisfies the full selection condition. For example, we may extract the simple condition (DEPARTMENT = 'Research') from the complex condition ((SALARY ≥ 30000) AND (DEPARTMENT = 'Research')); each record satisfying (DEPARTMENT = 'Research') is located and then tested to see if it also satisfies (SALARY ≥ 30000).

When several file records satisfy a search condition, the *first* record—with respect to the physical sequence of file records—is initially located and designated the **current record.** Subsequent search operations commence from this record and locate the *next* record in the file that satisfies the condition.

Actual operations for locating and accessing file records vary from system to system. Below, we present a set of representative operations. Typically, high-level programs, such as DBMS software programs, access the records by using these commands, so we sometimes refer to **program variables** in the following descriptions:

- *Open:* Prepares the file for reading or writing. Allocates appropriate buffers (typically at least two) to hold file blocks from disk, and retrieves the file header. Sets the file pointer to the beginning of the file.

- *Reset:* Sets the file pointer of an open file to the beginning of the file.

- *Find* (or *Locate*): Searches for the first record that satisfies a search condition. Transfers the block containing that record into a main memory buffer (if it is not already there). The file pointer points to the record in the buffer and it becomes the *current record.* Sometimes, different verbs are used to indicate whether the located record is to be retrieved or updated.

- *Read* (or *Get*): Copies the current record from the buffer to a program variable in the user program. This command may also advance the current record pointer to the next record in the file, which may necessitate reading the next file block from disk.

- *FindNext:* Searches for the next record in the file that satisfies the search condition. Transfers the block containing that record into a main memory buffer (if it is not already there). The record is located in the buffer and becomes the current record.

- *Delete:* Deletes the current record and (eventually) updates the file on disk to reflect the deletion.

- *Modify:* Modifies some field values for the current record and (eventually) updates the file on disk to reflect the modification.

- *Insert:* Inserts a new record in the file by locating the block where the record is to be inserted, transferring that block into a main memory buffer (if it is not already there), writing the record into the buffer, and (eventually) writing the buffer to disk to reflect the insertion.

- *Close:* Completes the file access by releasing the buffers and performing any other needed cleanup operations.

The preceding (except for Open and Close) are called **record-at-a-time** operations, because each operation applies to a single record. It is possible to streamline the operations Find, FindNext, and Read into a single operation, Scan, whose description is as follows:

- *Scan:* If the file has just been opened or reset, *Scan* returns the first record; otherwise it returns the next record. If a condition is specified with the operation, the returned record is the first or next record satisfying the condition.

In database systems, additional **set-at-a-time** higher-level operations may be applied to a file. Examples of these are as follows:

- *FindAll:* Locates *all* the records in the file that satisfy a search condition.

- *FindOrdered:* Retrieves all the records in the file in some specified order.

- *Reorganize:* Starts the reorganization process. As we shall see, some file organizations require periodic reorganization. An example is to reorder the file records by sorting them on a specified field.

At this point, it is worthwhile to note the difference between the terms *file organization* and *access method*. A **file organization** refers to the organization of the data of a file into records, blocks, and access structures; this includes the way records and blocks are placed on the storage medium and interlinked. An **access method,** on the other hand, provides a group of operations—such as those listed earlier—that can be applied to a file. In general, it is possible to apply several access methods to a file organization. Some access methods, though, can be applied only to files organized in certain ways. For example, we cannot apply an indexed access method to a file without an index (see Chapter 6).

Usually, we expect to use some search conditions more than others. Some files may be **static,** meaning that update operations are rarely performed; other, more **dynamic** files may change frequently, so update operations are constantly applied to them. A successful file organization should perform as efficiently as possible the operations we expect to *apply frequently* to the file. For example, consider the EMPLOYEE file (Figure 5.7a), which stores the records for current employees in a company. We expect to insert records (when employees are hired), delete records (when employees leave the company), and modify records (say, when an employee's salary or job is changed). Deleting or modifying a record requires a selection condition to identify a particular record or set of records. Retrieving one or more records also requires a selection condition.

If users expect mainly to apply a search condition based on SSN, the designer must choose a file organization that facilitates locating a record given its SSN value. This may involve physically ordering the records by SSN value or defining an index on SSN (see Chapter 6). Suppose that a second application uses the file to generate employees' paychecks and requires that paychecks be grouped by department. For this application, it is best to store all employee records having the same department value contiguously, clustering them into blocks and perhaps ordering them by name within each department. However, this arrangement conflicts with ordering the records by SSN values. If both applications are important, the designer should choose an organization that allows both operations to be done efficiently. Unfortunately, in many cases there may not be an organization that allows all needed operations on a file to be implemented efficiently. In such cases a compromise must be chosen that takes into account the expected importance and mix of retrieval and update operations.

In the following sections and in Chapter 6, we discuss methods for organizing records of a file on disk. Several general techniques, such as ordering, hashing, and indexing, are used to create access methods. In addition, various general techniques for handling insertions and deletions work with many file organizations.

5.7 Files of Unordered Records (Heap Files)

In this simplest and most basic type of organization, records are placed in the file in the order in which they are inserted, so new records are inserted at the end of the file. Such an organization is called a **heap** or **pile file.**[9] This organization is often used with additional access paths, such as the secondary indexes discussed in Chapter 6. It is also used to collect and store data records for future use.

Inserting a new record is *very efficient*: the last disk block of the file is copied into a buffer; the new record is added; and the block is then **rewritten** back to disk. The address of the last file block is kept in the file header. However, searching for a record using any search condition involves a **linear search** through the file block by block—an expensive procedure. If only one record satisfies the search condition, then, on the average, a program will read into memory and search half the file blocks before it finds the record. For a file of b blocks, this requires searching $(b/2)$ blocks, on average. If no records or several records satisfy the search condition, the program must read and search all b blocks in the file.

To delete a record, a program must first find its block, copy the block into a buffer, then delete the record from the buffer, and finally **rewrite the block** back to the disk. This leaves unused space in the disk block. Deleting a large number of records in this way results in wasted storage space. Another technique used for record deletion is to have an

---

9. Sometimes this organization is called a **sequential file.**

extra byte or bit, called a **deletion marker,** stored with each record. A record is deleted by setting the deletion marker to a certain value. A different value of the marker indicates a valid (not deleted) record. Search programs consider only valid records in a block when conducting their search. Both of these deletion techniques require periodic **reorganization** of the file to reclaim the unused space of deleted records. During reorganization, the file blocks are accessed consecutively, and records are packed by removing deleted records. After such a reorganization, the blocks are filled to capacity once more. Another possibility is to use the space of deleted records when inserting new records, although this requires extra bookkeeping to keep track of empty locations.

We can use either spanned or unspanned organization for an unordered file, and it may be used with either fixed-length or variable-length records. Modifying a variable-length record may require deleting the old record and inserting a modified record, because the modified record may not fit in its old space on disk.

To read all records in order of the values of some field, we create a sorted copy of the file. Sorting is an expensive operation for a large disk file, and special techniques for **external sorting** are used (see Chapter 18).

For a file of unordered *fixed-length records* using *unspanned blocks* and *contiguous allocation*, it is straightforward to access any record by its **position** in the file. If the file records are numbered $0, 1, 2, \ldots, r - 1$ and the records in each block are numbered $0, 1, \ldots, bfr - 1$, where bfr is the blocking factor, then the ith record of the file is located in block $\lfloor (i/bfr) \rfloor$ and is the $(i \bmod bfr)^{th}$ record in that block. Such a file is often called a **relative** or **direct file** because records can easily be accessed directly by their relative positions. Accessing a record by its position does not help locate a record based on a search condition; however, it facilitates the construction of access paths on the file, such as the indexes discussed in Chapter 6.

5.8 Files of Ordered Records (Sorted Files)

We can physically order the records of a file on disk based on the values of one of their fields—called the **ordering field.** This leads to an **ordered** or **sequential** file.[10] If the ordering field is also a **key field** of the file—a field guaranteed to have a unique value in each record—then the field is called the **ordering key** for the file. Figure 5.9 shows an ordered file with NAME as the ordering key field (assuming that employees have distinct names).

Ordered records have some advantages over unordered files. First, reading the records in order of the ordering key values becomes extremely efficient, because no sorting is required. Second, finding the next record from the current one in order of the ordering key usually requires no additional block accesses, because the next record is in the same block as the current one (unless the current record is the last one in the block). Third, using a search condition based on the value of an ordering key field results in faster access when the binary search technique is used, which constitutes an improvement over linear searches, although it is not often used for disk files.

---

10. The term *sequential file* has also been used to refer to unordered files.

	NAME	SSN	BIRTHDATE	JOB	SALARY	SEX
block 1	Aaron, Ed					
	Abbott, Diane					
	⋮					
	Acosta, Marc					
block 2	Adams, John					
	Adams, Robin					
	⋮					
	Akers, Jan					
block 3	Alexander, Ed					
	Alfred, Bob					
	⋮					
	Allen, Sam					
block 4	Allen, Troy					
	Anders, Keith					
	⋮					
	Anderson, Rob					
block 5	Anderson, Zach					
	Angeli, Joe					
	⋮					
	Archer, Sue					
block 6	Arnold, Mack					
	Arnold, Steven					
	⋮					
	Atkins, Timothy					
⋮						
block n −1	Wong, James					
	Wood, Donald					
	⋮					
	Woods, Manny					
block n	Wright, Pam					
	Wyatt, Charles					
	⋮					
	Zimmer, Byron					

Figure 5.9 Some blocks of an ordered (sequential) file of EMPLOYEE records with NAME as the ordering key field.

A **binary search** for disk files can be done on the blocks rather than on the records. Suppose that the file has b blocks numbered $1, 2, \ldots, b$; the records are ordered by ascending value of their ordering key field; and we are searching for a record whose ordering key field value is K. Assuming that disk addresses of the file blocks are available in the file header, the binary search can be described by Algorithm 5.1. A binary search usually accesses $\log_2(b)$ blocks, whether the record is found or not—an improvement over linear searches, where, on the average, $(b/2)$ blocks are accessed when the record is found and b blocks are accessed when the record is not found.

ALGORITHM 5.1 Binary search on an ordering key of a disk file.

```
l ← 1; u ← b; (* b is the number of file blocks*)
while (u ≥ l) do
  begin i ← (l + u) div 2;
  read block i of the file into the buffer;
  if K < (ordering key field value of the first record in block i)
  then u ← i - 1
  else if K > (ordering key field value of the last record in block i)
      then l ← i + 1
      else if the record with ordering key field value = K is in the buffer
          then goto found
          else goto notfound;
  end;
goto notfound;
```

A search criterion involving the conditions $>$, $<$, $\geq$, and $\leq$ on the ordering field is quite efficient, since the physical ordering of records means that all records satisfying the condition are contiguous in the file. For example, referring to Figure 5.9, if the search criterion is (NAME < 'G')—where < means *alphabetically before*—the records satisfying the search criterion are those from the beginning of the file up to the first record that has a NAME value starting with the letter G.

Ordering does not provide any advantages for random or ordered access of the records based on values of the other *nonordering fields* of the file. In these cases we do a linear search for random access. To access the records in order based on a nonordering field, it is necessary to create another sorted copy—in a different order—of the file.

Inserting and deleting records are expensive operations for an ordered file because the records must remain physically ordered. To insert a record, we must find its correct position in the file, based on its ordering field value, and then make space in the file to insert the record in that position. For a large file this can be very time-consuming because, on the average, half the records of the file must be moved to make space for the new record. This means that half the file blocks must be read and rewritten after records are moved among them. For record deletion, the problem is less severe if deletion markers and periodic reorganization are used.

One option for making insertion more efficient is to keep some unused space in each block for new records. However, once this space is used up, the original problem resurfaces. Another frequently used method is to create a temporary *unordered* file called an

overflow or **transaction** file. With this technique, the actual ordered file is called the **main** or **master** file. New records are inserted at the end of the overflow file rather than in their correct position in the main file. Periodically, the overflow file is sorted and merged with the master file during file reorganization. Insertion becomes very efficient, but at the cost of increased complexity in the search algorithm. The overflow file must be searched using a linear search if, after the binary search, the record is not found in the main file. For applications that do not require the most up-to-date information, overflow records can be ignored during a search.

Modifying a field value of a record depends on two factors: (1) the search condition to locate the record and (2) the field to be modified. If the search condition involves the ordering key field, we can locate the record using a binary search; otherwise we must do a linear search. A nonordering field can be modified by changing the record and rewriting it in the same physical location on disk—assuming fixed-length records. Modifying the ordering field means that the record can change its position in the file, which requires deletion of the old record followed by insertion of the modified record.

Reading the file records in order of the ordering field is quite efficient if we ignore the records in overflow, since the blocks can be read consecutively using double buffering. To include the records in overflow, we must merge them in their correct positions; in this case, we can first reorganize the file, and then read its blocks sequentially. To reorganize the file, first sort the records in the overflow file, and then merge them with the master file. The records marked for deletion are removed during the reorganization.

Ordered files are rarely used in database applications unless an additional access path, called a **primary index,** is used; this results in an **indexed-sequential file.** This further improves the random access time on the ordering key field. We discuss indexes in Chapter 6.

5.9 Hashing Techniques

Another type of primary file organization is based on hashing, which provides very fast access to records on certain search conditions. This organization is usually called a **hash file.**[11] The search condition must be an equality condition on a single field, called the **hash field** of the file. In most cases, the hash field is also a key field of the file, in which case it is called the **hash key.** The idea behind hashing is to provide a function h, called a **hash function** or **randomizing function,** that is applied to the hash field value of a record and yields the *address* of the disk block in which the record is stored. A search for the record within the block can be carried out in a main memory buffer. For most records, we need only a single-block access to retrieve that record.

Hashing is also used as an internal search structure within a program whenever a group of records is accessed exclusively by using the value of one field. We describe the use of hashing for internal files in Section 5.9.1; then we show how it is modified to store external files on disk in Section 5.9.2. In Section 5.9.3 we discuss techniques for extending hashing to dynamically growing files.

---

11. A hash file has also been called a *direct file*.

5.9.1 Internal Hashing

For internal files, hashing is typically implemented as a **hash table** through the use of an array of records. Suppose that the array index range is from 0 to $M - 1$ (Figure 5.10a); then we have M **slots** whose addresses correspond to the array indexes. We choose a hash function that transforms the hash field value into an integer between 0 and $M - 1$. One common hash function is the $h(K) = K$ **mod M** function, which returns the remainder of

Figure 5.10   Internal hashing data structures. (a) Array of M positions for use in internal hashing. (b) Collision resolution by chaining records.

an integer hash field value K after division by M; this value is then used for the record address.

Noninteger hash field values can be transformed into integers before the mod function is applied. For character strings, the numeric (ASCII) codes associated with characters can be used in the transformation—for example, by multiplying those code values. For a hash field whose data type is a string of 20 characters, Algorithm 5.2(a) can be used to calculate the hash address. We assume that the code function returns the numeric code of a character and that we are given a hash field value K of type K: *array [1..20] of char* (in PASCAL) or *char K[20]* (in C).

ALGORITHM 5.2 Two simple hashing algorithms. (a) Applying the mod hash function to a character string K. (b) Collision resolution by open addressing.

```
(a) temp ← 1;
    for i ← 1 to 20 do temp ← temp * code(K[i]) mod M;
    hash_address ← temp mod M;
(b) i ← hash_address(K); a ← i;
    if location i is occupied
        then begin i ← (i + 1) mod M;
            while (i ≠ a) and location i is occupied
                do i ← (i + 1) mod M;
            if (i = a) then all positions are full
                else new_hash_address ← i;
        end;
```

Other hashing functions can be used. One technique, called **folding,** involves applying an arithmetic function such as *addition* or a logical function such as *exclusive or* to different portions of the hash field value to calculate the hash address. Another technique involves picking some digits of the hash field value—for example, the third, fifth, and eighth digits—to form the hash address.[12] The problem with most hashing functions is that they do not guarantee that distinct values will hash to distinct addresses, because the **hash field space**—the number of possible values a hash field can take—is usually much larger than the **address space**—the number of available addresses for records. The hashing function maps the hash field space to the address space.

A **collision** occurs when the hash field value of a record that is being inserted hashes to an address that already contains a different record. In this situation, we must insert the new record in some other position, since its hash address is occupied. The process of finding another position is called **collision resolution.** There are numerous methods for collision resolution, including the following:

- *Open addressing:* Proceeding from the occupied position specified by the hash address, the program checks the subsequent positions in order until an unused (empty) position is found. Algorithm 5.2(b) may be used for this purpose.

---

12. A detailed discussion of hashing functions is outside the scope of our presentation.

- *Chaining:* For this method, various overflow locations are kept, usually by extending the array with a number of overflow positions. In addition, a pointer field is added to each record location. A collision is resolved by placing the new record in an unused overflow location and setting the pointer of the occupied hash address location to the address of that overflow location. A linked list of overflow records for each hash address is thus maintained, as shown in Figure 5.10(b).

- *Multiple hashing:* The program applies a second hash function if the first results in a collision. If another collision results, the program uses open addressing or applies a third hash function and then uses open addressing if necessary.

Each collision resolution method requires its own algorithms for insertion, retrieval, and deletion of records. The algorithms for chaining are the simplest. Deletion algorithms for open addressing are rather tricky. Data structures textbooks discuss internal hashing algorithms in more detail.

The goal of a good hashing function is to distribute the records uniformly over the address space so as to minimize collisions while not leaving many unused locations. Simulation and analysis studies have shown that it is usually best to keep a hash table between 70 and 90 percent full so that the number of collisions remains low and we do not waste too much space. Hence, if we expect to have r records to store in the table, we should choose M locations for the address space such that (r/M) is between 0.7 and 0.9. It may also be useful to choose a prime number for M, since it has been demonstrated that this distributes the hash addresses better over the address space when the mod hashing function is used. Other hash functions may require M to be a power of 2.

5.9.2   External Hashing for Disk Files

Hashing for disk files is called **external hashing.** To suit the characteristics of disk storage, the target address space is made of **buckets,** each of which holds multiple records. A bucket is either one disk block or a cluster of contiguous blocks. The hashing function maps a key into a relative bucket number, rather than assign an absolute block address to the bucket. A table maintained in the file header converts the bucket number into the corresponding disk block address, as illustrated in Figure 5.11.

The collision problem is less severe with buckets, because as many records as will fit in a bucket can hash to the same bucket without causing problems. However, we must make provisions for the case where a bucket is filled to capacity and a new record being inserted hashes to that bucket. We can use a variation of chaining in which a pointer is maintained in each bucket to a linked list of overflow records for the bucket, as shown in Figure 5.12. The pointers in the linked list should be **record pointers,** which include both a block address and a relative record position within the block.

Hashing provides the fastest possible access for retrieving an arbitrary record given the value of its hash field. Although most good hash functions do not maintain records in order of hash field values, some functions—called **order preserving**—do. A simple example of an order preserving hash function is to take the leftmost three digits of an invoice number field as the hash address and keep the records sorted by invoice number within

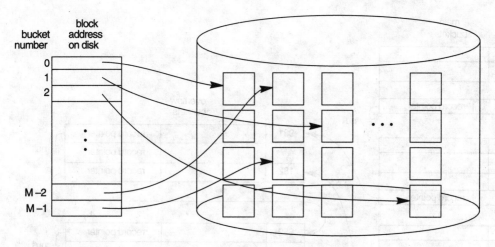

bucket
number

block
address
on disk

0
1
2

M −2
M −1

Figure 5.11   Matching bucket numbers to disk block addresses.

each bucket. Another example is to use an integer hash key directly as an index to a relative file, if the hash key values fill up a particular interval; for example, if employee numbers in a company are assigned as 1, 2, 3, . . . up to the total number of employees, we can use the identity hash function that maintains order. Unfortunately, this only works if keys are generated in order by some application.

The hashing scheme described is called **static hashing** because a fixed number of buckets M is allocated. This can be a serious drawback for dynamic files. Suppose that we allocate M buckets for the address space and let m be the maximum number of records that can fit in one bucket; then at most $(m * M)$ records will fit in the allocated space. If the number of records turns out to be substantially fewer than $(m * M)$, we are left with a lot of unused space. On the other hand, if the number of records increases to substantially more than $(m * M)$, numerous collisions will result and retrieval will be slowed down because of the long lists of overflow records. In either case, we may have to change the number of blocks M allocated and then use a new hashing function (based on the new value of M) to redistribute the records. These reorganizations can be quite time consuming for large files. Newer dynamic file organizations based on hashing allow the number of buckets to vary dynamically with only localized reorganization (see Section 5.9.3).

When using external hashing, searching for a record given a value of some field other than the hash field is as expensive as in the case of an unordered file. Record deletion can be implemented by removing the record from its bucket. If the bucket has an overflow chain, we can move one of the overflow records into the bucket to replace the deleted record. If the record to be deleted is already in overflow, we simply remove it from the linked list. Notice that removing an overflow record implies that we should keep track of empty positions in overflow. This is done easily by maintaining a linked list of unused overflow locations.

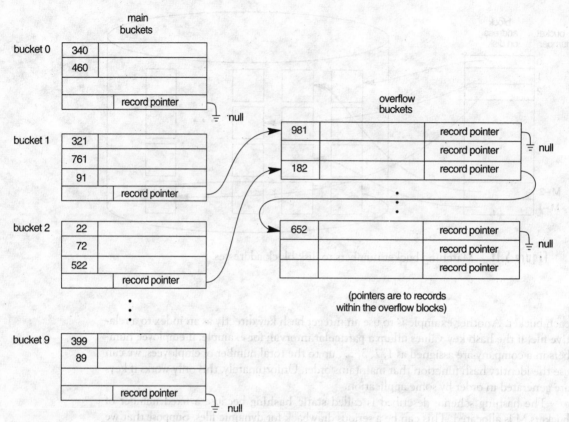

Figure 5.12   Handling overflow for buckets by chaining.

Modifying a record's field value depends on two factors: (1) the search condition to locate the record and (2) the field to be modified. If the search condition is an equality comparison on the hash field, we can locate the record efficiently by using the hashing function; otherwise, we must do a linear search. A nonhash field can be modified by changing the record and rewriting it in the same bucket. Modifying the hash field means that the record can move to another bucket, which requires deletion of the old record followed by insertion of the modified record.

5.9.3   Hashing Techniques That Allow Dynamic File Expansion

A major drawback of the *static* hashing scheme just discussed is that the hash address space is fixed. Hence, it is difficult to expand or shrink the file dynamically. The schemes described in this section attempt to remedy this situation. The first scheme—extendible hashing—stores an access structure in addition to the file, and hence is somewhat similar to indexing (Chapter 6). The main difference is that the access structure is based on the values that result after application of the hash function to the search field. In indexing, the access structure is based on the values of the search field itself. The second technique, called linear hashing, does not require additional access structures.

These hashing schemes take advantage of the fact that the result of applying a hashing function is a nonnegative integer and hence can be represented as a binary number. The access structure is built on the **binary representation** of the hashing function result, which is a string of **bits.** We call this the **hash value** of a record. Records are distributed among buckets based on the values of the *leading bits* in their hash values.

Extendible Hashing. In extendible hashing, a type of **directory**—an array of 2^d bucket addresses—is maintained, where d is called the **global depth** of the directory. The integer value corresponding to the first (high-order) d bits of a hash value is used as an index to the array to determine a directory entry, and the address in that entry determines the bucket in which the corresponding records are stored. However, there does not have to be a distinct bucket for each of the 2^d directory locations. Several directory locations with the same first d' bits for their hash values may contain the same bucket address if all the records that hash to these locations fit in a single bucket. A **local depth d'**—stored with each bucket—specifies the number of bits on which the bucket contents are based. Figure 5.13 shows a directory with global depth $d = 3$.

The value of d can be increased or decreased by one at a time, thus doubling or halving the number of entries in the directory array. Doubling is needed if a bucket, whose local depth d' is equal to the global depth d, overflows. Halving occurs if $d > d'$ for all the buckets after some deletions occur. Most record retrievals require two block accesses—one to the directory and the other to the bucket.

To illustrate bucket splitting, suppose that a new inserted record causes overflow in the bucket whose hash values start with 01—the third bucket in Figure 5.13. The records will be distributed between two buckets: the first contains all records whose hash values start with 010, and the second all those whose hash values start with 011. Now the two directory locations for 010 and 011 point to the two new distinct buckets. Before the split, they pointed to the same bucket. The local depth d' of the two new buckets is 3, which is one more than the local depth of the old bucket.

If a bucket that overflows and is split used to have a local depth d' equal to the global depth d of the directory, then the size of the directory must now be doubled so that we can use an extra bit to distinguish the two new buckets. For example, if the bucket for records whose hash values start with 111 in Figure 5.13 overflows, the two new buckets need a directory with global depth $d = 4$, because the two buckets are now labeled 1110 and 1111, and hence their local depths are both 4. The directory size is hence doubled, and each of the other original locations in the directory is also split into two locations, both of which have the same pointer value as did the original location.

The main advantage of extendible hashing that makes it attractive is that the performance of the file does not degrade as the file grows, as opposed to static external hashing where collisions increase and the corresponding chaining causes additional accesses. In addition, no space is allocated in extendible hashing for future growth, but additional buckets can be allocated dynamically as needed. The space overhead for the directory

DATA FILE BUCKETS

local depth of
each bucket

DIRECTORY

d' = 3   bucket for records
            whose hash values
            start with 000

d' = 3   bucket for records
            whose hash values
            start with 001

000
001
010
011
100
101
110
111

d' = 2   bucket for records
            whose hash values
            start with 01

d' = 2   bucket for records
            whose hash values
            start with 10

global depth
d = 3

d' = 3   bucket for records
            whose hash values
            start with 110

d' = 3   bucket for records
            whose hash values
            start with 111

Figure 5.13   Structure of the extendible hashing scheme.

table is negligible. The maximum directory size is 2^k, where k is the number of bits in the hash value. Another advantage is that splitting causes minor reorganization in most cases, since only the records in one bucket are redistributed to the two new buckets. The only time a reorganization is more expensive is when the directory has to be doubled (or halved). A disadvantage is that the directory must be searched before accessing the buckets themselves, resulting in two block accesses instead of one in static hashing. This performance penalty is considered minor and hence the scheme is considered quite desirable for dynamic files.

Linear Hashing.   The idea behind linear hashing is to allow a hash file to expand and shrink its number of buckets dynamically *without* needing a directory. Suppose that the file starts with M buckets numbered 0, 1, . . . , M − 1 and uses the mod hash function $h(K) = K \bmod M$; this hash function is called the initial hash function h_i. Overflow because of collisions is still needed and can be handled by maintaining individual over-flow chains for each bucket. However, when a collision leads to an overflow record in *any* file bucket, the *first* bucket in the file—bucket 0—is split into two buckets: the original bucket 0 and a new bucket M at the end of the file. The records originally in bucket 0 are distributed between the two buckets based on a different hashing function $h_{i+1}(K) = K$ mod 2M. A key property of the two hash functions h_i and h_{i+1} is that any records that hashed to bucket 0 based on h_i will hash to either bucket 0 or bucket M based on h_{i+1}; this is necessary for linear hashing to work.

As further collisions lead to overflow records, additional buckets are split in the *linear* order 1, 2, 3, ... If enough overflows occur, all the original file buckets 0, 1, . . . , M − 1 will have been split, so the file now has 2M instead of M buckets, and all buckets use the hash function h_{i+1}. Hence, the records in overflow are eventually redistributed into regular buckets, using the function h_{i+1} via a *delayed split* of their buckets. There is no direc-tory; only a value n—which is initially set to 0 and is incremented by 1 whenever a split occurs—is needed to determine which buckets have been split. To retrieve a record with hash key value K, first apply the function h_i to K; if $h_i(K) < n$, then apply the function h_{i+1} on K because the bucket is already split. Initially, n = 0, indicating that the function h_i applies to all buckets; n grows linearly as buckets are split.

When n = M after being incremented, this signifies that all the original buckets have been split and the hash function h_{i+1} applies to all records in the file. At this point, n is reset to 0 (zero), and any new collisions that cause overflow lead to the use of a new hash-ing function $h_{i+2}(K) = K$ mod 4M. In general, a sequence of hashing functions $h_{i+j}(K) = K$ mod $(2^j M)$ is used, where j = 0, 1, 2, . . . ; a new hashing function h_{i+j+1} is needed when-ever all the buckets 0, 1, . . . , $(2^j M) − 1$ have been split and n is reset to 0. The search for a record with hash key value K is given by Algorithm 5.3.

Splitting can be controlled by monitoring the file load factor instead of by splitting when-ever an overflow occurs. In general, the **file load factor** *l* can be defined as $l = r/(bfr * N)$, where r is the current number of file records, *bfr* is the maximum number of records that can fit in a bucket, and N is the current number of file buckets. Buckets that have been split can also be recombined if the load of the file falls below a certain threshold. Blocks are combined linearly, and N is decremented appropriately. The file load can be used to trigger both splits and combinations; in this manner the file load can be kept within a desired range. Splits can be triggered when the load exceeds a certain threshold—say, 0.9—and combinations can be triggered when the load falls below another threshold—say, 0.7.

ALGORITHM 5.3 The search procedure for linear hashing.

```
if n = 0
    then m ← hⱼ(K) (* m is the hash value of record with hash key K *)
    else begin
        m ← hⱼ(K);
        if m < n then m ← hⱼ₊₁ (K)
        end;
search the bucket whose hash value is m (and its overflow, if any);
```

5.10   Other Primary File Organizations

5.10.1   Files of Mixed Records

The file organizations we have studied so far assume that all records of a particular file are of the same record type. The records could be of EMPLOYEES, PROJECTS, STUDENTS, or DEPARTMENTS, but each file contains records of only one type. In most database applications, we encounter situations in which numerous types of entities are interrelated in various ways, as we saw in Chapter 3. Relationships among records in various files can be represented by **connecting fields**.[13] For example, a STUDENT record can have a connecting field MAJORDEPT whose value gives the name of the DEPARTMENT in which the student is majoring. This MAJORDEPT field *refers* to a DEPARTMENT entity, which should be represented by a record of its own in the DEPARTMENT file. If we want to retrieve field values from two related records, we must retrieve one of the records first. Then we can use its connecting field value to retrieve the related record in the other file. Hence, relationships are implemented by **logical field references** among the records in distinct files.

File organizations in object DBMSs, as well as legacy systems such as hierarchical and network DBMSs, often implement relationships among records as **physical relationships** realized by physical contiguity (or clustering) of related records or by physical pointers. These file organizations typically assign an **area** of the disk to hold records of more than one type so that records of different types can be **physically clustered** on disk. If a particular relationship is expected to be used very frequently, implementing the relationship physically can increase the system's efficiency at retrieving related records. For example, if the query to retrieve a DEPARTMENT record and all records for STUDENTs majoring in that department is very frequent, it would be desirable to place each DEPARTMENT record and its cluster of STUDENT records contiguously on disk in a mixed file. The concept of **physical clustering** of object types is used in object DBMSs to store related objects together in a mixed file.

To distinguish the records in a mixed file, each record has—in addition to its field values—a **record type** field, which specifies the type of record. This is typically the first field in each record and is used by the system software to determine the type of record it is about to process. Using the catalog information, the DBMS can determine the fields of that record type and their sizes, in order to interpret the data values in the record.

5.10.2   B-Trees and Other Data Structures

Other data structures can be used for primary file organizations. For example, if both the record size and the number of records in a file are small, some DBMSs offer the option of a B-tree data structure as the primary file organization. We will describe B-trees in Section 6.3.1, when we discuss the use of the B-tree data structure for indexing. In general, any data structure that can be adapted to the characteristics of disk devices can be used as a primary file organization for record placement on disk.

---

13. The concept of foreign keys in the relational model (Chapter 7) and references among objects in object-oriented models (Chapter 11) are examples of connecting fields.

5.11   Summary

We began this chapter by discussing the characteristics of memory hierarchies and then concentrated on secondary storage devices. In particular, we focused on magnetic disks because they are used most often to store on-line database files. We reviewed the recent advances in disk technology represented by RAID (Redundant Arrays of Inexpensive [Independent] Disks).

Data on disk is stored in blocks; accessing a disk block is expensive because of the seek time, rotational delay, and block transfer time. Double buffering can be used when accessing consecutive disk blocks, to reduce the average block access time. Other disk parameters are discussed in Appendix B. We presented different ways of storing records of a file on disk. Records of a file are grouped into disk blocks and can be of fixed length or variable length, spanned or unspanned, and of the same record type or mixed-types. We discussed the file header, which describes the record formats and keeps track of the disk addresses of the file blocks. Information in the file header is used by system software accessing the file records.

We then presented a set of typical commands for accessing individual file records and discussed the concept of the current record of a file. We discussed how complex record search conditions are transformed into simple search conditions that are used to locate records in the file.

Three primary file organizations were then discussed: unordered, ordered, and hashed. Unordered files require a linear search to locate records, but record insertion is very simple. We discussed the deletion problem and the use of deletion markers.

Ordered files shorten the time required to read records in order of the ordering field. The time required to search for an arbitrary record, given the value of its ordering key field, is also reduced if a binary search is used. However, maintaining the records in order makes insertion very expensive; thus the technique of using an unordered overflow file to reduce the cost of record insertion was discussed. Overflow records are merged with the master file periodically during file reorganization.

Hashing provides very fast access to an arbitrary record of a file, given the value of its hash key. The most suitable method for external hashing is the bucket technique, with one or more contiguous blocks corresponding to each bucket. Collisions causing bucket overflow are handled by chaining. Access on any nonhash field is slow, and so is ordered access of the records on any field. We then discussed two hashing techniques for files that grow and shrink in the number of records dynamically—namely, extendible and linear hashing.

Finally, we briefly discussed other possibilities for primary file organizations, such as B-trees, and files of mixed records, which implement relationships among records of different types physically as part of the storage structure.

Review Questions

5.1. What is the difference between primary and secondary storage?

5.2. Why are disks, not tapes, used to store on-line database files?

5.3. Define the following terms: *disk, disk pack, track, block, cylinder, sector, interblock gap, read/write head.*

5.4. Discuss the process of disk initialization.

5.5. Discuss the mechanism used to read data from or write data to the disk.

5.6. What are the components of a disk block address?

5.7. Why is accessing a disk block expensive? Discuss the time components involved in accessing a disk block.

5.8. Describe the mismatch between processor and disk technologies.

5.9. What are the main goals of the RAID technology? How does it achieve them?

5.10. How does disk mirroring help improve reliability? Give a quantitative example.

5.11. What are the techniques used to improve performance of disks in RAID?

5.12. What characterizes the levels in RAID organization?

5.13. How does double buffering improve block access time?

5.14. What are the reasons for having variable-length records? What types of separator characters are needed for each?

5.15. Discuss the techniques for allocating file blocks on disk.

5.16. What is the difference between a file organization and an access method?

5.17. What is the difference between static and dynamic files?

5.18. What are the typical record-at-a-time operations for accessing a file? Which of these depend on the current record of a file?

5.19. Discuss the techniques for record deletion.

5.20. Discuss the advantages and disadvantages of using (a) an unordered file, (b) an ordered file, and (c) a static hash file with buckets and chaining. Which operations can be performed efficiently on each of these organizations, and which operations are expensive?

5.21. Discuss the techniques for allowing a hash file to expand and shrink dynamically. What are the advantages and disadvantages of each?

5.22. What are mixed files used for? What are other types of primary file organizations?

Exercises

5.23. Consider a disk with the following characteristics (these are not parameters of any particular disk unit): block size $B = 512$ bytes; interblock gap size $G = 128$ bytes; number of blocks per track = 20; number of tracks per surface = 400. A disk pack consists of 15 double-sided disks.

a. What is the total capacity of a track, and what is its useful capacity (excluding interblock gaps)?

b. How many cylinders are there?

c. What are the total capacity and the useful capacity of a cylinder?

d. What are the total capacity and the useful capacity of a disk pack?

e. Suppose that the disk drive rotates the disk pack at a speed of 2400 rpm (revolutions per minute); what are the transfer rate (tr) in bytes/msec and the block transfer time (btt) in msec? What is the average rotational delay (rd) in msec? What is the bulk transfer rate? (See Appendix B.)

f. Suppose that the average seek time is 30 msec. How much time does it take (on the average) in msec to locate and transfer a single block, given its block address?

g. Calculate the average time it would take to transfer 20 random blocks, and compare this with the time it would take to transfer 20 consecutive blocks using double buffering to save seek time and rotational delay.

5.24. A file has r = 20,000 STUDENT records of *fixed length*. Each record has the following fields: NAME (30 bytes), SSN (9 bytes), ADDRESS (40 bytes), PHONE (9 bytes), BIRTHDATE (8 bytes), SEX (1 byte), MAJORDEPTCODE (4 bytes), MINORDEPTCODE (4 bytes), CLASSCODE (4 bytes, integer), and DEGREEPROGRAM (3 bytes). An additional byte is used as a deletion marker. The file is stored on the disk whose parameters are given in Exercise 5.23.

a. Calculate the record size R in bytes.

b. Calculate the blocking factor *bfr* and the number of file blocks b, assuming an unspanned organization.

c. Calculate the average time it takes to find a record by doing a linear search on the file if (i) the file blocks are stored contiguously, and double buffering is used; (ii) the file blocks are not stored contiguously.

d. Assume that the file is ordered by SSN; calculate the time it takes to search for a record given its SSN value, by doing a binary search.

5.25. Suppose that only 80 percent of the STUDENT records from Exercise 5.24 have a value for PHONE, 85 percent for MAJORDEPTCODE, 15 percent for MINORDEPTCODE, and 90 percent for DEGREEPROGRAM; and suppose that we use a variable-length record file. Each record has a 1-byte *field type* for each field in the record, plus the 1-byte deletion marker and a 1-byte end-of-record marker. Suppose that we use a *spanned* record organization, where each block has a 5-byte pointer to the next block (this space is not used for record storage).

a. Calculate the average record length R in bytes.

b. Calculate the number of blocks needed for the file.

5.26. Suppose that a disk unit has the following parameters: seek time s = 20 msec; rotational delay rd = 10 msec; block transfer time btt = 1 msec; block size B = 2400 bytes; interblock gap size G = 600 bytes. An EMPLOYEE file has the following fields: SSN, 9 bytes; LASTNAME, 20 bytes; FIRSTNAME, 20 bytes; MIDDLE INIT, 1 byte; BIRTHDATE, 10 bytes; ADDRESS, 35 bytes; PHONE, 12 bytes; SUPERVISORSSN, 9 bytes; DEPARTMENT, 4 bytes; JOBCODE, 4 bytes; *deletion marker*, 1 byte. The EMPLOYEE file has r = 30,000 records, fixed-length format, and unspanned blocking. Write appropriate formulas *and* calculate the following values for the above EMPLOYEE file:

a. The record size R (including the deletion marker), the blocking factor *bfr*, and the number of disk blocks b.

b. Calculate the wasted space in each disk block because of the unspanned organization.

c. Calculate the transfer rate tr and the bulk transfer rate btr for this disk unit (see Appendix B for definitions of tr and btr).

d. Calculate the average *number of block accesses* needed to search for an arbitrary record in the file, using linear search.

e. Calculate in msec the average *time* needed to search for an arbitrary record in the file, using linear search, if the file blocks are stored on consecutive disk blocks and double buffering is used.

f. Calculate in msec the average *time* needed to search for an arbitrary record in the file, using linear search, if the file blocks are *not* stored on consecutive disk blocks.

g. Assume that the records are ordered via some key field. Calculate the average *number of block accesses* and the *average time* needed to search for an arbitrary record in the file, using binary search.

5.27. A PARTS file with Part# as hash key includes records with the following Part# values: 2369, 3760, 4692, 4871, 5659, 1821, 1074, 7115, 1620, 2428, 3943, 4750, 6975, 4981, 9208. The file uses eight buckets, numbered 0 to 7. Each bucket is one disk block and holds two records. Load these records into the file in the given order, using the hash function $h(K) = K \mod 8$. Calculate the average number of block accesses for a random retrieval on Part#.

5.28. Load the records of Exercise 5.27 into expandable hash files based on extendible hashing. Show the structure of the directory at each step, and the global and local depths. Use the hash function $h(K) = K \mod 128$.

5.29. Load the records of Exercise 5.27 into an expandable hash file, using linear hashing. Start with a single disk block, using the hash function $h_0 = K \mod 2^0$, and show how the file grows and how the hash functions change as the records are inserted. Assume that blocks are split whenever an overflow occurs, and show the value of n at each stage.

5.30. Compare the file commands listed in Section 5.6 to those available on a file access method you are familiar with.

5.31. Suppose that we have an unordered file of fixed-length records that uses an unspanned record organization. Outline algorithms for insertion, deletion, and modification of a file record. State any assumptions you make.

5.32. Suppose that we have an ordered file of fixed-length records and an unordered overflow file to handle insertion. Both files use unspanned records. Outline algorithms for insertion, deletion, and modification of a file record and for reorganizing the file. State any assumptions you make.

5.33. Can you think of techniques other than an unordered overflow file that can be used to make insertions in an ordered file more efficient?

5.34. Suppose that we have a hash file of fixed-length records, and suppose that overflow is handled by chaining. Outline algorithms for insertion, deletion, and modification of a file record. State any assumptions you make.

5.35. Can you think of techniques other than chaining to handle bucket overflow in external hashing?

5.36. Write pseudocode for the insertion algorithms for linear hashing and for extendible hashing.

5.37. Write program code to access individual fields of records under each of the following circumstances. For each case, state the assumptions you make concerning pointers, separator characters, and so forth. Determine the type of information needed in the file header in order for your code to be general in each case.

a. Fixed-length records with unspanned blocking.

b. Fixed-length records with spanned blocking.

c. Variable-length records with variable-length fields and spanned blocking.

d. Variable-length records with repeating groups and spanned blocking.

e. Variable-length records with optional fields and spanned blocking.

f. Variable-length records that allow all three cases in parts c, d, and e.

5.38. Suppose that a file initially contains r = 120,000 records of R = 200 bytes each in an unsorted (heap) file. The block size B = 2400 bytes, the average seek time s = 16 ms, the average rotational latency rd = 8.3 ms and the block transfer time btt = 0.8 ms. Assume that 1 record is deleted for every 2 records added until the total number of active records is 240,000.

a. How many block transfers are needed to reorganize the file?

b. How long does it take to find a record right before reorganization?

c. How long does it take to find a record right after reorganization?

5.39. Suppose we have a sequential (ordered) file of 100,000 records where each record is 240 bytes. Assume that B = 2400 bytes, s = 16 ms, rd = 8.3 ms, and btt = 0.8 ms. Suppose we want to make X independent random record reads from the file. We could make X random block reads or we could perform one exhaustive read of the entire file looking for those X records. The question is to decide when it would be more efficient to perform one exhaustive read of the entire file than to perform X individual random reads. That is, what is the value for X when an exhaustive read of the file is more efficient than random X reads? Develop this as a function of X.

5.40. Suppose that a static hash file initially has 600 buckets in the primary area and that records are inserted that create an overflow area of 600 buckets. If we reorganize the hash file, we can assume that the overflow is eliminated. If the cost of reorganizing the file is the cost of the bucket transfers (reading and writing all of the buckets) and the only periodic file operation is the fetch operation, then how many times would we have to perform a fetch (successfully) to make the reorganization cost-effective? That is, the reorganization cost and subsequent search cost are less than the search cost before reorganization. Support your answer. Assume s = 16 ms, rd = 8.3 ms, btt = 1 ms.

5.41. Suppose we want to create a linear hash file with a file load factor of 0.7 and a blocking factor of 20 records per bucket, which is to contain 112,000 records initially.

a. How many buckets should we allocate in the primary area?

b. What should be the number of bits used for bucket addresses?

Selected Bibliography

Wiederhold (1983) has a detailed discussion and analysis of secondary storage devices and file organizations. Optical disks are described in Berg and Roth (1989) and analyzed in Ford and Christodoulakis [1991]. Flash memory is discussed by Dippert and Levy (1993). Ruemmler and Wilkes (1994) present a survey of the magnetic-disk technology. Most textbooks on databases include discussions of the material presented here. Most data structures textbooks, including Knuth (1973), discuss static hashing in more detail; Knuth has a complete discussion of hash functions and collision resolution techniques, as well as of their performance comparison. Knuth also offers a detailed discussion of techniques for sorting external files. Textbooks on file structures include Claybrook (1983), Smith and Barnes (1987), and Salzberg (1988); they discuss additional file organizations including tree structured files, and have detailed algorithms for operations on files. Additional textbooks on file organizations include Miller (1987), and Livadas (1989). Salzberg et al. (1990) describes a distributed external sorting algorithm. File organizations with a high degree of fault tolerance are described by Bitton and Gray (1988) and by Gray et al. (1990). Disk striping is proposed in Salem and Garcia Molina (1986). The first paper on redundant arrays of inexpensive disks (RAID) is by Patterson et al. (1988). Chen and Patterson (1990) and the excellent survey of RAID by Chen et al. (1994) are additional references. Grochowski and Hoyt (1996) discuss future trends in disk drives. Various formulas for the RAID architecture appear in Chen et al. (1994).

Morris (1968) is an early paper on hashing. Extendible hashing is described in Fagin et al. (1979). Linear hashing is described by Litwin (1980). Dynamic hashing, which we did not discuss in detail, was proposed by Larson (1978). There are many proposed variations for extendible and linear hashing; for examples, see Cesarini and Soda (1991), Du and Tong (1991), and Hachem and Berra (1992).

CHAPTER 6 | Index Structures for Files

In this chapter, we assume that a file already exists with some primary organization such as the unordered, ordered, or a hashed organizations that were described in Chapter 5. We will describe additional auxiliary **access structures** called **indexes**, which are used to speed up the retrieval of records in response to certain search conditions. The index structures typically provide **secondary access paths**, which provide alternative ways of accessing the records without affecting the physical placement of records on disk. They enable efficient access to records based on the **indexing fields** that are used to construct the index. Basically, *any field* of the file can be used to create an index and *multiple indexes* on different fields can be constructed on the same file. A variety of indexes are possible; each of them uses a particular data structure to speed up the search. To find a record or records in the file based on a certain selection criterion on an indexing field, one has to initially access the index, which points to one or more blocks in the file where the required records are located. The most prevalent types of indexes are based on ordered files (single-level indexes) and tree data structures (multilevel indexes, B+-trees). Indexes can also be constructed based on hashing or other search data structures.

We describe different types of single-level ordered indexes—primary, secondary, and clustering—in Section 6.1. By viewing a single-level index as an ordered file, one can develop additional indexes for it, giving rise to the concept of multilevel indexes. A popular indexing scheme called ISAM (Indexed Sequential Access Method) is based on this idea. We discuss multilevel indexes in Section 6.2. In Section 6.3 we describe B-trees and B+-trees, which are data structures that are commonly used in DBMSs to implement dynamically changing multilevel indexes: B[+]-trees have become a commonly accepted default structure for generating indexes on demand in most relational DBMSs. Section 6.4 is devoted to the alternative ways of accessing data based on a combination of multiple keys. In Section 6.5, we discuss how other data structures—such as hashing—can be used to construct indexes. We also briefly introduce the concept of logical indexes, which give an additional level of indirection from physical indexes, allowing for the physical index to be flexible and extensible in its organization. Section 6.6 summarizes the chapter.

6.1 Types of Single-Level Ordered Indexes

The idea behind an ordered index access structure is similar to that behind the index used in a textbook, which lists important terms at the end of the book in alphabetical order along with a list of page numbers where the term appears in the book. We can search an index to find a list of *addresses*—page numbers in this case—and use these addresses to locate a term in the textbook by *searching* the specified pages. The alternative, if no other guidance is given, would be to sift slowly through the whole textbook word by word to find the term we are interested in; this corresponds to doing a linear search on a file. Of course, most books do have additional information, such as chapter and section titles, that can help us find a term without having to search through the whole book. However, the index is the only exact indication of where each term occurs in the book.

For a file with a given record structure consisting of several fields (or attributes), an index access structure is usually defined on a single field of a file, called an **indexing field** (or **indexing attribute**).[1] The index typically stores each value of the index field along with a list of pointers to all disk blocks that contain records with that field value. The values in the index are *ordered* so that we can do a binary search on the index. The index file is much smaller than the data file, so searching the index using a binary search is reasonably efficient. Multilevel indexing (see Section 6.2) does away with the need for a binary search at the expense of creating indexes to the index itself.

There are several types of ordered indexes. A **primary index** is specified on the *ordering key field* of an ordered file of records. Recall from Section 5.8 that an ordering key field is used to *physically order* the file records on disk, and every record has a *unique value* for that field. If the ordering field is not a key field—that is, if numerous records in the file can have the same value for the ordering field—another type of index, called a **clustering index**, can be used. Notice that a file can have at most one physical ordering field, so it can have at most one primary index or one clustering index, *but not both*. A third type of index, called a **secondary index**, can be specified on any *nonordering* field of a file. A file can have several secondary indexes in addition to its primary access method. In the next three subsections we discuss these three types of single-level indexes.

---

1. We will use the terms *field* and *attribute* interchangeably in this chapter.

6.1.1 Primary Indexes

A **primary index** is an ordered file whose records are of fixed length with two fields. The first field is of the same data type as the ordering key field—called the **primary key**—of the data file, and the second field is a pointer to a disk block (a block address). There is one **index entry** (or **index record**) in the index file for each *block* in the data file. Each index entry has the value of the primary key field for the *first* record in a block and a pointer to that block as its two field values. We will refer to the two field values of index entry i as <K(i), P(i)>.

To create a primary index on the ordered file shown in Figure 5.9, we use the NAME field as primary key, because that is the ordering key field of the file (assuming that each value of NAME is unique). Each entry in the index has a NAME value and a pointer. The first three index entries are as follows:

<K(1) = (Aaron,Ed), P(1) = address of block 1>

<K(2) = (Adams,John), P(2) = address of block 2>

<K(3) = (Alexander,Ed), P(3) = address of block 3>

Figure 6.1 illustrates this primary index. The total number of entries in the index is the same as the *number of disk blocks* in the ordered data file. The first record in each block of the data file is called the **anchor record** of the block, or simply the **block anchor**.[2]

Indexes can also be characterized as dense or sparse. A **dense index** has an index entry for *every search key value* (and hence every record) in the data file. A **sparse (or non-dense) index**, on the other hand, has index entries for only some of the search values. A primary index is hence a nondense (sparse) index, since it includes an entry for each disk block of the data file rather than for every search value (or every record).

The index file for a primary index needs substantially fewer blocks than does the data file, for two reasons. First, there are *fewer index entries* than there are records in the data file. Second, each index entry is typically *smaller in size* than a data record because it has only two fields; consequently, more index entries than data records can fit in one block. A binary search on the index file hence requires fewer block accesses than a binary search on the data file.

A record whose primary key value is K lies in the block whose address is P(i), where K(i) ≤ K < K(i + 1). The ith block in the data file contains all such records because of the physical ordering of the file records on the primary key field. To retrieve a record, given the value K of its primary key field, we do a binary search on the index file to find the appropriate index entry i, and then retrieve the data file block whose address is P(i).[3]

---

2. We can use a scheme similar to the one described here, with the last record in each block (rather than the first) as the block anchor. This slightly improves the efficiency of the search algorithm.

3. Notice that the above formula would not be correct if the data file were ordered on a *nonkey field*; in that case the same index value in the block anchor could be repeated in the last records of the previous block.

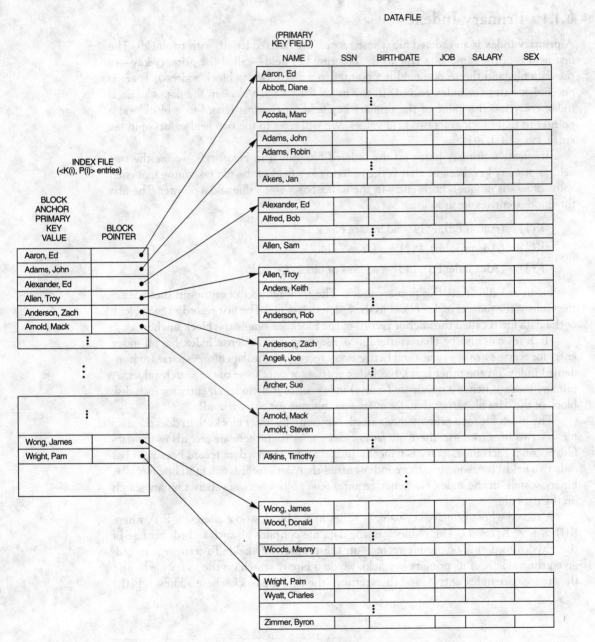

Figure 6.1 Primary index on the ordering key field of the file shown in Figure 5.9.

Example 1 illustrates the saving in block accesses that is attainable when a primary index is used to search for a record.

EXAMPLE 1: Suppose that we have an ordered file with r = 30,000 records stored on a disk with block size B = 1024 bytes. File records are of fixed size and are unspanned, with record length R = 100 bytes. The blocking factor for the file would be bfr = $\lfloor (B/R) \rfloor$ = $\lfloor (1024/100) \rfloor$ = 10 records per block. The number of blocks needed for the file is b = $\lceil (r/bfr) \rceil$ = $\lceil (30,000/10) \rceil$ = 3000 blocks. A binary search on the data file would need approximately $\lceil \log_2 b \rceil$ = $\lceil (\log_2 3000) \rceil$ = 12 block accesses.

Now suppose that the ordering key field of the file is V = 9 bytes long, a block pointer is P = 6 bytes long, and we have constructed a primary index for the file. The size of each index entry is R_i = (9 + 6) = 15 bytes, so the blocking factor for the index is bfr_i = $\lfloor (B/R_i) \rfloor$ = $\lfloor (1024/15) \rfloor$ = 68 entries per block. The total number of index entries r_i is equal to the number of blocks in the data file, which is 3000. The number of index blocks is hence b_i = $\lceil (r_i/bfr_i) \rceil$ = $\lceil (3000/68) \rceil$ = 45 blocks. To perform a binary search on the index file would need $\lceil (\log_2 b_i) \rceil$ = $\lceil (\log_2 45) \rceil$ = 6 block accesses. To search for a record using the index, we need one additional block access to the data file for a total of 6 + 1 = 7 block accesses—an improvement over binary search on the data file, which required 12 block accesses.

A major problem with a primary index—as with any ordered file—is insertion and deletion of records. With a primary index, the problem is compounded because, if we attempt to insert a record in its correct position in the data file, we have to not only move records to make space for the new record but also change some index entries, since moving records will change the anchor records of some blocks. Using an unordered overflow file, as discussed in Section 5.8, can reduce this problem. Another possibility is to use a linked list of overflow records for each block in the data file. This is similar to the method of dealing with overflow records described with hashing in Section 5.9.2. Records within each block and its overflow linked list can be sorted to improve retrieval time. Record deletion is handled using deletion markers.

6.1.2   Clustering Indexes

If records of a file are physically ordered on a nonkey field—which *does not* have a distinct value for each record—that field is called the **clustering field**. We can create a different type of index, called a **clustering index**, to speed up retrieval of records that have the same value for the clustering field. This differs from a primary index, which requires that the ordering field of the data file have a *distinct value* for each record.

A clustering index is also an ordered file with two fields; the first field is of the same type as the clustering field of the data file, and the second field is a block pointer. There is one entry in the clustering index for each *distinct value* of the clustering field, containing the value and a pointer to the *first block* in the data file that has a record with that value for its clustering field. Figure 6.2 shows an example. Notice that record insertion and deletion still cause problems, because the data records are physically ordered. To alleviate the problem of insertion, it is common to reserve a whole block (or a cluster of contiguous

Figure 6.2   A clustering index on the DEPTNUMBER ordering nonkey field of an EMPLOYEE file.

blocks) for *each value* of the clustering field; all records with that value are placed in the block (or block cluster). This makes insertion and deletion relatively straightforward. Figure 6.3 shows this scheme.

A clustering index is another example of a *nondense* index, because it has an entry for every *distinct value* of the indexing field rather than for every record in the file. There is some similarity between Figures 6.1 to 6.3, on the one hand, and Figure 5.13, on the other. An index is somewhat similar to the directory structures used for extendible hashing,

Figure 6.3 Clustering index with a separate block cluster for each group of records that share the same value for the clustering field.

described in Section 5.9.3. Both are searched to find a pointer to the data block containing the desired record. A main difference is that an index search uses the values of the search field itself, whereas a hash directory search uses the hash value that is calculated by applying the hash function to the search field.

6.1.3   Secondary Indexes

A **secondary index** is also an ordered file with two fields. The first field is of the same data type as some *nonordering field* of the data file that is an **indexing field**. The second field is either a *block* pointer or a *record* pointer. There can be *many* secondary indexes (and hence, indexing fields) for the same file.

We first consider a secondary index access structure on a key field that has a *distinct value* for every record. Such a field is sometimes called a **secondary key**. In this case there is one index entry for *each record* in the data file, which contains the value of the secondary key for the record and a pointer either to the block in which the record is stored or to the record itself. Hence, such an index is **dense**.

We again refer to the two field values of index entry i as $<K(i), P(i)>$. The entries are **ordered** by value of $K(i)$, so we can perform a binary search. Because the records of the data file are *not* physically ordered by values of the secondary key field, we cannot use block anchors. That is why an index entry is created for each record in the data file, rather than for each block, as in the case of a primary index. Figure 6.4 illustrates a secondary index in which the pointers $P(i)$ in the index entries are *block pointers*, not record pointers. Once the appropriate block is transferred to main memory, a search for the desired record within the block can be carried out.

A secondary index usually needs more storage space and longer search time than does a primary index, because of its larger number of entries. However, the *improvement* in search time for an arbitrary record is much greater for a secondary index than for a primary index, since we would have to do a *linear search* on the data file if the secondary index did not exist. For a primary index, we could still use a binary search on the main file, even if the index did not exist. Example 2 illustrates the improvement in number of blocks accessed.

EXAMPLE 2: Consider the file of Example 1 with r = 30,000 fixed-length records of size R = 100 bytes stored on a disk with block size B = 1024 bytes. The file has b = 3000 blocks, as calculated in Example 1. To do a linear search on the file, we would require b/2 = 3000/2 = 1500 block accesses on the average. Suppose that we construct a secondary index on a nonordering key field of the file that is V = 9 bytes long. As in Example 1, a block pointer is P = 6 bytes long, so each index entry is $R_i = (9 + 6) = 15$ bytes, and the blocking factor for the index is $bfr_i = \lfloor (B/R_i) \rfloor = \lfloor (1024/15) \rfloor = 68$ entries per block. In a dense secondary index such as this, the total number of index entries r_i is equal to the *number of records* in the data file, which is 30,000. The number of blocks needed for the index is hence $b_i = \lceil (r_i/bfr_i) \rceil = \lceil (30,000/68) \rceil = 442$ blocks.

Figure 6.4 A dense secondary index (with block pointers) on a nonordering key field of a file.

A binary search on this secondary index needs $\lceil (\log_2 b_i) \rceil = \lceil (\log_2 442) \rceil = 9$ block accesses. To search for a record using the index, we need an additional block access to the data file for a total of $9 + 1 = 10$ block accesses—a vast improvement over the 1500 block accesses needed on the average for a linear search, but slightly worse than the seven block accesses required for the primary index.

We can also create a secondary index on a *nonkey field* of a file. In this case, numerous records in the data file can have the same value for the indexing field. There are several options for implementing such an index:

- Option 1 is to include several index entries with the same $K(i)$ value—one for each record. This would be a dense index.

- Option 2 is to have variable-length records for the index entries, with a repeating field for the pointer. We keep a list of pointers $<P(i,1), ..., P(i,k)>$ in the index entry for $K(i)$—one pointer to each block that contains a record whose indexing field value equals $K(i)$. In either option 1 or option 2, the binary search algorithm on the index must be modified appropriately.

- Option 3, which is more commonly used, is to keep the index entries themselves at a fixed length and have a single entry for each *index field value* but to create an extra level of indirection to handle the multiple pointers. In this nondense scheme, the pointer $P(i)$ in index entry $<K(i), P(i)>$ points to a *block of record pointers*; each record pointer in that block points to one of the data file records with value $K(i)$ for the indexing field. If some value $K(i)$ occurs in too many records, so that their record pointers cannot fit in a single disk block, a cluster or linked list of blocks is used. This technique is illustrated in Figure 6.5. Retrieval via the index requires one or more additional block access because of the extra level, but the algorithms for searching the index and (more importantly) for inserting of new records in the data file are straightforward. In addition, retrievals on complex selection conditions may be handled by referring to the record pointers, without having to retrieve many unnecessary file records (see Exercise 6.19).

Notice that a secondary index provides a **logical ordering** on the records by the indexing field. If we access the records in order of the entries in the secondary index, we get them in order of the indexing field.

6.1.4 Summary

To conclude this section, we summarize the discussion on index types in two tables. Table 6.1 shows the index field characteristics of each type of ordered single-level index discussed—primary, clustering, and secondary. Table 6.2 summarizes the properties of each type of index by comparing the number of index entries and specifying which indexes are dense and which use block anchors of the data file.

Figure 6.5 A secondary index (with record pointers) on a nonkey field implemented using one level of indirection so that index entries are of fixed length and have unique field values.

Table 6.1 Types of Indexes

	Ordering Field	**Nonordering field**
Key field	Primary index	Secondary index (key)
Nonkey field	Clustering index	Secondary index (nonkey)

Table 6.2　Properties of Index Types

		Number of (First-level) Index Entries	Dense or Nondense	Block Anchoring on the Data File
Type of Index	**Primary**	Number of blocks in data file	Nondense	Yes
	Clustering	Number of distinct index field values	Nondense	Yes/no[a]
	Secondary (key)	Number of records in data file	Dense	No
	Secondary (nonkey)	Number of records[b] or Number of distinct index field values[c]	Dense or Nondense	No

[a]Yes if every distinct value of the ordering field starts a new block; no otherwise.
[b]For option 1.
[c]For options 2 and 3.

6.2　Multilevel Indexes

The indexing schemes we have described thus far involve an ordered index file. A binary search is applied to the index to locate pointers to a disk block or to a record (or records) in the file having a specific index field value. A binary search requires approximately $(\log_2 b_i)$ block accesses for an index with b_i blocks, because each step of the algorithm reduces the part of the index file that we continue to search by a factor of 2. This is why we take the log function to the base 2. The idea behind a **multilevel index** is to reduce the part of the index that we continue to search by bfr_i, the blocking factor for the index, which is larger than 2. Hence, the search space is reduced much faster. The value bfr_i is called the **fan-out** of the multilevel index, and we will refer to it by the symbol **fo**. Searching a multilevel index requires approximately $(\log_{fo} b_i)$ block accesses, which is a smaller number than for binary search if the fan-out is larger than 2.

A multilevel index considers the index file, which we will now refer to as the **first** (or **base**) **level** of a multilevel index, as an *ordered file* with a *distinct value* for each K(i). Hence we can create a primary index for the first level; this index to the first level is called the **second level** of the multilevel index. Because the second level is a primary index, we can use block anchors so that the second level has one entry for *each block* of the first level. The blocking factor bfr_i for the second level—and for all subsequent levels—is the same as that for the first-level index, because all index entries are the same size; each has one field value and one block address. If the first level has r_1 entries, and the blocking factor—which is also the fan-out—for the index is $bfr_i = fo$, then the first level needs $\lceil (r_1/fo) \rceil$ blocks, which is therefore the number of entries r_2 needed at the second level of the index.

We can repeat this process for the second level. The **third level**, which is a primary index for the second level, has an entry for each second-level block, so the number of third-level entries is $r_3 = \lceil (r_2/fo) \rceil$. Notice that we require a second level only if the first level needs more than one block of disk storage, and, similarly, we require a third level only if the second level needs more than one block. We can repeat the preceding process until all the entries of some index level t fit in a single block. This block at the tth level is called the **top** index level.[4] Each level reduces the number of entries at the previous level by a factor of fo—the index fan-out—so we can use the formula $1 \leq (r_1/((fo)^t))$ to calculate t. Hence, a multilevel index with r_1 first-level entries will have approximately t levels, where $t = \lceil (\log_{fo}(r_1)) \rceil$.

The multilevel scheme described here can be used on any type of index, whether it is primary, clustering, or secondary—as long as the first-level index has *distinct values for K(i) and fixed-length entries*. Figure 6.6 shows a multilevel index built over a primary index. Example 3 illustrates the improvement in number of blocks accessed when a multilevel index is used to search for a record.

EXAMPLE 3: Suppose that the dense secondary index of Example 2 is converted into a multilevel index. We calculated the index blocking factor $bfr_i = 68$ index entries per block, which is also the fan-out fo for the multilevel index; the number of first-level blocks $b_1 = 442$ blocks was also calculated. The number of second-level blocks will be $b_2 = \lceil (b_1/fo) \rceil = \lceil (442/68) \rceil = 7$ blocks, and the number of third-level blocks will be $b_3 = \lceil (b_2/fo) \rceil = \lceil (7/68) \rceil = 1$ block. Hence, the third level is the top level of the index, and $t = 3$. To access a record by searching the multilevel index, we must access one block at each level plus one block from the data file, so we need $t + 1 = 3 + 1 = 4$ block accesses. Compare this to Example 2, where 10 block accesses were needed when a single-level index and binary search were used.

Notice that we could also have a multilevel primary index, which would be nondense. Exercise 6.14(c) illustrates this case, where we *must* access the data block from the file before we can determine whether the record being searched for is in the file. For a dense index, this can be determined by accessing the first index level (without having to access a data block), since there is an index entry for *every* record in the file.

A common file organization used in business data processing is an ordered file with a multilevel primary index on its ordering key field. Such an organization is called an **indexed sequential file** and was used in a large number of early IBM systems. Insertion is handled by some form of overflow file that is merged periodically with the data file. The index is re-created during file reorganization. IBM's **ISAM** organization incorporates a twolevel index that is closely related to the organization of the disk. The first level is a cylinder index, which has the key value of an anchor record for each cylinder of a disk pack and a pointer to the track index for the cylinder. The track index has the key value of an anchor record for each track in the cylinder and a pointer to the track. The track can then be searched sequentially for the desired record or block.

---

4. The numbering scheme for index levels used here is the reverse of the way levels are commonly defined for tree data structures. In tree data structures, t is referred to as level 0 (zero), $t - 1$ is level 1, etc.

Figure 6.6 A two-level primary index resembling ISAM (Indexed Sequential Access Method) organization.

Algorithm 6.1 outlines the search procedure for a record in a data file that uses a nondense multilevel primary index with t levels. We refer to entry i at level j of the index as $<K_j(i), P_j(i)>$, and we search for a record whose primary key value is K. We assume that any overflow records are ignored. If the record is in the file, there must be some entry at level 1 with $K_1(i) \leq K < K_1(i + 1)$ and the record will be in the block of the data file whose address is $P_1(i)$. Exercise 6.19 discusses modifying the search algorithm for other types of indexes.

ALGORITHM 6.1 Searching a nondense multilevel primary index with t levels.

```
p ← address of top level block of index;
for j ← t step - 1 to 1 do
  begin
  read the index block (at jᵗʰ index level) whose address is p;
  search block p for entry i such that Kⱼ(i) ≤ K < Kⱼ(i + 1) (if Kⱼ(i)
    is the last entry in the block, it is sufficient to satisfy Kⱼ(i)
    ≤ K);
  p ← Pⱼ(i) (* picks appropriate pointer at jᵗʰ index level *)
  end;
read the data file block whose address is p;
search block p for record with key = K;
```

As we have seen, a multilevel index reduces the number of blocks accessed when searching for a record, given its indexing field value. We are still faced with the problems of dealing with index insertions and deletions, because all index levels are *physically ordered files*. To retain the benefits of using multilevel indexing while reducing index insertion and deletion problems, designers adopted a multilevel index that leaves some space in each of its blocks for inserting new entries. This is called a **dynamic multilevel index** and is often implemented by using data structures called B-trees and B⁺-trees, which we describe in the next section.

6.3 Dynamic Multilevel Indexes Using B-Trees and B⁺-Trees

B-trees and B⁺-trees are special cases of the well-known tree data structure. We introduce very briefly the terminology used in discussing tree data structures. A **tree** is formed of **nodes**. Each node in the tree, except for a special node called the **root**, has one **parent** node and several—zero or more—**child** nodes. The root node has no parent. A node that does not have any child nodes is called a **leaf** node; a nonleaf node is called an **internal** node. The **level** of a node is always one more than the level of its parent, with the level of the root node being zero.[5] A **subtree** of a node consists of that node and all its **descendant** nodes—its child nodes, the child nodes of its child nodes, and so on. A precise recursive definition of a subtree is that it consists of a node n and the subtrees of all the child nodes of n. Figure 6.7 illustrates a tree data structure. In this figure the root node is A, and its child nodes are B, C, and D. Nodes E, J, C, G, H, and K are leaf nodes.

Usually, we display a tree with the root node at the top, as shown in Figure 6.7. One way to implement a tree is to have as many pointers in each node as there are child nodes of that node. In some cases, a parent pointer is also stored in each node. In addition to pointers, a node usually contains some kind of stored information. When a multilevel

---

5. This standard definition of the level of a tree node, which we use throughout Section 6.3, is different from the one we gave for multilevel indexes in Section 6.2.

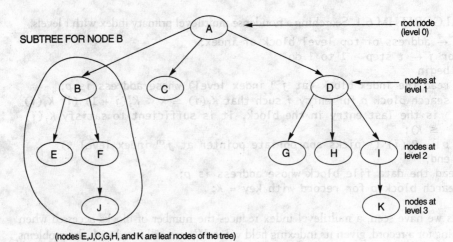

SUBTREE FOR NODE B

(nodes E,J,C,G,H, and K are leaf nodes of the tree)

Figure 6.7   A tree data structure that shows an unbalanced tree.

index is implemented as a tree structure, this information includes the values of the file's indexing field that are used to guide the search for a particular record.

In Section 6.3.1, we introduce search trees and then discuss B-trees, which can be used as dynamic multilevel indexes to guide the search for records in a data file. B-tree nodes are kept between 50 and 100 percent full, and pointers to the data blocks are stored in both internal nodes and leaf nodes of the B-tree structure. In Section 6.3.2 we discuss B$^+$-trees, a variation of B-trees in which pointers to the data blocks of a file are stored only in leaf nodes; this can lead to fewer levels and higher-capacity indexes.

6.3.1   Search Trees and B-Trees

A search tree is a special type of tree that is used to guide the search for a record, given the value of one of the record's fields. The multilevel indexes discussed in Section 6.2 can be thought of as a variation of a search tree; each node in the multilevel index can have as many as *fo* pointers and *fo* key values, where *fo* is the index fan-out. The index field values in each node guide us to the next node, until we reach the data file block that contains the required records. By following a pointer, we restrict our search at each level to a subtree of the search tree and ignore all nodes not in this subtree.

Search Trees.   A search tree is slightly different from a multilevel index. A **search tree** of order p is a tree such that each node contains *at most* p − 1 search values and p pointers in the order $<P_1, K_1, P_2, K_2, ..., P_{q-1}, K_{q-1}, P_q>$, where q ≤ p; each P_i is a pointer to a child node (or a null pointer); and each K_i is a search value from some ordered set of val-

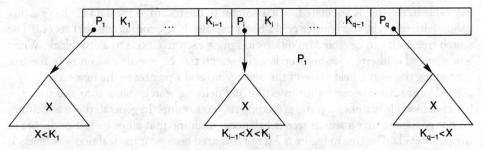

Figure 6.8   A node in a search tree with subtrees below it.

ues. All search values are assumed to be unique.[6] Figure 6.8 illustrates a node in a search tree. Two constraints must hold at all times on the search tree:

1. Within each node, $K_1 < K_2 < ... < K_{q-1}$.
2. For all values X in the subtree pointed at by P_i, we have $K_{i-1} < X < K_i$ for $1 < i < q$; $X < K_i$ for $i = 1$; and $K_{i-1} < X$ for $i = q$ (see Figure 6.8).

Whenever we search for a value X, we follow the appropriate pointer P_i according to the formulas in condition 2 above. Figure 6.9 illustrates a search tree of order $p = 3$ and integer search values. Notice that some of the pointers P_i in a node may be null pointers.

We can use a search tree as a mechanism to search for records stored in a disk file. The values in the tree can be the values of one of the fields of the file, called the **search field** (which is the same as the index field if a multilevel index guides the search). Each

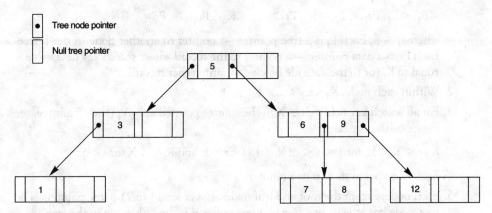

Figure 6.9   A search tree of order $p = 3$.

6. This restriction can be relaxed, but then the formulas that follow must be modified.

key value in the tree is associated with a pointer to the record in the data file having that value. Alternatively, the pointer could be to the disk block containing that record. The search tree itself can be stored on disk by assigning each tree node to a disk block. When a new record is inserted, we must update the search tree by inserting an entry in the tree containing the search field value of the new record and a pointer to the new record.

Algorithms are necessary for inserting and deleting search values into and from the search tree while maintaining the preceding two constraints. In general, these algorithms do not guarantee that a search tree is **balanced**, meaning that all of its leaf nodes are at the same level.[7] The tree in Figure 6.7 is not balanced because it has leaf nodes at levels 1, 2, and 3. Keeping a search tree balanced is important because it guarantees that no nodes will be at very high levels and hence require many block accesses during a tree search. Another problem with search trees is that record deletion may leave some nodes in the tree nearly empty, thus wasting storage space and increasing the number of levels. The B-tree addresses both of these problems by specifying additional constraints on the search tree.

B-Trees.   The B-tree has additional constraints that ensure that the tree is always balanced and that the space wasted by deletion, if any, never becomes excessive. The algorithms for insertion and deletion, though, become more complex in order to maintain these constraints. Nonetheless, most insertions and deletions are simple processes; they become complicated only under special circumstances—namely, whenever we attempt an insertion into a node that is already full or a deletion from a node that makes it less than half full. More formally, a **B-tree** of **order p,** when used as an access structure on a *key field* to search for records in a data file, can be defined as follows:

1. Each internal node in the B-tree (Figure 6.10a) is of the form

   $<P_1, <K_1, Pr_1>, P_2, <K_2, Pr_2>, ..., <K_{q-1}, Pr_{q-1}>, P_q>$

   where $q \leq p$. Each P_i is a **tree pointer**—a pointer to another node in the B-tree. Each Pr_i is a **data pointer**[8]—a pointer to the record whose search key field value is equal to K_i (or to the data file block containing that record).

2. Within each node, $K_1 < K_2 < ... < K_{q-1}$.

3. For all search key field values X in the subtree pointed at by P_i (the ith subtree, see Figure 6.10a), we have:

   $K_{i-1} < X < K_i$ for $1 < i < q$; $X < K_i$ for i = 1; and $K_{i-1} < X$ for i = q.

4. Each node has at most p tree pointers.

5. Each node, except the root and leaf nodes, has at least $\lceil (p/2) \rceil$ tree pointers. The root node has at least two tree pointers unless it is the only node in the tree.

---

7. The definition of *balanced* is different for binary trees. Balanced binary trees are known as AVL trees.

8. A data pointer is either a block address, or a record address; the latter is essentially a block address and a record offset within the block.

Figure 6.10   B-tree structures. (a) A node in a B-tree with q – 1 search values.
(b) A B-tree of order p = 3. The values were inserted in the order 8, 5, 1, 7, 3, 12, 9, 6.

6. A node with q tree pointers, q $\leq$ p , has q − 1 search key field values (and hence has q − 1 data pointers).

7. All leaf nodes are at the same level. Leaf nodes have the same structure as internal nodes except that all of their *tree pointers* P_i are null.

Figure 6.10(b) illustrates a B-tree of order p = 3. Notice that all search values K in the B-tree are unique because we assumed that the tree is used as an access structure on a key field. If we use a B-tree *on a nonkey field*, we must change the definition of the file pointers Pr_i to point to a block—or cluster of blocks—that contain the pointers to the file records. This extra level of indirection is similar to Option 3, discussed in Section 6.1.3, for secondary indexes.

A B-tree starts with a single root node (which is also a leaf node) at level 0 (zero). Once the root node is full with p − 1 search key values and we attempt to insert another entry in the tree, the root node splits into two nodes at level 1. Only the middle value is kept in the root node, and the rest of the values are split evenly between the other two nodes. When a nonroot node is full and a new entry is inserted into it, that node is split into two nodes at the same level, and the middle entry is moved to the parent node along with two pointers to the new split nodes. If the parent node is full, it is also split. Splitting can propagate all the way to the root node, creating a new level if the root is split. We do not discuss algorithms for B-trees in detail here; rather, we outline search and insertion procedures for B⁺-trees in the next section.

If deletion of a value causes a node to be less than half full, it is combined with its neighboring nodes, and this can also propagate all the way to the root. Hence, deletion can reduce the number of tree levels. It has been shown by analysis and simulation that, after numerous random insertions and deletions on a B-tree, the nodes are approximately 69 percent full when the number of values in the tree stabilizes. This is also true of B$^+$-trees. If this happens, node splitting and combining will occur only rarely, so insertion and deletion become quite efficient. If the number of values grows, the tree will expand without a problem—although splitting of nodes may occur, so some insertions will take more time. Example 4 illustrates how we calculate the order p of a B-tree stored on disk.

EXAMPLE 4: Suppose the search field is V = 9 bytes long, the disk block size is B = 512 bytes, a record (data) pointer is P_r = 7 bytes, and a block pointer is P = 6 bytes. Each B-tree node can have *at most* p tree pointers, p − 1 data pointers, and p − 1 search key field values (see Figure 6.10a). These must fit into a single disk block if each B-tree node is to correspond to a disk block. Hence, we must have:

$$(p * P) + ((p - 1) * (P_r + V)) \leq B$$
$$(p * 6) + ((p - 1) * (7 + 9)) \leq 512$$
$$(22 * p) \leq 528$$

We can choose p to be a large value that satisfies the above inequality, which gives p = 23 (p = 24 is not chosen because of the reasons given next).

In general, a B-tree node may contain additional information needed by the algorithms that manipulate the tree, such as the number of entries q in the node and a pointer to the parent node. Hence, before we do the preceding calculation for p, we should reduce the block size by the amount of space needed for all such information. Next, we illustrate how to calculate the number of blocks and levels for a B-tree.

EXAMPLE 5: Suppose that the search field of Example 4 is a nonordering key field, and we construct a B-tree on this field. Assume that each node of the B-tree is 69 percent full. Each node, on the average, will have p * 0.69 = 23 * 0.69 or approximately 16 pointers and, hence, 15 search key field values. The **average fan-out** fo =16. We can start at the root and see how many values and pointers can exist, on the average, at each subsequent level:

Root:	1 node	15 entries	16 pointers
Level 1:	16 nodes	240 entries	256 pointers
Level 2:	256 nodes	3840 entries	4096 pointers
Level 3:	4096 nodes	61,440 entries	

At each level, we calculated the number of entries by multiplying the total number of pointers at the previous level by 15, the average number of entries in each node. Hence, for the given block size, pointer size, and search key field size, a two-level B-tree holds 3840 + 240 + 15 = 4095 entries on the average; a three-level B-tree holds 65,535 entries on the average.

B-trees are sometimes used as primary file organizations. In this case, whole records are stored within the B-tree nodes rather than just the <search key, record pointer> entries. This works well for files with a relatively *small number of records*, and a *small record size.* Otherwise, the fan-out and the number of levels become too great to permit efficient access.

In summary, B-trees provide a multilevel access structure that is a balanced tree structure in which each node is at least half full. Each node in a B-tree of order p can have at most p−1 search values.

6.3.2   B⁺-Trees

Most implementations of a dynamic multilevel index use a variation of the B-tree data structure called a **B⁺-tree**. In a B-tree, every value of the search field appears once at some level in the tree, along with a data pointer. In a B⁺-tree, data pointers are stored *only at the leaf nodes* of the tree; hence, the structure of leaf nodes differs from the structure of internal nodes. The leaf nodes have an entry for *every* value of the search field, along with a data pointer to the record (or to the block that contains this record) if the search field is a key field. For a nonkey search field, the pointer points to a block containing pointers to the data file records, creating an extra level of indirection.

The leaf nodes of the B⁺-tree are usually linked together to provide ordered access on the search field to the records. These leaf nodes are similar to the first (base) level of an index. Internal nodes of the B⁺-tree correspond to the other levels of a multilevel index. Some search field values from the leaf nodes are *repeated* in the internal nodes of the B⁺-tree to guide the search. The structure of the *internal nodes* of a B⁺-tree of order p (Figure 6.11a) is as follows:

1. Each internal node is of the form

   $<P_1, K_1, P_2, K_2, ..., P_{q-1}, K_{q-1}, P_q>$

   where $q \leq p$ and each P_i is a **tree pointer**.

2. Within each internal node, $K_1 < K_2 < ... < K_{q-1}$.

3. For all search field values X in the subtree pointed at by P_i, we have $K_{i-1} < X \leq K_i$ for $1 < i < q$; $X \leq K_i$ for i = 1; and $K_{i-1} < X$ for i = q (see Figure 6.11a).[9]

4. Each internal node has at most p tree pointers.

5. Each internal node, except the root, has at least $\lceil (p/2) \rceil$ tree pointers. The root node has at least two tree pointers if it is an internal node.

6. An internal node with q pointers, $q \leq p$, has q − 1 search field values.

The structure of the *leaf nodes* of a B⁺-tree of order p (Figure 6.11b) is as follows:

1. Each leaf node is of the form

   $<<K_1, Pr_1>, <K_2, Pr_2>, ..., <K_{q-1}, Pr_{q-1}>, P_{next}>$

---

9. Our definition follows Knuth (1973). One can define a B⁺-tree differently by exchanging the $<$ and $\leq$ symbols ($K_{i-1} \leq X < K_i$; $X < K_1$; $K_{q-1} \leq X$), but the principles remain the same.

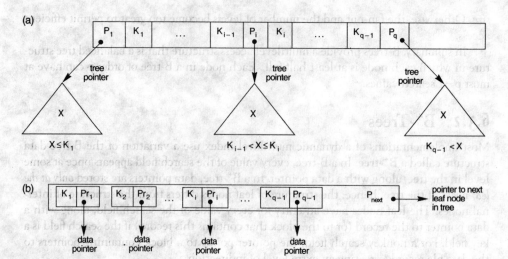

Figure 6.11   The nodes of a B$^+$-tree. (a) Internal node of a B$^+$-tree with q − 1 search values. (b) Leaf node of a B$^+$-tree with q−1 search values and q−1 data pointers.

where q ≤ p, each Pr_i is a data pointer, and P_{next} points to the next *leaf node* of the B$^+$-tree.

2. Within each leaf node, $K_1 < K_2 < ... < K_{q-1}$, q ≤ p.

3. Each Pr_i is a **data pointer** that points to the record whose search field value is K_i or to a file block containing the record (or to a block of record pointers that point to records whose search field value is K_i if the search field is not a key).

4. Each leaf node has at least $\lceil (p/2) \rceil$ values.

5. All leaf nodes are at the same level.

The pointers in internal nodes are *tree pointers* to blocks that are tree nodes, whereas the pointers in leaf nodes are *data pointers* to the data file records or blocks—except for the P_{next} pointer, which is a tree pointer to the next leaf node. By starting at the leftmost leaf node, it is possible to traverse leaf nodes as a linked list, using the P_{next} pointers. This provides ordered access to the data records on the indexing field. A $P_{previous}$ pointer can also be included. For a B$^+$-tree on a nonkey field, an extra level of indirection is needed similar to the one shown in Figure 6.5, so the Pr pointers are block pointers to blocks that contain a set of record pointers to the actual records in the data file, as discussed in Option 3 of Section 6.1.3.

Because entries in the *internal nodes* of a B$^+$-tree include search values and tree pointers without any data pointers, more entries can be packed into an internal node of a B$^+$-tree than for a similar B-tree. Thus, for the same block (node) size, the order p will be larger for the B$^+$-tree than for the B-tree, as we illustrate in Example 6. This can lead to fewer B$^+$-tree levels, improving search time. Because the structures for internal and for leaf nodes of a B⁺-tree are different, the order p can be different. We will use p to denote the order for *internal nodes* and p_{leaf} to denote the order for *leaf nodes*, which we define as being the maximum number of data pointers in a leaf node.

EXAMPLE 6: To calculate the order p of a B⁺-tree, suppose that the search key field is V = 9 bytes long, the block size is B = 512 bytes, a record pointer is P_r = 7 bytes, and a block pointer is P = 6 bytes, as in Example 4. An internal node of the B⁺-tree can have up to p tree pointers and p − 1 search field values; these must fit into a single block. Hence, we have:

$$(p * P) + ((p - 1) * V) \leq B$$
$$(p * 6) + ((p - 1) * 9) \leq 512$$
$$(15 * p) \leq 521$$

We can choose p to be the largest value satisfying the above inequality, which gives p = 34. This is larger than the value of 23 for the B-tree, resulting in a larger fan-out and more entries in each internal node of a B⁺-tree than in the corresponding B-tree. The leaf nodes of the B⁺-tree will have the same number of values and pointers, except that the pointers are data pointers and a next pointer. Hence, the order p_{leaf} for the leaf nodes can be calculated as follows:

$$(p_{leaf} * (P_r + V)) + P \leq B$$
$$(p_{leaf} * (7 + 9)) + 6 \leq 512$$
$$(16 * p_{leaf}) \leq 506$$

It follows that each leaf node can hold up to p_{leaf} = 31 key value/data pointer combinations, assuming that the data pointers are record pointers.

As with the B-tree, we may need additional information—to implement the insertion and deletion algorithms—in each node. This information can include the type of node (internal or leaf), the number of current entries q in the node, and pointers to the parent and sibling nodes. Hence, before we do the above calculations for p and p_{leaf}, we should reduce the block size by the amount of space needed for all such information. The next example illustrates how we can calculate the number of entries in a B⁺-tree.

EXAMPLE 7: Suppose that we construct a B⁺-tree on the field of Example 6. To calculate the approximate number of entries of the B⁺-tree, we assume that each node is 69 percent full. On the average, each internal node will have 34 * 0.69 or approximately 23 pointers, and hence 22 values. Each leaf node, on the average, will hold 0.69 * p_{leaf} = 0.69 * 31 or approximately 21 data record pointers. A B⁺-tree will have the following average number of entries at each level:

Root:	1 node	22 entries	23 pointers
Level 1:	23 nodes	506 entries	529 pointers
Level 2:	529 nodes	11,638 entries	12,167 pointers
Leaf level:	12,167 nodes	255,507 record pointers	

For the block size, pointer size, and search field size given above, a three-level B⁺-tree holds up to 255,507 record pointers, on the average. Compare this to the 65,535 entries for the corresponding B-tree in Example 5.

Search, Insertion, and Deletion with B⁺-Trees.   Algorithm 6.2 outlines the procedure using the B⁺-tree as access structure to search for a record. Algorithm 6.3 illustrates the procedure for inserting a record in a file with a B⁺-tree access structure. These algorithms assume the existence of a key search field, and they must be modified appropriately for the case of a B⁺-tree on a nonkey field. We now illustrate insertion and deletion with an example.

ALGORITHM 6.2 Searching for a record with search key field value K, using a B⁺-tree.

```
n ← block containing root node of B⁺-tree;
read block n;
while (n is not a leaf node of the B⁺-tree) do
   begin
   q ← number of tree pointers in node n;
   if K ≤ n.K₁ (*n.Kᵢ refers to the iᵗʰ search field value in node n*)
      then n ← n.P₁ (*n.Pᵢ refers to the iᵗʰ tree pointer in node n*)
      else if K > n.K_{q-1}
         then n ← n.P_q
         else begin
            search node n for an entry i such that n.K_{i-1} < K ≤ n.Kᵢ;
            n ← n.Pᵢ
            end;
   read block n
   end;
search block n for entry (Kᵢ,Prᵢ) with K = Kᵢ; (* search leaf node *)
if found
   then read data file block with address Prᵢ and retrieve record
   else record with search field value K is not in the data file;
```

ALGORITHM 6.3 Inserting a record with search key field value K in a B⁺-tree of order p.

```
n ← block containing root node of B⁺-tree;
read block n; set stack S to empty;
while (n is not a leaf node of the B⁺-tree) do
   begin
   push address of n on stack S;
      (*stack S holds parent nodes that are needed in case of split*)
   q ← number of tree pointers in node n;
   if K ≤ n.K₁ (*n.Kᵢ refers to the iᵗʰ search field value in node n*)
      then n ← n.P₁ (*n.Pᵢ refers to the iᵗʰ tree pointer in node n*)
      else if K > n.K_{q-1}
```

```
        then n ← n.P_q
        else begin
        search node n for an entry i such that n.K_{i-1} < K ≤ n.K_i;
        n ← n.P_i
        end;
    read block n
    end;
search block n for entry (K_i, Pr_i) with K = K_i;  (*search leaf node n*)
if found
    then record already in file—cannot insert
    else (*insert entry in B^+-tree to point to record*)
    begin
    create entry (K,Pr) where Pr points to the new record;
    if leaf node n is not full
    then insert entry (K, Pr) in correct position in leaf node n
    else
    begin (*leaf node n is full with p_leaf record pointers—is split*)
    copy n to temp (*temp is an oversize leaf node to hold extra entry*);
    insert entry (K, Pr) in temp in correct position;
        (*temp now holds p_leaf + 1 entries of the form (K_i, Pr_i)*)
    new ← a new empty leaf node for the tree; new.P_next ← n.P_next;
    j ← ⌈(p_leaf + 1)/2⌉;
    n ← first j entries in temp (up to entry (K_j,Pr_j)); n.P_next ← new;
    new ← remaining entries in temp; K ← K_j;
(*now we must move (K,new) and insert in parent internal node
  —however, if parent is full, split may propagate*)
    finished ← false;
    repeat
    if stack S is empty
        then (*no parent node—new root node is created for the tree*)
        begin
        root ← a new empty internal node for the tree;
        root ← <n, K, new>; finished ← true;
    end
    else
    begin
    n ← pop stack S;
    if internal node n is not full
        then
        begin (*parent node not full—no split*)
        insert (K, new) in correct position in internal node n;
        finished ← true
        end
        else
        begin (*internal node n is full with p tree pointers—is split*)
            copy n to temp (*temp is an oversize internal node*);
            insert (K,new) in temp in correct position;
                (*temp now has p+1 tree pointers*)
```

```
        new ← a new empty internal node for the tree;
        j ← ⌊((p + 1)/2)⌋;
        n ← entries up to tree pointer Pⱼ in temp;
            (*n contains <P₁, K₁, P₂, K₂, ..., Pⱼ₋₁, Kⱼ₋₁, Pⱼ >*)
        new ← entries from tree pointer Pⱼ₊₁ in temp;
            (*new contains < Pⱼ₊₁, Kⱼ₊₁, ..., Kₚ₋₁, Pₚ, Kₚ, Pₚ₊₁ >*)
        K ← Kⱼ
    (*now we must move (K,new) and insert in parent internal node*)
        end
      end
  until finished
  end;
end;
```

Figure 6.12 illustrates insertion of records in a B^+-tree of order $p = 3$ and $p_{leaf} = 2$. First, we observe that the root is the only node in the tree, so it is also a leaf node. As soon as more than one level is created, the tree is divided into internal nodes and leaf nodes. Notice that *every key value must exist at the leaf level*, because all data pointers are at the leaf level. However, only some values exist in internal nodes to guide the search. Notice also that every value appearing in an internal node also appears as *the rightmost value* in the leaf level of the subtree pointed at by the tree pointer to the left of the value.

When a *leaf node* is full and a new entry is inserted there, the node **overflows** and must be split. The first $j = \lceil ((p_{leaf} + 1)/2) \rceil$ entries in the original node are kept there, and the remaining entries are moved to a new leaf node. The jth search value is replicated in the parent internal node, and an extra pointer to the new node is created in the parent. These must be inserted in the parent node in their correct sequence. If the parent internal node is full, the new value will cause it to overflow also, so it must be split. The entries in the internal node up to P_j—the jth tree pointer after inserting the new value and pointer, where $j = \lfloor ((p + 1)/2) \rfloor$—are kept, while the jth search value is *moved* to the parent, not replicated. A new internal node will hold the entries from P_{j+1} to the end of the entries in the node (see Algorithm 6.3). This splitting can propagate all the way up to create a new root node and hence a new level for the B^+-tree.

Figure 6.13 illustrates deletion from a B^+-tree. When an entry is deleted, it is always removed from the leaf level. If it happens to occur in an internal node, it must also be removed from there. In the latter case, the value to its left in the leaf node must replace it in the internal node, because that value is now the rightmost entry in the subtree. Deletion may cause **underflow** by reducing the number of entries in the leaf node to below the minimum required. In this case we try to find a **sibling** leaf node—a leaf node directly to the left or to the right of the node with underflow—and **redistribute** the entries among the node and its sibling so that both are at least half full; otherwise, the node is merged with its siblings and the number of leaf nodes is reduced. A common method is to try redistributing entries with the left sibling; if this is not possible, an attempt to redistribute with the right sibling is made. If this is not possible either, the three nodes are merged into two leaf nodes. In such a case, underflow may propagate to **internal** nodes because

INSERTION SEQUENCE: 8, 5, 1, 7, 3, 12, 9, 6

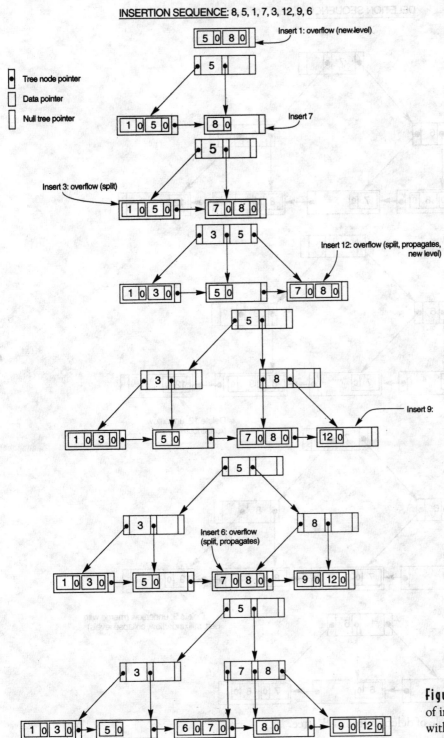

Figure 6.12 An example of insertion in a B⁺-tree with p = 3 and p_leaf = 2.

DELETION SEQUENCE: 5, 12, 9

Figure 6.13   An example of deletion from a B+-tree.

one fewer tree pointer and search value are needed. This can propagate and reduce the tree levels.

Notice that implementing the insertion and deletion algorithms may require parent and sibling pointers for each node, or the use of a stack as in Algorithm 6.3. Each node should also include the number of entries in it and its type (leaf or internal). Another alternative is to implement insertion and deletion as recursive procedures.

Variations of B-Trees and B⁺-Trees. To conclude this section, we briefly mention some variations of B-trees and B⁺-trees. In some cases, constraint 5 on the B-tree (or B⁺-tree), which requires each node to be at least half full, can be changed to require each node to be at least two-thirds full. In this case the B-tree has been called a **B*-tree**. In general, some systems allow the user to choose a **fill factor** between 0.5 and 1.0, where the latter means that the B-tree (index) nodes are to be completely full. It is also possible to specify two fill factors for a B⁺-tree: one for the leaf level and one for the internal nodes of the tree. When the index is first constructed, each node is filled up to approximately the fill factors specified. Recently, investigators have suggested relaxing the requirement that a node be half full, and instead allow a node to become completely empty before merging, to simplify the deletion algorithm. Simulation studies show that this does not waste too much additional space under randomly distributed insertions and deletions.

6.4 Indexes on Multiple Keys

In our discussion so far, we assumed that the primary or secondary keys on which files were accessed were single attributes (fields). In many retrieval and update requests, multiple attributes are involved. If a certain combination of attributes is used very frequently, it is advantageous to set up an access structure to provide efficient access by a key value that is a combination of those attributes.

For example, consider an EMPLOYEE file containing attributes DNO (department number), AGE, STREET, CITY, ZIPCODE, SALARY and SKILL_CODE, with the key of SSN (social security number). Consider the query: "List the employees in department number 4 whose age is 59." Note that both DNO and AGE are nonkey attributes, which means that a search value for either of these will point to multiple records. The following alternative search strategies may be considered:

1. Assuming DNO has an index, but AGE does not, access the records having DNO = 4 using the index then select from among them those records that satisfy AGE = 59.

2. Alternately, if AGE is indexed but DNO is not, access the records having AGE = 59 using the index then select from among them those records that satisfy DNO = 4 .

3. If indexes have been created on both DNO and AGE, both indexes may be used; each gives a set of records or a set of pointers (to blocks or records). An intersection of these sets of records or pointers yields those records that satisfy both conditions.

All of these alternatives eventually give the correct result. However, if the set of records that meet each condition (DNO = 4 or AGE =59) individually are large, yet only a few records satisfy the combined condition, then none of the above is a very efficient technique for the given search request. A number of possibilities exist that would treat the combination <DNO, AGE>, or <AGE, DNO> as a search key made up of multiple attributes. We briefly outline these techniques below. We will refer to keys containing multiple attributes as **composite keys**.

6.4.1   Ordered Index on Multiple Attributes

All the discussion in this chapter so far applies if we create an index on a search key field that is a combination of <DNO, AGE>. The search key is a pair of values <4, 59> in the above example. In general, if an index is created on attributes $<A_1, A_2, ..., A_n>$, the search key values are tuples with n values: $<v_1, v_2,......, v_n>$.

A lexicographic ordering of these tuple values establishes an order on this composite search key. For our example, all of department keys for department number 3 precede those for department 4. Thus <3, n> precedes <4, m> for any values of m and n. The ascending key order for keys with DNO = 4 would be <4, 18>, <4, 19>, <4, 20>, and so on. Lexicographic ordering works similarly to ordering of character strings. An index on a composite key of n attributes works similarly to any index discussed in this chapter so far.

6.4.2   Partitioned Hashing

Partitioned hashing is an extension of static external hashing (Section 5.9.2) that allows access on multiple keys. It is suitable only for equality comparisons; range queries are not supported. In partitioned hashing, for a key consisting of n components, the hash function is designed to produce a result with n separate hash addresses. The bucket address is a concatenation of these n addresses. It is then possible to search for the required composite search key by looking up the appropriate buckets that match the parts of the address in which we are interested.

For example, consider the composite search key <DNO, AGE>. If DNO and AGE are hashed into a 3-bit and 5-bit address respectively, we get an 8-bit bucket address. Suppose that DNO = 4 has a hash address "100" and AGE = 59 has hash address "10101". Then to search for the combined search value, DNO = 4 and AGE = 59, one goes to bucket address 100 10101; just to search for all employees with AGE = 59, all buckets (eight of them) will be searched whose addresses are "000 10101", "001 10101", ... etc. An advantage of partitioned hashing is that it can be easily extended to any number of attributes. The bucket addresses can be designed so that high order bits in the addresses correspond to more frequently accessed attributes. Additionally, no separate access structure needs to be maintained for the individual attributes. The main drawback of partitioned hashing is that it cannot handle range queries on any of the component attributes.

6.4.3   Grid Files

Another alternative is to organize the EMPLOYEE file as a grid file. If we want to access a file on two keys, say DNO and AGE as in our example, we can construct a grid array with one linear scale (or dimension) for each of the search attributes. Figure 6.14 shows a grid array for the EMPLOYEE file with one linear scale for DNO and another for the AGE attribute. The scales are made in a way as to achieve a uniform distribution of that attribute. Thus, in our example, we show that the linear scale for DNO has DNO = 1, 2 combined as one value 0 on the scale, while DNO = 5 corresponds to the value 2 on that scale. Similarly, AGE is divided into its scale of 0 to 5 by grouping ages so as to distribute the employees uniformly by age. The grid array shown for this file has a total of 36 cells. Each cell points to some bucket address where the records corresponding to that cell are stored. Figure 6.14 also shows assignment of cells to buckets (only partially).

Thus our request for DNO = 4 and AGE = 59 maps into the cell (1, 5) corresponding to the grid array. The records for this combination will be found in the corresponding bucket. This method is particularly useful for range queries that would map into a set of cells corresponding to a group of values along the linear scales. Conceptually, the grid file concept may be applied to any number of search keys. For n search keys, the grid array would have n dimensions. The grid array thus allows a partitioning of the file along the dimensions of the search key attributes and provides an access by combinations of values along those dimensions. Grid files perform well in terms of reduction in time for multiple key access. However, they represent a space overhead in terms of the grid array structure.

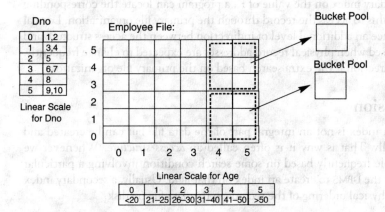

Figure 6.14   Example of a grid array on DNO and AGE attributes.

Moreover, with dynamic files, a frequent reorganization of the file adds to the maintenance cost.[10]

6.5 Other Types of Indexes

6.5.1 Using Hashing and Other Data Structures as Indexes

It is also possible to create access structures similar to indexes that are based on *hashing*. The index entries <K, Pr> (or <K, P>) can be organized as a dynamically expandable hash file, using one of the techniques described in Section 5.9.3; searching for an entry uses the hash search algorithm on K. Once an entry is found, the pointer Pr (or P) is used to locate the corresponding record in the data file. Other search structures can also be used as indexes.

6.5.2 Logical versus Physical Indexes

So far, we have assumed that the index entries <K, Pr> (or <K, P>) always include a physical pointer Pr (or P) that specifies the physical record address on disk as a block number and offset. This is sometimes called a **physical index**, and it has the disadvantage that the pointer must be changed if the record is moved to another disk location. For example, suppose that a primary file organization is based on linear hashing or extendible hashing; then, each time a bucket is split, some records are allocated to new buckets and hence have new physical addresses. If there was a secondary index on the file, the pointers to those records would have to be found and updated—a difficult task.

To remedy this situation, we can use a structure called a **logical index**, whose index entries are of the form <K, K_p>. Each entry has one value K for the secondary indexing field matched with the value K_p of the field used for the primary file organization. By searching the secondary index on the value of K, a program can locate the corresponding value of K_p and use this to access the record through the primary file organization. Logical indexes thus introduce an additional level of indirection between the access structure and the data. They are used when physical record addresses are expected to change frequently. The cost of this indirection is the extra search based on the primary file organization.

6.5.3 Discussion

In many systems, an index is not an integral part of the data file but can be created and discarded dynamically. That is why it is often called an *access structure*. Whenever we expect to access a file frequently based on some search condition involving a particular field, we can request the DBMS to create an index on that field. Usually, a secondary index is created to avoid physical ordering of the records in the data file on disk.

---

10. Insertion/deletion algorithms for grid files may be found in Nievergelt [1984].

The main advantage of secondary indexes is that—theoretically, at least—they can be created in conjunction with *virtually any primary record organization*. Hence, a secondary index could be used to complement other primary access methods such as ordering or hashing, or it could even be used with mixed files. To create a B$^+$-tree secondary index on some field of a file, we must go through all records in the file to create the entries at the leaf level of the tree. These entries are then sorted and filled according to the specified fill factor; simultaneously, the other index levels are created. It is more expensive and much harder to create primary indexes and clustering indexes dynamically, because the records of the data file must be physically sorted on disk in order of the indexing field. However, some systems allow users to create these indexes dynamically on their files by sorting the file during index creation.

It is common to use an index to enforce a *key constraint* on an attribute. While searching the index to insert a new record, it is straightforward to check at the same time whether another record in the file—and hence in the index tree—has the same key attribute value as the new record. If so, the insertion can be rejected.

A file that has a secondary index on every one of its fields is often called a **fully inverted file**. Because all indexes are secondary, new records are inserted at the end of the file; therefore, the data file itself is an unordered (heap) file. The indexes are usually implemented as B$^+$-trees, so they are updated dynamically to reflect insertion or deletion of records. Some commercial DBMSs, such as ADABAS of Software-AG, use this method extensively.

We referred to the popular IBM file organization called ISAM in Section 6.2. Another IBM method, the **virtual storage access method** (VSAM), is somewhat similar to the B$^+$-tree access structure.

6.6   Summary

In this chapter we presented file organizations that involve additional access structures, called indexes, to improve the efficiency of retrieval of records from a data file. These access structures may be used *in conjunction with* the primary file organizations discussed in Chapter 5, which are used to organize the file records themselves on disk.

Three types of ordered single-level indexes were introduced: (1) primary, (2) clustering, and (3) secondary. Each index is specified on a field of the file. Primary and clustering indexes are constructed on the physical ordering field of a file, whereas secondary indexes are specified on non-ordering fields. The field for a primary index must also be a key of the file, whereas it is a non-key field for a clustering index. A single-level index is an ordered file and is searched using a binary search. We showed how multilevel indexes can be constructed to improve the efficiency of searching an index.

We then showed how multilevel indexes can be implemented as B-trees and B$^+$-trees, which are dynamic structures that allow an index to expand and shrink dynamically. The nodes (blocks) of these index structures are kept between half full and completely full by the insertion and deletion algorithms. Nodes eventually stabilize at an average occupancy of 69 percent full, allowing space for insertions without requiring reorganization of the index for the majority of insertions. B$^+$-trees can generally hold more entries in their internal nodes than can B-trees, so they may have fewer levels or hold more entries than does a corresponding B-tree.

We gave an overview of multiple key access methods, and showed how an index can be constructed based on hash data structures. We then introduced the concept of a logical index, and compared it with the physical indexes we described before. Finally, we discussed how combinations of the above organizations can be used. For example, secondary indexes are often used with mixed files, as well as with unordered and ordered files. Secondary indexes can also be created for hash files and dynamic hash files.

Review Questions

6.1. Define the following terms: *indexing field*, *primary key field*, *clustering field*, *secondary key field*, *block anchor*, *dense index*, and *non-dense (sparse) index*.

6.2. What are the differences among primary, secondary, and clustering indexes? How do these differences affect the ways in which these indexes are implemented? Which of the indexes are dense, and which are not?

6.3. Why can we have at most one primary or clustering index on a file, but several secondary indexes?

6.4. How does multilevel indexing improve the efficiency of searching an index file?

6.5. What is the order p of a B-tree? Describe the structure of B-tree nodes.

6.6. What is the order p of a B^+-tree? Describe the structure of both internal and leaf nodes of a B^+-tree.

6.7. How does a B-tree differ from a B^+-tree? Why is a B^+-tree usually preferred as an access structure to a data file?

6.8. Explain what alternative choices exist for accessing a file based on multiple search keys.

6.9. What is partitioned hashing? How does it work? What are its limitations?

6.10. What is a grid file? What are its advantages and disadvantages?

6.11. Show an example of constructing a grid array on two attributes on some file.

6.12. What is a fully inverted file? What is an indexed sequential file?

6.13. How can hashing be used to construct an index? What is the difference between a logical index and a physical index?

Exercises

6.14. Consider a disk with block size B = 512 bytes. A block pointer is P = 6 bytes long, and a record pointer is P_R = 7 bytes long. A file has r = 30,000 EMPLOYEE records of *fixed length*. Each record has the following fields: NAME (30 bytes), SSN (9 bytes), DEPARTMENTCODE (9 bytes), ADDRESS (40 bytes), PHONE (9 bytes), BIRTHDATE (8 bytes), SEX (1 byte), JOBCODE (4 bytes), SALARY (4 bytes, real number). An additional byte is used as a deletion marker.

   a. Calculate the record size R in bytes.

   b. Calculate the blocking factor bfr and the number of file blocks b, assuming an unspanned organization.

c. Suppose that the file is *ordered* by the key field SSN and we want to construct a *primary index* on SSN. Calculate (i) the index blocking factor bfr_i (which is also the index fan-out fo); (ii) the number of first-level index entries and the number of first-level index blocks; (iii) the number of levels needed if we make it into a multilevel index; (iv) the total number of blocks required by the multilevel index; and (v) the number of block accesses needed to search for and retrieve a record from the file—given its SSN value—using the primary index.

d. Suppose that the file is *not ordered* by the key field SSN and we want to construct a *secondary index* on SSN. Repeat the previous exercise (part c) for the secondary index and compare with the primary index.

e. Suppose that the file is *not ordered* by the nonkey field DEPARTMENTCODE and we want to construct a *secondary index* on DEPARTMENTCODE, using option 3 of Section 6.1.3, with an extra level of indirection that stores record pointers. Assume there are 1000 distinct values of DEPARTMENTCODE and that the EMPLOYEE records are evenly distributed among these values. Calculate (i) the index blocking factor bfr_i (which is also the index fan-out fo); (ii) the number of blocks needed by the level of indirection that stores record pointers; (iii) the number of first-level index entries and the number of first-level index blocks; (iv) the number of levels needed if we make it into a multilevel index; (v) the total number of blocks required by the multilevel index and the blocks used in the extra level of indirection; and (vi) the approximate number of block accesses needed to search for and retrieve all records in the file that have a specific DEPARTMENTCODE value, using the index.

f. Suppose that the file is *ordered* by the nonkey field DEPARTMENTCODE and we want to construct a *clustering index* on DEPARTMENTCODE that uses block anchors (every new value of DEPARTMENTCODE starts at the beginning of a new block). Assume there are 1000 distinct values of DEPARTMENTCODE and that the EMPLOYEE records are evenly distributed among these values. Calculate (i) the index blocking factor bfr_i (which is also the index fan-out fo); (ii) the number of first-level index entries and the number of first-level index blocks; (iii) the number of levels needed if we make it into a multilevel index; (iv) the total number of blocks required by the multilevel index; and (v) the number of block accesses needed to search for and retrieve all records in the file that have a specific DEPARTMENT-CODE value, using the clustering index (assume that multiple blocks in a cluster are contiguous).

g. Suppose that the file is *not ordered* by the key field SSN and we want to construct a B^+-tree access structure (index) on SSN. Calculate (i) the orders p and p_{leaf} of the B^+-tree; (ii) the number of leaf-level blocks needed if blocks are approximately 69 percent full (rounded up for convenience); (iii) the number of levels needed if internal nodes are also 69 percent full (rounded up for convenience); (iv) the total number of blocks required by the B^+-tree; and (v) the number of block accesses needed to search for and retrieve a record from the file—given its SSN value—using the B^+-tree.

h. Repeat part g, but for a B-tree rather than for a B^+-tree. Compare your results for the B-tree and for the B^+-tree.

6.15. A PARTS file with Part# as key field includes records with the following Part# values: 23, 65, 37, 60, 46, 92, 48, 71, 56, 59, 18, 21, 10, 74, 78, 15, 16, 20, 24, 28, 39, 43, 47, 50, 69, 75, 8, 49, 33, 38. Suppose that the search field values are inserted in the given order in a B$^+$-tree of order p = 4 and p_{leaf} = 3; show how the tree will expand and what the final tree will look like.

6.16. Repeat Exercise 6.15, but use a B-tree of order p = 4 instead of a B$^+$-tree.

6.17. Suppose that the following search field values are deleted, in the given order, from the B$^+$-tree of Exercise 6.15; show how the tree will shrink and show the final tree. The deleted values are 65, 75, 43, 18, 20, 92, 59, 37.

6.18. Repeat Exercise 6.17, but for the B-tree of Exercise 6.16.

6.19. Algorithm 6.1 outlines the procedure for searching a nondense multilevel primary index to retrieve a file record. Adapt the algorithm for each of the following cases:

a. A multilevel secondary index on a nonkey nonordering field of a file. Assume that option 3 of Section 6.1.3 is used, where an extra level of indirection stores pointers to the individual records with the corresponding index field value.

b. A multilevel secondary index on a nonordering key field of a file.

c. A multilevel clustering index on a nonkey ordering field of a file.

6.20. Suppose that several secondary indexes exist on nonkey fields of a file, implemented using option 3 of Section 6.1.3; for example, we could have secondary indexes on the fields DEPARTMENTCODE, JOBCODE, and SALARY of the EMPLOYEE file of Exercise 6.14. Describe an efficient way to search for and retrieve records satisfying a complex selection condition on these fields, such as (DEPARTMENTCODE = 5 AND JOBCODE = 12 AND SALARY = 50,000), using the record pointers in the indirection level.

6.21. Adapt Algorithms 6.2 and 6.3, which outline search and insertion procedures for a B$^+$-tree, to a B-tree.

6.22. It is possible to modify the B$^+$-tree insertion algorithm to delay the case where a new level is produced by checking for a possible *redistribution* of values among the leaf nodes. Figure 6.15 illustrates how this could be done for our example in Figure 6.12; rather than splitting the leftmost leaf node when 12 is inserted, we do a *left redistribution* by moving 7 to the leaf node to its left (if there is space in this node). Figure 6.15 shows how the tree would look when redistribution is considered. It is also possible to consider *right redistribution*. Try to modify the B$^+$-tree insertion algorithm to take redistribution into account.

6.23. Outline an algorithm for deletion from a B$^+$-tree.

6.24. Repeat Exercise 6.23 for a B-tree.

Selected Bibliography

Bayer and McCreight (1972) introduced B-trees and associated algorithms. Comer (1979) provides an excellent survey of B-trees and their history, and variations of B-trees. Knuth (1973) provides detailed analysis of many search techniques, including B-trees and some of their variations. Nievergelt (1974) discusses the use of binary search trees for file organization. Textbooks on file structures including Wirth (1972), Claybrook (1983),

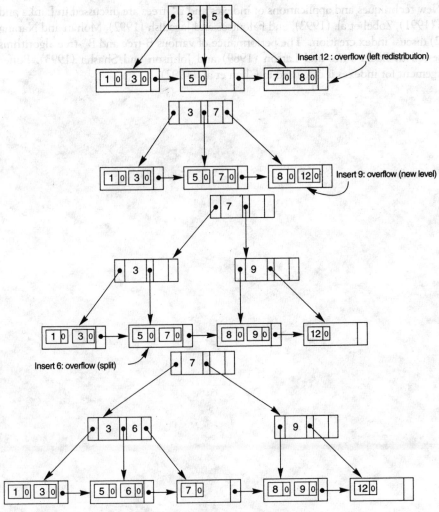

Figure 6.15   B⁺-tree insertion with left redistribution.

Smith and Barnes (1987), Miller (1987), and Salzberg (1988) discuss indexing in detail and may be consulted for search, insertion, and deletion algorithms for B-trees and B⁺-trees. Larson (1981) analyzes index-sequential files, and Held and Stonebraker (1978) compares static multilevel indexes with B-tree dynamic indexes. Lehman and Yao (1981) and Srinivasan and Carey (1991) did further analysis of concurrent access to B-trees. The books by Wiederhold (1983), Smith and Barnes (1987), and Salzberg (1988) among others, discuss many of the search techniques described in this chapter. Grid files are introduced in Nievergelt (1984). Partial-match retrieval, which uses partitioned hashing, is discussed in Burkhard (1976, 1979).

New techniques and applications of indexes and B+-trees are discussed in Lanka and Mays (1991), Zobel et al. (1992), and Faloutsos and Jagadish (1992). Mohan and Narang (1992) discuss index creation. The performance of various B-tree and B+-tree algorithms is assessed in Baeza-Yates and Larson (1989) and Johnson and Shasha (1993). Buffer management for indexes is discussed in Chan et al. (1992).

PART 2

Relational Model, Languages, and Systems

CHAPTER 7

The Relational Data Model, Relational Constraints, and the Relational Algebra

This chapter opens Part II of the book on relational databases. The relational model was first introduced by Ted Codd of IBM Research in 1970 in a classic paper [Codd 1970], and attracted immediate attention due to its simplicity and mathematical foundations. The model uses the concept of a *mathematical relation*—which looks somewhat like a table of values—as its basic building block, and has its theoretical basis in set theory and first order predicate logic. In this chapter we discuss the basic characteristics of the model, its constraints, and the relational algebra, which is a set of operations for the relational model. The model has been implemented in a large number of commercial systems over the last twenty or so years.

Because of the amount of material related to the relational model, we have devoted the whole of Part II of this textbook to it. In Chapter 8, we will describe the SQL query language, which is the *standard* for commercial relational DBMSs. Chapter 9 presents additional topics concerning relational databases. Sections 9.1 and 9.2 present algorithms for designing a relational database schema by mapping a conceptual schema in the ER or EER model (see Chapters 3 and 4) into a relational representation. These mappings are incorporated into many database design and CASE[1] tools. The remainder of Chapter 9 presents some other relational languages. Chapter 10 presents an overview of two commercial relational DBMSs—ORACLE and Microsoft ACCESS. Chapters 14 and 15 in Part IV of the

---

1. CASE stands for Computer Aided Software Engineering.

book present another aspect of the relational model, namely the formal constraints of functional and multivalued dependencies; these dependencies are used to develop a relational database design theory based on the concept known as *normalization*.

Data models that preceded the relational model include the hierarchical and network models. They were proposed in the sixties and were implemented in early DBMSs during the seventies and eighties. Because of their historical importance and the large existing user base for these DBMSs, we have included a summary of the highlights of these models in Appendices C and D. These models and systems will be with us for many years and are today being called *legacy systems*.

In this chapter, we will concentrate on describing the basic principles of the relational model of data. We begin by defining the modeling concepts and notation of the relational model in Section 7.1. Section 7.2 is devoted to a discussion of relational constraints that are now considered an important part of the relational model and are automatically enforced in most relational DBMSs. Section 7.3 defines the update operations of the relational model and discusses how violations of integrity constraints are handled.

In Section 7.4 we present a detailed discussion of the relational algebra, which is a collection of operations for manipulating relations and specifying queries. The relational algebra is an integral part of the relational data model. Section 7.5 defines additional relational operations that were added to the basic relational algebra because of their importance to many database applications. We give examples of specifying queries that use relational operations in Section 7.6. The same queries are used in subsequent chapters to illustrate various languages. Section 7.7 summarizes the chapter.

For the reader who is interested in a less detailed introduction to relational concepts, Sections 7.1.2, 7.4.7, and 7.5 may be skipped.

7.1   Relational Model Concepts

The relational model represents the database as a collection of *relations*. Informally, each relation resembles a table of values or, to some extent, a "flat" file of records. For example, the database of files that was shown in Figure 1.2 is considered to be in the relational model. However, there are important differences between relations and files, as we shall soon see.

When a relation is thought of as a **table** of values, each row in the table represents a collection of related data values. We introduced entity types and relationship types as concepts for modeling real-world data in Chapter 3. In the relational model, each row in the table represents a fact that typically corresponds to a real-world entity or relationship. The table name and column names are used to help in interpreting the meaning of the values in each row. For example, the first table of Figure 1.2 is called STUDENT because each row represents facts about a particular student entity. The column names—Name, StudentNumber, Class, Major—specify how to interpret the data values in each row, based on the column each value is in. All values in a column are of the same data type.

In the formal relational model terminology, a row is called a *tuple*, a column header is called an *attribute*, and the table is called a *relation*. The data type describing the types of values that can appear in each column is called a *domain*. We now define these terms—*domain*, *tuple*, *attribute*, and *relation*—more precisely.

7.1.1 Domains, Attributes, Tuples, and Relations

A **domain** D is a set of atomic values. By **atomic** we mean that each value in the domain is indivisible as far as the relational model is concerned. A common method of specifying a domain is to specify a data type from which the data values forming the domain are drawn. It is also useful to specify a name for the domain, to help in interpreting its values. Some examples of domains follow:

- USA_phone_numbers: The set of 10-digit phone numbers valid in the United States.
- Local_phone_numbers: The set of 7-digit phone numbers valid within a particular area code in the United States.
- Social_security_numbers: The set of valid 9-digit social security numbers.
- Names: The set of names of persons.
- Grade_point_averages: Possible values of computed grade point averages; each must be a real (floating point) number between 0 and 4.
- Employee_ages: Possible ages of employees of a company; each must be a value between 15 and 80 years old.
- Academic_department_names: The set of academic department names, such as Computer Science, Economics, and Physics, in a university.
- Academic_department_codes: The set of academic department codes, such as CS, ECON, and PHYS, in a university.

The preceding are called *logical* definitions of domains. A **data type** or **format** is also specified for each domain. For example, the data type for the domain USA_phone_numbers can be declared as a character string of the form (ddd)ddd-dddd, where each d is a numeric (decimal) digit and the first three digits form a valid telephone area code. The data type for Employee_ages is an integer number between 15 and 80. For Academic_department_names, the data type is the set of all character strings that represent valid department names. A domain is thus given a name, data type, and format. Additional information for interpreting the values of a domain can also be given; for example, a numeric domain such as Person_weights should have the units of measurement—pounds or kilograms.

A **relation schema** R, denoted by $R(A_1, A_2, \ldots, A_n)$, is made up of a relation name R and a list of attributes $A_1, A_2, \ldots, A_n$. Each **attribute** A_i is the name of a role played by some domain D in the relation schema R. D is called the **domain** of A_i and is denoted by $dom(A_i)$. A relation schema is used to *describe* a relation; R is called the **name** of this relation. The **degree** of a relation is the number of attributes n of its relation schema.

An example of a relation schema for a relation of degree 7, which describes university students, is the following:

STUDENT(Name, SSN, HomePhone, Address, OfficePhone, Age, GPA)

STUDENT	Name	SSN	HomePhone	Address	OfficePhone	Age	GPA
	Benjamin Bayer	305-61-2435	373-1616	2918 Bluebonnet Lane	null	19	3.21
	Katherine Ashly	381-62-1245	375-4409	125 Kirby Road	null	18	2.89
	Dick Davidson	422-11-2320	null	3452 Elgin Road	749-1253	25	3.53
	Charles Cooper	489-22-1100	376-9821	265 Lark Lane	749-6492	28	3.93
	Barbara Benson	533-69-1238	839-8461	7384 Fontana Lane	null	19	3.25

Figure 7.1   The attributes and tuples of a relation STUDENT.

For this relation schema, STUDENT is the name of the relation, which has seven attributes. We can specify the following previously defined domains for some of the attributes of the STUDENT relation: dom(Name) = Names; dom(SSN) = Social_security_numbers; dom(HomePhone) = Local_phone_numbers, dom(OfficePhone) = Local_phone_numbers, and dom(GPA) = Grade_point_averages.

A **relation** (or **relation state**)[2] r of the relation schema $R(A_1, A_2, \ldots, A_n)$, also denoted by r(R), is a set of n-tuples $r = \{t_1, t_2, \ldots, t_m\}$. Each **n-tuple** t is an ordered list of n values $t = <v_1, v_2, \ldots, v_n>$, where each value v_i, $1 \leq i \leq n$, is an element of dom(A_i) or is a special **null** value. The ith value in tuple t, which corresponds to the attribute A_i, is referred to as $t[A_i]$. The terms relation **intension** for the schema R and relation **extension** for a relation state r(R) are also commonly used.

Figure 7.1 shows an example of a STUDENT relation, which corresponds to the STUDENT schema specified above. Each tuple in the relation represents a particular student entity. We display the relation as a table, where each tuple is shown as a row and each attribute corresponds to a column header indicating a role or interpretation of the values in that column. *Null values* represent attributes whose values are unknown or do not exist for some individual STUDENT tuples.

The above definition of a relation can be *restated* as follows. A relation r(R) is a **mathematical relation** of degree n on the domains dom(A_1), dom(A_2), $\ldots$, dom(A_n), which is a **subset** of the **Cartesian product** of the domains that define R:

$$r(R) \subseteq (\text{dom} (A_1) \times \text{dom}(A_2) \times \ldots \times \text{dom}(A_n))$$

The Cartesian product specifies all possible combinations of values from the underlying domains. Hence, if we denote the number of values or **cardinality** of a domain D by $|D|$, and assume that all domains are finite, the total number of tuples in the Cartesian product is:

$$|\text{dom}(A_1)| * |\text{dom}(A_2)| * \ldots * |\text{dom}(A_n)|$$

---

2. This has also been called a **relation instance.** We will not use this term because *instance* is also used to refer to a single tuple or row.

Out of all these possible combinations, a relation state at a given time—the **current relation state**—reflects only the valid tuples that represent a particular state of the real world. In general, as the state of the real world changes, so does the relation, by being transformed into another relation state. However, the schema R is relatively static and does *not* change except very infrequently—for example, as a result of adding an attribute to represent new information that was not originally stored in the relation.

It is possible for several attributes to *have the same domain*. The attributes indicate different **roles,** or interpretations, for the domain. For example, in the STUDENT relation, the same domain Local_phone_numbers plays the role of HomePhone, referring to the "home phone of a student," and the role of OfficePhone, referring to the "office phone of the student."

7.1.2 Characteristics of Relations

The earlier definition of relations implies certain characteristics that make a relation different from a file or a table. We now discuss some of these characteristics.

Ordering of Tuples in a Relation. A *relation* is defined as a set of tuples. Mathematically, elements of a set have *no order* among them; hence tuples in a relation do not have any particular order. However, in a file, records are physically stored on disk so there always is an order among the records. This ordering indicates first, second, ith, and last records in the file. Similarly, when we display a relation as a table, the rows are displayed in a certain order.

Tuple ordering is not part of a relation definition, because a relation attempts to represent facts at a logical or abstract level. Many logical orders can be specified on a relation; for example, tuples in the STUDENT relation in Figure 7.1 could be logically ordered by values of Name, SSN, Age, or some other attribute. The definition of a relation does not specify any order: there is *no preference* for one logical ordering over another. Hence,.the relation displayed in Figure 7.2 is considered *identical* to the one shown in Figure 7.1. When a relation is implemented as a file, a physical ordering may be specified on the records of the file.

Ordering of Values within a Tuple, and an Alternative Definition of a Relation. According to the preceding definition of a relation, an n-tuple is an *ordered list* of n values, so the ordering of values in a tuple—and hence of attributes in a relation schema

STUDENT	Name	SSN	HomePhone	Address	OfficePhone	Age	GPA
	Dick Davidson	422-11-2320	null	3452 Elgin Road	749-1253	25	3.53
	Barbara Benson	533-69-1238	839-8461	7384 Fontana Lane	null	19	3.25
	Charles Cooper	489-22-1100	376-9821	265 Lark Lane	749-6492	28	3.93
	Katherine Ashly	381-62-1245	375-4409	125 Kirby Road	null	18	2.89
	Benjamin Bayer	305-61-2435	373-1616	2918 Bluebonnet Lane	null	19	3.21

Figure 7.2 The relation STUDENT from Figure 7.1, with a different order of tuples.

t = < (Name, Dick Davidson),(SSN, 422-11-2320),(HomePhone, null),(Address, 3452 Elgin Road),
                    (OfficePhone, 749-1253),(Age, 25),(GPA, 3.53)>

t = < (Address, 3452 Elgin Road),(Name, Dick Davidson),(SSN, 422-11-2320),(Age, 25),
                    (OfficePhone,749-1253),(GPA, 3.53),(HomePhone, null)>

Figure 7.3   Two identical tuples when order of attributes and values is not part of the
              definition of a relation.

definition—is important. However, at a logical level, the order of attributes and their values are *not* really important as long as the correspondence between attributes and values is
maintained.

An **alternative definition** of a relation can be given, making the ordering of values in
a tuple *unnecessary*. In this definition, a relation schema R = {A_1, A_2, . . ., A_n} is a *set* of
attributes, and a relation r(R) is a finite set of **mappings** r = {t_1, t_2, . . ., t_m}, where each
tuple t_i is a mapping from R to D, and D is the union of the attribute domains; that is, D =
dom(A_1) $\cup$ dom(A_2) $\cup$ . . . $\cup$ dom(A_n). In this definition, t[A_i] must be in dom(A_i) for
$1 \leq i \leq n$ for each mapping t in r. Each mapping t_i is called a tuple.

According to this definition, a **tuple** can be considered as a **set** of (<attribute>,
<value>) pairs, where each pair gives the value of the mapping from an attribute A_i to a
value v_i from dom(A_i). The ordering of attributes is *not* important, because the attribute
name appears with its value. By this definition, the two tuples shown in Figure 7.3 are
identical. This makes sense at an abstract or logical level, since there really is no reason to
prefer having one attribute value appear before another in a tuple.

When a relation is implemented as a file, the attributes are physically ordered as
fields within a record. We will use the **first definition** of relation, where the attributes and
the values within tuples *are ordered*, because it simplifies much of the notation. However,
the alternative definition given here is more general.

Values in the Tuples.   Each value in a tuple is an **atomic** value; that is, it is not divisible
into components within the framework of the basic relational model. Hence, composite
and multivalued attributes (see Chapter 3) are not allowed. Much of the theory behind
the relational model was developed with this assumption in mind, which is called the
first normal form assumption.[3] Multivalued attributes must be represented by separate
relations, and composite attributes are represented only by their simple component
attributes. Recent research in the relational model attempts to remove these restrictions
by using the concept of **nonfirst normal form** or **nested** relations (see Chapter 13).

The values of some attributes within a particular tuple may be unknown or may not
apply to that tuple. A special value, called **null,** is used for these cases. For example, in
Figure 7.1, some student tuples have null for their office phones because they do not have
an office (that is, office phone *does not apply* to these students). Another student has a

---

3. We discuss this assumption in more detail in Chapter 14.

null for home phone, presumably because either he does not have a home phone or he has one but we do not know it (value is *unknown*). In general, we can have *several types* of null values, such as "value unknown," "value exists but not available," or "attribute does not apply to this tuple." It is possible to devise different codes for different types of null values. Incorporating different types of null values into relational model operations has proved difficult, and a full discussion is outside the scope of this book.

Interpretation of a Relation. The relation schema can be interpreted as a declaration or a type of **assertion.** For example, the schema of the STUDENT relation of Figure 7.1 asserts that, in general, a student entity has a Name, SSN, HomePhone, Address, OfficePhone, Age, and GPA. Each tuple in the relation can then be interpreted as a **fact** or a particular instance of the assertion. For example, the first tuple in Figure 7.1 asserts the fact that there is a STUDENT whose name is Benjamin Bayer, SSN is 305-61-2435, Age is 19, and so on.

Notice that some relations may represent facts about *entities*, whereas other relations may represent facts about *relationships*. For example, a relation schema MAJORS (StudentSSN, DepartmentCode) asserts that students major in academic departments; a tuple in this relation relates a student to his or her major department. Hence, the relational model represents facts about both entities and relationships *uniformly* as relations.

An alternative interpretation of a relation schema is as a **predicate;** in this case, the values in each tuple are interpreted as values that *satisfy* the predicate. This interpretation is quite useful in the context of logic programming languages, such as PROLOG, because it allows the relational model to be used within these languages. This is further discussed in Chapter 25 when we discuss deductive databases.

7.1.3 Relational Model Notation

We will use the following notation in our presentation:

- A relation schema R of degree n is denoted by $R(A_1, A_2, \ldots, A_n)$.
- An n-tuple t in a relation r(R) is denoted by $t = <v_1, v_2, \ldots, v_n>$, where v_i is the value corresponding to attribute A_i. The following notation refers to **component values** of tuples:
  - Both $t[A_i]$ and $t.A_i$ refer to the value v_i in t for attribute A_i.
  - Both $t[A_u, A_w, \ldots, A_z]$ and $t.(A_u, A_w, \ldots, A_z)$, where $A_u, A_w, \ldots, A_z$ is a list of attributes from R, refer to the subtuple of values $<v_u, v_w, \ldots, v_z>$ from t corresponding to the attributes specified in the list.
- The letters Q, R, S denote relation names.
- The letters q, r, s denote relation states.
- The letters t, u, v denote tuples.
- In general, the name of a relation schema such as STUDENT *also indicates* the current set of tuples in that relation—the *current relation state*—whereas STUDENT(Name, SSN, . . .) refers *only* to the relation schema.

- An attribute A can be qualified with the relation name R to which it belongs by using the *dot notation* R.A—for example, STUDENT.Name or STUDENT.Age. This is because the same name may be used for two attributes in different relations. However, all attribute names *in a particular relation* must be distinct.

As an example, consider the tuple t = <'Barbara Benson', '533-69-1238', '839-8461', '7384 Fontana Lane', null, 19, 3.25> from the STUDENT relation in Figure 7.1; we have t[Name] = <'Barbara Benson'>, and t[SSN, GPA, Age] = <'533-69-1238', 3.25, 19>.

7.2 Relational Constraints and Relational Database Schemas

In this section, we discuss the various restrictions on data that can be specified on a relational database schema in the form of constraints. These include domain constraints, key constraints, entity integrity, and referential integrity constraints. Other types of constraints, called *data dependencies* (which include *functional dependencies* and *multivalued dependencies*), are used mainly for database design by normalization and will be discussed in Chapters 14 and 15.

7.2.1 Domain Constraints

Domain constraints specify that the value of each attribute A must be an atomic value from the domain dom(A). We have already discussed the ways in which domains can be specified in Section 7.1.1. The data types associated with domains typically include standard numeric data types for integers (such as short-integer, integer, long-integer) and real numbers (float and double-precision float). Characters, fixed-length strings, and variable-length strings are also available, as are date, time, timestamp, and money data types. Other possible domains may be described by a subrange of values from a data type or as an enumerated data type where all possible values are explicitly listed. Rather than describe these in detail here, we discuss the data types offered by the SQL2 relational standard in Section 8.1.2.

7.2.2 Key Constraints and Constraints on Null

A *relation* is defined as a *set of tuples*. By definition, all elements of a set are distinct; hence, all tuples in a relation must also be distinct. This means that no two tuples can have the same combination of values for *all* their attributes. Usually, there are other **subsets of attributes** of a relation schema R with the property that no two tuples in any relation state r of R should have the same combination of values for these attributes. Suppose that we denote one such subset of attributes by SK; then for any two *distinct* tuples t_1 and t_2 in a relation state r of R, we have the constraint that

$$t_1[SK] \neq t_2[SK]$$

Any such set of attributes SK is called a **superkey** of the relation schema R. A superkey SK specifies a *uniqueness constraint* that no two distinct tuples in a state r of R can have the same value for SK. Every relation has at least one default superkey—the set of all its attributes. A superkey can have redundant attributes, however, so a more useful concept is that of a *key*, which has no redundancy. A **key** K of a relation schema R is a superkey of R with the additional property that removing any attribute A from K leaves a set of attributes K' that is not a superkey of R. Hence, a key is a *minimal superkey*—that is, a superkey from which we cannot remove any attributes and still have the uniqueness constraint hold.

For example, consider the STUDENT relation of Figure 7.1. The attribute set {SSN} is a key of STUDENT because no two student tuples can have the same value for SSN.[4] Any set of attributes that includes SSN—for example, {SSN, Name, Age}—is a superkey. However, the superkey {SSN, Name, Age} is not a key of STUDENT, because removing Name or Age or both from the set still leaves us with a superkey.

The value of a key attribute can be used to identify uniquely each tuple in the relation. For example, the SSN value 305-61-2435 identifies uniquely the tuple corresponding to Benjamin Bayer in the STUDENT relation. Notice that a set of attributes constituting a key is a property of the relation schema; it is a constraint that should hold on *every* relation state of the schema. A key is determined from the meaning of the attributes, and the property is *time-invariant*; it must continue to hold when we insert new tuples in the relation. For example, we cannot and should not designate the Name attribute of the STUDENT relation in Figure 7.1 as a key, because there is no guarantee that two students with identical names will never exist.[5]

In general, a relation schema may have more than one key. In this case, each of the keys is called a **candidate key.** For example, the CAR relation in Figure 7.4 has two candidate keys: LicenseNumber and EngineSerialNumber. It is common to designate one of the candidate keys as the **primary key** of the relation. This is the candidate key whose values are used to *identify* tuples in the relation. We use the convention that the attributes that form the primary key of a relation schema are <u>underlined</u>, as shown in Figure 7.4. Notice that, when a relation schema has several candidate keys, the choice of one to

CAR	LicenseNumber	EngineSerialNumber	Make	Model	Year
	Texas ABC-739	A69352	Ford	Mustang	96
	Florida TVP-347	B43696	Oldsmobile	Cutlass	99
	New York MPO-22	X83554	Oldsmobile	Delta	95
	California 432-TFY	C43742	Mercedes	190-D	93
	California RSK-629	Y82935	Toyota	Camry	98
	Texas RSK-629	U028365	Jaguar	XJS	98

Figure 7.4   The CAR relation with two candidate keys: LicenseNumber and Engine-SerialNumber.

---

4. Note that SSN is also a superkey.

5. Names are sometimes used as keys, but then some artifact—such as appending an ordinal number—must be used to distinguish between identical names.

become primary key is arbitrary; however, it is usually better to choose a primary key with a single attribute or a small number of attributes.

Another constraint on attributes specifies whether null values are or are not permitted. For example, if every STUDENT tuple must have a valid, non-null value for the Name attribute, then Name of STUDENT is constrained to be NOT NULL.

7.2.3 Relational Databases and Relational Database Schemas

So far, we have discussed single relations and single relation schemas. A relational database usually contains many relations, with tuples in relations that are related in various ways. In this section we define a relational database and a relational database schema. A **relational database schema** S is a set of relation schemas $S = \{R_1, R_2, \ldots, R_m\}$ and a set of **integrity constraints** IC. A **relational database state**[6] DB of S is a set of relation states DB $= \{r_1, r_2, \ldots, r_m\}$ such that each r_i is a state of R_i and such that the r_i relation states satisfy the integrity constraints specified in IC. Figure 7.5 shows a relational database schema

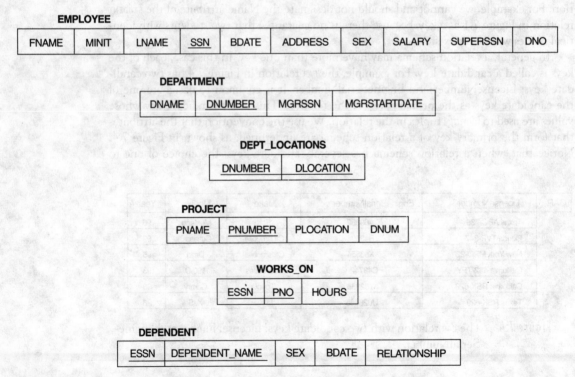

Figure 7.5   Schema diagram for the COMPANY relational database schema; the primary keys are underlined.

---

6. A relational database *state* is also called a relational database *instance*.

EMPLOYEE	FNAME	MINIT	LNAME	SSN	BDATE	ADDRESS	SEX	SALARY	SUPERSSN	DNO
	John	B	Smith	123456789	1965-01-09	731 Fondren, Houston, TX	M	30000	333445555	5
	Franklin	T	Wong	333445555	1955-12-08	638 Voss, Houston, TX	M	40000	888665555	5
	Alicia	J	Zelaya	999887777	1968-07-19	3321 Castle, Spring, TX	F	25000	987654321	4
	Jennifer	S	Wallace	987654321	1941-06-20	291 Berry, Bellaire, TX	F	43000	888665555	4
	Ramesh	K	Narayan	666884444	1962-09-15	975 Fire Oak, Humble, TX	M	38000	333445555	5
	Joyce	A	English	453453453	1972-07-31	5631 Rice, Houston, TX	F	25000	333445555	5
	Ahmad	V	Jabbar	987987987	1969-03-29	980 Dallas, Houston, TX	M	25000	987654321	4
	James	E	Borg	888665555	1937-11-10	450 Stone, Houston, TX	M	55000	null	1

DEPT_LOCATIONS	DNUMBER	DLOCATION
	1	Houston
	4	Stafford
	5	Bellaire
	5	Sugarland
	5	Houston

DEPARTMENT	DNAME	DNUMBER	MGRSSN	MGRSTARTDATE
	Research	5	333445555	1988-05-22
	Administration	4	987654321	1995-01-01
	Headquarters	1	888665555	1981-06-19

WORKS_ON	ESSN	PNO	HOURS
	123456789	1	32.5
	123456789	2	7.5
	666884444	3	40.0
	453453453	1	20.0
	453453453	2	20.0
	333445555	2	10.0
	333445555	3	10.0
	333445555	10	10.0
	333445555	20	10.0
	999887777	30	30.0
	999887777	10	10.0
	987987987	10	35.0
	987987987	30	5.0
	987654321	30	20.0
	987654321	20	15.0
	888665555	20	null

PROJECT	PNAME	PNUMBER	PLOCATION	DNUM
	ProductX	1	Bellaire	5
	ProductY	2	Sugarland	5
	ProductZ	3	Houston	5
	Computerization	10	Stafford	4
	Reorganization	20	Houston	1
	Newbenefits	30	Stafford	4

DEPENDENT	ESSN	DEPENDENT_NAME	SEX	BDATE	RELATIONSHIP
	333445555	Alice	F	1986-04-05	DAUGHTER
	333445555	Theodore	M	1983-10-25	SON
	333445555	Joy	F	1958-05-03	SPOUSE
	987654321	Abner	M	1942-02-28	SPOUSE
	123456789	Michael	M	1988-01-04	SON
	123456789	Alice	F	1988-12-30	DAUGHTER
	123456789	Elizabeth	F	1967-05-05	SPOUSE

Figure 7.6 One possible relational database state corresponding to the COMPANY schema.

that we call COMPANY = {EMPLOYEE, DEPARTMENT, DEPT_LOCATIONS, PROJECT, WORKS_ON, DEPENDENT}. Figure 7.6 shows a relational database state corresponding to the COMPANY schema. We will use this schema and database state in this chapter and in Chapters 8 through 10 for developing example queries in different relational languages. When we refer to a relational database, we implicitly include both its schema and its current state.

In Figure 7.5, the DNUMBER attribute in both DEPARTMENT and DEPT_LOCATIONS stands for the same real-world concept—the number given to a department. That same concept is called DNO in EMPLOYEE and DNUM in PROJECT. Attributes that represent the same real-world concept may or may not have identical names in different relations. Alternatively, attributes that represent different concepts may have the same name in different relations. For example, we could have used the attribute name NAME for both PNAME of PROJECT and DNAME of DEPARTMENT; in this case, we would have two attributes that share the same name but represent different real-world concepts—project names and department names.

In some early versions of the relational model, an assumption was made that the same real-world concept, when represented by an attribute, would have *identical* attribute names in all relations. This creates problems when the same real-world concept is used in different roles (meanings) in the same relation. For example, the concept of social security number appears twice in the EMPLOYEE relation of Figure 7.5: once in the role of the employee's social security number, and once in the role of the supervisor's social security number. We gave them distinct attribute names—SSN and SUPERSSN, respectively—in order to distinguish their meaning.

Each relational DBMS must have a Data Definition Language (DDL) for defining a relational database schema. Current relational DBMSs are mostly using SQL for this purpose. We present the SQL DDL in Section 8.1.

Integrity constraints are specified on a database schema and are expected to hold on every database state of that schema. In addition to domain and key constraints, two other types of constraints are considered part of the relational model: entity integrity and referential integrity.

7.2.4 Entity Integrity, Referential Integrity, and Foreign Keys

The **entity integrity constraint** states that no primary key value can be null. This is because the primary key value is used to identify individual tuples in a relation; having null values for the primary key implies that we cannot identify some tuples. For example, if two or more tuples had null for their primary keys, we might not be able to distinguish them.

Key constraints and entity integrity constraints are specified on individual relations. The **referential integrity constraint** is specified between two relations and is used to maintain the consistency among tuples of the two relations. Informally, the referential integrity constraint states that a tuple in one relation that refers to another relation must refer to an *existing tuple* in that relation. For example, in Figure 7.6, the attribute DNO of EMPLOYEE gives the department number for which each employee works; hence, its value in every EMPLOYEE tuple must match the DNUMBER value of some tuple in the DEPARTMENT relation.

To define referential integrity more formally, we first define the concept of a *foreign key*. The conditions for a foreign key, given below, specify a referential integrity constraint between the two relation schemas R_1 and R_2. A set of attributes FK in relation schema R_1 is a **foreign key** of R_1 that references relation R_2 if it satisfies the following two rules:

1. The attributes in FK have the same domain(s) as the primary key attributes PK of R_2; the attributes FK are said to **reference** or **refer to** the relation R_2.
2. A value of FK in a tuple t_1 of the current state $r_1(R_1)$ either occurs as a value of PK for some tuple t_2 in the current state $r_2(R_2)$ or is null. In the former case, we have $t_1[FK] = t_2[PK]$, and we say that the tuple t_1 **references** or **refers to** the tuple t_2. R_1 is called the **referencing relation** and R_2 is the **referenced relation.**

In a database of many relations, there are usually many referential integrity constraints. To specify these constraints, we must first have a clear understanding of the meaning or role that each set of attributes plays in the various relation schemas of the database. Referential integrity constraints typically arise from the *relationships among the entities* represented by the relation schemas. For example, consider the database shown in Figure 7.6. In the EMPLOYEE relation, the attribute DNO refers to the department for which an employee works; hence, we designate DNO to be a foreign key of EMPLOYEE, referring to the DEPARTMENT relation. This means that a value of DNO in any tuple t_1 of the EMPLOYEE relation must match a value of the primary key of DEPARTMENT—the DNUMBER attribute—in some tuple t_2 of the DEPARTMENT relation, or the value of DNO *can be null* if the employee does not belong to a department. In Figure 7.6 the tuple for employee 'John Smith' references the tuple for the 'Research' department, indicating that 'John Smith' works for this department.

Notice that a foreign key can *refer to its own relation.* For example, the attribute SUPERSSN in EMPLOYEE refers to the supervisor of an employee; this is another employee, represented by a tuple in the EMPLOYEE relation. Hence, SUPERSSN is a foreign key that references the EMPLOYEE relation itself. In Figure 7.6 the tuple for employee 'John Smith' references the tuple for employee 'Franklin Wong,' indicating that 'Franklin Wong' is the supervisor of 'John Smith.'

We can *diagrammatically display referential integrity constraints* by drawing a directed arc from each foreign key to the relation it references. For clarity, the arrowhead may point to the primary key of the referenced relation. Figure 7.7 shows the schema in Figure 7.5 with the referential integrity constraints displayed in this manner.

All integrity constraints should be specified on the relational database schema if we want to enforce these constraints on the database states. Hence, the DDL includes provisions for specifying the various types of constraints so that the DBMS can automatically enforce them. Most relational DBMSs support key and entity integrity constraints, and make provisions to support referential integrity. These constraints are specified as a part of data definition.

The preceding integrity constraints do not include a large class of general constraints, sometimes called *semantic integrity constraints*, that may have to be specified and enforced on a relational database. Examples of such constraints are "the salary of an employee should not exceed the salary of the employee's supervisor" and "the maximum number of hours an employee can work on all projects per week is 56." Such constraints can be specified and enforced by using a general purpose **constraint specification language.** Mechanisms called

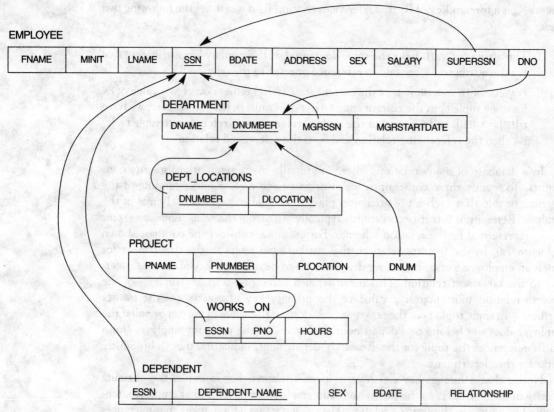

Figure 7.7   Referential integrity constraints displayed on the COMPANY relational database schema diagram.

triggers and assertions can be used. In SQL2, a CREATE ASSERTION statement is used for this purpose (see Chapters 8 and 23).

The types of constraints we discussed above may be termed as *state constraints*, because they define the constraints that a *valid state* of the database must satisfy. Another type of constraints, called *transition constraints*, can be defined to deal with state changes in the database.[7] An example of a transition constraint is: "the salary of an employee can only increase." Such constraints are typically specified using active rules and triggers, as we shall discuss in Chapter 23.

---

7. State constraints are also called *static constraints*, and transition constraints are called *dynamic constraints*.

7.3 Update Operations and Dealing with Constraint Violations

The operations of the relational model can be categorized into *retrievals* and *updates*. The relational algebra operations, which can be used to specify retrievals, are discussed in detail in Section 7.4. In this section, we concentrate on the update operations. There are three basic update operations on relations: (1) insert, (2) delete, and (3) modify. **Insert** is used to insert a new tuple or tuples in a relation; **Delete** is used to delete tuples; and **Update** (or **Modify**) is used to change the values of some attributes in existing tuples. Whenever update operations are applied, the integrity constraints specified on the relational database schema should not be violated. In this section we discuss the types of constraints that may be violated by each update operation and the types of actions that may be taken if an update does cause a violation. We use the database shown in Figure 7.6 for examples and discuss only key constraints, entity integrity constraints, and the referential integrity constraints shown in Figure 7.7. For each type of update, we give some example operations and discuss any constraints that each operation may violate.

7.3.1 The Insert Operation

The **Insert** operation provides a list of attribute values for a new tuple t that is to be inserted into a relation R. Insert can violate any of the four types of constraints discussed in the previous section. Domain constraints can be violated if an attribute value is given that does not appear in the corresponding domain. Key constraints can be violated if a key value in the new tuple t already exists in another tuple in the relation r(R). Entity integrity can be violated if the primary key of the new tuple t is null. Referential integrity can be violated if the value of any foreign key in t refers to a tuple that does not exist in the referenced relation. Here are some examples to illustrate this discussion.

1. Insert <'Cecilia', 'F', 'Kolonsky', null, '1960-04-05', '6357 Windy Lane, Katy, TX', F, 28000, null, 4> into EMPLOYEE.

   - This insertion violates the entity integrity constraint (null for the primary key SSN), so it is rejected.

2. Insert <'Alicia', 'J', 'Zelaya', '999887777', '1960-04-05', '6357 Windy Lane, Katy, TX', F, 28000, '987654321', 4> into EMPLOYEE.

   - This insertion violates the key constraint because another tuple with the same SSN value already exists in the EMPLOYEE relation, and so it is rejected.

3. Insert <'Cecilia', 'F', 'Kolonsky', '677678989', '1960-04-05', '6357 Windswept, Katy, TX', F, 28000, '987654321', 7> into EMPLOYEE.

   - This insertion violates the referential integrity constraint specified on DNO because no DEPARTMENT tuple exists with DNUMBER = 7.

4. Insert <'Cecilia', 'F', 'Kolonsky', '677678989', '1960-04-05', '6357 Windy Lane, Katy, TX', F, 28000, null, 4> into EMPLOYEE.

   • This insertion satisfies all constraints, so it is acceptable.

If an insertion violates one or more constraints, the default option is to *reject the insertion*. In this case, it would be useful if the DBMS could explain to the user why the insertion was rejected. Another option is to attempt to *correct the reason for rejecting the insertion,* but this is typically not used for violations caused by Insert; rather, it is used more often in correcting violations for Delete and Update. The following examples illustrate how this option may be used for Insert violations. In operation 1 above, the DBMS could ask the user to provide a value for SSN and could accept the insertion if a valid SSN value were provided. In operation 3, the DBMS could either ask the user to change the value of DNO to some valid value (or set it to null), or it could ask the user to insert a DEPARTMENT tuple with DNUMBER = 7 and could accept the insertion only after such an operation was accepted. Notice that in the latter case the insertion can **cascade** back to the EMPLOYEE relation if the user attempts to insert a tuple for department 7 with a value for MGRSSN that does not exist in the EMPLOYEE relation.

7.3.2   The Delete Operation

The **Delete** operation can violate only referential integrity, if the tuple being deleted is referenced by the foreign keys from other tuples in the database. To specify deletion, a condition on the attributes of the relation selects the tuple (or tuples) to be deleted. Here are some examples.

1. Delete the WORKS_ON tuple with ESSN = '999887777' and PNO = 10.

   • This deletion is acceptable.

2. Delete the EMPLOYEE tuple with SSN = '999887777'.

   • This deletion is not acceptable, because tuples in WORKS_ON refer to this tuple. Hence, if the tuple is deleted, referential integrity violations will result.

3. Delete the EMPLOYEE tuple with SSN = '333445555'.

   • This deletion will result in even worse referential integrity violations, because the tuple involved is referenced by tuples from the EMPLOYEE, DEPARTMENT, WORKS_ON, and DEPENDENT relations.

Three options are available if a deletion operation causes a violation. The first option is to *reject the deletion*. The second option is to *attempt to cascade (or propagate) the deletion* by deleting tuples that reference the tuple that is being deleted. For example, in operation 2, the DBMS could automatically delete the offending tuples from WORKS_ON with ESSN = '999887777'. A third option is to *modify the referencing attribute values* that cause the violation; each such value is either set to null or changed to reference another valid tuple. Notice that, if a referencing attribute that causes a violation is *part of the primary key,* it *cannot be* set to null; otherwise, it would violate entity integrity.

Combinations of these three options are also possible. For example, to avoid having operation 3 cause a violation, the DBMS may automatically delete all tuples from WORKS_ON and DEPENDENT with ESSN = '333445555'. Tuples in EMPLOYEE with SUPERSSN = '333445555' and the tuple in DEPARTMENT with MGRSSN = '333445555' can have their SUPERSSN and MGRSSN values changed to other valid values or to null. Although it may make sense to delete automatically the WORKS_ON and DEPENDENT tuples that refer to an EMPLOYEE tuple, it may not make sense to delete other EMPLOYEE tuples or a DEPARTMENT tuple. In general, when a referential integrity constraint is specified, the DBMS should allow the user to *specify which of the three options* applies in case of a violation of the constraint. We discuss how to specify these options in SQL2 DDL in Chapter 8.

7.3.3   The Update Operation

The **Update** operation is used to change the values of one or more attributes in a tuple (or tuples) of some relation R. It is necessary to specify a condition on the attributes of the relation to select the tuple (or tuples) to be modified. Here are some examples.

1. Update the SALARY of the EMPLOYEE tuple with SSN = '999887777' to 28000.

   • Acceptable.

2. Update the DNO of the EMPLOYEE tuple with SSN = '999887777' to 1.

   • Acceptable.

3. Update the DNO of the EMPLOYEE tuple with SSN = '999887777' to 7.

   • Unacceptable, because it violates referential integrity.

4. Update the SSN of the EMPLOYEE tuple with SSN = '999887777' to '987654321'.

   • Unacceptable, because it violates primary key and referential integrity constraints.

Updating an attribute that is neither a primary key nor a foreign key usually causes no problems; the DBMS need only check to confirm that the new value is of the correct data type and domain. Modifying a primary key value is similar to deleting one tuple and inserting another in its place, because we use the primary key to identify tuples. Hence, the issues discussed earlier under both Insert and Delete come into play. If a foreign key attribute is modified, the DBMS must make sure that the new value refers to an existing tuple in the referenced relation (or is null).

7.4   Basic Relational Algebra Operations

In addition to defining the database structure and constraints, a data model must include a set of operations to manipulate the data. A basic set of relational model operations constitute the **relational algebra.** These operations enable the user to specify basic retrieval requests. The result of a retrieval is a new relation, which may have been formed from one or more relations. The algebra operations thus produce new relations, which can be further manipulated using operations of the same algebra. A sequence of relational algebra operations forms a **relational algebra expression,** whose result will also be a relation.

The relational algebra operations are usually divided into two groups. One group includes set operations from mathematical set theory; these are applicable because each relation is defined to be a set of tuples. Set operations include UNION, INTERSECTION, SET DIFFERENCE, and CARTESIAN PRODUCT. The other group consists of operations developed specifically for relational databases; these include SELECT, PROJECT, and JOIN, among others. The SELECT and PROJECT operations are discussed first, because they are the simplest. Then we discuss set operations. Finally, we discuss JOIN and other complex operations. The relational database shown in Figure 7.6 is used for our examples.

Some common database requests cannot be performed with the basic relational algebra operations, so additional operations are needed to express these requests. Some of these additional operations are described in Section 7.5.

7.4.1   The SELECT Operation

The SELECT operation is used to select a *subset* of the tuples from a relation that satisfy a **selection condition.** One can consider the SELECT operation to be a *filter* that keeps only those tuples that satisfy a qualifying condition. For example, to select the EMPLOYEE tuples whose department is 4, or those whose salary is greater than $30,000, we can individually specify each of these two conditions with a SELECT operation as follows:

$$\sigma_{DNO=4}(\text{EMPLOYEE})$$

$$\sigma_{SALARY>30000}(\text{EMPLOYEE})$$

In general, the SELECT operation is denoted by

$$\sigma_{<\text{selection condition}>}(R)$$

where the symbol σ (sigma) is used to denote the SELECT operator, and the selection condition is a Boolean expression specified on the attributes of relation R. Notice that R is generally a *relational algebra expression* whose result is a relation; the simplest expression is just the name of a database relation. The relation resulting from the SELECT operation has the *same attributes* as R. The Boolean expression specified in <selection condition> is made up of a number of **clauses** of the form

<attribute name> <comparison op> <constant value>, or

<attribute name> <comparison op> <attribute name>

where <attribute name> is the name of an attribute of R, <comparison op> is normally one of the operators $\{=, <, \leq, >, \geq, \neq\}$, and <constant value> is a constant value from the attribute domain. Clauses can be arbitrarily connected by the Boolean operators AND, OR, and NOT to form a general selection condition. For example, to select the tuples for all employees who either work in department 4 and make over $25,000 per year, or work in department 5 and make over $30,000, we can specify the following SELECT operation:

$$\sigma_{(DNO=4 \text{ AND } SALARY>25000) \text{ OR } (DNO=5 \text{ AND } SALARY>30000)}(\text{EMPLOYEE})$$

(a)

FNAME	MINIT	LNAME	SSN	BDATE	ADDRESS	SEX	SALARY	SUPERSSN	DNO
Franklin	T	Wong	333445555	1955-12-08	638 Voss,Houston,TX	M	40000	888665555	5
Jennifer	S	Wallace	987654321	1941-06-20	291 Berry,Bellaire,TX	F	43000	888665555	4
Ramesh	K	Narayan	666884444	1962-09-15	975 FireOak,Humble,TX	M	38000	333445555	5

(b)

LNAME	FNAME	SALARY
Smith	John	30000
Wong	Franklin	40000
Zelaya	Alicia	25000
Wallace	Jennifer	43000
Narayan	Ramesh	38000
English	Joyce	25000
Jabbar	Ahmad	25000
Borg	James	55000

(c)

SEX	SALARY
M	30000
M	40000
F	25000
F	43000
M	38000
M	25000
M	55000

Figure 7.8 Results of SELECT and PROJECT operations. (a) $\sigma_{(DNO=4\ AND\ SALARY>25000)\ OR\ (DNO=5\ AND\ SALARY>30000)}(EMPLOYEE)$. (b) $\pi_{LNAME,\ FNAME,\ SALARY}(EMPLOYEE)$. (c) $\pi_{SEX,\ SALARY}(EMPLOYEE)$

The result is shown in Figure 7.8(a). Notice that the comparison operators in the set $\{=, <, \leq, >, \geq, \neq\}$ apply to attributes whose domains are *ordered values*, such as numeric or date domains. Domains of strings of characters are considered ordered based on the collating sequence of the characters. If the domain of an attribute is a set of *unordered values*, then only the comparison operators in the set $\{=, \neq\}$ can be used. An example of an unordered domain is the domain Color = {red, blue, green, white, yellow, . . .} where no order is specified among the various colors. Some domains allow additional types of comparison operators; for example, a domain of character strings may allow the comparison operator SUBSTRING_OF.

In general, the result of a SELECT operation can be determined as follows. The <selection condition> is applied independently to each tuple t in R. This is done by substituting each occurrence of an attribute A_i in the selection condition with its value in the tuple $t[A_i]$. If the condition evaluates to true, then tuple t is **selected.** All the selected tuples appear in the result of the SELECT operation. The Boolean conditions AND, OR, and NOT have their normal interpretation as follows:

- (cond1 AND cond2) is true if both (cond1) and (cond2) are true; otherwise, it is false.
- (cond1 OR cond2) is true if either (cond1) or (cond2) or both are true; otherwise, it is false.
- (NOT cond) is true if cond is false; otherwise, it is false.

The SELECT operator is unary; that is, it is applied to a single relation. Moreover, the selection operation is applied to *each tuple individually*; hence, selection conditions cannot involve more than one tuple. The **degree** of the relation resulting from a SELECT operation is the same as that of R. The number of tuples in the resulting relation is always *less than or equal to* the number of tuples in R. That is, $|\sigma_c(R)| \leq |R|$ for any condition C.

The fraction of tuples selected by a selection condition is referred to as the **selectivity** of the condition.

Notice that the SELECT operation is **commutative**; that is,

$$\sigma_{<cond1>}(\sigma_{<cond2>}(R)) = \sigma_{<cond2>}(\sigma_{<cond1>}(R))$$

Hence, a sequence of SELECTs can be applied in any order. In addition, we can always combine a **cascade** of SELECT operations into a single SELECT operation with a conjunctive (AND) condition; that is:

$$\sigma_{<cond1>}(\sigma_{<cond2>}(\ldots(\sigma_{<condn>}(R))\ldots)) = \sigma_{<cond1>\ AND\ <cond2>\ AND\ \ldots\ AND\ <condn>}(R)$$

7.4.2   The PROJECT Operation

If we think of a relation as a table, the SELECT operation selects some of the *rows* from the table while discarding other rows. The **PROJECT** operation, on the other hand, selects certain *columns* from the table and discards the other columns. If we are interested in only certain attributes of a relation, we use the PROJECT operation to *project* the relation over these attributes only. For example, to list each employee's first and last name and salary, we can use the PROJECT operation as follows:

$$\pi_{LNAME,\ FNAME,\ SALARY}(EMPLOYEE)$$

The resulting relation is shown in Figure 7.8(b). The general form of the PROJECT operation is

$$\pi_{<attribute\ list>}(R)$$

where π (pi) is the symbol used to represent the PROJECT operation and <attribute list> is a list of attributes from the attributes of relation R. Again, notice that R is, in general, a *relational algebra expression* whose result is a relation, which in the simplest case is just the name of a database relation. The result of the PROJECT operation has only the attributes specified in <attribute list> and *in the same order as they appear in the list*. Hence, its **degree** is equal to the number of attributes in <attribute list>.

If the attribute list includes only nonkey attributes of R, duplicate tuples are likely to occur; the PROJECT operation *removes any duplicate tuples*, so the result of the PROJECT operation is a set of tuples and hence a valid relation.[8] This is known as **duplicate elimination.** For example, consider the following PROJECT operation:

$$\pi_{SEX,\ SALARY}(EMPLOYEE)$$

The result is shown in Figure 7.8(c). Notice that the tuple <F, 25000> appears only once in Figure 7.8(c), even though this combination of values appears twice in the EMPLOYEE relation.

---

8. If duplicates are not eliminated, the result would be a **multiset** or **bag** of tuples rather than a set. As we shall see in Chapter 8, the SQL language allows the user to specify whether duplicates should be eliminated or not.

The number of tuples in a relation resulting from a PROJECT operation is always less than or equal to the number of tuples in R. If the projection list is a superkey of R—that is, it includes some key of R—the resulting relation has the *same number* of tuples as R. Moreover,

$$\pi_{<list1>}(\pi_{<list2>}(R)) = \pi_{<list1>}(R)$$

as long as <list2> contains the attributes in <list1>; otherwise, the left-hand side is an incorrect expression. It is also noteworthy that commutativity *does not* hold on PROJECT.

7.4.3 Sequences of Operations and the RENAME Operation

The relations shown in Figure 7.8 do not have any names. In general, we may want to apply several relational algebra operations one after the other. Either we can write the operations as a single **relational algebra expression** by nesting the operations, or we can apply one operation at a time and create intermediate result relations. In the latter case, we must name the relations that hold the intermediate results. For example, to retrieve the first name, last name, and salary of all employees who work in department number 5, we must apply a SELECT and a PROJECT operation. We can write a single relational algebra expression as follows:

$$\pi_{FNAME, LNAME, SALARY}(\sigma_{DNO=5}(EMPLOYEE))$$

Figure 7.9(a) shows the result of this relational algebra expression. Alternatively, we can explicitly show the sequence of operations, giving a name to each intermediate relation:

$$DEP5\_EMPS \leftarrow \sigma_{DNO=5}(EMPLOYEE)$$

$$RESULT \leftarrow \pi_{FNAME, LNAME, SALARY}(DEP5\_EMPS)$$

It is often simpler to break down a complex sequence of operations by specifying intermediate result relations than to write a single relational algebra expression. We can also use this technique to **rename** the attributes in the intermediate and result relations. This can be useful in connection with more complex operations such as UNION and JOIN, as we shall see. To rename the attributes in a relation, we simply list the new attribute names in parentheses, as in the following example:

$$TEMP \leftarrow \sigma_{DNO=5}(EMPLOYEE)$$

$$R(FIRSTNAME, LASTNAME, SALARY) \leftarrow \pi_{FNAME, LNAME, SALARY}(TEMP)$$

The above two operations are illustrated in Figure 7.9(b). If no renaming is applied, the names of the attributes in the resulting relation of a SELECT operation are the same as those in the original relation and in the same order. For a PROJECT operation with no renaming, the resulting relation has the same attribute names as those in the projection list and in the same order in which they appear in the list.

We can also define a **RENAME** operation—which can rename either the relation name, or the attribute names, or both—in a manner similar to the way we defined SELECT

(a)

FNAME	LNAME	SALARY
John	Smith	30000
Franklin	Wong	40000
Ramesh	Narayan	38000
Joyce	English	25000

(b)

TEMP	FNAME	MINIT	LNAME	SSN	BDATE	ADDRESS	SEX	SALARY	SUPERSSN	DNO
	John	B	Smith	123456789	1965-01-09	731 Fondren,Houston,TX	M	30000	333445555	5
	Franklin	T	Wong	333445555	1955-12-08	638 Voss,Houston,TX	M	40000	888665555	5
	Ramesh	K	Narayan	666884444	1962-09-15	975 Fire Oak,Humble,TX	M	38000	333445555	5
	Joyce	A	English	453453453	1972-07-31	5631 Rice,Houston,TX	F	25000	333445555	5

R	FIRSTNAME	LASTNAME	SALARY
	John	Smith	30000
	Franklin	Wong	40000
	Ramesh	Narayan	38000
	Joyce	English	25000

Figure 7.9   Results of relational algebra expressions.

(a) $\pi_{\text{LNAME, FNAME, SALARY}} (\sigma_{\text{DNO}=5}(\text{EMPLOYEE}))$.

(b) The same expression using intermediate relations and renaming of attributes.

and PROJECT. The general RENAME operation when applied to a relation R of degree n is denoted by

$$\rho_{S(B1, B2, ..., Bn)}(R) \text{ or } \rho_S(R) \text{ or } \rho_{(B1, B2, ..., Bn)}(R)$$

where the symbol ρ (rho) is used to denote the RENAME operator, S is the new relation name, and B_1, B_2, . . ., B_n are the new attribute names. The first expression renames both the relation and its attributes; the second renames the relation only; and the third renames the attributes only. If the attributes of R are $(A_1, A_2, . . ., A_n)$ in that order, then each A_i is renamed as B_i.

7.4.4 Set Theoretic Operations

The next group of relational algebra operations are the standard mathematical operations on sets. For example, to retrieve the social security numbers of all employees who either work in department 5 or directly supervise an employee who works in department 5, we can use the UNION operation as follows:

DEP5_EMPS←$\sigma_{\text{DNO}=5}$(EMPLOYEE)

RESULT1←π_{SSN}(DEP5_EMPS)

RESULT2(SSN)←π_{SUPERSSN}(DEP5_EMPS)

RESULT← RESULT1 $\cup$ RESULT2

The relation RESULT1 has the social security numbers of all employees who work in department 5, whereas RESULT2 has the social security numbers of all employees who

RESULT1	SSN
	123456789
	333445555
	666884444
	453453453

RESULT2	SSN
	333445555
	888665555

RESULT	SSN
	123456789
	333445555
	666884444
	453453453
	888665555

Figure 7.10   Query result after the UNION operation: RESULT ← RESULT1 ∪ RESULT2.

directly supervise an employee who works in department 5. The UNION operation produces the tuples that are in either RESULT1 or RESULT2 or both (see Figure 7.10).

Several set theoretic operations are used to merge the elements of two sets in various ways, including **UNION, INTERSECTION,** and **SET DIFFERENCE.** These are binary operations; that is, each is applied to two sets. When these operations are adapted to relational databases, the two relations on which any of the above three operations are applied must have the same **type of tuples;** this condition is called *union compatibility.* Two relations $R(A_1, A_2, \ldots, A_n)$ and $S(B_1, B_2, \ldots, B_n)$ are said to be **union compatible** if they have the same degree n, and if $dom(A_i) = dom(B_i)$ for $1 \leq i \leq n$. This means that the two relations have the same number of attributes and that each pair of corresponding attributes have the same domain.

We can define the three operations UNION, INTERSECTION, and SET DIFFERENCE on two union-compatible relations R and S as follows:

- **UNION:** The result of this operation, denoted by R ∪ S, is a relation that includes all tuples that are either in R or in S or in both R and S. Duplicate tuples are eliminated.

- **INTERSECTION:** The result of this operation, denoted by R ∩ S, is a relation that includes all tuples that are in both R and S.

- **SET DIFFERENCE:** The result of this operation, denoted by R − S, is a relation that includes all tuples that are in R but not in S.

We will adopt the convention that the resulting relation has the same attribute names as the *first* relation R. Figure 7.11 illustrates the three operations. The relations STUDENT and INSTRUCTOR in Figure 7.11(a) are union compatible, and their tuples represent the names of students and instructors, respectively. The result of the UNION operation in Figure 7.11(b) shows the names of all students and instructors. Note that duplicate tuples appear only once in the result. The result of the INTERSECTION operation (Figure 7.11c) includes only those who are both students and instructors. Notice that both UNION and INTERSECTION are *commutative operations;* that is

R ∪ S = S ∪ R, and R ∩ S = S ∩ R

Both union and intersection can be treated as n-ary operations applicable to any number of relations as both are *associative operations;* that is

R ∪ (S ∪ T) = (R ∪ S) ∪ T, and (R ∩ S) ∩ T = R ∩ (S ∩ T)

(a)

STUDENT	FN	LN
	Susan	Yao
	Ramesh	Shah
	Johnny	Kohler
	Barbara	Jones
	Amy	Ford
	Jimmy	Wang
	Ernest	Gilbert

INSTRUCTOR	FNAME	LNAME
	John	Smith
	Ricardo	Browne
	Susan	Yao
	Francis	Johnson
	Ramesh	Shah

(b)

FN	LN
Susan	Yao
Ramesh	Shah
Johnny	Kohler
Barbara	Jones
Amy	Ford
Jimmy	Wang
Ernest	Gilbert
John	Smith
Ricardo	Browne
Francis	Johnson

(c)

FN	LN
Susan	Yao
Ramesh	Shah

(d)

FN	LN
Johnny	Kohler
Barbara	Jones
Amy	Ford
Jimmy	Wang
Ernest	Gilbert

(e)

FNAME	LNAME
John	Smith
Ricardo	Browne
Francis	Johnson

Figure 7.11   Illustrating the set operations UNION, INTERSECTION, and DIFFERENCE. (a) Two union compatible relations. (b) STUDENT ∪ INSTRUCTOR. (c) STUDENT ∩ INSTRUCTOR. (d) STUDENT − INSTRUCTOR. (e) INSTRUCTOR − STUDENT.

The DIFFERENCE operation is *not commutative*; that is, in general

R − S ≠ S − R

Figure 7.11(d) shows the names of students who are not instructors, and Figure 7.11(e) shows the names of instructors who are not students.

Next we discuss the **CARTESIAN PRODUCT** operation—also known as **CROSS PRODUCT** or **CROSS JOIN**—denoted by **X**, which is also a binary set operation, but the relations on which it is applied do *not* have to be union compatible. This operation is used to combine tuples from two relations in a combinatorial fashion. In general, the result of $R(A_1,$

$A_2, \ldots, A_n) \times S(B_1, B_2, \ldots, B_m)$ is a relation Q with n + m attributes $Q(A_1, A_2, \ldots, A_n,$ $B_1, B_2, \ldots, B_m)$, in that order. The resulting relation Q has one tuple for each combination of tuples—one from R and one from S. Hence, if R has n_R tuples and S has n_S tuples, then R **x** S will have $n_R * n_S$ tuples. The operation applied by itself is generally meaningless. It is useful when followed by a selection that matches values of attributes coming from the component relations. For example, suppose that we want to retrieve for each female employee a list of the names of her dependents; we can do this as follows:

FEMALE_EMPS←$\sigma_{SEX='F'}$(EMPLOYEE)

EMPNAMES←$\pi_{FNAME, LNAME, SSN}$(FEMALE_EMPS)

EMP_DEPENDENTS← EMPNAMES **X** DEPENDENT

ACTUAL_DEPENDENTS←$\sigma_{SSN=ESSN}$(EMP_DEPENDENTS)

RESULT←$\pi_{FNAME, LNAME, DEPENDENT\_NAME}$(ACTUAL_DEPENDENTS)

The resulting relations from the above sequence of operations are shown in Figure 7.12. The EMP_DEPENDENTS relation is the result of applying the CARTESIAN PRODUCT operation to EMPNAMES from Figure 7.12 with DEPENDENT from Figure 7.6. In EMP_DEPENDENTS, every tuple from EMPNAMES is combined with every tuple from DEPENDENT, giving a result that is not very meaningful. We only want to combine a female employee tuple with her dependents—namely, the DEPENDENT tuples whose ESSN values match the SSN value of the EMPLOYEE tuple. The ACTUAL_DEPENDENTS relation accomplishes this.

The CARTESIAN PRODUCT creates tuples with the combined attributes of two relations. We can then SELECT only related tuples from the two relations by specifying an appropriate selection condition, as we did in the preceding example. Because this sequence of CARTESIAN PRODUCT followed by SELECT is used quite commonly to identify and select related tuples from two relations, a special operation, called JOIN, was created to specify this sequence as a single operation. We discuss the JOIN operation next.

7.4.5 The JOIN Operation

The JOIN operation, denoted by $\bowtie$, is used to combine *related tuples* from two relations into single tuples. This operation is very important for any relational database with more than a single relation, because it allows us to process relationships among relations. To illustrate join, suppose that we want to retrieve the name of the manager of each department. To get the manager's name, we need to combine each department tuple with the employee tuple whose SSN value matches the MGRSSN value in the department tuple. We do this by using the JOIN operation, and then projecting the result over the necessary attributes, as follows:

DEPT_MGR ← DEPARTMENT $\bowtie_{MGRSSN=SSN}$ EMPLOYEE

RESULT←$\pi_{DNAME, LNAME, FNAME}$(DEPT_MGR)

The first operation is illustrated in Figure 7.13. Note that MGRSSN is a foreign key and that the referential integrity constraint plays a role in having matching tuples in the

FEMALE_EMPS	FNAME	MINIT	LNAME	SSN	BDATE	ADDRESS	SEX	SALARY	SUPERSSN	DNO
	Alicia	J	Zelaya	999887777	1968-07-19	3321 Castle,Spring,TX	F	25000	987654321	4
	Jennifer	S	Wallace	987654321	1941-06-20	291 Berry,Bellaire,TX	F	43000	888665555	4
	Joyce	A	English	453453453	1972-07-31	5631 Rice,Houston,TX	F	25000	333445555	5

EMPNAMES	FNAME	LNAME	SSN
	Alicia	Zelaya	999887777
	Jennifer	Wallace	987654321
	Joyce	English	453453453

EMP_DEPENDENTS	FNAME	LNAME	SSN	ESSN	DEPENDENT_NAME	SEX	BDATE	• • •
	Alicia	Zelaya	999887777	333445555	Alice	F	1986-04-05	• • •
	Alicia	Zelaya	999887777	333445555	Theodore	M	1983-10-25	• • •
	Alicia	Zelaya	999887777	333445555	Joy	F	1958-05-03	• • •
	Alicia	Zelaya	999887777	987654321	Abner	M	1942-02-28	• • •
	Alicia	Zelaya	999887777	123456789	Michael	M	1988-01-04	• • •
	Alicia	Zelaya	999887777	123456789	Alice	F	1988-12-30	• • •
	Alicia	Zelaya	999887777	123456789	Elizabeth	F	1967-05-05	• • •
	Jennifer	Wallace	987654321	333445555	Alice	F	1986-04-05	• • •
	Jennifer	Wallace	987654321	333445555	Theodore	M	1983-10-25	• • •
	Jennifer	Wallace	987654321	333445555	Joy	F	1958-05-03	• • •
	Jennifer	Wallace	987654321	987654321	Abner	M	1942-02-28	• • •
	Jennifer	Wallace	987654321	123456789	Michael	M	1988-01-04	• • •
	Jennifer	Wallace	987654321	123456789	Alice	F	1988-12-30	• • •
	Jennifer	Wallace	987654321	123456789	Elizabeth	F	1967-05-05	• • •
	Joyce	English	453453453	333445555	Alice	F	1986-04-05	• • •
	Joyce	English	453453453	333445555	Theodore	M	1983-10-25	• • •
	Joyce	English	453453453	333445555	Joy	F	1958-05-03	• • •
	Joyce	English	453453453	987654321	Abner	M	1942-02-28	• • •
	Joyce	English	453453453	123456789	Michael	M	1988-01-04	• • •
	Joyce	English	453453453	123456789	Alice	F	1988-12-30	• • •
	Joyce	English	453453453	123456789	Elizabeth	F	1967-05-05	• • •

ACTUAL_DEPENDENTS	FNAME	LNAME	SSN	ESSN	DEPENDENT_NAME	SEX	BDATE	• • •
	Jennifer	Wallace	987654321	987654321	Abner	M	1942-02-28	• • •

RESULT	FNAME	LNAME	DEPENDENT_NAME
	Jennifer	Wallace	Abner

Figure 7.12   An illustration of the CARTESIAN PRODUCT operation.

DEPT_MGR	DNAME	DNUMBER	MGRSSN	• • •	FNAME	MINIT	LNAME	SSN	• • •
	Research	5	333445555	• • •	Franklin	T	Wong	333445555	• • •
	Administration	4	987654321	• • •	Jennifer	S	Wallace	987654321	• • •
	Headquarters	1	888665555	• • •	James	E	Borg	888665555	• • •

Figure 7.13   Illustrating the JOIN operation.

referenced relation EMPLOYEE. The example we gave earlier to illustrate the CARTESIAN PRODUCT operation can be specified, using the JOIN operation, by replacing the two operations:

EMP_DEPENDENTS ← EMPNAMES **X** DEPENDENT

ACTUAL_DEPENDENTS ← $\sigma_{SSN=ESSN}$(EMP_DEPENDENTS)

with a single JOIN operation:

ACTUAL_DEPENDENTS ← EMPNAMES $\bowtie$ $_{SSN=ESSN}$ DEPENDENT

The general form of a JOIN operation on two relations[9] $R(A_1, A_2, \ldots, A_n)$ and $S(B_1, B_2, \ldots, B_m)$ is:

$R \bowtie _{<join\ condition>} S$

The result of the JOIN is a relation Q with $n + m$ attributes $Q(A_1, A_2, \ldots, A_n, B_1, B_2, \ldots, B_m)$ in that order; Q has one tuple for each combination of tuples—one from R and one from S—*whenever the combination satisfies the join condition*. This is the main difference between CARTESIAN PRODUCT and JOIN: in JOIN, only combinations of tuples *satisfying the join condition* appear in the result, whereas in the CARTESIAN PRODUCT *all* combinations of tuples are included in the result. The join condition is specified on attributes from the two relations R and S and is evaluated for each combination of tuples. Each tuple combination for which the join condition evaluates to true is included in the resulting relation Q *as a single combined tuple*.

A general join condition is of the form:

<condition> AND <condition> AND . . . AND <condition>

where each condition is of the form $A_i \theta B_j$, A_i is an attribute of R, B_j is an attribute of S, A_i and B_j have the same domain, and θ (theta) is one of the comparison operators $\{=, <, \leq, >, \geq, \neq\}$. A JOIN operation with such a general join condition is called a **THETA JOIN**. Tuples whose join attributes are null *do not* appear in the result. In that sense, the join operation does *not* necessarily preserve all of the information in the participating relations.

The most common JOIN involves join conditions with equality comparisons only. Such a JOIN, where the only comparison operator used is =, is called an **EQUIJOIN**. Both examples we have considered were EQUIJOINs. Notice that in the result of an EQUIJOIN we always have one or more pairs of attributes that have *identical values* in every tuple. For example, in Figure 7.13, the values of the attributes MGRSSN and SSN are identical in every tuple of DEPT_MGR because of the equality join condition specified on these two attributes. Because one of each pair of attributes with identical values is superfluous, a new operation called **NATURAL JOIN**—denoted by * —was created to get rid of the second (superfluous) attribute in an EQUIJOIN condition.[10] The standard definition of NATURAL JOIN requires that the two join attributes (or each pair of join attributes) have

---

9. Again, notice that R and S can be the relations that result from general *relational algebra expressions*.

10. **NATURAL JOIN** is basically an EQUIJOIN followed by removal of the superfluous attributes.

(a)

PROJ_DEPT	PNAME	PNUMBER	PLOCATION	DNUM	DNAME	MGRSSN	MGRSTARTDATE
	ProductX	1	Bellaire	5	Research	333445555	1988-05-22
	ProductY	2	Sugarland	5	Research	333445555	1988-05-22
	ProductZ	3	Houston	5	Research	333445555	1988-05-22
	Computerization	10	Stafford	4	Administration	987654321	1995-01-01
	Reorganization	20	Houston	1	Headquarters	888665555	1981-06-19
	Newbenefits	30	Stafford	4	Administration	987654321	1995-01-01

(b)

DEPT_LOCS	DNAME	DNUMBER	MGRSSN	MGRSTARTDATE	LOCATION
	Headquarters	1	888665555	1981-06-19	Houston
	Administration	4	987654321	1995-01-01	Stafford
	Research	5	333445555	1988-05-22	Bellaire
	Research	5	333445555	1988-05-22	Sugarland
	Research	5	333445555	1988-05-22	Houston

Figure 7.14   An illustration of the NATURAL JOIN operation. (a) PROJ_DEPT ← PROJECT * DEPT. (b) DEPT_LOCS ← DEPARTMENT * DEPT_LOCATIONS.

the same name in both relations. If this is not the case, a renaming operation is applied first. In the following example, we first rename the DNUMBER attribute of DEPARTMENT to DNUM—so that it has the same name as the DNUM attribute in PROJECT—then apply NATURAL JOIN:

$$\text{PROJ\_DEPT} \leftarrow \text{PROJECT} * \rho_{(\text{DNAME,DNUM,MGRSSN,MGRSTARTDATE})}(\text{DEPARTMENT})$$

The attribute DNUM is called the **join attribute.** The resulting relation is illustrated in Figure 7.14(a). In the PROJ_DEPT relation, each tuple combines a PROJECT tuple with the DEPARTMENT tuple for the department that controls the project, but *only one join attribute* is kept.

If the attributes on which the natural join is specified *have the same names in both relations,* renaming is unnecessary. For example, to apply a natural join on the DNUMBER attributes of DEPARTMENT and DEPT_LOCATIONS, it is sufficient to write:

$$\text{DEPT\_LOCS} \leftarrow \text{DEPARTMENT} * \text{DEPT\_LOCATIONS}$$

The resulting relation is shown in Figure 7.14(b), which combines each department with its locations and has one tuple for each location. In general, NATURAL JOIN is performed by equating *all* attribute pairs that have the same name in the two relations. There can be a list of join attributes from each relation, and each corresponding pair must have the same name.

A more general but non-standard definition for NATURAL JOIN is

$$Q \leftarrow R *_{(<\text{list1}>),(<\text{list2}>)} S$$

In this case, <list1> specifies a list of i attributes from R, and <list2> specifies a list of i attributes from S. The lists are used to form equality comparison conditions between pairs of corresponding attributes; the conditions are then ANDed together. Only the list corresponding to attributes of the first relation R—<list 1>—is kept in the result Q.

Notice that if no combination of tuples satisfies the join condition, the result of a JOIN is an empty relation with zero tuples. In general, if R has n_R tuples and S has n_S tuples, the result of a JOIN operation $R \bowtie_{<join\ condition>} S$ will have between zero and n_R * n_S tuples. The expected size of the join result divided by the maximum size n_R * n_S leads to a ratio called **join selectivity,** which is a property of each join condition. If there is no join condition, all combinations of tuples qualify and the JOIN becomes a CARTESIAN PRODUCT, also called CROSS PRODUCT or CROSS JOIN.

The join operation is used to combine data from multiple relations so that related information can be presented in a single table. Note that sometimes a join may be specified between a relation and itself, as we shall illustrate in Section 7.5.2. The natural join or equijoin operation can also be specified among multiple tables, leading to an *n-way join*. For example, consider the following three-way join:

$$((\text{PROJECT} \bowtie_{\text{DNUM=DNUMBER}} \text{DEPARTMENT}) \bowtie_{\text{MGRSSN=SSN}} \text{EMPLOYEE})$$

This links each project to its controlling department, and then relates the department to its manager employee. The net result is a consolidated relation where each tuple contains this project-department-manager information.

7.4.6 A Complete Set of Relational Algebra Operations

It has been shown that the set of relational algebra operations $\{\sigma, \pi, \cup, -, \times\}$ is a **complete** set; that is, any of the other relational algebra operations can be expressed as a *sequence of operations from this set*. For example, the INTERSECTION operation can be expressed by using UNION and DIFFERENCE as follows:

$$R \cap S \equiv (R \cup S) - ((R - S) \cup (S - R))$$

Although, strictly speaking, INTERSECTION is not required, it is inconvenient to specify this complex expression every time we wish to specify an intersection. As another example, a JOIN operation can be specified as a CARTESIAN PRODUCT followed by a SELECT operation, as we discussed:

$$R \bowtie_{<condition>} S \equiv \sigma_{<condition>} (R \times S)$$

Similarly, a NATURAL JOIN can be specified as a CARTESIAN PRODUCT preceded by RENAME and followed by SELECT and PROJECT operations. Hence, the various JOIN operations are also *not strictly necessary* for the expressive power of the relational algebra; however, they are very important because they are convenient to use and are very commonly applied in database applications. Other operations have been included in the relational algebra for convenience rather than necessity. We discuss one of these—the DIVISION operation—in the next section.

7.4.7 The DIVISION Operation

The DIVISION operation is useful for a special kind of query that sometimes occurs in database applications. An example is "Retrieve the names of employees who work on *all* the projects that 'John Smith' works on." To express this query using the DIVISION operation, proceed as follows. First, retrieve the list of project numbers that 'John Smith' works on in the intermediate relation SMITH_PNOS:

$$\text{SMITH} \leftarrow \sigma_{\text{FNAME='John' AND LNAME='Smith'}}(\text{EMPLOYEE})$$
$$\text{SMITH\_PNOS} \leftarrow \pi_{\text{PNO}}(\text{WORKS\_ON} \bowtie_{\text{ESSN=SSN}} \text{SMITH})$$

Next, create a relation that includes a tuple <PNO, ESSN> whenever the employee whose social security number is ESSN works on the project whose number is PNO in the intermediate relation SSN_PNOS:

$$\text{SSN\_PNOS} \leftarrow \pi_{\text{ESSN,PNO}}(\text{WORKS\_ON})$$

Finally, apply the DIVISION operation to the two relations, which gives the desired employees' social security numbers:

$$\text{SSNS(SSN)} \leftarrow \text{SSN\_PNOS} \div \text{SMITH\_PNOS}$$
$$\text{RESULT} \leftarrow \pi_{\text{FNAME, LNAME}}(\text{SSNS} * \text{EMPLOYEE})$$

The previous operations are shown in Figure 7.15(a). In general, the DIVISION operation is applied to two relations $R(Z) \div S(X)$, where $X \subseteq Z$. Let $Y = Z - X$ (and hence $Z = X \cup Y$); that is, let Y be the set of attributes of R that are not attributes of S. The result of DIVISION is a relation $T(Y)$ that includes a tuple t if tuples t_R appear in R with $t_R[Y] = t$, and with $t_R[X] = t_S$ *for every tuple* t_S in S. This means that, for a tuple t to appear in the result T of the DIVISION, the values in t must appear in R in combination with *every* tuple in S.

Figure 7.15(b) illustrates a DIVISION operator where $X = \{A\}$, $Y = \{B\}$, and $Z = \{A, B\}$. Notice that the tuples (values) b_1 and b_4 appear in R in combination with all three tuples in S; that is why they appear in the resulting relation T. All other values of B in R do not appear with all the tuples in S and are not selected: b_2 does not appear with a_2 and b_3 does not appear with a_1.

The DIVISION operator can be expressed as a sequence of π, x, and $-$ operations as follows:

$$T_1 \leftarrow \pi_Y(R)$$
$$T_2 \leftarrow \pi_Y((S \times T_1) - R)$$
$$T \leftarrow T_1 - T_2$$

(a)

SSN_PNOS	ESSN	PNO
	123456789	1
	123456789	2
	666884444	3
	453453453	1
	453453453	2
	333445555	2
	333445555	3
	333445555	10
	333445555	20
	999887777	30
	999887777	10
	987987987	10
	987987987	30
	987654321	30
	987654321	20
	888665555	20

SMITH_PNOS	PNO
	1
	2

SSNS	SSN
	123456789
	453453453

(b)

R	A	B
	a1	b1
	a2	b1
	a3	b1
	a4	b1
	a1	b2
	a3	b2
	a2	b3
	a3	b3
	a4	b3
	a1	b4
	a2	b4
	a3	b4

S	A
	a1
	a2
	a3

T	B
	b1
	b4

Figure 7.15 Illustrating the DIVISION operation. (a) Dividing SSN_PNOS by SMITH_PNOS. (b) T ← R ÷ S.

7.5 Additional Relational Operations

Some common database requests—which are needed in commercial query languages for relational DBMSs—cannot be performed with the basic relational algebra operations described in Section 7.4. In this section we define additional operations to express these requests. These operations enhance the expressive power of the relational algebra.

7.5.1 Aggregate Functions and Grouping

The first type of request that cannot be expressed in the basic relational algebra is to specify mathematical **aggregate functions** on collections of values from the database. Examples of such functions include retrieving the average or total salary of all employees or the number of employee tuples. Common functions applied to collections of numeric values include SUM, AVERAGE, MAXIMUM, and MINIMUM. The COUNT function is used for counting tuples or values.

Another common type of request involves grouping the tuples in a relation by the value of some of their attributes and then applying an aggregate function independently to each group. An example would be to group employee tuples by DNO, so that each group includes the tuples for employees working in the same department. We can then list each DNO value along with, say, the average salary of employees within the department.

We can define an AGGREGATE FUNCTION operation, using the symbol $\mathcal{F}$ (pronounced "script F"),[11] to specify these types of requests as follows:

$$\text{<grouping attributes>} \; \mathcal{F} \; \text{<function list>} \; (R)$$

where <grouping attributes> is a list of attributes of the relation specified in R, and <function list> is a list of (<function> <attribute>) pairs. In each such pair, <function> is one of the allowed functions—such as SUM, AVERAGE, MAXIMUM, MINIMUM, COUNT—and <attribute> is an attribute of the relation specified by R. The resulting relation has the grouping attributes plus one attribute for each element in the function list. For example, to retrieve each department number, the number of employees in the department, and their average salary, while renaming the resulting attributes as indicated below, we write:

$$\rho_{R(DNO, NO\_OF\_EMPLOYEES, AVERAGE\_SAL)} \; (_{DNO} \; \mathcal{F} \; _{COUNT\ SSN,\ AVERAGE\ SALARY} \; (EMPLOYEE))$$

The result of this operation is shown in Figure 7.16(a).

In the above example, we specified a list of attribute names—between parentheses in the rename operation—for the resulting relation R. If no renaming is applied, then the attributes of the resulting relation that correspond to the function list will each be the concatenation of the function name with the attribute name in the form <function>_<attribute>. For example, Figure 7.16(b) shows the result of the following operation:

$$_{DNO} \; \mathcal{F} \; _{COUNT\ SSN,\ AVERAGE\ SALARY} (EMPLOYEE)$$

---

11. There is no single agreed-upon notation for specifying aggregate functions. In some cases a "script A" is used.

(a)

R	DNO	NO_OF_EMPLOYEES	AVERAGE_SAL
	5	4	33250
	4	3	31000
	1	1	55000

(b)

DNO	COUNT_SSN	AVERAGE_SALARY
5	4	33250
4	3	31000
1	1	55000

(c)

COUNT_SSN	AVERAGE_SALARY
8	35125

Figure 7.16   An illustration of the AGGREGATE FUNCTION operation.
(a) R(DNO, NO_OF_EMPLOYEES, AVERAGE_SAL) $\leftarrow$ $_{DNO}\Im$
COUNT SSN,AVERAGE SALARY (EMPLOYEE). (b) $_{DNO}\Im$ COUNT SSN,AVERAGE
SALARY(EMPLOYEE). (c) $\Im$ COUNT SSN,AVERAGE SALARY(EMPLOYEE).

If no grouping attributes are specified, the functions are applied to the attribute values of *all the tuples* in the relation, so the resulting relation has a *single tuple only*. For example, Figure 7.16(c) shows the result of the following operation:

$\Im$ COUNT SSN, AVERAGE SALARY(EMPLOYEE)

It is important to note that, in general, duplicates are *not eliminated* when an aggregate function is applied; this way, the normal interpretation of functions such as SUM and AVERAGE is computed.[12] It is worth emphasizing that the result of applying an aggregate function is a relation, not a scalar number—even if it has a single value.

7.5.2 Recursive Closure Operations

Another type of operation that, in general, cannot be specified in the basic relational algebra is **recursive closure**. This operation is applied to a **recursive relationship** between tuples of the same type, such as the relationship between an employee and a supervisor. This relationship is described by the foreign key SUPERSSN of the EMPLOYEE relation in Figures 7.6 and 7.7, which relates each employee tuple (in the role of supervisee) to another employee tuple (in the role of supervisor). An example of a recursive operation is to retrieve all supervisees of an employee e at all levels—that is, all employees e′ directly supervised by e; all employees e″ directly supervised by each employee e′; all employees e‴ directly supervised by each employee e″; and so on. Although it is

---

12. In SQL, the option of eliminating duplicates before applying the aggregate function is available by including the keyword DISTINCT (see Chapter 8).

straightforward in the relational algebra to specify all employees supervised by e *at a specific level*, it is difficult to specify all supervisees at *all* levels. For example, to specify the SSNs of all employees e′ directly supervised—*at level one*—by the employee e whose name is 'James Borg' (see Figure 7.6), we can apply the following operation:

$$\text{BORG\_SSN} \leftarrow \pi_{SSN}(\sigma_{FNAME='James'\ AND\ LNAME='Borg'}(\text{EMPLOYEE}))$$

$$\text{SUPERVISION(SSN1, SSN2)} \leftarrow \pi_{SSN,\ SUPERSSN}(\text{EMPLOYEE})$$

$$\text{RESULT1(SSN)} \leftarrow \pi_{SSN1}(\text{SUPERVISION} \bowtie_{SSN2=SSN} \text{BORG\_SSN})$$

To retrieve all employees supervised by Borg at level 2—that is, all employees e″ supervised by some employee e′ who is directly supervised by Borg—we can apply another JOIN to the result of the first query, as follows:

$$\text{RESULT2(SSN)} \leftarrow \pi_{SSN1}(\text{SUPERVISION} \bowtie_{SSN2=SSN} \text{RESULT1})$$

To get both sets of employees supervised at levels 1 and 2 by 'James Borg,' we can apply the UNION operation to the two results, as follows:

$$\text{RESULT} \leftarrow \text{RESULT2} \cup \text{RESULT1}$$

The results of these queries are illustrated in Figure 7.17. Although it is possible to retrieve employees at each level and then take their UNION, we cannot, in general, specify a query such as "retrieve the supervisees of 'James Borg' at all levels" without utilizing a looping mechanism.[13] An operation called the *transitive closure* of relations has been proposed to compute the recursive relationship as far as the recursion proceeds.

7.5.3   OUTER JOIN and OUTER UNION Operations

Finally, we discuss some extensions of the JOIN and UNION operations. The JOIN operations described earlier match tuples that satisfy the join condition. For example, for a NATURAL JOIN operation R * S, only tuples from R that have matching tuples in S—and vice versa—appear in the result. Hence, tuples without a *matching* (or *related*) tuple are eliminated from the JOIN result. Tuples with null in the join attributes are also eliminated. A set of operations, called OUTER JOINs, can be used when we want to keep all the tuples in R, or those in S, or those in both relations in the result of the JOIN, whether or not they have matching tuples in the other relation. This satisfies the need of queries where tuples from two tables are to be combined by matching corresponding rows, but some tuples are liable to be lost for lack of matching values. In such cases an operation is desirable that would preserve all the tuples whether or not they produce a match.

For example, suppose that we want a list of all employee names and also the name of the departments they manage *if they happen to manage a department;* we can apply an operation **LEFT OUTER JOIN,** denoted by $⟕$, to retrieve the result as follows:

$$\text{TEMP} \leftarrow (\text{EMPLOYEE} ⟕_{SSN=MGRSSN} \text{DEPARTMENT})$$

$$\text{RESULT} \leftarrow \pi_{FNAME,\ MINIT,\ LNAME,\ DNAME}(\text{TEMP})$$

---

13. We will discuss recursive queries further in Chapter 25 when we give an overview of deductive databases. Also, the SQL3 standard includes syntax for recursive closure.

(Borg's SSN is 888665555)

	(SSN)	(SUPERSSN)
SUPERVISION	**SSN1**	**SSN2**
	123456789	333445555
	333445555	888665555
	999887777	987654321
	987654321	888665555
	666884444	333445555
	453453453	333445555
	987987987	987654321
	888665555	null

RESULT 1	**SSN**
	333445555
	987654321

(Supervised by Borg)

RESULT 2	**SSN**
	123456789
	999887777
	666884444
	453453453
	987987987

(Supervised by Borg's subordinates)

RESULT	**SSN**
	123456789
	999887777
	666884444
	453453453
	987987987
	333445555
	987654321

(RESULT1 ∪ RESULT2)

Figure 7.17 A two-level recursive query.

The LEFT OUTER JOIN operation keeps every tuple in the *first* or *left* relation R in R ⋈ S; if no matching tuple is found in S, then the attributes of S in the join result are filled or "padded" with null values. The result of these operations is shown in Figure 7.18.

A similar operation, **RIGHT OUTER JOIN**, denoted by ⋈, keeps every tuple in the *second* or right relation S in the result of R ⋈ S. A third operation, **FULL OUTER JOIN**, denoted by ⋈, keeps all tuples in both the left and the right relations when no matching tuples are found, padding them with null values as needed. The three outer join operations are part of the SQL2 standard (see Chapter 8).

The **OUTER UNION** operation was developed to take the union of tuples from two relations if the relations are *not union compatible*. This operation will take the UNION of tuples in two relations that are **partially compatible,** meaning that only some of their attributes are union compatible. It is expected that the list of compatible attributes includes a key for both relations. Tuples from the component relations with the same key are represented only once in the result and have values for all attributes in the result. The attributes that are not union compatible from either relation are kept in the result, and tuples that have no values for these attributes are padded with null values. For example, an OUTER UNION can be applied to two relations whose schemas are STUDENT(Name, SSN, Department, Advisor) and FACULTY(Name, SSN, Department, Rank). The resulting relation schema is R(Name, SSN, Department, Advisor, Rank), and all the tuples from both

RESULT	FNAME	MINIT	LNAME	DNAME
	John	B	Smith	null
	Franklin	T	Wong	Research
	Alicia	J	Zelaya	null
	Jennifer	S	Wallace	Administration
	Ramesh	K	Narayan	null
	Joyce	A	English	null
	Ahmad	V	Jabbar	null
	James	E	Borg	Headquarters

Figure 7.18   The LEFT OUTER JOIN operation.

relations are included in the result. Student tuples will have a null for the Rank attribute, whereas faculty tuples will have a null for the Advisor attribute. A tuple that exists in both will have values for all its attributes.[14]

Another capability that exists in most commercial languages (but not in the basic relational algebra) is that of specifying operations on values after they are extracted from the database. For example, arithmetic operations such as +, −, and * can be applied to numeric values.

7.6   Examples of Queries in Relational Algebra

We now give additional examples to illustrate the use of the relational algebra operations. All examples refer to the database of Figure 7.6. In general, the same query can be stated in numerous ways using the various operations. We will state each query in one way and leave it to the reader to come up with equivalent formulations.

QUERY 1

Retrieve the name and address of all employees who work for the 'Research' department.

$$\text{RESEARCH\_DEPT} \leftarrow \sigma_{\text{DNAME}='\text{Research}'}(\text{DEPARTMENT})$$

$$\text{RESEARCH\_EMPS} \leftarrow (\text{RESEARCH\_DEPT} \bowtie_{\text{DNUMBER}=\text{DNO}} \text{EMPLOYEE})$$

$$\text{RESULT} \leftarrow \pi_{\text{FNAME, LNAME, ADDRESS}}(\text{RESEARCH\_EMPS})$$

This query could be specified in other ways; for example, the order of the JOIN and SELECT operations could be reversed, or the JOIN could be replaced by a NATURAL JOIN (after renaming).

---

14. Notice that OUTER UNION is equivalent to a FULL OUTER JOIN if the join attributes are *all* the common attributes of the two relations.

QUERY 2

For every project located in 'Stafford', list the project number, the controlling department number, and the department manager's last name, address, and birthdate.

STAFFORD_PROJS ← $\sigma_{\text{PLOCATION='Stafford'}}$(PROJECT)

CONTR_DEPT ← (STAFFORD_PROJS $\bowtie_{\text{DNUM=DNUMBER}}$ DEPARTMENT)

PROJ_DEPT_MGR ← (CONTR_DEPT $\bowtie_{\text{MGRSSN=SSN}}$ EMPLOYEE)

RESULT ← $\pi_{\text{PNUMBER, DNUM, LNAME, ADDRESS, BDATE}}$(PROJ_DEPT_MGR)

QUERY 3

Find the names of employees who work on *all* the projects controlled by department number 5.

DEPT5_PROJS(PNO) ← $\pi_{\text{PNUMBER}}(\sigma_{\text{DNUM=5}}$(PROJECT))

EMP_PRJO(SSN, PNO) ← $\pi_{\text{ESSN, PNO}}$(WORKS_ON)

RESULT_EMP_SSNS ← EMP_PRJO ÷ DEPT5_PROJS

RESULT ← $\pi_{\text{LNAME, FNAME}}$(RESULT_EMP_SSNS * EMPLOYEE)

QUERY 4

Make a list of project numbers for projects that involve an employee whose last name is 'Smith', either as a worker or as a manager of the department that controls the project.

SMITHS(ESSN) ← $\pi_{\text{SSN}}(\sigma_{\text{LNAME='Smith'}}$(EMPLOYEE))

SMITH_WORKER_PROJ ← π_{PNO}(WORKS_ON * SMITHS)

MGRS ← $\pi_{\text{LNAME, DNUMBER}}$(EMPLOYEE $\bowtie_{\text{SSN=MGRSSN}}$ DEPARTMENT)

SMITH_MANAGED_DEPTS(DNUM) ← $\pi_{\text{DNUMBER}}(\sigma_{\text{LNAME='Smith'}}$(MGRS))

SMITH_MGR_PROJS(PNO) ← π_{PNUMBER}(SMITH_MANAGED_DEPTS * PROJECT)

RESULT ← (SMITH_WORKER_PROJS $\cup$ SMITH_MGR_PROJS)

QUERY 5

List the names of all employees with two or more dependents.

Strictly speaking, this query cannot be done in the *basic relational algebra*. We have to use the AGGREGATE FUNCTION operation with the COUNT aggregate function. We assume that dependents of the *same* employee have *distinct* DEPENDENT_NAME values.

T_1(SSN, NO_OF_DEPTS) ← $_{\text{ESSN}}\mathfrak{I}$ COUNT DEPENDENT_NAME(DEPENDENT)

T_2 ← $\sigma_{\text{NO_OF_DEPS}\geq 2}(T_1)$

RESULT ← $\pi_{\text{LNAME, FNAME}}(T_2$ * EMPLOYEE)

QUERY 6

Retrieve the names of employees who have no dependents.

ALL_EMPS ← π_{SSN}(EMPLOYEE)

EMPS_WITH_DEPS(SSN) ← π_{ESSN}(DEPENDENT)

EMPS_WITHOUT_DEPS ← (ALL_EMPS − EMPS_WITH_DEPS)

RESULT ← $\pi_{LNAME, FNAME}$(EMPS_WITHOUT_DEPS * EMPLOYEE)

QUERY 7

List the names of managers who have at least one dependent.

MGRS(SSN) ← π_{MGRSSN}(DEPARTMENT)

EMPS_WITH_DEPS(SSN) ← π_{ESSN}(DEPENDENT)

MGRS_WITH_DEPS ← (MGRS ∩ EMPS_WITH_DEPS)

RESULT ← $\pi_{LNAME, FNAME}$(MGRS_WITH_DEPS * EMPLOYEE)

As we mentioned earlier, the same query can in general be specified in many different ways. For example, the operations can often be applied in various sequences. In addition, some operations can be used to replace others; for example, the INTERSECTION operation in Query 7 can be replaced by a NATURAL JOIN. As an exercise, try to do each of the above example queries using different operations.[15] In Chapters 8 and 9 we will show how these queries are written in other relational languages.

7.7 Summary

In this chapter we presented the modeling concepts provided by the relational model of data. We also discussed the relational algebra and additional operations that can be used to manipulate relations. We started by introducing the concepts of domains, attributes, and tuples. We then defined a relation schema as a list of attributes that describe the structure of a relation. A relation, or relation state, is a set of tuples that conform to the schema.

Several characteristics differentiate relations from ordinary tables or files. The first is that tuples in a relation are not ordered. The second involves the ordering of attributes in a relation schema and the corresponding ordering of values within a tuple. We gave an alternative definition of relation that does not require these two orderings, but we continued to use the first definition, which requires attributes and tuple values to be ordered, for convenience. We then discussed values in tuples and introduced null values to represent missing or unknown information.

---

15. When queries are optimized (see Chapter 18), the system will choose a particular sequence of operations that corresponds to an execution strategy that can be executed efficiently.

We then discussed the relational model constraints, starting with domain constraints, then key constraints, including the concepts of superkey, candidate key, and primary key, and the NOT NULL constraint on attributes. We then defined relational databases and relational database schemas. Additional relational constraints include the entity integrity constraint, which prohibits primary key attributes from being null. The interrelation constraint of referential integrity was then described, which is used to maintain consistency of references among tuples from different relations.

The modification operations on the relational model are Insert, Delete, and Update. Each operation may violate certain types of constraints. Whenever an operation is applied, the database state after the operation is executed must be checked to ensure that no constraints are violated.

We then described the basic relational algebra, which is a set of operations for manipulating relations that can be used to specify queries. We presented the various operations and illustrated the types of queries for which each is used. Table 7.1 lists the various relational algebra operations we discussed. The unary relational operators SELECT and PROJECT, as well as the RENAME operation, were discussed first. Then we discussed binary set theoretic operations requiring that relations on which they are applied be union compatible; these include UNION, INTERSECTION, and SET DIFFERENCE. The CARTESIAN PRODUCT operation is another set operation that can be used to combine tuples from two relations, producing all possible combinations. We showed how CARTESIAN PRODUCT followed by SELECT can identify related tuples from two relations. The JOIN operations can directly identify and combine related tuples. Join operations include THETA JOIN, EQUIJOIN, and NATURAL JOIN.

We then discussed some important types of queries that *cannot* be stated with the basic relational algebra operations. We introduced the AGGREGATE FUNCTION operation to deal with aggregate types of requests. We discussed recursive queries and showed how some types of recursive queries can be specified. We then presented the OUTER JOIN and OUTER UNION operations, which extend JOIN and UNION.

Review Questions

7.1. Define the following terms: *domain, attribute, n-tuple, relation schema, relation state, degree of a relation, relational database schema, relational database state.*

7.2. Why are tuples in a relation not ordered?

7.3. Why are duplicate tuples not allowed in a relation?

7.4. What is the difference between a key and a superkey?

7.5. Why do we designate one of the candidate keys of a relation to be the primary key?

7.6. Discuss the characteristics of relations that make them different from ordinary tables and files.

7.7. Discuss the various reasons that lead to the occurrence of null values in relations.

7.8. Discuss the entity integrity and referential integrity constraints. Why is each considered important?

7.9. Define *foreign key*. What is this concept used for? How does it play a role in the join operation?

Table 7.1   Operations of Relational Algebra

Operation	Purpose	Notation
SELECT	Selects all tuples that satisfy the selection condition from a relation R.	$\sigma_{<selection\ condition>}(R)$
PROJECT	Produces a new relation with only some of the attributes of R, and removes duplicate tuples.	$\pi_{<attribute\ list>}(R)$
THETA JOIN	Produces all combinations of tuples from R_1 and R_2 that satisfy the join condition.	$R_1 \bowtie_{<join\ condition>} R_2$
EQUIJOIN	Produces all the combinations of tuples from R_1 and R_2 that satisfy a join condition with only equality comparisons.	$R_1 \bowtie_{<join\ condition>} R_2$, or $R_1 \bowtie_{(<join\ attributes\ 1>),\ (<join\ attributes\ 2>)} R_2$
NATURAL JOIN	Same as EQUIJOIN except that the join attributes of R_2 are not included in the resulting relation; if the join attributes have the same names, they do not have to be specified at all.	$R_1 *_{<join\ condition>} R_2$, or $R_1 *_{(<join\ attributes\ 1>),\ (<join\ attributes\ 2>)} R_2$ or $R_1 * R_2$
UNION	Produces a relation that includes all the tuples in R_1 or R_2 or both R_1 and R_2; R_1 and R_2 must be union compatible.	$R_1 \cup R_2$
INTERSECTION	Produces a relation that includes all the tuples in both R_1 and R_2; R_1 and R_2 must be union compatible.	$R_1 \cap R_2$
DIFFERENCE	Produces a relation that includes all the tuples in R_1 that are not in R_2; R_1 and R_2 must be union compatible.	$R_1 - R_2$
CARTESIAN PRODUCT	Produces a relation that has the attributes of R_1 and R_2 and includes as tuples all possible combinations of tuples from R_1 and R_2.	$R_1 \times R_2$
DIVISION	Produces a relation R(X) that includes all tuples $t[X]$ in $R_1(Z)$ that appear in R_1 in combination with every tuple from $R_2(Y)$, where $Z = X \cup Y$.	$R_1(Z) \div R_2(Y)$

7.10. Discuss the various update operations on relations and the types of integrity constraints that must be checked for each update operation.

7.11. List the operations of relational algebra and the purpose of each.

7.12. What is union compatibility? Why do the UNION, INTERSECTION, and DIFFERENCE operations require that the relations on which they are applied be union compatible?

7.13. Discuss some types of queries for which renaming of attributes is necessary in order to specify the query unambiguously.

7.14. Discuss the various types of JOIN operations. Why is theta join required?

7.15. What is the FUNCTION operation? What is it used for?

7.16. How are the OUTER JOIN operations different from the (inner) JOIN operations? How is the OUTER UNION operation different from UNION?

Exercises

7.17. Show the result of each of the example queries in Section 7.6 as it would apply to the database of Figure 7.6.

7.18. Specify the following queries on the database schema shown in Figure 7.5, using the relational operators discussed in this chapter. Also show the result of each query as it would apply to the database of Figure 7.6.

    a. Retrieve the names of all employees in department 5 who work more than 10 hours per week on the 'ProductX' project.

    b. List the names of all employees who have a dependent with the same first name as themselves.

    c. Find the names of all employees who are directly supervised by 'Franklin Wong'.

    d. For each project, list the project name and the total hours per week (by all employees) spent on that project.

    e. Retrieve the names of all employees who work on every project.

    f. Retrieve the names of all employees who do not work on any project.

    g. For each department, retrieve the department name and the average salary of all employees working in that department.

    h. Retrieve the average salary of all female employees.

    i. Find the names and addresses of all employees who work on at least one project located in Houston but whose department has no location in Houston.

    j. List the last names of all department managers who have no dependents.

7.19. Suppose that each of the following update operations is applied directly to the database of Figure 7.7. Discuss *all* integrity constraints violated by each operation, if any, and the different ways of enforcing these constraints.

    a. Insert <'Robert', 'F', 'Scott', '943775543', '1952-06-21', '2365 Newcastle Rd, Bellaire, TX', M, 58000, '888665555', 1> into EMPLOYEE.

    b. Insert <'ProductA', 4, 'Bellaire', 2> into PROJECT.

    c. Insert <'Production', 4, '943775543', '1998-10-01'> into DEPARTMENT.

    d. Insert <'677678989', null, '40.0'> into WORKS_ON.

    e. Insert <'453453453', 'John', M, '1970-12-12', 'SPOUSE'> into DEPENDENT.

    f. Delete the WORKS_ON tuples with ESSN = '333445555'.

    g. Delete the EMPLOYEE tuple with SSN = '987654321'.

    h. Delete the PROJECT tuple with PNAME = 'ProductX'.

    i. Modify the MGRSSN and MGRSTARTDATE of the DEPARTMENT tuple with DNUMBER = 5 to '123456789' and '1999-10-01', respectively.

    j. Modify the SUPERSSN attribute of the EMPLOYEE tuple with SSN = '999887777' to '943775543'.

    k. Modify the HOURS attribute of the WORKS_ON tuple with ESSN = '999887777' and PNO = 10 to '5.0'.

AIRPORT

AIRPORT_CODE	NAME	CITY	STATE

FLIGHT

NUMBER	AIRLINE	WEEKDAYS

FLIGHT_LEG

FLIGHT_NUMBER	LEG_NUMBER	DEPARTURE_AIRPORT_CODE	SCHEDULED_DEPARTURE_TIME

		ARRIVAL_AIRPORT_CODE	SCHEDULED_ARRIVAL_TIME

LEG_INSTANCE

FLIGHT_NUMBER	LEG_NUMBER	DATE	NUMBER_OF_AVAILABLE_SEATS	AIRPLANE_ID

	DEPARTURE_AIRPORT_CODE	DEPARTURE_TIME	ARRIVAL_AIRPORT_CODE	ARRIVAL_TIME

FARES

FLIGHT_NUMBER	FARE_CODE	AMOUNT	RESTRICTIONS

AIRPLANE_TYPE

TYPE_NAME	MAX_SEATS	COMPANY

CAN_LAND

AIRPLANE_TYPE_NAME	AIRPORT_CODE

AIRPLANE

AIRPLANE_ID	TOTAL_NUMBER_OF_SEATS	AIRPLANE_TYPE

SEAT_RESERVATION

FLIGHT_NUMBER	LEG_NUMBER	DATE	SEAT_NUMBER	CUSTOMER_NAME	CUSTOMER_PHONE

Figure 7.19   The AIRLINE relational database schema.

7.20. Consider the AIRLINE relational database schema shown in Figure 7.19, which describes a database for airline flight information. Each FLIGHT is identified by a flight NUMBER, and consists of one or more FLIGHT_LEGS with LEG_NUMBERS 1, 2, 3, etc. Each leg has scheduled arrival and departure times and airports and has many LEG_INSTANCES—one for each DATE on which the flight travels. FARES are kept for each flight. For each leg instance, SEAT_RESERVATIONS are kept, as are the AIRPLANE used on the leg and the actual arrival and departure times and airports. An AIRPLANE is identified by an AIRPLANE_ID and is of a particular AIRPLANE_TYPE. CAN_LAND relates

AIRPLANE_TYPES to the AIRPORTS in which they can land. An AIRPORT is identified by an AIRPORT_CODE. Specify the following queries in relational algebra:

a. For each flight, list the flight number, the departure airport for the first leg of the flight, and the arrival airport for the last leg of the flight.

b. List the flight numbers and weekdays of all flights or flight legs that depart from Houston Intercontinental Airport (airport code 'IAH') and arrive in Los Angeles International Airport (airport code 'LAX').

c. List the flight number, departure airport code, scheduled departure time, arrival airport code, scheduled arrival time, and weekdays of all flights or flight legs that depart from some airport in the city of Houston and arrive at some airport in the city of Los Angeles.

d. List all fare information for flight number 'CO197'.

e. Retrieve the number of available seats for flight number 'CO197' on '1999-10-09'.

7.21. Consider an update for the AIRLINE database to enter a reservation on a particular flight or flight leg on a given date.

a. Give the operations for this update.

b. What types of constraints would you expect to check?

c. Which of these constraints are key, entity integrity, and referential integrity constraints, and which are not?

d. Specify all the referential integrity constraints on Figure 7.19.

7.22. Consider the relation

CLASS(Course#, Univ_Section#, InstructorName, Semester, BuildingCode, Room#, TimePeriod, Weekdays, CreditHours).

This represents classes taught in a university, with unique Univ_Section#. Identify what you think should be various candidate keys, and write in your own words the constraints under which each candidate key would be valid.

7.23. Consider the LIBRARY relational schema shown in Figure 7.20, which is used to keep track of books, borrowers, and book loans. Referential integrity constraints are shown as directed arcs in Figure 7.20, as in the notation of Figure 7.7. Write down relational expressions for the following queries on the LIBRARY database:

a. How many copies of the book titled *The Lost Tribe* are owned by the library branch whose name is 'Sharpstown'?

b. How many copies of the book titled *The Lost Tribe* are owned by each library branch?

c. Retrieve the names of all borrowers who do not have any books checked out.

d. For each book that is loaned out from the 'Sharpstown' branch and whose DueDate is today, retrieve the book title, the borrower's name, and the borrower's address.

e. For each library branch, retrieve the branch name and the total number of books loaned out from that branch.

f. Retrieve the names, addresses, and number of books checked out for all borrowers who have more than five books checked out.

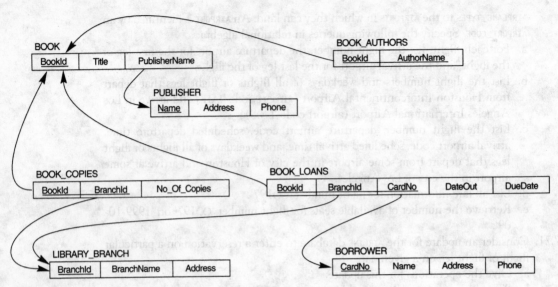

Figure 7.20   A relational database schema for a LIBRARY database.

g. For each book authored (or coauthored) by 'Stephen King,' retrieve the title and the number of copies owned by the library branch whose name is 'Central.'

7.24. Consider the following six relations for an order processing database application in a company:

CUSTOMER(Cust#, Cname, City)

ORDER(Order#, Odate, Cust#, Ord_Amt)

ORDER_ITEM(Order#, Item#, Qty)

ITEM(Item#, Unit_price)

SHIPMENT(Order#, Warehouse#, Ship_date)

WAREHOUSE(Warehouse#, City)

Here, Ord_Amt refers to total dollar amount of an order; Odate is the date the order was placed; Shjp_date is the date an order is shipped from the warehouse. Assume that an order can be shipped from several warehouses. Specify the foreign keys for the above schema, stating any assumptions you make. Then specify the following queries in relational algebra:

a. List the Order# and Ship_date for all orders shipped from Warehouse number 'W2'.

b. List the Warehouse information from which the Customer named 'Jose Lopez' was supplied his orders. Produce a listing: Order#, Warehouse#.

c. Produce a listing: CUSTNAME, #OFORDERS, AVG_ORDER_AMT, where the middle column is the total number of orders by the customer and the last column is the average order amount for that customer.

d. List the orders that were not shipped within 30 days of ordering.

e. List the Order# for orders that were shipped from *all* warehouses that the company has in New York.

7.25. Consider the following relations for a database that keeps track of business trips of salespersons in a sales office:

SALESPERSON(SSN, Name, Start_Year, Dept_No)

TRIP(SSN, From_City, To_City, Departure_Date, Return_Date, Trip_ID)

EXPENSE(Trip_ID, Account#, Amount)

Specify the foreign keys for the above schema, stating any assumptions you make. Then specify the following queries in relational algebra:

a. Give the details (all attributes of TRIP relation) for trips that exceeded $2000 in expenses.

b. Print the SSN of salesman who took trips to 'Honolulu'.

c. Print the total trip expenses incurred by the salesman with SSN = '234-56-7890'.

7.26. Consider the following relations for a database that keeps track of student enrollment in courses and the books adopted for each course:

STUDENT(SSN, Name, Major, Bdate)

COURSE(Course#, Cname, Dept)

ENROLL(SSN, Course#, Quarter, Grade)

BOOK_ADOPTION(Course#, Quarter, Book_ISBN)

TEXT(Book_ISBN, Book_Title, Publisher, Author) ·

Specify the foreign keys for the above schema, stating any assumptions you make. Then specify the following queries in relational algebra:

a. List the number of courses taken by all students named 'John Smith' in Winter 1999 (i.e., Quarter = 'W99').

b. Produce a list of textbooks (include Course#, Book_ISBN, Book_Title) for courses offered by the 'CS' department that have used more than two books.

c. List any department that has *all* its adopted books published by 'BC Publishing'.

7.27. Consider the two tables T1 and T2 shown in Figure 7.21. Show the results of the following operations:

a. $T1 \bowtie_{T1.P = T2.A} T2$

b. $T1 \bowtie_{T1.Q = T2.B} T2$

c. $T1 \bowtie_{T1.P = T2.A} T2$

d. $T1 \bowtie_{T1.Q = T2.B} T2$

e. $T1 \cup T2$

f. $T1 \bowtie_{(T1.P = T2.A \text{ AND } T1.R = T2.C)} T2$

7.28. Consider the following relations for a database that keeps track of auto sales in a car dealership (Option refers to some optional equipment installed on an auto):

CAR(Serial-No, Model, Manufacturer, Price)

Table T1

P	Q	R
10	a	5
15	b	8
25	a	6

Table T2

A	B	C
10	b	6
25	c	3
10	b	5

Figure 7.21   A database state for the relations T1 and T2.

OPTIONS(<u>Serial-No</u>, <u>Option-Name</u>, Price)

SALES(<u>Salesperson-id</u>, <u>Serial-No</u>, Date, Sale-price)

SALESPERSON(<u>Salesperson-id</u>, Name, Phone)

First, specify the foreign keys for the above schema, stating any assumptions you make. Next, populate the relations with a few example tuples, and then show an example of an insertion in the SALES and SALESPERSON relations that *violates* the referential integrity constraints and another insertion that does not. Then specify the following queries in relational algebra:

a. For the salesperson named 'Jane Doe', list the following information for all the cars she sold: Serial#, Manufacturer, Sale-price.

b. List the Serial# and Model of cars that have no options.

c. Consider the natural join operation between SALESPERSON and SALES. What is the meaning of a left outer join for these tables (do not change the order of relations). Explain with an example.

d. Write a query in relational algebra involving selection and one set operation and say in words what the query does.

Selected Bibliography

The relational model was introduced by Codd (1970) in a classic paper. Codd also introduced relational algebra and laid the theoretical foundations for the relational model in a series of papers (Codd 1971, 1972, 1972a, 1974); he was later given the Turing award, the highest honor of the ACM, for his work on the relational model. In a later paper, Codd (1979) discussed extending the relational model to incorporate more meta-data and semantics about the relations; he also proposed a three-valued logic to deal with uncertainty in relations and incorporating NULLs in the relational algebra. The resulting model is known as RM/T. Childs (1968) had earlier used set theory to model databases. More recently, Codd (1990) published a book examining over 300 features of the relational data model and database systems.

Since Codd's pioneering work, much research has been conducted on various aspects of the relational model. Todd (1976) describes an experimental DBMS called PRTV that directly implements the relational algebra operations. Date (1983a) discusses outer joins.

Schmidt and Swenson (1975) introduces additional semantics into the relational model by classifying different types of relations. Chen's (1976) Entity Relationship model, which was discussed in Chapter 3, was a means to communicate the real-world semantics of a relational database at the conceptual level. Wiederhold and Elmasri (1979) introduces various types of connections between relations to enhance its constraints. Work on extending relational operations is discussed by Carlis (1986) and Ozsoyoglu et al. (1985). Cammarata et al. (1989) extends the relational model integrity constraints and joins. Extensions of the relational model are discussed in Chapter 13. Additional bibliographic notes for other aspects of the relational model and its languages, systems, extensions, and theory are given in Chapters 8, 9, 10, 13, 14, 15, 18, 22, 23, and 24.

CHAPTER 8

SQL–The Relational Database Standard

The SQL language may be considered one of the major reasons for the success of relational databases in the commercial world. Because it became a standard for relational databases, users were less concerned about migrating their database applications from other types of database systems—for example, network or hierarchical systems—to relational systems. The reason is that even if the user became dissatisfied with the particular relational DBMS product they chose to use, converting to another relational DBMS would not be expected to be too expensive and time consuming, since both systems would follow the same language standards. In practice, of course, there are many differences between various commercial relational DBMS packages. However, if the user is diligent in using only those features that are part of the standard, and if both relational systems faithfully support the standard, then conversion between the two systems should be much simplified. Another advantage of having such a standard is that users may write statements in a database application program that can access data stored in two or more relational DBMSs without having to change the database sub-language (SQL) if both relational DBMSs support standard SQL.

This chapter presents the main features of the SQL standard for *commercial relational DBMSs*, whereas Chapter 7 presented the most important *formalisms* underlying the relational data model. In Chapter 7 we discussed the relational algebra operations; these operations are very important for understanding the types of requests that may be specified on a relational database. They are also important for query processing and optimization in a relational DBMS, as we shall see in Chapter 18. However, the relational algebra operations are considered to be too technical for most commercial DBMS users. One reason is because a query in relational algebra is written as a sequence of operations that, when executed, produce the required result. Hence, the user must specify how—that is, *in what order*—to execute the query operations. On the other hand, the SQL language provides a high-level *declarative* language interface, so the user only specifies *what* the result is to be, leaving the actual optimization and decisions on how to execute the query to the DBMS. SQL includes some features from relational algebra, but it is based to a greater extent on the *tuple relational calculus*, which is another formal query language for relational databases that we shall describe in Section 9.3. The SQL syntax is more user-friendly than either of the two formal languages.

The name SQL is derived from Structured Query Language. Originally, SQL was called SEQUEL (for Structured English QUEry Language) and was designed and implemented at IBM Research as the interface for an experimental relational database system called SYSTEM R. SQL is now the standard language for commercial relational DBMSs. A joint effort by ANSI (the American National Standards Institute) and ISO (the International Standards Organization) has led to a standard version of SQL (ANSI 1986), called SQL-86 or SQL1. A revised and much expanded standard called SQL2 (also referred to as SQL-92) has subsequently been developed. Plans are already well underway for SQL3, which will further extend SQL with object-oriented and other recent database concepts.

SQL is a comprehensive database language; it has statements for data definition, query, and update. Hence, it is both a DDL *and* a DML. In addition, it has facilities for defining views on the database, for specifying security and authorization, for defining integrity constraints, and for specifying transaction controls. It also has rules for embedding SQL statements into a general-purpose programming language such as C or PASCAL.[1] We will discuss most of these topics in the following subsections. In our discussion, we will mostly follow SQL2. Features of SQL3 are overviewed in Section 13.4.

Section 8.1 describes the SQL2 DDL commands for creating and modifying schemas, tables, and constraints. Sections 8.2 describes the basic SQL constructs for specifying retrieval queries and Section 8.3 goes over more complex features. Section 8.4 describes the SQL commands for inserting, deleting and updating, and Section 8.5 discusses the concept of views (virtual tables). Section 8.6 shows how general constraints may be specified as assertions or triggers. Section 8.7 lists some SQL features that are presented in other chapters of the book; these include embedded SQL in Chapter 10, transaction control in Chapter 19, and security/authorization in Chapter 22. Section 8.8 summarizes the chapter.

For the reader who desires a less comprehensive introduction to SQL, parts or all of the following sections may be skipped: 8.2.5, 8.3, 8.5, 8.6, and 8.7.

---

1. Originally, SQL had statements for creating and dropping indexes on the files that represent relations, but these have been dropped from the current SQL2 standard.

8.1   Data Definition, Constraints, and Schema Changes in SQL2

SQL uses the terms **table, row,** and **column** for relation, tuple, and attribute, respectively. We will use the corresponding terms interchangeably. The SQL2 commands for data definition are CREATE, ALTER, and DROP; these are discussed in Sections 8.1.2 to 8.1.4. First, however, we discuss schema and catalog concepts in Section 8.1.1. Section 8.1.2 describes how tables are created, the available data types for attributes, and how constraints are specified. Sections 8.1.3 and 8.1.4 describe the **schema evolution commands** available in SQL2, which can be used to alter the schema by adding or dropping tables, attributes, and constraints. We only give an overview of the most important features. Details can be found in the SQL2 document.

8.1.1   Schema and Catalog Concepts in SQL2

Early versions of SQL did not include the concept of a relational database schema; all tables (relations) were considered part of the same schema. The concept of an SQL schema was incorporated into SQL2 in order to group together tables and other constructs that belong to the same database application. An SQL **schema** is identified by a **schema name,** and includes an authorization identifier to indicate the user or account who owns the schema, as well as **descriptors** for *each element* in the schema. Schema **elements** include the tables, constraints, views, domains, and other constructs (such as authorization grants) that describe the schema. A schema is created via the CREATE SCHEMA statement, which can include all the schema elements' definitions. Alternatively, the schema can be assigned a name and authorization identifier, and the elements can be defined later. For example, the following statement creates a schema called COMPANY, owned by the user with authorization identifier JSMITH:

CREATE SCHEMA COMPANY **AUTHORIZATION** JSMITH;

In addition to the concept of schema, SQL2 uses the concept of **catalog**—a named collection of schemas in an SQL environment. A catalog always contains a special schema called INFORMATION_SCHEMA, which provides information on all the element descriptors of all the schemas in the catalog to authorized users. Integrity constraints such as referential integrity can be defined between relations only if they exist in schemas within the same catalog. Schemas within the same catalog can also share certain elements, such as domain definitions.

8.1.2   The CREATE TABLE Command and SQL2 Data Types and Constraints

The CREATE TABLE command is used to specify a new relation by giving it a name and specifying its attributes and constraints. The attributes are specified first, and each attribute is given a name, a data type to specify its domain of values, and any attribute constraints such as NOT NULL. The key, entity integrity, and referential integrity constraints can be specified—within the CREATE TABLE statement—after the attributes are declared, or they can be added later using the ALTER TABLE command (see Section 8.1.4). Figure 8.1(a) shows sample data definition statements in SQL for the relational database schema shown in Figure 7.7. Typically, the SQL schema in which the relations are declared is implicitly specified in the environment in which the CREATE TABLE statements are executed. Alternatively, we can explicitly attach the schema name to the relation name, separated by a period. For example, by writing:

CREATE TABLE COMPANY.EMPLOYEE ...

rather than

CREATE TABLE EMPLOYEE ...

as in Figure 8.1(a), we can explicitly (rather than implicitly) make the EMPLOYEE table part of the COMPANY schema.

Data Types and Domains in SQL2. The **data types** available for attributes include numeric, character-string, bit-string, date, and time. **Numeric** data types include integer numbers of various sizes (INTEGER or INT, and SMALLINT), and real numbers of various precision (FLOAT, REAL, DOUBLE PRECISION). Formatted numbers can be declared by using DECIMAL(i,j)—or DEC(i,j) or NUMERIC(i,j)—where i, the *precision*, is the total number of decimal digits and j, the *scale*, is the number of digits after the decimal point. The default for scale is zero, and the default for precision is implementation-defined.

Character-string data types are either fixed-length—CHAR(n) or CHARACTER(n), where n is the number of characters—or varying-length—VARCHAR(n) or CHAR VARYING(n) or CHARACTER VARYING(n), where n is the maximum number of characters. **Bit-string** data types are either of fixed length n—BIT(n)—or varying length—BIT VARYING(n), where n is the maximum number of bits. The default for n, the length of a character string or bit string, is one.

There are new data types for **date** and **time** in SQL2. The DATE data type has ten positions, and its components are YEAR, MONTH, and DAY typically in the form YYYY-MM-DD. The TIME data type has at least eight positions, with the components HOUR, MINUTE, and SECOND, typically in the form HH:MM:SS. Only valid dates and times should be allowed by the SQL implementation. In addition, a data type TIME(i), where i is called *time fractional seconds precision*, specifies $i + 1$ additional positions for TIME—one position for an additional separator character, and i positions for specifying decimal fractions of a second. A TIME WITH TIME ZONE data type includes an additional six positions for specifying the *displacement* from the standard universal time zone, which is in the range $+13{:}00$ to $-12{:}59$ in units of HOURS:MINUTES. If WITH TIME ZONE is not included, the default is the local time zone for the SQL session. Finally, a **timestamp** data type (TIMESTAMP) includes both the DATE and TIME fields, plus a minimum of six positions for fractions of seconds and an optional WITH TIME ZONE qualifier.

Another data type related to DATE, TIME, and TIMESTAMP is the INTERVAL data type. This specifies an **interval**—a *relative value* that can be used to increment or decrement an absolute value of a date, time, or timestamp. Intervals are qualified to be either YEAR/MONTH intervals or DAY/TIME intervals.

In SQL2, it is possible to specify the data type of each attribute directly, as in Figure 8.1(a); alternatively, a domain can be declared, and the domain name used. This makes it

```
CREATE TABLE EMPLOYEE
     ( FNAME             VARCHAR(15)      NOT NULL ,
       MINIT             CHAR ,
       LNAME             VARCHAR(15)      NOT NULL ,
       SSN               CHAR(9)          NOT NULL ,
       BDATE             DATE
       ADDRESS           VARCHAR(30) ,
       SEX               CHAR ,
       SALARY            DECIMAL(10,2) ,
       SUPERSSN          CHAR(9) ,
       DNO               INT              NOT NULL ,
     PRIMARY KEY (SSN) ,
     FOREIGN KEY (SUPERSSN) REFERENCES EMPLOYEE(SSN) ,
     FOREIGN KEY (DNO) REFERENCES DEPARTMENT(DNUMBER) ) ;

CREATE TABLE DEPARTMENT
     ( DNAME             VARCHAR(15)      NOT NULL ,
       DNUMBER           INT              NOT NULL ,
       MGRSSN            CHAR(9)          NOT NULL ,
       MGRSTARTDATE      DATE ,
     PRIMARY KEY (DNUMBER) ,
     UNIQUE (DNAME) ,
     FOREIGN KEY (MGRSSN) REFERENCES EMPLOYEE(SSN) ) ;

CREATE TABLE DEPT_LOCATIONS
     ( DNUMBER           INT              NOT NULL ,
       DLOCATION         VARCHAR(15)      NOT NULL ,
     PRIMARY KEY (DNUMBER, DLOCATION) ,
     FOREIGN KEY (DNUMBER) REFERENCES DEPARTMENT(DNUMBER) ) ;

CREATE TABLE PROJECT
     ( PNAME             VARCHAR(15)      NOT NULL ,
       PNUMBER           INT              NOT NULL ,
       PLOCATION         VARCHAR(15) ,
       DNUM              INT              NOT NULL ,
     PRIMARY KEY (PNUMBER) ,
     UNIQUE (PNAME) ,
     FOREIGN KEY (DNUM) REFERENCES DEPARTMENT(DNUMBER) ) ;

CREATE TABLE WORKS_ON
     ( ESSN              CHAR(9)          NOT NULL ,
       PNO               INT              NOT NULL ,
       HOURS             DECIMAL(3,1)     NOT NULL ,
     PRIMARY KEY (ESSN, PNO) ,
     FOREIGN KEY (ESSN) REFERENCES EMPLOYEE(SSN) ,
     FOREIGN KEY (PNO) REFERENCES PROJECT(PNUMBER) ) ;

CREATE TABLE DEPENDENT
     ( ESSN              CHAR(9)          NOT NULL ,
       DEPENDENT_NAME    VARCHAR(15)      NOT NULL ,
       SEX               CHAR ,
       BDATE             DATE ,
       RELATIONSHIP      VARCHAR(8) ,
     PRIMARY KEY (ESSN, DEPENDENT_NAME) ,
     FOREIGN KEY (ESSN) REFERENCES EMPLOYEE(SSN) ) ;
```

Figure 8.1(a)   An illustration of SQL2 data definition. SQL2 statements defining
                 the COMPANY schema of Figure 7.7.

easier to change the data type for a domain that is used by numerous attributes in a schema, and improves schema readability. For example, we can create a domain SSN_TYPE by the following statement:

CREATE DOMAIN SSN_TYPE **AS** CHAR(9);

We can use SSN_TYPE in place of CHAR(9) in Figure 8.1(a) for the attributes SSN and SUPERSSN of EMPLOYEE, MGRSSN of DEPARTMENT, ESSN of WORKS_ON, and ESSN of DEPENDENT. A domain can also have an optional default specification via a DEFAULT clause, as we will discuss later for attributes.

Specifying Constraints and Default Values in SQL2. Because SQL allows NULLs as attribute values, a *constraint* NOT NULL may be specified if NULL is not permitted for a particular attribute. This should always be specified for the primary key attributes of each relation, as well as for any other attributes whose values are required not to be NULL, as shown in Figure 8.1(a). It is also possible to define a *default value* for an attribute by appending the clause DEFAULT <value> to an attribute definition. The default value is included in any new tuple if an explicit value is not provided for that attribute. Figure 8.1(b) illustrates an example of specifying a default manager for a new department and a default department for a new employee. If no default clause is specified, the default *default value* (!) is NULL.

Following the attribute (or column) specifications, additional *table constraints* can be specified on a table, including keys and referential integrity, as illustrated in Figure 8.1(a).[2] The **PRIMARY KEY** clause specifies one or more attributes that make up the primary key of a relation. The **UNIQUE** clause specifies alternate (or secondary) keys. Referential integrity is specified via the **FOREIGN KEY** clause.

As we discussed in Section 7.2.4, a referential integrity constraint can be violated when tuples are inserted or deleted or when a foreign key attribute value is modified. In SQL2, the schema designer can specify the action to be taken if a referential integrity constraint is violated upon deletion of a referenced tuple or upon modification of a referenced primary key value, by attaching a **referential triggered action** clause to any foreign key constraint. The options include SET NULL, CASCADE, and SET DEFAULT. An option must be qualified with either ON DELETE or ON UPDATE. We illustrate this with the example shown in Figure 8.1(b). Here, the database designer chooses SET NULL ON DELETE and CASCADE ON UPDATE for the foreign key SUPERSSN of EMPLOYEE. This means that if the tuple for a supervising employee is *deleted*, the value of SUPERSSN is automatically set to NULL for all employee tuples that were referencing the deleted employee tuple. On the other hand, if the SSN value for a supervising employee is *updated* (say, because it was entered incorrectly), the new value is *cascaded* to SUPERSSN for all employee tuples referencing the updated employee tuple.

---

2. Key and referential integrity constraints were not included in earlier versions of SQL. In some earlier implementations, keys were specified implicitly at the internal level via the CREATE INDEX command.

In general, the action taken by the DBMS for SET NULL or SET DEFAULT is the same for both ON DELETE or ON UPDATE; the value of the affected referencing attributes is changed to NULL for SET NULL, and to the specified default value for SET DEFAULT. The action for CASCADE ON DELETE is to delete all the referencing tuples, whereas the action for CASCADE ON UPDATE is to change the value of the foreign key to the updated (new) primary key value for all referencing tuples. It is the responsibility of the database designer to choose the appropriate action and to specify it in the DDL. As a general rule, the CASCADE option is suitable for "relationship" relations such as WORKS_ON, for relations that represent multivalued attributes such as DEPT_LOCATIONS, and for relations that represent weak entity types such as DEPENDENT.

Figure 8.1(b) also illustrates how a constraint may be given a name, following the keyword CONSTRAINT. The names of all constraints within a particular schema must be

```
CREATE TABLE EMPLOYEE
    ( . . . ,
     DNO              INT   NOT NULL   DEFAULT 1,
     CONSTRAINT EMPPK
      PRIMARY KEY (SSN) ,
     CONSTRAINT EMPSUPERFK
      FOREIGN KEY (SUPERSSN) REFERENCES EMPLOYEE(SSN)
                   ON DELETE SET NULL   ON UPDATE CASCADE ,
     CONSTRAINT EMPDEPTFK
      FOREIGN KEY (DNO) REFERENCES DEPARTMENT(DNUMBER)
                   ON DELETE SET DEFAULT   ON UPDATE CASCADE );

CREATE TABLE DEPARTMENT
    ( . . . ,
     MGRSSN   CHAR(9) NOT NULL DEFAULT '888665555' ,
     . . . ,
     CONSTRAINT DEPTPK
      PRIMARY KEY (DNUMBER) ,
     CONSTRAINT DEPTSK
      UNIQUE (DNAME),
     CONSTRAINT DEPTMGRFK
      FOREIGN KEY (MGRSSN) REFERENCES EMPLOYEE(SSN)
       ON DELETE SET DEFAULT   ON UPDATE CASCADE );

CREATE TABLE DEPT_LOCATIONS
    ( . . . ,
     PRIMARY KEY (DNUMBER, DLOCATION),
     FOREIGN KEY (DNUMBER) REFERENCES DEPARTMENT(DNUMBER)
      ON DELETE CASCADE   ON UPDATE CASCADE ) ;
```

Figure 8.1(b)   An illustration of SQL2 data definition. Specifying default attribute values and referential triggered actions.

unique. A constraint name is used to identify a particular constraint in case the constraint must be dropped later and replaced with another constraint, as we shall discuss in Section 8.1.4. Giving names to constraints is optional.

The relations declared through CREATE TABLE statements are called **base tables** (or base relations); this means that the relation and its tuples are actually created and stored as a file by the DBMS. Base relations are distinguished from **virtual relations,** created through the CREATE VIEW statement (see Section 8.5), which may or may not correspond to an actual physical file. In SQL the attributes in a base table are considered to be *ordered in the sequence in which they are specified* in the CREATE TABLE statement. However, rows (tuples) are not considered to be ordered within a relation.

8.1.3   The DROP SCHEMA and DROP TABLE Commands

If a whole schema is not needed any more, the DROP SCHEMA command can be used. There are two *drop behavior* options: CASCADE and RESTRICT. For example, to remove the COMPANY database schema and all its tables, domains, and other elements, the CASCADE option is used as follows:

DROP SCHEMA COMPANY **CASCADE;**

If the RESTRICT option is chosen in place of CASCADE, the schema is dropped only if it has *no elements* in it; otherwise, the DROP command will not be executed.

If a base relation within a schema is not needed any longer, the relation and its definition can be deleted by using the DROP TABLE command. For example, if we no longer wish to keep track of dependents of employees in the COMPANY database of Figure 7.6, we can get rid of the DEPENDENT relation by issuing the command:

DROP TABLE DEPENDENT **CASCADE;**

If the RESTRICT option is chosen instead of CASCADE, a table is dropped only if it is *not referenced* in any constraints (for example, by foreign key definitions in another relation) or views (see Section 8.5). With the CASCADE option, all such constraints and views that reference the table are dropped automatically from the schema, along with the table itself.

8.1.4   The ALTER TABLE Command

The definition of a base table can be changed by using the ALTER TABLE command, which is a **schema evolution** command. The possible *alter table actions* include adding or dropping a column (attribute), changing a column definition, and adding or dropping table constraints. For example, to add an attribute for keeping track of jobs of employees to the EMPLOYEE base relations in the COMPANY schema, we can use the command:

ALTER TABLE COMPANY.EMPLOYEE **ADD** JOB VARCHAR(12);

We must still enter a value for the new attribute JOB for each individual EMPLOYEE tuple. This can be done either by specifying a default clause or by using the UPDATE command (see Section 8.4). If no default clause is specified, the new attribute will have NULLs in all the tuples of the relation immediately after the command is executed; hence, the NOT NULL constraint is *not allowed* in this case.

To drop a column, we must choose either CASCADE or RESTRICT for drop behavior. If CASCADE is chosen, all constraints and views that reference the column are dropped automatically from the schema, along with the column. If RESTRICT is chosen, the command is successful only if no views or constraints reference the column. For example, the following command removes the attribute ADDRESS from the EMPLOYEE base table:

ALTER TABLE COMPANY.EMPLOYEE **DROP** ADDRESS **CASCADE;**

It is also possible to alter a column definition by dropping an existing default clause or by defining a new default clause. The following examples illustrate this clause:

ALTER TABLE COMPANY.DEPARTMENT **ALTER** MGRSSN **DROP DEFAULT;**

ALTER TABLE COMPANY.DEPARTMENT **ALTER** MGRSSN **SET DEFAULT** "333445555";

Finally, one can change the constraints specified on a table by adding or dropping a constraint. To be dropped, a constraint must have been given a name when it was specified. For example, to drop the constraint named EMPSUPERFK in Figure 8.1(b) from the EMPLOYEE relation, we write

ALTER TABLE COMPANY.EMPLOYEE
DROP CONSTRAINT EMPSUPERFK **CASCADE;**

Once this is done, we can redefine a replacement constraint by adding a new constraint to the relation, if needed. This is specified by using the **ADD** keyword followed by the new constraint, which can be named or unnamed and can be of any of the table constraint types discussed in Section 8.1.2.

The preceding subsections gave an overview of the data definition and schema evolution commands of SQL2. There are many other details and options, and we refer the interested reader to the SQL and SQL2 documents listed in the bibliographical notes. The next two sections discuss the querying capabilities of SQL.

8.2 Basic Queries in SQL

SQL has one basic statement for retrieving information from a database: the **SELECT statement.** The SELECT statement *has no relationship* to the SELECT operation of relational algebra, which was discussed in Chapter 7. There are many options and flavors to the SELECT statement in SQL, so we will introduce its features gradually. We will use example queries specified on the schema of Figure 7.5 and will refer to the sample database state shown in Figure 7.6 to show the results of some of the example queries.

Before proceeding, we must point out an important distinction between SQL and the formal relational model discussed in Chapter 7: SQL allows a table (relation) to have two or more tuples that are identical in all their attribute values. Hence, in general, an SQL **table** is not a *set of tuples*, because a set does not allow two identical members; rather it is a **multiset** (sometimes called a *bag*) of tuples. Some SQL relations are constrained to be sets because a key constraint has been declared or because the DISTINCT option has been used with the SELECT statement (described later in this section). We should be aware of this distinction as we discuss the examples.

8.2.1   The SELECT-FROM-WHERE Structure of SQL Queries

The basic form of the SELECT statement, sometimes called a **mapping** or a **select-from-where block,** is formed of the three clauses SELECT, FROM, and WHERE and has the following form:

> **SELECT** <attribute list>
> **FROM**   <table list>
> **WHERE** <condition>;

where:

- <attribute list> is a list of attribute names whose values are to be retrieved by the query.
- <table list> is a list of the relation names required to process the query.
- <condition> is a conditional (Boolean) expression that identifies the tuples to be retrieved by the query.

We now illustrate the basic SELECT statement with some example queries. We will label the queries here with the same query numbers that appear in Chapters 7 and 9 for easy cross reference.

QUERY 0

Retrieve the birthdate and address of the employee(s) whose name is 'John B. Smith'[3]

> **Q0: SELECT** BDATE, ADDRESS
> **FROM**   EMPLOYEE
> **WHERE** FNAME='John' **AND** MINIT='B' **AND** LNAME='Smith';

This query involves only the EMPLOYEE relation listed in the FROM-clause. The query *selects* the EMPLOYEE tuples that satisfy the condition of the WHERE-clause, then *projects* the result on the BDATE and ADDRESS attributes listed in the SELECT-clause. Q0 is similar to the following relational algebra expression—except that duplicates, if any, would not be eliminated:

$$\pi_{BDATE,ADDRESS}(\sigma_{FNAME='John'\ AND\ MINIT='B'\ AND\ LNAME='Smith'}(EMPLOYEE))$$

---

3. This is a new query that did not appear in Chapter 7.

Hence, a simple SQL query with a single relation name in the FROM-clause is similar to a SELECT-PROJECT pair of relational algebra operations. The SELECT-clause of SQL specifies the *projection attributes*, and the WHERE-clause specifies the *selection condition*. The only difference is that in the SQL query we may get duplicate tuples in the result of the query, because the constraint that a relation is a set is not enforced. Figure 8.2(a) shows the result of query Q0 on the database of Figure 7.6.

(a)
BDATE	ADDRESS
1965-01-09	731 Fondren, Houston, TX

(b)
FNAME	LNAME	ADDRESS
John	Smith	731 Fondren, Houston, TX
Franklin	Wong	638 Voss, Houston, TX
Ramesh	Narayan	975 Fire Oak, Humble, TX
Joyce	English	5631 Rice, Houston, TX

(c)
PNUMBER	DNUM	LNAME	ADDRESS	BDATE
10	4	Wallace	291 Berry, Bellaire, TX	1941-06-20
30	4	Wallace	291 Berry, Bellaire, TX	1941-06-20

(d)
E.FNAME	E.LNAME	S.FNAME	S.LNAME
John	Smith	Franklin	Wong
Franklin	Wong	James	Borg
Alicia	Zelaya	Jennifer	Wallace
Jennifer	Wallace	James	Borg
Ramesh	Narayan	Franklin	Wong
Joyce	English	Franklin	Wong
Ahmad	Jabbar	Jennifer	Wallace

(e)
SSN
123456789
333445555
999887777
987654321
666884444
453453453
987987987
888665555

(f)
SSN	DNAME
123456789	Research
333445555	Research
999887777	Research
987654321	Research
666884444	Research
453453453	Research
987987987	Research
888665555	Research
123456789	Administration
333445555	Administration
999887777	Administration
987654321	Administration
666884444	Administration
453453453	Administration
987987987	Administration
888665555	Administration
123456789	Headquarters
333445555	Headquarters
999887777	Headquarters
987654321	Headquarters
666884444	Headquarters
453453453	Headquarters
987987987	Headquarters
888665555	Headquarters

(g)
FNAME	MINIT	LNAME	SSN	BDATE	ADDRESS	SEX	SALARY	SUPERSSN	DNO
John	B	Smith	123456789	1965-09-01	731 Fondren, Houston, TX	M	30000	333445555	5
Franklin	T	Wong	333445555	1955-12-08	638 Voss, Houston, TX	M	40000	888665555	5
Ramesh	K	Narayan	666884444	1962-09-15	975 Fire Oak, Humble, TX	M	38000	333445555	5
Joyce	A	English	453453453	1972-07-31	5631 Rice, Houston, TX	F	25000	333445555	5

Figure 8.2 Results of queries specified on the database of Figure 7.6. (a) Result of Q0. (b) Result of Q1. (c) Result of Q2. (d) Result of Q8. (e) Result of Q9. (f) Result of Q10. (g) Result of Q1C.

QUERY 1

Retrieve the name and address of all employees who work for the 'Research' department.

Q1: **SELECT**   FNAME, LNAME, ADDRESS
      FROM   EMPLOYEE, DEPARTMENT
      WHERE   DNAME='Research' **AND** DNUMBER=DNO;

Query Q1 is similar to a SELECT–PROJECT–JOIN sequence of relational algebra operations. Such queries are often called **select–project–join queries.** In the WHERE-clause of Q1, the condition DNAME = 'Research' is a **selection condition** and corresponds to a SELECT operation in the relational algebra. The condition DNUMBER = DNO is a **join condition,** which corresponds to a JOIN condition in the relational algebra. The result of query Q1 is shown in Figure 8.2(b). In general, any number of select and join conditions may be specified in a single SQL query. The next example is a select–project–join query with *two* join conditions.

QUERY 2

For every project located in 'Stafford', list the project number, the controlling department number, and the department manager's last name, address, and birthdate.

Q2: **SELECT**   PNUMBER, DNUM, LNAME, ADDRESS, BDATE
      FROM   PROJECT, DEPARTMENT, EMPLOYEE
      WHERE   DNUM=DNUMBER **AND** MGRSSN=SSN **AND**
              PLOCATION='Stafford';

The join condition DNUM = DNUMBER relates a project to its controlling department, whereas the join condition MGRSSN = SSN relates the controlling department to the employee who manages that department. The result of query Q2 is shown in Figure 8.2(c).

8.2.2 Dealing with Ambiguous Attribute Names and Renaming (Aliasing)

In SQL the same name can be used for two (or more) attributes as long as the attributes are in *different relations*. If this is the case, and a query refers to two or more attributes with the same name, we must **qualify** the attribute name with the relation name, to prevent ambiguity. This is done by *prefixing* the relation name to the attribute name and separating the two by a period. To illustrate this, suppose that in Figures 7.5 and 7.6 the DNO and LNAME attributes of the EMPLOYEE relation were called DNUMBER and NAME and the DNAME attribute of DEPARTMENT was also called NAME; then, to prevent ambiguity, query Q1 would be rephrased as shown in Q1A. We must prefix the attributes NAME and DNUMBER in Q1A to specify which ones we are referring to, because the attribute names are used in both relations:

Q1A: SELECT   FNAME, EMPLOYEE.NAME, ADDRESS
       FROM   EMPLOYEE, DEPARTMENT
       WHERE   DEPARTMENT.NAME='Research' AND
                  DEPARTMENT.DNUMBER=EMPLOYEE.DNUMBER;

Ambiguity also arises in the case of queries that refer to the same relation twice, as in the following example.

QUERY 8

For each employee, retrieve the employee's first and last name and the first and last name of his or her immediate supervisor.[4]

Q8: SELECT   E.FNAME, E.LNAME, S.FNAME, S.LNAME
     FROM   EMPLOYEE AS E, EMPLOYEE AS S
     WHERE   E.SUPERSSN=S.SSN;

In this case, we are allowed to declare alternative relation names E and S, called **aliases** or **tuple variables,** for the EMPLOYEE relation. An alias can follow the keyword AS, as shown above in Q8, or it can directly follow the relation name—for example, by writing EMPLOYEE E, EMPLOYEE S in the WHERE-clause of Q8. It is also possible to rename the relation attributes within the query in SQL2 by giving them aliases; for example, if we write

EMPLOYEE **AS** E(FN, MI, LN, SSN, BD, ADDR, SEX, SAL, SSSN, DNO)

in the FROM-clause, FN becomes an alias for FNAME, MI for MINIT, LN for LNAME, and so on. In Q8, we can think of E and S as two *different copies* of the EMPLOYEE relation; the first, E, represents employees in the role of supervisees; and the second, S, represents employees in the role of supervisors. We can now join the two copies. Of course, in reality there is *only one* EMPLOYEE relation, and the join condition is meant to join the relation with itself by matching the tuples that satisfy the join condition E.SUPERSSN = S.SSN. Notice that this is an example of a one-level recursive query, as we discussed in Section 7.5.2. As in relational algebra, we *cannot* specify a general recursive query, with an unknown number of levels, in a single SQL2 statement.[5]

The result of query Q8 is shown in Figure 8.2(d). Whenever one or more aliases are given to a relation, we can use these names to represent different references to that relation. This permits multiple references to the same relation within a query. Notice that, if we want to, we can use this alias-naming mechanism in any SQL query, whether or not the same relation needs to be referenced more than once. For example, we could specify query

---

4. This query did not appear in Chapter 7; hence it is given the number 8 to distinguish it from queries 1 through 7 of Section 7.6.
5. A construct for specifying recursive queries is planned for SQL3.

Q1A as in Q1B just for convenience to shorten the relation names that prefix the attributes:

Q1B: **SELECT** E.FNAME, E.NAME, E.ADDRESS
            FROM EMPLOYEE E, DEPARTMENT D
            WHERE D.NAME='Research' **AND** D.DNUMBER=E.DNUMBER;

8.2.3 Unspecified WHERE-Clause and Use of Asterisk (*)

We discuss two more features of SQL here. A *missing WHERE-clause* indicates no condition on tuple selection; hence, *all tuples* of the relation specified in the FROM-clause qualify and are selected for the query result.[6] If more than one relation is specified in the FROM-clause and there is no WHERE-clause, then the CROSS PRODUCT—*all possible tuple combinations*—of these relations is selected. For example, Query 9 selects all EMPLOYEE SSNs (Figure 8.2e), and Query 10 selects all combinations of an EMPLOYEE SSN and a DEPARTMENT DNAME (Figure 8.2f).

QUERIES 9 and 10

Select all EMPLOYEE SSNs (Q9), and all combinations of EMPLOYEE SSN and DEPARTMENT DNAME (Q10) in the database.

Q9: **SELECT** SSN
        FROM EMPLOYEE;

Q10: **SELECT** SSN, DNAME
        FROM EMPLOYEE, DEPARTMENT;

It is extremely important to specify every selection and join condition in the WHERE-clause; if any such condition is overlooked, incorrect and very large relations may result. Notice that Q10 is similar to a CROSS PRODUCT operation followed by a PROJECT operation in relational algebra. If we specify all the attributes of EMPLOYEE and DEPARTMENT in Q10, we get the CROSS PRODUCT.

To retrieve all the attribute values of the selected tuples, we do not have to list the attribute names explicitly in SQL; we just specify an *asterisk* (*), which stands for *all the attributes*. For example, query Q1C retrieves all the attribute values of EMPLOYEE tuples who work in DEPARTMENT number 5 (Figure 8.2g); query Q1D retrieves all the attributes of an EMPLOYEE and the attributes of the DEPARTMENT he or she works in for every employee of the 'Research' department; and Q10A specifies the CROSS PRODUCT of the EMPLOYEE and DEPARTMENT relations.

Q1C: **SELECT** *
        FROM EMPLOYEE
        WHERE DNO=5;

---

6. This is equivalent to the condition WHERE TRUE, which means *every row in the table is selected*.

Q1D:	SELECT	*
	FROM	EMPLOYEE, DEPARTMENT
	WHERE	DNAME='Research' **AND** DNO=DNUMBER;
Q10A:	SELECT	*
	FROM	EMPLOYEE, DEPARTMENT;

8.2.4 Tables as Sets in SQL

As we mentioned earlier, SQL usually treats a table not as a set but rather as a **multiset;** *duplicate tuples can appear more than once* in a table, and in the result of a query. SQL does not automatically eliminate duplicate tuples in the results of queries, for the following reasons:

- Duplicate elimination is an expensive operation. One way to implement it is to sort the tuples first and then eliminate duplicates.

- The user may want to see duplicate tuples in the result of a query.

- When an aggregate function (see Section 8.3.5) is applied to tuples, in most cases we do not want to eliminate duplicates.

An SQL table with a key is restricted to being a set, since the key value must be distinct in each tuple.[7] If we *do want* to eliminate duplicate tuples from the result of an SQL query, we use the keyword **DISTINCT** in the SELECT-clause, meaning that only distinct tuples should remain in the result. In general, a query with SELECT DISTINCT eliminates duplicates whereas a query with SELECT ALL does not (specifying SELECT with neither ALL nor DIS-TINCT is equivalent to SELECT ALL). For example, Query 11 retrieves the salary of every employee; if several employees have the same salary, that salary value will appear as many times in the result of the query, as shown in Figure 8.3(a). If we are interested only in distinct salary values, we want each value to appear only once, regardless of how many employees earn that salary. By using the keyword **DISTINCT** as in Q11A we accomplish this, as shown in Figure 8.3(b).

QUERY 11

Retrieve the salary of every employee (Q11) and all distinct salary values (Q11A).

Q11:	SELECT ALL	SALARY
	FROM	EMPLOYEE;
Q11A:	SELECT DISTINCT	SALARY
	FROM	EMPLOYEE;

---

7. In general, an SQL table is not required to have a key although in most cases there will be one.

(a)   SALARY

    30000
    40000
    25000
    43000
    38000
    25000
    25000
    55000

(b)   SALARY

    30000
    40000
    25000
    43000
    38000
    55000

(c)   FNAME   LNAME

(d)   FNAME   LNAME
       James   Borg

Figure 8.3   Results of some other queries specified on the database shown in
                 Figure 7.6. (a) Result of Q11. (b) Result of Q11A. (c) Result of
                 Q16. (d) Result of Q18.

SQL has directly incorporated some of the set operations of relational algebra. There is a
set union operation (**UNION**), and in SQL2 there are also set difference (**EXCEPT**) and set
intersection (**INTERSECT**) operations.[8] The relations resulting from these set operations are
sets of tuples; that is, *duplicate tuples are eliminated from the result*. Because these set operations apply only to *union-compatible relations*, we must make sure that the two relations on
which we apply the operation have the same attributes and that the attributes appear in the
same order in both relations. The next example illustrates the use of UNION.

QUERY 4

Make a list of all project numbers for projects that involve an employee whose last
name is 'Smith', either as a worker or as a manager of the department that controls
the project.

Q4: (SELECT   **DISTINCT** PNUMBER
     FROM   PROJECT, DEPARTMENT, EMPLOYEE
     WHERE   DNUM=DNUMBER **AND** MGRSSN=SSN **AND**
                LNAME='Smith')

     UNION
     (SELECT   **DISTINCT** PNUMBER
     FROM   PROJECT, WORKS_ON, EMPLOYEE
     WHERE   PNUMBER=PNO **AND** ESSN=SSN **AND** LNAME='Smith');

The first SELECT query retrieves the projects that involve a 'Smith' as manager of the
department that controls the project, and the second retrieves the projects that involve a

---

8. SQL2 also has corresponding multiset operations, which are followed by the keyword **ALL** (**UNION
ALL, EXCEPT ALL, INTERSECT ALL**). Their results are multisets.

'Smith' as a worker on the project. Notice that, if several employees have the last name 'Smith', the project names involving any of them will be retrieved. Applying the UNION operation to the two SELECT queries gives the desired result.

8.2.5 Substring Comparisons, Arithmetic Operators, and Ordering

In this section we discuss several more features of SQL. The first feature allows comparison conditions on only parts of a character string, using the LIKE comparison operator. Partial strings are specified by using two reserved characters: '%' replaces an arbitrary number of characters, and the underscore (_) replaces a single character. For example, consider the following query.

QUERY 12

Retrieve all employees whose address is in Houston, Texas.

Q12: SELECT   FNAME, LNAME
      FROM   EMPLOYEE
      WHERE   ADDRESS LIKE '%Houston,TX%';

To retrieve all employees who were born during the 1950s, we can use Query 26. Here, '5' must be the third character of the string (according to our format for date), so we use the value '_ _ 5 _ _ _ _ _ _ _ _', with each underscore[9] serving as a placeholder for an arbitrary character.

QUERY 12A

Find all employees who were born during the 1950s.

Q12A: SELECT   FNAME, LNAME
      FROM   EMPLOYEE
      WHERE   BDATE LIKE '_ _ 5 _ _ _ _ _ _ _';

Another feature allows the use of arithmetic in queries. The standard arithmetic operators for addition (+), subtraction (−), multiplication (*), and division (/) can be applied to numeric values or attributes with numeric domains. For example, suppose that we want to see the effect of giving all employees who work on the 'ProductX' project a 10 percent raise; we can issue Query 13 to see what their salaries would become.

---

9. If underscore or % are literal characters in the string, they should be preceded with an *escape character*, which is specified after the string; for example, 'AB_CD\%EF' ESC '\' represents the literal string 'AB_CD%EF'.

QUERY 13

Show the resulting salaries if every employee working on the 'ProductX' project is given a 10 percent raise.

Q13: SELECT   FNAME, LNAME, 1.1*SALARY
      FROM   EMPLOYEE, WORKS_ON, PROJECT
      WHERE   SSN=ESSN AND PNO=PNUMBER AND
                PNAME='ProductX';

For string data types, the concatenate operator '| |' can be used in a query to append two string values. For date, time, timestamp, and interval data types, operators include incrementing ('+') or decrementing ('–') a date, time, or timestamp by a type-compatible interval. In addition, an interval value can be specified as the difference between two date, time, or timestamp values. Another comparison operator that can be used for convenience is BETWEEN, which is illustrated in Query 14.[10]

QUERY 14

Retrieve all employees in department 5 whose salary is between $30,000 and $40,000.

Q14: SELECT   *
      FROM   EMPLOYEE
      WHERE   (SALARY BETWEEN 30000 AND 40000) AND DNO = 5;

SQL allows the user to order the tuples in the result of a query by the values of one or more attributes, using the ORDER BY-clause. This is illustrated by Query 15.

QUERY 15

Retrieve a list of employees and the projects they are working on, ordered by department and, within each department, ordered alphabetically by last name, first name.

Q15: SELECT   DNAME, LNAME, FNAME, PNAME
      FROM   DEPARTMENT, EMPLOYEE, WORKS_ON, PROJECT
      WHERE   DNUMBER=DNO AND SSN=ESSN AND
                PNO=PNUMBER
      ORDER BY DNAME, LNAME, FNAME;

The default order is in ascending order of values. We can specify the keyword DESC if we want a descending order of values. The keyword ASC can be used to specify ascending

---

10. The condition (SALARY BETWEEN 30000 AND 40000) is equivalent to ((SALARY ≥ 30000) AND (SALARY ≤ 40000)).

order explicitly. If we want descending order on DNAME and ascending order on LNAME, FNAME, the ORDER BY-clause of Q15 becomes

ORDER BY DNAME **DESC**, LNAME **ASC**, FNAME **ASC**

8.3 More Complex SQL Queries

In the previous section, we described the basic types of queries in SQL. Because of the generality and expressive power of the language, there are many additional features that allow users to specify more complex queries. We discuss several of these features in this section.

8.3.1 Nested Queries and Set Comparisons

Some queries require that existing values in the database be fetched and then used in a comparison condition. Such queries can be conveniently formulated by using **nested queries,** which are complete SELECT . . . FROM . . . WHERE . . . blocks within the WHERE-clause of another query. That other query is called the **outer query.** Query 4 is formulated in Q4 without a nested query, but it can be rephrased to use nested queries as shown in Q4A:

Q4A: **SELECT** **DISTINCT** PNUMBER
    FROM PROJECT
    WHERE PNUMBER **IN** (**SELECT** PNUMBER
            FROM PROJECT, DEPARTMENT, EMPLOYEE
            WHERE DNUM=DNUMBER **AND** MGRSSN=SSN **AND** LNAME='Smith')
        OR
        PNUMBER **IN** (**SELECT** PNO
            FROM WORKS_ON, EMPLOYEE
            WHERE ESSN=SSN **AND** LNAME='Smith');

The first nested query selects the project numbers of projects that have a 'Smith' involved as manager, while the second selects the project numbers of projects that have a 'Smith' involved as worker. In the outer query, we select a PROJECT tuple if the PNUMBER value of that tuple is in the result of either nested query. The comparison operator **IN** compares a value v with a set (or multiset) of values V and evaluates to **TRUE** if v is one of the elements in V.

The IN operator can also compare a tuple of values in parentheses with a set or multiset of union-compatible tuples. For example, the query:

SELECT DISTINCT ESSN
FROM WORKS_ON

WHERE   (PNO, HOURS) **IN** (**SELECT** PNO, HOURS **FROM** WORKS_ON
                 WHERE SSN='123456789');

will select the social security numbers of all employees who work the same (project, hours) combination on some project that employee 'John Smith' (whose SSN = '123456789') works on.

In addition to the IN operator, a number of other comparison operators can be used to compare a single value v (typically an attribute name) to a set or multiset V (typically a nested query). The = ANY (or = SOME) operator returns TRUE if the value v is equal to *some* value in the set V and is hence equivalent to IN. The keywords ANY and SOME have the same meaning. Other operators that can be combined with ANY (or SOME) include >, >=, <, <=, and <>. The keyword ALL can also be combined with each of these operators. For example, the comparison condition (v > ALL V) returns TRUE if the value v is greater than *all* the values in the set V. An example is the following query, which returns the names of employees whose salary is greater than the salary of all the employees in department 5:

SELECT   LNAME, FNAME
FROM   EMPLOYEE
WHERE   SALARY > **ALL** (**SELECT** SALARY **FROM** EMPLOYEE **WHERE**
             DNO=5);

In general, we can have several levels of nested queries. We can once again be faced with possible ambiguity among attribute names if attributes of the same name exist—once in a relation in the FROM-clause of the *outer query*, and the other in a relation in the FROM-clause of the *nested query*. The rule is that a reference to an *unqualified attribute* refers to the relation declared in the **innermost nested query.** For example, in the SELECT-clause and WHERE-clause of the first nested query of Q4A, a reference to any unqualified attribute of the PROJECT relation refers to the PROJECT relation specified in the FROM-clause of the nested query. To refer to an attribute of the PROJECT relation specified in the outer query, we can specify and refer to an *alias* for that relation. These rules are similar to scope rules for program variables in a programming language such as PASCAL, which allows nested procedures and functions. To illustrate the potential ambiguity of attribute names in nested queries, consider Query 16, whose result is shown in Figure 8.3(c).

QUERY 16

Retrieve the name of each employee who has a dependent with the same first name and same sex as the employee.

Q16:   **SELECT**   E.FNAME, E.LNAME
       FROM   EMPLOYEE **AS** E
       WHERE   E.SSN **IN** (**SELECT**   ESSN
                          FROM   DEPENDENT
                          WHERE   E.FNAME=DEPENDENT_NAME
                                   AND E.SEX=SEX);

In the nested query of Q16, we must qualify E.SEX because it refers to the SEX attribute of EMPLOYEE from the outer query, and DEPENDENT also has an attribute called SEX. All unqualified references to SEX in the nested query refer to SEX of DEPENDENT. However, we do not *have* *to* qualify FNAME and SSN because the DEPENDENT relation does not have attributes called FNAME and SSN, so there is no ambiguity.

Correlated Nested Queries. Whenever a condition in the WHERE-clause of a nested query references some attribute of a relation declared in the outer query, the two queries are said to be **correlated.** We can understand a correlated query better by considering that the *nested query is evaluated once for each tuple (or combination of tuples) in the outer query.* For example, we can think of Q16 as follows: for *each* EMPLOYEE tuple, evaluate the nested query, which retrieves the ESSN values for all DEPENDENT tuples with the same sex and name as the EMPLOYEE tuple; if the SSN value of the EMPLOYEE tuple is *in* the result of the nested query, then select that EMPLOYEE tuple.

In general, a query written with nested SELECT . . . FROM . . . WHERE . . . blocks and using the = or IN comparison operators can *always* be expressed as a single block query. For example, Q16 may be written as in Q16A:

```
Q16A: SELECT   E.FNAME, E.LNAME
      FROM     EMPLOYEE AS E, DEPENDENT AS D
      WHERE    E.SSN=D.ESSN AND E.SEX=D.SEX AND
               E.FNAME=D.DEPENDENT_NAME;
```

The original SQL implementation on SYSTEM R also had a **CONTAINS** comparison operator, which is used to compare two sets or multisets. This operator was subsequently dropped from the language, possibly because of the difficulty in implementing it efficiently. Most commercial implementations of SQL do *not* have this operator. The CONTAINS operator compares two sets of values and returns TRUE if one set contains all values in the other set. Query 3 illustrates the use of the CONTAINS operator.

QUERY 3

Retrieve the name of each employee who works on *all* the projects controlled by department number 5.

```
Q3:   SELECT   FNAME, LNAME
      FROM     EMPLOYEE
      WHERE    (  (SELECT   PNO
                   FROM     WORKS_ON
                   WHERE    SSN=ESSN)
                CONTAINS
                  (SELECT   PNUMBER
                   FROM     PROJECT
                   WHERE    DNUM=5) );
```

In Q3, the second nested query (which is not correlated with the outer query) retrieves the project numbers of all projects controlled by department 5. For *each* employee tuple, the first nested query (which is correlated) retrieves the project numbers on which the employee works; if these contain all projects controlled by department 5, the employee tuple is selected and the name of that employee is retrieved. Notice that the CONTAINS comparison operator is similar in function to the DIVISION operation of the relational algebra, described in Section 7.4.7. Because the CONTAINS operation is not part of SQL, we use the EXISTS function to specify these types of queries, as will be shown in Section 8.3.2.

8.3.2   The EXISTS and UNIQUE Functions in SQL

The EXISTS function in SQL is used to check whether the result of a correlated nested query is empty (contains no tuples) or not. We illustrate the use of EXISTS—and also NOT EXISTS—with some examples. First, we formulate Query 16 in an alternative form that uses EXISTS. This is shown as Q16B:

Q16B: SELECT   E.FNAME, E.LNAME
        FROM   EMPLOYEE AS E
        WHERE   EXISTS (SELECT   *
                         FROM   DEPENDENT
                         WHERE   E.SSN=ESSN AND E.SEX=SEX AND
                                   E.FNAME=DEPENDENT_NAME);

EXISTS and NOT EXISTS are usually used in conjunction with a correlated nested query. In Q16B, the nested query references the SSN, FNAME, and SEX attributes of the EMPLOYEE relation from the outer query. We can think of Q16B as follows: for each EMPLOYEE tuple, evaluate the nested query, which retrieves all DEPENDENT tuples with the same social security number, sex, and name as the EMPLOYEE tuple; if at least one tuple EXISTS in the result of the nested query, then select that EMPLOYEE tuple. In general, EXISTS(Q) returns TRUE if there is *at least one tuple* in the result of query Q, and it returns FALSE otherwise. On the other hand, NOT EXISTS(Q) returns TRUE if there are *no tuples* in the result of query Q, and it returns FALSE otherwise. Next, we illustrate the use of NOT EXISTS.

QUERY 6

Retrieve the names of employees who have no dependents.

Q6:   SELECT   FNAME, LNAME
        FROM   EMPLOYEE
        WHERE   NOT EXISTS   (SELECT   *
                               FROM   DEPENDENT
                               WHERE   SSN=ESSN);

In Q6, the correlated nested query retrieves all DEPENDENT tuples related to an EMPLOYEE tuple. If *none exist*, the EMPLOYEE tuple is selected. We can explain Q6 as follows: for *each* EMPLOYEE tuple, the correlated nested query selects all DEPENDENT tuples whose ESSN value matches the EMPLOYEE SSN; if the result is empty, no dependents are related to the employee, so we select that EMPLOYEE tuple and retrieve its FNAME and LNAME. There is another SQL function UNIQUE(Q) that returns TRUE if there are no duplicate tuples in the result of query Q; otherwise, it returns FALSE.

QUERY 7

List the names of managers who have at least one dependent.

```
Q7:   SELECT   FNAME, LNAME
      FROM     EMPLOYEE
      WHERE    EXISTS   (SELECT   *
                         FROM     DEPENDENT
                         WHERE    SSN=ESSN)
               AND
               EXISTS   (SELECT   *
                         FROM     DEPARTMENT
                         WHERE    SSN=MGRSSN);
```

One way to write this query is shown in Q7, where we specify two nested correlated queries; the first selects all DEPENDENT tuples related to an EMPLOYEE, and the second selects all DEPARTMENT tuples managed by the EMPLOYEE. If at least one of the first and at least one of the second exist, we select the EMPLOYEE tuple. Can you rewrite this query using only a single nested query or no nested queries?

Query 3, which we used to illustrate the CONTAINS comparison operator, can be stated using EXISTS and NOT EXISTS in SQL systems. There are two options. The first is to use the well known set theory transformation that *(S1 CONTAINS S2) is logically equiva-lent to (S2 EXCEPT S1) is empty*;[11] this is shown as Q3A.

```
Q3A:  SELECT   FNAME, LNAME
      FROM     EMPLOYEE
      WHERE    NOT EXISTS
               (   (SELECT   PNUMBER
                    FROM     PROJECT
                    WHERE    DNUM=5)
                   EXCEPT
                   (SELECT   PNO
                    FROM     WORKS_ON
                    WHERE    SSN=ESSN) );
```

---

11. Recall that EXCEPT is the set difference operator.

The second option is shown as Q3B below. Notice that we need two-level nesting in Q3B and that this formulation is quite a bit more complex than Q3, which used the CONTAINS comparison operator, and Q3A, which uses NOT EXISTS and EXCEPT. However, CONTAINS is not part of SQL, and not all relational systems have the EXCEPT operator even though it is part of SQL2:

```
Q3B:   SELECT   LNAME, FNAME
       FROM     EMPLOYEE
       WHERE    NOT EXISTS
                (SELECT *
                FROM      WORKS_ON B
                WHERE     (B.PNO IN    (SELECT   PNUMBER
                                        FROM      PROJECT
                                        WHERE     DNUM=5) )
                          AND
                NOT EXISTS (SELECT    *
                            FROM      WORKS_ON C
                            WHERE     C.ESSN=SSN
                                      AND
                                      C.PNO=B.PNO) );
```

In Q3B, the outer nested query selects any WORKS_ON (B) tuples whose PNO is of a project controlled by department 5, *if* there is not a WORKS_ON (C) tuple with the same PNO and the same SSN as that of the EMPLOYEE tuple under consideration in the outer query. If no such tuple exists, we select the EMPLOYEE tuple. The form of Q3B matches the following rephrasing of Query 3: select each employee such that there does not exist a project controlled by department 5 that the employee does not work on.

Notice that Query 3 is typically stated in relational algebra by using the DIVISION operation. Moreover, Query 3 requires a type of quantifier called a **universal quantifier** in the relational calculus (see Section 9.3.5). The negated existential quantifier NOT EXISTS can be used to express a universally quantified query, as we shall discuss in Chapter 9.

8.3.3   Explicit Sets and NULLS in SQL

We have seen several queries with a nested query in the WHERE-clause. It is also possible to use an **explicit set of values** in the WHERE-clause, rather than a nested query. Such a set is enclosed in parentheses in SQL.

QUERY 17

Retrieve the social security numbers of all employees who work on project number 1, 2, or 3.

Q17:   **SELECT DISTINCT** ESSN
        FROM   WORKS_ON
        WHERE   PNO **IN** (1, 2, 3);

SQL allows queries that check whether a value is NULL—missing or undefined or not applicable. However, rather than using = or ≠ to compare an attribute to NULL, SQL uses IS or IS NOT. This is because SQL considers each null value as being distinct from every other null value, so equality comparison is not appropriate. It follows that, when a join condition is specified, tuples with null values for the join attributes are not included in the result (unless it is an OUTER JOIN; see Section 8.3.4). Query 18 illustrates this; its result is shown in Figure 8.3(d).

QUERY 18

Retrieve the names of all employees who do not have supervisors.

Q18:   **SELECT** FNAME, LNAME
        FROM   EMPLOYEE
        WHERE   SUPERSSN **IS NULL**;

8.3.4 Renaming Attributes and Joined Tables

It is possible to rename any attribute that appears in the result of a query by adding the qualifier AS followed by the desired new name. Hence, the AS construct can be used to alias both attribute and relation names, and it can be used in both the SELECT and FROM clauses. For example, Q8A below shows how query Q8 can be slightly changed to retrieve the last name of each employee and his or her supervisor, while renaming the resulting attribute names as EMPLOYEE_NAME and SUPERVISOR_NAME. The new names will appear as column headers in the query result:

Q8A: **SELECT** E.LNAME **AS** EMPLOYEE_NAME, S.LNAME **AS**
                SUPERVISOR_NAME
        FROM   EMPLOYEE **AS** E, EMPLOYEE **AS** S
        WHERE   E.SUPERSSN=S.SSN;

The concept of a **joined table** (or **joined relation**) was incorporated into SQL2 to permit users to specify a table resulting from a join operation *in the FROM-clause* of a query. This construct may be easier to comprehend than mixing together all the select and join conditions in the WHERE-clause. For example, consider query Q1, which retrieves the name and address of every employee who works for the 'Research' department. It may be easier first to specify the join of the EMPLOYEE and DEPARTMENT relations, and then to select the desired tuples and attributes. This can be written in SQL2 as in Q1A:

Q1A: **SELECT** FNAME, LNAME, ADDRESS
        FROM   (EMPLOYEE **JOIN** DEPARTMENT **ON** DNO=DNUMBER)
        WHERE   DNAME='Research';

The FROM-clause in Q1A contains a single *joined table*. The attributes of such a table are all the attributes of the first table, EMPLOYEE, followed by all the attributes of the second table, DEPARTMENT. The concept of a joined table also allows the user to specify different types of join, such as NATURAL JOIN and various types of OUTER JOIN. In a NATURAL JOIN on two relations R and S, no join condition is specified; an implicit equi-join condition for *each pair of attributes with the same name* from R and S is created. Each such pair of attributes is included only once in the resulting relation (see Section 7.4.5.)

If the names of the join attributes are not the same in the base relations, it is possible to rename the attributes so that they match, and then to apply NATURAL JOIN. In this case, the AS construct can be used to rename a relation and all its attributes in the FROM clause. This is illustrated in Q1B, where the DEPARTMENT relation is renamed as DEPT and its attributes are renamed as DNAME, DNO (to match the name of the desired join attribute DNO in EMPLOYEE), MSSN, and MSDATE. The implied join condition for this NATURAL JOIN is EMPLOYEE.DNO = DEPT.DNO, because this is the only pair of attributes with the same name after renaming:

Q1B: SELECT   FNAME, LNAME, ADDRESS
        FROM   (EMPLOYEE **NATURAL JOIN**
                  (DEPARTMENT **AS** DEPT (DNAME, DNO, MSSN,
                  MSDATE)))
        WHERE   DNAME='Research;

The default type of join in a joined table is an **inner** join, where a tuple is included in the result only if a matching tuple exists in the other relation. For example, in query Q8A, only employees that *have a supervisor* are included in the result; an EMPLOYEE tuple whose value for SUPERSSN is NULL is excluded. If the user requires that all employees be included, an outer join must be used explicitly (see Section 7.5.3 for a definition of OUTER JOIN). In SQL2, this is handled by explicitly specifying the OUTER JOIN in a joined table, as illustrated in Q8B:

Q8B: SELECT   E.LNAME **AS** EMPLOYEE_NAME, S.LNAME **AS**
                  SUPERVISOR_NAME
        FROM   (EMPLOYEE **AS** E **LEFT OUTER JOIN** EMPLOYEE **AS** S
                  ON E.SUPERSSN=S.SSN);

The options available for specifying joined tables in SQL2 include INNER JOIN (same as JOIN), LEFT OUTER JOIN, RIGHT OUTER JOIN, and FULL OUTER JOIN. In the latter three, the keyword OUTER may be omitted. It is also possible to *nest* join specifications; that is, one of the tables in a join may itself be a joined table. This is illustrated by Q2A, which is a different way of specifying query Q2, using the concept of a joined table:

Q2A: SELECT   PNUMBER, DNUM, LNAME, ADDRESS, BDATE
        FROM   ((PROJECT **JOIN** DEPARTMENT **ON** DNUM=
                  DNUMBER) **JOIN** EMPLOYEE **ON** MGRSSN=SSN)
        WHERE   PLOCATION='Stafford';

8.3.5 Aggregate Functions and Grouping

In Section 7.5.1, we introduced the concept of an aggregate function as a relational operation. Because grouping and aggregation are required in many database applications, SQL has features that incorporate these concepts. The first of these is a number of built-in functions: COUNT, SUM, MAX, MIN, and AVG. The COUNT function returns the number of tuples or values as specified in a query. The functions SUM, MAX, MIN, and AVG are applied to a set or multiset of numeric values and return, respectively, the sum, maximum value, minimum value, and average (mean) of those values. These functions can be used in the SELECT-clause or in a HAVING-clause (which we will introduce later). The functions MAX and MIN can also be used with attributes that have nonnumeric domains if the domain values have a *total ordering* among one another.[12] We illustrate the use of these functions with example queries.

QUERY 19

Find the sum of the salaries of all employees, the maximum salary, the minimum salary, and the average salary.

Q19: **SELECT** **SUM** (SALARY), **MAX** (SALARY), **MIN** (SALARY),
                    AVG (SALARY)

         FROM EMPLOYEE;

If we want to get the preceding function values for employees of a specific department—say the 'Research' department—we can write Query 20, where the EMPLOYEE tuples are restricted by the WHERE-clause to those employees who work for the 'Research' department.

QUERY 20

Find the sum of the salaries of all employees of the 'Research' department, as well as the maximum salary, the minimum salary, and the average salary in this department.

Q20: **SELECT** **SUM** (SALARY), **MAX** (SALARY), **MIN** (SALARY),
                    AVG (SALARY)

         FROM EMPLOYEE, DEPARTMENT

         WHERE DNO=DNUMBER **AND** DNAME='Research';

QUERIES 21 and 22

Retrieve the total number of employees in the company (Q21) and the number of employees in the 'Research' department (Q22).

---

12. Total order means that for any two values in the domain, it can be determined that one appears before the other in the defined order; for example, DATE, TIME and TIMESTAMP domains have total orderings on their values, as do alphabetic strings.

Q21:   SELECT   COUNT (*)
        FROM   EMPLOYEE;

Q22:   SELECT   COUNT (*)
        FROM   EMPLOYEE, DEPARTMENT
        WHERE   DNO=DNUMBER AND DNAME='Research';

Here the asterisk (*) refers to the *rows* (tuples), so COUNT (*) returns the number of rows in the result of the query. We may also use the COUNT function to count values in a column rather than tuples, as in the next example.

QUERY 23

Count the number of distinct salary values in the database.

Q23:   SELECT   COUNT (DISTINCT SALARY)
        FROM   EMPLOYEE;

Notice that, if we write COUNT(SALARY) instead of COUNT(DISTINCT SALARY) in Q23, we *get the same result* as COUNT(*) because duplicate values will not be eliminated, and so the number of values will be the same as the number of tuples.[13] The preceding examples show how functions are applied to retrieve a summary value from the database. In some cases we may need to use functions to select particular tuples. In such cases we specify a correlated nested query with the desired function, and we use that nested query in the WHERE-clause of an outer query. For example, to retrieve the names of all employees who have two or more dependents (Query 5), we can write:

Q5:   SELECT   LNAME, FNAME
        FROM   EMPLOYEE
        WHERE   (SELECT COUNT (*)
                  FROM   DEPENDENT
                  WHERE   SSN=ESSN) >= 2;

The correlated nested query counts the number of dependents that each employee has; if this is greater than or equal to 2, the employee tuple is selected.

In many cases we want to apply the aggregate functions *to subgroups of tuples in a relation,* based on some attribute values. For example, we may want to find the average salary of employees in each department or the number of employees who work on each project. In these cases we need to group the tuples that have the same value of some attribute(s), called the **grouping attribute(s),** and we need to apply the function to each such group independently. SQL has a **GROUP BY-clause** for this purpose. The GROUP BY-clause specifies the grouping attributes, which should *also appear in the* SELECT-*clause,* so that the value resulting from applying each function to a group of tuples appears along with the value of the grouping attribute(s).

---

13. Unless some tuples have NULL for SALARY, in which case they are not counted.

QUERY 24

For each department, retrieve the department number, the number of employees in the department, and their average salary.

Q24:   SELECT   DNO, **COUNT** (*), **AVG** (SALARY)
       FROM   EMPLOYEE
       GROUP BY DNO;

In Q24, the EMPLOYEE tuples are divided into groups—each group having the same value for the grouping attribute DNO. The COUNT and AVG functions are applied to each such group of tuples. Notice that the SELECT-clause includes only the grouping attribute and the functions to be applied on each group of tuples. Figure 8.4(a) illustrates how grouping works on Q24, and it also shows the result of Q24.

QUERY 25

For each project, retrieve the project number, the project name, and the number of employees who work on that project.

Q25:   SELECT   PNUMBER, PNAME, **COUNT** (*)
       FROM   PROJECT, WORKS_ON
       WHERE   PNUMBER=PNO
       GROUP BY PNUMBER, PNAME;

Q25 shows how we can use a join condition in conjunction with GROUP BY. In this case, the grouping and functions are applied *after* the joining of the two relations. Sometimes we want to retrieve the values of these functions only for *groups that satisfy certain conditions*. For example, suppose that we want to modify Query 25 so that only projects with more than two employees appear in the result. SQL provides a **HAVING-clause,** which can appear in conjunction with a GROUP BY-clause, for this purpose. HAVING provides a condition on the group of tuples associated with each value of the grouping attributes; and only the groups that satisfy the condition are retrieved in the result of the query. This is illustrated by Query 26.

QUERY 26

For each project *on which more than two employees work*, retrieve the project number, the project name, and the number of employees who work on the project.

Q26:   SELECT   PNUMBER, PNAME, **COUNT** (*)
       FROM   PROJECT, WORKS_ON
       WHERE   PNUMBER=PNO
       GROUP BY PNUMBER, PNAME
       HAVING COUNT (*) > 2;

(a)

FNAME	MINIT	LNAME	SSN	• • •	SALARY	SUPERSSN	DNO
John	B	Smith	123456789		30000	333445555	5
Franklin		Wong	333445555		40000	888665555	5
Ramesh	K	Narayan	666884444		38000	333445555	5
Joyce	A	English	453453453	• • •	25000	333445555	5
Alicia	J	Zelaya	999887777		25000	987654321	4
Jennifer	S	Wallace	987654321		43000	888665555	4
Ahmad		Jabbar	987987987		25000	987654321	4
James		Bong	888665555		55000	null	1

DNO	COUNT (*)	AVG (SALARY)
5	4	33250
4	3	31000
1	1	55000

Result of Q24.

Grouping EMPLOYEE tuples by the value of DNO.

(b)

PNAME	PNUMBER		ESSN	PNO	HOURS
ProductX	1		123456789	1	32.5
ProductX	1		453453453	1	20.0
ProductY	2		123456789	2	7.5
ProductY	2		453453453	2	20.0
ProductY	2		333445555	2	10.0
ProductZ	3		666884444	3	40.0
ProductZ	3		333445555	3	10.0
Computerization	10	• • •	333445555	10	10.0
Computerization	10		999887777	10	10.0
Computerization	10		987987987	10	35.0
Reorganization	20		333445555	20	10.0
Reorganization	20		987654321	20	15.0
Reorganization	20		888665555	20	null
Newbenefits	30		987987987	30	5.0
Newbenefits	30		987654321	30	20.0
Newbenefits	30		999887777	30	30.0

These groups are not selected by the HAVING condition of Q26.

After applying the WHERE clause but before applying HAVING.

PNAME	PNUMBER		ESSN	PNO	HOURS
ProductY	2		123456789	2	7.5
ProductY	2		453453453	2	20.0
ProductY	2		333445555	2	10.0
Computerization	10	• • •	333445555	10	10.0
Computerization	10		999887777	10	10.0
Computerization	10		987987987	10	35.0
Reorganization	20		333445555	20	10.0
Reorganization	20		987654321	20	15.0
Reorganization	20		888665555	20	null
Newbenefits	30		987987987	30	5.0
Newbenefits	30		987654321	30	20.0
Newbenefits	30		999887777	30	30.0

PNAME	COUNT (*)
ProductY	3
Computerization	3
Reorganization	3
Newbenefits	3

Result of Q26
(PNUMBER not shown).

After applying the HAVING clause condition.

Figure 8.4   Results of GROUP BY and HAVING. (a) Results for Query 24. (b) Results for Query 26.

Notice that, while selection conditions in the WHERE-clause limit the *tuples* to which functions are applied, the HAVING-clause serves to choose *whole groups*. Figure 8.4(b) illustrates the use of HAVING and displays the result of Q26.

QUERY 27

For each project, retrieve the project number, the project name, and the number of employees from department 5 who work on the project.

Q27: SELECT   PNUMBER, PNAME, COUNT (*)
      FROM   PROJECT, WORKS_ON, EMPLOYEE
      WHERE   PNUMBER=PNO AND SSN=ESSN AND DNO=5
      GROUP BY   PNUMBER, PNAME;

Here we restrict the tuples in the relation (and hence the tuples in each group) to those that satisfy the condition specified in the WHERE-clause—namely, that they work in department number 5. Notice that we must be extra careful when two different conditions apply (one to the function in the SELECT-clause and another to the function in the HAVING-clause). For example, suppose that we want to count the *total* number of employees whose salaries exceed $40,000 in each department, but only for departments where more than five employees work. Here, the condition (SALARY > 40000) applies only to the COUNT function in the SELECT-clause. Suppose that we write the following *incorrect* query:

SELECT   DNAME, COUNT (*)
FROM   DEPARTMENT, EMPLOYEE
WHERE   DNUMBER=DNO AND SALARY>40000
GROUP BY   DNAME
HAVING   COUNT (*) > 5;

This is incorrect because it will select only departments that have more than five employees *who each earn more than* $40,000. The rule is that the WHERE-clause is executed first, to select individual tuples; the HAVING-clause is applied later, to select individual groups of tuples. Hence, the tuples are already restricted to employees who earn more than $40,000, *before* the function in the HAVING-clause is applied. One way to write the query correctly is to use a nested query, as shown in Query 28.

QUERY 28

For each department that has more than five employees, retrieve the department number and the number of its employees who are making more than $40,000.

Q28: SELECT   DNUMBER, COUNT (*)
      FROM   DEPARTMENT, EMPLOYEE
      WHERE   DNUMBER=DNO AND SALARY>40000 AND
                  DNO IN (SELECT   DNO

```
        FROM        EMPLOYEE
        GROUP BY    DNO
        HAVING      COUNT (*) > 5)
GROUP BY    DNUMBER;
```

8.3.6 Discussion and Summary of SQL Queries

A query in SQL can consist of up to six clauses, but only the first two—SELECT and FROM—are mandatory. The clauses are specified in the following order, with the clauses between square brackets [. . .] being optional:

SELECT <attribute and function list>
FROM <table list>
[WHERE <condition>]
[GROUP BY <grouping attribute(s)>]
[HAVING <group condition>]
[ORDER BY <attribute list>];

The SELECT-clause lists the attributes or functions to be retrieved. The FROM-clause specifies all relations (tables) needed in the query, including joined relations, but not those in nested queries. The WHERE-clause specifies the conditions for selection of tuples from these relations, including join conditions if needed. GROUP BY specifies grouping attributes, whereas HAVING specifies a condition on the groups being selected rather than on the individual tuples. The built-in aggregate functions COUNT, SUM, MIN, MAX, and AVG are used in conjunction with grouping, but they can also be applied to all the selected tuples in a query without a GROUP BY clause. Finally, ORDER BY specifies an order for displaying the result of a query.

A query is evaluated *conceptually* by applying first the FROM-clause (to identify all tables involved in the query or to materialize any joined tables), followed by the WHERE-clause, and then GROUP BY and HAVING. Conceptually, ORDER BY is applied at the end to sort the query result. If none of the last three clauses (GROUP BY, HAVING, ORDER BY) are specified, we can *think conceptually* of a query as being executed as follows: for *each combination of tuples*—one from each of the relations specified in the FROM-clause—evaluate the WHERE-clause; if it evaluates to TRUE, place the values of the attributes specified in the SELECT-clause from this tuple combination in the result of the query. Of course, this is not an efficient way to implement the query in a real system, and each DBMS has special query optimization routines to decide on an execution plan that is efficient. We discuss query processing and optimization in Chapter 18.

In general, there are numerous ways to specify the same query in SQL. This flexibility in specifying queries has advantages and disadvantages. The main advantage is that users can choose the technique they are most comfortable with when specifying a query. For example, many queries may be specified with join conditions in the WHERE-clause, or by using joined relations in the FROM-clause, or with some form of nested queries and the IN comparison operator. Some users may be more comfortable with one approach, whereas others may be more comfortable with another. From the programmer's and the system's query optimization point of view, it is generally preferable to write a query with as little nesting and implied ordering as possible.

The disadvantage of having numerous ways of specifying the same query is that this may confuse the user, who may not know which technique to use to specify particular types of queries. Another problem is that it may be more efficient to execute a query specified in one way than the same query specified in an alternative way. Ideally, this should not be the case: the DBMS should process the same query in the same way, regardless of how the query is specified. But this is quite difficult in practice, as each DBMS has different methods for processing queries specified in different ways. Thus, an additional burden on the user is to determine which of the alternative specifications is the most efficient. Ideally, the user should worry only about specifying the query correctly. It is the responsibility of the DBMS to execute the query efficiently. In practice, however, it helps if the user is aware of which types of constructs in a query are more expensive to process than others.

8.4 Insert, Delete, and Update Statements in SQL

In SQL three commands can be used to modify the database: INSERT, DELETE, and UPDATE. We discuss each of these in turn.

8.4.1 The INSERT Command

In its simplest form, INSERT is used to add a single tuple to a relation. We must specify the relation name and a list of values for the tuple. The values should be listed *in the same order* in which the corresponding attributes were specified in the CREATE TABLE command. For example, to add a new tuple to the EMPLOYEE relation shown in Figure 7.5 and specified in the CREATE TABLE EMPLOYEE . . . command in Figure 8.1, we can use U1:

U1:   **INSERT INTO** EMPLOYEE

       VALUES   ('Richard', 'K', 'Marini', '653298653', '1962-12-30','98 Oak Forest,Katy,TX','M', 37000, '987654321', 4);

A second form of the INSERT statement allows the user to specify explicit attribute names that correspond to the values provided in the INSERT command. This is useful if a relation has many attributes, but only a few of those attributes are assigned values in the new tuple. These attributes must include all attributes with NOT NULL specification and no default value; attributes with NULL allowed or DEFAULT values are the ones that can be *left out*. For example, to enter a tuple for a new EMPLOYEE for whom we know only the FNAME, LNAME, DNO, and SSN attributes, we can use U1A:

U1A: **INSERT INTO** EMPLOYEE (FNAME, LNAME, DNO, SSN)

       VALUES   ('Richard', 'Marini', 4, '653298653');

Attributes not specified in U1A are set to their DEFAULT or to NULL, and the values are listed in the same order as the *attributes are listed in the* INSERT *command itself*. It is also possible to insert into a relation *multiple tuples* separated by commas in a single INSERT command. The attribute values forming *each tuple* are enclosed in parentheses.

A DBMS that fully implements SQL2 should support and enforce all the integrity constraints that can be specified in the DDL. However, some DBMSs do not incorporate all the constraints, in order to maintain the efficiency of the DBMS and because of the complexity of enforcing all constraints. If a system does not support some constraint—say, referential integrity—the users or programmers must enforce the constraint. For example, if we issue the command in U2 on the database shown in Figure 7.6, a DBMS not supporting referential integrity will do the insertion even though no DEPARTMENT tuple exists in the database with DNUMBER = 2. It is the responsibility of the user to check that any such constraints *whose checks are not implemented by the* DBMS are not violated. However, the DBMS must implement checks to enforce all the SQL integrity constraints *it supports*. A DBMS enforcing NOT NULL will reject an INSERT command in which an attribute declared to be NOT NULL does not have a value; for example, U2A would be *rejected* because no SSN value is provided.

U2:	INSERT INTO	EMPLOYEE (FNAME, LNAME, SSN, DNO)
	VALUES	('Robert', 'Hatcher', '980760540', 2);
		(* U2 is rejected if referential integrity checking is provided by DBMS *)

U2A:	INSERT INTO	EMPLOYEE (FNAME, LNAME, DNO)
	VALUES	('Robert', 'Hatcher', 5);
		(* U2A is rejected if NOT NULL checking is provided by DBMS *)

A variation of the INSERT command inserts multiple tuples into a relation in conjunction with creating the relation and loading it with the *result of a query*. For example, to create a temporary table that has the name, number of employees, and total salaries for each department, we can write the statements in U3A and U3B:

U3A:	CREATE TABLE	DEPTS_INFO
	(DEPT_NAME	VARCHAR(15),
	NO_OF_EMPS	INTEGER,
	TOTAL_SAL	INTEGER);

U3B:	INSERT INTO	DEPTS_INFO (DEPT_NAME, NO_OF_EMPS, TOTAL_SAL)
	SELECT	DNAME, COUNT (*), SUM (SALARY)
	FROM	(DEPARTMENT JOIN EMPLOYEE ON DNUMBER=DNO)
	GROUP BY	DNAME;

A table DEPTS_INFO is created by U3A and is loaded with the summary information retrieved from the database by the query in U3B. We can now query DEPTS_INFO as we could any other relation; and when we do not need it any more, we can remove it by using the DROP TABLE command. Notice that the DEPTS_INFO table may not be up to date;

that is, if we update either the DEPARTMENT or the EMPLOYEE relations after issuing U3B, the information in DEPTS_INFO *becomes outdated*. We have to create a view (see Section 8.5) to keep such a table up to date.

8.4.2 The DELETE Command

The DELETE command removes tuples from a relation. It includes a WHERE-clause, similar to that used in an SQL query, to select the tuples to be deleted. Tuples are explicitly deleted from only one table at a time. However, the deletion may propagate to tuples in other relations if *referential triggered actions* are specified in the referential integrity constraints of the DDL (see Section 8.1.2). Depending on the number of tuples selected by the condition in the WHERE-clause, zero, one, or several tuples can be deleted by a single DELETE command. A missing WHERE-clause specifies that all tuples in the relation are to be deleted; however, the table remains in the database as an empty table.[14] The DELETE commands in U4A to U4D, if applied independently to the database of Figure 7.6, will delete zero, one, four, and all tuples, respectively, from the EMPLOYEE relation:

U4A: **DELETE FROM** EMPLOYEE
            WHERE   LNAME='Brown';

U4B: **DELETE FROM** EMPLOYEE
            WHERE   SSN='123456789';

U4C: **DELETE FROM** EMPLOYEE
            WHERE   DNO **IN** (**SELECT**   DNUMBER
                                        FROM   DEPARTMENT
                                        WHERE   DNAME='Research');

U4D: **DELETE FROM** EMPLOYEE;

8.4.3 The UPDATE Command

The UPDATE command is used to modify attribute values of one or more selected tuples. As in the DELETE command, a WHERE-clause in the UPDATE command selects the tuples to be modified from a single relation. However, updating a primary key value may propagate to the foreign key values of tuples in other relations if such a *referential triggered action* is specified in the referential integrity constraints of the DDL (see Section 8.1.2). An additional SET-**clause** specifies the attributes to be modified and their new values. For example, to change the location and controlling department number of project number 10 to 'Bellaire' and 5, respectively, we use U5:

U5:   **UPDATE**   PROJECT
          SET   PLOCATION = 'Bellaire', DNUM = 5
          WHERE   PNUMBER=10;

---

14. We must use the DROP TABLE command to remove the table completely.

Several tuples can be modified with a single UPDATE command. An example is to give all employees in the 'Research' department a 10 percent raise in salary, as shown in U6. In this request, the modified SALARY value depends on the original SALARY value in each tuple, so two references to the SALARY attribute are needed. In the SET-clause, the reference to the SALARY attribute on the right refers to the old SALARY value *before modification*, and the one on the left refers to the new SALARY value *after modification*:

U6:	UPDATE	EMPLOYEE
	SET	SALARY = SALARY *1.1
	WHERE	DNO IN (SELECT DNUMBER
		FROM DEPARTMENT
		WHERE DNAME='Research');

It is also possible to specify NULL or DEFAULT as the new attribute value. Notice that each UPDATE command explicitly specifies a single relation only. To modify multiple relations, we must issue several UPDATE commands. These (and other SQL commands) could be embedded in a general-purpose program, as we shall discuss in Chapter 10.

8.5 Views (Virtual Tables) in SQL

In this section we introduce the concept of a view in SQL. We then show how views are specified, and we discuss the problem of updating a view, and how a view can be implemented by the DBMS.

8.5.1 Concept of a View in SQL

A **view** in SQL terminology is a single table that is derived from other tables.[15] These other tables could be base tables or previously defined views. A view does not necessarily exist in physical form; it is considered a **virtual table,** in contrast to base tables whose tuples are actually stored in the database. This limits the possible update operations that can be applied to views, but it does not provide any limitations on querying a view.

We can think of a view as a way of specifying a table that we need to reference frequently, even though it may not exist physically. For example, in Figure 7.5 we may frequently issue queries that retrieve the employee name and the project names that the employee works on. Rather than having to specify the join of the EMPLOYEE, WORKS_ON, and PROJECT tables every time we issue that query, we can define a view that is a result of these joins. We can then issue queries on the view, which are specified as single-table retrievals rather than as retrievals involving two joins on three tables. We call the tables EMPLOYEE, WORKS_ON, and PROJECT the **defining tables** of the view.

---

15. As used here, the term *view* is more limited than the term *user views* discussed in Chapters 1 and 2, since a user view would possibly include many relations.

8.5.2 Specification of Views in SQL

The command to specify a view is CREATE VIEW. The view is given a (virtual) table name (or view name), a list of attribute names, and a query to specify the contents of the view. If none of the view attributes result from applying functions or arithmetic operations, we do not have to specify attribute names for the view, as they would be the same as the names of the attributes of the defining tables in the default case. The views in V1 and V2 create virtual tables whose schemas are illustrated in Figure 8.5 when applied to the database schema of Figure 7.5.

V1:	CREATE VIEW	WORKS_ON1
	AS SELECT	FNAME, LNAME, PNAME, HOURS
	FROM	EMPLOYEE, PROJECT, WORKS_ON
	WHERE	SSN=ESSN **AND** PNO=PNUMBER;
V2:	CREATE VIEW	DEPT_INFO(DEPT_NAME, NO_OF_EMPS, TOTAL_ SAL)
	AS SELECT	DNAME, **COUNT** (*), **SUM** (SALARY)
	FROM	DEPARTMENT, EMPLOYEE
	WHERE	DNUMBER=DNO
	GROUP BY	DNAME;

In V1, we did not specify any new attribute names for the view WORKS_ON1 (although we could have); in this case, WORKS_ON1 inherits the names of the view attributes from the defining tables EMPLOYEE, PROJECT, and WORKS_ON. View V2 explicitly specifies new attribute names for the view DEPT_INFO, using a one-to-one correspondence between the attributes specified in the CREATE VIEW clause and those specified in the SELECT-clause of the query that defines the view. We can now specify SQL queries on a view—or virtual table—in the same way we specify queries involving base tables. For example, to retrieve the last name

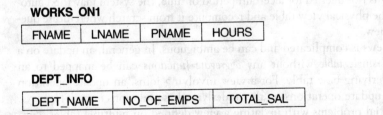

WORKS_ON1

FNAME	LNAME	PNAME	HOURS

DEPT_INFO

DEPT_NAME	NO_OF_EMPS	TOTAL_SAL

Figure 8.5 Two views specified on the database schema of Figure 7.5.

and first name of all employees who work on 'ProjectX', we can utilize the WORKS_ON1 view and specify the query as in QV1:

QV1:   SELECT   FNAME, LNAME
        FROM   WORKS_ON1
        WHERE   PNAME='ProjectX';

The same query would require the specification of two joins if specified on the base relations; one of the main advantages of a view is to simplify the specification of certain queries. Views are also used as a security and authorization mechanism (see Chapter 22).

A view is *always up to date*; if we modify the tuples in the base tables on which the view is defined, the view must automatically reflect these changes. Hence, the view is not realized at the time of *view definition* but rather at the time we *specify a query* on the view. It is the responsibility of the DBMS and not the user to make sure that the view is up to date.

If we do not need a view any more, we can use the DROP VIEW command to dispose of it. For example, to get rid of the view V1, we can use the SQL statements in V1A:

V1A: DROP VIEW   WORKS_ON1;

8.5.3 View Implementation and View Update

The problem of efficiently implementing a view for querying is complex. Two main approaches have been suggested. One strategy, called **query modification,** involves modifying the view query into a query on the underlying base tables. The disadvantage of this approach is that it is inefficient for views defined via complex queries that are time-consuming to execute, especially if multiple queries are applied to the view within a short period of time. The other strategy, called **view materialization,** involves physically creating a temporary view table when the view is first queried and keeping that table on the assumption that other queries on the view will follow. In this case, an efficient strategy for automatically updating the view table when the base tables are updated must be developed in order to keep the view up to date. Techniques using the concept of **incremental update** have been developed for this purpose, where it is determined what new tuples must be inserted, deleted, or modified in a materialized view table when a change is applied to one of the defining base tables. The view is generally kept as long as it is being queried. If the view is not queried for a certain period of time, the system may then automatically remove the physical view table and recompute it from scratch when future queries reference the view.

Updating of views is complicated and can be ambiguous. In general, an update on a view defined on a *single table* without any *aggregate functions* can be mapped to an update on the underlying base table. For a view involving joins, an update operation may be mapped to update operations on the underlying base relations *in multiple ways*. To illustrate potential problems with updating a view defined on multiple tables, consider the WORKS_ON1 view, and suppose that we issue the command to update the PNAME attribute of 'John Smith' from 'ProductX' to 'ProductY'. This view update is shown in UV1:

> UV1:   **UPDATE** WORKS_ON1
>   **SET** PNAME = 'ProductY'
>   **WHERE** LNAME='Smith' **AND** FNAME='John' **AND**
>   PNAME='ProductX';

This query can be mapped into several updates on the base relations to give the desired update effect on the view. Two possible updates (a) and (b) on the base relations corresponding to UV1 are shown here:

> **(a):** **UPDATE** WORKS_ON
>   **SET** PNO = (SELECT PNUMBER **FROM** PROJECT
>   **WHERE** PNAME='ProductY')
>   **WHERE** ESSN IN (SELECT SSN **FROM** EMPLOYEE
>   **WHERE** LNAME='Smith' **AND** FNAME='John')
>   **AND**
>   PNO **IN** (SELECT PNUMBER **FROM** PROJECT
>   **WHERE** PNAME='ProductX');

> **(b):** **UPDATE** PROJECT
>   **SET** PNAME = 'ProductY'
>   **WHERE** PNAME = 'ProductX';

Update (a) relates 'John Smith' to the 'ProductY' PROJECT tuple in place of the 'ProductX' PROJECT tuple and is the most likely desired update. However, (b) would also give the desired update effect on the view, but it accomplishes this by changing the name of the 'ProductX' tuple in the PROJECT relation to 'ProductY'. It is quite unlikely that the user who specified the view update UV1 wants the update to be interpreted as in (b), since it also has the effect of changing all the view tuples with PNAME = 'ProductX'.

Some view updates may not make much sense; for example, modifying the TOTAL_SAL attribute of the DEPT_INFO view does not make sense because TOTAL_SAL is defined to be the sum of the individual employee salaries. This request is shown as UV2:

> UV2:   **UPDATE** DEPT_INFO
>   **SET** TOTAL_SAL=100000
>   **WHERE** DNAME='Research';

A large number of updates on the underlying base relations can satisfy this view update. A view update is feasible when only *one possible update* on the base relations can accomplish the desired update effect on the view. Whenever an update on the view can be mapped to *more than one update* on the underlying base relations, we must have a certain procedure to choose the desired update. Some researchers have developed methods for choosing the most likely update, while other researchers prefer to have the user choose the desired update mapping during view definition.

In summary, we can make the following observations:

- A view with a single defining table is updatable if the view attributes contain the primary key (or possibly some other candidate key) of the base relation, because this maps each (virtual) view tuple to a single base tuple.
- Views defined on multiple tables using joins are generally not updatable.
- Views defined using grouping and aggregate functions are not updatable.

In SQL2, the clause WITH CHECK OPTION must be added at the end of the view definition if a view is to be updated. This allows the system to check for view updatability and to plan an execution strategy for view updates.

8.6 Specifying General Constraints as Assertions

In SQL2, users can specify more general constraints—those that do not fall into any of the categories described in Section 8.1.2—via **declarative assertions,** using the CREATE ASSERTION **statement** of the DDL. Each assertion is given a constraint name and is specified via a condition similar to the WHERE-clause of an SQL query. For example, to specify the constraint that "the salary of an employee must not be greater than the salary of the manager of the department that the employee works for" in SQL2, we can write the following assertion:

    CREATE ASSERTION SALARY_CONSTRAINT
    CHECK (NOT EXISTS (SELECT * FROM EMPLOYEE E, EMPLOYEE M,
                                   DEPARTMENT D
                 WHERE E.SALARY>M.SALARY **AND**
                       E.DNO=D.DNUMBER **AND**
                       D.MGRSSN=M.SSN));

The constraint name SALARY_CONSTRAINT is followed by the keyword CHECK, which is followed by a **condition** in parentheses that must hold true on every database state for the assertion to be satisfied. The constraint name can be used later to refer to the constraint or to modify or drop it. The DBMS is responsible for ensuring that the condition is not violated. Any WHERE-clause condition can be used, but many constraints can be specified using the EXISTS and NOT EXISTS style of conditions. Whenever some tuples in the database cause the condition of an ASSERTION statement to evaluate to FALSE, the constraint is **violated.** The constraint is **satisfied** by a database state if *no combination of tuples* in that database state violates the constraint.

Note that the CHECK clause and constraint condition can also be used in conjunction with the CREATE DOMAIN statement (see Section 8.1.2) to specify constraints on a particular domain, such as restricting the values of a domain to a *subrange* of the data type for the domain. For example, to restrict the values of department numbers to an integer number between 1 and 20, we can write the following statement:

CREATE DOMAIN D_NUM **AS** INTEGER
CHECK (D_NUM > 0 **AND** D_NUM < 21);

Earlier versions of SQL had two types of statements to declare constraints: ASSERT and TRIGGER. The **ASSERT statement** is somewhat similar to CREATE ASSERTION of SQL2 with a different syntax. The **TRIGGER statement** is used in a different way. In many cases it is convenient to specify the type of action to be taken in case of a constraint violation. Rather than offering users only the option of aborting the transaction that causes a violation, the DBMS should make other options available. For example, it may be useful to specify a constraint that, if violated, causes some user to be informed of the violation. A manager may want to be informed if an employee's travel expenses exceed a certain limit by receiving a message whenever this occurs. The action that the DBMS must take in this case is to send an appropriate message to that user, and the constraint is thus used to **monitor** the database. Other actions may be specified, such as executing a specific procedure or triggering other updates. A mechanism called a *trigger* has been proposed to implement such actions in earlier versions of SQL. A **trigger** specifies a **condition** and an **action** to be taken in case that condition is satisfied. The condition is usually specified as an assertion that invokes or "triggers" the action when it becomes TRUE. We will discuss triggers in more detail in Chapter 23 when we describe *active databases*.

8.7 Additional Features of SQL

There are a number of additional features of SQL that we have not described in this chapter, but will discuss elsewhere in the book. These are as follows:

- SQL has language constructs for specifying the *granting and revoking of privileges* to users. Privileges typically correspond to the right to use certain SQL commands to access certain relations. Each relation is assigned an owner, and either the owner or the DBA staff can grant to selected users the privilege to use an SQL statement—such as SELECT, INSERT, DELETE, or UPDATE—to access the relation. In addition, the DBA staff can grant the privileges to create schemas, tables, or views to certain users. These SQL commands—called **GRANT** and **REVOKE**—are discussed in Chapter 22 where we discuss database security and authorization.

- SQL has a methodology for embedding SQL statements in a general purpose programming language, such as C, C++, COBOL, or PASCAL. SQL also has **language bindings** to various programming languages that specify the correspondence of SQL data types to the data types of each of the programming languages. **Embedded SQL** is based on the concept of a **cursor** that can range over the query result one tuple at a time. We will discuss embedded SQL, and give examples of how it is used in relational database programming, in Chapter 10.

- SQL has transaction control commands. These are used to specify units of database processing for concurrency control and recovery purposes. We will discuss these commands in Chapter 19.

- Each commercial DBMS will have, in addition to the SQL commands, a set of commands for specifying physical database design parameters, file structures for relations, and access paths such as indexes. We called these commands a *storage definition language* (SDL) in Chapter 2. Earlier versions of SQL had commands for **creating indexes,** but these were removed from the language because they were not at the conceptual schema level (see Chapter 2). We will discuss these commands for a specific commercial relational DBMS in Chapter 10.

8.8 Summary

In this chapter we presented the SQL database language. This language or variations of it have been implemented as interfaces to many commercial relational DBMSs, including IBM's DB2 and SQL/DS, ORACLE, INGRES, INFORMIX, and SYBASE. The original version of SQL was implemented in the experimental DBMS called SYSTEM R, which was developed at IBM Research. SQL is designed to be a comprehensive language that includes statements for data definition, queries, updates, view definition, and constraint specification. We discussed each of these in separate sections of this chapter. In the final section we discussed additional features that are described elsewhere in the book. Our emphasis was on the SQL2 standard. The next version of the standard, called SQL3, is well underway. It will incorporate object-oriented and other advanced database features into the standard. We discuss some of the proposed features of SQL3 in Chapter 13.

Table 8.1 shows a summary of the syntax (or structure) of various SQL statements. This summary is not meant to be comprehensive nor to describe every possible SQL construct; rather, it is meant to serve as a quick reference to the major types of constructs available in SQL. We use BNF notation, where nonterminal symbols are shown in angled brackets < . . . >, optional parts are shown in square brackets [. . .], repetitions are shown in braces { . . . }, and alternatives are shown in parentheses (. . . | . . . | . . .).[16]

Review Questions

8.1. How do the relations (tables) in SQL differ from the relations defined formally in Chapter 7? Discuss the other differences in terminology. Why does SQL allow duplicate tuples in a table or in a query result?

8.2. List the data types that are allowed for SQL2 attributes.

8.3. How does SQL allow implementation of the entity integrity and referential integrity constraints described in Chapter 7? What about general integrity constraints?

---

16. The full syntax of SQL2 is described in a document of over 500 pages.

Table 8.1   Summary of SQL Syntax

CREATE TABLE <table name> (<column name> <column type> [<attribute constraint>]
                        {, <column name> <column type> [<attribute constraint>] }
                        [<table constraint> {,<table constraint>}])

DROP TABLE <table name>

ALTER TABLE <table name> ADD <column name> <column type>

SELECT [DISTINCT] <attribute list>
FROM (<table name> { <alias>} | <joined table>) {, (<table name> { <alias>} | <joined table>) }
[WHERE <condition>]
[GROUP BY <grouping attributes> [HAVING <group selection condition>]]
[ORDER BY <column name> [<order>] {, <column name> [<order>] }]

<attribute list>::= (* | (<column name> | <function>(([DISTINCT]<column name> | *)))
                        {,(<column name> | <function>(([DISTINCT] <column name> | *)) }))
<grouping attributes>::= <column name> { , <column name>}
<order>::= (ASC | DESC)

INSERT INTO <table name> [(<column name>{, <column name>})]
(VALUES (<constant value> , { <constant value>}){,(<constant value>{,<constant value>})}
 | <select statement>)

DELETE FROM <table name>
[WHERE <selection condition>]

UPDATE <table name>
SET <column name>=<value expression> { , <column name>=<value expression> }
[WHERE <selection condition>]

CREATE [UNIQUE] INDEX <index name>*
ON <table name> (<column name> [<order>] {, <column name> [<order>] })
[CLUSTER]

DROP INDEX <index name>

CREATE VIEW <view name> [(<column name> { , <column name> })]
AS <select statement>

DROP VIEW <view name>

---

*These last two commands are not part of standard SQL2.

8.4. What is a view in SQL, and how is it defined? Discuss the problems that may arise when one attempts to update a view. How are views typically implemented?

8.5. Describe the six clauses in the syntax of an SQL query, and show what type of constructs can be specified in each of the six clauses. Which of the six clauses are required and which are optional?

8.6. Describe conceptually how an SQL query will be executed by specifying the conceptual order of executing each of the six clauses.

Exercises

8.7. Consider the database shown in Figure 1.2, whose schema is shown in Figure 2.1. What are the referential integrity constraints that should hold on the schema? Write appropriate SQL DDL statements to define the database.

8.8. Repeat Exercise 8.7, but use the AIRLINE database schema of Figure 7.19.

8.9. Consider the LIBRARY relational database schema of Figure 7.20. Choose the appropriate action (reject, cascade, set to null, set to default) for each referential integrity constraint, both for *delete* of a referenced tuple, and for *update* of a primary key attribute value in a referenced tuple. Justify your choices.

8.10. Write appropriate SQL DDL statements for declaring the LIBRARY relational database schema of Figure 7.20. Use the referential actions chosen in Exercise 8.9.

8.11. Write SQL queries for the LIBRARY database queries given in Exercise 7.23.

8.12. How can the key and foreign key constraints be enforced by the DBMS? Is the enforcement technique you suggest difficult to implement? Can the constraint checks be executed efficiently when updates are applied to the database?

8.13. Specify the queries of Exercise 7.18 in SQL. Show the result of each query if it is applied to the COMPANY database of Figure 7.6.

8.14. Specify the following additional queries on the database of Figure 7.5 in SQL. Show the query results if each query is applied to the database of Figure 7.6.

  a. For each department whose average employee salary is more than $30,000, retrieve the department name and the number of employees working for that department.

  b. Suppose that we want the number of *male* employees in each department rather than all employees (as in Exercise 8.14a). Can we specify this query in SQL? Why or why not?

8.15. Specify the updates of Exercise 7.19, using the SQL update commands.

8.16. Specify the following queries in SQL on the database schema of Figure 1.2.

  a. Retrieve the names of all senior students majoring in 'CS' (computer science).

  b. Retrieve the names of all courses taught by Professor King in 1998 and 1999.

  c. For each section taught by Professor King, retrieve the course number, semester, year, and number of students who took the section.

  d. Retrieve the name and transcript of each senior student (Class = 5) majoring in CS. A transcript includes course name, course number, credit hours, semester, year, and grade for each course completed by the student.

  e. Retrieve the names and major departments of all straight-A students (students who have a grade of A in all their courses).

    f. Retrieve the names and major departments of all students who do not have a grade of A in any of their courses.

8.17. Write SQL update statements to do the following on the database schema shown in Figure 1.2.

    a. Insert a new student <'Johnson', 25, 1, 'MATH'> in the database.

    b. Change the class of student 'Smith' to 2.

    c. Insert a new course <'Knowledge Engineering','CS4390', 3,'CS'>.

    d. Delete the record for the student whose name is 'Smith' and whose student number is 17.

8.18. Specify the following views in SQL on the COMPANY database schema shown in Figure 7.5.

    a. A view that has the department name, manager name, and manager salary for every department.

    b. A view that has the employee name, supervisor name, and employee salary for each employee who works in the 'Research' department.

    c. A view that has project name, controlling department name, number of employees, and total hours worked per week on the project for each project.

    d. A view that has project name, controlling department name, number of employees, and total hours worked per week on the project for each project *with more than one employee working on it.*

8.19. Consider the following view DEPT_SUMMARY, defined on the COMPANY database of Figure 7.6:

CREATE VIEW DEPT_SUMMARY (D, C, TOTAL_S, AVERAGE_S)

AS SELECT   DNO, COUNT (*), SUM (SALARY), AVG (SALARY)

    FROM   EMPLOYEE

    GROUP BY DNO;

State which of the following queries and updates would be allowed on the view. If a query or update would be allowed, show what the corresponding query or update on the base relations would look like, and give its result when applied to the database of Figure 7.6.

    a. **SELECT** *
       FROM   DEPT_SUMMARY;

    b. **SELECT** D, C
       FROM   DEPT_SUMMARY
       WHERE TOTAL_S > 100000;

    c. **SELECT** D, AVERAGE_S
       FROM   DEPT_SUMMARY
       WHERE C > (**SELECT** C **FROM** DEPT_SUMMARY **WHERE** D=4);

    d. **UPDATE** DEPT_SUMMARY
       SET   D=3
       WHERE D=4;

    e. **DELETE FROM** DEPT_SUMMARY
       WHERE C > 4;

8.20. Consider the relation schema CONTAINS(Parent_part#, Sub_part#); a tuple $<P_i, P_j>$ in CONTAINS means that part P_i contains part P_j as a direct component. Suppose that we choose a part P_k that contains no other parts, and we want to find the part numbers of all parts that contain P_k, directly or indirectly at any level; this is a *recursive query* that requires computing the **transitive closure** of CONTAINS. Show that this query cannot be directly specified as a single SQL query. Can you suggest extensions to SQL to allow the specification of such queries?

8.21. Specify the queries and updates of Exercises 7.20 and 7.21, which refer to the AIRLINE database, in SQL.

8.22. Choose some database application that you are familiar with.
    a. Design a relational database schema for your database application.
    b. Declare your relations, using the SQL DDL.
    c. Specify a number of queries in SQL that are needed by your database application.
    d. Based on your expected use of the database, choose some attributes that should have indexes specified on them.
    e. Implement your database, if you have a DBMS that supports SQL.

8.23. Specify the answers to Exercises 7.24 through 7.28 in SQL.

Selected Bibliography

The SQL language, originally named SEQUEL, was based on the language SQUARE (Specifying Queries as Relational Expressions), described by Boyce et al. (1975). The syntax of SQUARE was modified into SEQUEL (Chamberlin and Boyce 1974) and then into SEQUEL 2 (Chamberlin et al. 1976), on which SQL is based. The original implementation of SEQUEL was done at IBM Research, San Jose, California.

Reisner (1977) describes a human factors evaluation of SEQUEL in which she found that users have some difficulty with specifying join conditions and grouping correctly. Date (1984b) contains a critique of the SQL language that points out its strengths and shortcomings. Date and Darwen (1993) describes SQL2. ANSI (1986) outlines the original SQL standard, and ANSI (1992) describes the SQL2 standard. Various vendor manuals describe the characteristics of SQL as implemented on DB2, SQL/DS, ORACLE, INGRES, INFORMIX, and other commercial DBMS products. Melton and Simon (1993) is a comprehensive treatment of SQL2. Horowitz (1992) discusses some of the problems related to referential integrity and propagation of updates in SQL2.

The question of view updates is addressed by Dayal and Bernstein (1978), Keller (1982), and Langerak (1990), among others. View implementation is discussed in Blakeley et al. (1989). Negri et al. (1991) describes formal semantics of SQL queries.

CHAPTER 9

ER- and EER-to-Relational Mapping, and Other Relational Languages

This chapter discusses two topics that are not directly related but serve to round out our presentation of the relational data model. The first topic focuses on **designing a relational database schema** based on a conceptual schema design. This is the logical database design (or data model mapping) step discussed in Section 3.1 (see Figure 3.1). This relates the concepts of the Entity-Relationship (ER) and Enhanced-ER (EER) models, presented in Chapters 3 and 4, to the concepts of the relational model, presented in Chapter 7. In Sections 9.1 and 9.2, we show how a relational database schema can be created from a conceptual schema developed using the ER or EER models. Many CASE (Computer-Aided Software Engineering) tools are based on the ER or EER or other similar models, as we have discussed in Chapters 3 and 4. These computerized tools are used interactively by database designers to develop an ER or EER schema for a database application. Many tools use ER diagrams or variations to develop the schema graphically, and then automatically convert it into a relational database schema in the DDL of a specific relational DBMS.

The second topic introduces some **other relational languages** that are important. These are presented in Sections 9.3 through 9.5. We first describe another formal language for relational databases, the **relational calculus.** There are two variations of relational calculus: the tuple relational calculus is described in Section 9.3, and the domain relational calculus is described in Section 9.4. Some of the SQL query language constructs discussed in Chapter 8 are based on the tuple relational calculus. The relational calculus is a formal language, based on the branch of mathematical logic called predicate calculus.[1] In tuple relational calculus, variables range over tuples; whereas in domain relational calculus, variables range over the domains (values) of attributes. Finally, in Section 9.5, we give an overview of the QBE (Query-By-Example) language, which is a graphical user-friendly relational language based on domain relational calculus. Section 9.6 summarizes the chapter.

Sections 9.1 and 9.2 on relational database design assume that the reader is familiar with the material in Chapters 3 and 4, respectively.

9.1   Relational Database Design Using ER-to-Relational Mapping

Section 9.1.1 provides an outline of an algorithm that can map an ER schema into the corresponding relational database schema. Section 9.1.2 summarizes the correspondences between ER and relational model constructs. Section 9.2 discusses the options for mapping the EER model constructs—such as generalization/specialization and categories—into relations.

9.1.1   ER-to-Relational Mapping Algorithm

We now describe the steps of an algorithm for ER-to-relational mapping. We will use the COMPANY relational database schema, shown in Figure 7.5, to illustrate the mapping steps.

STEP 1: For each regular (strong) entity type E in the ER schema, create a relation R that includes all the simple attributes of E. Include only the simple component attributes of a composite attribute. Choose one of the key attributes of E as primary key for R. If the chosen key of E is composite, the set of simple attributes that form it will together form the primary key of R.

In our example, we create the relations EMPLOYEE, DEPARTMENT, and PROJECT in Figure 7.5 to correspond to the regular entity types EMPLOYEE, DEPARTMENT, and PROJECT from Figure 3.2.[2] The foreign key and relationship attributes, if any, are not included yet; they will be added during subsequent steps. These include the attributes SUPERSSN and DNO of EMPLOYEE; MGRSSN and MGRSTARTDATE of DEPARTMENT; and DNUM of PROJECT. In our example, we choose SSN, DNUMBER, and PNUMBER as primary keys for the relations EMPLOYEE, DEPARTMENT, and PROJECT, respectively.

STEP 2: For each weak entity type W in the ER schema with owner entity type E, create a relation R, and include all simple attributes (or simple components of com-

---

1. In this chapter no familiarity with first-order predicate calculus, which deals with quantified variables and values, is assumed.

2. These are sometimes called *entity relations* because each tuple (row) represents an entity instance.

posite attributes) of W as attributes of R. In addition, include as foreign key attributes of R the primary key attribute(s) of the relation(s) that correspond to the owner entity type(s); this takes care of the identifying relationship type of W. The primary key of R is the combination of the primary key(s) of the owner(s) and the partial key of the weak entity type W, if any.

In our example, we create the relation DEPENDENT in this step to correspond to the weak entity type DEPENDENT. We include the primary key SSN of the EMPLOYEE relation—which corresponds to the owner entity type—as a foreign key attribute of DEPENDENT; we renamed it ESSN, although this is not necessary. The primary key of the DEPENDENT relation is the combination {ESSN, DEPENDENT_NAME} because DEPENDENT_NAME is the partial key of DEPENDENT.

It is common to choose the propagate (CASCADE) option for the referential triggered action (see Section 8.1) on the foreign key in the relation corresponding to the weak entity type, since a weak entity has an existence dependency on its owner entity. This can be used for both ON UPDATE and ON DELETE.

STEP 3: For each binary 1:1 relationship type R in the ER schema, identify the relations S and T that correspond to the entity types participating in R. Choose one of the relations—S, say—and include as foreign key in S the primary key of T. It is better to choose an entity type with *total participation* in R in the role of S. Include all the simple attributes (or simple components of composite attributes) of the 1:1 relationship type R as attributes of S.

In our example, we map the 1:1 relationship type MANAGES from Figure 3.2 by choosing the participating entity type DEPARTMENT to serve in the role of S, because its participation in the MANAGES relationship type is total (every department has a manager). We include the primary key of the EMPLOYEE relation as foreign key in the DEPARTMENT relation and rename it MGRSSN. We also include the simple attribute Start-Date of the MANAGES relationship type in the DEPARTMENT relation and rename it MGRSTARTDATE.

Notice that an alternative mapping of a 1:1 relationship type is possible by merging the two entity types and the relationship into a single relation. This is appropriate when *both participations are total*.

STEP 4: For each regular binary 1:N relationship type R, identify the relation S that represents the participating entity type at the *N-side* of the relationship type. Include as foreign key in S the primary key of the relation T that represents the other entity type participating in R; this is because each entity instance on the N-side is related to at most one entity instance on the 1-side of the relationship type. Include any simple attributes (or simple components of composite attributes) of the 1:N relationship type as attributes of S.

In our example, we now map the 1:N relationship types WORKS_FOR, CONTROLS, and SUPERVISION from Figure 3.2. For WORKS_FOR we include the primary key DNUMBER of the DEPARTMENT relation as foreign key in the EMPLOYEE relation and call it DNO. For SUPERVISION we include the primary key of the EMPLOYEE relation as foreign key in the EMPLOYEE relation itself—because the relationship is recursive—and call it SUPERSSN. The CONTROLS relationship is mapped to the foreign key attribute DNUM of PROJECT, which references the primary key DNUMBER of the DEPARTMENT relation.

STEP 5: For each binary M:N relationship type R, create a new relation S to represent R. Include as foreign key attributes in S the primary keys of the relations that represent the participating entity types; their combination will form the primary key of S. Also include any simple attributes of the M:N relationship type (or simple components of composite attributes) as attributes of S. Notice that we cannot represent an M:N relationship type by a single foreign key attribute in one of the participating relations—as we did for 1:1 or 1:N relationship types—because of the M:N cardinality ratio.

In our example, we map the M:N relationship type WORKS_ON from Figure 3.2 by creating the relation WORKS_ON in Figure 7.5.[3] We include the primary keys of the PROJECT and EMPLOYEE relations as foreign keys in WORKS_ON and rename them PNO and ESSN, respectively. We also include an attribute HOURS in WORKS_ON to represent the Hours attribute of the relationship type. The primary key of the WORKS_ON relation is the combination of the foreign key attributes {ESSN, PNO}.

The propagate (CASCADE) option for the referential triggered action (see Section 8.1) should be specified on the foreign keys in the relation corresponding to the relationship R, since each relationship instance has an existence dependency on each of the entities it relates. This can be used for both ON UPDATE and ON DELETE.

Notice that we can always map 1:1 or 1:N relationships in a manner similar to M:N relationships. This alternative is particularly useful when few relationship instances exist, in order to avoid null values in foreign keys. In this case, the primary key of the "relationship" relation will be *only one* of the foreign keys that reference the participating "entity" relations. For a 1:N relationship, this will be the foreign key that references the entity relation on the N-side. For a 1:1 relationship, the foreign key that references the entity relation with total participation (if any) is chosen as primary key.

STEP 6: For each multivalued attribute A, create a new relation R. This relation R will include an attribute corresponding to A, plus the primary key attribute K—as a foreign key in R—of the relation that represents the entity type or relationship type that has A as an attribute. The primary key of R is the combination of A and K. If the multivalued attribute is composite, we include its simple components.[4]

In our example, we create a relation DEPT_LOCATIONS. The attribute DLOCATION represents the multivalued attribute Locations of DEPARTMENT, while DNUMBER—as foreign key—represents the primary key of the DEPARTMENT relation. The primary key of

---

3. These are sometimes called *relationship relations* because each tuple (row) corresponds to a relationship instance.

4. In some cases when a multivalued attribute is composite, only some of the component attributes are required in the key of R; these attributes are similar to a partial key of a weak entity type that corresponds to the multivalued attribute.

DEPT_LOCATIONS is the combination of {DNUMBER, DLOCATION}. A separate tuple will exist in DEPT_LOCATIONS for each location that a department has.

The propagate (CASCADE) option for the referential triggered action (see Section 8.1) should be specified on the foreign key in the relation corresponding to the multivalued attribute for both ON UPDATE and ON DELETE.

Figure 7.5 (and 7.7) shows the relational database schema obtained through the preceding steps, and Figure 7.6 shows a sample database state. Notice that we did not discuss the mapping of n-ary relationship types (n > 2), because none exist in Figure 3.2; these are mapped in a similar way to M:N relationship types by including the following additional step in the mapping algorithm.

STEP 7: For each n-ary relationship type R, where n > 2, create a new relation S to represent R. Include as foreign key attributes in S the primary keys of the relations that represent the participating entity types. Also include any simple attributes of the n-ary relationship type (or simple components of composite attributes) as attributes of S. The primary key of S is usually a combination of all the foreign keys that reference the relations representing the participating entity types. However, if the cardinality constraints on any of the entity types E participating in R is 1, then the primary key of S should not include the foreign key attribute that references the relation E' corresponding to E (see Section 4.7). This concludes the mapping procedure.

For example, consider the relationship type SUPPLY of Figure 4.13(a). This can be mapped to the relation SUPPLY shown in Figure 9.1, whose primary key is the combination of foreign keys {SNAME, PARTNO, PROJNAME}.

The main point to note in a relational schema, in contrast to an ER schema, is that relationship types are not represented explicitly; instead, they are represented by having

SUPPLIER

SNAME	
	. . .

PROJECT

PROJNAME	
	. . .

PART

PARTNO	
	. . .

SUPPLY

SNAME	PROJNAME	PARTNO	QUANTITY

Figure 9.1   Mapping the n-ary relationship type SUPPLY from Figure 4.13(a).

two attributes A and B, one a primary key and the other a foreign key—over the same domain—included in two relations S and T. Two tuples in S and T are related when they have the same value for A and B. By using the EQUIJOIN (or NATURAL JOIN) operation over S.A and T.B, we can combine all pairs of related tuples from S and T and materialize the relationship. When a binary 1:1 or 1:N relationship type is involved, a single join operation is usually needed. For a binary M:N relationship type, two join operations are needed, whereas for n-ary relationship types, n joins are needed.

For example, to form a relation that includes the employee name, project name, and hours that the employee works on each project, we need to connect each EMPLOYEE tuple to the related PROJECT tuples via the WORKS_ON relation of Figure 7.5. Hence, we must apply the EQUIJOIN operation to the EMPLOYEE and WORKS_ON relations with the join condition SSN = ESSN, and then apply another EQUIJOIN operation to the resulting relation and the PROJECT relation with join condition PNO = PNUMBER. In general, when multiple relationships need to be traversed, numerous join operations must be specified. A relational database user must always be aware of the foreign key attributes in order to use them correctly in combining related tuples from two or more relations. If an equijoin is performed among attributes of two relations that do not represent a foreign key/primary key relationship, the result can often be meaningless and may lead to spurious (invalid) data. For example, the reader can try joining PROJECT and DEPT_LOCATIONS relations on the condition DLOCATION = PLOCATION and examine the result (see also Chapter 14).

Another point to note in the relational schema is that we create a separate relation for *each* multivalued attribute. For a particular entity with a set of values for the multivalued attribute, the key attribute value of the entity is repeated once for each value of the multivalued attribute in a separate tuple. This is because the basic relational model does *not* allow multiple values (a list, or a set of values) for an attribute in a single tuple. For example, because department 5 has three locations, three tuples exist in the DEPT_LOCATIONS relation of Figure 7.6; each tuple specifies one of the locations. In our example, we apply EQUIJOIN to DEPT_LOCATIONS and DEPARTMENT on the DNUMBER attribute to get the values of all locations along with other DEPARTMENT attributes. In the resulting relation, the values of the other department attributes are repeated in separate tuples for every location that a department has.

The basic relational algebra does not have a NEST or COMPRESS operation that would produce from the DEPT_LOCATIONS relation of Figure 7.6 a set of tuples of the form {<1, Houston>, <4, Stafford>, <5, {Bellaire, Sugarland, Houston}>}. This is a serious drawback of the basic normalized or "flat" version of the relational model. On this score, the object-oriented, hierarchical, and network models have better facilities than does the relational model. The nested relational model (see Section 13.6) attempts to remedy this.

9.1.2   Summary of Mapping for Model Constructs and Constraints

We now summarize the correspondences between ER and relational model constructs and constraints in Table 9.1.

Table 9.1 Correspondence between ER and Relational Models

ER Model	Relational Model
Entity type	"Entity" relation
1:1 or 1:N relationship type	Foreign key (or "relationship" relation)
M:N relationship type	"Relationship" relation and two foreign keys
n-ary relationship type	"Relationship" relation and n foreign keys
Simple attribute	Attribute
Composite attribute	Set of simple component attributes
Multivalued attribute	Relation and foreign key
Value set	Domain
Key attribute	Primary (or secondary) key

9.2 Mapping EER Model Concepts to Relations

We now discuss the mapping of EER model concepts to relations by extending the ER-to-relational mapping algorithm that was presented in Section 9.1 above.

9.2.1 Superclass/Subclass Relationships and Specialization (or Generalization)

There are several options for mapping a number of subclasses that together form a specialization (or alternatively, that are generalized into a superclass), such as the {SECRETARY, TECHNICIAN, ENGINEER} subclasses of EMPLOYEE in Figure 4.4. We can add a further step to our ER-to-relational mapping algorithm from Section 9.1, which has seven steps, to handle the mapping of specialization. Step 8, which follows, gives the most common options; other mappings are also possible. We then discuss the conditions under which each option should be used. We use Attrs(R) to denote the attributes of relation R and PK(R) to denote the primary key of R.

STEP 8: Convert each specialization with m subclasses $\{S_1, S_2, \ldots, S_m\}$ and (generalized) superclass C, where the attributes of C are $\{k, a_1, \ldots, a_n\}$ and k is the (primary) key, into relation schemas using one of the four following options:

   Option 8A: Create a relation L for C with attributes Attrs(L) = $\{k, a_1, \ldots, a_n\}$ and PK(L) = k. Create a relation L_i for each subclass S_i, $1 \le i \le m$, with the attributes Attrs(L_i) = $\{k\} \cup \{$attributes of $S_i\}$ and PK(L_i) = k.

   Option 8B: Create a relation L_i for each subclass S_i, $1 \le i \le m$, with the attributes Attrs(L_i) = {attributes of S_i} $\cup \{k, a_1, \ldots, a_n\}$ and PK(L_i) = k.

Option 8C: Create a single relation L with attributes Attrs(L) = {k, a_1, . . ., a_n} ∪ {attributes of S_1} ∪ . . . ∪ {attributes of S_m} ∪ {t} and PK(L) = k. This option is for a specialization whose subclasses are *disjoint*, and t is a **type** (or **discriminating**) attribute that indicates the subclass to which each tuple belongs, if any. This option has the potential for generating a large number of null values.

Option 8D: Create a single relation schema L with attributes Attrs(L) = {k, a_1, . . ., a_n} ∪ {attributes of S_1} ∪ . . . ∪ {attributes of S_m} ∪ {t_1, t_2, . . ., t_m} and PK(L) = k. This option is for a specialization whose subclasses are *overlapping* (but will also work for a disjoint specialization), and each t_i, $1 \leq i \leq m$, is a Boolean attribute indicating whether a tuple belongs to subclass S_i.

Options 8A and 8B can be called the *multiple relation options*, whereas options 8C and 8D can be called the *single relation options*. Option 8A creates a relation L for the superclass C and its attributes, plus a relation L_i for each subclass S_i; each L_i includes the specific (or local) attributes of S_i, plus the primary key of the superclass C, which is propagated to L_i and becomes its primary key. An EQUIJOIN operation on the primary key between any L_i and L produces all the specific and inherited attributes of the entities in S_i. This option is illustrated in Figure 9.2(a) for the EER schema in Figure 4.4. Option 8A

(a) EMPLOYEE

SSN	FName	MInit	LName	BirthDate	Address	JobType

SECRETARY

SSN	TypingSpeed

TECHNICIAN

SSN	TGrade

ENGINEER

SSN	EngType

(b) CAR

VehicleId	LicensePlateNo	Price	MaxSpeed	NoOfPassengers

TRUCK

VehicleId	LicensePlateNo	Price	NoOfAxles	Tonnage

(c) EMPLOYEE

SSN	FName	MInit	LName	BirthDate	Address	JobType	TypingSpeed	TGrade	EngType

(d) PART

PartNo	Description	MFlag	DrawingNo	ManufactureDate	BatchNo	PFlag	SupplierName	ListPrice

Figure 9.2   Options for mapping specializations (or generalizations) to relations. (a) Mapping the EER schema of Figure 4.4 to relations by using Option A. (b) Mapping the EER schema of Figure 4.3(b) into relations by using Option B. (c) Mapping the EER schema of Figure 4.4 by using Option C, with JobType playing the role of type attribute. (d) Mapping the EER schema of Figure 4.5 by using Option D, with two Boolean type fields Mflag and Pflag.

works for any constraints on the specialization: disjoint or overlapping, total or partial. Notice that the constraint

$$\pi_{<k>}(L_i) \subseteq \pi_{<k>}(L)$$

must hold for each L_i. This specifies an *inclusion dependency* $L_i.k<L.k$ (see Section 15.4).

In option 8B, the EQUIJOIN operation is *built into* the schema and the relation L is done away with, as illustrated in Figure 9.2(b) for the EER specialization in Figure 4.3(b). This option works well only when *both* the disjoint and total constraints hold. If the specialization is not total, an entity that does not belong to any of the subclasses S_i is lost. If the specialization is not disjoint, an entity belonging to more than one subclass will have its inherited attributes from the superclass C stored redundantly in more than one L_i. With option 8B, no relation holds all the entities in the superclass C; consequently, we must apply an OUTER UNION (or FULL OUTER JOIN) operation to the L_i relations to retrieve all the entities in C. The result of the outer union will be similar to the relations under options 8C and 8D except that the type fields will be missing. Whenever we search for an arbitrary entity in C, we must search all the m relations L_i.

Options 8C and 8D create a single relation to represent the superclass C and all its subclasses. An entity that does not belong to some of the subclasses will have null values for the specific attributes of these subclasses. These options are hence not recommended if many specific attributes are defined for the subclasses. If few specific subclass attributes exist, however, these mappings are preferable to options 8A and 8B because they do away with the need to specify EQUIJOIN and OUTER UNION operations and hence can yield a more efficient implementation. Option 8C is used to handle disjoint subclasses by including a single **type** (or **image** or **discriminating**) **attribute** t to indicate the subclass to which each tuple belongs; hence, the domain of t could be $\{1, 2, \ldots, m\}$. If the specialization is partial, t can have null values in tuples that do not belong to any subclass. If the specialization is attribute-defined, that attribute serves the purpose of t and t is not needed; this option is illustrated in Figure 9.2(c) for the EER specialization in Figure 4.4. Option 8D is used to handle overlapping subclasses by including m *Boolean* type fields, one for *each* subclass. It can also be used for disjoint classes. Each type field t_i can have a domain {yes, no}, where a value of yes indicates that the tuple is a member of subclass S_i. This option is illustrated in Figure 9.2(d) for the EER specialization in Figure 4.5, where Mflag and Pflag are the type fields. Notice that it is also possible to create a single type of m bits instead of the m type fields.

When we have a multilevel specialization (or generalization) hierarchy or lattice, we do not have to follow the same mapping option for all the specializations. Instead, we can use one mapping option for part of the hierarchy or lattice and other options for other parts. Figure 9.3 shows one possible mapping into relations for the lattice of Figure 4.7. Here we used option 8A for PERSON/ {EMPLOYEE, ALUMNUS, STUDENT}, option 8C for EMPLOYEE/{STAFF, FACULTY, STUDENT_ASSISTANT}, and option 8D for both STUDENT_ASSISTANT/{RESEARCH_ASSISTANT, TEACHING_ASSISTANT}, STUDENT/STUDENT_ASSISTANT (in STUDENT), and STUDENT/{GRADUATE_STUDENT, UNDERGRADUATE_STUDENT}. In Figure 9.3, all attributes whose names end with 'Type' or 'Flag' are type fields.

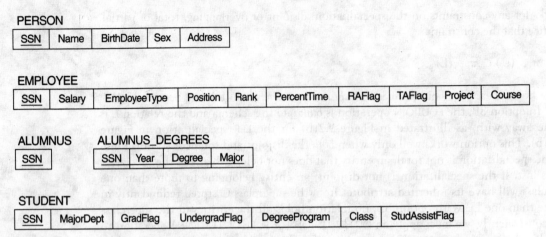

PERSON

SSN	Name	BirthDate	Sex	Address

EMPLOYEE

SSN	Salary	EmployeeType	Position	Rank	PercentTime	RAFlag	TAFlag	Project	Course

ALUMNUS   ALUMNUS_DEGREES

SSN

SSN	Year	Degree	Major

STUDENT

SSN	MajorDept	GradFlag	UndergradFlag	DegreeProgram	Class	StudAssistFlag

Figure 9.3   Mapping the EER specialization lattice shown in Figure 4.7 using multiple options.

9.2.2 Mapping of Shared Subclasses

A shared subclass, such as ENGINEERING_MANAGER of Figure 4.6, is a subclass of several super-classes. These classes must all have the same key attribute; otherwise, the shared subclass would be modeled as a category. We can apply any of the options discussed in step 8 to a shared subclass, although usually option 8A is used. In Figure 9.3, options 8C and 8D are used for the shared subclass STUDENT_ASSISTANT in EMPLOYEE and STUDENT, respectively.

9.2.3 Mapping of Categories

A category is a subclass of the *union* of two or more superclasses that can have different keys because they can be of different entity types. An example is the OWNER category shown in Figure 4.8, which is a subset of the union of three entity types PERSON, BANK, and COMPANY. The other category in that figure, REGISTERED_VEHICLE, has two superclasses that have the same key attribute.

For mapping a category whose defining superclasses have different keys, it is custom-ary to specify a new key attribute, called a **surrogate key,** when creating a relation to cor-respond to the category. This is because the keys of the defining classes are different, so we cannot use any one of them exclusively to identify all entities in the category. We can now create a relation schema OWNER to correspond to the OWNER category, as illustrated in Figure 9.4, and include any attributes of the category in this relation. The primary key of OWNER is the surrogate key OwnerId. We also add the surrogate key attribute OwnerId as foreign key to each relation corresponding to a superclass of the category, to specify the correspondence in values between the surrogate key and the key of each superclass.

For a category whose superclasses have the same key, such as VEHICLE in Figure 4.8, there is no need for a surrogate key. The mapping of the REGISTERED_VEHICLE category, which illustrates this case, is also shown in Figure 9.4.

The next three sections discuss some relational query languages that are important both theoretically and in practice.

PERSON

SSN	DriverLicenseNo	Name	Address	OwnerId

BANK

BName	BAddress	OwnerId

COMPANY

CName	CAddress	OwnerId

OWNER

OwnerId	OwnerType

REGISTERED_VEHICLE

VehicleId	LicensePlateNumber

CAR

VehicleId	CStyle	CMake	CModel	CYear

TRUCK

VehicleId	TMake	TModel	Tonnage	TYear

OWNS

OwnerId	VehicleId	PurchaseDate	LienOrRegular

Figure 9.4 Mapping the categories of Figure 4.8 to relations.

9.3 The Tuple Relational Calculus

Relational calculus is a formal query language where we write one **declarative** expression to specify a retrieval request and hence there is no description of how to evaluate a query; a calculus expression specifies *what* is to be retrieved rather than *how* to retrieve it. Therefore, the relational calculus is considered to be a **nonprocedural** language. This differs from relational algebra, where we must write a *sequence of operations* to specify a retrieval request; hence it can be considered as a **procedural** way of stating a query. It is possible to nest algebra operations to form a single expression; however, a certain order among the operations is always explicitly specified in a relational algebra expression. This order also influences the strategy for evaluating the query.

It has been shown that any retrieval that can be specified in the relational algebra can also be specified in the relational calculus, and vice versa; in other words, the **expressive power** of the two languages is *identical*. This has led to the definition of the concept of a relationally complete language. A relational query language L is considered **relationally complete** if we can express in L any query that can be expressed in relational calculus. Relational completeness has become an important basis for comparing the expressive power of high-level query languages. However, as we saw in Section 7.5, certain frequently required queries in database applications cannot be expressed in relational algebra or calculus. Most relational query languages are relationally complete but have *more expressive power* than relational algebra or relational calculus because of additional operations such as aggregate functions, grouping, and ordering. All our examples will again refer to the database shown in Figures 7.5 and 7.6. The queries are the same as those we presented in relational algebra in Chapter 7.

9.3.1   Tuple Variables and Range Relations

The tuple relational calculus is based on specifying a number of **tuple variables.** Each tuple variable usually **ranges over** a particular database relation, meaning that the variable may take as its value any individual tuple from that relation. A simple tuple relational calculus query is of the form

{t | COND(t)}

where t is a tuple variable and COND(t) is a conditional expression involving t. The result of such a query is the set of all tuples t that satisfy COND(t). For example, to find all employees whose salary is above $50,000, we can write the following tuple calculus expression:

{t | EMPLOYEE(t) **and** t.SALARY>50000}

The condition EMPLOYEE(t) specifies that the *range relation* of tuple variable t is EMPLOYEE. Each EMPLOYEE tuple t that satisfies the condition t.SALARY>50000 will be retrieved. Notice that t.SALARY references attribute SALARY of tuple variable t; this notation resembles how attribute names are qualified with relation names or aliases in SQL. In the notation of Chapter 7, t.SALARY is the same as writing t[SALARY].

The above query retrieves all attribute values for each selected EMPLOYEE tuple t. To retrieve only *some* of the attributes—say, the first and last names—we write

{t.FNAME, t.LNAME | EMPLOYEE(t) **and** t.SALARY>50000}

This is equivalent to the following SQL query:

SELECT   T.FNAME, T.LNAME
FROM   EMPLOYEE **AS** T
WHERE   T.SALARY>50000 ;

Informally, we need to specify the following information in a tuple calculus expression:

1. For each tuple variable t, the **range relation** R of t. This value is specified by a condition of the form R(t).

2. A condition to select particular combinations of tuples. As tuple variables range over their respective range relations, the condition is evaluated for every possible combination of tuples to identify the **selected combinations** for which the condition evaluates to TRUE.

3. A set of attributes to be retrieved, the **requested attributes.** The values of these attributes are retrieved for each selected combination of tuples.

Observe the correspondence of the preceding items to a simple SQL query: item 1 corresponds to the FROM-clause relation names; item 2 corresponds to the WHERE-clause condition; and item 3 corresponds to the SELECT-clause attribute list. Before we discuss the formal syntax of tuple relational calculus, consider another query we have seen before.

QUERY 0

Retrieve the birthdate and address of the employee (or employees) whose name is 'John B. Smith'.

QO : {t.BDATE, t.ADDRESS | EMPLOYEE(t) **and** t.FNAME='John' **and** t.MINIT='B' **and** t.LNAME='Smith'}

In tuple relational calculus, we first specify the requested attributes t.BDATE and t.ADDRESS for each selected tuple t. Then we specify the condition for selecting a tuple following the bar (|)—namely, that t be a tuple of the EMPLOYEE relation whose FNAME, MINIT, and LNAME attribute values are 'John', 'B', and 'Smith', respectively.

9.3.2   Expressions and Formulas in Tuple Relational Calculus

A general **expression** of the tuple relational calculus is of the form

$$\{t_1.A_1, t_2.A_2, \ldots, t_n.A_n \mid COND(t_1, t_2, \ldots, t_n, t_{n+1}, t_{n+2}, \ldots, t_{n+m})\}$$

where $t_1, t_2, \ldots, t_n, t_{n+1}, \ldots, t_{n+m}$ are tuple variables, each A_i is an attribute of the relation on which t_i ranges, and COND is a **condition** or **formula**[5] of the tuple relational calculus. A formula is made up of predicate calculus atoms, which can be one of the following:

1. An atom of the form $R(t_i)$, where R is a relation name and t_i is a tuple variable. This atom identifies the range of the tuple variable t_i as the relation whose name is R.

2. An atom of the form $t_i.A$ **op** $t_j.B$, where **op** is one of the comparison operators in the set $\{=, >, \geq, <, \leq, \neq\}$, t_i and t_j are tuple variables, A is an attribute of the relation on which t_i ranges, and B is an attribute of the relation on which t_j ranges.

3. An atom of the form $t_i.A$ **op** c or c **op** $t_j.B$, where **op** is one of the comparison operators in the set $\{=, >, \geq, <, \leq, \neq\}$, t_i and t_j are tuple variables, A is an attribute of the relation on which t_i ranges, B is an attribute of the relation on which t_j ranges, and c is a constant value.

---

5. Also called a **well-formed formula** or **wff** in mathematical logic.

Each of the preceding atoms evaluates to either TRUE or FALSE for a specific combination of tuples; this is called the **truth value** of an atom. In general, a tuple variable ranges over all possible tuples "in the universe." For atoms of type 1, if the tuple variable is assigned a tuple that is a *member of the specified relation* R, the atom is TRUE; otherwise it is FALSE. In atoms of types 2 and 3, if the tuple variables are assigned to tuples such that the values of the specified attributes of the tuples satisfy the condition, then the atom is TRUE.

A **formula** (condition) is made up of one or more atoms connected via the logical operators **and, or,** and **not** and is defined recursively as follows:

1. Every atom is a formula.

2. If F_1 and F_2 are formulas, then so are (F_1 **and** F_2), (F_1 **or** F_2), **not**(F_1), and **not** (F_2). The truth values of these four formulas are derived from their component formulas F_1 and F_2 as follows:

   a. (F_1 **and** F_2) is TRUE if both F_1 and F_2 are TRUE; otherwise, it is FALSE.
   b. (F_1 **or** F_2) is FALSE if both F_1 and F_2 are FALSE; otherwise it is TRUE.
   c. **not**(F_1) is TRUE if F_1 is FALSE; it is FALSE if F_1 is TRUE.
   d. **not**(F_2) is TRUE if F_2 is FALSE; it is FALSE if F_2 is TRUE.

9.3.3   The Existential and Universal Quantifiers

In addition, two special symbols called **quantifiers** can appear in formulas; these are the **universal quantifier** ($\forall$) and the existential quantifier ($\exists$). Truth values for formulas with quantifiers are described in 3 and 4 below; first, however, we need to define the concepts of free and bound tuple variables in a formula. Informally, a tuple variable t is bound if it is quantified, meaning that it appears in an ($\exists$ t) or ($\forall$ t) clause; otherwise, it is free. Formally, we define a tuple variable in a formula as **free** or **bound** according to the following rules:

- An occurrence of a tuple variable in a formula F that *is an atom* is free in F.
- An occurrence of a tuple variable t is free or bound in a formula made up of logical connectives—(F_1 **and** F_2), (F_1 **or** F_2), **not**(F_1), and **not**(F_2)—depending on whether it is free or bound in F_1 or F_2 (if it occurs in either). Notice that in a formula of the form F = (F_1 **and** F_2) or F = (F_1 **or** F_2), a tuple variable may be free in F_1 and bound in F_2, or vice versa. In this case, one occurrence of the tuple variable is bound and the other is free in F.
- All *free* occurrences of a tuple variable t in F are **bound** in a formula F' of the form F' = ($\exists$ t)(F) or F' = ($\forall$ t)(F). The tuple variable is bound to the quantifier specified in F'. For example, consider the formulas:

F_1 : d.DNAME='Research'

F_2 : ($\exists$t)(d.DNUMBER=t.DNO)

F_3 : ($\forall$d)(d.MGRSSN='333445555')

The tuple variable d is free in both F_1 and F_2, whereas it is bound to the universal quantifier in F_3. Variable t is bound to the ($\exists$) quantifier in F_2.

We can now give rules 3 and 4 for the definition of a formula we started earlier:

3. If F is a formula, then so is $(\exists t)(F)$, where t is a tuple variable. The formula $(\exists t)(F)$ is TRUE if the formula F evaluates to TRUE for *some* (at least one) tuple assigned to free occurrences of t in F; otherwise $(\exists t)(F)$ is FALSE.

4. If F is a formula, then so is $(\forall t)(F)$, where t is a tuple variable. The formula $(\forall t)(F)$ is TRUE if the formula F evaluates to TRUE for *every tuple* (in the universe) assigned to free occurrences of t in F; otherwise $(\forall t)(F)$ is FALSE.

The $(\exists)$ quantifier is called an existential quantifier because a formula $(\exists t)(F)$ is true if "there exists" some tuple that makes F TRUE. For the universal quantifier, $(\forall t)(F)$ is TRUE if every possible tuple that can be assigned to free occurrences of t in F is substituted for t, and F is TRUE for *every such substitution*. It is called the universal (or for all) quantifier because every tuple in "the universe of" tuples must make F TRUE to make the quantified formula TRUE.

9.3.4 Example Queries Using the Existential Quantifier

We will use some of the same queries shown in Chapter 7 to give a flavor of how the same queries are specified in relational algebra and in relational calculus. Notice that some queries are easier to specify in the relational algebra than in the relational calculus, and vice versa.

QUERY 1

Retrieve the name and address of all employees who work for the 'Research' department.

Q1 : {t.FNAME, t.LNAME, t.ADDRESS | EMPLOYEE(t) **and** $(\exists d)$
(DEPARTMENT(d) **and** d.DNAME='Research' **and** d.DNUMBER=t.DNO) }

The *only free tuple variables* in a relational calculus expression should be those that appear to the left of the bar (|). In Q1, t is the only free variable; it is then *bound successively* to each tuple. If a tuple *satisfies the conditions* specified in Q1, the attributes FNAME, LNAME, and ADDRESS are retrieved for each such tuple. The conditions EMPLOYEE(t) and DEPARTMENT(d) specify the range relations for t and d. The condition d.DNAME = 'Research' is a **selection condition** and corresponds to a SELECT operation in the relational algebra, whereas the condition d.DNUMBER = t.DNO is a **join condition** and serves a similar purpose to the JOIN operation (see Chapter 7).

QUERY 2

For every project located in 'Stafford', list the project number, the controlling department number, and the department manager's last name, birthdate, and address.

Q2 : {p.PNUMBER, p.DNUM, m.LNAME, m.BDATE, m.ADDRESS | PROJECT(p) and
EMPLOYEE(m) and p.PLOCATION='Stafford' and
((∃d)(DEPARTMENT(d) and p.DNUM=d.DNUMBER and
d.MGRSSN=m.SSN)) }

In Q2 there are two free tuple variables, p and m. Tuple variable d is bound to the existential quantifier. The query condition is evaluated for every combination of tuples assigned to p and m; and out of all possible combinations of tuples to which p and m are bound, only the combinations that satisfy the condition are selected.

Several tuple variables in a query can range over the same relation. For example, to specify the query Q8—for each employee, retrieve the employee's first and last name and the first and last name of his or her immediate supervisor—we specify two tuple variables e and s that both range over the EMPLOYEE relation:

Q8 : {e.FNAME, e.LNAME, s.FNAME, s.LNAME | EMPLOYEE(e) and EMPLOYEE(s) and
e.SUPERSSN=s.SSN}

QUERY 3'

Find the name of each employee who works on *some* project controlled by department number 5. This is a variation of query 3 in which "all" is changed to "some." In this case we need two join conditions and two existential quantifiers.

Q3' : {e.LNAME, e.FNAME | EMPLOYEE(e) and ((∃ x)(∃ w)

(PROJECT(x) and WORKS_ON(w) and x.DNUM=5 and w.ESSN=e.SSN and
x.PNUMBER=w.PNO)) }

QUERY 4

Make a list of project numbers for projects that involve an employee whose last name is 'Smith', either as a worker or as manager of the controlling department for the project.

Q4 : {p.PNUMBER | PROJECT(p) and
(((∃ e)(∃ w)(EMPLOYEE(e) and WORKS_ON(w) and
w.PNO=p.PNUMBER and e.LNAME='Smith' and e.SSN=w.ESSN))
or
((∃ m)(∃ d)(EMPLOYEE(m) and DEPARTMENT(d) and
p.DNUM=d.DNUMBER and d.MGRSSN=m.SSN and m.LNAME='Smith'))) }

Compare this with the relational algebra version of this query in Chapter 7. The UNION operation in relational algebra can usually be substituted with an **or** connective in relational calculus. In the next section we discuss the relationship between the universal and existential quantifiers and show how one can be transformed into the other.

9.3.5 Transforming the Universal and Existential Quantifiers

We now introduce some well-known transformations from mathematical logic that relate the universal and existential quantifiers. It is possible to transform a universal quantifier into an existential quantifier, and vice versa, and to get an equivalent expression. One general transformation can be described informally as follows: transform one type of quantifier into the other with negation (preceded by **not**); **and** and **or** replace one another; a negated formula becomes unnegated; and an unnegated formula becomes negated. Some special cases of this transformation can be stated as follows:

$(\forall x) (P(x)) \equiv$ **not** $(\exists x) ($**not** $(P(x)))$

$(\exists x) (P(x)) \equiv$ **not** $(\forall x) ($**not** $(P(x)))$

$(\forall x) (P(x)$ **and** $Q(x)) \equiv$ **not** $(\exists x) ($**not** $(P(x))$ **or not** $(Q(x)))$

$(\forall x) (P(x)$ **or** $Q(x)) \equiv$ **not** $(\exists x) ($**not** $(P(x))$ **and not** $(Q(x)))$

$(\exists x) (P(x))$ **or** $Q(x)) \equiv$ **not** $(\forall x) ($**not** $(P(x))$ **and not** $(Q(x)))$

$(\exists x) (P(x)$ **and** $Q(x)) \equiv$ **not** $(\forall x) ($**not** $(P(x))$ **or not** $(Q(x)))$

Notice also that the following is true, where the $\Rightarrow$ symbol stands for **implies**:

$(\forall x) (P(x)) \Rightarrow (\exists x) (P(x))$

not $(\exists x) (P(x)) \Rightarrow$ **not** $(\forall x) (P(x))$

9.3.6 Using the Universal Quantifier

Whenever we use a universal quantifier, it is quite judicious to follow a few rules to ensure that our expression makes sense. We discuss these rules with respect to Query 3.

QUERY 3

Find the names of employees who work on *all* the projects controlled by department number 5. One way of specifying this query is by using the universal quantifier as shown.

Q3 : {e.LNAME, e.FNAME | EMPLOYEE(e) **and** (($\forall$ x)(**not**(PROJECT(x)) **or not**(x.DNUM=5)
or (($\exists$ w)(WORKS_ON(w) **and** w.ESSN=e.SSN **and** x.PNUMBER=w.PNO)))) }

We can break up Q3 into its basic components as follows:

Q3 : {e.LNAME, e.FNAME | EMPLOYEE(e) **and** F' }

F' = (($\forall$ x)(**not**(PROJECT(x)) **or** F_1))

F_1 = **not** (x.DNUM=5) **or** F_2

F_2 = (($\exists$ w)(WORKS_ON(w) **and** w.ESSN = e.SSN **and** x.PNUMBER=w.PNO))

We want to make sure that a selected employee e works on *all the projects* controlled by department 5, but the definition of universal quantifier says that to make the quantified formula true, the inner formula must be true *for all tuples in the universe*. The trick is to exclude from the universal quantification all tuples that we are not interested in by making the condition TRUE *for all such tuples*. This is necessary because a universally quantified tuple variable, such as x in Q3, must evaluate to TRUE *for every possible tuple* assigned to it to make the quantified formula TRUE. The first tuples to exclude are those that are not in the relation R of interest. Then we exclude the tuples we are not interested in from R itself. Finally, we specify a condition F_2 that must hold on all the remaining tuples in R. Hence, we can explain Q3 as follows:

1. For the formula F' = ($\forall$ x)(F) to be TRUE, we must have the formula F be TRUE *for all tuples in the universe that can be assigned to x*. However, in Q3 we are only interested in F being TRUE for all tuples of the PROJECT relation that are controlled by department 5. Hence, the formula F is of the form (**not**(PROJECT(x)) **or** F_1). The '**not**(PROJECT(x)) **or** . . .' condition is TRUE for all tuples *not in the PROJECT relation* and has the effect of eliminating these tuples from consideration in the truth value of F_1. For every tuple in the project relation, F_1 must be TRUE if F' is to be TRUE.

2. Using the same line of reasoning, we do not want to consider tuples in the PROJECT relation that are not controlled by department number 5, since we are only interested in PROJECT tuples whose DNUM = 5. We can therefore write:

   if (x.DNUM=5) **then** F_2

   which is equivalent to

   (**not** (x.DNUM=5) **or** F_2)

   Formula F_1, hence, is of the form **not**(x.DNUM=5) **or** F_2. In the context of Q3, this means that, for a tuple x in the PROJECT relation, either its DNUM $\neq$ 5 or it must satisfy F_2.

3. Finally, F_2 gives the condition that we want to hold for a selected EMPLOYEE tuple: that the employee works on *every PROJECT tuple that has not been excluded yet*. Such employee tuples are selected by the query.

In English, Q3 gives the following condition for selecting an EMPLOYEE tuple e: for every tuple x in the PROJECT relation with x.DNUM = 5, there must exist a tuple w in WORKS_ON such that w.ESSN = e.SSN and w.PNO = x.PNUMBER. This is equivalent to saying that EMPLOYEE e works on every PROJECT x in DEPARTMENT number 5. (Whew!)

Using the general transformation from universal to existential quantifiers given in Section 9.3.5, we can rephrase the query in Q3 as shown in Q3A:

Q3A : {e.LNAME, e.FNAME | EMPLOYEE(e) **and** (**not** ($\exists$ x) (PROJECT(x) **and** (x.DNUM=5) **and**

(**not** ($\exists$ w)(WORKS_ON(w) **and** w.ESSN=e.SSN **and** x.PNUMBER=w.PNO)))))}

We now give some additional examples of queries that use quantifiers.

QUERY 6

Find the names of employees who have no dependents.

Q6 : {e.FNAME, e.LNAME | EMPLOYEE(e) and (not (∃d)(DEPENDENT(d) and e.SSN=d.ESSN))}

Using the general transformation rule, we can rephrase Q6 as follows:

Q6A : {e.FNAME, e.LNAME | EMPLOYEE(e) and ((∀ d) (not (DEPENDENT(d)) or not (e.SSN=d.ESSN)))}

QUERY 7

List the names of managers who have at least one dependent.

Q7 : {e.FNAME, e.LNAME | EMPLOYEE(e) and ((∃ d) (∃ p)
(DEPARTMENT(d) and DEPENDENT(p) and e.SSN=d.MGRSSN and
p.ESSN=e.SSN))}

The above query is handled by interpreting "managers who have at least one dependent" as "managers for whom there exists some dependent."

9.3.7 Safe Expressions

Whenever we use universal quantifiers, existential quantifiers, or negation of predicates in a calculus expression, we must make sure that the resulting expression makes sense. A **safe expression** in relational calculus is one that is guaranteed to yield a *finite number of tuples* as its result; otherwise, the expression is called **unsafe.** For example, the expression

{t | **not** (EMPLOYEE(t))}

is *unsafe* because it yields all tuples in the universe that are *not* EMPLOYEE tuples, which are infinitely numerous. If we follow the rules for Q3 discussed earlier, we will get a safe expression when using universal quantifiers. We can define safe expressions more precisely by introducing the concept of the *domain of a tuple relational calculus expression*: This is the set of all values that either appear as constant values in the expression or exist in any tuple of the relations referenced in the expression. The domain of {t | not(EMPLOYEE(t))} is the set of all attribute values appearing in some tuple of the EMPLOYEE relation (for any attribute). The domain of the expression Q3A would include all values appearing in EMPLOYEE, PROJECT, and WORKS_ON (unioned with the value 5 appearing in the query itself).

An expression is said to be **safe** if all values in its result are from the domain of the expression. Notice that the result of {t | **not**(EMPLOYEE(t))} is unsafe, since it will, in general, include tuples (and hence values) from outside the EMPLOYEE relation; such values are not in the domain of the expression. All of our other examples are safe expressions.

9.3.8 Quantifiers in SQL

The EXISTS function in SQL is similar to the existential quantifier of the relational calculus. When we write:

SELECT . . .

FROM . . .

WHERE EXISTS (SELECT *

                FROM   R AS X

                WHERE   P(X))

in SQL, it is equivalent to saying that a tuple variable X ranging over the relation R is existentially quantified. The nested query on which the EXISTS function is applied is normally correlated with the outer query; that is, the condition P(X) includes some attribute from the outer query relations. The WHERE condition of the outer query evaluates to TRUE if the nested query returns a nonempty result that contains one or more tuples.

SQL does not include a universal quantifier. Use of a negated existential quantifier **not** $(\exists\ x)$ by writing NOT EXISTS is how SQL supports universal quantification, as illustrated by Q3 in Chapter 8.

9.4 The Domain Relational Calculus

There is another type of relational calculus called the domain relational calculus, or simply, **domain calculus.** The language QBE that is related to domain calculus was developed almost concurrently with SQL at IBM Research, Yorktown Heights. The formal specification of the domain calculus was proposed after the development of the QBE system.

The domain calculus differs from the tuple calculus in the *type of variables* used in formulas: rather than having variables range over tuples, the variables range over single values from domains of attributes. To form a relation of degree n for a query result, we must have n of these **domain variables**—one for each attribute. An expression of the domain calculus is of the form

$$\{x_1, x_2, \ldots, x_n \mid COND(x_1, x_2, \ldots, x_n, x_{n+1}, x_{n+2}, \ldots, x_{n+m})\}$$

where $x_1, x_2, \ldots, x_n, x_{n+1}, x_{n+2}, \ldots, x_{n+m}$ are domain variables that range over domains (of attributes) and COND is a **condition** or **formula** of the domain relational calculus. A formula is made up of **atoms.** The atoms of a formula are slightly different from those for the tuple calculus and can be one of the following:

1. An atom of the form $R(x_1, x_2, \ldots, x_j)$, where R is the name of a relation of degree j and each x_i, $1 \leq i \leq j$, is a domain variable. This atom states that a list of values of $<x_1, x_2, \ldots, x_j>$ must be a tuple in the relation whose name is R, where x_i is the value of the ith attribute value of the tuple. To make a domain calculus expression more concise, we *drop the commas* in a list of variables; thus we write

   $$\{x_1, x_2, \ldots, x_n \mid R(x_1\ x_2\ x_3)\ \textbf{and}\ \ldots\}$$

instead of:

$$\{x_1, x_2, \ldots, x_n \mid R(x_1, x_2, x_3) \textbf{ and } \ldots\}$$

2. An atom of the form x_i **op** x_j, where **op** is one of the comparison operators in the set $\{=, >, \geq, <, \leq, \neq\}$ and x_i and x_j are domain variables.

3. An atom of the form x_i **op** c or c **op** x_j, where **op** is one of the comparison operators in the set $\{=, >, \geq, <, \leq, \neq\}$, x_i and x_j are domain variables, and c is a constant value.

As in tuple calculus, atoms evaluate to either TRUE or FALSE for a specific set of values, called the **truth values** of the atoms. In case 1, if the domain variables are assigned values corresponding to a tuple of the specified relation R, then the atom is TRUE. In cases 2 and 3, if the domain variables are assigned values that satisfy the condition, then the atom is TRUE.

In a similar way to the tuple relational calculus, formulas are made up of atoms, variables, and quantifiers, so we will not repeat the specifications for formulas here. Some examples of queries specified in the domain calculus follow. We will use lowercase letters l, m, n, ..., x, y, z for domain variables.

QUERY 0

Retrieve the birthdate and address of the employee whose name is 'John B. Smith'.

Q0 : $\{uv \mid (\exists q) (\exists r) (\exists s) (\exists t) (\exists w) (\exists x) (\exists y) (\exists z)$

(EMPLOYEE(qrstuvwxyz) **and** q='John' **and** r='B' **and** s='Smith')}

We need ten variables for the EMPLOYEE relation, one to range over the domain of each attribute in order. Of the ten variables q, r, s, ..., z, only u and v are free. We first specify the *requested attributes*, BDATE and ADDRESS, by the domain variables u for BDATE and v for ADDRESS. Then we specify the condition for selecting a tuple following the bar (|)—namely, that the sequence of values assigned to the variables qrstuvwxyz be a tuple of the EMPLOYEE relation and that the values for q (FNAME), r (MINIT), and s (LNAME) be 'John', 'B', and 'Smith', respectively. For convenience, we will quantify only those variables *actually appearing in a condition* (these would be q, r, and s in Q0) in the rest of our examples.

An alternative notation for writing this query is to assign the constants 'John', 'B', and 'Smith' directly as shown in Q0A, where all variables are free:

Q0A : $\{uv \mid$ EMPLOYEE('John','B','Smith',t,u,v,w,x,y,z) $\}$

QUERY 1

Retrieve the name and address of all employees who work for the 'Research' department.

Q1 : $\{qsv \mid (\exists z) (\exists l) (\exists m)$ (EMPLOYEE(qrstuvwxyz) **and**

DEPARTMENT(lmno) **and** l='Research' **and** m=z)}

A condition relating two domain variables that range over attributes from two relations, such as m = z in Q1, is a **join condition**; whereas a condition that relates a domain variable to a constant, such as l = 'Research', is a **selection condition.**

QUERY 2

For every project located in 'Stafford', list the project number, the controlling department number, and the department manager's last name, birthdate, and address.

Q2 : {iksuv | (∃ j) (∃ m)(∃ n) (∃ t)(PROJECT(hijk) **and** EMPLOYEE(qrstuvwxyz) **and** DEPARTMENT(lmno) **and** k=m **and** n=t **and** j='Stafford')}

QUERY 6

Find the names of employees who have no dependents.

Q6 : {qs | (∃ t) (EMPLOYEE(qrstuvwxyz) **and** (**not**(∃ l) (DEPENDENT(lmnop) **and** t=l)))}

Query 6 can be restated using universal quantifiers instead of the existential quantifiers, as shown in Q6A:

Q6A : {qs | (∃ t) (EMPLOYEE(qrstuvwxyz) **and** ((∀ l) (**not**(DEPENDENT(lmnop)) **or** **not**(t=l))))}

QUERY 7

List the names of managers who have at least one dependent.

Q7 : {sq | (∃ t) (∃ j) (∃ l)(EMPLOYEE(qrstuvwxyz) **and** DEPARTMENT(hijk) **and** DEPENDENT(lmnop) **and** t=j **and** l=t)}

As we mentioned earlier, it can be shown that any query that can be expressed in the relational algebra can also be expressed in the domain or tuple relational calculus. Also, any safe expression in the domain or tuple relational calculus can be expressed in the relational algebra.

9.5 Overview of the QBE Language

The Query-By-Example (QBE) language is important because it is one of the first graphical query languages with minimum syntax developed for database systems. It was developed at IBM Research and is available as an IBM commercial product as part of the QMF (Query Management Facility) interface option to DB2. The language was also implemented in the PARADOX DBMS, and is related to a point-and-click type interface in the ACCESS DBMS (see Chapter 10). It differs from SQL in that the user does not have to specify a structured query explicitly; rather, the query is formulated by filling in **templates** of relations that are displayed on a monitor screen. Figure 9.5 shows how these templates

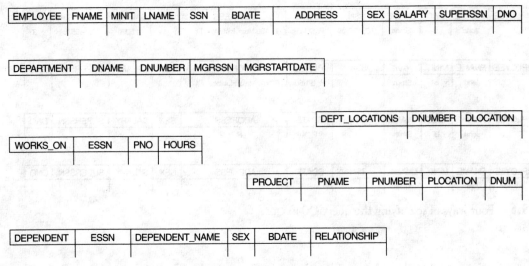

Figure 9.5   The relational schema of Figure 7.6 as it may be displayed by QBE.

may look for the database of Figure 7.6. The user does not have to remember the names of attributes or relations, because they are displayed as part of these templates. In addition, the user does not have to follow any rigid syntax rules for query specification; rather, constants and variables are entered in the columns of the templates to construct an **example** related to the retrieval or update request. QBE is related to the domain relational calculus, as we shall see, and its original specification has been shown to be relationally complete.

9.5.1 Basic Retrievals in QBE

In QBE, retrieval queries are specified by filling in one or more rows in the templates of the tables. For a single relation query, we enter either constants or **example elements** (a QBE term) in the columns of the template of that relation. An example element stands for a domain variable and is specified as an example value preceded by the underscore character (_). Additionally, a P. prefix (called the P dot operator) is entered in certain columns to indicate that we would like to print (or display) values in those columns for our result. The constants specify values that must be exactly matched in those columns.

For example, consider the query QO: "Retrieve the birthdate and address of John B. Smith." We show in Figures 9.6(a) through 9.6(d) how this query can be specified in a progressively more terse form in QBE. In Figure 9.6(a) an example of an employee is presented as the type of row that we are interested in. By leaving John B. Smith as constants in the FNAME, MINIT, and LNAME columns, we are specifying an exact match in those columns. All the rest of the columns are preceded by an underscore indicating that they are domain variables (example elements). The P. prefix is placed in the BDATE and ADDRESS columns to indicate that we would like to output value(s) in those columns.

(a)

EMPLOYEE	FNAME	MINIT	LNAME	SSN	BDATE	ADDRESS	SEX	SALARY	SUPERSSN	DNO
	John	B	Smith	_123456789	P._9/1/60	P._100 Main, Houston, TX	_M	_25000	_123456789	_3

(b)

EMPLOYEE	FNAME	MINIT	LNAME	SSN	BDATE	ADDRESS	SEX	SALARY	SUPERSSN	DNO
	John	B	Smith		P._9/1/60	P._100 Main, Houston, TX				

(c)

EMPLOYEE	FNAME	MINIT	LNAME	SSN	BDATE	ADDRESS	SEX	SALARY	SUPERSSN	DNO
	John	B	Smith		P._X	P._Y				

(d)

EMPLOYEE	FNAME	MINIT	LNAME	SSN	BDATE	ADDRESS	SEX	SALARY	SUPERSSN	DNO
	John	B	Smith		P.	P.				

Figure 9.6   Four ways of specifying the query Q0 in QBE.

Q0 can be abbreviated as shown in Figure 9.6(b). There is no need to specify example values for columns in which we are not interested. Moreover, because example values are completely arbitrary, we can just specify variable names for them, as shown in Figure 9.6(c). Finally, we can also leave out the example values entirely, as shown in Figure 9.6(d), and just specify a P. under the columns to be retrieved.

To see how retrieval queries in QBE are similar to the domain relational calculus, compare Figure 9.6(d) with Q0 (simplified) in domain calculus, which is as follows:

Q0 : { uv | EMPLOYEE(qrstuvwxyz) **and** q='John' **and** r='B' **and** s='Smith'}

We can think of each column in a QBE template as an *implicit domain variable*; hence, FNAME corresponds to the domain variable q, MINIT corresponds to r, . . ., and DNO corresponds to z. In the QBE query, the columns with P. correspond to variables specified to the left of the bar in domain calculus, whereas the columns with constant values correspond to tuple variables with equality selection conditions on them. The condition EMPLOYEE(qrstuvwxyz) and the existential quantifiers are implicit in the QBE query because the template corresponding to the EMPLOYEE relation is used.

In QBE, the user interface first allows the user to choose the tables (relations) needed to formulate a query by displaying a list of all relation names. The templates for the chosen relations are then displayed. The user moves to the appropriate columns in the templates and specifies the query. Special function keys were provided to move among templates and perform certain functions.

We now give examples to illustrate basic facilities of QBE. Comparison operators other than = (such as > or ≥) may be entered in a column before typing a constant value. For example, the query Q0A: "List the social security numbers of employees who work more than 20 hours per week on project number 1," can be specified as shown in Figure 9.7(a). For more complex conditions, the user can ask for a **condition box,** which is created by pressing a particular function key. The user can then type the complex condi-

(a)

WORKS_ON	ESSN	PNO	HOURS
	P.		>20

(b)

WORKS_ON	ESSN	PNO	HOURS
	P.	_PX	_HX

CONDITIONS

_HX>20 AND (_PX = 1 OR _PX = 2)

(c)

WORKS_ON	ESSN	PNO	HOURS
	P.	1	>20
	P.	2	>20

Figure 9.7 Specifying complex conditions in QBE. (a) The same query Q0A. (b) The query Q0B with a condition box. (c) The query Q0B without a condition box.

tion.[6] For example, the query Q0B—"List the social security numbers of employees who work more than 20 hours per week on either project 1 or project 2"—can be specified as shown in Figure 9.7(b).

Some complex conditions can be specified without a condition box. The rule is that all conditions specified on the same row of a relation template are connected by the **and** logical connective (*all* must be satisfied by a selected tuple), whereas conditions specified on distinct rows are connected by **or** (*at least one* must be satisfied). Hence, Q0B can also be specified, as shown in Figure 9.7(c), by entering two distinct rows in the template.

Now consider query Q0C: "List the social security numbers of employees who work on *both* project 1 and project 2"; this cannot be specified as in Figure 9.8(a), which lists those who work on *either* project 1 or project 2. The example variable _ES will bind itself to ESSN values in <−, 1, −> tuples *as well as* to those in <−, 2, −> tuples. Figure 9.8(b) shows how to specify Q0C correctly, where the condition (_EX = _EY) in the box makes the _EX and _EY variables bind only to identical ESSN values.

In general, once a query is specified, the resulting values are displayed in the template under the appropriate columns. If the result contains more rows than can be displayed on the screen, most QBE implementations have function keys to allow scrolling up and down

---

6. Negation with the ¬ symbol is *not* allowed in a condition box.

(a)

WORKS_ON	ESSN	PNO	HOURS
	P._ES	1	
	P._ES	2	

(b)

WORKS_ON	ESSN	PNO	HOURS
	P._EX	1	
	P._EY	2	

CONDITIONS

_EX = _EY

Figure 9.8   Specifying EMPLOYEES who work on both projects. (a) Incorrect specification of an AND condition. (b) Correct specification.

the rows. Similarly, if a template or several templates are too wide to appear on the
screen, it is possible to scroll sideways to examine all the templates.

A join operation is specified in QBE by using the *same variable*[7] in the columns to be
joined. For example, the query Q1: "List the name and address of all employees who work
for the 'Research' department," can be specified as shown in Figure 9.9(a). Any number of
joins can be specified in a single query. We can also specify a **result table** to display the
result of the join query, as shown in Figure 9.9(a); this is needed if the result includes
attributes from two or more relations. If no result table is specified, the system provides
the query result in the columns of the various relations, which may make it difficult to
interpret. Figure 9.9(a) also illustrates the feature of QBE for specifying that all attributes
of a relation should be retrieved, by placing the P. operator under the relation name in the
relation template.

To join a table with itself, we specify different variables to represent the different references to the table. For example, query Q8—"For each employee retrieve the employee's
first and last name as well as the first and last name of his or her immediate supervisor"—
can be specified as shown in Figure 9.9(b), where the variables starting with E refer to an
employee and those starting with S refer to a supervisor.

9.5.2   Grouping, Aggregation, and Database Modification in QBE

Next, consider the types of queries that require grouping or aggregate functions. A grouping operator G. can be specified in a column to indicate that tuples should be grouped by

---

7. A variable is called an **example element** in QBE manuals.

Figure 9.9   Illustrating JOIN and result relations in QBE. (a) The query Q1. (b) The query Q8.

the value of that column. Common functions can be specified, such as AVG., SUM., CNT. (count), MAX., and MIN. In QBE the functions AVG., SUM., and CNT. are applied to distinct values within a group in the default case. If we want these functions to apply to all values, we must use the prefix ALL.[8] This convention is *different* in SQL, where the default is to apply a function to all values.

Figure 9.10(a) shows query Q23, which counts the number of *distinct* salary values in the EMPLOYEE relation. Query Q23A (Figure 9.10b) counts all salary values, which is the same as counting the number of employees. Figure 9.10(c) shows Q24, which retrieves each department number and the number of employees and average salary within each department; hence, the DNO column is used for grouping as indicated by the G. function. Several of the operators G., P., and ALL can be specified in a single column. Figure 9.10(d) shows query Q26, which displays each project name and the number of employees working on it for projects on which more than two employees work.

QBE has a negation symbol, ¬, which is used in a manner similar to the NOT EXISTS function in SQL. Figure 9.11 shows query Q6, which lists the names of employees who have no dependents. The negation symbol ¬ says that we will select values of the _SX variable from the EMPLOYEE relation only if they do not occur in the DEPENDENT relation. The same effect can be produced by placing a ¬ _SX in the ESSN column.

Although the QBE language as originally proposed was shown to support the equivalent of the EXISTS and NOT EXISTS functions of SQL, the QBE implementation in QMF (under the DB2 system) does *not* provide this support. Hence, the QMF version of QBE, which we discuss here, is *not relationally complete*. Queries such as Q3—"Find employees who work on *all* projects controlled by department 5"—*cannot* be specified.

---

8. ALL in QBE is unrelated to the universal quantifier.

(a) EMPLOYEE	FNAME	MINIT	LNAME	SSN	BDATE	ADDRESS	SEX	SALARY	SUPERSSN	DNO
								P.CNT.		

(b) EMPLOYEE	FNAME	MINIT	LNAME	SSN	BDATE	ADDRESS	SEX	SALARY	SUPERSSN	DNO
								P.CNT.ALL		

(c) EMPLOYEE	FNAME	MINIT	LNAME	SSN	BDATE	ADDRESS	SEX	SALARY	SUPERSSN	DNO
				P.CNT.ALL				P.AVG.ALL		P.G.

(d) PROJECT	PNAME	PNUMBER	PLOCATION	DNUM
	P.	_PX		

WORKS_ON	ESSN	PNO	HOURS
	P.CNT._EX	G._PX	

CONDITIONS

CNT._EX>2

Figure 9.10   Functions and grouping in QBE. (a) The query Q23. (b) The query Q23A. (c) The query Q24. (d) The query Q26.

EMPLOYEE	FNAME	MINIT	LNAME	SSN	BDATE	ADDRESS	SEX	SALARY	SUPERSSN	DNO
	P.		P.	_SX						

DEPENDENT	ESSN	DEPENDENT_NAME	SEX	BDATE	RELATIONSHIP
¬	_SX				

Figure 9.11   Illustrating negation by the query Q6.

There are three QBE operators for modifying the database: I. for insert, D. for delete, and U. for update. The insert and delete operators are specified in the template column under the relation name, whereas the update operator is specified under the columns to be updated. Figure 9.12(a) shows how to insert a new EMPLOYEE tuple. For deletion, we first enter the D. operator and then specify the tuples to be deleted by a condition (Figure 9.12b). To update a tuple, we specify the U. operator under the attribute name, followed by the new value of the attribute. We should also select the tuple or tuples to be updated in the usual way. Figure 9.12(c) shows an update request to increase the salary of 'John Smith' by 10 percent and also to reassign him to department number 4.

QBE also has data definition capabilities. The tables of a database can be specified interactively, and a table definition can also be updated by adding, renaming, or removing a column. We can also specify various characteristics for each column, such as whether it is a key of the relation, what its data type is, and whether an index should be created on

(a)	EMPLOYEE	FNAME	MINIT	LNAME	SSN	BDATE	ADDRESS	SEX	SALARY	SUPERSSN	DNO
	I.	Richard	K	Marini	653298653	30-DEC-52	98 Oak Forest, Katy, TX	M	37000	987654321	4

(b)	EMPLOYEE	FNAME	MINIT	LNAME	SSN	BDATE	ADDRESS	SEX	SALARY	SUPERSSN	DNO
	D.				653298653						

(c)	EMPLOYEE	FNAME	MINIT	LNAME	SSN	BDATE	ADDRESS	SEX	SALARY	SUPERSSN	DNO
		John		Smith					U._S*1.1		U.4

Figure 9.12 Modifying the database in QBE. (a) Insertion. (b) Deletion. (c) Update in QBE.

that field. QBE also has facilities for view definition, authorization, storing query definitions for later use, and so on.

QBE does not use the "linear" style of SQL; rather, it is a "two-dimensional" language, because users specify a query moving around the full area of the screen. Tests on users have shown that QBE is easier to learn than SQL, especially for nonspecialists. In this sense, QBE was the first user-friendly "visual" relational database language.

More recently, numerous other user-friendly interfaces have been developed for commercial database systems. The use of menus, graphics, and forms is now becoming quite common. Visual query languages, which are still not so common, are likely to be offered with commercial relational databases in the future.

9.6 Summary

This chapter covered two topics that are not directly related: relational schema design by ER-to-relational mapping and other relational languages. The reason they were grouped in one chapter is to conclude our conceptual coverage of the relational model. In Section 9.1, we showed how a conceptual schema design in the ER model can be mapped to a relational database schema. An algorithm for ER-to-relational mapping was given and illustrated by examples from the COMPANY database. Table 9.1 summarized the correspondences between the ER and relational model constructs and constraints. We then showed additional steps for mapping the constructs from the EER model into the relational model.

We then presented the basic concepts behind relational calculus, a declarative formal query language for the relational model, which is based on the branch of mathematical logic called predicate calculus. There are two types of relational calculi: (1) the tuple relational calculus, which uses tuple variables that range over tuples (rows) of relations, and (2) the domain relational calculus, which uses domain variables that range over domains (columns of relations).

In relational calculus, a query is specified in a single declarative statement, without specifying any order or method for retrieving the query result. In contrast, a relational algebra expression implicitly specifies a sequence of operations with an ordering to retrieve the result of a query. Hence, relational calculus is often considered to be a higher-level language than the relational algebra because a relational calculus expression states *what* we want to retrieve regardless of *how* the query may be executed.

We discussed the syntax of relational calculus queries using both tuple and domain variables. We also discussed the existential quantifier ($\exists$) and the universal quantifier ($\forall$). We saw that relational calculus variables are bound by these quantifiers. We saw in detail how queries with universal quantification are written, and we discussed the problem of specifying safe queries whose results are finite. We also discussed rules for transforming universal into existential quantifiers, and vice versa. It is the quantifiers that give expressive power to the relational calculus, making it equivalent to relational algebra.

The SQL language, described in Chapter 8, has its roots in the tuple relational calculus. A SELECT–PROJECT–JOIN query in SQL is similar to a tuple relational calculus expression, if we consider each relation name in the FROM clause of the SQL query to be a tuple variable with an implicit existential quantifier. The EXISTS function in SQL is equivalent to the existential quantifier and can be used in its negated form (NOT EXISTS) to specify universal quantification. There is no explicit equivalent of a universal quantifier in SQL. There is no analog to grouping and aggregation functions in relational calculus.

We then gave an overview of the QBE language, which is the first graphical query language with minimal syntax and is based on the domain relational calculus. We discussed it with several examples.

Review Questions

9.1. Discuss the correspondences between the ER model constructs and the relational model constructs. Show how each ER model construct can be mapped to the relational model, and discuss any alternative mappings. Discuss the options for mapping EER model constructs.

9.2. In what sense does relational calculus differ from relational algebra, and in what sense are they similar?

9.3. How does tuple relational calculus differ from domain relational calculus?

9.4. Discuss the meanings of the existential quantifier ($\exists$) and the universal quantifier ($\forall$).

9.5. Define the following terms with respect to the tuple calculus: *tuple variable*, *range relation*, *atom*, *formula*, *expression*.

9.6. Define the following terms with respect to the domain calculus: *domain variable*, *range relation*, *atom*, *formula*, *expression*.

9.7. What is meant by a *safe expression* in relational calculus?

9.8. When is a query language called relationally complete?

9.9. Why must the insert I. and delete D. operators of QBE appear under the relation name in a relation template, not under a column name?

9.10. Why must the update U. operators of QBE appear under a column name in a relation template, not under the relation name?

Exercises

9.11. Try to map the relational schema of Figure 7.20 into an ER schema. This is part of a process known as *reverse engineering*, where a conceptual schema is created for an existing implemented database. State any assumption you make.

9.12. Figure 9.13 shows an ER schema for a database that may be used to keep track of transport ships and their locations for maritime authorities. Map this schema into a relational schema, and specify all primary keys and foreign keys.

9.13. Map the BANK ER schema of Exercise 3.23 (shown in Figure 3.17) into a relational schema. Specify all primary keys and foreign keys. Repeat for the AIRLINE schema (Figure 3.16) of Exercise 3.19 and for the other schemas for Exercises 3.16 through 3.24.

9.14. Specify queries a, b, c, e, f, i, and j of Exercise 7.18 in both the tuple relational calculus and the domain relational calculus.

9.15. Specify queries a, b, c, and d of Exercise 7.20 in both the tuple relational calculus and the domain relational calculus.

9.16. Specify queries of Exercise 8.16 in both the tuple relational calculus and the domain relational calculus. Also specify these queries in the relational algebra.

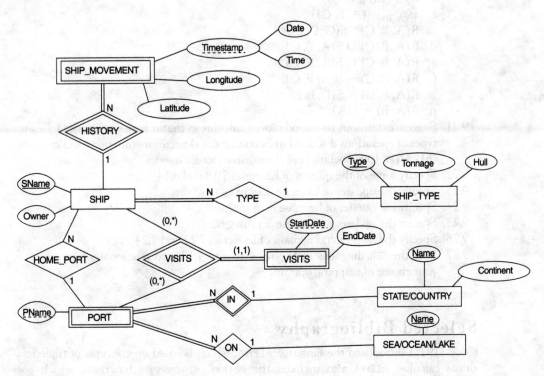

Figure 9.13   An ER schema for a SHIP_TRACKING database.

9.17. In a tuple relational calculus query with n tuple variables, what would be the typical minimum number of join conditions? Why? What is the effect of having a smaller number of join conditions?

9.18. Rewrite the domain relational calculus queries that followed Q0 in Section 9.5 in the style of the abbreviated notation of Q0A, where the objective is to minimize the number of domain variables by writing constants in place of variables wherever possible.

9.19. Consider this query: Retrieve the SSNs of employees who work on at least those projects on which the employee with SSN = 123456789 works. This may be stated as (FORALL x) (IF P THEN Q), where

- x is a tuple variable that ranges over the PROJECT relation.
- P ≡ employee with SSN = 123456789 works on project x.
- Q ≡ employee e works on project x.

Express the query in tuple relational calculus, using the rules

- $(\forall x)(P(x)) \equiv not(\exists x)(not(P(x)))$.
- (IF P THEN Q) ≡ (not(P) or Q).

9.20. Show how you may specify the following relational algebra operations in both tuple and domain relational calculus.

a. $\sigma_{A=C}(R(A, B, C))$.
b. $\pi_{<A, B>}(R(A, B, C))$.
c. $R(A, B, C) * S(C, D, E)$.
d. $R(A, B, C) \cup S(A, B, C)$.
e. $R(A, B, C) \cap S(A, B, C)$.
f. $R(A, B, C) - S(A, B, C)$.
g. $R(A, B, C) \times S(D, E, F)$.
h. $R(A, B) \div S(A)$.

9.21. Suggest extensions to the relational calculus so that it may express the following types of operations discussed in Section 6.6: (a) aggregate functions and grouping; (b) OUTER JOIN operations; (c) recursive closure queries.

9.22. Specify some of the queries of Exercises 7.18 and 8.14 in QBE.

9.23. Specify the updates of Exercise 7.19 in QBE.

9.24. Specify the queries of Exercise 8.16 in QBE.

9.25. Specify the updates of Exercise 8.17 in QBE.

9.26. Specify the queries and updates of Exercises 7.23 and 7.24 in QBE.

9.27. Map the EER diagrams in Figures 4.10 and 4.17 into relational schemas. Justify your choice of mapping options.

Selected Bibliography

Codd (1971) introduced the language ALPHA, which is based on concepts of tuple relational calculus. ALPHA also includes the notion of aggregate functions, which goes beyond relational calculus. The original formal definition of relational calculus was given by Codd (1972), which also provided an algorithm that transforms any tuple relational calculus expression to relational algebra. Codd defined relational completeness of a query language to mean at least as powerful as relational calculus. Ullman (1988) describes a formal proof of the equivalence of relational algebra with the safe expressions of tuple and domain relational calculus. Abiteboul et al. (1995) and Atzeni and deAntonellis (1993) give a detailed treatment of formal relational languages.

Although ideas of domain relational calculus were initially proposed in the QBE language (Zloof 1975), the concept was formally defined by Lacroix and Pirotte (1977). The experimental version of the Query-By-Example system is described in (Zloof 1977). The ILL language (Lacroix and Pirotte 1977a) is based on domain relational calculus. Whang et al. (1990) extends QBE with universal quantifiers. The QUEL language (Stonebraker et al. 1976) is based on tuple relational calculus, with implicit existential quantifiers but no universal quantifiers, and was implemented in the INGRES system. Thomas and Gould (1975) report the results of experiments comparing the ease of use of QBE to SQL. The commercial QBE functions are described in an IBM manual (1978), and a quick reference card is available (IBM 1978a). Appropriate DB2 reference manuals discuss the QBE implementation for that system. Visual query languages of which QBE is an example are being proposed as a means of querying databases; conferences such as the Visual Database Systems Workshop (e.g., Spaccapietra and Jain 1995) have a number of proposals for such languages.

CHAPTER 10

Examples of Relational Database Management Systems: Oracle and Microsoft Access

In this chapter we turn our attention to the implementation of the relational data model in commercial systems. Because the relational database management system (RDBMS) family encompasses such a large number of products, we cannot within the scope of this book compare the features or evaluate all of them; rather, we focus in depth on two representative systems: Oracle, which is representative of the larger products that originated from mainframe computers, and Microsoft Access, a product that is appealing to the PC platform user. Our goal here will be to show how these products have a similar set of RDBMS features and functionality yet have different ways of packaging and offering them.

Section 10.1 presents a historical overview of the development of RDBMSs, and Sections 10.2 through 10.5 describe the Oracle RDBMS. Section 10.2 describes the architecture and main functions of the Oracle system. The data modeling in terms of schema objects, the languages, and the facilities of methods and triggers are presented in Section 10.3. Section 10.4 describes how Oracle organizes storage in the system. Section 10.5 presents some examples of programming in Oracle. Section 10.6 presents an overview of the tools available in Oracle for database design and application development. Later in the book we will discuss the distributed version of Oracle (Section 24.6) and in Chapter 13 we will highlight the object-relational features in Oracle 8, which extend Oracle with object-oriented features.

The Microsoft Access product presently comes bundled with Office 97 to be used on Windows and Windows NT machines. In Section 10.7 we give an overview of Microsoft Access including data definition and manipulation, and its graphic interactive facilities for ease of querying. Section 10.8 gives a summary of the features and functionality of Access related to forms, reports, and macros and briefly discusses some additional facilities available in Access.

10.1   Relational Database Management Systems: A Historical Perspective

After the relational model was introduced in 1970, there was a flurry of experimentation with relational ideas. A major research and development effort was initiated at IBM's San Jose (now called Almaden) Research Center. It led to the announcement of two commercial relational DBMS products by IBM in the 1980s: SQL/DS for DOS/VSE (disk operating system/virtual storage extended) and for VM/CMS (virtual machine/conversational monitoring system) environments, introduced in 1981; and DB2 for the MVS operating system, introduced in 1983. Another relational DBMS, INGRES, was developed at the University of California, Berkeley, in the early 1970s and commercialized by Relational Technology, Inc., in the late 1970s. INGRES became a commercial RDBMS marketed by Ingres, Inc., a subsidiary of ASK, Inc., and is presently marketed by Computer Associates. Other popular commercial RDBMSs include Oracle of Oracle, Inc.; Sybase of Sybase, Inc.; RDB of Digital Equipment Corp, now owned by Compaq; INFORMIX of Informix, Inc.; and UNIFY of Unify, Inc.

Besides the RDBMSs mentioned above, many implementations of the relational data model appeared on the personal computer (PC) platform in the 1980s. These include RIM, RBASE 5000, PARADOX, OS/2 Database Manager, DBase IV, XDB, WATCOM SQL, SQL Server (of Sybase, Inc.), SQL Server (of Microsoft), and most recently Access (also of Microsoft, Inc.). They were initially single-user systems, but more recently they have started offering the client/server database architecture (see Chapters 17 and 24) and are becoming compliant with Microsoft's *Open Database Connectivity* (ODBC), a standard that permits the use of many front-end tools with these systems.

The word *relational* is also used somewhat inappropriately by several vendors to refer to their products as a marketing gimmick. To qualify as a genuine relational DBMS, a system must have at least the following properties:[1]

1. It must store data as relations such that each column is independently identified by its column name and the ordering of rows is immaterial.

2. The operations available to the user, as well as those used internally by the system, should be true relational operations; that is, they should be able to generate new relations from old relations.

3. The system must support at least one variant of the JOIN operation.

---

1. Codd (1985) specified 12 rules for determining whether a DBMS is relational. Codd (1990) presents a treatise on extended relational models and systems, identifying more than 330 features of relational systems, divided into 18 categories.

Although we could add to the above list, we propose these criteria as a very minimal set for testing whether a system is relational. It is easy to see that some of the so-called relational DBMSs do not satisfy these criteria.

We begin with a description of Oracle, currently one of the more widely used RDBMSs. Because some concepts in the discussion may not have been introduced yet, we will give references to later chapters in the book when necessary. Those interested in getting a deeper understanding may review the appropriate concepts in those sections and should refer to the system manuals.

10.2 The Basic Structure of the Oracle System

Traditionally, RDBMS vendors have chosen to use their own terminology in describing products in their documentation. In this section we will thus describe the organization of the Oracle system in its own nomenclature. We will try to relate this terminology to our own wherever possible. It is interesting to see how the RDBMS vendors have designed software packages that basically follow the relational model yet offer a whole variety of features needed to accomplish the design and implementation of large databases and their applications.

An **Oracle server** consists of an **Oracle database**—the collection of stored data, including log and control files—and the **Oracle Instance**—the processes, including Oracle (system) processes and user processes taken together, created for a specific instance of the database operation. Oracle server supports SQL to define and manipulate data. In addition, it has a procedural language—called PL/SQL—to control the flow of SQL, to use variables, and to provide error-handling procedures. Oracle can also be accessed through general purpose programming languages such as C or JAVA.

10.2.1 Oracle Database Structure

The Oracle database has two primary structures: (1) a *physical structure*—referring to the actual stored data—and (2) a *logical structure*—corresponding to an abstract representation of the stored data, which roughly corresponds to the conceptual schema of the database.[2] The database contains the following types of files:

- One or more *data files*; these contain the actual data.
- Two or more log files called *redo log files* (see Chapter 21 on database recovery); these record all changes made to data and are used in the process of recovering, if certain changes do not get written to permanent storage.

---

2. Some of the discussion in this section uses terms that have not been introduced yet. They are essential for a discussion of the complete architecture of Oracle. Readers may refer to the appropriate chapters where these terms are defined and explained.

- One or more *control files*; these contain control information such as database name, file names and locations, and a database creation timestamp. This file is also needed for recovery purposes.
- *Trace files* and an *alert log*; background processes have a trace file associated with them and the alert log maintains major database events (see Chapter 23 on active databases).

Both the log file and control files may be multiplexed—that is, multiple copies may be written to multiple devices.

The structure of an Oracle database consists of the definition of the database in terms of **schema objects** and one or more **tablespaces.** The schema objects contain definitions of tables, views, sequences, stored procedures, indexes, clusters, and database links. Tablespaces, segments, and extents are the terms used to describe *physical storage structures*; they govern how the physical space of the database is used (see Section 10.4).

Oracle Instance.   As we described earlier, the set of processes that constitute an instance of the server's operation is called an Oracle Instance, which consists of a System Global Area and a set of background processes. Figure 10.1 is a standard architecture diagram for Oracle, showing a number of user processes in the foreground and an Oracle process in the background. It has the following components:

- *System global area* (SGA): This area of memory is used for database information shared by users. Oracle assigns an SGA area when an instance starts. For optimal performance, the SGA is generally made as large as possible, while still fitting in real memory. The SGA in turn is divided into several types of memory structures:

  1. *Database buffer cache:* This keeps the most recently accessed data blocks from the database. By keeping most frequently accessed data blocks in this cache, the disk I/O activity can be significantly reduced.
  2. Redo log buffer, which is the buffer for the redo log file and is used for recovery purposes.
  3. Shared pool, which contains shared memory constructs; these include shared SQL areas, which contain parse trees of SQL queries and execution plans for executing SQL statements (see Chapter 18).

- *User processes:* Each user process corresponds to the execution of some application (for example, an Oracle Forms application) or some tool.
- *Program global area* (PGA) (not shown in Figure 10.1): This is a memory buffer that contains data and control information for a server process. A PGA is created by Oracle when a server process is started.
- *Oracle processes:* A process (sometimes called a job or task) is a "thread of control" or a mechanism in an operating system that can execute a series of steps. A process has its own private memory area where it runs. Oracle processes are divided into server processes and background processes. We review the types of Oracle processes and their specific functions next.

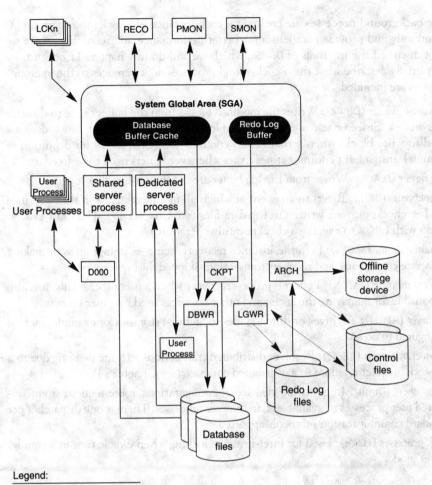

Legend:

LCKn   Lock process
RECO   Recoverer process
PMON   Process monitor
SMON   System monitor
CKPT   Checkpoint
ARCH   Archiver
DBWR   Database writer
LGWR   Log writer

Figure 10.1 An Oracle instance. (From Oracle (1997a).)

10.2.2 Oracle Processes

Oracle creates **server processes** to handle requests from connected user processes. In a *dedicated server configuration*, a server process handles requests for a single user process. A more efficient alternative is a *multithreaded server configuration*, in which many user processes share a small number of server processes.

The **background processes** are created for each instance of Oracle; they perform I/O asynchronously and provide parallelism for better performance and reliability. Since we have not discussed the internals of DBMSs, which we will do in Chapters 17 onward, we can only briefly describe what these background processes do; references to the appropriate chapters are included.

- *Database Writer (DBWR)*: Writes the modified blocks from the buffer cache to the data files on disk. Since Oracle uses write-ahead logging (see Chapter 21), DBWR does *not* need to write blocks when a transaction commits (see Chapter 19 for definition of commit). Instead, it performs *batched writes* whenever buffers need to be freed up.

- *Log writer (LGWR)*: Writes from the log buffer area to the on-line disk log file.

- *Checkpoint (CKPT)*: Refers to an event at which all modified buffers in the SGA since the last checkpoint are written to the data files (see Chapter 19). The CKPT process works with DBWR to execute a checkpointing operation.

- *System monitor (SMON)*: Performs instance recovery, manages storage areas by making the space contiguous, and recovers transactions skipped during recovery.

- *Process monitor (PMON)*: Performs process recovery when a user process fails. It is also responsible for managing the cache and other resources used by a user process.

- *Archiver (ARCH)*: Archives on-line log files to archival storage (for example, tape) if configured to do so.

- *Recoverer process (RECO)*: Resolves distributed transactions that are pending due to a network or systems failure in a distributed database (see Chapter 24).

- *Dispatchers (Dnnn)*: In multithreaded server configurations, route requests from connected user processes to available shared server processes. There is one dispatcher per standard communication protocol supported.

- *Lock processes (LCKn)*: Used for inter-instance locking when Oracle runs in a parallel server mode.

10.2.3   Oracle Startup and Shutdown

An Oracle database is not available to users until the Oracle server has been started up and the database has been opened. Starting a database and making it available system wide requires the following steps:

1. **Starting an instance of the database:** The SGA is allocated and background processes are created in this step. A parameter file controlling the size of the SGA, the name of the database to which the instance can connect, etc., are set up to govern the initialization of the instance.

2. **Mounting a database:** This associates a previously started Oracle instance with a database. Until then it is available only to administrators. Multiple instances of Oracle may mount the same database concurrently. The database administrator chooses whether to run the database in exclusive or parallel mode. When an Oracle instance mounts a database in an *exclusive mode*, only that instance can access the database. On the other hand, if the instance is started in a *parallel or shared mode*, other instances that are started in parallel mode can also mount the database.

3. *Opening a database:* This is a database administration activity. Opening a mounted database makes it available for normal database operations by having Oracle open the on-line data files and log files.

The reverse of the above operations will shut down an Oracle instance as follows:

1. Close the database.

2. Dismount the database.

3. Shut down the Oracle instance.

The parameter file that governs the creation of an Oracle instance contains parameters of the following types:

- Parameters that name things (for example, name of database, name and location of database's control files, names of private rollback segments[3]).

- Parameters that set limits such as maximums (for example, maximum allowable size for SGA, maximum buffer size).

- Parameters that affect capacity, called *variable parameters* (for example, the DB_BLOCK_BUFFERS parameter sets the number of data blocks to allocate in the SGA).

The database administrator may vary the parameters as part of continuous database monitoring and maintenance.

10.3 Database Structure and Its Manipulation in Oracle

Oracle was designed originally as a relational database management system (RDBMS). Starting with version 8 of the product, Oracle is being positioned as an object-relational database management system (ORDBMS). Our goal here is to review the features of Oracle including its relational and object-relational modeling facilities.[4] The main differences between Oracle 8 and the previous versions of Oracle are highlighted in Section 10.6.

10.3.1 Schema Objects

In Oracle, the term *schema* refers to a collection of data definition objects. Schema objects are the individual objects that describe tables, views, etc. There is a distinction between the logical schema objects and the physical storage components called *tablespaces*. The following schema objects are supported in Oracle. Notice that Oracle uses its own terminology that goes beyond the basic definitions of the relational model.

- *Tables:* Basic units of data that conform to the relational model discussed in Chapters 7 and 8. Each column (attribute) has a column name, datatype, and width (which depends on the type and precision).

---

3. For a discussion of *rollback*, see Chapter 21.

4. We will discuss object databases in Chapters 11 and 12, and object-relational systems in Chapter 13.

- *Views* (see Chapter 8): Virtual tables that may be defined on base tables or on other views. If the key of the result of the join in a **join view**—that is, a view whose defining query includes a join operation—matches the key of a base table, that base table is considered **key preserved** in that view. Updating of a join view is allowed if the update applies to attributes of a base table that is key preserved. For example, consider a join of the EMPLOYEE and DEPARTMENT tables in our COMPANY database (from Figure 7.5) to yield a join view EMP_DEPT. This join table has key SSN, which matches the key of EMPLOYEE but does *not* match the key of DEPARTMENT. Hence, the EMPLOYEE base table is considered to be key preserved, but DEPARTMENT is *not*. The update on the view

```
UPDATE  EMP_DEPT
SET     Salary = Salary * 1.07
WHERE   DNO = 5 ;
```

  is acceptable because it modifies the salary attribute from the key preserved EMPLOYEE table, but the update

```
UPDATE  EMP_DEPT
SET     Mgrssn = '987654321'
WHERE   Dname = 'Research' ;
```

  fails with an error code because DEPARTMENT is not key preserved.

- *Synonyms:* Direct references to objects.[5] They are used to provide public access to an object, mask the real name or owner of an object, etc. A user may create a private synonym that is available to only that user.

- *Program units:* A function, stored procedure, or package. Procedures or functions are written in SQL or PL/SQL, which is a procedural language extension to SQL in Oracle. The term **stored procedure** is commonly used to refer to a procedure that is considered to be a part of the data definition and implements some integrity rule or business rule or a policy when it is invoked. Functions return single values. Packages provide a method of encapsulating and storing related procedures for easier management and control.

- *Sequence:* A special provision of a data type in Oracle for attribute value generation. An attribute may derive its value from a sequence, which is an automatically generated internal number. The same sequence may be used for one or more tables. As an example, an attribute EMPID for the EMPLOYEE table may be internally generated as a sequence.

- *Indexes* (see Chapter 6): An index can be generated on one or more columns of a table as requested via SQL.

- *Cluster:* A group of records from one or more tables physically stored in a mixed file (see Chapter 5). Related rows from multiple tables are physically stored together on disk blocks to improve performance.[6] By creating an **index cluster,**[7] the EMPLOYEE and DEPARTMENT tables may be clustered by the **cluster key** DNUMBER and the data is grouped

---

5. This is somewhat similar to naming in object databases (see Chapters 11 and 12).

6. Clustering is also often used in object databases.

7. This type of structure has also been called a *join index,* since the records to be joined together from the two files are clustered.

so that the row for the DEPARTMENT with DNUMBER = 1 from the DEPARTMENT table is followed by the rows from EMPLOYEE table for all employees in that department. **Hash clusters** also group records; however, the cluster key value is hashed first, and all rows belonging to this hash value (from the different tables being clustered) are stored under the same hash bucket address.

- *Database links:* Named objects in Oracle that establish paths from one database to another. These are used in distributed databases (see Chapter 24).

10.3.2   Oracle Data Dictionary

The Oracle data dictionary is a read-only set of tables that keeps the metadata—that is, the schema description—for a database. It is composed of base tables that contain encrypted data stored by the system. User-accessible views of the dictionary decode, summarize, and conveniently display the information for users. Users are rarely given access to base tables. The special prefixes USER, ALL, and DBA are used respectively to refer to the user's view (schema objects that the user owns), expanded user view objects (objects that a user has authorization to access), and a complete set of information (for the DBA's use). We will be discussing system catalogs in detail in Chapter 17. Oracle dictionary, which is a system catalog, has the following type of information:

- Names of users.
- Security information (privileges and roles) about which users have access to what data (see Chapter 22).
- Schema objects information.
- Integrity constraints.
- Space allocation and utilization of the database objects.
- Statistics on attributes, tables, and predicates.
- Access audit trail information.

It is possible to query the data dictionary using SQL. For example, the query:

```
SELECT object_name, object_type FROM user-objects;
```

returns the information about schema objects owned by the user.

```
SELECT owner, object_name, object_type FROM all-objects;
```

returns information on all objects to which the user has access.

In addition to the above dictionary information, Oracle constantly monitors database activity and records it in tables called **dynamic performance tables.** The DBA has access to those tables to monitor system performance and may grant access to views over these tables to some users.

10.3.3   SQL in Oracle

The SQL implemented in Oracle is compliant with the SQL ANSI/ISO standard. It is similar to the SQL facilities discussed in Chapter 8 with some variations. All operations on a database in Oracle are performed using SQL **statements**—that is, any string of SQL language given to Oracle for execution. A complete SQL query is referred to as an SQL **sentence.** The following SQL statements are handled (see Chapter 8):

- *DDL statements:* Define schema objects discussed in Section 10.2.1, and also grant and revoke privileges (see Chapter 22).

- *DML statements:* Specify querying, insert, delete, and update operations. In addition, locking a table or view (see Chapter 20) or examining the execution plan of a query (see Chapter 18) are also DML operations.

- *Transaction control statements:* Specify units of work. A **transaction** is a logical unit of work (we will discuss transactions in detail in Chapter 19) that begins with an executable statement and ends when the changes made to the database are either *committed* (written to permanent storage) or *rolled back* (aborted). Transaction control statements in SQL include COMMIT (WORK), SAVEPOINT, and ROLLBACK.

- *Session control statements:* Allow users to control the properties of their current session by enabling or disabling roles of users and changing language settings. Examples: ALTER SESSION, CREATE ROLE.

- *System control statements:* Allow the administrator to change settings such as the minimum number of shared servers, or to kill a session. The only statement of this type is ALTER SYSTEM.

- *Embedded SQL statements:* Allow SQL statements to be embedded in a procedural programming language, such as PL/SQL of Oracle or the C language. In the latter case, Oracle uses the PRO*C precompiler to process SQL statements in the C program. Statements include cursor management operations like OPEN, FETCH, CLOSE, and other operations like EXECUTE.

The PL/SQL language is Oracle's procedural language extension that adds procedural functionality to SQL. By compiling and storing PL/SQL code in a database as a stored procedure, network traffic between applications and the database is reduced. PL/SQL blocks can also be sent by an application to a database for performing complex operations without excessive network traffic.

10.3.4   Methods in Oracle 8

Methods (operations) have been added to Oracle 8 as a part of the object-relational extension. A **method** is a procedure or function that is part of the definition of a user-defined **abstract data type.** Methods are written in PL/SQL and stored in the database or written in a language like C and stored externally.[8] Methods differ from stored procedures in the following ways:

- A program invokes a method by referring to an object of its associated type.

---

8. We will discuss methods that define the behavioral specification of classes in object databases in Chapters 11 and 12.

- An Oracle method has complete access to the attributes of its associated object and to the information about its type. Note that this is not true in general for object data models.

Every (abstract) data type has a system-defined **constructor method,** which is a method that constructs a new object according to the data type's specification. The name of the constructor method is identical to the name of the user-defined type; it behaves as a function and returns the new object as its value. Oracle supports certain special kinds of methods:

- Comparison methods define an order relationship among objects of a given data type.

- Map methods are functions defined on built-in types to compare them. For example, a map method called area may be used to compare rectangles based on their areas.

- Order methods use their own logic to return a value that encodes the ordering among two objects of the same type. For example, for an object type insurance_policy, two different order methods may be defined: one that orders policies by (issue_date, last-name, firstname) and another by policy_number.

10.3.5   Triggers

In Oracle, active rule capability is provided by a database **trigger**—stored procedure (or rule) that is implicitly executed (or fired) when the table with which it is associated has an insert, delete, or update performed on it.[9] Triggers can be used to enforce additional constraints or to automatically perform additional actions that are required by business rules or policies that go beyond the standard key, entity integrity, and referential integrity constraints imposed by the system.

10.4   Storage Organization in Oracle

A database is divided into logical storage units called **tablespaces,** with the following characteristics:

- Each database is divided into one or more tablespaces.

- There is system tablespace and users tablespace.

- One or more **datafiles** (which correspond to stored base tables) are created in each tablespace. A datafile can be associated with only one database. When requested data is not available in the memory cache for the database, it is read from the appropriate datafile. To reduce the total disk access activity, data is pooled in memory and written to datafiles all at once under the control of the DBWR background process.

- The combined storage capacity of a database's tablespace is the total storage capacity of the database.

---

9. We discuss active database concepts in Chapter 23.

Every Oracle database contains a tablespace named SYSTEM (to hold the data dictionary's objects), which Oracle creates automatically when the database is created. At least one user tablespace is needed to reduce contention between the system's internal dictionary objects and schema objects.

Physical storage is organized in terms of data blocks, extents, and segments. The finest level of granularity of storage is a **data block** (also called *logical block, page,* or *Oracle block*), which is a fixed number of bytes. An **extent** is a specific number of contiguous data blocks. A **segment** is a set of extents allocated to a specific data structure. For a given table, the data may be stored in a **data segment** and the index may be stored in an **index segment.** The relationships among these terms are shown in Figure 10.2.

Figure 10.2   Data blocks, extents, and segments in Oracle. (From Oracle (1997a).)

10.4.1 Data Blocks

For an Oracle database, the data block—not an operating system block—represents the smallest unit of I/O. Its size would typically be a multiple of the operating system block size. A data block has the following components:

- *Header:* Contains general block information such as block address and type of segment.
- *Table directory:* Contains information about tables that have data in the data block.
- *Row directory:* Contains information about the actual rows. Oracle reuses the space on insertion of rows but does not reclaim it when rows are deleted.
- *Row data:* Uses the bulk of the space in the data block. A row can span blocks (that is, occupy multiple blocks).
- *Free space:* Space allocated for row updates and new rows.

Two space management parameters PCTFREE and PCTUSED enable the DBA/designer to control the use of free space in data blocks. PCTFREE sets the minimum percentage of a data block to be preserved as free space for possible updates to rows. For example:

PCTFREE 30

states that 30 percent of each data block will be kept as free space. After a data block is filled to 70 percent, Oracle would consider it unavailable for the insertion of new rows. The PCTUSED parameter sets the *minimum* percentage of a block's space that must be reached—due to DELETE and UPDATE statements that reduce the size of data—before new rows can be added to the block. For example, if in the CREATE TABLE statement, we set

PCTUSED 50

a data block used for this table's data segment—which has already reached 70 percent of its storage space as determined by PCTFREE—is considered unavailable for the insertion of new rows until the amount of used space in the block falls below 50 percent.[10] This way, 30 percent of the block remains open for updates of existing rows; new rows can be inserted only when the amount of used space falls below 50 percent, and then insertions can proceed until 70 percent of the space is utilized.

When using Oracle data types such as LONG or LONG RAW, or in some other situations of using large objects, a row may not fit in a data block. In such a case, Oracle stores the data for the row in a chain of data blocks reserved for that segment. This is called **row chaining.** If a row originally fits in one block but is updated so that it does not fit any longer, Oracle uses **migration**—moving an entire row to a new data block and trying to fit it there. The original row leaves a pointer to the new data block. With row chaining and migration, multiple data blocks are required to be accessed and as a result performance degrades.

---

10. These statements are examples of what we called *storage definition language* in Chapter 2, which specify physical storage parameters. They are *not* part of the SQL standard.

10.4.2   Extents

When a table is created, Oracle allocates it an initial extent. Incremental extents are automatically allocated when the initial extent becomes full. The STORAGE clause of CREATE TABLE is used to define for every type of segment how much space to allocate initially as well as the maximum amount of space and the number of extents.[11] All extents allocated in index segments remain allocated as long as the index exists. When an index associated with a table or cluster is dropped, Oracle reclaims the space.

10.4.3   Segments

A segment is made up of a number of extents and belongs to a tablespace. Oracle uses the following four types of segments:

- *Data segments:* Each nonclustered table and each cluster has a single data segment to hold all its data. Oracle creates the data segment when the application creates the table or cluster with the CREATE command. Storage parameters can be set and altered with appropriate CREATE and ALTER commands.

- *Index segments:* Each index in an Oracle database has a single index segment, which is created with the CREATE INDEX command. The statement names the tablespace and specifies storage parameters for the segment.

- *Temporary segments:* Temporary segments are created by Oracle for use by SQL statements that need a temporary work area. When the statement completes execution, the statement's extents are returned to the system for future use. The statements that require a temporary segment are CREATE INDEX, SELECT . . . {ORDER BY | GROUP BY}, SELECT DISTINCT, and (SELECT . . .) {UNION | MINUS[12] | INTERSECT} (SELECT . . .). Some unindexed joins and correlated subqueries may also require temporary segments. Queries with ORDER BY, GROUP BY, or DISTINCT clauses, which require a sort operation, may be helped by using the SORT_AREA_SIZE parameter.

- *Rollback segments:* Each database must contain one or more rollback segments, which are used for "undoing" transactions. A rollback segment records old values of data (whether or not it commits) that are used to provide read consistency (when using multiversion control) to roll back a transaction and for recovering a database.[13] Oracle creates an initial rollback segment called SYSTEM whenever a database is created. This segment is in the SYSTEM tablespace and uses that tablespace's default storage parameters.

---

11. The details of the exact allocation and the deallocation algorithms for extents are described in Oracle (1997a).

12. MINUS is the same as EXCEPT (see Chapter 8).

13. See Chapters 20 and 21 for further details on these concepts.

10.5 Programming Oracle Applications

Programming in Oracle is done in several ways:

- Writing interactive SQL queries in the SQL query mode.
- Writing programs in a host language like COBOL, C, or PASCAL, and embedding SQL within the program. A precompiler such as PRO*COBOL or PRO*C is used to link the application to Oracle.
- Writing in PL/SQL, which is Oracle's own procedural language.
- Using Oracle Call Interface (OCI) and the Oracle runtime library SQLLIB.

10.5.1 Programming in PL/SQL

PL/SQL is Oracle's procedural language extension to SQL. PL/SQL offers software engineering features such as data encapsulation, information hiding, overloading, and exception handling to the developers. It is the most heavily used technique for application development in Oracle.

PL/SQL is a block-structured language. That is, the basic units—procedures, functions and anonymous blocks—that make up a PL/SQL program are logical blocks, which can contain any number of nested subblocks. A block or subblock groups logically related declarations and statements. The declarations are local to the block and cease to exist when the block completes. As illustrated below, a PL/SQL block has three parts: (1) a **declaration part** where variables and objects are declared, (2) an **executable part** where these variables are manipulated, and (3) an **exception part** where exceptions or errors raised during execution can be handled.

```
[ DECLARE
        ---declarations ]
BEGIN
        ---statements
[ EXCEPTION
        ---handlers ]
END ;
```

In the declaration part—which is optional—variables are declared. Variables can have any SQL data type as well as additional PL/SQL data types. Variables can also be assigned values in this section. Objects are manipulated in the executable part, which is the only required part. Here data can be processed using conditional, iterative, and sequential flow-of-control statements such as IF-THEN-ELSE, FOR-LOOP, WHILE-LOOP, EXIT-WHEN, and GO-TO. The exception part handles any error conditions raised in the executable part. The exception could be user-defined errors or database errors or exceptions. When an error or exception occurs, an exception is raised and the normal execution stops and control transfers to the exception-handling part of the PL/SQL block or subprogram.

Suppose we want to write PL/SQL programs to process the database of Figure 7.5. As a first example, E1, we write a program segment that prints out some information about an employee who has the highest salary as follows:

```
E1:
DECLARE
        v_fname      employee.fname%TYPE;
        v_minit      employee.minit%TYPE;
        v_lname      employee.lname%TYPE;
        v_address    employee.address%TYPE;
        v_salary     employee.salary%TYPE;

BEGIN
        SELECT  fname, minit, lname, address, salary
        INTO    v_fname, v_minit, v_lname, v_address , v_salary
        FROM    EMPLOYEE
        WHERE   salary = (select max (salary) from employee) ;

        DBMS_OUTPUT.PUT_LINE (v_fname, v_minit, v_lname, v_address,
                              v_salary);

EXCEPTION
        WHEN OTHERS
        DBMS_OUTPUT.PUT_LINE ('Error Detected');
END;
```

In E1, we need to declare program variables to match the types of the database attributes that the program will process. These program variables may or may not have names that are identical to their corresponding attributes. The %TYPE in each variable declaration means that that variable is of the same type as the corresponding column in the table. DBMS_OUTPUT.PUT_LINE is PL/SQL's print function. The error handling part prints out an error message if Oracle detects an error—in this case, if more than one employee is selected—while executing the SQL. The program needs an INTO clause, which specifies the program variables into which attribute values from the database are retrieved.

In the next example, E2, we write a simple program to increase the salary of employees whose salaries are less than the average salary by 10 percent. The program recomputes and prints out the average salary if it exceeds 50000 after the above update.

```
E2:
DECLARE
        avg_salary NUMBER;

BEGIN
        SELECT avg(salary) INTO avg_salary
        FROM employee;

        UPDATE employee
          SET salary = salary*1.1
```

```
     WHERE salary < avg_salary;

     SELECT avg(salary) INTO avg_salary
     FROM employee;

     IF avg_salary > 50000 THEN
     dbms_output.put_line ('Average Salary is ' || avg_salary) ;
     END IF;

     COMMIT;

EXCEPTION
     WHEN OTHERS THEN
     dbms_output.put_line ('Error in Salary update ')
     ROLLBACK;

END;
```

In E2, `avg_salary` is defined as a variable and it gets the value of the average of the employees' salary from the first SELECT statement and this value is used to choose which of the employees will have their salaries updated. The EXCEPTION part rolls back the whole transaction (that is, removes any effect of the transaction on the database) if an error of any type occurs during execution.

10.5.2 Cursors in PL/SQL

The set of rows returned by a query can consist of zero, one, or multiple rows, depending on how many rows meet the search criteria. When a query returns multiple rows, it is necessary to explicitly declare a **cursor** to process the rows. A cursor is similar to a *file variable* or *file pointer,* which points to a single row (tuple) from the result of a query. Cursors should be declared in the declarative part and are controlled by three commands: OPEN, FETCH, and CLOSE. The cursor is initialized with the OPEN statement, which executes the query, retrieves the resulting set of rows, and sets the cursor to a position before the first row in the result of the query. This becomes the current row for the cursor. The FETCH statement, when executed for the first time, retrieves the first row into the program variables and sets the cursor to point to that row. Subsequent executions of FETCH advance the cursor to the next row in the result set, and retrieve that row into the program variables. This is similar to the traditional record-at-a-time file processing. When the last row has been processed, the cursor is released with the CLOSE statement. Example E3 displays the SSN of employees whose salary is greater than their supervisor's salary.

```
E3:
DECLARE
     emp_salary NUMBER;
     emp_super_salary NUMBER;
     emp_ssn CHAR (9);
     emp_superssn CHAR (9);
     CURSOR salary_cursor IS
```

```
         SELECT ssn, salary, superssn FROM employee;
BEGIN
   OPEN salary_cursor;

   LOOP
      FETCH salary_cursor INTO emp_ssn, emp_salary, emp_superssn;
      EXIT WHEN salary_cursor%NOTFOUND;

      IF emp_superssn is NOT NULL THEN
          SELECT salary INTO emp_super_salary
          FROM employee
          WHERE ssn = emp_superssn;

          IF emp_salary > emp_super_salary THEN
          dbms_output.put_line(emp_ssn);
          END IF;
      END IF;
   END LOOP;
   IF salary_cursor%ISOPEN THEN CLOSE salary_cursor;

   EXCEPTION
      WHEN NO_DATA_FOUND THEN
      dbms_output.put_line ('Errors with ssn ' || emp_ssn);
      IF salary_cursor%ISOPEN THEN CLOSE salary_cursor;

END;
```

In the above example, the SALARY_CURSOR loops through the entire employee table until the cursor fetches no further rows. The exception part handles the situation where an incorrect supervisor ssn may be assigned to an employee. The %NOTFOUND is one of the four cursor attributes, which are the following:

- %ISOPEN returns TRUE if the cursor is already open.

- %FOUND returns TRUE if the last FETCH returned a row, and returns FALSE if the last FETCH failed to return a row.

- %NOTFOUND is the logical opposite of %FOUND.

- %ROWCOUNT yields the number of rows fetched.

As a final example, E4 shows a program segment that gets a list of all the employees, increments each employee's salary by 10 percent, and displays the old and the new salary.

```
E4:
DECLARE
   v_fname     employee.fname%TYPE;
   v_minit     employee.minit%TYPE;
   v_lname     employee.lname%TYPE;
   v_address   employee.address%TYPE;
   v_salary    employee.salary%TYPE;
```

```
        CURSOR EMP IS
            SELECT ssn, fname, minit, lname, salary
            FROM employee;

    BEGIN
      OPEN EMP ;

      LOOP
          FETCH EMP INTO v_ssn, v_fname, v_minit, v_lname,
           v_salary ;
          EXIT WHEN EMP%NOTFOUND;

          dbms_output.putline('SSN:' || v_ssn || 'Old salary :'
                              || v_salary);

          UPDATE employee
          SET    salary = salary*1.1
          WHERE  ssn = v_ssn;
          COMMIT;
          dbms_output.putline('SSN:' || v_ssn || ' New salary :'
                              || v_salary*1.1);

      END LOOP;
      CLOSE EMP;

    EXCEPTION
      WHEN OTHERS
      dbms_output.put_line ('Error Detected');
    END:
```

10.5.3 An Example in PRO*C

An Oracle precompiler is a programming tool that allows the programmer to embed SQL statements in a source program of some programming language. The precompiler accepts the source program as input, translates the embedded SQL statements into standard Oracle runtime library calls, and generates a modified source program that can be compiled, linked, and executed. The languages that Oracle provides precompilers for include C, C++, and COBOL, among others. Here, we will discuss an application programming example using PRO*C, the precompiler for the C language.

Using PRO*C provides automatic conversion between Oracle and C language data types. Both SQL statements and PL/SQL blocks can be embedded in a C host program. This combines the power of the C language with the convenience of using SQL for database access. To write a PRO*C program to process the database of Figure 7.5, we need to declare program variables to match the types of the database attributes that the program will process. The error-handling function SQL_ERROR prints out an error message if Oracle detects an error while executing the SQL. The first PRO*C example E5 (same as E1 in PL/SQL) is a program segment that prints out some information about an employee who has the highest salary (assuming only one employee is selected). Here VARCHAR is an Oracle-supplied structure. The program connects to the database as the user "Scott" with a password of "TIGER".

```
E5:
#include <stdio.h>
#include <string.h>

VARCHAR username[30] ;
VARCHAR password[10] ;
VARCHAR v_fname[15] ;
VARCHAR v_minit[1] ;
VARCHAR v_lname[15] ;
VARCHAR v_address[30] ;
char    v_ssn[9] ;
float   f_salary ;

main ()
{
strcpy (username.arr , "Scott") ;
username.len = strlen(username.arr) ;
strcpy(password.arr,"TIGER") ;
password.len = strlen(password.arr) ;

EXEC SQL WHENEVER SQLERROR DO sql_error() ;
EXEC SQL CONNECT :username IDENTIFIED BY :password ;
EXEC SQL SELECT fname, minit, lname, address, salary
     INTO :v_fname, :v_minit, :v_lname, :v_address , :f_salary
     FROM EMPLOYEE
     WHERE salary = (select max (salary) from employee) ;

printf (" Employee first name, Middle Initial, Last Name, Address, Sal-
ary \n") ;
printf ("%s %s %s %s %f \n ", v_fname.arr, v_minit.arr,
v_lname.arr, v_address.arr , f_salary) ;
}

sql_error()
{
EXEC SQL WHENEVER SQLERROR CONTINUE;
printf(" Error detected \n");
}
```

Cursors are used in PRO*C in a manner similar to their use in PL/SQL (see Section 10.5.2). Example E6 (same as E4 in PL/SQL) illustrates their use, where the EMP cursor is explicitly declared. The program segment in E6 gets a list of all the employees, increments the salaries by 10 percent, and displays the old and new salary. Implicit cursor attributes return information about the execution of an INSERT, UPDATE, DELETE, or SELECT INTO statement. The values of these cursor attributes always refer to the most recently executed SQL statement. In E6, the NOTFOUND cursor attribute is an implicit variable that returns TRUE if the SQL statement returned no rows.

```
E6:
. . . /* same include statements and variable declarations as E5

main ()
{
strcpy (username.arr , "Scott") ;
username.len= strlen(username.arr);
strcpy(password.arr,"TIGER") ;
password.len = strlen(password.arr);

EXEC SQL WHENEVER SQLERROR DO sql_error();
EXEC SQL CONNECT :username IDENTIFIED BY :password ;
EXEC SQL DECLARE EMP CURSOR FOR
     SELECT   ssn, fname, minit, lname, salary
     FROM     employee ;

EXEC SQL OPEN EMP ;
EXEC SQL WHENEVER NOTFOUND DO BREAK ;

for (;;)
{
EXEC SQL FETCH EMP INTO :v_ssn, :v_fname, :v_minit, :v_lname,
       :f_salary ;
printf ("Social Security Number : %d , Old Salary : %f " ,
        v_ssn, f_salary) ;

EXEC SQL  UPDATE  employee
          SET     salary = salary*1.1
          WHERE   ssn = :v_ssn ;
EXEC SQL  COMMIT;
   printf ("Social Security Number : %d New Salary : %f " ,
        v_ssn, f_salary*1.1) ;
}
}

sql_error()
{
EXEC SQL WHENEVER SQLERROR CONTINUE;
printf(" Error detected \n");
}
```

10.6 Oracle Tools

Various tools have been offered to develop applications and to design databases in
RDBMSs.[14] Many tools exist that take the designer through all phases of database design
starting with conceptual modeling using variations of extended entity-relationship

---

14. It is not our intention to survey these tools in detail here.

diagrams through physical design. Oracle offers its own tool called Designer 2000 for this purpose.

Designer 2000 facilitates rapid model-based development and provides *Entity-Relationship diagrams* for data modeling, *Function Hierarchy approach* for process modeling, and *Dataflow techniques* to capture information flows within an information system.[15] The Entity-Relationship Diagrammer unit of Designer 2000 supports the creation, display, and manipulation of all entities and relationships. Each of these constructs are defined in terms of properties, including attributes. Various properties of attributes are displayed using default symbols for mandatory, optional, and uniquely identifying (key) attributes. The entities and relationships are displayed diagrammatically for better visual understanding.

The Function Hierarchy Diagrammer unit represents the activities (processes) carried out by a business. It uses the technique of functional decomposition, whereby a high-level statement of an enterprise or departmental business function is broken down into progressively more detailed functions. This helps to identify candidate business functions for computerization and areas of commonality across the organization.

The Matrix Diagrammer unit is a general-purpose cross-referencing tool that can be used to support project scoping, impact analysis, network planning, and quality control for a database application development project. It also provides information about the different network nodes where the database tables are residing and the modules using these tables.

For developing applications, there are a number of prototyping tools available including Powerbuilder by Sybase. Oracle provides its own tool called Developer 2000, which lets the user design graphical user interfaces (GUIs), and enables the user to interactively develop actual programs with queries and transactions. The tool interacts with Oracle databases as the back end. Developer 2000 offers a set of builders for database-derived forms, reports, queries, objects, charts, and procedures that make it simpler for developers to build database-driven applications. Version 2.0 includes graphical wizards to automate application creation. A new object library lets developers reuse components by dragging them into their applications. Object partitioning lets developers move code from client to server to cut down on network traffic. Developer 2000 includes a project builder tool to manage team development, and a debugger that works across all tiers of the application. It integrates with Oracle's Designer 2000, offers access to all major databases, and allows the embedding of ActiveX controls in applications.

10.7   An Overview of Microsoft Access

Access is one of the well-known implementations of the relational data model on the PC platform. It is considered as part of an integrated set of tools for creating and managing databases on the PC Windows platform. The database applications for Access may range

---

15. For a better understanding of the information system design and the database design process, see Sections 16.1 and 16.2. Features of design tools are discussed in Section 16.5.

from personal applications, such as maintaining an inventory of your personal audio and video collection, to small business applications, such as maintaining business-specific customer information. With compliance to the Microsoft Open Database Connectivity (ODBC) standard and the prevalence of today's client-server architectures, PC relational databases may be used as a front-end to databases stored on non-PC platforms. For example, an end user can specify ad hoc queries graphically in Access over an Oracle database stored on a UNIX server.

Access provides a database engine and a graphical user interface (GUI) for data definition and manipulation, with the power of SQL. It also provides a programming language called Access Basic. Users can quickly develop forms and reports for input/output operations against the database through the use of **Wizards,** which are interactive programs that guide the user through a series of questions in a dialog mode. The definition of the forms and reports is interactively accomplished when the user designs the layout and links the different fields on the form or report to items in the database. Access 97 (the latest release of Access at the time of this writing) also provides the database developer with hyperlinks as a native data type, extending the functionality of the database with the ability to share information on the Internet.

10.7.1 Architecture of Access

Access is an RDBMS that has several components. One component is the underlying database engine, called the **Microsoft Jet engine,**[16] which is responsible for managing the data. Another component is the user interface, which calls the engine to provide data services, such as storage and retrieval of data. The engine stores all the application data (tables, indexes, forms, reports, macros, and modules) in a single Microsoft database file (.mdb file). The engine also provides advanced capabilities, such as heterogeneous data access through ODBC, data validation, concurrency control using locks, and query optimization.

Access works like a complete application development environment, with the internal engine serving to provide the user with RDBMS capabilities. The Access user interface provides Wizards and Builders to aid the user in designing a database application. Builders are interactive programs that help the user build syntactically correct expressions. The programming model used by Access is event-driven. The user builds a sequence of simple operations, called **macros,** to be performed in response to actions that occur during the use of the database application. While some applications can be written in their entirety using macros, others may require the extended capabilities of **Access Basic,** the programming language provided by Access.

There are different ways in which an application with multiple components that includes Access can be integrated. A **component** (in Microsoft terminology) is an application or development tool that makes its objects available to other applications. Using **automation** in Visual Basic, it is possible to work with objects from other components to construct a seamless integrated application. Using the **Object Linking and Embedding**

---

16. We will refer to this simply as the *engine* in the remainder of this discussion.

(OLE) technology, a user can include documents created in another component on a report or form within Access. Automation and OLE are distinct technologies, which are a part of the **Component Object Model** (COM), a standard proposed by Microsoft.

10.7.2 Data Definition of Access Databases

Although Access provides a programmatic approach to data definition through **Access SQL,** its dialect of SQL, the Access GUI provides a graphical approach to defining tables and relationships among them. A table can be created directly in a **design view** or it can be created interactively under the guidance of a table wizard. Table definition contains not only the structure of the table but also the formatting of the field layout and masks for field inputs, validation rules, captions, default values, indexing, and so on. The data types for fields include text, number, date/time, currency, Yes/no (boolean), hyperlink, and AutoNumber, which automatically generates sequential numbers for new records. Access also provides the capability to import data from external tables and to link to external tables.

Figure 10.3 shows the EMPLOYEE table from the COMPANY relational database schema, when opened in the design view. The SSN field is selected (highlighted), so its properties are displayed in a **Field Properties window** at the bottom left of the screen. The **format property** provides for a default display format, where SSN has hyphens located after the third and fifth positions as per convention. The **input mask** provides automatic formatting characters for display during data input in order to validate the input data. For

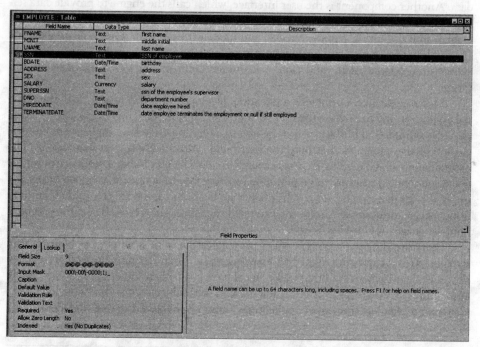

Figure 10.3   Defining the EMPLOYEE relation using the Access user interface.

example, the input mask for SSN displays the hyphen positions and indicates that the other characters are digits. The **caption property** specifies the name to be used on forms and reports for this field. A blank caption specifies the default, which is the field name itself. A **default value** can be specified if appropriate for a particular field. Field validation includes the specification of **validation rules** and **validation text**—the latter displayed when a validation rule is violated. For the SSN example, the input mask provides the necessary field validation rule. However, other fields may require additional validation rules—for example, the SALARY field may be required to be greater than a certain minimum. Other field properties include specifying whether the field is **required**—that is, NULL is not allowed—and whether textual fields allow zero length strings. Another field property includes the **index specification,** which allows for three possibilities: (1) no index, (2) an index with duplicates, or (3) an index without duplicates. Since SSN is the primary key of EMPLOYEE, the field is indexed with no duplicates allowed.

In addition to the Field Properties window, Access also provides a **Table Properties window.** This is used to specify **table validation rules,** which are integrity constraints across multiple columns of a table or across tables. For example, the user can define a table validation rule on the EMPLOYEE table specifying that an employee cannot be his or her own supervisor.

10.7.3 Defining Relationships and Referential Integrity Constraints

Access allows interactive definition of relationships between tables—which can specify referential integrity constraints—via the **Relationships window.** To define a relationship, the user first adds the two tables involved to the window display and then selects the primary key of one table and drags it to where it appears as a foreign key in the other table. For example, to define the relationship between DNUMBER of DEPARTMENT and DNO of EMPLOYEE, the user selects DEPARTMENT.DNUMBER and drags it over to EMPLOYEE.DNO. This action pops up another window that prompts the user for further information regarding the establishment of the relationship, as shown in Figure 10.4. The user checks the "Enforce Referential Integrity" box if Access is to automatically enforce the referential integrity specified by the relationship. The user may also specify the automatic cascading of updates to related fields and deletions of related records by selecting the appropriate boxes. The "Relationship Type" is automatically determined by Access based on the definition of the related fields. If only one of the related fields is a primary key or has a unique index, then Access creates a one-to-many relationship, indicating that an instance (value) of the primary key can appear many times as an instance of the foreign key in the related table. This is the case in our example because DNUMBER is the primary key of DEPARTMENT and DNO is not the primary key of EMPLOYEE nor does it have a unique index defined on it. If both fields are either keys or have unique indexes, then Access creates a one-to-one relationship. For example, consider the definition of a relationship between EMPLOYEE.SSN and DEPARTMENT.MGRSSN. If the MGRSSN of DEPARTMENT is defined to have an index with no duplicates (a unique index) and SSN is the primary key of EMPLOYEE, then Access creates a one-to-one relationship.

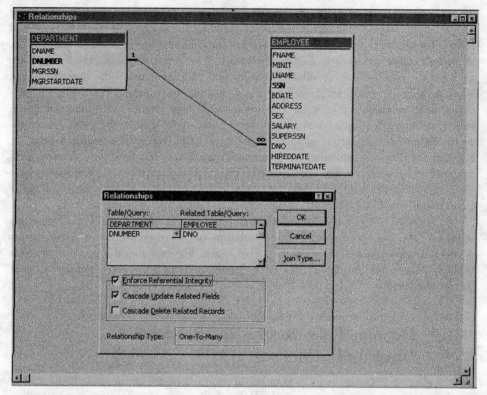

Figure 10.4   Establishing referential integrity between DNUMBER and DNO.

Although specifying a relationship is the mechanism used to specify referential integrity between tables, the user need not choose the option to enforce referential integrity because relationships are also used to specify implicit join conditions for queries. For example, if no relationship is pre-specified during the graphical design of a query, then a default join of the related fields is performed if related tables are selected for that query, regardless of whether referential integrity is enforced or not.[17] Access chooses an inner join as the default join type but the user may choose a right or left outer join by clicking on the "Join Type" box (see Figure 10.4) and selecting the appropriate join type.

Figure 10.5 shows the Relationships window for the COMPANY database schema in Access. Note the similarity to Figure 7.7, which shows the eight referential integrity constraints of the COMPANY database. One difference is that Access displays the cardinality ratio associated with each relationship.[18] Another difference is the duplicate display of the

---

17. Hence, specifying a relationship is similar to defining an *implicit join condition* for queries that involve the two tables, unless a different relationship (join condition) is established during query specification.

18. The cardinality ratios are similar to those used in ER diagrams (see Figure 3.2), but the *infinity symbol* is used in Access instead of N.

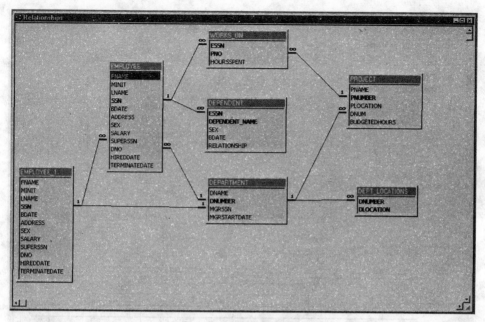

Figure 10.5   Relationships Window for the COMPANY schema.

EMPLOYEE relation, as EMPLOYEE and EMPLOYEE_1, in Figure 10.5. This duplication is needed when defining multiple relationships between two tables or a recursive relationship (between a table and itself). In Figure 10.5, in order to define the recursive relationship between the EMPLOYEE.SSN and EMPLOYEE.SUPERSSN, the user first adds another copy of the EMPLOYEE table to the Relationships window before dragging the primary key SSN to the foreign key SUPERSSN. Even if the recursive relationship did not exist in the COMPANY schema, we would need to duplicate EMPLOYEE (or, alternatively, DEPARTMENT) because two relationships exist between EMPLOYEE and DEPARTMENT: SSN to MGRSSN and DNUMBER to DNO.

10.7.4   Data Manipulation in Access

The data manipulation operations of the relational model are categorized into retrieval queries and updates (insert, delete, and modify operations). Access provides for query definition either graphically through a QBE interface or programmatically through Access SQL. The user has the ability to design a graphical query and then switch to the SQL view to examine the SQL query generated by Access. Access provides for update operations through forms that are built by the application programmer, by direct manipulation of the table data in Datasheet view, or through the Access Basic programming language.

Retrieval operations are easily specified graphically in the Access QBE interface. Consider Query 1 over the COMPANY database that retrieves the names and addresses of all employees who work for the "Research" department. Figure 10.6 shows the query both in

(a)

(b)

Figure 10.6   Defining Query 1 in (a) Access QBE and (b) Access SQL.

QBE and SQL. To define the query in QBE, the user first adds the EMPLOYEE and DEPARTMENT tables to the query window. The default join between DEPARTMENT.DNUMBER and EMPLOYEE.DNO that was established via the Relationships window at data definition is automatically incorporated into the query definition as illustrated by the line shown between the related fields. If such a predefined join is not needed for a query, the user needs to highlight the link in the query window and hit the Delete key. To establish a join that had not been prespecified, the user selects the join attribute from one table and drags it over to the join attribute in the other table. To include an attribute in the query, the user drags it from the top window to the bottom window. For attributes to be displayed in the query result, the user checks the "Show" box. To specify a selection condition on an attribute, the user can type an expression directly in the "Criteria" grid or use the aid of an Expression Builder. To see the equivalent query in Access SQL, the user switches from the QBE Design View to the SQL View.[19]

The above example illustrates how a user builds a query using the Design View Query window. Multiple join queries beyond two tables can be developed in a similar way. Wizards are available to guide the user in defining queries—although the ease of use of Access QBE makes them unnecessary.

Update operations on the database are typically guided by the use of forms that incorporate the business rules of the application. There is also a Datasheet view of a table that the sophisticated end user can use to insert, delete, or modify data directly by choosing "open table" from a database window. These updates are subject to the constraints specified through the data definition process, including data types, input masks, field and table validation rules, and relationships.

10.8 Features and Functionality of Access

This section presents an overview of some of the other features of Access, including forms, reports, macros, and Access Basic.

10.8.1 Forms

Access provides Form Wizards to assist the database programmer with the development of forms. A typical scenario with a Form Wizard involves the following:

- Choosing a table or query where the form's data comes from.
- Selecting the fields in the form.
- Choosing the desired layout (for example, columnar, tabular, Datasheet, or justified).
- Choosing a style for the headings.
- Specifying a form title.

Use of queries in the above process is equivalent to treating them as views. The Wizard then generates a form based on the above input. This form can then be opened in Design View for modification, if desired. Figure 10.7 shows a form, titled "Employee," which was created using a Form Wizard. This form chooses all the fields of the EMPLOYEE table. A justified layout was chosen with a standard style for headings. The form shown is essentially that provided by the Wizard with a few exceptions. The size of some of the fields were modified easily in Design View by selecting the box with the mouse and dragging it to the appropriate size. This simple form allows the user to view, insert, delete and modify EMPLOYEE records, subject to the defined constraints. The user views the data in the EMPLOYEE relation by repeatedly scrolling the page (using Page Down or > on the bottom line). The user can find a given employee record using the "Find" function in the Access "Edit" menu. Once an

---

19. Note that Access SQL allows join specifications in the FROM clause, which is supported in the SQL2 standard.

Figure 10.7   A Form for the EMPLOYEE table.

employee is found, the user can directly update the employee data or choose to delete the employee using the "Delete Record" function, which is also found on the "Edit" menu. To insert a new employee, the user inserts data into an empty record, which can be accessed by paging down (or using > on the bottom line) beyond the last record in the table.

The Access user interface provides a sophisticated Design View for creating more complicated forms. The form designer has a "Toolbox" that provides various controls for incorporation into a form—for example, buttons, check boxes, combo boxes, and subforms. Buttons and check boxes support the ease of use of choosing a built-in option on a form. A "Combo Box" provides a mechanism for the user to select an item from a list of possible values, ensuring the correctness of the entered data. For example, a combo box can be used to choose the department number for an employee. Subforms are forms within forms, allowing a form to include information from multiple tables. For example, on the Project form a subform can be used to display information about the employees that work on that project. There are "Control Wizards" that guide the form designer through the incorporation of the selected controls on the form.

10.8.2   Reports

Reports are integral components to any database system, providing various ways to group, sort, and summarize data for printing based on a user's needs. Like forms, reports are bound to underlying tables or queries. Access provides Report Wizards to assist the database programmer with the development of reports. A typical scenario with a Report Wizard involves the following:

- Choosing a table or query where the report's data comes from.
- Selecting the fields in the report.
- Specifying the grouping levels within the report.
- Indicating the sort order and summary information for the report.
- Choosing a report layout and orientation.
- Specifying a style for the report title.

The Wizard then generates a report based on the above input. This report can then be opened in Design View for modification, if desired.

Figure 10.8 shows a report, titled "Salaries by Department," which was created with Report Wizard by using data from the EMPLOYEE relation and choosing the fields in the

Salaries by Department

DNO	LNAME	FNAME	SALARY
1			
	BORG	James	$55,000.00
			$55,000.00
4			
	JABBAR	Ahmad	$25,000.00
	WALLACE	Jennifer	$43,000.00
	ZELAYA	Alicia	$25,000.00
			$93,000.00
5			
	ENGLISH	Joyce	$25,000.00
	NARAYAN	Ramesh	$38,000.00
	SMITH	John	$30,000.00
	WONG	Franklin	$40,000.00
			$133,000.00
Total Salaries			**$281,000.00**

Figure 10.8 An Access report titled Salaries by Department.

order that they were to appear on the report: DNO, LNAME, FNAME, and SALARY. A grouping level on DNO was specified to group the salaries by department number (DNO). The sorting of the detailed record on LNAME was indicated, as was the summary for the grouping as a SUM of the SALARY field (shown in boldface). A default report layout, orientation, and style was chosen from the ones provided by Access. The report shown is essentially that provided by the Wizard with a few exceptions. The headings for the group footer and report footer were modified from the defaults with a point and click in Design View.

The Access user interface also provides a sophisticated Design View for creating more complicated reports. Similar to the form designer's toolbox, a toolbox is provided to the report designer with "Control Wizards" that guide the report designer through the incorporation of the selected controls on the report. For example, a "Subreport" control combines multiple reports into one. This can be used, for example, to specify a report for departments that includes as a subreport the information on the projects controlled by that department.

10.8.3 Macros and Access Basic

The programming model of Access is event-driven. Access is responsible for recognizing various events and the user can specify how to respond to an event by writing a **macro,** which is a sequence of simple operations called **actions.** Examples of event categories include changes to data, performing actions on a window, typing on the keyboard, or a mouse action. Consider the example of coding a macro in response to the event of closing a window that uses the "OpenForm" action to open another window. Access provides various actions to the macro programmer for building a powerful database application.

While some applications can be written in their entirety using macros, other applications may require the extended capabilities of Access Basic, the complete programming language provided by Access and a subset of Visual Basic. Access Basic provides the power of a programming language, allowing for the use of flow-of-control constructs, the ability to use and pass arguments to customized Access Basic procedures, and record-at-a-time manipulation of records versus the set-at-a-time manipulation provided by macros and queries. Modules on the main toolbar refer to preprogrammed Access Basic procedures.

10.8.4   Additional Features

Access supports certain advanced queries, one of which is the **crosstab query**—a way of grouping the data by values in one column and performing aggregation functions within the group. Excel calls these queries as pivot tables.

OLE (object linking and embedding) is a Microsoft standard for linking and embedding objects in documents. Access enables the user to exchange information between applications. Use of Active X controls in Access extends the use of an application with little or no new programming.

Security.   Access has a user-level security model similar to Microsoft Windows-NT Server where users provide a login and password when they start Access and their userid and groupids determine privileges, which can be set using a Wizard. In addition, Access has the following methods to protect an application:

* The startup option of Access application can be made to restrict access to the Database Window and special keys.
* An application can be saved as an MDE file to remove Visual Basic source code and prevent changes to the design of forms, reports, and modules.

Replication.   Access also supports database replication. The tools menu provides for full or partial replication of a database. An Access database must be converted to a "Design Master" before the replication commands can be used. Two or more copies of the database called **replicas** can be created; each replica may also contain additional local objects. A **Design Master** is the replica for which changes can be made to the database design and objects. The Replication command available on the tools menu allows creation of a replica and the synchronization of the replica with another member of the replica set. Synchronization among replicas is available by a menu command or programmatically in Visual Basic. There is also a menu command for Resolving Conflicts. Additional software called **replication manager** is used to provide a visual interface for converting databases, making additional replicas, viewing relationships between replicas, setting their properties, etc. Replication manager also allows synchronization of data over the Internet or Intranet, an internal network in an organization.

Multiuser Operation. To make an application available for multiuser access, the application is made available on a network server. For concurrent updates, locking is provided. Locking can be done programmatically in Visual Basic, but it is done automatically by Access when bound forms are used, where a form is bound to a table. Access maintains an LDB file that contains the current locking information. The locking options are "No Locks," "All Records," and "Edited Record." The RecordLocks property can be set for a given form or for the entire database (from the Tools menu, choose the Options command and then the Advanced command).

Developer's Edition. An Access database can be saved as an MDE file, which compiles the Visual Basic source code. With the Developer's Edition the MDE file allows the distribution of the application to multiple desktops without requiring a copy of Access at each desktop. It also provides for a setup capability. Without the developer's edition, an MDE file is just a compiled and compacted version of the database application.

10.9   Summary

In this chapter we reviewed two representative and very popular relational database management system (RDBMS) products: Oracle and Microsoft Access. Our goal was to introduce the reader to the typical architecture and functionality of a high-end product like Oracle and a PC-based smaller RDBMS like Access. While we may call Oracle a full-fledged RDBMS, we may call Access a data management tool that is geared for the less sophisticated user. We gave a historical overview of the development of relational database management systems, then described the architecture and main functions of the Oracle system. We discussed how Oracle represents a database and manipulates it, and the storage organization in the system. We then gave examples of programming in Oracle using PL/SQL, which is Oracle's own programming language with embedded SQL, and using PRO*C, which is a pre-compiler for the C language. We reviewed some of the tools available in Oracle for database design and application development. We then provided an overview of Microsoft Access, its architecture, definition of data, defining relationships, and database manipulation using QBE and SQL. We reviewed some additional features and functionality of Access.

Selected Bibliography

Many manuals describe the Oracle system. Oracle (1997a) through (1997f) are particularly relevant to our coverage. Sunderraman (1999) is a good reference for programming in Oracle. Oracle press has published many books on different aspects of the system, and there is a publication called *Oracle System Journal* that reports on the constant development of the product. Access also has a number of manuals, and Microsoft (1996) is relevant to our coverage. Many popular books have been written on how to use the system.

PART 3

Object-Oriented and Extended Relational Database Technology

CHAPTER 11 | Concepts for Object-Oriented Databases

In this chapter and the next, we discuss object-oriented data models and database systems.[1] Traditional data models and systems, such as relational, network, and hierarchical, have been quite successful in developing the database technology required for many traditional business database applications. However, they have certain shortcomings when more complex database applications must be designed and implemented—for example, databases for engineering design and manufacturing (CAD/CAM and CIM[2]), scientific experiments, telecommunications, geographic information systems, and multimedia.[3] These newer applications have requirements and characteristics that differ from those of traditional business applications, such as more complex structures for objects, longer-duration transactions, new data types for storing images or large textual items, and the need to define nonstandard application-specific operations. Object-oriented databases were proposed to meet the needs of these more complex applications. The object-oriented approach offers the flexibility to handle some of these requirements without being

---

1. These databases are often referred to as **Object Databases** and the systems are referred to as **Object Database Management Systems** (ODBMS). However, because this chapter discusses many general object-oriented concepts, we will use the term *object-oriented* instead of just *object*.

2. Computer-Aided Design/Computer-Aided Manufacturing and Computer-Integrated Manufacturing.

3. Multimedia databases must store various types of multimedia objects, such as video, audio, images, graphics, documents (see Chapter 23).

limited by the data types and query languages available in traditional database systems. A key feature of object-oriented databases is the power they give the designer to specify both the *structure* of complex objects and the *operations* that can be applied to these objects.

Another reason for the creation of object-oriented databases is the increasing use of object-oriented programming languages in developing software applications. Databases are now becoming fundamental components in many software systems, and traditional databases are difficult to use when embedded in object-oriented software applications that are developed in an object-oriented programming language such as C++, SMALLTALK, or JAVA. Object-oriented databases are designed so they can be directly—or *seamlessly*—integrated with software that is developed using object-oriented programming languages.

The need for additional data modeling features has also been recognized by relational DBMS vendors, and the newer versions of relational systems are incorporating many of the features that were proposed for object-oriented databases. This has led to systems that are characterized as *object-relational* or *extended relational* DBMSs (see Chapter 13). The next version of the SQL standard for relational DBMSs, SQL3, will include some of these features.

In the past few years, many experimental prototypes and commercial object-oriented database systems have been created. The experimental prototypes include the ORION system developed at MCC,[4] OPENOODB at Texas Instruments, the IRIS system at Hewlett-Packard laboratories, the ODE system at AT&T Bell Labs,[5] and the ENCORE/ObServer project at Brown University. Commercially available systems include GEMSTONE/OPAL of GemStone Systems, ONTOS of Ontos, Objectivity of Objectivity Inc., Versant of Versant Object Technology, ObjectStore of Object Design, ARDENT of ARDENT Software,[6] and POET of POET Software. These represent only a partial list of the experimental prototypes and the commercially available object-oriented database systems.

As commercial object-oriented DBMSs became available, the need for a standard model and language was recognized. Because the formal procedure for approval of standards normally takes a number of years, a consortium of object-oriented DBMS vendors and users, called ODMG,[7] proposed a standard that is known as the ODMG-93 standard, which has since been revised with the latest version being ODMG version 2.0. We will describe many features of the ODMG standard in Chapter 12.

Object-oriented databases have adopted many of the concepts that were developed originally for object-oriented programming languages.[8] In Section 11.1, we examine the origins of the object-oriented approach and discuss how it applies to database systems. Then, in Sections 11.2 through 11.6, we describe the key concepts utilized in many object-oriented database systems. Section 11.2 discusses *object identity*, *object structure*, and *type*

---

4. Microelectronics and Computer Technology Corporation, Austin, Texas.

5. Now called Lucent Technologies.

6. Formerly O2 of O2 Technology.

7. Object Database Management Group.

8. Similar concepts were also developed in the fields of semantic data modeling and knowledge representation.

constructors. Section 11.3 presents the concepts of *encapsulation of operations* and definition of *methods* as part of class declarations, and also discusses the mechanisms for storing objects in a database by making them *persistent*. Section 11.4 describes *type and class hierarchies* and *inheritance* in object-oriented databases, and Section 11.5 provides an overview of the issues that arise when *complex objects* need to be represented and stored. Section 11.6 discusses additional concepts, including *polymorphism, operator overloading, dynamic binding, multiple and selective inheritance*, and *versioning* and *configuration* of objects.

This chapter presents the general concepts of object-oriented databases, whereas Chapter 12 will present specific examples of how these concepts are realized. The topics covered in Chapter 12 include the ODMG 2.0 standard; object-oriented database design; examples of two commercial Object Database Management Systems (ARDENT and ObjectStore); and an overview of the CORBA standard for distributed objects.

The reader may skip Sections 11.5 and 11.6 of this chapter if a less detailed introduction to the topic is desired.

11.1 Overview of Object-Oriented Concepts

This section gives a quick overview of the history and main concepts of object-oriented databases, or OODBs for short. The OODB concepts are then explained in more detail in Sections 11.2 through 11.6. The term *object-oriented*—abbreviated by OO or O-O—has its origins in OO programming languages, or OOPLs. Today OO concepts are applied in the areas of databases, software engineering, knowledge bases, artificial intelligence, and computer systems in general. OOPLs have their roots in the SIMULA language, which was proposed in the late 1960s. In SIMULA, the concept of a *class* groups together the internal data structure of an object in a class declaration. Subsequently, researchers proposed the concept of *abstract data type*, which hides the internal data structures and specifies all possible external operations that can be applied to an object, leading to the concept of *encapsulation*. The programming language SMALLTALK, developed at Xerox PARC[9] in the 1970s, was one of the first languages to explicitly incorporate additional OO concepts, such as message passing and inheritance. It is known as a *pure* OO programming language, meaning that it was explicitly designed to be object-oriented. This contrasts with *hybrid* OO programming languages, which incorporate OO concepts into an already existing language. An example of the latter is C++, which incorporates OO concepts into the popular C programming language.

An **object** typically has two components: state (value) and behavior (operations). Hence, it is somewhat similar to a *program variable* in a programming language, except that it will typically have a *complex data structure* as well as *specific operations* defined by the programmer.[10] Objects in an OOPL exist only during program execution and are hence called *transient objects*. An OO database can extend the existence of objects so that they are stored permanently, and hence the objects *persist* beyond program termination and

---

9. Palo Alto Research Center, Palo Alto, California.

10. Objects have many other characteristics, as we discuss in the rest of this chapter.

can be retrieved later and shared by other programs. In other words, OO databases store *persistent objects* permanently on secondary storage, and allow the sharing of these objects among multiple programs and applications. This requires the incorporation of other well-known features of database management systems, such as indexing mechanisms, concurrency control, and recovery. An OO database system interfaces with one or more OO programming languages to provide persistent and shared object capabilities.

One goal of OO databases is to maintain a direct correspondence between real-world and database objects so that objects do not lose their integrity and identity and can easily be identified and operated upon. Hence, OO databases provide a unique system-generated *object identifier* (OID) for each object. We can compare this with the relational model where each relation must have a primary key attribute whose value identifies each tuple uniquely. In the relational model, if the value of the primary key is changed, the tuple will have a new identity, even though it may still represent the same real-world object. Alternatively, a real-world object may have different names for key attributes in different relations, making it difficult to ascertain that the keys represent the same object (for example, the object identifier may be represented as EMP_ID in one relation and as SSN in another).

Another feature of OO databases is that objects may have an *object structure* of *arbitrary complexity* in order to contain all of the necessary information that describes the object. In contrast, in traditional database systems, information about a complex object is often *scattered* over many relations or records, leading to loss of direct correspondence between a real-world object and its database representation.

The internal structure of an object in OOPLs includes the specification of **instance variables,** which hold the values that define the internal state of the object. Hence, an instance variable is similar to the concept of an *attribute*, except that instance variables may be encapsulated within the object and thus are not necessarily visible to external users. Instance variables may also be of arbitrarily complex data types. Object-oriented systems allow definition of the operations or functions (behavior) that can be applied to objects of a particular type. In fact, some OO models insist that all operations a user can apply to an object must be predefined. This forces a *complete encapsulation* of objects. This rigid approach has been relaxed in most OO data models for several reasons. First, the database user often needs to know the attribute names so they can specify selection conditions on the attributes to retrieve specific objects. Second, complete encapsulation implies that any simple retrieval requires a predefined operation, thus making ad hoc queries difficult to specify on the fly.

To encourage encapsulation, an operation is defined in two parts. The first part, called the *signature* or *interface* of the operation, specifies the operation name and arguments (or parameters). The second part, called the *method* or *body*, specifies the *implementation* of the operation. Operations can be invoked by passing a *message* to an object, which includes the operation name and the parameters. The object then executes the method for that operation. This encapsulation permits modification of the internal structure of an object, as well as the implementation of its operations, without the need to disturb the external programs that invoke these operations. Hence, encapsulation provides a form of data and operation independence (see Chapter 2).

Another key concept in OO systems is that of type and class hierarchies and *inheritance.* This permits specification of new types or classes that inherit much of their structure and operations from previously defined types or classes. Hence, specification of object types can proceed systematically. This makes it easier to develop the data types of a system incrementally, and to *reuse* existing type definitions when creating new types of objects.

One problem in early OO database systems involved representing *relationships* among objects. The insistence on complete encapsulation in early OO data models led to the argument that relationships should not be explicitly represented, but should instead be described by defining appropriate methods that locate related objects. However, this approach does not work very well for complex databases with many relationships, because it is useful to identify these relationships and make them visible to users. The ODMG 2.0 standard has recognized this need and it explicitly represents binary relationships via a pair of *inverse references*—that is, by placing the OIDs of related objects within the objects themselves, and maintaining referential integrity, as we shall describe in Chapter 12.

Some OO systems provide capabilities for dealing with *multiple versions* of the same object—a feature that is essential in design and engineering applications. For example, an old version of an object that represents a tested and verified design should be retained until the new version is tested and verified. A new version of a complex object may include only a few new versions of its component objects, whereas other components remain unchanged. In addition to permitting versioning, OO databases should also allow for *schema evolution*, which occurs when type declarations are changed or when new types or relationships are created. These two features are not specific to OODBs and should ideally be included in all types of DBMSs.[11]

Another OO concept is *operator polymorphism*, which refers to an operation's ability to be applied to different types of objects; in such a situation, an *operation name* may refer to several distinct *implementations*, depending on the type of objects it is applied to. This feature is also called *operator overloading*. For example, an operation to calculate the area of a geometric object may differ in its method (implementation), depending on whether the object is of type triangle, circle, or rectangle. This may require the use of *late binding* of the operation name to the appropriate method at run-time, when the type of object to which the operation is applied becomes known.

This section provided an overview of the main concepts of OO databases. In Sections 11.2 through 11.6, we discuss these concepts in more detail.

11.2   Object Identity, Object Structure, and Type Constructors

In this section we first discuss the concept of object identity, and then we present the typical structuring operations for defining the structure of the state of an object. These structuring operations are often called **type constructors.** They define basic data-structuring operations that can be combined to form complex object structures.

---

11. Several schema evolution operations, such as ALTER TABLE, are already defined in the relational SQL2 standard (see Section 8.1).

11.2.1   Object Identity

An OO database system provides a **unique identity** to each independent object stored in the database. This unique identity is typically implemented via a unique, system-generated **object identifier,** or **OID.** The value of an OID is not visible to the external user, but it is used internally by the system to identify each object uniquely and to create and manage inter-object references.

The main property required of an OID is that it be **immutable;** that is, the OID value of a particular object should not change. This preserves the identity of the real-world object being represented. Hence, an OO database system must have some mechanism for generating OIDs and preserving the immutability property. It is also desirable that each OID be used only once; that is, even if an object is removed from the database, its OID should not be assigned to another object. These two properties imply that the OID should not depend on any attribute values of the object, since the value of an attribute may be changed or corrected. It is also generally considered inappropriate to base the OID on the physical address of the object in storage, since the physical address can change after a physical reorganization of the database. However, some systems do use the physical address as OID to increase the efficiency of object retrieval. If the physical address of the object changes, an *indirect pointer* can be placed at the former address, which gives the new physical location of the object. It is more common to use long integers as OIDs and then to use some form of hash table to map the OID value to the physical address of the object.

Some early OO data models required that everything—from a simple value to a complex object—be represented as an object; hence, every basic value, such as an integer, string, or Boolean value, has an OID. This allows two basic values to have different OIDs, which can be useful in some cases. For example, the integer value 50 can be used sometimes to mean a weight in kilograms and at other times to mean the age of a person. Then, two basic objects with distinct OIDs could be created, but both objects would represent the integer value 50. Although useful as a theoretical model, this is not very practical, since it may lead to the generation of too many OIDs. Hence, most OO database systems allow for the representation of both objects and **values.** Every object must have an immutable OID, whereas a value has no OID and just stands for itself. Hence, a value is typically stored within an object and *cannot be referenced* from other objects. In some systems, complex structured values can also be created without having a corresponding OID if needed.

11.2.2   Object Structure

In OO databases, the state (current value) of a complex object may be constructed from other objects (or other values) by using certain **type constructors.** One formal way of representing such objects is to view each object as a triple (i, c, v), where i is a unique *object identifier* (the OID), c is a *type constructor*[12] (that is, an indication of how the object state is constructed), and v is the object state (or *current value*). The data model will typically

---

12. This is different from the constructor operation that is used in C++ and other OOPLs.

include several type constructors. The three most basic constructors are **atom, tuple,** and **set.** Other commonly used constructors include **list, bag,** and **array.** The atom constructor is used to represent all basic atomic values, such as integers, real numbers, character strings, Booleans, and any other basic data types that the system supports directly.

The object state v of an object (i, c, v) is interpreted based on the constructor c. If $c =$ atom, the state (value) v is an atomic value from the domain of basic values supported by the system. If $c =$ set, the state v is a *set of object identifiers* $\{i_1, i_2, \ldots, i_n\}$, which are the OIDs for a set of objects that are typically of the same type. If $c =$ tuple, the state v is a tuple of the form $<a_1{:}i_1, a_2{:}i_2, \ldots, a_n{:}i_n>$, where each a_j is an attribute name[13] and each i_j is an OID. If $c =$ list, the value v is an *ordered list* $[i_1, i_2, \ldots, i_n]$ of OIDs of objects of the same type. A list is similar to a set except that the OIDs in a list are *ordered*, and hence we can refer to the first, second, or j^{th} object in a list. For $c =$ array, the state of the object is a single-dimensional array of object identifiers. The main difference between array and list is that a list can have an arbitrary number of elements whereas an array typically has a maximum size. The difference between *set* and *bag*[14] is that all elements in a set must be distinct whereas a bag can have duplicate elements.

This model of objects allows arbitrary nesting of the set, list, tuple, and other constructors. The state of an object that is not of type atom will refer to other objects by their object identifiers. Hence, the only case where an actual value appears is in *the state of an object of type atom.*[15]

The type constructors **set, list, array,** and **bag** are called **collection types** (or **bulk types**), to distinguish them from basic types and tuple types. The main characteristic of a collection type is that the state of the object will be a *collection of objects* that may be unordered (such as a set or a bag) or ordered (such as a list or an array). The **tuple** type constructor is often called a **structured type,** since it corresponds to the **struct** construct in the C and C++ programming languages.

EXAMPLE 1: A Complex Object

We now represent some objects from the relational database shown in Figure 7.6, using the preceding model, where an object is defined by a triple (OID, type constructor, state) and the available type constuctors are atom, set, and tuple. We use $i_1, i_2, i_3, \ldots$ to stand for unique system-generated object identifiers. Consider the following objects:

$o_1 = (i_1,$ atom, 'Houston')

$o_2 = (i_2,$ atom, 'Bellaire')

$o_3 = (i_3,$ atom, 'Sugarland')

---

13. Also called an *instance variable name* in OO terminology.

14. Also called a multiset.

15. As we noted earlier, it is not practical to generate a unique system identifier for every value, so real systems allow for both OIDs and *structured value*, which can be structured by using the same type constructors as objects, except that a value *does not have* an OID.

$o_4 = (i_4, \text{atom}, 5)$

$o_5 = (i_5, \text{atom}, \text{'Research'})$

$o_6 = (i_6, \text{atom}, \text{'1988-05-22'})$

$o_7 = (i_7, \text{set}, \{i_1, i_2, i_3\})$

$o_8 = (i_8, \text{tuple}, <\text{DNAME}:i_5, \text{DNUMBER}:i_4, \text{MGR}:i_9, \text{LOCATIONS}:i_7, \text{EMPLOYEES}:i_{10}, \text{PROJECTS}:i_{11}>)$

$o_9 = (i_9, \text{tuple}, <\text{MANAGER}:i_{12}, \text{MANAGER\_START\_DATE}:i_6>)$

$o_{10} = (i_{10}, \text{set}, \{i_{12}, i_{13}, i_{14}\})$

$o_{11} = (i_{11}, \text{set } \{i_{15}, i_{16}, i_{17}\})$

$o_{12} = (i_{12}, \text{tuple}, <\text{FNAME}:i_{18}, \text{MINIT}:i_{19}, \text{LNAME}:i_{20}, \text{SSN}:i_{21}, \ldots, \text{SALARY}:i_{26}, \text{SUPERVISOR}:i_{27}, \text{DEPT}:i_8>)$

. . .

The first six objects (o_1–o_6) listed here represent atomic values. There will be many similar objects, one for each distinct constant atomic value in the database.[16] Object o_7 is a set-valued object that represents the set of locations for department 5; the set $\{i_1, i_2, i_3\}$ refers to the atomic objects with values {'Houston', 'Bellaire', 'Sugarland'}. Object o_8 is a tuple-valued object that represents department 5 itself, and has the attributes DNAME, DNUMBER, MGR, LOCATIONS, and so on. The first two attributes DNAME and DNUMBER have atomic objects o_5 and o_4 as their values. The MGR attribute has a tuple object o_9 as its value, which in turn has two attributes. The value of the MANAGER attribute is the object whose OID is i_{12}, which represents the employee 'John B. Smith' who manages the department, whereas the value of MANAGER_START_DATE is another atomic object whose value is a date. The value of the EMPLOYEES attribute of o_8 is a set object with OID = i_{10}, whose value is the set of object identifiers for the employees who work for the DEPARTMENT (objects i_{12}, plus i_{13} and i_{14}, which are not shown). Similarly, the value of the PROJECTS attribute of o_8 is a set object with OID = i_{11}, whose value is the set of object identifiers for the projects that are controlled by department number 5 (objects i_{15}, i_{16}, and i_{17}, which are not shown). The object whose OID = i_{12} represents the employee 'John B. Smith' with all its atomic attributes (FNAME, MINIT, LNAME, SSN, . . ., SALARY, that are referencing the atomic objects i_{18}, i_{19}, i_{20}, i_{21}, . . ., i_{26}, respectively (not shown)) plus SUPERVISOR which references the employee object with OID = i_{27} (this represents 'James E. Borg' who supervises 'John B. Smith' but is not shown) and DEPT which references the department object with OID = i_8 (this represents department number 5 where 'John B. Smith' works). ∎

In this model, an object can be represented as a graph structure that can be constructed by recursively applying the type constructors. The graph representing an object o_i can be constructed by first creating a node for the object o_i itself. The node for o_i is labeled with the OID and the object constructor c. We also create a node in the graph for each basic atomic value. If an object o_i has an atomic value, we draw a directed arc from

---

16. These atomic objects are the ones that may cause a problem, due to the use of too many object identifiers, if this model is implemented directly.

the node representing o_i to the node representing its basic value. If the object value is constructed, we draw directed arcs from the object node to a node that represents the constructed value. Figure 11.1 shows the graph for the example DEPARTMENT object o_8 given earlier.

The preceding model permits two types of definitions in a comparison of the *states of two objects* for equality. Two objects are said to have **identical states** (deep equality) if the graphs representing their states are identical in every respect, including the OIDs at every level. Another, weaker definition of equality is when two objects have **equal states** (shallow equality). In this case, the graph structures must be the same, and all the corresponding atomic values in the graphs should also be the same. However, some corresponding internal nodes in the two graphs may have objects with *different OIDs*.

EXAMPLE 2: Identical Versus Equal Objects

A example can illustrate the difference between the two definitions for comparing object states for equality. Consider the following objects o_1, o_2, o_3, o_4, o_5, and o_6:

$o_1 = (i_1, \text{tuple}, <a_1{:}i_4, a_2{:}i_6>)$

$o_2 = (i_2, \text{tuple}, <a_1{:}i_5, a_2{:}i_6>)$

$o_3 = (i_3, \text{tuple}, <a_1{:}i_4, a_2{:}i_6>)$

$o_4 = (i_4, \text{atom}, 10)$

$o_5 = (i_5, \text{atom}, 10)$

$o_6 = (i_6, \text{atom}, 20)$

The objects o_1 and o_2 have *equal* states, since their states at the atomic level are the same but the values are reached through distinct objects o_4 and o_5. However, the states of objects o_1 and o_3 are *identical*, even though the objects themselves are not because they have distinct OIDs. Similarly, although the states of o_4 and o_5 are identical, the actual objects o_4 and o_5 are equal but not identical, because they have distinct OIDs.

11.2.3 Type Constructors

An **object definition language** (ODL)[17] that incorporates the preceding type constructors can be used to define the object types for a particular database application. In Chapter 12, we shall describe the standard ODL of ODMG, but we first introduce the concepts gradually in this section using a simpler notation. The type constructors can be used to define the *data structures* for an OO *database schema*. In Section 11.3 we will see how to incorporate the definition of *operations* (or methods) into the OO schema. Figure 11.2 shows how we may declare Employee and Department types corresponding to the object instances shown in Figure 11.1. In Figure 11.2, the Date type is defined as a tuple rather than an atomic value as in Figure 11.1. We use the keywords tuple, set, and list for the type con-

---

17. This would correspond to the DDL (Data Definition Language) of the database system (see Chapter 2).

LEGEND:

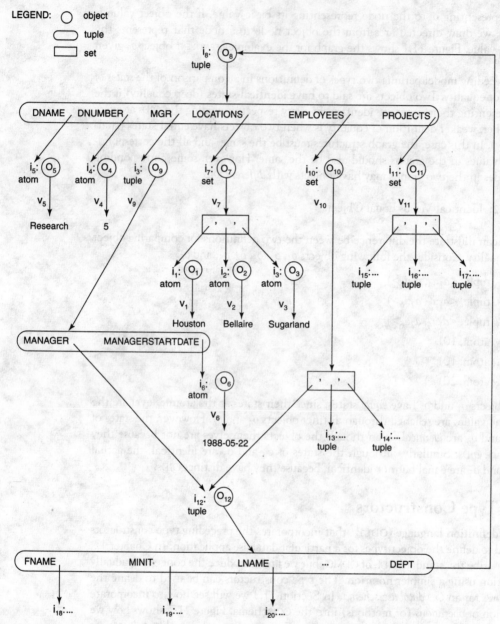

Figure 11.1   Representation of a DEPARTMENT complex object as a graph.

structors, and the available standard data types (integer, string, float, and so on) for atomic types.

Attributes that refer to other objects—such as dept of Employee or projects of Department—are basically **references** to other objects and hence serve to represent *rela-*

```
define type Employee:
    tuple (      fname:          string;
                 minit:          char;
                 lname:          string;
                 ssn:            string;
                 birthdate:      Date;
                 address:        string;
                 sex:            char;
                 salary:         float;
                 supervisor:     Employee;
                 dept:           Department;        );
define type Date
    tuple (      year:           integer;
                 month:          integer;
                 day:            integer;    );
define type Department
    tuple (      dname:          string;
                 dnumber:        integer;
                 mgr:            tuple (    manager:     Employee;
                                           startdate:   Date;        );
                 locations:      set(string);
                 employees:      set(Employee);
                 projects        set(Project);   );
```

Figure 11.2 Specifying the object types Employee, Date, and Department using type constructors.

tionships among the object types. For example, the attribute dept of Employee is of type Department, and hence is used to refer to a specific Department object (where the Employee works). The value of such an attribute would be an OID for a specific Department object. A binary relationship can be represented in one direction, or it can have an *inverse reference*. The latter representation makes it easy to traverse the relationship in both directions. For example, the attribute employees of Department has as its value a *set of references* (that is, a set of OIDs) to objects of type Employee; these are the employees who work for the department. The inverse is the reference attribute dept of Employee. We will see in Chapter 12 how the ODMG 2.0 standard allows inverses to be explicitly declared as relationship attributes to ensure that inverse references are consistent.

11.3 Encapsulation of Operations, Methods, and Persistence

The concept of *encapsulation* is one of the main characteristics of OO languages and systems. It is also related to the concepts of *abstract data types* and *information hiding* in programming languages. In traditional database models and systems, this concept was not applied, since it is customary to make the structure of database objects visible to users and external programs. In these traditional models, a number of standard database operations are applicable to objects of all types. For example, in the relational model, the operations for selecting, inserting, deleting, and modifying tuples are generic and may be applied to *any relation* in the database. The relation and its attributes are visible to users and to external programs that access the relation by using these operations.

11.3.1   Specifying Object Behavior via Class Operations

The concepts of information hiding and encapsulation can be applied to database objects. The main idea is to define the **behavior** of a type of object based on the **operations** that can be externally applied to objects of that type. The internal structure of the object is hidden, and the object is accessible only through a number of predefined operations. Some operations may be used to create (insert) or destroy (delete) objects; other operations may update the object state; and others may be used to retrieve parts of the object state or to apply some calculations. Still other operations may perform a combination of retrieval, calculation, and update. In general, the **implementation** of an operation can be specified in a *general-purpose programming language* that provides flexibility and power in defining the operations.

The external users of the object are only made aware of the **interface** of the object type, which defines the name and arguments (parameters) of each operation. The implementation is hidden from the external users; it includes the definition of the internal data structures of the object and the implementation of the operations that access these structures. In OO terminology, the interface part of each operation is called the **signature,** and the operation implementation is called a **method.** Typically, a method is invoked by sending a **message** to the object to execute the corresponding method. Notice that, as part of executing a method, a subsequent message to another object may be sent, and this mechanism may be used to return values from the objects to the external environment or to other objects.

For database applications, the requirement that all objects be completely encapsulated is too stringent. One way of relaxing this requirement is to divide the structure of an object into **visible** and **hidden** attributes (instance variables). Visible attributes may be directly accessed for reading by external operators, or by a high-level query language. The hidden attributes of an object are completely encapsulated and can be accessed only through predefined operations. Most OODBMSs employ high-level query languages for accessing visible attributes. In Chapter 12, we will describe the OQL query language that is proposed as a standard query language for OODBs.

In most cases, operations that *update* the state of an object are encapsulated. This is a way of defining the update semantics of the objects, given that in many OO data models, few integrity constraints are predefined in the schema. Each type of object has its integrity constraints *programmed into the methods* that create, delete, and update the objects by explicitly writing code to check for constraint violations and to handle exceptions. In such cases, all update operations are implemented by encapsulated operations. More recently, the ODL for the ODMG 2.0 standard allows the specification of some constraints such as keys and inverse relationships (referential integrity) so that the system can automatically enforce these constraints (see Chapter 12).

```
    define class Employee:
        type tuple(   fname:              string;
                      minit:              char;
                      lname:              string;
                      ssn:                string;
                      birthdate:          Date;
                      address:            string;
                      sex:                char;
                      salary:             float;
                      supervisor:         Employee;
                      dept:               Department;          );
        operations    age:                integer;
                      create_emp:         Employee;
                      destroy_emp:        boolean;
    end Employee;


    define class Department
        type tuple(   dname:              string;
                      dnumber:            integer;
                      mgr:                tuple (    manager: Employee;
                                                     startdate: Date;        );
                      locations:          set(string);
                      employees:          set(Employee);
                      projects:           set(Project);        );
        operations    no_of_emps:         integer;
                      create_dept:        Department;
                      destroy_dept:       boolean;
                      assign_emp(e: Employee): boolean;
                      (* adds an employee to the department *)
                      remove_emp(e: Employee): boolean;
                      (* removes an employee from the department *)
    end Department;
```

Figure 11.3 Adding operations to the definitions of Employee and Department.

The term **class** is often used to refer to an object type definition, along with the definitions of the operations for that type.[18] Figure 11.3 shows how the type definitions of Figure 11.2 may be extended with operations to define classes. A number of operations are declared for each class, and the signature (interface) of each operation is included in the class definition. A method (implementation) for each operation must be defined elsewhere, using a programming language. Typical operations include the **object constructor** operation, which is used to create a new object, and the **destructor** operation, which is used to destroy an object. A number of **object modifier** operations can also be declared to modify various attributes of an object. Additional operations can **retrieve** information about the object.

---

18. This definition of *class* is similar to how it is used in the popular C++ programming language. The ODMG standard uses the word *interface* in addition to *class* (see Chapter 12). In the EER model, the term *class* was used to refer to an object type, along with the set of all objects of that type (see Chapter 4).

An operation is typically applied to an object by using the **dot notation.** For example, if d is a reference to a department object, we can invoke an operation such as no_of_emps by writing d.no_of_emps. Similarly, by writing d.destroy_dept, the object referenced by d is destroyed (deleted). The only exception is the constructor operation, which returns a reference to a new Department object. Hence, it is customary to have a default name for the constructor operation that is the name of the class itself, although this was not used in Figure 11.3.[19] The dot notation is also used to refer to attributes of an object—for example, by writing d.dnumber or d.mgr.startdate.

11.3.2   Specifying Object Persistence via Naming and Reachability

An OODBMS is often closely coupled with an OOPL. The OOPL is used to specify the method implementations as well as other application code. An object is typically created by some executing application program, by invoking the object constructor operation. Not all objects are meant to be stored permanently in the database. **Transient objects** exist in the executing program and disappear once the program terminates. **Persistent objects** are stored in the database and persist after program termination. The typical mechanisms for making an object persistent are *naming* and *reachability*.

The **naming mechanism** involves giving an object a unique persistent name through which it can be retrieved by this and other programs. This persistent object name can be given via a specific statement or operation in the program, as illustrated in Figure 11.4. All such names given to objects must be unique within a particular database. Hence, the named persistent objects are used as **entry points** to the database through which users and applications can start their database access. Obviously, it is not practical to give names to all objects in a large database that includes thousands of objects, so most objects are made persistent by using the second mechanism, called **reachability.** The reachability mechanism works by making the object reachable from some persistent object. An object B is said to be **reachable** from an object A if a sequence of references in the object graph lead from object A to object B. For example, all the objects in Figure 11.1 are reachable from object o_8; hence, if o_8 is made persistent, all the other objects in Figure 11.1 also become persistent.

If we first create a named persistent object N, whose state is a *set* or *list* of objects of some class C, we can make objects of C persistent by *adding them* to the set or list, and thus making them reachable from N. Hence, N defines a **persistent collection** of objects of class C. For example, we can define a class DepartmentSet (see Figure 11.4) whose objects are of type **set**(Department).[20] Suppose that an object of type DepartmentSet is

---

19. Default names for the constructor and destructor operations exist in the C++ programming language. For example, for class Employee, the *default constructor name* is Employee and the *default constructor name* is ~Employee. It is also common to use the *new* operation to create new objects.

20. As we shall see in Chapter 12, the ODMG ODL syntax uses **set<Department>** instead of **set**(Department).

```
define class DepartmentSet:
    type          set(Department);
    operations    add_dept(d: Department): boolean;
          (* adds a department to the DepartmentSet object *)
              remove_dept(d: Department): boolean;
          (* removes a department from the DepartmentSet object *)
              create_dept_set:        DepartmentSet;
              destroy_dept_set:       boolean;
end DepartmentSet;

    ...


persistent name AllDepartments: DepartmentSet;
(* AllDepartments is a persistent named object of type DepartmentSet *)

    ...

d:= create_dept;
(* create a new Department object in the variable d *)

    ...

b:= AllDepartments.add_dept(d);
(* make d persistent by adding it to the persistent set AllDepartments *)

    ...
```

Figure 11.4   Creating persistent objects by naming and reachability.

created, and suppose that it is named AllDepartments and thus made persistent, as illustrated in Figure 11.4. Any Department object that is added to the set of AllDepartments by using the add_dept operation becomes persistent by virtue of its being reachable from AllDepartments. The AllDepartments object is often called the **extent** of the class Department, as it will hold all persistent objects of type Department. As we shall see in Chapter 12, the ODMG ODL standard gives the schema designer the option of naming an extent as part of class definition.

Notice the difference between traditional database models and OO databases in this respect. In traditional database models, such as the relational model or the EER model, *all* objects are assumed to be persistent. Hence, when an entity type or class such as EMPLOYEE is defined in the EER model, it represents both the *type declaration* for EMPLOYEE and a *persistent set of all* EMPLOYEE objects. In the OO approach, a class declaration of EMPLOYEE specifies only the type and operations for a class of objects. The user must separately define a persistent object of type set(EMPLOYEE) or list(EMPLOYEE) whose value is the *collection of references* to all persistent EMPLOYEE objects, if this is desired, as illustrated in Figure 11.4.[21] In fact, it is possible to define several persistent collections for the same class definition, if desired. This allows transient and persistent objects to follow the same type and class declarations of the ODL and the OOPL.

---

21. Some systems, such as POET, automatically create the extent for a class.

11.4   Type Hierarchies and Inheritance

Another main characteristic of OO database systems is that they allow type hierarchies and inheritance. Type hierarchies in databases usually imply a constraint on the extents corresponding to the types in the hierarchy. We first discuss type hierarchies (in Section 11.4.1), and then the constraints on the extents (in Section 11.4.2). We use a different OO model in this section—a model in which attributes and operations are treated uniformly—since both attributes and operations can be inherited.

11.4.1   Type Hierarchies and Inheritance

In most database applications, there are numerous objects of the same type or class. Hence, OO databases must provide a capability for classifying objects based on their type, as do other database systems. But in OO databases, a further requirement is that the system permit the definition of new types based on other predefined types, leading to a **type** (or **class**) **hierarchy.**

Typically, a type is defined by assigning it a type name and then defining a number of attributes (instance variables) and operations (methods) for the type.[22] In some cases, the attributes and operations are together called *functions*, since attributes resemble functions with zero arguments. A function name can be used to refer to the value of an attribute or to refer to the resulting value of an operation (method). In this section, we use the term **function** to refer to both attributes *and* operations of an object type, since they are treated similarly in a basic introduction to inheritance.[23]

A type in its simplest form can be defined by giving it a **type name** and then listing the names of its visible (*public*) **functions.** When specifying a type in this section, we use the following format, which does not specify arguments of functions, to simplify the discussion:

```
TYPE_NAME: function, function, . . . , function
```

For example, a type that describes characteristics of a PERSON may be defined as follows:

```
PERSON: Name, Address, Birthdate, Age, SSN
```

In the PERSON type, the Name, Address, SSN, and Birthdate functions can be implemented as stored attributes, whereas the Age function can be implemented as a method that calculates the Age from the value of the Birthdate attribute and the current date.

The concept of **subtype** is useful when the designer or user must create a new type that is similar but not identical to an already defined type. The subtype then inherits all

---

22. In this section, we will use the terms *type* and *class* as meaning the same thing—namely, the attributes *and* operations of some type of object.

23. We will see in Chapter 12 that types with functions are similar to the interfaces used in ODMG ODL.

the functions of the predefined type, which we shall call the **supertype.** For example, suppose that we want to define two new types EMPLOYEE and STUDENT as follows:

> EMPLOYEE: Name, Address, Birthdate, Age, SSN, Salary, HireDate, Seniority
>
> STUDENT: Name, Address, Birthdate, Age, SSN, Major, GPA

Since both STUDENT and EMPLOYEE include all the functions defined for PERSON plus some additional functions of their own, we can declare them to be **subtypes** of PERSON. Each will inherit the previously defined functions of PERSON—namely, Name, Address, Birthdate, Age, and SSN. For STUDENT, it is only necessary to define the new (local) functions Major and GPA, which are not inherited. Presumably, Major can be defined as a stored attribute, whereas GPA may be implemented as a method that calculates the student's grade point average by accessing the Grade values that are internally stored (hidden) within each STUDENT object as *private attributes*. For EMPLOYEE, the Salary and HireDate functions may be stored attributes, whereas Seniority may be a method that calculates Seniority from the value of HireDate.

The idea of defining a type involves defining all of its functions and implementing them either as attributes or as methods. When a subtype is defined, it can then inherit all of these functions and their implementations. Only functions that are specific or **local** to the subtype, and hence are not implemented in the supertype, need to be defined and implemented. Therefore, we can declare EMPLOYEE and STUDENT as follows:

> EMPLOYEE **subtype-of** PERSON: Salary, HireDate, Seniority
>
> STUDENT **subtype-of** PERSON: Major, GPA

In general, a subtype includes *all* of the functions that are defined for its supertype plus some additional functions that are specific only to the subtype. Hence, it is possible to generate a **type hierarchy** to show the supertype/subtype relationships among all the types declared in the system.

As another example, consider a type that describes objects in plane geometry, which may be defined as follows:

> GEOMETRY_OBJECT: Shape, Area, ReferencePoint

For the GEOMETRY_OBJECT type, Shape is implemented as an attribute (its domain can be an enumerated type with values 'triangle', 'rectangle', 'circle', and so on), and Area is a method that is applied to calculate the area. Now suppose that we want to define a number of subtypes for the GEOMETRY_OBJECT type, as follows:

> RECTANGLE **subtype-of** GEOMETRY_OBJECT: Width, Height
>
> TRIANGLE **subtype-of** GEOMETRY_OBJECT: Side1, Side2, Angle
>
> CIRCLE **subtype-of** GEOMETRY_OBJECT: Radius

Notice that the Area operation may be implemented by a different method for each subtype, since the procedure for area calculation is different for rectangles, triangles, and circles. Similarly, the attribute ReferencePoint may have a different meaning for each subtype; it might be the center point for RECTANGLE and CIRCLE objects, and the vertex point between the two given sides for a TRIANGLE object. Some OO database systems allow the **renaming** of inherited functions in different subtypes to reflect the meaning more closely.

An alternative way of declaring these three subtypes is to specify the value of the Shape attribute as a condition that must be satisfied for objects of each subtype:

```
RECTANGLE subtype-of GEOMETRY_OBJECT (Shape='rectangle'): Width,
Height
TRIANGLE subtype-of GEOMETRY_OBJECT (Shape='triangle'): Side1, Side2,
Angle
CIRCLE subtype-of GEOMETRY_OBJECT (Shape='circle'): Radius
```

Here, only GEOMETRY_OBJECT objects whose Shape='rectangle' are of the subtype RECTANGLE, and similarly for the other two subtypes. In this case, all functions of the GEOMETRY_OBJECT supertype are inherited by each of the three subtypes, but the value of the Shape attribute is restricted to a specific value for each.

Notice that type definitions describe objects but *do not* generate objects on their own. They are just declarations of certain types; and as part of that declaration, the implementation of the functions of each type is specified. In a database application, there are many objects of each type. When an object is created, it typically belongs to one or more of these types that have been declared. For example, a circle object is of type CIRCLE and GEOMETRY_OBJECT (by inheritance). Each object also becomes a member of one or more persistent collections of objects (or extents), which are used to group together collections of objects that are meaningful to the database application.

11.4.2 Constraints on Extents Corresponding to a Type Hierarchy[24]

In most OO databases, the collection of objects in an extent has the same type or class. However, this is not a necessary condition. For example, SMALLTALK, a so-called *typeless* OO language, allows a collection of objects to contain objects of different types. This can also be the case when other non-object-oriented typeless languages, such as LISP, are extended with OO concepts. However, since the majority of OO databases support types, we will assume that **extents** are collections of objects of the same type for the remainder of this section.

It is common in database applications that each type or subtype will have an extent associated with it, which holds the collection of all persistent objects of that type or subtype. In this case, the constraint is that every object in an extent that corresponds to a subtype must also be a member of the *extent* that corresponds to its supertype. Some OO database systems have a predefined system type (called the ROOT class or the OBJECT class) whose extent contains all the objects in the system.[25] Classification then proceeds by

---

24. In the second edition of this book, we used the title *Class Hierarchies* to describe these extent constraints. Because the word *class* has too many different meanings, *extent* is used in this edition. This is also more consistent with ODMG 2.0 terminology (see Chapter 12).

25. This is called OBJECT in the ODMG model (see Chapter 12).

assigning objects into additional subtypes that are meaningful to the application, creating a **type hierarchy** or **class hierarchy** for the system. All extents for system- and user-defined classes are subsets of the extent corresponding to the class OBJECT, directly or indirectly. In the ODMG model (see Chapter 12), the user may or may not specify an extent for each class (type), depending on the application.

In most OO systems, a distinction is made between persistent and transient objects and collections. A **persistent collection** holds a collection of objects that is stored permanently in the database and hence can be accessed and shared by multiple programs. A **transient collection** exists temporarily during the execution of a program but is not kept when the program terminates. For example, a transient collection may be created in a program to hold the result of a query that selects some objects from a persistent collection and copies those objects into the transient collection. The transient collection holds the same type of objects as the persistent collection. The program can then manipulate the objects in the transient collection, and once the program terminates, the transient collection ceases to exist. In general, numerous collections—transient or persistent—may contain objects of the same type.

Notice that the type constructors discussed in Section 11.2 permit the state of one object to be a collection of objects. Hence, collection objects whose types are based on the *set constructor* can define a number of collections—one corresponding to each object. The set-valued objects themselves are members of another collection. This allows for multilevel classification schemes, where an object in one collection has as its state a collection of objects of a different class.

As we shall see in Chapter 12, the ODMG 2.0 model distinguishes between type inheritance—called interface inheritance and denoted by the ":" symbol—and the extent inheritance constraint—denoted by the keyword EXTEND.

11.5 Complex Objects

A principal motivation that led to the development of OO systems was the desire to represent complex objects. There are two main types of complex objects: structured and unstructured. A structured complex object is made up of components and is defined by applying the available type constructors recursively at various levels. An unstructured complex object typically is a data type that requires a large amount of storage, such as a data type that represents an image or a large textual object.

11.5.1 Unstructured Complex Objects and Type Extensibility

An **unstructured complex object** facility provided by a DBMS permits the storage and retrieval of large objects that are needed by the database application. Typical examples of such objects are *bitmap images* and *long text strings* (such as documents); they are also known as **binary large objects,** or **BLOBs** for short. These objects are unstructured in the sense that the DBMS does not know what their structure is—only the application that uses them can interpret their meaning. For example, the application may have functions to display an image or to search for certain keywords in a long text string. The objects are considered complex because they require a large area of storage and are not part of the standard data types provided by traditional DBMSs. Because the object size is quite large, a DBMS may retrieve a portion of the object and provide it to the application program before the whole object is retrieved. The DBMS may also use buffering and caching techniques to prefetch portions of the object before the application program needs to access them.

The DBMS software does not have the capability to directly process selection conditions and other operations based on values of these objects, unless the application provides the code to do the comparison operations needed for the selection. In an OODBMS, this can be accomplished by defining a new abstract data type for the uninterpreted objects and by providing the methods for selecting, comparing, and displaying such objects. For example, consider objects that are two-dimensional bitmap images. Suppose that the application needs to select from a collection of such objects only those that include a certain pattern. In this case, the user must provide the pattern recognition program as a method on objects of the bitmap type. The OODBMS then retrieves an object from the database and runs the method for pattern recognition on it to determine whether the object includes the required pattern.

Because an OODBMS allows users to create new types, and because a type includes both structure and operations, we can view an OODBMS as having an **extensible type system.** We can create libraries of new types by defining their structure and operations, including complex types. Applications can then use or modify these types, in the latter case by creating subtypes of the types provided in the libraries. However, the DBMS internals must provide the underlying storage and retrieval capabilities for objects that require large amounts of storage so that the operations may be applied efficiently. Many OODBMSs provide for the storage and retrieval of large unstructured objects such as character strings or bit strings, which can be passed "as is" to the application program for interpretation. Recently, relational and extended relational DBMSs have also been able to provide such capabilities.

11.5.2   Structured Complex Objects

A **structured complex object** differs from an unstructured complex object in that the object's structure is defined by repeated application of the type constructors provided by the OODBMS. Hence, the object structure is defined and known to the OODBMS. As an example, consider the DEPARTMENT object shown in Figure 11.1. At the first level, the object has a tuple structure with six attributes: DNAME, DNUMBER, MGR, LOCATIONS, EMPLOYEES, and PROJECTS. However, only two of these attributes—namely, DNAME and DNUMBER—have basic values; the other four have complex values and hence build the second level of the complex object structure. One of these four (MGR) has a tuple structure, and the other three (LOCATIONS, EMPLOYEES, PROJECTS) have set structures. At the third level, for a MGR tuple value, we have one basic attribute (MANAGERSTARTDATE) and one attribute (MANAGER) that refers to an employee object, which has a tuple structure. For a LOCATIONS set, we have a set of basic values, but for both the EMPLOYEES and the PROJECTS sets, we have sets of tuple-structured objects.

Two types of reference semantics exist between a complex object and its components at each level. The first type, which we can call **ownership semantics,** applies when the sub-objects of a complex object are encapsulated within the complex object and are hence considered part of the complex object. The second type, which we can call **reference semantics,** applies when the components of the complex object are themselves independent objects but may be referenced from the complex object. For example, we may consider the DNAME, DNUMBER, MGR, and LOCATIONS attributes to be owned by a DEPARTMENT, whereas EMPLOYEES and PROJECTS are references because they reference independent objects. The first type is also referred to as the *is-part-of* or *is-component-of* relationship; and the second type is called the *is-associated-with* relationship, since it describes an equal association between two independent objects. The is-part-of relationship (ownership semantics) for constructing complex objects has the property that the component objects are encapsulated within the complex object and are considered part of the internal object state. They need not have object identifiers and can only be accessed by methods of that object. They are deleted if the object itself is deleted. On the other hand, a complex object whose components are referenced is considered to consist of independent objects that can have their own identity and methods. When a complex object needs to access its referenced components, it must do so by invoking the appropriate methods of the components, since they are not encapsulated within the complex object. Hence, reference semantics represents *relationships* among independent objects. In addition, a referenced component object may be referenced by more than one complex object and hence is not automatically deleted when the complex object is deleted.

An OODBMS should provide storage options for **clustering** the component objects of a complex object together on secondary storage in order to increase the efficiency of operations that access the complex object. In many cases, the object structure is stored on disk pages in an uninterpreted fashion. When a disk page that includes an object is retrieved into memory, the OODBMS can build up the structured complex object from the information on the disk pages, which may refer to additional disk pages that must be retrieved. This is known as **complex object assembly.**

11.6   Other Objected-Oriented Concepts

In this section we give an overview of some additional OO concepts, including polymorphism (operator overloading), multiple inheritance, selective inheritance, versioning, and configurations.

11.6.1   Polymorphism (Operator Overloading)

Another characteristic of OO systems is that they provide for **polymorphism** of operations, which is also sometimes referred to as **operator overloading.** This concept allows the same *operator name* or *symbol* to be bound to two or more different *implementations* of the operator, depending on the type of objects to which the operator is applied. A simple example from programming languages can illustrate this concept. In some languages, the operator symbol "+" can mean different things when applied to operands (objects) of different types. If the operands of "+" are of type *integer*, the operation invoked is integer addition. If the operands of "+" are of type *floating point*, the operation invoked is floating point addition. If the operands of "+" are of type *set*, the operation invoked is set union. The compiler can determine which operation to execute based on the types of operands supplied.

In OO databases, a similar situation may occur. We can use the GEOMETRY_OBJECT example discussed in Section 11.4 to illustrate polymorphism[26] in OO databases. Suppose that we declare GEOMETRY_OBJECT and its subtypes as follows:

```
GEOMETRY_OBJECT: Shape, Area, ReferencePoint
RECTANGLE subtype-of GEOMETRY_OBJECT (Shape='rectangle'): Width,
Height
TRIANGLE subtype-of GEOMETRY_OBJECT (Shape='triangle'): Side1, Side2,
Angle
CIRCLE subtype-of GEOMETRY_OBJECT (Shape='circle'): Radius
```

Here, the function Area is declared for all objects of type GEOMETRY_OBJECT. However, the implementation of the method for Area may differ for each subtype of GEOMETRY_OBJECT. One possibility is to have a general implementation for calculating the area of a generalized GEOMETRY_OBJECT (for example, by writing a general algorithm to calculate the area of a polygon) and then to rewrite more efficient algorithms to calculate the areas of specific types of geometric objects, such as a circle, a rectangle, a triangle, and so on. In this case, the Area function is *overloaded* by different implementations.

The OODBMS must now select the appropriate method for the Area function based on the type of geometric object to which it is applied. In strongly typed systems, this can be done at compile time, since the object types must be known. This is termed **early (or static) binding.** However, in systems with weak typing or no typing (such as SMALLTALK and LISP), the type of the object to which a function is applied may not be known until run-time. In this case, the function must check the type of object at run-time and then invoke the appropriate method. This is often referred to as **late (or dynamic) binding.**

11.6.2   Multiple Inheritance and Selective Inheritance

Multiple inheritance in a type hierarchy occurs when a certain subtype T is a subtype of two (or more) types and hence inherits the functions (attributes and methods) of both supertypes. For example, we may create a subtype ENGINEERING_MANAGER that is a subtype of both MANAGER and ENGINEER. This leads to the creation of a **type lattice** rather than a type hierarchy. One problem that can occur with multiple inheritance is that the supertypes from which the subtype inherits may have distinct functions of the same name, creating an ambiguity. For example, both MANAGER and ENGINEER may have a function called Salary. If

---

26. In programming languages, there are several kinds of polymorphism. The interested reader is referred to the bibliographic notes for works that include a more thorough discussion.

the Salary function is implemented by different methods in the MANAGER and ENGINEER super-types, an ambiguity exists as to which of the two is inherited by the subtype ENGINEERING_MANAGER. It is possible, however, that both ENGINEER and MANAGER inherit Salary from the same supertype (such as EMPLOYEE) higher up in the lattice. The general rule is that if a function is inherited from some *common supertype*, then it is inherited only once. In such a case, there is no ambiguity; the problem only arises if the functions are distinct in the two supertypes.

There are several techniques for dealing with ambiguity in multiple inheritance. One solution is to have the system check for ambiguity when the subtype is created, and to let the user explicitly choose which function is to be inherited at this time. Another solution is to use some system default. A third solution is to disallow multiple inheritance alto-gether if name ambiguity occurs, instead forcing the user to change the name of one of the functions in one of the supertypes. Indeed, some OO systems do not permit multiple inheritance at all.

Selective inheritance occurs when a subtype inherits only some of the functions of a supertype. Other functions are not inherited. In this case, an EXCEPT clause may be used to list the functions in a supertype that are *not* to be inherited by the subtype. The mech-anism of selective inheritance is not typically provided in OO database systems, but it is used more frequently in artificial intelligence applications.[27]

11.6.3 Versions and Configurations

Many database applications that use OO systems require the existence of several **versions** of the same object.[28] For example, consider a database application for a software engi-neering environment that stores various software artifacts, such as *design modules, source code modules,* and *configuration information* to describe which modules should be linked together to form a complex program, and *test cases* for testing the system. Commonly, *maintenance activities* are applied to a software system as its requirements evolve. Mainte-nance usually involves changing some of the design and implementation modules. If the system is already operational, and if one or more of the modules must be changed, the designer should create a **new version** of each of these modules to implement the changes. Similarly, new versions of the test cases may have to be generated to test the new versions of the modules. However, the existing versions should not be discarded until the new ver-sions have been thoroughly tested and approved; only then should the new versions replace the older ones.

Notice that there may be more than two versions of an object. For example, consider two programmers working to update the same software module concurrently. In this case, two versions, in addition to the original module, are needed. The programmers can

---

27. In the ODMG 2.0 model, type inheritance refers to inheritance of operations only, not attributes (see Chapter 12).

28. Versioning is not a problem that is unique to OODBs but can be applied to relational or other types of DBMSs.

update their own versions of the same software module concurrently. This is often referred to as **concurrent engineering.** However, it eventually becomes necessary to merge these two versions together so that the new (hybrid) version can include the changes made by both programmers. During merging, it is also necessary to make sure that their changes are compatible. This necessitates creating yet another version of the object: one that is the result of merging the two independently updated versions.

As can be seen from the preceding discussion, an OODBMS should be able to store and manage multiple versions of the same conceptual object. Several systems do provide this capability, by allowing the application to maintain multiple versions of an object and to refer explicitly to particular versions as needed. However, the problem of merging and reconciling changes made to two different versions is typically left to the application developers, who know the semantics of the application. Some DBMSs have certain facilities that can compare the two versions with the original object and determine whether any changes made are incompatible, in order to assist with the merging process. Other systems maintain a **version graph** that shows the relationships among versions. Whenever a version v_1 originates by copying another version v, a directed arc can be drawn from v to v_1. Similarly, if two versions v_2 and v_3 are merged to create a new version v_4, directed arcs are drawn from v_2 and v_3 to v_4. The version graph can help users understand the relationships among the various versions and can be used internally by the system to manage the creation and deletion of versions.

When versioning is applied to complex objects, further issues arise that must be resolved. A complex object, such as a software system, may consist of many modules. When versioning is allowed, each of these modules may have a number of different versions and a version graph. A **configuration** of the complex object is a collection consisting of one version of each module arranged in such a way that the module versions in the configuration are compatible and together form a valid version of the complex object. A new version or configuration of the complex object does not have to include new versions for every module. Hence, certain module versions that have not been changed may belong to more than one configuration of the complex object. Notice that a configuration is a collection of versions of *different* objects that together make up a complex object, whereas the version graph describes versions of the *same* object. A configuration should follow the type structure of a complex object; multiple configurations of the same complex object are analogous to multiple versions of a component object.

11.7 Summary

In this chapter we discussed the concepts of the object-oriented approach to database systems, which was proposed to meet the needs of complex database applications and to add database functionality to object-oriented programming languages such as C++. We first discussed the main concepts used in OO databases, which include the following:

- *Object identity:* Objects have unique identities that are independent of their attribute values.

- *Type constructors:* Complex object structures can be constructed by recursively applying a set of basic constructors, such as tuple, set, list, and bag.

- *Encapsulation of operations:* Both the object structure and the operations that can be applied to objects are included in the object class definitions.

- *Programming language compatibility:* Both persistent and transient objects are handled uniformly. Objects are made persistent by being attached to a persistent collection.

- *Type hierarchies and inheritance:* Object types can be specified by using a type hierarchy, which allows the inheritance of both attributes and methods of previously defined types.

- *Extents:* All persistent objects of a particular type can be stored in an extent. Extents corresponding to a type hierarchy have set/subset constraints enforced on them.

- *Support for complex objects:* Both structured and unstructured complex objects can be stored and manipulated.

- *Polymorphism and operator overloading:* Operations and method names can be overloaded to apply to different object types with different implementations.

- *Versioning:* Some OO systems provide support for maintaining several versions of the same object.

In the next chapter, we show how some of these concepts are realized in the ODMG standard and give examples of specific OODBMSs. We also discuss object-oriented database design and a standard for distributed objects called CORBA.

Review Questions

11.1. What are the origins of the object-oriented approach?

11.2. What primary characteristics should an OID possess?

11.3. Discuss the various type constructors. How are they used to create complex object structures?

11.4. Discuss the concept of encapsulation, and tell how it is used to create abstract data types.

11.5. Explain what the following terms mean in object-oriented database terminology: *method, signature, message, collection, extent.*

11.6. What is the relationship between a type and its subtype in a type hierarchy? What is the constraint that is enforced on extents corresponding to types in the type hierarchy?

11.7. What is the difference between persistent and transient objects? How is persistence handled in typical OO database systems?

11.8. How do regular inheritance, multiple inheritance, and selective inheritance differ?

11.9. Discuss the concept of polymorphism/operator overloading.

11.10. What is the difference between structured and unstructured complex objects?

11.11. What is the difference between ownership semantics and reference semantics in structured complex objects?

11.12. What is versioning? Why is it important? What is the difference between versions and configurations?

Exercises

11.13. Convert the example of GEOMETRY_OBJECTS given in Section 11.4.1 from the functional notation to the notation given in Figure 11.3 that distinguishes between attributes and operations. Use the keyword INHERIT to show that one class inherits from another class.

11.14. Compare inheritance in the EER model (see Chapter 4) to inheritance in the OO model described in Section 11.4.

11.15. Consider the UNIVERSITY EER schema of Figure 4.10. Think of what operations are needed for the entity types/classes in the schema. Do not consider constructor and destructor operations.

11.16. Consider the COMPANY ER schema of Figure 3.2. Think of what operations are needed for the entity types/classes in the schema. Do not consider constructor and destructor operations.

Selected Bibliography

Object-oriented database concepts are an amalgam of concepts from OO programming languages and from database systems and conceptual data models. A number of textbooks describe OO programming languages—for example, Stroustrup (1986) and Pohl (1991) for C++, and Goldberg (1989) for SMALLTALK. Recent books by Cattell (1994) and Lausen and Vossen (1997) describes OO database concepts.

There is a vast bibliography on OO databases, so we can only provide a representative sample here. The October 1991 issue of CACM and the December 1990 issue of *IEEE Computer* describe object-oriented database concepts and systems. Dittrich (1986) and Zaniolo et al. (1986) survey the basic concepts of object-oriented data models. An early paper on object-oriented databases is Baroody and DeWitt (1981). Su et al. (1988) presents an object-oriented data model that is being used in CAD/CAM applications. Mitschang (1989) extends the relational algebra to cover complex objects. Query languages and graphical user interfaces for OO are described in Gyssens et al. (1990), Kim (1989), Alashqur et al. (1989), Bertino et al. (1992), Agrawal et al. (1990), and Cruz (1992).

Polymorphism in databases and object-oriented programming languages is discussed in Osborn (1989), Atkinson and Buneman (1987), and Danforth and Tomlinson (1988). Object identity is discussed in Abiteboul and Kanellakis (1989). OO programming languages for databases are discussed in Kent (1991). Object constraints are discussed in Delcambre et al. (1991) and Elmasri et al. (1993). Authorization and security in OO databases are examined in Rabitti et al. (1991) and Bertino (1992).

Additional references will be given at the end of Chapter 12.

CHAPTER 12 | Object Database Standards, Languages, and Design

As we discussed at the beginning of Chapter 8, having a standard for a particular type of database system is very important, because it provides support for portability of database applications. **Portability** is generally defined as the capability to execute a particular application program on different systems with minimal modifications to the program itself. In the object database field,[1] portability would allow a program written to access one Object Database Management System (ODBMS) package, say ObjectStore, to access another ODBMS package, say O2 (now called ARDENT), as long as both the ObjectStore and O2 systems support the standard faithfully. This is important to database users because they are generally wary of investing in a new technology if the different vendors do not adhere to a standard. To illustrate why portability is important, suppose that a particular user invests thousands of dollars in creating an application that runs on a particular vendor's product and is then dissatisfied with that product for some reason—say the performance does not meet their requirements. If the application was written using the standard language constructs, it is possible for the user to convert the application to a different vendor's product—which adheres to the same language standards but may have better performance for that user's application—without having to do major modifications that require time and a major monetary investment.

---

1. In this chapter, we will use *object* database instead of *object-oriented* database (as in the previous chapter), since this is now more commonly accepted terminology for standards.

A second potential advantage of having and adhering to standards is that it helps in achieving **interoperability,** which generally refers to the ability of an application to access multiple distinct systems. In database terms, this means that the same application program may access some data stored under one ODBMS package, and other data stored under another package. There are different levels of interoperability. For example, the DBMSs could be two distinct DBMS packages of the same type—for example, two object database systems—or they could be two DBMS packages of different types—say one relational DBMS and one object DBMS. A third advantage of standards is that it allows customers to *compare commercial products* more easily by determining which parts of the standard are supported by each product.

As we discussed in the introduction to Chapter 8, one of the reasons for the success of commercial relational DBMSs is the SQL standard. The lack of a standard for ODBMSs until recently may have caused some potential users to shy away from converting to this new technology. A consortium of ODBMS vendors, called ODMG (Object Data Management Group), proposed a standard that is known as the ODMG-93 or ODMG 1.0 standard. This was revised into ODMG 2.0, which we will describe in this chapter. The standard is made up of several parts: the **object model,** the **object definition language** (ODL), the **object query language** (OQL), and the **bindings** to object-oriented programming languages. Language bindings have been specified for three object-oriented programming languages—namely, C++, SMALLTALK, and JAVA. Some vendors only offer specific language bindings, without offering the full capabilities of ODL and OQL. We will describe the ODMG object model in Section 12.1, ODL in Section 12.2, OQL in Section 12.3, and the C++ language binding in Section 12.4. Examples of how to use ODL, OQL, and the C++ language binding will use the UNIVERSITY database example introduced in Chapter 4. In our description, we will follow the ODMG 2.0 object model as described in Cattell et al. (1997).[2] It is important to note that many of the ideas embodied in the ODMG object model are based on two decades of research into conceptual modeling and object-oriented databases by many researchers.

Following the description of the ODMG model, we will describe a technique for object database conceptual design in Section 12.5. We will discuss how object-oriented databases differ from relational databases and show how to map a conceptual database design in the EER model to the ODL statements of the ODMG model. Then in Section 12.6, we give overviews of two commercial ODBMSs—namely, O2 and ObjectStore. Finally, in Section 12.7, we will give an overview of the CORBA (Common Object Request Broker Architecture) standard for supporting interoperability among distributed object systems.

The reader may skip Sections 12.3 through 12.7 if a less detailed introduction to the topic is desired.

12.1 Overview of the Object Model of ODMG

The ODMG **object model** is the data model upon which the object definition language (ODL) and object query language (OQL) are based. In fact, this object model provides the data types, type constructors, and other concepts that can be utilized in the ODL to specify

---

2. The earlier version of the object model was published in 1993.

object database schemas. Hence, it is meant to provide a standard data model for object-oriented databases, just as the SQL report describes a standard data model for relational databases. It also provides a standard terminology in a field where the same terms were sometimes used to describe different concepts. We will try to adhere to the ODMG terminology in this chapter. Many of the concepts in the ODMG model have already been discussed in Chapter 11, and we assume the reader has already gone through Sections 11.1 through 11.5. We will point out whenever the ODMG terminology differs from that used in Chapter 11.

12.1.1 Objects and Literals

Objects and literals are the basic building blocks of the object model. The main difference between the two is that an object has both an object identifier and a **state** (or current value), whereas a literal has only a value but *no object identifier*.[3] In either case, the value can have a complex structure. The object state can change over time by modifying the object value. A literal is basically a constant value, possibly having a complex structure, that does not change.

An **object** is described by four characteristics: (1) identifier, (2) name, (3) lifetime, and (4) structure. The **object identifier** is a unique system-wide identifier (or `Object_Id`).[4] Every object must have an object identifier. In addition to the `Object_Id`, some objects may optionally be given a unique **name** within a particular database—this name can be used to refer to the object in a program, and the system should be able to locate the object given that name.[5] Obviously, not all individual objects will have unique names. Typically, a few objects, mainly those that hold collections of objects of a particular object type—such as extents—will have a name. These names are used as **entry points** to the database; that is, by locating these objects by their unique name, the user can then locate other objects that are referenced from these objects. Other important objects in the application may also have unique names. All such names within a particular database must be unique. The **lifetime** of an object specifies whether it is a *persistent object* (that is, a database object) or *transient object* (that is, an object in an executing program that disappears after the program terminates). Finally, the **structure** of an object specifies how the object is constructed by using the type constructors. The structure specifies whether an object is *atomic* or a *collection object*.[6] The term *atomic object* is different than the way we defined the *atom constructor* in Section 11.2.2, and it is quite different from an atomic literal (see below). In the ODMG model, an atomic object is any object that is not a collection, so this also covers *structured objects* created using the *struct* constructor.[7] We will discuss collection objects in Section 12.1.2 and atomic objects in Section 12.1.3. First, we define the concept of a literal.

---

3. We will use the terms *value* and *state* interchangeably here.

4. Corresponds to the OID of Chapter 11.

5. This corresponds to the naming mechanism described in Section 11.3.

6. In the ODMG model, *atomic objects* do not correspond to objects whose values are basic data types. All basic values (integers, reals, etc.) are considered to be *literals*.

7. The *struct* construct corresponds to the *tuple constructor* of Chapter 11.

In the object model, a **literal** is a value that *does not have* an object identifier. However, the value may have a simple or complex structure. There are three types of literals: (1) atomic, (2) collection, and (3) structured. **Atomic literals**[8] correspond to the values of basic data types and are predefined. The basic data types of the object model include long, short, and unsigned integer numbers (these are specified by the keywords Long, Short, Unsigned Long, Unsigned Short in ODL), regular and double precision floating point numbers (Float, Double), boolean values (Boolean), single characters (Char), character strings (String), and enumeration types (Enum), among others. **Structured literals** correspond roughly to values that are constructed using the tuple constructor described in Section 11.2.2. They include Date, Interval, Time, and Timestamp as built-in structures (see Figure 12.1b), as well as any additional user-defined type structures as needed by each application.[9] User-defined structures are created using the **Struct** keyword in ODL, as in the C and C++ programming languages. **Collection literals** specify a value that is a collection of objects or values but the collection itself does not have an `Object_Id`. The collections in the object model are `Set<t>`, `Bag<t>`, `List<t>`, and `Array<t>`, where t is the type of objects or values in the collection.[10] Another collection type is Dictionary `<k,v>`, which is a collection of associations `<k,v>` where each k is a key (a unique search value) associated with a value v; this can be used to create an index on a collection of values.

Figure 12.1 gives a simplified view of the basic components of the object model. The notation of ODMG uses the keyword interface where we had used the keywords *type* and *class* in Chapter 11. In fact, interface is a more appropriate term, since it describes the interface of types of objects—namely, their visible attributes, relationships, and operations.[11] These interfaces are typically noninstantiable (that is, no objects are created for an interface) but they serve to define operations that can be *inherited* by the user-defined objects for a particular application. The keyword *class* in the object model is reserved for user-specified class declarations that form a database schema and are used for creating application objects. Figure 12.1 is a simplified version of the object model. For the full

```
interface Object {
    ...
    boolean      same_as(in Object other_object);
    Object       copy();
    void         delete();
};
```

Figure 12.1a   Overview of the interface definitions for part of the ODMG object model. The basic `Object` interface, inherited by all objects.

---

8. The use of the word atomic in *atomic literal* **does** correspond to the way we used *atom constructor* in Section 11.2.2.

9. The structures for Date, Interval, Time, and Timestamp can be used to create either literal values or objects with identifiers.

10. These are similar to the corresponding type constructors described in Section 11.2.2.

11. Interface is also the keyword used in the CORBA standard (see Section 12.5) and the JAVA programming language.

```
interface Date : Object {
    enum            Weekday
    {Sunday, Monday, Tuesday, Wednesday, Thursday, Friday, Saturday};
    enum            Month
    {January, February, March, April, May, June, July, August, September, October, November, December};
    unsigned short  year();
    unsigned short  month();
    unsigned short  day();
    ...
    boolean         is_equal(in Date other_Date);
    boolean         is_greater(in Date other_Date);
    ...
};

interface Time : Object {
    ...
    unsigned short  hour();
    unsigned short  minute();
    unsigned short  second();
    unsigned short  millisecond();
    ...
    boolean         is_equal(in Time other_Time);
    boolean         is_greater(in Time other_Time);
    ...
    Time            add_interval(in Interval some_Interval);
    Time            subtract_interval(in Interval some_Interval);
    Interval        subtract_time(in Time other_Time);
};

interface Timestamp : Object {
    ...
    unsigned short  year();
    unsigned short  month();
    unsigned short  day();
    unsigned short  hour();
    unsigned short  minute();
    unsigned short  second();
    unsigned short  millisecond();
    ...
    Timestamp       plus(in Interval some_Interval);
    Timestamp       minus(in Interval some_Interval);
    boolean         is_equal(in Timestamp other_Timestamp);
    boolean         is_greater(in Timestamp other_Timestamp);
    ...
};

interface Interval : Object {
    unsigned short  day();
    unsigned short  hour();
    unsigned short  minute();
    unsigned short  second();
    unsigned short  millisecond();
    ...
    Interval        plus(in Interval some_Interval);
    Interval        minus(in Interval some_Interval);
    Interval        product(in long some_value);
    Interval        quotient(in long some_value);
    boolean         is_equal(in Interval other_Interval);
    boolean         is_greater(in Interval other_Interval);
    ...
};
```

Figure 12.1b Overview of the interface definitions for part of the ODMG object model.
Some standard interfaces for structured literals.

389

```
interface Collection : Object {
    ...
    exception       ElementNotFound{any element; };
    unsigned long   cardinality();
    boolean         is_empty();
    ...
    boolean         contains_element(in any element);
    void            insert_element(in any element);
    void            remove_element(in any element)
                        raises(ElementNotFound);
    Iterator        create_iterator(in boolean stable);
    ...
};

interface Iterator {
    exception       NoMoreElements();
    ...
    boolean         is_stable();
    boolean         at_end();
    void            reset();
    any             get_element() raises(NoMoreElements);
    void            next_position() raises(NoMoreElements);
    ...
};

interface Set : Collection {
    Set             create_union(in Set other_set);
    ...
    boolean         is_subset_of(in Set other_set);
    ...
};

interface Bag : Collection {
    unsigned long   occurrences_of(in any element);
    Bag             create_union(in Bag other_bag);
    ...
};

interface List : Collection {
    exception       Invalid_Index{unsigned_long index; };
    void            remove_element_at(in unsigned long position)
                        raises(InvalidIndex);
    any             retrieve_element_at(in unsigned long position)
                        raises(InvalidIndex);
    void            replace_element_at(in any element, in unsigned long position)
                        raises(InvalidIndex);
    void            insert_element_after(in any element, in unsigned long position)
                        raises(InvalidIndex);
    ...
    void            insert_element_first(in any element);
    ...
    void            remove_first_element() raises(InvalidIndex);
    ...
    any             retrieve_first_element() raises(InvalidIndex);
    ...
    List            concat(in List other_list);
    void            append(in List other_list);
};
```

Figure 12.1c   Overview of the interface definitions for part of the ODMG object
model. Interface definitions for collection objects.

```
interface Array : Collection {
    exception        Invalid_Index{unsigned_long index; };
    void             remove_element_at(in unsigned long index)
                         raises(InvalidIndex);
    any              retrieve_element_at(in unsigned long index)
                         raises(InvalidIndex);
    void             replace_element_at(in unsigned long index, in any element)
                         raises(InvalidIndex);
    void             resize(in unsigned long new_size);
};

struct Association {any key; any value; };

interface Dictionary : Collection {
    exception        KeyNotFound{any key; };
    void             bind(in any key, in any value);
    void             unbind(in any key) raises(KeyNotFound);
    any              lookup(in any key) raises(KeyNotFound);
    boolean          contains_key(in any key);
};
```

Figure 12.1c   *(continued)*

specifications, see Cattell et al. (1997). We will describe the constructs shown in Figure 12.1 as we describe the object model.

In the object model, all objects inherit the basic interface of Object, shown in Figure 12.1(a). Hence, the basic operations that are inherited by all objects (from the Object interface) are copy (creates a new copy of the object), delete (deletes the object), and same_as (compares the object's identity to another object).[12] In general, operations are applied to objects using the **dot notation.** For example, given an object o, to compare it with another object p, we write

    o.same_as(p)

The result returned by this expression is Boolean and would be true if the identity of p is the same as that of o, and false otherwise. Similarly, to create a copy p of object o, we write

    p = o.copy()

An alternative to the dot notation is the **arrow notation:** o->same_as(p) or o->copy().

Type inheritance, which is used to define type/subtype relationships, is specified in the object model using the colon (:) notation, as in the C++ programming language. Hence, in Figure 12.1, we can see that all interfaces, such as Collection, Date, and Time, inherit the basic Object interface. In the object model, there are two main types of objects: (1) collection objects, described in Section 12.1.2, and (2) atomic (and structured) objects, described in Section 12.1.3.

---

12. Additional operations are defined on objects for *locking* purposes, which are not shown in Figure 12.1. We discuss locking concepts for databases in Chapter 20.

12.1.2   Built-in Interfaces for Collection Objects

Any **collection object** inherits the basic Collection interface shown in Figure 12.1(c), which shows the operations for all collection objects. Given a collection object o, the o.cardinality() operation returns the number of elements in the collection. The operation o.is_empty() returns true if the collection o is empty, and false otherwise. The operations o.insert_element(e) and o.remove_element(e) insert or remove an element e from the collection o. Finally, the operation o.contains_element(e) returns true if the collection o includes element e, and returns false otherwise. The operation i = o.create_iterator() creates an **iterator object** i for the collection object o, which can iterate over each element in the collection. The interface for iterator objects is also shown in Figure 12.1(c). The i.reset() operation sets the iterator at the first element in a collection (for an unordered collection, this would be some arbitrary element), and i.next_position() sets the iterator to the next element. The i.get_element() retrieves the **current element,** which is the element at which the iterator is currently positioned.

The ODMG object model uses **exceptions** for reporting errors or particular conditions. For example, the ElementNotFound exception in the Collection interface would be raised by the o.remove_element(e) operation if e is not an element in the collection o. The NoMoreElements exception in the iterator interface would be raised by the i.next_position() operation if the iterator is currently positioned at the last element in the collection, and hence no more elements exist for the iterator to point to.

Collection objects are further specialized into Set, List, Bag, Array, and Dictionary, which inherit the operations of the Collection interface. A **Set<t>** object type can be used to create objects such that the value of object o is a *set whose elements are of type t*. The Set interface includes the additional operation p = o.create_union(s) (see Figure 12.1c), which returns a new object p of type Set<t> that is the union of the two sets o and s. Other operations similar to create_union (not shown in Figure 12.1c) are create_intersection(s) and create_difference(s). Operations for set comparison include the o.is_subset_of(s) operation, which returns true if the set object o is a subset of some other set object s, and returns false otherwise. Similar operations (not shown in Figure 12.1c) are is_proper_subset_of(s), is_superset_of(s), and is_proper_superset_of(s). The **Bag<t>** object type allows duplicate elements in the collection and also inherits the Collection interface. It has three operations—create_union(b), create_intersection(b), and create_difference(b)—that all return a new object of type Bag<t>. For example, p = o.create_union(b) returns a Bag object p that is the union of o and b (keeping duplicates). The o.occurrences_of(e) operation returns the number of duplicate occurrences of element e in bag o.

A **List<t>** object type inherits the Collection operations and can be used to create collections where the order of the elements is important. The value of each such object o is an *ordered list whose elements are of type t*. Hence, we can refer to the first, last, and i^{th} element in the list. Also, when we add an element to the list, we must specify the position in the list where the element is inserted. Some of the List operations are shown in Figure 12.1(c). If o is an object of type List<t>, the operation o.insert_element_first(e) (see Figure 12.1c) inserts the element e before the first element in the list o, so that e becomes the first element in the list. A similar operation (not shown) is o.insert_element_last(e). The operation o.insert_element_after(e,i) in Figure 12.1(c) inserts the element e after the ith element in the list o and will raise the exception InvalidIndex if no i^{th} element exists in o. A similar operation (not shown) is o.insert_element_before(e,i). To remove elements from the list, the operations are e = o.remove_first_element(), e = o.remove_last_element(), and e = o.remove_element_at(i); these operations remove the indicated element from the list *and* return the element as the operation's result. Other operations retrieve an element without removing it from the list. These are e = o.retrieve_first_element(), e = o.retrieve_last_element(), and e = o.retrieve_element_at(i). Finally, two operations to manipulate lists are defined. These are p = o.concat(l), which creates a new list p that is the concatenation of lists o and l (the elements in list o followed by those in list l), and o.append(l), which appends the elements of list l to the end of list o (without creating a new list object).

The **Array<t>** object type also inherits the Collection operations. It is similar to a list except that an array has a fixed number of elements. The specific operations for an Array object o are o.replace_element_at(i,e), which replaces the array element at position i with element e; e = o.remove_element_at(i), which retrieves the ith element and replaces it with a null value; and e = o.retrieve_element_at(i), which simply retrieves the ith element of the array. Any of these operations can raise the exception InvalidIndex if i is greater than the array's size. The operation o.resize(n) changes the number of array elements to n.

The last type of collection objects are of type **Dictionary<k, v>.** This allows the creation of a collection of association pairs <k, v>, where all k (key) values are unique. This allows for associative retrieval of a particular pair given its key value (similar to an index). If o is a collection object of type Dictionary<k,v>, then o.bind(k,v) binds value v to the key k as an association <k,v> in the collection, whereas o.unbind(k) removes the association with key k from o, and v = o.lookup(k) returns the value v associated with key k in o. The latter two operations can raise the exception KeyNotFound. Finally, o.contains_key(k) returns true if key k exists in o, and returns false —otherwise.

Figure 12.2 is a diagram that illustrates the inheritance hierarchy of the built-in constructs of the object model. Operations are inherited from the supertype to the subtype. The collection object interfaces described above are *not directly instantiable*; that is, one cannot directly create objects based on these interfaces. Rather, the interfaces can be used to specify user-defined collection objects—of type Set, Bag, List, Array, or Dictionary—for a particular database application. When a user designs a database schema, they will declare their own object interfaces and classes that are relevant to the database application. If an interface or class is one of the collection objects, say a Set, then it will inherit the operations of the Set interface. For example, in a UNIVERSITY database application, the user can specify a class for Set<Student>, whose objects would be sets of Student objects. The programmer can then use the operations for Set<t> to manipulate an object of type Set<Student>. Creating application classes is typically done by utilizing the object definition language ODL (see Section 12.2).

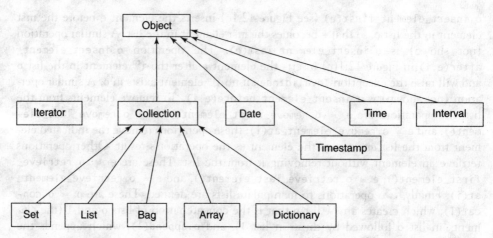

Figure 12.2   Inheritance hierarchy for the built-in interfaces of the object model.

It is important to note that all objects in a particular collection *must be of the same type*. Hence, although the keyword **any** appears in the specifications of collection interfaces in Figure 12.1(c), this does not mean that objects of any type can be intermixed within the same collection. Rather, it means that any type can be used when specifying the type of elements for a particular collection (including other collection types!).

12.1.3   Atomic (User-Defined) Objects

The previous section described the built-in collection types of the object model. We now discuss how object types for *atomic objects* can be constructed. These are specified using the keyword **class** in ODL. In the object model, any user-defined object that is not a collection object is called an **atomic object.**[13] For example, in a UNIVERSITY database application, the user can specify an object type (class) for Student objects. Most such objects will be **structured objects;** for example, a Student object will have a complex structure, with many attributes, relationships, and operations, but it is still considered atomic because it is not a collection. Such a user-defined atomic object type is defined as a class by specifying its **properties** and **operations.** The properties define the state of the object and are further distinguished into **attributes** and **relationships.** In this subsection, we elaborate on the three types of components—attributes, relationships, and operations—that a user-defined object type for atomic (structured) objects can include. We illustrate our discussion with the two classes `Employee` and `Department` shown in Figure 12.3.

An **attribute** is a property that describes some aspect of an object. Attributes have values, which are typically literals having a simple or complex structure, that are stored within the object. However, attribute values can also be `Object_Ids` of other objects.

---

13. As mentioned earlier, this definition of *atomic object* in the ODMG object model is different from the definition of atom constructor given in Chapter 11, which is the definition used in much of the object-oriented database literature.

```
class Employee
(  extent   all_employees
   key      ssn )
{
   attribute      string                          name;
   attribute      string                          ssn;
   attribute      date                  birthdate;
   attribute      enum Gender{M, F}     sex;
   attribute      short                 age;
   relationship   Department            works_for
                       inverse Department::has_emps;
   void           reassign_emp(in string new_dname)
                       raises(dname_not_valid);
};


class Department
(  extent   all_departments
   key      dname, dnumber   )
{
   attribute      string                    dname;
   attribute      short                     dnumber;
   attribute      struct Dept_Mgr {Employee manager, date startdate}
                                  mgr;
   attribute      set<string>           locations;
   attribute      struct Projs {string projname, time weekly_hours}
                                  projs;
   relationship   set<Employee>     has_emps inverse Employee::works_for;
   void           add_emp(in string new_ename) raises(ename_not_valid);
   void           change_manager(in string new_mgr_name; in date startdate);
};
```

Figure 12.3   The attributes, relationships, and operations in a class definition.

Attribute values can even be specified via methods that are used to calculate the attribute value. In Figure 12.3,[14] the attributes for Employee are name, ssn, birthdate, sex, and age, and those for Department are dname, dnumber, mgr, locations, and projs. The mgr and projs attributes of Department have complex structure and are defined via **struct,** which corresponds to the *tuple constructor* of Chapter 11. Hence, the value of mgr in each Department object will have two components: manager, whose value is an Object_Id that references the Employee object that manages the Department, and startdate, whose value is a date. The locations attribute of Department is defined via the **set** constructor, since each Department object can have a set of locations.

A **relationship** is a property that specifies that two objects in the database are related together. In the object model of ODMG, only binary relationships (see Chapter 3) are explicitly represented, and each binary relationship is represented by a *pair of inverse*

---

14. We are using the Object Definition Language (ODL) notation in Figure 12.3, which will be discussed in more detail in Section 12.2.

references specified via the keyword relationship. In Figure 12.3, one relationship exists that relates each `Employee` to the `Department` in which he or she works—the `works_for` relationship of `Employee`. In the inverse direction, each `Department` is related to the set of `Employees` that work in the `Department`—the `has_emps` relationship of `Department`. The keyword `inverse` specifies that these two properties specify a single conceptual relationship in inverse directions.[15] By specifying inverses, the database system can maintain the referential integrity of the relationship automatically. That is, if the value of `works_for` for a particular `Employee` e refers to `Department` d, then the value of `has_emps` for `Department` d must include a reference to e in its set of `Employee` references. If the database designer desires to have a relationship to be represented in *only one direction*, then it has to be modeled as an attribute (or operation). An example is the manager component of the `mgr` attribute in `Department`.

In addition to attributes and relationships, the designer can include **operations** in object type (class) specifications. Each object type can have a number of **operation signatures,** which specify the operation name, its argument types, and its returned value, if applicable. Operation names are unique within each object type, but they can be overloaded by having the same operation name appear in distinct object types. The operation signature can also specify the names of **exceptions** that can occur during operation execution. The implementation of the operation will include the code to raise these exceptions. In Figure 12.3, the `Employee` class has one operation, `reassign_emp`, and the `Department` class has two operations, `add_emp` and `change_manager`.

12.1.4   Interfaces, Classes, and Inheritance

In the ODMG 2.0 object model, two concepts exist for specifying object types: interfaces and classes. In addition, two types of inheritance relationships exist. In this section, we discuss the differences and similarities among these concepts. Following the ODMG 2.0 terminology, we use the word **behavior** to refer to *operations*, and **state** to refer to *properties* (attributes and relationships).

An **interface** is a specification of the abstract behavior of an object type, which specifies the operation signatures. Although an interface may have state properties (attributes and relationships) as part of its specifications, these *cannot* be inherited from the interface, as we shall see. An interface also is **noninstantiable**—that is, one cannot create objects that correspond to an interface definition.[16]

A **class** is a specification of both the abstract behavior and abstract state of an object type, and is **instantiable**—that is, one can create individual object instances corresponding to a class definition. Because interfaces are noninstantiable, they are mainly used to specify abstract operations that can be inherited by classes or by other interfaces. This is

---

15. Chapter 3 discussed how a relationship can be represented by two attributes in inverse directions.

16. This is somewhat similar to the concept of abstract class in the C++ programming language.

called **behavior inheritance** and is specified by the ":" symbol.[17] Hence, in the ODMG 2.0 object model, behavior inheritance requires the supertype to be an interface, whereas the subtype could be either a class or another interface.

Another inheritance relationship, called EXTENDS and specified by the **extends** keyword, is used to inherit both state and behavior strictly among classes. In an EXTENDS inheritance, both the supertype and the subtype must be classes. Multiple inheritance via EXTENDS is not permitted. However, multiple inheritance is allowed for behavior inheritance via ":". Hence, an interface may inherit behavior from several other interfaces. A class may also inherit behavior from several interfaces via ":", in addition to inheriting behavior and state from *at most one* other class via EXTENDS. We will give examples in Section 12.2 of how these two inheritance relationships—":" and EXTENDS—may be used.

12.1.5   Extents, Keys, and Factory Objects

In the ODMG 2.0 object model, the database designer can declare an **extent** for any object type that is defined via a **class** declaration. The extent is given a name, and it will contain all persistent objects of that class. Hence, the extent behaves as a *set object* that holds all persistent objects of the class. In Figure 12.3, the Employee and Department classes have extents called all_employees and all_departments, respectively. This is similar to creating two objects—one of type Set<Employee> and the second of type Set<Department>—and making them persistent by naming them all_employees and all_departments. Extents are also used to automatically enforce the set/subset relationship between the extents of a supertype and its subtype. If two classes A and B have extents all_A and all_B, and class B is a subtype of class A (that is, class B EXTENDS class A), then the collection of objects in all_B must be a subset of those in all_A at any point in time. This constraint is automatically enforced by the database system.

A class with an extent can have one or more keys. A **key** consists of one or more properties (attributes or relationships) whose values are constrained to be unique for each object in the extent. For example, in Figure 12.3, the Employee class has the ssn attribute as key (each Employee object in the extent must have a unique ssn value), and the Department class has two distinct keys: dname and dnumber (each Department must have a unique dname and a unique dnumber). For a composite key[18] that is made of several properties, the properties that form the key are contained in parentheses. For example, if a class Vehicle with an extent all_vehicles has a key made up of a combination of two attributes state and license_number, they would be placed in parentheses as (state, license_number) in the key declaration.

---

17. The ODMG 2.0 report also calls interface inheritance as type/subtype, is-a, and generalization/ specialization relationships, although, in the literature, these terms have been used to describe inheritance of both state and operations (see Chapters 4 and 11).

18. A composite key is called a *compound key* in the ODMG 2.0 report.

Next, we present the concept of **factory object**—an object that can be used to generate or create individual objects via its operations. Some of the interfaces of factory objects that are part of the ODMG 2.0 object model are shown in Figure 12.4. The interface `ObjectFactory` has a single operation, `new()`, which returns a new object with an `Object_Id`. By inheriting this interface, users can create their own factory interfaces for each user-defined (atomic) object type, and the programmer can implement the operation *new* differently for each type of object. Figure 12.4 also shows a `DateFactory` interface, which has additional operations for creating a new `calendar_date`, and for creating an object whose value is the `current_date`, among other operations (not shown in Figure 12.4). As we can see, a factory object basically provides the **constructor operations** for new objects.

Finally, we discuss the concept of a **database.** Because a ODBMS can create many different databases, each with its own schema, the ODMG 2.0 object model has interfaces for `DatabaseFactory` and `Database` objects, as shown in Figure 12.4. Each database has its own *database name*, and the **bind** operation can be used to assign individual unique names to persistent objects in a particular database. The **lookup** operation returns an object from the database that has the specified `object_name`, and the **unbind** operation removes the name of a persistent named object from the database.

```
interface ObjectFactory {
    Object            new();
};

interface DateFactory : ObjectFactory {
    exception         InvalidDate{};
    ...
    Date              calendar_date(   in unsigned short year,
                                       in unsigned short month,
                                       in unsigned short day)
                      raises(InvalidDate);
    ...
    Date              current();
};

interface DatabaseFactory {
    Database          new();
};

interface Database {
    void              open(in string database_name);
    void              close();
    void              bind(in any some_object, in string object_name);
    Object            unbind(in string name);
    Object            lookup(in string object_name)
                          raises(ElementNotFound);
    ...
};
```

Figure 12.4   Interfaces to illustrate factory objects and database objects.

12.2 The Object Definition Language

After our overview of the ODMG 2.0 object model in the previous section, we now show how these concepts can be utilized to create an object database schema using the object definition language ODL.[19] The ODL is designed to support the semantic constructs of the ODMG 2.0 object model and is independent of any particular programming language. Its main use is to create object specifications—that is, classes and interfaces. Hence, ODL is not a full programming language. A user can specify a database schema in ODL independently of any programming language, then use the specific language bindings to specify how ODL constructs can be mapped to constructs in specific programming languages, such as C++, SMALLTALK, and JAVA. We will give an overview of the C++ binding in Section 12.4.

Figure 12.5(b) shows a possible object schema for part of the UNIVERSITY database, which was presented in Chapter 4. We will describe the concepts of ODL using this example, and the one in Figure 12.7. The graphical notation for Figure 12.5(b) is described in Figure 12.5(a) and can be considered as a variation of EER diagrams (see Chapter 4) with the added concept of interface inheritance but without several EER concepts, such as categories (union types) and attributes of relationships.

Figure 12.6 shows one possible set of ODL class definitions for the UNIVERSITY database. In general, there may be several possible mappings from an object schema diagram (or EER schema diagram) into ODL classes. We will discuss these options further in Section 12.5.

Figure 12.6 shows the straightforward way of mapping part of the UNIVERSITY database from Chapter 4. Entity types are mapped into ODL classes, and inheritance is done using EXTENDS. However, there is no direct way to map categories (union types) or to do multiple inheritance. In Figure 12.6, the classes Person, Faculty, Student, and GradStudent have the extents persons, faculty, students, and grad_students, respectively. Both Faculty and Student EXTENDS Person, and GradStudent EXTENDS Student. Hence, the collection of students (and the collection of faculty) will be constrained to be a subset of the collection of persons at any point in time. Similarly, the collection of grad_students will be a subset of students. At the same time, individual Student and Faculty objects will inherit the properties (attributes and relationships) and operations of Person, and individual GradStudent objects will inherit those of Student.

The classes Department, Course, Section, and CurrSection in Figure 12.6 are straightforward mappings of the corresponding entity types in Figure 12.5(b). However, the class Grade requires some explanation. The Grade class corresponds to the M:N relationship between Student and Section in Figure 12.5(b). The reason it was made into a separate class (rather than as a pair of inverse relationships) is because it includes the relationship attribute grade.[20] Hence, the M:N relationship is mapped to the class Grade, and a pair of 1:N relationships, one between Student and Grade and the other between

---

19. The ODL syntax and data types are meant to be compatible with the Interface Definition Language (IDL) of CORBA (Common Object Request Broker Architecture), with extensions for relationships and other database concepts.

20. We will discuss alternative mappings for attributes of relationships in Section 12.5.

(a)

(b)

Figure 12.5   An example of a database schema. (a) Graphical notation for representing ODL schemas. (b) A graphical object database schema for part of the UNIVERSITY database.

```
class Person
(   extent   persons
    key       ssn )
{
    attribute      struct Pname {string fname, string mname, string lname }
                                name;
    attribute      string              ssn;
    attribute      date                birthdate;
    attribute      enum Gender{M, F}  sex;
    attribute      struct Address
                      {short no, string street, short aptno, string city, string state, short zip }
                                address;
    short    age();
};

class Faculty extends Person
(   extent  faculty  )
{
    attribute      string              rank;
    attribute      float               salary;
    attribute      string              office;
    attribute      string              phone;
    relationship Department            works_in inverse Department::has_faculty;
    relationship set<GradStudent> advises inverse GradStudent::advisor;
    relationship set<GradStudent> on_committee_of
                                inverse GradStudent::committee;
    void     give_raise(in float raise);
    void     promote(in string new_rank);
};

class Grade
(   extent  grades  )
{
    attribute      enum GradeValues{A,B,C,D,F,I,P}
                                grade;
    relationship Section section inverse Section::students;
    relationship Student student inverse Student::completed_sections;
};

class Student extends Person
(   extent  students  )
{
    attribute      string              class;
    attribute      Department          minors_in;
    relationship Department majors_in inverse Department::has_majors;
    relationship set<Grade> completed_sections inverse Grade::student;
    relationship set<CurrSection> registered_in
                                inverse CurrSection::registered_students;
    void     change_major(in string dname) raises(dname_not_valid);
    float    gpa();
    void     register(in short secno) raises(section_not_valid);
    void     assign_grade(in short secno; in GradeValue grade)
                                raises(section_not_valid,grade_not_valid);
};
```

Figure 12.6 Possible ODL schema for the UNIVERSITY database of Figure 12.5(b).

```
class Degree
{
    attribute     string          college;
    attribute     string          degree;
    attribute     string          year;
};


class GradStudent extends Student
(   extent  grad_students   )
{
    attribute       set<Degree>     degrees;
    relationship Faculty advisor inverse Faculty::advises;
    relationship set<Faculty> committee inverse Faculty::on_committee_of;
    void    assign_advisor(in string lname; in string fname)
                              raises(faculty_not_valid);
    void    assign_committee_member(in string lname; in string fname)
                              raises(faculty_not_valid);
};


class Department
(   extent  departments key dname   )
{
    attribute     string          dname;
    attribute     string          dphone;
    attribute     string          doffice;
    attribute     string          college;
    attribute     Faculty         chair;
    relationship set<Faculty> has_faculty inverse Faculty::works_in;
    relationship set<Student> has_majors inverse Student::majors_in;
    relationship set<Course> offers inverse Course::offered_by;
};


class Course
(   extent  courses key cno   )
{
    attribute     string          cname;
    attribute     string          cno;
    attribute     string          description;
    relationship set<Section> has_sections inverse Section::of_course;
    relationship Department offered_by inverse Department::offers;
};


class Section
(   extent  sections   )
{
    attribute     short           secno;
    attribute     string          year;
    attribute     enum Quarter{Fall, Winter, Spring, Summer} qtr;
    relationship set<Grade> students inverse Grade::section;
    relationship Course of_course inverse Course::has_sections;
};


class CurrSection extends Section
(   extent  current_sections      )
{
    relationship set<Student> registered_students inverse Student::registered_in
    void    register_student(in string ssn)
              raises(student_not_valid, section_not_valid, section_full);
};
```

Figure 12.6   (continued)

402

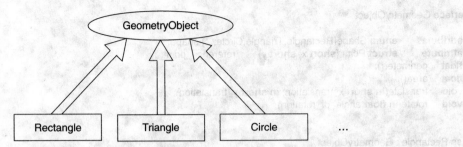

Figure 12.7a   An illustration of interface inheritance via ":". Graphical schema representation.

Section and Grade.[21] These two relationships are represented by the following relationship properties: completed_sections of Student; section and student of Grade; and students of Section (see Figure 12.6). Finally, the class Degree is used to represent the composite, multivalued attribute degrees of GradStudent (see Figure 4.10).

Because the previous example did not include any interfaces, only classes, we now utilize a different example to illustrate interfaces and interface (behavior) inheritance. Figure 12.7 is part of a database schema for storing geometric objects. An interface GeometryObject is specified, with operations to calculate the perimeter and area of a geometric object, plus operations to translate (move) and rotate an object. Several classes (Rectangle, Triangle, Circle, . . .) inherit the GeometryObject interface. Since GeometryObject is an interface, it is *noninstantiable*—that is, no objects can be created based on this interface directly. However, objects of type Rectangle, Triangle, Circle, . . . can be created, and these objects inherit all the operations of the GeometryObject interface. Note that with interface inheritance, only operations are inherited, not properties (attributes, relationships). Hence, if a property is needed in the inheriting class, it must be repeated in the class definition, as with the reference_point attribute in Figure 12.7. Notice that the inherited operations can have different implementations in each class. For example, the implementations of the area and perimeter operations may be different for Rectangle, Triangle, and Circle.

Multiple inheritance of interfaces by a class is allowed, as is multiple inheritance of interfaces by another interface. However, with the EXTENDS (class) inheritance, multiple inheritance is *not permitted*. Hence, a class can inherit via EXTENDS from at most one class (in addition to inheriting from zero or more interfaces).

---

21. This is similar to how an M:N relationship is mapped in the relational model (see Chapter 9) and in the legacy network model (see Appendix C).

```
interface GeometryObject
{
    attribute        enum Shape{Rectangle,Triangle,Circle,...} shape;
    attribute        struct Point {short x, short y}        reference_point;
    float    perimeter();
    float    area();
    void     translate(in short x_translation; in short y_translation);
    void     rotate(in float angle_of_rotation);
};

class Rectangle : GeometryObject
(   extent   rectangles       )
{
    attribute        struct Point {short x, short y}        reference_point;
    attribute        short                 length;
    attribute        short                 height;
    attribute        float                 orientation_angle;
};

class Triangle : GeometryObject
(   extent   triangles  )
{
    attribute        struct Point {short x, short y}        reference_point;
    attribute        short                 side_1;
    attribute        short                 side_2;
    attribute        float                 side1_side2_angle;
    attribute        float                 side1_orientation_angle;
};

class Circle : GeometryObject
(   extent   circles   )
{
    attribute        struct Point {short x, short y}        reference_point;
    attribute        short                 radius;
};
```

Figure 12.7b   An illustration of interface inheritance via ":". Corresponding interface and class definitions in ODL.

12.3   The Object Query Language

The object query language (OQL) is the query language proposed for the ODMG object model. It is designed to work closely with the programming languages for which an ODMG binding is defined, such as C++, SMALLTALK, and JAVA. Hence, an OQL query embedded into one of these programming languages can return objects that match the type system of that language. In addition, the implementations of class operations in an ODMG schema can have their code written in these programming languages. The OQL syntax for queries is similar to the syntax of the relational standard query language SQL, with additional features for ODMG concepts, such as object identity, complex objects, operations, inheritance, polymorphism, and relationships.

We will first discuss the syntax of simple OQL queries and the concept of using named objects or extents as database entry points in Section 12.3.1. Then in Section 12.3.2, we discuss the structure of query results and the use of path expressions to traverse relationships among objects. Other OQL features for handling object identity, inheritance, polymorphism, and other object oriented concepts are discussed in Section 12.3.3. The examples to illustrate OQL queries are based on the UNIVERSITY database schema given in Figure 12.6.

12.3.1 Simple OQL Queries, Database Entry Points, and Iterator Variables

The basic OQL syntax is a **select** ... **from** ... **where** ... structure, as for SQL. For example, the query to retrieve the names of all departments in the college of 'Engineering' can be written as follows:

```
Q0:   SELECT   d.dname
      FROM     d in departments
      WHERE    d.college = 'Engineering';
```

In general, an **entry point** to the database is needed for each query, which can be any *named persistent object*. For many queries, the entry point is the name of the **extent** of a class. Recall that the extent name is considered to be the name of a persistent object whose type is a collection (in most cases, a set) of objects from the class. Looking at the extent names in Figure 12.6, the named object departments is of type set<Department>; persons is of type set<Person>; faculty is of type set<Faculty>; and so on.

The use of an extent name—departments in Q0—as an entry point refers to a persistent collection of objects. Whenever a collection is referenced in an OQL query, we should define an **iterator variable**[22]—d in Q0—that ranges over each object in the collection. In many cases, as in Q0, the query will select certain objects from the collection, based on the conditions specified in the where-clause. In Q0, only persistent objects d in the collection of departments that satisfy the condition d.college = 'Engineering' are selected for the query result. For each selected object d, the value of d.dname is retrieved in the query result. Hence, the *type of the result* for Q0 is bag<string>, because the type of each dname value is string (even though the actual result is a set because dname is a key attribute). In general, the result of a query would be of type *bag* for **select** ... **from** ... and of type *set* for **select distinct** ... **from** ..., as in SQL (adding the keyword distinct eliminates duplicates).

Using the example in Q0, there are three syntactic options for specifying iterator variables:

d **in** departments

departments d

departments **as** d

---

22. This is similar to the tuple variables that range over tuples in SQL queries.

We will use the first construct in our examples.[23]

The named objects used as database entry points for OQL queries are not limited to the names of extents. Any named persistent object, whether it refers to an atomic (single) object or to a collection object can be used as a database entry point.

12.3.2 Query Results and Path Expressions

The result of a query can in general be of any type that can be expressed in the ODMG object model. A query does not have to follow the **select** ... **from** ... **where** ... structure; in the simplest case, any persistent name on its own is a query, whose result is a reference to that persistent object. For example, the query

    Q1: departments;

returns a reference to the collection of all persistent department objects, whose type is set<Department>. Similarly, suppose we had given (via the database bind operation, see Figure 12.4) a persistent name csdepartment to a single department object (the computer science department); then, the query:

    Q1a: csdepartment;

returns a reference to that individual object of type Department. Once an entry point is specified, the concept of a **path expression** can be used to specify a *path* to related attributes and objects. A path expression typically starts at a *persistent object name,* or at the iterator variable that ranges over individual objects in a collection. This name will be followed by zero or more relationship names or attribute names connected using the *dot notation.* For example, referring to the UNIVERSITY database of Figure 12.6, the following are examples of path expressions, which are also valid queries in OQL:

    Q2: csdepartment.chair;
    Q2a: csdepartment.chair.rank;
    Q2b: csdepartment.has_faculty;

The first expression Q2 returns an object of type Faculty, because that is the type of the attribute chair of the Department class. This will be a reference to the Faculty object that is related to the department object whose persistent name is csdepartment via the attribute chair; that is, a reference to the Faculty object who is chairperson of the computer science department. The second expression Q2a is similar, except that it returns the rank of this Faculty object (the computer science chair) rather than the object reference; hence, the type returned by Q2a is string, which is the data type for the rank attribute of the Faculty class.

Path expressions Q2 and Q2a return single values, because the attributes chair (of Department) and rank (of Faculty) are both single-valued and they are applied to a single object. The third expression Q2b is different; it returns an object of type set<Faculty> even when applied to a single object, because that is the type of the relationship has_faculty of the Department class. The collection returned will include ref-

---

23. Note that the latter two options are similar to the syntax for specifying tuple variables in SQL queries.

erences to all `Faculty` objects that are related to the department object whose persistent name is `csdepartment` via the relationship `has_faculty`; that is, references to all `Faculty` objects who are working in the computer science department. Now, to return the ranks of computer science faculty, we *cannot* write

    Q3': csdepartment.has_faculty.rank;

This is because it is not clear whether the object returned would be of type `set<string>` or `bag<string>` (the latter being more likely, since multiple faculty may share the same rank). Because of this type of ambiguity problem, OQL does not allow expressions such as Q3'. Rather, one must use an iterator variable over these collections, as in Q3a or Q3b below:

    Q3a: select f.rank
          from   f in csdepartment.has_faculty;
    Q3b: select distinct f.rank
          from   f in csdepartment.has_faculty;

Here, Q3a returns `bag<string>` (duplicate rank values appear in the result), whereas Q3b returns `set<string>` (duplicates are eliminated via the **distinct** keyword). Both Q3a and Q3b illustrate how an iterator variable can be defined in the `from`-clause to range over a restricted collection specified in the query. The variable `f` in Q3a and Q3b ranges over the elements of the collection `csdepartment.has_faculty`, which is of type `set<Faculty>`, and includes only those faculty that are members of the computer science department.

In general, an OQL query can return a result with a complex structure specified in the query itself by utilizing the `struct` keyword. Consider the following two examples:

    Q4:   csdepartment.chair.advises;
    Q4a: select struct (name:struct(last_name: s.name.lname,
                                     first_name: s.name.fname),
                  degrees:(select struct (deg: d.degree,
                                          yr: d.year,
                                          college: d.college)
                          from d in s.degrees)
          from s in csdepartment.chair.advises;

Here, Q4 is straightforward, returning an object of type `set<GradStudent>` as its result; this is the collection of graduate students that are advised by the chair of the computer science department. Now, suppose that a query is needed to retrieve the last and first names of these graduate students, plus the list of previous degrees of each. This can be written as in Q4a, where the variable `s` ranges over the collection of graduate students advised by the chairperson, and the variable `d` ranges over the degrees of each such student `s`. The type of the result of Q4a is a collection of (first-level) `struct`s where each struct has two components: `name` and `degrees`.[24] The `name` component is a further struct made up of `last_name` and `first_name`, each being a single string. The degrees component is defined by an embedded query and is itself a

---

24. As mentioned earlier, `struct` corresponds to the tuple constructor discussed in Chapter 11.

collection of further (second level) structs, each with three string components: deg, yr, and college.

Note that OQL is *orthogonal* with respect to specifying path expressions. That is, attributes, relationships, and operation names (methods) can be used interchangeably within the path expressions, as long as the type system of OQL is not compromised. For example, one can write the following queries to retrieve the grade point average of all senior students majoring in computer science, with the result ordered by gpa, and within that by last and first name:

```
Q5a:  select struct (last_name: s.name.lname, first_name:
                            s.name.fname, gpa: s.gpa)
      from s in csdepartment.has_majors
      where s.class = 'senior'
      order by gpa desc, last_name asc, first_name asc;
Q5b:  select struct (last_name: s.name.lname, first_name:
                            s.name.fname, gpa: s.gpa)
      from s in students
      where s.majors_in.dname = 'Computer Science' and
            s.class = 'senior'
      order by gpa desc, last_name asc, first_name asc;
```

Q5a used the named entry point csdepartment to directly locate the reference to the computer science department and then locate the students via the relationship has_majors, whereas Q5b searches the students extent to locate all students majoring in that department. Notice how attribute names, relationship names, and operation (method) names are all used interchangeably (in an orthogonal manner) in the path expressions: gpa is an operation; majors_in and has_majors are relationships; and class, name, dname, lname, and fname are attributes. The implementation of the gpa operation computes the grade point average and returns its value as a float type for each selected student.

The order by clause is similar to the corresponding SQL construct, and specifies in which order the query result is to be displayed. Hence, the collection returned by a query with an order by clause is of type *list*.

12.3.3   Other Features of OQL

Specifying Views as Named Queries.   The view mechanism in OQL uses the concept of a **named query.** The *define* keyword is used to specify an identifier of the named query, which must be a unique name among all named objects, class names, method names, or function names in the schema. If the identifier has the same name as an existing named query, then the new definition replaces the previous definition. Once defined, a query definition is persistent until it is redefined or deleted. A view can also have parameters (arguments) in its definition.

For example, the following view V1 defines a named query has_minors to retrieve the set of objects for students minoring in a given department:

```
V1: define has_minors(deptname) as
    select s
    from s in students
    where s.minors_in.dname = deptname;
```

Because the ODL schema in Figure 12.6 only provided a unidirectional minors_in attribute for a Student, we can use the above view to represent its inverse without having to explicitly define a relationship. This type of view can be used to represent inverse relationships that are not expected to be used frequently. The user can now utilize the above view to write queries such as

```
has_minors('Computer Science');
```

which would return a bag of students minoring in the Computer Science department. Note that in Figure 12.6, we did define has_majors as an explicit relationship, presumably because it is expected to be used more often.

Extracting Single Elements from Singleton Collections. An OQL query will, in general, return a collection as its result, such as a bag, set (if distinct is specified), or list (if the order by clause is used). If the user requires that a query only return a single element, there is an *element* operator in OQL that is guaranteed to return a single element e from a singleton collection c that contains only one element. If c contains more than one element or if c is empty, then the element operator *raises an exception*. For example, Q6 returns the single object reference to the computer science department:

```
Q6: element (select d
             from d in departments
             where d.dname = 'Computer Science');
```

Since a department name is unique across all departments, the result should be one department. The type of the result is d:Department.

Collection Operators (Aggregate Functions, Quantifiers). Because many query expressions specify collections as their result, a number of operators have been defined that are applied to such collections. These include aggregate operators as well as membership and quantification (universal and existential) over a collection.

The aggregate operators (min, max, count, sum, and avg) operate over a collection.[25] The operator count returns an integer type. The remaining aggregate operators (min, max, sum, avg) return the same type as the type of the operand collection. Two examples follow. The query Q7 returns the number of students minoring in 'Computer Science,' while Q8 returns the average gpa of all seniors majoring in computer science.

---

25. These correspond to aggregate functions in SQL.

```
Q7:   count (s in has_minors('Computer Science'));
Q8:   avg (select s.gpa
            from s in students
            where s.majors_in.dname = 'Computer Science' and
                  s.class = 'senior');
```

Notice that aggregate operations can be applied to any collection of the appropriate type and can be used in any part of a query. For example, the query to retrieve all department names that have more that 100 majors can be written as in Q9:

```
Q9:   select d.dname
      from   d in departments
      where  count (d.has_majors) > 100;
```

The *membership* and *quantification* expressions return a boolean type—that is, true or false. Let v be a variable, c a collection expression, b an expression of type boolean (that is, a boolean condition), and e an element of the type of elements in collection c. Then:

(**e in** c) returns true if element e is a member of collection c.

(**for all** v **in** c: b) returns true if *all* the elements of collection c satisfy b.

(**exists** v **in** c: b) returns true if there is at least one element in c satisfying b.

To illustrate the membership condition, suppose we want to retrieve the names of all students who completed the course called 'Database Systems I'. This can be written as in Q10, where the nested query returns the collection of course names that each student s has completed, and the membership condition returns true if 'Database Systems I' is in the collection for a particular student s:

```
Q10: select s.name.lname, s.name.fname
     from s in students
     where 'Database Systems I' in
           (select c.cname
            from c in s.completed_sections.section.of_course);
```

Q10 also illustrates a simpler way to specify the select clause of queries that return a collection of structs; the type returned by Q10 is bag<struct(string, string)>.

One can also write queries that return true/false results. As an example, let us assume that there is a named object called Jeremy of type Student. Then, query Q11 answers the following question: "Is Jeremy a computer science minor?" Similarly, Q12 answers the question "Are all computer science graduate students advised by computer science faculty?". Both Q11 and Q12 return true or false, which are interpreted as yes or no answers to the above questions:

```
Q11: Jeremy in has_minors('Computer Science');
Q12: for all g in
       (select s
        from s in grad_students
        where s.majors_in.dname = 'Computer Science')
     : g.advisor in csdepartment.has_faculty;
```

Note that query Q12 also illustrates how attribute, relationship, and operation inheritance applies to queries. Although s is an iterator that ranges over the extent grad_students, we can write s.majors_in because the majors_in relationship is inherited by GradStudent from Student via EXTENDS (see Figure 12.6). Finally, to illustrate the exists quantifier, query Q13 answers the following question: "Does any graduate computer science major have a 4.0 gpa?" Here, again, the operation gpa is inherited by GradStudent from Student via EXTENDS.

```
Q13: exists g in
       (select s
        from s in grad_students
        where s.majors_in.dname = 'Computer Science')
      : g.gpa = 4;
```

Ordered (Indexed) Collection Expressions.   As we discussed in Section 12.1.2, collections that are lists and arrays have additional operations, such as retrieving the ith, first and last elements. In addition, operations exist for extracting a subcollection and concatenating two lists. Hence, query expressions that involve lists or arrays can invoke these operations. We will illustrate a few of these operations using example queries. Q14 retrieves the last name of the faculty member who earns the highest salary:

```
Q14: first (select    struct(faculty: f.name.lname, salary:
                              f.salary)
            from      f in faculty
            order by  f.salary desc);
```

Q14 illustrates the use of the *first* operator on a list collection that contains the salaries of faculty members sorted in descending order on salary. Thus the first element in this sorted list contains the faculty member with the highest salary. This query assumes that only one faculty member earns the maximum salary. The next query, Q15, retrieves the top three computer science majors based on gpa.

```
Q15: (select struct(last_name: s.name.lname, first_name:
                    s.name.fname, gpa: s.gpa)
      from s in csdepartment.has_majors
      order by gpa desc) [0:2];
```

The select-from-order-by query returns a list of computer science students ordered by gpa in descending order. The first element of an ordered collection has an index position of 0, so the expression [0:2] returns a list containing the first, second and third elements of the select-from-order-by result.

The Grouping Operator.   The group by clause in OQL, although similar to the corresponding clause in SQL, provides explicit reference to the collection of objects within each *group* or *partition*. First we give an example, then describe the general form of these queries.

Q16 retrieves the number of majors in each department. In this query, the students are grouped into the same partition (group) if they have the same major; that is, the same value for s.majors_in.dname:

```
Q16: select     struct(deptname, number_of_majors:
                        count (partition))
     from       s in students
     group by   deptname: s.majors_in.dname;
```

The result of the grouping specification is of type set<struct(deptname: string, partition: bag<struct(s:Student)>)>, which contains a struct for each group (partition) that has two components: the grouping attribute value (deptname) and the bag of the student objects in the group (partition). The select clause returns the grouping attribute (name of the department), and a count of the number of elements in each partition (that is, the number of students in each department), where partition is the keyword used to refer to each partition. The result type of the select clause is set<struct(deptname: string, number_of_majors: integer)>. In general, the syntax for the group by clause is

$$\text{group by } f_1: e_1, \ f_2: e_2, \ \ldots, \ f_k: e_k$$

where $f_1: e_1, \ f_2: e_2, \ \ldots, \ f_k: e_k$ is a list of partitioning (grouping) attributes and each partitioning attribute specification $f_i: e_i$ defines an attribute (field) name f_i and an expression e_i. The result of applying the grouping (specified in the group by clause) is a set of structures:

$$\text{set<struct}(f_1: t_1, \ f_2: t_2, \ \ldots, \ f_k: t_k, \ \text{partition: bag<B>})>$$

where t_i is the type returned by the expression e_i, partition is a distinguished field name (a keyword), and B is a structure whose fields are the iterator variables (s in Q16) declared in the from clause having the appropriate type.

Just as in SQL, a *having* clause can be used to filter the partitioned sets (that is, select only some of the groups based on group conditions). In Q17, the previous query is modified to illustrate the having clause (and also shows the simplified syntax for the select clause). Q17 retrieves for each department having more than 100 majors, the average gpa of its majors. The having clause in Q17 selects only those partitions (groups) that have more than 100 elements (that is, departments with more than 100 students).

```
Q17: select     deptname, avg_gpa: avg (select p.s.gpa from p
                                            in partition)
     from       s in students
     group by   deptname: s.majors_in.dname
     having     count (partition) > 100;
```

Note that the select clause of Q17 returns the average gpa of the students in the partition. The expression

```
select p.s.gpa from p in partition
```

returns a bag of student gpas for that partition. The from clause declares an iterator variable p over the partition collection, which is of type bag<struct(s: Student)>.

Then the path expression **p.s.gpa** is used to access the gpa of each student in the partition.

12.4 Overview of the C++ Language Binding

The C++ language binding specifies how ODL constructs are mapped to C++ constructs. This is done via a C++ class library that provides classes and operations that implement the ODL constructs. An Object Manipulation Language (OML) is needed to specify how database objects are retrieved and manipulated within a C++ program, and this is based on the C++ programming language syntax and semantics. In addition to the ODL/OML bindings, a set of constructs called *physical pragmas* are defined to allow the programmer some control over physical storage issues, such as clustering of objects, utilizing indices, and memory management.

The class library added to C++ for the ODMG standard uses the prefix **d_** for class declarations that deal with database concepts.[26] The goal is that the programmer should think that only one language is being used, not two separate languages. For the programmer to refer to database objects in a program, a class **d_Ref<T>** is defined for each database class **T** in the schema. Hence, program variables of type **d_Ref<T>** can refer to both persistent and transient objects of class **T**.

In order to utilize the various built-in types in the ODMG Object Model such as collection types, various template classes are specified in the library. For example, an abstract class **d_Object<T>** specifies the operations to be inherited by all objects. Similarly, an abstract class **d_Collection<T>** specifies the operations of collections. These classes are not instantiable, but only specify the operations that can be inherited by all objects and by collection objects, respectively. A template class is specified for each type of collection; these include **d_Set<T>**, **d_List<T>**, **d_Bag<T>**, **d_Varray<T>**, and **d_Dictionary<T>**, and correspond to the collection types in the Object Model (see Section 12.1). Hence, the programmer can create classes of types such as **d_Set<d_Ref<Student>>** whose instances would be sets of references to **Student** objects, or **d_Set<String>** whose instances would be sets of Strings. In addition, a class **d_Iterator** corresponds to the Iterator class of the Object Model.

The C++ ODL allows a user to specify the classes of a database schema using the constructs of C++ as well as the constructs provided by the object database library. For specifying the data types of attributes,[27] basic types such as **d_Short** (short integer), **d_UShort** (unsigned short integer), **d_Long** (long integer), and **d_Float** (floating point number) are provided. In addition to the basic data types, several structured literal types are provided to correspond to the structured literal types of the ODMG Object Model. These include **d_String**, **d_Interval**, **d_Date**, **d_Time**, and **d_Timestamp** (see Figure 12.1b).

---

26. Presumably, **d_** stands for *database* classes.

27. That is, *member variables* in object-oriented programming terminology.

To specify relationships, the keyword `_Rel_` is used within the prefix of type names; for example, by writing

```
d_Rel_Ref<Department, _has_majors> majors_in;
```

in the Student class, and

```
d_Rel_Set<Student, _majors_in> has_majors;
```

in the Department class, we are declaring that majors_in and has_majors are relationship properties that are inverses of one another and hence represent a 1:N binary relationship between Department and Student.

For the OML, the binding overloads the operation *new* so that it can be used to create either persistent or transient objects. To create persistent objects, one must provide the database name and the persistent name of the object. For example, by writing

```
d_Ref<Student> s = new(DB1, 'John_Smith') Student;
```

the programmer creates a named persistent object of type Student in database DB1 with persistent name John_Smith. Another operation, delete_object() can be used to delete objects. Object modification is done by the operations (methods) defined in each class by the programmer.

The C++ binding also allows the creation of extents by using the library class d_Extent. For example, by writing

```
d_Extent<Person> AllPersons(DB1);
```

the programmer would create a named collection object AllPersons—whose type would be d_Set<Person>—in the database DB1 that would hold persistent objects of type Person. However, key constraints are not supported in the C++ binding, and any key checks must be programmed in the class methods.[28] Also, the C++ binding does not support persistence via reachability; the object must be statically declared to be persistent at the time it is created.

12.5   Object Database Conceptual Design

Section 12.5.1 discusses how Object Database (ODB) design differs from Relational Database (RDB) design. Section 12.5.2 outlines a mapping algorithm that can be used to create an ODB schema, made of ODMG ODL class definitions, from a conceptual EER schema.

12.5.1   Differences Between Conceptual Design of ODB and RDB

One of the main differences between ODB and RDB design is how relationships are handled. In ODB, relationships are typically handled by having relationship properties or reference attributes that include OID(s) of the related objects. These can be considered as

---

28. We have only provided a brief overview of the C++ binding. For full details, see Cattell et al. (1997), Ch. 5.

OID *references* to the related objects. Both single references and collections of references are allowed. References for a binary relationship can be declared in a single direction, or in both directions, depending on the types of access expected. If declared in both directions, they may be specified as inverses of one another, thus enforcing the ODB equivalent of the relational referential integrity constraint.

In RDB, relationships among tuples (records) are specified by attributes with matching values. These can be considered as *value references* and are specified via *foreign keys*, which are values of primary key attributes repeated in tuples of the referencing relation. These are limited to being single-valued in each record because multivalued attributes are not permitted in the basic relational model. Thus, M:N relationships must be represented not directly but as a separate relation (table), as discussed in Section 9.1.

Mapping binary relationships that contain attributes is not straightforward in ODBs, since the designer must choose in which direction the attributes should be included. If the attributes are included in both directions, then redundancy in storage will exist and may lead to inconsistent data. Hence, it is sometimes preferable to use the relational approach of creating a separate table by creating a separate class to represent the relationship. This approach can also be used for *n*-ary relationships, with degree $n > 2$.

Another major area of difference between ODB and RDB design is how inheritance is handled. In ODB, these structures are built into the model, so the mapping is achieved by using the inheritance constructs, such as *derived* (:) and *EXTENDS*. In relational design, as we discussed in Section 9.2, there are several options to choose from since no built-in construct exists for inheritance in the basic relational model. It is important to note, though, that object-relational and extended-relational systems are adding features to directly model these constructs as well as to include operation specifications in abstract data types (see Chapter 13).

The third major difference is that in ODB design, it is necessary to specify the operations early on in the design since they are part of the class specifications. Although it is important to specify operations during the design phase for all types of databases, it may be delayed in RDB design as it is not strictly required until the implementation phase.

12.5.2 Mapping an EER Schema to an ODB Schema

It is relatively straightforward to design the type declarations of object classes for an ODBMS from an EER schema that contains *neither* categories *nor n*-ary relationships with $n > 2$. However, the operations of classes are not specified in the EER diagram and must be added to the class declarations after the structural mapping is completed. The outline of the mapping from EER to ODL is as follows:

Step 1: Create an ODL *class* for each EER entity type or subclass. The type of the ODL class should include all the attributes of the EER class.[29] *Multivalued attributes* are

---

29. This implicitly uses a tuple constructor at the top level of the type declaration, but in general, the tuple constructor is not explicitly shown in the ODL class declarations.

declared by using the set, bag, or list constructors.[30] If the values of the multivalued attribute for an object should be ordered, the list constructor is chosen; if duplicates are allowed, the bag constructor should be chosen; otherwise, the set constructor is chosen. *Composite attributes* are mapped into a tuple constructor (by using a struct declaration in ODL).

Declare an extent for each class, and specify any key attributes as keys of the extent. (This is possible only if an extent facility and key constraint declarations are available in the ODBMS.)

Step 2: Add relationship properties or reference attributes for each *binary relationship* into the ODL classes that participate in the relationship. These may be created in one or both directions. If a binary relationship is represented by references in *both* directions, declare the references to be relationship properties that are inverses of one another, if such a facility exists.[31] If a binary relationship is represented by a reference in only *one* direction, declare the reference to be an attribute in the referencing class whose type is the referenced class name.

Depending on the cardinality ratio of the binary relationship, the relationship properties or reference attributes may be single-valued or collection types. They will be single-valued for binary relationships in the 1:1 or N:1 directions; they are collection types (set-valued or list-valued[32]) for relationships in the 1:N or M:N direction. An alternative way for mapping binary M:N relationships is discussed in Step 7 below.

If relationship attributes exist, a tuple constructor (struct) can be used to create a structure of the form <reference, relationship attributes>, which may be included instead of the reference attribute. However, this does not allow the use of the inverse constraint. In addition, if this choice is represented in *both directions*, the attribute values will be represented twice, creating redundancy.

Step 3: Include appropriate operations for each class. These are not available from the EER schema and must be added to the database design by referring to the original requirements. A constructor method should include program code that checks any constraints that must hold when a new object is created. A destructor method should check any constraints that may be violated when an object is deleted. Other methods should include any further constraint checks that are relevant.

Step 4: An ODL class that corresponds to a subclass in the EER schema inherits (via EXTENDS) the type and methods of its superclass in the ODL schema. Its *specific* (non-inherited) attributes, relationship references, and operations are specified, as discussed in Steps 1, 2, and 3.

---

30. Further analysis of the application domain is needed to decide on which constructor to use because this information is not available from the EER schema.

31. The ODL standard provides for the explicit definition of inverse relationships. Some ODBMS products may not provide this support; in such a case, the programmers must maintain every relationship explicitly by coding the methods that update the objects appropriately.

32. The decision whether to use set or list is not available from the EER schema and must be determined from the requirements.

Step 5: Weak entity types can be mapped in the same way as regular entity types. An alternative mapping is possible for weak entity types that do not participate in any relationships except their identifying relationship; these can be mapped as though they were *composite multivalued attributes* of the owner entity type, by using the `set<struct<...>>` or `list<struct<...>>` constructors. The attributes of the weak entity are included in the `struct<...>` construct, which corresponds to a tuple constructor. Attributes are mapped as discussed in Steps 1 and 2.

Step 6: Categories (union types) in an EER schema are difficult to map to ODL. It is possible to create a mapping similar to the EER-to-relational mapping (see Section 9.2) by declaring a class to represent the category and defining 1:1 relationships between the category and each of its superclasses. Another option is to use a *union type*, if it is available.

Step 7: An n-ary relationship with degree $n > 2$ can be mapped into a separate class, with appropriate references to each participating class. These references are based on mapping a 1:N relationship from each class that represents a participating entity type to the class that represents the n-ary relationship. An M:N binary relationship, especially if it contains relationship attributes, may also use this mapping option, if desired.

The mapping has been applied to a subset of the UNIVERSITY database schema of Figure 4.10 in the context of the ODMG object database standard. The mapped object schema using the ODL notation is shown in Figure 12.6.

12.6 Examples of ODBMSs

We now illustrate the concepts discussed in this and the previous chapter by examining two ODBMSs. Section 12.6.1 presents an overview of the O2 system (now called Ardent) by Ardent Software, and Section 12.6.2 gives an overview of the ObjectStore system produced by Object Design Inc. As we mentioned at the beginning of this chapter, there are many other commercial and prototype ODBMSs; we use these two as examples to illustrate specific systems.

12.6.1 Overview of the O2 System

In our overview of the O2 system, we first illustrate data definition and then consider examples of data manipulation in O2. Following that, we give a brief discussion of the system architecture of O2.

Data Definition in O2.   In O2, the schema definition uses the C++ or JAVA language bindings for ODL as defined by ODMG. Section 12.4 provided an overview of the ODMG C++ language binding. Figure 12.8(a) shows example definitions in the C++ O2 binding for part of the UNIVERSITY database given in ODL in Figure 12.6. Note that the C++ O2 binding for defining relationships has chosen to be compliant with the simpler syntax of

```
struct Ename {
    d_String                fname;
    d_String                mname;
    d_String                lname;
};

struct Address {
    d_UShort                no;
    d_String                street;
    d_UShort                aptno;
    d_String                city;
    d_String                state;
    d_UShort                zip;
};

class Person : public d_Object {
public:
// Attributes
    Ename                   ename;
    d_String                ssn;
    d_Date                  birthdate;
    enum Gender {M,F}       sex;
    Address                 address;
// Operations
    Person(const char * pname);
    d_UShort age;
// Extent
static d_Set<d_Ref<Person>>         persons;
static const char * const           extent_name;
};

class Faculty: public Person {
public:
// Attributes
    d_String                rank;
    d_Float                 salary;
    d_String                office;
    d_String                phone;
// Relationships (syntax is ODMG 1.1 compliant)
    d_Ref<Department>       works_in
                            inverse Department::has_faculty;
    d_Set<d_Ref<GradStudent>>       advises
                            inverse GradStudent::advisor;
    d_Set<d_Ref<GradStudent>>   on_committee_of
                            inverse GradStudent::committee;
// Operations
    Faculty(const char * fname, d_Float salary);
    void give_raise(in d_Float raise);
    void promote(in d_String new_rank);
// Extent
static d_Set<d_Ref<Faculty>>        faculty;
static const char * const           extent_name;
};
```

Figure 12.8a   Example illustrating O2. Defining part of the UNIVERSITY schema using the C++ O2 binding.

ODMG 1.1 for defining inverse relationships rather than the ODMG 2.0 described in Section 12.2.

Data Manipulation in O2. Applications for O2 can be developed using the C++ (or JAVA) O2 binding, which provides an ODMG-compliant native language binding to the O2 database. The binding enhances the programming language by providing the following: persistent pointers; generic collections; persistent named objects; relationships; queries; and database system support for sessions, databases, and transactions.

We now illustrate the use of the C++ O2 binding for writing methods for classes. Figure 12.8(b) shows example definitions for the implementation of the schema related to the Faculty class, including the constructor and the member functions (operations) to give a raise and to promote a faculty member. The default constructor for Faculty automatically maintains the extent. The programmer-specified constructor for Faculty shown in Figure 12.8(b) adds the new faculty object to its extent. Both member functions (operations) give_raise and promote modify attributes of persistent faculty objects. Although the ODMG C++ language binding indicates that a mark_modified member function of d_Object is to be called before the object is modified, the C++ O2 binding provides this functionality automatically.

In the C++ ODMG model, persistence is declared when creating the object. Persistence is an immutable property; a transient object cannot become persistent. Referential integrity is not guaranteed; if subobjects of a persistent object are not persistent, the application will fail traversal of references. Also, if an object is deleted, references to it will fail when traversing them.

```
// Faculty Class

const char * const Faculty::extent_name = "faculty";

// Faculty constructor here
Faculty::Faculty(const char * fname, d_Float fsalary) :
    Person(fname)
{
    salary = fsalary;
    // Put this new faculty into the extension
    faculty->insert_element(this);
}

void Faculty::give_raise(d_Float raise);
{
    salary += raise;
}

void Faculty::promote(d_String new_rank);
{
    rank = new_rank;
}
```

Figure 12.8b Example illustrating O2. C++ O2 schema implementation for the Faculty class.

By comparison, the O2 ODBMS supports persistence by reachability, which simplifies application programming and enforces referential integrity. When an object or value becomes persistent, so do all of its subobjects, freeing the programmer from performing this task explicitly. At any time, an object can switch from persistent to transient and back again. During object creation, the programmer does not need to decide whether the object will be persistent. Objects are made persistent when instantiated and continue to retain their identity. Objects no longer referenced are garbage-collected automatically.

O2 also supports the object query language (OQL) as both an ad hoc interactive query language and as an embedded function in a programming language. Section 12.3 discussed the OQL standard in depth. When mapped into the C++ programming language, there are two alternatives for using OQL queries. The first approach is the use of a query member function (operation) on a collection; in this case, a selection predicate is specified, with the syntax of the where clause of OQL, to filter the collection by selecting the tuples satisfying the where condition. For example, suppose that the class Department has an extent departments; the following operation then uses the predicate specified as the second argument to filter the collection of departments and assigns the result to the first argument engineering_depts.

```
d_Bag<d_Ref<Department>> engineering_depts;
departments->query(engineering_depts, "this.college =
              \"Engineering\" ");
```

In the example, the keyword this refers to the object to which the operation is applied (the departments collection in this case). The condition (college="Engineering") filters the collection, returning a bag of references to departments in the college of "Engineering".[33]

The second approach provides complete functionality of OQL from a C++ program through the use of the d_oql_execute function, which executes a constructed query of type d_OQL_Query as given in its first argument and returns the result into the C++ collection specified in its second argument. The following embedded OQL example is identical to Q0, returning the names of departments in the college of Engineering into the C++ collection engineering_dept_names.

```
d_Bag<d_String> engineering_dept_names;
d_OQL_Query      q0(
  "select d.dname from d in departments where d.college =
      \"Engineering\"");
d_oql_execute(q0, engineering_dept_names);
```

Queries may contain parameters, specified by the syntax $i, where i is a number referring to the ith operand in the query. The << operator is used to pass parameters to the query, before calling the d_oql_execute function.

Overview of the O2 System Architecture.   In this section, we give a brief overview of the O2 system architecture. The kernel of the O2 system, called O2Engine, is responsible

---

33. Note that because the condition itself is a string specified between quotation marks ". . .", we must place \" if a quote character appears literally within that string.

for much of the ODBMS functionality. This includes providing support for storing, retrieving, and updating persistently stored objects that may be shared by multiple programs. O2Engine implements the concurrency control, recovery, and security mechanisms that are typical in database systems. In addition, O2Engine implements a transaction management model, schema evolution mechanisms, versioning, notification management as well as a replication mechanism.

The implementation of O2Engine at the system level is based on a *client/server architecture* to accommodate the current trend toward networked and distributed computer systems (see Chapters 17 and 24). The *server component*, which can be a file server machine, is responsible for retrieving data efficiently when requested by a client and to maintain the appropriate concurrency control and recovery information. In O2, concurrency control uses locking, and recovery is based on a write-ahead logging technique (see Chapter 21). O2 provides adaptive locking. By default, locking is at the page level but is moved down to the object level when a conflict occurs on the page. The server also does a certain amount of page caching to reduce disk I/O, and it is accessed via a remote procedure call (RPC) interface from the clients. A *client* is typically a workstation or PC and most of the O2 functionality is provided at the client level.

At the functional level, O2Engine has three main components: (1) the storage component, (2) the object manager, and (3) the schema manager. The *storage component* is at the lowest level. The implementation of this layer is split between the client and the server. The server process provides disk management, page storage and retrieval, concurrency control, and recovery. The client process caches pages and locks that have been provided by the server and makes them available to the higher-level functional modules of the O2 client.

The next functional component, called the *object manager*, deals with structuring objects and values, clustering related objects on disk pages, indexing objects, maintaining object identity, performing operations on objects, and so on. Object identifiers were implemented in O2 as the physical disk address of an object, to avoid the overhead of logical-to-physical OID mapping. The OID includes a disk volume identifier, a page number within the volume, and a slot number within the page. O2 also provides a logical permanent identifier for any persistent object or collection to allow external applications or databases to keep object identifiers that will always be valid even if the objects are moved. External identifiers are never reused. The system manages a special B-tree to store external identifiers, therefore accessing an object using its external ID is done in constant time. Structured complex objects are broken down into record components, and indexes are used to access set-structured or list-structured components of an object.

The top functional level of O2Engine is called the *schema manager*. It keeps track of class, type, and method definitions; provides the inheritance mechanisms; checks the consistency of class declarations; and provides for schema evolution, which includes the creation, modification, and deletion of class declarations incrementally. When an application accesses an object whose class has changed, the object manager automatically adapts its structure to the current definition of the class, without introducing any new overhead for up-to-date objects. For the interested reader, references to material that discusses various aspects of the O2 system are given in the selected bibliography at the end of this chapter.

12.6.2   Overview of the ObjectStore System

In this section, we give an overview of the ObjectStore ODBMS. First we illustrate data definition in ObjectStore, and then we give examples of queries and data manipulation.

Data Definition in ObjectStore.   The ObjectStore system has different packages that can be acquired separately. One package provides persistent storage for the JAVA programming language and another for the C++ programming language. We will describe only the C++ package, which is closely integrated with the C++ language and provides persistent storage capabilities for C++ objects. ObjectStore uses C++ class declarations as its data definition language, with an extended C++ syntax that includes additional constructs specifically useful in database applications. Objects of a class can be transient in the program, or they can be persistently stored by ObjectStore. Persistent objects can be shared by multiple programs. A pointer to an object has the same syntax regardless of whether the object is persistent or transient, so persistence is somewhat transparent to the programmers and users.

Figure 12.9 shows possible ObjectStore C++ class declarations for a portion of the UNIVERSITY database, whose EER schema was given in Figure 4.10. ObjectStore's extended C++ compiler supports inverse relationship declarations and additional functions.[34] In C++, an asterisk (*) specifies a reference (pointer), and the type of field (attribute) is listed before the attribute name. For example, the declaration

```
Faculty *advisor
```

in the Grad_Student class specifies that the attribute *advisor* has the type pointer to a Faculty object. The basic types in C++ include character (char), integer (int), and real number (float). A character string can be declared to be of type char* (a pointer to an array of characters).

In C++, a *derived* class E' inherits the description of a *base* class E by including the name of E in the definition of E' following a colon (:) and either the keyword **public** or the keyword **private**.[35] For example, in Figure 12.9, both the Faculty and the Student classes are derived from the Person class, and both inherit the fields (attributes) and the functions (methods) declared in the description of Person. Functions are distinguished from attributes by including parameters between parentheses after the function name. If a function has no parameters, we just include the parentheses (). A function that does not return a value has the type **void**. ObjectStore adds its own **set constructor** to C++ by using the keyword **os_Set** (for ObjectStore set). For example, the declaration

```
os_Set<Transcript*> transcript
```

within the Student class specifies that the value of the attribute transcript in each Student object is a *set of pointers* to objects of type Transcript. The tuple constructor is

---

34. ObjectStore can also be used with other C++ compilers, by including ObjectStore's C++ library interface.

35. C++ has two types of derivations: public and private. We will consider only public derivations here.

```
/* this is the file univ_schema.H that includes the database class declarations */

struct Phone {
    int area_code ;
    int number ;
}

struct Date {
    int year ;
    int month ;
    int day ;
}

class Person {
public:
    char  ssn[9] ;
    struct {
        char* firstname ;
        char* middlename ;
        char* lastname ;
        } name ;
    struct {
        int     number
        char* street ;
        char* apt_no ;
        char* city ;
        char* state ;
        char* zipcode ;
        } address ;
    Date birthdate ;
    char sex ;

    int age () ;
}

struct Transcript {
    char     grade;
    float    ngrade;
    Section  *Section;
}

class Student: public Person {
    /* Student inherits (is derived from) Person */ public:
    char*                   class;
    Department              *majors_in;
    Department              *minors_in;
    os_Set<Section*>        registered_in;
    os_Set<Transcript*>     transcript;

    float grade_point_average () ;
    void change_class () ;
    void change_major (Department *new_major) ;
}
```

Figure 12.9   ObjectStore C++ class declarations for part of the UNIVERSITY database.

```
struct Degree {
    char* college ;
    char* degree ;
    int    year ;
}

class Grad_student: public Student {
    /* Grad_student inherits (is derived from) Student */public :
    os_Set<Degree*>        degrees ;
    Faculty                *advisor ;
}

class Faculty: public Person {    /* Faculty inherits (is derived from) Person */
    float    salary;
    char*    rank;
    char*    foffice;
    char*    fphone;
    os_Set<Department*>    belongs_to;
    Department             *chairs;
    os_Set<Grant*>         grants;
    os_Set<Student*>       advises;

    void promote_faculty () ;
    void give_raise (float  percent) ;
}

class Department {
    char*    dname;
    char*    office;
    Phone  dphone;
    os_Set<Faculty*>    members;
    os_Set<Student*>    majors;
    Faculty             chairperson;
    os_Set<Course*>     courses;

    void add_major (Student  *s) ;
    void remove_major (Student  *s) ;
}
```

Figure 12.9   (continued)

implicit in C++ declarations whenever various attributes are declared in a class. Object-Store also has bag and list constructors, called os_Bag and os_List, respectively.

The class declarations in Figure 12.9 include reference attributes in both directions for the relationships from Figure 4.10. ObjectStore includes a **relationship facility** permitting the specification of inverse attributes that represent a binary relationship. Figure 12.10 illustrates the syntax of this facility.

Figure 12.10 also illustrates another C++ feature: the **constructor** function for a class. A class can have a function with the same name as the class name, which is used to create new objects of the class. In Figure 12.10, the constructor for Faculty supplies only the ssn value for a Faculty object (ssn is inherited from Person), and the constructor for Department supplies only the dname value. The values of other attributes can be added to the objects later, although in a real system the constructor function would include more

```
extern database *univ_db ;

class Person ;

class Faculty: public Person {    /* Faculty inherits (is derived from) Person */
    float   salary ;
    char* rank ;
    char* foffice ;
    char* fphone ;
    os_relationship_m_m (Faculty, belongs_to, Department, members, os_Set<Department*>),
    os_relationship_1_1 (Faculty, chairs, Department, chairperson, Department*);
    os_Set<Grant*>     grants ;
    os_Set<Student*> advises ;

    Faculty (char  s[9]) { ssn = new (univ_db) char[9] ; strcpy(ssn,  s) ; }
        /* the ssn attribute is inherited from Person */
    void promote_faculty () ;
    void give_raise (float  percent) ;
}

class Department {
    char*   dname ;
    char*   office ;
    Phone  dphone ;
    os_relationship_m_m (Department, members, Faculty, belongs_to, os_Set<Faculty*>);
    os_Set<Student*> majors ;
    os_relationship_1_1 (Department, chairperson, Faculty, chairs, Faculty*);
    os_Set<Course*> courses ;

    Department (char*  d) { dname = new (univ_db) char[strlen(d)+1] ; strcpy(dname,  d) ; }
    void add_faculty (Faculty  *f) ;
    void add_major (Student  *s) ;
    int   remove_major (Student  *s) ;
    os_rel_m_m_body (Faculty, belongs_to, Department, members);
    os_rel_m_m_body (Department, members, Faculty, belongs_to);
    os_rel_1_1_body (Faculty, chairs, Department, chairperson);
    os_rel_1_1_body (Department, chairperson, Faculty, chairs);
}
```

Figure 12.10 Declaring inverse relationships in ObjectStore C++.

parameters to construct a more complete object. We discuss how constructors can be used to create persistent objects next.

Data Manipulation in ObjectStore.   The ObjectStore collection types os_Set, os_Bag, and os_List can have additional functions applied to them. These include the functions **insert**(e), **remove**(e), and **create**, which can be used to insert an element e into a collection, to remove an element e from a collection, and to create a new collection, respectively. In addition, a **for** programming construct creates a cursor iterator c to loop over each element c in a collection. These functions are illustrated in Figure 12.11(a), which shows how a few of the methods declared in Figure 12.9 may be specified in ObjectStore.

```
(a)
int Person::age () {
      Date d = today() ; int a = d.year - birthdate.year ;
      if ( d.month < birthdate.month ) ||
        ( d.month == birthdate.month ) && ( d.day < birthdate.day ) ) --a ;
      return a;
} ;

float Student::grade_point_average () {
    float sum = 0.0 ; int count = 0 ; Transcript* t ;
    os_Cursor<Transcript*> cur(transcript);
    for (t = cur.first(); cur.more(); t = cur.next
        sum += t->ngrade ; ++count ;  /* increments sum by ngrade, count by 1 */
        }
    return sum/count ;
} ;

void Student::change_major (Department  *new_major) {majors_in = new_major ; }
void Department::remove_major (Student  *s) {majors->remove(s) ; }
void Department::add_faculty (Faculty  *f) { members->insert (f) ; }
void Department::add_major (Student* s) { majors->insert(s) ; }


(b)
main () {
    database  *univ_db = database::open ("/database/univ" ) ;

    transaction::begin () ;
/* create two persistent sets to hold all Faculty and all Department objects *
    os_Set<Faculty*>  &all_faculty = os_Set<Faculty*>::create(univ_db) ;
    os_Set<Department*>  &all_depts = os_Set<Department*>::create(univ_db) ;

/* create a new Faculty object and a new Department object using the constructors */
    Faculty    *f = new (univ_db) Faculty ("123456789") ;
    Department    *d = new (univ_db) Department ("Computer Science") ;
/* relate the objects by invoking the appropriate method */
    d->add_faculty (f) ;
/* add the objects to their persistent sets */
    all_faculty.insert(f) ; all_depts.insert(d) ;

    transaction::commit () ;
}
```

Figure 12.11   ObjectStore C++ programming. (a) Code for some of the member functions (operations) in Figure 12.9. (b) Creating persistent objects.

The function add_major adds a (pointer to a) student to the set attribute majors of the **Department** class, by invoking the insert function via the statement majors->insert. Similarly, the remove_major function removes a student pointer from the same set. Here, we assume that the appropriate declarations of relationships have been made, so any inverse attributes are automatically maintained by the system. In the grade_point_ average function, the for loop is used to iterate over the set of transcript records within a Student object to calculate the GPA.

In C++, functional reference to components within an object o uses the *arrow notation* when a pointer to o is provided, and uses the *dot notation* when a variable whose value is the object o itself is provided. These references can be used to refer to both attributes and functions of an object. For example, the references d.year and t–>ngrade in the age and grade_point_average functions refer to component attributes, whereas the reference to majors+>remove in remove_major invokes the remove function of ObjectStore on the majors set.

To create persistent objects and collections in ObjectStore, the programmer or user must assign a **name,** which is also called a *persistent variable.* The persistent variable can be viewed as a shorthand reference to the object, and it is permanently "remembered" by ObjectStore. For example, in Figure 12.11(b), we created two persistent set-valued objects all_faculty and all_depts and made them persistent in the database called univ_db. These objects are used by the application to hold pointers to all persistent objects of type faculty and department, respectively. An object that is a member of a defined class may be created by invoking the object constructor function for that class, with the keyword **new.** For example, in Figure 12.11(b), we created a Faculty object and a Department object, and then related them by invoking the method add_faculty. Finally, we added them to the all_faculty and all_dept sets to make them persistent.

ObjectStore also has a query facility, which can be used to select a set of objects from a collection by specifying a selection condition. The result of a query is a collection of pointers to the objects that satisfy the query. Queries can be embedded within a C++ program and can be considered a means of associative high-level access to select objects that avoids the need to create an explicit looping construct. Figure 12.12 illustrates a few queries, each of which returns a subset of objects from the all_faculty collection that satisfy a particular condition. The first query in Figure 12.12 selects all Faculty objects from the all_faculty collection whose rank is Assistant Professor. The second query retrieves professors whose salary is greater than $5,000.00. The third query retrieves department chairs, and the fourth query retrieves computer science faculty.

```
os_Set<Faculty*>  &asst_profs =
    all_faculty -> query ("Faculty*", "!strcmp (rank, \"Assistant Professor\")", db);
os_Set<Faculty*>  &rich_asst_profs =
    all_faculty -> query ("Faculty*", "salary>5000.00", db);
os_Set<Faculty*>  &dept_chairs =
    all_faculty -> query ("Faculty*", "chairs != NULL", db);
os_Set<Faculty*>  &cs_faculty =
    all_faculty -> query ("Faculty*", "belongs_to [:dname==\"Computer Science\"]", db);
```

Figure 12.12   Queries in ObjectStore C++.

12.7 Overview of the CORBA Standard for Distributed Objects

A guiding principle of the ODMG 2.0 object database standard was to be compatible with the Common Object Request Broker Architecture (CORBA) standards of the Object Management Group (OMG). CORBA is an object management standard that allows objects to communicate in a distributed, heterogeneous environment, providing transparency across network, operating system, and programming language boundaries. Since the OMG object model is a common model for object-oriented systems, including ODBMS, the ODMG has defined its object model to be a superset of the OMG object model. Although the OMG has not yet standardized the use of an ODBMS within CORBA, the ODMG has addressed this issue in a position statement, defining an architecture within the OMG environment for the use of ODBMS. This section includes a brief overview of CORBA to facilitate a discussion on the relationship of the ODMG 2.0 object database standard to the OMG CORBA standard.

CORBA uses objects as a unifying paradigm for distributed components written in different programming languages and running on various operating systems and networks. CORBA objects can reside anywhere on the network. It is the responsibility of an Object Request Broker (ORB) to provide the transparency across network, operating system, and programming language boundaries by receiving method invocations from one object, called the **client,** and delivering them to the appropriate target object, called the **server.** The client object is only aware of the server object's interface, which is specified in a standard definition language.

The OMG's Interface Definition Language (IDL) is a programming language independent specification of the public interface of a CORBA object. IDL is part of the CORBA specification and describes only the functionality, not the implementation, of an object. Therefore, IDL provides programming language interoperability by specifying only the attributes and operations belonging to an interface. The methods specified in an interface definition can be implemented in and invoked from a programming language that provides CORBA bindings, such as C, C++, ADA, SMALLTALK, and JAVA.

An interface definition in IDL strongly resembles an interface definition in ODL, since ODL was designed with IDL compatibility as a guiding principle. ODL, however, extends IDL with relationships and class definitions. IDL cannot declare member variables. The attribute declarations in an IDL interface definition do not indicate storage, but they are mapped to get and set methods to retrieve and modify the attribute value. This is why ODL classes that inherit behavior only from an interface must duplicate the inherited attribute declarations since attribute specifications in classes define member variables. IDL method specifications must include the name and mode (input, output) of parameters and the return type of the method. IDL method specifications do not include the specification of constructors or destructors, and operation name overloading is not allowed.

The IDL specification is compiled to verify the interface definition and to map the IDL interface into the target programming language of the compiler. An IDL compiler generates three files: (1) a header file, (2) a client source file, and (3) a server source file. The *header file* defines the programming language specific view of the IDL interface definition, which is included in both the server and its clients. The *client source file*. called the **stub**

code, is included in the source code of the client to transmit requests to the server for the interfaces defined in the compiled IDL file. The *server source file,* called the **skeleton code,** is included in the source code of the server to accept requests from a client. Since the same programmer does not in general write the client and server implementations at the same time in the same programming language, not all of the generated files are necessarily used. The programmer writing the client implementation uses the header and stub code. The programmer writing the server implementation uses the header and skeleton code.

The above compilation scenario illustrates *static definitions of method invocations* at compile time, providing strong type checking. CORBA also provides the flexibility of *dynamic method invocations at run time.* The CORBA Interface Repository contains the metadata or descriptions of the registered component interfaces. The capability to retrieve, store, and modify metadata information is provided by the Interface Repository Application Program Interfaces (APIs). The Dynamic Invocation Interface (DII) allows the client at run-time to discover objects and their interfaces, to construct and invoke these methods, and to receive the results from these dynamic invocations. The Dynamic Skeleton Interface (DSI) allows the ORB to deliver requests to registered objects that do not have a static skeleton defined. This extensive use of metadata makes CORBA a self-describing system.

Figure 12.13 shows the structure of a CORBA 2.0 ORB. Most of the components of the diagram have already been explained in our discussion thus far, except for the Object Adapter, the Implementation Repository (not shown in figure), and the ORB Interface.

The Object Adapter (OA) acts as a liaison between the ORB and object implementations, which provide the state and behavior of an object. An object adapter is responsible for the following: registering object implementations; generating and mapping object references; registering activation and deactivation of object implementations; and invoking methods, either statically or dynamically. The CORBA standard requires that an ORB support a standard adapter known as the Basic Object Adapter (BOA). The ORB may support

*Really the Basic Object Adaptor

Figure 12.13   The CORBA 2.0 ORB Architecture. Pearson Education Ltd. from CORBA *Distributed Objects* by Sean Baker © 1997 Addison Wesley Longman.

Figure 12.14   The CORBA Object Management Architecture (OMA). Pearson
Education Ltd. from CORBA *Distributed Objects* by Sean Baker
© 1997 Addison Wesley Longman.

other object adapters. Two other object adapters have been proposed but not standardized: a Library Object Adapter and an Object-Oriented Database Adapter.

The Object Adapter registers the object implementations in an Implementation
Repository. This registration typically includes a mapping from the name of the server
object to the name of the executable code of the object implementation.

The ORB Interface provides operations on object references. There are two types of
object references: (1) an invocable reference that is valid within the session it is obtained,
and (2) a stringified reference that is valid across session boundaries.[36] The ORB Interface
provides operations to convert between these forms of object references.

The Object Management Architecture (OMA), shown in Figure 12.14, is built on top
of the core CORBA infrastructure. The OMA provides optional CORBAservices and COR-
BAfacilities for support of distributed applications through a collection of interfaces
specified in IDL. CORBAservices provide system-level services to objects, such as naming
and event services. CORBAfacilities provide higher-level services for application objects.
The CORBAfacilities are categorized as either horizontal or vertical. *Horizontal facilities*
span application domains—for example, services that facilitate user interface programming for any application domain. *Vertical facilities* are specific to an application domain—
for example, specific services needed in the telecommunications application domain.

Some of the CORBAservices are database related, such as concurrency and query services, and thus overlap with the facilities of a DBMS. The OMG has not yet standardized

---

36. A *stringified reference* is a reference (pointer, ObjectId) that has been converted to a string so it
can be passed among heterogeneous systems. The ORB will convert it back to a reference when
required.

the use of an ODBMS within CORBA. The ODMG has addressed this issue in a position statement, indicating that the integration of an ODBMS in an OMG ORB environment must respect the goals of distribution and heterogeneity while allowing the ODBMS to be responsible for its multiple objects. The relationship between the ORB and the ODBMS should be reciprocal; the ORB should be able to use the ODBMS as a repository and the ODBMS should be able to use the services provided by the ORB.

It is unrealistic to expect every object within an ODBMS to be individually registered with the ORB since the overhead would be prohibitive. The ODMG proposes the use of an alternative adapter, called an Object Database Adapter (ODA), to provide the desired flexibility and performance. The ODBMS should have the capability to manage both ORB registered and unregistered objects, to register subspaces of object identifiers within the ORB, and to allow direct access to the objects managed by the ODBMS. To access objects in the database that are not registered with the ORB, an ORB request is made to the database object, making the objects in the database directly accessible to the application. From the client's view, access to objects in the database that are registered with the ORB should not be different than any other ORB-accessible object.

12.8 Summary

In this chapter we discussed the proposed standard for object-oriented databases. We started by describing the various constructs of the ODMG object model. The various built-in types, such as Object, Collection, Iterator, Set, List, and so on were described by their interfaces, which specify the built-in operations of each type. These built-in types are the foundation upon which the object definition language (ODL) and object query language (OQL) are based. We also described the difference between objects, which have an ObjectId, and literals, which are values with no OID. Users can declare classes for their application that inherit operations from the appropriate built-in interfaces. Two types of properties can be specified in a user-defined class—attributes and relationships—in addition to the operations that can be applied to objects of the class. The ODL allows users to specify both interfaces and classes, and permits two different types of inheritance—interface inheritance via ":" and class inheritance via EXTENDS. A class can have an extent and keys.

A description of ODL then followed, and an example database schema for the UNI-VERSITY database was used to illustrate the ODL constructs. We then presented an overview of the object query language (OQL). The OQL follows the concept of orthogonality in constructing queries, meaning that an operation can be applied to the result of another operation as long as the type of the result is of the correct input type for the operation. The OQL syntax follows many of the constructs of SQL but includes additional concepts such as path expressions, inheritance, methods, relationships, and collections. Examples of how to use OQL over the UNIVERSITY database were given.

We then gave an overview of the C++ language binding, which extends C++ class declarations with the ODL type constructors but permits seamless integration of C++ with the ODBMS.

Following the description of the ODMG model, we described a general technique for designing object-oriented database schemas. We discussed how object-oriented databases differ from relational databases in three main areas: references to represent relationships, inclusion of operations, and inheritance. We showed how to map a conceptual database design in the EER model to the constructs of object databases. We then gave overviews of two ODBMSs, O2 and Object Store. Finally, we gave an overview of the CORBA (Common Object Request Broker Architecture) standard for supporting interoperability among distributed object systems, and how it relates to the object database standard.

Review Questions

12.1. What are the differences and similarities between objects and literals in the ODMG Object Model?

12.2. List the basic operations of the following built-in interfaces of the ODMG Object Model: Object, Collection, Iterator, Set, List, Bag, Array, and Dictionary.

12.3. Describe the built-in structured literals of the ODMG Object Model and the operations of each.

12.4. What are the differences and similarities of attribute and relationship properties of a user-defined (atomic) class?

12.5. What are the differences and similarities of EXTENDS and interface ":" inheritance?

12.6. Discuss how persistence is specified in the ODMG Object Model in the C++ binding.

12.7. Why are the concepts of extents and keys important in database applications?

12.8. Describe the following OQL concepts: *database entry points, path expressions, iterator variables, named queries (views), aggregate functions, grouping,* and *quantifiers.*

12.9. What is meant by the type orthogonality of OQL?

12.10. Discuss the general principles behind the C++ binding of the ODMG standard.

12.11. What are the main differences between designing a relational database and an object database?

12.12. Describe the steps of the algorithm for object database design by EER-to-OO mapping.

12.13. What is the objective of CORBA? Why is it relevant to the ODMG standard?

12.14. Describe the following CORBA concepts: IDL, stub code, skeleton code, DII (Dynamic Invocation Interface), and DSI (Dynamic Skeleton Interface).

Exercises

12.15. Design an OO schema for a database application that you are interested in. First construct an EER schema for the application; then create the corresponding classes in ODL. Specify a number of methods for each class, and then specify queries in OQL for your database application.

12.16. Consider the AIRPORT database described in Exercise 4.21. Specify a number of operations/methods that you think should be applicable to that application. Specify the ODL classes and methods for the database.

12.17. Map the COMPANY ER schema of Figure 3.2 into ODL classes. Include appropriate methods for each class.

12.18. Specify in OQL the queries in the exercises to Chapters 7 and 8 that apply to the COMPANY database.

Selected Bibliography

Cattell et al. (1997) describes the ODMG 2.0 standard and Cattell et al. (1993) describes the earlier versions of the standard. Several books describe the CORBA architecture—for example, Baker (1996). Other general references to object-oriented databases were given in the bibliographic notes to Chapter 11.

The O2 system is described in Deux et al. (1991) and Bancilhon et al. (1992) includes a list of references to other publications describing various aspects of O2. The O2 model was formalized in Velez et al. (1989). The ObjectStore system is described in Lamb et al. (1991). Fishman et al. (1987) and Wilkinson et al. (1990) discuss IRIS, an object-oriented DBMS developed at Hewlett-Packard laboratories. Maier et al. (1986) and Butterworth et al. (1991) describe the design of GEMSTONE. An OO system supporting open architecture developed at Texas Instruments is described in Thompson et al. (1993). The ODE system developed at ATT Bell Labs is described in Agrawal and Gehani (1989). The ORION system developed at MCC is described in Kim et al. (1990). Morsi et al. (1992) describes an OO testbed.

CHAPTER 13

Object Relational and Extended Relational Database Systems

In the preceding chapters we have primarily discussed three data models—the Entity-Relationship (ER) model and its enhanced version, the EER model, in Chapters 3 and 4; the relational data model and its languages and systems in Chapters 7 through 10; and the object-oriented data model and object database languages and standards in Chapters 11 and 12. We discussed how all these data models have been thoroughly developed in terms of the following features:

- Modeling constructs for developing schemas for database applications.
- Constraints facilities for expressing certain types of relationships and constraints on the data as determined by application semantics.
- Operations and language facilities to manipulate the database.

Out of these three models, the ER model has been primarily employed in CASE tools that are used for database and software design, whereas the other two models have been used as the basis for commercial DBMSs. This chapter discusses the emerging class of commercial DBMSs that are called *object-relational* or *enhanced relational systems*, and some of the conceptual foundations for these systems. These systems—which are often called object-relational DBMSs (ORDBMSs)—emerged as a way of enhancing the capabilities of relational DBMSs (RDBMSs) with some of the features that appeared in object DBMSs (ODBMSs).

We start in Section 13.1 by giving a historical perspective of database technology evolution and current trends to understand why these systems emerged. Section 13.2

gives an overview of the Informix database server as an example of a commercial extended ORDBMS. Section 13.3 discusses the object-relational and extended features of Oracle, which was described in Chapter 10 as an example of a commercial RDBMS. We then turn our attention to the issue of standards in Section 13.4 by giving an overview of the SQL3 standard, which provides extended and object capabilities to the SQL standard for RDBMS. Section 13.5 discusses some issues related to the implementation of extended relational systems and Section 13.6 presents an overview of the nested relational model, which provides some of the theoretical foundations behind extending the relational model with complex objects. Section 13.7 is a summary.

Readers interested in typical features of ORDBMS may read Sections 13.1 through 13.3 and be familiar with features of SQL3 from Section 13.4. Those interested in the trends for the SQL standard may read only Section 13.4. Other sections may be skipped in an introductory course.

13.1 Evolution and Current Trends of Database Technology

Section 13.1.1 gives a historical overview of the evolution of database systems technology, while Section 13.1.2 gives an overview of current trends.

13.1.1 The Evolution of Database Systems Technology

In the commercial world today, there are several families of DBMS products available. Two of the most dominant ones are RDBMS and ODBMS, which subscribe to the relational and the object data models respectively. Two other major types of DBMS products—hierarchical and network—are now being referred to as **legacy DBMSs**; these are based on the hierarchical and the network data models, both of which were introduced in the mid-1960s. The hierarchical family primarily has one dominant product—IMS of IBM, whereas the network family includes a large number of DBMSs, such as IDS II (Honeywell), IDMS (Computer Associates), IMAGE (Hewlett Packard), VAX-DBMS (Digital), and TOTAL/SUPRA (Cincom), to name a few. The hierarchical and network data models are summarized in Appendixes C and D.[1]

As database technology evolves, the legacy DBMSs will be gradually replaced by newer offerings. In the interim, we must face the major problem of **interoperability**—the interoperation of a number of databases belonging to all of the disparate families of DBMSs—as well as to legacy file management systems. A whole series of new systems and tools to deal with this problem are emerging as well. Chapter 12 outlined standards like ODMG and CORBA, which are bringing interoperability and portability to applications involving databases from different models and systems.

---

1. Those chapters devoted to the Network Data Model and the Hierarchical Data Model are available at the Web site for this book.

13.1.2 The Current Drivers of Database Systems Technology

The main forces behind the development of extended ORDBMSs stem from the inability of the legacy DBMSs and the basic relational data model as well as the earlier RDBMSs to meet the challenges of new applications.[2] These are primarily in areas that involve a variety of types of data—for example, text in computer-aided desktop publishing; images in satellite imaging or weather forecasting; complex nonconventional data in engineering designs, in the biological genome information, and in architectural drawings; time series data in history of stock market transactions or sales histories; and spatial and geographic data in maps, air/water pollution data, and traffic data. Hence there is a clear need to design databases that can develop, manipulate, and maintain the complex objects arising from such applications. Furthermore, it is becoming necessary to handle digitized information that represents audio and video data streams (partitioned into individual frames) requiring the storage of BLOBs (binary large objects) in DBMSs.

The popularity of the relational model is helped by a very robust infrastructure in terms of the commercial DBMSs that have been designed to support it. However, the basic relational model and earlier versions of its SQL language proved inadequate to meet the above challenges. Legacy data models like the network data model have a facility to model relationships explicitly, but they suffer from a heavy use of pointers in the implementation and have no concepts like object identity, inheritance, encapsulation, or the support for multiple data types and complex objects. The hierarchical model fits well with some naturally occurring hierarchies in nature and in organizations, but it is too limited and rigid in terms of built-in hierarchical paths in the data. Hence, a trend was started to combine the best features of the object data model and languages into the relational data model so that it can be extended to deal with the challenging applications of today.

In most of this chapter we highlight the features of two representative DBMSs that exemplify the ORDBMS approach: Informix Universal Server and Oracle 8.[3] We then discuss features of the SQL3 language—the next version of the SQL standard—which extends SQL2 (or SQL-92) by incorporating object database and other features such as extended data types. We conclude by briefly discussing the nested relational model, which has its origin in a series of research proposals and prototype implementations; this provides a means of embedding hierarchically structured complex objects within the relational framework.

---

2. In Chapters 26 and 27, we summarize the latest trends in decision support and other emerging applications, and the corresponding challenges they pose to database technology.

3. An ORDBMS called Illustra was acquired by Informix and integrated into Informix's Universal Database Server; the IBM DB2 Universal Server—called UDB—has similar ORDBMS features, as do other systems, but we do not discuss these due to space limitations.

13.2   The Informix Universal Server[4]

The Informix Universal Server is an ORDBMS that combines relational and object database technologies from two previously existing products: Informix and Illustra. The latter system originated from the POSTGRES DBMS, which was a research project at the University of California at Berkeley that was commercialized as the Montage DBMS and went through the name Miro before being named Illustra. Illustra was then acquired by Informix, integrated into its RDBMS, and introduced as the Informix Universal Server—an ORDBMS.

To see why ORDBMSs emerged, we start by focusing on one way of classifying DBMS applications according to two dimensions or axes: (1) complexity of data—the X-dimension—and (2) complexity of querying—the Y-dimension. We can arrange these axes into a simple 0-1 space having four quadrants:

Quadrant 1 ($X = 0$, $Y = 0$): Simple data, simple querying

Quadrant 2 ($X = 0$, $Y = 1$): Simple data, complex querying

Quadrant 3 ($X = 1$, $Y = 0$): Complex data, simple querying

Quadrant 4 ($X = 1$, $Y = 1$): Complex data, complex querying

Traditional RDBMSs belong to Quadrant 2. Although they support complex ad hoc queries and updates (as well as transaction processing), they can deal only with simple data that can be modeled as a set of rows in a table. Many object databases (ODBMSs) fall in Quadrant 3, since they concentrate on managing complex data but have somewhat limited querying capabilities based on navigation.[5] In order to move into the fourth quadrant to support both complex data and querying, RDBMSs have been incorporating more complex data objects (as we shall describe here) while ODBMSs have been incorporating more complex querying (for example, the OQL high-level query language, discussed in Chapter 12). The Informix Universal Server belongs to Quadrant 4 because it has extended its basic relational model by incorporating a variety of features that make it object-relational.

Other current ORDBMSs that evolved from RDBMSs include Oracle 8 from Oracle Corporation, Universal DB (UDB) from IBM, Odapter by Hewlett Packard (HP) (which extends Oracle's DBMS), and Open ODB from HP (which extends HP's own Allbase/SQL product). The more successful products seem to be those that maintain the option of working as an RDBMS while introducing the additional functionality. Another system, UniSQL from UniSQL Inc., was developed from scratch as an ORDBMS product. Our intent here is *not* to provide a comparative analysis of these products but only to give an overview of two representative systems.

---

4. The discussion in this section is primarily based on the book *Object-Relational DBMSs* by Michael Stonebraker and Dorothy Moore (1996), and on the input provided by Magdi Morsi of Informix, Inc.

5. Quadrant 1 includes any software packages that deal with data handling without sophisticated data retrieval and manipulation features. These include spreadsheets like EXCEL, word processors like Microsoft Word, or any file management software.

How Informix Universal Server Extends the Relational Data Model. The extensions to the relational data model provided by Illustra and incorporated into Informix Universal Server fall into the following categories:

- Support for additional or extensible data types.
- Support for user-defined routines (procedures or functions).
- Implicit notion of inheritance.
- Support for indexing extensions.
- Data Blades Application Programming Interface (API).[6]

We give an overview of each of these features in the following sections. We have already introduced in a general way the concepts of data types, type constructors, complex objects, and inheritance in the context of object-oriented models (see Chapter 11).

13.2.1 Extensible Data Types

The architecture of Informix Universal Server comprises the basic DBMS plus a number of **Data Blade modules.** The idea is to treat the DBMS as a razor into which a particular blade is inserted for the support of a specific data type. A number of data types have been provided, including two-dimensional geometric objects (such as points, lines, circles, and ellipses), images, time series, text, and Web pages. When Informix announced the Universal Server, 29 Data Blades were already available.[7] It is also possible for an application to create its own types, thus making the data type notion fully extendible. In addition to the built-in types, Informix Universal Server provides the user with the following four constructs to declare additional types:[8]

1. Opaque type.
2. Distinct type.
3. Row type.
4. Collection type.

When creating a type based on one of the first three options, the user has to provide functions and routines for manipulation and conversion, including built-in, aggregate, and operator functions as well as any additional user-defined functions and routines. The details of these four types are presented in the following sections.

Opaque Type. The opaque type has its internal representation hidden, so it is used for encapsulating a type. The user has to provide casting functions to convert an opaque object between its hidden representation in the server (database) and its visible represen-

---

6. Data Blades provides extensions to the basic system, as we shall discuss later in Section 13.2.6.

7. For more information on the Data Blades for Informix Universal Server, consult the Web site http://www.informix.com/informix/.

8. These roughly correspond to type constructors (see Chapter 11).

tation as seen by the client (calling program). The user functions *send/receive* are needed to convert to/from the server internal representation from/to the client representation. Similarly, *import/export* functions are used to convert to/from an external representation for bulk copy from/to the internal representation. Several other functions may be defined for processing the opaque types, including *assign()*, *destroy()*, and *compare()*.

The specification of an opaque type includes its name, internal length if fixed, maximum internal length if it is variable length, alignment (which is the byte boundary), as well as whether or not it is hashable (for creating a hash access structure). If we write

```
CREATE OPAQUE TYPE fixed_opaque_udt (INTERNALLENGTH = 8,
    ALIGNMENT = 4, CANNOTHASH);
CREATE OPAQUE TYPE var_opaque_udt (INTERNALLENGTH = variable,
    MAXLEN=1024, ALIGNMENT = 8);
```

then the first statement creates a fixed-length user-defined opaque type, named `fixed_opaque_udt`, and the second statement creates a variable length one, named `var_opaque_udt`. Both are described in an implementation with internal parameters that are not visible to the client.

Distinct Type.   The distinct data type is used to extend an existing type through inheritance. The newly defined type inherits the functions/routines of its base type, if they are not overridden. For example, the statement

```
CREATE DISTINCT TYPE hiring_date AS DATE;
```

creates a new user-defined type, `hiring_date`, which can be used like any other built-in type.

Row Type.   The row type, which represents a composite attribute, is analogous to a *struct* type in the C programming language.[9] It is a composite type that contains one or more fields. Row type is also used to support inheritance by using the keyword UNDER, but the type system supports single inheritance only. By creating tables whose tuples are of a particular row type, it is possible to treat a relation as part of an object-oriented schema and establish inheritance relationships among the relations. In the following row type declarations, `employee_t` and `student_t` inherit (or are *declared under*) `person_t`:

```
CREATE ROW TYPE person_t(name VARCHAR(60), social_security
    NUMERIC(9), birth_date DATE);
CREATE ROW TYPE employee_t(salary NUMERIC(10,2), hired_on
    hiring_date) UNDER person_t;
CREATE ROW TYPE student_t(gpa NUMERIC(4,2), address
    VARCHAR(200)) UNDER person_t;
```

Collection Type.   Informix Universal Server collections include lists, sets, and multisets (bags) of built-in types as well as user-defined types.[10] A collection can be the type of

---

9. This is similar to the *tuple constructor* discussed in Chapter 11.

10. These are similar to the *collection types* discussed in Chapters 11 and 12.

either a field in a row type or a column in a table. The elements of a **set** collection cannot contain duplicate values, and have no specific order. The **list** may contain duplicate elements, and order is significant. Finally, the **multiset** may include duplicates and has no specific order. Consider the following example:

```
CREATE TABLE employee (name VARCHAR(50) NOT NULL, commission
   MULTISET (MONEY));
```

Here, the `employee` table contains the commission column, which is of type multiset.

13.2.2 Support for User-Defined Routines

Informix Universal Server supports user-defined functions and routines to manipulate the user defined types. The implementation of these functions can be in either Stored Procedure Language (SPL), or in the C or JAVA programming languages. User-defined functions enable the user to define operator functions such as *plus()*, *minus()*, *times()*, *divide()*, *positive()*, and *negate()*, built-in functions such as *cos()* and *sin()*, aggregate functions such as *sum()* and *avg()*, and user-defined routines. This enables Informix Universal Server to handle user-defined types as a built-in type whenever the required functions are defined. The following example specifies an equal function to compare two objects of the `fixed_opaque_udt` type declared earlier:

```
CREATE FUNCTION equal (arg1 fixed_opaque_udt, arg2
    fixed_opaque_udt) RETURNING BOOLEAN;
EXTERNAL NAME "/usr/lib/informix/libopaque.so
    (fixed_opaque_udt_equal)" LANGUAGE C;
END FUNCTION;
```

Informix Universal Server also supports **cast**—a function that converts objects from a source type to a target type. There are two types of user-defined casts: (1) implicit and (2) explicit. Implicit casts are invoked automatically, whereas explicit casts are invoked only when the cast operator is specified explicitly by using "::" or CAST AS. If the source and target types have the same internal structure (such as when using the *distinct types* specification), no user-defined functions are needed.

Consider the following example to illustrate explicit casting, where the employee table has a `col1` column of type `var_opaque_udt` and a `col2` column of type `fixed_opaque_udt`.

```
SELECT col1 FROM employee WHERE fixed_opaque_udt::col1 = col2;
```

In order to compare `col1` with `col2`, the cast operator is applied to `col1` to convert it from `var_opaque_udt` to `fixed_opaque_udt`.

13.2.3 Support for Inheritance

Inheritance is addressed at two levels in Informix Universal Server: (1) data inheritance and (2) function inheritance.

Data Inheritance. To create subtypes under existing row types, we use the UNDER keyword as discussed earlier. Consider the following example:

```
CREATE ROW TYPE employee_type (
    ename VARCHAR(25),
    ssn CHAR(9),
    salary INT) ;

CREATE ROW TYPE engineer_type (
    degree VARCHAR(10),
    license VARCHAR(20))
    UNDER employee_type;

CREATE ROW TYPE engr_mgr_type (
    manager_start_date VARCHAR(10),
    dept_managed VARCHAR(20))
    UNDER engineer_type;
```

The above statements create an employee_type and a subtype called engineer_type, which represents employees who are engineers and hence inherits all attributes of employees and has additional properties of degree and license. Another type called engr_mgr_type is a subtype under engineer_type, and hence inherits from engineer_type and implicitly from employee_type as well. Informix Universal Server does not support multiple inheritance. We can now create tables called employee, engineer, and engr_mgr based on these row types.

Note that storage options for storing type hierarchies in tables vary. Informix Universal Server provides the option to store instances in different combinations—for example, one instance (record) at each level or one instance that consolidates all levels—these correspond to the mapping options in Section 9.2. The inherited attributes are either represented repeatedly in the tables at lower levels or are represented with a reference to the object of the supertype. The processing of SQL commands is appropriately modified based on the type hierarchy. For example, the query

```
SELECT *
FROM employee
WHERE salary > 100000;
```

returns the employee information from *all* tables where each selected employee is represented. Thus the scope of the employee table extends to all tuples under employee. As a default, queries on the supertable return columns from the supertable as well as those from the subtables that inherit from that supertable. In contrast, the query

```
SELECT *
FROM ONLY (employee)
WHERE salary > 100000;
```

returns instances from only the employee table because of the keyword ONLY.

It is possible to query a supertable using a *correlation variable* so that the result contains not only supertable_type columns of the subtables but also subtype-specific columns of the subtables. Such a query returns rows of different sizes; the result is called a

jagged row result. Retrieving all information about an employee from all levels in a "jagged form" is accomplished by

```
SELECT e
FROM employee e ;
```

For each employee, depending on whether he or she is an engineer or some other subtype(s), it will return additional sets of attributes from the appropriate subtype tables.

Views defined over supertables cannot be updated because placement of inserted rows is ambiguous.

Function Inheritance.   In the same way that data is inherited among tables along a type hierarchy, functions can also be inherited in an ORDBMS. For example, a function over-paid may be defined on employee_type to select those employees making a higher salary than Bill Brown as follows:

```
CREATE FUNCTION overpaid (employee_type)
RETURNS BOOLEAN AS
RETURN $1.salary > (SELECT salary
                    FROM employee
                    WHERE ename = 'Bill Brown');
```

The tables under the employee table automatically inherit this function. However, the same function may be redefined for the engr_mgr_type as those employees making a higher salary than Jack Jones as follows:

```
CREATE FUNCTION overpaid (engr_mgr_type)
RETURNS BOOLEAN AS
RETURN $1.salary > (SELECT salary
                    FROM employee
                    WHERE ename = 'Jack Jones');
```

For example, consider the query

```
SELECT e.ename
FROM ONLY (employee) e
WHERE overpaid (e);
```

which is evaluated with the first definition of overpaid. The query

```
SELECT g.ename
FROM engineer g
WHERE overpaid (g);
```

also uses the first definition of overpaid (because it was not redefined for engineer), whereas

```
SELECT gm.ename
FROM engr_mgr gm
WHERE overpaid (gm);
```

uses the second definition of overpaid, which overrides the first. This is called **operation** (or **function**) **overloading,** as was discussed in Section 11.6 under polymorphism. Note that overpaid—and other functions—can also be treated as *virtual attributes*; hence overpaid may be referenced as `employee.overpaid` or `engr_mgr.overpaid` in a query.

13.2.4 Support for Indexing Extensions

Informix Universal Server supports indexing on user-defined routines on either a single table or a table hierarchy. For example,

```
CREATE INDEX empl_city ON employee (city (address));
```

creates an index on the table employee using the value of the city function.

In order to support user-defined indexes, Informix Universal Server supports operator classes, which are used to support user-defined data types in the generic B-tree as well as other secondary access methods such as R-trees.

13.2.5 Support for External Data Source

Informix Universal Server supports external data sources (such as data stored in a file system) that are mapped to a table in the database called the **virtual table interface.** This interface enables the user to define operations that can be used as *proxies* for the other operations, which are needed to access and manipulate the row or rows associated with the underlying data source. These operations include `open`, `close`, `fetch`, `insert`, and `delete`. Informix Universal Server also supports a set of functions that enables calling SQL statements within a user-defined routine without the overhead of going through a client interface.

13.2.6 Support for Data Blades Application Programming Interface

The Data Blades Application Programming Interface (API) of Informix Universal Server provides new data types and functions for specific types of applications. We will review the extensible data types for two-dimensional operations (required in GIS or CAD applications),[11] the data types related to image storage and management, the time series data type, and a few features of the text data type. The strength of ORDBMSs to deal with the new unconventional applications is largely attributed to these special data types and the tailored functionality that they provide.

Two-Dimensional Data Types.   For a two-dimensional application, the relevant data types would include the following:

- A **point** defined by (X, Y) coordinates.
- A **line** defined by its two end points.

---

11. Recall that GIS stands for Geographic Information Systems and CAD for Computer Aided Design.

- A **polygon** defined by an ordered list of n points that form its vertices.
- A **path** defined by a sequence (ordered list) of points.
- A **circle** defined by its center point and radius.

Given the above as data types, a function such as *distance* may be defined between two points, a point and a line, a line and a circle, and so on, by implementing the appropriate mathematical expressions for distance in a programming language. Similarly, a Boolean cross function—which returns true or false depending on whether two geometric objects cross (or intersect)—can be defined between a line and a polygon, a path and a polygon, a line and a circle, and so on. Other relevant Boolean functions for GIS applications would be *overlap* (polygon, polygon), *contains* (polygon, polygon), *contains* (point, polygon), and so on. Note that the concept of overloading (operation polymorphism) applies when the same function name is used with different argument types.

Image Data Types. Images are stored in a variety of standard formats—such as TIFF, GIF, JPEG, photoCD, GROUP 4, and FAX—so one may define a data type for each of these formats and use appropriate library functions to input images from other media or to render images for display. Alternately, IMAGE can be regarded as a single data type with a large number of options for storage of data. The latter option would allow a column in a table to be of type IMAGE and yet accept images in a variety of different formats. The following are some possible functions (operations) on images:

```
rotate (image, angle) returns image.
crop (image, polygon) returns image.
enhance (image) returns image.
```

The *crop* function extracts the portion of an image that intersects with a polygon. The *enhance* function improves the quality of an image by performing contrast enhancement. Multiple images may be supplied as parameters to the following functions:

```
common (image1, image2) returns image.
union (image1, image2) returns image.
similarity. (image1, image2) returns number.
```

The *similarity* function typically takes into account the distance between two vectors with components <color, shape, texture, edge> that describe the content of the two images. The VIR Data Blade in Informix Universal Server can be used to accomplish a search on images by content based on the above similarity measure.[12]

Time Series Data Type. Informix Universal Server supports a time series data type that makes the handling of time series data much more simplified than storing it in multiple tables. For example, consider storing the closing stock price on the New York Stock

---

12. Another product of this variety is QBIC (Query By Image Content), supplied with IBM's DB2/6000.

Exchange for more than 3,000 stocks for each workday when the market is open. Such a table can be defined as follows:

```
CREATE TABLE stockprices (
company-name VARCHAR(30),
symbol VARCHAR(5),
prices TIME_SERIES OF FLOAT);
```

Regarding the stock price data for all 3,000 companies over an entire period of, say, several years, only one relation is adequate thanks to the time series data type for the prices attribute. Without this data type, each company would need one table. For example, a table for the `coca_cola` company (symbol KO) may be declared as follows:

```
CREATE TABLE coca_cola (
recording_date DATE,
price FLOAT);
```

In this table, there would be approximately 260 tuples per year—one for each business day. The time series data type takes into account the calendar, starting time, recording interval (for example, daily, weekly, monthly), and so on. Functions such as extracting a subset of the time series (for example, closing prices during January 1999), summarizing at a coarser granularity (for example, average weekly closing price from the daily closing prices), and constructing moving averages are appropriate.

A query on the stockprices table that gives the moving average for 30 days starting at June 1, 1999 for the `coca_cola` stock can use the MOVING-AVG function as follows:

```
SELECT MOVING-AVG(prices, 30, '1999-06-01')
FROM stockprices
WHERE symbol = "KO";
```

The same query in SQL on the table `coca_cola` would be much more complicated to write and would access numerous tuples, whereas the above query on the stockprices table deals with a single row in the table corresponding to this company. It is claimed that using the time series data type provides an order of magnitude performance gain in processing such queries.

Text Data Type. The text DataBlade supports storage, search, and retrieval for text objects. It defines a single data type called **doc,** whose instances are stored as large objects that belong to the built-in data type `large-text`. We will briefly discuss a few important features of this data type.

The underlying storage for `large-text` is the same as that for the `large-object` data type. References to a single large object are recorded in the 'refcount' system table, which stores information such as number of rows referring to the large object, its OID, its storage manager, its last modification time, and its archive storage manager. Automatic conversion between `large-text` and `text` data types enables any functions with text arguments to be applied to `large-text` objects. Thus concatenation of `large-text` objects as strings as well as extraction of substrings from a `large-text` object are possible.

The Text DataBlade parameters include format for which the default is ASCII, with other possibilities such as postscript, dvipostscript, nroff, troff, and text. A Text Conversion DataBlade, which is separate from the Text DataBlade, is needed to convert documents among the various formats. An External File parameter instructs the internal representation of doc to store a pointer to an external file rather than copying it to a large object.[13]

For manipulation of doc objects, functions such as the following are used:

```
Import_doc (doc, text) returns doc.
Export_doc (doc, text) returns text.
Assign (doc) returns doc.
Destroy (doc) returns void.
```

The Assign and Destroy functions already exist for the built-in large-object and large-text data types, but they must be redefined by the user for objects of type doc. The following statement creates a table called legaldocuments, where each row has a title of the document in one column and the document itself as the other column:

```
CREATE TABLE legaldocuments(
title TEXT,
document DOC);
```

To insert a new row into this table of a document called 'lease.contract,' the following statement can be used:

```
INSERT INTO legaldocuments (title, document)
VALUES ('lease.contract', 'format {troff}:/user/local/
    documents/lease');
```

The second value in the values clause is the path name specifying the file location of this document; the format specification signifies that it is a troff document. To search the text, an index must be created, as in the following statement:

```
CREATE INDEX legalindex
ON legaldocuments
USING dtree(document text_ops);
```

In the above, text_ops is an op-class (operator class) applicable to an access structure called a dtree index, which is a special index structure for documents. When a document of the doc data type is inserted into a table, the text is parsed into individual words. The Text DataBlade is case insensitive; hence, Housenumber, HouseNumber, or housenumber are all considered the same word. Words are *stemmed* according to the WORDNET thesaurus. For example, houses or housing would be stemmed to house, quickly to quick, and talked to talk. A stopword file is kept, which contains insignifi-

---

13. As we will see in Section 13.4, SQL3 is trying to go away from the notion of external files and would like to incorporate LOBs (large objects) as an integral part of the database managed by the DBMS.

cant words such as articles or prepositions that are ignored in the searches. Examples of stopwords include is, not, a, the, but, for, and, if, and so on.

Informix Universal Server provides two sets of routines—the **contains routines** and **text-string functions**—to enable applications to determine which documents contain a certain word or words and which documents are similar. When these functions are used in a search condition, the data is returned in descending order of how well the condition matches the documents, with the best match showing first. There is WeightContains(index to use, tuple-id of the document, input string) function and a similar WeightContainsWords function that returns a precision number between 0 and 1 indicating the closeness of the match between the input string or input words and the specific document for that tuple-id. To illustrate the use of these functions, consider the following query: Find the titles of legal documents that contain the top ten terms in the document titled 'lease contract', which can be specified as follows:

```
SELECT d.title
FROM legaldocuments d, legaldocuments l
WHERE contains (d.doc, AndTerms (TopNTerms(l,document,10))) AND
l.title = 'lease.contract' AND d.title <> 'lease.contract';
```

This query illustrates how SQL can be enhanced with these data type specific functions to yield a very powerful capability of handing text-related functions. In this query, variable d refers to the entire legal corpus whereas l refers to the specific document whose title is 'lease.contract'. TopNTerms extracts the top ten terms from the 'lease.contract' document (l); AndTerms combines these terms into a list; and contains compares the terms in that list with the stemwords in every other document (d) in the table legaldocuments.

Summary of Data Blades.   As we can see, Data Blades enhance an RDBMS by providing various constructors for abstract data types (ADTs) that allow a user to operate on the data as if it were stored in an ODBMS using the ADTs as classes. This makes the relational system *behave* as an ODBMS, and drastically cuts down the programming effort needed when compared with achieving the same functionality with just SQL embedded in a programming language.

13.3 Object-Relational Features of Oracle 8

In this section we will review a number of features related to the version of the Oracle DBMS product called Release 8.X, which has been enhanced to incorporate object-relational features. At the same time, the robust underlying relational framework, data model, schema features, and storage organization described in Chapter 10 have been retained and continue as a strength of this system. A number of additional data types with related manipulation facilities called **cartridges** have been added.[14] For example, the spatial cartridge allows map-based and geographic information to be handled.[15] Manage-

---

14. Cartridges in Oracle are somewhat similar to Data Blades in Informix.

15. See the Section 23.3 for a brief discussion of spatial data modeling and Section 27.4 on Geographic Information Systems.

ment of multimedia data has been facilitated with new data types.[16] Here we highlight the differences between the release 8.X of Oracle (as available at the time of this writing) from the preceding version in terms of the new object-oriented features and data types as well as some storage options. Portions of the language SQL3, which we will introduce in Section 13.4, will be applicable to Oracle. We do not discuss these SQL3 features here.

13.3.1 Some Examples of Object-Relational Features of Oracle

As an ORDBMS, Oracle 8 continues to provide the capabilities of an RDBMS and additionally supports object-oriented concepts. This provides higher levels of abstraction so that application developers can manipulate application objects as opposed to constructing the objects from relational data. The complex information about an object can be hidden, but the properties (attributes, relationships) and methods (operations) of the object can be identified in the data model. Moreover, object type declarations can be reused via inheritance, thereby reducing application development time and effort. To facilitate object modeling, Oracle introduced the following features (as well as some of the SQL3 features in Section 13.4).

Representing Multivalued Attributes Using VARRAY.   Some attributes of an object/ entity could be multivalued. In the relational model, the multivalued attributes would have to be handled by forming a new table (see Section 9.1 and Section 14.3.2 on first normal form). If ten attributes of a large table were multivalued, we would have eleven tables generated from a single table after normalization. To get the data back, the developer would have to do ten joins across these tables. This does not happen in an object model since all the attributes of an object—including multivalued ones—are encapsulated within the object. Oracle 8 achieves this by using a varying length array (VARRAY) data type, which has the following properties:

1. COUNT: Current number of elements.
2. LIMIT: Maximum number of elements the VARRAY can contain. This is user defined.

Consider the example of a customer VARRAY entity with attributes name and phone_ numbers, where phone_numbers is multivalued. First, we need to define an object type representing a phone_number as follows:

```
CREATE TYPE phone_num_type AS OBJECT (phone_number CHAR(10));
```

Then we define a VARRAY whose elements would be objects of type phone_num_type:

```
CREATE TYPE phone_list_type as VARRAY (5) OF phone_num_type;
```

---

16. We will review multimedia databases in Sections 23.3 and 27.2.

Now we can create the `customer_type` data type as an object with attributes `customer_name` and `phone_numbers`:

```
CREATE TYPE customer_type AS
OBJECT (customer_name VARCHAR(20),
        phone_numbers phone_list_type);
```

It is now possible to create the `customer` table as

```
CREATE TABLE customer OF customer_type;
```

To retrieve a list of all customers and their phone numbers, we can issue a simple query without any joins:

```
SELECT customer_name, phone_numbers
FROM customers;
```

Using Nested Tables to Represent Complex Objects.   In object modeling, some attributes of an object could be objects themselves. Oracle 8 accomplishes this by having **nested tables** (see Section 13.6). Here, columns (equivalent to object attributes) can be declared as tables. In the above example let us assume that we have a description attached to every phone number (for example, home, office, cellular). This could be modeled using a nested table by first redefining `phone_num_type` as follows:

```
CREATE TYPE phone_num_type AS
OBJECT (phone_number CHAR(10), description CHAR(30));
```

We next redefine `phone_list_type` as a table of `phone_number_type` as follows:

```
CREATE TYPE phone_list_type AS TABLE OF phone_number_type;
```

We can then create the type `customer_type` and the `customer` table as before. The only difference is that `phone_list_type` is now a nested table instead of a VARRAY. Both structures have similar functions with a few differences. Nested tables do *not* have an upper bound on the number of items whereas VARRAYs do have a limit. Individual items can be retrieved from the nested tables, but this is not possible with VARRAYs. Additional indexes can also be built on nested tables for faster data access.

Object Views.   Object views can be used to build virtual objects from relational data, thereby enabling programmers to evolve existing schemas to support objects. This allows relational and object applications to coexist on the same database. In our example, let us say that we had modeled our customer database using a relational model, but management decided to do all future applications in the object model. Moving over to the object view of the same existing relational data would thus facilitate the transition.

13.3.2 Managing Large Objects and Other Storage Features

Oracle can now store extremely large objects like video, audio, and text documents. New data types have been introduced for this purpose. These include the following:

- BLOB (binary large object).
- CLOB (character large object).

- BFILE (binary file stored outside the database).
- NCLOB (fixed-width multibyte CLOB).

All of the above except for BFILE, which is stored outside the database, are stored inside the database along with other data. Only the directory name for a BFILE is stored in the database.

Index Only Tables.   Standard Oracle 7.X involves keeping indexes as a B$^+$-tree that contains pointers to data blocks (see Chapter 6). This gives good performance in most situations. However, both the index and the data block must be accessed to read the data. Moreover, key values are stored twice—in the table and in the index—increasing the storage costs. Oracle 8 supports both the standard indexing scheme and also **index only tables,** where the data records and index are kept together in a B-tree structure (see Chapter 6). This allows faster data retrieval and requires less storage space for small- to medium-sized files where the record size is not too large.

Partitioned Tables and Indexes.   Large tables and indexes can be broken down into smaller partitions. The table now becomes a logical structure and the partitions become the actual physical structures that hold the data. This gives the following advantages:

- Continued data availability in the event of partial failures of some partitions.
- Scalable performance allowing substantial growth in data volumes.
- Overall performance improvement in query and transaction processing.

13.4   An Overview of SQL3

We introduced SQL as the standard language for RDBMSs in Chapter 8. As we discussed, SQL was first specified in the 1970s and underwent enhancements in 1989 and 1992. Chapter 8 covered the syntax and facilities of SQL-92, also known as SQL2. The language is continuing its evolution toward a new standard called SQL3, which adds object-oriented and other features. We already illustrated through various examples in Informix Universal Server and Oracle 8 how SQL can be extended to deal simultaneously with tables from the relational model and classes and objects from the object model. This section highlights some of the features of SQL3 with a particular emphasis on the object-relational concepts.

13.4.1   The SQL3 Standard and Its Components

We will briefly point out what each part of the SQL3 standard deals with, then describe some SQL3 features that are relevant to the object extensions to SQL. The SQL3 standard includes the following parts:[17]

- SQL/Framework, SQL/Foundation, SQL/Bindings, SQL/Object.
- New parts addressing temporal, transaction aspects of SQL.

---

17. The discussion about the standard is largely based on Melton and Mattos (1996).

- SQL/CLI (Call Level Interface).
- SQL/PSM (Persistent Stored Modules).

SQL/Foundation deals with new data types, new predicates, relational operations, cursors, rules and triggers, user-defined types, transaction capabilities, and stored routines. SQL/CLI (Call Level Interface) provides rules that allow execution of application code without providing source code and avoids the need for preprocessing. It provides a new type of language binding and is analogous to dynamic SQL in SQL-92. Based on Microsoft ODBC (Open Database Connectivity) and SQL Access Group's standard, it contains about 50 routines for tasks such as connection to the SQL server, allocating and deallocating resources, obtaining diagnostic and implementation information, and controlling termination of transactions. SQL/PSM (Persistent Stored Modules) specifies facilities for partitioning an application between a client and a server. The goal is to enhance performance by minimizing network traffic. SQL/Bindings includes Embedded SQL and Direct Invocation as in SQL-92. Embedded SQL has been enhanced to include additional exception declarations. SQL/Temporal deals with historical data, time series data, and other temporal extensions, and it is being proposed by the TSQL2 committee.[18] SQL/Transaction specification formalizes the XA interface for use by SQL implementors.

13.4.2   Some New Operations and Features in SQL3

New types of operations have been added to SQL3. These include SIMILAR, which allows the use of regular expressions to match character strings. Boolean values have been extended with UNKNOWN when a comparison yields neither true nor false because some values may be null. A major new operation is **linear recursion** for specifying recursive queries (see Section 7.6). To illustrate this, suppose we have a table called PART_TABLE(Part1, Part2), which contains a tuple <p1, p2> whenever part p1 contains part p2 as a component. A query to produce the **bill of materials** for some part p1 (that is, all component parts needed to produce p1) is written as a recursive query as follows:

```
WITH RECURSIVE
BILL_MATERIAL (Part1, Part2) AS
    (SELECT Part1, Part2
    FROM PART_TABLE
    WHERE Part1 = 'p1'
        UNION ALL
    SELECT PART_TABLE(Part1), PART_TABLE(Part2)
    FROM BILL_MATERIAL, PART_TABLE
    WHERE PART_TABLE.Part1 = BILL_MATERIAL(Part2))

SELECT * FROM BILL_MATERIAL
ORDER BY Part1, Part2;
```

---

18. The full proposal appears in Snodgrass and Jensen (1996). We discuss temporal modeling and introduce TSQL2 in Chapter 23.

The final result is contained in BILL_MATERIAL(Part1, Part2). The UNION ALL operation is evaluated by taking a union of all tuples generated by the inner block until no new tuples can be generated. Because SQL2 lacks recursion, it was left to the programmer to accomplish it by appropriate iteration. We discuss recursion in relational queries in more detail in Chapter 25.

For security in SQL3, the concept of **role** is introduced, which is similar to a "job description" and is subject to authorization of privileges. The actual persons (user accounts) that are assigned to a role may change, but the role authorization itself does not have to be changed. SQL3 also includes syntax for the specification and use of **triggers** (see Chapter 23) as active rules. Triggering events include the INSERT, DELETE, and UPDATE operations on a table. The trigger can be specified to be considered BEFORE or AFTER the triggering event. This feature is present in both of the ORDBMS systems we discussed. The concept of **trigger granularity** is included in SQL3, which allows the specification of both row-level triggers (the trigger is considered for each affected row) or statement-level trigger (the trigger is considered only once for each triggering event).[19] For distributed (client-server) databases (see Chapter 24), the concept of a **client module** is included in SQL3. A client module may contain externally invoked procedures, cursors, and temporary tables, which can be specified using SQL3 syntax.

SQL3 also is being extended with programming language facilities. Routines written in computationally complete SQL with full matching of data types and an integrated environment are referred to as **SQL routines.** To make the language computationally complete, the following programming control structures are included in the SQL3 syntax: CALL/RETURN, BEGIN/END, FOR/END_FOR, IF/THEN/ELSE/END_IF, CASE/END_CASE, LOOP/END_LOOP, WHILE/END_WHILE, REPEAT/UNTIL/END_REPEAT, and LEAVE. Variables are declared using DECLARE, and assignments are specified using SET. **External routines** refer to programs written in a host language (ADA, C, COBOL, PASCAL, etc.), possibly containing embedded SQL and having possible type mismatches. The advantage of external routines is that there are existing libraries of such routines that are broadly used, which can cut down a lot of implementation effort for applications. On the other hand, SQL routines are more "pure," but they have not been in wide use. SQL routines can be used for server routines (schema-level routines or modules) or as client modules, and they may be procedures or functions that return values.

A number of built-in functions enhance the capability of SQL3. They are used to manage **handles,** which in turn are classified into **environment handles** that refer to capabilities, **connection handles** that are connections to servers, and **statement handles** that manage SQL statements and cursors. There are also functions to manage descriptors and diagnostics as well as help functions.

13.4.3 Object-Relational Support in SQL3

The SQL/Object specification extends SQL-92 to include object-oriented capabilities. New data types include Boolean, character, and binary large objects (LOBs), and large object locators. We saw in Section 13.3 how large objects are used in Oracle 8.

---

19. These concepts are discussed in more detail in Chapter 23.

SQL3 proposes LOB manipulation within the DBMS without having to use external files.[20] Certain operators do not apply to LOB-valued attributes—for example, arithmetic comparisons, group by, and order by. On the other hand, retrieval of partial value, LIKE comparison, concatenation, substring, position, and length are operations that can be applied to LOBs.

Objects in SQL3. Under SQL/Foundation and SQL/Object Specification, SQL allows user-defined data types, type constructors, collection types, user-defined functions and procedures, support for large objects, and triggers. Objects in SQL3 are of two types:

- Row or tuple types whose instances are tuples in tables.
- Abstract Data Types (shortened as ADT or value ADT), which are any general types used as components of tuples.

A **row type** may be defined using the syntax

```
CREATE ROW TYPE row_type_name (<component declarations>);
```

An example is

```
CREATE ROW TYPE Emp_row_type (
  name VARCHAR (35),
  age INTEGER
  );
CREATE ROW TYPE Comp_row_type (
  compname VARCHAR (20),
  location VARCHAR (20)
  );
```

A table can then be created based on the row type declaration as follows:

```
CREATE TABLE Employee OF TYPE Emp_row_type;
CREATE TABLE Company OF TYPE Comp_row_type;
```

A component attribute of one tuple may be a **reference** (specified using the keyword REF) to a tuple of another (or possibly the same) relation. Thus we can define

```
CREATE ROW TYPE Employment_row_type (
  employee REF (Emp_row_type),
  company REF (Comp_row_type)
  );

CREATE TABLE Employment OF TYPE Employment_row_type;
```

SQL3 uses a **double dot notation** to build path expressions that refer to the components of tuples. For example, the query below retrieves employees working in New York from the Employment table.

```
SELECT Employment..employee..name
FROM Employment
WHERE Employment..company..location = 'New York';
```

---

20. Note that external files for storing LOB data are allowed in current systems.

In SQL3, → is used for **dereferencing** and has the same meaning assigned to it in C. Thus if r is a reference to a tuple and a is a component attribute in that tuple, $r \rightarrow a$ is the value of attribute a in that tuple. **Object identifiers** can be explicitly declared and accessed. For example, the definition of Emp_row_type may be changed as follows:

```
CREATE ROW TYPE Emp_row_type (
   name CHAR (35),
   age INTEGER,
   emp_id REF (Emp_row_type)
);
```

In the above example, the emp_id values may be system generated by using

```
CREATE TABLE Employee OF TYPE Emp_row_type
VALUES FOR emp_id ARE SYSTEM GENERATED;
```

If several relations of the same row type exist, SQL3 provides a mechanism by which a reference attribute may be made to point to a specific table of that type by using

```
SCOPE FOR <attribute> IS <relation>
```

Although the row types discussed above provide the functionality of objects and eventually allow construction of complex object types by combining row types, they do not provide for encapsulation as discussed in Section 11.3, which is an essential feature of object modeling. Encapsulation is provided through abstract data types in SQL3.

Abstract Data Types in SQL3.   In SQL3 a construct similar to class definition is provided whereby the user can create a named user-defined type with its own behavioral specification and internal structure; it is known as an **Abstract Data Type (ADT)**. The general form of an ADT specification is:

```
CREATE TYPE <type-name> (
   list of component attributes with individual types
   declaration of EQUAL and LESS THAN functions
   declaration of other functions (methods)
);
```

SQL3 provides certain built-in functions for ADTs. For an ADT called Type_T, the **constructor function** Type_T() returns a new object of that type. In the new ADT object, every attribute is initialized to its default value. An **observer function** A is implicitly created for each attribute A to read its value. Hence, A(X) returns the value of attribute A of Type_T if X is of type Type_T. A **mutator function** for updating an attribute sets the value of the attribute to a new value. SQL3 allows these functions to be blocked from public use; an EXECUTE privilege is needed to have access to these functions.

An ADT has a number of user-defined functions associated with it. The syntax is

```
FUNCTION <name> (<argument_list>) RETURNS <type>;
```

Two types of functions can be defined: internal SQL3 and external. Internal functions are written in the extended (computationally complete) version of SQL. External functions are written in a host language, with only their signature (interface) appearing in the ADT definition. The form of an external function definition is

```
DECLARE EXTERNAL <function_name> <signature>
LANGUAGE <language_name>;
```

Many ORBDMSs have taken the approach of defining a set of ADTs and associated functions for specific application domains, and packaging them together. For example, the Data Blades in Informix Universal Server and the cartridges in Oracle can be considered as such packages or libraries of ADTs for specific application domains.

ADTs can be used as the types for attributes in SQL3 and the parameter types in a function or procedure, and as a source type in a distinct type. **Type Equivalence** is defined in SQL3 at two levels. Two types are **name equivalent** if and only if they have the same name. Two types are **structurally equivalent** if and only if they have the same number of components and the components are pairwise type equivalent. Under SQL-92, the definition of UNION-compatibility among two tables is based on the tables being structurally equivalent. Operations on columns, however, are based on name equivalence. Thus the operation

```
UPDATE table_t
SET c1 = c2
WHERE <condition>
```

would be acceptable if the types of c1 and c2 are name equivalent (or are implicitly convertible). Attributes and functions in ADTs are divided into three categories:

- PUBLIC (visible at the ADT interface).
- PRIVATE (not visible at the ADT interface).
- PROTECTED (visible only to subtypes).

It is also possible to define virtual attributes as part of ADTs, which are computed and updated using functions. SQL3 has rules for dealing with inheritance (specified via the UNDER keyword), overloading, and resolution of functions. They can be summarized as follows:

Inheritance

- All attributes are inherited.
- The order of supertypes in the UNDER clause determines the inheritance hierarchy.
- An instance of a subtype can be used in every context in which a supertype instance is used.

Overloading

- A subtype can redefine any function that is defined in its supertype, with the restriction that the signature be the same.

Resolution of Functions

- When a function is called, the best match is selected based on the types of all arguments.
- For dynamic linking, the runtime types of parameters is considered.

SQL3 supports constructors for collection types, which can be used for creating nested structures for complex objects. List, set, and multiset are supported as built-in type constructors. Arguments for these type constructors can be any other type, including row types, ADTs, and other collection types. Instances of these types can be treated as tables for query purposes. Collections can be **unnested** by correlating derived tables in SQL3.[21] For example, to return the elements of the set hobbies for employee John Smith, we first define an attribute in the table `employee` as follows:

```
hobbies SET (VARCHAR(20))
```

We can then write

```
THE (SELECT e.hobbies
     FROM employee e
     WHERE e.name = "John Smith")
```

Another facility in SQL3 is the supertable/subtable facility, which is not equivalent to super and subtypes and no substitutability is assumed. However, a subtable inherits every column from its supertable; every row of a subtable corresponds to one and only one row in the supertable; every row in the supertable corresponds to at most one row in a subtable. INSERT, DELETE, and UPDATE operations are appropriately propagated. For example, consider the `real_estate_info` table defined as follows:

```
CREATE TABLE real_estate_info (
   property real_estate,
   owner CHAR(25),
   price MONEY,
);
```

The following subtables can be defined:

```
CREATE TABLE american_real_estate UNDER real_estate_info;
CREATE TABLE georgia_real_estate UNDER american_real_estate;
CREATE TABLE atlanta_real_estate UNDER georgia_real_estate;
```

We have given an overview of the proposed facilities in SQL3. At this time, both the SQL/Foundations and SQL/Object specification have reached the third step of the standardization process called the Committee Draft status. It is evident that the facilities that make SQL3 object-oriented closely follow what has been implemented in commercial ORDBMSs. The next two steps of standardization are called Draft International Standard and International Standard, respectively. SQL/MM (multimedia) is being proposed as a separate standard for multimedia database management with multiple parts: framework, full text, spatial, general purpose facilities, and still image. It is being pursued by a separate committee. We already saw the use of the two-dimensional data types and the image and text Datablades in Informix Universal Server that have considered issues relevant to this standard.

---

21. We will discuss nesting and unnesting of tables when we discuss the nested relational model in Section 13.6.

13.5   Implementation and Related Issues for Extended Type Systems

There are various implementation issues regarding the support of an extended type system with associated functions (operations). We briefly summarize them here.[22]

- The ORDBMS must dynamically link a user-defined function in its address space only when it is required. As we saw in the case of the two ORDBMSs, numerous functions are required to operate on two- or three-dimensional spatial data, images, text, and so on. With a static linking of all function libraries, the DBMS address space may increase by an order of magnitude. Dynamic linking is available in the two ORDBMSs that we studied.

- Client-server issues deal with the placement and activation of functions.[23] If the server needs to perform a function, it is best to do so in the DBMS address space rather than remotely, due to the large amount of overhead. If the function demands computation that is too intensive or if the server is attending to a very large number of clients, the server may ship the function to a separate client machine. For security reasons, it is better to run functions at the client using the user ID of the client. In the future functions are likely to be written in interpreted languages like JAVA.

- It should be possible to run queries inside functions. A function must operate the same way whether it is used from an application using the application program interface (API), or whether it is invoked by the DBMS as a part of executing SQL with the function embedded in an SQL statement. Systems should support a nesting of these "callbacks."

- Because of the variety in the data types in an ORDBMS and associated operators, efficient storage and access of the data is important. For spatial data or multidimensional data, new storage structures such as R-trees, quad trees, or Grid files may be used. The ORDBMS must allow new types to be defined with new access structures. Dealing with large text strings or binary files also opens up a number of storage and search options. It should be possible to explore such new options by defining new data types within the ORDBMS.

Other Issues Concerning Object-Relational Systems.   In the above discussion of Informix Universal Server and Oracle 8, we have concentrated on how an ORDBMS extends the relational model. We discussed the features and facilities it provides to operate on relational data stored as tables as if it were an object database. There are other obvious problems to consider in the context of an ORDBMS:

- *Object-relational database design:* We described a procedure for designing object schemas in Section 12.5. Object-relational design is more complicated because we have to consider not only the underlying design considerations of application semantics

---

22. This discussion is derived largely from Stonebraker and Moore (1996).
23. We discuss the client-server approach in Chapters 17 and 24.

and dependencies in the relational data model (which will be discussed in Chapters 14 and 15) but also the object-oriented nature of the extended features that we have just discussed.

- *Query processing and optimization:* By extending SQL with functions and rules, this problem is further compounded beyond the query optimization overview that we will discuss for the relational model in Chapter 18.

- *Interaction of rules with transactions:* Rule processing as implied in SQL3 covers more than just the update-update rules (see Section 23.1), which are implemented in RDBMSs as triggers. Moreover, RDBMSs currently implement only immediate execution of triggers. A deferred execution of triggers involves additional processing.

13.6   The Nested Relational Data Model

To complete this discussion, we summarize in this section an approach that proposes the use of nested tables, also known as nonnormal form relations. No commercial DBMS has chosen to implement this concept in its original form. The **nested relational model** removes the restriction of first normal form (1NF, see Chapter 14) from the basic relational model, and thus is also known as the **Non-1NF** or **Non-First Normal Form (NFNF)** or **NF^2** relational model. In the basic relational model—also called the **flat relational model**—attributes are required to be single-valued and to have atomic domains. The nested relational model allows composite and multivalued attributes, thus leading to complex tuples with a hierarchical structure. This is useful for representing objects that are naturally hierarchically structured. In Figure 13.1, part (a) shows a nested relation schema DEPT based on part of the COMPANY database, and part (b) gives an example of a Non-1NF tuple in DEPT.

To define the DEPT schema as a nested structure, we can write the following:

```
DEPT = (DNO, DNAME, MANAGER, EMPLOYEES, PROJECTS, LOCATIONS)
EMPLOYEES = (ENAME, DEPENDENTS)
PROJECTS = (PNAME, PLOC)
LOCATIONS = (DLOC)
DEPENDENTS = (DNAME, AGE)
```

First, all attributes of the DEPT relation are defined. Next, any nested attributes of DEPT—namely, EMPLOYEES, PROJECTS, and LOCATIONS—are themselves defined. Next, any second-level nested attributes, such as DEPENDENTS of EMPLOYEES, are defined, and so on. All attribute names must be distinct in the nested relation definition. Notice that a nested attribute is typically a **multivalued composite attribute,** thus leading to a "nested relation" *within each tuple.* For example, the value of the PROJECTS attribute within each DEPT tuple is a relation with two attributes (PNAME, PLOC). In the DEPT tuple of Figure 13.1(b), the PROJECTS attribute contains three tuples as its value. Other nested attributes may be **multivalued simple attributes,** such as LOCATIONS of DEPT. It is also possible to have a nested attribute that is **single-valued and composite,** although most nested relational models treat such an attribute as though it were multivalued.

(a)

DNO	DNAME	MANAGER	EMPLOYEES		PROJECTS		LOCATIONS
			ENAME	DEPENDENTS	PNAME	PLOC	DLOC
				DNAME	AGE			

(b)

4	Administration	Wallace	Zelaya	Thomas	8	New benefits	Stafford	Stafford
				Jennifer	6	Computerization	Stafford	Greenway
			Wallace	Jack	18	Phone System	Greenway	
				Robert	15			
				Mary	10			
			Jabbar					

(c)

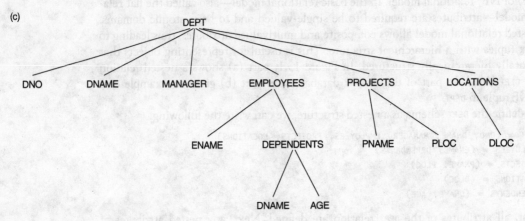

Figure 13.1 Illustrating a nested relation. (a) DEPT schema. (b) Example of a Non-1NF tuple of DEPT. (c) Tree representation of DEPT schema.

When a nested relational database schema is defined, it consists of a number of external relation schemas; these define the top level of the individual nested relations. In addition, nested attributes are called **internal relation schemas,** since they define relational structures that are nested inside another relation. In our example, DEPT is the only external relation. All the others—EMPLOYEES, PROJECTS, LOCATIONS, and DEPENDENTS—are internal relations. Finally, **simple attributes** appear at the leaf level and are not nested. We can represent each relation schema by means of a tree structure, as shown in Figure 13.1(c), where the root is an external relation schema, the leaves are simple attributes, and the internal nodes are internal relation schemas. Notice the similarity between this representation and a hierarchical schema (see Appendix D).

It is important to be aware that the three first-level nested relations in DEPT represent *independent information*. Hence, EMPLOYEES represents the employees *working for* the department, PROJECTS represents the projects *controlled by* the department, and LOCATIONS represents the various department locations. The relationship between EMPLOYEES and PROJECTS is not represented in the schema; this is an M:N relationship, which is difficult to represent in a hierarchical structure.

Extensions to the relational algebra and to the relational calculus, as well as to SQL, have been proposed for nested relations. The interested reader is referred to the selected bibliography at the end of this chapter for details. Here, we illustrate two operations, NEST and UNNEST, that can be used to augment standard relational algebra operations for converting between nested and flat relations. Consider the flat EMP_PROJ relation of Figure 14.4, and suppose that we project it over the attributes SSN, PNUMBER, HOURS, ENAME as follows:

$$\text{EMP\_PROJ\_FLAT} \leftarrow \pi_{\text{SSN, ENAME, PNUMBER, HOURS}}(\text{EMP\_PROJ})$$

To create a nested version of this relation, where one tuple exists for each employee and the (PNUMBER, HOURS) are nested, we use the NEST operation as follows:

$$\text{EMP\_PROJ\_NESTED} \leftarrow \text{NEST}_{\text{PROJS = (PNUMBER, HOURS)}}(\text{EMP\_PROJ\_FLAT})$$

The effect of this operation is to create an internal nested relation PROJS = (PNUMBER, HOURS) within the external relation EMP_PROJ_NESTED. Hence, NEST groups together the tuples *with the same value* for the attributes that are *not specified* in the NEST operation; these are the SSN and ENAME attributes in our example. For each such group, which represents one employee in our example, a single nested tuple is created with an internal nested relation PROJS = (PNUMBER, HOURS). Hence, the EMP_PROJ_NESTED relation looks like the EMP_PROJ relation shown in Figure 14.9(a) and (b).

Notice the similarity between nesting and grouping for aggregate functions. In the former, each group of tuples becomes a single nested tuple; in the latter, each group becomes a single summary tuple after an aggregate function is applied to the group.

The UNNEST operation is the inverse of NEST. We can reconvert EMP_PROJ_NESTED to EMP_PROJ_FLAT as follows:

$$\text{EMP\_PROJ\_FLAT} \leftarrow \text{UNNEST}_{\text{PROJS = (PNUMBER, HOURS)}}(\text{EMP\_PROJ\_NESTED})$$

Here, the PROJS nested attribute is flattened into its components PNUMBER, HOURS.

We saw in our SQL3 discussion above that nest and unnest facilities are proposed to create these nested relations. Nested tuples resemble complex objects, with a strictly hierarchical structure.

13.7 Summary

In this chapter, we first gave an overview of the history and current trends in database management systems that led to the development of object-relational DBMSs (ORDBMSs). We then focused on some of the features of Informix Universal Server and of Oracle 8 in order to illustrate how commercial RDBMSs are being extended with object features. Other commercial RDBMSs are providing similar extensions. We saw that these systems also provide Data Blades (Informix) or Cartridges (Oracle) that provide specific type extensions for newer application domains, such as spatial, time series, or text/document databases. Because of the extendibility of ORDBMSs, these packages can be included as abstract data type (ADT) libraries whenever the users need to implement the types of applications they support. Users can also implement their own extensions as needed by using the ADT facilities of these systems.

We then looked at some of the features that have been added to the SQL standard in SQL3 to provide object database features and abstract data types. We briefly discussed some implementation issues for ADTs. Finally, we gave an overview of the nested relational model, which extends the flat relational model with hierarchically structured complex objects.

Selected Bibliography

The references provided for the object-oriented database approach in Chapters 11 and 12 are also relevant for object-relational systems. Stonebraker and Moore (1996) provides a comprehensive reference for object-relational DBMSs. The discussion about concepts related to Illustra in that book are mostly applicable to the current Informix Universal Server. Kim (1995) discusses many issues related to modern database systems that include object orientation. For the most current information on Informix and Oracle, consult, their Web sites: www.informix.com and www.oracle.com, respectively.

The SQL3 standard is described in various publications of the ISO WG3 (Working Group 3) reports; for example, see Kulkarni et al. (1995) and Melton et al. (1991). An excellent tutorial on SQL3 was given at the Very Large Data Bases Conference by Melton and Mattos (1996). Ullman and Widom (1997) have a good discussion of SQL3 with examples.

For issues related to rules and triggers, Widom and Ceri (1995) have a collection of chapters on active databases. Some comparative studies—for example, Ketabchi et al. (1990)—compare relational DBMSs with object DBMSs; their conclusion shows the superiority of the object-oriented approach for nonconventional applications. The nested relational model is discussed in Schek and Scholl (1985), Jaeshke and Schek (1982), Chen and Kambayashi (1991), and Makinouchi (1977), among others. Algebras and query languages for nested relations are presented in Paredaens and VanGucht (1992), Pistor and Andersen (1986), Roth et al. (1988), and Ozsoyoglu et al. (1987), among others. Implementation of prototype nested relational systems is described in Dadam et al. (1986), Deshpande and VanGucht (1988), and Schek and Scholl (1989).

PART 4

Database Design Theory and Methodology

CHAPTER 14

Functional Dependencies and Normalization for Relational Databases

In Chapters 7 through 10, we presented various aspects of the relational model. Each *relation schema* consists of a number of attributes and the *relational database schema* consists of a number of relation schemas. So far, we have assumed that attributes are grouped to form a relation schema by using the common sense of the database designer or by mapping a schema specified in the Entity-Relationship (ER) or Enhanced-ER (EER) model (or some other similar conceptual data model) into a relational schema. The EER model makes the designer identify entity types and relationship types and their respective attributes, which leads to a natural and logical grouping of the attributes into relations when the mapping procedures in Sections 9.1 and 9.2 are followed. However, we still need some formal measure of why one grouping of attributes into a relation schema may be better than another. So far in our discussion of conceptual design in Chapters 3 and 4 and its mapping into the relational model in Chapter 9, we have not developed any measure of the appropriateness, "goodness," or quality of the design, other than the intuition of the designer.

In this chapter we discuss some of the theory that has been developed in an attempt to choose "good" relation schemas—that is, to measure formally why one set of groupings of attributes into relation schemas is better than another. There are two levels at which we can discuss the "goodness" of relation schemas. The first is the **logical** (or **conceptual**) **level**—how users interpret the relation schemas and the meaning of their attributes. Having good relation schemas at this level enables users to understand clearly the meaning of the data in the relations, and hence to formulate their queries correctly. The second is the **implementation** (or **storage**) **level**—how the tuples in a base relation are stored and updated. This level applies only to schemas of base relations—which will be physically stored as files—whereas at the logical level we are interested in schemas of both base relations and views (virtual relations). The relational database design theory developed in this chapter applies mainly to *base relations*, although some criteria of appropriateness also apply to views, as will be shown in Section 14.1.

Moreover, as with any design problem, database design may be performed using two approaches: (1) bottom-up or (2) top-down. A **bottom-up design methodology** would consider the basic relationships *among individual attributes* as the starting point, and it would use those to build up relations. Other than the binary relational model,[1] this approach is not very popular in practice and suffers from the problem of collecting a large number of binary attribute relationships as the starting point. This approach is also called *design by synthesis*. In contrast, a **top-down design methodology** would start with a number of groupings of attributes into relations that have already been obtained from conceptual design and mapping activities. *Design by analysis* is then applied to the relations individually and collectively, leading to further decomposition until all desirable properties are met.

The theory described in this chapter is applicable to both the top-down and bottom-up approaches, but it is more practical when applied to the top-down approach. We start in Section 14.1 by informally discussing some criteria for good and bad relation schemas. Section 14.2 then defines the concept of *functional dependency*, a formal constraint among attributes that is the main tool for formally measuring the appropriateness of attribute groupings into relation schemas. Properties of functional dependencies are also studied and analyzed. In Section 14.3 we show how functional dependencies can be used to group attributes into relation schemas that are in a *normal form*. A relation schema is in a normal form when it satisfies certain desirable properties. The process of *normalization* consists of analyzing relations to meet increasingly more stringent requirements leading to progressively better groupings, or higher normal forms. We show how the functional dependencies—which are identified by the database designer—can be used to analyze a relation with a designated primary key to determine what normal form it is in and how it should be further decomposed to achieve the next higher normal form. In Section 14.4 we discuss more general definitions of normal forms that do not require step-by-step analysis and normalization.

Chapter 15 will continue the development of the theory related to the design of good relational schemas. Whereas in Chapter 14 we concentrate on the normal forms for single relation schemas, in Chapter 15 we discuss measures of appropriateness for a whole set of relation schemas that together form a *relational database schema*. We specify two such properties—the nonadditive (lossless) join property and the dependency preservation property—and discuss algorithms for relational database design that are based on functional dependencies, normal forms, and the aforementioned properties. In Chapter 15 we also define additional types of dependencies and advanced normal forms that further enhance the "goodness" of relation schemas.

---

1. For example, the NIAM methodology; see Verheijen and VanBekkum (1982).

For the reader interested in only an informal introduction to normalization, Sections 14.2.3, 14.2.4, and 14.5 may be skipped.

14.1 Informal Design Guidelines for Relation Schemas

We discuss four *informal measures* of quality for relation schema design in this section:

1. Semantics of the attributes.
2. Reducing the redundant values in tuples.
3. Reducing the null values in tuples.
4. Disallowing the possibility of generating spurious tuples.

These measures are not always independent of one another, as we shall see.

14.1.1 Semantics of the Relation Attributes

Whenever we group attributes to form a relation schema, we assume that a certain meaning is associated with the attributes. In Chapter 7 we discussed how each relation can be interpreted as a set of facts or statements. This meaning, or **semantics,** specifies how to interpret the attribute values stored in a tuple of the relation—in other words, how the attribute values in a tuple relate to one another. If the conceptual design is done carefully, followed by a mapping into relations, most of the semantics would have been accounted for and the resulting design should have a clear meaning.

In general, the easier it is to explain the semantics of the relation, the better the relation schema design will be. To illustrate this, consider Figure 14.1, a simplified version of the COMPANY relational database schema of Figure 7.5, and Figure 14.2, which presents an example of populated relations of this schema. The meaning of the EMPLOYEE relation schema is quite simple: each tuple represents an employee, with values for the employee's name (ENAME), social security number (SSN), birthdate (BDATE), and address (ADDRESS), and the number of the department that the employee works for (DNUMBER). The DNUMBER attribute is a foreign key that represents an *implicit relationship* between EMPLOYEE and DEPARTMENT. The semantics of the DEPARTMENT and PROJECT schemas are also straightforward; each DEPARTMENT tuple represents a department entity, and each PROJECT tuple represents a project entity. The attribute DMGRSSN of DEPARTMENT relates a department to the employee who is its manager, while DNUM of PROJECT relates a project to its controlling department; both are foreign key attributes.

The semantics of the other two relation schemas in Figure 14.1 are slightly more complex. Each tuple in DEPT_LOCATIONS gives a department number (DNUMBER) and *one of* the locations of the department (DLOCATION). Each tuple in WORKS_ON gives an employee social security number (SSN), the project number of *one of* the projects that the employee works on (PNUMBER), and the number of hours per week that the employee works on that project (HOURS). However, both schemas have a well-defined and unambiguous interpretation. The schema DEPT_LOCATIONS represents a multivalued attribute of DEPARTMENT, whereas WORKS_

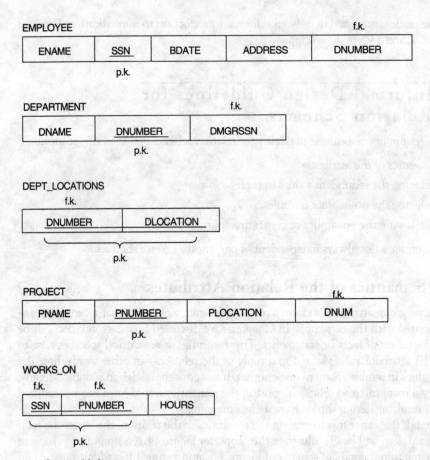

EMPLOYEE

ENAME	SSN	BDATE	ADDRESS	DNUMBER (f.k.)
	p.k.			

DEPARTMENT

DNAME	DNUMBER	DMGRSSN (f.k.)
	p.k.	

DEPT_LOCATIONS

DNUMBER (f.k.)	DLOCATION

p.k.

PROJECT

PNAME	PNUMBER	PLOCATION	DNUM (f.k.)
	p.k.		

WORKS_ON

SSN (f.k.)	PNUMBER (f.k.)	HOURS

p.k.

Figure 14.1 Simplified version of the COMPANY relational database schema.

ON represents an M:N relationship between EMPLOYEE and PROJECT. Hence, all the relation schemas in Figure 14.1 may be considered good from the standpoint of having clear semantics. The following informal guideline further elaborates the relation schema design.

GUIDELINE 1: Design a relation schema so that it is easy to explain its meaning. Do not combine attributes from multiple entity types and relationship types into a single relation. Intuitively, if a relation schema corresponds to one entity type or one relationship type, the meaning tends to be clear. Otherwise, the relation corresponds to a mixture of multiple entities and relationships and hence becomes semantically unclear.

The relation schemas in Figures 14.3(a) and (b) also have clear semantics. (The reader should ignore the lines under the relations for now, as they are used to illustrate functional dependency notation in Section 14.2.) A tuple in the EMP_DEPT relation schema

EMPLOYEE

ENAME	SSN	BDATE	ADDRESS	DNUMBER
Smith,John B.	123456789	1965-01-09	731 Fondren,Houston,TX	5
Wong,Franklin T.	333445555	1955-12-08	638 Voss,Houston,TX	5
Zelaya,Alicia J.	999887777	1968-07-19	3321 Castle,Spring,TX	4
Wallace,Jennifer S.	987654321	1941-06-20	291 Berry,Bellaire,TX	4
Narayan,Remesh K.	666884444	1962-09-15	975 Fire Oak,Humble,TX	5
English,Joyce A.	453453453	1972-07-31	5631 Rice,Houston,TX	5
Jabbar,Ahmad V.	987987987	1969-03-29	980 Dallas,Houston,TX	4
Borg,James E.	888665555	1937-11-10	450 Stone,Houston,TX	1

DEPT_LOCATIONS

DNUMBER	DLOCATION
1	Houston
4	Stafford
5	Bellaire
5	Sugarland
5	Houston

DEPARTMENT

DNAME	DNUMBER	DMGRSSN
Research	5	333445555
Administration	4	987654321
Headquarters	1	888665555

WORKS_ON

SSN	PNUMBER	HOURS
123456789	1	32.5
123456789	2	7.5
666884444	3	40.0
453453453	1	20.0
453453453	2	20.0
333445555	2	10.0
333445555	3	10.0
333445555	10	10.0
333445555	20	10.0
999887777	30	30.0
999887777	10	10.0
987987987	10	35.0
987987987	30	5.0
987654321	30	20.0
987654321	20	15.0
888665555	20	null

PROJECT

PNAME	PNUMBER	PLOCATION	DNUM
ProductX	1	Bellaire	5
ProductY	2	Sugarland	5
ProductZ	3	Houston	5
Computerization	10	Stafford	4
Reorganization	20	Houston	1
Newbenefits	30	Stafford	4

Figure 14.2 Example relations for the schema of Figure 14.1.

of Figure 14.3(a) represents a single employee but includes additional information—namely, the name (DNAME) of the department for which the employee works and the social security number (DMGRSSN) of the department manager. For the EMP_PROJ relation of Figure 14.3(b), each tuple relates an employee to a project but also includes the employee name (ENAME), project name (PNAME), and project location (PLOCATION). Although there is nothing wrong logically with these two relations, they are considered poor designs because they violate Guideline 1 by mixing attributes from distinct real-world entities; EMP_DEPT mixes attributes of employees and departments, and EMP_PROJ mixes attributes of employees and

Figure 14.3 Two relation schemas and their functional dependencies. Both suffer from update anomalies. (a) The EMP_DEPT relation schema. (b) The EMP_PROJ relation schema.

projects. They may be used as views, but they cause problems when used as base relations, as we shall discuss in the following section.

14.1.2 Redundant Information in Tuples and Update Anomalies

One goal of schema design is to minimize the storage space that the base relations (files) occupy. Grouping attributes into relation schemas has a significant effect on storage space. For example, compare the space used by the two base relations EMPLOYEE and DEPARTMENT in Figure 14.2 with the space for an EMP_DEPT base relation in Figure 14.4, which is the result of applying the NATURAL JOIN operation to EMPLOYEE and DEPARTMENT. In EMP_DEPT, the attribute values pertaining to a particular department (DNUMBER, DNAME, DMGRSSN) are repeated for *every employee who works for that department*. In contrast, each department's information appears only once in the DEPARTMENT relation in Figure 14.2. Only the department number (DNUMBER) is repeated in the EMPLOYEE relation for each employee who works in that department. Similar comments apply to the EMP_PROJ relation (Figure 14.4), which augments the WORKS_ON relation with additional attributes from EMPLOYEE and PROJECT.

Another serious problem with using the relations in Figure 14.4 as base relations is the problem of **update anomalies.** These can be classified into insertion anomalies, deletion anomalies, and modification anomalies.[2]

---

2. These anomalies were identified by Codd (1972a) to justify the need for normalization of relations, as we shall discuss in Section 14.3.

EMP_DEPT

ENAME	SSN	BDATE	ADDRESS	DNUMBER	DNAME	DMGRSSN
Smith,John B.	123456789	1965-01-09	731 Fondren,Houston,TX	5	Research	333445555
Wong,Franklin T.	333445555	1955-12-08	638 Voss,Houston,TX	5	Research	333445555
Zelaya, Alicia J.	999887777	1968-07-19	3321 Castle,Spring,TX	4	Administration	987654321
Wallace,Jennifer S.	987654321	1941-06-20	291 Berry,Bellaire,TX	4	Administration	987654321
Narayan,Ramesh K.	666884444	1962-09-15	975 FireOak,Humble,TX	5	Research	333445555
English,Joyce A.	453453453	1972-07-31	5631 Rice,Houston,TX	5	Research	333445555
Jabbar,Ahmad V.	987987987	1969-03-29	980 Dallas,Houston,TX	4	Administration	987654321
Borg,James E.	888665555	1937-11-10	450 Stone,Houston,TX	1	Headquarters	888665555

EMP_PROJ

SSN	PNUMBER	HOURS	ENAME	PNAME	PLOCATION
123456789	1	32.5	Smith,John B.	ProductX	Bellaire
123456789	2	7.5	Smith,John B.	ProductY	Sugarland
666884444	3	40.0	Narayan,Ramesh K.	ProductZ	Houston
453453453	1	20.0	English,Joyce A.	ProductX	Bellaire
453453453	2	20.0	English,Joyce A.	ProductY	Sugarland
333445555	2	10.0	Wong,Franklin T.	ProductY	Sugarland
333445555	3	10.0	Wong,Franklin T.	ProductZ	Houston
333445555	10	10.0	Wong,Franklin T.	Computerization	Stafford
333445555	20	10.0	Wong,Franklin T.	Reorganization	Houston
999887777	30	30.0	Zelaya,Alicia J.	Newbenefits	Stafford
999887777	10	10.0	Zelaya,Alicia J.	Computerization	Stafford
987987987	10	35.0	Jabbar,Ahmad V.	Computerization	Stafford
987987987	30	5.0	Jabbar,Ahmad V.	Newbenefits	Stafford
987654321	30	20.0	Wallace,Jennifer S.	Newbenefits	Stafford
987654321	20	15.0	Wallace,Jennifer S.	Reorganization	Houston
888665555	20	null	Borg,James E.	Reorganization	Houston

Figure 14.4 Example relations for the schemas in Figure 14.3 that result from applying NATURAL JOIN to the relations in Figure 14.2. These may be stored as base relations for performance reasons.

Insertion Anomalies. These can be differentiated into two types, illustrated by the following examples based on the EMP_DEPT relation:

- To insert a new employee tuple into EMP_DEPT, we must include either the attribute values for the department that the employee works for, or nulls (if the employee does not work for a department as yet). For example, to insert a new tuple for an employee who works in department number 5, we must enter the attribute values of department 5 correctly so that they are *consistent* with values for department 5 in other tuples in EMP_DEPT. In the design of Figure 14.2 we do not have to worry about this consistency problem because we enter only the department number in the employee tuple; all other attribute values of department 5 are recorded only once in the database, as a single tuple in the DEPARTMENT relation.

- It is difficult to insert a new department that has no employees as yet in the EMP_DEPT relation. The only way to do this is to place null values in the attributes for employee.

This causes a problem because SSN is the primary key of EMP_DEPT, and each tuple is supposed to represent an employee entity—not a department entity. Moreover, when the first employee is assigned to that department, we do not need the tuple with null values any more. This problem does not occur in the design of Figure 14.2, because a department is entered in the DEPARTMENT relation whether or not any employees work for it, and whenever an employee is assigned to that department, a corresponding tuple is inserted in EMPLOYEE.

Deletion Anomalies.   This problem is related to the second insertion anomaly situation discussed above. If we delete from EMP_DEPT an employee tuple that happens to represent the last employee working for a particular department, the information concerning that department is lost from the database. This problem does not occur in the database of Figure 14.2 because DEPARTMENT tuples are stored separately.

Modification Anomalies.   In EMP_DEPT, if we change the value of one of the attributes of a particular department—say, the manager of department 5—we must update the tuples of all employees who work in that department; otherwise, the database will become inconsistent. If we fail to update some tuples, the same department will be shown to have two different values for manager in different employee tuples, which should not be the case.

Based on the preceding three anomalies, we can state the guideline that follows.

GUIDELINE 2: Design the base relation schemas so that no insertion, deletion, or modification anomalies are present in the relations. If any anomalies are present, note them clearly and make sure that the programs that update the database will operate correctly.

The second guideline is consistent with and, in a way, a restatement of the first guideline. We can also see the need for a more formal approach to evaluating whether a design meets these guidelines. Sections 14.2 through 14.4 provide these needed formal concepts. It is important to note that these guidelines may sometimes *have to be violated* in order to *improve the performance* of certain queries. For example, if an important query retrieves information concerning the department of an employee, along with employee attributes, the EMP_DEPT schema may be used as a base relation. However, the anomalies in EMP_DEPT must be noted and well understood so that, whenever the base relation is updated, we do not end up with inconsistencies. In general, it is advisable to use anomaly-free base relations and to specify views that include the JOINs for placing together the attributes frequently referenced in important queries. This reduces the number of JOIN terms specified in the query, making it simpler to write the query correctly, and in many cases it improves the performance.[3]

---

3. The performance of a query specified on a view that is the JOIN of several base relations depends on how the DBMS implements the view. Many relational DBMSS materialize a frequently used view so that they do not have to perform the JOINs often. The DBMS remains responsible for updating the materialized view (either immediately or periodically) whenever the base relations are updated.

14.1.3 Null Values in Tuples

In some schema designs we may group many attributes together into a "fat" relation. If many of the attributes do not apply to all tuples in the relation, we end up with many nulls in those tuples. This can waste space at the storage level and may also lead to problems with understanding the meaning of the attributes and with specifying JOIN operations at the logical level.[4] Another problem with nulls is how to account for them when aggregate operations such as COUNT or SUM are applied. Moreover, nulls can have multiple interpretations, such as the following:

- The attribute *does not apply* to this tuple.
- The attribute value for this tuple is *unknown*.
- The value is *known but absent*; that is, it has not been recorded yet.

Having the same representation for all nulls compromises the different meanings they may have. Therefore, we may state another guideline.

GUIDELINE 3: As far as possible, avoid placing attributes in a base relation whose values may frequently be null. If nulls are unavoidable, make sure that they apply in exceptional cases only and do not apply to a majority of tuples in the relation.

For example, if only 10 percent of employees have individual offices, there is little justification for including an attribute OFFICE_NUMBER in the EMPLOYEE relation; rather, a relation EMP_OFFICES(ESSN, OFFICE_NUMBER) can be created to include tuples for only the employees with individual offices.

14.1.4 Generation of Spurious Tuples

Consider the two relation schemas EMP_LOCS and EMP_PROJ1 in Figure 14.5(a), which can be used instead of the EMP_PROJ relation of Figure 14.3(b). A tuple in EMP_LOCS means that the employee whose name is ENAME works on *some project* whose location is PLOCATION. A tuple in EMP_PROJ1 means that the employee whose social security number is SSN works HOURS per week on the project whose name, number, and location are PNAME, PNUMBER, and PLOCATION. Figure 14.5(b) shows relation extensions of EMP_LOCS and EMP_PROJ1 corresponding to the EMP_PROJ relation of Figure 14.4, which are obtained by applying the appropriate PROJECT (π) operations to EMP_PROJ (ignore the dotted lines in Figure 14.5b for now).

Suppose that we used EMP_PROJ1 and EMP_LOCS as the base relations instead of EMP_PROJ. This produces a particularly bad schema design, because we cannot recover the information that was originally in EMP_PROJ from EMP_PROJ1 and EMP_LOCS. If we attempt a NATURAL JOIN operation on EMP_PROJ1 and EMP_LOCS, the result produces many more tuples than the original population of tuples in EMP_PROJ. In Figure 14.6, the result of applying the join to

---

4. This is because inner and outer joins produce different results when nulls are involved in joins. The users must thus be aware of the different meanings of the various types of joins. Although this is reasonable for sophisticated users, it may be difficult for others.

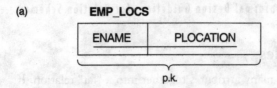

(a)

EMP_LOCS

ENAME	PLOCATION

‿‿‿‿‿ p.k. ‿‿‿‿‿

EMP_PROJ1

SSN	PNUMBER	HOURS	PNAME	PLOCATION

‿‿‿‿‿ p.k. ‿‿‿‿‿

(b)

EMP_LOCS

ENAME	PLOCATION
Smith, John B.	Bellaire
Smith, John B.	Sugarland
Narayan, Ramesh K.	Houston
English, Joyce A.	Bellaire
English, Joyce A.	Sugarland
Wong, Franklin T.	Sugarland
Wong, Franklin T.	Houston
Wong, Franklin T.	Stafford
Zelaya, Alicia J.	Stafford
Jabbar, Ahmad V.	Stafford
Wallace, Jennifer S.	Stafford
Wallace, Jennifer S.	Houston
Borg,James E.	Houston

EMP_PROJ1

SSN	PNUMBER	HOURS	PNAME	PLOCATION
123456789	1	32.5	Product X	Bellaire
123456789	2	7.5	Product Y	Sugarland
666884444	3	40.0	Product Z	Houston
453453453	1	20.0	Product X	Bellaire
453453453	2	20.0	Product Y	Sugarland
333445555	2	10.0	Product Y	Sugarland
333445555	3	10.0	Product Z	Houston
333445555	10	10.0	Computerization	Stafford
333445555	20	10.0	Reorganization	Houston
999887777	30	30.0	Newbenefits	Stafford
999887777	10	10.0	Computerization	Stafford
987987987	10	35.0	Computerization	Stafford
987987987	30	5.0	Newbenefits	Stafford
987654321	30	20.0	Newbenefits	Stafford
987654321	20	15.0	Reorganization	Houston
888665555	20	null	Reorganization	Houston

Figure 14.5 Alternative (bad) representation of the EMP_PROJ relation. (a) Representing EMP_PROJ of Figure 14.3(b) by two relation schemas: EMP_LOCS and EMP_PROJ1. (b) Result of projecting the populated relation EMP_PROJ of Figure 14.4 on the attributes of EMP_LOCS and EMP_PROJ1.

SSN	PNUMBER	HOURS	PNAME	PLOCATION	
123456789	1	32.5	ProductX	Bellaire	Smith,John B.
* 123456789	1	32.5	ProductX	Bellaire	English,Joyce A.
123456789	2	7.5	ProductY	Sugarland	Smith,John B.
* 123456789	2	7.5	ProductY	Sugarland	English,Joyce A.
* 123456789	2	7.5	ProductY	Sugarland	Wong,Franklin T.
666884444	3	40.0	ProductZ	Houston	Narayan,Ramesh K.
* 666884444	3	40.0	ProductZ	Houston	Wong,Franklin T.
453453453	1	20.0	ProductX	Bellaire	Smith,John B.
453453453	1	20.0	ProductX	Bellaire	English,Joyce A.
* 453453453	2	20.0	ProductY	Sugarland	Smith,John B.
453453453	2	20.0	ProductY	Sugarland	English,Joyce A.
* 453453453	2	20.0	ProductY	Sugarland	Wong,Franklin T.
* 333445555	2	10.0	ProductY	Sugarland	Smith,John B.
* 333445555	2	10.0	ProductY	Sugarland	English,Joyce A.
333445555	2	10.0	ProductY	Sugarland	Wong,Franklin T.
* 333445555	3	10.0	ProductZ	Houston	Narayan,Ramesh K.
333445555	3	10.0	ProductZ	Houston	Wong,Franklin T.
333445555	10	10.0	Computerization	Stafford	Wong,Franklin T.
* 333445555	20	10.0	Reorganization	Houston	Narayan,Ramesh K.
333445555	20	10.0	Reorganization	Houston	Wong,Franklin T.

Figure 14.6 Result of applying the NATURAL JOIN operation to the tuples above dotted lines in EMP_PROJ1 and EMP_LOCS, with generated spurious tuples marked by an asterisk.

only the tuples *above* the dotted lines in Figure 14.5(b) is shown (to reduce the size of the resulting relation). Additional tuples that were not in EMP_PROJ are called **spurious tuples** because they represent spurious or *wrong* information that is not valid. The spurious tuples are marked by asterisks (*) in Figure 14.6.

Decomposing EMP_PROJ into EMP_LOCS and EMP_PROJ1 is undesirable because, when we JOIN them back using NATURAL JOIN, we do not get the correct original information. This is because in this case PLOCATION is the attribute that relates EMP_LOCS and EMP_PROJ1, and PLOCATION is neither a primary key nor a foreign key in either EMP_LOCS or EMP_PROJ1. We can now informally state another design guideline.

GUIDELINE 4: Design relation schemas so that they can be JOINed with equality conditions on attributes that are either primary keys or foreign keys in a way that guarantees that no spurious tuples are generated. Do not have relations that contain matching attributes other than foreign key-primary key combinations. If such relations are unavoidable, do not join them on such attributes, because the join may produce spurious tuples.

This informal guideline obviously needs to be stated more formally. In Chapter 15 we discuss a formal condition, called the nonadditive (or lossless) join property, which guarantees that certain joins do not produce spurious tuples.

14.1.5   Summary and Discussion of Design Guidelines

In Sections 14.1.1 through 14.1.4, we informally discussed situations that lead to problematic relation schemas, and we proposed informal guidelines for a good relational design. The problems we pointed out, which can be detected without additional tools of analysis, are as follows:

- Anomalies that imply additional work to be done during insertion into and modification of a relation, and that may cause accidental loss of information during a deletion from a relation.
- Waste of storage space due to nulls and difficulty of performing aggregation operations and joins due to null values.
- Generation of invalid and spurious data during joins on improperly related base relations.

In the rest of this chapter we present formal concepts and theory that may be used to define concepts of the "goodness" and the "badness" of *individual* relation schemas more precisely. We first discuss functional dependency as a tool for analysis. Then we specify the three normal forms and the Boyce-Codd normal form (BCNF) for relation schemas. In Chapter 15 we give additional criteria for determining that a set of relation schemas together forms a good relational database schema. We also present algorithms that are a part of this theory to design relational databases and define additional normal forms beyond BCNF. The normal forms defined in this chapter are based on the concept of a functional dependency, which we describe next, whereas the normal forms discussed in Chapter 15 use additional types of data dependencies called multivalued dependencies and join dependencies.

14.2   Functional Dependencies

The single most important concept in relational schema design is that of a functional dependency. In this section we formally define the concept, and in Section 14.3 we see how it can be used to define normal forms for relation schemas.

14.2.1   Definition of Functional Dependency

A functional dependency is a constraint between two sets of attributes from the database. Suppose that our relational database schema has n attributes $A_1, A_2, \ldots A_n$; let us think of the whole database as being described by a single **universal** relation schema $R = \{A_1, A_2, \ldots A_n\}$.[5] We do not imply that we will actually store the database as a single universal table; we use this concept only in developing the formal theory of data dependencies.[6]

---

5. This concept of a universal relation is important when we discuss the algorithms for relational database design in Chapter 15.

6. This assumption means that every attribute in the database should have a *distinct name*. In Chapter 7 we prefixed attribute names by relation names to achieve uniqueness whenever attributes in distinct relations had the same name.

A **functional dependency,** denoted by $X \rightarrow Y$, between two sets of attributes X and Y that are subsets of R specifies a *constraint* on the possible tuples that can form a relation state r of R. The constraint is that, for any two tuples t_1 and t_2 in r that have $t_1[X] = t_2[X]$, we must also have $t_1[Y] = t_2[Y]$. This means that the values of the Y component of a tuple in r depend on, or are *determined by*, the values of the X component; or alternatively, the values of the X component of a tuple uniquely (or **functionally**) **determine** the values of the Y component. We also say that there is a functional dependency from X to Y or that Y is **functionally dependent** on X. The abbreviation for functional dependency is **FD** or **f.d.** The set of attributes X is called the **left-hand side** of the FD, and Y is called the **right-hand side.**

Thus X functionally determines Y in a relation schema R if and only if, whenever two tuples of $r(R)$ agree on their X-value, they must necessarily agree on their Y-value. Notice the following:

- If a constraint on R states that there cannot be more than one tuple with a given X-value in any relation instance $r(R)$—that is, X is a **candidate key** of R—this implies that $X \rightarrow Y$ for any subset of attributes Y of R (because the key constraint implies that no two tuples in any legal state $r(R)$ will have the same value of X).

- If $X \rightarrow Y$ in R, this does not say whether or not $Y \rightarrow X$ in R.

A functional dependency is a property of the **semantics** or **meaning of the attributes.** The database designers will use their understanding of the semantics of the attributes of R—that is, how they relate to one another—to specify the functional dependencies that should hold on *all* relation states (extensions) r of R. Whenever the semantics of two sets of attributes in R indicate that a functional dependency should hold, we specify the dependency as a constraint. Relation extensions $r(R)$ that satisfy the functional dependency constraints are called **legal extensions** (or **legal relation states**) of R, because they obey the functional dependency constraints. Hence, the main use of functional dependencies is to describe further a relation schema R by specifying constraints on its attributes that must hold *at all times*. Certain FDs can be specified without referring to a specific relation, but as a property of those attributes. For example, {State, Driver_license_number} → SSN should hold for any adult in the United States. It is also possible that certain functional dependencies may cease to exist in the real world if the relationship changes. For example, the FD Zip_code → Area_code used to exist as a relationship between postal codes and telephone number codes in the United States, but with the proliferation of telephone area codes it is no longer true.

Consider the relation schema EMP_PROJ in Figure 14.3(b); from the semantics of the attributes, we know that the following functional dependencies should hold:

a. SSN → ENAME
b. PNUMBER → {PNAME, PLOCATION}
c. {SSN, PNUMBER} → HOURS

These functional dependencies specify that (a) the value of an employee's social security number (SSN) uniquely determines the employee name (ENAME), (b) the value of a project's number (PNUMBER) uniquely determines the project name (PNAME) and location

TEACH

TEACHER	COURSE	TEXT
Smith	Data Structures	Bartram
Smith	Data Management	Al-Nour
Hall	Compilers	Hoffman
Brown	Data Structures	Augenthaler

Figure 14.7   The TEACH relation state with an apparent functional dependency TEXT → COURSE. However, COURSE → TEXT is ruled out.

(PLOCATION), and (c) a combination of SSN and PNUMBER values uniquely determines the number of hours the employee works on the project per week (HOURS). Alternatively, we say that ENAME is functionally determined by (or functionally dependent on) SSN, or "given a value of SSN, we know the value of ENAME," and so on.

A functional dependency is a *property of the relation schema* (intension) R, not of a particular legal relation state (extension) r of R. Hence, an FD *cannot* be inferred automatically from a given relation extension r but must be defined explicitly by someone who knows the semantics of the attributes of R. For example, Figure 14.7 shows a particular state of the TEACH relation schema. Although at first glance we may think that TEXT → COURSE, we cannot confirm this unless we know that it is true *for all possible legal states* of TEACH. It is, however, sufficient to demonstrate a single counterexample to disprove a functional dependency. For example, because 'Smith' teaches both 'Data Structures' and 'Data Management', we can conclude that TEACHER does *not* functionally determine COURSE.

Figure 14.3 introduces a **diagrammatic notation** for displaying FDs: Each FD is displayed as a horizontal line. The left-hand side attributes of the FD are connected by vertical lines to the line representing the FD, while the right-hand-side attributes are connected by arrows pointing toward the attributes, as shown in Figures 14.3(a) and (b).

14.2.2   Inference Rules for Functional Dependencies

We denote by F the set of functional dependencies that are specified on relation schema R. Typically, the schema designer specifies the functional dependencies that are *semantically obvious*; usually, however, numerous other functional dependencies hold in *all* legal relation instances that satisfy the dependencies in F. Those other dependencies can be *inferred* or *deduced* from the FDs in F. For real-life examples, it is practically impossible to specify all possible functional dependencies that may hold. The set of all such dependencies is called the **closure** of F and is denoted by F^+. For example, suppose that we specify the following set F of obvious functional dependencies on the relation schema of Figure 14.3(a):

F = {SSN → {ENAME, BDATE, ADDRESS, DNUMBER},

    DNUMBER → {DNAME, DMGRSSN}}

We can *infer* the following additional functional dependencies from F:

SSN → {DNAME, DMGRSSN},

SSN → SSN,

DNUMBER → DNAME

An FD $X \rightarrow Y$ is **inferred from** a set of dependencies F specified on R if $X \rightarrow Y$ holds in *every* relation state r that is a legal extension of R; that is, whenever r satisfies all the dependencies in F, $X \rightarrow Y$ also holds in r. The closure F^+ of F is the set of all functional dependencies that can be inferred from F. To determine a systematic way to infer dependencies, we must discover a set of **inference rules** that can be used to infer new dependencies from a given set of dependencies. We consider some of these inference rules next. We use the notation $F \vDash X \rightarrow Y$ to denote that the functional dependency $X \rightarrow Y$ is inferred from the set of functional dependencies F.

In the following discussion, we use an abbreviated notation when discussing functional dependencies. We concatenate attribute variables and drop the commas for convenience. Hence, the FD $\{X,Y\} \rightarrow Z$ is abbreviated to $XY \rightarrow Z$, and the FD $\{X,Y,Z\} \rightarrow \{U,V\}$ is abbreviated to $XYZ \rightarrow UV$. The following six rules (IR1 through IR6) are well-known inference rules for functional dependencies:

IR1 (reflexive rule[7]): If $X \supseteq Y$, then $X \rightarrow Y$.

IR2 (augmentation rule[8]): $\{ X \rightarrow Y \} \vDash XZ \rightarrow YZ$.

IR3 (transitive rule): $\{ X \rightarrow Y, Y \rightarrow Z \} \vDash X \rightarrow Z$.

IR4 (decomposition, or projective, rule): $\{ X \rightarrow YZ \} \vDash X \rightarrow Y$.

IR5 (union, or additive, rule): $\{ X \rightarrow Y, X \rightarrow Z \} \vDash X \rightarrow YZ$.

IR6 (pseudotransitive rule): $\{ X \rightarrow Y, WY \rightarrow Z \} \vDash WX \rightarrow Z$.

The reflexive rule (IR1) states that a set of attributes always determines itself or any of its subsets, which is obvious. Because IR1 generates dependencies that are always true, such dependencies are called trivial. Formally, a functional dependency $X \rightarrow Y$ is **trivial** if $X \supseteq Y$; otherwise, it is **nontrivial.** The augmentation rule (IR2) says that adding the same set of attributes to both the left- and right-hand sides of a dependency results in another valid dependency. According to IR3, functional dependencies are transitive. The decomposition rule (IR4) says that we can remove attributes from the right-hand side of a dependency; applying this rule repeatedly can decompose the FD $X \rightarrow \{A_1, A_2, ..., A_n\}$ into the set of dependencies $\{X \rightarrow A_1, X \rightarrow A_2, ..., X \rightarrow A_n\}$. The union rule (IR5) allows us to do the opposite; we can combine a set of dependencies $\{X \rightarrow A_1, X \rightarrow A_2, ..., X \rightarrow A_n\}$ into the single FD $X \rightarrow \{A_1, A_2, ..., A_n\}$.

Each of the preceding inference rules can be proved from the definition of functional dependency, either by direct proof or **by contradiction.** A proof by contradiction assumes

---

7. The reflexive rule can also be stated as $X \rightarrow X$; that is, any set of attributes functionally determines itself.

8. The augmentation rule can also be stated as $\{ X \rightarrow Y \} \vDash XZ \rightarrow Y$; that is, augmenting the left-hand side attributes of an FD produces another valid FD.

that the rule does not hold and shows that this is not possible. We now prove that the first three rules (IR1 through IR3) are valid. The second proof is by contradiction.

PROOF OF IR1

Suppose that $X \supseteq Y$ and that two tuples t_1 and t_2 exist in some relation instance r of R such that $t_1 [X] = t_2 [X]$. Then $t_1[Y] = t_2[Y]$ because $X \supseteq Y$; hence, $X \rightarrow Y$ must hold in r.

PROOF OF IR2 (BY CONTRADICTION)

Assume that $X \rightarrow Y$ holds in a relation instance r of R but that $XZ \rightarrow YZ$ does not hold. Then there must exist two tuples t_1 and t_2 in r such that (1) $t_1 [X] = t_2 [X]$, (2) $t_1 [Y] = t_2 [Y]$, (3) $t_1 [XZ] = t_2 [XZ]$, and (4) $t_1 [YZ] \neq t_2 [YZ]$. This is not possible because from (1) and (3) we deduce (5) $t_1 [Z] = t_2 [Z]$, and from (2) and (5) we deduce (6) $t_1 [YZ] = t_2 [YZ]$, contradicting (4).

PROOF OF IR3

Assume that (1) $X \rightarrow Y$ and (2) $Y \rightarrow Z$ both hold in a relation r. Then for any two tuples t_1 and t_2 in r such that $t_1 [X] = t_2 [X]$, we must have (3) $t_1 [Y] = t_2 [Y]$, from assumption (1); hence we must also have (4) $t_1 [Z] = t_2 [Z]$, from (3) and assumption (2); hence $X \rightarrow Z$ must hold in r.

Using similar proof arguments, we can prove the inference rules IR4 to IR6 and any additional valid inference rules. However, a simpler way to prove that an inference rule for functional dependencies is valid is to prove it by using inference rules that have already been shown to be valid. For example, we can prove IR4 through IR6 by using IR1 through IR3 as follows:

PROOF OF IR4 (USING IR1 THROUGH IR3)

1. $X \rightarrow YZ$ (given).
2. $YZ \rightarrow Y$ (using IR1 and knowing that $YZ \supseteq Y$).
3. $X \rightarrow Y$ (using IR3 on 1 and 2).

PROOF OF IR5 (USING IR1 THROUGH IR3)

1. $X \rightarrow Y$ (given).
2. $X \rightarrow Z$ (given).
3. $X \rightarrow XY$ (using IR2 on 1 by augmenting with X; notice that $XX = X$).
4. $XY \rightarrow YZ$ (using IR2 on 2 by augmenting with Y).
5. $X \rightarrow YZ$ (using IR3 on 3 and 4).

PROOF OF IR6 (USING IR1 THROUGH IR3)

1. $X \rightarrow Y$ (given).
2. $WY \rightarrow Z$ (given).

3. $WX \rightarrow WY$ (using IR2 on 1 by augmenting with W).

4. $WX \rightarrow Z$ (using IR3 on 3 and 2).

It has been shown by Armstrong (1974) that inference rules IR1 through IR3 are sound and complete. By sound, we mean that, given a set of functional dependencies F specified on a relation schema R, any dependency that we can infer from F by using IR1 through IR3 holds in every relation state r of R that *satisfies the dependencies* in F. By complete, we mean that using IR1 through IR3 repeatedly to infer dependencies until no more dependencies can be inferred results in the complete set of *all possible dependencies* that can be inferred from F. In other words, the set of dependencies F^+, which we called the closure of F, can be determined from F by using only inference rules IR1 through IR3. Inference rules IR1 through IR3 are known as **Armstrong's inference rules.**[9]

Typically, database designers first specify the set of functional dependencies F that can easily be determined from the semantics of the attributes of R; then IR1, IR2, and IR3 are used to infer additional functional dependencies that will also hold on R. A systematic way to determine these additional functional dependencies is first to determine each set of attributes X that appears as a left-hand side of some functional dependency in F and then to determine the set of *all attributes* that are dependent on X. Thus for each such set of attributes X, we determine the set X^+ of attributes that are functionally determined by X based on F; X^+ is called the **closure of X under F.** Algorithm 14.1 can be used to calculate X^+.

Algorithm 14.1 Determining X^+, the closure of X under F

```
X+ := X;
repeat
    oldX+ := X+;
    for each functional dependency Y → Z in F do
        if X+ ⊇ Y then X+ := X+ ∪ Z;
until (X+ = oldX+);
```

Algorithm 14.1 starts by setting X^+ to all the attributes in X. By IR1, we know that all these attributes 'are functionally dependent on X. Using inference rules IR3 and IR4, we add attributes to X^+, using each functional dependency in F. We keep going through all the dependencies in F (the repeat loop) until no more attributes are added to X^+ *during a complete cycle* (the for loop) through the dependencies in F. For example, consider the relation schema EMP_PROJ in Figure 14.3(b); from the semantics of the attributes, we specify the following set F of functional dependencies that should hold on EMP_PROJ:

$F = \{$SSN $\rightarrow$ ENAME,

PNUMBER $\rightarrow$ {PNAME, PLOCATION},

{SSN, PNUMBER} $\rightarrow$ HOURS}

---

9. They are actually known as **Armstrong's axioms.** In the strict mathematical sense, the *axioms* (given facts) are the functional dependencies in F, since we assume that they are correct, while IR1 through IR3 are the *inference rules* for inferring new functional dependencies (new facts).

Using Algorithm 14.1, we calculate the following closure sets with respect to F:

$\{ \text{SSN} \}^+ = \{ \text{SSN, ENAME} \}$

$\{ \text{PNUMBER} \}^+ = \{ \text{PNUMBER, PNAME, PLOCATION} \}$

$\{ \text{SSN, PNUMBER} \}^+ = \{ \text{SSN, PNUMBER, ENAME, PNAME, PLOCATION, HOURS} \}$

14.2.3 Equivalence of Sets of Functional Dependencies

In this section we discuss the equivalence of two sets of functional dependencies. First, we give some preliminary definitions. A set of functional dependencies E is **covered by** a set of functional dependencies F—or alternatively, F is said to **cover** E—if every FD in E is also in F^+; that is, if every dependency in E can be inferred from F. Two sets of functional dependencies E and F are **equivalent** if $E^+ = F^+$. Hence, equivalence means that every FD in E can be inferred from F, and every FD in F can be inferred from E; that is, E is equivalent to F if both the conditions E covers F *and* F covers E hold.

We can determine whether F covers E by calculating X^+ with respect to F for each FD $X \rightarrow Y$ in E, and then checking whether this X^+ includes the attributes in Y. If this is the case for *every* FD in E, then F covers E. We determine whether E and F are equivalent by checking that E covers F and F covers E.

14.2.4 Minimal Sets of Functional Dependencies

A set of functional dependencies F is **minimal** if it satisfies the following conditions:

1. Every dependency in F has a single attribute for its right-hand side.
2. We cannot replace any dependency $X \rightarrow A$ in F with a dependency $Y \rightarrow A$, where Y is a proper subset of X, and still have a set of dependencies that is equivalent to F.
3. We cannot remove any dependency from F and still have a set of dependencies that is equivalent to F.

We can think of a minimal set of dependencies as being a set of dependencies in a *standard or canonical form* and with *no redundancies*. Condition 1 ensures that every dependency is in a canonical form with a single attribute on the right-hand side.[10] Conditions 2 and 3 ensure that there are no redundancies in the dependencies either by having redundant attributes on the left-hand side of a dependency (Condition 2), or by having a dependency that can be inferred from the remaining FDs in F (Condition 3). A **minimal cover** of a set of functional dependencies F is a minimal set of dependencies F_{min} that is equivalent to F. Unfortunately, there can be several minimal covers for a set of functional dependencies. We can always find *at least one* minimal cover G for any set of dependencies F using Algorithm 14.2.

---

10. This is a standard form, not a requirement, to simplify the conditions and algorithms that ensure no redundancy exists in F. By using the inference rules IR4 and IR5, we can convert a single dependency with multiple attributes on the right-hand side into a set of dependencies, and vice versa.

Algorithm 14.2 Finding a minimal cover G for F

1. Set `G := F`.

2. Replace each functional dependency $X \rightarrow \{A_1, A_2, \ldots, A_n\}$ in `G` by the
   `n` functional dependencies $X \rightarrow A_1$, $X \rightarrow A_2$, . . ., $X \rightarrow A_n$.

3. For each functional dependency $X \rightarrow A$ in `G`

   for each attribute `B` that is an element of `X`

   if $((G - \{X \rightarrow A\}) \cup \{(X - \{B\}) \rightarrow A\})$ is equivalent to
   `G`,

   then replace $X \rightarrow A$ with $(X - \{B\}) \rightarrow A$ in `G`.

4. For each remaining functional dependency $X \rightarrow A$ in `G`

   if $(G - \{X \rightarrow A\})$ is equivalent to `G`,

   then remove $X \rightarrow A$ from `G`.

14.3 Normal Forms Based on Primary Keys

Having studied functional dependencies and some of their properties, we are now ready to use them as information about the semantics of the relation schemas. We assume that a set of functional dependencies is given for each relation, and that each relation has a designated primary key; this information combined with the tests (conditions) for normal forms drives the normalization process. We will focus on the first three normal forms for relation schemas and the intuition behind them, and discuss how they were developed historically. More general definitions of these normal forms, which take into account all candidate keys of a relation rather than just the primary key, are deferred to Section 14.4. In Section 14.5 we define Boyce-Codd normal form (BCNF), and in Chapter 15 we define further normal forms that are based on other types of data dependencies.

We start in Section 14.3.1 by informally discussing normal forms and the motivation behind their development, as well as reviewing some definitions from Chapter 7 that are needed here. We then discuss first normal form (1NF) in Section 14.3.2, and present the definitions of second normal form (2NF) and third normal form (3NF) that are based on primary keys in Sections 14.3.3 and 14.3.4.

14.3.1 Introduction to Normalization

The normalization process, as first proposed by Codd (1972a), takes a relation schema through a series of tests to "certify" whether it satisfies a certain **normal form.** The process, which proceeds in a top-down fashion by evaluating each relation against the criteria for normal forms and decomposing relations as necessary, can thus be considered as *relational design by analysis.* Initially, Codd proposed three normal forms, which he called first, second, and third normal form. A stronger definition of 3NF—called Boyce-Codd normal form (BCNF)—was proposed later by Boyce and Codd. All these normal forms are based on the functional dependencies among the attributes of a relation. Later, a fourth normal form (4NF) and a fifth normal form (5NF) were proposed, based on the concepts of multivalued dependencies and join dependencies, respectively; these are discussed in

Chapter 15. At the beginning of Chapter 15, we also discuss how 3NF relations may be synthesized from a given set of FDs. This approach is called *relational design by synthesis*.

Normalization of data can hence be looked upon as a process of analyzing the given relation schemas based on their FDs and primary keys to achieve the desirable properties of (1) minimizing redundancy and (2) minimizing the insertion, deletion, and update anomalies discussed in Section 14.1.2. Unsatisfactory relation schemas that do not meet certain conditions—the **normal form tests**—are decomposed into smaller relation schemas that meet the tests and hence possess the desirable properties. Thus, the normalization procedure provides database designers with:

- A formal framework for analyzing relation schemas based on their keys and on the functional dependencies among their attributes.

- A series of normal form tests that can be carried out on individual relation schemas so that the relational database can be **normalized** to any desired degree.

The **normal form** of a relation refers to the highest normal form condition that it meets, and hence indicates the degree to which it has been normalized. Normal forms, when considered *in isolation* from other factors, do not guarantee a good database design. It is generally not sufficient to check separately that each relation schema in the database is, say, in BCNF or 3NF. Rather, the process of normalization through decomposition must also confirm the existence of additional properties that the relational schemas, taken together, should possess. These would include two properties:

- The **lossless join** or **nonadditive join property,** which guarantees that the spurious tuple generation problem discussed in Section 14.1.4 does not occur with respect to the relation schemas created after decomposition.

- The **dependency preservation property,** which ensures that each functional dependency is represented in some individual relations resulting after decomposition.

The nonadditive join property is extremely critical and must be achieved at any cost, whereas the dependency preservation property, although desirable, is sometimes sacrificed, as we shall see in Section 15.1.2. We defer the presentation of the formal concepts and techniques that guarantee the above two properties to Chapter 15.

Additional normal forms may be defined to meet other desirable criteria, based on additional types of constraints, as we shall see in Chapter 15. However, the practical utility of normal forms becomes questionable when the constraints on which they are based are hard to understand or to detect by the database designers and users who must discover these constraints. Thus database design as practiced in industry today pays particular attention to normalization up to BCNF or 4NF.

Another point worth noting is that the database designers *need not* normalize to the highest possible normal form. Relations may be left in a lower normalization status for performance reasons, such as those discussed at the end of Section 14.1.2. The process of storing the join of higher normal form relations as a base relation—which is in a lower normal form—is known as **denormalization.**

Before proceeding further, let us look again at the definitions of keys of a relation schema from Chapter 7. A **superkey** of a relation schema $R = \{A_1, A_2, ..., A_n\}$ is a set of attributes $S \subseteq R$ with the property that no two tuples t_1 and t_2 in any legal relation state r of

R will have $t_1[S] = t_2[S]$. A **key** K is a superkey with the *additional property* that removal of any attribute from K will cause K not to be a superkey any more. The difference between a key and a superkey is that a key has to be *minimal*; that is, if we have a key $K = \{A_1, A_2, ..., A_k\}$ of R, then $K - \{A_i\}$ is *not a key* of R for any i, $1 \le i \le k$. In Figure 14.1 {SSN} is a key for EMPLOYEE, whereas {SSN}, {SSN, ENAME}, {SSN, ENAME, BDATE}, etc. are all superkeys.

If a relation schema has more than one key, each is called a **candidate key.** One of the candidate keys is *arbitrarily* designated to be the **primary key,** and the others are called secondary keys. Each relation schema must have a primary key. In Figure 14.1 {SSN} is the only candidate key for EMPLOYEE, so it is also the primary key.

An attribute of relation schema R is called a **prime attribute** of R if it is a member of *some candidate key* of R. An attribute is called **nonprime** if it is not a prime attribute—that is, if it is not a member of any candidate key. In Figure 14.1 both SSN and PNUMBER are prime attributes of WORKS_ON, whereas other attributes of WORKS_ON are nonprime.

We now present the first three normal forms: 1NF, 2NF, and 3NF. These were proposed by Codd (1972a) as a sequence to achieve the desirable state of 3NF relations by progressing through the intermediate states of 1NF and 2NF if needed.

14.3.2 First Normal Form

First normal form (1NF) is now considered to be part of the formal definition of a relation in the basic (flat) relational model;[11] historically, it was defined to disallow multivalued attributes, composite attributes, and their combinations. It states that the domain of an attribute must include only *atomic* (simple, indivisible) *values* and that the value of any attribute in a tuple must be a *single value* from the domain of that attribute. Hence, 1NF disallows having a set of values, a tuple of values, or a combination of both as an attribute value for a *single tuple*. In other words, 1NF disallows "relations within relations" or "relations as attributes of tuples." The only attribute values permitted by 1NF are single **atomic** (or **indivisible) values.**

Consider the DEPARTMENT relation schema shown in Figure 14.1, whose primary key is DNUMBER, and suppose that we extend it by including the DLOCATIONS attribute as shown in Figure 14.8(a). We assume that each department can have *a number of* locations. The DEPARTMENT schema and an example extension are shown in Figure 14.8. As we can see, this is not in 1NF because DLOCATIONS is not an atomic attribute, as illustrated by the first tuple in Figure 14.8(b). There are two ways we can look at the DLOCATIONS attribute:

- The domain of DLOCATIONS contains atomic values, but some tuples can have a set of these values. In this case, DLOCATIONS *is not* functionally dependent on DNUMBER.

- The domain of DLOCATIONS contains sets of values and hence is nonatomic. In this case, DNUMBER $\rightarrow$ DLOCATIONS, because each set is considered a single member of the attribute domain.[12]

---

11. This condition is removed in the *nested relational model* and in *object-relational systems* (ORDBMSs), both of which allow *unnormalized relations* (see Chapter 13).

12. In this case we can consider the domain of DLOCATIONS to be the **power set** of the set of single locations; that is, the domain is made up of *all possible subsets* of the set of single locations.

(a)   DEPARTMENT

DNAME	DNUMBER	DMGRSSN	DLOCATIONS

(b)   DEPARTMENT

DNAME	DNUMBER	DMGRSSN	DLOCATIONS
Research	5	333445555	{Bellaire, Sugarland, Houston}
Administration	4	987654321	{Stafford}
Headquarters	1	888665555	{Houston}

(c)   DEPARTMENT

DNAME	DNUMBER	DMGRSSN	DLOCATION
Research	5	333445555	Bellaire
Research	5	333445555	Sugarland
Research	5	333445555	Houston
Administration	4	987654321	Stafford
Headquarters	1	888665555	Houston

Figure 14.8   Normalization into 1NF. (a) Relation schema that is not in 1NF. (b) Example relation instance. (c) 1NF relation with redundancy.

In either case, the DEPARTMENT relation of Figure 14.8 is not in 1NF; in fact, it does not even qualify as a relation, according to our definition of relation in Section 7.1. There are three main techniques to achieve first normal form for such a relation:

1. Remove the attribute DLOCATIONS that violates 1NF and place it in a separate relation DEPT_LOCATIONS along with the primary key DNUMBER of DEPARTMENT. The primary key of this relation is the combination {DNUMBER, DLOCATION}, as shown in Figure 14.2. A distinct tuple in DEPT_LOCATIONS exists for *each location* of a department. This decomposes the non-1NF relation into two 1NF relations.

2. Expand the key so that there will be a separate tuple in the original DEPARTMENT relation for each location of a DEPARTMENT, as shown in Figure 14.8(c). In this case, the primary key becomes the combination {DNUMBER, DLOCATION}. This solution has the disadvantage of introducing *redundancy* in the relation.

3. If a *maximum number of values* is known for the attribute—for example, if it is known that *at most three locations* can exist for a department—replace the DLOCATIONS attribute by three atomic attributes: DLOCATION1, DLOCATION2, and DLOCATION3. This solution has the disadvantage of introducing *null values* if most departments have fewer than three locations.

Of the three solutions above, the first is superior because it does not suffer from redundancy and it is completely general, having no limit placed on a maximum number of values. In fact, if we choose the second solution, it will be decomposed further during subsequent normalization steps into the first solution.

The first normal form also disallows multivalued attributes that are themselves composite. These are called **nested relations** because each tuple can have a relation *within it*. Figure 14.9 shows how the EMP_PROJ relation could appear if nesting is allowed. Each tuple represents an employee entity, and a relation PROJS(PNUMBER, HOURS) *within each tuple* represents the

(a)

EMP_PROJ

SSN	ENAME	PROJS	
		PNUMBER	HOURS

(b)

EMP_PROJ

SSN	ENAME	PNUMBER	HOURS
123456789	Smith,John B.	1	32.5
		2	7.5
666884444	Narayan,Ramesh K.	3	40.0
453453453	English,Joyce A.	1	20.0
		2	20.0
333445555	Wong,Franklin T.	2	10.0
		3	10.0
		10	10.0
		20	10.0
999887777	Zelaya,Alicia J.	30	30.0
		10	10.0
987987987	Jabbar,Ahmad V.	10	35.0
		30	5.0
987654321	Wallace,Jennifer S.	30	20.0
		20	15.0
888665555	Borg,James E.	20	null

(c)

EMP_PROJ1

SSN	ENAME

EMP_PROJ2

SSN	PNUMBER	HOURS

Figure 14.9 Normalizing nested relations into 1NF. (a) Schema of the EMP_PROJ relation with a "nested relation" PROJS. (b) Example extension of the EMP_PROJ relation showing nested relations within each tuple. (c) Decomposing EMP_PROJ into 1NF relations EMP_PROJ1 and EMP_PROJ2 by propagating the primary key.

employee's projects and the hours per week that employee works on each project. The schema of this EMP_PROJ relation can be represented as follows:

    EMP_PROJ(SSN, ENAME, {PROJS(PNUMBER, HOURS)})

The set braces { } identify the attribute PROJS as multivalued, and we list the component attributes that form PROJS between parentheses ( ). Interestingly, recent research into the relational model is attempting to allow and formalize nested relations (see Section 13.6), which were disallowed early on by 1NF.

Notice that SSN is the primary key of the EMP_PROJ relation in Figures 14.9(a) and (b), while PNUMBER is the **partial** primary key of the nested relation; that is, within each tuple, the nested relation must have unique values of PNUMBER. To normalize this into 1NF, we remove the nested relation attributes into a new relation and *propagate the primary key* into it; the primary key of the new relation will combine the partial key with the primary key of the original relation. Decomposition and primary key propagation yield the schemas EMP_PROJ1 and EMP_PROJ2 shown in Figure 14.9(c).

This procedure can be applied recursively to a relation with multiple-level nesting to **unnest** the relation into a set of 1NF relations. This is useful in converting an unnormalized relation schema with many levels of nesting into 1NF relations, as we saw in Section 13.6. We also saw in that section that the unnest operator is a part of the nested relational model. Chapter 15 will show that restricting relations to 1NF leads to the problems associated with multivalued dependencies and 4NF.

14.3.3   Second Normal Form

Second normal form (2NF) is based on the concept of *full functional dependency*. A functional dependency $X \rightarrow Y$ is a **full functional dependency** if removal of any attribute A from X means that the dependency does not hold any more; that is, for any attribute $A \in X$, $(X - \{A\})$ *does not* functionally determine Y. A functional dependency $X \rightarrow Y$ is a **partial dependency** if some attribute $A \in X$ can be removed from X and the dependency still holds; that is, for some $A \in X$, $(X - \{A\}) \rightarrow Y$. In Figure 14.3(b), {SSN, PNUMBER} $\rightarrow$ HOURS is a full dependency (neither SSN $\rightarrow$ HOURS nor PNUMBER $\rightarrow$ HOURS holds). However, the dependency {SSN, PNUMBER} $\rightarrow$ ENAME is partial because SSN $\rightarrow$ ENAME holds.

The test for 2NF involves testing for functional dependencies whose left-hand side attributes are part of the primary key. If the primary key contains a single attribute, the test need not be applied at all. A relation schema R is in **2NF** if every nonprime attribute A in R is *fully functionally dependent* on the primary key of R. The EMP_PROJ relation in Figure 14.3(b) is in 1NF but is not in 2NF. The nonprime attribute ENAME violates 2NF because of FD2, as do the nonprime attributes PNAME and PLOCATION because of FD3. The functional dependencies FD2 and FD3 make ENAME, PNAME, and PLOCATION partially dependent on the primary key {SSN, PNUMBER} of EMP_PROJ, thus violating the 2NF test.

If a relation schema is not in 2NF, it can be "second normalized" or "2NF normalized" into a number of 2NF relations in which nonprime attributes are associated only with the part of the primary key on which they are fully functionally dependent. The functional dependencies FD1, FD2, and FD3 in Figure 14.3(b) hence lead to the decomposition of EMP_PROJ into the three relation schemas EP1, EP2, and EP3 shown in Figure 14.10(a), each of which is in 2NF.

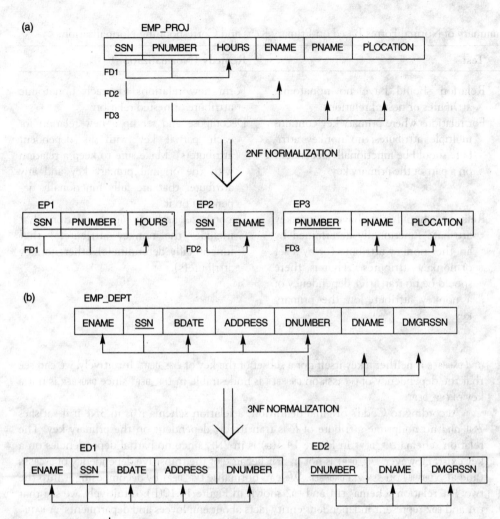

Figure 14.10 The normalization process. (a) Normalizing EMP_PROJ into 2NF relations. (b) Normalizing EMP_DEPT into 3NF relations.

14.3.4 Third Normal Form

Third normal form (3NF) is based on the concept of *transitive dependency*. A functional dependency $X \rightarrow Y$ in a relation schema R is a **transitive dependency** if there is a set of attributes Z that is neither a candidate key nor a subset of any key of R,[13] and both $X \rightarrow Z$ and $Z \rightarrow Y$ hold. The dependency SSN → DMGRSSN is transitive through DNUMBER in EMP_DEPT of Figure 14.3(a) because both the dependencies SSN → DNUMBER and DNUMBER → DMGRSSN hold

---

13. This is the general definition of transitive dependency. Because we are concerned only with primary keys in this section, we allow transitive dependencies where X is the primary key but Z may be (a subset of) a candidate key.

Table 14.1   Summary of Normal Forms Based on Primary Keys and Corresponding Normalization.

Normal Form	Test	Remedy (Normalization)
First (1NF)	Relation should have no nonatomic attributes or nested relations	Form new relations for each nonatomic attribute or nested relation
Second (2NF)	For relations where primary key contains multiple attributes, no nonkey attribute should be functionally dependent on a part of the primary key	Decompose and set up a new relation for each partial key with its dependent attribute(s). Make sure to keep a relation with the original primary key and any attributes that are fully functionally dependent on it.
Third (3NF)	Relation should not have a nonkey attribute functionally determined by another nonkey attribute (or by a set of nonkey attributes.) That is, there should be no transitive dependency of a nonkey attribute on the primary key.	Decompose and set up a relation that includes the nonkey attribute(s) that functionally determine(s) other nonkey attribute(s).

and DNUMBER is neither a key itself nor a subset of the key of EMP_DEPT. Intuitively, we can see that the dependency of DMGRSSN on DNUMBER is undesirable in EMP_DEPT since DNUMBER is not a key of EMP_DEPT.

According to Codd's original definition, a relation schema R is in **3NF** if it satisfies 2NF *and* no nonprime attribute of R is transitively dependent on the primary key. The relation schema EMP_DEPT in Figure 14.3(a) is in 2NF, since no partial dependencies on a key exist. However, EMP_DEPT is not in 3NF because of the transitive dependency of DMGRSSN (and also DNAME) on SSN via DNUMBER. We can normalize EMP_DEPT by decomposing it into the two 3NF relation schemas ED1 and ED2 shown in Figure 14.10(b). Intuitively, we see that ED1 and ED2 represent independent entity facts about employees and departments. A NATURAL JOIN operation on ED1 and ED2 will recover the original relation EMP_DEPT without generating spurious tuples.

Table 14.1 informally summarizes the three normal forms based on primary keys, the tests used in each case, and the corresponding "remedy" or normalization to achieve the normal form.

14.4   General Definitions of Second and Third Normal Forms

In general, we want to design our relation schemas so that they have neither partial nor transitive dependencies, because these types of dependencies cause the update anomalies discussed in Section 14.1.2. The steps for normalization into 3NF relations that we discussed so far disallow partial and transitive dependencies on the *primary key*. These definitions, however, do not take other candidate keys of a relation, if any, into account. In this section we give the more general definitions of 2NF and 3NF that take *all* candidate keys of a relation into account. Notice that this does not affect the definition of 1NF, since it is independent of keys and functional dependencies. As a general definition of **prime attribute,** an attribute that is part of *any candidate key* will be considered as prime. Partial and full functional dependencies and transitive dependencies will now be *with respect to all candidate keys* of a relation.

14.4.1 General Definition of Second Normal Form

A relation schema R is in **second normal form (2NF)** if every nonprime attribute A in R is not partially dependent on *any* key of R.[14] Consider the relation schema LOTS shown in Figure 14.11(a), which describes parcels of land for sale in various counties of a state. Suppose that there are two candidate keys: PROPERTY_ID# and {COUNTY_NAME, LOT#}; that is, lot numbers are unique only within each county but PROPERTY_ID numbers are unique across counties for the entire state.

Based on the two candidate keys PROPERTY_ID# and {COUNTY_NAME, LOT#}, we know that the functional dependencies FD1 and FD2 of Figure 14.11(a) hold. We choose PROPERTY_ID# as the primary key, so it is underlined in Figure 14.11(a); but no special consideration will be given to this key over the other candidate key. Suppose that the following two additional functional dependencies hold in LOTS:

FD3: COUNTRY_NAME → TAX_RATE

FD4: AREA → PRICE

In words, the dependency FD3 says that the tax rate is fixed for a given county (does not vary lot by lot within the same county), while FD4 says that the price of a lot is determined by its area regardless of which county it is in. (Assume that this is the price of the lot for tax purposes.) The LOTS relation schema violates the general definition of 2NF because TAX_RATE is partially dependent on the candidate key {COUNTY_NAME, LOT#}, due to FD3. To normalize LOTS into 2NF, we decompose it into the two relations LOTS1 and LOTS2, shown in Figure 14.11(b). We construct LOTS1 by removing the attribute TAX_RATE that violates 2NF from LOTS and placing it with COUNTY_NAME (the left-hand side of FD3 that causes the partial dependency) into another relation LOTS2. Both LOTS1 and LOTS2 are in 2NF. Notice that FD4 does not violate 2NF and is carried over to LOTS1.

14.4.2 General Definition of Third Normal Form

A relation schema R is in **third normal form (3NF)** if, whenever a *nontrivial* functional dependency $X \rightarrow A$ holds in R, either (a) X is a superkey of R, or (b) A is a prime attribute of R. According to this definition, LOTS2 (Figure 14.11b) is in 3NF. However, FD4 in LOTS1 violates 3NF because AREA is not a superkey and PRICE is not a prime attribute in LOTS1. To

---

14. This definition can be restated as follows: A relation schema R is in 2NF if every nonprime attribute A in R is fully functionally dependent on *every* key of R.

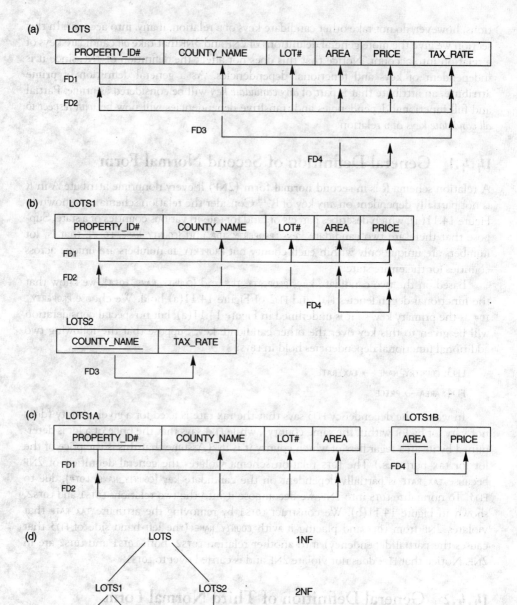

Figure 14.11 Normalization to 2NF and 3NF. (a) The LOTS relation schema and its functional dependencies FD1 through FD4. (b) Decomposing LOTS into the 2NF relations LOTS1 and LOTS2. (c) Decomposing LOTS1 into the 3NF relations LOTS1A and LOTS1B. (d) Summary of normalization of LOTS.

normalize LOTS1 into 3NF, we decompose it into the relation schemas LOTS1A and LOTS1B shown in Figure 14.11(c). We construct LOTS1A by removing the attribute PRICE that violates 3NF from LOTS1 and placing it with AREA (the left-hand side of FD4 that causes the transitive dependency) into another relation LOTS1B. Both LOTS1A and LOTS1B are in 3NF. Two points are worth noting about the general definition of 3NF:

- LOTS1 violates 3NF because PRICE is transitively dependent on each of the candidate keys of LOTS1 via the nonprime attribute AREA.
- This definition can be applied *directly* to test whether a relation schema is in 3NF; it does *not* have to go through 2NF first. If we apply the above 3NF definition to LOTS with the dependencies FD1 through FD4, we find that *both* FD3 and FD4 violate 3NF. We could hence decompose LOTS into LOTS1A, LOTS1B, and LOTS2 directly. Hence the transitive and partial dependencies that violate 3NF can be removed *in any order*.

14.4.3 Interpreting the General Definition of 3NF

A relation schema R violates the general definition of 3NF if a functional dependency $X \rightarrow A$ holds in R that violates *both* conditions (a) and (b) of 3NF. Violating (b) means that A is a nonprime attribute. Violating (a) means that X is not a superset of any key of R; hence, X could be nonprime or it could be a proper subset of a key of R. If X is nonprime, we typically have a transitive dependency that violates 3NF, whereas if X is a proper subset of a key of R we have a partial dependency that violates 3NF (and also 2NF). Hence, we can state a **general alternative definition of 3NF** as follows: A relation schema R is in 3NF if every nonprime attribute of R meets both of the following terms:

- It is fully functionally dependent on every key of R.
- It is nontransitively dependent on every key of R.

14.5 Boyce-Codd Normal Form

Boyce-Codd normal form (BCNF) was proposed as a simpler form of 3NF, but it was found to be stricter than 3NF, because every relation in BCNF is also in 3NF; however, a relation in 3NF is *not necessarily* in BCNF. Intuitively, we can see the need for a stronger normal form than 3NF by going back to the LOTS relation schema of Figure 14.11(a) with its four functional dependencies, FD1 through FD4. Suppose that we have thousands of lots in the relation but the lots are from only two counties: Dekalb and Fulton. Suppose also that lot sizes in Dekalb County are only 0.5, 0.6, 0.7, 0.8, 0.9, and 1.0 acres, whereas lot sizes in Fulton County are restricted to 1.1, 1.2, ..., 1.9, and 2.0 acres. In such a situation we would have the additional functional dependency FD5: AREA $\rightarrow$ COUNTY_NAME. If we add this to the other dependencies, the relation schema LOTS1A still is in 3NF because COUNTY_NAME is a prime attribute.

The area of a lot that determines the county, as specified by FD5, can be represented by 16 tuples in a separate relation R(AREA, COUNTY_NAME), since there are only 16 possible AREA values. This representation reduces the redundancy of repeating the same information in the thousands of LOTS1A tuples. BCNF is a *stronger normal form* that would disallow LOTS1A and suggest the need for decomposing it.

The formal definition of BCNF differs slightly from the definition of 3NF. A relation schema R is in **BCNF** if whenever a *nontrivial* functional dependency $X \rightarrow A$ holds in R, then X is a superkey of R. The only difference between the definitions of BCNF and 3NF is that condition (b) of 3NF, which allows A to be prime, is absent from BCNF.

In our example, FD5 violates BCNF in LOTS1A because AREA is not a superkey of LOTS1A. Note that FD5 satisfies 3NF in LOTS1A because COUNTY_NAME is a prime attribute (condition b), but this condition does not exist in the definition of BCNF. We can decompose LOTS1A into two BCNF relations LOTS1AX and LOTS1AY, shown in Figure 14.12(a). This decomposition loses the functional dependency FD2 because its attributes no longer coexist in the same relation.

In practice, most relation schemas that are in 3NF are also in BCNF. Only if $X \rightarrow A$ holds in a relation schema R with X not being a superkey *and* A being a prime attribute will R be in 3NF but not in BCNF. The relation schema R shown in Figure 14.12(b) illustrates the general case of such a relation. Ideally, relational database design should strive to achieve BCNF or 3NF for every relation schema. Achieving the normalization

Figure 14.12   Boyce-Codd normal form. (a) BCNF normalization with the dependency of FD2 being "lost" in the decomposition. (b) A relation R in 3NF but not in BCNF.

TEACH

STUDENT	COURSE	INSTRUCTOR
Narayan	Database	Mark
Smith	Database	Navathe
Smith	Operating Systems	Ammar
Smith	Theory	Schulman
Wallace	Database	Mark
Wallace	Operating Systems	Ahamad
Wong	Database	Omiecinski
Zelaya	Database	Navathe

Figure 14.13 A relation TEACH that is in 3NF but not in BCNF.

status of just 1NF or 2NF is not considered adequate, as they were developed historically as stepping stones to 3NF and BCNF. Figure 14.13 shows a relation TEACH with the following dependencies:

FD1: {STUDENT, COURSE} → INSTRUCTOR

FD2:[15] INSTRUCTOR → COURSE

Note that {STUDENT, COURSE} is a candidate key for this relation and that the dependencies shown follow the pattern in Figure 14.12(b). Hence this relation is in 3NF but not BCNF. Decomposition of this relation schema into two schemas is not straightforward because it may be decomposed in one of the three possible pairs:

1. {STUDENT, INSTRUCTOR} and {STUDENT, COURSE}.
2. {COURSE, INSTRUCTOR} and {COURSE, STUDENT}
3. {INSTRUCTOR, COURSE} and {INSTRUCTOR, STUDENT}.

All three decompositions "lose" the functional dependency FD1. The desirable decomposition out of the above three is the third one, because it will not generate spurious tuples after a join. A test to determine whether a decomposition is nonadditive (lossless) is discussed in Section 15.1.3 under Property LJ1. In general, a relation not in BCNF should be decomposed so as to meet this property, while possibly forgoing the preservation of all functional dependencies in the decomposed relations, as is the case in this example. Algorithm 15.3 in the next chapter does that and could have been used above to give the same decomposition for TEACH.

---

15. This assumes that "each instructor teaches one course" is a constraint for this application.

14.6 Summary

In this chapter we discussed on an intuitive basis several pitfalls in relational database design, identified informally some of the measures for indicating whether a relation schema is "good" or "bad," and provided informal guidelines for a good design. We then presented some formal concepts that allow us to do relational design in a top-down fashion by analyzing relations individually. We defined this process of design by analysis and decomposition by introducing the process of normalization. The topics discussed in this chapter will be continued in Chapter 15, where we discuss more advanced concepts in relational design theory.

We discussed the problems of update anomalies that occur when redundancies are present in relations. Informal measures of good relation schemas include simple and clear attribute semantics and few nulls in the extensions of relations. A good decomposition should also avoid the problem of generation of spurious tuples as a result of the join operation.

We defined the concept of functional dependency and discussed some of its properties. Functional dependencies are the fundamental source of semantic information about the attributes of a relation schema. We showed how from a given set of functional dependencies, additional dependencies can be inferred using a set of inference rules. We defined the concepts of closure and minimal cover of a set of dependencies, and we provided an algorithm to compute a minimal cover. We also showed how to check whether two sets of functional dependencies are equivalent.

We then described the normalization process for achieving good designs by testing relations for undesirable types of functional dependencies. We provided a treatment of successive normalization based on a predefined primary key in each relation, then relaxed this requirement and provided more general definitions of second normal form (2NF) and third normal form (3NF) that take all candidate keys of a relation into account. We presented examples to illustrate how using the general definition of 3NF a given relation may be analyzed and decomposed to eventually yield a set of relations in 3NF.

Finally, we presented Boyce-Codd normal form (BCNF) and discussed how it is a stronger form of 3NF. We also illustrated how the decomposition of a non-BCNF relation must be done by considering the nonadditive decomposition requirement.

Chapter 15 will present synthesis as well as decomposition algorithms for relational database design based on functional dependencies. Related to decomposition, we will discuss the concepts of *lossless (nonadditive) join* and *dependency preservation*, which are enforced by some of these algorithms. Other topics in Chapter 15 include multivalued dependencies, join dependencies, and additional normal forms that take these dependencies into account.

Review Questions

14.1. Discuss the attribute semantics as an informal measure of goodness for a relation schema.

14.2. Discuss insertion, deletion, and modification anomalies. Why are they considered bad? Illustrate with examples.

14.3. Why are many nulls in a relation considered bad?

14.4. Discuss the problem of spurious tuples and how we may prevent it.

14.5. State the informal guidelines for relation schema design that we discussed. Illustrate how violation of these guidelines may be harmful.

14.6. What is a functional dependency? Who specifies the functional dependencies that hold among the attributes of a relation schema?

14.7. Why can we not infer a functional dependency from a particular relation state?

14.8. Why are Armstrong's inference rules—the three inference rules IR1 through IR3—important?

14.9. What is meant by the completeness and soundness of Armstrong's inference rules?

14.10. What is meant by the closure of a set of functional dependencies?

14.11. When are two sets of functional dependencies equivalent? How can we determine their equivalence?

14.12. What is a minimal set of functional dependencies? Does every set of dependencies have a minimal equivalent set?

14.13. What does the term *unnormalized relation* refer to? How did the normal forms develop historically?

14.14. Define first, second, and third normal forms when only primary keys are considered. How do the general definitions of 2NF and 3NF, which consider all keys of a relation, differ from those that consider only primary keys?

14.15. What undesirable dependencies are avoided when a relation is in 3NF?

14.16. Define Boyce-Codd normal form. How does it differ from 3NF? Why is it considered a stronger form of 3NF?

Exercises

14.17. Suppose that we have the following requirements for a university database that is used to keep track of students' transcripts:

a. The university keeps track of each student's name (SNAME); student number (SNUM); social security number (SSN); current address (SCADDR) and phone (SCPHONE); permanent address (SPADDR) and phone (SPPHONE); birth date (BDATE); sex (SEX); class (CLASS) (freshman, sophomore, ..., graduate); major department (MAJORCODE); minor department (MINORCODE) (if any); and degree program (PROG) (B.A., B.S., ..., PH.D.). Both SSSN and student number have unique values for each student.

b. Each department is described by a name (DNAME), department code (DCODE), office number (DOFFICE), office phone (DPHONE), and college (DCOLLEGE). Both name and code have unique values for each department.

c. Each course has a course name (CNAME), description (CDESC), course number (CNUM), number of semester hours (CREDIT), level (LEVEL), and offering department (CDEPT). The course number is unique for each course.

d. Each section has an instructor (INAME), semester (SEMESTER), year (YEAR), course (SECCOURSE), and section number (SECNUM). The section number distinguishes different sections of the same course that are taught during the same semester/year; its values are 1, 2, 3, ..., up to the total number of sections taught during each semester.

e. A grade record refers to a student (SSN), a particular section, and a grade (GRADE).

Design a relational database schema for this database application. First show all the functional dependencies that should hold among the attributes. Then design relation schemas for the database that are each in 3NF or BCNF. Specify the key attributes of each relation. Note any unspecified requirements, and make appropriate assumptions to render the specification complete.

14.18. Prove or disprove the following inference rules for functional dependencies. A proof can be made either by a proof argument or by using inference rules IR1 through IR3. A disproof should be performed by demonstrating a relation instance that satisfies the conditions and functional dependencies in the left-hand side of the inference rule but does not satisfy the dependencies in the right-hand side.

a. $\{W \to Y, X \to Z\} \models \{WX \to Y\}$.
b. $\{X \to Y\}$ and $Y \supseteq Z \models \{X \to Z\}$.
c. $\{X \to Y, X \to W, WY \to Z\} \models \{X \to Z\}$.
d. $\{XY \to Z, Y \to W\} \models \{XW \to Z\}$.
e. $\{X \to Z, Y \to Z\} \models \{X \to Y\}$.
f. $\{X \to Y, XY \to Z\} \models \{X \to Z\}$.
g. $\{X \to Y, Z \to W\} \models \{XZ \to YW\}$.
h. $\{XY \to Z, Z \to X\} \models \{Z \to Y\}$.
i. $\{X \to Y, Y \to Z\} \models \{X \to YZ\}$.
j. $\{XY \to Z, Z \to W\} \models \{X \to W\}$.

14.19. Consider the following two sets of functional dependencies: $F = \{A \to C, AC \to D, E \to AD, E \to H\}$ and $G = \{A \to CD, E \to AH\}$. Check whether they are equivalent.

14.20. Consider the relation schema EMP_DEPT in Figure 14.3(a) and the following set G of functional dependencies on EMP_DEPT: $G = \{SSN \to \{ENAME, BDATE, ADDRESS, DNUMBER\}, DNUMBER \to \{DNAME, DMGRSSN\}\}$. Calculate the closures $\{SSN\}^+$ and $\{DNUMBER\}^+$ with respect to G.

14.21. Is the set of functional dependencies G in Exercise 14.20 minimal? If not, try to find a minimal set of functional dependencies that is equivalent to G. Prove that your set is equivalent to G.

14.22. What update anomalies occur in the EMP_PROJ and EMP_DEPT relations of Figures 14.3 and 14.4?

14.23. In what normal form is the LOTS relation schema in Figure 14.11(a) with respect to the restrictive interpretations of normal form that take *only the primary key* into account? Would it be in the same normal form if the general definitions of normal form were used?

14.24. Prove that any relation schema with two attributes is in BCNF.

14.25. Why do spurious tuples occur in the result of joining the EMP_PROJ1 and EMP_ LOCS relations of Figure 14.5 (result shown in Figure 14.6)?

14.26. Consider the universal relation $R = \{A, B, C, D, E, F, G, H, I, J\}$ and the set of functional dependencies $F = \{\{A, B\} \to \{C\}, \{A\} \to \{D, E\}, \{B\} \to \{F\}, \{F\} \to \{G, H\}, \{D\} \to \{I, J\}\}$. What is the key for R? Decompose R into 2NF, then 3NF relations.

14.27. Repeat exercise 14.26 for the following different set of functional dependencies
$G = \{\{A, B\} \to \{C\}, \{B, D\} \to \{E, F\}, \{A, D\} \to \{G, H\}, \{A\} \to \{I\}, \{H\} \to \{J\}\}$.

14.28. Consider the following relation:

A	B	C	TUPLE#
10	b1	c1	#1
10	b2	c2	#2
11	b4	c1	#3
12	b3	c4	#4
13	b1	c1	#5
14	b3	c4	#6

a. Given the above extension (state), which of the following dependencies *may hold* in the above relation? If the dependency cannot hold, explain why *by specifying the tuples that cause the violation.*

  i. $A \to B$, ii. $B \to C$, iii. $C \to B$, iv. $B \to A$, v. $C \to A$

b. Does the above relation have a *potential* candidate key? If it does, what is it? If it does not, why not?

14.29. Consider a relation $R(A, B, C, D, E)$ with the following dependencies:

$AB \to C, CD \to E, DE \to B$

Is AB a candidate key of this relation? If not, is ABD? Explain your answer.

14.30. Consider the relation R, which has attributes that hold schedules of courses and sections at a university; $R = \{$CourseNo, SecNo, OfferingDept, Credit-Hours, CourseLevel, InstructorSSN, Semester, Year, Days_Hours, RoomNo, NoOfStudents$\}$. Suppose that the following functional dependencies hold on R:

$\{$CourseNo$\} \to \{$OfferingDept, CreditHours, CourseLevel$\}$

$\{$CourseNo, SecNo, Semester, Year$\} \to$

   $\{$Days_Hours, RoomNo, NoOfStudents, InstructorSSN$\}$

$\{$RoomNo, Days_Hours, Semester, Year$\} \to$

   $\{$InstructorSSN, CourseNo, SecNo$\}$

Try to determine which sets of attributes form keys of R. How would you normalize this relation?

14.31. Consider the following relations for an order-processing application database in ABC Inc.

ORDER (O#, Odate, Cust#, Total_amount)
ORDER-ITEM(O#,I#, Qty_ordered, Total_price, Discount%)

Assume that each item has a different discount; the `Total_price` refers to one item, `Odate` is the date on which the order was placed, the `Total_amount` is the amount of the order. If we apply natural join on the relations `ORDER-ITEM` and `ORDER` in the above database, what does the resulting relation schema look like? What will be its key? Show the FDs in this resulting relation. Is it in 2NF Is it in 3NF? Why or why not? (State assumptions, if you make any.)

14.32. Consider the following relation:

`CAR_SALE (Car #, Date_sold, Salesman#, Commission%, Discount_amt)`

Assume that a car may be sold by multiple salesmen and hence {`Car#`, `Salesman#`} is the primary key. Additional dependencies are

`Date_sold → Discount_amt and Salesman# → Commission%`.

Based on the given primary key, is this relation in 1NF, 2NF, or 3NF? Why or why not? How would you successively normalize it completely?

14.33. Consider the relation for published books:

`BOOK (Book_title, Authorname, Book_type, Listprice, Author_affil, Publisher)`

`Author_affil` refers to the affiliation of author. Suppose the following dependencies exist:

`Book_title → Publisher, Book_type`

`Book_type → Listprice`

`Authorname → Author-affil`

a. What normal form is the relation in? Explain your answer.

b. Apply normalization until you cannot decompose the relations further. State the reasons behind each decomposition.

Selected Bibliography

Functional dependencies were originally introduced by Codd (1970). The original definitions of first, second, and third normal form were also defined in Codd (1972a), where a discussion on update anomalies can be found. Boyce-Codd normal form was defined in Codd (1974). The alternative definition of third normal form is given in Ullman (1988), as is the definition of BCNF that we give here. Ullman (1988), Maier (1983), and Atzeni and De Antonellis (1993) contain many of the theorems and proofs concerning functional dependencies.

Armstrong (1974) shows the soundness and completeness of the inference rules IR1 through IR3. Additional references to relational design theory are given in Chapter 15.

CHAPTER 15

Relational Database Design Algorithms and Further Dependencies

As we discussed in Chapter 14, there are two main approaches for relational database design. The first approach is a **top-down design,** a technique that is currently used most extensively in commercial database application design; this involves designing a conceptual schema in a high-level data model, such as the EER model, and then mapping the conceptual schema into a set of relations using mapping procedures such as the ones discussed in Sections 9.1 and 9.2. Following this, each of the relations is analyzed based on the functional dependencies and assigned primary keys, by applying the normalization procedure in Section 14.3 to remove partial and transitive dependencies if any remain. Analyzing for undesirable dependencies can also be done during the conceptual design itself by analyzing the functional dependencies among attributes within the entity types and relationship types, thereby obviating the need for additional normalization after the mapping is performed.

The second approach is **bottom-up design,** a technique that is a more purist approach and views relational database schema design strictly in terms of functional and other types of dependencies specified on the database attributes. After the database designer specifies the dependencies, a **normalization algorithm** is applied to synthesize the relation schemas. Each individual relation schema should possess the measures of goodness associated with 3NF or BCNF or with some higher normal form. In this chapter, we describe some of these normalization algorithms as well as the other types of dependencies. We also describe the two desirable properties of nonadditive (lossless) joins and dependency preservation in more detail. The normalization algorithms typically start by synthesizing one giant relation schema, called the **universal relation,** which includes all the database attributes. We then repeatedly perform decomposition until it is no longer feasible or no longer desirable, based on the functional and other dependencies specified by the database designer.

Section 15.1 presents several normalization algorithms based on functional dependencies alone that can be used to synthesize 3NF and BCNF schemas. We first describe the two desirable **properties of decompositions**—namely, the dependency preservation property and the lossless (or nonadditive) join property, which are both used by the design algorithms to achieve desirable decompositions. We also show that normal forms are *insufficient on their own* as criteria for a good relational database schema design. The relations must collectively satisfy these two additional properties to qualify as a good design.

We then introduce other types of data dependencies, including multivalued dependencies and join dependencies, which specify constraints that *cannot be* expressed by functional dependencies. Presence of these dependencies leads to the definition of fourth normal form (4NF) and fifth normal form (5NF) respectively. We also define inclusion dependencies and template dependencies (which have not led to any new normal forms so far). We then briefly discuss domain-key normal form (DKNF), which is considered the most general normal form.

It is possible to skip some or all of Sections 15.3, 15.4, and 15.5.

15.1   Algorithms for Relational Database Schema Design

In Section 15.1.1 we give examples to show that looking at an *individual* relation to test whether it is in a higher normal form does not, on its own, guarantee a good design; rather, a *set of relations* that together form the relational database schema must possess certain additional properties to ensure a good design. In Sections 15.1.2 and 15.1.3 we discuss two of these properties: the dependency preservation property and the lossless or nonadditive join property. We present decomposition algorithms that guarantee these properties (which are formal concepts), as well as guaranteeing that the individual relations are normalized appropriately. Section 15.1.4 discusses problems associated with null values, and Section 15.1.5 summarizes the design algorithms and their properties.

15.1.1   Relation Decomposition and Insufficiency of Normal Forms

The relational database design algorithms that we present here start from a single **universal relation schema** $R = \{A_1, A_2, ..., A_n\}$ that includes *all* the attributes of the database. We implicitly make the **universal relation assumption,** which states that every attribute name is unique. The set F of functional dependencies that should hold on the attributes of R is specified by the database designers and is made available to the design algorithms. Using the functional dependencies, the algorithms decompose the universal relation schema R into a set of relation schemas $D = \{R_1, R_2, ..., R_m\}$ that will become the relational database schema; D is called a **decomposition** of R.

We must make sure that each attribute in R will appear in at least one relation schema R_i in the decomposition so that no attributes are "lost"; formally we have

$$\bigcup_{i=1}^{m} R_i = R$$

This is called the **attribute preservation** condition of a decomposition.

Another goal is to have each individual relation R_i in the decomposition D be in BCNF (or 3NF). However, this condition is not sufficient to guarantee a good database design on its own. We must consider the decomposition as a whole, in addition to looking at the individual relations. To illustrate this point, consider the EMP_LOCS(ENAME, PLOCATION) relation of Figure 14.5, which is in 3NF and also in BCNF. In fact, any relation schema with only two attributes is automatically in BCNF.[1] Although EMP_LOCS is in BCNF, it still gives rise to spurious tuples when joined with EMP_PROJ1(SSN, PNUMBER, HOURS, PNAME, PLOCATION), which is not in BCNF (see the result of the natural join in Figure 14.6). Hence, EMP_LOCS represents a particularly bad relation schema because of its convoluted semantics by which PLOCATION gives the location of *one of the projects* on which an employee works. Joining EMP_LOCS with PROJECT(PNAME, PNUMBER, PLOCATION, DNUM) of Figure 14.2—which *is* in BCNF—also gives rise to spurious tuples. We need other criteria that, together with the conditions of 3NF or BCNF, prevent such bad designs. In the next three subsections we discuss such additional conditions that should hold on a decomposition D as a whole.

15.1.2 Decomposition and Dependency Preservation

It would be useful if each functional dependency $X \rightarrow Y$ specified in F either appeared directly in one of the relation schemas R_i in the decomposition D or could be inferred from the dependencies that appear in some R_i. Informally, this is the *dependency preservation condition*. We want to preserve the dependencies because each dependency in F represents a constraint on the database. If one of the dependencies is not represented in some individual relation R_i of the decomposition, we cannot enforce this constraint by dealing with an individual relation; instead, we have to join two or more of the relations in the decomposition and then check that the functional dependency holds in the result of the join operation. This is clearly an inefficient and impractical procedure.

It is not necessary that the exact dependencies specified in F appear themselves in individual relations of the decomposition D. It is sufficient that the union of the dependencies that hold on the individual relations in D be equivalent to F. We now define these concepts more formally.

First we need a preliminary definition. Given a set of dependencies F on R, the **projection** of F on R_i, denoted by $\pi_{R_i}(F)$ where R_i is a subset of R,[2] is the set of dependencies $X \rightarrow Y$ in F^+ such that the attributes in $X \cup Y$ are all contained in R_i. Hence, the projection of F on each relation schema R_i in the decomposition D is the set of functional dependencies in

---

1. As an exercise, the reader should prove that this statement is true.

2. In the second edition of this book, we used the notation $\pi_F(R_i)$ (instead of $\pi_{R_i}(F)$) to denote the projection of F on R_i.

F^+, the closure of F, such that all their left- and right-hand-side attributes are in R_i. We say that a decomposition $D = \{R_1, R_2, ..., R_m\}$ of R is **dependency-preserving** with respect to F if the union of the projections of F on each R_i in D is equivalent to F; that is

$$((\pi_{R1}(F)) \cup ... \cup (\pi_{Rm}(F)))^+ = F^+$$

If a decomposition is not dependency-preserving, some dependency is **lost** in the decomposition. As we mentioned earlier, to check that a lost dependency holds, we must take the JOIN of two or more relations in the decomposition to get a relation that includes all left- and right-hand-side attributes of the lost dependency, and then check that the dependency holds on the result of the JOIN—an option that is not practical.

An example of a decomposition that does not preserve dependencies is shown in Figure 14.12(a), where the functional dependency FD2 is lost when LOTS1A is decomposed into {LOTS1AX, LOTS1AY}. The decompositions in Figure 14.11, however, are dependency-preserving. Similarly, for the example in Figure 14.13, no matter what decomposition is chosen for the relation TEACH(STUDENT, COURSE, INSTRUCTOR) out of the three shown, one or both of the dependencies originally present are lost. We state a claim below related to this property without providing any proof.

Claim 1: It is always possible to find a dependency-preserving decomposition D with respect to F such that each relation R_i in D is in 3NF.

Algorithm 15.1 creates a dependency-preserving decomposition $D = \{R_1, R_2, ..., R_m\}$ of a universal relation R based on a set of functional dependencies F, such that each R_i in D is in 3NF. It guarantees only the dependency-preserving property; it does *not* guarantee the lossless join property that will be discussed in the next section. The first step of Algorithm 15.1 is to find a minimal cover G for F; Algorithm 14.2 can be used for this step.

Algorithm 15.1 Relational synthesis algorithm with dependency preservation

Input: A universal relation R and a set of functional dependencies F on the attributes of R.

1. Find a minimal cover G for F (use Algorithm 14.2);
2. For each left-hand-side X of a functional dependency that appears in G, create a relation schema in D with attributes $\{X \cup \{A_1\} \cup \{A_2\} ... \cup \{A_k\}\}$, where $X \rightarrow A_1$, $X \rightarrow A_2$, ..., $X \rightarrow A_k$ are the only dependencies in G with X as left-hand-side (X is the *key* of this relation);
3. Place any remaining attributes (that have not been placed in any relation) in a single relation schema to ensure the attribute preservation property.

Claim 1A: Every relation schema created by Algorithm 15.1 is in 3NF. (We will not provide a formal proof here;[3] the proof depends on G being a minimal set of dependencies).

---

3. See Maier (1983) or Ullman (1982) for a proof.

It is obvious that all the dependencies in G are preserved by the algorithm because each dependency appears in one of the relations R_i in the decomposition D. Since G is equivalent to F, all the dependencies in F are either preserved directly in the decomposition or are derivable from those in the resulting relations, thus ensuring the dependency preservation property. Algorithm 15.1 is called the **relational synthesis algorithm,** because each relation schema R_i in the decomposition is *synthesized* (constructed) from the set of functional dependencies in G with the same left-hand-side X.

15.1.3 Decomposition and Lossless (Nonadditive) Joins

Another property a decomposition D should possess is the lossless join or nonadditive join property, which ensures that no spurious tuples are generated when a NATURAL JOIN operation is applied to the relations in the decomposition. We already illustrated this problem in Section 14.1.4 with the example of Figures 14.5 and 14.6. Because this is a property of a decomposition of relation *schemas*, the condition of no spurious tuples should hold on *every legal relation state*—that is, every relation state that satisfies the functional dependencies in F. Hence, the lossless join property is always defined with respect to a specific set F of dependencies. Formally, a decomposition $D = \{R_1, R_2, ..., R_m\}$ of R has the **lossless (nonadditive) join property** with respect to the set of dependencies F on R if, for *every* relation state r of R that satisfies F, the following holds, where $*$ is the NATURAL JOIN of all the relations in D:

$$* (\pi_{R1}(r), ..., \pi_{Rm}(r)) = r$$

The word loss in *lossless* refers to *loss of information*, not to loss of tuples. If a decomposition does not have the lossless join property, we may get additional spurious tuples after the PROJECT(π) and NATURAL JOIN($*$) operations are applied; these additional tuples represent erroneous information. We prefer the term **nonadditive join** because it describes the situation more accurately; if the property holds on a decomposition, we are guaranteed that no spurious tuples bearing wrong information are *added* to the result after the PROJECT and NATURAL JOIN operations are applied.

The decomposition of EMP_PROJ(SSN, PNUMBER, HOURS, ENAME, PNAME, PLOCATION) from Figure 14.3 into EMP_LOCS(ENAME, PLOCATION) and EMP_PROJ1(SSN, PNUMBER, HOURS, PNAME, PLOCATION) in Figure 14.5 obviously does not have the lossless join property as illustrated in Figure 14.6. We can use Algorithm 15.2 to check whether a given decomposition D has the lossless join property with respect to a set of functional dependencies F.

Algorithm 15.2 Testing for the lossless (nonadditive) join property

Input: A universal relation R, a decomposition $D = \{R_1, R_2, ..., R_m\}$ of R, and a set F of functional dependencies.

```
1. Create an initial matrix S with one row i for each relation R_i in D,
   and one column j for each attribute A_j in R.
2. Set S(i,j):=b_{ij} for all matrix entries.
   (* each b_{ij} is a distinct symbol associated with indices (i,j) *)
```

3. For each row i representing relation schema R_i
   {for each column j representing attribute A_j
      {if (relation R_i includes attribute A_j) then set $S(i,j) := a_j$;};};
   (* each a_j is a distinct symbol associated with index (j) *)
4. Repeat the following loop until a *complete loop execution* results in no changes to S
      {for each functional dependency $X \rightarrow Y$ in F

         {for all rows in S *which have the same symbols* in the columns corresponding to attributes in X

               {make the symbols in each column that correspond to an attribute in Y be the same in all these rows as follows: if any of the rows has an "a" symbol for the column, set the other rows to that *same* "a" symbol in the column. If no "a" symbol exists for the attribute in any of the rows, choose one of the "b" symbols that appear in one of the rows for the attribute and set the other rows to that same "b" symbol in the column ;};};};
5. If a row is made up entirely of "a" symbols, then the decomposition has the lossless join property; otherwise it does not.

Given a relation R that is decomposed into a number of relations R_1, R_2, ..., R_m, Algorithm 15.2 begins by creating a relation state r in the matrix S. Row i in S represents a tuple t_i (corresponding to relation R_i) which has "a" symbols in the columns that correspond to the attributes of R_i and "b" symbols in the remaining columns. The algorithm then transforms the rows of this matrix (during the loop of step 4) so that they represent tuples that satisfy all the functional dependencies in F. At the end of the loop of applying functional dependencies, any two rows in S—which represent two tuples in r—that agree in their values for the left-hand-side attributes X of a functional dependency $X \rightarrow Y$ in F will also agree in their values for the right-hand-side attributes Y. It can be shown that after applying the loop of Step 4, if any row in S ends up with all "a" symbols, then the decomposition D has the lossless join property with respect to F. If, on the other hand, no row ends up being all "a" symbols, D does not satisfy the lossless join property. In the latter case, the relation state r represented by S at the end of the algorithm will be an example of a relation state r of R that satisfies the dependencies in F but does not satisfy the lossless join condition; thus, this relation serves as a counterexample that proves that D does not have the lossless join property with respect to F. Note that the "a" and "b" symbols have no special meaning at the end of the algorithm.

Figure 15.1(a) shows how we apply Algorithm 15.2 to the decomposition of the EMP_PROJ relation schema from Figure 14.3(b) into the two relation schemas EMP_PROJ1 and EMP_LOCS of Figure 14.5(a). The loop in Step 4 of the algorithm cannot change any "b" symbols to "a" symbols; hence, the resulting matrix S does not have a row with all "a" symbols, and so the decomposition does not have the lossless join property.

Figure 15.1(b) shows another decomposition of EMP_PROJ into EMP, PROJECT, and WORKS_ON that does have the lossless join property, and Figure 15.1(c) shows how we apply the algorithm to that decomposition. Once a row consists only of "a" symbols, we know that

(a) R={SSN, ENAME, PNUMBER, PNAME, PLOCATION, HOURS}   D={R₁, R₂}
     R₁=EMP_LOCS={ENAME, PLOCATION}
     R₂=EMP_PROJ1={SSN, PNUMBER, HOURS, PNAME, PLOCATION}

F={SSN→ENAME;PNUMBER→{PNAME, PLOCATION} ;{SSN,PNUMBER}→HOURS}

	SSN	ENAME	PNUMBER	PNAME	PLOCATION	HOURS
R₁	b_1	a_2	b_{13}	b_{14}	a_5	b_{16}
R₂	a_1	b_{22}	a_3	a_4	a_5	a_6

(no changes to matrix after applying functional dependencies)

(b)

EMP	
SSN	ENAME

PROJECT		
PNUMBER	PNAME	PLOCATION

WORKS_ON		
SSN	PNUMBER	HOURS

(c) R={SSN, ENAME, PNUMBER, PNAME, PLOCATION, HOURS}   D={R₁, R₂, R₃}
     R₁=EMP={SSN, ENAME}
     R₂=PROJ={PNUMBER, PNAME, PLOCATION}
     R₃=WORKS_ON={SSN, PNUMBER, HOURS}

F={SSN→ENAME;PNUMBER→{PNAME, PLOCATION} ;{SSN,PNUMBER}→HOURS}

	SSN	ENAME	PNUMBER	PNAME	PLOCATION	HOURS
R₁	a_1	a_2	b_{13}	b_{14}	b_{15}	b_{16}
R₂	b_{21}	b_{22}	a_3	a_4	a_5	b_{26}
R₃	a_1	b_{32}	a_3	b_{34}	b_{35}	a_6

(original matrix S at start of algorithm)

	SSN	ENAME	PNUMBER	PNAME	PLOCATION	HOURS
R₁	a_1	a_2	b_{13}	b_{14}	b_{15}	b_{16}
R₂	b_{21}	b_{22}	a_3	a_4	a_5	b_{26}
R₃	a_1	b_{32} a_2	a_3	b_{34} a_4	b_{35} a_5	a_6

(matrix S after applying the first two functional dependencies -
last row is all "a" symbols, so we stop)

Figure 15.1 The lossless join testing algorithm. (a) Applying the algorithm to test the
decomposition of EMP_PROJ into EMP_PROJ1 and EMP_LOCS. (b) Another decomposition of EMP_PROJ. (c) Applying the algorithm to the decomposition in
Figure 15.1(b).

the decomposition has the lossless join property, and we can stop applying the functional dependencies (Step 4 of the algorithm) to the matrix S.

Algorithm 15.2 allows us to test whether a particular decomposition D obeys the lossless join property with respect to a set of functional dependencies F. The next question is whether there is an algorithm to decompose a universal relation schema $R = \{A_1, A_2, ..., A_n\}$ into a decomposition $D = \{R_1, R_2, ..., R_m\}$ such that each R_i is in BCNF *and* the decomposition D has the lossless join property with respect to F. The answer is yes, but we need to present some properties of lossless join decompositions in general before describing the algorithm. The first property deals with **binary decompositions**—decomposition of a relation R into two relations. It gives an easier test to apply than Algorithm 15.2, but it is *limited* to binary decompositions only.

PROPERTY LJ1

A decomposition $D = \{R_1, R_2\}$ of R has the lossless join property with respect to a set of functional dependencies F on R *if and only if* either

- The FD $((R_1 \cap R_2) \rightarrow (R_1 - R_2))$ is in F^+, or
- The FD $((R_1 \cap R_2) \rightarrow (R_2 - R_1))$ is in F^+.

You should verify that this property holds with respect to our informal successive normalization examples in Sections 14.3 and 14.4. The second property deals with applying successive decompositions.

PROPERTY LJ2

If a decomposition $D = \{R_1, R_2, ..., R_m\}$ of R has the lossless join property with respect to a set of functional dependencies F on R, and if a decomposition $D_1 = \{Q_1, Q_2, ..., Q_k\}$ of R_i has the lossless join property with respect to the projection of F on R_i, then the decomposition $D_2 = \{R_1, R_2, ..., R_{i-1}, Q_1, Q_2, ..., Q_k, R_{i+1}, ..., R_m\}$ of R has the lossless join property with respect to F.

Property LJ2 says that, *if* a decomposition D already has the lossless join property—with respect to F—and we further decompose one of the relation schemas R_i in D into another decomposition D_1 that has the lossless join property—with respect to $\pi_{Ri}(F)$—*then* replacing R_i in D by D_1 will result in a decomposition that also has the lossless join property—with respect to F. We implicitly assumed this property in the informal normalization examples of Sections 14.3 and 14.4. For example, in Figure 14.11, as we normalized the LOTS relation into LOTS1 and LOTS2, this decomposition was assumed to be lossless. Decomposing LOTS1 further into LOTS1A and LOTS1B results in three relations: LOTS1A, LOTS1B, and LOTS2; this eventual decomposition maintains the losslessness by virtue of Property LJ2 above.

Algorithm 15.3 utilizes properties LJ1 and LJ2 to create a lossless join decomposition $D = \{R_1, R_2, ..., R_m\}$ of a universal relation R based on a set of functional dependencies F, such that each R_i in D is in BCNF.

Algorithm 15.3 Relational decomposition into BCNF relations with lossless join property

Input: A universal relation R and a set of functional dependencies F on the attributes of R.

1. Set D := {R};
2. While there is a relation schema Q in D that is not in BCNF do
   {
   choose a relation schema Q in D that is not in BCNF;
   find a functional dependency X → Y in Q that violates BCNF;
   replace Q in D by two relation schemas (Q − Y) and (X ∪ Y);
   };

Each time through the loop in Algorithm 15.3, we decompose one relation schema Q that is not in BCNF into two relation schemas. According to properties LJ1 and LJ2, the decomposition D has the lossless join property. At the end of the algorithm, all relation schemas in D will be in BCNF. The reader can check that the normalization example in Figures 14.11 and 14.12 basically follows this algorithm. The functional dependencies FD3, FD4, and later FD5 violate BCNF, so the LOTS relation is decomposed appropriately into BCNF relations and the decomposition then satisfies the lossless join property. Similarly, if we apply the algorithm to the TEACH relation schema from Figure 14.13, it is decomposed into TEACH1(INSTRUCTOR, STUDENT) and TEACH2(INSTRUCTOR, COURSE) because the dependency FD2 : INSTRUCTOR → COURSE violates BCNF.

In Step 2 of Algorithm 15.3, it is necessary to determine whether a relation schema Q is in BCNF or not. One method for doing this is to test, for each functional dependency $X \rightarrow Y$ in Q, whether X^+ fails to include all the attributes in Q. If that is the case, then $X \rightarrow Y$ violates BCNF because X cannot then be a (super)key of Q. Another technique is based on an observation that whenever a relation schema Q violates BCNF, there exists a pair of attributes A and B in Q such that $\{Q - \{A, B\}\} \rightarrow A$; by computing the closure $\{Q - \{A, B\}\}^+$ for each pair of attributes $\{A, B\}$ of Q, and checking whether the closure includes A (or B), we can determine whether Q is in BCNF.

If we want a decomposition to have the lossless join property *and* to preserve dependencies, we have to be satisfied with relation schemas in 3NF rather than BCNF. A simple modification to Algorithm 15.1, shown as Algorithm 15.4, yields a decomposition D of R that does the following:

- Preserves dependencies.
- Has the lossless join property.
- Is such that each resulting relation schema in the decomposition is in 3NF.

Algorithm 15.4 Relational synthesis algorithm with dependency preservation and lossless join property

Input: A universal relation R and a set of functional dependencies F on the attributes of R.

1. Find a minimal cover G for F (use Algorithm 14.2).
2. For each left-hand-side X of a functional dependency that appears in G create a relation schema in D with attributes $\{X \cup \{A_1\} \cup \{A_2\}$ ... $\cup \{A_k\}\}$, where $X \rightarrow A_1$, $X \rightarrow A_2$, ..., $X \rightarrow A_k$ are the only dependencies in G with X as left-hand-side (X is the *key* of this relation).
3. If none of the relation schemas in D contains a key of R, then create one more relation schema in D that contains attributes that form a key of R.

It can be shown that the decomposition formed from the set of relation schemas created by the preceding algorithm is dependency-preserving *and* has the lossless join property. In addition, each relation schema in the decomposition is in 3NF. This algorithm is an improvement over Algorithm 15.1 in that the former guaranteed only dependency preservation.[4]

Step 3 of Algorithm 15.4 involves identifying a key K of R. Algorithm 15.4a can be used to identify a key K of R based on the set of given functional dependencies F. We start by setting K to all the attributes of R; we then remove one attribute at a time and check whether the remaining attributes still form a superkey. Notice that the set of functional dependencies used to determine a key in Algorithm 15.4a could be either F or G, since they are equivalent. Notice, too, that Algorithm 15.4a determines only *one key* out of the possible candidate keys for R; the key returned depends on the order in which attributes are removed from R in Step 2.

Algorithm 15.4a Finding a key K for relation schema R based on a set F of functional dependencies

1. Set $K := R$.
2. For each attribute A in K
   {compute $(K - A)^+$ with respect to F;
   If $(K - A)^+$ contains all the attributes in R, then set $K := K - \{A\}$};

It is not always possible to find a decomposition into relation schemas that preserves dependencies and allows each relation schema in the decomposition to be in BCNF (instead of 3NF as in Algorithm 15.4). We can check the 3NF relation schemas in the decomposition individually to see whether each satisfies BCNF. If some relation schema R_i is not in BCNF, we can choose to decompose it further or to leave it as it is in 3NF (with some possible update anomalies). The fact that we cannot always find a decomposition into relation schemas in BCNF that preserves dependencies can be illustrated by the examples in Figure 14.12. The relations LOTS1A (Figure 14.12a) and TEACH (Figure 14.13) are not in BCNF but are in 3NF. Any attempt to decompose either relation further into BCNF rela-

---

4. Step 3 of Algorithm 15.1 is not needed in Algorithm 15.4 to preserve attributes because the key will include any unplaced attributes; these are the attributes that do not participate in any functional dependency.

tions results in loss of the dependency FD2 : {COUNTY_NAME, LOT#} → {PROPERTY_ID#, AREA} in LOTS1A or loss of FD1: {STUDENT, COURSE} → INSTRUCTOR in TEACH.

It is important to note that the theory of lossless join decompositions is based on the assumption that *no null values are allowed for the join attributes*. The next section discusses some of the problems that nulls may cause in relational decompositions.

15.1.4 Problems with Null Values and Dangling Tuples

We must carefully consider the problems associated with nulls when designing a relational database schema. There is no fully satisfactory relational design theory as yet that includes null values. One problem occurs when some tuples have null values for attributes that will be used to JOIN individual relations in the decomposition. To illustrate this, consider the database shown in Figure 15.2(a), where two relations EMPLOYEE and DEPARTMENT are shown. The last two employee tuples—Berger and Benitez—represent newly hired employees who have not yet been assigned to a department (assume that this does not violate any integrity constraints). Now suppose that we want to retrieve a list of (ENAME, DNAME) values for all the employees. If we apply the NATURAL JOIN operation on EMPLOYEE and DEPARTMENT (Figure 15.2b), the two aforementioned tuples will *not* appear in the result. The OUTER JOIN operation, discussed in Chapter 7, can deal with this problem. Recall that, if we take the LEFT OUTER JOIN of EMPLOYEE with DEPARTMENT, tuples in EMPLOYEE that have null for the join attribute will still appear in the result, joined with an "imaginary" tuple in DEPARTMENT that has nulls for all its attribute values. Figure 15.2(c) shows the result.

In general, whenever a relational database schema is designed where two or more relations are interrelated via foreign keys, particular care must be devoted to watching for potential null values in foreign keys. This can cause unexpected loss of information in queries that involve joins on that foreign key. Moreover, if nulls occur in other attributes, such as SALARY, their effect on built-in functions such as SUM and AVERAGE must be carefully evaluated.

A related problem is that of **dangling tuples**, which may occur if we carry a decomposition too far. Suppose that we decompose the EMPLOYEE relation of Figure 15.2(a) further into EMPLOYEE_1 and EMPLOYEE_2, shown in Figure 15.3(a) and 15.3(b).[5] If we apply the NATURAL JOIN operation to EMPLOYEE_1 and EMPLOYEE_2, we get the original EMPLOYEE relation. However, we may use the alternative representation, shown in Figure 15.3(c), where we *do not include a tuple* in EMPLOYEE_3 if the employee has not been assigned a department (instead of including a tuple with null for DNUM as in EMPLOYEE_2). If we use EMPLOYEE_3 instead of EMPLOYEE_2 and apply a NATURAL JOIN on EMPLOYEE_1 and EMPLOYEE_3, the tuples for Berger and Benitez will not appear in the result; these are called **dangling tuples** because they are represented in only one of the two relations that represent employees and hence are lost if we apply an (inner) join operation.

---

5. This sometimes happens when we apply vertical fragmentation to a relation in the context of a distributed database (see Chapter 24).

(a)

EMPLOYEE

ENAME	SSN	BDATE	ADDRESS	DNUM
Smith, John B.	123456789	1965-01-09	731 Fondren, Houston, TX	5
Wong, Franklin T.	333445555	1955-12-08	638 Voss, Houston, TX	5
Zelaya, Alicia J.	999887777	1968-07-19	3321 Castle, Spring, TX	4
Wallace, Jennifer S.	987654321	1941-06-20	291 Berry, Bellaire, TX	4
Narayan, Ramesh K.	666884444	1962-09-15	975 Fire Oak, Humble, TX	5
English, Joyce A.	453453453	1972-07-31	5631 Rice, Houston, TX	5
Jabbar, Ahmad V.	987987987	1969-03-29	980 Dallas, Houston, TX	4
Borg, James E.	888665555	1937-11-10	450 Stone, Houston, TX	1
Berger, Anders C.	999775555	1965-04-26	6530 Braes, Bellaire, TX	null
Benitez, Carlos M.	888664444	1963-01-09	7654 Beech, Houston, TX	null

DEPARTMENT

DNAME	DNUM	DMGRSSN
Research	5	333445555
Administration	4	987654321
Headquarters	1	888665555

(b)

ENAME	SSN	BDATE	ADDRSS	DNUM	DNAME	DMGRSSN
Smith, John B.	123456789	1965-01-09	731 Fondren, Houston, TX	5	Research	333445555
Wong, Franklin T.	333445555	1955-12-08	638 Voss, Houston, TX	5	Research	333445555
Zelaya, Alicia J.	999887777	1968-07-19	3321 Castle, Spring, TX	4	Administration	987654321
Wallace, Jennifer S.	987654321	1941-06-20	291 Berry, Bellaire, TX	4	Administration	987654321
Narayan, Ramesh K.	666884444	1962-09-15	975 Fire Oak, Humble, TX	5	Research	333445555
English, Joyce A.	453453453	1972-07-31	5631 Rice, Houston, TX	5	Research	333445555
Jabbar, Ahmad V.	987987987	1969-03-29	980 Dallas, Houston, TX	4	Administration	987654321
Borg, James E.	888665555	1937-11-10	450 Stone, Houston, TX	1	Headquarters	888665555

(c)

ENAME	SSN	BDATE	ADDRSS	DNUM	DNAME	DMGRSSN
Smith, John B.	123456789	1965-01-09	731 Fondren, Houston, TX	5	Research	333445555
Wong, Franklin T.	333445555	1955-12-08	638 Voss, Houston, TX	5	Research	333445555
Zelaya, Alicia J.	999887777	1968-07-19	3321 Castle, Spring, TX	4	Administration	987654321
Wallace, Jennifer S.	987654321	1941-06-20	291 Berry, Bellaire, TX	4	Administration	987654321
Narayan, Ramesh K.	666884444	1962-09-15	975 Fire Oak, Humble, TX	5	Research	333445555
English, Joyce A.	453453453	1972-07-31	5631 Rice, Houston, TX	5	Research	333445555
Jabbar, Ahmad V.	987987987	1969-03-29	980 Dallas, Houston, TX	4	Administration	987654321
Borg, James E.	888665555	1937-11-10	450 Stone, Houston, TX	1	Headquarters	888665555
Berger, Anders C.	999775555	1965-04-26	6530 Braes, Bellaire, TX	null	null	null
Benitez, Carlos M.	888664444	1963-01-09	7654 Beech, Houston, TX	null	null	null

Figure 15.2   Illustrating null value join issues. (a) A database with nulls for some join attributes. (b) Result of applying NATURAL JOIN to the EMPLOYEE and DEPARTMENT relations. (c) Result of applying OUTER JOIN to EMPLOYEE and DEPARTMENT.

(a) **EMPLOYEE_1**

ENAME	SSN	BDATE	ADDRESS
Smith, John B.	123456789	1965-01-09	731 Fondren, Houston, TX
Wong, Franklin T.	333445555	1955-12-08	638 Voss, Houston, TX
Zelaya, Alicia J.	999887777	1968-07-19	3321 Castle, Spring, TX
Wallace, Jennifer S.	987654321	1941-06-20	291 Berry, Bellaire, TX
Narayan, Ramesh K.	666884444	1962-09-15	975 Fire Oak, Humble, TX
English, Joyce A.	453453453	1972-07-31	5631 Rice, Houston, TX
Jabbar, Ahmad V.	987987987	1969-03-29	980 Dallas, Houston, TX
Borg, James E.	888665555	1937-11-10	450 Stone, Houston, TX
Berger, Anders C.	999775555	1965-04-26	6530 Braes, Bellaire, TX
Benitez, Carlos M.	888664444	1963-01-09	7654 Beech, Houston, TX

(b) **EMPLOYEE_2**

SSN	DNUM
123456789	5
333445555	5
999887777	4
987654321	4
666884444	5
453453453	5
987987987	4
888665555	1
999775555	null
888664444	null

(c) **EMPLOYEE_3**

SSN	DNUM
123456789	5
333445555	5
999887777	4
987654321	4
666884444	5
453453453	5
987987987	4
888665555	1

Figure 15.3 The "dangling tuple" problem. (a) The relation EMPLOYEE_1 (includes all attributes of EMPLOYEE except DNUMBER). (b) The relation EMPLOYEE_2 (includes DNUMBER attribute with null values). (c) The relation EMPLOYEE_3 (includes DNUMBER attribute but does not include tuples for which DNUMBER has null values).

15.1.5 Discussion of Normalization Algorithms

One of the problems with the normalization algorithms we described is that the database designer must first specify *all* the relevant functional dependencies among the database attributes. This is not a simple task for a large database with hundreds of attributes. Failure to specify one or two important dependencies may result in an undesirable design. Another problem is that these algorithms are not deterministic in general. For example, the *synthesis algorithms* (Algorithms 15.1 and 15.4) require the specification of a minimal cover G for the set of functional dependencies F. Because there may be in general many minimal covers corresponding to F, the algorithm can give different designs depending on the particular minimal cover used. Some of these designs may not be desirable. The *decomposition algorithm* (Algorithm 15.3) depends on the order in which the functional dependencies are supplied to the algorithm; again it is possible that many different designs may arise corresponding to the same set of functional dependencies, depending on the order in which such dependencies are considered for violation of BCNF. Again, some of the designs may be quite superior while others may be undesirable.

15.2 Multivalued Dependencies and Fourth Normal Form

So far we have discussed only functional dependency, which is by far the most important type of dependency in relational database design theory. However, in many cases relations have constraints that cannot be specified as functional dependencies. In this section, we discuss the concept of *multivalued dependency* (MVD) and define *fourth normal form*, which is based on this dependency. Multivalued dependencies are a consequence of first normal form (1NF) (see Section 14.3.2), which disallowed an attribute in a tuple to have a *set of values*. If we have two or more multivalued *independent* attributes in the same relation schema, we get into a problem of having to repeat every value of one of the attributes with every value of the other attribute to keep the relation state consistent and to maintain the independence among the attributes involved. This constraint is specified by a multivalued dependency.

For example, consider the relation EMP shown in Figure 15.4(a). A tuple in this EMP relation represents the fact that an employee whose name is ENAME works on the project whose name is PNAME and has a dependent whose name is DNAME. An employee may work on several projects and may have several dependents, and the employee's projects and dependents are independent of one another.[6] To keep the relation state consistent, we must have a separate tuple to represent every combination of an employee's dependent and an employee's project. This constraint is specified as a multivalued dependency on the EMP relation. Informally, whenever two *independent* 1:N relationships A:B and A:C are mixed in the same relation, an MVD may arise.

15.2.1 Formal Definition of Multivalued Dependency

Formally, a **multivalued dependency** (MVD) $X \twoheadrightarrow Y$ specified on relation schema R, where X and Y are both subsets of R, specifies the following constraint on any relation state r of R: If two tuples t_1 and t_2 exist in r such that $t_1[X] = t_2[X]$, then two tuples t_3 and t_4 should also exist in r with the following properties,[7] where we use Z to denote $(R - (X \cup Y))$:[8]

- $t_3[X] = t_4[X] = t_1[X] = t_2[X]$.
- $t_3[Y] = t_1[Y]$ and $t_4[Y] = t_2[Y]$.
- $t_3[Z] = t_2[Z]$ and $t_4[Z] = t_1[Z]$.

---

6. In an ER diagram, each would be represented as a multivalued attribute or as a weak entity type (see Chapter 3).

7. The tuples t_1, t_2, t_3, and t_4 are not necessarily distinct.

8. Z is shorthand for the attributes remaining in R after the attributes in $(X \cup Y)$ are removed from R.

(a) **EMP**

ENAME	PNAME	DNAME
Smith	X	John
Smith	Y	Anna
Smith	X	Anna
Smith	Y	John

(b) **EMP_PROJECTS**

ENAME	PNAME
Smith	X
Smith	Y

EMP_DEPENDENTS

ENAME	DNAME
Smith	John
Smith	Anna

(c) **SUPPLY**

SNAME	PARTNAME	PROJNAME
Smith	Bolt	ProjX
Smith	Nut	ProjY
Adamsky	Bolt	ProjY
Walton	Nut	ProjZ
Adamsky	Nail	ProjX
Adamsky	Bolt	ProjX
Smith	Bolt	ProjY

(d) **R1**

SNAME	PARTNAME
Smith	Bolt
Smith	Nut
Adamsky	Bolt
Walton	Nut
Adamsky	Nail

R2

SNAME	PROJNAME
Smith	ProjX
Smith	ProjY
Adamsky	ProjY
Walton	ProjZ
Adamsky	ProjX

R3

PARTNAME	PROJNAME
Bolt	ProjX
Nut	ProjY
Bolt	ProjY
Nut	ProjZ
Nail	ProjX

Figure 15.4   Fourth and fifth normal form. (a) The EMP relation with two MVDs: ENAME $\longrightarrow\!\!\!\!\rightarrow$ PNAME and ENAME $\longrightarrow\!\!\!\!\rightarrow$ DNAME. (b) Decomposing EMP into two relations in 4NF. (c) The relation SUPPLY with no MVDs satisfies 4NF but does not satisfy 5NF if the JD(R1, R2, R3) holds. (d) Decomposing SUPPLY into three 5NF relations.

Whenever $X \longrightarrow\!\!\!\!\rightarrow Y$ holds, we say that X **multidetermines** Y. Because of the symmetry in the definition, whenever $X \longrightarrow\!\!\!\!\rightarrow Y$ holds in R, so does $X \longrightarrow\!\!\!\!\rightarrow Z$. Hence, $X \longrightarrow\!\!\!\!\rightarrow Y$ implies $X \longrightarrow\!\!\!\!\rightarrow Z$, and therefore it is sometimes written as $X \longrightarrow\!\!\!\!\rightarrow Y | Z$.

The formal definition specifies that, given a particular value of X, the set of values of Y determined by this value of X is completely determined by X alone and *does not depend* on the values of the remaining attributes Z of R. Hence, whenever two tuples exist that have distinct values of Y but the same value of X, these values of Y must be repeated in separate tuples with *every distinct value of* Z that occurs with that same value of X. This informally corresponds to Y being a multivalued attribute of the entities represented by tuples in R.

In Figure 15.4(a) the MVDs ENAME $\twoheadrightarrow$ PNAME and ENAME $\twoheadrightarrow$ DNAME (or ENAME $\twoheadrightarrow$ PNAME|DNAME) hold in the EMP relation. The employee with ENAME 'Smith' works on projects with PNAME 'X' and 'Y' and has two dependents with DNAME 'John' and 'Anna'. If we stored only the first two tuples in EMP (<'Smith', 'X', 'John'> and <'Smith', 'Y', 'Anna'>), we would incorrectly show associations between project 'X' and 'John' and between project 'Y' and 'Anna'; these should not be conveyed, because no such meaning is intended in this relation. Hence, we must store the other two tuples (<'Smith', 'X', 'Anna'> and <'Smith', 'Y', 'John'>) to show that {'X', 'Y'} and {'John', 'Anna'} are associated only with 'Smith'; that is, there is no association between PNAME and DNAME— which means that the two attributes are independent.

An MVD X $\twoheadrightarrow$ Y in R is called a **trivial MVD** if (a) Y is a subset of X, or (b) X ∪ Y = R. For example, the relation EMP_PROJECTS in Figure 15.4(b) has the trivial MVD ENAME $\twoheadrightarrow$ PNAME. An MVD that satisfies neither (a) nor (b) is called a **nontrivial MVD**. A trivial MVD will hold in *any* relation state r of R; it is called trivial because it does not specify any significant or meaningful constraint on R.

If we have a nontrivial MVD in a relation, we may have to repeat values redundantly in the tuples. In the EMP relation of Figure 15.4(a), the values 'X' and 'Y' of PNAME are repeated with each value of DNAME (or by symmetry, the values 'John' and 'Anna' of DNAME are repeated with each value of PNAME). This redundancy is clearly undesirable. However, the EMP schema is in BCNF because *no* functional dependencies hold in EMP. Therefore, we need to define a fourth normal form that is stronger than BCNF and disallows relation schemas such as EMP. We first discuss some of the properties of MVDs and consider how they are related to functional dependencies.

15.2.2 Inference Rules for Functional and Multivalued Dependencies

As with functional dependencies (FDs), inference rules for multivalued dependencies (MVDs) have been developed. It is better, though, to develop a unified framework that includes both FDs and MVDs so that both types of constraints can be considered together. The following inference rules IR1 through IR8 form a sound and complete set for inferring functional and multivalued dependencies from a given set of dependencies. Assume that all attributes are included in a "universal" relation schema $R = \{A_1, A_2, ..., A_n\}$ and that X, Y, Z, and W are subsets of R.

IR1 (reflexive rule for FDs): If $X \supseteq Y$, then $X \rightarrow Y$.

IR2 (augmentation rule for FDs): $\{X \rightarrow Y\} \vDash XZ \rightarrow YZ$.

IR3 (transitive rule for FDs): $\{X \rightarrow Y, Y \rightarrow Z\} \vDash X \rightarrow Z$.

IR4 (complementation rule for MVDs): $\{X \twoheadrightarrow Y\} \vDash \{X \twoheadrightarrow (R - (X \cup Y))\}$.

IR5 (augmentation rule for MVDs): If $X \twoheadrightarrow Y$ and $W \supseteq Z$ then $WX \twoheadrightarrow YZ$.

IR6 (transitive rule for MVDs): $\{X \twoheadrightarrow Y, Y \twoheadrightarrow Z\} \models X \twoheadrightarrow (Z - Y)$.

IR7 (replication rule for FD to MVD): $\{X \to Y\} \models X \twoheadrightarrow Y$.

IR8 (coalescence rule for FDs and MVDs): If $X \twoheadrightarrow Y$ and there exists W with the properties that (a) $W \cap Y$ is empty, (b) $W \to Z$, and (c) $Y \supseteq Z$, then $X \to Z$.

IR1 through IR3 are Armstrong's inference rules for FDs alone. IR4 through IR6 are inference rules pertaining to MVDs only. IR7 and IR8 relate FDs and MVDs. In particular, IR7 says that a functional dependency is a *special case* of a multivalued dependency; that is, every FD is also an MVD because it satisfies the formal definition of MVD. Basically, an FD $X \to Y$ is an MVD $X \twoheadrightarrow Y$ with the *additional restriction* that at most one value of Y is associated with each value of X.[9] Given a set F of functional and multivalued dependencies specified on $R = \{A_1, A_2, ..., A_n\}$, we can use IR1 through IR8 to infer the (complete) set of all dependencies (functional or multivalued) F^+ that will hold in every relation state r of R that satisfies F. We again call F^+ the **closure** of F.

15.2.3 Fourth Normal Form

We now present the definition of **fourth normal form (4NF),** which is violated when a relation has undesirable multivalued dependencies, and hence can be used to identify and decompose such relations. A relation schema R is in 4NF with respect to a set of dependencies F (that includes functional dependencies and multivalued dependencies) if, for every *nontrivial* multivalued dependency $X \twoheadrightarrow Y$ in F^+, X is a superkey for R.

The EMP relation of Figure 15.4(a) is not in 4NF because in the nontrivial MVDs ENAME $\twoheadrightarrow$ PNAME and ENAME $\twoheadrightarrow$ DNAME, ENAME is not a superkey of EMP. We decompose EMP into EMP_PROJECTS and EMP_DEPENDENTS, shown in Figure 15.4(b). Both EMP_PROJECTS and EMP_DEPENDENTS are in 4NF, because the MVDs ENAME $\twoheadrightarrow$ PNAME in EMP_PROJECTS and ENAME $\twoheadrightarrow$ DNAME in EMP_DEPENDENTS are trivial MVDs. No other nontrivial MVDs hold in either EMP_PROJECTS or EMP_DEPENDENTS. No FDs hold in these relation schemas either.

To illustrate the importance of 4NF, Figure 15.5(a) shows the EMP relation with an additional employee, 'Brown', who has three dependents ('Jim', 'Joan', and 'Bob') and works on four different projects ('W', 'X', 'Y', and 'Z'). There are 16 tuples in EMP in Figure 15.5(a). If we decompose EMP into EMP_PROJECTS and EMP_DEPENDENTS, as shown in Figure 15.5(b), we need to store a total of only 11 tuples in both relations. Not only would the decomposition save on storage, but also the update anomalies associated with multivalued dependencies are avoided. For example, if Brown starts working on another project, we must insert three tuples in EMP—one for each dependent. If we forget to insert any one of those, the relation violates the MVD and becomes inconsistent in that it incorrectly implies a relationship between project and dependent. However, only a single tuple need be inserted in the 4NF relation EMP_PROJECTS. Similar problems occur with deletion and modification anomalies if a relation is not in 4NF.

---

9. That is, the set of values of Y determined by a value of X is restricted to being a *singleton set* with only one value.

(a) **EMP**

ENAME	PNAME	DNAME
Smith	X	John
Smith	Y	Anna
Smith	X	Anna
Smith	Y	John
Brown	W	Jim
Brown	X	Jim
Brown	Y	Jim
Brown	Z	Jim
Brown	W	Joan
Brown	X	Joan
Brown	Y	Joan
Brown	Z	Joan
Brown	W	Bob
Brown	X	Bob
Brown	Y	Bob
Brown	Z	Bob

(b) **EMP_PROJECTS**

ENAME	PNAME
Smith	X
Smith	Y
Brown	W
Brown	X
Brown	Y
Brown	Z

EMP_DEPENDENTS

ENAME	DNAME
Smith	Anna
Smith	John
Brown	Jim
Brown	Joan
Brown	Bob

Figure 15.5   Benefits of 4NF. (a) The EMP relation with some additional tuples. (b) Projecting EMP on EMP_PROJECTS and EMP_DEPENDENTS.

The EMP relation in Figure 15.4(a) is not in 4NF, because it represents two *independent* 1:N relationships—one between employees and the projects they work on and the other between employees and their dependents. We sometimes have a relationship between three entities that depends on all three participating entities, such as the SUPPLY relation shown in Figure 15.4(c). (Consider only the tuples in Figure 15.4(c) *above* the dotted line for now.) In this case a tuple represents a supplier supplying a specific part *to a particular project*, so there are *no* nontrivial MVDs. The SUPPLY relation is already in 4NF and should not be decomposed. Notice that relations containing nontrivial MVDs tend to be **all key relations**—that is, their key is all their attributes taken together.

15.2.4   Lossless Join Decomposition into 4NF Relations

Whenever we decompose a relation schema R into $R_1 = (X \cup Y)$ and $R_2 = (R - Y)$ based on an MVD $X \twoheadrightarrow Y$ that holds in R, the decomposition has the lossless join property. It can be shown that this is a necessary and sufficient condition for decomposing a schema into two schemas that have the lossless join property, as given by property LJ1′.

PROPERTY LJ1′

The relation schemas R_1 and R_2 form a lossless join decomposition of R if and only if $(R_1 \cap R_2) \twoheadrightarrow (R_1 - R_2)$ (or by symmetry, if and only if $(R_1 \cap R_2) \twoheadrightarrow (R_2 - R_1)$).

This is similar to property LJ1 of Section 15.1.3, except that LJ1 dealt with FDs only, whereas LJ1′ deals with both FDs and MVDs (recall that an FD is also an MVD). We can use a slight modification of Algorithm 15.3 to develop Algorithm 15.5, which creates a lossless join decomposition into relation schemas that are in 4NF (rather than in BCNF). As with Algorithm 15.3, Algorithm 15.5 does *not* necessarily produce a decomposition that preserves FDs.

Algorithm 15.5 Relational decomposition into 4NF relations with lossless join property

Input: A universal relation R and a set of functional and multivalued dependencies F.

```
1. Set D := { R };
2. While there is a relation schema Q in D that is not in 4NF do
   {
   choose a relation schema Q in D that is not in 4NF;
   find a nontrivial MVD X ⟶⟶ Y in Q that violates 4NF;
   replace Q in D by two relation schemas (Q − Y) and (X ∪ Y);
   };
```

15.3 Join Dependencies and Fifth Normal Form

We saw that LJ1 and LJ1' give the condition for a relation schema R to be decomposed into two schemas R_1 and R_2, where the decomposition has the lossless join property. However, in some cases there may be no lossless join decomposition of R into *two* relation schemas but there may be a lossless join decomposition into *more than two* relation schemas. Moreover, there may be no functional dependency in R that violates any normal form up to BCNF and there may be no nontrivial MVD present in R either that violates 4NF. We then resort to another dependency called the join dependency and if it is present, carry out a *multiway decomposition* into fifth normal form (5NF). It is important to note that such a dependency is very difficult to detect in practice and therefore, normalization into 5NF is considered very rarely in practice.

A **join dependency** (JD), denoted by $JD(R_1, R_2, ..., R_n)$, specified on relation schema R, specifies a constraint on the states r of R. The constraint states that every legal state r of R should have a lossless join decomposition into $R_1, R_2, ..., R_n$; that is, for every such r we have

$$* (\pi_{R1}(r), \pi_{R2}(r), ..., \pi_{Rn}(r)) = r$$

Notice that an MVD is a special case of a JD where $n = 2$. That is, a JD denoted as $JD(R_1, R_2)$ implies an MVD $(R_1 \cap R_2) \twoheadrightarrow (R_1 - R_2)$ (or by symmetry, $(R_1 \cap R_2) \twoheadrightarrow (R_2 - R_1)$). A join dependency $JD(R_1, R_2, ..., R_n)$, specified on relation schema R, is a **trivial** JD if one of the relation schemas R_i in $JD(R_1, R_2, ..., R_n)$ is equal to R. Such a dependency is called trivial because it has the lossless join property for *any* relation state r of R and hence does not specify any constraint on R. We can now define *fifth normal form*, which is also called *project-join normal form*. A relation schema R is in **fifth normal form (5NF)** (or **project-join normal form (PJNF)**) with respect to a set F of functional, multivalued, and join dependencies if, for every nontrivial join dependency $JD(R_1, R_2, ..., R_n)$ in F^+ (that is, implied by F), every R_i is a superkey of R.

For an example of a JD, consider once again the SUPPLY all-key relation of Figure 15.4(c). Suppose that the following additional constraint always holds: Whenever a supplier *s* supplies part *p*, *and* a project *j* uses part *p*, *and* the supplier *s* supplies *at least one* part to project *j*, *then* supplier *s* will also be supplying part *p* to project *j*. This constraint can be restated in other ways and specifies a join dependency JD(R1, R2, R3) among the three projections R1(SNAME, PARTNAME), R2(SNAME, PROJNAME), and R3(PARTNAME, PROJNAME) of SUPPLY. If this constraint holds, the tuples below the dotted line in Figure 15.4(c) must exist in any legal state of the SUPPLY relation that also contains the tuples above the dotted line. Figure 15.4(d) shows how the SUPPLY relation *with the join dependency* is decomposed into three relations R1, R2, and R3 that are each in 5NF. Notice that applying NATURAL JOIN to *any two* of these relations *produces spurious tuples*, but applying NATURAL JOIN to *all three together* does not. The reader should verify this on the example relation of Figure 15.4(c) and its projections in Figure 15.4(d). This is because only the JD exists, but no MVDs are specified. Notice, too, that the JD(R1, R2, R3) is specified on all legal relation states, not just on the one shown in Figure 15.4(c).

Discovering JDs in practical databases with hundreds of attributes is possible only with a great degree of intuition about the data on the part of the designer. Hence, current practice of database design pays scant attention to them.

15.4 Inclusion Dependencies

Inclusion dependencies were defined in order to formalize certain interrelational constraints. For example, the foreign key (or referential integrity) constraint cannot be specified as a functional or multivalued dependency because it relates attributes across relations; but it can be specified as an inclusion dependency. Moreover, inclusion dependencies can also be used to represent the constraint between two relations that represent a class/subclass relationship (see Chapter 4). Formally, an **inclusion dependency** $R.X < S.Y$ between two sets of attributes—X of relation schema R, and Y of relation schema S—specifies the constraint that, at any specific time when r is a relation state of R and s a relation state of S, we must have

$$\pi_X(r(R)) \subseteq \pi_Y(s(S))$$

The $\subseteq$ (subset) relationship does not necessarily have to be a proper subset. Obviously, the sets of attributes on which the inclusion dependency is specified—X of R and Y of S—must have the same number of attributes. In addition, the domains for each pair of corresponding attributes should be compatible. For example, if $X = \{A_1, A_2, ..., A_n\}$ and $Y = \{B_1, B_2, ..., B_n\}$, one possible correspondence is to have dom(A_i) COMPATIBLE-WITH dom(B_i) for $1 \leq i \leq n$. In this case we say that A_i **corresponds-to** B_i.

For example, we can specify the following inclusion dependencies on the relational schema in Figure 14.1:

```
DEPARTMENT.DMGRSSN < EMPLOYEE.SSN

WORKS_ON.SSN < EMPLOYEE.SSN
```

EMPLOYEE.DNUMBER < DEPARTMENT.DNUMBER

PROJECT.DNUM < DEPARTMENT.DNUMBER

WORKS_ON.PNUMBER < PROJECT.PNUMBER

DEPT_LOCATIONS.DNUMBER < DEPARTMENT.DNUMBER

All the preceding inclusion dependencies represent **referential integrity constraints.** We can also use inclusion dependencies to represent **class/subclass relationships.** For example, in the relational schema of Figure 9.3, we can specify the following inclusion dependencies:

EMPLOYEE.SSN < PERSON.SSN

ALUMNUS.SSN < PERSON.SSN

STUDENT.SSN < PERSON.SSN

Inference rules exist for inclusion dependencies. The following are three examples:

IDIR1 (reflexivity): $R.X < R.X$.

IDIR2 (attribute correspondence): If $R.X < S.Y$ where $X = \{A_1, A_2, ..., A_n\}$ and $Y = \{B_1, B_2, ..., B_n\}$ and A_i CORRESPONDS-TO B_i, then $R.A_i < S.B_i$ for $1 \leq i \leq n$.

IDIR3 (transitivity): If $R.X < S.Y$ and $S.Y < T.Z$, then $R.X < T.Z$.

The preceding inference rules were shown to be sound and complete for inclusion dependencies. So far, no normal forms have been developed based on inclusion dependencies.

15.5   Other Dependencies and Normal Forms

15.5.1   Template Dependencies

No matter how many types of dependencies we develop, some peculiar constraint may come up based on the semantics of attributes within relations that cannot be represented by any of them. The idea behind template dependencies is to specify a template—or example—that defines each constraint or dependency. There are two types of templates: tuple-generating templates and constraint-generating templates. A template consists of a number of **hypothesis tuples** that are meant to show an example of the tuples that may appear in one or more relations. The other part of the template is the **template conclusion.** For tuple-generating templates, the conclusion is a *set of tuples* that must also exist in the relations if the hypothesis tuples are there. For constraint-generating templates, the template conclusion is a *condition* that must hold on the hypothesis tuples.

Figure 15.6 shows how we may define functional, multivalued, and inclusion dependencies by templates. Figure 15.7 shows how we may specify the constraint that "an employee's salary cannot be higher than the salary of his or her direct supervisor" on the relation schema EMPLOYEE in Figure 7.5.

(a)

$R = \{ A , B , C , D \}$

hypothesis

$a_1 \quad b_1 \quad c_1 \quad d_1$ $X = \{ A , B \}$

$a_1 \quad b_1 \quad c_2 \quad d_2$ $Y = \{ C , D \}$

conclusion $c_1 = c_2$ and $d_1 = d_2$

(b)

$R = \{ A , B , C , D \}$

hypothesis

$a_1 \quad b_1 \quad c_1 \quad d_1$ $X = \{ A , B \}$

$a_1 \quad b_1 \quad c_2 \quad d_2$ $Y = \{ C \}$

conclusion

$a_1 \quad b_1 \quad c_2 \quad d_1$

$a_1 \quad b_1 \quad c_1 \quad d_2$

(c)

$R = \{ A , B , C , D \}$ $S = \{ E , F , G \}$

$X = \{ C , D \}$

hypothesis $a_1 \quad b_1 \quad c_1 \quad d_1$ $Y = \{ E , F \}$

conclusion $c_1 \quad d_1 \quad g$

Figure 15.6   Templates for common types of dependencies. (a) Template for the functional dependency $X \rightarrow Y$. (b) Template for the multivalued dependency $X \twoheadrightarrow Y$. (c) Template for the inclusion dependency $R.X < S.Y$.

EMPLOYEE = { NAME , SSN , ... , SALARY , SUPERVISORSSN }

	a	b	c	d
hypothesis	e	d		f	g

conclusion   c < f

Figure 15.7   Templates for the constraint that an employee's salary must be less than the supervisor's salary.

15.5.2 Domain-Key Normal Form (DKNF)

There is no hard and fast rule about defining normal forms only up to 5NF. Historically, the process of normalization and the process of discovering undesirable dependencies was carried through 5NF as a meaningful design activity, but it has been possible to define stricter normal forms that take into account additional types of dependencies and constraints. The idea behind **domain-key normal form (DKNF)** is to specify (theoretically, at least) the "ultimate normal form" that takes into account all possible types of dependencies and constraints. A relation is said to be in DKNF if all constraints and dependencies that should hold on the relation can be enforced simply by enforcing the domain constraints and key constraints on the relation. For a relation in DKNF, it becomes very straightforward to enforce all database constraints by simply checking that each attribute value in a tuple is of the appropriate domain and that every key constraint is enforced.

However, because of the difficulty of including complex constraints in a DKNF relation, its practical utility is limited, since it may be quite difficult to specify general integrity constraints. For example, consider a relation CAR(MAKE, VIN#) (where VIN# is the vehicle identification number) and another relation MANUFACTURE(VIN#, COUNTRY) (where COUNTRY is the country of manufacture). A general constraint may be of the following form: "If the MAKE is either Toyota or Lexus, then the first character of the VIN# is a "J" if the country of manufacture is Japan; if the MAKE is Honda or Acura, the second character of the VIN# is a "J" if the country of manufacture is Japan." There is no simplified way to represent such constraints short of writing a procedure (or general assertions) to test them.

15.6 Summary

In this chapter we presented several normalization algorithms. The *relational synthesis algorithms* create 3NF relations from a universal relation schema based on a given set of functional dependencies that has been specified by the database designer. The relational decomposition algorithms create BCNF (or 4NF) relations by successive lossless decomposition of unnormalized relations into two component relations at a time. We first discussed two important properties of decompositions: the lossless (nonadditive) join property, and the dependency-preserving property. An algorithm to test for lossless decomposition, and a simpler test for checking the losslessness of binary decompositions, were described. We saw that it is possible to synthesize 3NF relation schemas that meet both of the above properties; however, in the case of BCNF, it is possible to aim only for losslessness; the dependency preservation *cannot* be necessarily guaranteed.

We then defined additional types of dependencies and some additional normal forms. Multivalued dependencies, which arise from an improper combination of two or more multivalued attributes in the same relation, are used to define fourth normal form (4NF). Join dependencies, which indicate a lossless multiway decomposition of a relation, lead to the definition of fifth normal form (5NF), which is also known as project-join normal form (PJNF). We also discussed inclusion dependencies, which are used to specify referential integrity and class/subclass constraints, and template dependencies, which can be used to specify arbitrary types of constraints. We concluded with a brief discussion of the domain-key normal form (DKNF).

Review Questions

15.1. What is meant by the attribute preservation condition on a decomposition?

15.2. Why are normal forms alone insufficient as a condition for a good schema design?

15.3. What is the dependency preservation property for a decomposition? Why is it important?

15.4. Why can we not guarantee that BCNF relation schemas be produced by dependency-preserving decompositions of non-BCNF relation schemas? Give a counterexample to illustrate this point.

15.5. What is the lossless (or nonadditive) join property of a decomposition? Why is it important?

15.6. Between the properties of dependency preservation and losslessness, which one must be definitely satisfied? Why?

15.7. Discuss the null value and dangling tuple problems.

15.8. What is a multivalued dependency? What type of constraint does it specify? When does it arise?

15.9. Illustrate how the process of creating first normal form relations may lead to multivalued dependencies. How should the first normalization be done properly so that MVDs are avoided?

15.10. Define fourth normal form. Why is it useful?

15.11. Define join dependencies and fifth normal form. Why is 5NF also called project-join normal form (PJNF)?

15.12. What types of constraints are inclusion dependencies meant to represent?

15.13. How do template dependencies differ from the other types of dependencies we discussed?

15.14. Why is the domain-key normal form (DKNF) known as the ultimate normal form?

Exercises

15.15. Show that the relation schemas produced by Algorithm 15.1 are in 3NF.

15.16. Show that, if the matrix S resulting from Algorithm 15.2 does not have a row that is all "a" symbols, projecting S on the decomposition and joining it back will always produce at least one spurious tuple.

15.17. Show that the relation schemas produced by Algorithm 15.3 are in BCNF.

15.18. Show that the relation schemas produced by Algorithm 15.4 are in 3NF.

15.19. Specify a template dependency for join dependencies.

15.20. Specify all the inclusion dependencies for the relational schema of Figure 7.5.

15.21. Prove that a functional dependency is also a multivalued dependency.

15.22. Consider the example of normalizing the LOTS relation in Section 14.4. Determine whether the decomposition of LOTS into {LOTS1AX, LOTS1AY, LOTS1B, LOTS2} has the lossless join property, by applying Algorithm 15.2 and also by using the test under property LJ1.

15.23. Show how the MVDs ENAME $\longrightarrow\!\!\!\!\rightarrow$ PNAME and ENAME $\longrightarrow\!\!\!\!\rightarrow$ DNAME in Figure 15.4(a) may arise during normalization into 1NF of a relation, where the attributes PNAME and DNAME are multivalued (nonsimple).

15.24. Apply Algorithm 15.4a to the relation in Exercise 14.26 to determine a key for R. Create a minimal set of dependencies G that is equivalent to F, and apply the synthesis algorithm (Algorithm 15.4) to decompose R into 3NF relations.

15.25. Repeat Exercise 15.24 for the functional dependencies in Exercise 14.27.

15.26. Apply the decomposition algorithm (Algorithm 15.3) to the relation R and the set of dependencies F in Exercise 14.26. Repeat for the dependencies G in Exercise 14.27.

15.27. Apply Algorithm 15.4a to the relation in Exercises 14.29 and 14.30 to determine a key for R. Apply the synthesis algorithm (Algorithm 15.4) to decompose R into 3NF relations and the decomposition algorithm (Algorithm 15.3) to decompose R into BCNF relations.

15.28. Write programs that implement Algorithms 15.3 and 15.4.

15.29. Consider the following decompositions for the relation schema R of Exercise 14.26. Determine whether each decomposition has (i) the dependency preservation property, and (ii) the lossless join property, with respect to F. Also determine which normal form each relation in the decomposition is in.

  a. $D_1 = \{R_1, R_2, R_3, R_4, R_5\}; R_1 = \{A, B, C\}, R_2 = \{A, D, E\}, R_3 = \{B, F\}, R_4 = \{F, G, H\}, R_5 = \{D, I, J\}$.

  b. $D_2 = \{R_1, R_2, R_3\}; R_1 = \{A, B, C, D, E\}, R_2 = \{B, F, G, H\}, R_3 = \{D, I, J\}$.

  c. $D_3 = \{R_1, R_2, R_3, R_4, R_5\}; R_1 = \{A, B, C, D\}, R_2 = \{D, E\}, R_3 = \{B, F\}, R_4 = \{F, G, H\}, R_5 = \{D, I, J\}$.

15.30. Consider the following relation REFRIG(Model#, Year, Price, Manuf_Plant, Color), which is abbreviated as REFRIG(M, Y, P, MP, C), and with the following set F of functional dependencies: $F = \{M \rightarrow MP, \{M, Y\} \rightarrow P, MP \rightarrow C\}$

  a. Evaluate each of the following as a candidate key for REFRIG, giving reasons why it can or cannot be a key: {M}, {M, Y}, {M, C}.

  b. Based on the above key determination, state whether the relation REFRIG is in 3NF and in BCNF, giving proper reasons.

  c. Consider the decomposition of REFRIG into D = {R1(M, Y, P), R2(M, MP, C)}. Is this decomposition lossless? Show why. (You may consult the test under property LJ1 in Section 15.1.3.)

Selected Bibliography

The books by Maier (1983) and Atzeni and De Antonellis (1992) include a comprehensive discussion of relational dependency theory. The decomposition algorithm (Algorithm 15.1) is due to Bernstein (1976). Algorithm 15.4 is based on the normalization algorithm presented in Biskup et al. (1979). Tsou and Fischer (1982) give a polynomial-time algorithm for BCNF decomposition.

The theory of dependency preservation and lossless joins is given in Ullman (1988), where proofs of some of the algorithms discussed here appear. The lossless join property is analyzed in Aho et al. (1979). Algorithms to determine the keys of a relation from functional dependencies are given in Osborn (1976); testing for BCNF is discussed in Osborn (1979). Testing for 3NF is discussed in Tsou and Fischer (1982). Algorithms for designing BCNF relations are given in Wang (1990) and Hernandez and Chan (1991).

Multivalued dependencies and fourth normal form are defined in Zaniolo (1976), and Nicolas (1978). Many of the advanced normal forms are due to Fagin: the fourth normal form in Fagin (1977), PJNF in Fagin (1979), and DKNF in Fagin (1981). The set of sound and complete rules for functional and multivalued dependencies was given by Beeri et al. (1977). Join dependencies are discussed by Rissanen (1977) and Aho et al. (1979). Inference rules for join dependencies are given by Sciore (1982). Inclusion dependencies are discussed by Casanova et al. (1981), and analyzed further in Cosmadakis et al. (1990). Their use in optimizing relational schemas is discussed in Casanova et al. (1989). Template dependencies are discussed by Sadri and Ullman (1982). Other dependencies are discussed in Nicolas (1978), Furtado (1978), and Mendelzon and Maier (1979). Abiteboul et al. (1995) provides a theoretical treatment of many of the ideas presented in this chapter and the last.

CHAPTER 16

Practical Database Design and Tuning

In this chapter we move from the theory to the practice of database design. We have already described in several chapters material that is relevant to the design of actual databases for practical real-world applications. This material includes Chapters 3 and 4 on database conceptual modeling; Chapters 7, 8, and 10 on the relational model, the SQL language, and relational systems (RDBMSs); Sections 9.1 and 9.2 on mapping a high-level conceptual ER or EER schema into a relational schema; Chapters 11 and 12 on the object data model, its associated languages, and object database systems (ODBMSs); Chapter 13 on object-relational systems (ORDBMSs); and Chapters 14 and 15 on data dependency theory and relational normalization algorithms. Unfortunately, there is no standard object database design theory comparable to the theory of relational database design. Section 12.5 discussed the differences between conceptual design in object versus relational databases and showed how EER schemas may be mapped into object database schemas.

The overall database design activity has to undergo a systematic process called the **design methodology,** whether the target database is managed by an RDBMS, ORDBMS, or ODBMS. Various design methodologies are implicit in the database design tools currently supplied by vendors. Popular tools include Designer 2000 by Oracle; ERWin, BPWin, and Paradigm Plus by Platinum Technology; Sybase enterprise application studio; ER Studio by Embarcadero Technologies; and System Architect by Popkin Software, among many others. Our goal in this chapter is to discuss not one specific methodology but rather database design in a broader context, as it is undertaken in large organizations for the design and implementation of applications catering to hundreds or thousands of users.

Generally, the design of small databases with perhaps up to 20 users need not be very complicated. But for medium-sized or large databases that serve several diverse application groups, each with tens or hundreds of users, a systematic approach to the overall database design activity becomes necessary. The sheer size of a populated database does not reflect the complexity of the design; it is the schema that is more important. Any database with a schema that includes more than 30 or 40 entity types and a similar number of relationship types requires a careful design methodology.

Using the term **large database** for databases with several tens of gigabytes of data and a schema with more than 30 or 40 distinct entity types, we can cover a wide array of databases in government, industry, and financial and commercial institutions. Service sector industries, including banking, hotels, airlines, insurance, utilities, and communications, use databases for their day-to-day operations 24 hours a day, 7 days a week—known in industry as *24 by 7* operation. Application systems for these databases are called *transaction processing systems* due to the large transaction volumes and rates that are required. In this chapter we will be concentrating on the database design for such medium- and large-scale databases where transaction processing dominates.

This chapter has a variety of objectives. Section 16.1 discusses the information system life cycle within organizations with a particular emphasis on the database system. Section 16.2 highlights the phases of a database design methodology in the organizational context. Section 16.3 emphasizes the need for joint database design/application design methodologies, and discusses physical database design. Section 16.4 provides the various forms of tuning of designs. Section 16.5 briefly discusses automated database design tools.

16.1   The Role of Information Systems in Organizations

16.1.1   The Organizational Context for Using Database Systems

Database systems have become a part of the information systems of many organizations. In the 1960s information systems were dominated by file systems, but since the early 1970s organizations have gradually moved to database systems. To accommodate such systems, many organizations have created the position of database administrator (DBA) or even database administration departments to oversee and control database life-cycle activities. Similarly, information resource management (IRM) has been recognized by large organizations to be a key to successful management of the business. There are several reasons for this:

- Data is regarded as a corporate resource, and its management and control is considered central to the effective working of the organization.

- More functions in organizations are computerized, increasing the need to keep large volumes of data available in an up-to-the-minute current state.

- As the complexity of the data and applications grows, complex relationships among the data need to be modeled and maintained.

- There is a tendency toward consolidation of information resources in many organizations.

Database systems satisfy the preceding four requirements in large measure. Two additional characteristics of database systems are also very valuable in this environment:

- *Data independence* protects application programs from changes in the underlying logical organization and in the physical access paths and storage structures.
- *External schemas* (views) allow the same data to be used for multiple applications, with each application having its own view of the data.

New capabilities provided by database systems and the following key features that they offer have made them integral components in computer-based information systems:

- Integration of data across multiple applications into a single database.
- Simplicity of developing new applications using high-level languages like SQL.
- Possibility of supporting casual access for browsing and querying by managers while supporting major production-level transaction processing.

From the early 1970s through the mid-1980s, the move was toward creating large centralized repositories of data managed by a single centralized DBMS. Over the last 10 to 15 years, this trend has been reversed because of the following developments:

1. Personal computers and database-like software products, such as EXCEL, FOXPRO, MSSQL, ACCESS (all of Microsoft), or SQL Anywhere (of Sybase) are being heavily utilized by users who previously belonged to the category of casual and occasional database users. Many administrators, secretaries, engineers, scientists, architects, and the like belong to this category. As a result, the practice of creating **personal databases** is gaining popularity. It is now possible to check out a copy of part of a large database from a mainframe computer or a database server, work on it from a personal workstation, and then re-store it on the mainframe. Similarly, users can design and create their own databases and then merge them into a larger one.

2. The advent of distributed and client-server DBMSs (see Chapters 17 and 24) is opening up the option of distributing the database over multiple computer systems for better local control and faster local processing. At the same time, local users can access remote data using the facilities provided by the DBMS as a client, or through the Web. Application development tools such as POWERBUILDER, or Developer 2000 (by Oracle) are being used heavily with built-in facilities to link applications to multiple back-end database servers.

3. Many organizations now use **data dictionary systems** or **information repositories,** which are mini DBMSs that manage **metadata**—that is, data that describes the database structure, constraints, applications, authorizations, and so on. These are often used as an integral tool for information resource management. A useful data dictionary system should store and manage the following types of information:

   a. Descriptions of the schemas of the database system.
   b. Detailed information on physical database design, such as storage structures, access paths, and file and record sizes.

    c. Descriptions of the database users, their responsibilities, and their access rights.

    d. High-level descriptions of the database transactions and applications and of the relationships of users to transactions.

    e. The relationship between database transactions and the data items referenced by them. This is useful in determining which transactions are affected when certain data definitions are changed.

    f. Usage statistics such as frequencies of queries and transactions and access counts to different portions of the database.

This metadata is available to DBAs, designers, and authorized users as on-line system documentation. This improves the control of DBAs over the information system and the users' understanding and use of the system. The advent of data warehousing technology has highlighted the importance of metadata. We discuss some of the system-maintained metadata in Chapter 17.

    When designing high-performance **transaction processing systems,** which require around-the-clock nonstop operation, performance becomes critical. These databases are often accessed by hundreds of transactions per minute from remote and local terminals. Transaction performance, in terms of the average number of transactions per minute and the average and maximum transaction response time, is critical. A careful physical database design that meets the organization's transaction processing needs is a must in such systems.

    Some organizations have committed their information resource management to certain DBMS and data dictionary products. Their investment in the design and implementation of large and complex systems makes it difficult for them to change to newer DBMS products, which means that the organizations become locked in to their current DBMS system. With regard to such large and complex databases, we cannot overemphasize the importance of a careful design that takes into account the need for possible system modifications—called tuning—to respond to changing requirements. The cost can be very high if a large and complex system cannot evolve, and it becomes necessary to move to other DBMS products.

16.1.2 The Information System Life Cycle

In a large organization, the database system is typically part of the **information system,** which includes all resources that are involved in the collection, management, use, and dissemination of the information resources of the organization. In a computerized environment, these resources include the data itself, the DBMS software, the computer system hardware and storage media, the personnel who use and manage the data (DBA, end users, parametric users, and so on), the applications software that accesses and updates the data, and the application programmers who develop these applications. Thus the database system is part of a much larger organizational information system.

    In this section we examine the typical life cycle of an information system and how the database system fits into this life cycle. The information system life cycle is often called the **macro life cycle,** whereas the database system life cycle is referred to as the **micro life cycle.** The distinction between these two is becoming fuzzy for information systems where databases are a major integral component. The macro life cycle typically includes the following phases:

1. *Feasibility analysis:* This phase is concerned with analyzing potential application areas, identifying the economics of information gathering and dissemination, performing preliminary cost-benefit studies, determining the complexity of data and processes, and setting up priorities among applications.

2. *Requirements collection and analysis:* Detailed requirements are collected by interacting with potential users and user groups to identify their particular problems and needs. Interapplication dependencies, communication, and reporting procedures are identified.

3. *Design:* This phase has two aspects: the design of the database system, and the design of the application systems (programs) that use and process the database.

4. *Implementation:* The information system is implemented, the database is loaded, and the database transactions are implemented and tested.

5. *Validation and acceptance testing:* The acceptability of the system in meeting users' requirements and performance criteria is validated. The system is tested against performance criteria and behavior specifications.

6. *Deployment, operation and maintenance:* This may be preceded by conversion of users from an older system as well as by user training. The operational phase starts when all system functions are operational and have been validated. As new requirements or applications crop up, they pass through all the previous phases until they are validated and incorporated into the system. Monitoring of system performance and system maintenance are important activities during the operational phase.

16.1.3 The Database Application System Life Cycle

Activities related to the database application system (micro) life cycle include the following phases:

1. *System definition:* The scope of the database system, its users, and its applications are defined. The interfaces for various categories of users, the response time constraints, and storage and processing needs are identified.

2. *Database design:* At the end of this phase, a complete logical and physical design of the database system on the chosen DBMS is ready.

3. *Database implementation:* This comprises the process of specifying the conceptual, external, and internal database definitions, creating empty database files, and implementing the software applications.

4. *Loading or data conversion:* The database is populated either by loading the data directly or by converting existing files into the database system format.

5. *Application conversion:* Any software applications from a previous system are converted to the new system.

6. *Testing and validation:* The new system is tested and validated.

7. *Operation:* The database system and its applications are put into operation. Usually, the old and the new systems are operated in parallel for some time.

8. *Monitoring and maintenance:* During the operational phase, the system is constantly monitored and maintained. Growth and expansion can occur in both data content and software applications. Major modifications and reorganizations may be needed from time to time.

Activities 2, 3, and 4 together are part of the design and implementation phases of the larger information system life cycle. Our emphasis in Section 16.2 is on activity 2, which covers the database design phase. Most databases in organizations undergo all of the preceding life-cycle activities. The conversion steps (4 and 5) are not applicable when both the database and the applications are new. When an organization moves from an established system to a new one, activities 4 and 5 tend to be the most time-consuming and the effort to accomplish them is often underestimated. In general, there is often feedback among the various steps because new requirements frequently arise at every stage. Figure 16.1 shows the feedback loop affecting the conceptual and logical design phases as a result of system implementation and tuning.

16.2   The Database Design Process

We now focus on Step 2 of the database application system life cycle, which is database design. The problem of database design can be stated as follows:

> *Design the logical and physical structure of one or more databases to accommodate the information needs of the users in an organization for a defined set of applications.*

The goals of database design are multiple:

- Satisfy the information content requirements of the specified users and applications.
- Provide a natural and easy-to-understand structuring of the information.
- Support processing requirements and any performance objectives such as response time, processing time, and storage space.

These goals are very hard to accomplish and measure, and they involve an inherent tradeoff: if one attempts to achieve more "naturalness" and "understandability" of the model, it may be at the cost of performance. The problem is aggravated because the database design process often begins with informal and poorly defined requirements. In contrast, the result of the design activity is a rigidly defined database schema that cannot easily be modified once the database is implemented. We can identify six main phases of the database design process:

1. Requirements collection and analysis.
2. Conceptual database design.
3. Choice of a DBMS.

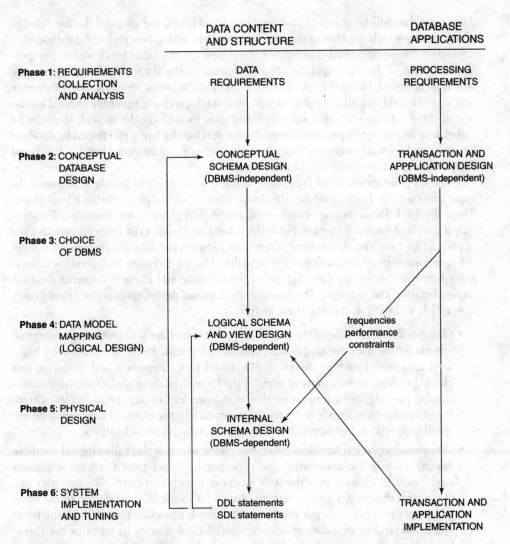

DATA CONTENT
AND STRUCTURE

DATABASE
APPLICATIONS

Phase 1: REQUIREMENTS
COLLECTION
AND ANALYSIS

DATA
REQUIREMENTS

PROCESSING
REQUIREMENTS

Phase 2: CONCEPTUAL
DATABASE
DESIGN

CONCEPTUAL
SCHEMA DESIGN
(DBMS-independent)

TRANSACTION AND
APPPLICATION DESIGN
(DBMS-independent)

Phase 3: CHOICE
OF DBMS

Phase 4: DATA MODEL
MAPPING
(LOGICAL DESIGN)

LOGICAL SCHEMA
AND VIEW DESIGN
(DBMS-dependent)

frequencies
performance
constraints

Phase 5: PHYSICAL
DESIGN

INTERNAL
SCHEMA DESIGN
(DBMS-dependent)

Phase 6: SYSTEM
IMPLEMENTATION
AND TUNING

DDL statements
SDL statements

TRANSACTION AND
APPLICATION
IMPLEMENTATION

Figure 16.1 Phases of database design for large databases.

4. Data model mapping (also called logical database design).

5. Physical database design.

6. Database system implementation and tuning.

The design process consists of two parallel activities, as illustrated in Figure 16.1. The first activity involves the design of the **data content and structure** of the database; the second relates to the design of **database applications.** To keep the figure simple, we have avoided showing most of the interactions among these two sides, but the two activities are closely intertwined. For example, by analyzing database applications, we can identify data items that will be stored in the database. In addition, the physical database design phase, during which we choose the storage structures and access paths of database files, depends on the applications that will use these files. On the other hand, we usually specify the design of database applications by referring to the database schema constructs, which are specified during the first activity. Clearly, these two activities strongly influence one another. Traditionally, database design methodologies have primarily focused on the first of these activities whereas software design has focused on the second; this may be called **data-driven** versus **process-driven design.** It is rapidly being recognized by database designers and software engineers that the two activities should proceed hand in hand, and design tools are increasingly combining them.

The six phases mentioned previously do not have to proceed strictly in sequence. In many cases we may have to modify the design from an earlier phase during a later phase. These **feedback loops** among phases—and also within phases—are common. We show only a couple of feedback loops in Figure 16.1, but many more exist between various pairs of phases. We have also shown some interaction between the data and the process sides of the figure; many more interactions exist in reality. Phase 1 in Figure 16.1 involves collecting information about the intended use of the database and Phase 6 concerns database implementation and redesign. The heart of the database design process comprises Phases 2, 4, and 5; we briefly summarize these phases:

- *Conceptual database design (Phase 2)*: The goal of this phase is to produce a conceptual schema for the database that is independent of a specific DBMS. We often use a high-level data model such as the ER or EER model (see Chapters 3 and 4) during this phase. In addition, we specify as many of the known database applications or transactions as possible, using a notation that is independent of any specific DBMS. Often, the DBMS choice is already made for the organization; the intent of conceptual design is still to keep it as free as possible from implementation considerations.

- *Data model mapping (Phase 4)*: During this phase, which is also called **logical database design,** we **map** (or **transform**) the conceptual schema from the high-level data model used in Phase 2 into the data model of the chosen DBMS. We can start this phase after choosing a specific type of DBMS—for example, if we decide to use some relational DBMS but have not yet decided on which particular one. We call the latter *system-independent* (but *data model-dependent*) logical design. In terms of the three-level DBMS architecture discussed in Chapter 2, the result of this phase is a *conceptual schema* in the chosen data model. In addition, the design of *external schemas* (views) for specific applications is often done during this phase.

- *Physical database design (Phase 5)*: During this phase, we design the specifications for the stored database in terms of physical storage structures, record placement, and indexes. This corresponds to designing the *internal schema* in the terminology of the three-level DBMS architecture.

- *Database system implementation and tuning (Phase 6)*: During this phase, the database and application programs are implemented, tested, and eventually deployed for service. Various transactions and applications are tested individually and then in conjunction with each other. This typically reveals opportunities for physical design changes, data indexing, reorganization, and different placement of data—an activity referred to as **database tuning.** Tuning is an ongoing activity—a part of system maintenance that continues for the life cycle of a database as long as the database and applications keep evolving and performance problems are detected.

In the following subsections we discuss each of the six phases of database design in more detail.

16.2.1 Phase 1: Requirements Collection and Analysis[1]

Before we can effectively design a database, we must know and analyze the expectations of the users and the intended uses of the database in as much detail as possible. This process is called **requirements collection and analysis.** To specify the requirements, we must first identify the other parts of the information system that will interact with the database system. These include new and existing users and applications, whose requirements are then collected and analyzed. Typically, the following activities are part of this phase:

1. The major application areas and user groups that will use the database or whose work will be affected by it are identified. Key individuals and committees within each group are chosen to carry out subsequent steps of requirements collection and specification.

2. Existing documentation concerning the applications is studied and analyzed. Other documentation—policy manuals, forms, reports, and organization charts—is reviewed to determine whether it has any influence on the requirements collection and specification process.

3. The current operating environment and planned use of the information is studied. This includes analysis of the types of transactions and their frequencies as well as of the flow of information within the system. Geographic characteristics regarding users, origin of transactions, destination of reports, and so forth, are studied. The input and output data for the transactions are specified.

4. Written responses to sets of questions are sometimes collected from the potential database users or user groups. These questions involve the users' priorities and the importance they place on various applications. Key individuals may be interviewed to help in assessing the worth of information and in setting up priorities.

Requirement analysis is carried out for the final users or "customers" of the database system by a team of analysts or requirement experts. The initial requirements are likely to be informal, incomplete, inconsistent, and partially incorrect. Much work therefore needs to be done to transform these early requirements into a specification of the application that can be used by developers and testers as the starting point for writing the implementation and test cases. Because the requirements reflect the initial understanding of a system that does not yet exist, they will inevitably change. It is therefore important to use techniques that help customers converge quickly on the implementation requirements.

There is a lot of evidence that customer participation in the development process increases customer satisfaction with the delivered system. For this reason, many practitioners now use meetings and workshops involving all stakeholders. One such methodology

---

1. A part of this section has been contributed by Colin Potts.

of refining initial system requirements is called Joint Application Design (JAD). More recently, techniques have been developed, such as Contextual Design, that involve the designers becoming immersed in the workplace in which the application is to be used. To help customer representatives better understand the proposed system, it is common to walk through workflow or transaction scenarios or to create a mock-up prototype of the application.

The preceding modes help structure and refine requirements but leave them still in an informal state. To transform requirements into a better structured form **requirements specification techniques** are used. These include OOA (object-oriented analysis), DFDs (data flow diagrams), and the refinement of application goals. These methods use diagramming techniques for organizing and presenting information-processing requirements. Additional documentation in the form of text, tables, charts, and decision requirements usually accompanies the diagrams. There are techniques that produce a formal specification that can be checked mathematically for consistency and "what-if" symbolic analyses. These methods are hardly used now but may become standard in the future for those parts of information systems that serve mission-critical functions and which therefore must work as planned. The model-based formal specification methods, of which the Z-notation and methodology is the most prominent, can be thought of as extensions of the ER model and are therefore the most applicable to information system design.

Some computer-aided techniques—called "Upper CASE" tools—have been proposed to help check the consistency and completeness of specifications, which are usually stored in a single repository and can be displayed and updated as the design progresses. Other tools are used to trace the links between requirements and other design entities, such as code modules and test cases. Such *traceability databases* are especially important in conjunction with enforced change-management procedures for systems where the requirements change frequently. They are also used in contractual projects where the development organization must provide documentary evidence to the customer that all the requirements have been implemented.

The requirements collection and analysis phase can be quite time-consuming, but it is crucial to the success of the information system. Correcting a requirements error is much more expensive than correcting an error made during implementation, because the effects of a requirements error are usually pervasive, and much more downstream work has to be re-implemented as a result. Not correcting the error means that the system will not satisfy the customer and may not even be used at all. Requirements gathering and analysis have been the subject of entire books.

16.2.2   Phase 2: Conceptual Database Design

The second phase of database design involves two parallel activities.[2] The first activity, **conceptual schema design,** examines the data requirements resulting from Phase 1 and produces a conceptual database schema. The second activity, **transaction and application**

---

2. This phase of design is discussed in great detail in the first seven chapters of Batini et al. (1992); we summarize that discussion here.

design, examines the database applications analyzed in Phase 1 and produces high-level specifications for these applications.

Phase 2a: Conceptual Schema Design. The conceptual schema produced by this phase is usually contained in a DBMS-independent high-level data model for the following reasons:

1. The goal of conceptual schema design is a complete understanding of the database structure, meaning (semantics), interrelationships, and constraints. This is best achieved independently of a specific DBMS because each DBMS typically has idiosyncrasies and restrictions that should not be allowed to influence the conceptual schema design.

2. The conceptual schema is invaluable as a *stable description* of the database contents. The choice of DBMS and later design decisions may change without changing the DBMS-independent conceptual schema.

3. A good understanding of the conceptual schema is crucial for database users and application designers. Use of a high-level data model that is more expressive and general than the data models of individual DBMSs is hence quite important.

4. The diagrammatic description of the conceptual schema can serve as an excellent vehicle of communication among database users, designers, and analysts. Because high-level data models usually rely on concepts that are easier to understand than lower-level DBMS-specific data models, or syntactic definitions of data, any communication concerning the schema design becomes more exact and more straightforward.

In this phase of database design, it is important to use a conceptual high-level data model with the following characteristics:

1. *Expressiveness:* The data model should be expressive enough to distinguish different types of data, relationships, and constraints.

2. *Simplicity and understandability:* The model should be simple enough for typical nonspecialist users to understand and use its concepts.

3. *Minimality:* The model should have a small number of basic concepts that are distinct and nonoverlapping in meaning.

4. *Diagrammatic representation:* The model should have a diagrammatic notation for displaying a conceptual schema that is easy to interpret.

5. *Formality:* A conceptual schema expressed in the data model must represent a formal unambiguous specification of the data. Hence, the model concepts must be defined accurately and unambiguously.

Many of these requirements—the first one in particular—sometimes conflict with other requirements. Many high-level conceptual models have been proposed for database design (see the selected bibliography for Chapter 4). In the following discussion, we will use the terminology of the Enhanced Entity-Relationship (EER) model presented in Chapter 4, and we will assume that it is being used in this phase. Conceptual schema design including data modeling is becoming an integral part of object-oriented analysis and design methodologies. The **Universal Modeling Language (UML)** has class diagrams that are largely based on extensions of the EER model.

Approaches to Conceptual Schema Design.   For conceptual schema design, we must identify the basic components of the schema: the entity types, relationship types, and attributes. We should also specify key attributes, cardinality and participation constraints on relationships, weak entity types, and specialization/generalization hierarchies/lattices. There are two approaches to designing the conceptual schema, which is derived from the requirements collected during Phase 1.

The first approach is the **centralized (or one-shot) schema design approach,** in which the requirements of the different applications and user groups from Phase 1 are merged into a single set of requirements *before* schema design begins. A single schema corresponding to the merged set of requirements is then designed. When many users and applications exist, merging all the requirements can be an arduous and time-consuming task. The assumption is that a centralized authority, the DBA, is responsible for deciding how to merge the requirements and for designing the conceptual schema for the whole database. Once the conceptual schema is designed and finalized, external schemas for the various user groups and applications can be specified by the DBA.

The second approach is the **view integration approach,** in which the requirements are not merged. Rather a schema (or view) is designed for each user group or application based only on its own requirements. Thus we develop one high-level schema (view) for each such user group or application. During a subsequent **view integration** phase, these schemas are merged or integrated into a **global conceptual schema** for the entire database. The individual views can be reconstructed as external schemas after view integration.

The main difference between the two approaches lies in the manner and stage in which multiple views or requirements of the many users and applications are reconciled and merged. In the centralized approach, the reconciliation is done manually by the DBA's staff prior to designing any schemas and is applied directly to the requirements collected in Phase 1. This places the burden to reconcile the differences and conflicts among user groups on the DBA's staff. The problem has been typically dealt with by using external consultants/design experts to bring in their own ways of resolving these conflicts. Because of the difficulties of managing this task, the view integration approach is now gaining more acceptance.

In the view integration approach, each user group or application actually designs its own conceptual (EER) schema from its requirements. Then an integration process is applied to these schemas (views) by the DBA to form the global integrated schema. Although view integration can be done manually, its application to a large database involving tens of user groups requires a methodology and the use of automated tools to help in carrying out the integration. The correspondences among the attributes, entity types, and relationship types in various views must be specified before the integration can be applied. In addition, problems such as integrating conflicting views and verifying the consistency of the specified interschema correspondences must be dealt with.

Strategies for Schema Design.   Given a set of requirements, whether for a single user or for a large user community, we must create a conceptual schema that satisfies these requirements. There are various strategies for designing such a schema. Most strategies follow an incremental approach—that is, they start with some schema constructs derived from the requirements and then they incrementally modify, refine, or build on them. We now discuss some of these strategies:

1. *Top-down strategy:* We start with a schema containing high-level abstractions and then apply successive top-down refinements. For example, we may specify only a few high-level entity types and then, as we specify their attributes, split them into lower-level entity types and relationships. The process of specialization to refine an entity type into subclasses that we illustrated in Sections 4.2 and 4.3 (see Figures 4.2, 4.4, and 4.5) is another example of a top-down design strategy.

2. *Bottom-up strategy:* Start with a schema containing basic abstractions and then combine or add to these abstractions. For example, we may start with the attributes and group these into entity types and relationships. We may add new relationships among entity types as the design progresses. The process of generalizing entity types into higher-level generalized superclasses (see Sections 4.2 and 4.3) is another example of a bottom-up design strategy.

3. *Inside-out strategy:* This is a special case of a bottom-up strategy, where attention is focused on a central set of concepts that are most evident. Modeling then *spreads outward* by considering new concepts in the vicinity of existing ones. We could specify a few clearly evident entity types in the schema and continue by adding other entity types and relationships that are related to each.

4. *Mixed strategy:* Instead of following any particular strategy throughout the design, the requirements are partitioned according to a top-down strategy, and part of the schema is designed for each partition according to a bottom-up strategy. The various schema parts are then combined.

Figures 16.2 and 16.3 illustrate top-down and bottom-up refinement, respectively. An example of a top-down refinement primitive is decomposition of an entity type into several entity types. Figure 16.2(a) shows a COURSE being refined into COURSE and SEMINAR, and the TEACHES relationship is correspondingly split into TEACHES and OFFERS. Figure 16.2(b) shows a COURSE_OFFERING entity type being refined into two entity types COURSE and INSTRUCTOR and a relationship between them. Refinement typically forces a designer to ask more questions and extract more constraints and details: for example, the (min, max) cardinality ratios between COURSE and INSTRUCTOR are obtained during refinement. Figure 16.3(a) shows the bottom-up refinement primitive of generating new relationships among entity types. The bottom-up refinement using categorization (union type) is illustrated in Figure 16.3(b), where the new concept of VEHICLE_OWNER is discovered from the existing entity types FACULTY, STAFF, and STUDENT; this process of creating a category and the related diagrammatic notation follows what we introduced in Section 4.4.

Schema (View) Integration.   For large databases with many expected users and applications, the view integration approach of designing individual schemas and then merging

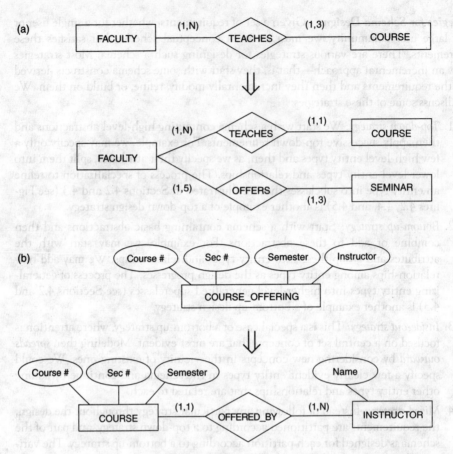

Figure 16.2   Examples of top-down refinement. (a) Generating a new entity type. (b) Decomposing an entity type into two entity types and a relationship.

them can be used. Because the individual views can be kept relatively small, design of the schemas is simplified. However, a methodology for integrating the views into a global database schema is needed. Schema integration can be divided into the following subtasks:

1. *Identifying correspondences and conflicts among the schemas:* Because the schemas are designed individually, it is necessary to specify constructs in the schemas that represent the same real-world concept. These correspondences must be identified before integration can proceed. During this process, several types of conflicts among the schemas may be discovered:

    a. *Naming conflicts:* These are of two types: synonyms and homonyms. A **synonym** occurs when two schemas use different names to describe the same

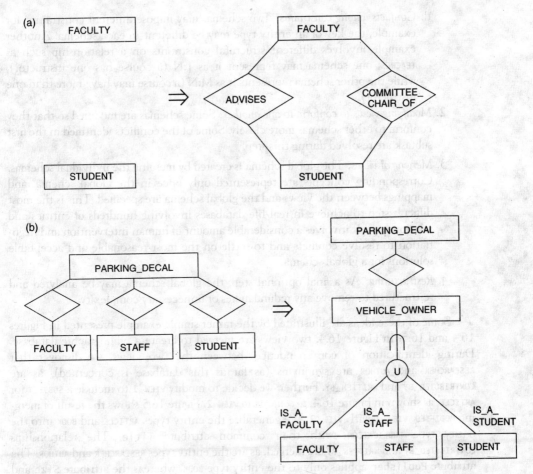

Figure 16.3 Examples of bottom-up refinement. (a) Discovering and adding new relationships. (b) Discovering a new category (union type) and relating it.

concept; for example, an entity type CUSTOMER in one schema may describe the same concept as an entity type CLIENT in another schema. A **homonym** occurs when two schemas use the same name to describe different concepts; for example, an entity type PART may represent computer parts in one schema and furniture parts in another schema.

b. *Type conflicts*: The same concept may be represented in two schemas by different modeling constructs. For example, the concept of a DEPARTMENT may be an entity type in one schema and an attribute in another.

c. *Domain (value set) conflicts*: An attribute may have different domains in two schemas. For example, SSN may be declared as an integer in one schema and as a character string in the other. A conflict of the unit of measure could occur if one schema represented WEIGHT in pounds and the other used kilograms.

  d. *Conflicts among constraints:* Two schemas may impose different constraints; for example, the key of an entity type may be different in each schema. Another example involves different structural constraints on a relationship such as TEACHES; one schema may represent it as 1:N (a course has one instructor), while the other schema represents it as M:N (a course may have more than one instructor).

2. *Modifying views to conform to one another:* Some schemas are modified so that they conform to other schemas more closely. Some of the conflicts identified in the first subtask are resolved during this step.

3. *Merging of views:* The global schema is created by merging the individual schemas. Corresponding concepts are represented only once in the global schema, and mappings between the views and the global schema are specified. This is the most difficult step to achieve in real-life databases involving hundreds of entities and relationships. It involves a considerable amount of human intervention and negotiation to resolve conflicts and to settle on the most reasonable and acceptable solutions for a global schema.

4. *Restructuring:* As a final optional step, the global schema may be analyzed and restructured to remove any redundancies or unnecessary complexity.

Some of these ideas are illustrated by the rather simple example presented in Figures 16.4 and 16.5. In Figure 16.4, two views are merged to create a bibliographic database. During identification of correspondences between the two views, we discover that RESEARCHER and AUTHOR are synonyms (as far as this database is concerned), as are CONTRIBUTED_BY and WRITTEN_BY. Further, we decide to modify VIEW 1 to include a SUBJECT for ARTICLE, as shown in Figure 16.4, *to conform to* VIEW 2. Figure 16.5 shows the result of merging MODIFIED VIEW 1 with VIEW 2. We generalize the entity types ARTICLE and BOOK into the entity type PUBLICATION, with their common attribute Title. The relationships CONTRIBUTED_BY and WRITTEN_BY are merged, as are the entity types RESEARCHER and AUTHOR. The attribute Publisher applies only to the entity type BOOK, whereas the attribute Size and the relationship type PUBLISHED_IN apply only to ARTICLE.

The above example illustrates the complexity of the merging process and how the meaning of the various concepts must be accounted for in simplifying the resultant schema design. For real-life designs, the process of schema integration requires a more disciplined and systematic approach. Several strategies have been proposed for the view integration process (Figure 16.6):

1. *Binary ladder integration:* Two schemas that are quite similar are integrated first. The resulting schema is then integrated with another schema, and the process is repeated until all schemas are integrated. The ordering of schemas for integration can be based on some measure of schema similarity. This strategy is suitable for manual integration because of its step-by-step approach.

2. *N-ary integration:* All the views are integrated in one procedure after an analysis and specification of their correspondences. This strategy requires computerized tools for large design problems. Such tools have been built as research prototypes but are not yet commercially available.

Figure 16.4 Modifying views to conform before integration.

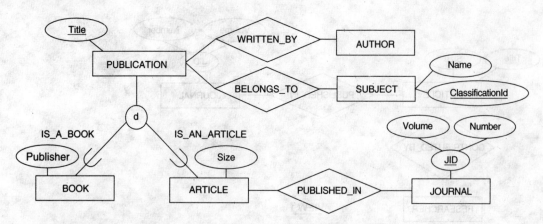

Figure 16.5   Integrated schema after merging views 1 and 2.

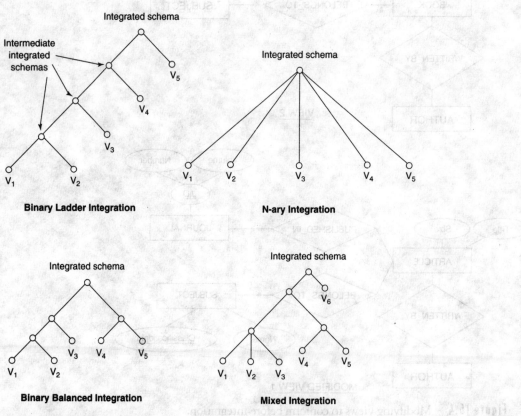

Figure 16.6   Different strategies for the view integration process.

3. *Binary balanced strategy:* Pairs of schemas are integrated first; then the resulting schemas are paired for further integration; the procedure is repeated until a final global schema results.

4. *Mixed strategy:* Initially, the schemas are partitioned into groups based on their similarity, and each group is integrated separately. The intermediate schemas are grouped again and integrated, and so on.

Phase 2b: Transaction Design. The purpose of Phase 2b, which proceeds in parallel with Phase 2a, is to design the characteristics of known database transactions (applications) in a DBMS-independent way. When a database system is being designed, the designers are aware of many known applications (or **transactions**) that will run on the database once it is implemented. An important part of database design is to specify the functional characteristics of these transactions early on in the design process. This ensures that the database schema will include all the information required by these transactions. In addition, knowing the relative importance of the various transactions and the expected rates of their invocation plays a crucial part in physical database design (Phase 5). Usually, only some of the database transactions are known at design time; after the database system is implemented, new transactions are continuously identified and implemented. However, the most important transactions are often known in advance of system implementation and should be specified at an early stage. The informal "80–20 rule" typically applies in this context: 80 percent of the workload is represented by 20 percent of the most frequently used transactions, which govern the design. In applications that are of the ad-hoc querying or batch processing variety, queries and applications that process a substantial amount of data must be identified.

A common technique for specifying transactions at a conceptual level is to identify their **input/output** and **functional behavior.** By specifying the input and output parameters (arguments), and internal functional flow of control, designers can specify a transaction in a conceptual and system-independent way. Transactions usually can be grouped into three categories: (1) **retrieval transactions,** which are used to retrieve data for display on a screen or for production of a report; (2) **update transactions,** which are used to enter new data or to modify existing data in the database; (3) **mixed transactions,** which are used for more complex applications that do some retrieval and some update. For example, consider an airline reservations database. A retrieval transaction could list all morning flights on a given date between two cities. An update transaction could be to book a seat on a particular flight. A mixed transaction may first display some data, such as showing a customer reservation on some flight, and then update the database, such as canceling the reservation by deleting it, or by adding a flight segment to an existing reservation. Transactions (applications) may originate in a front-end tool such as POWER-BUILDER (from Sybase) or Developer 2000 (from Oracle), which collect parameters online and then send a transaction to the DBMS as a backend.[3]

---

3. This philosophy has been followed for over 20 years in popular products like CICS, which serves as a tool to generate transactions for legacy DBMSs like IMS.

Several techniques for requirements specification include notation for specifying **processes,** which in this context are more complex operations that can consist of several transactions. Process modeling tools like BPWin as well as workflow modeling tools are becoming popular to identify information flows in organizations. The UML language, which provides for data modeling via class and object diagrams, has a variety of process modeling diagrams including state transition diagrams, activity diagrams, sequence diagrams, and collaboration diagrams. All of these refer to activities, events, and operations within the information system, the inputs and outputs of the processes, and the sequencing or synchronization requirements, and other conditions. It is possible to refine these specifications and extract individual transactions from them. Other proposals for specifying transactions include TAXIS, GALILEO, and GORDAS (see the selected bibliography at the end of this chapter). Some of these have been implemented into prototype systems and tools. Process modeling still remains an active area of research.

Transaction design is just as important as schema design, but it is often considered to be part of software engineering rather than database design. Many current design methodologies emphasize one over the other. One should go through Phases 2a and 2b in parallel, using feedback loops for refinement, until a stable design of schema and transactions is reached.[4]

16.2.3   Phase 3: Choice of a DBMS

The choice of a DBMS is governed by a number of factors—some technical, others economic, and still others concerned with the politics of the organization. The technical factors are concerned with the suitability of the DBMS for the task at hand. Issues to consider here are the type of DBMS (relational, object-relational, object, other), the storage structures and access paths that the DBMS supports, the user and programmer interfaces available, the types of high-level query languages, the availability of development tools, ability to interface with other DBMSs via standard interfaces, architectural options related to client-server operation, and so on. Nontechnical factors include the financial status and the support organization of the vendor. In this section we concentrate on discussing the economic and organizational factors that affect the choice of DBMS. The following costs must be considered:

1. *Software acquisition cost:* This is the "up-front" cost of buying the software, including language options, different interface options such as forms, menu, and Web-based graphic user interface (GUI) tools, recovery/backup options, special access methods, and documentation. The correct DBMS version for a specific operating system must be selected. Typically, the development tools, design tools, and additional language support are not included in basic pricing.

2. *Maintenance cost:* This is the recurring cost of receiving standard maintenance service from the vendor and for keeping the DBMS version up to date.

3. *Hardware acquisition cost:* New hardware may be needed, such as additional memory, terminals, disk drives and controllers, or specialized DBMS storage and archival storage.

---

4. High-level transaction modeling is covered in Batini et al. (1992, chaps. 8, 9, and 11). The joint functional and data analysis philosophy is advocated throughout that book.

4. *Database creation and conversion cost:* This is the cost of either creating the database system from scratch or converting an existing system to the new DBMS software. In the latter case it is customary to operate the existing system in parallel with the new system until all the new applications are fully implemented and tested. This cost is hard to project and is often underestimated.

5. *Personnel cost:* Acquisition of DBMS software for the first time by an organization is often accompanied by a reorganization of the data-processing department. Positions of DBA and staff exist in most companies that have adopted DBMSs.

6. *Training cost:* Because DBMSs are often complex systems, personnel must often be trained to use and program the DBMS. Training is required at all levels, including programming, application development, and database administration.

7. *Operating cost:* The cost of continued operation of the database system is typically not worked into an evaluation of alternatives because it is incurred regardless of the DBMS selected.

The benefits of acquiring a DBMS are not so easy to measure and quantify. A DBMS has several intangible advantages over traditional file systems, such as ease of use, consolidation of company-wide information, wider availability of data, and faster access to information. With Web-based access, certain parts of the data can be made globally accessible to employees as well as external users. More tangible benefits include reduced application development cost, reduced redundancy of data, and better control and security. Although databases have been firmly entrenched in most organizations, the decision of whether to move an application from a file-based to a database-centered approach comes up frequently. This move is generally driven by the following factors:

1. *Data complexity:* As data relationships become more complex, the need for a DBMS is felt more strongly.

2. *Sharing among applications:* The greater the sharing among applications, the more the redundancy among files, and hence the greater the need for a DBMS.

3. *Dynamically evolving or growing data:* If the data changes constantly, it is easier to cope with these changes using a DBMS than using a file system.

4. *Frequency of ad hoc requests for data:* File systems are not at all suitable for ad hoc retrieval of data.

5. *Data volume and need for control:* The sheer volume of data and the need to control it sometimes demands a DBMS.

It is difficult to develop a generic set of guidelines for adopting a single approach to data management within an organization—whether relational, object-oriented, or object-relational. If the data to be stored in the database has a high level of complexity and deals with multiple data types, the typical approach may be to consider an object or object-relational DBMS.[5] Also, the benefits of inheritance among classes and the corresponding advantage of

---

5. See the discussion in Section 13.1 concerning this issue.

reuse favors these approaches. Finally, several economic and organizational factors affect the choice of one DBMS over another:

1. *Organization-wide adoption of a certain philosophy:* This is often a dominant factor affecting the acceptability of a certain data model (for example, relational versus object), a certain vendor, or a certain development methodology and tools (for example, use of an object-oriented analysis and design tool and methodology may be required of all new applications).

2. *Familiarity of personnel with the system:* If the programming staff within the organization is familiar with a particular DBMS, it may be favored to reduce training cost and learning time.

3. *Availability of vendor services:* The availability of vendor assistance in solving problems with the system is important, since moving from a non-DBMS to a DBMS environment is generally a major undertaking and requires much vendor assistance at the start.

Another factor to consider is the DBMS portability among different types of hardware. Many commercial DBMSs now have versions that run on many hardware/software configurations (or **platforms**). The need of applications for backup, recovery, performance, integrity, and security must also be considered. Many DBMSs are currently being designed as *total solutions* to the information-processing and information resource management needs within organizations. Most DBMS vendors are combining their products with the following options or built-in features:

- Text editors and browsers.
- Report generators and listing utilities.
- Communication software (often called teleprocessing monitors).
- Data entry and display features such as forms, screens, and menus with automatic editing features.
- Inquiry and access tools that can be used on the World Wide Web (Web enabling tools).
- Graphical database design tools.

A large amount of "third-party" software is available that provides added functionality to a DBMS in each of the above areas. In rare cases it may be preferable to develop in-house software rather than use a DBMS—for example, if the applications are very well defined and are *all* known beforehand. Under such circumstances, an in-house custom-designed system may be appropriate to implement the known applications in the most efficient way. In most cases, however, new applications that were not foreseen at design time come up *after* system implementation. This is precisely why DBMSs have become very popular: They facilitate the incorporation of new applications with only incremental modifications to the existing design of a database. Such design evolution—or **schema evolution**—is a feature present to various degrees in commercial DBMSs.

16.2.4 Phase 4: Data Model Mapping (Logical Database Design)

The next phase of database design is to create a conceptual schema and external schemas in the data model of the selected DBMS by mapping those schemas produced in Phase 2a. The mapping can proceed in two stages:

1. *System-independent mapping:* In this stage, the mapping does not consider any specific characteristics or special cases that apply to the DBMS implementation of the data model. We already discussed DBMS-independent mapping of an ER schema to a relational schema in Section 9.1 and of EER schemas to relational and object-oriented schemas in Sections 9.2 and 12.5, respectively.

2. *Tailoring the schemas to a specific DBMS:* Different DBMSs implement a data model by using specific modeling features and constraints. We may have to adjust the schemas obtained in Step 1 to conform to the specific implementation features of a data model as used in the selected DBMS.

The result of this phase should be DDL statements in the language of the chosen DBMS that specify the conceptual and external level schemas of the database system. But if the DDL statements include some physical design parameters, a complete DDL specification must wait until after the physical database design phase is completed. Many automated CASE (computer-assisted software engineering) design tools (see Section 16.5) can generate DDL for commercial systems from a conceptual schema design.

16.2.5 Phase 5: Physical Database Design

Physical database design is the process of choosing specific storage structures and access paths for the database files to achieve good performance for the various database applications. Each DBMS offers a variety of options for file organization and access paths. These usually include various types of indexing, clustering of related records on disk blocks, linking related records via pointers, and various types of hashing. Once a specific DBMS is chosen, the physical database design process is restricted to choosing the most appropriate structures for the database files from among the options offered by that DBMS. In this section we give generic guidelines for physical design decisions; they hold for any type of DBMS. The following criteria are often used to guide the choice of physical database design options:

1. *Response time:* This is the elapsed time between submitting a database transaction for execution and receiving a response. A major influence on response time that is under the control of the DBMS is the database access time for data items referenced by the transaction. Response time is also influenced by factors not under DBMS control, such as system load, operating system scheduling, or communication delays.

2. *Space utilization:* This is the amount of storage space used by the database files and their access path structures on disk, including indexes and other access paths.

3. *Transaction throughput:* This is the average number of transactions that can be processed per minute; it is a critical parameter of transaction systems such as those used for airline reservations or banking. Transaction throughput must be measured under peak conditions on the system.

Typically, average and worst-case limits on the preceding parameters are specified as part of the system performance requirements. Analytical or experimental techniques, which can include prototyping and simulation, are used to estimate the average and worst-case values under different physical design decisions, to determine whether they meet the specified performance requirements.

Performance depends on record size and number of records in the file. Hence, we must estimate these parameters for each file. In addition, we should estimate the update and retrieval patterns for the file cumulatively from all the transactions. Attributes used for selecting records should have primary access paths and secondary indexes constructed for them. Estimates of file growth, either in the record size because of new attributes or in the number of records, should also be taken into account during physical database design.

The result of the physical database design phase is an *initial* determination of storage structures and access paths for the database files. It is almost always necessary to modify the design on the basis of its observed performance after the database system is implemented. We include this activity of **database tuning** in the next phase and cover it in a separate section. In Section 16.3 we will briefly discuss physical design issues related to relational DBMSs.

16.2.6 Phase 6: Database System Implementation and Tuning

After the logical and physical designs are completed, we can implement the database system. This is typically the responsibility of the DBA and is carried out in conjunction with the database designers. Language statements in the DDL (data definition language) including the SDL (storage definition language) of the selected DBMS are compiled and used to create the database schemas and (empty) database files. The database can then be **loaded** (populated) with the data. If data is to be converted from an earlier computerized system, **conversion routines** may be needed to reformat the data for loading into the new database.

Database transactions must be implemented by the application programmers by referring to the conceptual specifications of transactions, and then writing and testing program code with embedded DML commands. Once the transactions are ready and the data is loaded into the database, the design and implementation phase is over and the operational phase of the database system begins.

Most systems include a monitoring utility to collect performance statistics, which are kept in the system catalog or data dictionary for later analysis. These include statistics on the number of invocations of predefined transactions or queries, input/output activity against files, counts of file pages or index records, and frequency of index usage. As the database system requirements change, it often becomes necessary to add or remove existing tables and to reorganize some files by changing primary access methods or by dropping old indexes and constructing new ones. Some queries or transactions may be rewritten for better performance. Database tuning continues as long as the database is in existence, as long as performance problems are discovered, and while the requirements keep changing.

16.3   Physical Database Design in Relational Databases

In this section we first discuss the physical design factors that affect the performance of applications and transactions; we then comment on the specific guidelines for RDBMSs. In Section 16.4 we discuss the variety of ways in which a design may be tuned once it has been in operation.

16.3.1   Factors That Influence Physical Database Design

Physical design is an activity where the goal is not only to come up with the appropriate structuring of data in storage but to do so in a way that guarantees good performance. For a given conceptual schema, there are many physical design alternatives in a given DBMS. It is not possible to make meaningful physical design decisions and performance analyses until we know the queries, transactions, and applications that are expected to run on the database. We must analyze these applications, their expected frequencies of invocation, any time constraints on their execution, and the expected frequency of update operations. We discuss each of these factors next.

A. Analyzing the Database Queries and Transactions.   Before undertaking physical database design, we must have a good idea of the intended use of the database by defining the queries and transactions that we expect to run on the database in a high-level form. For each query, we should specify the following:

1. The files that will be accessed by the query.[6]
2. The attributes on which any selection conditions for the query are specified.
3. The attributes on which any join conditions or conditions to link multiple tables or objects for the query are specified.
4. The attributes whose values will be retrieved by the query.

The attributes listed in items 2 and 3 above are candidates for definition of access structures. For each update transaction or operation, we should specify the following:

1. The files that will be updated.
2. The type of operation on each file (insert, update, or delete).
3. The attributes on which selection conditions for a delete or update are specified.
4. The attributes whose values will be changed by an update operation.

---

6. For simplicity we use the term *files*. This can be substituted by tables or classes or objects.

Again, the attributes listed previously in item 3 are candidates for access structures. On the other hand, the attributes listed in item 4 are candidates for avoiding an access structure, since modifying them will require updating the access structures.

B. Analyzing the Expected Frequency of Invocation of Queries and Transactions. Besides identifying the characteristics of expected queries and transactions, we must consider their expected rates of invocation. This frequency information, along with the attribute information collected on each query and transaction, is used to compile a cumulative list of expected frequency of use for all queries and transactions. This is expressed as the expected frequency of using each attribute in each file as a selection attribute or a join attribute, over all the queries and transactions. Generally, for large volumes of processing, the informal "80–20 rule" applies, which states that approximately 80 percent of the processing is accounted for by only 20 percent of the queries and transactions. Therefore, in practical situations it is rarely necessary to collect exhaustive statistics and invocation rates on all the queries and transactions; it is sufficient to determine the 20 percent or so most important ones.

C. Analyzing the Time Constraints of Queries and Transactions. Some queries and transactions may have stringent performance constraints. For example, a transaction may have the constraint that it should terminate within 5 seconds on 95 percent of the occasions when it is invoked and that it should never take more than 20 seconds. Such performance constraints place further priorities on the attributes that are candidates for access paths. The selection attributes used by queries and transactions with time constraints become higher-priority candidates for primary access structures.

D. Analyzing the Expected Frequencies of Update Operations. A minimum number of access paths should be specified for a file that is updated frequently, because updating the access paths themselves slows down the update operations.

E. Analyzing the Uniqueness Constraints on Attributes. Access paths should be specified on all candidate key attributes—or sets of attributes—that are either the primary key or constrained to be unique. The existence of an index (or other access path) makes it sufficient to search only the index when checking this constraint, since all values of the attribute will exist in the leaf nodes of the index.

Once we have compiled the preceding information, we can address the physical database design decisions, which consist mainly of deciding on the storage structures and access paths for the database files.

16.3.2 Physical Database Design Decisions

Most relational systems represent each base relation as a physical database file. The access path options include specifying the type of file for each relation and the attributes on which indexes should be defined. At most one of the indexes on each file may be a primary or clustering index. Any number of additional secondary indexes can be created.[7]

Design Decisions about Indexing.   The attributes whose values are required in equality or range conditions (selection operation) and those that are keys or that participate in join conditions (join operation) require access paths.

The performance of queries largely depends upon what indexes or hashing schemes exist to expedite the processing of selections and joins. On the other hand, during insert, delete, or update operations, existence of indexes adds to the overhead. This overhead must be justified in terms of the gain in efficiency by expediting queries and transactions.

The physical design decisions for indexing fall into the following categories:

1. *Whether to index an attribute:* The attribute must be a key, or there must be some query that uses that attribute either in a selection condition (equality or range of values) or in a join. One factor in favor of setting up many indexes is that some queries can be processed by just scanning the indexes without retrieving any data.

2. *What attribute or attributes to index on:* An index can be constructed on one or multiple attributes. If multiple attributes from one relation are involved together in several queries, (for example, (garment_style_#, color) in a garment inventory database), a multiattribute index is warranted. The ordering of attributes within a multiattribute index must correspond to the queries. For example, the above index assumes that queries would be based on an ordering of colors within a garment_style_# rather than vice versa.

3. *Whether to set up a clustered index:* At most one index per table can be a primary or clustering index, because this implies that the file be physically ordered on that attribute. In most RDBMSs, this is specified by the keyword CLUSTER. (If the attribute is a key, a primary index is created, whereas a clustering index is created if the attribute is not a key.) If a table requires several indexes, the decision about which one should be a clustered index depends upon whether keeping the table ordered on that attribute is needed. Range queries benefit a great deal from clustering. If several attributes require range queries, relative benefits must be evaluated before deciding which attribute to cluster on. If a query is to be answered by doing an index search only (without retrieving data records), the corresponding index should *not* be clustered, since the main benefit of clustering is achieved when retrieving the records themselves.

4. *Whether to use a hash index over a tree index:* In general, RDBMSs use B[+]-trees for indexing. However, ISAM and hash indexes are also provided in some systems (see Chapter 6). B[+]-trees support both equality and range queries on the attribute used as the search key. Hash indexes work well with equality conditions, particularly during joins to find a matching record(s).

---

7. The reader should review the various types of indexes described in Section 6.1. For a clearer understanding of this discussion, it is also useful to be familiar with the algorithms for query processing discussed in Chapter 18.

5. *Whether to use dynamic hashing for the file:* For files that are very volatile—that is, those that grow and shrink continuously—one of the dynamic hashing schemes discussed in Section 5.9 would be suitable. Currently, they are not offered by most commercial RDBMSs.

Denormalization as a Design Decision for Speeding Up Queries.   The ultimate goal during normalization (see Chapters 14 and 15) was to separate the logically related attributes into tables to minimize redundancy, and thereby avoid the update anomalies that lead to an extra processing overhead to maintain consistency in the database.

The above ideals are sometimes sacrificed in favor of faster execution of frequently occurring queries and transactions. This process of storing the logical database design (which may be in BCNF or 4NF) in a weaker normal form, say 2NF or 1NF, is called **denormalization.** Typically, the designer adds to a table attributes that are needed for answering queries or producing reports so that a join with another table, which contains the newly added attribute, is avoided. This reintroduces a partial functional dependency or a transitive dependency into the table, thereby creating the associated redundancy problems (see Chapter 14).

Other forms of denormalization consist of storing extra tables to maintain original functional dependencies that are lost during a BCNF decomposition. For example, Figure 14.13 showed the TEACH(STUDENT, COURSE, INSTRUCTOR) relation with the functional dependencies {{STUDENT, COURSE} → INSTRUCTOR, INSTRUCTOR → COURSE}. A lossless decomposition of TEACH into T1(STUDENT, INSTRUCTOR) and T2(INSTRUCTOR, COURSE) does *not* allow queries of the form "what course did student Smith take from Instructor Navathe" to be answered without joining T1 and T2. Therefore, storing T1, T2, and TEACH may be a possible solution, which reduces the design from BCNF to 3NF. Here, TEACH is a materialized join of the other two tables, representing an extreme redundancy. Any updates to T1 and T2 would have to be applied to TEACH. An alternate strategy is to consider T1 and T2 as updatable base tables whereas TEACH can be created as a view.

16.4   An Overview of Database Tuning in Relational Systems

After a database is deployed and is in operation, actual use of the applications, transactions, queries, and views reveals factors and problem areas that may not have been accounted for during the initial physical design. The inputs to physical design listed in Section 16.3.1 can be revised by gathering actual statistics about usage patterns. Resource utilization as well as internal DBMS processing—such as query optimization—can be monitored to reveal bottlenecks, such as contention for the same data or devices. Volumes of activity and sizes of data can be better estimated. It is therefore necessary to monitor and revise the physical database design constantly. The goals of tuning are as follows:

- To make applications run faster.
- To lower the response time of queries/transactions.
- To improve the overall throughput of transactions.

The dividing line between physical design and tuning is very thin. The same design decisions that we discussed in Section 16.3.3 are revisited during the tuning phase, which is a continued adjustment of design. We give only a brief overview of the tuning process below.[8] The inputs to the tuning process include statistics related to the factors mentioned in Section 16.3.1. In particular, DBMSs can internally collect the following statistics:

- Sizes of individual tables.
- Number of distinct values in a column.
- The number of times a particular query or transaction is submitted/executed in an interval of time.
- The times required for different phases of query and transaction processing (for a given set of queries or transactions).

These and other statistics create a profile of the contents and use of the database. Other information obtained from monitoring the database system activities and processes includes the following:

- *Storage statistics:* Data about allocation of storage into tablespaces, indexspaces, and buffer ports.[9]
- *I/O and device performance statistics:* Total read/write activity (paging) on disk extents and disk hot spots.
- *Query/transaction processing statistics:* Execution times of queries and transactions, optimization times during query optimization.
- *Locking/logging related statistics:* Rates of issuing different types of locks, transaction throughput rates, and log records activity.[10]
- *Index statistics:* Number of levels in an index, number of noncontiguous leaf pages, etc.

Many of the above statistics relate to transactions, concurrency control, and recovery, which are to be discussed in Chapters 19 through 21. Tuning a database involves dealing with the following types of problems:

- How to avoid excessive lock contention, thereby increasing concurrency among transactions.
- How to minimize overheard of logging and unnecessary dumping of data.
- How to optimize buffer size and scheduling of processes.
- How to allocate resources such as disks, RAM, and processes for most efficient utilization.

---

8. Interested readers should consult Shasha (1992) for a detailed discussion of tuning.

9. See Chapter 10 for explanation of these terms.

10. The reader will need to look ahead and review Chapters 19-21 for explanation of these terms.

Most of the previously mentioned problems can be solved by setting appropriate physical DBMS parameters, changing configurations of devices, changing operating system parameters, and other similar activities. The solutions tend to be closely tied to specific systems. The DBAs are typically trained to handle these problems of tuning for the specific DBMS. We briefly discuss the tuning of various physical database design decisions below.

16.4.1   Tuning Indexes

The initial choice of indexes may have to be revised for the following reasons:

- Certain queries may take too long to run for lack of an index.
- Certain indexes may not get utilized at all.
- Certain indexes may be causing excessive overhead because the index is on an attribute that undergoes frequent changes.

Most DBMSs have a command or trace facility, which can be used by the DBA to ask the system to show how a query was executed—what operations were performed in what order and what secondary access structures were used. By analyzing these execution plans, it is possible to diagnose the causes of the above problems. Some indexes may be dropped and some new indexes may be created based on the tuning analysis.

The goal of tuning is to dynamically evaluate the requirements, which sometimes fluctuate seasonally or during different times of the month or week, and to reorganize the indexes to yield the best overall performance. Dropping and building new indexes is an overhead that can be justified in terms of performance improvements. Updating of a table is generally suspended while an index is dropped or created; this loss of service must be accounted for. Besides dropping or creating indexes and changing from a nonclustered to a clustered index and vice versa, **rebuilding the index** may improve performance. Most RDBMSs use B^+-trees for an index. If there are many deletions on the index key, index pages may contain wasted space, which can be claimed during a rebuild operation. Similarly, too many insertions may cause overflows in a clustered index that affect performance. Rebuilding a clustered index amounts to reorganizing the entire table ordered on that key.

The available options for indexing and the way they are defined, created, and reorganized varies from system to system. Just for illustration, consider the sparse and dense indexes of Chapter 6. Sparse indexes have one index pointer for each page (disk block) in the data file; dense indexes have an index pointer for each record. Sybase provides clustering indexes as sparse indexes in the form of B^+-trees whereas INGRES provides sparse clustering indexes as ISAM files, and dense clustering indexes as B^+-trees. In some versions of Oracle and DB2, the option of setting up a clustering index is limited to a dense index (with many more index entries), and the DBA has to work with this limitation.

16.4.2   Tuning the Database Design

We already discussed in Section 16.3.2 the need for a possible denormalization, which is a departure from keeping all tables as BCNF relations. If a given physical database design does not meet the expected objectives, we may revert to the logical database design, make adjustments to the logical schema, and remap it to a new set of physical tables and indexes.

As we pointed out in Section 16.2, the entire database design has to be driven by the processing requirements as much as by data requirements. If the processing requirements are dynamically changing, the design needs to respond by making changes to the conceptual schema if necessary and to reflect those changes into the logical schema and physical design. These changes may be of the following nature:

- Existing tables may be joined (denormalized) because certain attributes from two or more tables are frequently needed together: This reduces the normalization level from BCNF to 3NF, 2NF, or 1NF.[11]

- For the given set of tables, there may be alternative design choices, all of which achieve 3NF or BCNF. One may be replaced by the other.

- A relation of the form R(K,A, B, C, D, ...)—with K as a set of key attributes—that is in BCNF can be stored into multiple tables that are also in BCNF—for example, R1(K, A, B), R2(K, C, D,), R3(K, ...)—by replicating the key K in each table. Each table groups sets of attributes that are accessed together. For example, the table EMPLOYEE(SSN, Name, Phone, Grade, Salary) may be split into two tables EMP1(SSN, Name, Phone) and EMP2(SSN, Grade, Salary). If the original table had a very large number of rows (say 100,000) and queries about phone numbers and salary information are totally distinct, this separation of tables may work better. This is also called **vertical partitioning.**

- Attribute(s) from one table may be repeated in another even though this creates redundancy and a potential anomaly. For example, Partname may be replicated in tables wherever the Part# appears (as foreign key), but there may be one master table called PART_MASTER(Part#, Partname, ...) where the Partname is guaranteed to be up-to-date.

- Just as vertical partitioning splits a table vertically into multiple tables, **horizontal partitioning** takes horizontal slices of a table and stores them as distinct tables. For example, product sales data may be separated into ten tables based on ten product lines. Each table has the same set of columns (attributes) but contains a distinct set of products (tuples). If a query or transaction applies to all product data, it may have to run against all the tables and the results may have to be combined.

These types of adjustments designed to meet the high volume queries or transactions, with or without sacrificing the normal forms, are commonplace in practice.

16.4.3 Tuning Queries

We already discussed how query performance is dependent upon appropriate selection of indexes and how indexes may have to be tuned after analyzing queries that give poor per-

---

11. Note that 3NF and 2NF address different types of problem dependencies which are independent of each other; hence the normalization (or denormalization) order between them is arbitrary.

formance by using the commands in the RDBMS that show the execution plan of the query. There are mainly two indications that suggest that query tuning may be needed:

1. A query issues too many disk accesses (for example, an exact match query scans an entire table).

2. The query plan shows that relevant indexes are not being used.

Some typical instances of situations prompting query tuning include the following:

1. Many query optimizers do not use indexes in the presence of arithmetic expressions (such as SALARY/365 > 10.50), numerical comparisons of attributes of different sizes and precision (such as AQTY = BQTY where AQTY is of type INTEGER and BQTY is of type SMALLINTEGER), NULL comparisons (such as BDATE IS NULL), and substring comparisons (such as LNAME LIKE "%MANN").

2. Indexes are often not used for nested queries using IN; for example, the query:

```
SELECT SSN FROM EMPLOYEE
WHERE DNO IN (SELECT DNUMBER FROM DEPARTMENT
             WHERE MGRSSN = '333445555');
```

may not use the index on DNO in EMPLOYEE, whereas using DNO = DNUMBER in the WHERE-clause with a single block query may cause the index to be used.

3. Some DISTINCTs may be redundant and can be avoided without changing the result. A DISTINCT often causes a sort operation and must be avoided as far as possible.

4. Unnecessary use of temporary result tables can be avoided by collapsing multiple queries into a single query *unless* the temporary relation is needed for some intermediate processing.

5. In some situations involving use of correlated queries, temporaries are useful. Consider the query:

```
SELECT SSN
FROM EMPLOYEE E
WHERE SALARY = SELECT MAX (SALARY)
              FROM EMPLOYEE AS M
              WHERE M.DNO = E.DNO;
```

This has the potential danger of searching all of the inner EMPLOYEE table M for *each* tuple from the outer EMPLOYEE table E. To make it more efficient, it can be broken into two queries where the first query just computes the maximum salary in each department as follows:

```
SELECT MAX (SALARY) AS HIGHSALARY, DNO INTO TEMP
FROM EMPLOYEE
GROUP BY DNO;

SELECT SSN
FROM EMPLOYEE, TEMP
WHERE SALARY = HIGHSALARY AND EMPLOYEE.DNO = TEMP.DNO;
```

6. If multiple options for join condition are possible, choose one that uses a clustering index and avoid those that contain string comparisons. For example, assuming

that the NAME attribute is a candidate key in EMPLOYEE and STUDENT, it is better to use EMPLOYEE.SSN = STUDENT.SSN as a join condition rather than EMPLOYEE.NAME = STUDENT.NAME if SSN has a clustering index in one or both tables.

7. One idiosyncrasy with query optimizers is that the order of tables in the FROM-clause may affect the join processing. If that is the case, one may have to switch this order so that the smaller of the two relations is scanned and the larger relation is used with an appropriate index.

8. Some query optimizers perform worse on nested queries compared to their equivalent unnested counterparts. There are four types of nested queries:

- Uncorrelated subqueries with aggregates in inner query.
- Uncorrelated subqueries without aggregates.
- Correlated subqueries with aggregates in inner query.
- Correlated subqueries without aggregates.

Out of the above four types, the first one typically presents no problem, since most query optimizers evaluate the inner query once. However, for a query of the second type, such as the example in (2) above, most query optimizers may not use an index on DNO in EMPLOYEE. The same optimizers may do so if the query is written as an unnested query. Transformation of correlated subqueries may involve setting temporary tables. Detailed examples are outside our scope here.[12]

9. Finally, many applications are based on views that define the data of interest to those applications. Sometimes, these views become an overkill, because a query may be posed directly against a base table, rather than going through a view that is defined by a join.

16.4.4   Additional Query Tuning Guidelines

Additional techniques for improving queries apply in certain situations:

1. A query with multiple selection conditions that are connected via OR may not be prompting the query optimizer to use any index. Such a query may be split up and expressed as a union of queries, each with a condition on an attribute that causes an index to be used. For example,

SELECT FNAME, LNAME, SALARY, AGE[13]
FROM EMPLOYEE
WHERE AGE > 45 **OR** SALARY < 50000;

may be executed using sequential scan giving poor performance. Splitting it up as

SELECT FNAME, LNAME, SALARY, AGE
FROM EMPLOYEE
WHERE AGE > 45

UNION

---

12. For further details, see Shasha (1992).

13. We modified the schema and used AGE in EMPLOYEE instead of BDATE.

```
SELECT FNAME, LNAME, SALARY, AGE
FROM EMPLOYEE
WHERE SALARY < 50000;
```

may utilize indexes on AGE as well as on SALARY.

2. To help in expediting a query, the following transformations may be tried:

   • NOT condition may be transformed into a positive expression.

   • Embedded SELECT blocks using IN, = ALL, = ANY, and = SOME may be replaced by joins.

   • If an equality join is set up between two tables, the range predicate (selection condition) on the joining attribute set up in one table may be repeated for the other table.

3. WHERE conditions may be rewritten to utilize the indexes on multiple columns. For example,

```
SELECT REGION#, PROD_TYPE, MONTH, SALES
FROM SALES_STATISTICS
WHERE REGION# = 3 AND ((PRODUCT_TYPE BETWEEN 1 AND 3) OR (PRODUCT_
TYPE BETWEEN 8 AND 10));
```

may use an index only on REGION# and search through all leaf pages of the index for a match on PRODUCT_TYPE. Instead, using

```
SELECT REGION#, PROD_TYPE, MONTH, SALES
FROM SALES_STATISTICS
WHERE (REGION# = 3 AND (PRODUCT_TYPE BETWEEN 1 AND 3)) OR (REGION# =
3 AND (PRODUCT_TYPE BETWEEN 8 AND 10));
```

can use a composite index on (REGION#, PRODUCT_TYPE) and work much more efficiently.

We have covered in this section most of the common opportunities where inefficiency of a query may be corrected by some simple corrective action such as using a temporary, avoiding certain types of constructs, or avoiding use of views. The problems and the remedies will depend upon the workings of a query optimizer within an RDBMS. Detailed literature exists in terms of individual manuals on database tuning guidelines for database administration by the RDBMS vendors.

16.5 Automated Design Tools

The database design activity predominantly spans Phase 2 (conceptual design), Phase 4 (data model mapping, or logical design) and Phase 5 (physical database design) in the design process that we discussed in Section 16.2. When database technology was first introduced, most database design was carried out manually by expert designers, who used their experience and knowledge in the design process.

However, at least two factors indicated that some form of automation had to be utilized if possible:

1. As an application involves more and more complexity of data in terms of relationships and constraints, the number of options or different designs to model the same information keeps increasing rapidly. It becomes difficult to deal with this complexity and the corresponding design alternatives manually.

2. The sheer size of some databases runs into hundreds of entity types and relationship types making the task of manually managing these designs almost impossible. The meta information related to the design process we described in Section 16.2 yields another database that must be created, maintained, and queried as a database in its own right.

The above factors have given rise to many tools on the market that come under the general category of CASE (Computer-Aided Software Engineering) tools for database design. They consist of a combination of the following facilities:

1. *Diagramming:* This allows the designer to draw a conceptual schema diagram, in some tool-specific notation. Most notations include entity types, relationship types that are shown either as separate boxes or simply as directed or undirected lines, cardinality constraints shown alongside the lines or in terms of the different types of arrowheads or min/max constraints, attributes, keys, and so on.[14] Some tools display inheritance hierarchies and use additional notation for showing the partial versus total and disjoint versus overlapping nature of the generalizations. The diagrams are internally stored as conceptual designs and are available for modification as well as generation of reports, cross reference listings, and other uses.

2. *Model mapping:* This implements mapping algorithms similar to the ones we presented in Sections 9.1 and 9.2. The mapping is system-specific—most tools generate schemas in SQL DDL for Oracle, DB2, Informix, Sybase, and other RDBMSs. This part of the tool is most amenable to automation. The designer can edit the produced DDL files if needed.

3. *Design normalization:* This utilizes a set of functional dependencies that are supplied at the conceptual design or after the relational schemas are produced during logical design. The design decomposition algorithms from Chapter 15 are applied to decompose existing relations into higher normal form relations. Typically, tools lack the approach of generating alternative 3NF or BCNF designs and allowing the designer to select among them based on some criteria like the minimum number of relations or least amount of storage.

Most tools incorporate some form of physical design including the choice of indexes. A whole range of separate tools exists for performance monitoring and measurement. The problem of tuning a design or the database implementation is still mostly handled as a human

---

14. We showed the ER, EER, and UML class diagram notations in Chapters 3 and 4. See Appendix A for an idea of the different types of diagrammatic notations used.

decision-making activity. Out of the phases of design described in this chapter, one area where there is hardly any commercial tool support is view integration (see Section 16.2.2).

We will not survey database design tools here, but only mention the following characteristics that a good design tool should possess:

1. *An easy-to-use interface:* This is critical because it enables designers to focus on the task at hand, not on understanding the tool. Graphical and point and click interfaces are commonly used. A few tools like the SECSI tool from France use natural language input. Different interfaces may be tailored to beginners or to expert designers.

2. *Analytical components:* Tools should provide analytical components for tasks that are difficult to perform manually, such as evaluating physical design alternatives or detecting conflicting constraints among views. This area is weak in most current tools.

3. *Heuristic components:* Aspects of the design that cannot be precisely quantified can be automated by entering heuristic rules in the design tool to evaluate design alternatives.

4. *Trade-off analysis:* A tool should present the designer with adequate comparative analysis whenever it presents multiple alternatives to choose from. Tools should ideally incorporate an analysis of a design change at the conceptual design level down to physical design. Because of the many alternatives possible for physical design in a given system, such tradeoff analysis is difficult to carry out and most current tools avoid it.

5. *Display of design results:* Design results, such as schemas, are often displayed in diagrammatic form. Aesthetically pleasing and well laid out diagrams are not easy to generate automatically. Multipage design layouts that are easy to read are another challenge. Other types of results of design may be shown as tables, lists, or reports that can be easily interpreted.

6. *Design verification:* This is a highly desirable feature. Its purpose is to verify that the resulting design satisfies the initial requirements. Unless the requirements are captured and internally represented in some analyzable form, the verification cannot be attempted.

Currently there is increasing awareness of the value of design tools, and they are becoming a must for dealing with large database design problems. There is also an increasing awareness that schema design and application design should go hand in hand, and the current trend among CASE tools is to address both areas. Some vendors like Platinum provide a tool for data modeling and schema design (ERWin) and another for process modeling and functional design (BPWin). Other tools (for example, SECSI) use expert system technology to guide the design process by including design expertise in the form of rules. Expert system technology is also useful in the requirements collection and analysis phase, which is typically a laborious and frustrating process. The trend is to use both metadata repositories and design tools to achieve better designs for complex databases. Without a claim of being exhaustive, Table 16.1 lists some popular database design and application modeling tools. Companies in the table are listed in alphabetical order.

Table 16.1 Some of the Currently Available Automated Database Design Tools

Company	Tool	Functionality
Embarcadero Technologies	ER Studio	Database Modeling in ER and IDEF1X
	DB Artisan	Database administration and space and security management
Oracle	Developer 2000 and Designer 2000	Database modeling, application development
Popkin Software	System Architect 2001	Data modeling, object modeling, process modeling, structured analysis/design
Platinum Technology	Platinum Enterprise Modeling Suite: ERwin, BPWin, Paradigm Plus	Data, process, and business component modeling
Persistence Inc.	Powertier	Mapping from O-O to relational model
Rational	Rational Rose	Modeling in UML and application generation in C++ and JAVA
Rogue Ware	RW Metro	Mapping from O-O to relational model
Resolution Ltd.	XCase	Conceptual modeling up to code maintenance
Sybase	Enterprise Application Suite	Data modeling, business logic modeling
Visio	Visio Enterprise	Data modeling, design and reengineering Visual Basic and Visual C++

16.6 Summary

We started this chapter by discussing the role of information systems in organizations; database systems are looked upon as a part of information systems in large-scale applications. We discussed how databases fit within an information system for information resource management in an organization and the life cycle they go through. We then discussed the six phases of the design process. The three phases commonly included as a part of database design are conceptual design, logical design (data model mapping), and physical design. We also discussed the initial phase of requirements collection and analysis, which is often considered to be a *predesign phase*. In addition, at some point during the design, a specific DBMS package must be chosen. We discussed some of the organizational criteria that come into play in selecting a DBMS. As performance problems are detected, and as new applications are added, designs have to be modified. For relational databases, we discussed the factors that affect physical database design decisions and provided guidelines for choosing among physical design alternatives. We discussed changes to logical design, modifications of indexing, and changes to queries as a part of database tuning.

The importance of designing both the schema and the applications (or transactions) was highlighted. We discussed different approaches to conceptual schema design and the difference between centralized schema design and the view integration approach. Finally, we briefly discussed the current functionality and desirable features of automated design tools.

Review Questions

16.1. What are the six phases of database design? Discuss each phase.

16.2. Which of the six phases are considered the main activities of the database design process itself? Why?

16.3. Why is it important to design the schemas and applications in parallel?

16.4. Why is it important to use an implementation-independent data model during conceptual schema design? What models are used in current design tools? Why?

16.5. Discuss the importance of Requirements Collection and Analysis.

16.6. Consider an actual application of a database system of interest. Define the requirements of the different levels of users in terms of data needed, types of queries, and transactions to be processed.

16.7. Discuss the characteristics that a data model for conceptual schema design should possess.

16.8. Compare and contrast the two main approaches to conceptual schema design.

16.9. Discuss the strategies for designing a single conceptual schema from its requirements.

16.10. What are the steps of the view integration approach to conceptual schema design? What are the difficulties during each step?

16.11. How would a view integration tool work? Design a sample modular architecture for such a tool.

16.12. What are the different strategies for view integration?

16.13. Discuss the factors that influence the choice of a DBMS package for the information system of an organization.

16.14. What is system-independent data model mapping? How is it different from system dependent data model mapping?

16.15. What are the important factors that influence physical database design?

16.16. Discuss the decisions made during physical database design.

16.17. Discuss the macro and micro life cycles of an information system.

16.18. Discuss the guidelines for physical database design in RDBMSs.

16.19. Discuss the types of modifications that may be applied to the logical database design of a relational database.

16.20. Under what situations would denormalization of a database schema be used? Give examples of denormalization.

16.21. Discuss the tuning of indexes for relational databases.

16.22. Discuss the considerations for reevaluating and modifying SQL queries.

16.23. Illustrate the types of changes to SQL queries that may be worth considering for improving the performance during database tuning.

16.24. What functions do the typical database design tools provide?

16.25. What type of functionality would be desirable in automated tools to support optimal design of large databases?

Selected Bibliography

There is a vast amount of literature on database design. We first list some of the books that address database design. Batini et al. (1992) is a comprehensive treatment of conceptual and logical database design. Wiederhold (1986) covers all phases of database design, with an emphasis on physical design. O'Neil (1994) has a detailed discussion of physical design and transaction issues in reference to commercial RDBMSs. A large body of work on conceptual modeling and design was done in the eighties. Brodie et al. (1984) gives a collection of chapters on conceptual modeling, constraint specification and analysis, and transaction design. Yao (1985) is a collection of works ranging from requirements specification techniques to schema restructuring. Teorey (1998) emphasizes EER modeling and discusses various aspects of conceptual and logical database design. McFadden and Hoffer (1997) is a good introduction to the business applications issues of database management.

Navathe and Kerschberg (1986) discuss all phases of database design and point out the role of data dictionaries. Goldfine and Konig (1988) and ANSI (1989) discuss the role of data dictionaries in database design. Rozen and Shasha (1991) and Carlis and March (1984) present different models for the problem of physical database design. Object-oriented database design is discussed in Schlaer and Mellor (1988), Rumbaugh et al. (1991), Martin and Odell (1991), and Jacobson (1992). Recent books by Blaha and Premerlani (1998) and Rumbaugh et al. (1999) consolidate the existing techniques in object-oriented design. Fowler and Scott (1997) is a quick introduction to UML.

Requirements collection and analysis is a heavily researched topic. Chatzoglu et al. (1997) and Lubars et al. (1993) present surveys of current practices in requirements capture, modeling, and analysis. Carroll (1995) provides a set of readings on the use of scenarios for requirements gathering in early stages of system development. Wood and Silver (1989) gives a good overview of the official Joint Application Design (JAD) process. Potter et al. (1991) describes the Z notation and methodology for formal specification of software. Zave (1997) has classified the research efforts in requirements engineering.

A large body of work has been produced on the problems of schema and view integration, which is becoming particularly relevant now because of the need to integrate a variety of existing databases. Navathe and Gadgil (1982) defined approaches to view integration. Schema integration methodologies are compared in Batini et al. (1986). Detailed work on n-ary view integration can be found in Navathe et al. (1986), Elmasri et al. (1986), and Larson et al. (1989). An integration tool based on Elmasri et al. (1986) is described in Sheth et al. (1988). Another view integration system is discussed in Hayne and Ram (1990). Casanova et al. (1991) describes a tool for modular database design. Motro (1987) discusses integration with respect to preexisting databases. The binary balanced strategy to view integration is discussed in Teorey and Fry (1982). A formal approach to view integration, which uses inclusion dependencies, is given in Casanova and Vidal (1982). Ramesh and Ram (1997) describe a methodology for integration of relationships in schemas utilizing the knowledge of integrity constraints; this extends the previous work of Navathe et al. (1984a). Sheth at al. (1993) describe the issues of building global schemas by reasoning about attribute relationships and entity equivalences. Navathe and Savasere (1996) describe a practical approach to building global schemas based on operators applied to schema components. Santucci (1998) provides a detailed treatment of refinement of EER schemas for integration. Castano et al. (1999) present a comprehensive survey of conceptual schema analysis techniques.

Transaction design is a relatively less thoroughly researched topic. Mylopoulos et al. (1980) proposed the TAXIS language, and Albano et al. (1987) developed the GALILEO system, both of which are comprehensive systems for specifying transactions. The GOR-DAS language for the ECR model (Elmasri et al. 1985) contains a transaction specification capability. Navathe and Balaraman (1991) and Ngu (1991) discuss transaction modeling in general for semantic data models. Elmagarmid (1992) discusses transaction models for advanced applications. Batini et al. (1992, chaps. 8, 9, and 11) discuss high level transaction design and joint analysis of data and functions. Shasha (1992) is an excellent source on database tuning.

Information about some well-known commercial database design tools can be found at the Web sites of the vendors (see company names in Table 16.1). Principles behind automated design tools are discussed in Batini et al. (1992, chap. 15). The SECSI tool from France is described in Metais et al. (1998). DKE (1997) is a special issue on natural language issues in databases.

PART 5

System Implementation Techniques

CHAPTER 17

Database System Architectures and the System Catalog

We now move into Part V of the book, on system implementation techniques. We start in this chapter by discussing two important aspects of database system implementation—system architectures and the system catalog. Although the two topics are not directly related, they provide a context and foundation for discussing the various DBMS system modules. Section 17.1 gives an overview of the basic system architectures that are used in DBMSs. In particular, we distinguish between the **centralized architectures** that were used in earlier systems, and the **client-server architectures**—which are prevalent in current systems. We discuss two different approaches to client-server architecture. The first, used in many relational DBMSs (RDBMSs), allows application programs to run at the client while most database functionality remains at the server. The second, used in many object DBMSs (ODBMSs), distributes some of the traditional DBMS functionality between the client and server. We will further discuss additional concepts and types of client-server architectures, as well as distributed database architectures, in Chapter 24.

We then turn our attention to the **system catalog,** which is at the heart of any general-purpose DBMS. It is a "minidatabase" itself, and one of its main functions is to store the **schemas,** or *descriptions*, of the databases that the DBMS maintains. Such information is often called **metadata.** It includes a description of the conceptual database schema, the internal schema, any external schemas, and the mappings between schemas at different levels. In addition, information needed by specific DBMS modules—for example, the query optimization module or the security and authorization module—is stored in the catalog.

569

In Section 17.2 we discuss general catalog information for relational DBMSs, and in Section 17.3 we focus on the catalog for a specific commercial DBMS, ORACLE. In Section 17.4 we discuss how a catalog is used by various modules of a DBMS, and we describe other types of information that may be stored in a catalog. In Section 17.5, we briefly discuss the types of systems called *data dictionaries* or *data repositories*, which maintain information similar to the catalog but of a more general nature.

17.1   System Architectures for DBMSs

17.1.1   Centralized DBMS Architecture

Architectures for DBMSs followed trends similar to those of general computer systems architectures. Earlier architectures used mainframe computers to provide the main processing for all functions of the system, including user application programs, user interface programs, as well as all the DBMS functionality. The reason was that most users accessed such systems via computer terminals that did not have processing power and only provided display capabilities. So, all processing was performed remotely, and only display information and controls were sent from the computer to the display terminals, which were connected to the central computer via various types of communications networks.

As the prices of hardware declined, most users replaced their terminals with personal computers (PCs) and workstations. At first, database systems used these computers in the same way as they had used display terminals, so that the DBMS itself was still a **centralized DBMS** where all the DBMS functionality, application program execution, and user interface processing were carried out in one machine. Figure 17.1(a) illustrates the physical components in a centralized architecture. Gradually DBMS systems started to exploit the available processing power at the user side, which led to client-server DBMS architectures.

17.1.2   Client-Server Architecture

We first discuss client-server architecture in general, then see how it is applied to DBMSs. The **client-server architecture** was developed to deal with computing environments where a large number of PCs, workstations, file servers, printers, database servers, Web servers, and other equipment are connected together via a network. The idea is to define **specialized servers** with specific functionalities. For example, it is possible to connect a number of PCs or small workstations as clients to a **file server** that maintains the files of the client machines. Another machine could be designated as a **printer server** by being connected to various printers; thereafter, all print requests by the clients are forwarded to this machine. **Web servers** or **E-mail servers** also fall into the specialized server category. In this way, the resources provided by specialized servers can be accessed by many client machines. The **client machines** provide the user with the appropriate interfaces to utilize these servers as well as with local processing power to run local applications. This concept

Figure 17.1(a) Diagrams to illustrate different architectures. Physical centralized architecture.

can be carried over to software, with specialized software—such as a DBMS or a CAD (computer-aided design) package—being stored on specific server machines and being made accessible to multiple clients. Figure 17.1(b) illustrates client-server architecture at the logical level, and Figure 17.1(c) is a simplified diagram that shows how the physical architecture would look. Some machines would be only client sites (for example, diskless workstations or workstations/PCs with disks that have only client software installed). Other machines would be dedicated servers. Still other machines would have both client and server functionality.

Figure 17.1(b) Diagrams to illustrate different architectures. Simplified logical client-server architecture.

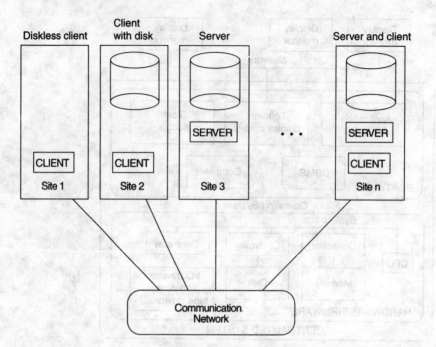

Figure 17.1(c)   Diagrams to illustrate different architectures. Simplified physical client-server architecture.

The concept of client-server architecture assumes an underlying framework that consists of many PCs and workstations as well as a smaller number of mainframe machines, connected via local area networks and other types of computer networks. A **client** in this framework is typically a user machine that provides user interface capabilities and local processing. When a client requires access to additional functionality—such as database access—that does not exist at that machine, it connects to a server that provides the needed functionality. A **server** is a machine that can provide services to the client machines, such as printing, archiving, or database access. Two main types of basic DBMS architectures were created on this underlying client-server framework.[1] We discuss those next.

17.1.3 Client-Server Architectures for DBMSs

The client-server architecture is increasingly being incorporated into commercial DBMS packages. In relational DBMSs, many of which started as centralized systems, the system components that were first moved to the client side were the user interface and application programs. Because SQL provided a standard language for RDBMSs, it created a logical dividing point between client and server. Hence, the query and transaction functionality remained at the server side. In such an architecture, the server is often called a **query**

---

1. There are many other variations of client-server architectures. We only discuss the two most basic ones here. In Chapter 24, we discuss additional client-server and distributed architectures.

server or transaction server, because it provided these two functionalities. In RDBMSs, the server is also often called an SQL server, since most RDBMS servers are based on the SQL language and standard.

In such a client-server architecture, the user interface programs and application programs can run at the client side. When DBMS access is required, the program establishes a connection to the DBMS—which is on the server side—and once the connection is created, the client program can communicate with the DBMS. A standard called Open Database Connectivity (ODBC) provides an Application Programming Interface (API), which allows client-side programs to call the DBMS, as long as both client and server machines have the necessary software installed. Most DBMS vendors provide ODBC drivers for their systems. Hence, a client program can actually connect to several RDBMSs and send query and transaction requests using the ODBC API, which are processed at the server sites. Any query results are sent back to the client program, which can process or display the results as needed. Another related standard for the JAVA programming language, called JDBC, has also been defined. This allows JAVA client programs to access the DBMS through a standard interface.

The second approach to client-server was taken by some object-oriented DBMSs. Because many of those systems were developed in the era of client-server architecture, the approach taken was to divide the software modules of the DBMS between client and server in a more integrated way. For example, the server level may include the part of the DBMS software responsible for handling data storage on disk pages, local concurrency control and recovery, buffering and caching of disk pages, and other such functions. Meanwhile, the client level may handle the user interface, data dictionary functions, DBMS interaction with programming language compilers, global query optimization/concurrency control/recovery, structuring of complex objects from the data in the buffers, and other such functions. In this approach, the client-server interaction is more tightly coupled and is done internally by the DBMS modules—some of which reside in the client—rather than by the users. The exact division of functionality varies from system to system. In such a client-server architecture, the server has been called a data server, because it provides data in disk pages to the client, which can then be structured into objects for the client programs by the client-side DBMS software itself.

We will further elaborate on client-server and distributed architectures in Chapter 24. After this brief introduction to system architectures, we discuss DBMS catalogs for the rest of this chapter.

17.2 Catalogs for Relational DBMSs

We now turn our attention to the second topic of this chapter, which is the DBMS catalog, and discuss catalogs for relational DBMSs.[2] The information stored in a catalog of an RDBMS includes the relation names, attribute names, and attribute domains (data types), as well as descriptions of constraints (primary keys, secondary keys, foreign keys, NULL/NOT NULL, and other types of constraints), views, and storage structures and indexes.

---

2. We discuss only relational systems here. Catalogs for other types of DBMSs will contain similar types of information, but the actual details will be different because of the differences between the data models.

REL_AND_ATTR_CATALOG

REL_NAME	ATTR_NAME	ATTR_TYPE	MEMBER_OF_PK	MEMBER_OF_FK	FK_RELATION
EMPLOYEE	FNAME	VSTR15	no	no	
EMPLOYEE	MINIT	CHAR	no	no	
EMPLOYEE	LNAME	VSTR15	no	no	
EMPLOYEE	SSN	STR9	yes	no	
EMPLOYEE	BDATE	STR9	no	no	
EMPLOYEE	ADDRESS	VSTR30	no	no	
EMPLOYEE	SEX	CHAR	no	no	
EMPLOYEE	SALARY	INTEGER	no	no	
EMPLOYEE	SUPERSSN	STR9	no	yes	
EMPLOYEE	DNO	INTEGER	no	yes	EMPLOYEE
DEPARTMENT	DNAME	VSTR10	no	no	DEPARTMENT
DEPARTMENT	DNUMBER	INTEGER	yes	no	
DEPARTMENT	MGRSSN	STR9	no	yes	
DEPARTMENT	MGRSTARTDATE	STR10	no	no	EMPLOYEE
DEPT_LOCATIONS	DNUMBER	INTEGER	yes	yes	
DEPT_LOCATIONS	DLOCATION	VSTR15	yes	no	DEPARTMENT
PROJECT	PNAME	VSTR10	no	no	
PROJECT	PNUMBER	INTEGER	yes	no	
PROJECT	PLOCATION	VSTR15	no	no	
PROJECT	DNUM	INTEGER	no	yes	DEPARTMENT
WORKS_ON	ESSN	STR9	yes	yes	EMPLOYEE
WORKS_ON	PNO	INTEGER	yes	yes	PROJECT
WORKS_ON	HOURS	REAL	no	no	
DEPENDENT	ESSN	STR9	yes	yes	EMPLOYEE
DEPENDENT	DEPENDENT_NAME	VSTR15	yes	no	
DEPENDENT	SEX	CHAR	no	no	
DEPENDENT	BDATE	STR9	no	no	

Figure 17.2   Basic catalog relation to describe the relation schemas in Figure 7.5.

Security and authorization information is also kept in the catalog; this describes each user's privileges to access specific database relations and views, and the creator or owner of each relation (see Chapter 22).

In relational DBMSs it is common practice to store the catalog itself as relations and to use the DBMS software for querying, updating, and maintaining the catalog. This allows DBMS routines (as well as users) to access the information stored in the catalog—whenever they are authorized to do so—using the query language of the DBMS, such as SQL.

A possible catalog structure for base relation information is shown in Figure 17.2, which stores relation names, attribute names, attribute types, and primary key information. Figure 17.2 also shows how foreign key constraints may be included. The description of the relational database schema in Figure 7.5 is shown as the tuples (contents) of the catalog relation in Figure 17.2, which we call REL_AND_ATTR_CATALOG. The primary key of REL_AND_ATTR_CATALOG is the combination of the attributes {REL_NAME, ATTR_NAME}, because all relation names should be unique and all attribute names *within a particular relation* should also be unique.[3] Another catalog relation can store information such as tuple size, current number of tuples, number of indexes, and creator name for each relation.

---

3. In general, the schema name should also be included in the REL_AND_ATTR_CATALOG catalog relation (and other catalog relations). It can also be part of the primary key, since a single DBMS can have multiple schemas. We left out the schema name to simplify the diagram in Figure 17.2.

To include information on secondary key attributes of a relation, we can simply extend the preceding catalog if we assume that an attribute can be a *member of one key only*. In this case we can replace the MEMBER_OF_PK attribute of REL_AND_ATTR_CATALOG with an attribute KEY_NUMBER; the value of KEY_NUMBER is 0 if the attribute is not a member of any key, 1 if it is a member of the primary key, and $i > 1$ for the ith secondary key, where the secondary keys of a relation are numbered 2, 3, ..., n. However, if an attribute can be a member of *more than one key*, which is the general case, the above representation is not sufficient. One possibility is to store information on key attributes separately in a second catalog relation RELATION_KEYS, with attributes {REL_NAME, KEY_NUMBER, MEMBER_ATTR}, which also together form the key of RELATION_KEYS. This is shown in Figure 17.3(a). The DDL compiler assigns the value 1 to KEY_NUMBER for the primary key and values 2, 3, ..., n for the secondary keys, if any. Each key will have a tuple in RELATION_KEYS for each attribute that is part of that key, and the value of MEMBER_ATTRIBUTE gives the name of that attribute. A similar structure can be used to store information involving foreign keys. If constraints are given names so they can be dropped later, then a unique attribute CONSTRAINT_NAME must be added to the catalog tables that describes constraints (including those that describe keys).

Next, let us consider information regarding indexes. In the general case where an attribute can be a member of more than one index, the RELATION_INDEXES catalog relation shown in Figure 17.3(b) can be used. The key of RELATION_INDEXES is the combination {INDEX_NAME, MEMBER_ATTR} (assuming that index names are unique). MEMBER_ATTR is the name of an attribute included in the index. For example, if we specify three indexes on the WORKS_ON relation of Figure 7.5—a clustering index on ESSN, a secondary index on PNO, and another secondary index on the combination {ESSN, PNO}—the attributes ESSN and PNO are

(a) RELATION_KEYS

REL_NAME	KEY_NUMBER	MEMBER_ATTR

(b) RELATION_INDEXES

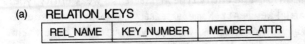

REL_NAME	INDEX_NAME	MEMBER_ATTR	INDEX_TYPE	ATTR_NO	ASC_DESC

(c) VIEW_QUERIES

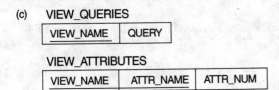

VIEW_NAME	QUERY

VIEW_ATTRIBUTES

VIEW_NAME	ATTR_NAME	ATTR_NUM

Figure 17.3 Other possible catalog relations for a relational system. (a) Possible catalog relation for storing general key information. (b) Possible catalog relation for storing index information. (c) Possible catalog relations for storing view information.

members of two indexes each. The ATTR_NO and ASC_DESC fields specify the order of each attribute within the index entries and specify whether the index entries are ordered in ascending or descending order in the index.[4]

The definitions of views must also be stored in the catalog. A view is specified by a query, with a possible renaming of the values appearing in the query result (see Chapter 8). We can use the two catalog relations shown in Figure 17.3(c) to store view definitions. The first, VIEW_QUERIES, has two attributes {VIEW_NAME, QUERY} and stores the query (as a text string) corresponding to the view. The second, VIEW_ATTRIBUTES, has attributes {VIEW_NAME, ATTR_NAME, ATTR_NUM} to store the names of the attributes of the view, where ATTR_NUM is an integer number greater than zero specifying the correspondence of each view attribute to the attributes in the query result. The key of VIEW_QUERIES is VIEW_NAME, and that of VIEW_ATTRIBUTES is the combination {VIEW_NAME, ATTR_NAME}.

The preceding examples illustrate the types of information stored in a catalog. In a real system, the catalog will typically include many more tables and information. Most relational systems store their catalog files as DBMS relations. However, because the catalog is accessed very frequently by the DBMS modules, it is important to implement catalog access as efficiently as possible. It may be more efficient to use a specialized set of data structures and access routines to implement the catalog, thus trading generality for efficiency. An additional problem is that of **system initialization;** the catalog tables must be created before the system can function!

In conclusion, we take a *conceptual* look at the basic information stored in the parts of a relational catalog for describing tables (relations). Figure 17.4 shows a high-level EER schema diagram (see Chapters 3 and 4) describing the information about schemas, relations, attributes, keys, views, and indexes. The SCHEMA entity type in the figure represents the schemas that have been defined in a RDBMS. The entity type RELATION is a weak entity type owned by (or identified by) SCHEMA—with partial key RelName—to represent the relations that appear in a particular schema. Two disjoint subclasses, BASE_RELATION and VIEW_RELATION, are created for RELATION. The entity type ATTRIBUTE is a weak entity type owned by BASE_RELATION, and its partial key is AttrName. BASE_RELATIONs also have general key and foreign key constraints, as well as indexes, whereas VIEW_RELATIONs have their defining query, as well as the AttrNum described earlier to specify correspondence of view attributes to query attributes. Notice that an additional unspecified constraint in Figure 17.4 is that all attributes related to a KEY or INDEX entity—via the relationships KEY_ATTRS or INDEX_ATTRS—must be related to the same BASE_RELATION entity to which the KEY or INDEX entity is related. KeyType specifies whether the key is a foreign, primary, or secondary key. FKEY is a subclass for foreign keys and is related to the referenced relation via the REFREL relationship.

We discuss additional information that must be stored in a catalog in Section 17.4.

---

4. This is necessary because the attributes in a composite index must be defined as an *ordered list*.

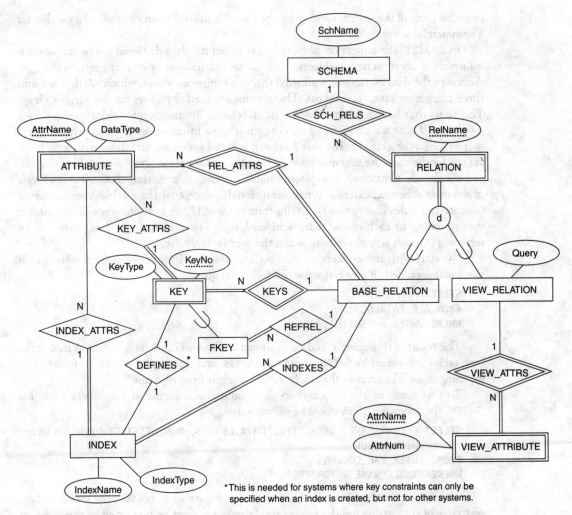

Figure 17.4 An example of an enhanced-ER (EER) diagram for part of a relational catalog.

*This is needed for systems where key constraints can only be specified when an index is created, but not for other systems.

17.3 System Catalog Information in ORACLE

The various commercial database products adopt different conventions and terminology with regard to their system catalog. However, in general, the catalogs contain similar metadata describing conceptual, internal, and external schemas. In this section, we examine parts of the system catalog for the ORACLE RDBMS as an example of a catalog for a commercial system.

In ORACLE, the collection of metadata is called the **data dictionary.** The metadata is information about **schema objects,** such as tables, indexes, views, triggers, and more. Access to the data dictionary is allowed through numerous **views,** which are divided into three categories: USER, ALL, and DBA. These terms are used as *prefixes* for the various views. The views that have a prefix of USER contain schema information for objects owned by a given user. Those with a prefix of ALL contain schema information for objects owned by a user as well as objects that the user has been granted access to, and those with a prefix of DBA are for the database administrator and contain information about all database objects.

As already mentioned, the system catalog contains information about all three levels of database schemas: external (view definitions), conceptual (base tables), and internal (storage and index descriptions). To illustrate in ORACLE, we examine some of the catalog views relating to each of the three schema levels. The catalog (metadata) data can be retrieved through SQL statements as can the user (actual) data.

We start with the conceptual schema information. To find the objects owned by a particular user, 'SMITH', we can write the following query:

```
SELECT *
FROM ALL_CATALOG
WHERE OWNER = 'SMITH';
```

The result of this query could be as shown in Figure 17.5, which indicates that three base tables are owned by SMITH: ACCOUNT, CUSTOMERS, and ORDERS, plus a view CUSTORDER. The meaning of each column in the result should be clear from its name.

To find some of the information describing the columns of the ORDERS table for 'SMITH', the following query could be submitted:

```
SELECT  COLUMN_NAME, DATA_TYPE, DATA_LENGTH, NUM_DISTINCT, LOW_VALUE,
        HIGH_VALUE
FROM    USER_TAB_COLUMNS
WHERE   TABLE_NAME = 'ORDERS';
```

The result of this query could be as shown in Figure 17.6. Because the USER_TAB_COL-UMNS table of the catalog has the prefix USER_, this query must be submitted by the *owner* of the ORDERS table. The last three columns specified in the SELECT-clause of the SQL query play an important role in the query optimization process, as we shall see in Chapter 18. The NUM_DISTINCT column specifies the number of distinct values for a given column and

OWNER	TABLE_NAME	TABLE_TYPE
SMITH	ACCOUNT	TABLE
SMITH	CUSTOMERS	TABLE
SMITH	CUSTORDER	VIEW
SMITH	ORDERS	TABLE

Figure 17.5   The result of querying ALL_CATALOG.

COLUMN_NAME	DATA_TYPE	DATA_LENGTH	NUM_DISTINCT	LOW_VALUE	HIGH_VALUE
ORDERNO	NUMBER	22	4	C102	C105
CUSTNO	NUMBER	22	3	C102	C106
ORDERDATE	DATE	7	4	77BF0A1E010101	77BF0B06010101

Figure 17.6   The result of querying USER_TAB_COLUMNS.

the LOW_VALUE and HIGH_VALUE specify the lowest and highest value, respectively, for the given column. We should note that these values, called **database statistics,** are not automatically updated when tuples are inserted/deleted/modified. Rather, the statistics are updated, either by exact computation or by estimation, whenever the ANALYZE SQL statement in ORACLE is executed as follows:

```
ANALYZE TABLE ORDERS
COMPUTE STATISTICS;
```

This SQL statement would update all statistics for the ORDERS relation and its associated indexes.

To access information about the internal schema, the USER_TABLES and USER_INDEXES catalog tables can be queried. For example, to find storage information about the ORDERS table, the following query can be submitted:

```
SELECT  PCT_FREE, INITIAL_EXTENT, NUM_ROWS, BLOCKS, EMPTY_BLOCKS,
        AVG_ROW_LENGTH
FROM    USER_TABLES
WHERE   TABLE_NAME = 'ORDERS';
```

The result of this query could be as shown in Figure 17.7, which contains a subset of the available storage information in the catalog. The information includes—from left to right—the minimum percentage of free space in a block, the size of the initial storage extent in bytes, the number of rows in the table, the number of used data blocks allocated to the table, the number of free data blocks allocated to the table, and the average length of a row in the table in bytes.

The information from USER_TABLES also plays a useful role in query processing and optimization. For example, in Figure 17.7, we see that the entire ORDERS table is stored in a single block of disk storage. So, processing a query that involves only the ORDERS relation

PCT_FREE	INITIAL_EXTENT	NUM_ROWS	BLOCKS	EMPTY_BLOCKS	AVG_ROW_LENGTH
10	10240	4	1	3	17

Figure 17.7   Result of querying USER_TABLES.

INDEX_NAME	UNIQUENESS	BLEVEL	LEAF_ BLOCKS	DISTINCT_ KEYS	AVG_LEAF_ BLOCKS_ PER_KEY	AVG_DATA_ BLOCKS_ PER_KEY
ORD_CUSTNO	NONUNIQUE	0	1	3	1	1

Figure 17.8   The result of querying USER_INDEXES.

can be done efficiently (without using an index) by accessing a single disk block. To retrieve information about the indexes for a specific table, the following query can be run:

```
SELECT  INDEX_NAME, UNIQUENESS, BLEVEL, LEAF_BLOCKS, DISTINCT_KEYS,
        AVG_LEAF_BLOCKS_PER_KEY, AVG_DATA_BLOCKS_PER_KEY
FROM    USER_INDEXES
WHERE   TABLE_NAME = 'ORDERS';
```

Figure 17.8 shows how the query result could look. The above table contains a subset of the available index storage information, which includes from left to right the name of the index, the uniqueness (whether the indexing attribute is unique—that is, a key—or not), the depth of the index from the root block to the leaf blocks (number of index levels), the number of leaf blocks, the number of distinct indexed values, the average number of leaf blocks for a specific value, and the average number of data blocks pointed to by a specific value in the index leaf blocks. Additional information on an index would include whether it is on a clustering (ordering) attribute in the table.

The storage information about the indexes is just as important to the query optimizer as the storage information about the relations. For example, the number of index blocks that have to be accessed when searching for a specific key can be computed as the sum of BLEVEL and LEAF_BLOCKS_PER_KEY.[5] This information is used by the optimizer in deciding how to execute a query efficiently (see Chapter 18).

For information about the external schema, the USER_VIEWS table can be queried as follows:

```
SELECT  *
FROM    USER_VIEWS;
```

The result could be as shown in Figure 17.9.

VIEW_NAME	TEXT_LENGTH	TEXT
CUSTORDER	101	select custname,city,orderno,orderdate from customers,orders where customers.custno=orders.custno;

Figure 17.9   The result of querying USER_VIEWS.

5. Note that BLEVEL is the number of index levels, and that LEAF_BLOCKS_PER_KEY is 1 if the indexing attribute is a key and is the number of indirect-level blocks otherwise (see Chapter 6).

COLUMN_NAME	DATA_TYPE	DATA_LENGTH
CITY	CHAR	20
ORDERNO	NUMBER	22
ORDERDATE	DATE	7
CUSTNAME	CHAR	20

Figure 17.10   Result of querying USER_TAB_COLUMNS about the CUSTORDER view.

Using the view name, CUSTORDER, the associated column information can be extracted from the USER_TAB_COLUMNS table. The query is shown below with the query results displayed in Figure 17.10.

```
SELECT  COLUMN_NAME, DATA_TYPE, DATA_LENGTH
FROM    USER_TAB_COLUMNS
WHERE   TABLE_NAME = 'CUSTORDER';
```

More detailed information about ORACLE's data dictionary facilities can be found in the ORACLE RDBMS Database Administrator's Guide and the ORACLE SQL Language Reference Manual.

17.4   Other Catalog Information Accessed by DBMS Software Modules

The DBMS modules use and access a catalog very frequently; that is why it is important to implement access to the catalog as efficiently as possible. In this section we discuss the different ways in which some of the DBMS software modules use and access the catalog. These include the following:

1. *DDL (and SDL) compilers:* These DBMS modules process and check the specification of a database schema in the data definition language (DDL) and store that description in the catalog. Schema constructs and constraints at all levels—conceptual, internal, and external—are extracted from the DDL and SDL (storage definition language) specifications and entered into the catalog, as is any mapping information among levels, if necessary. Hence, these software modules actually **populate** (load) the catalog's minidatabase (or **metadatabase**) with data, the data being the descriptions of database schemas.

2. *Query and DML parser and verifier:* These modules parse queries, DML retrieval statements, and database update statements; they also check the catalog to verify whether all the schema names referenced in these statements are valid. For example, in a relational system, a query parser would check that all the relation names specified in the query exist in the catalog and that the attributes specified belong to the appropriate relations and have the appropriate type.

3. *Query and DML compilers:* These compilers convert high-level queries and DML commands into low-level file access commands. The mapping between the conceptual schema and the internal schema file structures is accessed from the catalog during this process. For example, the catalog must include a description of each file and its fields and the correspondences between fields and conceptual-level attributes.

4. *Query and DML optimizer:*[6] The query optimizer accesses the catalog for access path, implementation information, and data statistics to determine the best way to execute a query or DML command (see Chapter 18). For example, the optimizer accesses the catalog to check which fields of a relation have hash access or indexes, before deciding how to execute a selection or join condition on the relation.

5. *Authorization and security checking:* The DBA has privileged commands to update the authorization and security portion of the catalog (see Chapter 22). All access by a user to a relation is checked by the DBMS for proper authorization by accessing the catalog.

6. *External-to-conceptual mapping of queries and DML commands:* Queries and DML commands specified with reference to an external view or schema must be transformed to refer to the conceptual schema before they can be processed by the DBMS. This is accomplished by accessing the catalog description of the view in order to perform the transformation.

17.5 Data Dictionary and Data Repository Systems

The terms data dictionary and data repository are used to indicate a more general software utility than a catalog. A **catalog** is closely coupled with the DBMS software; it provides the information stored in it to users and the DBA, but it is *mainly* accessed by the various software modules of the DBMS itself, such as DDL and DML compilers, the query optimizer, the transaction processor, report generators, and the constraint enforcer. On the other hand, the software package for a *stand-alone* **data dictionary** or **data repository** may interact with the software modules of the DBMS, but it is *mainly* used by the designers, users, and administrators of a computer system for information resource management. These systems are used to maintain information on system hardware and software configurations, documentation, applications, and users, as well as other information relevant to system administration.

If a data dictionary system is used *only* by designers, users, and administrators, not by the DBMS software, it is called a **passive data dictionary;** otherwise, it is called an **active data dictionary** or **data directory.** Figure 17.11 illustrates the types of active data dictionary interfaces. Data dictionaries are also used to document the database design process

---

6. As we shall see in Chapter 18, items 3 and 4 are generally processed by the same DBMS module.

Figure 17.11   Human and software interfaces to a data dictionary.

itself, by storing documentation on the results of every design phase and the design decisions. This helps in automating the design process by making the design decisions and changes available to all the database designers. Modifications to the database description are made by changing the data dictionary contents. Using the data dictionary during database design means that, at the conclusion of the design phase, the metadata is already in the data dictionary.

17.6 Summary

In this chapter we first gave an overview of the centralized versus client-server system architectures, and described how these architectures are used in the database context. We discussed how earlier database systems were centralized, and how the emergence of the environment of networked workstations, PCs, and mainframes led to client-server computing. We showed how relational systems evolved into SQL servers (also called query servers or transaction servers), and discussed how the newer object databases further divide basic functionality between client and server, leading to data servers.

We then discussed the type of information that is included in a DBMS catalog. We discussed catalog structure for a relational DBMS and showed how it can store the constructs of the relational model, including information concerning key constraints, indexes, and views. We also gave a conceptual description—in the form of an EER schema diagram—of the relational model constructs and how they are related to one another. We covered some specifics about the system catalog in the ORACLE RDBMS. We then discussed how different DBMS modules access the information stored in a DBMS catalog, and gave an overview of other types of information stored in a catalog. Finally, we briefly discussed data dictionary/repository systems and how they differ from catalogs.

Review Questions

17.1. What is the difference between centralized and client-server architectures in general?

17.2. How did relational DBMSs evolve from the centralized architecture to the client-server architecture? What is ODBC used for in this context?

17.3. How do object databases differ from relational systems in a client-server system architecture?

17.4. What is meant by the term *metadata*?

17.5. How are relational DBMS catalogs usually implemented?

17.6. Discuss the types of information included in a relational catalog at the conceptual, internal, and external levels.

17.7. Discuss how some of the different DBMS modules access a catalog and the type of information each accesses.

17.8. Why is it important to have efficient access to a DBMS catalog?

17.9. What are the three different view categories for catalog information in ORACLE and why are they important?

Exercises

17.10. Expand the relational catalog of Figure 17.3 to include a more complete description of a relational schema plus internal descriptions of storage files and any needed mapping information.

17.11. For the EER diagrams shown in Figure 17.4, use the mapping algorithms discussed in Chapter 9 to create an equivalent relational schema to represent a relational catalog.

17.12. Write (in English) sample queries against the EER schema of Figures 17.4 that would retrieve meaningful information about the database schemas from the catalog.

17.13. Using the relational schemas from Exercise 17.11, write the queries you specified in 17.12 in some relational query language (SQL, relational algebra).

17.14. Suppose that we have a "generalized" DBMS that uses the EER model at the conceptual schema level and relation-like files at the internal level. Draw an EER diagram to represent the basic information for a catalog that represents such an EER database system. First describe the EER concepts as an EER schema (!), and then add mapping information from the conceptual schema to the internal schema in the catalog.

17.15. Why are database statistics, such as those stored in ORACLE, not updated automatically after every insert/delete/update to a table?

Selected Bibliography

Detailed information about the system catalog for the ORACLE relational database system can be found in the ORACLE RDBMS Database Administrator's Guide (1992a).

CHAPTER 18

Query Processing and Optimization

In this chapter we discuss the techniques used by a DBMS to process, optimize, and execute high-level queries. A query expressed in a high-level query language such as SQL must first be scanned, parsed, and validated.[1] The **scanner** identifies the language tokens—such as SQL keywords, attribute names, and relation names—in the text of the query, whereas the **parser** checks the query syntax to determine whether it is formulated according to the syntax rules (rules of grammar) of the query language. The query must also be **validated,** by checking that all attribute and relation names are valid and semantically meaningful names in the schema of the particular database being queried. An internal representation of the query is then created, usually as a tree data structure called a **query tree.** It is also possible to represent the query using a graph data structure called a **query graph.** The DBMS must then devise an **execution strategy** for retrieving the result of the query from the database files. A query typically has many possible execution strategies, and the process of choosing a suitable one for processing a query is known as **query optimization.**

Figure 18.1 shows the different steps of processing a high-level query. The **query optimizer** module has the task of producing an execution plan, and the **code generator** generates the code to execute that plan. The **runtime database processor** has the task of running

---

1. We will not discuss the parsing and syntax-checking phase of query processing here; this material is discussed in compiler textbooks.

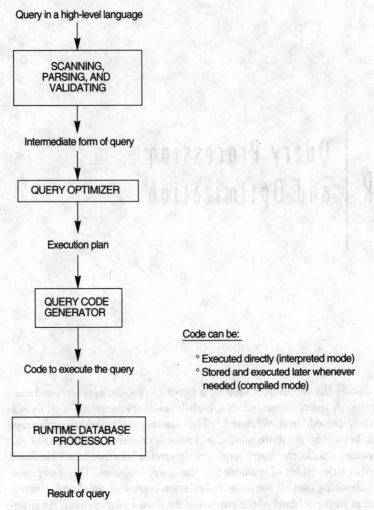

Query in a high-level language

SCANNING,
PARSING, AND
VALIDATING

Intermediate form of query

QUERY OPTIMIZER

Execution plan

QUERY CODE
GENERATOR

Code can be:

° Executed directly (interpreted mode)
° Stored and executed later whenever
  needed (compiled mode)

Code to execute the query

RUNTIME DATABASE
PROCESSOR

Result of query

Figure 18.1   Typical steps when processing a high-level query.

the query code, whether in compiled or interpreted mode, to produce the query result. If a runtime error results, an error message is generated by the runtime database processor.

The term *optimization* is actually a misnomer because in some cases the chosen execution plan is not the optimal (best) strategy—it is just a *reasonably efficient strategy* for executing the query. Finding the optimal strategy is usually too time-consuming except for the simplest of queries and may require information on how the files are implemented and even on the contents of the files—information that may not be fully available in the DBMS catalog. Hence, *planning of an execution strategy* may be a more accurate description than *query optimization*.

For lower-level navigational database languages in legacy systems—such as the network DML or the hierarchical HDML (see Appendixes C and D)—the programmer must choose the query execution strategy while writing a database program. If a DBMS provides only a navigational language, there is *limited need or opportunity* for extensive query optimization by the DBMS; instead, the programmer is given the capability to choose the "optimal" execution strategy. On the other hand, a high-level query language—such as SQL for relational DBMSs (RDBMSs) or OQL for object DBMSs (ODBMSs)—is more declarative in nature because it specifies what the intended results of the query are, rather than identifying the details of *how* the result should be obtained. Query optimization is thus necessary for queries that are specified in a high-level query language.

We will concentrate on describing query optimization in the context of an RDBMS because many of the techniques we describe have been adapted for ODBMSs.[2] A relational DBMS must systematically evaluate alternative query execution strategies and choose a reasonably efficient or optimal strategy. Each DBMS typically has a number of general database access algorithms that implement relational operations such as SELECT or JOIN or combinations of these operations. Only execution strategies that can be implemented by the DBMS access algorithms and that apply to the particular query and particular physical database design can be considered by the query optimization module.

We start in Section 18.1 with a general discussion of how SQL queries are typically translated into relational algebra queries and then optimized. We then discuss algorithms for implementing relational operations in Section 18.2. Following this, we give an overview of query optimization strategies. There are two main techniques for implementing query optimization. The first technique is based on **heuristic rules** for ordering the operations in a query execution strategy. A heuristic is a rule that works well in most cases but is not guaranteed to work well in every possible case. The rules typically reorder the operations in a query tree. The second technique involves **systematically estimating** the cost of different execution strategies and choosing the execution plan with the lowest cost estimate. The two techniques are usually combined in a query optimizer.[3] We discuss heuristic optimization in Section 18.3 and cost estimation in Section 18.4. We then provide a brief overview of the factors considered during query optimization in the ORACLE commercial RDBMS in Section 18.5. Section 18.6 introduces the topic of semantic query optimization, in which known constraints are used to devise efficient query execution strategies.

18.1 Translating SQL Queries into Relational Algebra

In practice, SQL is the query language that is used in most commercial RDBMSs. An SQL query is first translated into an equivalent extended relational algebra expression—represented as a query tree data structure—that is then optimized. Typically, SQL queries are decomposed into **query blocks,** which form the basic units that can be translated into the

---

2. There are some query optimization problems and techniques that are pertinent only to ODBMSs. However, we do not discuss these here as we can give only an introduction to query optimization.

3. In addition to query optimization, similar optimization techniques are also used for constraint enforcement by the DBMS.

algebraic operators and optimized. A query block contains a single SELECT-FROM-WHERE expression, as well as GROUP BY and HAVING clauses if these are part of the block. Hence, nested queries within a query are identified as separate query blocks. Because SQL includes aggregate operators—such as MAX, MIN, SUM, AND COUNT—these operators must also be included in the extended algebra, as we discussed in Section 7.5.

Consider the following SQL query on the EMPLOYEE relation in Figure 7.5:

```
SELECT   LNAME, FNAME
FROM     EMPLOYEE
WHERE    SALARY >   (SELECT   MAX (SALARY)
                     FROM     EMPLOYEE
                     WHERE    DNO=5) ;
```

This query includes a nested subquery and hence would be decomposed into two blocks. The inner block is

```
(SELECT MAX (SALARY)
FROM     EMPLOYEE
WHERE    DNO=5)
```

and the outer block is

```
SELECT LNAME, FNAME
FROM     EMPLOYEE
WHERE    SALARY > c
```

where c represents the result returned from the inner block. The inner block could be translated into the extended relational algebra expression

$$\Im_{\text{MAX SALARY}}(\sigma_{\text{DNO}=5}(\text{EMPLOYEE}))$$

and the outer block into the expression

$$\pi_{\text{LNAME},\text{FNAME}}(\sigma_{\text{SALARY}>c}(\text{EMPLOYEE}))$$

The *query optimizer* would then choose an execution plan for each block. We should note that in the above example, the inner block needs to be evaluated only once to produce the maximum salary, which is then used—as the constant c—by the outer block. We called this an *uncorrelated nested query* in Chapter 8. It is much harder to optimize the more complex *correlated nested queries* (see Section 8.3), where a tuple variable from the outer block appears in the WHERE-clause of the inner block.

18.2 Basic Algorithms for Executing Query Operations

An RDBMS must include **algorithms** for implementing the different types of relational operations (as well as other types of operations) that can appear in a query execution strategy. These operations include the basic and extended relational algebra operations discussed in Chapter 7 and, in many cases, combinations of these operations. For each such operation or combination of operations, one or more algorithms would typically be available to execute the operation(s). An algorithm may apply only to particular storage structures and access paths; if so, it can only be used if the files involved in the operation include these access paths (see Chapters 5 and 6). In this section we discuss typical algorithms used to implement SELECT, JOIN, and other relational operations. We begin by discussing *external sorting* in Section 18.2.1, which is at the heart of many relational operations that utilize *sort-merge strategies*. Then we discuss algorithms for implementing the SELECT operation in Section 18.2.2; the JOIN operation in Section 18.2.3; the PROJECT operation and the set operations (UNION, INTERSECTION, SET DIFFERENCE) in Section 18.2.4; and aggregate operations (MIN, MAX, COUNT, AVERAGE, SUM) in Section 18.2.5.[4]

18.2.1 External Sorting

Sorting is one of the primary algorithms used in query processing. For example, whenever an SQL query specifies an ORDER BY-clause, the query result must be sorted. Sorting is also a key component in sort-merge algorithms used for JOIN and other operations (such as UNION and INTERSECTION), and in duplicate elimination algorithms for the PROJECT operation (when an SQL query specifies the DISTINCT option in the SELECT clause). We will discuss some of these algorithms in Sections 18.2.3 and 18.2.4. Note that sorting may be avoided if an appropriate index exists to allow ordered access to the records.

External sorting refers to sorting algorithms that are suitable for large files of records stored on disk that do not fit entirely in main memory, such as most database files.[5] The typical external sorting algorithm uses a **sort-merge strategy,** which starts by sorting small subfiles—called **runs**—of the main file and then merges the sorted runs, creating larger sorted subfiles that are merged in turn. The sort-merge algorithm, like other database algorithms, requires *buffer space* in main memory, where the actual sorting and merging of the runs is performed. The basic algorithm, outlined in Figure 18.2, consists of two phases: (1) the sorting phase and (2) the merging phase.

In the **sorting phase,** runs (portions or pieces) of the file that can fit in the available buffer space are read into main memory, sorted using an internal sorting algorithm, and written back to disk as temporary sorted subfiles (or runs). The size of a run and **number of initial runs (n_R)** is dictated by the **number of file blocks (b)** and the **available buffer space (n_B).** For example, if n_B = 5 blocks and the size of the file b = 1024 blocks, then n_R = $\lceil (b/n_B) \rceil$, or 205 initial runs each of size 5 blocks (except the last run which will have 4 blocks). Hence, after the sort phase, 205 sorted runs are stored as temporary subfiles on disk.

In the **merging phase,** the sorted runs are merged during one or more **passes.** The **degree of merging (d_M)** is the number of runs that can be merged together in each pass. In each pass, one buffer block is needed to hold one block from each of the runs being merged, and one block is needed for containing one block of the merge result. Hence, d_M

---

4. Similarly, algorithms must also be available for implementing OUTER JOINs, correlated subqueries, and other more complex operations but we do not discuss those here.

5. *Internal sorting algorithms* are suitable for sorting data structures that can fit entirely in memory.

```
set    i ← 1;
       j ← b;      {size of the file in blocks}
       k ← nB;     {size of buffer in blocks}
       m ← ⌈(j/k)⌉;
{Sort Phase}
while (i <= m)
      do {
            read next k blocks of the file into the buffer or if there are less than k blocks remaining,
                then read in the remaining blocks;
            sort the records in the buffer and write as a temporary subfile;
            i ← i + 1;
          }
{Merge Phase: merge subfiles until only 1 remains}
set    i ← 1;
       p ← ⌈logk-1 m⌉;   {p is the number of passes for the merging phase}
       j ← m;
while (i <= p)
      do {
            n ← 1;
            q ← ⌈(j/ (k-1))⌉;   {number of subfiles to write in this pass}
            while (n <= q)
                  do {
                        read next k-1 subfiles or remaining subfiles (from previous pass) one block at a time;
                        merge and write as new subfile;
                        n ← n + 1;
                      }
            j ← q;
            i ← i + 1;
          }
```

Figure 18.2   Outline of the sort-merge algorithm for external sorting.

is the smaller of $(n_B - 1)$ and n_R, and the number of passes is $\lceil (log_{dM}(n_R)) \rceil$. In our example, $d_M = 4$ (four-way merging), so the 205 initial sorted runs would be merged into 52 at the end of the first pass, which are then merged into 13, then 4, then 1 run, which means that *four passes* are needed. The minimum d_M of 2 gives the worst-case performance of the algorithm, which is

$$(2 * b) + (2 * (b * (\log_2 b)))$$

The first term represents the number of block accesses for the sort phase, since each file block is accessed twice—once for reading into memory and once for writing the records back to disk after sorting. The second term represents the number of block accesses for the merge phase, assuming the worst-case d_M of 2. In general, the log is taken to the base d_M and the expression for number of block accesses becomes

$$(2 * b) + (2 * (b * (\log_{dM} b)))$$

18.2.2 Implementing the SELECT Operation

There are many options for executing a SELECT operation; some depend on the file having specific access paths and may apply only to certain types of selection conditions. We discuss some of the algorithms for implementing SELECT in this section. We will use the following operations, specified on the relational database of Figure 7.5, to illustrate our discussion:

(OP1): $\sigma_{SSN='123456789'}(\text{EMPLOYEE})$

(OP2): $\sigma_{DNUMBER>5}(\text{DEPARTMENT})$

(OP3): $\sigma_{DNO=5}(\text{EMPLOYEE})$

(OP4): $\sigma_{DNO=5 \text{ AND } SALARY>30000 \text{ AND } SEX='F'}(\text{EMPLOYEE})$

(OP5): $\sigma_{ESSN='123456789' \text{ AND } PNO=10}(\text{WORKS\_ON})$

Search Methods for Simple Selection. A number of search algorithms are possible for selecting records from a file. These are also known as **file scans,** because they scan the records of a file to search for and retrieve records that satisfy a selection condition.[6] If the search algorithm involves the use of an index, the index search is called an **index scan.** The following search methods (S1 through S6) are examples of some of the search algorithms that can be used to implement a select operation:

- S1. *Linear search (brute force):* Retrieve *every record* in the file, and test whether its attribute values satisfy the selection condition.

- S2. *Binary search:* If the selection condition involves an equality comparison on a key attribute on which the file is ordered, binary search—which is more efficient than linear search—can be used. An example is OP1 if SSN is the ordering attribute for the EMPLOYEE file.[7]

- S3. *Using a primary index (or hash key):* If the selection condition involves an equality comparison on a **key attribute** with a primary index (or hash key)—for example, SSN = '123456789' in OP1—use the primary index (or hash key) to retrieve the record. Note that this condition retrieves a single record (at most).

- S4. *Using a primary index to retrieve multiple records:* If the comparison condition is >, >=, <, or <= on a key field with a primary index—for example, DNUMBER > 5 in OP2—use the index to find the record satisfying the corresponding equality condition (DNUMBER = 5), then retrieve all subsequent records in the (ordered) file. For the condition DNUMBER < 5, retrieve all the preceding records.

- S5. *Using a clustering index to retrieve multiple records:* If the selection condition involves an equality comparison on a **non-key attribute** with a clustering index—for example, DNO = 5 in OP3—use the index to retrieve all the records satisfying the condition.

---

6. A selection operation is sometimes called a **filter,** since it filters out the records in the file that *do not* satisfy the selection condition.

7. Generally, binary search is not used in database search because ordered files are not used unless they also have a corresponding primary index.

- S6. *Using a secondary (B$^+$-tree) index on an equality comparison:* This search method can be used to retrieve a single record if the indexing field is a **key** (has unique values) or to retrieve multiple records if the indexing field is **not a key.** This can also be used for comparisons involving $>$, $>=$, $<$, or $<=$.

In Section 18.4.3, we discuss how to develop formulas that estimate the access cost of these search methods in terms of number of block accesses and access time. Method S1 applies to any file, but all the other methods depend on having the appropriate access path on the attribute used in the selection condition. Methods S4 and S6 can be used to retrieve records in a certain *range*—for example, 30000<=SALARY<=35000. Queries involving such conditions are called **range queries.**

Search Methods for Complex Selection. If a condition of a SELECT operation is a **conjunctive condition**—that is, if it is made up of several simple conditions connected with the AND logical connective such as OP4 above—the DBMS can use the following additional methods to implement the operation:

- S7. *Conjunctive selection using an individual index:* If an attribute involved in any **single simple condition** in the conjunctive condition has an access path that permits the use of one of the Methods S2 to S6, use that condition to retrieve the records and then check whether each retrieved record *satisfies the remaining simple conditions* in the conjunctive condition.

- S8. *Conjunctive selection using a composite index:* If two or more attributes are involved in equality conditions in the conjunctive condition and a composite index (or hash structure) exists on the combined fields—for example, if an index has been created on the composite key (ESSN, PNO) of the WORKS_ON file for OP5— we can use the index directly.

- S9. *Conjunctive selection by intersection of record pointers:*[8] If secondary indexes (or other access paths) are available on more than one of the fields involved in simple conditions in the conjunctive condition, and if the indexes include record pointers (rather than block pointers), then each index can be used to retrieve the **set of record pointers** that satisfy the individual condition. The **intersection** of these sets of record pointers gives the record pointers that satisfy the conjunctive condition, which are then used to retrieve those records directly. If only some of the conditions have secondary indexes, each retrieved record is further tested to determine whether it satisfies the remaining conditions.[9]

---

8. A record pointer uniquely identifies a record and provides the address of the record on disk; hence, it is also called the **record identifier** or **record id.**

9. The technique can have many variations—for example, if the indexes are *logical indexes* that store primary key values instead of record pointers.

Whenever a single condition specifies the selection—such as OP1, OP2, or OP3—we can only check whether an access path exists on the attribute involved in that condition If an access path exists, the method corresponding to that access path is used; otherwise, the brute force linear search approach of method S1 can be used. Query optimization for a SELECT operation is needed mostly for conjunctive select conditions whenever *more than one* of the attributes involved in the conditions have an access path. The optimizer should choose the access path that *retrieves the fewest records* in the most efficient way by estimating the different costs (see Section 18.4) and choosing the method with the least estimated cost.

When the optimizer is choosing between multiple simple conditions in a conjunctive select condition, it typically considers the selectivity of each condition. The **selectivity (s)** is defined as the ratio of the number of records (tuples) that satisfy the condition to the total number of records (tuples) in the file (relation), and thus is a number between zero and 1—zero selectivity means no records satisfy the condition and 1 means all the records satisfy the condition. Although exact selectivities of all conditions may not be available, **estimates of selectivities** are often kept in the DBMS catalog and are used by the optimizer. For example, for an equality condition on a key attribute of relation $r(R)$, $s = 1/|r(R)|$, where $|r(R)|$ is the number of tuples in relation $r(R)$. For an equality condition on an attribute with i *distinct values*, s is estimated by $(|r(R)|/i)/|r(R)|$ or $1/i$, assuming that the records are evenly distributed among the distinct values.[10] Under this assumption, $|r(R)|/i$ records will satisfy an equality condition on this attribute. In general, the number of records satisfying a selection condition with selectivity s is estimated to be $|r(R)| * s$. The smaller this estimate is, the higher the desirability of using that condition first to retrieve records.

Compared to a conjunctive selection condition, a **disjunctive condition** (where simple conditions are connected by the OR logical connective rather than by AND) is much harder to process and optimize. For example, consider OP4':

(OP49): $\sigma_{\text{DNO}=5 \text{ OR } \text{SALARY}>30000 \text{ OR } \text{SEX}='F'}(\text{EMPLOYEE})$

With such a condition, little optimization can be done, because the records satisfying the disjunctive condition are the *union* of the records satisfying the individual conditions. Hence, if any *one* of the conditions does not have an access path, we are compelled to use the brute force linear search approach. Only if an access path exists on *every* condition can we optimize the selection by retrieving the records satisfying each condition—or their record ids—and then applying the union operation to eliminate duplicates.

A DBMS will have available many of the methods discussed above, and typically many additional methods. The query optimizer must choose the appropriate one for executing each SELECT operation in a query. This optimization uses formulas that estimate the costs for each available access method, as we shall discuss in Section 18.4. The optimizer chooses the access method with the lowest estimated cost.

---

10. In more sophisticated optimizers, histograms representing the distribution of the records among the different attribute values can be kept in the catalog.

18.2.3   Implementing the JOIN Operation

The JOIN operation is one of the most time-consuming operations in query processing. Many of the join operations encountered in queries are of the EQUIJOIN and NATURAL JOIN varieties, so we consider only these two here. For the remainder of this chapter, the term **join** refers to an EQUIJOIN (or NATURAL JOIN). There are many possible ways to implement a **two-way join,** which is a join on two files. Joins involving more than two files are called **multiway joins.** The number of possible ways to execute multiway joins grows very rapidly. In this section we discuss techniques for implementing only two-way joins. To illustrate our discussion, we refer to the relational schema of Figure 7.5 once more—specifically, to the EMPLOYEE, DEPARTMENT, and PROJECT relations. The algorithms we consider are for join operations of the form

$$R \bowtie_{A=B} S$$

where A and B are domain-compatible attributes of R and S, respectively. The methods we discuss can be extended to more general forms of join. We illustrate four of the most common techniques for performing such a join, using the following example operations:

(OP6):   EMPLOYEE $\bowtie_{DNO=DNUMBER}$ DEPARTMENT

(OP7):   DEPARTMENT $\bowtie_{MGRSSN=SSN}$ EMPLOYEE

Methods for Implementing Joins

- J1. *Nested-loop join (brute force)*: For each record t in R (outer loop), retrieve every record s from S (inner loop) and test whether the two records satisfy the join condition $t[A] = s[B]$.[11]

- J2. *Single-loop join (using an access structure to retrieve the matching records)*: If an index (or hash key) exists for one of the two join attributes—say, B of S—retrieve each record t in R, one at a time (single loop), and then use the access structure to retrieve directly all matching records s from S that satisfy $s[B] = t[A]$.

- J3. *Sort–merge join*: If the records of R and S are *physically sorted* (ordered) by value of the join attributes A and B, respectively, we can implement the join in the most efficient way possible. Both files are scanned concurrently in order of the join attributes, matching the records that have the same values for A and B. If the files are not sorted, they may be sorted first by using external sorting (see Section 18.2.1). In this method, pairs of file blocks are copied into memory buffers in order and the records of each file are scanned only once each for matching with the other file—unless both A and B are nonkey attributes, in which case the method needs to be modified slightly. A sketch of the sort-merge join algorithm is given in Figure 18.3(a). We use $R(i)$ to refer to the ith record in R. A variation of the sort-merge join can be used when secondary indexes exist on both join attributes. The indexes provide the ability to access (scan) the records in order of the join attributes, but the records themselves are physically scattered all over the

---

11. For disk files, it is obvious that the loops will be over disk blocks so this technique has also been called *nested-block join*.

(a)   sort the tuples in R on attribute A; (*assume R has n tuples (records) *)
       sort the tuples in S on attribute B; (*assume S has m tuples (records) *)
       set $i \leftarrow 1, j \leftarrow 1$;
       while $(i \leq n)$ and $(j \leq m)$
       do{   if $R(i)[A] > S(j)[B]$
                then   set $j \leftarrow j+1$
            elseif $R(i)[A] < S(j)[B]$
                then   set $i \leftarrow i+1$
                else {   (* $R(i)[A] = S(j)[B]$, so we output a matched tuple*)
                          output the combined tuple $<R(i), S(j)>$ to T;
                              (*output other tuples that match R(i), if any*)
                          set $l \leftarrow j+1$;
                          while $(l \leq m)$ and $(R(i)[A] = S(l)[B])$
                          do   {   output the combined tuple $<R(i), S(l)>$ to T;
                                      set $l \leftarrow l+1$
                            }
                          (*output other tuples that match S(j), if any*)
                          set $k \leftarrow i+1$;
                          •while $(k \leq n)$ and $(R(k)[A] = S(j)[B])$
                          do   {   output the combined tuple $<R(k), S(j)>$ to T;
                                      set $k \leftarrow k+1$
                            }
                        set $i \leftarrow k, j \leftarrow l$
                  }
       }

(b)   create a tuple t[<attribute list>] in T' for each tuple t in R;
          (*T' contains the projection result <u>before</u> duplicate elimination*)
       if <attribute list> includes a key of R
          then $T \leftarrow T'$
          else {   sort the tuples in T';
                   set $i \leftarrow 1, j \leftarrow 2$;
                   while $i \leq n$
                      do   {   output the tuple T'[i] to T;
                              while T'[i] = T'[j] and $j \leq n$ do $j \leftarrow j+1$; (*eliminate duplicates*)
                              $i \leftarrow j; j \leftarrow i+1$
                      }
          }
       (* T contains the projection result after duplicate elimination *)

Figure 18.3   Implementing JOIN, PROJECT, UNION, INTERSECTION, and SET DIFFERENCE by using sort-merge, where R has n tuples and S has m tuples. (a) Implementing the operation $T \leftarrow R \bowtie_{A=B} S$. (b) Implementing the operation $T \leftarrow \pi_{<\text{attribute list}>}(R)$.

file blocks, so this method may be quite inefficient, as every record access may involve accessing a different disk block.

- J4. *Hash-join:* The records of files R and S are both hashed to the same hash file, using the same hashing function on the join attributes A of R and B of S as hash keys. First, a single pass through the file with fewer records (say, R) hashes its records to the hash file buckets; this is called the **partitioning phase,** since the records of R

(c)   sort the tuples in R and S using the same unique sort attributes;
      set $i \leftarrow 1, j \leftarrow 1$;
      while $(i \leq n)$ and $(j \leq m)$
      do {   if $R(i) > S(j)$
                   then   {   output $S(j)$ to T;
                                 set $j \leftarrow j+1$
                          }
                   elseif $R(i) < S(j)$
                   then   {   output $R(i)$ to T;
                                 set $i \leftarrow i+1$
                          }
                   else set $j \leftarrow j+1$ (*$R(i)=S(j)$, so we skip one of the duplicate tuples*)
          }
      if $(i \leq n)$ then add tuples $R(i)$ to $R(n)$ to T;
      if $(j \leq m)$ then add tuples $S(j)$ to $S(m)$ to T;

(d)   sort the tuples in R and R using the same unique sort attributes;
      set $i \leftarrow 1, j \leftarrow 1$;
      while $(i \leq n)$ and $(j \leq m)$
      do {   if $R(i) > S(j)$
                   then   set $j \leftarrow j+1$
                   elseif $R(i) < S(j)$
                   then   set $i \leftarrow i+1$
                   else   {   output $R(i)$ to T; (* $R(i)=S(j)$, so we output the tuple *)
                                 set $i \leftarrow i+1, j \leftarrow j+1$
                          }
          }

(e)   sort the tuples in R and S using the same unique sort attributes;
      set $i \leftarrow 1, j \leftarrow 1$;
      while $(i \leq n)$ and $(j \leq m)$
      do {   if $R(i) > S(j)$
                   then   set $j \leftarrow j+1$
                   elseif $R(i) < S(j)$
                   then   {   output $R(i)$ to T; (* $R(i)$ has no matching $S(j)$, so output $R(i)$*)
                                 set $i \leftarrow i+1$
                          }
                   else   set $i \leftarrow i+1, j \leftarrow j+1$
          }
      if $(i \leq n)$ then add tuples $R(i)$ to $R(n)$ to T;

Figure 18.3   Implementing JOIN, PROJECT, UNION, INTERSECTION, and SET
DIFFERENCE by using sort-merge, where R has n tuples and S has
m tuples. (c) Implementing the operation $T \leftarrow R \cup S$.
(d) Implementing the operation $T \leftarrow R \cap S$. (e) Implementing
the operation $T \leftarrow R - S$.

are partitioned into the hash buckets. In the second phase, called the **probing
phase,** a single pass through the other file (S) then hashes each of its records to
probe the appropriate bucket, and that record is combined with all matching
records from R in that bucket. This simplified description of hash-join assumes
that the smaller of the two files *fits entirely into memory buckets* after the first

phase. We will discuss variations of hash-join that do not require this assumption below.

In practice, techniques J1 to J4 are implemented by accessing *whole disk blocks* of a file, rather than individual records. Depending on the available buffer space in memory, the number of blocks read in from the file can be adjusted.

Effects of Available Buffer Space and Join Selection Factor on Join Performance. The buffer space available has an important effect on the various join algorithms. First, let us consider the nested-loop approach (J1). Looking again at the operation OP6 above, assume that the number of buffers available in main memory for implementing the join is $n_B = 7$ blocks (buffers). For illustration, assume that the DEPARTMENT file consists of $r_D = 50$ records stored in $b_D = 10$ disk blocks and that the EMPLOYEE file consists of $r_E = 6000$ records stored in $b_E = 2000$ disk blocks. It is advantageous to read as many blocks as possible at a time into memory from the file whose records are used for the outer loop (that is, $n_B - 2$ blocks). The algorithm can then read one block at a time for the inner-loop file and use its records to **probe** (that is, search) the outer loop blocks in memory for matching records. This reduces the total number of block accesses. An extra buffer block is needed to contain the resulting records after they are joined, and the contents of this buffer block are appended to the **result file**—the disk file that contains the join result—whenever it is filled. This buffer block is then is reused to hold additional result records.

In the nested-loop join, it makes a difference which file is chosen for the outer loop and which for the inner loop. If EMPLOYEE is used for the outer loop, each block of EMPLOYEE is read once, and the entire DEPARTMENT file (each of its blocks) is read once for *each time* we read in $(n_B - 2)$ blocks of the EMPLOYEE file. We get the following:

Total number of blocks accessed for outer file = b_E

Number of times $(n_B - 2)$ blocks of outer file are loaded = $\lceil b_E / (n_B - 2) \rceil$

Total number of blocks accessed for inner file = $b_D * \lceil b_E / (n_B - 2) \rceil$

Hence, we get the following total number of block accesses:

$$b_E + (\lceil b_E / (n_B - 2) \rceil * b_D) = 2000 + (\lceil (2000/5) \rceil * 10) = 6000 \text{ block accesses}$$

On the other hand, if we use the DEPARTMENT records in the outer loop, by symmetry we get the following total number of block accesses:

$$b_D + (\lceil b_D / (n_B - 2) \rceil * b_E) = 10 + (\lceil (10/5) \rceil * 2000) = 4010 \text{ block accesses}$$

The join algorithm uses a buffer to hold the joined records of the result file. Once the buffer is filled, it is written to disk and reused.[12] If the result file of the join operation has b_{RES} disk blocks, each block is written once, so an additional b_{RES} block access should be added to the preceding formulas in order to estimate the total cost of the join operation. The same holds for the formulas developed later for other join algorithms. As this

---

12. If we reserve two buffers for the result file, double buffering can be used to speed the algorithm (see Section 5.4).

example shows, it is advantageous to use the file *with fewer blocks* as the outer-loop file in the nested-loop join.

Another factor that affects the performance of a join, particularly the single-loop method J2, is the percentage of records in a file that will be joined with records in the other file. We call this the **join selection factor**[13] of a file with respect to an equijoin condition with another file. This factor depends on the particular equijoin condition between the two files. To illustrate this, consider the operation OP7, which joins each DEPARTMENT record with the EMPLOYEE record for the manager of that department. Here, each DEPARTMENT record (there are 50 such records in our example) is expected to be joined with a *single* EMPLOYEE record, but many EMPLOYEE records (the 4950 of them that do not manage a department) will not be joined.

Suppose that secondary indexes exist on both the attributes SSN of EMPLOYEE and MGRSSN of DEPARTMENT, with the number of index levels $x_{SSN} = 4$ and $x_{MGRSSN} = 2$, respectively. We have two options for implementing method J2. The first retrieves each EMPLOYEE record and then uses the index on MGRSSN of DEPARTMENT to find a matching DEPARTMENT record. In this case, no matching record will be found for employees who do not manage a department. The number of block accesses for this case is approximately

$$b_E + (r_R * (x_{MGRSSN} + 1)) = 2000 + (5000 * 3) = 17{,}000 \text{ block accesses}$$

The second option retrieves each DEPARTMENT record and then uses the index on SSN of EMPLOYEE to find a matching manager EMPLOYEE record. In this case, every DEPARTMENT record will have one matching EMPLOYEE record. The number of block accesses for this case is approximately

$$b_D + (r_D * (x_{SSN} + 1)) = 10 + (50 * 5) = 260 \text{ block accesses}$$

The second option is more efficient because the join selection factor of DEPARTMENT with respect to the join condition SSN = MGRSSN is 1, whereas the join selection factor of EMPLOYEE with respect to the same join condition is (50/5000), or 0.01. For method J2, either the smaller file or the file that has a match for every record (that is, the file with the high join selection factor) should be used in the (outer) join loop. It is also possible to create an index specifically for performing the join operation if one does not already exist.

The sort-merge join J3 is quite efficient if both files are already sorted by their join attribute. Only a single pass is made through each file. Hence, the number of blocks accessed is equal to the sum of the numbers of blocks in both files. For this method, both OP6 and OP7 would need $b_E + b_D = 2000 + 10 = 2010$ block accesses. However, both files are required to be ordered by the join attributes; if one or both are not, they may be sorted specifically for performing the join operation. If we estimate the cost of sorting an external file by ($b \log_2 b$) block accesses, and if both files need to be sorted, the total cost of a sort-merge join can be estimated by ($b_E + b_D + b_E \log_2 b_E + b_D \log_2 b_D$).

---

13. This is different from the *join selectivity*, which we shall discuss in Section 18.4.

Partition Hash Join and Hybrid Hash Join.   The hash-join method J4 is also quite efficient. In this case only a single pass is made through each file, whether or not the files are ordered. If the hash table for the smaller of the two files can be kept entirely in main memory after hashing (partitioning) on its join attribute, the implementation is straightforward. If, however, parts of the hash file must be stored on disk, the method becomes more complex, and a number of variations to improve the efficiency have been proposed. We discuss two techniques: partition hash join and a variation called hybrid hash join, which has been shown to be quite efficient.

In the **partition hash join** algorithm, each file is first partitioned into M partitions using a **partitioning hash function** on the join attributes. Then, each pair of partitions is joined. For example, suppose we are joining relations R and S on the join attributes $R.A$ and $S.B$:

$$R \bowtie_{A=B} S$$

In the **partitioning phase,** R is partitioned into the M partitions $R_1, R_2, ..., R_M$, and S into the M partitions $S_1, S_2, ..., S_M$. The property of each pair of corresponding partitions R_i, S_i is that records in R_i *only need to be joined* with records in S_i, and vice versa. This property is ensured by using the *same hash function* to partition both files on their join attributes—attribute A for R and attribute B for S. The minimum number of in-memory buffers needed for the partitioning phase is M. Each of the files R and S are partitioned separately. For each of the partitions, a single in-memory buffer—whose size is one disk block—is allocated to store the records that hash to this partition. Whenever the in-memory buffer for a partition gets filled, its contents are appended to a **disk subfile** that stores this partition. The partitioning phase has *two iterations*. After the first iteration, the first file R is partitioned into the subfiles $R_1, R_2, ..., R_M$, where all the records that hashed to the same buffer are in the same partition. After the second iteration, the second file S is similarly partitioned.

In the second phase, called the **joining** or **probing phase,** M *iterations* are needed. During iteration i, the two partitions R_i and S_i are joined. The minimum number of buffers needed for iteration i is the number of blocks in the smaller of the two partitions, say R_i, plus two additional buffers. If we use a nested loop join during iteration i, the records from the smaller of the two partitions R_i are copied into memory buffers; then all blocks from the other partition S_i are read—one at a time—and each record is used to **probe** (that is, search) partition R_i for matching record(s). Any matching records are joined and written into the result file. To improve the efficiency of in-memory probing, it is common to use an *in-memory hash table* for storing the records in partition R_i by using a *different* hash function from the partitioning hash function.[14]

We can approximate the cost of this partition hash-join as $3 * (b_R + b_S) + b_{RES}$ for our example, since each record is read once and written back to disk once during the partitioning phase. During the joining (probing) phase, each record is read a second time to

---

14. If the hash function used for partitioning is used again, all records in a partition will hash to the same bucket again.

perform the join. The *main difficulty* of this algorithm is to ensure that the partitioning hash function is **uniform**—that is, the partition sizes are nearly equal in size. If the partitioning function is **skewed** (nonuniform), then some partitions may be too large to fit in the available memory space for the second joining phase.

Notice that if the available in-memory buffer space $n_B > (b_R + 2)$, where b_R is the number of blocks for the *smaller* of the two files being joined, say R, then there is no reason to do partitioning since in this case the join can be performed entirely in memory using some variation of the nested-loop join based on hashing and probing. For illustration, assume we are performing the join operation OP6, repeated below:

(OP6): EMPLOYEE ⋈ DNO=DNUMBER DEPARTMENT

In this example, the smaller file is the DEPARTMENT file; hence, if the number of available memory buffers $n_B > (b_D + 2)$, the whole DEPARTMENT file can be read into main memory and organized into a hash table on the join attribute. Each EMPLOYEE block is then read into a buffer, and each EMPLOYEE record in the buffer is hashed on its join attribute and is used to *probe* the corresponding in-memory bucket in the DEPARTMENT hash table. If a matching record is found, the records are joined, and the result record(s) are written to the result buffer and eventually to the result file on disk. The cost in terms of block accesses is hence $(b_D + b_E)$, plus b_{RES}—the cost of writing the result file.

The **hybrid hash-join algorithm** is a variation of partition hash join, where the *joining* phase for *one of the partitions* is included in the *partitioning* phase. To illustrate this, let us assume that the size of a memory buffer is one disk block; that n_B such buffers are *available*; and that the hash function used is $h(K) = K \bmod M$ so that M partitions are being created, where $M < n_B$. For illustration, assume we are performing the join operation OP6. In the *first pass* of the partitioning phase, when the hybrid hash-join algorithm is partitioning the smaller of the two files (DEPARTMENT in OP6), the algorithm divides the buffer space among the M partitions such that all the blocks of the *first partition* of DEPARTMENT completely reside in main memory. For each of the other partitions, only a single in-memory buffer—whose size is one disk block—is allocated; the remainder of the partition is written to disk as in the regular partition hash join. Hence, at the end of the *first pass of the partitioning phase*, the first partition of DEPARTMENT resides wholly in main memory, whereas each of the other partitions of DEPARTMENT resides in a disk subfile.

For the second pass of the partitioning phase, the records of the second file being joined—the larger file, EMPLOYEE in OP6—are being partitioned. If a record hashes to the *first partition*, it is joined with the matching record in DEPARTMENT and the joined records are written to the result buffer (and eventually to disk). If an EMPLOYEE record hashes to a partition other than the first, it is partitioned normally. Hence, at the end of the second pass of the partitioning phase, all records that hash to the first partition have been joined. Now there are $M - 1$ pairs of partitions on disk. Therefore, during the second **joining** or **probing** phase, $M - 1$ *iterations* are needed instead of M. The goal is to join as many records during the partitioning phase so as to save the cost of storing those records back to disk and rereading them a second time during the joining phase.

18.2.4 Implementing PROJECT and Set Operations

A PROJECT operation $\pi_{<attribute\ list>}(R)$ is straightforward to implement if <attribute list> includes a key of relation R, because in this case the result of the operation will have the same number of tuples as R, but with only the values for the attributes in <attribute list> in each tuple. If <attribute list> does not include a key of R, *duplicate tuples must be eliminated*. This is usually done by sorting the result of the operation and then eliminating duplicate tuples, which appear consecutively after sorting. A sketch of the algorithm is given in Figure 18.3(b). Hashing can also be used to eliminate duplicates: as each record is hashed and inserted into a bucket of the hash file in memory, it is checked against those already in the bucket; if it is a duplicate, it is not inserted. It is useful to recall here that in SQL queries, the default is not to eliminate duplicates from the query result; only if the keyword DISTINCT is included are duplicates eliminated from the query result.

Set operations—UNION, INTERSECTION, SET DIFFERENCE, and CARTESIAN PRODUCT—are sometimes expensive to implement. In particular, the CARTESIAN PRODUCT operation $R \times S$ is quite expensive, because its result includes a record for each combination of records from R and S. In addition, the attributes of the result include all attributes of R and S. If R has n records and j attributes and S has m records and k attributes, the result relation will have $n * m$ records and $j + k$ attributes. Hence, it is important to avoid the CARTESIAN PRODUCT operation and to substitute other equivalent operations during query optimization (see Section 18.3).

The other three set operations—UNION, INTERSECTION, and SET DIFFERENCE[15]—apply only to union-compatible relations, which have the same number of attributes and the same attribute domains. The customary way to implement these operations is to use variations of the **sort-merge technique:** the two relations are sorted on the same attributes, and, after sorting, a single scan through each relation is sufficient to produce the result. For example, we can implement the UNION operation, $R \cup S$, by scanning and merging both sorted files concurrently, and whenever the same tuple exists in both relations, only one is kept in the merged result. For the INTERSECTION operation, $R \cap S$, we keep in the merged result only those tuples that appear in *both relations*. Figure 18.3(c) to (e) sketches the implementation of these operations by sorting and merging. If sorting is done on unique key attributes, the operations are further simplified.

Hashing can also be used to implement UNION, INTERSECTION, and SET DIFFERENCE. One table is partitioned and the other is used to probe the appropriate partition. For example, to implement $R \cup S$, first hash (partition) the records of R; then, hash (probe) the records of S, but do not insert duplicate records in the buckets. To implement $R \cap S$, first partition the records of R to the hash file. Then, while hashing each record of S, probe to check if an identical record from R is found in the bucket, and if so add the record to the result file. To implement $R - S$, first hash the records of R to the hash file

---

15. SET DIFFERENCE is called EXCEPT in SQL.

buckets. While hashing (probing) each record of S, if an identical record is found in the bucket, remove that record from the bucket.

18.2.5 Implementing Aggregate Operations

The aggregate operators (MIN, MAX, COUNT, AVERAGE, SUM), when applied to an entire table, can be computed by a table scan or by using an appropriate index, if available. For example, consider the following SQL query:

```
SELECT  MAX(SALARY)
FROM    EMPLOYEE;
```

If an (ascending) index on SALARY exists for the EMPLOYEE relation, then the optimizer can decide on using the index to search for the largest value by following the *rightmost* pointer in each index node from the root to the rightmost leaf. That node would include the largest SALARY value as its *last* entry. In most cases, this would be more efficient than a full table scan of EMPLOYEE, since no actual records need to be retrieved. The MIN aggregate can be handled in a similar manner, except that the *leftmost* pointer is followed from the root to leftmost leaf. That node would include the smallest SALARY value as its *first* entry.

The index could also be used for the COUNT, AVERAGE, and SUM aggregates, but only if it is a **dense index**—that is, if there is an index entry for every record in the main file. In this case, the associated computation would be applied to the values in the index. For a **nondense index,** the actual number of records associated with each index entry must be used for a correct computation (except for COUNT DISTINCT, where the number of distinct values can be counted from the index itself).

When a GROUP BY clause is used in a query, the aggregate operator must be applied separately to each group of tuples. Hence, the table must first be partitioned into subsets of tuples, where each partition (group) has the same value for the grouping attributes. In this case, the computation is more complex. Consider the following query:

```
SELECT   DNO, AVG(SALARY)
FROM     EMPLOYEE
GROUP BY DNO;
```

The usual technique for such queries is to first use either **sorting** or **hashing** on the grouping attributes to partition the file into the appropriate groups. Then the algorithm computes the aggregate function for the tuples in each group, which have the same grouping attribute(s) value. In the example query, the set of tuples for each department number would be grouped together in a partition and the average computed for each group.

Notice that if a **clustering index** (see Chapter 6) exists on the grouping attribute(s), then the records are *already partitioned* (grouped) into the appropriate subsets. In this case, it is only necessary to apply the computation to each group.

18.2.6 Implementing Outer Join

In Section 7.5.3, the *outer join operation* was introduced, with its three variations: left outer join, right outer join, and full outer join. We also discussed in Chapter 8 how these operations can be specified in SQL2. The following is an example of a left outer join operation in SQL2:

```
SELECT LNAME, FNAME, DNAME
FROM (EMPLOYEE LEFT OUTER JOIN DEPARTMENT ON DNO=DNUMBER);
```

The result of this query is a table of employee names and their associated departments. It is similar to a regular (inner) join result, with the exception that if an EMPLOYEE tuple (a tuple in the *left* relation) *does not have an associated department*, the employee's name will still appear in the resulting table, but the department name would be *null* for such tuples in the query result.

Outer join can be computed by modifying one of the join algorithms, such as nested-loop join or single-loop join. For example, to compute a *left* outer join, we use the left relation as the outer loop or single-loop because every tuple in the left relation must appear in the result. If there are matching tuples in the other relation, the joined tuples are produced and saved in the result. However, if no matching tuple is found, the tuple is still included in the result but is padded with null value(s). The sort-merge and hash-join algorithms can also be extended to compute outer joins.

Alternatively, outer join can be computed by executing a combination of relational algebra operators. For example, the left outer join operation shown above is equivalent to the following sequence of relational operations:

1. Compute the (inner) JOIN of the EMPLOYEE and DEPARTMENT tables.

$$\text{TEMP1} \leftarrow \pi_{\text{LNAME,FNAME,DNAME}} (\text{EMPLOYEE} \bowtie_{\text{DNO=DNUMBER}} \text{DEPARTMENT})$$

2. Find the EMPLOYEE tuples that do not appear in the (inner) JOIN result.

$$\text{TEMP2} \leftarrow \pi_{\text{LNAME,FNAME}} (\text{EMPLOYEE}) - \pi_{\text{LNAME,FNAME}} (\text{TEMP1})$$

3. Pad each tuple in TEMP2 with a null DNAME field.

$$\text{TEMP2} \leftarrow \text{TEMP2} \times \text{'null'}$$

4. Apply the UNION operation to TEMP1, TEMP2 to produce the LEFT OUTER JOIN result.

$$\text{RESULT} \leftarrow \text{TEMP1} \cup \text{TEMP2}$$

The cost of the outer join as computed above would be the sum of the costs of the associated steps (inner join, projections, and union). However, note that Step 3 can be done as the temporary relation is being constructed in Step 2; that is, we can simply pad each resulting tuple with a null. In addition, in Step 4, we know that the two operands of the union are disjoint (no common tuples), so there is no need for duplicate elimination.

18.2.7 Combining Operations Using Pipelining

A query specified in SQL will typically be translated into a relational algebra expression that is *a sequence of relational operations*. If we execute a single operation at a time, we must generate temporary files on disk to hold the results of these temporary operations, creating excessive overhead. Generating and storing large temporary files on disk is time-consuming and can be unnecessary in many cases, since these files will immediately be used as input to the next operation. To reduce the number of temporary files, it is common to generate query execution code that correspond to algorithms for combinations of operations in a query.

For example, rather than being implemented separately, a JOIN can be combined with two SELECT operations on the input files and a final PROJECT operation on the resulting file; all this is implemented by one algorithm with two input files and a single output file. Rather than creating four temporary files, we apply the algorithm directly and get just one result file. In Section 18.3.1 we discuss how heuristic relational algebra optimization can group operations together for execution. This is called **pipelining** or **stream-based processing.**

It is common to create the query execution code dynamically to implement multiple operations. The generated code for producing the query combines several algorithms that correspond to individual operations. As the result tuples from one operation are produced, they are provided as input for subsequent operations. For example, if a join operation follows two select operations on base relations, the tuples resulting from each select are provided as input for the join algorithm in a **stream** or **pipeline** as they are produced.

18.3   Using Heuristics in Query Optimization

In this section we discuss optimization techniques that apply heuristic rules to modify the internal representation of a query—which is usually in the form of a query tree or a query graph data structure—to improve its expected performance. The parser of a high-level query first generates an *initial internal representation*, which is then optimized according to heuristic rules. Following that, a query execution plan is generated to execute groups of operations based on the access paths available on the files involved in the query.

One of the main **heuristic rules** is to apply SELECT and PROJECT operations *before* applying the JOIN or other binary operations. This is because the size of the file resulting from a binary operation—such as JOIN—is usually a multiplicative function of the sizes of the input files. The SELECT and PROJECT operations reduce the size of a file and hence should be applied *before* a join or other binary operation.

We start in Section 18.3.1 by introducing the query tree and query graph notations. These can be used as the basis for the data structures that are used for internal representation of queries. A query tree is used to represent a relational algebra or extended relational algebra expression, whereas a query graph is used to represent a relational calculus expression. We then show in Section 18.3.2 how heuristic optimization rules are applied to convert a query tree into an **equivalent query tree,** which represents a different relational algebra expression that is more efficient to execute but gives the same result as the original one. We also discuss the equivalence of various relational algebra expressions. Finally, Section 18.3.3 discusses the generation of query execution plans.

18.3.1   Notation for Query Trees and Query Graphs

A **query tree** is a tree data structure that corresponds to a relational algebra expression. It represents the input relations of the query as *leaf nodes* of the tree, and represents the relational algebra operations as internal nodes. An execution of the query tree consists of executing an internal node operation whenever its operands are available and then replacing that internal node by the relation that results from executing the operation. The execution terminates when the root node is executed and produces the result relation for the query.

Figure 18.4(a) shows a query tree for query Q2 of Chapters 7 to 9: For every project located in 'Stafford', retrieve the project number, the controlling department number,

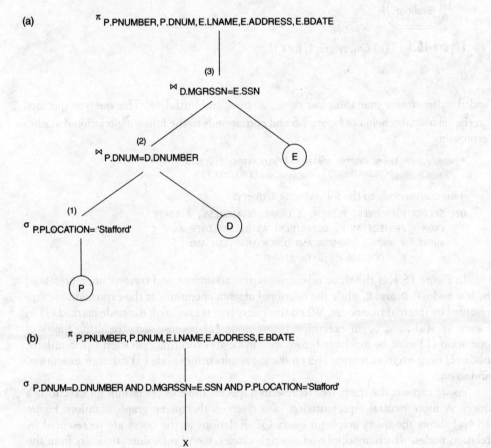

(a) π P.PNUMBER, P.DNUM, E.LNAME, E.ADDRESS, E.BDATE

(3)

$\bowtie$ D.MGRSSN=E.SSN

(2)

$\bowtie$ P.DNUM=D.DNUMBER

E

(1)

σ P.PLOCATION= 'Stafford'

D

P

(b) π P.PNUMBER, P.DNUM, E.LNAME, E.ADDRESS, E.BDATE

σ P.DNUM=D.DNUMBER AND D.MGRSSN=E.SSN AND P.PLOCATION='Stafford'

X

X   E

P   D

Figure 18.4   Two query trees for the query Q2. (a) Query tree corresponding to the relational algebra expression for Q2. (b) Initial (canonical) query tree for SQL query Q2.

(c)   [P.PNUMBER,P.DNUM]   [E.LNAME,E.ADDRESS,E.BDATE]

Figure 18.4   (c) Query graph for Q2.

and the department manager's last name, address, and birthdate. This query is specified on the relational schema of Figure 7.5 and corresponds to the following relational algebra expression:

$$\pi_{PNUMBER,DNUM,LNAME,ADDRESS,BDATE} \ (((\sigma_{PLOCATION='Stafford'}(PROJECT))$$
$$\bowtie_{DNUM=DNUMBER}(DEPARTMENT)) \ \bowtie_{MGRSSN=SSN}(EMPLOYEE))$$

This corresponds to the following SQL query:

```
Q2: SELECT  P.PNUMBER, P.DNUM, E.LNAME, E.ADDRESS, E.BDATE
    FROM    PROJECT AS P, DEPARTMENT AS D, EMPLOYEE AS E
    WHERE   P.DNUM=D.DNUMBER AND D.MGRSSN=E.SSN AND
            P.PLOCATION='Stafford';
```

In Figure 18.4(a) the three relations PROJECT, DEPARTMENT, and EMPLOYEE are represented by leaf nodes P, D, and E, while the relational algebra operations of the expression are represented by internal tree nodes. When this query tree is executed, the node marked (1) in Figure 18.4(a) must begin execution before node (2) because some resulting tuples of operation (1) must be available before we can begin executing operation (2). Similarly, node (2) must begin executing and producing results before node (3) can start execution, and so on.

As we can see, the query tree represents a specific order of operations for executing a query. A more neutral representation of a query is the **query graph** notation. Figure 18.4(c) shows the query graph for query Q2. Relations in the query are represented by **relation nodes,** which are displayed as single circles. Constant values, typically from the query selection conditions, are represented by **constant nodes,** which are displayed as double circles. Selection and join conditions are represented by the graph **edges,** as shown in Figure 18.4(c). Finally, the attributes to be retrieved from each relation are displayed in square brackets above each relation.

The query graph representation does not indicate an order on which operations to perform first. There is only a single graph corresponding to each query.[16] Although some

---

16. Hence, a query graph corresponds to a *relational calculus* expression (see Chapter 9).

optimization techniques were based on query graphs, it is now generally accepted that query trees are preferable because, in practice, the query optimizer needs to show the order of operations for query execution, which is not possible in query graphs.

18.3.2 Heuristic Optimization of Query Trees

In general, many different relational algebra expressions—and hence many different query trees—can be equivalent; that is, they can correspond to the same query.[17] The query parser will typically generate a standard **initial query tree** to correspond to an SQL query, without doing any optimization. For example, for a select–project–join query, such as Q2, the initial tree is shown in Figure 18.4(b). The CARTESIAN PRODUCT of the relations specified in the FROM clause is first applied; then the selection and join conditions of the WHERE clause are applied, followed by the projection on the SELECT clause attributes. Such a canonical query tree represents a relational algebra expression that is *very ineffi-cient if executed directly*, because of the CARTESIAN PRODUCT (×) operations. For example, if the PROJECT, DEPARTMENT, and EMPLOYEE relations had record sizes of 100, 50, and 150 bytes and contained 100, 20, and 5000 tuples, respectively, the result of the CARTESIAN PRODUCT would contain 10 million tuples of record size 300 bytes each. However, the query tree in Figure 18.4(b) is in a simple standard form that can be easily created. It is now the job of the heuristic query optimizer to transform this initial query tree into a **final query tree** that is efficient to execute.

The optimizer must include rules for equivalence among relational algebra expressions that can be applied to the initial tree. The heuristic query optimization rules then utilize these equivalence expressions to transform the initial tree into the final, optimized query tree. We first discuss informally how a query tree is transformed by using heuristics. Then we discuss general transformation rules and show how they may be used in an algebraic heuristic optimizer.

Example of Transforming a Query.   Consider the following query Q on the database of Figure 7.5: "Find the last names of employees born after 1957 who work on a project named 'Aquarius'." This query can be specified in SQL as follows:

```
Q:  SELECT LNAME
    FROM   EMPLOYEE, WORKS_ON, PROJECT
    WHERE  PNAME='Aquarius' AND PNUMBER=PNO AND ESSN=SSN
           AND BDATE.'1957-12-31';
```

The initial query tree for Q is shown in Figure 18.5(a). Executing this tree directly first creates a very large file containing the CARTESIAN PRODUCT of the entire EMPLOYEE, WORKS_ON, and PROJECT files. However, this query needs only one record from the PROJECT relation—for the 'Aquarius' project—and only the EMPLOYEE records for those whose date of birth is after '1957-12-31'. Figure 18.5(b) shows an improved query tree that first

---

17. A query may also be stated in various ways in a high-level query language such as SQL (see Chapter 8).

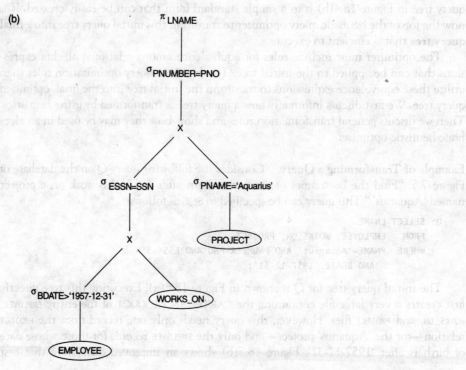

Figure 18.5 Steps in converting a query tree during heuristic optimization.
(a) Initial (canonical) query tree for SQL query Q. (b) Moving
SELECT operations down the query tree.

(c)

(d)

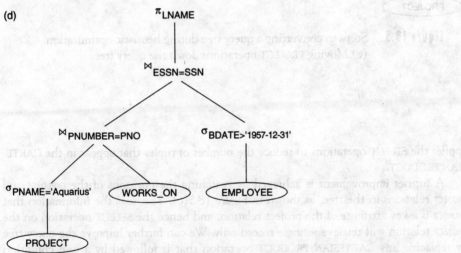

Figure 18.5 Steps in converting a query tree during heuristic optimization.
(c) Applying the more restrictive SELECT operation first.
(d) Replacing CARTESIAN PRODUCT and SELECT with JOIN operations.

(e)

Figure 18.5   Steps in converting a query tree during heuristic optimization.
(e) Moving PROJECT operations down the query tree.

applies the SELECT operations to reduce the number of tuples that appear in the CARTE-
SIAN PRODUCT.

A further improvement is achieved by switching the positions of the EMPLOYEE and
PROJECT relations in the tree, as shown in Figure 18.5(c). This uses the information that
PNUMBER is a key attribute of the project relation, and hence the SELECT operation on the
PROJECT relation will retrieve a single record only. We can further improve the query tree
by replacing any CARTESIAN PRODUCT operation that is followed by a join condition
with a JOIN operation, as shown in Figure 18.5(d). Another improvement is to keep only
the attributes needed by subsequent operations in the intermediate relations, by including
PROJECT (π) operations as early as possible in the query tree, as shown in Figure 18.5(e).
This reduces the attributes (columns) of the intermediate relations, whereas the SELECT
operations reduce the number of tuples (records).

As the preceding example demonstrates, a query tree can be transformed step by step
into another query tree that is more efficient to execute. However, we must make sure
that the transformation steps always lead to an equivalent query tree. To do this, the

query optimizer must know which transformation rules preserve this equivalence. We discuss some of these transformation rules next.

General Transformation Rules for Relational Algebra Operations. There are many rules for transforming relational algebra operations into equivalent ones. Here we are interested in the meaning of the operations and the resulting relations. Hence, if two relations have the same set of attributes in a *different order* but the two relations represent the same information, we consider the relations equivalent. In Section 7.1.2 we gave an alternative definition of *relation* that makes order of attributes unimportant; we will use this definition here. We now state some transformation rules that are useful in query optimization, without proving them:

1. Cascade of σ: A conjunctive selection condition can be broken up into a cascade (that is, a sequence) of individual σ operations:

   $$\sigma_{c1 \text{ AND } c2 \text{ AND } \dots \text{ AND } cn}(R) \equiv \sigma_{c1}(\sigma_{c2}(\dots(\sigma_{cn}(R))\dots))$$

2. Commutativity of σ: The σ operation is commutative:

   $$\sigma_{c1}(\sigma_{c2}(R)) \equiv \sigma_{c2}(\sigma_{c1}(R))$$

3. Cascade of π: In a cascade (sequence) of π operations, all but the last one can be ignored:

   $$\pi_{List1}(\pi_{List2}(\dots(\pi_{Listm}(R))\dots)) \equiv \pi_{List1}(R)$$

4. Commuting σ with π: If the selection condition c involves only those attributes $A1, \dots, An$ in the projection list, the two operations can be commuted:

   $$\pi_{A1, A2, \dots, An}(\sigma_c(R)) \equiv \sigma_c(\pi_{A1, A2, \dots, An}(R))$$

5. Commutativity of $\bowtie$ (and $\times$): The $\bowtie$ operation is commutative, as is the $\times$ operation:

   $$R \bowtie_c S \equiv S \bowtie_c R$$
   $$R \times S \equiv S \times R$$

   Notice that, although the order of attributes may not be the same in the relations resulting from the two joins (or two cartesian products), the "meaning" is the same because order of attributes is not important in the alternative definition of relation.

6. Commuting σ with $\bowtie$ (or $\times$): If all the attributes in the selection condition c involve only the attributes of one of the relations being joined—say, R—the two operations can be commuted as follows:

   $$\sigma_c(R \bowtie S) \equiv (\sigma_c(R)) \bowtie S$$

   Alternatively, if the selection condition c can be written as ($c1$ AND $c2$), where condition $c1$ involves only the attributes of R and condition $c2$ involves only the attributes of S, the operations commute as follows:

   $$\sigma_c(R \bowtie S) \equiv (\sigma_{c1}(R)) \bowtie (\sigma_{c2}(S))$$

The same rules apply if the $\bowtie$ is replaced by a $\times$ operation.

7. Commuting π with $\bowtie$ (or $\times$): Suppose that the projection list is $L = \{A_1, ..., A_n, B_1, ..., B_m\}$, where $A_1, ..., A_n$ are attributes of R and $B_1, ..., B_m$ are attributes of S. If the join condition c involves only attributes in L, the two operations can be commuted as follows:

$$\pi_L (R \bowtie_c S) \equiv (\pi_{A1, ..., An} (R)) \bowtie_c (\pi_{B1, ..., Bm} (S))$$

If the join condition c contains additional attributes not in L, these must be added to the projection list, and a final π operation is needed. For example, if attributes $A_{n+1}, ..., A_{n+k}$ of R and $B_{m+1}, ..., B_{m+p}$ of S are involved in the join condition c but are not in the projection list L, the operations commute as follows:

$$\pi_L (R \bowtie_c S) \equiv \pi_L ((\pi_{A1,...,An,An+1,...,An+k}(R)) \bowtie_c (\pi_{B1,...,Bm,Bm+1,...,Bm+p} (S)))$$

For $\times$, there is no condition c, so the first transformation rule always applies by replacing $\bowtie_c$ with $\times$.

8. Commutativity of set operations: The set operations $\cup$ and $\cap$ are commutative but $-$ is not.

9. Associativity of $\bowtie$, $\times$, $\cup$, and $\cap$: These four operations are individually associative; that is, if θ stands for any one of these four operations (throughout the expression), we have:

$$(R \theta S) \theta T \equiv R \theta (S \theta T)$$

10. Commuting σ with set operations: The σ operation commutes with $\cup$, $\cap$, and $-$. If θ stands for any one of these three operations (throughout the expression), we have:

$$\sigma_c (R \theta S) \equiv (\sigma_c (R)) \theta (\sigma_c (S))$$

11. The π operation commutes with $\cup$:

$$\pi_L (R \cup S) \equiv (\pi_L (R)) \cup (\pi_L (S))$$

12. Converting a $(\sigma, \times)$ sequence into $\bowtie$: If the condition c of a σ that follows a $\times$ corresponds to a join condition, convert the $(\sigma, \times)$ sequence into a $\bowtie$ as follows:

$$(\sigma_c (R \times S)) \equiv (R \bowtie_c S)$$

There are other possible transformations. For example, a selection or join condition c can be converted into an equivalent condition by using the following rules (DeMorgan's laws):

```
NOT (c1 AND c2)  ≡  (NOT c1) OR  (NOT c2)
NOT (c1 OR  c2)  ≡  (NOT c1) AND (NOT c2)
```

Additional transformations discussed in Chapters 7 and 9 are not repeated here. We discuss next how transformations can be used in heuristic optimization.

Outline of a Heuristic Algebraic Optimization Algorithm. We can now outline the steps of an algorithm that utilizes some of the above rules to transform an initial query tree into an optimized tree that is more efficient to execute (in most cases). The algorithm will lead to transformations similar to those discussed in our example of Figure 18.5. The steps of the algorithm are as follows:

1. Using Rule 1, break up any SELECT operations with conjunctive conditions into a cascade of SELECT operations. This permits a greater degree of freedom in moving SELECT operations down different branches of the tree.

2. Using Rules 2, 4, 6, and 10 concerning the commutativity of SELECT with other operations, move each SELECT operation as far down the query tree as is permitted by the attributes involved in the select condition.

3. Using Rules 5 and 9 concerning commutativity and associativity of binary operations, rearrange the leaf nodes of the tree using the following criteria. First, position the leaf node relations with the most restrictive SELECT operations so they are executed first in the query tree representation. The definition of *most restrictive* SELECT can mean either the ones that produce a relation with the fewest tuples or with the smallest absolute size.[18] Another possibility is to define the most restrictive SELECT as the one with the smallest selectivity; this is more practical because estimates of selectivities are often available in the DBMS catalog. Second, make sure that the ordering of leaf nodes does not cause CARTESIAN PRODUCT operations; for example, if the two relations with the most restrictive SELECT do not have a direct join condition between them, it may be desirable to change the order of leaf nodes to avoid Cartesian products.[19]

4. Using Rule 12, combine a CARTESIAN PRODUCT operation with a subsequent SELECT operation in the tree into a JOIN operation, if the condition represents a join condition.

5. Using Rules 3, 4, 7, and 11 concerning the cascading of PROJECT and the commuting of PROJECT with other operations, break down and move lists of projection attributes down the tree as far as possible by creating new PROJECT operations as needed. Only those attributes needed in the query result and in subsequent operations in the query tree should be kept after each PROJECT operation.

6. Identify subtrees that represent groups of operations that can be executed by a single algorithm.

In our example, Figure 18.5(b) shows the tree of Figure 18.5(a) after applying Steps 1 and 2 of the algorithm; Figure 18.5(c) shows the tree after Step 3; Figure 18.5(d) after Step 4; and Figure 18.5(e) after Step 5. In Step 6 we may group together the operations in the subtree whose root is the operation π_{ESSN} into a single algorithm. We may also group the remaining operations into another subtree, where the tuples resulting from the first algorithm replace the subtree whose root is the operation π_{ESSN}, because the first grouping means that this subtree is executed first.

---

18. Either definition can be used, since these rules are heuristic.

19. Note that a Cartesian product is acceptable in some cases—for example, if each relation has only a single tuple because each had a previous select condition on a key field.

Summary of Heuristics for Algebraic Optimization. We now summarize the basic heuristics for algebraic optimization. The main heuristic is to apply first the operations that reduce the size of intermediate results. This includes performing as early as possible SELECT operations to reduce the number of tuples and PROJECT operations to reduce the number of attributes. This is done by moving SELECT and PROJECT operations as far down the tree as possible. In addition, the SELECT and JOIN operations that are most restrictive—that is, result in relations with the fewest tuples or with the smallest absolute size—should be executed before other similar operations. This is done by reordering the leaf nodes of the tree among themselves while avoiding Cartesian products, and adjusting the rest of the tree appropriately.

18.3.3 Converting Query Trees into Query Execution Plans

An execution plan for a relational algebra expression represented as a query tree includes information about the access methods available for each relation as well as the algorithms to be used in computing the relational operators represented in the tree. As a simple example, consider query Q1 from Chapter 7, whose corresponding relational algebra expression is

$$\pi_{\text{FNAME, LNAME, ADDRESS}}(\sigma_{\text{DNAME='RESEARCH'}}(\text{DEPARTMENT})$$

$$\bowtie_{\text{DNUMBER=DNO}} \text{EMPLOYEE})$$

The query tree is shown in Figure 18.6. To convert this into an execution plan, the optimizer might choose an index search for the SELECT operation (assuming one exists), a table scan as access method for EMPLOYEE, a nested-loop join algorithm for the join, and a scan of the JOIN result for the PROJECT operator. In addition, the approach taken for executing the query may specify a materialized or a pipelined evaluation.

With **materialized evaluation,** the result of an operation is stored as a temporary relation (that is, the result is *physically materialized*). For instance, the join operation can be computed and the entire result stored as a temporary relation, which is then read as input by the algorithm that computes the PROJECT operation, which would produce the query

Figure 18.6   A query tree for query Q1.

result table. On the other hand, with **pipelined evaluation,** as the resulting tuples of an operation are produced, they are forwarded directly to the next operation in the query sequence. For example, as the selected tuples from DEPARTMENT are produced by the SELECT operation, they are placed in a buffer; the JOIN operation algorithm would then consume the tuples from the buffer, and those tuples that result from the JOIN operation are pipelined to the projection operation algorithm. The advantage of pipelining is the cost savings in not having to write the intermediate results to disk and not having to read them back for the next operation.

18.4   Using Selectivity and Cost Estimates in Query Optimization

A query optimizer should not depend solely on heuristic rules; it should also estimate and compare the costs of executing a query using different execution strategies and should choose the strategy with the *lowest cost estimate*. For this approach to work, accurate cost estimates are required so that different strategies are compared fairly and realistically. In addition, we must limit the number of execution strategies to be considered; otherwise, too much time will be spent making cost estimates for the many possible execution strategies. Hence, this approach is more suitable for **compiled queries** where the optimization is done at compile time and the resulting execution strategy code is stored and executed directly at runtime. For **interpreted queries,** where the entire process shown in Figure 18.1 occurs at runtime, a full-scale optimization may slow down the response time. A more elaborate optimization is indicated for compiled queries, whereas a partial, less time-consuming optimization works best for interpreted queries.

We call this approach **cost-based query optimization,**[20] and it uses traditional optimization techniques that search the *solution space* to a problem for a solution that minimizes an objective (cost) function. The cost functions used in query optimization are estimates and not exact cost functions, so the optimization may select a query execution strategy that is not the optimal one. In Section 18.4.1 we discuss the components of query execution cost. In Section 18.4.2 we discuss the type of information needed in cost functions. This information is kept in the DBMS catalog. In Section 18.4.3 we give examples of cost functions for the SELECT operation, and in Section 18.4.4 we discuss cost functions for two-way JOIN operations. Section 18.4.5 discusses multiway joins, and Section 18.4.6 gives an example.

18.4.1   Cost Components for Query Execution

The cost of executing a query includes the following components:

1. *Access cost to secondary storage:* This is the cost of searching for, reading, and writing data blocks that reside on secondary storage, mainly on disk. The cost of

---

20. This approach was first used in the optimizer for the SYSTEM R experimental DBMS developed at IBM.

searching for records in a file depends on the type of access structures on that file, such as ordering, hashing, and primary or secondary indexes. In addition, factors such as whether the file blocks are allocated contiguously on the same disk cylinder or scattered on the disk affect the access cost.

2. *Storage cost:* This is the cost of storing any intermediate files that are generated by an execution strategy for the query.

3. *Computation cost:* This is the cost of performing in-memory operations on the data buffers during query execution. Such operations include searching for and sorting records, merging records for a join, and performing computations on field values.

4. *Memory usage cost:* This is the cost pertaining to the number of memory buffers needed during query execution.

5. *Communication cost:* This is the cost of shipping the query and its results from the database site to the site or terminal where the query originated.

For large databases, the main emphasis is on minimizing the access cost to secondary storage. Simple cost functions ignore other factors and compare different query execution strategies in terms of the number of block transfers between disk and main memory. For smaller databases, where most of the data in the files involved in the query can be completely stored in memory, the emphasis is on minimizing computation cost. In distributed databases, where many sites are involved (see Chapter 24), communication cost must be minimized also. It is difficult to include all the cost components in a (weighted) cost function because of the difficulty of assigning suitable weights to the cost components. That is why some cost functions consider a single factor only—disk access. In the next section we discuss some of the information that is needed for formulating cost functions.

18.4.2   Catalog Information Used in Cost Functions

To estimate the costs of various execution strategies, we must keep track of any information that is needed for the cost functions. This information may be stored in the DBMS catalog, where it is accessed by the query optimizer. First, we must know the size of each file. For a file whose records are all of the same type, the **number of records (tuples) (r),** the (average) **record size (R),** and the **number of blocks (b)** (or close estimates of them) are needed. The **blocking factor (bfr)** for the file may also be needed. We must also keep track of the *primary access method* and the *primary access attributes* for each file. The file records may be unordered, ordered by an attribute with or without a primary or clustering index, or hashed on a key attribute. Information is kept on all secondary indexes and indexing attributes. The **number of levels (x)** of each multilevel index (primary, secondary, or clustering) is needed for cost functions that estimate the number of block accesses that occur during query execution. In some cost functions the **number of first-level index blocks (b_{I1})** is needed.

Another important parameter is the **number of distinct values (d)** of an attribute and its **selectivity (sl),** which is the fraction of records satisfying an equality condition on the attribute. This allows estimation of the **selection cardinality ($s = sl * r$)** of an attribute, which is the *average* number of records that will satisfy an equality selection condition on that attribute. For a *key attribute*, $d = r$, $sl = 1/r$ and $s = 1$. For a *nonkey attribute*, by making an assumption that the d distinct values are uniformly distributed among the records, we estimate $sl = (1/d)$ and so $s = (r/d)$.[21]

Information such as the number of index levels is easy to maintain because it does not change very often. However, other information may change frequently; for example, the number of records r in a file changes every time a record is inserted or deleted. The query optimizer will need reasonably close but not necessarily completely up-to-the-minute values of these parameters for use in estimating the cost of various execution strategies. In the next two sections we examine how some of these parameters are used in cost functions for a cost-based query optimizer.

18.4.3 Examples of Cost Functions for SELECT

We now give cost functions for the selection algorithms S1 to S8 discussed in Section 18.2.2 in terms of *number of block transfers* between memory and disk. These cost functions are estimates that ignore computation time, storage cost, and other factors. The cost for method Si is referred to as C_{Si} block accesses.

- S1. *Linear search (brute force) approach:* We search all the file blocks to retrieve all records satisfying the selection condition; hence, $C_{S1a} = b$. For an equality condition on a key, only half the file blocks are searched on the average before finding the record, so $C_{S1b} = (b/2)$ if the record is found; if no record satisfies the condition, $C_{S1b} = b$.

- S2. *Binary search:* This search accesses approximately $C_{S2} = \log_2 b + \lceil (s/bfr) \rceil - 1$ file blocks. This reduces to $\log_2 b$ if the equality condition is on a unique (key) attribute, because $s = 1$ in this case.

- S3. *Using a primary index (S3a) or hash key (S3b) to retrieve a single record:* For a primary index, retrieve one more block than the number of index levels; hence, $C_{S3a} = x + 1$. For hashing, the cost function is approximately $C_{S3b} = 1$ for static hashing or linear hashing, and it is 2 for extendible hashing (see Chapter 5).

- S4. *Using an ordering index to retrieve multiple records:* If the comparison condition is $>$, $>=$, $<$, or $<=$ on a key field with an ordering index, roughly half the file records will satisfy the condition. This gives a cost function of $C_{S4} = x + (b/2)$. This is a very rough estimate, and although it may be correct on the average, it may be quite inaccurate in individual cases.

- S5. *Using a clustering index to retrieve multiple records:* Given an equality condition, s records will satisfy the condition, where s is the selection cardinality of the indexing attribute. This means that $\lceil (s/bfr) \rceil$ file blocks will be accessed, giving $C_{S5} = x + \lceil (s/bfr) \rceil$.

- S6. *Using a secondary (B^+-tree) index:* On an *equality* comparison, s records will satisfy the condition, where s is the selection cardinality of the indexing attribute.

---

21. As we mentioned earlier, more accurate optimizers may store histograms of the distribution of records over the data values for an attribute.

However, because the index is nonclustering, each of the records may reside on a different block, so the (worst case) cost estimate is $C_{S6a} = x + s$. This reduces to $x + 1$ for a key indexing attribute. If the comparison condition is $>$, $>=$, $<$, or $<=$ and half the file records are assumed to satisfy the condition, then (very roughly) half the first-level index blocks are accessed, plus half the file records via the index. The cost estimate for this case, approximately, is $C_{S6b} = x + (b_{I1}/2) + (r/2)$. The $r/2$ factor can be refined if better selectivity estimates are available.

- S7. *Conjunctive selection*: We can use either S1 or one of the methods S2 to S6 discussed above. In the latter case, we use one condition to retrieve the records and then check in the memory buffer whether each retrieved record satisfies the remaining conditions in the conjunction.

- S8. *Conjunctive selection using a composite index*: Same as S3a, S5, or S6a, depending on the type of index.

Example of Using the Cost Functions.   In a query optimizer, it is common to enumerate the various possible strategies for executing a query and to estimate the costs for different strategies. An optimization technique, such as dynamic programming, may be used to find the optimal (least) cost estimate efficiently, without having to consider all possible execution strategies. We do not discuss optimization algorithms here; rather, we use a simple example to illustrate how cost estimates may be used. Suppose that the EMPLOYEE file of Figure 7.5 has $r_E = 10,000$ records stored in $b_E = 2000$ disk blocks with blocking factor $bfr_E = 5$ records/block and the following access paths:

1. A clustering index on SALARY, with levels $x_{SALARY} = 3$ and average selection cardinality $s_{SALARY} = 20$.

2. A secondary index on the key attribute SSN, with $x_{SSN} = 4$ ($s_{SSN} = 1$).

3. A secondary index on the nonkey attribute DNO, with $x_{DNO} = 2$ and first-level index blocks $b_{I1DNO} = 4$. There are $d_{DNO} = 125$ distinct values for DNO, so the selection cardinality of DNO is $s_{DNO} = (r_E/d_{DNO}) = 80$.

4. A secondary index on SEX, with $x_{SEX} = 1$. There are $d_{SEX} = 2$ values for the sex attribute, so the average selection cardinality is $s_{SEX} = (r_E/d_{SEX}) = 5000$.

We illustrate the use of cost functions with the following examples:

(OP1): $\sigma_{SSN='123456789'}$(EMPLOYEE)

(OP2): $\sigma_{DNO>5}$(EMPLOYEE)

(OP3): $\sigma_{DNO=5}$(EMPLOYEE)

(OP4): $\sigma_{DNO=5 \text{ AND } SALARY>30000 \text{ AND } SEX='F'}$(EMPLOYEE)

The cost of the brute force (linear search) option S1 will be estimated as $C_{S1a} = b_E = 2000$ (for a selection on a nonkey attribute) or $C_{S1b} = (b_E/2) = 1000$ (average cost for a selection on a key attribute). For OP1 we can use either method S1 or method S6a; the cost estimate for S6a is $C_{S6a} = x_{SSN} + 1 = 4 + 1 = 5$, and it is chosen over Method S1, whose average cost is $C_{S1b} = 1000$. For OP2 we can use either method S1 (with estimated cost C_{S1a} = 2000) or method S6b (with estimated cost C_{S6b} = x_{DNO} + $(b_{I1DNO}/2)$ + $(r_E/2)$ = 2 + (4/2) + (10,000/2) = 5004), so we choose the brute force approach for OP2. For OP3 we can use either method S1 (with estimated cost C_{S1a} = 2000) or method S6a (with estimated cost C_{S6a} = x_{DNO} + s_{DNO} = 2 + 80 = 82), so we choose method S6a.

Finally, consider OP4, which has a conjunctive selection condition. We need to estimate the cost of using any one of the three components of the selection condition to retrieve the records, plus the brute force approach. The latter gives cost estimate C_{S1a} = 2000. Using the condition (DNO = 5) first gives the cost estimate C_{S6a} = 82. Using the condition (SALARY > 30,000) first gives a cost estimate C_{S4} = x_{SALARY} + $(b_E/2)$ = 3 + (2000/2) = 1003. Using the condition (SEX = 'F') first gives a cost estimate C_{S6a} = x_{SEX} + s_{SEX} = 1 + 5000 = 5001. The optimizer would then choose method S6a on the secondary index on DNO because it has the lowest cost estimate. The condition (DNO = 5) is used to retrieve the records, and the remaining part of the conjunctive condition (SALARY > 30,000 AND SEX = 'F') is checked for each selected record after it is retrieved into memory.

18.4.4 Examples of Cost Functions for JOIN

To develop reasonably accurate cost functions for JOIN operations, we need to have an estimate for the size (number of tuples) of the file that results *after* the JOIN operation. This is usually kept as a ratio of the size (number of tuples) of the resulting join file to the size of the Cartesian product file, if both are applied to the same input files, and it is called the **join selectivity (js).** If we denote the number of tuples of a relation R by $|R|$, we have

$$js = |(R \bowtie_c S)| \, / \, |(R \times S)| = |(R \bowtie_c S)| \, / \, (|R| * |S|)$$

If there is no join condition c, then $js = 1$ and the join is the same as the CARTESIAN PRODUCT. If no tuples from the relations satisfy the join condition, then $js = 0$. In general, $0 \leq js \leq 1$. For a join where the condition c is an equality comparison $R.A = S.B$, we get the following two special cases:

1. If A is a key of R, then $|(R \bowtie_c S)| \leq |S|$, so $js \leq (1/|R|)$.
2. If B is a key of S, then $|(R \bowtie_c S)| \leq |R|$, so $js \leq (1/|S|)$.

Having an estimate of the join selectivity for commonly occurring join conditions enables the query optimizer to estimate the size of the resulting file after the join operation, given the sizes of the two input files, by using the formula $|(R \bowtie_c S)| = js * |R| * |S|$. We can now give some sample *approximate* cost functions for estimating the cost of some of the join algorithms given in Section 18.2.3. The join operations are of the form

$$R \bowtie_{A=B} S$$

where A and B are domain-compatible attributes of R and S, respectively. Assume that R has b_R blocks and that S has b_S blocks:

- J1. *Nested-loop join:* Suppose that we use R for the outer loop; then we get the following cost function to estimate the number of block accesses for this method, assuming *three memory buffers*. We assume that the blocking factor for the resulting file is bfr_{RS} and that the join selectivity is known:

$$C_{J1} = b_R + (b_R * b_S) + ((js * |R| * |S|)/bfr_{RS})$$

The last part of the formula is the cost of writing the resulting file to disk. This cost formula can be modified to take into account different numbers of memory buffers, as discussed in Section 18.2.3.

- J2. *Single-loop join (using an access structure to retrieve the matching record(s))*: If an index exists for the join attribute B of S with index levels x_B, we can retrieve each record s in R and then use the index to retrieve all the matching records t from S that satisfy $t[B] = s[A]$. The cost depends on the type of index. For a secondary index where s_B is the selection cardinality for the join attribute B of S,[22] we get

$$C_{J2a} = b_R + (|R| * (x_B + s_B)) + ((js * |R| * |S|)/bfr_{RS})$$

For a clustering index where s_B is the selection cardinality of B, we get

$$C_{J2b} = b_R + (|R| * (x_B + (s_B/bfr_B))) + ((js * |R| * |S|)/bfr_{RS})$$

For a primary index, we get

$$C_{J2c} = b_R + (|R| * (x_B + 1)) + ((js * |R| * |S|)/bfr_{RS})$$

If a hash key exists for one of the two join attributes—say, B of S—we get

$$C_{J2d} = b_R + (|R| * h) + ((js * |R| * |S|)/bfr_{RS})$$

where $h \geq 1$ is the average number of block accesses to retrieve a record, given its hash key value.

- J3. *Sort–merge join*: If the files are already sorted on the join attributes, the cost function for this method is

$$C_{J3a} = b_R + b_S + ((js * |R| * |S|)/bfr_{RS})$$

If we must sort the files, the cost of sorting must be added. We can approximate the sorting cost by $(2 * b) + (2 * b * \log_2 b)$ for a file of b blocks (see Section 18.2.1). Hence, we get the following cost function:

$$C_{J3b} = (2 * b_R * (1 + \log_2 b_R)) + (2 * b_S * (1 + \log_2 b_S)) + b_R + b_S + ((js * |R| * |S|)/bfr_{RS})$$

Example of Using the Cost Functions. Suppose that we have the EMPLOYEE file described in the example of the previous section, and assume that the DEPARTMENT file of

---

22. *Selection cardinality* was defined as the average number of records that satisfy an equality condition on an attribute, which is the average number of records that have the same value for the attribute and hence will be joined to a single record in the other file.

Figure 7.5 consists of $r_D = 125$ records stored in $b_D = 13$ disk blocks. Consider the join operations

(OP6): EMPLOYEE $\bowtie_{DNO=DNUMBER}$ DEPARTMENT
(OP7): DEPARTMENT $\bowtie_{MGRSSN=SSN}$ EMPLOYEE

Suppose that we have a primary index on DNUMBER of DEPARTMENT with $x_{DNUMBER} = 1$ level and a secondary index on MGRSSN of DEPARTMENT with selection cardinality $s_{MGRSSN} = 1$ and levels $x_{MGRSSN} = 2$. Assume that the join selectivity for OP6 is $js_{OP6} = (1/|\text{DEPARTMENT}|) = 1/125$ because DNUMBER is a key of DEPARTMENT. Also assume that the blocking factor for the resulting join file $bfr_{ED} = 4$ records per block. We can estimate the costs for the JOIN operation OP6 using the applicable methods J1 and J2 as follows:

1. Using Method J1 with EMPLOYEE as outer loop:

$$C_{J1} = b_E + (b_E * b_D) + ((js_{OP6} * r_E * r_D)/bfr_{ED})$$
$$= 2000 + (2000 * 13) + (((1/125) * 10,000 * 125)/4) = 30,500$$

2. Using Method J1 with DEPARTMENT as outer loop:

$$C_{J1} = b_D + (b_E * b_D) + ((js_{OP6} * r_E * r_D)/bfr_{ED})$$
$$= 13 + (13 * 2000) + (((1/125) * 10,000 * 125/4) = 28,513$$

3. Using Method J2 with EMPLOYEE as outer loop:

$$C_{J2c} = b_E + (r_E * (x_{DNUMBER} + 1)) + ((js_{OP6} * r_E * r_D)/bfr_{ED}$$
$$= 2000 + (10,000 * 2) + (((1/125) * 10,000 * 125/4) = 24,500$$

4. Using Method J2 with DEPARTMENT as outer loop:

$$C_{J2a} b_D + (r_D * (x_{DNO} + s_{DNO})) + ((js_{OP6} * r_E * r_D)/bfr_{ED}$$
$$= 13 + (125 * (2 + 80)) + (((1/125) * 10,000 * 125/4) = 12,763$$

Case 4 has the lowest cost estimate and will be chosen. Notice that if 15 memory buffers (or more) were available for executing the join instead of just two, 13 of them could be used to hold the entire DEPARTMENT relation in memory, one could be used as buffer for the result, and the cost for Case 2 could be drastically reduced to just $b_E + b_D + ((js_{OP6} * r_E * r_D)/bfr_{ED})$ or 4513, as discussed in Section 18.2.3. As an exercise, the reader should perform a similar analysis for OP7.

18.4.5 Multiple Relation Queries and Join Ordering

The algebraic transformation rules in Section 18.3.2 include a commutative rule and an associative rule for the join operation. With these rules, many equivalent join expressions can be produced. As a result, the number of alternative query trees grows very rapidly as the number of joins in a query increases. In general, a query that joins n relations will have $n - 1$ join operations, and hence can have a large number of different join orders.

Figure 18.7   Two left-deep (join) query trees.

Estimating the cost of every possible join tree for a query with a large number of joins will require a substantial amount of time by the query optimizer. Hence, some pruning of the possible query trees is needed. Query optimizers typically limit the structure of a (join) query tree to that of left-deep (or right-deep) trees. A **left-deep tree** is a binary tree where the right child of each nonleaf node is always a base relation. The optimizer would choose the particular left-deep tree with the lowest estimated cost. Two examples of left-deep trees are shown in Figure 18.7. (Note that the trees in Figure 18.5 are also left-deep trees.)

With left-deep trees, the right child is considered to be the inner relation when executing a nested-loop join. One advantage of left-deep (or right-deep) trees is that they are amenable to pipelining, as discussed in Section 18.3.3. For instance, consider the first left-deep tree in Figure 18.7 and assume that the join algorithm is the single-loop method; in this case, a disk page of tuples of the outer relation is used to probe the inner relation for matching tuples. As a resulting block of tuples is produced from the join of R1 and R2, it could be used to probe R3. Likewise, as a resulting page of tuples is produced from this join, it could be used to probe R4. Another advantage of left-deep (or right-deep) trees is that having a base relation as one of the inputs of each join allows the optimizer to utilize any access paths on that relation that may be useful in executing the join.

If materialization is used instead of pipelining (see Section 18.3.3), the join results could be materialized and stored as temporary relations. The key idea from the optimizer's standpoint with respect to join ordering is to find an ordering that will reduce the size of the temporary results, since the temporary results (pipelined or materialized) are used by subsequent operators and hence affect the execution cost of those operators.

18.4.6   Example to Illustrate Cost-Based Query Optimization

We will consider query Q2 and its query tree shown in Figure 18.4 (a) to illustrate cost-based query optimization:

```
Q2: SELECT PNUMBER, DNUM, LNAME, ADDRESS, BDATE
    FROM   PROJECT, DEPARTMENT, EMPLOYEE
    WHERE  DNUM=DNUMBER AND MGRSSN=SSN AND PLOCATION='Stafford';
```

(a)

TABLE_NAME	COLUMN_NAME	NUM_DISTINCT	LOW_VALUE	HIGH_VALUE
PROJECT	PLOCATION	200	1	200
PROJECT	PNUMBER	2000	1	2000
PROJECT	DNUM	50	1	50
DEPARTMENT	DNUMBER	50	1	50
DEPARTMENT	MGRSSN	50	1	50
EMPLOYEE	SSN	10000	1	10000
EMPLOYEE	DNO	50	1	50
EMPLOYEE	SALARY	500	1	500

(b)

TABLE_NAME	NUM_ROWS	BLOCKS
PROJECT	2000	100
DEPARTMENT	50	5
EMPLOYEE	10000	2000

(c)

INDEX_NAME	UNIQUENESS	BLEVEL*	LEAF_ BLOCKS	DISTINCT _KEYS
PROJ_PLOC	NONUNIQUE	1	4	200
EMP_SSN	UNIQUE	1	50	10000
EMP_SAL	NONUNIQUE	1	50	500

*BLEVEL is the number of levels without the leaf level.

Figure 18.8 Sample statistical information for relations in Q2. (a) Column information. (b) Table information. (c) Index information.

Suppose we have the statistical information about the relations shown in Figure 18.8. The format of the information follows the catalog presentation in Section 17.3. The LOW_VALUE and HIGH_VALUE statistics have been normalized for clarity. The tree in Figure 18.4(a) is assumed to represent the result of the algebraic heuristic optimization process and the start of cost-based optimization (in this example, we assume that the heuristic optimizer does not push the projection operations down the tree).

The first cost-based optimization to consider is join ordering. As previously mentioned, we assume the optimizer considers only left-deep trees, so the potential join orders—without Cartesian product—are

1. PROJECT ⋈ DEPARTMENT ⋈ EMPLOYEE
2. DEPARTMENT ⋈ PROJECT ⋈ EMPLOYEE
3. DEPARTMENT ⋈ EMPLOYEE ⋈ PROJECT
4. EMPLOYEE ⋈ DEPARTMENT ⋈ PROJECT

Assume that the selection operation has already been applied to the PROJECT relation. If we assume a materialized approach, then a new temporary relation is created after each join operation. To examine the cost of join order (1), the first join is between PROJECT and DEPARTMENT. Both the join method and the access methods for the input relations must be determined. Since DEPARTMENT has no index according to Figure 18.8, the only available access method is a table scan (that is, a linear search). The PROJECT relation will have the selection operation performed before the join, so two options exist: table scan (linear search) or utilizing its PROJ_PLOC index, so the optimizer must compare their estimated costs. The statistical information on the PROJ_PLOC index (see Figure 18.8) shows the number of index levels $x = 2$ (root plus leaf levels). The index is nonunique (because PLOCATION is not a key of PROJECT), so the optimizer assumes a uniform data distribution and estimates the number of record pointers for each PLOCATION value to be 10. This is computed from the tables in Figure 18.8 by multiplying SELECTIVITY * NUM_ROWS, where SELECTIVITY is estimated by 1/NUM_DISTINCT. So the cost of using the index and accessing the records is estimated to be 12 block accesses (2 for the index and 10 for the data blocks). The cost of a table scan is estimated to be 100 block accesses, so the index access is more efficient as expected.

In the materialized approach, a temporary file TEMP1 of size 1 block is created to hold the result of the selection operation. The file size is calculated by determining the blocking factor using the formula NUM_ROWS/BLOCKS, which gives 2000/100 or 20 rows per block. Hence, the 10 records selected from the PROJECT relation will fit into a single block. Now we can compute the estimated cost of the first join. We will consider only the nested-loop join method, where the outer relation is the temporary file, TEMP1, and the inner relation is DEPARTMENT. Since the entire TEMP1 file fits in available buffer space, we need to read each of the DEPARTMENT table's five blocks only once, so the join cost is six block accesses plus the cost of writing the temporary result file, TEMP2. The optimizer would have to determine the size of TEMP2. Since the join attribute DNUMBER is the key for DEPARTMENT, any DNUM value from TEMP1 will join with at most one record from DEPARTMENT, so the number of rows in the TEMP2 will be equal to the number of rows in TEMP1, which is 10. The optimizer would determine the record size for TEMP2 and the number of blocks needed to store these 10 rows. For brevity, assume that the blocking factor for TEMP2 is five rows per block, so a total of two blocks are needed to store TEMP2.

Finally, the cost of the last join needs to be estimated. We can use a single-loop join on TEMP2 since in this case the index EMP_SSN (see Figure 18.8) can be used to probe and locate matching records from EMPLOYEE. Hence, the join method would involve reading in each block of TEMP2 and looking up each of the five MGRSSN values using the EMP_SSN index. Each index lookup would require a root access, a leaf access, and a data block access ($x+1$, where the number of levels x is 2). So, 10 lookups require 30 block accesses. Adding the two block accesses for TEMP2 gives a total of 32 block accesses for this join.

For the final projection, assume pipelining is used to produce the final result, which does not require additional block accesses, so the total cost for join order (1) is estimated as the sum of the previous costs. The optimizer would then estimate costs in a similar manner for the other three join orders and choose the one with the lowest estimate. We leave this as an exercise for the reader.

18.5 Overview of Query Optimization in ORACLE

The ORACLE DBMS (Version 7) provides two different approaches to query optimization: rule-based and cost-based. With the rule-based approach, the optimizer chooses execution plans based on heuristically ranked operations. ORACLE maintains a table of 15 ranked access paths, where a lower ranking implies a more efficient approach. The access paths range from table access by ROWID (most efficient)—where ROWID specifies the record's physical address that includes the data file, data block, and row offset within the block—to a full table scan (least efficient)—where all rows in the table are searched by doing multiblock reads. However, the rule-based approach is being phased out in favor of the cost-based approach, where the optimizer examines alternative access paths and operator algorithms and chooses the execution plan with lowest estimated cost. The catalog tables containing statistical information are used in a similar fashion, as described in Section 18.4.6. The estimated query cost is proportional to the expected elapsed time needed to execute the query with the given execution plan. The ORACLE optimizer calculates this cost based on the estimated usage of resources, such as I/O, CPU time, and memory needed. The goal of cost-based optimization in ORACLE is to minimize the elapsed time to process the entire query.

An interesting addition to the ORACLE query optimizer is the capability for an application developer to specify **hints** to the optimizer.[23] The idea is that an application developer might know more information about the data than the optimizer. For example, consider the EMPLOYEE table shown in Figure 7.5. The SEX column of that table has only two distinct values. If there are 10,000 employees, then the optimizer would estimate that half are male and half are female, assuming a uniform data distribution. If a secondary index exists, it would more than likely not be used. However, if the application developer knows that there are only 100 male employees, a hint could be specified in an SQL query whose WHERE-clause condition is SEX = 'M' so that the associated index would be used in processing the query. Various hints can be specified, such as:

- The optimization approach for an SQL statement.
- The access path for a table accessed by the statement.
- The join order for a join statement.
- A particular join operation in a join statement.

The cost-based optimization of ORACLE 8 is a good example of the sophisticated approach taken to optimize SQL queries in commercial RDBMSs.

18.6 Semantic Query Optimization

A different approach to query optimization, called **semantic query optimization,** has been suggested. This technique, which may be used in combination with the techniques discussed previously, uses constraints specified on the database schema—such as unique attributes and other more complex constraints—in order to modify one query into another query that is more efficient to execute. We will not discuss this approach in detail but only illustrate it with a simple example. Consider the SQL query:

```
SELECT  E.LNAME, M.LNAME
FROM    EMPLOYEE AS E, EMPLOYEE AS M
WHERE   E.SUPERSSN=M.SSN AND E.SALARY.M.SALARY
```

---

23. Such hints have also been called query *annotations.*

This query retrieves the names of employees who earn more than their supervisors. Suppose that we had a constraint on the database schema that stated that no employee can earn more than his or her direct supervisor. If the semantic query optimizer checks for the existence of this constraint, it need not execute the query at all because it knows that the result of the query will be empty. This may save considerable time if the constraint checking can be done efficiently. However, searching through many constraints to find those that are applicable to a given query and that may semantically optimize it can also be quite time-consuming. With the inclusion of active rules in database systems (see Chapter 23), semantic query optimization techniques may eventually be fully incorporated into the DBMSs of the future.

18.7   Summary

In this chapter we gave an overview of the techniques used by DBMSs in processing and optimizing high-level queries. We first discussed how SQL queries are translated into relational algebra and then how various relational algebra operations may be executed by a DBMS. We saw that some operations, particularly SELECT and JOIN, may have many execution options. We also discussed how operations can be combined during query processing to create pipelined or stream-based execution instead of materialized execution.

Following that, we described heuristic approaches to query optimization, which use heuristic rules and algebraic techniques to improve the efficiency of query execution. We showed how a query tree that represents a relational algebra expression can be heuristically optimized by reorganizing the tree nodes and transforming it into another equivalent query tree that is more efficient to execute. We also gave equivalence-preserving transformation rules that may be applied to a query tree. Then we introduced query execution plans for SQL queries, which add method execution plans to the query tree operations.

We then discussed the cost-based approach to query optimization. We showed how cost functions are developed for some database access algorithms and how these cost functions are used to estimate the costs of different execution strategies. We presented an overview of the ORACLE query optimizer, and we mentioned the technique of semantic query optimization.

Review Questions

18.1. Discuss the reasons for converting SQL queries into relational algebra queries before optimization is done.

18.2. Discuss the different algorithms for implementing each of the following relational operators and the circumstances under which each algorithm can be used: SELECT, JOIN, PROJECT, UNION, INTERSECT, SET DIFFERENCE, CARTESIAN PRODUCT.

18.3. What is a query execution plan?

18.4. What is meant by the term *heuristic optimization*? Discuss the main heuristics that are applied during query optimization.

18.5. How does a query tree represent a relational algebra expression? What is meant by an execution of a query tree? Discuss the rules for transformation of query trees, and identify when each rule should be applied during optimization.

18.6. How many different join orders are there for a query that joins 10 relations?

18.7. What is meant by *cost-based query optimization*?

18.8. What is the difference between *pipelining* and *materialization*?

18.9. Discuss the cost components for a cost function that is used to estimate query execution cost. Which cost components are used most often as the basis for cost functions?

18.10. Discuss the different types of parameters that are used in cost functions. Where is this information kept?

18.11. List the cost functions for the SELECT and JOIN methods discussed in Section 18.2.

18.12. What is meant by semantic query optimization? How does it differ from other query optimization techniques?

Exercises

18.13. Consider SQL queries Q1, Q8, Q1B, Q4, and Q27 from Chapter 8.
  a. Draw at least two query trees that can represent *each* of these queries. Under what circumstances would you use each of your query trees?
  b. Draw the initial query tree for each of these queries, then show how the query tree is optimized by the algorithm outlined in Section 18.3.2.
  c. For each query, compare your own query trees of part (a) and the initial and final query trees of part (b).

18.14. A file of 4096 blocks is to be sorted with an available buffer space of 64 blocks. How many passes will be needed in the merge phase of the external sort-merge algorithm?

18.15. Develop cost functions for the PROJECT, UNION, INTERSECTION, SET DIFFERENCE, and CARTESIAN PRODUCT algorithms discussed in Sections 18.2.3 and 18.2.4.

18.16. Develop cost functions for an algorithm that consists of two SELECTs, a JOIN, and a final PROJECT, in terms of the cost functions for the individual operations.

18.17. Can a nondense index be used in the implementation of an aggregate operator? Why or why not?

18.18. Calculate the cost functions for different options of executing the JOIN operation OP7 discussed in Section 18.2.3.

18.19. Develop formulas for the hybrid hash join algorithm for calculating the size of the buffer for the first bucket. Develop more accurate cost estimation formulas for the algorithm.

18.20. Estimate the cost of operations OP6 and OP7, using the formulas developed in Exercise 18.19.

18.21. Extend the sort-merge join algorithm to implement the left outer join operation.

18.22. Compare the cost of two different query plans for the following query:

$$\sigma_{\text{SALARY}.40000}(\text{EMPLOYEE} \bowtie_{\text{DNO=DNUMBER}} \text{DEPARTMENT})$$

Use the database statistics in Figure 18.8.

Selected Bibliography

A survey by Graefe (1993) discusses query execution in database systems and includes an extensive bibliography. A survey paper by Jarke and Koch (1984) gives a taxonomy of query optimization and includes a bibliography of work in this area. A detailed algorithm for relational algebra optimization is given by Smith and Chang (1975). The Ph.D. thesis of Kooi (1980) provides a foundation for query processing techniques.

Whang (1985) discusses query optimization in OBE (Office-By-Example), which is a system based on QBE. Cost-based optimization was introduced in the SYSTEM R experimental DBMS and is discussed in Astrahan et al. (1976). Selinger et al. (1979) discuss the optimization of multiway joins in SYSTEM R. Join algorithms are discussed in Gotlieb (1975), Blasgen and Eswaran (1976), and Whang et al. (1982). Hashing algorithms for implementing joins are described and analyzed in DeWitt et al. (1984), Bratbergsengen (1984), Shapiro (1986), Kitsuregawa et al. (1989), and Blakeley and Martin (1990), among others. Approaches to finding a good join order are presented in Ioannidis and Kang (1990) and in Swami and Gupta (1989). A discussion of the implications of left-deep and bushy join trees is presented in Ioannidis and Kang (1991). Kim (1982) discusses transformations of nested SQL queries into canonical representations. Optimization of aggregate functions is discussed in Klug (1982) and Muralikrishna (1992). Salzberg et al. (1990) describe a fast external sorting algorithm. Estimating the size of temporary relations is crucial for query optimization. Sampling-based estimation schemes are presented in Haas et al. (1995) and in Haas and Swami (1995). Lipton et al. (1990) also discuss selectivity estimation. Having the database system store and use more detailed statistics in the form of histograms is the topic of Muralikrishna and DeWitt (1988) and Poosala et al. (1996).

Kim et al. (1985) discuss advanced topics in query optimization. Semantic query optimization is discussed in King (1981) and Malley and Zdonick (1986). More recent work on semantic query optimization is reported in Chakravarthy et al. (1990), Shenoy and Ozsoyoglu (1989), and Siegel et al. (1992).

CHAPTER 19 | Transaction Processing Concepts

19.1 Introduction to Transaction Processing

The concept of transaction provides a mechanism for describing logical units of database processing. **Transaction processing systems** are systems with large databases and hundreds of concurrent users that are executing database transactions. Examples of such systems include systems for reservations, banking, credit card processing, stock markets, supermarket checkout, and other similar systems. They require high availability and fast response time for hundreds of concurrent users. In this chapter we present the concepts that are needed in transaction processing systems. We define the concept of a transaction, which is used to represent a logical unit of database processing that must be completed in its entirety to ensure correctness. We discuss the concurrency control problem, which occurs when multiple transactions submitted by various users interfere with one another in a way that produces incorrect results. We also discuss recovery from transaction failures.

Section 19.1 informally discusses why concurrency control and recovery are necessary in a database system. Section 19.2 introduces the concept of a transaction and discusses additional concepts related to transaction processing in database systems. Section 19.3 presents the concepts of atomicity, consistency preservation, isolation, and durability or permanency—called the ACID properties—that are considered desirable in transactions. Section 19.4 introduces the concept of schedules (or histories) of executing transactions and characterizes the recoverability of schedules. Section 19.5 discusses the concept of serializability of concurrent transaction executions, which can be used to define correct execution sequences (or schedules) of concurrent transactions. Section 19.6 presents the facilities that support the transaction concept in SQL2.

The two subsequent chapters continue with more details on the techniques used to support transaction processing. Chapter 20 describes the basic concurrency control techniques, and Chapter 21 presents an overview of recovery techniques.

19.1   Introduction to Transaction Processing

In this section we informally introduce the concepts of concurrent execution of transactions and recovery from transaction failures. Section 19.1.1 compares single-user and multiuser database systems and demonstrates how concurrent execution of transactions can take place in multiuser systems. Section 19.1.2 defines the concept of transaction and presents a simple model of transaction execution, based on read and write database operations, that is used to formalize concurrency control and recovery concepts. Section 19.1.3 shows by informal examples why concurrency control techniques are needed in multiuser systems. Finally, Section 19.1.4 discusses why techniques are needed to permit recovery from failure by discussing the different ways in which transactions can fail while executing.

19.1.1   Single-User Versus Multiuser Systems

One criterion for classifying a database system is according to the number of users who can use the system **concurrently**—that is, at the same time. A DBMS is **single-user** if at most one user at a time can use the system, and it is **multiuser** if many users can use the system—and hence access the database—concurrently. Single-user DBMSs are mostly restricted to some microcomputer systems; most other DBMSs are multiuser. For example, an airline reservations system is used by hundreds of travel agents and reservation clerks concurrently. Systems in banks, insurance agencies, stock exchanges, supermarkets, and the like are also operated on by many users who submit transactions concurrently to the system.

Multiple users can access databases—and use computer systems—simultaneously because of the concept of **multiprogramming,** which allows the computer to execute multiple programs—or **processes**—at the same time. If only a single central processing unit (CPU) exists, it can actually execute at most one process at a time. However, **multiprogramming operating systems** execute some commands from one process, then suspend that process and execute some commands from the next process, and so on. A process is resumed at the point where it was suspended whenever it gets its turn to use the CPU again. Hence, concurrent execution of processes is actually **interleaved,** as illustrated in Figure 19.1, which shows two processes A and B executing concurrently in an interleaved fashion. Interleaving keeps the CPU busy when a process requires an input or output (I/O) operation, such as reading a block from disk. The CPU is switched to execute another process rather than remaining idle during I/O time. Interleaving also prevents a long process from delaying other processes.

If the computer system has multiple hardware processors (CPUs), **parallel processing** of multiple processes is possible, as illustrated by processes C and D in Figure 19.1. Most of the theory concerning concurrency control in databases is developed in terms of **interleaved concurrency,** so for the remainder of this chapter we assume this model. In a multiuser DBMS, the stored data items are the primary resources that may be accessed

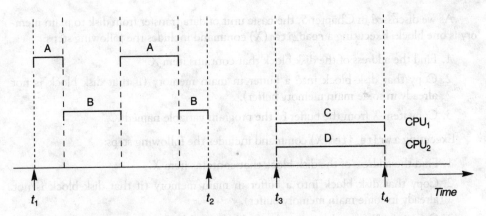

Figure 19.1   Interleaved processing versus parallel processing of concurrent transactions.

concurrently by interactive users or application programs, which are constantly retrieving information from and modifying the database.

19.1.2 Transactions, Read and Write Operations, and DBMS Buffers

A **transaction** is a logical unit of database processing that includes one or more database access operations—these can include insertion, deletion, modification, or retrieval operations. The database operations that form a transaction can either be embedded within an application program or they can be specified interactively via a high-level query language such as SQL. One way of specifying the transaction boundaries is by specifying explicit **begin transaction** and **end transaction** statements in an application program; in this case, all database access operations between the two are considered as forming one transaction. A single application program may contain more than one transaction if it contains several transaction boundaries. If the database operations in a transaction do not update the database but only retrieve data, the transaction is called a **read-only transaction.**

The model of a database that is used to explain transaction processing concepts is much simplified. A **database** is basically represented as a collection of **named data items.** The size of a data item is called its **granularity,** and it can be a field of some record in the database, or it may be a larger unit such as a record or even a whole disk block, but the concepts we discuss are independent of the data item granularity. Using this simplified database model, the basic database access operations that a transaction can include are as follows:

- **read_item(X):** Reads a database item named X into a program variable. To simplify our notation, we assume that *the program variable is also named X.*

- **write_item(X):** Writes the value of program variable X into the database item named X.

As we discussed in Chapter 5, the basic unit of data transfer from disk to main memory is one block. Executing a read_item(X) command includes the following steps:

1. Find the address of the disk block that contains item X.
2. Copy that disk block into a buffer in main memory (if that disk block is not already in some main memory buffer).
3. .Copy item X from the buffer to the program variable named X.

Executing a write_item(X) command includes the following steps:

1. Find the address of the disk block that contains item X.
2. Copy that disk block into a buffer in main memory (if that disk block is not already in some main memory buffer).
3. Copy item X from the program variable named X into its correct location in the buffer.
4. Store the updated block from the buffer back to disk (either immediately or at some later point in time).

Step 4 is the one that actually updates the database on disk. In some cases the buffer is not immediately stored to disk, in case additional changes are to be made to the buffer. Usually, the decision about when to store back a modified disk block that is in a main memory buffer is handled by the recovery manager of the DBMS in cooperation with the underlying operating system. The DBMS will generally maintain a number of **buffers** in main memory that hold database disk blocks containing the database items being processed. When these buffers are all occupied, and additional database blocks must be copied into memory, some buffer replacement policy is used to choose which of the current buffers is to be replaced. If the chosen buffer has been modified, it must be written back to disk before it is reused.[1]

A transaction includes read_item and write_item operations to access and update the database. Figure 19.2 shows examples of two very simple transactions. The **read-set** of a transaction is the set of all items that the transaction reads, and the **write-set** is the set

(a)	T_1	(b)	T_2
	read_item (X);		read_item (X);
	X:=X-N;		X:=X+M;
	write_item (X);		write_item (X);
	read_item (Y);		
	Y:=Y+N;		
	write_item (Y);		

Figure 19.2   Two sample transactions. (a) Transaction T_1. (b) Transaction T_2

---

1. We will not discuss buffer replacement policies here as these are typically discussed in operating systems textbooks.

of all items that the transaction writes. For example, the read-set of T_1 in Figure 19.2 is $\{X, Y\}$ and its write-set is also $\{X, Y\}$.

Concurrency control and recovery mechanisms are mainly concerned with the database access commands in a transaction. Transactions submitted by the various users may execute concurrently and may access and update the same database items. If this concurrent execution is uncontrolled, it may lead to problems, such as an inconsistent database. In the next section we informally introduce three of the problems that may occur.

19.1.3   Why Concurrency Control Is Needed

Several problems can occur when concurrent transactions execute in an uncontrolled manner. We illustrate some of these problems by referring to a much simplified airline reservations database in which a record is stored for each airline flight. Each record includes the number of reserved seats on that flight as a *named data item*, among other information. Figure 19.2(a) shows a transaction T_1 that *transfers* N reservations from one flight whose number of reserved seats is stored in the database item named X to another flight whose number of reserved seats is stored in the database item named Y. Figure 19.2(b) shows a simpler transaction T_2 that just *reserves* M seats on the first flight (X) referenced in transaction T_1.[2] To simplify our example, we do not show additional portions of the transactions, such as checking whether a flight has enough seats available before reserving additional seats.

When a database access program is written, it has the flight numbers, their dates, and the number of seats to be booked as parameters; hence, the same program can be used to execute many transactions, each with different flights and numbers of seats to be booked. For concurrency control purposes, a transaction is a *particular execution* of a program on a specific date, flight, and number of seats. In Figure 19.2(a) and (b), the transactions T_1 and T_2 are *specific executions* of the programs that refer to the specific flights whose numbers of seats are stored in data items X and Y in the database. We now discuss the types of problems we may encounter with these two transactions if they run concurrently.

The Lost Update Problem.   This problem occurs when two transactions that access the same database items have their operations interleaved in a way that makes the value of some database item incorrect. Suppose that transactions T_1 and T_2 are submitted at approximately the same time, and suppose that their operations are interleaved as shown in Figure 19.3(a); then the final value of item X is incorrect, because T_2 reads the value of X *before* T_1 changes it in the database, and hence the updated value resulting from T_1 is lost. For example, if X = 80 at the start (originally there were 80 reservations on the flight), N = 5 (T_1 transfers 5 seat reservations from the flight corresponding to X to the flight corresponding to Y), and M = 4 (T_2 reserves 4 seats on X), the final result should be

---

2. A similar, more commonly used example assumes a bank database, with one transaction doing a transfer of funds from account X to account Y and the other transaction doing a deposit to account X.

$X = 79$; but in the interleaving of operations shown in Figure 19.3(a), it is $X = 84$ because the update in T_1 that removed the five seats from X was *lost*.

The Temporary Update (or Dirty Read) Problem. This problem occurs when one transaction updates a database item and then the transaction fails for some reason (see Section 19.1.4). The updated item is accessed by another transaction before it is changed back to its original value. Figure 19.3(b) shows an example where T_1 updates item X and then fails before completion, so the system must change X back to its original value. Before it can do so, however, transaction T_2 reads the "temporary" value of X, which will

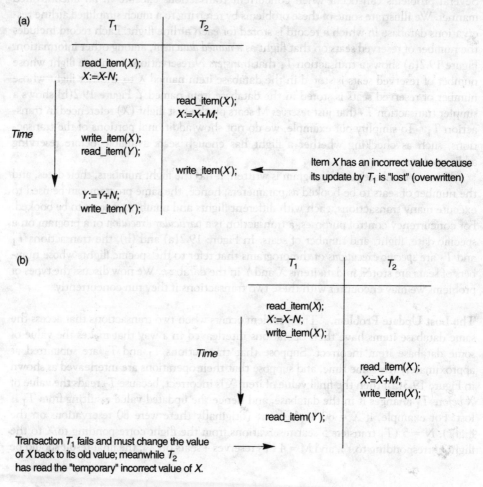

(a)

T_1	T_2
read_item(X);	
X:=X-N;	
	read_item(X);
	X:=X+M;
write_item(X);	
read_item(Y);	
	write_item(X); ← Item X has an incorrect value because its update by T_1 is "lost" (overwritten)
Y:=Y+N;	
write_item(Y);	

Time ↓

(b)

T_1	T_2
read_item(X);	
X:=X-N;	
write_item(X);	
	read_item(X);
	X:=X+M;
	write_item(X);
read_item(Y);	

Time ↓

Transaction T_1 fails and must change the value of X back to its old value; meanwhile T_2 has read the "temporary" incorrect value of X.

Figure 19.3   Some problems that occur when concurrent execution is uncontrolled. (a) The lost update problem. (b) The temporary update problem.

(c)

T_1	T_3
	sum:=0;
	read_item(A);
	sum:=sum+A;
	⋮
read_item(X);	
X:=X-N;	
write_item(X);	
	read_item(X);
	sum:=sum+X;
	read_item(Y);
	sum:=sum+Y;
read_item(Y);	
Y:=Y+N;	
write_item(Y);	

T_3 reads X after N is subtracted and reads Y before N is added; a wrong summary is the result (off by N).

Figure 19.3   Some problems that occur when concurrent execution is uncontrolled. (c) The incorrect summary problem.

not be recorded permanently in the database because of the failure of T_1. The value of item X that is read by T_2 is called *dirty data*, because it has been created by a transaction that has not completed and committed yet; hence, this problem is also known as the *dirty read problem*.

The Incorrect Summary Problem. If one transaction is calculating an aggregate summary function on a number of records while other transactions are updating some of these records, the aggregate function may calculate some values before they are updated and others after they are updated. For example, suppose that a transaction T_3 is calculating the total number of reservations on all the flights; meanwhile, transaction T_1 is executing. If the interleaving of operations shown in Figure 19.3(c) occurs, the result of T_3 will be off by an amount N because T_3 reads the value of X *after* N seats have been subtracted from it but reads the value of Y *before* those N seats have been added to it.

Another problem that may occur is called **unrepeatable read,** where a transaction T reads an item twice and the item is changed by another transaction T' between the two reads. Hence, T receives *different values* for its two reads of the same item. This may occur, for example, if during an airline reservation transaction, a customer is inquiring about seat availability on several flights. When the customer decides on a particular flight, the transaction then reads the number of seats on that flight a second time before completing the reservation.

19.1.4   Why Recovery Is Needed

Whenever a transaction is submitted to a DBMS for execution, the system is responsible for making sure that either (1) all the operations in the transaction are completed successfully and their effect is recorded permanently in the database, or (2) the transaction has no effect whatsoever on the database or on any other transactions. The DBMS must not permit some operations of a transaction T to be applied to the database while other operations of T are not. This may happen if a transaction **fails** after executing some of its operations but before executing all of them.

Types of Failures.   Failures are generally classified as transaction, system, and media failures. There are several possible reasons for a transaction to fail in the middle of execution:

1. *A computer failure (system crash)*: A hardware, software, or network error occurs in the computer system during transaction execution. Hardware crashes are usually media failures—for example, main memory failure.

2. *A transaction or system error*: Some operation in the transaction may cause it to fail, such as integer overflow or division by zero. Transaction failure may also occur because of erroneous parameter values or because of a logical programming error.[3] In addition, the user may interrupt the transaction during its execution.

3. *Local errors or exception conditions detected by the transaction*: During transaction execution, certain conditions may occur that necessitate cancellation of the transaction. For example, data for the transaction may not be found. Notice that an exception condition,[4] such as insufficient account balance in a banking database, may cause a transaction, such as a fund withdrawal, to be canceled. This exception should be programmed in the transaction itself, and hence would not be considered a failure.

4. *Concurrency control enforcement*: The concurrency control method (see Chapter 20) may decide to abort the transaction, to be restarted later, because it violates serializability (see Section 19.5) or because several transactions are in a state of deadlock.

5. *Disk failure*: Some disk blocks may lose their data because of a read or write malfunction or because of a disk read/write head crash. This may happen during a read or a write operation of the transaction.

6. *Physical problems and catastrophes*: This refers to an endless list of problems that includes power or air-conditioning failure, fire, theft, sabotage, overwriting disks or tapes by mistake, and mounting of a wrong tape by the operator.

---

3. In general, a transaction should be thoroughly tested to ensure that it has no bugs (logical programming errors).

4. Exception conditions, if programmed correctly, *do not* constitute transaction failures.

Failures of types 1, 2, 3, and 4 are more common than those of types 5 or 6. Whenever a failure of type 1 through 4 occurs, the system must keep sufficient information to recover from the failure. Disk failure or other catastrophic failures of type 5 or 6 do not happen frequently; if they do occur, recovery is a major task. We discuss recovery from failure in Chapter 21.

The concept of transaction is fundamental to many techniques for concurrency control and recovery from failures.

19.2   Transaction and System Concepts

In this section we discuss additional concepts relevant to transaction processing. Section 19.2.1 describes the various states a transaction can be in, and discusses additional relevant operations needed in transaction processing. Section 19.2.2 discusses the system log, which keeps information needed for recovery. Section 19.2.3 describes the concept of commit points of transactions, and why they are important in transaction processing.

19.2.1   Transaction States and Additional Operations

A transaction is an atomic unit of work that is either completed in its entirety or not done at all. For recovery purposes, the system needs to keep track of when the transaction starts, terminates, and commits or aborts (see below). Hence, the recovery manager keeps track of the following operations:

- BEGIN_TRANSACTION: This marks the beginning of transaction execution.

- READ or WRITE: These specify read or write operations on the database items that are executed as part of a transaction.

- END_TRANSACTION: This specifies that READ and WRITE transaction operations have ended and marks the end of transaction execution. However, at this point it may be necessary to check whether the changes introduced by the transaction can be permanently applied to the database (committed) or whether the transaction has to be aborted because it violates serializability (see Section 19.5) or for some other reason.

- COMMIT_TRANSACTION: This signals a *successful end* of the transaction so that any changes (updates) executed by the transaction can be safely **committed** to the database and will not be undone.

- ROLLBACK (or ABORT): This signals that the transaction has *ended unsuccessfully*, so that any changes or effects that the transaction may have applied to the database must be *undone*.

Figure 19.4 shows a state transition diagram that describes how a transaction moves through its execution states. A transaction goes into an **active state** immediately after it starts execution, where it can issue READ and WRITE operations. When the transaction ends, it moves to the **partially committed state.** At this point, some recovery protocols need to ensure that a system failure will not result in an inability to record the changes of the transaction permanently (usually by recording changes in the system log, discussed in the

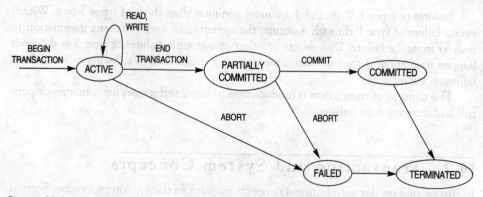

Figure 19.4   State transition diagram illustrating the states for transaction execution.

next section).[5] Once this check is successful, the transaction is said to have reached its commit point and enters the **committed state.** Commit points are discussed in more detail in Section 19.2.3. Once a transaction is committed, it has concluded its execution successfully and all its changes must be recorded permanently in the database.

However, a transaction can go to the **failed state** if one of the checks fails or if the transaction is aborted during its active state. The transaction may then have to be rolled back to undo the effect of its WRITE operations on the database. The **terminated state** corresponds to the transaction leaving the system. The transaction information that is maintained in system tables while the transaction has been running is removed when the transaction terminates. Failed or aborted transactions may be *restarted* later—either automatically or after being resubmitted by the user—as brand new transactions.

19.2.2   The System Log

To be able to recover from failures that affect transactions, the system maintains a **log**[6] to keep track of all transaction operations that affect the values of database items. This information may be needed to permit recovery from failures. The log is kept on disk, so it is not affected by any type of failure except for disk or catastrophic failure. In addition, the log is periodically backed up to archival storage (tape) to guard against such catastrophic failures. We now list the types of entries—called **log records**—that are written to the log and the action each performs. In these entries, T refers to a unique **transaction-id** that is generated automatically by the system and is used to identify each transaction:

1. [start_transaction,T]: Indicates that transaction T has started execution.
2. [write_item,T,X,*old_value*,*new_value*]: Indicates that transaction T has changed the value of database item X from *old_value* to *new_value*.

---

5. Optimistic concurrency control (see Section 20.4) also requires that certain checks be made at this point to ensure that the transaction did not interfere with other executing transactions.

6. The log has sometimes been called the DBMS journal.

3. [read_item,T,X]: Indicates that transaction T has read the value of database item X.

4. [commit,T]: Indicates that transaction T has completed successfully, and affirms that its effect can be committed (recorded permanently) to the database.

5. [abort,T]: Indicates that transaction T has been aborted.

Protocols for recovery that avoid cascading rollbacks (see Section 19.4.2)—which include all practical protocols—do not require that READ operations be written to the system log. However, if the log is also used for other purposes—such as auditing (keeping track of all database operations)—then such entries can be included. In addition, some recovery protocols require simpler WRITE entries that do not include new_value (see Section 19.4.2).

Notice that we assume here that *all* permanent changes to the database occur within transactions, so the notion of recovery from a transaction failure amounts to either undoing or redoing transaction operations individually from the log. If the system crashes, we can recover to a consistent database state by examining the log and using one of the techniques described in Chapter 21. Because the log contains a record of every WRITE operation that changes the value of some database item, it is possible to **undo** the effect of these WRITE operations of a transaction T by tracing backward through the log and resetting all items changed by a WRITE operation of T to their old_values. **Redoing** the operations of a transaction may also be needed if all its updates are recorded in the log but a failure occurs before we can be sure that all these new_values have been written permanently in the actual database on disk.[7] Redoing the operations of transaction T is applied by tracing forward through the log and setting all items changed by a WRITE operation of T to their new_values.

19.2.3 Commit Point of a Transaction

A transaction T reaches its **commit point** when all its operations that access the database have been executed successfully *and* the effect of all the transaction operations on the database have been recorded in the log. Beyond the commit point, the transaction is said to be **committed,** and its effect is assumed to be *permanently recorded* in the database. The transaction then writes a commit record [commit,T] into the log. If a system failure occurs, we search back in the log for all transactions T that have written a [start_transaction,T] record into the log but have not written their [commit,T] record yet; these transactions may have to be *rolled back* to undo their effect on the database during the recovery process. Transactions that have written their commit record in the log must also have recorded all their WRITE operations in the log, so their effect on the database can be *redone* from the log records.

Notice that the log file must be kept on disk. As discussed in Chapter 5, updating a disk file involves copying the appropriate block of the file from disk to a buffer in main memory, updating the buffer in main memory, and copying the buffer to disk. It is common to keep

---

7. Undo and redo are discussed more fully in Chapter 21.

one or more blocks of the log file in main memory buffers until they are filled with log entries and then to write them back to disk only once, rather than writing to disk every time a log entry is added. This saves the overhead of multiple disk writes of the same log file block. At the time of a system crash, only the log entries that have been *written back to disk* are considered in the recovery process because the contents of main memory may be lost. Hence, *before* a transaction reaches its commit point, any portion of the log that has not been written to the disk yet must now be written to the disk. This process is called **force-writing** the log file before committing a transaction.

19.3   Desirable Properties of Transactions

Transactions should possess several properties. These are often called the ACID **properties,** and they should be enforced by the concurrency control and recovery methods of the DBMS. The following are the ACID properties:

1. **Atomicity:** A transaction is an atomic unit of processing; it is either performed in its entirety or not performed at all.

2. **Consistency preservation:** A transaction is consistency preserving if its complete execution take(s) the database from one consistent state to another.

3. **Isolation:** A transaction should appear as though it is being executed in isolation from other transactions. That is, the execution of a transaction should not be interfered with by any other transactions executing concurrently.

4. **Durability or permanency:** The changes applied to the database by a committed transaction must persist in the database. These changes must not be lost because of any failure.

The atomicity property requires that we execute a transaction to completion. It is the responsibility of the transaction recovery subsystem of a DBMS to ensure atomicity. If a transaction fails to complete for some reason, such as a system crash in the midst of transaction execution, the recovery technique must undo any effects of the transaction on the database.

The preservation of consistency is generally considered to be the responsibility of the programmers who write the database programs or of the DBMS module that enforces integrity constraints. Recall that a **database state** is a collection of all the stored data items (values) in the database at a given point in time. A **consistent state** of the database satisfies the constraints specified in the schema as well as any other constraints that should hold on the database. A database program should be written in a way that guarantees that, if the database is in a consistent state before executing the transaction, it will be in a consistent state after the *complete* execution of the transaction, assuming that *no interference with other transactions* occurs.

Isolation is enforced by the concurrency control subsystem of the DBMS.[8] If every transaction does not make its updates visible to other transactions until it is committed,

---

8. We will discuss concurrency control protocols in Chapter 20.

one form of isolation is enforced that solves the temporary update problem and eliminates cascading rollbacks (see Chapter 21). There have been attempts to define the *level of isolation* of a transaction. A transaction is said to have level 0 (zero) isolation if it does not overwrite the dirty reads of higher-level transactions. A level 1 (one) isolation transaction has no lost updates; and level 2 isolation has no lost updates and no dirty reads. Finally, level 3 isolation (also called *true isolation*) has, in addition to degree 2 properties, repeatable reads.

Finally, the durability property is the responsibility of the recovery subsystem of the DBMS. We will discuss how recovery protocols enforce durability and atomicity in Chapter 21.

19.4 Schedules and Recoverability

When transactions are executing concurrently in an interleaved fashion, then the order of execution of operations from the various transactions is known as a **schedule** (or **history**). In this section, we first define the concept of schedule, and then we characterize the types of schedules that facilitate recovery when failures occur. In Section 19.5, we characterize schedules in terms of the interference of participating transactions, leading to the concepts of serializability and serializable schedules.

19.4.1 Schedules (Histories) of Transactions

A **schedule** (or **history**) S of n transactions $T_1, T_2, ..., T_n$ is an ordering of the operations of the transactions subject to the constraint that, for each transaction T_i that participates in S, the operations of T_i in S must appear in the same order in which they occur in T_i. Note, however, that operations from other transactions T_j can be interleaved with the operations of T_i in S. For now, consider the order of operations in S to be a *total ordering*, although it is possible theoretically to deal with schedules whose operations form *partial orders* (as we discuss later).

For the purpose of recovery and concurrency control, we are mainly interested in the `read_item` and `write_item` operations of the transactions, as well as the `commit` and `abort` operations. A shorthand notation for describing a schedule uses the symbols r, w, c, and a for the operations `read_item`, `write_item`, `commit`, and `abort`, respectively, and appends as subscript the transaction id (transaction number) to each operation in the schedule. In this notation, the database item X that is read or written follows the r and w operations in parentheses. For example, the schedule of Figure 19.3(a), which we shall call S_a, can be written as follows in this notation:

S_a: $r_1(X); r_2(X); w_1(X); r_1(Y); w_2(X); w_1(Y);$

Similarly, the schedule for Figure 19.3(b), which we call S_b, can be written as follows, if we assume that transaction T_1 aborted after its `read_item(Y)` operation:

S_b: $r_1(X); w_1(X); r_2(X); w_2(X); r_1(Y); a_1;$

Two operations in a schedule are said to **conflict** if they satisfy all three of the following conditions: (1) they belong to different transactions; (2) they access the same item X; and (3) at least one of the operations is a write_item(X). For example, in schedule S_a, the operations $r_1(X)$ and $w_2(X)$ conflict, as do the operations $r_2(X)$ and $w_1(X)$, and the operations $w_1(X)$ and $w_2(X)$. However, the operations $r_1(X)$ and $r_2(X)$ do not conflict, since they are both read operations; the operations $w_2(X)$ and $w_1(Y)$ do not conflict, because they operate on distinct data items X and Y; and the operations $r_1(X)$ and $w_1(X)$ do not conflict, because they belong to the same transaction.

A schedule S of n transactions $T_1, T_2, ..., T_n$, is said to be a **complete schedule** if the following conditions hold:

1. The operations in S are exactly those operations in $T_1, T_2, ..., T_n$, including a commit or abort operation as the last operation for each transaction in the schedule.

2. For any pair of operations from the same transaction T_i, their order of appearance in S is the same as their order of appearance in T_i.

3. For any two conflicting operations, one of the two must occur before the other in the schedule.[9]

The preceding condition (3) allows for two *nonconflicting operations* to occur in the schedule without defining which occurs first, thus leading to the definition of a schedule as a **partial order** of the operations in the n transactions.[10] However, a total order must be specified in the schedule for any pair of conflicting operations (condition 3) and for any pair of operations from the same transaction (condition 2). Condition 1 simply states that all operations in the transactions must appear in the complete schedule. Since every transaction has either committed or aborted, a complete schedule will not contain any active transactions at the end of the schedule.

In general, it is difficult to encounter complete schedules in a transaction processing system, because new transactions are continually being submitted to the system. Hence, it is useful to define the concept of the **committed projection** $C(S)$ of a schedule S, which includes only the operations in S that belong to committed transactions—that is, transactions T_i whose commit operation c_i is in S.

19.4.2 Characterizing Schedules Based on Recoverability

For some schedules it is easy to recover from transaction failures, whereas for other schedules the recovery process can be quite involved. Hence, it is important to characterize the types of schedules for which recovery is possible, as well as those for which recovery is relatively simple. These characterizations do not actually provide the recovery algorithm but instead only attempt to theoretically characterize the different types of schedules.

---

9. Theoretically, it is not necessary to determine an order between pairs of *nonconflicting* operations.

10. In practice, most schedules have a total order of operations. If parallel processing is employed, it is theoretically possible to have schedules with partially-ordered non-conflicting operations.

First, we would like to ensure that, once a transaction T is committed, it should *never* be necessary to roll back T. The schedules that theoretically meet this criterion are called *recoverable schedules* and those that do not are called **nonrecoverable,** and hence should not be permitted. A schedule S is recoverable if no transaction T in S commits until all transactions T' that have written an item that T reads have committed. A transaction T **reads** from transaction T' in a schedule S if some item X is first written by T' and later read by T. In addition, T' should not have been aborted before T reads item X, and there should be no transactions that write X after T' writes it and before T reads it (unless those transactions, if any, have aborted before T reads X).

Recoverable schedules require a complex recovery process as we shall see, but if sufficient information is kept (in the log), a recovery algorithm can be devised. The (partial) schedules S_a and S_b from the preceding section are both recoverable, since they satisfy the above definition. Consider the schedule S_a' given below, which is the same as schedule S_a except that two commit operations have been added to S_a:

S_a': $r_1(X)$; $r_2(X)$; $w_1(X)$; $r_1(Y)$; $w_2(X)$; c_2; $w_1(Y)$; c_1;

S_a' is recoverable, even though it suffers from the lost update problem. However, consider the two (partial) schedules S_c and S_d that follow:

S_c: $r_1(X)$; $w_1(X)$; $r_2(X)$; $r_1(Y)$; $w_2(X)$; c_2; a_1;
S_d: $r_1(X)$; $w_1(X)$; $r_2(X)$; $r_1(Y)$; $w_2(X)$; $w_1(Y)$; c_1; c_2;
S_e: $r_1(X)$; $w_1(X)$; $r_2(X)$; $r_1(Y)$; $w_2(X)$; $w_1(Y)$; a_1; a_2;

S_c is not recoverable, because T_2 reads item X from T_1, and then T_2 commits before T_1 commits. If T_1 aborts after the c_2 operation in S_c, then the value of X that T_2 read is no longer valid and T_2 must be aborted *after* it had been committed, leading to a schedule that is not recoverable. For the schedule to be recoverable, the c_2 operation in S_c must be postponed until after T_1 commits, as shown in S_d; if T_1 aborts instead of committing, then T_2 should also abort as shown in S_e, because the value of X it read is no longer valid.

In a recoverable schedule, no committed transaction ever needs to be rolled back. However, it is possible for a phenomenon known as **cascading rollback (or cascading abort)** to occur, where an *uncommitted* transaction has to be rolled back because it read an item from a transaction that failed. This is illustrated in schedule S_e, where transaction T_2 has to be rolled back because it read item X from T_1, and T_1 then aborted.

Because cascading rollback can be quite time-consuming—since numerous transactions can be rolled back (see Chapter 21)—it is important to characterize the schedules where this phenomenon is guaranteed not to occur. A schedule is said to be **cascadeless,** or **avoid cascading rollback,** if every transaction in the schedule reads only items that were written by committed transactions. In this case, all items read will not be discarded, so no cascading rollback will occur. To satisfy this criterion, the $r_2(X)$ command in schedule S_e must be postponed until after T_1 has committed (or aborted), thus delaying T_2 but ensuring no cascading rollback if T_1 aborts.

Finally, there is a third, more restrictive type of schedule, called a **strict schedule,** in which transactions can neither read nor write an item X until the last transaction that wrote X has committed (or aborted). Strict schedules simplify the recovery process. In a strict schedule, the process of undoing a `write_item(X)` operation of an aborted transaction is simply to restore the **before image** (*old_value* or BFIM) of data item X. This simple procedure always works correctly for strict schedules, but it may not work for recoverable or cascadeless schedules. For example, consider schedule S_f:

$$S_f: w_1(X, 5); w_2(X, 8); a_1;$$

Suppose that the value of X was originally 9, which is the before image stored in the system log along with the $w_1(X, 5)$ operation. If T_1 aborts, as in S_f, the recovery procedure that restores the before image of an aborted write operation will restore the value of X to 9, even though it has already been changed to 8 by transaction T_2, thus leading to potentially incorrect results. Although schedule S_f is cascadeless, it is not a strict schedule, since it permits T_2 to write item X even though the transaction T_1 that last wrote X had not yet committed (or aborted). A strict schedule does not have this problem.

We have now characterized schedules according to the following terms: (1) recoverability, (2) avoidance of cascading rollback, and (3) strictness. We have thus seen that those properties of schedules are successively more stringent conditions. Thus condition (2) implies condition (1), and condition (3) implies both (2) and (1), but the reverse is not always true.

19.5 Serializability of Schedules

In the previous section, we characterized schedules based on their recoverability properties. We now characterize the types of schedules that are considered correct when concurrent transactions are executing. Suppose that two users—two airline reservation clerks—submit to the DBMS transactions T_1 and T_2 of Figure 19.2 at approximately the same time. If no interleaving of operations is permitted, there are only two possible outcomes:

1. Execute all the operations of transaction T_1 (in sequence) followed by all the operations of transaction T_2 (in sequence).
2. Execute all the operations of transaction T_2 (in sequence) followed by all the operations of transaction T_1 (in sequence).

These alternatives are shown in Figure 19.5(a) and (b), respectively. If interleaving of operations is allowed, there will be many possible orders in which the system can execute the individual operations of the transactions. Two possible schedules are shown in Figure 19.5(c). The concept of **serializability of schedules** is used to identify which schedules are correct when transaction executions have interleaving of their operations in the schedules. This section defines serializability and discusses how it may be used in practice.

19.5.1 Serial, Nonserial, and Conflict-Serializable Schedules

Schedules A and B in Figure 19.5(a) and (b) are called *serial* because the operations of each transaction are executed consecutively, without any interleaved operations from the other transaction. In a serial schedule, entire transactions are performed in serial order:

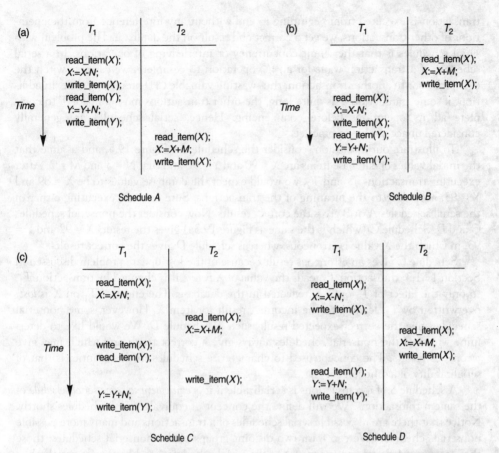

Figure 19.5 Examples of serial and nonserial schedules involving transactions T_1 and T_2. (a) Serial schedule A: T_1 followed by T_2. (b) Serial schedule B: T_2 followed by T_1. (c) Two nonserial schedules C and D with interleaving of operations.

T_1 and then T_2 in Figure 19.5(a), and T_2 and then T_1 in Figure 19.5(b). Schedules C and D in Figure 19.5(c) are called *nonserial* because each sequence interleaves operations from the two transactions.

Formally, a schedule S is **serial** if, for every transaction T participating in the schedule, all the operations of T are executed consecutively in the schedule; otherwise, the schedule is called **nonserial.** Hence, in a serial schedule, only one transaction at a time is active—the commit (or abort) of the active transaction initiates execution of the next transaction. No interleaving occurs in a serial schedule. One reasonable assumption we can make, if we consider the transactions to be *independent,* is that every serial schedule is considered correct. We can assume this because every transaction is assumed to be correct if executed on its own (according to the consistency preservation property of Section 19.3). Hence, it does not matter which transaction is executed first. As long as every transaction is executed from beginning to end without any interference from the operations of other transactions, we get a correct end result on the database. The problem with serial schedules is that they limit concurrency or interleaving of operations. In a serial schedule, if a transaction waits for an I/O operation to complete, we cannot switch the CPU processor to another transaction, thus wasting valuable CPU processing time. In addition, if some transaction T is quite long, the other transactions must wait for T to complete all its operations before commencing. Hence, serial schedules are generally considered unacceptable in practice.

To illustrate our discussion, consider the schedules in Figure 19.5, and assume that the initial values of database items are $X = 90$ and $Y = 90$ and that $N = 3$ and $M = 2$. After executing transactions T_1 and T_2, we would expect the database values to be $X = 89$ and $Y = 93$, according to the meaning of the transactions. Sure enough, executing either of the serial schedules A or B gives the correct results. Now consider the nonserial schedules C and D. Schedule C (which is the same as Figure 19.3a) gives the results $X = 92$ and $Y = 93$, in which the X value is erroneous, whereas schedule D gives the correct results.

Schedule C gives an erroneous result because of the lost update problem discussed in Section 19.1.3; transaction T_2 reads the value of X *before* it is changed by transaction T_1, so only the effect of T_2 on X is reflected in the database. The effect of T_1 on X is *lost*, overwritten by T_2, leading to the incorrect result for item X. However, some nonserial schedules give the correct expected result, such as schedule D. We would like to determine which of the nonserial schedules *always* give a correct result and which may give erroneous results. The concept used to characterize schedules in this manner is that of serializability of a schedule.

A schedule S of n transactions is **serializable** if it is *equivalent to some serial schedule* of the same n transactions. We will define the concept of equivalence of schedules shortly. Notice that there are $n!$ possible serial schedules of n transactions and many more possible nonserial schedules. We can form two disjoint groups of the nonserial schedules: those that are equivalent to one (or more) of the serial schedules, and hence are serializable; and those that are not equivalent to *any* serial schedule and hence are not serializable.

Saying that a nonserial schedule S is serializable is equivalent to saying that it is correct, because it is equivalent to a serial schedule, which is considered correct. The remaining question is: When are two schedules considered "equivalent"? There are several ways to define equivalence of schedules. The simplest, but least satisfactory, definition of schedule equivalence involves comparing the effects of the schedules on the database. Two schedules are, called **result equivalent** if they produce the same final state of the database. However, two different schedules may accidentally produce the same final state. For example, in Figure 19.6, schedules S_1 and S_2 will produce the same final

S_1	S_2
read_item(X);	read_item(X);
$X:=X+10$;	$X:=X*1.1$;
write_item(X);	write_item(X);

Figure 19.6   Two schedules that are result equivalent for the initial value of $X = 100$ but are not result equivalent in general.

database state if they execute on a database with an initial value of $X = 100$; but for other initial values of X, the schedules are *not* result equivalent. In addition, these two schedules execute different transactions, so they definitely should not be considered equivalent. Hence, result equivalence alone cannot be used to define equivalence of schedules. The safest and most general approach to defining schedule equivalence is not to make any assumption about the types of operations included in the transactions. For two schedules to be equivalent, the operations applied to each data item affected by the schedules should be applied to that item in both schedules *in the same order*. Two definitions of equivalence of schedules are generally used: *conflict equivalence* and *view equivalence*. We discuss conflict equivalence next, which is the more commonly used definition.

Two schedules are said to be **conflict equivalent** if the order of any two *conflicting operations* is the same in both schedules. Recall from Section 19.4.1 that two operations in a schedule are said to *conflict* if they belong to different transactions, access the same database item, and at least one of the two operations is a `write_item` operation. If two conflicting operations are applied in *different orders* in two schedules, the effect can be different on the database or on other transactions in the schedule, and hence the schedules are not conflict equivalent. For example, if a read and write operation occur in the order $r_1(X)$, $w_2(X)$ in schedule S_1, and in the reverse order $w_2(X)$, $r_1(X)$ in schedule S_2, the value read by $r_1(X)$ can be different in the two schedules. Similarly, if two write operations occur in the order $w_1(X)$, $w_2(X)$ in S_1, and in the reverse order $w_2(X)$, $w_1(X)$ in S_2, the next $r(X)$ operation in the two schedules will read potentially different values; or if these are the last operations writing item X in the schedules, the final value of item X in the database will be different.

Using the notion of conflict equivalence, we define a schedule S to be **conflict serializable**[11] if it is (conflict) equivalent to some serial schedule S'. In such a case, we can reorder the *nonconflicting* operations in S until we form the equivalent serial schedule S'. According to this definition, schedule D of Figure 19.5(c) is equivalent to the serial schedule A of Figure 19.5(a). In both schedules, the `read_item`(X) of T_2 reads the value of X written by T_1, while the other `read_item` operations read the database values from the initial database state. In addition, T_1 is the last transaction to write Y, and T_2 is the last transaction to write X in both schedules. Because A is a serial schedule and schedule D is equivalent to A, D is a *serializable schedule*. Notice that the operations $r_1(Y)$ and $w_1(Y)$ of schedule D do not conflict with the operations $r_2(X)$ and $w_2(X)$, since they access different data items. Hence, we can move $r_1(Y)$, $w_1(Y)$ before $r_2(X)$, $w_2(X)$, leading to the equivalent serial schedule T_1, T_2.

Schedule C of Figure 19.5(c) is not equivalent to either of the two possible serial schedules A and B, and hence is *not serializable*. Trying to reorder the operations of schedule C to find an equivalent serial schedule fails, because $r_2(X)$ and $w_1(X)$ conflict, which means that we cannot move $r_2(X)$ down to get the equivalent serial schedule T_1, T_2. Sim-

---

11. We will use *serializable* to mean conflict serializable. Another definition of serializable used in practice (see Section 19.6) is to have repeatable reads, no dirty reads, and no phantom records (see Section 20.7.1 for a discussion on phantoms).

ilarly, because $w_1(X)$ and $w_2(X)$ conflict, we cannot move $w_1(X)$ down to get the equivalent serial schedule T_2, T_1.

Another, more complex definition of equivalence—called *view equivalence*, which leads to the concept of *view serializability*—is discussed in Section 19.5.4.

19.5.2   Testing for Conflict Serializability of a Schedule

There is a simple algorithm for determining the conflict serializability of a schedule. Most concurrency control methods *do not* actually test for serializability. Rather protocols, or rules, are developed that guarantee that a schedule will be serializable. We discuss the algorithm for testing conflict serializability of schedules here to gain a better understanding of these concurrency control protocols, which are discussed in Chapter 20.

Algorithm 19.1 can be used to test a schedule for conflict serializability. The algorithm looks at only the `read_item` and `write_item` operations in a schedule to construct a **precedence graph** (or **serialization graph**), which is a **directed graph** $G = (N, E)$ that consists of a set of nodes $N = \{T_1, T_2, ..., T_n\}$ and a set of directed edges $E = \{e_1, e_2, ..., e_m\}$. There is one node in the graph for each transaction T_i in the schedule. Each edge e_i in the graph is of the form $(T_j \rightarrow T_k)$, $1 \leq j \leq n$, $1 \leq k \leq n$, where T_j is the **starting node** of e_i and T_k is the **ending node** of e_i. Such an edge is created if one of the operations in T_j appears in the schedule *before* some *conflicting operation* in T_k.

> **ALGORITHM 19.1** Testing conflict serializability of a schedule S.
>
> 1. For each transaction T_i participating in schedule S, create a node labeled T_i in the precedence graph.
> 2. For each case in S where T_j executes a `read_item(X)` after T_i executes a `write_item(X)`, create an edge $(T_i \rightarrow T_j)$ in the precedence graph.
> 3. For each case in S where T_j executes a `write_item(X)` after T_i executes a `read_item(X)`, create an edge $(T_i \rightarrow T_j)$ in the precedence graph.
> 4. For each case in S where T_j executes a `write_item(X)` after T_i executes a `write_item(X)`, create an edge $(T_i \rightarrow T_j)$ in the precedence graph.
> 5. The schedule S is serializable if and only if the precedence graph has no cycles.

The precedence graph is constructed as described in Algorithm 19.1. If there is a cycle in the precedence graph, schedule S is not (conflict) serializable; if there is no cycle, S is serializable. A **cycle** in a directed graph is a **sequence of edges** $C = ((T_j \rightarrow T_k), (T_k \rightarrow T_p), ..., (T_i \rightarrow T_j))$ with the property that the starting node of each edge—except the first edge—is the same as the ending node of the previous edge, and the starting node of the first edge is the same as the ending node of the last edge (the sequence starts and ends at the same node).

In the precedence graph, an edge from T_i to T_j means that transaction T_i must come before transaction T_j in any serial schedule that is equivalent to S, because two conflicting operations appear in the schedule in that order. If there is no cycle in the precedence graph, we can create an **equivalent serial schedule** S' that is equivalent to S, by ordering the transactions that participate in S as follows: Whenever an edge exists in the prece-

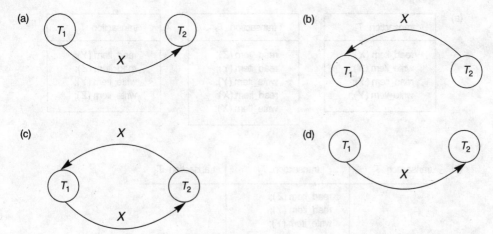

Figure 19.7 Constructing the precedence graphs for schedules A to D from Figure 19.5 to test for conflict serializability. (a) Precedence graph for serial schedule A. (b) Precedence graph for serial schedule B. (c) Precedence graph for schedule C (not serializable). (d) Precedence graph for schedule D (serializable, equivalent to schedule A).

dence graph from T_i to T_j, T_i must appear before T_j in the equivalent serial schedule S'.[12] Notice that the edges $(T_i \rightarrow T_j)$ in a precedence graph can optionally be labeled by the name(s) of the data item(s) that led to creating the edge. Figure 19.7 shows such labels on the edges.

In general, several serial schedules can be equivalent to S if the precedence graph for S has no cycle. However, if the precedence graph has a cycle, it is easy to show that we cannot create any equivalent serial schedule, so S is not serializable. The precedence graphs created for schedules A to D, respectively, of Figure 19.5 appear in Figure 19.7(a) to (d). The graph for schedule C has a cycle, so it is not serializable. The graph for schedule D has no cycle, so it is serializable, and the equivalent serial schedule is T_1 followed by T_2. The graphs for schedules A and B have no cycles, as expected, because the schedules are *serial* and hence serializable.

Another example, in which three transactions participate, is shown in Figure 19.8. Figure 19.8(a) shows the read_item and write_item operations in each transaction. Two schedules E and F for these transactions are shown in Figure 19.8(b) and (c), respectively, and the precedence graphs for schedules E and F are shown in parts (d) and (e). Schedule E is not serializable, because the corresponding precedence graph has cycles. Schedule F is serializable, and the serial schedule equivalent to F is shown in Figure 19.8(e). Although only one equivalent serial schedule exists for F, in general there may be *more than one equivalent serial schedule* for a serializable schedule. Figure 19.8(f) shows a precedence graph representing a schedule that has two equivalent serial schedules.

---

12. This process of ordering the nodes of an acyclic graph is known as topological sorting.

(a)

transaction T_1	transaction T_2	transaction T_3
read_item (X); write_item (X); read_item (Y); write_item (Y);	read_item (Z); read_item (Y); write_item (Y); read_item (X); write_item (X);	read_item (Y); read_item (Z); write_item (Y); write_item (Z);

(b)

transaction T_1	transaction T_2	transaction T_3
	read_item (Z); read_item (Y); write_item (Y);	
		read_item (Y); read_item (Z);
read_item (X); write_item (X);		write_item (Y); write_item (Z);
	read_item (X);	
read_item (Y); write_item (Y);		
	write_item (X);	

Time ↓

Schedule *E*

(c)

transaction T_1	transaction T_2	transaction T_3
		read_item (Y); read_item (Z);
read_item (X); write_item (X);		write_item (Y); write_item (Z);
	read_item (Z);	
read_item (Y); write_item (Y);		
	read_item (Y); write_item (Y); read_item (X); write_item (X);	

Time ↓

Schedule *F*

Figure 19.8   Another example of serializability testing. (a) The READ and WRITE operations of three transactions T_1, T_2, and T_3. (b) Schedule *E*. (c) Schedule *F*.

(d)

Equivalent serial schedules

None

Reason

cycle $X(T_1 \rightarrow T_2)$, $Y(T_2 \rightarrow T_1)$
cycle $X(T_1 \rightarrow T_2)$, $YZ(T_2 \rightarrow T_3)$, $Y(T_3 \rightarrow T_1)$

(e)

Equivalent serial schedules

$T_3 \longrightarrow T_1 \longrightarrow T_2$

(f)

Equivalent serial schedules

$T_3 \longrightarrow T_1 \longrightarrow T_2$
$T_3 \longrightarrow T_2 \longrightarrow T_1$

Figure 19.8 Another example of serializability testing. (d) Precedence graph for schedule E. (e) Precedence graph for schedule F. (f) Precedence graph with two equivalent serial schedules.

19.5.3 Uses of Serializability

As we discussed earlier, saying that a schedule S is (conflict) serializable—that is, S is (conflict) equivalent to a serial schedule—is tantamount to saying that S is correct. Being *serializable* is distinct from being *serial*, however. A serial schedule represents inefficient processing because no interleaving of operations from different transactions is permitted. This can lead to low CPU utilization while a transaction waits for disk I/O, or for another transaction to terminate, thus slowing down processing considerably. A serializable schedule gives the benefits of concurrent execution without giving up any correctness. In practice, it is quite difficult to test for the serializability of a schedule. The interleaving of operations from concurrent transactions—which are usually executed as processes by the operating system—is typically determined by the operating system scheduler, which allocates resources to all processes. Factors such as system load, time of transaction submission, and priorities of processes contribute to the ordering of operations in a schedule. Hence, it is difficult to determine how the operations of a schedule will be interleaved beforehand to ensure serializability.

If transactions are executed at will and then the resulting schedule is tested for serializability, we must cancel the effect of the schedule if it turns out not to be serializable. This is a serious problem that makes this approach impractical. Hence, the approach taken in most practical systems is to determine methods that ensure serializability, without having to test the schedules themselves. The approach taken in most commercial DBMSs is to design **protocols** (sets of rules) that—if followed by *every* individual transaction or if enforced by a DBMS concurrency control subsystem—will ensure serializability of *all schedules in which the transactions participate*.

Another problem appears here: When transactions are submitted continuously to the system, it is difficult to determine when a schedule begins and when it ends. Serializability theory can be adapted to deal with this problem by considering only the committed projection of a schedule S. Recall from Section 19.4.1 that the *committed projection* $C(S)$ of a schedule S includes only the operations in S that belong to committed transactions. We can theoretically define a schedule S to be serializable if its committed projection $C(S)$ is equivalent to some serial schedule, since only committed transactions are guaranteed by the DBMS.

In Chapter 20, we discuss a number of different concurrency control protocols that guarantee serializability. The most common technique, called *two-phase locking*, is based on locking data items to prevent concurrent transactions from interfering with one another, and enforcing an additional condition that guarantees serializability. This is used in the majority of commercial DBMSs. Other protocols have been proposed;[13] these include *timestamp ordering*, where each transaction is assigned a unique timestamp and the protocol ensures that any conflicting operations are executed in the order of the transaction timestamps; *multiversion protocols*, which are based on maintaining multiple versions of data items; and *optimistic* (also called *certification* or *validation*) *protocols*, which check for possible serializability violations after the transactions terminate but before they are permitted to commit.

19.5.4   View Equivalence and View Serializability

In Section 19.5.1, we defined the concepts of conflict equivalence of schedules and conflict serializability. Another less restrictive definition of equivalence of schedules is called *view equivalence*. This leads to another definition of serializability called *view serializability*.

---

13. These other protocols have not been used much in practice so far; most systems use some variation of the two-phase locking protocol.

Two schedules S and S' are said to be **view equivalent** if the following three conditions hold:

1. The same set of transactions participates in S and S', and S and S' include the same operations of those transactions.

2. For any operation $r_i(X)$ of T_i in S, if the value of X read by the operation has been written by an operation $w_j(X)$ of T_j (or if it is the original value of X before the schedule started), the same condition must hold for the value of X read by operation $r_i(X)$ of T_i in S'.

3. If the operation $w_k(Y)$ of T_k is the last operation to write item Y in S, then $w_k(Y)$ of T_k must also be the last operation to write item Y in S'.

The idea behind view equivalence is that, as long as each read operation of a transaction reads the result of the same write operation in both schedules, the write operations of each transaction must produce the same results. The read operations are hence said to *see the same view* in both schedules. Condition 3 ensures that the final write operation on each data item is the same in both schedules, so the database state should be the same at the end of both schedules. A schedule S is said to be **view serializable** if it is view equivalent to a serial schedule.

The definitions of conflict serializability and view serializability are similar if a condition known as the **constrained write assumption** holds on all transactions in the schedule. This condition states that any write operation $w_i(X)$ in T_i is preceded by a $r_i(X)$ in T_i *and* that the value written by $w_i(X)$ in T_i depends only on the value of X read by $r_i(X)$. This assumes that computation of the new value of X is a function $f(X)$ based on the old value of X read from the database. However, the definition of view serializability is less restrictive than that of conflict serializability under the **unconstrained write assumption,** where the value written by an operation $w_i(X)$ in T_i can be independent of its old value from the database. This is called a **blind write,** and it is illustrated by the following schedule S_g of three transactions $T_1: r_1(X), w_1(X); T_2: w_2(X);$ and $T_3: w_3(X)$:

$S_g: r_1(X); w_2(X); w_1(X); w_3(X); c_1; c_2; c_3;$

In S_g the operations $w_2(X)$ and $w_3(X)$ are blind writes, since T_2 and T_3 do not read the value of X. The schedule S_g is view serializable, since it is view equivalent to the serial schedule T_1, T_2, T_3. However, S_g is not conflict serializable, since it is not conflict equivalent to any serial schedule. It has been shown that any conflict-serializable schedule is also view serializable but not vice versa, as illustrated by the preceding example. There is an algorithm to test whether a schedule S is view serializable or not. However, the problem of testing for view serializability has been shown to be NP-complete, meaning that finding an efficient polynomial time algorithm for this problem is highly unlikely.

19.5.5 Other Types of Equivalence of Schedules

Serializability of schedules is sometimes considered to be too restrictive as a condition for ensuring the correctness of concurrent executions. Some applications can produce schedules that are correct by satisfying conditions less stringent than either conflict serializability or view serializability. An example is the type of transactions known as **debit-credit transactions**—for example, those that apply deposits and withdrawals to a data item whose value is the current balance of a bank account. The semantics of debit-credit operations is that they update the value of a data item X by either subtracting from or adding to the value of the data item. Because addition and subtraction operations are commutative—that is, they can be applied in any order—it is possible to produce correct schedules that are not serializable. For example, consider the following two transactions, each of which may be used to transfer an amount of money between two bank accounts:

T_1: $r_1(X)$; $X := X - 10$; $w_1(X)$; $r_1(Y)$; $Y := Y + 10$; $w_1(Y)$;

T_2: $r_2(Y)$; $Y := Y - 20$; $w_2(Y)$; $r_2(X)$; $X := X + 20$; $w_2(X)$;

Consider the following non-serializable schedule S_h for the two transactions:

S_h: $r_1(X)$; $w_1(X)$; $r_2(Y)$; $w_2(Y)$; $r_1(Y)$; $w_1(Y)$; $r_2(X)$; $w_2(X)$;

With the additional knowledge, or **semantics,** that the operations between each $r_i(I)$ and $w_i(I)$ are commutative, we know that the order of executing the sequences consisting of (read, update, write) is not important as long as each (read, update, write) sequence by a particular transaction T_i on a particular item I is not interrupted by conflicting operations. Hence, the schedule S_h is considered to be correct even though it is not serializable. Researchers have been working on extending concurrency control theory to deal with cases where serializability is considered to be too restrictive as a condition for correctness of schedules.

19.6 Transaction Support in SQL

The definition of an SQL-transaction is similar to our already defined concept of a transaction. That is, it is a logical unit of work and is guaranteed to be atomic. A single SQL statement is always considered to be atomic—either it completes execution without error or it fails and leaves the database unchanged.

With SQL, there is no explicit Begin_Transaction statement. Transaction initiation is done implicitly when particular SQL statements are encountered. However, every transaction must have an explicit end statement, which is either a COMMIT or a ROLLBACK. Every transaction has certain characteristics attributed to it. These characteristics are specified by a SET TRANSACTION statement in SQL2. The characteristics are the *access mode*, the *diagnostic area size*, and the *isolation level*.

The **access mode** can be specified as READ ONLY or READ WRITE. The default is READ WRITE, unless the isolation level of READ UNCOMMITTED is specified (see below), in which case READ ONLY is assumed. A mode of READ WRITE allows update, insert, delete and create commands to be executed. A mode of READ ONLY, as the name implies, is simply for data retrieval.

The **diagnostic area size** option, DIAGNOSTIC SIZE n, specifies an integer value n, indicating the number of conditions that can be held simultaneously in the diagnostic area. These conditions supply feedback information (errors or exceptions) to the user on the most recently executed SQL statement.

The **isolation level** option is specified using the statement ISOLATION LEVEL <isolation>, where the value for <isolation> can be READ UNCOMMITTED, READ COMMITTED, REPEATABLE READ, or SERIALIZABLE.[14] The default isolation level is SERIALIZABLE, although some systems use as READ COMMITTED their default. The use of the term SERIALIZABLE here is based on not allowing violations that cause dirty read, unrepeatable read, and phantoms,[15] and it is thus not identical to the way serializability was defined earlier in Section 19.5. If a transaction executes at a lower isolation level than SERIALIZABLE, then one or more of the following three violations may occur:

1. **Dirty read:** A transaction T_1 may read the update of a transaction T_2, which has not yet committed. If T_2 fails and is aborted, then T_1 would have read a value that does not exist and is incorrect.

2. **Nonrepeatable read:** A transaction T_1 may read a given value from a table. If another transaction T_2 later updates that value and T_1 reads that value again, T_1 will see a different value.

3. **Phantoms:** A transaction T_1 may read a set of rows from a table, perhaps based on some condition specified in the SQL WHERE-clause. Now suppose that a transaction T_2 inserts a new row that also satisfies the WHERE-clause condition used in T_1, into the table used by T_1. If T_1 is repeated, then T_1 will see a phantom, a row that previously did not exist.

Table 19.1 summarizes the possible violations for the different isolation levels. An entry of "yes" indicates that a violation is possible and an entry of "no" indicates that it is not possible.

A sample SQL transaction might look like the following:

```
EXEC SQL WHENEVER SQLERROR GOTO UNDO;
EXEC SQL SET TRANSACTION
    READ WRITE
    DIAGNOSTICS SIZE 5
```

Table 19.1 Possible Violations Based on Isolation Levels as Defined in SQL

Isolation level	Type of Violation		
	Dirty read	Nonrepeatable read	Phantom
READ UNCOMMITTTED	yes	yes	yes
READ COMMITTED	no	yes	yes
REPEATABLE READ	no	no	yes
SERIALIZABLE	no	no	no

14. These are similar to the *isolation levels* discussed briefly at the end of Section 19.3.

15. The dirty read and unrepeatable read problems were discussed in Section 19.1.3. Phantoms are discussed in Section 20.6.1.

```
          ISOLATION LEVEL SERIALIZABLE;
EXEC SQL INSERT INTO EMPLOYEE (FNAME, LNAME, SSN, DNO, SALARY)
          VALUES ('Robert', 'Smith', '991004321', 2, 35000);
EXEC SQL UPDATE EMPLOYEE
          SET SALARY = SALARY * 1.1 WHERE DNO = 2;
EXEC SQL COMMIT;
GOTO THE_END;
UNDO: EXEC SQL ROLLBACK;
THE_END: ...;
```

The above transaction consists of first inserting a new row in the EMPLOYEE table and then updating the salary of all employees who work in department 2. If an error occurs on any of the SQL statements, the entire transaction is rolled back. This implies that any updated salary (by this transaction) would be restored to its previous value and that the newly inserted row would be removed.

As we have seen, SQL provides a number of transaction-oriented features. The DBA or database programmers can take advantage of these options to try improving transaction performance by relaxing serializability if that is acceptable for their applications.

19.7 Summary

In this chapter we discussed DBMS concepts for transaction processing. We introduced the concept of a database transaction and the operations relevant to transaction processing. We compared single-user systems to multiuser systems and then presented examples of how uncontrolled execution of concurrent transactions in a multiuser system can lead to incorrect results and database values. We also discussed the various types of failures that may occur during transaction execution.

We then introduced the typical states that a transaction passes through during execution, and discussed several concepts that are used in recovery and concurrency control methods. The system log keeps track of database accesses, and the system uses this information to recover from failures. A transaction either succeeds and reaches its commit point or it fails and has to be rolled back. A committed transaction has its changes permanently recorded in the database. We presented an overview of the desirable properties of transactions—namely, atomicity, consistency preservation, isolation, and durability—which are often referred to as the ACID properties.

We then defined a schedule (or history) as an execution sequence of the operations of several transactions with possible interleaving. We characterized schedules in terms of their recoverability. Recoverable schedules ensure that, once a transaction commits, it never needs to be undone. Cascadeless schedules add the additional condition to ensure that no aborted transaction requires the cascading abort of other transactions. Strict schedules provide an even stronger condition that allows a simple recovery scheme consisting of restoring the old values of items that have been changed by an aborted transaction.

We then defined equivalence of schedules and saw that a serializable schedule is equivalent to some serial schedule. We defined the concepts of conflict equivalence and view equivalence, which led to definitions for conflict serializability and view serializability. A serializable schedule is considered correct. We then presented algorithms for testing the (conflict) serializability of a schedule. We discussed why testing for serializability is impractical in a real system, although it can be used to define and verify concurrency control protocols, and we briefly mentioned less restrictive definitions of schedule equivalence. Finally, we gave a brief overview of how transaction concepts are used in practice within SQL.

We will discuss concurrency control protocols in Chapter 20, and recovery protocols in Chapter 21.

Review Questions

19.1. What is meant by the concurrent execution of database transactions in a multiuser system? Discuss why concurrency control is needed, and give informal examples.

19.2. Discuss the different types of failures. What is meant by catastrophic failure?

19.3. Discuss the actions taken by the read_item and write_item operations on a database.

19.4. Draw a state diagram, and discuss the typical states that a transaction goes through during execution.

19.5. What is the system log used for? What are the typical kinds of records in a system log? What are transaction commit points, and why are they important?

19.6. Discuss the atomicity, durability, isolation, and consistency preservation properties of a database transaction.

19.7. What is a schedule (history)? Define the concepts of recoverable, cascadeless, and strict schedules, and compare them in terms of their recoverability.

19.8. Discuss the different measures of transaction equivalence. What is the difference between conflict equivalence and view equivalence?

19.9. What is a serial schedule? What is a serializable schedule? Why is a serial schedule considered correct? Why is a serializable schedule considered correct?

19.10. What is the difference between the constrained write and the unconstrained write assumptions? Which is more realistic?

19.11. Discuss how serializability is used to enforce concurrency control in a database system. Why is serializability sometimes considered too restrictive as a measure of correctness for schedules?

19.12. Describe the four levels of isolation in SQL2.

19.13. Define the violations caused by each of the following: dirty read, nonrepeatable read, and phantoms.

Exercises

19.14. Change transaction T_2 in Figure 19.2b to read

```
read_item(X);
X:= X+M;
if X > 90 then exit
else write_item(X);
```

Discuss the final result of the different schedules in Figure 19.3(a) and (b), where $M = 2$ and $N = 2$, with respect to the following questions. Does adding the above condition change the final outcome? Does the outcome obey the implied consistency rule (that the capacity of X is 90)?

19.15. Repeat Exercise 19.12, adding a check in T_1 so that Y does not exceed 90.

19.16. Add the operation commit at the end of each of the transactions T_1 and T_2 from Figure 19.2; then list all possible schedules for the modified transactions. Determine which of the schedules are recoverable, which are cascadeless, and which are strict.

19.17. List all possible schedules for transactions T_1 and T_2 from Figure 19.2, and determine which are conflict serializable (correct) and which are not.

19.18. How many *serial* schedules exist for the three transactions in Figure 19.8(a)? What are they? What is the total number of possible schedules?

19.19. Write a program to create all possible schedules for the three transactions in Figure 19.8(a), and to determine which of those schedules are conflict serializable and which are not. For each conflict serializable schedule, your program should print the schedule and list all equivalent serial schedules.

19.20. Why is an explicit transaction end statement needed in SQL2 but not an explicit begin statement?

19.21. Describe situations where each of the different isolation levels would be useful for transaction processing.

19.22. Which of the following schedules is (conflict) serializable? For each serializable schedule, determine the equivalent serial schedules.
   a. $r_1(X); r_3(X); w_1(X); r_2(X); w_3(X);$
   b. $r_1(X); r_3(X); w_3(X); w_1(X); r_2(X);$
   c. $r_3(X); r_2(X); w_3(X); r_1(X); w_1(X);$
   d. $r_3(X); r_2(X); r_1(X); w_3(X); w_1(X);$

19.23. Consider the three transactions T_1, T_2, and T_3, and the schedules S_1 and S_2 given below. Draw the serializability (precedence) graphs for S_1 and S_2, and state whether each schedule is serializable or not. If a schedule is serializable, write down the equivalent serial schedule(s).

T_1: $r_1(X); r_1(Z); w_1(X);$

T_2: $r_2(Z); r_2(Y); w_2(Z); w_2(Y);$

T_3: $r_3(X); r_3(Y); w_3(Y);$

S_1: $r_1(X); r_2(Z); r_1(Z); r_3(X); r_3(Y); w_1(X); w_3(Y); r_2(Y); w_2(Z); w_2(Y);$

S_2: $r_1(X); r_2(Z); r_3(X); r_1(Z); r_2(Y); r_3(Y); w_1(X); w_2(Z); w_3(Y); w_2(Y);$

19.24. Consider schedules S_3, S_4, and S_5 below. Determine whether each schedule is strict, cascadeless, recoverable, or nonrecoverable. (Determine the strictest recoverability condition that each schedule satisfies.)

S_3: $r_1(X); r_2(Z); r_1(Z); r_3(X); r_3(Y); w_1(X); c_1; w_3(Y); c_3; r_2(Y); w_2(Z); w_2(Y); c_2;$

S_4: $r_1(X); r_2(Z); r_1(Z); r_3(X); r_3(Y); w_1(X); w_3(Y); r_2(Y); w_2(Z); w_2(Y); c_1; c_2; c_3;$

S_5: $r_1(X); r_2(Z); r_3(X); r_1(Z); r_2(Y); r_3(Y); w_1(X); c_1; w_2(Z); w_3(Y); w_2(Y); c_3; c_2;$

Selected Bibliography

The concept of transaction is discussed in Gray (1981). Bernstein, Hadzilacos, and Goodman (1987) focus on concurrency control and recovery techniques in both centralized and distributed database systems; it is an excellent reference. Papadimitriou (1986) offers a more theoretical perspective. A large reference book of more than a thousand pages by Gray and Reuter (1993) offers a more practical perspective of transaction processing concepts and techniques. Elmagarmid (1992) and Bhargava (1989) offer collections of research papers on transaction processing. Transaction support in SQL2 is described in Date and Darwen (1993). The concepts of serializability are introduced in Gray et al. (1975). View serializability is defined in Yannakakis (1984). Recoverability of schedules is discussed in Hadzilacos (1983, 1988).

Selected Bibliography

The concept of transaction...

CHAPTER 20

Concurrency Control Techniques

In this chapter, we discuss a number of concurrency control techniques that are used to ensure the noninterference or isolation property of concurrently executing transactions. Most of these techniques ensure serializability of schedules (see Section 19.5), using **protocols** (that is, sets of rules) that guarantee serializability. One important set of protocols employs the technique of **locking** data items to prevent multiple transactions from accessing the items concurrently; a number of locking protocols are described in Section 20.1. Locking protocols are used in most commercial DBMSs. Another set of concurrency control protocols use **timestamps.** A timestamp is a unique identifier for each transaction, generated by the system. Concurrency control protocols that use timestamp ordering to ensure serializability are described in Section 20.2. In Section 20.3, we discuss **multiversion** concurrency control protocols that use multiple versions of a data item. In Section 20.4, we present a protocol based on the concept of **validation** or **certification** of a transaction after it executes its operations; these are sometimes called **optimistic protocols.**

Another factor that affects concurrency control is the **granularity** of the data items—that is, what portion of the database a data item represents. An item can be as small as a single attribute (field) value or as large as a disk block, or even a whole file or the entire database. We discuss granularity of items in Section 20.5. In Section 20.6, we discuss concurrency control issues that arise when indexes are used to process transactions. Finally, in Section 20.7 we discuss some additional concurrency control issues.

It is sufficient to cover Sections 20.1, 20.5, 20.6, and 20.7, and possibly 20.3.2, if the main emphasis is on introducing the concurrency control techniques that are used most often in practice. The other techniques are mainly of theoretical interest.

20.1   Locking Techniques for Concurrency Control

Some of the main techniques used to control concurrent execution of transactions are based on the concept of locking data items. A **lock** is a variable associated with a data item that describes the status of the item with respect to possible operations that can be applied to it. Generally, there is one lock for each data item in the database. Locks are used as a means of synchronizing the access by concurrent transactions to the database items. In Section 20.1.1 we discuss the nature and types of locks. Then, in Section 20.1.2, we present protocols that use locking to guarantee serializability of transaction schedules. Finally, in Section 20.1.3 we discuss two problems associated with the use of locks—namely, deadlock and starvation—and show how these problems are handled.

20.1.1   Types of Locks and System Lock Tables

Several types of locks are used in concurrency control. To introduce locking concepts gradually, we first discuss binary locks, which are simple but restrictive and so are not used in practice. We then discuss shared/exclusive locks, which provide more general locking capabilities and are used in practical database locking schemes. In Section 20.3.2, we describe a certify lock and show how it can be used to improve performance of locking protocols.

Binary Locks.   A **binary lock** can have two **states** or **values:** locked and unlocked (or 1 and 0, for simplicity). A distinct lock is associated with each database item X. If the value of the lock on X is 1, item X *cannot be accessed* by a database operation that requests the item. If the value of the lock on X is 0, the item can be accessed when requested. We refer to the current value (or state) of the lock associated with item X as LOCK(X).

Two operations, lock_item and unlock_item, are used with binary locking. A transaction requests access to an item X by first issuing a **lock_item(X)** operation. If LOCK(X) = 1, the transaction is forced to wait. If LOCK(X) = 0, it is set to 1 (the transaction **locks** the item) and the transaction is allowed to access item X. When the transaction is through using the item, it issues an **unlock_item(X)** operation, which sets LOCK(X) to 0 (**unlocks** the item) so that X may be accessed by other transactions. Hence, a binary lock enforces **mutual exclusion** on the data item. A description of the lock_item(X) and unlock_item(X) operations is shown in Figure 20.1.

Notice that the lock_item and unlock_item operations must be implemented as indivisible units (known as **critical sections** in operating systems); that is, no interleaving should be allowed once a lock or unlock operation is started until the operation terminates or the transaction waits. In Figure 20.1, the wait command within the lock_item(X) operation is usually implemented by putting the transaction on a waiting queue for item X until X is unlocked and the transaction can be granted access to it. Other lock_item (X):

B: if LOCK (X)=0   (* item is unlocked *)
   then LOCK (X)←1   (* lock the item *)
   else begin
     wait (until lock (X)=0 and
        the lock manager wakes up the transaction);
     go to B
     end;

unlock_item (X):

   LOCK (X)←0; (* unlock the item *)
   if any transactions are waiting
     then wakeup one of the waiting transactions;

Figure 20.1   Lock and unlock operations for binary locks.

transactions that also want to access X are placed on the same queue. Hence, the wait command is considered to be outside the lock_item operation.

Notice that it is quite simple to implement a binary lock; all that is needed is a binary-valued variable, LOCK, associated with each data item X in the database. In its simplest form, each lock can be a record with three fields: <data item name, LOCK, locking transaction> plus a queue for transactions that are waiting to access the item. The system needs to maintain only these records for the items that are currently locked in a **lock table,** which could be organized as a hash file. Items not in the lock table are considered to be unlocked. The DBMS has a **lock manager subsystem** to keep track of and control access to locks.

If the simple binary locking scheme described here is used, every transaction must obey the following rules:

1. A transaction T must issue the operation lock_item(X) before any read_item(X) or write_item(X) operations are performed in T.

2. A transaction T must issue the operation unlock_item(X) after all read_item(X) and write_item(X) operations are completed in T.

3. A transaction T will not issue a lock_item(X) operation if it already holds the lock on item X.[1]

4. A transaction T will not issue an unlock_item(X) operation unless it already holds the lock on item X.

These rules can be enforced by the lock manager module of the DBMS. Between the lock_item(X) and unlock_item(X) operations in transaction T, T is said to **hold the lock** on item X. At most one transaction can hold the lock on a particular item. Thus no two transactions can access the same item concurrently.

---

1. This rule may be removed if we modify the lock_item(X) operation in Figure 18.1 so that if the item is currently locked *by the requesting transaction*, the lock is granted.

Shared/Exclusive (or Read/Write) Locks. The preceding binary locking scheme is too restrictive for database items, because at most one transaction can hold a lock on a given item. We should allow several transactions to access the same item X if they all access X for *reading purposes only*. However, if a transaction is to write an item X, it must have exclusive access to X. For this purpose, a different type of lock called a **multiple-mode lock** is used. In this scheme—called **shared/exclusive** or **read/write locks**—there are three locking operations: `read_lock(X)`, `write_lock(X)`, and `unlock(X)`. A lock associated with an item X, LOCK(X), now has three possible states: "read-locked," "write-locked," or "unlocked." A **read-locked item** is also called **share-locked,** because other transactions are allowed to read the item, whereas a **write-locked item** is called **exclusive-locked,** because a single transaction exclusively holds the lock on the item.

One method for implementing the preceding three operations on a read/write lock is to keep track of the number of transactions that hold a shared (read) lock on an item in the lock table. Each record in the lock table will have four fields: <data item name, LOCK, no_of_reads, locking_transaction(s)>. Again, to save space, the system need maintain lock records only for locked items in the lock table. The value (state) of LOCK is either read-locked or write-locked, suitably coded (if we assume no records are kept in the lock table for unlocked items). If LOCK(X)=write-locked, the value of locking_transaction(s) is a single transaction that holds the exclusive (write) lock on X. If LOCK(X)=read-locked, the value of locking transaction(s) is a list of one or more transactions that hold the shared (read) lock on X. The three operations `read_lock(X)`, `write_lock(X)`, and `unlock(X)` are described in Figure 20.2.[2] As before, each of the three operations should be considered indivisible; no interleaving should be allowed once one of the operations is started until either the operation terminates by granting the lock or the transaction is placed on a waiting queue for the item.

When we use the shared/exclusive locking scheme, the system must enforce the following rules:

1. A transaction T must issue the operation `read_lock(X)` or `write_lock(X)` before any `read_item(X)` operation is performed in T.

2. A transaction T must issue the operation `write_lock(X)` before any `write_item(X)` operation is performed in T.

3. A transaction T must issue the operation `unlock(X)` after all `read_item(X)` and `write_item(X)` operations are completed in T.[3]

4. A transaction T will not issue a `read_lock(X)` operation if it already holds a read (shared) lock or a write (exclusive) lock on item X. This rule may be relaxed, as we discuss shortly.

5. A transaction T will not issue a `write_lock(X)` operation if it already holds a read (shared) lock or write (exclusive) lock on item X. This rule may be relaxed, as we discuss shortly.

---

2. These algorithms do not allow *upgrading* or *downgrading* of locks, as described later in this section. The reader can extend the algorithms to allow these additional operations.

3. This rule may be relaxed to allow a transaction to unlock an item, then lock it again later.

read_lock (X):
   B: if LOCK (X)="unlocked"
      then begin LOCK (X)← "read-locked";
                     no_of_reads(X)← 1
         end
      else if LOCK(X)="read-locked"
            then no_of_reads(X)← no_of _reads(X) + 1
            else begin wait (until LOCK (X)="unlocked" and
                        the lock manager wakes up the transaction);
                  go to **B**
                  end;

write_lock (X):
   B: if LOCK (X)="unlocked"
      then LOCK (X)← "write-locked"
      else begin
            wait (until LOCK(X)="unlocked" and
               the lock manager wakes up the transaction);
            go to **B**
            end;

unlock (X):
   if LOCK (X)="write-locked"
      then begin LOCK (X)← "unlocked;"
            wakeup one of the waiting transactions, if any
            end
      else if LOCK(X)="read-locked"
            then begin
                  no_of_reads(X)← no_of_reads(X) – 1;
                  if no_of_reads(X)=0
                     then begin LOCK (X)="unlocked";
                           wakeup one of the waiting transactions, if any
                           end
                  end;

Figure 20.2   Locking and unlocking operations for two-mode (read-write or shared-exclusive) locks.

6. A transaction T will not issue an unlock(X) operation unless it already holds a read (shared) lock or a write (exclusive) lock on item X.

Conversion of Locks.   Sometimes it is desirable to relax conditions 4 and 5 in the preceding list in order to allow **lock conversion**; that is, a transaction that already holds a lock on item X is allowed under certain conditions to **convert** the lock from one locked state to another. For example, it is possible for a transaction T to issue a read_lock(X) and then later on to **upgrade** the lock by issuing a write_lock(X) operation. If T is the only transaction holding a read lock on X at the time it issues the write_lock(X) operation, the lock can be upgraded; otherwise, the transaction must wait. It is also possible for a transaction T to issue a write_lock(X) and then later on to **downgrade** the lock by issuing a read_lock(X) operation. When upgrading and downgrading of locks is used, the lock table must include transaction identifiers in the record structure for each lock (in the locking_transaction(s) field) to store the information on which transactions hold locks on the item. The descriptions of the read_lock(X) and write_lock(X) operations in Figure 20.2 must be changed appropriately. We leave this as an exercise for the reader.

Using binary locks or read/write locks in transactions, as described earlier, *does not guarantee serializability* of schedules on its own. Figure 20.3 shows an example where the preceding locking rules are followed but a nonserializable schedule may result. This is because in Figure 20.3(a) the items Y in T_1 and X in T_2 were *unlocked too early*. This

(a)

T_1	T_2
read_lock(Y);	read_lock(X);
read_item(Y);	read_item(X);
unlock(Y);	unlock(X);
write_lock(X);	write_lock(Y);
read_item(X);	read_item(Y);
X:=X+Y;	Y:=X+Y;
write_item(X);	write_item(Y);
unlock(X);	unlock(Y);

(b) Initial values: X=20, Y=30
Result of serial schedule T_1 followed by T_2 :
  X=50, Y=80
Result of serial schedule T_2 followed by T_1 :
  X=70, Y=50

(c)

T_1	T_2
read_lock(Y);	
read_item(Y);	
unlock(Y);	
	read_lock(X);
	read_item(X);
	unlock(X);
	write_lock(Y);
	read_item(Y);
	Y:=X+Y;
	write_item(Y);
	unlock(Y);
write_lock(X);	
read_item(X);	
X:=X+Y;	
write_item(X);	
unlock(X);	

Time

Result of schedule S:
X=50, Y=50
(nonserializable)

Figure 20.3 Transactions that do not obey two-phase locking. (a) Two transactions T_1 and T_2. (b) Results of possible serial schedules of T_1 and T_2. (c) A nonserializable schedule S that uses locks.

allows a schedule such as the one shown in Figure 20.3(c) to occur, which is not a serializable schedule and hence gives incorrect results. To guarantee serializability, we must follow *an additional protocol* concerning the positioning of locking and unlocking operations in every transaction. The best known protocol, two-phase locking, is described in the next section.

20.1.2   Guaranteeing Serializability by Two-Phase Locking

A transaction is said to follow the **two-phase locking protocol** if *all* locking operations (read_lock, write_lock) precede the *first* unlock operation in the transaction.[4] Such a transaction can be divided into two phases: an **expanding** or **growing (first) phase,** during which new locks on items can be acquired but none can be released; and a **shrinking (second) phase,** during which existing locks can be released but no new locks can be acquired. If lock conversion is allowed, then upgrading of locks (from read-locked to write-locked) must be done during the expanding phase, and downgrading of locks (from write-locked to read-locked) must be done in the shrinking phase. Hence, a read_lock(X) operation that downgrades an already held write lock on X can appear only in the shrinking phase.

Transactions T_1 and T_2 of Figure 20.3(a) do not follow the two-phase locking protocol. This is because the write_lock(X) operation follows the unlock(Y) operation in T_1, and similarly the write_lock(Y) operation follows the unlock(X) operation in T_2. If we enforce two-phase locking, the transactions can be rewritten as T_1' and T_2', as shown in Figure 20.4. Now, the schedule shown in Figure 20.3(c) is not permitted for T_1' and T_2' (with their modified order of locking and unlocking operations) under the rules of locking described in Section 20.1.1. This is because T_1' will issue its write_lock(X) *before* it

T_1'	T_2'
read_lock (Y);	read_lock (X);
read_item (Y);	read_item (X);
write_lock (X);	write_lock (Y);
unlock (Y);	unlock (X);
read_item (X);	read_item (Y);
X:=X+Y;	Y:=X+Y;
write_item (X);	write_item (Y);
unlock (X);	unlock (Y);

Figure 20.4   Transactions T_1' and T_2', which are the same as T_1 and T_2 of Figure 20.3 but which follow the two-phase locking protocol. Note that they can produce a deadlock.

---

4. This is unrelated to the two-phase commit protocol for recovery in distributed databases (see Chapter 24).

unlocks item Y; consequently, when T_2' issues its read_lock(X), it is forced to wait until T_1' releases the lock by issuing an unlock (X) in the schedule.

It can be proved that, if *every* transaction in a schedule follows the two-phase locking protocol, the schedule is *guaranteed to be serializable*, obviating the need to test for serializability of schedules any more. The locking mechanism, by enforcing two-phase locking rules, also enforces serializability.

Two-phase locking may limit the amount of concurrency that can occur in a schedule. This is because a transaction T may not be able to release an item X after it is through using it if T must lock an additional item Y later on; or conversely, T must lock the additional item Y before it needs it so that it can release X. Hence, X must remain locked by T until all items that the transaction needs to read or write have been locked; only then can X be released by T. Meanwhile, another transaction seeking to access X may be forced to wait, even though T is done with X; conversely, if Y is locked earlier than it is needed, another transaction seeking to access Y is forced to wait even though T is not using Y yet. This is the price for guaranteeing serializability of all schedules without having to check the schedules themselves.

Basic, Conservative, Strict, and Rigorous Two-Phase Locking.   There are a number of variations of two-phase locking (2PL). The technique just described is known as **basic 2PL.** A variation known as **conservative 2PL** (or **static 2PL**) requires a transaction to lock all the items it accesses *before the transaction begins execution*, by **predeclaring** its *read-set* and *write-set*. Recall from Section 19.1.2 that the **read-set** of a transaction is the set of all items that the transaction reads, and the **write-set** is the set of all items that it writes. If any of the predeclared items needed cannot be locked, the transaction does not lock any item; instead, it waits until all the items are available for locking. Conservative 2PL is a deadlock-free protocol, as we shall see in Section 20.1.3 when we discuss the deadlock problem. However, it is difficult to use in practice because of the need to predeclare the read-set and write-set, which is not possible in most situations.

In practice, the most popular variation of 2PL is **strict 2PL,** which guarantees strict schedules (see Section 19.4). In this variation, a transaction T does not release any of its exclusive (write) locks until after it commits or aborts. Hence, no other transaction can read or write an item that is written by T unless T has committed, leading to a strict schedule for recoverability. Strict 2PL is not deadlock-free. A more restrictive variation of strict 2PL is **rigorous 2PL,** which also guarantees strict schedules. In this variation, a transaction T does not release any of its locks (exclusive or shared) until after it commits or aborts, and so it is easier to implement than strict 2PL. Notice the difference between conservative and rigorous 2PL; the former must lock all its items *before it starts* so once the transaction starts it is in its shrinking phase, whereas the latter does not unlock any of its items until *after it terminates* (by committing or aborting) so the transaction is in its expanding phase until it ends.

In many cases, the **concurrency control subsystem** itself is responsible for generating the read_lock and write_lock requests. For example, suppose the system is to enforce the strict 2PL protocol. Then, whenever transaction T issues a read_item(X), the system calls the read_lock(X) operation on behalf of T. If the state of LOCK(X) is write_locked by some other transaction T', the system places T on the waiting queue for item X; otherwise, it grants the read_lock(X) request and permits the read_item(X) operation of T to execute. On the other hand, if transaction T issues a write_item(X), the system calls the write_lock(X) operation on behalf of T. If the state of LOCK(X) is write_locked or read_locked by some other transaction T', the system places T on the waiting queue for item X; if the state of LOCK(X) is read_locked *and* T itself is the only transaction holding the read lock on X, the system upgrades the lock to write locked and permits the write_item(X) operation by T; finally, if the state of LOCK(X) is unlocked, the system grants the write_lock(X) request and permits the write_item(X) operation to execute. After each action, the system must update its lock table appropriately.

Although the two-phase locking protocol guarantees serializability (that is, every schedule that is permitted is serializable), it does not permit *all possible* serializable schedules (that is, some serializable schedules will be prohibited by the protocol). In addition, the use of locks can cause two additional problems: deadlock and starvation. We discuss these problems and their solutions in the next section.

20.1.3 Dealing with Deadlock and Starvation

Deadlock occurs when *each* transaction T in a set of *two or more transactions* is waiting for some item that is locked by some other transaction T' in the set. Hence, each transaction in the set is on a waiting queue, waiting for one of the other transactions in the set to release the lock on an item. A simple example is shown in Figure 20.5(a), where the two transactions T_1' and T_2' are deadlocked in a partial schedule; T_1' is on the waiting queue for X, which is locked by T_2', while T_2' is on the waiting queue for Y, which is locked by T_1'. Meanwhile, neither T_1' nor T_2' nor any other transaction can access items X and Y.

Deadlock Prevention Protocols. One way to prevent deadlock is to use a **deadlock prevention protocol.**[5] One deadlock prevention protocol, which is used in conservative two-phase locking, requires that every transaction *lock all the items it needs in advance* (which is generally not a practical assumption)—if any of the items cannot be obtained, none of the items are locked. Rather, the transaction waits and then tries again to lock all the

Figure 20.5 Illustrating the deadlock problem. (a) A partial schedule of T_1' and T_2' that is in a state of deadlock. (b) A wait-for graph for the partial schedule in (a).

---

5. These protocols are not generally used in practice, either because of unrealistic assumptions or because of their possible overhead. Deadlock detection and timeouts (see below) are more practical.

items it needs. This solution obviously further limits concurrency. A second protocol, which also limits concurrency, involves *ordering all the items* in the database and making sure that a transaction that needs several items will lock them according to that order. This requires that the programmer (or the system) be aware of the chosen order of the items, which is also not practical in the database context.

A number of other deadlock prevention schemes have been proposed that make a decision about what to do with a transaction involved in a possible deadlock situation: Should it be blocked and made to wait or should it be aborted, or should the transaction preempt and abort another transaction? These techniques use the concept of **transaction timestamp** TS(T), which is a unique identifier assigned to each transaction. The timestamps are typically based on the order in which transactions are started; hence, if transaction T_1 starts before transaction T_2, then $TS(T_1) < TS(T_2)$. Notice that the *older* transaction has the *smaller* timestamp value. Two schemes that prevent deadlock are called wait-die and wound-wait. Suppose that transaction T_i tries to lock an item X but is not able to because X is locked by some other transaction T_j with a conflicting lock. The rules followed by these schemes are as follows:

- **Wait-die:** If $TS(T_i) < TS(T_j)$, then (T_i older than T_j) T_i is allowed to wait; otherwise (T_i younger than T_j) abort T_i (T_i *dies*) and restart it later *with the same timestamp*.

- **Wound-wait:** If $TS(T_i) < TS(T_j)$, then (T_i older than T_j) abort T_j (T_i *wounds* T_j) and restart it later *with the same timestamp*; otherwise (T_i younger than T_j) T_i is allowed to wait.

In wait-die, an older transaction is allowed to wait on a younger transaction, whereas a younger transaction requesting an item held by an older transaction is aborted and restarted. The wound-wait approach does the opposite: A younger transaction is allowed to wait on an older one, whereas an older transaction requesting an item held by a younger transaction *preempts* the younger transaction by aborting it. Both schemes end up aborting the *younger* of the two transactions that *may be involved* in a deadlock. It can be shown that these two techniques are deadlock-free, since in wait-die, transactions only wait on younger transactions so no cycle is created. Similarly, in wound-wait, transactions only wait on older transactions so no cycle is created. However, both techniques may cause some transactions to be aborted and restarted needlessly, even though those transactions may *never actually cause a deadlock*.

Another group of protocols that prevent deadlock do not require timestamps. These include the no waiting (NW) and cautious waiting (CW) algorithms. In the **no waiting algorithm,** if a transaction is unable to obtain a lock, it is immediately aborted and then restarted after a certain time delay without checking whether a deadlock will actually occur or not. Because this scheme can cause transactions to abort and restart needlessly, the **cautious waiting** algorithm was proposed to try to reduce the number of needless aborts/restarts. Suppose that transaction T_i tries to lock an item X but is not able to do so because X is locked by some other transaction T_j with a conflicting lock. The cautious waiting rules are as follows:

- **Cautious waiting:** If T_j is not blocked (not waiting for some other locked item), then T_i is blocked and allowed to wait; otherwise abort T_i.

It can be shown that cautious waiting is deadlock-free, by considering the time $b(T)$ at which each blocked transaction T was blocked. If the two transactions T_i and T_j above both become blocked, and T_i is waiting on T_j, then $b(T_i) < b(T_j)$, since T_i can only wait on T_j at a time when T_j is not blocked. Hence, the blocking times form a total ordering on all blocked transactions, so no cycle that causes deadlock can occur.

Deadlock Detection and Timeouts. A second—more practical—approach to dealing with deadlock is **deadlock detection,** where the system checks if a state of deadlock actually exists. This solution is attractive if we know there will be little interference among the transactions—that is, if different transactions will rarely access the same items at the same time. This can happen if the transactions are short and each transaction locks only a few items, or if the transaction load is light. On the other hand, if transactions are long and each transaction uses many items, or if the transaction load is quite heavy, it may be advantageous to use a deadlock prevention scheme.

A simple way to detect a state of deadlock is for the system to construct and maintain a **wait-for graph.** One node is created in the wait-for graph for each transaction that is currently executing. Whenever a transaction T_i is waiting to lock an item X that is currently locked by a transaction T_j, a directed edge $(T_i \rightarrow T_j)$ is created in the wait-for graph. When T_j releases the lock(s) on the items that T_i was waiting for, the directed edge is dropped from the wait-for graph. We have a state of deadlock if and only if the wait-for graph has a cycle. One problem with this approach is the matter of determining *when* the system should check for a deadlock. Criteria such as the number of currently executing transactions or the period of time several transactions have been waiting to lock items may be used. Figure 20.5(b) shows the wait-for graph for the (partial) schedule shown in Figure 20.5(a). If the system is in a state of deadlock, some of the transactions causing the deadlock must be aborted. Choosing which transactions to abort is known as **victim selection.** The algorithm for victim selection should generally avoid selecting transactions that have been running for a long time and that have performed many updates, and it should try instead to select transactions that have not made many changes.

Another simple scheme to deal with deadlock is the use of **timeouts.** This method is practical because of its low overhead and simplicity. In this method, if a transaction waits for a period longer than a system-defined timeout period, the system assumes that the transaction may be deadlocked and aborts it—regardless of whether a deadlock actually exists or not.

Starvation. Another problem that may occur when we use locking is **starvation,** which occurs when a transaction cannot proceed for an indefinite period of time while other transactions in the system continue normally. This may occur if the waiting scheme for locked items is unfair, giving priority to some transactions over others. One solution for starvation is to have a fair waiting scheme, such as using a **first-come-first-serve** queue; transactions are enabled to lock an item in the order in which they originally requested the lock. Another scheme allows some transactions to have priority over others but increases the priority of a transaction the longer it waits, until it eventually gets the highest priority and proceeds. Starvation can also occur because of victim selection if the algorithm selects the same transaction as victim repeatedly, thus causing it to abort and never finish execution. The algorithm can use higher priorities for transactions that have been aborted multiple times to avoid this problem. The wait-die and wound-wait schemes discussed above avoid starvation.

20.2   Concurrency Control Based on Timestamp Ordering

The use of locks, combined with the 2PL protocol, guarantees serializability of schedules. The serializable schedules produced by 2PL have their equivalent serial schedules based on the order in which executing transactions lock the items they acquire. If a transaction needs an item that is already locked, it may be forced to wait until the item is released. A different approach that guarantees serializability involves using transaction timestamps to order transaction execution for an equivalent serial schedule. In Section 20.2.1 we discuss timestamps and in Section 20.2.2 we discuss how serializability is enforced by ordering transactions based on their timestamps.

20.2.1   Timestamps

Recall that a **timestamp** is a unique identifier created by the DBMS to identify a transaction. Typically, timestamp values are assigned in the order in which the transactions are submitted to the system, so a timestamp can be thought of as the *transaction start time*. We will refer to the timestamp of transaction T as **TS(T)**. Concurrency control techniques based on timestamp ordering do not use locks; hence, *deadlocks cannot occur*.

Timestamps can be generated in several ways. One possibility is to use a counter that is incremented each time its value is assigned to a transaction. The transaction timestamps are numbered 1, 2, 3, . . . in this scheme. A computer counter has a finite maximum value, so the system must periodically reset the counter to zero when no transactions are executing for some short period of time. Another way to implement timestamps is to use the current date/time value of the system clock and ensure that no two timestamp values are generated during the same tick of the clock.

20.2.2   The Timestamp Ordering Algorithm

The idea for this scheme is to order the transactions based on their timestamps. A schedule in which the transactions participate is then serializable, and the equivalent serial schedule has the transactions in order of their timestamp values. This is called **timestamp ordering (TO)**. Notice how this differs from 2PL, where a schedule is serializable by being equivalent to *some* serial schedule allowed by the locking protocols. In timestamp ordering, however, the schedule is equivalent to the *particular serial order* corresponding to the order of the transaction timestamps. The algorithm must ensure that, for each item accessed by *conflicting operations* in the schedule, the order in which the item is accessed does not violate the serializability order. To do this, the algorithm associates with each database item X two timestamp (**TS**) values:

1. **Read_TS(X):** The **read timestamp** of item X; this is the largest timestamp among all the timestamps of transactions that have successfully read item X—that is, read_TS(X) = TS(T), where T is the *youngest* transaction that has read X successfully.

2. **Write_TS(X):** The **write timestamp** of item X; this is the largest of all the timestamps of transactions that have successfully written item X—that is, write_TS(X) = TS(T), where T is the *youngest* transaction that has written X successfully.

Basic Timestamp Ordering. Whenever some transaction T tries to issue a `read_item(X)` or a `write_item(X)` operation, the **basic TO** algorithm compares the timestamp of T with read_TS(X) and write_TS(X) to ensure that the timestamp order of transaction execution is not violated. If this order is violated, then transaction T is aborted and resubmitted to the system as a new transaction with a *new timestamp*. If T is aborted and rolled back, any transaction T_1 that may have used a value written by T must also be rolled back. Similarly, any transaction T_2 that may have used a value written by T_1 must also be rolled back, and so on. This effect is known as **cascading rollback** and is one of the problems associated with basic TO, since the schedules produced are not recoverable. An *additional protocol* must be enforced to ensure that the schedules are recoverable, cascadeless, or strict. We first describe the basic TO algorithm here. The concurrency control algorithm must check whether conflicting operations violate the timestamp ordering in the following two cases:

1. Transaction T issues a `write_item(X)` operation:
   a. If read_TS(X) > TS(T) or if write_TS(X) > TS(T), then abort and roll back T and reject the operation. This should be done because some younger transaction with a timestamp greater than TS(T)—and hence *after* T in the timestamp ordering—has already read or written the value of item X before T had a chance to write X, thus violating the timestamp ordering.
   b. If the condition in part (a) does not occur, then execute the `write_item(X)` operation of T and set write_TS(X) to TS(T).

2. Transaction T issues a `read_item(X)` operation:
   a. If write_TS(X) > TS(T), then abort and roll back T and reject the operation. This should be done because some younger transaction with timestamp greater than TS(T)—and hence *after* T in the timestamp ordering—has already written the value of item X before T had a chance to read X.
   b. If write_TS(X) <= TS(T), then execute the read_item(X) operation of T and set read_TS(X) to the *larger* of TS(T) and the current read_TS(X).

Hence, whenever the basic TO algorithm detects two *conflicting operations* that occur in the incorrect order, it rejects the later of the two operations by aborting the transaction that issued it. The schedules produced by basic TO are hence guaranteed to be conflict serializable, like the 2PL protocol. However, some schedules are possible under each protocol that are not allowed under the other. Hence, neither protocol allows *all possible* serializable schedules. As mentioned earlier, deadlock does not occur with timestamp ordering. However, cyclic restart (and hence starvation) may occur if a transaction is continually aborted and restarted.

Strict Timestamp Ordering.   A variation of basic TO called **strict** TO ensures that the schedules are both **strict** (for easy recoverability) and (conflict) serializable. In this variation, a transaction T that issues a read_item(X) or write_item(X) such that $TS(T) >$ write_TS(X) has its read or write operation *delayed* until the transaction T' that *wrote* the value of X (hence $TS(T') =$ write_TS(X)) has committed or aborted. To implement this algorithm, it is necessary to simulate the locking of an item X that has been written by transaction T' until T' is either committed or aborted. This algorithm does not cause deadlock, since T waits for T' only if $TS(T) > TS(T')$.

Thomas's Write Rule.   A modification of the basic TO algorithm, known as **Thomas's write rule,** does not enforce conflict serializability; but it rejects fewer write operations, by modifying the checks for the write_item(X) operation as follows:

1. If read_TS(X) $> TS(T)$, then abort and roll back T and reject the operation.
2. If write_TS(X) $> TS(T)$, then do not execute the write operation but continue processing. This is because some transaction with timestamp greater than $TS(T)$—and hence after T in the timestamp ordering—has already written the value of X. Hence, we must ignore the write_item(X) operation of T because it is already outdated and obsolete. Notice that any conflict arising from this situation would be detected by case (1).
3. If neither the condition in part (1) nor the condition in part (2) occurs, then execute the write_item(X) operation of T and set write_TS(X) to TS(T).

20.3 Multiversion Concurrency Control Techniques

Other protocols for concurrency control keep the old values of a data item when the item is updated. These are known as **multiversion concurrency control,** because several versions (values) of an item are maintained. When a transaction requires access to an item, an *appropriate* version is chosen to maintain the serializability of the currently executing schedule, if possible. The idea is that some read operations that would be rejected in other techniques can still be accepted by reading an *older version* of the item to maintain serializability. When a transaction writes an item, it writes a *new version* and the old version of the item is retained. Some multiversion concurrency control algorithms use the concept of view serializability rather than conflict serializability.

An obvious drawback of multiversion techniques is that more storage is needed to maintain multiple versions of the database items. However, older versions may have to be maintained anyway—for example, for recovery purposes. In addition, some database applications require older versions to be kept to maintain a history of the evolution of data item values. The extreme case is a *temporal database* (see Chapter 23), which keeps track of all changes and the times at which they occurred. In such cases, there is no additional storage penalty for multiversion techniques, since older versions are already maintained.

Several multiversion concurrency control schemes have been proposed. We discuss two schemes here, one based on timestamp ordering and the other based on 2PL.

20.3.1 Multiversion Technique Based on Timestamp Ordering

In this method, several versions X_1, X_2, ..., X_k of each data item X are maintained. For *each version*, the value of version X_i and the following two timestamps are kept:

1. **read_TS(X_i):** The **read timestamp** of X_i is the largest of all the timestamps of transactions that have successfully read version X_i.

2. **write_TS(X_i):** The **write timestamp** of X_i is the timestamp of the transaction that wrote the value of version X_i.

Whenever a transaction T is allowed to execute a `write_item(X)` operation, a new version X_{k+1} of item X is created, with both the write_TS(X_{k+1}) and the read_TS(X_{k+1}) set to TS(T). Correspondingly, when a transaction T is allowed to read the value of version X_i, the value of read_TS(X_i) is set to the larger of the current read_TS(X_i) and TS(T).

To ensure serializability, the following two rules are used:

1. If transaction T issues a `write_item(X)` operation, and version i of X has the highest write_TS(X_i) of all versions of X that is also *less than or equal to* TS(T), and read_TS(X_i) > TS(T), then abort and roll back transaction T; otherwise, create a new version X_j of X with read_TS(X_j) = write_TS(X_j) = TS(T).

2. If transaction T issues a `read_item(X)` operation, find the version i of X that has the highest write_TS(X_i) of all versions of X that is also *less than or equal to* TS(T); then return the value of X_i to transaction T, and set the value of read_TS(X_i) to the larger of TS(T) and the current read_TS(X_i).

As we can see in case 2, a `read_item(X)` is always successful, since it finds the appropriate version X_i to read based on the write_TS of the various existing versions of X. In case 1, however, transaction T may be aborted and rolled back. This happens if T is attempting to write a version of X that should have been read by another transaction T' whose timestamp is read_TS(X_i); however, T' has already read version X_i, which was written by the transaction with timestamp equal to write_TS(X_i). If this conflict occurs, T is rolled back; otherwise, a new version of X, written by transaction T, is created. Notice that, if T is rolled back, cascading rollback may occur. Hence, to ensure recoverability, a transaction T should not be allowed to commit until after all the transactions that have written some version that T has read have committed.

20.3.2 Multiversion Two-Phase Locking Using Certify Locks

In this multiple-mode locking scheme, there are *three locking modes* for an item: read, write, and certify, instead of just the two modes (read, write) discussed previously. Hence, the state of LOCK(X) for an item X can be one of read-locked, write-locked, certify-locked, or unlocked. In the standard locking scheme with only read and write locks (see Section 20.1.1), a write lock is an exclusive lock. We can describe the relationship between read and write locks in the standard scheme by means of the **lock compatibility table** shown in Figure 20.6(a). An entry of *yes* means that, if a transaction T holds the type of lock specified in the column header on item X and if transaction T' requests the type of lock specified in the row header on the same item X, then T' can *obtain the lock* because the locking modes are compatible. On the other hand, an entry of *no* in the table indicates that the locks are not compatible, so T' must wait until T releases the lock.

In the standard locking scheme, once a transaction obtains a write lock on an item, no other transactions can access that item. The idea behind multiversion 2PL is to allow other transactions T' to read an item X while a single transaction T holds a write lock on X. This is accomplished by allowing *two versions* for each item X; one version must always have been written by some committed transaction. The second version X' is created when a transaction T acquires a write lock on the item. Other transactions can continue to read the *committed version* of X while T holds the write lock. Transaction T can write the value of X' as needed, without affecting the value of the committed version X. How-

(a)

	Read	Write
Read	yes	no
Write	no	no

(b)

	Read	Write	Certify
Read	yes	yes	no
Write	yes	no	no
Certify	no	no	no

Figure 20.6   Lock compatibility tables. (a) A compatibility table for read/write locking scheme. (b) A compatibility table for read/write/certify locking scheme.

ever, once T is ready to commit, it must obtain a **certify lock** on all items that it currently holds write locks on before it can commit. The certify lock is not compatible with read locks, so the transaction may have to delay its commit until all its write-locked items are released by any reading transactions in order to obtain the certify locks. Once the certify locks—which are exclusive locks—are acquired, the committed version X of the data item is set to the value of version X', version X' is discarded, and the certify locks are then released. The lock compatibility table for this scheme is shown in Figure 20.6(b).

In this multiversion 2PL scheme, reads can proceed concurrently with a single write operation—an arrangement not permitted under the standard 2PL schemes. The cost is that a transaction may have to delay its commit until it obtains exclusive certify locks on *all the items* it has updated. It can be shown that this scheme avoids cascading aborts, since transactions are only allowed to read the version X that was written by a committed transaction. However, deadlocks may occur if upgrading of a read lock to a write lock is allowed, and these must be handled by variations of the techniques discussed in Section 20.1.3.

20.4 Validation (Optimistic) Concurrency Control Techniques

In all the concurrency control techniques we have discussed so far, a certain degree of checking is done *before* a database operation can be executed. For example, in locking, a check is done to determine whether the item being accessed is locked. In timestamp ordering, the transaction timestamp is checked against the read and write timestamps of the item. Such checking represents overhead during transaction execution, with the effect of slowing down the transactions.

In **optimistic concurrency control techniques,** also known as **validation** or **certification techniques,** *no checking* is done while the transaction is executing. Several proposed concurrency control methods use the validation technique. We will describe only one scheme here. In this scheme, updates in the transaction are *not* applied directly to the database items until the transaction reaches its end. During transaction execution, all updates are applied to *local copies* of the data items that are kept for the transaction.[6] At the end of transaction execution, a **validation phase** checks whether any of the transaction's updates violate serializability. Certain information needed by the validation phase must be kept by the system. If serializability is not violated, the transaction is committed and the database is updated from the local copies; otherwise, the transaction is aborted and then restarted later.

There are three phases for this concurrency control protocol:

1. **Read phase:** A transaction can read values of committed data items from the database. However, updates are applied only to local copies (versions) of the data items kept in the transaction workspace.

---

6. Note that this can be considered as keeping multiple versions of items!

2. **Validation phase:** Checking is performed to ensure that serializability will not be violated if the transaction updates are applied to the database.

3. **Write phase:** If the validation phase is successful, the transaction updates are applied to the database; otherwise, the updates are discarded and the transaction is restarted.

The idea behind optimistic concurrency control is to do all the checks at once; hence, transaction execution proceeds with a minimum of overhead until the validation phase is reached. If there is little interference among transactions, most will be validated successfully. However, if there is much interference, many transactions that execute to completion will have their results discarded and must be restarted later. Under these circumstances, optimistic techniques do not work well. The techniques are called "optimistic" because they assume that little interference will occur and hence that there is no need to do checking during transaction execution.

The optimistic protocol we describe uses transaction timestamps and also requires that the write_sets and read_sets of the transactions be kept by the system. In addition, *start* and *end* times for some of the three phases need to be kept for each transaction. Recall that the **write_set** of a transaction is the set of items it writes, and the **read_set** is the set of items it reads. In the validation phase for transaction T_i, the protocol checks that T_i does not interfere with any committed transactions or with any other transactions currently in their validation phase. The validation phase for T_i checks that, for each such transaction T_j that is either committed or is in its validation phase, *one* of the following conditions holds:

1. Transaction T_j completes its write phase before T_i starts its read phase.

2. T_i starts its write phase after T_j completes its write phase, and the read_set of T_i has no items in common with the write_set of T_j.

3. Both the read_set and write_set of T_i have no items in common with the write_set of T_j, and T_j completes its read phase before T_i completes its read phase.

When validating transaction T_i, the first condition is checked first for each transaction T_j, since (1) is the simplest condition to check. Only if condition (1) is false is condition (2) checked, and only if (2) is false is condition (3)—the most complex to evaluate—checked. If any one of these three conditions holds, there is no interference and T_i is validated successfully. If none of these three conditions holds, the validation of transaction T_i fails and it is aborted and restarted later because interference *may* have occurred.

20.5 Granularity of Data Items and Multiple Granularity Locking

All concurrency control techniques assumed that the database was formed of a number of named data items. A database item could be chosen to be one of the following:

- A database record.
- A field value of a database record.

- A disk block.
- A whole file.
- The whole database.

The granularity can affect the performance of concurrency control and recovery. In Section 20.5.1, we discuss some of the tradeoffs with regard to choosing the granularity level used for locking, and, in Section 20.5.2, we discuss a multiple granularity locking scheme, where the granularity level (size of the data item) may be changed dynamically.

20.5.1 Granularity Level Considerations for Locking

The size of data items is often called the **data item granularity.** *Fine granularity* refers to small item sizes, whereas *coarse granularity* refers to large item sizes. Several tradeoffs must be considered in choosing the data item size. We shall discuss data item size in the context of locking, although similar arguments can be made for other concurrency control techniques.

First, notice that the larger the data item size is, the lower the degree of concurrency permitted. For example, if the data item size is a disk block, a transaction T that needs to lock a record B must lock the whole disk block X that contains B because a lock is associated with the whole data item (block). Now, if another transaction S wants to lock a different record C that happens to reside in the same block X in a conflicting lock mode, it is forced to wait. If the data item size was a single record, transaction S would be able to proceed, because it would be locking a different data item (record).

On the other hand, the smaller the data item size is, the more the number of items in the database. Because every item is associated with a lock, the system will have a larger number of active locks to be handled by the lock manager. More lock and unlock operations will be performed, causing a higher overhead. In addition, more storage space will be required for the lock table. For timestamps, storage is required for the read_TS and write_ TS for each data item, and there will be similar overhead for handling a large number of items.

Given the above tradeoffs, an obvious question can be asked: What is the best item size? The answer is that *it depends on the types of transactions involved.* If a typical transaction accesses a small number of records, it is advantageous to have the data item granularity be one record. On the other hand, if a transaction typically accesses many records in the same file, it may be better to have block or file granularity so that the transaction will consider all those records as one (or a few) data items.

20.5.2 Multiple Granularity Level Locking

Since the best granularity size depends on the given transaction, it seems appropriate that a database system support multiple levels of granularity, where the granularity level can be different for various mixes of transactions. Figure 20.7 shows a simple granularity hierarchy with a database containing two files, each file containing several pages, and each page containing several records. This can be used to illustrate a **multiple granularity level** 2PL protocol, where a lock can be requested at any level. However, additional types of locks will be needed to efficiently support such a protocol.

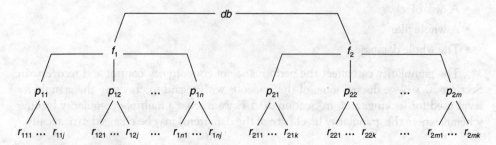

Figure 20.7   A granularity hierarchy for illustrating multiple granularity level locking.

Consider the following scenario, with only shared and exclusive lock types, that refers to the example in Figure 20.7. Suppose transaction T_1 wants to update *all the records* in file f_1, and T_1 requests and is granted an exclusive lock for f_1. Then all of f_1's pages (p_{11} through p_{1n})—and the records contained on those pages—are locked in exclusive mode. This is beneficial for T_1 because setting a single file-level lock is more efficient than setting n page-level locks or having to lock each individual record. Now suppose another transaction T_2 only wants to read record r_{1nj} from page p_{1n} of file f_1; then T_2 would request a shared record-level lock on r_{1nj}. However, the database system (that is, the transaction manager or more specifically the lock manager) must verify the compatibility of the requested lock with already held locks. One way to verify this is to traverse the tree from the leaf r_{1nj} to p_{1n} to f_1 to *db*. If at any time a conflicting lock is held on any of those items, then the lock request for r_{1nj} is denied and T_2 is blocked and must wait. This traversal would be fairly efficient.

However, what if transaction T_2's request came *before* transaction T_1's request? In this case, the shared record lock is granted to T_2 for r_{1nj}, but when T_1's file-level lock is requested, it is quite difficult for the lock manger to check all nodes (pages and records) that are descendants of node f_1 for a lock conflict. This would be very inefficient and would defeat the purpose of having multiple granularity level locks.

To make multiple granularity level locking practical, additional types of locks, called **intention locks,** are needed. The idea behind intention locks is for a transaction to indicate, along the path from the root to the desired node, what type of lock (shared or exclusive) it will require from one of the node's descendants. There are three types of intention locks:

1. Intention-shared (IS) indicates that a shared lock(s) will be requested on some descendant node(s).

2. Intention-exclusive (IX) indicates that an exclusive lock(s) will be requested on some descendant node(s).

3. Shared-intention-exclusive (SIX) indicates that the current node is locked in shared mode but an exclusive lock(s) will be requested on some descendant node(s).

	IS	IX	S	SIX	X
IS	yes	yes	yes	yes	no
IX	yes	yes	no	no	no
S	yes	no	yes	no	no
SIX	yes	no	no	no	no
X	no	no	no	no	no

Figure 20.8 Lock compatibility matrix for multiple granularity locking.

The compatibility table of the three intention locks, and the shared and exclusive locks, is shown in Figure 20.8. Besides the introduction of the three types of intention locks, an appropriate locking protocol must be used. The **multiple granularity locking** (MGL) protocol consists of the following rules:

1. The lock compatibility (based on Figure 20.8) must be adhered to.
2. The root of the tree must be locked first, in any mode.
3. A node N can be locked by a transaction T in S or IS mode only if the parent node N is already locked by transaction T in either IS or IX mode.
4. A node N can be locked by a transaction T in X, IX, or SIX mode only if the parent of node N is already locked by transaction T in either IX or SIX mode.
5. A transaction T can lock a node only if it has not unlocked any node (to enforce the 2PL protocol).
6. A transaction T can unlock a node, N, only if none of the children of node N are currently locked by T.

Rule 1 simply states that conflicting locks cannot be granted. Rules 2, 3, and 4 state the conditions when a transaction may lock a given node in any of the lock modes. Rules 5 and 6 of the MGL protocol enforce 2PL rules to produce serializable schedules. To illustrate the MGL protocol with the database hierarchy in Figure 20.7, consider the following three transactions:

1. T_1 wants to update record r_{111} and record r_{211}.
2. T_2 wants to update all records on page p_{12}.
3. T_3 wants to read record r_{11j} and the entire f_2 file.

Figure 20.9 shows a possible serializable schedule for these three transactions. Only the lock operations are shown. The notation <lock_type>(<item>) is used to display the locking operations in the schedule.

T_1	T_2	T_3
IX(db)		
IX(f_1)		
	IX(db)	
		IS(db)
		IS(f_1)
		IS(p_{11})
IX(p_{11})		
X(r_{111})		
	IX(f_1)	
	X(p_{12})	
		S(r_{11j})
IX(f_2)		
IX(p_{21})		
X(r_{211})		
unlock(r_{211})		
unlock(p_{21})		
unlock(f_2)		
		S(f_2)
	unlock(p_{12})	
	unlock(f_1)	
	unlock(db)	
unlock(r_{111})		
unlock(p_{11})		
unlock(f_1)		
unlock(db)		
		unlock(r_{11j})
		unlock(p_{11})
		unlock(f_1)
		unlock(f_2)
		unlock(db)

Figure 20.9   Lock operations to illustrate a serializable schedule.

The multiple granularity level protocol is especially suited when processing a mix of transactions that include: (1) short transactions that access only a few items (records or fields), and (2) long transactions that access entire files. In this environment, less transaction blocking and less locking overhead is incurred by such protocol when compared to a single level granularity locking approach.

20.6   Using Locks for Concurrency Control in Indexes

Two-phase locking can also be applied to indexes (see Chapter 6), where the nodes of an index correspond to disk pages. However, holding locks on index pages until the shrinking phase of 2PL could cause an undue amount of transaction blocking. This is because searching an index always *starts at the root,* so if a transaction wants to insert a record (write operation), the root would be locked in exclusive mode, so all other conflicting lock requests for the index must wait until the transaction enters its shrinking phase. This blocks all other transactions from accessing the index, so in practice other approaches to locking an index must be used.

The tree structure of the index can be taken advantage of when developing a concurrency control scheme. For example, when an index search (read operation) is being executed, a path in the tree is traversed from the root to a leaf. Once a lower-level node in the path has been accessed, the higher-level nodes in that path will not be used again. So once a read lock on a child node is obtained, the lock on the parent can be released. Second, when an insertion is being applied to a leaf node (that is, when a key and a pointer are inserted), then a specific leaf node must be locked in exclusive mode. However, if that node is not full, the insertion will not cause changes to higher-level index nodes, which implies that they need not be locked exclusively.

A conservative approach for insertions would be to lock the root node in exclusive mode and then to access the appropriate child node of the root. If the child node is not full, then the lock on the root node can be released. This approach can be applied all the way down the tree to the leaf, which is typically three or four levels from the root. Although exclusive locks are held, they are soon released. An alternative, more optimistic approach would be to request and hold shared locks on the nodes leading to the leaf node, with an exclusive lock on the leaf. If the insertion causes the leaf to split, insertion will propagate to a higher level node(s). Then, the locks on the higher level node(s) can be upgraded to exclusive mode.

Another approach to index locking is to use a variant of the B^+-tree, called the **B-link tree.** In a B-link tree, sibling nodes on the same level are linked together at every level. This allows shared locks to be used when requesting a page and requires that the lock be released before accessing the child node. For an insert operation, the shared lock on a node would be upgraded to exclusive mode. If a split occurs, the parent node must be relocked in exclusive mode. One complication is for search operations executed concurrently with the update. Suppose that a concurrent update operation follows the same path as the search, and inserts a new entry into the leaf node. In addition, suppose that the insert causes that leaf node to split. When the insert is done, the search process resumes, following the pointer to the desired leaf, only to find that the key it is looking for is not present because the split has moved that key into a new leaf node, which would be the *right sibling* of the original leaf node. However, the search process can still succeed if it follows the pointer (link) in the original leaf node to its right sibling, where the desired key has been moved.

Handling the deletion case, where two or more nodes from the index tree merge, is also part of the B-link tree concurrency protocol. In this case, locks on the nodes to be merged are held as well as a lock on the parent of the two nodes to be merged.

20.7   Other Concurrency Control Issues

In this section, we discuss some other issues relevant to concurrency control. In Section 20.7.1, we discuss problems associated with insertion and deletion of records and the so-called *phantom problem*, which may occur when records are inserted. This problem was described as a potential problem requiring a concurrency control measure in Section 19.6. Then, in Section 20.7.2, we discuss problems that may occur when a transaction outputs some data to a monitor before it commits, and then the transaction is later aborted.

20.7.1   Insertion, Deletion, and Phantom Records

When a new data item is **inserted** in the database, it obviously cannot be accessed until after the item is created and the insert operation is completed. In a locking environment, a lock for the item can be created and set to exclusive (write) mode; the lock can be released at the same time as other write locks would be released, based on the concurrency control protocol being used. For a timestamp-based protocol, the read and write timestamps of the new item are set to the timestamp of the creating transaction.

A **deletion operation** is applied on an existing data item. For locking protocols, again an exclusive (write) lock must be obtained before the transaction can delete the item. For timestamp ordering, the protocol must ensure that no later transaction has read or written the item before allowing the item to be deleted.

A situation known as the **phantom problem** can occur when a new record that is being inserted by some transaction T satisfies a condition that a set of records accessed by another transaction T' must satisfy. For example, suppose that transaction T is inserting a new EMPLOYEE record whose DNO = 5, while transaction T' is accessing all EMPLOYEE records whose DNO = 5 (say, to add up all their SALARY values to calculate the personnel budget for department 5). If the equivalent serial order is T followed by T', then T' must read the new EMPLOYEE record and include its SALARY in the sum calculation. For the equivalent serial order T' followed by T, the new salary should not be included. Notice that although the transactions logically conflict, in the latter case there is really no record (data item) in common between the two transactions, since T' may have locked all the records with DNO = 5 *before* T inserted the new record. This is because the record that causes the conflict is a **phantom record** that has suddenly appeared in the database on being inserted. If other operations in the two transactions conflict, the conflict due to the phantom record may not be recognized by the concurrency control protocol.

One solution to the phantom record problem is to use **index locking,** as discussed in Section 20.6. Recall from Chapter 6 that an index includes entries that have an attribute value, plus a set of pointers to all records in the file with that value. For example, an index on DNO of EMPLOYEE would include an entry for each distinct DNO value, plus a set of pointers to all EMPLOYEE records with that value. If the index entry is locked *before* the record itself can be accessed, then the conflict on the phantom record can be detected. This is because transaction T′ would request a read lock on the *index entry* for DNO = 5, and T would request a write lock on the same entry *before* they could place the locks on the actual records. Since the index locks conflict, the phantom conflict would be detected.

A more general technique, called **predicate locking,** would lock access to all records that satisfy an *arbitrary predicate* (condition) in a similar manner; however predicate locks have proved to be difficult to implement efficiently.

20.7.2 Interactive Transactions

Another problem occurs when interactive transactions read input and write output to an interactive device, such as a monitor screen, before they are committed. The problem is that a user can input a value of a data item to a transaction T that is based on some value written to the screen by transaction T′, which may not have committed. This dependency between T and T′ cannot be modeled by the system concurrency control method, since it is only based on the user interacting with the two transactions.

An approach to dealing with this problem is to postpone output of transactions to the screen until they have committed.

20.7.3 Latches

Locks held for a short duration are typically called **latches.** Latches do not follow the usual concurrency control protocol such as two-phase locking. For example, a latch can be used to guarantee the physical integrity of a page when that page is being written from the buffer to disk. A latch would be acquired for the page, the page written to disk, and then the latch is released.

20.8 Summary

In this chapter we discussed DBMS techniques for concurrency control. We started by discussing lock-based protocols, which are by far the most commonly used in practice. We described the two-phase locking (2PL) protocol and a number of its variations: basic 2PL, strict 2PL, conservative 2PL, and rigorous 2PL. The strict and rigorous variations are more common because of their better recoverability properties. We introduced the concepts of shared (read) and exclusive (write) locks, and showed how locking can guarantee serializability when used in conjunction with the two-phase locking rule. We also presented various techniques for dealing with the deadlock problem, which can occur with locking. In practice, it is common to use timeouts and deadlock detection (wait-for graphs).

We then presented other concurrency control protocols that are not used often in practice but are important for the theoretical alternatives they show for solving this problem. These include the timestamp ordering protocol, which ensures serializability based on the order of transaction timestamps. Timestamps are unique, system-generated transaction identifiers. We discussed Thomas's write rule, which improves performance but does not guarantee conflict serializability. The strict timestamp ordering protocol was also presented. We then discussed two multiversion protocols, which assume that older versions of data items can be kept in the database. One technique, called multiversion two-phase locking (which has been used in practice), assumes that two versions can exist for an item and attempts to increase concurrency by making write and read locks compatible (at the cost of introducing an additional certify lock mode). We also presented a multiversion protocol based on timestamp ordering. We then presented an example of an optimistic protocol, which is also known as a certification or validation protocol.

We then turned our attention to the important practical issue of data item granularity. We described a multigranularity locking protocol that allows the change of granularity (item size) based on the current transaction mix, with the goal of improving the performance of concurrency control. An important practical issue was then presented, which is to develop locking protocols for indexes so that indexes do not become a hindrance to concurrent access. Finally, we introduced the phantom problem and problems with interactive transactions, and briefly described the concept of latches and how it differs from locks.

In the next chapter, we give an overview of recovery techniques.

Review Questions

20.1. What is the two-phase locking protocol? How does it guarantee serializability?

20.2. What are some variations of the two-phase locking protocol? Why is strict or rigorous two-phase locking often preferred?

20.3. Discuss the problems of deadlock and starvation, and the different approaches to dealing with these problems.

20.4. Compare binary locks to exclusive/shared locks. Why is the latter type of locks preferable?

20.5. Describe the wait-die and wound-wait protocols for deadlock prevention.

20.6. Describe the cautious waiting, no waiting, and timeout protocols for deadlock prevention.

20.7. What is a timestamp? How does the system generate timestamps?

20.8. Discuss the timestamp ordering protocol for concurrency control. How does strict timestamp ordering differ from basic timestamp ordering?

20.9. Discuss two multiversion techniques for concurrency control.

20.10. What is a certify lock? What are the advantages and disadvantages of using certify locks?

20.11. How do optimistic concurrency control techniques differ from other concurrency control techniques? Why are they also called validation or certification techniques? Discuss the typical phases of an optimistic concurrency control method.

20.12. How does the granularity of data items affect the performance of concurrency control? What factors affect selection of granularity size for data items?

20.13. What type of locks are needed for insert and delete operations?

20.14. What is multiple granularity locking? Under what circumstances is it used?

20.15. What are intention locks?

20.16. When are latches used?

20.17. What is a phantom record? Discuss the problem that a phantom record can cause for concurrency control.

20.18. How does index locking resolve the phantom problem?

20.19. What is a predicate lock?

Exercises

20.20. Prove that the basic two-phase locking protocol guarantees conflict serializability of schedules. (*Hint:* Show that, if a serializability graph for a schedule has a cycle, then at least one of the transactions participating in the schedule does not obey the two-phase locking protocol.)

20.21. Modify the data structures for multiple-mode locks and the algorithms for `read_lock(X)`, `write_lock(X)`, and `unlock(X)` so that upgrading and downgrading of locks are possible. (*Hint:* The lock needs to check the transaction id(s) that hold the lock, if any.)

20.22. Prove that strict two-phase locking guarantees strict schedules.

20.23. Prove that the wait-die and wound-wait protocols avoid deadlock and starvation.

20.24. Prove that cautious waiting avoids deadlock.

20.25. Apply the timestamp ordering algorithm to the schedules of Figure 19.8(b) and (c), and determine whether the algorithm will allow the execution of the schedules.

20.26. Repeat Exercise 20.25, but use the multiversion timestamp ordering method.

20.27. Why is two-phase locking not used as a concurrency control method for indexes such as B^+-trees?

20.28. The compatibility matrix of Figure 20.8 shows that IS and IX locks are compatible. Explain why this is valid.

20.29. The MGL protocol states that a transaction T can unlock a node N, only if none of the children of node N are still locked by transaction T. Show that without this condition, the MGL protocol would be incorrect.

Selected Bibliography

The two-phase locking protocol, and the concept of predicate locks was first proposed by Eswaran et al. (1976). Bernstein et al. (1987), Gray and Reuter (1993), and Papadimitriou (1986) focus on concurrency control and recovery. Kumar (1996) focuses on performance of concurrency control methods. Locking is discussed in Gray et al. (1975), Lien and Weinberger (1978), Kedem and Silbershatz (1980), and Korth (1983). Deadlocks and wait-for graphs were formalized by Holt (1972), and the wait-wound and wound-die schemes are presented in Rosenkrantz et al. (1978). Cautious waiting is discussed in Hsu et al. (1992). Helal et al. (1993) compares various locking approaches. Timestamp-based concurrency control techniques are discussed in Bernstein and Goodman (1980) and Reed (1983). Optimistic concurrency control is discussed in Kung and Robinson (1981) and Bassiouni (1988). Papadimitriou and Kanellakis (1979) and

Bernstein and Goodman (1983) discuss multiversion techniques. Multiversion timestamp ordering was proposed in Reed (1978, 1983), and multiversion two-phase locking is discussed in Lai and Wilkinson (1984). A method for multiple locking granularities was proposed in Gray et al. (1975), and the effects of locking granularities are analyzed in Ries and Stonebraker (1977). Bhargava and Reidl (1988) presents an approach for dynamically choosing among various concurrency control and recovery methods. Concurrency control methods for indexes are presented in Lehman and Yao (1981) and in Shasha and Goodman (1988). A performance study of various B+ tree concurrency control algorithms is presented in Srinivasan and Carey (1991).

Other recent work on concurrency control includes semantic-based concurrency control (Badrinath and Ramamritham, 1992), transaction models for long running activities (Dayal et al., 1991), and multilevel transaction management (Hasse and Weikum, 1991).

CHAPTER 21

Database Recovery Techniques

In this chapter we discuss some of the techniques that can be used for database recovery from failures. We have already discussed the different causes of failure, such as system crashes and transaction errors, in Section 19.1.4. We have also covered many of the concepts that are used by recovery processes, such as the system log and commit points, in Section 19.2.

We start Section 21.1 with an outline of a typical recovery procedures and a categorization of recovery algorithms, and then discuss several recovery concepts, including write-ahead logging, in-place versus shadow updates, and the process of rolling back (undoing) the effect of an incomplete or failed transaction. In Section 21.2, we present recovery techniques based on *deferred update*, also known as the NO-UNDO/REDO technique. In Section 21.3, we discuss recovery techniques based on immediate update; these include the UNDO/REDO and UNDO/NO-REDO algorithms. We discuss the technique known as shadowing or shadow paging, which can be categorized as a NO-UNDO/NO-REDO algorithm in Section 21.4. An example of a practical DBMS recovery scheme, called ARIES, is presented in Section 21.5. Recovery in multidatabases is briefly discussed in Section 21.6. Finally, techniques for recovery from catastrophic failure are discussed in Section 21.7.

Our emphasis is on conceptually describing several different approaches to recovery. For descriptions of recovery features in specific systems, the reader should consult the bibliographic notes and the user manuals for those systems. Recovery techniques are often intertwined with the concurrency control mechanisms. Certain recovery techniques are best used with specific concurrency control methods. We will attempt to discuss recovery concepts independently of concurrency control mechanisms, but we will discuss the circumstances under which a particular recovery mechanism is best used with a certain concurrency control protocol.

21.1 Recovery Concepts

21.1.1 Recovery Outline and Categorization of Recovery Algorithms

Recovery from transaction failures usually means that the database is *restored* to the most recent consistent state just before the time of failure. To do this, the system must keep information about the changes that were applied to data items by the various transactions. This information is typically kept in the **system log,** as we discussed in Section 19.2.2. A typical strategy for recovery may be summarized informally as follows:

1. If there is extensive damage to a wide portion of the database due to catastrophic failure, such as a disk crash, the recovery method restores a past copy of the database that was *backed up* to archival storage (typically tape) and reconstructs a more current state by reapplying or *redoing* the operations of committed transactions from the *backed up* log, up to the time of failure.

2. When the database is not physically damaged but has become inconsistent due to noncatastrophic failures of types 1 through 4 of Section 19.1.4, the strategy is to reverse any changes that caused the inconsistency by *undoing* some operations. It may also be necessary to *redo* some operations in order to restore a consistent state of the database, as we shall see. In this case we do not need a complete archival copy of the database. Rather, the entries kept in the on-line system log are consulted during recovery.

Conceptually, we can distinguish two main techniques for recovery from noncatastrophic transaction failures: (1) deferred update and (2) immediate update. The **deferred update** techniques do not physically update the database on disk until *after* a transaction reaches its commit point; then the updates are recorded in the database. Before reaching commit, all transaction updates are recorded in the local transaction workspace (or buffers). During commit, the updates are first recorded persistently in the log and then written to the database. If a transaction fails before reaching its commit point, it will not have changed the database in any way, so UNDO is not needed. It may be necessary to REDO the effect of the operations of a committed transaction from the log, because their effect may not yet have been recorded in the database. Hence, deferred update is also known as the NO-UNDO/REDO **algorithm.** We discuss this technique in Section 21.2.

In the **immediate update** techniques, the database may be updated by some operations of a transaction *before* the transaction reaches its commit point. However, these operations are typically recorded in the log *on disk* by force writing *before* they are applied to the database, making recovery still possible. If a transaction fails after recording some changes in the database but before reaching its commit point, the effect of its operations on the database must be undone; that is, the transaction must be rolled back. In the general case of immediate update, both *undo* and *redo* may be required during recovery. This technique, known as the UNDO/REDO algorithm, requires both operations, and is used most often in practice. A variation of the algorithm where all updates are recorded in the database before a transaction commits requires *undo* only, so it is known as the UNDO/NO-REDO algorithm. We discuss these techniques in Section 21.3.

21.1.2 Caching of Disk Blocks

The recovery process is often closely intertwined with operating system functions—in particular, the buffering and caching of disk pages in main memory. Typically, one or more disk pages that include the data items to be updated are **cached** into main memory buffers and then updated in memory before being written back to disk. The caching of disk pages is traditionally an operating system function, but because of its importance to the efficiency of recovery procedures, it is handled by the DBMS by calling low-level operating systems routines.

In general, it is convenient to consider recovery in terms of the database disk pages (blocks). Typically a collection of in-memory buffers, called the DBMS **cache,** is kept under the control of the DBMS for the purpose of holding these buffers. A **directory** for the cache is used to keep track of which database items are in the buffers.[1] This can be a table of <disk page address, buffer location> entries. When the DBMS requests action on some item, it first checks the cache directory to determine whether the disk page containing the item is in the cache. If it is not, then the item must be located on disk, and the appropriate disk pages are copied into the cache. It may be necessary to **replace** (or **flush**) some of the cache buffers to make space available for the new item. Some page-replacement strategy from operating systems, such as least recently used (LRU) or first-in-first-out (FIFO), can be used to select the buffers for replacement.

Associated with each buffer in the cache is a **dirty bit,** which can be included in the directory entry, to indicate whether or not the buffer has been modified. When a page is first read from the database disk into a cache buffer, the cache directory is updated with the new disk page address, and the dirty bit is set to 0 (zero). As soon as the buffer is modified, the dirty bit for the corresponding directory entry is set to 1 (one). When the buffer contents are replaced (flushed) from the cache, the contents must first be written back to the corresponding disk page *only if its dirty bit is 1*. Another bit, called the **pin-unpin** bit, is also needed—a page in the cache is **pinned** (bit value 1 (one)) if it cannot be written back to disk as yet.

Two main strategies can be employed when flushing a modified buffer back to disk. The first strategy, known as **in-place updating,** writes the buffer back to the *same original disk location*, thus overwriting the old value of any changed data items on disk.[2] Hence, a single copy of each database disk block is maintained. The second strategy, known as

---

1. This is somewhat similar to the concept of *page tables* used by the operating system.

2. In-place updating is used in most systems in practice.

shadowing, writes an updated buffer at a different disk location, so multiple versions of data items can be maintained. In general, the old value of the data item before updating is called the **before image (BFIM),** and the new value after updating is called the **after image (AFIM).** In shadowing, both the BFIM and the AFIM can be kept on disk; hence, it is not strictly necessary to maintain a log for recovering. We briefly discuss recovery based on shadowing in Section 21.4.

21.1.3   Write-Ahead Logging, Steal/No-Steal, and Force/No-Force

When in-place updating is used, it is necessary to use a log for recovery (see Section 19.2.2). In this case, the recovery mechanism must ensure that the BFIM of the data item is recorded in the appropriate log entry and that the log entry is flushed to disk before the BFIM is overwritten with the AFIM in the database on disk. This process is generally known as **write-ahead logging.** Before we can describe a protocol for write-ahead logging, we need to distinguish between two types of log entry information included for a write command: (1) the information needed for UNDO and (2) that needed for REDO. A **REDO-type log entry** includes the **new value** (AFIM) of the item written by the operation since this is needed to *redo* the effect of the operation from the log (by setting the item value in the database to its AFIM). The **UNDO-type log entries** include the **old value** (BFIM) of the item since this is needed to *undo* the effect of the operation from the log (by setting the item value in the database back to its BFIM). In an UNDO/REDO algorithm, both types of log entries are combined. In addition, when cascading rollback is possible, `read_item` entries in the log are considered to be UNDO-type entries (see Section 21.1.5).

As mentioned, the DBMS cache holds the cached database disk blocks, which include not only *data blocks* but also *index blocks* and *log blocks* from the disk. When a log record is written, it is stored in the current log block in the DBMS cache. The log is simply a sequential (append-only) disk file and the DBMS cache may contain several log blocks (for example, the last *n* log blocks) that will be written to disk. When an update to a data block—stored in the DBMS cache—is made, an associated log record is written to the last log block in the DBMS cache. With the write-ahead logging approach, the log blocks that contain the associated log records for a particular data block update must first be written to disk before the data block itself can be written back to disk.

Standard DBMS recovery terminology includes the terms **steal/no-steal** and **force/no-force,** which specify when a page from the database can be written to disk from the cache:

1. If a cache page updated by a transaction *cannot* be written to disk before the transaction commits, this is called a **no-steal approach.** The pin-unpin bit indicates if a page cannot be written back to disk. Otherwise, if the protocol allows writing an updated buffer *before* the transaction commits, it is called **steal.** Steal is used when the DBMS cache (buffer) manager needs a buffer frame for another transaction and the buffer manager replaces an existing page that had been updated but whose transaction has not committed.

2. If all pages updated by a transaction are immediately written to disk when the transaction commits, this is called a **force approach.** Otherwise, it is called **no-force.**

The deferred update recovery scheme in Section 21.2 follows a *no-steal* approach. However, typical database systems employ a *steal/no-force* strategy. The advantage of steal is that it avoids the need for a very large buffer space to store all updated pages in memory. The advantage of no-force is that an updated page of a committed transaction may still be in the buffer when another transaction needs to update it, thus eliminating the I/O cost to read that page again from disk. This may provide a substantial saving in the number of I/O operations when a specific page is updated heavily by multiple transactions.

To permit recovery when in-place updating is used, the appropriate entries required for recovery must be permanently recorded in the log on disk before changes are applied to the database. For example, consider the following **write-ahead logging (WAL)** protocol for a recovery algorithm that requires both UNDO and REDO:

1. The before image of an item cannot be overwritten by its after image in the data-base on disk until all UNDO-type log records for the updating transaction—up to this point in time—have been force-written to disk.

2. The commit operation of a transaction cannot be completed until all the REDO-type and UNDO-type log records for that transaction have been force-written to disk.

To facilitate the recovery process, the DBMS recovery subsystem may need to main-tain a number of lists related to the transactions being processed in the system. These include a list for **active transactions** that have started but not committed as yet, and it may also include lists of all **committed** and **aborted transactions** since the last checkpoint (see next section). Maintaining these lists makes the recovery process more efficient.

21.1.4 Checkpoints in the System Log and Fuzzy Checkpointing

Another type of entry in the log is called a **checkpoint**.[3] A [checkpoint] record is writ-ten into the log periodically at that point when the system writes out to the database on disk all DBMS buffers that have been modified. As a consequence of this, all transactions that have their [commit,T] entries in the log before a [checkpoint] entry do not need to have their WRITE operations *redone* in case of a system crash, since all their updates will be recorded in the database on disk during checkpointing.

The recovery manager of a DBMS must decide at what intervals to take a checkpoint. The interval may be measured in time—say, every m minutes—or in the number t of com-mitted transactions since the last checkpoint, where the values of m or t are system parameters. Taking a checkpoint consists of the following actions:

1. Suspend execution of transactions temporarily.

2. Force-write all main memory buffers that have been modified to disk.

3. Write a [checkpoint] record to the log, and force-write the log to disk.

4. Resume executing transactions.

---

3. The term *checkpoint* has been used to describe more restrictive situations in some systems, such as DB2. It has also been used in the literature to describe entirely different concepts.

As a consequence of Step 2, a checkpoint record in the log may also include additional information, such as a list of active transaction ids, and the locations (addresses) of the first and most recent (last) records in the log for each active transaction. This can facilitate undoing transaction operations in the event that a transaction must be rolled back.

The time needed to force-write all modified memory buffers may delay transaction processing because of Step 1. To reduce this delay, it is common to use a technique called **fuzzy checkpointing** in practice. In this technique, the system can resume transaction processing after the [checkpoint] record is written to the log without having to wait for Step 2 to finish. However, until Step 2 is completed, the previous [checkpoint] record should remain to be valid. To accomplish this, the system maintains a pointer to the valid checkpoint, which continues to point to the previous [checkpoint] record in the log. Once Step 2 is concluded, that pointer is changed to point to the new checkpoint in the log.

21.1.5 Transaction Rollback

If a transaction fails for whatever reason after updating the database, it may be necessary to **roll back** the transaction. If any data item values have been changed by the transaction and written to the database, they must be restored to their previous values (BFIMs). The undo-type log entries are used to restore the old values of data items that must be rolled back.

If a transaction T is rolled back, any transaction S that has, in the interim, read the value of some data item X written by T must also be rolled back. Similarly, once S is rolled back, any transaction R that has read the value of some data item Y written by S must also be rolled back; and so on. This phenomenon is called **cascading rollback,** and can occur when the recovery protocol ensures *recoverable* schedules but does not ensure *strict* or *cascadeless* schedules (see Section 19.4.2). Cascading rollback, understandably, can be quite complex and time-consuming. That is why almost all recovery mechanisms are designed such that cascading rollback *is never required*.

Figure 21.1 shows an example where cascading rollback is required. The read and write operations of three individual transactions are shown in Figure 21.1(a). Figure 21.1(b) shows the system log at the point of a system crash for a particular execution schedule of these transactions. The values of data items A, B, C, and D, which are used by the transactions, are shown to the right of the system log entries. We assume that the original item values, shown in the first line, are $A = 30$, $B = 15$, $C = 40$, and $D = 20$. At the point of system failure, transaction T_3 has not reached its conclusion and must be rolled back. The WRITE operations of T_3, marked by a single * in Figure 21.1(b), are the T_3 operations that are undone during transaction rollback. Figure 21.1(c) graphically shows the operations of the different transactions along the time axis.

We must now check for cascading rollback. From Figure 21.1(c) we see that transaction T_2 reads the value of item B that was written by transaction T_3; this can also be determined by examining the log. Because T_3 is rolled back, T_2 must now be rolled back, too. The WRITE operations of T_2, marked by ** in the log, are the ones that are undone. Note that only write_item operations need to be undone during transaction rollback;

(a)

T_1	T_2	T_3
read_item(A)	read_item(B)	read_item(C)
read_item(D)	write_item(B)	write_item(B)
write_item(D)	read_item(D)	read_item(A)
	write_item(D)	write_item(A)

(b)

	A	B	C	D
	30	15	40	20
[start_transaction, T_3]				
[read_item, T_3, C]				
* [write_item, T_3, B, 15, 12]		12		
[start_transaction, T_2]				
[read_item, T_2, B]				
** [write_item, T_2, B, 12, 18]		18		
[start_transaction, T_1]				
[read_item, T_1, A]				
[read_item, T_1, D]				
[write_item, T_1, D, 20, 25]				25
[read_item, T_2, D]				
** [write_item, T_2, D, 25, 26]				26
[read_item, T_3, A]				

← system crash

* T_3 is rolled back because it did not reach its commit point.
** T_2 is rolled back because it reads the value of item B written by T_3.

(c)

Figure 21.1   Illustrating cascading rollback (a process that never occurs in strict or cascadeless schedules). (a) The read and write operations of three transactions. (b) System log at point of crash. (c) Operations before the crash.

`read_item` operations are recorded in the log only to determine whether cascading roll-back of additional transactions is necessary.

In practice, cascading rollback of transactions is *never* required because practical recovery methods guarantee cascadeless or strict schedules. Hence, there is also no need to record any `read_item` operations in the log, because these are needed only for deter-mining cascading rollback.

21.2 Recovery Techniques Based on Deferred Update

The idea behind deferred update techniques is to defer or postpone any actual updates to the database until the transaction completes its execution successfully and reaches its commit point.[4] During transaction execution, the updates are recorded only in the log and in the cache buffers. After the transaction reaches its commit point and the log is force-written to disk, the updates are recorded in the database. If a transaction fails before reaching its commit point, there is no need to undo any operations, because the transac-tion has not affected the database on disk in any way. Although this may simplify recov-ery, it cannot be used in practice unless transactions are short and each transaction changes few items. For other types of transactions, there is the potential for running out of buffer space because transaction changes must be held in the cache buffers until the commit point.

We can state a typical deferred update protocol as follows:

1. A transaction cannot change the database on disk until it reaches its commit point.

2. A transaction does not reach its commit point until all its update operations are recorded in the log *and* the log is force-written to disk.

Notice that Step 2 of this protocol is a restatement of the write-ahead logging (WAL) protocol. Because the database is never updated on disk until after the transaction com-mits, there is never a need to UNDO any operations. Hence, this is known as the **NO-UNDO/REDO recovery algorithm.** REDO is needed in case the system fails after a transac-tion commits but before all its changes are recorded in the database on disk. In this case, the transaction operations are redone from the log entries.

Usually, the method of recovery from failure is closely related to the concurrency control method in multiuser systems. First we discuss recovery in single-user systems, where no concurrency control is needed, so that we can understand the recovery process independently of any concurrency control method. We then discuss how concurrency control may affect the recovery process.

---

4. Hence deferred update can generally be characterized as a *no-steal approach*.

21.2.1 Recovery Using Deferred Update in a Single-User Environment

In such an environment, the recovery algorithm can be rather simple. The algorithm RDU_S (Recovery using Deferred Update in a Single-user environment) uses a REDO procedure, given subsequently, for redoing certain `write_item` operations; it works as follows:

PROCEDURE **RDU_S**: Use two lists of transactions: the committed transactions since the last checkpoint, and the active transactions (at most one transaction will fall in this category, because the system is single-user). Apply the REDO operation to all the `write_item` operations of the committed transactions from the log in the order in which they were written to the log. Restart the active transactions.

The REDO procedure is defined as follows:

REDO(**WRITE_OP**): Redoing a `write_item` operation WRITE_OP consists of examining its log entry [write_item, T, X, new_value] and setting the value of item X in the database to `new_value`, which is the after image (AFIM).

The REDO operation is required to be **idempotent**—that is, executing it over and over is equivalent to executing it just once. In fact, the whole recovery process should be idempotent. This is so because, if the system were to fail during the recovery process, the next recovery attempt might REDO certain `write_item` operations that had already been redone during the first recovery process. The result of recovery from a system crash *during recovery* should be the same as the result of recovering *when there is no crash during recovery!*

Notice that the only transaction in the active list will have had no effect on the database because of the deferred update protocol, and it is ignored completely by the recovery process because none of its operations were reflected in the database on disk. However, this transaction must now be restarted, either automatically by the recovery process or manually by the user.

Figure 21.2 shows an example of recovery in a single-user environment, where the first failure occurs during execution of transaction T_2, as shown in Figure 21.2(b). The recovery process will redo the [write_item, T_1, D, 20] entry in the log by resetting the value of item D to 20 (its new value). The [write, T_2, ...] entries in the log are ignored by the recovery process because T_2 is not committed. If a second failure occurs during recovery from the first failure, the same recovery process is repeated from start to finish, with identical results.

21.2.2 Deferred Update with Concurrent Execution in a Multiuser Environment

For multiuser systems with concurrency control, the recovery process may be more complex, depending on the protocols used for concurrency control. In many cases, the concurrency control and recovery processes are interrelated. In general, the greater the

(a)

T_1	T_2
read_item(A)	read_item(B)
read_item(D)	write_item(B)
write_item(D)	read_item(D)
	write_item(D)

(b)   [start_transaction, T_1]
      [write_item, T_1,D,20]
      [commit, T_1]
      [start_transaction, T_2]
      [write_item, T_2,B,10]
      [write_item, T_2,D,25] ←—system crash

The [write_item,....] operations of T_1 are redone.
T_2 log entries are ignored by the recovery process.

Figure 21.2   An example of recovery using deferred update in a single-user
environment. (a) The read and write operations of two transactions. (b) The system log at the point of crash.

degree of concurrency we wish to achieve, the more time consuming the task of recovery
becomes.

Consider a system in which concurrency control uses strict two-phase locking, so the
locks on items remain in effect *until the transaction reaches its commit point*. After that, the
locks can be released. This ensures strict and serializable schedules. Assuming that
[checkpoint] entries are included in the log, a possible recovery algorithm for this case,
which we call RDU_M (Recovery using Deferred Update in a Multi-user environment), is
given next. This procedure uses the REDO procedure defined earlier.

PROCEDURE RDU_M (WITH CHECKPOINTS): Use two lists of transactions maintained by the system: the committed transactions T since the last checkpoint (**commit list**), and the active transactions T' (**active list**). REDO all the WRITE operations
of the committed transactions from the log, *in the order in which they were written into
the log*. The transactions that are active and did not commit are effectively canceled
and must be resubmitted.

Figure 21.3 shows a possible schedule of executing transactions. When the checkpoint was taken at time t_1, transaction T_1 had committed, whereas transactions T_3 and T_4
had not. Before the system crash at time t_2, T_3 and T_2 were committed but not T_4 and T_5.
According to the RDU_M method, there is no need to redo the write_item operations of
transaction T_1—or any transactions committed before the last checkpoint time t_1.
Write_item operations of T_2 and T_3 must be redone, however, because both transactions
reached their commit points after the last checkpoint. Recall that the log is force-written
before committing a transaction. Transactions T_4 and T_5 are ignored: They are effectively
canceled or rolled back because none of their write_item operations were recorded in

Figure 21.3 An example of recovery in a multiuser environment.

the database under the deferred update protocol. We will refer to Figure 21.3 later to illustrate other recovery protocols.

We can make the NO-UNDO/REDO recovery algorithm *more efficient* by noting that, if a data item X has been updated—as indicated in the log entries—more than once by committed transactions since the last checkpoint, it is only necessary to REDO *the last update of* X from the log during recovery. The other updates would be overwritten by this last REDO in any case. In this case, we start from *the end of the log*; then, whenever an item is redone, it is added to a list of redone items. Before REDO is applied to an item, the list is checked; if the item appears on the list, it is not redone again, since its last value has already been recovered.

If a transaction is aborted for any reason (say, by the deadlock detection method), it is simply resubmitted, since it has not changed the database on disk. A drawback of the method described here is that it limits the concurrent execution of transactions because *all items remain locked until the transaction reaches its commit point*. In addition, it may require excessive buffer space to hold all updated items until the transactions commit. The method's main benefit is that transaction operations *never need to be undone*, for two reasons:

1. A transaction does not record any changes in the database on disk until after it reaches its commit point—that is, until it completes its execution successfully. Hence, a transaction is never rolled back because of failure during transaction execution.

2. A transaction will never read the value of an item that is written by an uncommitted transaction, because items remain locked until a transaction reaches its commit point. Hence, no cascading rollback will occur.

Figure 21.4 shows an example of recovery for a multiuser system that utilizes the recovery and concurrency control method just described.

	T_1	T_2	T_3	T_4
(a)	read_item(A)	read_item(B)	read_item(A)	read_item(B)
	read_item(D)	write_item(B)	write_item(A)	write_item(B)
	write_item(D)	read_item(D)	read_item(C)	read_item(A)
		write_item(D)	write_item(C)	write_item(A)

(b)   [start_transaction, T_1]

     [write_item, T_1, D, 20]

     [commit, T_1]

     [checkpoint]

     [start_transaction, T_4]

     [write_item, T_4, B, 15]

     [write_item, T_4, A, 20]

     [commit, T_4]

     [start_transaction, T_2]

     [write_item, T_2, B, 12]

     [start_transaction, T_3]

     [write_item, T_3, A, 30]

     [write_item, T_2, D, 25] ← system crash

T_2 and T_3 are ignored because they did not reach their commit points.
T_4 is redone because its commit point is after the last system checkpoint.

Figure 21.4 An example of recovery using deferred update with concurrent transactions. (a) The read and write operations of four transactions. (b) System log at the point of crash.

21.2.3 Transaction Actions That Do Not Affect the Database

In general, a transaction will have actions that do not affect the database, such as generating and printing messages or reports from information retrieved from the database. If a transaction fails before completion, we may not want the user to get these reports, since the transaction has failed to complete. If such erroneous reports are produced, part of the recovery process would have to inform the user that these reports are wrong, since the user may take an action based on these reports that affects the database. Hence, such reports should be generated only *after the transaction reaches its commit point*. A common method of dealing with such actions is to issue the commands that generate the reports but keep them as batch jobs, which are executed only after the transaction reaches its commit point. If the transaction fails, the batch jobs are canceled.

21.3   Recovery Techniques Based on Immediate Update

In these techniques, when a transaction issues an update command, the database can be updated "immediately," without any need to wait for the transaction to reach its commit point. In these techniques, however, an update operation must still be recorded in the log (on disk) *before* it is applied to the database—using the write-ahead logging protocol—so that we can recover in case of failure.

Provisions must be made for *undoing* the effect of update operations that have been applied to the database by a *failed transaction*. This is accomplished by rolling back the transaction and undoing the effect of the transaction's write_item operations. Theoretically, we can distinguish two main categories of immediate update algorithms. If the recovery technique ensures that all updates of a transaction are recorded in the database on disk *before the transaction commits*, there is never a need to REDO any operations of committed transactions. This is called the **UNDO/NO-REDO recovery algorithm.** On the other hand, if the transaction is allowed to commit before all its changes are written to the database, we have the most general case, known as the **UNDO/REDO recovery algorithm.** This is also the most complex technique. Next, we discuss two examples of UNDO/REDO algorithms and leave it as an exercise for the reader to develop the UNDO/NO-REDO variation. In Section 21.5, we describe a more practical approach known as the ARIES recovery technique.

21.3.1   UNDO/REDO Recovery Based on Immediate Update in a Single-User Environment

In a single-user system, if a failure occurs, the executing (active) transaction at the time of failure may have recorded some changes in the database. The effect of all such operations must be undone. The recovery algorithm RIU_S (Recovery using Immediate Update in a Single-user environment) uses the REDO procedure defined earlier, as well as the UNDO procedure defined below.

PROCEDURE RIU_S

1. Use two lists of transactions maintained by the system: the committed transactions since the last checkpoint and the active transactions (at most one transaction will fall in this category, because the system is single-user).

2. Undo all the write_item operations of the *active* transaction from the log, using the UNDO procedure described below.

3. Redo the write_item operations of the *committed* transactions from the log, in the order in which they were written in the log, using the REDO procedure described earlier.

The UNDO procedure is defined as follows:

UNDO(WRITE_OP): Undoing a `write_item` operation `WRITE_OP` consists of examining its log entry [`write_item`, T, X, `old_value`, `new_value`] and setting the value of item X in the database to `old_value` which is the before image (BFIM). Undoing a number of `write_item` operations from one or more transactions from the log must proceed in the *reverse order* from the order in which the operations were written in the log.

21.3.2 UNDO/REDO Recovery Based on Immediate Update with Concurrent Execution

When concurrent execution is permitted, the recovery process again depends on the protocols used for concurrency control. The procedure RIU_M (Recovery using Immediate Updates for a Multiuser environment) outlines a recovery algorithm for concurrent transactions with immediate update. Assume that the log includes checkpoints and that the concurrency control protocol produces *strict schedules*—as, for example, the strict two-phase locking protocol does. Recall that a strict schedule does not allow a transaction to read or write an item unless the transaction that last wrote the item has committed (or aborted and rolled back). However, deadlocks can occur in strict two-phase locking, thus requiring abort and UNDO of transactions. For a strict schedule, UNDO of an operation requires changing the item back to its old value (BFIM).

PROCEDURE RIU_M

1. Use two lists of transactions maintained by the system: the committed transactions since the last checkpoint and the active transactions.

2. Undo all the `write_item` operations of the *active* (uncommitted) transactions, using the UNDO procedure. The operations should be undone in the reverse of the order in which they were written into the log.

3. Redo all the `write_item` operations of the *committed* transactions from the log, in the order in which they were written into the log.

As we discussed in Section 21.2.2, Step 3 is more efficiently done by starting from the *end of the log* and redoing only *the last update of each item* X. Whenever an item is redone, it is added to a list of redone items and is not redone again.

21.4 Shadow Paging

This recovery scheme does not require the use of a log in a single-user environment. In a multiuser environment, a log may be needed for the concurrency control method. Shadow paging considers the database to be made up of a number of fixed-size disk pages

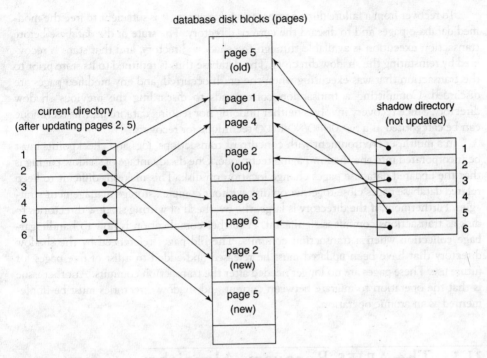

database disk blocks (pages)

current directory
(after updating pages 2, 5)

shadow directory
(not updated)

1	
2	
3	
4	
5	
6	

page 5
(old)

page 1

page 4

page 2
(old)

page 3

page 6

page 2
(new)

page 5
(new)

	1
	2
	3
	4
	5
	6

Figure 21.5   An example of shadow paging.

(or disk blocks)—say, n—for recovery purposes. A **directory** with n entries[5] is constructed, where the ith entry points to the ith database page on disk. The directory is kept in main memory if it is not too large, and all references—reads or writes—to database pages on disk go through it. When a transaction begins executing, the **current directory**—whose entries point to the most recent or current database pages on disk—is copied into a **shadow directory.** The shadow directory is then saved on disk while the current directory is used by the transaction.

During transaction execution, the shadow directory is *never* modified. When a write_item operation is performed, a new copy of the modified database page is created, but the old copy of that page is *not overwritten*. Instead, the new page is written elsewhere—on some previously unused disk block. The current directory entry is modified to point to the new disk block, whereas the shadow directory is not modified and continues to point to the old unmodified disk block. Figure 21.5 illustrates the concepts of shadow and current directories. For pages updated by the transaction, two versions are kept. The old version is referenced by the shadow directory, and the new version by the current directory.

---

5. The directory is similar to the **page table** maintained by the operating system for each process.

To recover from a failure during transaction execution, it is sufficient to free the modified database pages and to discard the current directory. The state of the database before transaction execution is available through the shadow directory, and that state is recovered by reinstating the shadow directory. The database thus is returned to its state prior to the transaction that was executing when the crash occurred, and any modified pages are discarded. Committing a transaction corresponds to discarding the previous shadow directory. Since recovery involves neither undoing nor redoing data items, this technique can be categorized as a NO-UNDO/NO-REDO technique for recovery.

In a multiuser environment with concurrent transactions, logs and checkpoints must be incorporated into the shadow paging technique. One disadvantage of shadow paging is that the updated database pages change location on disk. This makes it difficult to keep related database pages close together on disk without complex storage management strategies. Furthermore, if the directory is large, the overhead of writing shadow directories to disk as transactions commit is significant. A further complication is how to handle **garbage collection** when a transaction commits. The old pages referenced by the shadow directory that have been updated must be released and added to a list of free pages for future use. These pages are no longer needed after the transaction commits. Another issue is that the operation to migrate between current and shadow directories must be implemented as an atomic operation.

21.5   The ARIES Recovery Algorithm

We now describe the ARIES algorithm as an example of a recovery algorithm used in database systems. ARIES uses a steal/no-force approach for writing, and it is based on three concepts: (1) write-ahead logging, (2) repeating history during redo, and (3) logging changes during undo. We already discussed write-ahead logging in Section 21.1.3. The second concept, **repeating history,** means that ARIES will retrace all actions of the database system prior to the crash to reconstruct the database state *when the crash occurred.* Transactions that were uncommitted at the time of the crash (active transactions) are undone. The third concept, **logging during undo,** will prevent ARIES from repeating the completed undo operations if a failure occurs during recovery, which causes a restart of the recovery process.

The ARIES recovery procedure consists of three main steps: (1) analysis, (2) REDO and (3) UNDO. The **analysis step** identifies the dirty (updated) pages in the buffer,[6] and the set of transactions active at the time of the crash. The appropriate point in the log where the REDO operation should start is also determined. The **REDO phase** actually reapplies updates from the log to the database. Generally, the REDO operation is applied to only committed transactions. However, in ARIES, this is not the case. Certain information in the ARIES log will provide the start point for REDO, from which REDO operations are

---

6. The actual buffers may be lost during a crash, since they are in main memory. Additional tables stored in the log during checkpointing (Dirty Page Table, Transaction Table) allow ARIES to identify this information (see below).

applied until the end of the log is reached. In addition, information stored by ARIES and in the data pages will allow ARIES to determine whether the operation to be redone has actually been applied to the database and hence need not be reapplied. Thus *only the necessary REDO operations* are applied during recovery. Finally, during the UNDO **phase,** the log is scanned backwards and the operations of transactions that were active at the time of the crash are undone in reverse order. The information needed for ARIES to accomplish its recovery procedure includes the log, the Transaction Table, and the Dirty Page Table. In addition, checkpointing is used. These two tables are maintained by the transaction manager and written to the log during checkpointing.

In ARIES, every log record has an associated **log sequence number (LSN)** that is monotonically increasing and indicates the address of the log record on disk. Each LSN corresponds to a *specific change* (action) of some transaction. In addition, each data page will store the LSN of the *latest log record corresponding to a change for that page*. A log record is written for any of the following actions: updating a page (write), committing a transaction (commit), aborting a transaction (abort), undoing an update (undo), and ending a transaction (end). The need for including the first three actions in the log has been discussed, but the last two need some explanation. When an update is undone, a *compensation log record* is written in the log. When a transaction ends, whether by committing or aborting, an *end log record* is written.

Common fields in all log records include: (1) the previous LSN for that transaction, (2) the transaction ID, and (3) the type of log record. The previous LSN is important because it links the log records (in reverse order) for each transaction. For an update (write) action, additional fields in the log record include: (4) the page ID for the page that includes the item, (5) the length of the updated item, (6) its offset from the beginning of the page, (7) the before image of the item, and (8) its after image.

Besides the log, two tables are needed for efficient recovery: the **Transaction Table** and the **Dirty Page Table,** which are maintained by the transaction manager. When a crash occurs, these tables are rebuilt in the analysis phase of recovery. The Transaction Table contains an entry for *each active transaction*, with information such as the transaction ID, transaction status, and the LSN of the most recent log record for the transaction. The Dirty Page Table contains an entry for each dirty page in the buffer, which includes the page ID and the LSN corresponding to the earliest update to that page.

Checkpointing in ARIES consists of the following: (1) writing a `begin_checkpoint` record to the log, (2) writing an `end_checkpoint` record to the log, and (3) writing *the LSN of* the `begin_checkpoint` record to a special file. This special file is accessed during recovery to locate the last checkpoint information. With the `end_checkpoint` record, the contents of both the Transaction Table and Dirty Page Table are appended to the end of the log. To reduce the cost, **fuzzy checkpointing** is used so that the DBMS can continue to execute transactions during checkpointing (see Section 21.1.4). In addition, the contents of the DBMS cache do not have to be flushed to disk during checkpoint, since the Transaction Table and Dirty Page Table—which are appended to the log on disk—contain the information needed for recovery. Notice that if a crash occurs during checkpointing, the special file will refer to the previous checkpoint, which is used for recovery.

After a crash, the ARIES recovery manager takes over. Information from the last checkpoint is first accessed through the special file. The **analysis phase** starts at the begin_checkpoint record and proceeds to the end of the log. When the end_checkpoint record is encountered, the Transaction Table and Dirty Page Table are accessed (recall that these tables were written in the log during checkpointing). During analysis, the log records being analyzed may cause modifications to these two tables. For instance, if an end log record was encountered for a transaction T in the Transaction Table, then the entry for T is deleted from that table. If some other type of log record is encountered for a transaction T', then an entry for T' is inserted into the Transaction Table, if not already present, and the last LSN field is modified. If the log record corresponds to a change for page P, then an entry would be made for page P (if not present in the table) and the associated LSN field would be modified. When the analysis phase is complete, the necessary information for REDO and UNDO has been compiled in the tables.

The **REDO phase** follows next. To reduce the amount of unnecessary work, ARIES starts redoing at a point in the log where it knows (for sure) that previous changes to dirty pages *have already been applied to the database on disk*. It can determine this by finding the smallest LSN, M, of all the dirty pages in the Dirty Page Table, which indicates the log position where ARIES needs to start the REDO phase. Any changes corresponding to a LSN $< M$, for redoable transactions, must have already been propagated to disk or already been overwritten in the buffer; otherwise, those dirty pages with that LSN would be in the buffer (and the Dirty Page Table). So, REDO starts at the log record with LSN = M and scans forward to the end of the log. For each change recorded in the log, the REDO algorithm would verify whether or not the change has to be reapplied. For example, if a change recorded in the log pertains to page P that is not in the Dirty Page Table, then this change is already on disk and need not be reapplied. Or, if a change recorded in the log (with LSN = N, say) pertains to page P and the Dirty Page Table contains an entry for P with LSN greater than N, then the change is already present. If neither of these two conditions hold, page P is read from disk and the LSN stored on that page, LSN(P), is compared with N. If $N <$ LSN(P), then the change has been applied and the page need not be rewritten to disk.

Once the REDO phase is finished, the database is in the exact state that it was in when the crash occurred. The set of active transactions—called the **undo_set**—has been identified in the Transaction Table during the analysis phase. Now, the UNDO **phase** proceeds by scanning backward from the end of the log and undoing the appropriate actions. A compensating log record is written for each action that is undone. The UNDO reads backward in the log until every action of the set of transactions in the undo_set has been undone. When this is completed, the recovery process is finished and normal processing can begin again.

Consider the recovery example shown in Figure 21.6. There are three transactions: T_1, T_2, and T_3. T_1 updates page C, T_2 updates pages B and C, and T_3 updates page A. Figure 21.6 (a) shows the partial contents of the log and (b) shows the contents of the Transaction Table and Dirty Page Table. Now, suppose that a crash occurs at this point. Since a checkpoint has occurred, the address of the associated begin_checkpoint record is retrieved, which is location 4. The analysis phase starts from location 4 until it reaches the end. The end_checkpoint record would contain the Transaction Table and Dirty Page table in Figure 21.6(b), and the analysis phase will further reconstruct these tables.

(a)

LSN	LAST_LSN	TRAN_ID	TYPE	PAGE_ID	OTHER INFORMATION
1	0	T1	update	C	...
2	0	T2	update	B	...
3	1	T1	commit		...
4	begin checkpoint				
5	end checkpoint				
6	0	T3	update	A	...
7	2	T2	update	C	...
8	7	T2	commit		...

(b)

TRANSACTION TABLE			DIRTY PAGE TABLE	
TRANSACTION ID	LAST LSN	STATUS	PAGE ID	LSN
T1	3	commit	C	1
T2	2	in progress	B	2

(c)

TRANSACTION TABLE			DIRTY PAGE TABLE	
TRANSACTION ID	LAST LSN	STATUS	PAGE ID	LSN
T1	3	commit	C	1
T2	8	commit	B	2
T3	6	in progress	A	6

Figure 21.6 An example of recovery in ARIES. (a) The log at point of crash.
(b) The Transaction and Dirty Page Tables at time of checkpoint.
(c) The Transaction and Dirty Page Tables after the analysis phase.

When the analysis phase encounters log record 6, a new entry for transaction T_3 is made in the Transaction Table and a new entry for page A is made in the Dirty Page table. After log record 8 is analyzed, the status of transaction T_2 is changed to committed in the Transaction Table. Figure 21.6(c) shows the two tables after the analysis phase.

For the REDO phase, the smallest LSN in the Dirty Page table is 1. Hence the REDO will start at log record 1 and proceed with the REDO of updates. The LSNs {1, 2, 6, 7} corresponding to the updates for pages C, B, A, and C, respectively, are not less than the LSNs of those pages (as shown in the Dirty Page table). So those data pages will be read again and the updates reapplied from the log (assuming the actual LSNs stored on those data pages are less then the corresponding log entry). At this point, the REDO phase is finished and the UNDO phase starts. From the Transaction Table (Figure 21.6c), UNDO is applied only to the active transaction T_3. The UNDO phase starts at log entry 6 (the last update for T_3) and proceeds backward in the log. The backward chain of updates for transaction T_3 (only log record 6 in this example) is followed and undone.

21.6   Recovery in Multidatabase Systems

So far, we have implicitly assumed that a transaction accesses a single database. In some cases a single transaction, called a **multidatabase transaction,** may require access to multiple databases. These databases may even be stored on different types of DBMSs; for example, some DBMSs may be relational, whereas others are object-oriented, hierarchical, or network DBMSs. In such a case, each DBMS involved in the multidatabase transaction may have its own recovery technique and transaction manager separate from those of the other DBMSs. This situation is somewhat similar to the case of a distributed database management system (see Chapter 24), where parts of the database reside at different sites that are connected by a communication network.

To maintain the atomicity of a multidatabase transaction, it is necessary to have a two-level recovery mechanism. A **global recovery manager,** or **coordinator,** is needed to maintain information needed for recovery, in addition to the local recovery managers and the information they maintain (log, tables). The coordinator usually follows a protocol called the **two-phase commit protocol,** whose two phases can be stated as follows:

- **Phase 1:** When all participating databases signal the coordinator that the part of the multidatabase transaction involving each has concluded, the coordinator sends a message "prepare for commit" to each participant to get ready for committing the transaction. Each participating database receiving that message will force-write all log records and needed information for local recovery to disk and then send a "ready to commit" or "OK" signal to the coordinator. If the force-writing to disk fails or the local transaction cannot commit for some reason, the participating database sends a "cannot commit" or "not OK" signal to the coordinator. If the coordinator does not receive a reply from a database within a certain time out interval, it assumes a "not OK" response.

- **Phase 2:** If *all* participating databases reply "OK," and the coordinator's vote is also "OK," the transaction is successful, and the coordinator sends a "commit" signal for the transaction to the participating databases. Because all the local effects of the transaction and information needed for local recovery have been recorded in the logs of the participating databases, recovery from failure is now possible. Each participating database completes transaction commit by writing a [commit] entry for the transaction in the log and permanently updating the database if needed. On the other hand, if one or more of the participating databases or the coordinator have a "not OK" response, the transaction has failed, and the coordinator sends a message to "roll back" or UNDO the local effect of the transaction to each participating database. This is done by undoing the transaction operations, using the log.

The net effect of the two-phase commit protocol is that either all participating databases commit the effect of the transaction or none of them do. In case any of the participants—or the coordinator—fails, it is always possible to recover to a state where either the transaction is committed or it is rolled back. A failure during or before Phase 1 usually requires the transaction to be rolled back, whereas a failure during Phase 2 means that a successful transaction can recover and commit.

21.7 Database Backup and Recovery from Catastrophic Failures

So far, all the techniques we have discussed apply to noncatastrophic failures. A key assumption has been that the system log is maintained on the disk and is not lost as a result of the failure. Similarly, the shadow directory must be stored on disk to allow recovery when shadow paging is used. The recovery techniques we have discussed use the entries in the system log or the shadow directory to recover from failure by bringing the database back to a consistent state.

The recovery manager of a DBMS must also be equipped to handle more catastrophic failures such as disk crashes. The main technique used to handle such crashes is that of **database backup.** The whole database and the log are periodically copied onto a cheap storage medium such as magnetic tapes. In case of a catastrophic system failure, the latest backup copy can be reloaded from the tape to the disk, and the system can be restarted.

To avoid losing all the effects of transactions that have been executed since the last backup, it is customary to back up the system log at more frequent intervals than full database backup by periodically copying it to magnetic tape. The system log is usually substantially smaller than the database itself and hence can be backed up more frequently. Thus users do not lose all transactions they have performed since the last database backup. All committed transactions recorded in the portion of the system log that has been backed up to tape can have their effect on the database redone. A new log is started after each database backup. Hence, to recover from disk failure, the database is first recreated on disk from its latest backup copy on tape. Following that, the effects of all the committed transactions whose operations have been recorded in the backed-up copies of the system log are reconstructed.

21.8 Summary

In this chapter we discussed the techniques for recovery from transaction failures. The main goal of recovery is to ensure the atomicity property of a transaction. If a transaction fails before completing its execution, the recovery mechanism has to make sure that the transaction has no lasting effects on the database. We first gave an informal outline for a recovery process and then discussed system concepts for recovery. These included a discussion of caching, in-place updating versus shadowing, before and after images of a data item, UNDO versus REDO recovery operations, steal/no-steal and force/no-force policies, system checkpointing, and the write-ahead logging protocol.

Next we discussed two different approaches to recovery: deferred update and immediate update. Deferred update techniques postpone any actual updating of the database on disk until a transaction reaches its commit point. The transaction force-writes the log to disk before recording the updates in the database. This approach, when used with certain concurrency control methods, is designed never to require transaction rollback, and recovery simply consists of redoing the operations of transactions committed after the last checkpoint from the log. The disadvantage is that too much buffer space may be needed, since updates are kept in the buffers and are not applied to disk until a transaction commits. Deferred update can lead to a recovery algorithm known as NO-UNDO/REDO. Immediate update techniques may apply changes to the database on disk before the transaction reaches a successful conclusion. Any changes applied to the database must first be recorded in the log and force-written to disk so that these operations can be undone if necessary. We also gave an overview of a recovery algorithm for immediate update known as UNDO/REDO. Another algorithm, known as UNDO/NO-REDO, can also be developed for immediate update if all transaction actions are recorded in the database before commit.

We discussed the shadow paging technique for recovery, which keeps track of old database pages by using a shadow directory. This technique, which is classified as NO-UNDO/NO-REDO, does not require a log in single-user systems but still needs the log for multiuser systems. We also presented ARIES, a specific recovery scheme used in some of IBM's relational database products. We then discussed the two-phase commit protocol, which is used for recovery from failures involving multidatabase transactions. Finally, we discussed recovery from catastrophic failures, which is typically done by backing up the database and the log to tape. The log can be backed up more frequently than the database, and the backup log can be used to redo operations starting from the last database backup.

Review Questions

21.1. Discuss the different types of transaction failures. What is meant by catastrophic failure?

21.2. Discuss the actions taken by the read_item and write_item operations on a database.

21.3. (*Review from Chapter 19*) What is the system log used for? What are the typical kinds of entries in a system log? What are checkpoints, and why are they important? What are transaction commit points, and why are they important?

21.4. How are buffering and caching techniques used by the recovery subsystem?

21.5. What are the before image (BFIM) and after image (AFIM) of a data item? What is the difference between in-place updating and shadowing, with respect to their handling of BFIM and AFIM?

21.6. What are UNDO-type and REDO-type log entries?

21.7. Describe the write-ahead logging protocol.

21.8. Identify three typical lists of transactions that are maintained by the recovery subsystem.

21.9. What is meant by transaction rollback? What is meant by cascading rollback? Why do practical recovery methods use protocols that do not permit cascading rollback? Which recovery techniques do not require any rollback?

21.10. Discuss the UNDO and REDO operations and the recovery techniques that use each.

21.11. Discuss the deferred update technique of recovery. What are the advantages and disadvantages of this technique? Why is it called the NO-UNDO/REDO method?

21.12. How can recovery handle transaction operations that do not affect the database, such as the printing of reports by a transaction?

21.13. Discuss the immediate update recovery technique in both single-user and multiuser environments. What are the advantages and disadvantages of immediate update?

21.14. What is the difference between the UNDO/REDO and the UNDO/NO-REDO algorithms for recovery with immediate update? Develop the outline for an UNDO/NO-REDO algorithm.

21.15. Describe the shadow paging recovery technique. Under what circumstances does it not require a log?

21.16. Describe the three phases of the ARIES recovery method.

21.17. What are log sequence numbers (LSNs) in ARIES? How are they used? What information does the Dirty Page Table and Transaction Table contain? Describe how fuzzy checkpointing is used in ARIES.

21.18. What do the terms steal/no-steal and force/no-force mean with regard to buffer management for transaction processing.

21.19. Describe the two-phase commit protocol for multidatabase transactions.

21.20. Discuss how recovery from catastrophic failures is handled.

Exercises

21.21. Suppose that the system crashes before the [read_item, T_3, A] entry is written to the log in Figure 21.1(b). Will that make any difference in the recovery process?

21.22. Suppose that the system crashes before the [write_item, T_2, D, 25, 26] entry is written to the log in Figure 21.1(b). Will that make any difference in the recovery process?

21.23. Figure 21.7 shows the log corresponding to a particular schedule at the point of a system crash for four transactions T_1, T_2, T_3, and T_4. Suppose that we use the *immediate update protocol* with checkpointing. Describe the recovery process from the system crash. Specify which transactions are rolled back, which operations in the log are redone and which (if any) are undone, and whether any cascading rollback takes place.

21.24. Suppose that we use the deferred update protocol for the example in Figure 21.7. Show how the log would be different in the case of deferred update by removing the unnecessary log entries; then describe the recovery process, using your modified log. Assume that only REDO operations are applied, and specify which operations in the log are redone and which are ignored.

21.25. How does checkpointing in ARIES differ from checkpointing as described in Section 21.1.4?

21.26. How are log sequence numbers used by ARIES to reduce the amount of REDO work needed for recovery? Illustrate with an example using the information shown in Figure 21.6. You can make your own assumptions as to when a page is written to disk.

21.27. What implications would a no-steal/force buffer management policy have on checkpointing and recovery?

[start_transaction, T_1]
[read_item, T_1, A]
[read_item, T_1, D]
[write_item, T_1, D, 20]
[commit, T_1]
[checkpoint]
[start_transaction, T_2]
[read_item, T_2, B]
[write_item, T_2, B, 12]
[start_transaction, T_4]
[read_item, T_4, D]
[write_item, T_4, D, 15]
[start_transaction, T_3]
[write_item, T_3, C, 30]
[read_item, T_4, A]
[write_item, T_4, A, 20]
[commit, T_4]
[read_item, T_2, D]
[write_item, T_2, D, 25] ← system crash

Figure 21.7   An example schedule and its corresponding log.

Choose the correct answer for each of the following multiple-choice questions:

21.28. Incremental logging with deferred updates implies that the recovery system must necessarily
   a. store the old value of the updated item in the log.
   b. store the new value of the updated item in the log.
   c. store both the old and new value of the updated item in the log.
   d. store only the Begin Transaction and Commit Transaction records in the log.

21.29. The write ahead logging (WAL) protocol simply means that
   a. the writing of a data item should be done ahead of any logging operation.
   b. the log record for an operation should be written before the actual data is written.
   c. all log records should be written before a new transaction begins execution.
   d. the log never needs to be written to disk.

21.30. In case of transaction failure under a deferred update incremental logging scheme, which of the following will be needed:
   a. an undo operation.
   b. a redo operation.
   c. an undo and redo operation.
   d. none of the above.

21.31. For incremental logging with immediate updates, a log record for a transaction would contain:
   a. a transaction name, data item name, old value of item, new value of item.
   b. a transaction name, data item name, old value of item.

c. a transaction name, data item name, new value of item.

d. a transaction name and a data item name.

21.32. For correct behavior during recovery, undo and redo operations must be

a. commutative.

b. associative.

c. idempotent.

d. distributive.

21.33. When a failure occurs, the log is consulted and each operation is either undone or redone. This is a problem because

a. searching the entire log is time consuming.

b. many redo's are unnecessary.

c. both (a) and (b).

d. none of the above.

21.34. When using a log based recovery scheme, it might improve performance as well as providing a recovery mechanism by

a. writing the log records to disk when each transaction commits.

b. writing the appropriate log records to disk during the transaction's execution.

c. waiting to write the log records until multiple transactions commit and writing them as a batch.

d. never writing the log records to disk.

21.35. There is a possibility of a cascading rollback when

a. a transaction writes items that have been written only by a committed transaction.

b. a transaction writes an item that is previously written by an uncommitted transaction.

c. a transaction reads an item that is previously written by an uncommitted transaction.

d. both (b) and (c).

21.36. To cope with media (disk) failures, it is necessary

a. for the DBMS to only execute transactions in a single user environment.

b. to keep a redundant copy of the database.

c. to never abort a transaction.

d. all of the above.

21.37. If the shadowing approach is used for flushing a data item back to disk, then

a. the item is written to disk only after the transaction commits.

b. the item is written to a different location on disk.

c. the item is written to disk before the transaction commits.

d. the item is written to the same disk location from which it was read.

Selected Bibliography

The books by Bernstein et al. (1987) and Papadimitriou (1986) are devoted to the theory and principles of concurrency control and recovery. The book by Gray and Reuter (1993) is an encyclopedic work on concurrency control, recovery, and other transaction-processing issues.

Verhofstad (1978) presents a tutorial and survey of recovery techniques in database systems. Categorizing algorithms based on their UNDO/REDO characteristics is discussed in Haerder and Reuter (1983) and in Bernstein et al. (1983). Gray (1978) discusses recovery, along with other system aspects of implementing operating systems for databases. The shadow paging technique is discussed in Lorie (1977), Verhofstad (1978), and Reuter (1980). Gray et al. (1981) discuss the recovery mechanism in SYSTEM R. Lockeman and Knutsen (1968), Davies (1972), and Bjork (1973) are early papers that discuss recovery. Chandy et al. (1975) discuss transaction rollback. Lilien and Bhargava (1985) discuss the concept of integrity block and its use to improve the efficiency of recovery.

Recovery using write-ahead logging is analyzed in Jhingran and Khedkar (1992) and is used in the ARIES system (Mohan et al. 1992a). More recent work on recovery includes compensating transactions (Korth et al. 1990) and main memory database recovery (Kumar 1991). The ARIES recovery algorithms (Mohan et al. 1992) have been quite successful in practice. Franklin et al. (1992) discusses recovery in the EXODUS system. Two recent books by Kumar and Hsu (1998) and Kumar and Son (1998) discuss recovery in detail and contain descriptions of recovery methods used in a number of existing relational database products.

persons. In the United States there are numerous laws governing privacy of information.

• Policy issues at the governmental, institutional, or corporate level as to what kinds of
information should not be made publicly available—for example, credit ratings and
personal medical records.

• System-related issues such as the system levels at which various security functions
should be enforced—for example, whether a security function should be handled at
the physical hardware level, the operating system level, or the DBMS level.

• The need in some organizations to identify multiple security levels and to categorize
the data and users based on these classifications—for example, top secret, secret, confidential, and unclassified. The security policy of the organization with respect to permitting access to various classifications of data must be enforced.

The multiple mechanisms provided by the DBMS that provide techniques to secure certain
areas relate to the access of selected portions of a database without a written authorization.
The security of a part of the database is particularly important when a large integrated database is
to be used by many different users within the same organization. For example, sensitive
information such as employee salaries or performance reviews should be kept confidential
from most of the database system's users. A DBMS typically includes a database security
and authorization subsystem that is responsible for ensuring the security of portions of a
database against unauthorized access. It is now customary to refer to two types of database
security mechanisms:

• The security mechanisms of hardware. These are used to grant privileges to users, including the capability to access specific data files, records, or fields in a specified mode
(such as read, insert, delete, or update).

• Mandatory security mechanisms serve to enforce multilevel security by classifying the
data and users into various security classes (or levels) and then implementing the
appropriate security policy of the organization. For example, a typical security policy
is to permit users at a certain classification level to see only the data items classified at
the user's own (or lower) classification level. As we shall see, an extension of this is the
role-based security, which enforces policies and privileges based on the concept of roles.

We first discuss the basic concepts of database security in Section 22.1. We then discuss the mechanisms used to grant and revoke privileges in relational database systems and
in SQL in Section 22.2—mechanisms that are often referred to as discretionary access control. In Section 22.3, we present an overview of the mechanisms for enforcing multiple levels of security—a more recent concern in database system security that is known as
mandatory access control. We also introduce the recently proposed technique for role-
based security. Section 22.4 briefly discusses the security problem in statistical databases.
In Section 22.5 we discuss the security issue of flow control, and in Section 22.6 we discuss
how to remove selected information and still preserve a certain degree of confidentiality.

22.1 Introduction to Database Security Issues

22.1.1 Types of Security

Database security is a very broad area that addresses many issues, including the following:

• Legal and ethical issues regarding the right to access certain information. Some information may be deemed to be private and cannot be accessed legally by unauthorized

persons. In the United States, there are numerous laws governing privacy of information.

- Policy issues at the governmental, institutional, or corporate level as to what kinds of information should not be made publicly available—for example, credit ratings and personal medical records.

- System-related issues such as the *system levels* at which various security functions should be enforced—for example, whether a security function should be handled at the physical hardware level, the operating system level, or the DBMS level.

- The need in some organizations to identify multiple *security levels* and to categorize the data and users based on these classifications—for example, top secret, secret, confidential, and unclassified. The security policy of the organization with respect to permitting access to various classifications of data must be enforced.

In a multiuser database system, the DBMS must provide techniques to enable certain users or user groups to access selected portions of a database without gaining access to the rest of the database. This is particularly important when a large integrated database is to be used by many different users within the same organization. For example, sensitive information such as employee salaries or performance reviews should be kept confidential from most of the database system's users. A DBMS typically includes a **database security and authorization subsystem** that is responsible for ensuring the security of portions of a database against unauthorized access. It is now customary to refer to two types of database security mechanisms:

- *Discretionary security mechanisms:* These are used to grant privileges to users, including the capability to access specific data files, records, or fields in a specified mode (such as read, insert, delete, or update).

- *Mandatory security mechanisms:* These are used to enforce multilevel security by classifying the data and users into various security classes (or levels) and then implementing the appropriate security policy of the organization. For example, a typical security policy is to permit users at a certain classification level to see only the data items classified at the user's own (or lower) classification level.

We discuss discretionary security in Section 22.2 and mandatory security in Section 22.3.

A second security problem common to all computer systems is that of preventing unauthorized persons from accessing the system itself—either to obtain information or to make malicious changes in a portion of the database. The security mechanism of a DBMS must include provisions for restricting access to the database system as a whole. This function is called **access control** and is handled by creating user accounts and passwords to control the log-in process by the DBMS. We discuss access control techniques in Section 22.1.3.

A third security problem associated with databases is that of controlling the access to a **statistical database,** which is used to provide statistical information or summaries of values based on various criteria. For example, a database for population statistics may provide statistics based on age groups, income levels, size of household, education levels, and other criteria. Statistical database users such as government statisticians or market research firms are allowed to access the database to retrieve statistical information about a population but not to access the detailed confidential information on specific individuals. Security for statistical databases must ensure that information on individuals cannot be accessed. It is sometimes possible to deduce certain facts concerning individuals from queries that involve only summary statistics on groups; consequently this must not be permitted either. This problem, called **statistical database security,** is discussed briefly in Section 22.4.

A fourth security issue is **data encryption,** which is used to protect sensitive data—such as credit card numbers—that is being transmitted via some type of communications network. Encryption can be used to provide additional protection for sensitive portions of a database as well. The data is **encoded** by using some coding algorithm. An unauthorized user who accesses encoded data will have difficulty deciphering it, but authorized users are given decoding or decrypting algorithms (or keys) to decipher the data. Encrypting techniques that are very difficult to decode without a key have been developed for military applications. We will not discuss encryption algorithms here.

A complete discussion of security in computer systems and databases is outside the scope of this textbook. We give only a brief overview of database security techniques here. The interested reader can refer to one of the references at the end of this chapter for a more comprehensive discussion.

22.1.2 Database Security and the DBA

As we discussed in Chapter 1, the database administrator (DBA) is the central authority for managing a database system. The DBA's responsibilities include granting privileges to users who need to use the system and classifying users and data in accordance with the policy of the organization. The DBA has a **DBA account** in the DBMS, sometimes called a **system** or **superuser account,** which provides powerful capabilities that are not made available to regular database accounts and users.[1] DBA privileged commands include commands for granting and revoking privileges to individual accounts, users, or user groups and for performing the following types of actions:

1. *Account creation:* This action creates a new account and password for a user or a group of users to enable them to access the DBMS.

2. *Privilege granting:* This action permits the DBA to grant certain privileges to certain accounts.

3. *Privilege revocation:* This action permits the DBA to revoke (cancel) certain privileges that were previously given to certain accounts.

4. *Security level assignment:* This action consists of assigning user accounts to the appropriate security classification level.

The DBA is responsible for the overall security of the database system. Action 1 in the preceding list is used to control access to the DBMS as a whole, whereas actions 2 and 3 are used to control *discretionary* database authorizations, and action 4 is used to control *mandatory* authorization.

---

1. This account is similar to the *root* or *superuser* accounts that are given to computer system administrators, allowing access to restricted operating systems commands.

22.1.3   Access Protection, User Accounts, and Database Audits

Whenever a person or a group of persons needs to access a database system, the individual or group must first apply for a user account. The DBA will then create a new **account number** and **password** for the user if there is a legitimate need to access the database. The user must **log in** to the DBMS by entering the account number and password whenever database access is needed. The DBMS checks that the account number and password are valid; if they are, the user is permitted to use the DBMS and to access the database. Application programs can also be considered as users and can be required to supply passwords.

It is straightforward to keep track of database users and their accounts and passwords by creating an encrypted table or file with the two fields AccountNumber and Password. This table can easily be maintained by the DBMS. Whenever a new account is created, a new record is inserted into the table. When an account is canceled, the corresponding record must be deleted from the table.

The database system must also keep track of all operations on the database that are applied by a certain user throughout each **log-in session,** which consists of the sequence of database interactions that a user performs from the time of logging in to the time of logging off. When a user logs in, the DBMS can record the user's account number and associate it with the terminal from which the user logged in. All operations applied from that terminal are attributed to the user's account until the user logs off. It is particularly important to keep track of update operations that are applied to the database so that, if the database is tampered with, the DBA can find out which user did the tampering.

To keep a record of all updates applied to the database and of the particular user who applied each update, we can modify the *system log*. Recall from Chapters 19 and 21 that the **system log** includes an entry for each operation applied to the database that may be required for recovery from a transaction failure or system crash. We can expand the log entries so that they also include the account number of the user and the on-line terminal ID that applied each operation recorded in the log. If any tampering with the database is suspected, a **database audit** is performed, which consists of reviewing the log to examine all accesses and operations applied to the database during a certain time period. When an illegal or unauthorized operation is found, the DBA can determine the account number used to perform this operation. Database audits are particularly important for sensitive databases that are updated by many transactions and users, such as a banking database that is updated by many bank tellers. A database log that is used mainly for security purposes is sometimes called an **audit trail.**

22.2   Discretionary Access Control Based on Granting/Revoking of Privileges

The typical method of enforcing **discretionary access control** in a database system is based on the granting and revoking of **privileges.** Let us consider privileges in the context of a relational DBMS. In particular, we will discuss a system of privileges somewhat similar to the one originally developed for the SQL language (see Chapter 8). Many current relational DBMSs use some variation of this technique. The main idea is to include additional statements in the query language that allow the DBA and selected users to grant and revoke privileges.

22.2.1 Types of Discretionary Privileges

In SQL2, the concept of **authorization identifier** is used to refer, roughly speaking, to a user account (or group of user accounts). For simplicity, we will use the words **user** or **account** interchangeably in place of authorization identifier. The DBMS must provide selective access to each relation in the database based on specific accounts. Operations may also be controlled; thus having an account does not necessarily entitle the account holder to all the functionality provided by the DBMS. Informally, there are two levels for assigning privileges to use the database system:

1. *The account level:* At this level, the DBA specifies the particular privileges that each account holds independently of the relations in the database.

2. *The relation (or table) level:* At this level, we can control the privilege to access each individual relation or view in the database.

The privileges at the **account level** apply to the capabilities provided to the account itself and can include the CREATE SCHEMA or CREATE TABLE privilege, to create a schema or base relation; the CREATE VIEW privilege; the ALTER privilege, to apply schema changes such as adding or removing attributes from relations; the DROP privilege, to delete relations or views; the MODIFY privilege, to insert, delete, or update tuples; and the SELECT privilege, to retrieve information from the database by using a SELECT query. Notice that these account privileges apply to the account in general. If a certain account does not have the CREATE TABLE privilege, no relations can be created from that account. Account-level privileges *are not* defined as part of SQL2; they are left to the DBMS implementers to define. In earlier versions of SQL, a CREATETAB privilege existed to give an account the privilege to create tables (relations).

The second level of privileges applies to the **relation level,** whether they are base relations or virtual (view) relations. These privileges *are* defined for SQL2. In the following discussion, the term *relation* may refer either to a base relation or to a view, unless we explicitly specify one or the other. Privileges at the relation level specify for each user the individual relations on which each type of command can be applied. Some privileges also refer to individual columns (attributes) of relations. SQL2 commands provide privileges at the *relation and attribute level only.* Although this is quite general, it makes it difficult to create accounts with limited privileges. The granting and revoking of privileges generally follows an authorization model for discretionary privileges known as the **access matrix model,** where the rows of a matrix M represent *subjects* (users, accounts, programs) and the columns represent *objects* (relations, records, columns, views, operations). Each position tion $M(i, j)$ in the matrix represents the types of privileges (read, write, update) that subject i holds on object j.

To control the granting and revoking of relation privileges, each relation R in a database is assigned an **owner account,** which is typically the account that was used when the relation was created in the first place. The owner of a relation is given *all* privileges on that relation. In SQL2, the DBA can assign an owner to a whole schema by creating the schema and associating the appropriate authorization identifier with that schema, using the CREATE SCHEMA command (see Section 8.1.1). The owner account holder can pass privileges on any of the owned relations to other users by **granting** privileges to their accounts. In SQL the following types of privileges can be granted on each individual relation R:

- SELECT (retrieval or read) privilege on R: Gives the account retrieval privilege. In SQL this gives the account the privilege to use the SELECT statement to retrieve tuples from R.

- MODIFY privileges on R: This gives the account the capability to modify tuples of R. In SQL this privilege is further divided into UPDATE, DELETE, and INSERT privileges to apply the corresponding SQL command to R. In addition, both the INSERT and UPDATE privileges can specify that only certain attributes of R can be updated by the account.

- REFERENCES privilege on R: This gives the account the capability to reference relation R when specifying integrity constraints. This privilege can also be restricted to specific attributes of R.

Notice that to create a view, the account must have SELECT privilege on *all relations* involved in the view definition.

22.2.2   Specifying Privileges Using Views

The mechanism of **views** is an important discretionary authorization mechanism in its own right. For example, if the owner A of a relation R wants another account B to be able to retrieve only some fields of R, then A can create a view V of R that includes only those attributes and then grant SELECT on V to B. The same applies to limiting B to retrieving only certain tuples of R; a view V′ can be created by defining the view by means of a query that selects only those tuples from R that A wants to allow B to access. We shall illustrate this discussion with the example given in Section 22.2.5.

22.2.3   Revoking Privileges

In some cases it is desirable to grant some privilege to a user temporarily. For example, the owner of a relation may want to grant the SELECT privilege to a user for a specific task and then revoke that privilege once the task is completed. Hence, a mechanism for **revoking** privileges is needed. In SQL a REVOKE command is included for the purpose of canceling privileges. We will see how the REVOKE command is used in the example in Section 22.2.5.

22.2.4   Propagation of Privileges Using the GRANT OPTION

Whenever the owner A of a relation R grants a privilege on R to another account B, the privilege can be given to B *with* or *without* the GRANT OPTION. If the GRANT OPTION is given, this means that B can also grant that privilege on R to other accounts. Suppose that B is given the GRANT OPTION by A and that B then grants the privilege on R to a third account C, also with GRANT OPTION. In this way, privileges on R can **propagate** to other accounts without the knowledge of the owner of R. If the owner account A now revokes the privilege granted to B, all the privileges that B propagated based on that privilege should automatically be revoked by the system.

It is possible for a user to receive a certain privilege from two or more sources. For example, $A4$ may receive a certain UPDATE R privilege from *both* $A2$ and $A3$. In such a case, if $A2$ revokes this privilege from $A4$, $A4$ will still continue to have the privilege by virtue of having been granted it from $A3$. If $A3$ later revokes the privilege from $A4$, $A4$ totally loses the privilege. Hence, a DBMS that allows propagation of privileges must keep track of how all the privileges were granted so that revoking of privileges can be done correctly and completely.

22.2.5 An Example

Suppose that the DBA creates four accounts—$A1$, $A2$, $A3$, and $A4$—and wants only $A1$ to be able to create base relations; then the DBA must issue the following GRANT command in SQL:

> **GRANT** CREATETAB **TO** A1;

The CREATETAB (create table) privilege gives account $A1$ the capability to create new database tables (base relations) and is hence an *account privilege*. This privilege was part of earlier versions of SQL but is now left to each individual system implementation to define. In SQL2, the same effect can be accomplished by having the DBA issue a CREATE SCHEMA command, as follows:

> **CREATE SCHEMA** EXAMPLE **AUTHORIZATION** A1;

Now user account $A1$ can create tables under the schema called EXAMPLE. To continue our example, suppose that $A1$ creates the two base relations EMPLOYEE and DEPARTMENT shown in Figure 22.1; then $A1$ is the **owner** of these two relations and hence has *all the relation privileges* on each of them.

Next, suppose that account $A1$ wants to grant to account $A2$ the privilege to insert and delete tuples in both of these relations. However, $A1$ does not want $A2$ to be able to

EMPLOYEE

NAME	SSN	BDATE	ADDRESS	SEX	SALARY	DNO

DEPARTMENT

DNUMBER	DNAME	MGRSSN

Figure 22.1 Schemas for the two relations EMPLOYEE and DEPARTMENT.

propagate these privileges to additional accounts. Then A1 can issue the following command:

> **GRANT** INSERT, DELETE **ON** EMPLOYEE, DEPARTMENT **TO** A2;

Notice that the owner account A1 of a relation automatically has the GRANT OPTION, allowing it to grant privileges on the relation to other accounts. However, account A2 cannot grant INSERT and DELETE privileges on the EMPLOYEE and DEPARTMENT tables, because A2 was not given the GRANT OPTION in the preceding command.

Next, suppose that A1 wants to allow account A3 to retrieve information from either of the two tables and also to be able to propagate the SELECT privilege to other accounts. Then A1 can issue the following command:

> **GRANT** SELECT **ON** EMPLOYEE, DEPARTMENT **TO** A3 **WITH GRANT OPTION**;

The clause WITH GRANT OPTION means that A3 can now propagate the privilege to other accounts by using GRANT. For example, A3 can grant the SELECT privilege on the EMPLOYEE relation to A4 by issuing the following command:

> **GRANT** SELECT **ON** EMPLOYEE **TO** A4;

Notice that A4 cannot propagate the SELECT privilege to other accounts because the GRANT OPTION was not given to A4. Now suppose that A1 decides to revoke the SELECT privilege on the EMPLOYEE relation from A3; A1 then can issue this command:

> **REVOKE** SELECT **ON** EMPLOYEE **FROM** A3;

The DBMS must now automatically revoke the SELECT privilege on EMPLOYEE from A4, too, because A3 granted that privilege to A4 and A3 does not have the privilege any more. Next, suppose that A1 wants to give back to A3 a limited capability to SELECT from the EMPLOYEE relation and wants to allow A3 to be able to propagate the privilege. The limitation is to retrieve only the NAME, BDATE, and ADDRESS attributes and only for the tuples with DNO = 5. A1 then can create the following view:

> **CREATE VIEW** A3EMPLOYEE **AS**
>   **SELECT** NAME, BDATE, ADDRESS
>   **FROM** EMPLOYEE
>   **WHERE** DNO = 5;

After the view is created, A1 can grant SELECT on the view A3EMPLOYEE to A3 as follows:

> **GRANT** SELECT **ON** A3EMPLOYEE **TO** A3 **WITH GRANT OPTION**;

Finally, suppose that A1 wants to allow A4 to update only the SALARY attribute of EMPLOYEE; A1 can then issue the following command:

> **GRANT** UPDATE **ON** EMPLOYEE (SALARY) **TO** A4;

The UPDATE or INSERT privilege can specify particular attributes that may be updated or inserted in a relation. Other privileges (SELECT, DELETE) are not attribute-specific, as this specificity can easily be controlled by creating the appropriate views that include only the desired attributes and granting the corresponding privileges on the views. However, because updating views is not always possible (see Chapter 8), the UPDATE and INSERT privileges are given the option to specify particular attributes of a base relation that may be updated.

22.2.6 Specifying Limits on Propagation of Privileges

Techniques to limit the propagation of privileges have been developed, although they have not yet been implemented in most DBMSs and are not a part of SQL. Limiting **horizontal propagation** to an integer number i means that an account B given the GRANT OPTION can grant the privilege to at most i other accounts. **Vertical propagation** is more complicated; it limits the depth of the granting of privileges. Granting a privilege with vertical propagation of zero is equivalent to granting the privilege with *no* GRANT OPTION. If account A grants a privilege to account B with vertical propagation set to an integer number $j > 0$, this means that the account B has the GRANT OPTION on that privilege, but B can grant the privilege to other accounts only with a vertical propagation *less than j*. In effect, vertical propagation limits the sequence of grant options that can be given from one account to the next based on a single original grant of the privilege.

We now briefly illustrate horizontal and vertical propagation limits—which are *not available* currently in SQL or other relational systems—with an example. Suppose that A1 grants SELECT to A2 on the EMPLOYEE relation with horizontal propagation = 1 and vertical propagation = 2. A2 can then grant SELECT to at most one account because the horizontal propagation limitation is set to 1. In addition, A2 cannot grant the privilege to another account except with vertical propagation = 0 (no GRANT OPTION) or 1; this is because A2 must reduce the vertical propagation by at least 1 when passing the privilege to others. As this example shows, horizontal and vertical propagation techniques are designed to limit the propagation of privileges.

22.3 Mandatory Access Control for Multilevel Security

The discretionary access control technique of granting and revoking privileges on relations has traditionally been the main security mechanism for relational database systems. This is an all-or-nothing method: a user either has or does not have a certain privilege. In many applications, an *additional security policy* is needed that classifies data and users based on security classes. This approach—known as **mandatory access control**—would typically be *combined* with the discretionary access control mechanisms described in Section 22.2. It is important to note that most commercial DBMSs currently provide mechanisms only for discretionary access control. However, the need for multilevel security exists in government, military, and intelligence applications, as well as in many industrial and corporate applications.

Typical **security classes** are top secret (TS), secret (S), confidential (C), and unclassified (U), where TS is the highest level and U the lowest. Other more complex security classification schemes exist, in which the security classes are organized in a lattice. For simplicity, we will use the system with four security classification levels, where TS ≥ S ≥ C ≥ U, to illustrate our discussion. The commonly used model for multilevel security, known as the Bell-LaPadula model, classifies each **subject** (user, account, program) and **object** (relation, tuple, column, view, operation) into one of the security classifications TS, S, C, or U. We will refer to the **clearance** (classification) of a subject S as **class(S)** and to the **classification** of an object O as **class(O).** Two restrictions are enforced on data access based on the subject/object classifications:

1. A subject S is not allowed read access to an object O unless class(S) ≥ class(O). This is known as the **simple security property.**
2. A subject S is not allowed to write an object O unless class(S) ≤ class(O). This is known as the ***-property** (or **star property**).

The first restriction is intuitive and enforces the obvious rule that no subject can read an object whose security classification is higher than the subject's security clearance. The second restriction is less intuitive. It prohibits a subject from writing an object at a lower security classification than the subject's security clearance. Violation of this rule would allow information to flow from higher to lower classifications, which violates a basic tenet of multilevel security. For example, a user (subject) with TS clearance may make a copy of an object with classification TS and then write it back as a new object with classification U, thus making it visible throughout the system.

To incorporate multilevel security notions into the relational database model, it is common to consider attribute values and tuples as data objects. Hence, each attribute A is associated with a **classification attribute** C in the schema, and each attribute value in a tuple is associated with a corresponding security classification. In addition, in some models, a **tuple classification** attribute TC is added to the relation attributes to provide a classification for each tuple as a whole. Hence, a **multilevel** relation schema R with n attributes would be represented as

$$R(A_1, C_1, A_2, C_2, ..., A_n, C_n, TC)$$

where each C_i represents the *classification attribute* associated with attribute A_i.

The value of the TC attribute in each tuple t—which is the *highest* of all attribute classification values within t—provides a general classification for the tuple itself, whereas each C_i provides a finer security classification for each attribute value within the tuple. The **apparent key** of a multilevel relation is the set of attributes that would have formed the primary key in a regular (single-level) relation. A multilevel relation will appear to contain different data to subjects (users) with different clearance levels. In some cases, it is possible to store a single tuple in the relation at a higher classification level and produce the corresponding tuples at a lower level classification through a process known as **filtering.** In other cases, it is necessary to store two or more tuples at different classification levels with the same value for the *apparent key*. This leads to the concept of **polyinstantiation,**[2] where several tuples can have the same apparent key value but have different attribute values for users at different classification levels.

---

2. This is similar to the notion of having multiple versions in the database that represent the same real-world object.

We illustrate these concepts with the simple example of a multilevel relation shown in Figure 22.2(a), where we display the classification attribute values next to each attribute's value. Assume that the Name attribute is the apparent key, and consider the query SELECT * FROM EMPLOYEE. A user with security clearance S would see the same relation shown in Figure 22.2(a), since all tuple classifications are less than or equal to S. However, a user with security clearance C would not be allowed to see values for Salary of Brown and JobPerformance of Smith, since they have higher classification. The tuples would be *filtered* to appear as shown in Figure 22.2(b), with Salary and JobPerformance *appearing as null*. For a user with security clearance U, the filtering allows only the name attribute of Smith to appear, with all the other attributes appearing as null (Figure 22.2c). Thus filtering introduces null values for attribute values whose security classification is higher than the user's security clearance.

In general, the **entity integrity** rule for multilevel relations states that all attributes that are members of the apparent key must not be null and must have the *same* security

(a)   EMPLOYEE

Name		Salary		JobPerformance		TC	
Smith	U	40000	C	Fair	S	S	
Brown	C	80000	S	Good	C	S	

(b)   EMPLOYEE

Name		Salary		JobPerformance		TC	
Smith	U	40000	C	null	C	C	
Brown	C	null	C	Good	C	C	

(c)   EMPLOYEE

Name		Salary		JobPerformance		TC	
Smith	U	null	U	null	U	U	

(d)   EMPLOYEE

Name		Salary		JobPerformance		TC	
Smith	U	40000	C	Fair	S	S	
Smith	U	40000	C	Excellent	C	C	
Brown	C	80000	S	Good	C	S	

Figure 22.2 A multilevel relation to illustrate multilevel security. (a) The original EMPLOYEE tuples. (b) Appearance of EMPLOYEE after filtering for classification C users. (c) Appearance of EMPLOYEE after filtering for classification U users. (d) Polyinstantiation of the Smith tuple.

classification within each individual tuple. In addition, all other attribute values in the tuple must have a security classification greater than or equal to that of the apparent key. This constraint ensures that a user can see the key if the user is permitted to see any part of the tuple at all. Other integrity rules, called **null integrity** and **interinstance integrity,** informally ensure that, if a tuple value at some security level can be filtered (derived) from a higher-classified tuple, then it is sufficient to store the higher-classified tuple in the multilevel relation.

To illustrate polyinstantiation further, suppose that a user with *security clearance* C tries to update the value of JobPerformance of Smith in Figure 22.2 to 'Excellent'; this corresponds to the following SQL update being issued:

```
UPDATE EMPLOYEE
SET JobPerformance = 'Excellent'
WHERE Name = 'Smith';
```

Since the view provided to users with security clearance C (see Figure 22.2b) permits such an update, the system should not reject it; otherwise, the user could infer that some nonnull value exists for the JobPerformance attribute of Smith rather than the null value that appears. This is an example of inferring information through what is known as a **covert channel,** which should not be permitted in highly secure systems. However, the user should not be allowed to overwrite the existing value of JobPerformance at the higher classification level. The solution is to create a **polyinstantiation** for the Smith tuple at the lower classification level C, as shown in Figure 22.2(d). This is necessary since the new tuple cannot be filtered from the existing tuple at classification S.

The basic update operations of the relational model (insert, delete, update) must be modified to handle this and similar situations, but this aspect of the problem is outside the scope of our presentation. We refer the interested reader to the end-of-chapter bibliography for further details.

22.4 Introduction to Statistical Database Security

Statistical databases are used mainly to produce statistics on various populations. The database may contain confidential data on individuals, which should be protected from user access. However, users are permitted to retrieve statistical information on the populations, such as averages, sums, counts, maximums, minimums, and standard deviations. The techniques that have been developed to protect the privacy of individual information are outside the scope of this book. We will only illustrate the problem with a very simple example, which refers to the relation shown in Figure 22.3. This is a PERSON relation with the attributes NAME, SSN, INCOME, ADDRESS, CITY, STATE, ZIP, SEX, and LAST_DEGREE.

A **population** is a set of tuples of a relation (table) that satisfy some selection condition. Hence each selection condition on the PERSON relation will specify a particular population of PERSON tuples. For example, the condition SEX = 'M' specifies the male

PERSON

NAME	SSN	INCOME	ADDRESS	CITY	STATE	ZIP	SEX	LAST_DEGREE

Figure 22.3 The PERSON relation schema for illustrating statistical database security.

population; the condition ((SEX = 'F') AND (LAST_DEGREE = 'M.S.' OR LAST_DEGREE = 'PH.D.')) specifies the female population that has an M.S. or PH.D. degree as their highest degree; and the condition CITY = 'Houston' specifies the population that lives in Houston.

Statistical queries involve applying statistical functions to a population of tuples. For example, we may want to retrieve the number of individuals in a population or the average income in the population. However, statistical users are not allowed to retrieve individual data, such as the income of a specific person. **Statistical database security** techniques must prohibit the retrieval of individual data. This can be controlled by prohibiting queries that retrieve attribute values and by allowing only queries that involve statistical aggregate functions such as COUNT, SUM, MIN, MAX, AVERAGE, and STANDARD DEVIATION. Such queries are sometimes called **statistical queries.**

In some cases it is possible to **infer** the values of individual tuples from a sequence of statistical queries. This is particularly true when the conditions result in a population consisting of a small number of tuples. As an illustration, consider the two statistical queries:

Q1: **SELECT COUNT** (*) **FROM** PERSON
     WHERE ,condition.;

Q2: **SELECT AVG** (INCOME) **FROM** PERSON
     WHERE ,condition.;

Now suppose that we are interested in finding the SALARY of 'Jane Smith', and we know that she has a PH.D. degree and that she lives in the city of Bellaire, Texas. We issue the statistical query Q1 with the following condition:

(LAST_DEGREE='PH.D.' AND SEX='F' AND CITY='Bellaire' AND STATE='Texas')

If we get a result of 1 for this query, we can issue Q2 with the same condition and find the INCOME of Jane Smith. Even if the result of Q1 on the preceding condition is not 1 but is a small number—say, 2 or 3—we can issue statistical queries using the functions MAX, MIN, and AVERAGE to identify the possible range of values for the INCOME of Jane Smith.

The possibility of inferring individual information from statistical queries is reduced if no statistical queries are permitted whenever the number of tuples in the population specified by the selection condition falls below some threshold. Another technique for prohibiting retrieval of individual information is to prohibit sequences of queries that refer repeatedly to the same population of tuples. It is also possible to introduce slight inaccuracies or "noise" into the results of statistical queries deliberately, to make it difficult to deduce individual information from the results. The interested reader is referred to the bibliography for a discussion of these techniques.

22.5 Summary

In this chapter we discussed several techniques for enforcing security in database systems. Security enforcement deals with controlling access to the database system as a whole and controlling authorization to access specific portions of a database. The former is usually done by assigning accounts with passwords to users. The latter can be accomplished by using a system of granting and revoking privileges to individual accounts for accessing specific parts of the database. This approach is generally referred to as discretionary access control. We presented some SQL commands for granting and revoking privileges, and we illustrated their use with examples. Then we gave an overview of mandatory access control mechanisms that enforce multilevel security. These require the classifications of users and data values into security classes and enforce the rules that prohibit flow of information from higher to lower security levels. Some of the key concepts underlying the multilevel relational model, including filtering and polyinstantiation, were presented. Finally, we briefly discussed the problem of controlling access to statistical databases to protect the privacy of individual information while concurrently providing statistical access to populations of records.

Review Questions

22.1. Discuss what is meant by each of the following terms: *database authorization, access control, data encryption, privileged (system) account, database audit, audit trail.*

22.2. Discuss the types of privileges at the account level and those at the relation level.

22.3. Which account is designated as the owner of a relation? What privileges does the owner of a relation have?

22.4. How is the view mechanism used as an authorization mechanism?

22.5. What is meant by granting a privilege?

22.6. What is meant by revoking a privilege?

22.7. Discuss the system of propagation of privileges and the restraints imposed by horizontal and vertical propagation limits.

22.8. List the types of privileges available in SQL.

22.9. What is the difference between *discretionary* and *mandatory* access control?

22.10. What are the typical security classifications? Discuss the simple security property and the *-property, and explain the justification behind these rules for enforcing multilevel security.

22.11. Describe the multilevel relational data model. Define the following terms: *apparent key, polyinstantiation, filtering.*

22.12. What is a statistical database? Discuss the problem of statistical database security.

Exercises

22.13. Consider the relational database schema of Figure 7.5. Suppose that all the relations were created by (and hence are owned by) user X, who wants to grant the following privileges to user accounts A, B, C, D, and E:

    a. Account A can retrieve or modify any relation except DEPENDENT and can grant any of these privileges to other users.

    b. Account B can retrieve all the attributes of EMPLOYEE and DEPARTMENT except for SALARY, MGRSSN, and MGRSTARTDATE.

    c. Account C can retrieve or modify WORKS_ON but can only retrieve the FNAME, MINIT, LNAME, SSN attributes of EMPLOYEE and the PNAME, PNUMBER attributes of PROJECT.

    d. Account D can retrieve any attribute of EMPLOYEE or DEPENDENT and can modify DEPENDENT.

    e. Account E can retrieve any attribute of EMPLOYEE but only for EMPLOYEE tuples that have DNO = 3.

    Write SQL statements to grant these privileges. Use views where appropriate.

22.14. Suppose that privilege (a) of Exercise 22.13 is to be given with GRANT OPTION but only so that account A can grant it to at most five accounts, and each of these accounts can propagate the privilege to other accounts but *without* the GRANT OPTION privilege. What would the horizontal and vertical propagation limits be in this case?

22.15. Consider the relation shown in Figure 22.2(d). How would it appear to a user with classification U? Suppose a classification U user tries to update the salary of 'Smith' to $50,000; what would be the result of this action?

Selected Bibliography

Authorization based on granting and revoking privileges was proposed for the SYSTEM R experimental DBMS and is presented in Griffiths and Wade (1976). Several books discuss security in databases and computer systems in general, including the books by Leiss (1982a) and Fernandez et al. (1981). Denning and Denning (1979) is a tutorial paper on data security.

Many papers discuss different techniques for the design and protection of statistical databases. These include McLeish (1989), Chin and Ozsoyoglu (1981), Leiss (1982), Wong (1984), and Denning (1980). Ghosh (1984) discusses the use of statistical databases for quality control. There are also many papers discussing cryptography and data encryption, including Diffie and Hellman (1979), Rivest et al. (1978), and Akl (1983).

Multilevel security is discussed in Jajodia and Sandhu (1991), Denning et al. (1987), Smith and Winslett (1992), Stachour and Thuraisingham (1990), and Lunt et al. (1990). Overviews of research issues in database security are given by Lunt and Fernandez (1990) and Jajodia and Sandhu (1991). The effects of multilevel security on concurrency control are discussed in Atluri et al. (1997). Security in next-generation, semantic, and object-oriented databases (see Chapters 11 through 13) is discussed in Rabbiti et al. (1991), Jajodia and Kogan (1990), and Smith (1990). Oh (1999) presents a model for both discretionary and mandatory security.

PART 6

Advanced Database Concepts & Emerging Applications

CHAPTER 23

Enhanced Data Models for Advanced Applications

As the use of database systems has grown, users have demanded additional functionality from these software packages, with the purpose of making it easier to implement more advanced and complex user applications. Object-oriented databases and object-relational systems do provide features that allow users to extend their systems by specifying additional abstract data types for each application. However, it is quite useful to identify certain common features for some of these advanced applications and to create models that can represent these common features. In addition, specialized storage structures and indexing methods can be implemented to improve the performance of these common features. These features can then be implemented as abstract data type or class libraries and separately purchased with the basic DBMS software package. The term **datablade** has been used in Informix and **cartridge** in Oracle (see Chapter 13) to refer to such optional submodules that can be included in a DBMS package. Users can utilize these features directly if they are suitable for their applications, without having to reinvent, reimplement, and reprogram such common features.

This chapter introduces database concepts for some of the common features that are needed by advanced applications and that are starting to have widespread use. The features we will cover are *active rules* that are used in active database applications, *temporal concepts* that are used in temporal database applications, and briefly some of the issues involving *multimedia databases*. It is important to note that each of these topics is very broad, and we can give only a brief introduction to each area. In fact, each of these areas can serve as the sole topic for a complete book.

In Section 23.1, we will introduce the topic of active databases, which provide additional functionality for specifying **active rules.** These rules can be automatically triggered by events that occur, such as a database update or a certain time being reached, and can initiate certain actions that have been specified in the rule declaration if certain conditions are met. Many commercial packages already have some of the functionality provided by active databases in the form of **triggers.**[1]

In Section 23.2, we will introduce the concepts of **temporal databases,** which permit the database system to store a history of changes, and allow users to query both current and past states of the database. Some temporal database models also allow users to store future expected information, such as planned schedules. It is important to note that many database applications are already temporal, but may have been implemented without having much temporal support from the DBMS package—that is, the temporal concepts were implemented in the application programs that access the database.

Section 23.3 will give a brief overview of spatial and multimedia databases. **Spatial databases** provide concepts for databases that keep track of objects in a multidimensional space. For example, cartographic databases that store maps include two-dimensional spatial positions of their objects, which include countries, states, rivers, cities, roads, seas, and so on. Other databases, such as meteorological databases for weather information are three-dimensional, since temperatures and other meteorological information are related to three-dimensional spatial points. **Multimedia databases** provide features that allow users to store and query different types of multimedia information, which includes **images** (such as pictures or drawings), **video clips** (such as movies, news reels, or home videos), **audio clips** (such as songs, phone messages, or speeches), and **documents** (such as books or articles).

Readers may choose to peruse the particular topics they are interested in, as the sections in this chapter are practically independent of one another.

23.1 Active Database Concepts

Rules that specify actions that are automatically triggered by certain events have been considered as important enhancements to a database system for quite some time. In fact, the concept of **triggers**—a technique for specifying certain types of active rules—has existed in early versions of the SQL specification for relational databases. Commercial relational DBMSs—such as Oracle, DB2, and SYBASE—have had various versions of triggers available. However, much research into what a general model for active databases should look like has been done since the early models of triggers were proposed. In Section 23.1.1, we will present the general concepts that have been proposed for specifying rules for active databases. We will use the syntax of the Oracle commercial relational DBMS to illustrate these concepts with specific examples, since Oracle triggers are close to the way rules will be specified in the SQL3 standard. Section 23.2 will discuss some general design and implementation issues for active databases. We then give examples of how

---

1. In fact, even some of the features in SQL2 can be considered active, such as the CASCADE actions specified on referential integrity constraints (see Chapter 8).

active databases are implemented in the STARBURST experimental DBMS in Section 23.1.3, since STARBURST provides for many of the concepts of generalized active databases within its framework. Section 23.1.4 discusses possible applications of active databases.

23.1.1 Generalized Model for Active Databases and Oracle Triggers

The model that has been used for specifying active database rules is referred to as the **Event-Condition-Action,** or ECA model. A rule in the ECA model has three components:

1. The **event** (or events) that trigger the rule: These events are usually database update operations that are explicitly applied to the database. However, in the general model, they could also be temporal events[2] or other kinds of external events.

2. The **condition** that determines whether the rule action should be executed: Once the triggering event has occurred, an *optional* condition may be evaluated. If *no condition* is specified, the action will be executed once the event occurs. If a condition is specified, it is first evaluated, and only *if it evaluates to true* will the rule action be executed.

3. The **action** to be taken: The action is usually a sequence of SQL statements, but it could also be a database transaction or an external program that will be automatically executed.

Let us consider some examples to illustrate these concepts. The examples are based on a much simplified variation of the COMPANY database application from Figure 7.7, which is shown in Figure 23.1, with each employee having a name (NAME), social security number (SSN), salary (SALARY), department to which they are currently assigned (DNO, a foreign key to DEPARTMENT), and a direct supervisor (SUPERVISOR_SSN, a (recursive) foreign key to EMPLOYEE). For this example, we assume that null is allowed for DNO, indicating that an

EMPLOYEE

NAME	SSN	SALARY	DNO	SUPERVISOR_SSN

DEPARTMENT

DNAME	DNO	TOTAL_SAL	MANAGER_SSN

Figure 23.1 A simplified COMPANY database used for active rule examples.

---

2. An example would be a temporal event specified as a periodic time, such as: Trigger this rule every day at 5:30 am.

employee may be temporarily unassigned to any department. Each department has a name (DNAME), number (DNO), the total salary of all employees assigned to the department (TOTAL_SAL), and a manager (MANAGER_SSN, a foreign key to EMPLOYEE).

Notice that the TOTAL_SAL attribute is really a derived attribute, whose value should be the sum of the salaries of all employees who are assigned to the particular department. Maintaining the correct value of such a derived attribute can be done via an active rule. We first have to determine the **events** that *may cause* a change in the value of TOTAL_SAL, which are as follows:

1. Inserting (one or more) new employee tuples.

2. Changing the salary of (one or more) existing employees.

3. Changing the assignment of existing employees from one department to another.

4. Deleting (one or more) employee tuples.

In the case of event 1, we only need to recompute TOTAL_SAL if the new employee is immediately assigned to a department—that is, if the value of the DNO attribute for the new employee tuple is not null (assuming null is allowed for DNO). Hence, this would be the **condition** to be checked. A similar condition could be checked for events 2 (and 4) to determine whether the employee whose salary is changed (or who is being deleted) is currently assigned to a department. For event 3, we will always execute an action to maintain the value of TOTAL_SAL correctly, so no condition is needed (the action is always executed).

The **action** for events 1, 2, and 4 is to automatically update the value of TOTAL_SAL for the employee's department to reflect the newly inserted, updated, or deleted employee's salary. In the case of event 3, a twofold action is needed; one to update the TOTAL_SAL of the employee's old department and the other to update the TOTAL_SAL of the employee's new department.

The four active rules R1, R2, R3, and R4—corresponding to the above situation—can be specified in the notation of the Oracle DBMS as shown in Figure 23.2(a). Let us consider rule R1 to illustrate the syntax of creating active rules in Oracle. The CREATE TRIGGER statement specifies a trigger (or active rule) name—TOTALSAL1 for R1. The AFTER-clause specifies that the rule will be triggered *after* the events that trigger the rule occur. The triggering events—an insert of a new employee in this example—are specified following the AFTER keyword.[3] The ON-clause specifies the relation on which the rule is specified—EMPLOYEE for R1. The *optional* keywords FOR EACH ROW specify that the rule will be triggered *once for each row* that is affected by the triggering event.[4] The *optional* WHEN-clause is used to specify any conditions that need to be checked after the rule is triggered but before the action is executed. Finally, the action(s) to be taken are specified as a PL/SQL block, which typically contains one or more SQL statements or calls to execute external procedures.

---

3. As we shall see later, it is also possible to specify BEFORE instead of AFTER, which indicates that the rule is triggered *before the triggering event is executed.*

4. Again, we shall see later that an alternative is to trigger the rule *only once* even if multiple rows (tuples) are affected by the triggering event.

(a)

R1:   **CREATE TRIGGER** TOTALSAL1
       AFTER INSERT ON EMPLOYEE
       FOR EACH ROW
       WHEN (**NEW**.DNO **IS NOT NULL**)
           UPDATE DEPARTMENT
           SET TOTAL_SAL=TOTAL_SAL + **NEW**.SALARY
           WHERE DNO=**NEW**.DNO;

R2:   **CREATE TRIGGER** TOTALSAL2
       AFTER UPDATE OF SALARY **ON** EMPLOYEE
       FOR EACH ROW
       WHEN (**NEW**.DNO **IS NOT NULL**)
           UPDATE DEPARTMENT
           SET TOTAL_SAL=TOTAL_SAL + **NEW**.SALARY – **OLD**.SALARY
           WHERE DNO=**NEW**.DNO;

R3:   **CREATE TRIGGER** TOTALSAL3
       AFTER UPDATE OF DNO **ON** EMPLOYEE
       FOR EACH ROW
       BEGIN
       UPDATE DEPARTMENT
       SET TOTAL_SAL=TOTAL_SAL + **NEW**.SALARY
       WHERE DNO=**NEW**.DNO;
       UPDATE DEPARTMENT
       SET TOTAL_SAL=TOTAL_SAL– **OLD**.SALARY
       WHERE DNO=**OLD**.DNO;
       END;

R4:   **CREATE TRIGGER** TOTALSAL4
       AFTER DELETE ON EMPLOYEE
       FOR EACH ROW
       WHEN (**OLD**.DNO **IS NOT NULL**)
           UPDATE DEPARTMENT
           SET TOTAL_SAL=TOTAL_SAL – **OLD**.SALARY
           WHERE DNO=**OLD**.DNO;

(b)

R5:   **CREATE TRIGGER** INFORM_SUPERVISOR1
       BEFORE INSERT OR UPDATE OF SALARY, SUPERVISOR_SSN **ON** EMPLOYEE
       FOR EACH ROW
       WHEN
       (**NEW**.SALARY > (**SELECT** SALARY **FROM** EMPLOYEE
               WHERE SSN=**NEW**.SUPERVISOR_SSN))
       INFORM_SUPERVISOR(**NEW**. SUPERVISOR_SSN, **NEW**.SSN);

Figure 23.2   Specifying active rules as triggers in Oracle notation. (a) Triggers
for automatically maintaining the consistency of TOTAL_SAL of
DEPARTMENT. (b) Trigger for comparing an employee's salary with that
of his or her supervisor.

The four triggers (active rules) R1, R2, R3, and R4 illustrate a number of features of active rules. First, the basic **events** that can be specified for triggering the rules are the standard SQL update commands: INSERT, DELETE, and UPDATE. These are specified by the keywords **INSERT, DELETE,** and **UPDATE** in Oracle notation. In the case of **UPDATE** one may specify the attributes to be updated—for example, by writing **UPDATE OF** SALARY, DNO. Second, the rule designer needs to have a way to refer to the tuples that have been inserted, deleted, or modified by the triggering event. The keywords **NEW** and **OLD** are used in Oracle notation; NEW is used to refer to a newly inserted or newly updated tuple, whereas OLD is used to refer to a deleted tuple or to a tuple before it was updated.

Thus rule R1 is triggered after an INSERT operation is applied to the EMPLOYEE relation. In R1, the condition (NEW.DNO IS NOT NULL) is checked, and if it evaluates to true, meaning that the newly inserted employee tuple is related to a department, then the action is executed. The action updates the DEPARTMENT tuple(s) related to the newly inserted employee by adding their salary (NEW.SALARY) to the TOTAL_SAL attribute of their related department.

Rule R2 is similar to R1, but it is triggered by an UPDATE operation that updates the SALARY of an employee rather than by an INSERT. Rule R3 is triggered by an update to the DNO attribute of EMPLOYEE, which signifies changing an employee's assignment from one department to another. There is no condition to check in R3, so the action is executed whenever the triggering event occurs. The action updates both the old department and new department of the reassigned employees by adding their salary to TOTAL_SAL of their *new* department and subtracting their salary from TOTAL_SAL of their *old* department. Note that this should work even if the value of DNO was null, because in this case no department will be selected for the rule action.[5]

It is important to note the effect of the optional FOR EACH ROW clause, which signifies that the rule is triggered separately *for each tuple*. This is known as a **row-level trigger.** If this clause was left out, the trigger would be known as a **statement-level trigger** and would be triggered once for each triggering statement. To see the difference, consider the following update operation, which gives a 10 percent raise to all employees assigned to department 5. This operation would be an event that triggers rule R2:

```
UPDATE      EMPLOYEE
SET         SALARY = 1.1 * SALARY
WHERE       DNO = 5;
```

Because the above statement could update multiple records, a rule using row-level semantics, such as R2 in Figure 23.2, would be triggered *once for each row*, whereas a rule using statement-level semantics is triggered *only once*. The Oracle system allows the user to choose which of the above two options is to be used for each rule. Including the optional FOR EACH ROW clause creates a row-level trigger, and leaving it out creates a statement-level trigger. Note that the keywords NEW and OLD can only be used with row-level triggers.

---

5. R1, R2, and R4 can also be written without a condition. However, they may be more efficient to execute with the condition since the action is not invoked unless it is required.

```
<trigger>  ::= CREATE TRIGGER <trigger name>
                (AFTER I BEFORE ) <triggering events> ON <table name>
                [ FOR EACH ROW ]
                [ WHEN <condition> ]
                <trigger actions> ;
<triggering events> ::=<trigger event> {OR <trigger event> }
<trigger event>::=INSERT I DELETE I UPDATE [ OF <column name> {, <column name>}] ]
<trigger action> ::=<PL/SQL block>
```

Figure 23.3 A syntax summary for specifying triggers in the Oracle system
(main options only).

As a second example, suppose we want to check whenever an employee's salary is greater than the salary of his or her direct supervisor. Several events can trigger this rule: inserting a new employee, changing an employee's salary, or changing an employee's supervisor. Suppose that the action to take would be to call an external procedure INFORM_ SUPERVISOR,[6] which will notify the supervisor. The rule could then be written as in R5 (see Figure 23.2b).

Figure 23.3 shows the syntax for specifying some of the main options available in Oracle triggers.

23.1.2 Design and Implementation Issues for Active Databases

The previous section gave an overview of the main concepts for specifying active rules. In this section, we discuss some additional issues concerning how rules are designed and implemented. The first issue concerns activation, deactivation, and grouping of rules. In addition to creating rules, an active database system should allow users to *activate*, *deactivate*, and *drop* rules by referring to their rule names. A **deactivated rule** will not be triggered by the triggering event. This feature allows users to selectively deactivate rules for certain periods of time when they are not needed. The **activate command** will make the rule active again. The **drop command** deletes the rule from the system. Another option is to group rules into named **rule sets,** so the whole set of rules could be activated, deactivated, or dropped. It is also useful to have a command that can trigger a rule or rule set via an explicit **PROCESS RULES** command issued by the user.

The second issue concerns whether the triggered action should be executed *before*, *after*, or *concurrently with* the triggering event. A related issue is whether the action being executed should be considered as a *separate transaction* or whether it should be part of the same transaction that triggered the rule. We will first try to categorize the various options.

---

6. Assuming that an appropriate external procedure has been declared. This is a feature that is available in SQL3.

It is important to note that not all options may be available for a particular active database system. In fact, most commercial systems are *limited to one or two of the options* that we will now discuss.

Let us assume that the triggering event occurs as part of a transaction execution. We should first consider the various options for how the triggering event is related to the evaluation of the rule's condition. The rule *condition evaluation* is also known as **rule consideration,** since the action is to be executed only after considering whether the condition evaluates to true or false. There are three main possibilities for rule consideration:

1. *Immediate consideration:* The condition is evaluated as part of the same transaction as the triggering event, and is evaluated *immediately*. This case can be further categorized into three options:
   - Evaluate the condition *before* executing the triggering event.
   - Evaluate the condition *after* executing the triggering event.
   - Evaluate the condition *instead of* executing the triggering event.

2. *Deferred consideration:* The condition is evaluated at the end of the transaction that included the triggering event. In this case, there could be many triggered rules waiting to have their conditions evaluated.

3. *Detached consideration:* The condition is evaluated as a separate transaction, spawned from the triggering transaction.

The next set of options concern the relationship between evaluating the rule condition and *executing* the rule action. Here, again, three options are possible: **immediate, deferred,** and **detached** execution. However, most active systems use the first option. That is, as soon as the condition is evaluated, if it returns true, the action is *immediately* executed.

The Oracle system (see Section 23.1.1) uses the *immediate consideration* model, but it allows the user to specify for each rule whether the *before* or *after* option is to be used with immediate condition evaluation. It also uses the *immediate execution* model. The STARBURST system (see Section 23.1.3) uses the *deferred consideration* option, meaning that all rules triggered by a transaction wait until the triggering transaction reaches its end and issues its COMMIT WORK command before the rule conditions are evaluated.[7]

Another issue concerning active database rules is the distinction between *row-level rules* versus *statement-level rules*. Because SQL update statements (which act as triggering events) can specify a set of tuples, one has to distinguish between whether the rule should be considered once for the *whole statement* or whether it should be considered separately *for each row* (that is, tuple) affected by the statement. The Oracle system (see Section 23.1.1) allows the user to choose which of the above two options is to be used for each rule, whereas STARBURST uses statement-level semantics only. We will give examples of how statement-level triggers can be specified in Section 23.1.3.

One of the difficulties that may have limited the widespread use of active rules, in spite of their potential to simplify database and software development, is that there are no

---

7. STARBURST also allows the user to explicitly start rule consideration via a PROCESS RULES command.

RI: **CREATE TRIGGER** T1
    AFTER INSERT ON TABLE1
    FOR EACH ROW
        UPDATE TABLE2
        SET ATTRIBUTE1=...;

R2:   **CREATE TRIGGER** T2
    AFTER UPDATE OF ATTRIBUTE1 **ON** TABLE2
    FOR EACH ROW
        INSERT INTO TABLE1 **VALUES** (...);

Figure 23.4   An example to illustrate the termination problem for active rules.

easy-to-use techniques for designing, writing, and verifying rules. For example, it is quite difficult to verify that a set of rules is **consistent,** meaning that two or more rules in the set do not contradict one another. It is also difficult to guarantee **termination** of a set of rules under all circumstances. To briefly illustrate the termination problem, consider the rules in Figure 23.4. Here, rule R1 is triggered by an INSERT event on TABLE1 and its action includes an update event on ATTRIBUTE1 of TABLE2. However, rule R2's triggering event is an UPDATE event on ATTRIBUTE1 of TABLE2, and its action includes an INSERT event on TABLE1. It is easy to see in this example that these two rules can trigger one another indefinitely, leading to nontermination. However, if dozens of rules are written, it is very difficult to determine whether termination is guaranteed or not.

If active rules are to reach their potential, it is necessary to develop tools for the design, debugging, and monitoring of active rules that can help users in designing and debugging their rules.

23.1.3 Examples of Statement-Level Active Rules in STARBURST

We now give some examples to illustrate how rules can be specified in the STARBURST experimental DBMS. This will allow us to demonstrate how statement-level rules can be written, since these are the only types of rules allowed in STARBURST.

The three active rules R1S, R2S, and R3S in Figure 23.5 correspond to the first three rules in Figure 23.2, but use STARBURST notation and statement-level semantics. We can explain the rule structure using rule R1S. The CREATE RULE statement specifies a rule name—TOTALSAL1 for R1S. The ON-clause specifies the relation on which the rule is specified—EMPLOYEE for R1S. The WHEN-clause is used to specify the **events** that trigger the rule.[8] The *optional* IF-clause is used to specify any **conditions** that need to be checked. Finally, the THEN-clause is used to specify the **action** (or actions) to be taken, which are typically one or more SQL statements.

---

8. Note that the WHEN keyword specifies *events* in STARBURST but is used to specify the rule *condition* in Oracle triggers.

RIS: **CREATE RULE** TOTALSAL1 **ON** EMPLOYEE
        WHEN INSERTED
        IF   **EXISTS(SELECT * FROM INSERTED WHERE** DNO **IS NOT NULL)**
        THEN   UPDATE   DEPARTMENT **AS** D
                 SET   D.TOTAL_SAL=D.TOTAL_SAL +
                         (SELECT SUM(I.SALARY) **FROM INSERTED AS** I **WHERE** D.DNO = I.DNO)
                 WHERE   D.DNO **IN (SELECT** DNO **FROM INSERTED)**;

R2S: **CREATE RULE** TOTALSAL2 **ON** EMPLOYEE
        WHEN   UPDATED (SALARY)
        IF   **EXISTS(SELECT * FROM NEW-UPDATED WHERE** DNO **IS NOT NULL)**
                 OR EXISTS(SELECT * FROM OLD-UPDATED WHERE DNO **IS NOT NULL)**
        THEN   UPDATE DEPARTMENT **AS** D
                 SET   D.TOTAL_SAL=D.TOTAL_SAL +
                         (SELECT SUM(N.SALARY) **FROM NEW-UPDATED AS** N **WHERE**
                            D.DNO =N.DNO) –
                         (SELECT SUM(O.SALARY) **FROM OLD-UPDATED AS** O **WHERE**
                            D.DNO=O.DNO)
                 WHERE   D.DNO **IN (SELECT** DNO **FROM NEW-UPDATED) OR**
                          D.DNO **IN (SELECT** DNO **FROM OLD-UPDATED)**;

R3S: **CREATE RULE** TOTALSAL3 **ON** EMPLOYEE
        WHEN   UPDATED(DNO)
        THEN   UPDATE DEPARTMENT **AS** D
                 SET   D.TOTAL_SAL=D.TOTAL_SAL +
                         (SELECT SUM(N.SALARY) **FROM NEW-UPDATED AS** N **WHERE**
                            D.DNO=N.DNO)
                 WHERE   D.DNO IN **(SELECT** DNO **FROM NEW-UPDATED)**;

                 UPDATE DEPARTMENT **AS** D
                 SET   D.TOTAL_SAL=D.TOTAL_SAL –
                         (SELECT SUM(O.SALARY) **FROM OLD-UPDATED AS** O **WHERE**
                            D.DNO=O.DNO)
                 WHERE   D.DNO **IN (SELECT** DNO **FROM OLD-UPDATED)**;

Figure 23.5   Active rules using statement-level semantics in STARBURST notation.

In STARBURST, the basic events that can be specified for triggering the rules are the standard SQL update commands: INSERT, DELETE, and UPDATE. These are specified by the keywords **INSERTED, DELETED,** and **UPDATED** in STARBURST notation. Second, the rule designer needs to have a way to refer to the tuples that have been modified. The keywords **INSERTED, DELETED, NEW-UPDATED,** and **OLD-UPDATED** are used in STARBURST notation to refer to four **transition tables** (relations) that include the newly inserted tuples, the deleted tuples, the updated tuples *before* they were updated, and the updated tuples *after* they were updated, respectively. Obviously, depending on the triggering events, only some of these transition tables may be available. The rule writer can refer to these tables when writing the condition and action parts of the rule. Transition tables contain tuples of the same type as those in the relation specified in the ON-clause of the rule—for R1S, R2S, and R3S, this is the EMPLOYEE relation.

In statement-level semantics, the rule designer can only refer to the transition tables as a whole and the rule is triggered only once, so the rules must be written differently than for row-level semantics. Because multiple employee tuples may be inserted in a single insert statement, we have to check if *at least one* of the newly inserted employee tuples is related to a department. In R1S, the condition

EXISTS(SELECT * FROM INSERTED WHERE DNO IS NOT NULL)

is checked, and if it evaluates to true, then the action is executed. The action updates in a single statement the DEPARTMENT tuple(s) related to the newly inserted employee(s) by adding their salaries to the TOTAL_SAL attribute of each related department. Because more than one newly inserted employee may belong to the same department, we use the SUM aggregate function to ensure that all their salaries are added.

Rule R2S is similar to R1S, but is triggered by an UPDATE operation that updates the salary of one or more employees rather than by an INSERT. Rule R3S is triggered by an update to the DNO attribute of EMPLOYEE, which signifies changing one or more employees' assignment from one department to another. There is no condition in R3S, so the action is executed whenever the triggering event occurs.[9] The action updates both the old department(s) and new department(s) of the reassigned employees by adding their salary to TOTAL_SAL of each *new* department and subtracting their salary from TOTAL_SAL of each *old* department.

In our example, it is more complex to write the statement-level rules than the row-level rules, as can be illustrated by comparing Figures 23.2 and 23.5. However, this is not a general rule, and other types of active rules may be easier to specify using statement-level notation than when using row-level notation.

The execution model for active rules in STARBURST uses **deferred consideration.** That is, all the rules that are triggered within a transaction are placed in a set—called the **conflict set**—which is not considered for evaluation of conditions and execution until the transaction ends (by issuing its COMMIT WORK command). STARBURST also allows the user to explicitly start rule consideration in the middle of a transaction via an explicit PROCESS RULES command. Because multiple rules must be evaluated, it is necessary to specify an order among the rules. The syntax for rule declaration in STARBURST allows the specification of *ordering* among the rules to instruct the system about the order in which a set of rules should be considered.[10] In addition, the transition tables—INSERTED, DELETED, NEW-UPDATED, and OLD-UPDATED—contain the *net effect* of all the operations within the transaction that affected each table, since multiple operations may have been applied to each table during the transaction.

---

9. As in the Oracle examples, rules R1S and R2S can be written without a condition. However, they may be more efficient to execute with the condition since the action is not invoked unless it is required.

10. If no order is specified between a pair of rules, the system default order is based on placing the rule declared first ahead of the other rule.

23.1.4   Potential Applications for Active Databases

Finally, we will briefly discuss some of the potential applications of active rules. Obviously, one important application is to allow **notification** of certain conditions that occur. For example, an active database may be used to monitor, say, the temperature of an industrial furnace. The application can periodically insert in the database the temperature reading records directly from temperature sensors, and active rules can be written that are triggered whenever a temperature record is inserted, with a condition that checks if the temperature exceeds the danger level, and the action to raise an alarm.

Active rules can also be used to **enforce integrity constraints** by specifying the types of events that may cause the constraints to be violated and then evaluating appropriate conditions that check whether the constraints are actually violated by the event or not. Hence, complex application constraints, often known as **business rules** may be enforced that way. For example, in the UNIVERSITY database application, one rule may monitor the grade point average of students whenever a new grade is entered, and it may alert the advisor if the GPA of a student falls below a certain threshold; another rule may check that course prerequisites are satisfied before allowing a student to enroll in a course; and so on.

Other applications include the automatic **maintenance of derived data**, such as the examples of rules R1 through R4 that maintain the derived attribute TOTAL_SAL whenever individual employee tuples are changed. A similar application is to use active rules to maintain the consistency of **materialized views** (see Chapter 8) whenever the base relations are modified. This application is also relevant to the new data warehousing technologies (see Chapter 26). A related application is to maintain **replicated tables** consistent by specifying rules that modify the replicas whenever the master table is modified.

23.2   Temporal Database Concepts

Temporal databases, in the broadest sense, encompass all database applications that require some aspect of time when organizing their information. Hence, they provide a good example to illustrate the need for developing a set of unifying concepts for application developers to use. Temporal database applications have been developed since the early days of database usage. However, in creating these applications, it was mainly left to the application designers and developers to discover, design, program, and implement the temporal concepts they need. There are many examples of applications where some aspect of time is needed to maintain the information in a database. These include *healthcare*, where patient histories need to be maintained; *insurance*, where claims and accident histories are required as well as information on the times when insurance policies are in effect; *reservation systems* in general (hotel, airline, car rental, train, etc.), where information on the dates and times when reservations are in effect are required; *scientific databases*, where data collected from experiments includes the time when each data is measured; an so on. Even the two examples used in this book may be easily expanded into temporal applications. In the COMPANY database, we may wish to keep SALARY, JOB, and PROJECT histories on each employee. In the UNIVERSITY database, time is already included in the SEMESTER and YEAR of each SECTION of a COURSE; the grade history of a STUDENT; and the information on research grants. In fact, it is realistic to conclude that the majority of database applications have some temporal information. Users often attempted to simplify or ignore temporal aspects because of the complexity that they add to their applications.

In this section, we will introduce some of the concepts that have been developed to deal with the complexity of temporal database applications. Section 23.2.1 gives an overview of how time is represented in databases, the different types of temporal information, and some of the different dimensions of time that may be needed. Section 23.2.2 discusses how time can be incorporated into relational databases. Section 23.2.3 gives some additional options for representing time that are possible in database models that allow complex-structured objects, such as object databases. Section 23.2.4 introduces operations for querying temporal databases, and gives a brief overview of the TSQL2 language, which extends SQL with temporal concepts. Section 23.2.5 focuses on time series data, which is a type of temporal data that is very important in practice.

23.2.1 Time Representation, Calendars, and Time Dimensions

For temporal databases, time is considered to be an *ordered sequence* of **points** in some **granularity** that is determined by the application. For example, suppose that some temporal application never requires time units that are less than one second. Then, each time point represents one second in time using this granularity. In reality, each second is a (short) *time duration*, not a point, since it may be further divided into milliseconds, microseconds, and so on. Temporal database researchers have used the term **chronon** instead of point to describe this minimal granularity for a particular application. The main consequence of choosing a minimum granularity—say, one second—is that events occurring within the same second will be considered to be *simultaneous events*, even though in reality they may not be.

Because there is no known beginning or ending of time, one needs a reference point from which to measure specific time points. Various calendars are used by various cultures (such as Gregorian (Western), Chinese, Islamic, Hindu, Jewish, Coptic, etc.) with different reference points. A **calendar** organizes time into different time units for convenience. Most calendars group 60 seconds into a minute, 60 minutes into an hour, 24 hours into a day (based on the physical time of earth's rotation around its axis), and 7 days into a week. Further grouping of days into months and months into years either follow solar or lunar natural phenomena, and are generally irregular. In the Gregorian calendar, which is used in most Western countries, days are grouped into months that are either 28, 29, 30, or 31 days, and 12 months are grouped into a year. Complex formulas are used to map the different time units to one another.

In SQL2, the temporal data types (see Chapter 8) include DATE (specifying Year, Month, and Day as YYYY-MM-DD), TIME (specifying Hour, Minute, and Second as HH:MM:SS), TIMESTAMP (specifying a Date/Time combination, with options for including sub-second divisions if they are needed), INTERVAL (a relative time duration, such as 10 days or 250 minutes), and PERIOD (an *anchored* time duration with a fixed starting point, such as the 10-day period from January 1, 1999 to January 10, 1999, inclusive).[11]

Event Information Versus Duration (or State) Information.   A temporal database will store information concerning when certain events occur, or when certain facts are considered to be true. There are several different types of temporal information. **Point events** or **facts** are typically associated in the database with a **single time point** in some granularity. For example, a bank deposit event may be associated with the timestamp when the deposit was made, or the total monthly sales of a product (fact) may be associated with a particular month (say, February 1999). Note that even though such events or facts may have different granularities, each is still associated with a *single time value* in the database. This type of information is often represented as **time series data** as we shall discuss in Section 23.2.5. **Duration events** or **facts,** on the other hand, are associated with a specific **time period** in the database.[12] For example, an employee may have worked in a company from August 15, 1993 till November 20, 1998.

A **time period** is represented by its **start** and **end time points** [start-time, end-time]. For example, the above period is represented as [1993-08-15, 1998-11-20]. Such a time period is often interpreted to mean the *set of all time points* from start-time to end-time, inclusive, in the specified granularity. Hence, assuming day granularity, the period [1993-08-15, 1998-11-20] represents the set of all days from August 15, 1993 until November 20, 1998, inclusive.[13]

Valid Time and Transaction Time Dimensions.   Given a particular event or fact that is associated with a particular time point or time period in the database, the association may be interpreted to mean different things. The most natural interpretation is that the associated time is the time that the event occurred, or the period during which the fact was considered to be true *in the real world*. If this interpretation is used, the associated time is often referred to as the **valid time.** A temporal database using this interpretation is called a **valid time database.**

However, a different interpretation can be used, where the associated time refers to the time when the information was actually stored in the database; that is, it is the value of the system time clock when the information is valid *in the system*.[14] In this case, the associated time is called the **transaction time.** A temporal database using this interpretation is called a **transaction time database.**

---

11. Unfortunately, the terminology has not been used consistently. For example, the term *interval* is often used to denote an anchored duration. For consistency, we shall use the SQL terminology.

12. This is the same as an anchored duration. It has also been frequently called a **time interval,** but to avoid confusion we will use **period** to be consistent with SQL terminology.

13. The representation [1993-08-15, 1998-11-20] is called a *closed interval* representation. One can also use an *open interval*, denoted [1993-08-15, 1998-11-21], where the set of points *does not include* the end point. Although the latter representation is sometimes more convenient, we shall use closed intervals throughout to avoid confusion.

14. The explanation is more involved, as we shall see in Section 23.2.3.

Other interpretations can also be intended, but these two are considered to be the most common ones, and they are referred to as **time dimensions.** In some applications, only one of the dimensions is needed and in other cases both time dimensions are required, in which case the temporal database is called a **bitemporal database.** If other interpretations are intended for time, the user can define the semantics and program the applications appropriately, and it is called a **user-defined time.**

The next section shows with examples how these concepts can be incorporated into relational databases, and Section 23.2.3 shows an approach to incorporate temporal concepts into object databases.

23.2.2 Incorporating Time in Relational Databases Using Tuple Versioning

Valid Time Relations.   Let us now see how the different types of temporal databases may be represented in the relational model. First, suppose that we would like to include the history of changes as they occur in the real world. Consider again the database in Figure 23.1, and let us assume that, for this application, the granularity is day. Then, we could convert the two relations EMPLOYEE and DEPARTMENT into **valid time relations** by adding the attributes VST (Valid Start Time) and VET (Valid End Time), whose data type is DATE in order to provide day granularity. This is shown in Figure 23.6(a), where the relations have been renamed EMP_VT and DEPT_VT, respectively.

Consider how the EMP_VT relation differs from the nontemporal EMPLOYEE relation (Figure 23.1).[15] In EMP_VT, each tuple v represents a **version** of an employee's information that is valid (in the real world) only during the time period· [v.VST,   v.VET], whereas in EMPLOYEE each tuple represents only the current state or current version of each employee. In EMP_VT, the **current version** of each employee typically has a special value, *now*, as its valid end time. This special value, *now,* is a **temporal variable** that implicitly represents the current time as time progresses. The nontemporal EMPLOYEE relation would only include those tuples from the EMP_VT relation whose VET is *now.*

Figure 23.7 shows a few tuple versions in the valid-time relations EMP_VT and DEPT_VT. There are two versions of Smith, three versions of Wong, one version of Brown, and one version of Narayan. We can now see how a valid time relation should behave when information is changed. Whenever one or more attributes of an employee are **updated,** rather than actually overwriting the old values, as would happen in a nontemporal relation, the system should create a new version and **close** the current version by changing its VET to the end time. Hence, when the user issued the command to update the salary of Smith effective on June 1, 1998 to $30000, the second version of Smith was created (see Figure 23.7). At the time of this update, the first version of Smith was the current version, with *now* as its VET, but after the update *now* was changed to May 31, 1998 (one less than June

---

15. A nontemporal relation is also called a **snapshot relation** as it shows only the *current snapshot* or *current state* of the database.

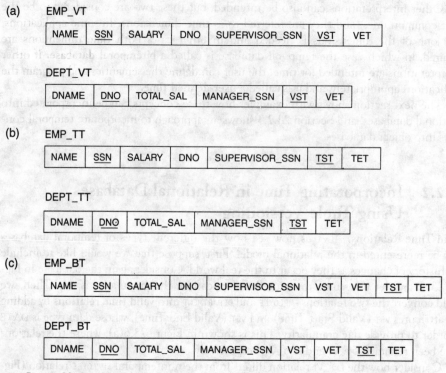

Figure 23.6   Different types of temporal relational databases. (a) Valid time database schema. (b) Transaction time database schema. (c) Bitemporal database schema.

1, 1998 in day granularity), to indicate that the version has become a **closed** or **history version** and that the new (second) version of Smith is now the current one.

It is important to note that in a valid time relation, the user must generally provide the valid time of an update. For example, the salary update of Smith may have been entered in the database on May 15, 1998 at 8:52:12am, say, even though the salary change in the real world is effective on June 1, 1998. This is called a **proactive update,** since it is applied to the database *before* it becomes effective in the real world. If the update was applied to the database *after* it became effective in the real world, it is called a **retroactive update.** An update that is applied at the same time when it becomes effective is called a **simultaneous update.**

The action that corresponds to **deleting** an employee in a nontemporal database would typically be applied to a valid time database by *closing the current version* of the employee being deleted. For example, if Smith leaves the company effective January 19, 1999, then this would be applied by changing VET of the current version of Smith from *now* to 1999-01-19. In Figure 23.7, there is no current version for Brown, because he pre-

EMP_VT

NAME	SSN	SALARY	DNO	SUPERVISOR_SSN	VST	VET
Smith	123456789	25000	5	333445555	1997-06-15	1998-05-31
Smith	123456789	30000	5	333445555	1998-06-01	now
Wong	333445555	25000	4	999887777	1994-08-20	1996-01-31
Wong	333445555	30000	5	999887777	1996-02-01	1997-03-31
Wong	333445555	40000	5	888665555	1997-04-01	now
Brown	222447777	28000	4	999887777	1996-05-01	1997-08-10
Narayan	666884444	38000	5	333445555	1998-08-01	now

. . .

DEPT_VT

DNAME	DNO	MANAGER_SSN	VST	VET
Research	5	888665555	1996-09-20	1997-03-31
Research	5	333445555	1997-04-01	now

. . .

Figure 23.7 Some tuple versions in the valid time relations EMP_VT and DEPT_VT.

sumably left the company on 1997-08-10 and was *logically deleted*. However, because the database is temporal, the old information on Brown is still there.

The operation to **insert** a new employee would correspond to *creating the first tuple version* for that employee, and making it the current version, with the VST being the effective (real world) time when the employee starts work. In Figure 23.7, the tuple on Narayan illustrates this, since the first version has not been updated yet.

Notice that in a valid time relation, the *nontemporal key*, such as SSN in EMPLOYEE, is no longer unique in each tuple (version). The new relation key for EMP_VT is a combination of the nontemporal key and the valid start time attribute VST,[16] so we use (SSN, VST) as primary key. This is because, at any point in time, there should be *at most one valid version* of each entity. Hence, the constraint that any two tuple versions representing the same entity should have *nonintersecting valid time periods* should hold on valid time relations. Notice that if the nontemporal primary key value may change over time, it is important to have a unique **surrogate key attribute,** whose value never changes for each real world entity, in order to relate together all versions of the same real world entity.

Valid time relations basically keep track of the history of changes as they become effective in the *real world*. Hence, if all real-world changes are applied, the database keeps a history of the *real-world states* that are represented. However, because updates,

---

16. A combination of the nontemporal key and the valid end time attribute VET could also be used.

insertions, and deletions may be applied retroactively or proactively, there is no record of the actual *database state* at any point in time. If the actual database states are more important to an application, then one should use *transaction time relations*.

Transaction Time Relations.   In a transaction time database, whenever a change is applied to the database, the actual **timestamp** of the transaction that applied the change (insert, delete, or update) is recorded. Such a database is most useful when changes are applied *simultaneously* in the majority of cases—for example, real-time stock trading or banking transactions. If we convert the nontemporal database of Figure 23.1 into a transaction time database, then the two relations EMPLOYEE and DEPARTMENT are converted into **transaction time relations** by adding the attributes TST (Transaction Start Time) and TET (Transaction End Time), whose data type is typically TIMESTAMP. This is shown in Figure 23.6(b), where the relations have been renamed EMP_TT and DEPT_TT, respectively.

In EMP_TT, each tuple v represents a *version* of an employee's information that was created at actual time v.TST and was (logically) removed at actual time v.TET (because the information was no longer correct). In EMP_TT, the *current version* of each employee typically has a special value, **uc (Until Changed),** as its transaction end time, which indicates that the tuple represents correct information *until it is changed* by some other transaction.[17] A transaction time database has also been called a **rollback database,**[18] because a user can logically roll back to the actual database state at any past point in time t by retrieving all tuple versions v whose transaction time period [v.TST, v.TET] includes time point t.

Bitemporal Relations.   Some applications require both valid time and transaction time, leading to **bitemporal relations.** In our example, Figure 23.6(c) shows how the EMPLOYEE and DEPARTMENT non-temporal relations in Figure 23.1 would appear as bitemporal relations EMP_BT and DEPT_BT, respectively. Figure 23.8 shows a few tuples in these relations. In these tables, tuples whose transaction end time TET is *uc* are the ones representing currently valid information, whereas tuples whose TET is an absolute timestamp are tuples that were valid until (just before) that timestamp. Hence, the tuples with *uc* in Figure 23.8 correspond to the valid time tuples in Figure 23.7. The transaction start time attribute TST in each tuple is the timestamp of the transaction that created that tuple.

Now consider how an **update operation** would be implemented on a bitemporal relation. In this model of bitemporal databases,[19] *no attributes are physically changed* in any tuple except for the transaction end time attribute TET with a value of *uc*.[20] To illustrate

---

17. The *uc* variable in transaction time relations corresponds to the *now* variable in valid time relations. The semantics are slightly different though.

18. The term rollback here does not have the same meaning as *transaction rollback* (see Chapter 21) during recovery, where the transaction updates are *physically undone*. Rather, here the updates can be *logically undone*, allowing the user to examine the database as it appeared at a previous time point.

19. There have been many proposed temporal database models. We are describing specific models here as examples to illustrate the concepts.

20. Some bitemporal models allow the VET attribute to be changed also, but the interpretations of the tuples are different in those models.

EMP_BT

	NAME	SSN	SALARY	DNO	SUPERVISOR_SSN	VST	VET	TST	TET
v1:	Smith	123456789	25000	5	333445555	1997-06-15	now	1997-06-08,13:05:58	1998-06-04,08:56:12
v2:	Smith	123456789	25000	5	333445555	1997-06-15	1998-05-31	1998-06-04,08:56:12	uc
v3:	Smith	123456789	30000	5	333445555	1998-06-01	now	1998-06-04,08:56:12	uc
v4:	Wong	333445555	25000	4	999887777	1994-08-20	now	1994-08-20,11:18:23	1996-01-07,14:33:02
v5:	Wong	333445555	25000	4	999887777	1994-08-20	1996-01-31	1996-01-07,14:33:02	uc
v6:	Wong	333445555	30000	5	999887777	1996-02-01	now	1996-01-07,14:33:02	1997-03-28,09:23:57
v7:	Wong	333445555	30000	5	999887777	1996-02-01	1997-03-31	1997-03-28,09:23:57	uc
v8:	Wong	333445555	40000	5	888665555	1997-04-01	now	1997-03-28,09:23:57	uc
v9:	Brown	222447777	28000	4	999887777	1996-05-01	now	1996-04-27,16:22:05	1997-08-12,10:11:07
v10:	Brown	222447777	28000	4	999887777	1996-05-01	1997-08-10	1997-08-12,10:11:07	uc
v11:	Narayan	666884444	38000	5	333445555	1998-08-01	now	1998-07-28,09:25:37	uc

. . .

DEPT_VT

	DNAME	DNO	MANAGER_SSN	VST	VET	TST	TET
v12:	Research	5	888665555	1996-09-20	now	1996-09-15,14:52:12	1996-03-28,09:23:57
v13:	Research	5	888665555	1996-09-20	1997-03-31	1997-03-28,09:23:57	uc
v14:	Research	5	333445555	1997-04-01	now	1997-03-28,09:23:57	uc

. . .

Figure 23.8 Some tuple versions in the bitemporal relations EMP_BT and DEPT_BT.

how tuples are created, consider the EMP_BT relation. The *current version* v of an employee has uc in its TET attribute and *now* in its VET attribute. If some attribute—say, SALARY—is updated, then the transaction T that performs the update should have two parameters: the new value of SALARY and the valid time VT when the new salary becomes effective (in the real world). Assume that VT− is the time point before VT in the given valid time granularity and that transaction T has a timestamp TS(T). Then, the following physical changes would be applied to the EMP_BT table:

1. Make a copy v2 of the current version v; set v2.VET to VT−, v2.TST to TS(T), v2.TET to uc, and insert v2 in EMP_BT; v2 is a copy of the previous current version v *after it is closed* at valid time VT−.

2. Make a copy v3 of the current version v; set v3.VST to VT, v3.VET to *now*, v3.SALARY to the new salary value, v3.TST to TS(T), v3.TET to uc, and insert v3 in EMP_BT; v3 represents the new current version.

3. Set v.TET to TS(T) since the current version is no longer representing correct information.

As an illustration, consider the first three tuples v1, v2, and v3 in EMP_BT in Figure 23.8. Before the update of Smith's salary from 25000 to 30000, only v1 was in EMP_BT and it was the current version and its TET was *uc*. Then, a transaction T whose timestamp TS(T) is 1998-06-04,08:56:12 updates the salary to 30000 with the effective valid time of 1998-06-01. The tuple v2 is created, which is a copy of v1 except that its VET is set to 1998-05-31, one day less than the new valid time and its TST is the timestamp of the updating transaction. The tuple v3 is also created, which has the new salary, its VST is set to 1998-06-01, and its TST is also the timestamp of the updating transaction. Finally, the TET of v1 is set to the timestamp of the updating transaction, 1998-06-04,08:56:12. Note that this is a *retroactive update*, since the updating transaction ran on June 4, 1998, but the salary change is effective on June 1, 1998.

Similarly, when Wong's salary and department are updated (at the same time) to 30000 and 5, the updating transaction's timestamp is 1996-01-07,14:33:02 and the effective valid time for the update is 1996-02-01. Hence, this is a *proactive update* because the transaction ran on January 7, 1996, but the effective date was February 1, 1996. In this case, tuple v4 is logically replaced by v5 and v6.

Next, let us illustrate how a **delete operation** would be implemented on a bitemporal relation by considering the tuples v9 and v10 in the EMP_BT relation of Figure 23.8. Here, employee Brown left the company effective August 10, 1997, and the logical delete is carried out by a transaction T with TS(T) = 1997-08-12,10:11:07. Before this, v9 was the current version of Brown, and its TET was *uc*. The logical delete is implemented by setting v9.TET to 1997-08-12,10:11:07 to invalidate it, and creating the *final version* v10 for Brown, with its VET = 1997-08-10 (see Figure 23.8). Finally, an **insert operation** is implemented by creating the *first version* as illustrated by v11 in the EMP_BT table.

Implementation Considerations.   There are various options for storing the tuples in a temporal relation. One is to store all the tuples in the same table, as in Figures 23.7 and 23.8. Another option is to create two tables: one for the currently valid information and the other for the rest of the tuples. For example, in the bitemporal EMP_BT relation, tuples with *uc* for their TET and *now* for their VET would be in one relation, the *current table*, since they are the ones currently valid (that is, represent the current snapshot), and all other tuples would be in another relation. This allows the database administrator to have different access paths, such as indexes for each relation, and keeps the size of the current table reasonable. Another possibility is to create a third table for corrected tuples whose TET is not *uc*.

Another option that is available is to *vertically partition* the attributes of the temporal relation into separate relations. The reason for this is that, if a relation has many attributes, a whole new tuple version is created whenever any one of the attributes is updated. If the attributes are updated asynchronously, each new version may differ in only one of the attributes, thus needlessly repeating the other attribute values. If a separate relation is created to contain only the attributes that *always change synchronously*, with the primary key replicated in each relation, the database is said to be in **temporal normal form.** However, to combine the information, a variation of join known as **temporal intersection join** would be needed, which is generally expensive to implement.

It is important to note that bitemporal databases allow a complete record of changes. Even a record of corrections is possible. For example, it is possible that two tuple versions of the same employee may have the same valid time but different attribute values as long as their transaction times are disjoint. In this case, the tuple with the later transaction time is a **correction** of the other tuple version. Even incorrectly entered valid times may be corrected this way. The incorrect state of the database will still be available as a previous database state for querying purposes. A database that keeps such a complete record of changes and corrections has been called an **append only database.**

23.2.3 Incorporating Time in Object-Oriented Databases Using Attribute Versioning

The previous section discussed the **tuple versioning approach** to implementing temporal databases. In this approach, whenever one attribute value is changed, a whole new tuple version is created, even though all the other attribute values will be identical to the previous tuple version. An alternative approach can be used in database systems that support **complex structured objects,** such as object databases (see Chapters 11 and 12) or object-relational systems (see Chapter 13). This approach is called **attribute versioning.**[21]

In attribute versioning, a single complex object is used to store all the temporal changes of the object. Each attribute that changes over time is called a **time-varying attribute,** and it has its values versioned over time by adding temporal periods to the attribute. The temporal periods may represent valid time, transaction time, or bitemporal, depending on the application requirements. Attributes that do not change are called **non-time-varying** and are not associated with the temporal periods. To illustrate this, consider the example in Figure 23.9, which is an attribute versioned valid time representation of EMPLOYEE using the ODL notation for object databases (see Chapter 12). Here, we assumed that name and social security number are non-time-varying attributes (they do not change over time), whereas salary, department, and supervisor are time-varying attributes (they may change over time). Each time-varying attribute is represented as a list of tuples <valid_start_time, valid_end_time, value>, ordered by valid start time.

Whenever an attribute is changed in this model, the current attribute version is *closed* and a **new attribute version** for this attribute only is appended to the list. This allows attributes to change asynchronously. The current value for each attribute has *now* for its valid_end_time. When using attribute versioning, it is useful to include a **lifespan temporal attribute** associated with the whole object whose value is one or more valid time periods that indicate the valid time of existence for the whole object. Logical deletion of the object is implemented by closing the lifespan. The constraint that any time period of an attribute within an object should be a subset of the object's lifespan should be enforced.

For bitemporal databases, each attribute version would have a tuple with five components:

<valid_start_time, valid_end_time, trans_start_time, trans_end_time, value>

The object lifespan would also include both valid and transaction time dimensions. The full capabilities of bitemporal databases can hence be available with attribute versioning. Mechanisms similar to those discussed earlier for updating tuple versions can be applied to updating attribute versions.

---

21. Attribute versioning can also be used in the nested relational model (see Chapter 13).

```
class Temporal_Salary
{
    attribute    Date            valid_start_time;
    attribute    Date            valid_end_time;
    attribute    float           salary;
};

class Temporal_Dept
{
    attribute    Date            valid_start_time;
    attribute    Date            valid_end_time;
    attribute    Department_VT   dept;
};

class Temporal_Supervisor
{
    attribute    Date            valid_start_time;
    attribute    Date            valid_end_time;
    attribute    Employee_VT     supervisor;
};

class Temporal_Lifespan
{
    attribute    Date            valid_ start_time;
    attribute    Date            valid_end_time;
};

class Employee_VT
(    extent    employees)
{
    attribute    list<Temporal_Lifespan>      lifespan;
    attribute    string                       name;
    attribute    string                       ssn;
    attribute    list<Temporal_Salary>        sal_history;
    attribute    list<Temporal_Dept>          dept_history;
    attribute    list<Temporal_Supervisor>    supervisor_history;
};
```

Figure 23.9   Possible ODL schema for a temporal valid time Employee_VT object class using attribute versioning.

23.2.4   Temporal Querying Constructs and the TSQL2 Language

So far, we have discussed how data models may be extended with temporal constructs. We now give a brief overview of how query operations need to be extended for temporal querying. Then we briefly discuss the TSQL2 language, which extends SQL for querying valid time, transaction time, and bitemporal relational databases.

In nontemporal relational databases, the typical selection conditions involve attribute conditions, and tuples that satisfy these conditions are selected from the set of *current tuples*. Following that, the attributes of interest to the query are specified by a *projection operation* (see Chapter 7). For example, in the query to retrieve the names of all employees working in department 5 whose salary is greater than 30000, the selection condition would be:

```
((SALARY > 30000) AND (DNO = 5))
```

The projected attribute would be NAME. In a temporal database, the conditions may involve time in addition to attributes. A **pure time condition** involves only time—for example, to select all employee tuple versions that were valid on a certain *time point* t or that were valid *during a certain time period* [t1, t2]. In this case, the specified time period is compared with the valid time period of each tuple version [t.VST, t.VET], and only those tuples that satisfy the condition are selected. In these operations, a period is considered to be equivalent to the set of time points from t1 to t2 inclusive, so the standard set comparison operations can be used. Additional operations, such as whether one time period ends *before* another starts are also needed.[22] Some of the more common operations used in queries are as follows:

[t.VST, t.VET] **INCLUDES** [t1, t2]	Equivalent to $t1 \geq t.VST$ AND $t2 \leq t.VET$
[t.VST, t.VET] **INCLUDED_IN** [t1, t2]	Equivalent to $t1 \leq t.VST$ AND $t2 \geq t.VET$
[t.VST, t.VET] **OVERLAPS** [t1, t2]	Equivalent to $(t1 \leq t.VET$ AND $t2 \geq t.VST)$[23]
[t.VST, t.VET] **BEFORE** [t1, t2]	Equivalent to $t1 \geq t.VET$
[t.VST, t.VET] **AFTER** [t1, t2]	Equivalent to $t2 \leq t.VST$
[t.VST, t.VET] **MEETS_BEFORE** [t1, t2]	Equivalent to $t1 = t.VET + 1$[24]
[t.VST, t.VET] **MEETS_AFTER** [t1, t2]	Equivalent to $t2 + 1 = t.VST$

In addition, operations are needed to manipulate time periods, such as computing the union or intersection of two time periods. The results of these operations may not themselves be periods, but rather **temporal elements**—a collection of one or more *disjoint* time periods such that no two time periods in a temporal element are directly adjacent. That is, for any two time periods [t1, t2] and [t3, t4] in a temporal element, the following three conditions must hold:

- [t1, t2] **intersection** [t3, t4] is empty.
- t3 is not the time point following t2 in the given granularity.
- t1 is not the time point following t4 in the given granularity.

---

22. A complete set of operations, known as **Allen's algebra,** has been defined for comparing time periods.

23. This operation returns true if the *intersection* of the two periods is not empty; it has also been called INTERSECTS_WITH.

24. Here, 1 (one) refers to one time point in the specified granularity. The MEETS operations basically specify if one period starts immediately after the other period ends.

The latter conditions are necessary to ensure unique representations of temporal elements. If two time periods [t1, t2] and [t3, t4] are adjacent, they are combined into a single time period [t1, t4]. This is called **coalescing** of time periods. Coalescing also combines intersecting time periods.

To illustrate how pure time conditions can be used, suppose a user wants to select all employee versions that were valid at any point during 1997. The appropriate selection condition applied to the relation in Figure 23.7 would be

[t.VST, t.VET] OVERLAPS [1997-01-01, 1997-12-31]

Typically, most temporal selections are applied to the valid time dimension. For a bitemporal database, one usually applies the conditions to the currently correct tuples with *uc* as their transaction end times. However, if the query needs to be applied to a previous database state, an AS_OF t clause is appended to the query, which means that the query is applied to the valid time tuples that were correct in the database at time t.

In addition to pure time conditions, other selections involve **attribute and time conditions.** For example, suppose we wish to retrieve all EMP_VT tuple versions t for employees who worked in department 5 at any time during 1997. In this case, the condition is

([t.VST, t.VET] OVERLAPS [1997-01-01, 1997-12-31]) AND (t.DNO = 5)

Finally, we give a brief overview of the TSQL2 query language, which extends SQL with constructs for temporal databases. The main idea behind TSQL2 is to allow users to specify whether a relation is nontemporal (that is, a standard SQL relation) or temporal. The CREATE TABLE statement is extended with an *optional* AS-clause to allow users to declare different temporal options. The following options are available:

- AS VALID STATE <granularity> (valid time relation with valid time period)
- AS VALID EVENT <granularity> (valid time relation with valid time point)
- AS TRANSACTION (transaction time relation with transaction time period)
- AS VALID STATE <granularity> AND TRANSACTION (bitemporal relation, valid time period)
- AS VALID EVENT <granularity> AND TRANSACTION (bitemporal relation, valid time point)

The keywords STATE and EVENT are used to specify whether a time *period* or time *point* is associated with the valid time dimension. In TSQL2, rather than have the user actually see how the temporal tables are implemented (as we discussed in the previous sections), the TSQL2 language adds query language constructs to specify various types of temporal selections, temporal projections, temporal aggregations, transformation among granularities, and many other concepts. The book by Snodgrass et al. (1995) describes the language.

23.2.5 Time Series Data

Time series data are used very often in financial, sales, and economics applications. They involve data values that are recorded according to a specific predefined sequence of time points. They are hence a special type of **valid event data,** where the event time points are predetermined according to a fixed calendar. Consider the example of closing daily stock prices of a particular company on the New York Stock Exchange. The granularity here is day, but the days that the stock market is open are known (nonholiday weekdays). Hence, it has been common to specify a computational procedure that calculates the particular **calendar** associated with a time series. Typical queries on time series involve **temporal aggregation** over higher granularity intervals—for example, finding the average or maximum *weekly* closing stock price or the maximum and minimum *monthly* closing stock price from the *daily* information.

As another example, consider the daily sales dollar amount at each store of a chain of stores owned by a particular company. Again, typical temporal aggregates would be retrieving the weekly, monthly, or yearly sales from the daily sales information (using the sum aggregate function), or comparing same store monthly sales with previous monthly sales, and so on.

Because of the specialized nature of time series data, and the lack of support in older DBMSs, it has been common to use specialized **time series management systems** rather that general purpose DBMSs for managing such information. In such systems, it has been common to store time series values in sequential order in a file, and apply specialized time series procedures to analyze the information. The problem with this approach is that the full power of high-level querying in languages such as SQL will not be available in such systems.

More recently, some commercial DBMS packages are offering time series extensions, such as the time series datablade of Informix Universal Server (see Chapter 13). In addition, the TSQL2 language provides some support for time series in the form of event tables.

23.3 Spatial and Multimedia Databases

Because the two topics discussed in this section are very broad, we can give only a very brief introduction to these fields. Section 23.3.1 introduces spatial databases, and Section 23.3.2 briefly discusses multimedia databases.

23.3.1 Introduction to Spatial Database Concepts

Spatial databases provide concepts for databases that keep track of objects in a multidimensional space. For example, cartographic databases that store maps include two-dimensional spatial descriptions of their objects—from countries and states to rivers, cities, roads, seas, and so on. These databases are used in many applications, such as environmental, emergency, and battle management. Other databases, such as meteorological databases for weather information, are three-dimensional, since temperatures and other meteorological information are related to three-dimensional spatial points. In general, a spatial database stores objects that have spatial characteristics that describe them. The spatial relationships among the objects are important, and they are often needed when querying the database. Although a spatial database can in general refer to an n-dimensional space for any n, we will limit our discussion to two dimensions as an illustration.

The main extensions that are needed for spatial databases are models that can interpret spatial characteristics. In addition, special indexing and storage structures are often needed to improve performance. Let us first discuss some of the model extensions for two-dimensional spatial databases. The basic extensions needed are to include two-dimensional geometric concepts, such as points, lines and line segments, circles, polygons, and arcs, in order to specify the spatial characteristics of objects. In addition, spatial operations are needed to operate on the objects' spatial characteristics—for example, to compute the distance between two objects—as well as spatial Boolean conditions—for example, to check whether two objects spatially overlap. To illustrate, consider a database that is used for emergency management applications. A description of the spatial positions of many types of objects would be needed. Some of these objects generally have static spatial characteristics, such as streets and highways, water pumps (for fire control), police stations, fire stations, and hospitals. Other objects have dynamic spatial characteristics that change over time, such as police vehicles, ambulances, or fire trucks.

The following categories illustrate three typical types of spatial queries:

- *Range query:* Finds the objects of a particular type that are within a given spatial area or within a particular distance from a given location. (For example, finds all hospitals within the Dallas city area, or finds all ambulances within five miles of an accident location.)

- *Nearest neighbor query:* Finds an object of a particular type that is closest to a given location. (For example, finds the police car that is closest to a particular location.)

- *Spatial joins or overlays:* Typically joins the objects of two types based on some spatial condition, such as the objects intersecting or overlapping spatially or being within a certain distance of one another. (For example, finds all cities that fall on a major highway or finds all homes that are within two miles of a lake.)

For these and other types of spatial queries to be answered efficiently, special techniques for spatial indexing are needed. One of the best known techniques is the use of **R-trees** and their variations. R-trees group together objects that are in close spatial physical proximity on the same leaf nodes of a tree-structured index. Since a leaf node can point to only a certain number of objects, algorithms for dividing the space into rectangular subspaces that include the objects are needed. Typical criteria for dividing the space include minimizing the rectangle areas, since this would lead to a quicker narrowing of the search space. Problems such as having objects with overlapping spatial areas are handled in different ways by the many different variations of R-trees. The internal nodes of R-trees are associated with rectangles whose area covers all the rectangles in its subtree. Hence, R-trees can easily answer queries, such as find all objects in a given area by limiting the tree search to those subtrees whose rectangles intersect with the area given in the query.

Other spatial storage structures include quadtrees and their variations. **Quadtrees** generally divide each space or subspace into equally sized areas, and proceed with the subdivisions of each subspace to identify the positions of various objects. Recently, many newer spatial access structures have been proposed, and this area is still an active research area.

23.3.2   Introduction to Multimedia Database Concepts

Multimedia databases provide features that allow users to store and query different types of multimedia information, which includes *images* (such as pictures or drawings), *video clips* (such as movies, newsreels, or home videos), *audio clips* (such as songs, phone messages, or speeches), and *documents* (such as books or articles). The main types of database queries that are needed involve locating multimedia sources that contain certain objects of interest. For example, one may want to locate all video clips in a video database that include a certain person in them, say Bill Clinton. One may also want to retrieve video clips based on certain activities included in them, such as a video clips were a goal is scored in a soccer game by a certain player or team.

The above types of queries are referred to as **content-based retrieval,** because the multimedia source is being retrieved based on its containing certain objects or activities. Hence, a multimedia database must use some model to organize and index the multimedia sources based on their contents. *Identifying the contents* of multimedia sources is a difficult and time-consuming task. There are two main approaches. The first is based on **automatic analysis** of the multimedia sources to identify certain mathematical characteristics of their contents. This approach uses different techniques depending on the type of multimedia source (image, text, video, or audio). The second approach depends on **manual identification** of the objects and activities of interest in each multimedia source and on using this information to index the sources. This approach can be applied to all the different multimedia sources, but it requires a manual preprocessing phase where a person has to scan each multimedia source to identify and catalog the objects and activities it contains so that they can be used to index these sources.

In the remainder of this section, we will very briefly discuss some of the characteristics of each type of multimedia source—images, video, audio, and text sources, in that order.

An **image** is typically stored either in raw form as a set of pixel or cell values, or in compressed form to save space. The image *shape descriptor* describes the geometric shape of the raw image, which is typically a rectangle of **cells** of a certain width and height. Hence, each image can be represented by an m by n grid of cells. Each cell contains a pixel value that describes the cell content. In black/white images, pixels can be one bit. In gray scale or color images, a pixel is multiple bits. Because images may require large amounts of space, they are often stored in compressed form. Compression standards, such as the GIF standard, use various mathematical transformations to reduce the number of cells stored but still maintain the main image characteristics. The mathematical transforms that can be used include Discrete Fourier Transform (DFT), Discrete Cosine Transform (DCT), and wavelet transforms.

To identify objects of interest in an image, the image is typically divided into homogeneous segments using a *homogeneity predicate*. For example, in a color image, cells that are adjacent to one another and whose pixel values are close are grouped into a segment. The homogeneity predicate defines the conditions for how to automatically group those cells. Segmentation and compression can hence identify the main characteristics of an image.

A typical image database query would be to find images in the database that are similar to a given image. The given image could be an isolated segment that contains, say, a pattern of interest, and the query is to locate other images that contain that same pattern. There are two main techniques for this type of search. The first approach uses a **distance function** to compare the given image with the stored images and their segments. If the distance value returned is small, the probability of a match is high. Indexes can be created to group together stored images that are close in the distance metric so as to limit the search space. The second approach, called the **transformation approach,** measures image similarity by having a small number of transformations that can transform one image's cells to match the other image. Transformations include rotations, translations, and scaling. Although the latter approach is more general, it is also more time consuming and difficult.

A **video source** is typically represented as a sequence of frames, where each frame is a still image. However, rather than identifying the objects and activities in every individual frame, the video is divided into **video segments,** where each segment is made up of a sequence of contiguous frames that includes the same objects/activities. Each segment is identified by its starting and ending frames. The objects and activities identified in each video segment can be used to index the segments. An indexing technique called *frame segment trees* has been proposed for video indexing. The index includes both objects, such as persons, houses, cars, and activities, such as a person *delivering* a speech or two people *talking*.

A **text/document source** is basically the full text of some article, book, or magazine. These sources are typically indexed by identifying the keywords that appear in the text and their relative frequencies. However, filler words are eliminated from that process. Because there could be too many keywords when attempting to index a collection of documents, techniques have been developed to reduce the number of keywords to those that are most relevant to the collection. A technique called *singular value decompositions* (SVD), which is based on matrix transformations, can be used for this purpose. An indexing technique called *telescoping vector trees*, or TV-trees, can then be used to group similar documents together.

Audio sources include stored recorded messages, such as speeches, class presentations, or even surveillance recording of phone messages or conversations by law enforcement. Here, discrete transforms can be used to identify the main characteristics of a certain person's voice in order to have similarity based indexing and retrieval. Audio characteristic features include loudness, intensity, pitch, and clarity.

23.4 Summary

In this chapter, we introduced database concepts for some of the common features that are needed by advanced applications: active databases, temporal databases, and spatial and multimedia databases. It is important to note that each of these topics is very broad and warrants a complete textbook.

We first introduced the topic of active databases, which provide additional functionality for specifying active rules. We introduced the event-condition-action or ECA model for active databases. The rules can be automatically triggered by events that occur—such as a database update—and they can initiate certain actions that have been specified in the rule declaration if certain conditions are true. Many commercial packages already have some of the functionality provided by active databases in the form of triggers. We discussed the different options for specifying rules, such as row-level versus statement-level, before versus after, and immediate versus deferred. We gave examples of row-level triggers in the Oracle commercial system, and statement-level rules in the STARBURST experimental system. We briefly discussed some design issues and some possible applications for active databases.

We then introduced some of the concepts of temporal databases, which permit the database system to store a history of changes and allows users to query both current and past states of the database. We discussed how time is represented and distinguished between the valid time and transaction time dimensions. We then discussed how valid time, transaction time, and bitemporal relations can be implemented using tuple versioning in the relational model, with examples to illustrate how updates, inserts, and deletes are implemented. We also showed how complex objects can be used to implement temporal databases using attribute versioning. We then looked at some of the querying operations for temporal relational databases and gave a very brief introduction to the TSQL2 language.

We then turned to spatial and multimedia databases. Spatial databases provide concepts for databases that keep track of objects that have spatial characteristics, and they require models for representing these spatial characteristics and operators for comparing and manipulating them. Multimedia databases provide features that allow users to store and query different types of multimedia information, which includes images (such as pictures or drawings), video clips (such as movies, news reels, or home videos), audio clips (such as songs, phone messages, or speeches), and documents (such as books or articles). We gave a very brief overview of the various types of media sources and how multimedia sources may be indexed.

Review Questions

23.1. What are the differences between row-level and statement-level active rules?

23.2. What are the differences among immediate, deferred, and detached *consideration* of active rule conditions?

23.3. What are the differences among immediate, deferred, and detached *execution* of active rule actions?

23.4. Briefly discuss the consistency and termination problems when designing a set of active rules.

23.5. Discuss some applications of active databases.

23.6. Discuss how time is represented in temporal databases and compare the different time dimensions.

23.7. What are the differences between valid time, transaction time, and bitemporal relations?

23.8. Describe how the insert, delete, and update commands should be implemented on a valid time relation.

23.9. Describe how the insert, delete, and update commands should be implemented on a bitemporal relation.

23.10. Describe how the insert, delete, and update commands should be implemented on a transaction time relation.

23.11. What are the main differences between tuple versioning and attribute versioning?

23.12. How do spatial databases differ from regular databases?

23.13. What are the different types of multimedia sources?

23.14. How are multimedia sources indexed for content-based retrieval?

Exercises

23.15. Consider the COMPANY database described in Figure 7.6. Using the syntax of Oracle triggers, write active rules to do the following:

    a. Whenever an employee's project assignments are changed, check if the total hours per week spent on the employee's projects are less than 30 or greater than 40; if so, notify the employee's direct supervisor.

    b. Whenever an EMPLOYEE is deleted, delete the PROJECT tuples and DEPENDENT tuples related to that employee, and if the employee is managing a department or supervising any employees, set the MGRSSN for that department to null and set the SUPERSSN for those employees to null.

23.16. Repeat 23.15 but use the syntax of STARBURST active rules.

23.17. Consider the relational schema shown in Figure 23.10. Write active rules for keeping the SUM_COMMISSIONS attribute of SALES_PERSON equal to the sum of the COMMISSION attribute in SALES for each sales person. Your rules should also check if the SUM_COMMISSIONS exceeds 100000; if it does, call a procedure notify_manager(S_ID). Write both statement-level rules in STARBURST notation and row-level rules in Oracle.

23.18. Consider the UNIVERSITY EER schema of Figure 4.10. Write some rules (in English) that could be implemented via active rules to enforce some common integrity constraints that you think are relevant to this application.

SALES

S_ID	V_ID	COMMISSION

SALES_PERSON

SALESPERSON_ID	NAME	TITLE	PHONE	SUM_COMMISSIONS

Figure 23.10 Database schema for sales and salesperson commissions in Exercise 23.17.

23.19. Discuss which of the updates that created each of the tuples shown in Figure 23.8 were applied retroactively and which were applied proactively.

23.20. Show how the following updates, if applied in sequence, would change the contents of the bitemporal EMP_BT relation in Figure 23.8. For each update, state whether it is a retroactive or proactive update.

    a. On 1999-03-10,17:30:00, the salary of Narayan is updated to 40000, effective on 1999-03-01.

    b. On 1998-07-30,08:31:00, the salary of Smith was corrected to show that it should have been entered as 31000 (instead of 30000 as shown), effective on 1998-06-01.

    c. On 1999-03-18,08:31:00, the database was changed to indicate that Narayan was leaving the company (i.e., logically deleted) effective 1999-03-31.

    d. On 1999-04-20,14:07:33, the database was changed to indicate the hiring of a new employee called Johnson, with the tuple <'Johnson', '334455667', 1, null> effective on 1999-04-20.

    e. On 1999-04-28,12:54:02, the database was changed to indicate that Wong was leaving the company (i.e. logically deleted) effective 1999-06-01.

    f. On 1999-05-05,13:07:33, the database was changed to indicate the rehiring of Brown, with the same department and supervisor but with salary 35000 effective on 1999-05-01.

23.21. Show how the updates given in Exercise 23.20, if applied in sequence, would change the contents of the valid time EMP_VT relation in Figure 23.7.

Selected Bibliography

The book by Zaniolo et al. (1997) consists of several parts, each describing an advanced database concept such as active, temporal, and spatial/text/multimedia databases. Widom and Ceri (1996) and Ceri and Fraternali (1997) focus on active database concepts and systems. Snodgrass et al. (1995) describe the TSQL2 language and data model. Khoshafian and Baker (1996), Faloutsos (1996), and Subrahmanian (1998) describe multimedia database concepts. Tansel et al. (1992) is a collection of chapters on temporal databases.

STARBURST rules are described in Widom and Finkelstein (1990). Early work on active databases includes the HiPAC project, discussed in Chakravarthy et al. (1989) and Chakravarthy (1990). A glossary for temporal databases is given in Jensen et al. (1994). Snodgrass (1987) focuses on TQuel, an early temporal query language.

Temporal normalization is defined in Navathe and Ahmed (1989). Paton (1999) and Paton and Diaz (1999) survey active databases. Chakravarthy et al. (1994) describe SENTINEL, and object-based active systems. Lee et al. (1998) discuss time series management.

CHAPTER 24

Distributed Databases and Client-Server Architecture

In this chapter we turn our attention to distributed databases (DDBs), distributed database management systems (DDBMSs), and how the client-server architecture is used as a platform for database application development. The DDB technology emerged as a merger of two technologies: (1) database technology, and (2) network and data communication technology. The latter has made tremendous strides in terms of wired and wireless technologies—from satellite and cellular communications and Metropolitan Area Networks (MANs) to the standardization of protocols like Ethernet, TCP/IP, and the Asynchronous Transfer Mode (ATM) as well as the explosion of the Internet, including the newly started Internet-2 development. While early databases moved toward centralization and resulted in monolithic gigantic databases in the seventies and early eighties, the trend reversed toward more decentralization and autonomy of processing in the late eighties. With advances in distributed processing and distributed computing that occurred in the operating systems arena, the database research community did considerable work to address the issues of data distribution, distributed query and transaction processing, distributed database metadata management, and other topics, and developed many research prototypes. However, a full-scale comprehensive DDBMS that implements the functionality and techniques proposed in DDB research never emerged as a commercially viable product. Most major vendors redirected their efforts from developing a "pure" DDBMS product into developing systems based on client-server, or toward developing active heterogeneous DBMSs.

Organizations, however, have been very interested in the *decentralization* of processing (at the system level) while achieving an *integration* of the information resources (at the logical level) within their geographically distributed systems of databases, applications, and users. Coupled with the advances in communications, there is now a general endorsement of the client-server approach to application development, which assumes many of the DDB issues.

In this chapter we discuss both distributed databases and client-server architectures,[1] in the development of database technology that is closely tied to advances in communications and network technology. Details of the latter are outside our scope; the reader is referred to a series of texts on data communications (see the Selected Bibliography at the end of this chapter).

Section 24.1 introduces distributed database management and related concepts. Detailed issues of distributed database design, involving fragmenting of data and distributing it over multiple sites with possible replication, are discussed in Section 24.2. Section 24.3 introduces different types of distributed database systems, including federated and multidatabase systems and highlights the problems of heterogeneity and the needs of autonomy in federated database systems, which will dominate for years to come. Sections 24.4 and 24.5 introduce distributed database query and transaction processing techniques, respectively. Section 24.6 discusses how the client-server architectural concepts are related to distributed databases. Section 24.7 elaborates on future issues in client-server architectures. Section 24.8 discusses distributed database features of the Oracle RDBMS.

For a short introduction to the topic, only sections 24.1, 24.3, and 24.6 may be covered.

24.1   Distributed Database Concepts

Distributed databases bring the advantages of distributed computing to the database management domain. A **distributed computing system** consists of a number of processing elements, not necessarily homogeneous, that are interconnected by a computer network, and that cooperate in performing certain assigned tasks. As a general goal, distributed computing systems partition a big, unmanageable problem into smaller pieces and solve it efficiently in a coordinated manner. The economic viability of this approach stems from two reasons: (1) more computer power is harnessed to solve a complex task, and (2) each autonomous processing element can be managed independently and develop its own applications.

We can define a **distributed database** (DDB) as a collection of multiple logically interrelated databases distributed over a computer network, and a **distributed database management system** (DDBMS) as a software system that manages a distributed database while making the distribution transparent to the user.[2] A collection of files stored at different nodes of a network and the maintaining of inter relationships among them via hyperlinks has become a common organization on the Internet, with files of Web pages.

---

1. The reader should review the introduction to client-server architecture in Section 17.1.

2. This definition and some of the discussion in this section is based on Ozsu and Valduriez (1999).

The common functions of database management, including uniform query processing and transaction processing, *do not* apply to this scenario yet. The technology is, however, moving in a direction such that distributed World Wide Web (WWW) databases will become a reality in the near future. We shall discuss issues of accessing databases on the Web in Section 27.1 and mobile and intermittently connected databases in Section 27.3. None of those qualify as DDB by the definition given earlier.

24.1.1 Parallel Versus Distributed Technology

Turning our attention to system architectures, there are two main types of multiprocessor system architectures that are commonplace:

- *Shared memory (tightly coupled) architecture:* Multiple processors share secondary (disk) storage and also share primary memory.
- *Shared disk (loosely coupled) architecture:* Multiple processors share secondary (disk) storage but each has their own primary memory.

These architectures enable processors to communicate without the overhead of exchanging messages over a network.[3] Database management systems developed using the above types of architectures are termed **parallel database management systems** rather than DDBMS, since they utilize parallel processor technology. Another type of multiprocessor architecture is called **shared nothing architecture.** In this architecture, every processor has its own primary and secondary (disk) memory, no common memory exists, and the processors communicate over a high-speed interconnection network (bus or switch). Although the shared nothing architecture resembles a distributed database computing environment, major differences exist in the mode of operation. In shared nothing multiprocessor systems, there is symmetry and homogeneity of nodes; this is not true of the distributed database environment where heterogeneity of hardware and operating system at each node is very common. Shared nothing architecture is also considered as an environment for parallel databases. Figure 24.1 contrasts these different architectures.

24.1.2 Advantages of Distributed Databases

Distributed database management has been proposed for various reasons ranging from organizational decentralization and economical processing to greater autonomy. We highlight some of these advantages here.

1. *Management of distributed data with different levels of transparency:* Ideally, a DBMS should be **distribution transparent** in the sense of hiding the details of where each file (table, relation) is physically stored within the system. Consider the company database in Figure 7.5 that we have been discussing throughout the book. The EMPLOYEE, PROJECT, and WORKS_ON tables may be fragmented horizontally

---

3. If both primary and secondary memories are shared, the architecture is also known as **shared everything architecture.**

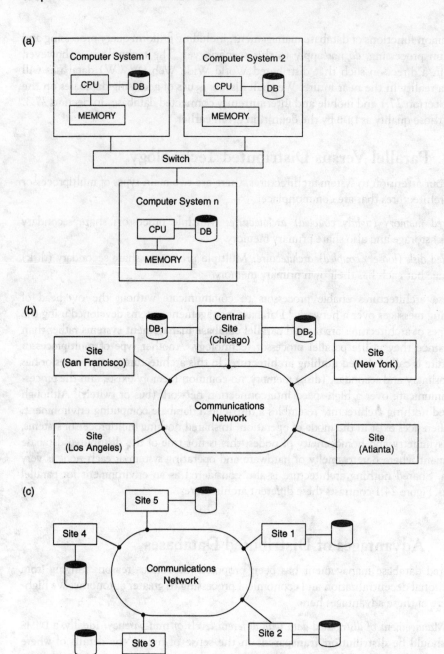

Figure 24.1   Some different database system architectures. (a) Shared nothing architecture. (b) A networked architecture with a centralized database at one of the sites. (c) A truly distributed database architecture.

(that is, into sets of rows, as we shall discuss in Section 24.2) and stored with possible replication as shown in Figure 24.2. The following types of transparencies are possible:

- *Distribution or network transparency:* This refers to freedom for the user from the operational details of the network. It may be divided into location transparency and naming transparency. **Location transparency** refers to the fact that the command used to perform a task is independent of the location of data and the location of the system where the command was issued. **Naming transparency** implies that once a name is specified, the named objects can be accessed unambiguously without additional specification.

- *Replication transparency:* As we show in Figure 24.2, copies of data may be stored at multiple sites for better availability, performance, and reliability. Replication transparency makes the user unaware of the existence of copies.

- *Fragmentation transparency:* Two types of fragmentation are possible. **Horizontal fragmentation** distributes a relation into sets of tuples (rows). **Vertical fragmentation** distributes a relation into subrelations where each subrelation is defined by a subset of the columns of the original relation. A global query by the user must be transformed into several fragment queries. Fragmentation transparency makes the user unaware of the existence of fragments.

2. *Increased reliability and availability:* These are two of the most common potential advantages cited for distributed databases. **Reliability** is broadly defined as the probability that a system is running (not down) at a certain time point, whereas

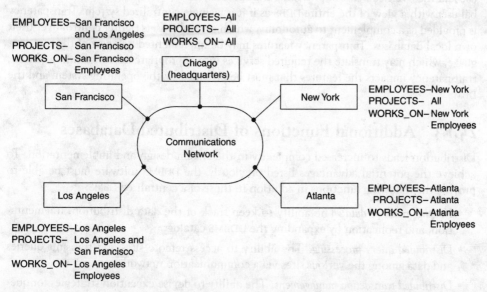

EMPLOYEES–San Francisco
    and Los Angeles
PROJECTS– San Francisco
WORKS_ON– San Francisco
    Employees

EMPLOYEES–All
PROJECTS– All
WORKS_ON– All

Chicago
(headquarters)

San Francisco

New York

EMPLOYEES–New York
PROJECTS– All
WORKS_ON– New York
    Employees

Communications
Network

Los Angeles

Atlanta

EMPLOYEES–Atlanta
PROJECTS– Atlanta
WORKS_ON– Atlanta
    Employees

EMPLOYEES–Los Angeles
PROJECTS– Los Angeles and
    San Francisco
WORKS_ON– Los Angeles
    Employees

Figure 24.2 Data distribution and replication among distributed databases

availability is the probability that the system is continuously available during a time interval. When the data and DBMS software are distributed over several sites, one site may fail while other sites continue to operate. Only the data and software that exist at the failed site cannot be accessed. This improves both reliability and availability. Further improvement is achieved by judiciously *replicating* data and software at more than one site. In a centralized system, failure at a single site makes the whole system unavailable to all users. In a distributed database, some of the data may be unreachable, but users may still be able to access other parts of the database.

3. *Improved performance:* A distributed DBMS fragments the database by keeping the data closer to where it is needed most. **Data localization** reduces the contention for CPU and I/O services and simultaneously reduces access delays involved in wide area networks. When a large database is distributed over multiple sites, smaller databases exist at each site. As a result, local queries and transactions accessing data at a single site have better performance because of the smaller local databases. In addition, each site has a smaller number of transactions executing than if all transactions are submitted to a single centralized database. Moreover, interquery and intraquery parallelism can be achieved by executing multiple queries at different sites, or by breaking up a query into a number of subqueries that execute in parallel. This contributes to improved performance.

4. *Easier expansion:* In a distributed environment, expansion of the system in terms of adding more data, increasing database sizes, or adding more processors is much easier.

The transparencies we discussed in (1) above lead to a compromise between ease of use and the overhead cost of providing transparency. Total transparency provides the global user with a view of the entire DDBS as if it is a single centralized system. Transparency is provided as a complement to **autonomy,** which gives the users tighter control over their own local databases. Transparency features may be implemented as a part of the user language, which may translate the required services into appropriate operations. In addition, transparency impacts the features that must be provided by the operating system and the DBMS.

24.1.3   Additional Functions of Distributed Databases

Distribution leads to increased complexity in the system design and implementation. To achieve the potential advantages listed previously, the DDBMS software must be able to provide the following functions in addition to those of a centralized DBMS:

- *Keeping track of data:* The ability to keep track of the data distribution, fragmentation, and replication by expanding the DDBMS catalog.

- *Distributed query processing:* The ability to access remote sites and transmit queries and data among the various sites via a communication network.

- *Distributed transaction management:* The ability to devise execution strategies for queries and transactions that access data from more than one site and to synchronize the access to distributed data and maintain integrity of the overall database.

- *Replicated data management:* The ability to decide which copy of a replicated data item to access and to maintain the consistency of copies of a replicated data item.

- *Distributed database recovery:* The ability to recover from individual site crashes and from new types of failures such as the failure of a communication links.

- *Security:* Distributed transactions must be executed with the proper management of the security of the data and the authorization/access privileges of users.

- *Distributed directory (catalog) management:* A directory contains information (metadata) about data in the database. The directory may be global for the entire DDB, or local for each site. The placement and distribution of the directory are design and policy issues.

These functions themselves increase the complexity of a DDBMS over a centralized DBMS. Before we can realize the full potential advantages of distribution, we must find satisfactory solutions to these design issues and problems. Including all this additional functionality is hard to accomplish, and finding optimal solutions is a step beyond that.

At the physical **hardware** level, the following main factors distinguish a DDBMS from a centralized system:

- There are multiple computers, called **sites** or **nodes.**

- These sites must be connected by some type of **communication network** to transmit data and commands among sites, as shown in Figure 24.1(c).

The sites may all be located in physical proximity—say, within the same building or group of adjacent buildings—and connected via a **local area network,** or they may be geographically distributed over large distances and connected via a **long-haul** or **wide area network.** Local area networks typically use cables, whereas long-haul networks use telephone lines or satellites. It is also possible to use a combination of the two types of networks.

Networks may have different **topologies** that define the direct communication paths among sites. The type and topology of the network used may have a significant effect on performance and hence on the strategies for distributed query processing and distributed database design. For high-level architectural issues, however, it does not matter which type of network is used; it only matters that each site is able to communicate, directly or indirectly, with every other site. For the remainder of this chapter, we assume that some type of communication network exists among sites, regardless of the particular topology. We will not address any network specific issues, although it is important to understand that for an efficient operation of a DDBS, network design and performance issues are very critical.

24.2 Data Fragmentation, Replication, and Allocation Techniques for Distributed Database Design

In this section we discuss techniques that are used to break up the database into logical units, called **fragments,** which may be assigned for storage at the various sites. We also discuss the use of **data replication,** which permits certain data to be stored in more than one site, and the process of **allocating** fragments—or replicas of fragments—for storage at the various sites. These techniques are used during the process of **distributed database design.** The information concerning data fragmentation, allocation, and replication is stored in a **global directory** that is accessed by the DDBS applications as needed.

24.2.1   Data Fragmentation

In a DDB, decisions must be made regarding which site should be used to store which portions of the database. For now, we will assume that there is *no replication;* that is, each relation—or portion of a relation—is to be stored at only one site. We discuss replication and its effects later in this section. We also use the terminology of relational databases—similar concepts apply to other data models. We assume that we are starting with a relational database schema and must decide on how to distribute the relations over the various sites. To illustrate our discussion, we use the relational database schema in Figure 7.5.

Before we decide on how to distribute the data, we must determine the *logical units* of the database that are to be distributed. The simplest logical units are the relations themselves; that is, each *whole* relation is to be stored at a particular site. In our example, we must decide on a site to store each of the relations EMPLOYEE, DEPARTMENT, PROJECT, WORKS_ON, and DEPENDENT of Figure 7.5. In many cases, however, a relation can be divided into smaller logical units for distribution. For example, consider the company database shown in Figure 7.6, and assume there are three computer sites—one for each department in the company.[4] We may want to store the database information relating to each department at the computer site for that department. A technique called *horizontal fragmentation* can be used to partition each relation by department.

Horizontal Fragmentation.   A **horizontal fragment** of a relation is a subset of the tuples in that relation. The tuples that belong to the horizontal fragment are specified by a condition on one or more attributes of the relation. Often, only a single attribute is involved. For example, we may define three horizontal fragments on the EMPLOYEE relation of Figure 7.6 with the following conditions: (DNO = 5), (DNO = 4), and (DNO = 1)—each fragment contains the EMPLOYEE tuples working for a particular department. Similarly, we may define three horizontal fragments for the PROJECT relation, with the conditions (DNUM = 5), (DNUM = 4), and (DNUM = 1)—each fragment contains the PROJECT tuples controlled by a particular department. **Horizontal fragmentation** divides a relation "horizontally" by grouping rows to create subsets of tuples, where each subset has a certain logical meaning. These fragments can then be assigned to different sites in the distributed system. **Derived horizontal fragmentation** applies the partitioning of a primary relation (DEPARTMENT in our example) to other secondary relations (EMPLOYEE and PROJECT in our example), which are related to the primary via a foreign key. This way, related data between the primary and the secondary relations gets fragmented in the same way.

Vertical Fragmentation.   Each site may not need all the attributes of a relation, which would indicate the need for a different type of fragmentation. **Vertical fragmentation**

---

4. Of course, in an actual situation, there will be many more tuples in the relations than those shown in Figure 7.6.

divides a relation "vertically" by columns. A **vertical fragment** of a relation keeps only certain attributes of the relation. For example, we may want to fragment the EMPLOYEE relation into two vertical fragments. The first fragment includes personal information—NAME, BDATE, ADDRESS, and SEX—and the second includes work-related information—SSN, SALARY, SUPERSSN, DNO. This vertical fragmentation is not quite proper because, if the two fragments are stored separately, we cannot put the original employee tuples back together, since there is *no common attribute* between the two fragments. It is necessary to include the primary key or some candidate key attribute in *every* vertical fragment so that the full relation can be reconstructed from the fragments. Hence, we must add the SSN attribute to the personal information fragment.

Notice that each horizontal fragment on a relation R can be specified by a $\sigma_{Ci}(R)$ operation in the relational algebra. A set of horizontal fragments whose conditions C1, C2, ..., Cn include all the tuples in R—that is, every tuple in R satisfies (C1 OR C2 OR $\cdots$ OR Cn)—is called a **complete horizontal fragmentation** of R. In many cases a complete horizontal fragmentation is also **disjoint;** that is, no tuple in R satisfies (Ci AND Cj) for any i $\neq$ j. Our two earlier examples of horizontal fragmentation for the EMPLOYEE and PROJECT relations were both complete and disjoint. To reconstruct the relation R from a *complete* horizontal fragmentation, we need to apply the UNION operation to the fragments.

A vertical fragment on a relation R can be specified by a $\pi_{Li}(R)$ operation in the relational algebra. A set of vertical fragments whose projection lists L1, L2, ..., Ln include all the attributes in R but share only the primary key attribute of R is called a **complete vertical fragmentation** of R. In this case the projection lists satisfy the following two conditions:

- L1 $\cup$ L2 $\cup$ ... $\cup$ Ln = ATTRS(R).
- Li $\cap$ Lj = PK(R) for any i $\neq$ j, where ATTRS(R) is the set of attributes of R and PK(R) is the primary key of R.

To reconstruct the relation R from a *complete* vertical fragmentation, we apply the OUTER UNION operation to the vertical fragments (assuming no horizontal fragmentation is used). Notice that we could also apply a FULL OUTER JOIN operation and get the same result for a complete vertical fragmentation, even when some horizontal fragmentation may also have been applied. The two vertical fragments of the EMPLOYEE relation with projection lists L1 = {SSN, NAME, BDATE, ADDRESS, SEX} and L2 = {SSN, SALARY, SUPERSSN, DNO} constitute a complete vertical fragmentation of EMPLOYEE.

Two horizontal fragments that are neither complete nor disjoint are those defined on the EMPLOYEE relation of Figure 7.5 by the conditions (SALARY > 50000) and (DNO = 4); they may not include all EMPLOYEE tuples, and they may include common tuples. Two vertical fragments that are not complete are those defined by the attribute lists L1 = {NAME, ADDRESS} and L2 = {SSN, NAME, SALARY}; these lists violate both conditions of a complete vertical fragmentation.

Mixed (Hybrid) Fragmentation.   We can intermix the two types of fragmentation, yielding a **mixed fragmentation.** For example, we may combine the horizontal and vertical fragmentations of the EMPLOYEE relation given earlier into a mixed fragmentation that includes six fragments. In this case the original relation can be reconstructed by applying UNION *and* OUTER UNION (or OUTER JOIN) operations in the appropriate order. In general, a **fragment** of a relation R can be specified by a SELECT-PROJECT combination of operations $\pi_L(\sigma_C(R))$. If C = TRUE (that is, all tuples are selected) and L $\neq$ ATTRS(R), we get a vertical fragment, and if C $\neq$ TRUE and L = ATTRS(R), we get a horizontal fragment. Finally, if C $\neq$ TRUE and L $\neq$ ATTRS(R), we get a mixed fragment. Notice that a relation can itself be considered a fragment with C = TRUE and L = ATTRS(R). In the following discussion, the term *fragment* is used to refer to a relation or to any of the preceding types of fragments.

A **fragmentation schema** of a database is a definition of a set of fragments that includes *all* attributes and tuples in the database and satisfies the condition that the whole database can be reconstructed from the fragments by applying some sequence of OUTER UNION (or OUTER JOIN) and UNION operations. It is also sometimes useful—although not necessary—to have all the fragments be disjoint except for the repetition of primary keys among vertical (or mixed) fragments. In the latter case, all replication and distribution of fragments is clearly specified at a subsequent stage, separately from fragmentation.

An **allocation schema** describes the allocation of fragments to sites of the DDBS; hence, it is a mapping that specifies for each fragment the site(s) at which it is stored. If a fragment is stored at more than one site, it is said to be **replicated.** We discuss data replication and allocation next.

24.2.2   Data Replication and Allocation

Replication is useful in improving the availability of data. The most extreme case is replication of the *whole database* at every site in the distributed system, thus creating a **fully replicated distributed database.** This can improve availability remarkably because the system can continue to operate as long as at least one site is up. It also improves performance of retrieval for global queries, because the result of such a query can be obtained locally from any one site; hence, a retrieval query can be processed at the local site where it is submitted, if that site includes a server module. The disadvantage of full replication is that it can slow down update operations drastically, since a single logical update must be performed on every copy of the database to keep the copies consistent. This is especially true if many copies of the database exist. Full replication makes the concurrency control and recovery techniques more expensive than they would be if there were no replication, as we shall see in Section 24.5.

The other extreme from full replication involves having **no replication**—that is, each fragment is stored at exactly one site. In this case all fragments *must be* disjoint, except for the repetition of primary keys among vertical (or mixed) fragments. This is also called **nonredundant allocation.**

Between these two extremes, we have a wide spectrum of **partial replication** of the data—that is, some fragments of the database may be replicated whereas others may not. The number of copies of each fragment can range from one up to the total number of sites in the distributed system. A special case of partial replication is occurring heavily in applications where mobile workers—such as sales forces, financial planners, and claims adjustors—carry partially replicated databases with them on laptops and personal digital assistants and synchronize them periodically with the server database.[5] A description of the replication of fragments is sometimes called a **replication schema.**

Each fragment—or each copy of a fragment—must be assigned to a particular site in the distributed system. This process is called **data distribution** (or **data allocation**). The choice of sites and the degree of replication depend on the performance and availability goals of the system and on the types and frequencies of transactions submitted at each site. For example, if high availability is required and transactions can be submitted at any site and if most transactions are retrieval only, a fully replicated database is a good choice. However, if certain transactions that access particular parts of the database are mostly submitted at a particular site, the corresponding set of fragments can be allocated at that site only. Data that is accessed at multiple sites can be replicated at those sites. If many updates are performed, it may be useful to limit replication. Finding an optimal or even a good solution to distributed data allocation is a complex optimization problem.

24.2.3 Example of Fragmentation, Allocation, and Replication

We now consider an example of fragmenting and distributing the company database of Figures 7.5 and 7.6. Suppose that the company has three computer sites—one for each current department. Sites 2 and 3 are for departments 5 and 4, respectively. At each of these sites, we expect frequent access to the EMPLOYEE and PROJECT information for the employees *who work in that department* and the projects *controlled by that department*. Further, we assume that these sites mainly access the NAME, SSN, SALARY, and SUPERSSN attributes of EMPLOYEE. Site 1 is used by company headquarters and accesses all employee and project information regularly, in addition to keeping track of DEPENDENT information for insurance purposes.

According to these requirements, the whole database of Figure 7.6 can be stored at site 1. To determine the fragments to be replicated at sites 2 and 3, we can first horizontally fragment DEPARTMENT by its key DNUMBER. We then apply derived fragmentation to the relations EMPLOYEE, PROJECT, and DEPT_LOCATIONS relations based on their foreign keys for department number—called DNO, DNUM, and DNUMBER, respectively, in Figure 7.5. We can then vertically fragment the resulting EMPLOYEE fragments to include only the attributes {NAME, SSN, SALARY, SUPERSSN, DNO}. Figure 24.3 shows the mixed fragments EMPD5 and EMPD4, which include the EMPLOYEE tuples satisfying the conditions DNO = 5 and DNO = 4, respectively. The horizontal fragments of PROJECT, DEPARTMENT, and DEPT_LOCATIONS are similarly fragmented by department number. All these fragments—stored at sites 2 and 3—are replicated because they are also stored at the headquarters site 1.

We must now fragment the WORKS_ON relation and decide which fragments of WORKS_ON to store at sites 2 and 3. We are confronted with the problem that no attribute of WORKS_ON directly indicates the department to which each tuple belongs. In fact, each tuple in WORKS_ON relates an employee **e** to a project **p**. We could fragment WORKS_ON based on the department **d** in which **e** works *or* based on the department **d'** that controls **p**. Fragmentation

---

5. For a scalable approach to synchronize partially replicated databases, see Mahajan et al. (1998).

(a)

EMPD5	FNAME	MINIT	LNAME	SSN	SALARY	SUPERSSN	DNO
	John	B	Smith	123456789	30000	333445555	5
	Franklin	T	Wong	333445555	40000	888665555	5
	Ramesh	K	Narayan	666884444	38000	333445555	5
	Joyce	A	English	453453453	25000	333445555	5

DEP5	DNAME	DNUMBER	MGRSSN	MGRSTARTDATE
	Research	5	333445555	1988-05-22

DEP5_LOCS	DNUMBER	LOCATION
	5	Bellaire
	5	Sugarland
	5	Houston

WORKS_ON5	ESSN	PNO	HOURS
	123456789	1	32.5
	123456789	2	7.5
	666884444	3	40.0
	453453453	1	20.0
	453453453	2	20.0
	333445555	2	10.0
	333445555	3	10.0
	333445555	10	10.0
	333445555	20	10.0

PROJS5	PNAME	PNUMBER	PLOCATION	DNUM
	Product X	1	Bellaire	5
	Product Y	2	Sugarland	5
	Product Z	3	Houston	5

Data at Site 2

(b)

EMPD4	FNAME	MINIT	LNAME	SSN	SALARY	SUPERSSN	DNO
	Alicia	J	Zelaya	999887777	25000	987654321	4
	Jennifer	S	Wallace	987654321	43000	888665555	4
	Ahmad	V	Jabbar	987987987	25000	987654321	4

DEP4	DNAME	DNUMBER	MGRSSN	MGRSTARTDATE
	Administration	4	987654321	1995-01-01

DEP4_LOCS	DNUMBER	LOCATION
	4	Stafford

WORKS_ON4	ESSN	PNO	HOURS
	333445555	10	10.0
	999887777	30	30.0
	999887777	10	10.0
	987987987	10	35.0
	987987987	30	5.0
	987654321	30	20.0
	987654321	20	15.0

PROJS4	PNAME	PNUMBER	PLOCATION	DNUM
	Computerization	10	Stafford	4
	Newbenefits	30	Stafford	4

Data at Site 3

Figure 24.3   Allocation of fragments to sites. (a) Relation fragments at site 2 corresponding to department 5. (b) Relation fragments at site 3 corresponding to department 4.

becomes easy if we have a constraint stating that d = d' for all WORKS_ON tuples—that is, if employees can work only on projects controlled by the department they work for. However, there is no such constraint in our database of Figure 7.6. For example, the WORKS_ON tuple <333445555, 10, 10.0> relates an employee who works for department 5 with a project controlled by department 4. In this case we could fragment WORKS_ON based on the department in which the employee works (which is expressed by the condition C) and then fragment further based on the department that controls the projects that employee is working on, as shown in Figure 24.4.

(a)

G1	ESSN	PNO	HOURS
	123456789	1	32.5
	123456789	2	7.5
	666884444	3	40.0
	453453453	1	20.0
	453453453	2	20.0
	333445555	2	10.0
	333445555	3	10.0

C1=C AND (PNO IN (SELECT PNUMBER
FROM PROJECT
WHERE DNUM=5))

G2	ESSN	PNO	HOURS
	333445555	10	10.0

C2=C AND (PNO IN (SELECT PNUMBER
FROM PROJECT
WHERE DNUM=4))

G3	ESSN	PNO	HOURS
	333445555	20	10.0

C3=C AND (PNO IN (SELECT PNUMBER
FROM PROJECT
WHERE DNUM=1))

Employees in Department 5

(b)

G4	ESSN	PNO	HOURS

C4=C AND (PNO IN (SELECT PNUMBER
FROM PROJECT
WHERE DNUM=5))

G5	ESSN	PNO	HOURS
	999887777	30	30.0
	999887777	10	10.0
	987987987	10	35.0
	987987987	30	5.0
	987654321	30	20.0

C5=C AND (PNO IN (SELECT PNUMBER
FROM PROJECT
WHERE DNUM=4))

G6	ESSN	PNO	HOURS
	987654321	20	15.0

C6=C AND (PNO IN (SELECT PNUMBER
FROM PROJECT
WHERE DNUM=1))

Employees in Department 4

(c)

G7	ESSN	PNO	HOURS

C7=C AND (PNO IN (SELECT PNUMBER
FROM PROJECT
WHERE DNUM=5))

G8	ESSN	PNO	HOURS

C8=C AND (PNO IN (SELECT PNUMBER
FROM PROJECT
WHERE DNUM=4))

G9	ESSN	PNO	HOURS
	888665555	20	null

C9=C AND (PNO IN (SELECT PNUMBER
FROM PROJECT
WHERE DNUM=1))

Employees in Department 1

Figure 24.4 Complete and disjoint fragments of the WORKS_ON relation. (a) Fragments of WORKS_ON for employees working in department 5 (C=[ESSN IN (SELECT SSN FROM EMPLOYEE WHERE DNO=5)]). (b) Fragments of WORKS_ON for employees working in department 4 (C=[ESSN IN (SELECT SSN FROM EMPLOYEE WHERE DNO=4)]). (c) Fragments of WORKS_ON for employees working in department 1 (C=[ESSN IN (SELECT SSN FROM EMPLOYEE WHERE DNO=1)]).

In Figure 24.4, the union of fragments G1, G2, and G3 gives all WORKS_ON tuples for employees who work for department 5. Similarly, the union of fragments G4, G5, and G6 gives all WORKS_ON tuples for employees who work for department 4. On the other hand, the union of fragments G1, G4, and G7 gives all WORKS_ON tuples for projects controlled by department 5. The condition for each of the fragments G1 through G9 is shown in Figure 24.4. The relations that represent M:N relationships, such as WORKS_ON, often have several possible logical fragmentations. In our distribution of Figure 24.3, we choose to include all fragments that can be joined to either an EMPLOYEE tuple or a PROJECT tuple at sites 2 and 3. Hence, we place the union of fragments G1, G2, G3, G4, and G7 at site 2 and the union of fragments G4, G5, G6, G2, and G8 at site 3. Notice that fragments G2 and G4 are replicated at both sites. This allocation strategy permits the join between the local EMPLOYEE or PROJECT fragments at site 2 or site 3 and the local WORKS_ON fragment to be performed completely locally. This clearly demonstrates how complex the problem of database fragmentation and allocation is for large databases. The Selected Bibliography at the end of this chapter discusses some of the work done in this area.

24.3   Types of Distributed Database Systems

The term distributed database management system can describe various systems that differ from one another in many respects. The main thing that all such systems have in common is the fact that data and software are distributed over multiple sites connected by some form of communication network. In this section we discuss a number of types of DDBMSs and the criteria and factors that make some of these systems different.

The first factor we consider is the **degree of homogeneity** of the DDBMS software. If all servers (or individual local DBMSs) use identical software and all users (clients) use identical software, the DDBMS is called **homogeneous;** otherwise, it is called **heterogeneous.** Another factor related to the degree of homogeneity is the **degree of local autonomy.** If there is no provision for the local site to function as a stand-alone DBMS, then the system has **no local autonomy.** On the other hand, if *direct access* by local transactions to a server is permitted, the system has some degree of local autonomy.

At one extreme of the autonomy spectrum, we have a DDBMS that "looks like" a centralized DBMS to the user. A single conceptual schema exists, and all access to the system is obtained through a site that is part of the DDBMS—which means that no local autonomy exists. At the other extreme we encounter a type of DDBMS called a *federated DDBMS* (or a *multidatabase system*). In such a system, each server is an independent and autonomous centralized DBMS that has its own local users, local transactions, and DBA and hence has a very high degree of *local autonomy.* The term **federated database system (FDBS)** is used when there is some global view or schema of the federation of databases that is shared by the applications. On the other hand, a **multidatabase system** does not have a global schema and interactively constructs one as needed by the application. Both systems are hybrids between distributed and centralized systems and the distinction we made between them is not strictly followed. We will refer to them as FDBSs in a generic sense.

In a heterogeneous FDBS, one server may be a relational DBMS, another a network DBMS, and a third an object or hierarchical DBMS; in such a case it is necessary to have a canonical system language and to include language translators to translate subqueries from the canonical language to the language of each server. We briefly discuss the issues affecting the design of FDBSs below.

Federated Database Management Systems Issues.   The type of heterogeneity present in FDBSs may arise from several sources. We discuss these sources first and then point out how the different types of autonomies contribute to a semantic heterogeneity that must be resolved in a heterogeneous FDBS.

- *Differences in data models:* Databases in an organization come from a variety of data models including the so-called legacy models (network and hierarchical, see Appendixes C and D), the relational data model, the object data model, and even files. The modeling capabilities of the models vary. Hence, to deal with them uniformly via a single global schema or to process them in a single language is challenging. Even if two databases are both from the RDBMS environment, the same information may be represented as an attribute name, as a relation name, or as a value in different databases. This calls for an intelligent query-processing mechanism that can relate information based on metadata.

- *Differences in constraints:* Constraint facilities for specification and implementation vary from system to system. There are comparable features that must be reconciled in the construction of a global schema. For example, the relationships from ER models are represented as referential integrity constraints in the relational model. Triggers may have to be used to implement certain constraints in the relational model. The global schema must also deal with potential conflicts among constraints.

- *Differences in query languages:* Even with the same data model, the languages and their versions vary. For example, SQL has multiple versions like SQL-89, SQL-92 (SQL2), and SQL3, and each system has its own set of data types, comparison operators, string manipulation features, and so on.

Semantic Heterogeneity.   Semantic heterogeneity occurs when there are differences in the meaning, interpretation, and intended use of the same or related data. Semantic heterogeneity among component database systems (DBSs) creates the biggest hurdle in designing global schemas of heterogeneous databases. The **design autonomy** of component DBSs refers to their freedom of choosing the following design parameters, which in turn affect the eventual complexity of the FDBS:

- *The universe of discourse from which the data is drawn:* For example, two customer accounts databases in the federation may be from United States and Japan with entirely different sets of attributes about customer accounts required by the accounting practices. Currency rate fluctuations would also present a problem. Hence, relations in these two databases which have identical names—CUSTOMER or ACCOUNT—may have some common and some entirely distinct information.

- *Representation and naming:* The representation and naming of data elements and the structure of the data model may be prespecified for each local database.

- *The understanding, meaning, and subjective interpretation of data.* This is a chief contributor to semantic heterogeneity.

- *Transaction and policy constraints:* These deal with serializability criteria, compensating transactions, and other transaction policies.

- *Derivation of summaries:* Aggregation, summarization, and other data-processing features and operations supported by the system.

Communication autonomy of a component DBS refers to its ability to decide whether to communicate with another component DBSs. **Execution autonomy** refers to the ability of a component DBS to execute local operations without interference from external operations by other component DBSs and its ability to decide the order in which to execute them. The **association autonomy** of a component DBS implies that it has the ability to decide whether and how much to share its functionality (operations it supports) and resources (data it manages) with other component DBSs. The major challenge of designing FDBSs is to let component DBSs interoperate while still providing the above types of autonomies to them.

A typical five-level schema architecture to support global applications in the FDBS environment is shown in Figure 24.5. In this architecture, the **local schema** is the conceptual schema (full database definition) of a component database, and the **component schema** is derived by translating the local schema into a canonical data model or common data model (CDM) for the FDBS. Schema translation from the local schema to the

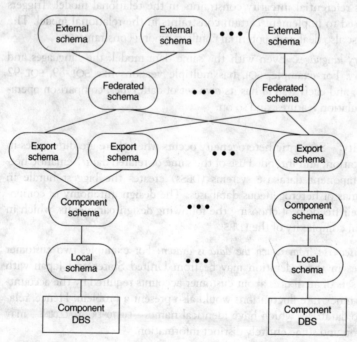

Figure 24.5   The five-level schema architecture in a federated database system (FDBS). *Source:* Adapted from Sheth and Larson, *Federated Database Systems for Managing Distributed Heterogeneous Autonomous Databases.* ACM *Computing Surveys* (Vol. 22: No. 3, September 1990).

component schema is accompanied by generation of mappings to transform commands on a component schema into commands on the corresponding local schema. The **export schema** represents the subset of a component schema that is available to the FDBS. The **federated schema** is the global schema or view, which is the result of integrating all the shareable export schemas. The **external schemas** define the schema for a user group or an application, as in the three-level schema architecture.[6]

All the problems related to query processing, transaction processing, and directory and metadata management and recovery apply to FDBSs with additional considerations. It is not within our scope to discuss them in detail here.

24.4 Query Processing in Distributed Databases

We now give an overview of how a DDBMS processes and optimizes a query. We first discuss the communication costs of processing a distributed query; we then discuss a special operation, called a *semijoin*, that is used in optimizing some types of queries in a DDBMS.

24.4.1 Data Transfer Costs of Distributed Query Processing

We discussed the issues involved in processing and optimizing a query in a centralized DBMS in Chapter 18. In a distributed system, several additional factors further complicate query processing. The first is the cost of transferring data over the network. This data includes intermediate files that are transferred to other sites for further processing, as well as the final result files that may have to be transferred to the site where the query result is needed. Although these costs may not be very high if the sites are connected via a high-performance local area network, they become quite significant in other types of networks. Hence, DDBMS query optimization algorithms consider the goal of reducing the *amount of data transfer* as an optimization criterion in choosing a distributed query execution strategy.

We illustrate this with two simple example queries. Suppose that the EMPLOYEE and DEPARTMENT relations of Figure 7.5 are distributed as shown in Figure 24.6. We will assume in this example that neither relation is fragmented. According to Figure 24.6, the size of the EMPLOYEE relation is $100 * 10,000 = 10^6$ bytes, and the size of the DEPARTMENT relation is $35 * 100 = 3500$ bytes. Consider the query Q: "For each employee, retrieve the employee name and the name of the department for which the employee works." This can be stated as follows in the relational algebra:

Q: $\pi_{\text{FNAME,LNAME,DNAME}}(\text{EMPLOYEE} \bowtie_{\text{DNO=DNUMBER}} \text{DEPARTMENT})$

The result of this query will include 10,000 records, assuming that every employee is related to a department. Suppose that each record in the query result is *40 bytes long*. The query is submitted at a distinct site 3, which is called the **result site** because the query result is needed there. Neither the EMPLOYEE nor the DEPARTMENT relations reside at site 3.

---

6. For a detailed discussion of the autonomies and the five-level architecture of FDBMSs, see Sheth and Larson (1990).

SITE 1:

EMPLOYEE

FNAME	MINIT	LNAME	SSN	BDATE	ADDRESS	SEX	SALARY	SUPERSSN	DNO

10,000 records
each record is 100 bytes long
SSN field is 9 bytes long   FNAME field is 15 bytes long
DNO field is 4 bytes long   LNAME field is 15 bytes long

SITE 2:

DEPARTMENT

DNAME	DNUMBER	MGRSSN	MGRSTARTDATE

100 records
each record is 35 bytes long
DNUMBER field is 4 bytes long   DNAME field is 10 bytes long
MGRSSN field is 9 bytes long

Figure 24.6   Example to illustrate volume of data transferred.

There are three simple strategies for executing this distributed query:

1. Transfer both the EMPLOYEE and the DEPARTMENT relations to the result site, and perform the join at site 3. In this case a total of 1,000,000 + 3500 = 1,003,500 bytes must be transferred.

2. Transfer the EMPLOYEE relation to site 2, execute the join at site 2, and send the result to site 3. The size of the query result is 40 * 10,000 = 400,000 bytes, so 400,000 + 1,000,000 = 1,400,000 bytes must be transferred.

3. Transfer the DEPARTMENT relation to site 1, execute the join at site 1, and send the result to site 3. In this case 400,000 + 3500 = 403,500 bytes must be transferred.

If minimizing the amount of data transfer is our optimization criterion, we should choose strategy 3. Now consider another query Q': "For each department, retrieve the department name and the name of the department manager." This can be stated as follows in the relational algebra:

$$Q': \pi_{FNAME, LNAME, DNAME}(DEPARTMENT \bowtie_{MGRSSN=SSN} EMPLOYEE)$$

Again, suppose that the query is submitted at site 3. The same three strategies for executing query Q apply to Q', except that the result of Q' includes only 100 records, assuming that each department has a manager:

1. Transfer both the EMPLOYEE and the DEPARTMENT relations to the result site, and perform the join at site 3. In this case a total of 1,000,000 + 3500 = 1,003,500 bytes must be transferred.

2. Transfer the EMPLOYEE relation to site 2, execute the join at site 2, and send the result to site 3. The size of the query result is 40 * 100 = 4000 bytes, so 4000 + 1,000,000 = 1,004,000 bytes must be transferred.

3. Transfer the DEPARTMENT relation to site 1, execute the join at site 1, and send the result to site 3. In this case 4000 + 3500 = 7500 bytes must be transferred.

Again, we would choose strategy 3—in this case by an overwhelming margin over strategies 1 and 2. The preceding three strategies are the most obvious ones for the case where the result site (site 3) is different from all the sites that contain files involved in the query (sites 1 and 2). However, suppose that the result site is site 2; then we have two simple strategies:

1. Transfer the EMPLOYEE relation to site 2, execute the query, and present the result to the user at site 2. Here, the same number of bytes—1,000,000—must be transferred for both Q and Q'.

2. Transfer the DEPARTMENT relation to site 1, execute the query at site 1, and send the result back to site 2. In this case 400,000 + 3500 = 403,500 bytes must be transferred for Q and 4000 + 3500 = 7500 bytes for Q'.

A more complex strategy, which sometimes works better than these simple strategies, uses an operation called **semijoin**. We introduce this operation and discuss distributed execution using semijoins next.

24.4.2 Distributed Query Processing Using Semijoin

The idea behind distributed query processing using the *semijoin operation* is to reduce the number of tuples in a relation before transferring it to another site. Intuitively, the idea is to send the *joining column* of one relation R to the site where the other relation S is located; this column is then joined with S. Following that, the join attributes, along with the attributes required in the result, are projected out and shipped back to the original site and joined with R. Hence, only the joining column of R is transferred in one direction, and a subset of S with no extraneous tuples or attributes is transferred in the other direction. If only a small fraction of the tuples in S participate in the join, this can be quite an efficient solution to minimizing data transfer.

To illustrate this, consider the following strategy for executing Q or Q':

1. Project the join attributes of DEPARTMENT at site 2, and transfer them to site 1. For Q, we transfer F = $\pi_{DNUMBER}$(DEPARTMENT), whose size is 4 * 100 = 400 bytes, whereas, for Q', we transfer F' = π_{MGRSSN}(DEPARTMENT), whose size is 9 * 100 = 900 bytes.

2. Join the transferred file with the EMPLOYEE relation at site 1, and transfer the required attributes from the resulting file to site 2. For Q, we transfer R = $\pi_{DNO, FNAME, LNAME}$(F $\bowtie_{DNUMBER=DNO}$ EMPLOYEE), whose size is 34 * 10,000 = 340,000 bytes, whereas, for Q', we transfer R' = $\pi_{MGRSSN, FNAME, LNAME}$(F' $\bowtie_{MGRSSN=SSN}$ EMPLOYEE), whose size is 39 * 100 = 3900 bytes.

3. Execute the query by joining the transferred file R or R' with DEPARTMENT, and present the result to the user at site 2.

Using this strategy, we transfer 340,400 bytes for Q and 4800 bytes for Q'. We limited the EMPLOYEE attributes and tuples transmitted to site 2 in step 2 to only those that will *actually be joined* with a DEPARTMENT tuple in step 3. For query Q, this turned out to include all EMPLOYEE tuples, so little improvement was achieved. However, for Q' only 100 out of the 10,000 EMPLOYEE tuples were needed.

The semijoin operation was devised to formalize this strategy. A **semijoin operation** $R \ltimes_{A=B} S$, where A and B are domain-compatible attributes of R and S, respectively, produces the same result as the relational algebra expression $\pi_R(R \bowtie_{A=B} S)$. In a distributed environment where R and S reside at different sites, the semijoin is typically implemented by first transferring $F = \pi_B(S)$ to the site where R resides and then joining F with R, thus leading to the strategy discussed here.

Notice that the semijoin operation is not commutative; that is,

$$R \ltimes S \neq S \ltimes R$$

24.4.3   Query and Update Decomposition

In a DDBMS with *no distribution transparency*, the user phrases a query directly in terms of specific fragments. For example, consider another query Q: "Retrieve the names and hours per week for each employee who works on some project controlled by department 5," which is specified on the distributed database where the relations at sites 2 and 3 are shown in Figure 24.3, and those at site 1 are shown in Figure 7.6, as in our earlier example. A user who submits such a query must specify whether it references the PROJS5 and WORKS_ON5 relations at site 2 (Figure 24.3) or the PROJECT and WORKS_ON relations at site 1 (Figure 7.6). The user must also maintain consistency of replicated data items when updating a DDBMS with *no replication transparency*.

On the other hand, a DDBMS that supports *full distribution, fragmentation,* and *replication transparency* allows the user to specify a query or update request on the schema of Figure 7.5 just as though the DBMS were centralized. For updates, the DDBMS is responsible for maintaining *consistency among replicated items* by using one of the distributed concurrency control algorithms to be discussed in Section 24.5. For queries, a **query decomposition** module must break up or **decompose** a query into **subqueries** that can be executed at the individual sites. In addition, a strategy for combining the results of the subqueries to form the query result must be generated. Whenever the DDBMS determines that an item referenced in the query is replicated, it must choose or **materialize** a particular replica during query execution.

To determine which replicas include the data items referenced in a query, the DDBMS refers to the fragmentation, replication, and distribution information stored in the DDBMS catalog. For vertical fragmentation, the attribute list for each fragment is kept in the catalog. For horizontal fragmentation, a condition, sometimes called a **guard,** is kept for each fragment. This is basically a selection condition that specifies which tuples exist in the fragment; it is called a guard because *only tuples that satisfy this condition* are permitted to be stored in the fragment. For mixed fragments, both the attribute list and the guard condition are kept in the catalog.

In our earlier example, the guard conditions for fragments at site 1 (Figure 7.6) are TRUE (all tuples), and the attribute lists are * (all attributes). For the fragments shown in Figure 24.3, we have the guard conditions and attribute lists shown in Figure 24.7. When

(a) EMPD5
     attribute list: FNAME,MINIT,LNAME,SSN,SALARY,SUPERSSN, DNO
     guard condition: DNO=5
   DEP5
     attribute list: * (all attributes DNAME,DNUMBER,MGRSSN,MGRSTARTDATE)
     guard condition: DNUMBER=5
   DEP5_LOCS
     attribute list: * (all attributes DNUMBER,LOCATION)
     guard condition: DNUMBER=5
   PROJS5
     attribute list: * (all attributes PNAME,PNUMBER,PLOCATION,DNUM)
     guard condition: DNUM=5
   WORKS_ON5
     attribute list: * (all attributes ESSN,PNO,HOURS)
     guard condition: ESSN IN (π_{SSN} (EMPD5)) OR PNO IN ($\pi_{PNUMBER}$ (PROJS5))

(b) EMPD4
     attribute list: FNAME,MINIT,LNAME,SSN,SALARY,SUPERSSN, DNO
     guard condition: DNO=4
   DEP4
     attribute list: * (all attributes DNAME,DNUMBER,MGRSSN,MGRSTARTDATE)
     guard condition: DNUMBER=4
   DEP4_LOCS
     attribute list: * (all attributes DNUMBER,LOCATION)
     guard condition: DNUMBER=4
   PROJS4
     attribute list: * (all attributes PNAME,PNUMBER,PLOCATION,DNUM)
     guard condition: DNUM=4
   WORKS_ON4
     attribute list: * (all attributes ESSN,PNO,HOURS)
     guard condition: ESSN IN (π_{SSN} (EMPD4)) OR PNO IN ($\pi_{PNUMBER}$ (PROJS4))

Figure 24.7   Guard conditions and attributes lists for fragments. (a) Site 2
fragments. (b) Site 3 fragments.

the DDBMS decomposes an update request, it can determine which fragments must be
updated by examining their guard conditions. For example, a user request to insert a new
EMPLOYEE tuple <'Alex', 'B', 'Coleman', '345671239', '22-APR-64', '3306 Sand-
stone, Houston, TX', M, 33000, '987654321', 4> would be decomposed by the
DDBMS into two insert requests: the first inserts the preceding tuple in the EMPLOYEE fragment at site 1, and the second inserts the projected tuple <'Alex', 'B', 'Coleman',
'345671239', 33000, '987654321', 4> in the EMPD4 fragment at site 3.

For query decomposition, the DDBMS can determine which fragments may contain
the required tuples by comparing the query condition with the guard conditions. For
example, consider the query Q: "Retrieve the names and hours per week for each
employee who works on some project controlled by department 5"; this can be specified
in SQL on the schema of Figure 7.5 as follows:

```
Q:  SELECT  FNAME, LNAME, HOURS
    FROM    EMPLOYEE, PROJECT, WORKS_ON
    WHERE   DNUM=5 AND PNUMBER=PNO AND ESSN=SSN;
```

Suppose that the query is submitted at site 2, which is where the query result will be needed. The DDBMS can determine from the guard condition on PROJS5 and WORKS_ON5 that all tuples satisfying the conditions (DNUM = 5 AND PNUMBER = PNO) reside at site 2. Hence, it may decompose the query into the following relational algebra subqueries:

T1 ← π_{ESSN}(PROJS5 $\bowtie_{PNUMBER=PNO}$ WORKS_ON5)
T2 ← $\pi_{ESSN, FNAME, LNAME}$(T1 $\bowtie_{ESSN=SSN}$ EMPLOYEE)
RESULT ← $\pi_{FNAME, LNAME, HOURS}$(T2 * WORKS_ON5)

This decomposition can be used to execute the query by using a semijoin strategy. The DDBMS knows from the guard conditions that PROJS5 contains exactly those tuples satisfying (DNUM = 5) and that WORKS_ON5 contains all tuples to be joined with PROJS5; hence, subquery T1 can be executed at site 2, and the projected column ESSN can be sent to site 1. Subquery T2 can then be executed at site 1, and the result can be sent back to site 2, where the final query result is calculated and displayed to the user. An alternative strategy would be to send the query Q itself to site 1, which includes all the database tuples, where it would be executed locally and from which the result would be sent back to site 2. The query optimizer would estimate the costs of both strategies and would choose the one with the lower cost estimate.

24.5 Overview of Concurrency Control and Recovery in Distributed Databases

For concurrency control and recovery purposes, numerous problems arise in a distributed DBMS environment that are not encountered in a centralized DBMS environment. These include the following:

- *Dealing with* **multiple copies** *of the data items:* The concurrency control method is responsible for maintaining consistency among these copies. The recovery method is responsible for making a copy consistent with other copies if the site on which the copy is stored fails and recovers later.

- *Failure of individual sites:* The DDBMS should continue to operate with its running sites, if possible, when one or more individual sites fail. When a site recovers, its local database must be brought up to date with the rest of the sites before it rejoins the system.

- *Failure of communication links:* The system must be able to deal with failure of one or more of the communication links that connect the sites. An extreme case of this problem is that **network partitioning** may occur. This breaks up the sites into two or more partitions, where the sites within each partition can communicate only with one another and not with sites in other partitions.

- *Distributed commit:* Problems can arise with committing a transaction that is accessing databases stored on multiple sites if some sites fail during the commit process. The **two-phase commit protocol** (see Chapter 21) is often used to deal with this problem.

- *Distributed deadlock:* Deadlock may occur among several sites, so techniques for dealing with deadlocks must be extended to take this into account.

Distributed concurrency control and recovery techniques must deal with these and other problems. In the following subsections, we review some of the techniques that have been suggested to deal with recovery and concurrency control in DDBMSs.

24.5.1 Distributed Concurrency Control Based on a Distinguished Copy of a Data Item

To deal with replicated data items in a distributed database, a number of concurrency control methods have been proposed that extend the concurrency control techniques for centralized databases. We discuss these techniques in the context of extending centralized *locking*. Similar extensions apply to other concurrency control techniques. The idea is to designate *a particular copy* of each data item as a **distinguished copy.** The locks for this data item are associated *with the distinguished copy,* and all locking and unlocking requests are sent to the site that contains that copy.

A number of different methods are based on this idea, but they differ in their method of choosing the distinguished copies. In the **primary site technique,** all distinguished copies are kept at the same site. A modification of this approach is the primary site with a **backup site.** Another approach is the **primary copy** method, where the distinguished copies of the various data items can be stored in different sites. A site that includes a distinguished copy of a data item basically acts as the **coordinator site** for concurrency control on that item. We discuss these techniques next.

Primary Site Technique. In this method a single **primary site** is designated to be the **coordinator site** *for all database items.* Hence, all locks are kept at that site, and all requests for locking or unlocking are sent there. This method is thus an extension of the centralized locking approach. For example, if all transactions follow the two-phase locking protocol, serializability is guaranteed. The advantage of this approach is that it is a simple extension of the centralized approach and hence is not overly complex. However, it has certain inherent disadvantages. One is that all locking requests are sent to a single site, possibly overloading that site and causing a system bottleneck. A second disadvantage is that failure of the primary site paralyzes the system, since all locking information is kept at that site. This can limit system reliability and availability.

Although all locks are accessed at the primary site, the items themselves can be accessed at any site at which they reside. For example, once a transaction obtains a read_lock on a data item from the primary site, it can access any copy of that data item. However, once a transaction obtains a write_lock and updates a data item, the DDBMS is responsible for updating *all copies* of the data item before releasing the lock.

Primary Site with Backup Site. This approach addresses the second disadvantage of the primary site method by designating a second site to be a **backup site.** All locking information is maintained at both the primary and the backup sites. In case of primary site failure, the backup site takes over as primary site, and a new backup site is chosen. This simplifies the process of recovery from failure of the primary site, since the backup site takes over and processing can resume after a new backup site is chosen and the lock status information is copied to that site. It slows down the process of acquiring locks, however, because all lock requests and granting of locks must be recorded at *both the primary and the backup sites* before a response is sent to the requesting transaction. The problem of the primary and backup sites becoming overloaded with requests and slowing down the system remains undiminished.

Primary Copy Technique. This method attempts to distribute the load of lock coordination among various sites by having the distinguished copies of different data items *stored at different sites*. Failure of one site affects any transactions that are accessing locks on items whose primary copies reside at that site, but other transactions are not affected. This method can also use backup sites to enhance reliability and availability.

Choosing a New Coordinator Site in Case of Failure. Whenever a coordinator site fails in any of the preceding techniques, the sites that are still running must choose a new coordinator. In the case of the primary site approach with *no* backup site, all executing transactions must be aborted and restarted in a tedious recovery process. Part of the recovery process involves choosing a new primary site and creating a lock manager process and a record of all lock information at that site. For methods that use backup sites, transaction processing is suspended while the backup site is designated as the new primary site and a new backup site is chosen and is sent copies of all the locking information from the new primary site.

If a backup site X is about to become the new primary site, X can choose the new backup site from among the system's running sites. However, if no backup site existed, or if both the primary and the backup sites are down, a process called **election** can be used to choose the new coordinator site. In this process, any site Y that attempts to communicate with the coordinator site repeatedly and fails to do so can assume that the coordinator is down and can start the election process by sending a message to all running sites proposing that Y become the new coordinator. As soon as Y receives a majority of yes votes, Y can declare that it is the new coordinator. The election algorithm itself is quite complex, but this is the main idea behind the election method. The algorithm also resolves any attempt by two or more sites to become coordinator at the same time. The references in the Selected Bibliography at the end of this chapter discuss the process in detail.

24.5.2 Distributed Concurrency Control Based on Voting

The concurrency control methods for replicated items discussed earlier all use the idea of a distinguished copy that maintains the locks for that item. In the **voting method,** there is no distinguished copy; rather, a lock request is sent to all sites that include a copy of the data item. Each copy maintains its own lock and can grant or deny the request for it. If a transaction that requests a lock is granted that lock by *a majority* of the copies, it holds the lock and informs *all copies* that it has been granted the lock. If a transaction does not receive a majority of votes granting it a lock within a certain *time-out period*, it cancels its request and informs all sites of the cancellation.

The voting method is considered a truly distributed concurrency control method, since the responsibility for a decision resides with all the sites involved. Simulation studies have shown that voting has higher message traffic among sites than do the distinguished copy methods. If the algorithm takes into account possible site failures during the voting process, it becomes extremely complex.

24.5.3 Distributed Recovery

The recovery process in distributed databases is quite involved. We give only a very brief idea of some of the issues here. In some cases it is quite difficult even to determine whether a site is down without exchanging numerous messages with other sites. For example, suppose that site X sends a message to site Y and expects a response from Y but does not receive it. There are several possible explanations:

- The message was not delivered to Y because of communication failure.
- Site Y is down and could not respond.
- Site Y is running and sent a response, but the response was not delivered.

Without additional information or the sending of additional messages, it is difficult to determine what actually happened.

Another problem with distributed recovery is distributed commit. When a transaction is updating data at several sites, it cannot commit until it is sure that the effect of the transaction on *every* site cannot be lost. This means that every site must first have recorded the local effects of the transactions permanently in the local site log on disk. The two-phase commit protocol, discussed in Section 20.6, is often used to ensure the correctness of distributed commit.

24.6 An Overview of Client-Server Architecture and Its Relationship to Distributed Databases

As we pointed out in the chapter introduction, full-scale DDBMSs have not been developed to support all the types of functionalities that we discussed so far. Instead, distributed database applications are being developed in the context of the client-server architecture, which we introduced in Section 17.1. The section further discusses client-server in the context of DDBMS.

Exactly how to divide the DBMS functionality between client and server has not yet been established. Different approaches have been proposed. One possibility is to include the functionality of a centralized DBMS at the server level. A number of relational DBMS products have taken this approach, where an SQL **server** is provided to the clients. Each client must then formulate the appropriate SQL queries and provide the user interface and programming language interface functions. Since SQL is a relational standard, various SQL servers, possibly provided by different vendors, can accept SQL commands. The client may also refer to a data dictionary that includes information on the distribution of data among the various SQL servers, as well as modules for decomposing a global query into a number of local queries that can be executed at the various sites. Interaction between client and server might proceed as follows during the processing of an SQL query:

1. The client parses a user query and decomposes it into a number of independent site queries. Each site query is sent to the appropriate server site.

2. Each server processes the local query and sends the resulting relation to the client site.

3. The client site combines the results of the subqueries to produce the result of the originally submitted query.

In this approach, the SQL server has also been called a **transaction server** (or a **database processor (DP)** or a **back-end machine**), whereas the client has been called an **application processor (AP)** (or a **front-end machine**). The interaction between client and server can be specified by the user at the client level or via a specialized DBMS client module that is part of the DBMS package. For example, the user may know what data is stored in each server, break down a query request into site subqueries manually, and submit individual subqueries to the various sites. The resulting tables may be combined explicitly by a further user query at the client level. The alternative is to have the client module undertake these actions automatically.

In a typical DDBMS, it is customary to divide the software modules into three levels:

1. The **server** software is responsible for local data management at a site, much like centralized DBMS software.

2. The **client** software is responsible for most of the distribution functions; it accesses data distribution information from the DDBMS catalog and processes all requests that require access to more than one site. It also handles all user interfaces.

3. The **communications software** (sometimes in conjunction with a **distributed operating system**) provides the communication primitives that are used by the client to transmit commands and data among the various sites as needed. This is not strictly part of the DDBMS, but it provides essential communication primitives and services.

The client is responsible for generating a distributed execution plan for a multisite query or transaction and for supervising distributed execution by sending commands to servers. These commands include local queries and transactions to be executed, as well as commands to transmit data to other clients or servers. Hence, client software should be included at any site where multisite queries are submitted. Another function controlled by the client (or coordinator) is that of ensuring consistency of replicated copies of a data item by employing distributed (or global) concurrency control techniques. The client must also ensure the atomicity of global transactions by performing global recovery when certain sites fail. We discussed distributed recovery and concurrency control in Section 24.5. One possible function of the client is to *hide* the details of data distribution from the user; that is, it enables the user to write global queries and transactions as though the database were centralized, without having to specify the sites at which the data referenced in the query or transaction resides. This property is called **distribution transparency.** Some DDBMSs do not provide distribution transparency, instead requiring that users be aware of the details of data distribution.

24.7 Distributed Databases in Oracle

In the client-server architecture, the Oracle database system is divided into two parts: (1) a front-end as the client portion, and (2) a back-end as the server portion. The client portion is the front-end database application that interacts with the user. The client has no data access responsibility and merely handles the requesting, processing, and presentation of data managed by the server. The server portion runs Oracle and handles the functions related to concurrent shared access. It accepts SQL and PL/SQL statements originating from client applications, processes them, and sends the results back to the client. Oracle client-server applications provide location transparency by making location of data transparent to users; several features like views, synonyms, and procedures contribute to this. Global naming is achieved by using `<tablename.@,databasename>` to refer to tables uniquely.

Oracle uses a two-phase commit protocol to deal with concurrent distributed transactions. The COMMIT statement triggers the two-phase commit mechanism. The RECO (recoverer) background process automatically resolves the outcome of those distributed transactions in which the commit was interrupted. The RECO of each local Oracle Server automatically commits or rolls back any "in-doubt" distributed transactions consistently on all involved nodes. For long-term failures, Oracle allows each local DBA to manually commit or roll back any in-doubt transactions and free up resources. Global consistency can be maintained by restoring the database at each site to a predetermined fixed point in the past.

Oracle's distributed database architecture is shown in Figure 24.8. A node in a distributed database system can act as a client, as a server, or both, depending on the situation. The figure shows two sites where databases called HQ (headquarters) and Sales are kept. For example, in the application shown running at the headquarters, for an SQL statement issued against local data (for example, DELETE FROM DEPT ...), the HQ computer acts as a server, whereas for a statement against remote data (for example, INSERT INTO EMP@SALES), the HQ computer acts as a client.

All Oracle databases in a distributed database system (DDBS) use Oracle's networking software Net8 for interdatabase communication. Net8 allows databases to communicate across networks to support remote and distributed transactions. It packages SQL statements into one of the many communication protocols to facilitate client to server communication and then packages the results back similarly to the client. Each database has a unique global name provided by a hierarchical arrangement of network domain names that is prefixed to the database name to make it unique.

Oracle supports database links that define a one-way communication path from one Oracle database to another. For example,

```
CREATE DATABASE LINK sales.us.americas;
```

establishes a connection to the sales database in Figure 24.8 under the network domain us that comes under domain americas.

Data in an Oracle DDBS can be replicated using snapshots or replicated master tables. Replication is provided at the following levels:

- *Basic replication:* Replicas of tables are managed for read-only access. For updates, data must be accessed at a single primary site.

Figure 24.8. Oracle distributed database systems. *Source:* From Oracle (1997a). Copyright © Oracle Corporation 1997. All rights reserved.

- *Advanced (symmetric) replication:* This extends beyond basic replication by allowing applications to update table replicas throughout a replicated DDBS. Data can be read and updated at any site. This requires additional software called Oracle's advanced replication option. A **snapshot** generates a copy of a part of the table by means of a query called the *snapshot defining query*. A simple snapshot definition looks like this:

```
CREATE SNAPSHOT sales.orders AS
SELECT * FROM sales.orders@hq.us.americas;
```

Oracle groups snapshots into refresh groups. By specifying a refresh interval, the snapshot is automatically refreshed periodically at that interval by up to ten **Snapshot**

Refresh Processes (SNPs). If the defining query of a snapshot contains a distinct or aggregate function, a GROUP BY or CONNECT BY clause, or join or set operations, the snapshot is termed a **complex snapshot** and requires additional processing. Oracle (up to version 7.3) also supports ROWID snapshots that are based on physical row identifiers of rows in the master table.

Heterogeneous Databases in Oracle.   In a heterogeneous DDBS, at least one database is a non-Oracle system. **Oracle Open Gateways** provides access to a non-Oracle database from an Oracle server, which uses a database link to access data or to execute remote procedures in the non-Oracle system. The Open Gateways feature includes the following:

- *Distributed transactions:* Under the two-phase commit mechanism, transactions may span Oracle and non-Oracle systems.
- *Transparent SQL access:* SQL statements issued by an application are transparently transformed into SQL statements understood by the non-Oracle system.
- *Pass-through SQL and stored procedures:* An application can directly access a non-Oracle system using that system's version of SQL. Stored procedures in a non-Oracle SQL based system are treated as if they were PL/SQL remote procedures.
- *Global query optimization:* Cardinality information, indexes, etc., at the non-Oracle system are accounted for by the Oracle Server query optimizer to perform global query optimization.
- *Procedural access:* Procedural systems like messaging or queuing systems are accessed by the Oracle server using PL/SQL remote procedure calls.

In addition to the above, data dictionary references are translated to make the non-Oracle data dictionary appear as a part of the Oracle Server's dictionary. Character set translations are done between national language character sets to connect multilingual databases.

24.8 Future Prospects of Client-Server Technology

Client-server computing is rapidly being shaped by advances in technology. Based on the technology available a few years ago, it is very difficult to say how many would have predicted the current state of client-server computing. It is equally difficult to predict where the technology will be in the next few years. Several factors play major roles in deciding the functionality of client or server or both: evolving hardware and software, network protocols, LAN/WAN technology, and communication pipelines. The declining cost of several of these factors make it continuously possible to have more computing power per dollar invested. These factors act as incentives for companies to constantly upgrade their computing environment.

Currently, the most common client-server architecture in industry is called as the **two-tier architecture.** The way we described DDBMSs conforms with this architecture. The server (or servers) store data, and clients access this data. The server plays a dominant role in this architecture. The advantage of this system is its simplicity and seamless compatibility with existing legacy systems. The emergence of powerful computing machines changed the role of both clients and server, thus gravitating slowly toward a three-tier system.

The emerging client-server architecture is called the **three-tier architecture.** In this model, the layers are represented by hosts, servers, and clients. The server plays an intermediary role by storing business rules (procedures or constraints) that are used to access data from the host. Clients contain GUI interfaces and some additional application-specific business rules. Thus the server acts as a conduit of passing (partially) processed data from host to clients where it may further be processed/filtered to be presented to users in GUI format. Thus *user interface*, *rules*, and *data access* act as three tiers. Clients are usually connected to the server via LAN, and the server is connected to the host via WAN. Remote clients may be connected to the server via WAN also. This system is well suited for big corporations where a centralized database can be stored on a corporate host and the costs of building LANs and WANs can be managed and optimized using the latest technologies for each within different parts of the organization.

Evolution of operating systems is playing an important role in defining the role of machines that act as clients. For example, a few years ago, Windows 3.x introduced a new way of computing to desktop computers, which has been followed by Windows 95 and Windows 98. Windows NT, though designed for servers, is increasingly being used on high-end clients in a networked business environment. Windows NT includes features for network administration and fault-tolerance, thus enhancing the stability of the system. This, combined with advances in computing power of hardware, make the desktop PC a formidable client today.

GUIs have become the de facto interface standard for clients. Now, smarter interfaces are the norm of the industry. Taking advantage of the technology, tools are being developed to make users do their jobs better and faster. An example is the Web-portal tools which allow managers to define the views of information they want to see as a Web-portal from which they can launch into detailed operations against a DDBS. In addition, the decreasing cost of computer memory and disk storage places increased computing and faster processing power in the hands of the users, thus changing the role of the clients. This will enable users to formulate data requests, locally store and analyze query results, display, and report information.

Multimedia is also playing a major role in applications development. The use of video, graphics, and voice as data demands larger amounts of storage and higher bandwidth for transmission. Advances in communications technology and deployment of fiber optic networks provide solution for the bandwidth bottleneck at servers. Metropolitan Area Networks (MANs) and Asynchronous Transfer Mode (ATM) are a couple of examples. Also, increased storage and faster processing enable a client to cache critical multimedia data locally, thereby reducing network traffic by reducing frequent lookups.

Servers too are constantly becoming more powerful with emerging technology. Now, a server, which could be a desktop machine, is capable of doing and even exceeding what a midrange computer was able to do a few years ago. Features such as parallel processing, multitasking, and multithreading make servers fast and efficient. Also, the decreasing cost of processors and disk storage makes it easier for servers to have dual processors and redundant disks making them more reliable and robust.

Advances in encryption and decryption technology make it safer to transfer encryption-sensitive data from server to client, where it will be decrypted. The latter can be done by the hardware or by advanced software. This technology gives higher levels of data security, but the network security issues remain a major concern. Various technologies for data compression are also helping in transferring large amounts of data from servers to clients over wired and wireless networks.

Future applications of client-server systems with high bandwidth networks will include video conferencing, telemedicine, and distance learning. We review several emerging technologies and applications of databases in Chapter 27 where client-server based DDBSs will be an integral part.

24.9 Summary

In this chapter we provided an introduction to distributed databases. This is a very broad topic, and we discussed only some of the basic techniques used with distributed databases. We first discussed the reasons for distribution and the potential advantages of distributed databases over centralized systems. We also defined the concept of distribution transparency and the related concepts of fragmentation transparency and replication transparency. We discussed the design issues related to data fragmentation, replication, and distribution, and we distinguished between horizontal and vertical fragments of relations. We discussed the use of data replication to improve system reliability and availability. We categorized DDBMSs by using criteria such as degree of homogeneity of software modules and degree of local autonomy. We discussed the issues of federated database management in some detail focusing on the needs of supporting various types of autonomies and dealing with semantic heterogeneity.

We illustrated some of the techniques used in distributed query processing, and discussed the cost of communication among sites, which is considered a major factor in distributed query optimization. We compared different techniques for executing joins and presented the semijoin technique for joining relations that reside on different sites. We briefly discussed the concurrency control and recovery techniques used in DDBMSs. We reviewed some of the additional problems that must be dealt with in a distributed environment that do not appear in a centralized environment.

We then discussed the client-server architecture concepts and related them to distributed databases, and we described some of the facilities in Oracle to support distributed databases. We concluded the chapter with some general remarks about the future of client-server technology.

Review Questions

24.1. What are the main reasons for and potential advantages of distributed databases?

24.2. What additional functions does a DDBMS have over a centralized DBMS?

24.3. What are the main software modules of a DDBMS? Discuss the main functions of each of these modules in the context of the client–server architecture.

24.4. What is a fragment of a relation? What are the main types of fragments? Why is fragmentation a useful concept in distributed database design?

24.5. Why is data replication useful in DDBMSs? What typical units of data are replicated?

24.6. What is meant by *data allocation* in distributed database design? What typical units of data are distributed over sites?

24.7. How is a horizontal partitioning of a relation specified? How can a relation be put back together from a complete horizontal partitioning?

24.8. How is a vertical partitioning of a relation specified? How can a relation be put back together from a complete vertical partitioning?

24.9. Discuss what is meant by the following terms: *degree of homogeneity of a* DDBMS, *degree of local autonomy of a* DDBMS, *federated* DBMS, *distribution transparency, fragmentation transparency, replication transparency, multidatabase system.*

24.10. Discuss the naming problem in distributed databases.

24.11. Discuss the different techniques for executing an equijoin of two files located at different sites. What main factors affect the cost of data transfer?

24.12. Discuss the semijoin method for executing an equijoin of two files located at different sites. Under what conditions is an equijoin strategy efficient?

24.13. Discuss the factors that affect query decomposition. How are guard conditions and attribute lists of fragments used during the query decomposition process?

24.14. How is the decomposition of an update request different from the decomposition of a query? How are guard conditions and attribute lists of fragments used during the decomposition of an update request?

24.15. Discuss the factors that do not appear in centralized systems that affect concurrency control and recovery in distributed systems.

24.16. Compare the primary site method with the primary copy method for distributed concurrency control. How does the use of backup sites affect each?

24.17. When are voting and elections used in distributed databases?

24.18. What are the software components in a client-server DDBMS? Compare the two-tier and three-tier client-server architectures.

Exercises

24.19. Consider the data distribution of the COMPANY database, where the fragments at sites 2 and 3 are as shown in Figure 24.3 and the fragments at site 1 are as shown in Figure 7.6. For each of the following queries, show at least two strategies of decomposing and executing the query. Under what conditions would each of your strategies work well?

a. For each employee in department 5, retrieve the employee name and the names of the employee's dependents.

b. Print the names of all employees who work in department 5 but who work on some project *not* controlled by department 5.

24.20. Consider the following relations:

```
BOOKS (Book#, Primary_author, Topic, Total_stock, $price)
BOOKSTORE (Store#, City, State, Zip, Inventory_value)
STOCK (Store#, Book#, Qty)
```

Total_stock is the total number of books in stock, and inventory_value is the total inventory value for the store in dollars.

a. Give an example of two simple predicates that would be meaningful for the BOOKSTORE relation for horizontal partitioning.

b. How would a derived horizontal partitioning of STOCK be defined based on the partitioning of BOOKSTORE?

c. Show predicates by which BOOKS may be horizontally partitioned by topic.

d. Show how the STOCK may be further partitioned from the partitions in (b) by adding the predicates in (c).

24.21. Consider a distributed database for a bookstore chain called National Books with 3 sites called EAST, MIDDLE, and WEST. The relation schemas are given in question 24.20. Consider that BOOKS are fragmented by $price amounts into:

B_1: BOOK1: up to $20.
B_2: BOOK2: from $20.01 to $50.
B_3: BOOK3: from $50.01 to $100.
B_4: BOOK4: $100.01 and above.

Similarly, BOOKSTORES are divided by Zipcodes into:

S_1: EAST: Zipcodes up to 35000.
S_2: MIDDLE: Zipcodes 35001 to 70000.
S_3: WEST: Zipcodes 70001 to 99999.

Assume that STOCK is a derived fragment based on BOOKSTORE only.

a. Consider the query:

```
SELECT Book#, Total_stock
FROM Books
WHERE $price > 15 and $price < 55;
```

Assume that fragments of BOOKSTORE are non-replicated and assigned based on region. Assume further that BOOKS are allocated as:

EAST: B_1, B_4
MIDDLE: B_1, B_2
WEST: B_1, B_2, B_3, B_4

Assuming the query was submitted in EAST, what remote subqueries does it generate? (write in SQL).

b. If the bookprice of Book#= 1234 is updated from $45 to $55 at site MIDDLE, what updates does that generate? Write in English and then in SQL.

c. Given an example query issued at WEST that will generate a subquery for MIDDLE.

d. Write a query involving selection and projection on the above relations and show two possible query trees that denote different ways of execution.

24.22. Consider that you have been asked to propose a database architecture in a large organization, General Motors, as an example, to consolidate all data including legacy databases (from Hierarchical and Network model,s which are explained in

Appendices C and D; no specific knowledge of these models is needed) as well as relational databases, which are geographically distributed so that global applications can be supported. Assume that alternative one is to keep all databases as they are, while alternative two is to first convert them to relational and then support the applications over a distributed integrated database.

a. Draw two schematic diagrams for the above alternatives showing the linkages among appropriate schemas. For alternative one, choose the approach of providing export schemas for each database and constructing unified schemas for each application.

b. List the steps one has to go through under each alternative from the present situation till global applications are viable.

c. Compare these from the issues of: (i) design time considerations, and (ii) runtime considerations.

Selected Bibliography

The textbooks by Ceri and Pelagatti (1984a) and Ozsu and Valduriez (1999) are devoted to distributed databases. Halsaal (1996), Tannenbaum (1996), and Stallings (1997) are textbooks on data communications and computer networks. Comer (1997) discusses networks and internets. Dewire (1993) is a textbook on client-server computing. Ozsu et al. (1994) has a collection of papers on distributed object management.

Distributed database design has been addressed in terms of horizontal and vertical fragmentation, allocation, and replication. Ceri et al. (1982) defined the concept of minterm horizontal fragments. Ceri et al. (1983) developed an integer programming based optimization model for horizontal fragmentation and allocation. Navathe et al. (1984) developed algorithms for vertical fragmentation based on attribute affinity and showed a variety of contexts for vertical fragment allocation. Wilson and Navathe (1986) present an analytical model for optimal allocation of fragments. Elmasri et al. (1987) discuss fragmentation for the ECR model; Karlapalem et al. (1994) discuss issues for distributed design of object databases. Navathe et al. (1996) discuss mixed fragmentation by combining horizontal and vertical fragmentation; Karlapalem et al. (1996) present a model for redesign of distributed databases.

Distributed query processing, optimization, and decomposition are discussed in Hevner and Yao (1979), Kerschberg et al. (1982), Apers et al. (1983), Ceri and Pelagatti (1984), and Bodorick et al. (1992). Bernstein and Goodman (1981) discuss the theory behind semijoin processing. Wong (1983) discusses the use of relationships in relation fragmentation. Concurrency control and recovery schemes are discussed in Bernstein and Goodman (1981a). Kumar and Hsu (1998) has some articles related to recovery in distributed databases. Elections in distributed systems are discussed in Garcia-Molina (1982). Lamport (1978) discusses problems with generating unique timestamps in a distributed system.

A concurrency control technique for replicated data that is based on voting is presented by Thomas (1979). Gifford (1979) proposes the use of weighted voting, and Paris (1986) describes a method called voting with witnesses. Jajodia and Mutchler (1990) discuss dynamic voting. A technique called *available copy* is proposed by Bernstein and Goodman (1984), and one that uses the idea of a group is presented in ElAbbadi and

Toueg (1988). Other recent work that discusses replicated data includes Gladney (1989), Agrawal and ElAbbadi (1990), ElAbbadi and Toueg (1990), Kumar and Segev (1993), Mukkamala (1989), and Wolfson and Milo (1991). Bassiouni (1988) discusses optimistic protocols for DDB concurrency control. Garcia-Molina (1983) and Kumar and Stonebraker (1987) discuss techniques that use the semantics of the transactions. Distributed concurrency control techniques based on locking and distinguished copies are presented by Menasce et al. (1980) and Minoura and Wiederhold (1982). Obermark (1982) presents algorithms for distributed deadlock detection.

A survey of recovery techniques in distributed systems is given by Kohler (1981). Reed (1983) discusses atomic actions on distributed data. A book edited by Bhargava (1987) presents various approaches and techniques for concurrency and reliability in distributed systems.

Federated database systems were first defined in McLeod and Heimbigner (1985). Techniques for schema integration in federated databases are presented by Elmasri et al. (1986), Batini et al. (1986), Hayne and Ram (1990), and Motro (1987). Elmagarmid and Helal (1988) and Gamal-Eldin et al. (1988) discuss the update problem in heterogeneous DDBSs. Heterogeneous distributed database issues are discussed in Hsiao and Kamel (1989). Sheth and Larson (1990) present an exhaustive survey of federated database management.

Recently, multidatabase systems and interoperability have become important topics. Techniques for dealing with semantic incompatibilities among multiple databases are examined in DeMichiel (1989), Siegel and Madnick (1991), Krishnamurthy et al. (1991), and Wang and Madnick (1989). Castano et al. (1998) presents an excellent survey of techniques for analysis of schemas. Pitoura et al. (1995) discuss object orientation in multidatabase systems.

Transaction processing in multidatabases is discussed in Mehrotra et al. (1992), Georgakopoulos et al. (1991), Elmagarmid et al. (1990), and Brietbart et al. (1990), among others. Elmagarmid et al. (1992) discuss transaction processing for advanced applications, including engineering applications discussed in Heiler et al. (1992).

The workflow systems, which are becoming popular to manage information in complex organizations, use multilevel and nested transactions in conjunction with distributed databases. Weikum (1991) discusses multilevel transaction management. Alonso et al. (1997) discuss limitations of current workflow systems.

A number of experimental distributed DBMSs have been implemented. These include distributed INGRES (Epstein et al., 1978), DDTS (Devor and Weeldreyer, 1980), SDD-1 (Rothnie et al., 1980), System R * (Lindsay et al., 1984), SIRIUS-DELTA (Ferrier and Stangret, 1982), and MULTIBASE (Smith et al., 1981). The OMNIBASE system (Rusinkiewicz et al., 1988) and the Federated Information Base developed using the Candide data model (Navathe et al. 1994) are examples of federated DDBMS. Pitoura et al. (1995) present a comparative survey of the federated database system prototypes. Most commercial DBMS vendors have products using the client-server approach and offer distributed versions of their systems. Some system issues concerning client-server DBMS architectures are discussed in Carey et al. (1991), DeWitt et al. (1990), and Wang and Rowe (1991). Khoshafian et al. (1992) discuss design issues for relational DBMSs in the client-server environment. Client-server management issues are discussed in many books, such as Zantinge and Adriaans (1996).

CHAPTER 25 | Deductive Databases

In this chapter, we discuss deductive databases, an area that is at the intersection of databases, logic, and artificial intelligence or knowledge bases. A **deductive database system** is a database system that includes capabilities to define **(deductive) rules,** which can deduce or infer additional information from the facts that are stored in a database. (These are different from the *active* rules discussed in Chapter 23.) Because part of the theoretical foundation for some deductive database systems is mathematical logic, such rules are often referred to as **logic databases.** Other types of systems, referred to as **expert database systems** or **knowledge-based systems,** also incorporate reasoning and inferencing capabilities; such systems use techniques that were developed in the field of artificial intelligence, including semantic networks, frames, production systems, or rules for capturing domain-specific knowledge. The main differences between these systems and the ones we discuss here are twofold:

1. Knowledge-based expert systems have traditionally assumed that the data needed resides in main memory; hence, secondary storage management is not an issue. Deductive database systems attempt to change this restriction so that either a DBMS is enhanced to handle an expert system interface or an expert system is enhanced to handle secondary storage resident data.

2. The knowledge in an expert or knowledge-based system is extracted from application experts and refers to an application domain rather than to knowledge inherent in the data.

801

Whereas a close relationship exists between these and the deductive databases we are about to discuss, a detailed discussion goes beyond our scope. In this chapter, we discuss only logic-based systems and give an overview of the formal foundations of deductive database systems.

For a brief introduction to deductive databases, the reader can cover only Sections 25.1 and 25.2. Those interested in applications of deductive databases may then go to Section 25.8.

25.1 Introduction to Deductive Databases

In a deductive database system, we typically specify rules through a **declarative language**—a language in which we specify what to achieve rather than how to achieve it. An **inference engine** (or **deduction mechanism**) within the system can deduce new facts from the database by interpreting these rules. The model used for deductive databases is closely related to the relational data model, and particularly to the domain relational calculus formalism (see Section 9.4). It is also related to the field of **logic programming** and the **Prolog** language. The deductive database work based on logic has used Prolog as a starting point. A variation of Prolog called **Datalog** is used to define rules declaratively in conjunction with an existing set of relations, which are themselves treated as literals in the language. Although the language structure of Datalog resembles that of Prolog, its operational semantics—that is, how a Datalog program is to be executed—is still a topic of active research.

A deductive database uses two main types of specifications: facts and rules. **Facts** are specified in a manner similar to the way relations are specified, except that it is not necessary to include the attribute names. Recall that a tuple in a relation describes some real-world fact whose meaning is partly determined by the attribute names. In a deductive database, the meaning of an attribute value in a tuple is determined solely by its *position* within the tuple. **Rules** are somewhat similar to relational views. They specify virtual relations that are not actually stored but that can be formed from the facts by applying inference mechanisms based on the rule specifications. The main difference between rules and views is that rules may involve recursion and hence may yield virtual relations that cannot be defined in terms of standard relational views.

The evaluation of Prolog programs is based on a technique called *backward chaining*, which involves a top-down evaluation of goals. In the deductive databases that use Datalog, attention has been devoted to handling large volumes of data stored in a relational database. Hence, evaluation techniques have been devised that resemble those for a bottom-up evaluation. Prolog suffers from the limitation that the order of specification of facts and rules is significant in evaluation; moreover, the order of literals (defined later in Section 25.2.2) within a rule is significant. The execution techniques for Datalog programs attempt to circumvent these problems.

We discussed object-oriented databases (OODBs) in Chapter 11. It is instructive to put deductive databases (DDBs) in a proper context with respect to OODBs. The emphasis in OODBs has been on providing a natural modeling mechanism for real-world objects by encapsulating their structure with behavior. The emphasis in DDBs, in contrast, has been on deriving new knowledge from existing data by supplying additional real-world relationships in the form of rules. A marriage of these two different enhancements to traditional databases has started appearing, in the form of adding deductive capabilities to OODBs and adding programming language interfaces like C++ to DDBs. This new breed of databases systems is referred to as deductive OODBs, or DOODs for short.[1]

The rest of this chapter is organized as follows. In Section 25.2, we introduce the Prolog/Datalog notation; Datalog is a deductive query language similar to Prolog but more suitable for database applications. In Section 25.3 we discuss theoretical interpretations of the meaning of rules. The two standard approaches to inference mechanisms in logic programming languages, called *forward chaining* and *backward chaining*, are discussed in Section 25.4. Section 25.5 presents concepts related to Datalog programs, their evaluation, and their execution. Section 25.6 discusses three examples of deductive database systems: a commercial system called LDL, and two university research systems called CORAL and NAIL! Section 25.7 is devoted to a discussion of object-oriented database systems (DOODs), and introduces VALIDITY, the latest commercial system in this family. Applications of commercial deductive databases—LDL and VALIDITY—are covered in Section 25.8.

25.2 Prolog/Datalog Notation

The notation used in Prolog/Datalog is based on providing predicates with unique names. A **predicate** has an implicit meaning, which is suggested by the predicate name, and a fixed number of **arguments.** If the arguments are all constant values, the predicate simply states that a certain fact is true. If, on the other hand, the predicate has variables as arguments, it is either considered as a query or as part of a rule or constraint. Throughout this chapter, we adopt the Prolog convention that all **constant values** in a predicate are either *numeric* or character strings; they are represented as identifiers (or names) starting with *lowercase letters* only, whereas **variable names** always start with an *uppercase letter*.

25.2.1 An Example

Consider the example shown in Figure 25.1, which is based on the relational database of Figure 7.6, but in a much simplified form. There are three predicate names: *supervise*, *superior*, and *subordinate*. The supervise predicate is defined via a set of facts, each of which has two arguments: a supervisor name, followed by the name of a *direct* supervisee (subordinate) of that supervisor. These facts correspond to the actual data that is stored in the database, and they can be considered as constituting a set of tuples in a relation SUPERVISE with two attributes whose schema is

SUPERVISE(Supervisor,Supervisee)

---

1. A historical perspective of these developments appears in Nicolas (1997).

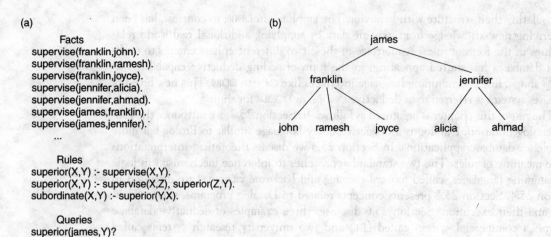

(a)

Facts
supervise(franklin,john).
supervise(franklin,ramesh).
supervise(franklin,joyce).
supervise(jennifer,alicia).
supervise(jennifer,ahmad).
supervise(james,franklin).
supervise(james,jennifer).
...

Rules
superior(X,Y) :- supervise(X,Y).
superior(X,Y) :- supervise(X,Z), superior(Z,Y).
subordinate(X,Y) :- superior(Y,X).

Queries
superior(james,Y)?
superior(james,joyce)?

Figure 25.1   (a) Prolog notation. (b) The supervisory tree.

Thus, supervise(X,Y) states the fact that "X supervises Y." Notice the omission of the attribute names in the Prolog notation. Attribute names are only represented by virtue of the position of each argument in a predicate: the first argument represents the supervisor, and the second argument represents a direct subordinate.

The other two predicate names are defined by rules. The main contribution of deductive databases is the ability to specify recursive rules, and to provide a framework for inferring new information based on the specified rules. A rule is of the form **head :- body,** where :- is read as "if and only if". A rule usually has a **single predicate** to the left of the :- symbol—called the **head** or **left-hand side** (LHS) or **conclusion** of the rule—and **one or more predicates** to the right of the :- symbol—called the **body** or **right-hand side** (RHS) or **premise(s)** of the rule. A predicate with constants as arguments is said to be **ground;** we also refer to it as an **instantiated predicate.** The arguments of the predicates that appear in a rule typically include a number of variable symbols, although predicates can also contain constants as arguments. A rule specifies that, if a particular assignment or **binding** of constant values to the variables in the body (RHS predicates) makes *all* the RHS predicates **true,** it also makes the head (LHS predicate) true by using the same assignment of constant values to variables. Hence, a rule provides us with a way of generating new facts that are instantiations of the head of the rule. These new facts are based on facts that already exist, corresponding to the instantiations (or bindings) of predicates in the body of the rule. Notice that by listing multiple predicates in the body of a rule we implicitly apply the **logical and** operator to these predicates. Hence, the commas between the RHS predicates may be read as meaning "and."

Consider the definition of the predicate superior in Figure 25.1, whose first argument is an employee name and whose second argument is an employee who is either a *direct* or an *indirect* subordinate of the first employee. By *indirect subordinate*, we mean the subordinate of some subordinate down to any number of levels. Thus superior(X,Y) stands for the fact that "X is a superior of Y" through direct or indirect supervision. We can write two rules that together specify the meaning of the new predicate. The first rule under Rules in the figure states that, for every value of X and Y, if supervise(X,Y)—the rule body—is true, then superior(X,Y)—the rule head—is also true, since Y would be a direct subordinate of X (at one level down). This rule can be used to generate all direct superior/subordinate relationships from the facts that define the supervise predicate. The second recursive rule states that, if supervise(X, Z) *and* superior(Z, Y) are *both* true, then superior(X,Y) is also true. This is an example of a **recursive rule,** where one of the rule body predicates in the RHS is the same as the rule head predicate in the LHS. In general, the rule body defines a number of premises such that, if they are all true, we can deduce that the conclusion in the rule head is also true. Notice that, if we have two (or more) rules with the same head (LHS predicate), it is equivalent to saying that the predicate is true (that is, that it can be instantiated) if *either one* of the bodies is true; hence, it is equivalent to a **logical or** operation. For example, if we have two rules X :- Y and X :- Z, they are equivalent to a rule X :- Y **or** Z. The latter form is not used in deductive systems, however, because it is not in the standard form of rule, called a Horn clause, as we discuss in Section 25.2.3.

A Prolog system contains a number of **built-in** predicates that the system can interpret directly. These typically include the equality comparison operator =(X,Y), which returns true if X and Y are identical and can also be written as X=Y by using the standard infix notation.[2] Other comparison operators for numbers, such as $<$, $<=$, $>$, and $>=$, can be treated as binary predicates. Arithmetic functions such as $+$, $-$, $*$, and $/$ can be used as arguments in predicates in Prolog. In contrast, Datalog (in its basic form) does *not* allow functions such as arithmetic operations as arguments; indeed, this is one of the main differences between Prolog and Datalog. However, later extensions to Datalog have been proposed to include functions.

A **query** typically involves a predicate symbol with some variable arguments, and its meaning (or "answer") is to deduce all the different constant combinations that, when **bound** (assigned) to the variables, can make the predicate true. For example, the first query in Figure 25.1 requests the names of all subordinates of "james" at any level. A different type of query, which has only constant symbols as arguments, returns either a true or a false result, depending on whether the arguments provided can be deduced from the facts and rules. For example, the second query in Figure 25.1 returns true, since superior(james, joyce) can be deduced.

---

2. A Prolog system typically has a number of different equality predicates that have different interpretations.

25.2.2   Datalog Notation

In Datalog, as in other logic-based languages, a program is built from basic objects called **atomic formulas.** It is customary to define the syntax of logic-based languages by describing the syntax of atomic formulas and identifying how they can be combined to form a program. In Datalog, atomic formulas are **literals** of the form $p(a_1, a_2, \ldots, a_n)$, where p is the predicate name and n is the number of arguments for predicate p. Different predicate symbols can have different numbers of arguments, and the number of arguments n of predicate p is sometimes called the **arity** or **degree** of p. The arguments can be either constant values or variable names. As mentioned earlier, we use the convention that constant values either are numeric or start with a *lowercase* character, whereas variable names always start with an *uppercase* character.

A number of **built-in predicates** are included in Datalog, which can also be used to construct atomic formulas. The built-in predicates are of two main types: the binary comparison predicates <(less), <=(less_or_equal), >(greater), and >= (greater_or_equal) over ordered domains; and the comparison predicates = (equal) and /= (not_equal) over ordered or unordered domains. These can be used as binary predicates with the same functional syntax as other predicates—for example by writing less(X, 3)—or they can be specified by using the customary infix notation X<3. Notice that, because the domains of these predicates are potentially infinite, they should be used with care in rule definitions. For example, the predicate greater(X, 3), if used alone, generates an infinite set of values for X that satisfy the predicate (all integer numbers greater than 3). We discuss this problem a bit later.

A **literal** is either an atomic formula as defined earlier—called a **positive literal**—or an atomic formula preceded by **not.** The latter is a negated atomic formula, called a **negative literal.** Datalog programs can be considered to be a *subset* of the **predicate calculus** formulas, which are somewhat similar to the formulas of the domain relational calculus (see Section 9.4). In Datalog, however, these formulas are first converted into what is known as **clausal form** before they are expressed in Datalog; and only formulas given in a restricted clausal form, called Horn clauses,[3] can be used in Datalog.

25.2.3   Clausal Form and Horn Clauses

Recall from Section 9.3.2 that a formula in the relational calculus is a condition that includes predicates called *atoms* (based on relation names). In addition, a formula can have quantifiers—namely, the *universal quantifier* (for all) and the *existential quantifier* (there exists). In clausal form, a formula must be transformed into another formula with the following characteristics:

- All variables in the formula are universally quantified. Hence, it is not necessary to include the universal quantifiers (for all) explicitly; the quantifiers are removed, and all variables in the formula are *implicitly* quantified by the universal quantifier.

---

3. Named after the mathematician Alfred Horn.

- In clausal form, the formula is made up of a number of clauses, where each **clause** is composed of a number of *literals* connected by OR logical connectives only. Hence, each clause is a *disjunction* of literals.

- The *clauses themselves* are connected by AND logical connectives only, to form a formula. Hence, the *clausal form of a formula* is a *conjunction* of clauses.

It can be shown that *any formula can be converted into clausal form*. For our purposes, we are mainly interested in the form of the individual clauses, each of which is a disjunction of literals. Recall that literals can be positive literals or negative literals. Consider a clause of the form:

$$not(P_1) \text{ OR } not(P_2) \text{ OR } ... \text{ OR } not(P_n) \text{ OR } Q_1 \text{ OR } Q_2 \text{ OR } ... \text{ OR } Q_m \qquad (1)$$

This clause has n negative literals and m positive literals. Such a clause can be transformed into the following equivalent logical formula:

$$P_1 \text{ AND } P_2 \text{ AND } ... \text{ AND } P_n => Q_1 \text{ OR } Q_2 \text{ OR } ... \text{ OR } Q_m \qquad (2)$$

where => is the **implies** symbol. The formulas (1) and (2) are equivalent, meaning that their truth values are always the same. This is the case because, if all the P_i literals ($i = 1$, $2, ..., n$) are true, the formula (2) is true only if at least one of the Q_i's is true, which is the meaning of the => (implies) symbol. Similarly, for formula (1), if all the P_i literals ($i = 1$, $2, ..., n$) are true, their negations are all false; so in this case formula (1) is true only if at least one of the Q_i's is true. In Datalog, rules are expressed as a restricted form of clauses called **Horn clauses,** in which a clause can contain *at most one* positive literal. Hence, a Horn clause is either of the form

$$not(P_1) \text{ OR } not(P_2) \text{ OR } ... \text{ OR } not(P_n) \text{ OR } Q \qquad (3)$$

or of the form

$$not(P_1) \text{ OR } not(P_2) \text{ OR } ... \text{ OR } not(P_n) \qquad (4)$$

The Horn clause in (3) can be transformed into the clause

$$P_1 \text{ AND } P_2 \text{ AND } ... \text{ AND } P_n => Q \qquad (5)$$

which is written in Datalog as the following rule

$$Q :- P_1, P_2, ..., P_n. \qquad (6)$$

The Horn clause in (4) can be transformed into

$$P_1 \text{ AND } P_2 \text{ AND } ... \text{ AND } P_n => \qquad (7)$$

which is written in Datalog as follows:

$$P_1, P_2, ..., P_n. \qquad (8)$$

A Datalog rule, as in (6), is hence a Horn clause, and its meaning, based on formula (5), is that if the predicates P_1 and P_2 and ... and P_n are all true for a particular binding to their variable arguments, then Q is also true and can hence be inferred. The Datalog expression (8) can be considered as an integrity constraint, where all the predicates must be true to satisfy the query.

In general, a query in Datalog consists of two components:

- A Datalog program, which is a finite set of rules.
- A literal $P(X_1, X_2, ..., X_n)$, where each X_i is a variable or a constant.

A Prolog or Datalog system has an internal **inference engine** that can be used to process and compute the results of such queries. Prolog inference engines typically return one result to the query (that is, one set of values for the variables in the query) at a time and must be prompted to return additional results. On the contrary, Datalog returns results set-at-a-time.

25.3 Interpretations of Rules

There are two main alternatives for interpreting the theoretical meaning of rules: *proof-theoretic* and *model-theoretic*. In practical systems, the inference mechanism within a system defines the exact interpretation, which may not coincide with either of the two theoretical interpretations. The inference mechanism is a computational procedure and hence provides a computational interpretation of the meaning of rules. In this section, we first discuss the two theoretical interpretations. Inference mechanisms are then discussed briefly as a way of defining the meaning of rules. We discuss specific inference mechanisms in more detail in Section 25.4.

In the **proof-theoretic** interpretation of rules, we consider the facts and rules to be true statements, or **axioms. Ground axioms** contain no variables. The facts are ground axioms that are given to be true. Rules are called **deductive axioms,** since they can be used to deduce new facts. The deductive axioms can be used to construct proofs that derive new facts from existing facts. For example, Figure 25.2 shows how to prove the fact superior(james, ahmad) from the rules and facts given in Figure 25.1. The proof-theoretic interpretation gives us a procedural or computational approach for computing an answer to the Datalog query. The process of proving whether a certain fact (theorem) holds is known as *theorem proving*.

The second type of interpretation is called the **model-theoretic** interpretation. Here, given a finite or an infinite domain of constant values,[4] we assign to a predicate every possible combination of values as arguments. We must then determine whether the predicate is true or false. In general, it is sufficient to specify the combinations of

1. superior(X,Y) :- supervise(X,Y).   (rule 1)
2. superior(X,Y) :- supervise(X,Z), superior(Z,Y).   (rule 2)

3. supervise(jennifer,ahmad).   (ground axiom, given)
4. supervise(james,jennifer).   (ground axiom, given)
5. superior(jennifer,ahmad).   (apply rule 1 on 3)
6. superior(james,ahmad).   (apply rule 2 on 4 and 5)

Figure 25.2   Proving a new fact.

---

4. The most commonly chosen domain is finite and is called the *Herbrand Universe*.

Rules

superior(X,Y) :- supervise(X,Y).
superior(X,Y) :- supervise(X,Z), superior(Z,Y).

Interpretation

Known Facts:

supervise(franklin,john) is **true**.
supervise(franklin,ramesh) is **true**.
supervise(franklin,joyce) is **true**.
supervise(jennifer,alicia) is **true**.
supervise(jennifer,ahmad) is **true**.
supervise(james,franklin) is **true**.
supervise(james,jennifer) is **true**.
supervise(X,Y) is **false** for all other possible (X,Y) combinations.

Derived Facts:

superior(franklin,john) is **true**.
superior(franklin,ramesh) is **true**.
superior(franklin,joyce) is **true**.
superior(jennifer,alicia) is **true**.
superior(jennifer,ahmad) is **true**.
superior(james,franklin) is **true**.
superior(james,jennifer) is **true**.
superior(james,john) is **true**.
superior(james,ramesh) is **true**.
superior(james,joyce) is **true**.
superior(james,alicia) is **true**.
superior(james,ahmad) is **true**.
superior(X,Y) is **false** for all other possible (X,Y) combinations.

Figure 25.3   An interpretation that is a minimal model.

arguments that make the predicate true, and to state that all other combinations make the predicate false. If this is done for every predicate, it is called an **interpretation** of the set of predicates. For example, consider the interpretation shown in Figure 25.3 for the predicates supervise and superior. This interpretation assigns a truth value (true or false) to every possible combination of argument values (from a finite domain) for the two predicates.

An interpretation is called a **model** for a *specific set of rules* if those rules are *always true* under that interpretation; that is, for any values assigned to the variables in the rules, the head of the rules is true when we substitute the truth values assigned to the predicates in the body of the rule by that interpretation. Hence, whenever a particular substitution (binding) to the variables in the rules is applied, if all the predicates in the body of a rule are true under the interpretation, the predicate in the head of the rule must also be true. The interpretation shown in Figure 25.3 is a model for the two rules shown, since it can never cause the rules to be violated. Notice that a rule is violated if a particular binding of constants to the variables makes all the predicates in the rule body true but makes the predicate in the rule head false. For example, if supervise(a,b) and superior(b,c) are both true under some interpretation, but superior(a,c) is not true, the interpretation cannot be a model for the recursive rule:

superior(X,Y) :- supervise(X,Z), superior(Z,Y)

In the model-theoretic approach, the meaning of the rules is established by providing a model for these rules. A model is called a **minimal model** for a set of rules if we cannot change any fact from true to false and still get a model for these rules. For example, consider the interpretation in Figure 25.3, and assume that the supervise predicate is defined by a set of known facts, whereas the superior predicate is defined as an interpretation (model) for the rules. Suppose that we add the predicate superior(james, bob) to the true predicates. This remains a model for the rules shown, but it is not a minimal model, since changing the truth value of superior(james, bob) from true to false still provides us with a model for the rules. The model shown in Figure 25.3 is the minimal model for the set of facts that are defined by the supervise predicate.

In general, the minimal model that corresponds to a given set of facts in the model-theoretic interpretation should be the same as the facts generated by the proof-theoretic interpretation for the same original set of ground and deductive axioms. However, this is generally true only for rules with a simple structure. Once we allow negation in the specification of rules, the correspondence between interpretations *does not* hold. In fact, with negation, numerous minimal models are possible for a given set of facts.

A third approach to interpreting the meaning of rules involves defining an inference mechanism that is used by the system to deduce facts from the rules. This inference mechanism would define a **computational interpretation** to the meaning of the rules. The Prolog logic programming language uses its inference mechanism to define the meaning of the rules and facts in a Prolog program. Not all Prolog programs correspond to the proof-theoretic or model-theoretic interpretations; it depends on the type of rules in the program. However, for many simple Prolog programs, the Prolog inference mechanism infers the facts that correspond either to the proof-theoretic interpretation or to a minimal model under the model-theoretic interpretation.

25.4 Basic Inference Mechanisms for Logic Programs

We now discuss the two main approaches to computational inference mechanisms that are based on the proof-theoretic interpretation of rules. These are the *bottom-up inference mechanisms*, where the inference starts from the given facts and generates additional facts that are matched to the goal of a query, and the *top-down inference mechanisms*, where the inference starts from the goal of a query and tries to find constant values that make it true. The latter approach has been used in Prolog.

25.4.1 Bottom-Up Inference Mechanisms (Forward Chaining)

In bottom-up inference, which is also called **forward chaining** or **bottom-up resolution**, the inference engine starts with the facts and applies the rules to generate new facts. As facts are generated, they are checked against the query predicate goal for a match. The term *forward chaining* indicates that the inference moves forward from the facts toward the goal. For example, consider the first query shown in Figure 25.1, and assume that the facts and rules shown are the only ones that hold. In bottom-up inference, the inference mechanism first checks whether any of the existing facts directly matches the query—superior(james, Y)?—that is given. Since all the facts are for the supervise predicate, no match is found; so the first rule is now applied to the existing facts to generate new facts. This causes the facts for the superior predicate to be generated by the first (nonrecursive) rule in the order shown in Figure 25.3. As each fact is generated, it is checked for a match against the query predicate. No matches are found until the fact superior(james, franklin) is generated, which results in the first answer to the query—namely, Y=franklin.

In a Prolog-like system, where one answer at a time is generated, additional prompts must be entered to search for the next answer; in this case, the system continues to generate new facts and returns the next answer, Y=jennifer, from the generated fact superior(james, jennifer). At this point, all possible applications of the first (nonrecursive) rule are exhausted, having generated the first seven facts of the superior predicate that are shown in Figure 25.3. If additional results are needed, the inference continues to the next (recursive) rule to generate additional facts. It must now match each supervise fact with each superior fact, searching for a match in the second argument of supervise with the first argument of superior, in order to satisfy both the RHS predicates: supervise(X, Z) *and* superior(Z,Y). This results in the generation of the subsequent facts listed in Figure 25.3, and the additional answers Y=john, Y=ramesh, Y=joyce, Y=alicia, and Y=ahmad.

In the bottom-up approach, a search strategy to generate only the facts that are relevant to a query should be used; otherwise, in a naive approach, all possible facts are generated in some order that is irrelevant to the particular query, which can be very inefficient for large sets of rules and facts.

25.4.2 Top-Down Inference Mechanisms (Backward Chaining)

The top-down inference mechanism—used in Prolog interpreters—is also called **backward chaining** and **top-down resolution**. It starts with the query predicate goal and attempts to find matches to the variables that lead to valid facts in the database. The term *backward chaining* indicates that the inference moves backward from the intended goal to determine facts that would satisfy the goal. In this approach, facts are not explicitly generated, as they are in forward chaining. For example, in processing the query superior(james,Y)?, the system first searches for any facts with the superior predicate whose first argument matches james. If any such facts exist, the system generates the results in the same order in which the facts were specified. Since there are no such facts in our example, the system then locates the first rule whose head (LHS) has the same predicate name as the query, leading to the (nonrecursive) rule:

superior(X,Y) :- supervise(X,Y)

The inference mechanism then matches X to james, leading to the rule:

superior(james,Y) :- supervise(james,Y)

The variable X is now said to be **bound** to the value james. The system proceeds to substitute superior(james,Y) with supervise(james,Y), and it searches for facts that match supervise(james,Y) to find an answer for Y. The facts are searched in the order in which they are listed in the program, leading to the first match Y=franklin, followed by the match Y=jennifer. At this point, the search using the first rule is exhausted, so the system searches for the next rule whose head (LHS) has the predicate name superior, which leads to the recursive rule. The inference mechanism then binds X to james, resulting in the modified rule:

superior(james,Y) :- supervise(james,Z), superior(Z,Y)

It then substitutes the LHS with the RHS and starts searching for facts that satisfy *both* of the RHS predicates. These are now called **subgoals** of the query. In this case, to find a match for the query, the system must find facts that satisfy more than one predicate— supervise(james, Z) *and* superior(Z, Y)—which is known as a **compound goal.** To satisfy a compound goal, a standard approach is to employ **depth-first** search, meaning that the program first tries to find a binding that makes the first predicate true, and then moves on to search for a corresponding match for the next predicate. If the first predicate binding does not result in any match that makes the second predicate true, the system **backtracks** and searches for the next binding that makes the first predicate true, and then continues the search as before.

In our example, the system finds the match supervise(james, franklin) for the first subgoal, which **binds** Z to franklin, resulting in Z=franklin. It then searches for a match to superior(franklin,Y) for the second subgoal, which continues the matching process by utilizing the first (nonrecursive) rule again and eventually returns Y=john, Y=ramesh, and Y=joyce. The process is then repeated with Z=jennifer, returning Y=alicia and Y=ahmad. These are shown pictorially in Figure 25.4.

In this example, there are no additional "third-level" superior relationships; but if there were, these would also be generated at their appropriate order in the inference process (see Exercise 25.1).[5]

There has been a lot of research in devising more efficient inference mechanisms in the field of logic programming. In particular, one can employ **breadth-first** search techniques instead of depth-first search for compound goals, where the search for matches to multiple subgoals can proceed in parallel. Optimization techniques designed to guide the search by using more promising rules early during inference have also been proposed.

The top-down, depth-first inference mechanism leads to certain problems because of its dependence on the order in which rules and facts are written. In particular, when rules are written to define a predicate recursively—for example, in the definition of the superior predicate—one must write the subgoals in the order shown so that no infinite recursion occurs during the inference process. Another problem occurs when rule definitions

---

5. Notice that, in our example, the order of search is quite similar for both forward and backward chaining. However, this is not generally the case.

Figure 25.4   Top-down evaluation of a query.

involve negation, which we will not be able to address in detail, except for a brief mention in Section 25.5.5. These problems have led to the definition of alternative inference mechanisms for Prolog, and query evaluation strategies for Datalog.

25.5 Datalog Programs and Their Evaluation

There are two main methods of defining the truth values of predicates in actual Datalog programs. **Fact-defined predicates** (or **relations**) are defined by listing all the combinations of values (the tuples) that make the predicate true. These correspond to base relations whose contents are stored in a database system. Figure 25.5 shows the fact-defined predicates employee, male, female, department, supervise, project, and workson, which correspond to part of the relational database shown in Figure 7.6. **Rule-defined predicates** (or **views**) are defined by being the head (LHS) of one or more Datalog rules; they correspond to *virtual relations* whose contents can be inferred by the inference engine. Figure 25.6 shows a number of rule-defined predicates.

25.5.1 Safety of Programs

A program or a rule is said to be **safe** if it generates a *finite* set of facts. The general theoretical problem of determining whether a set of rules is safe is undecidable. However, one can determine the safety of restricted forms of rules. For example, the rules shown in Figure 25.6 are safe. One situation where we get unsafe rules that can generate an infinite

employee(john).
employee(franklin).
employee(alicia).
employee(jennifer).
employee(ramesh).
employee(joyce).
employee(ahmad).
employee(james).

salary(john,30000).
salary(franklin,40000).
salary(alicia,25000).
salary(jennifer,43000).
salary(ramesh,38000).
salary(joyce,25000).
salary(ahmad,25000).
salary(james,55000).

department(john,research).
department(franklin,research).
department(alicia,administration).
department(jennifer,administration).
department(ramesh,research).
department(joyce,research).
department(ahmad,administration).
department(james,headquarters).

supervise(franklin,john).
supervise(franklin,ramesh).
supervise(franklin,joyce).
supervise(jennifer,alicia).
supervise(jennifer,ahmad).
supervise(james,franklin).
supervise(james,jennifer).

male(john).
male(franklin).
male(ramesh).
male(ahmad).
male(james).

female(alicia).
female(jennifer).
female(joyce).

project(productx).
project(producty).
project(productz).
project(computerization).
project(reorganization).
project(newbenefits).

workson(john,productx,32).
workson(john,producty,8).
workson(ramesh,productz,40).
workson(joyce,productx,20).
workson(joyce,producty,20).
workson(franklin,producty,10).
workson(franklin,productz,10).
workson(franklin,computerization,10).
workson(franklin,reorganization,10).
workson(alicia,newbenefits,30).
workson(alicia,computerization,10).
workson(ahmad,computerization,35).
workson(ahmad,newbenefits,5).
workson(jennifer,newbenefits,20).
workson(jennifer,reorganization,15).
workson(james,reorganization,10).

Figure 25.5   Fact predicates for part of the database from Figure 7.6.

superior(X,Y) :- supervise(X,Y).
superior(X,Y) :- supervise(X,Z), superior(Z,Y).

subordinate(X,Y) :- superior(Y,X).

supervisor(X) :- employee(X), supervise(X,Y).

over_40K_emp(X) :- employee(X), salary(X,Y), Y>=40000.
under_40K_supervisor(X) :- supervisor(X), not(over_40K_emp(X)).
main_productx_emp(X) :- employee(X), workson(X,productx,Y), Y>=20.
president(X) :- employee(X), not(supervise(Y,X)).

Figure 25.6   Rule-defined predicates.

number of facts arises when one of the variables in the rule can range over an infinite domain of values, and that variable is not limited to ranging over a finite relation. For example, consider the rule

big_salary(Y) :- Y>60000

Here, we can get an infinite result if Y ranges over all possible integers. But suppose that we change the rule as follows:

big_salary(Y) :- employee(X), salary(X,Y), Y>60000

In the second rule, the result is not infinite, since the values that Y can be bound to are now restricted to values that are the salary of some employee in the database—presumably, a finite set of values. We can also rewrite the rule as follows:

big_salary(Y) :- Y>60000, employee(X), salary(X,Y)

In this case, the rule is still theoretically safe. However, in Prolog or any other system that uses a top-down, depth-first inference mechanism, the rule creates an infinite loop, since we first search for a value for Y and then check whether it is a salary of an employee. The result is generation of an infinite number of Y values, even though these, after a certain point, cannot lead to a set of true RHS predicates. One definition of Datalog considers both rules to be safe, since it does not depend on a particular inference mechanism. Nonetheless, it is generally advisable to write such a rule in the safest form, with the predicates that restrict possible bindings of variables placed first. As another example of an unsafe rule, consider the following rule:

has_something(X,Y) :- employee(X)

Here, an infinite number of Y values can again be generated, since the variable Y appears only in the head of the rule and hence is not limited to a finite set of values. To define safe rules more formally, we use the concept of a limited variable. A variable X is **limited** in a rule if (1) it appears in a regular (not built-in) predicate in the body of the rule; (2) it appears in a predicate of the form X=c or c=X or (c1<=X and X<=c2) in the rule body, where c, c1, and c2 are constant values; or (3) it appears in a predicate of the form X=Y or Y=X in the rule body, where Y is a limited variable. A rule is said to be **safe** if all its variables are limited.

25.5.2 Use of Relational Operations

It is straightforward to specify many operations of the relational algebra in the form of Datalog rules that define the result of applying these operations on the database relations (fact predicates). This means that relational queries and views can easily be specified in Datalog. The additional power that Datalog provides is in the specification of recursive queries, and views based on recursive queries. In this section, we show how some of the standard relational operations can be specified as Datalog rules. Our examples will use the base relations (fact-defined predicates) rel_one, rel_two, and rel_three, whose schemas are shown in Figure 25.7. In Datalog, we do not need to specify the attribute names

```
rel_one(A,B,C).
rel_two(D,E,F).
rel_three(G,H,I,J).

select_one_A_eq_c(X,Y,Z) :- rel_one(c,Y,Z).
select_one_B_less_5(X,Y,Z) :- rel_one(X,Y,Z), Y<5.
select_one_A_eq_c_and_B_less_5(X,Y,Z) :- rel_one(c,Y,Z), Y<5.

select_one_A_eq_c_or_B_less_5(X,Y,Z) :- rel_one(c,Y,Z).
select_one_A_eq_c_or_B_less_5(X,Y,Z) :- rel_one(X,Y,Z), Y<5.

project_three_on_G_H(W,X) :- rel_three(W,X,Y,Z).

union_one_two(X,Y,Z) :- rel_one(X,Y,Z).
union_one_two(X,Y,Z) :- rel_two(X,Y,Z).

intersect_one_two(X,Y,Z) :- rel_one(X,Y,Z), rel_two(X,Y,Z).

difference_two_one(X,Y,Z) :- rel_two(X,Y,Z), not(rel_one(X,Y,Z)).

cart_prod_one_three(T,U,V,W,X,Y,Z) :-
              rel_one(T,U,V), rel_three(W,X,Y,Z).

natural_join_one_three_C_eq_G(U,V,W,X,Y,Z) :-
              rel_one(U,V,W), rel_three(W,X,Y,Z).
```

Figure 25.7   Predicates for illustrating relational operations.

as in Figure 25.7; rather, the arity (degree) of each predicate is the important aspect. In a practical system, the domain (data type) of each attribute is also important for operations such as UNION, INTERSECTION, and JOIN, and we assume that the attribute types are compatible for the various operations, as discussed in Chapter 7.

Figure 25.7 illustrates a number of basic relational operations. Notice that, if the Datalog model is based on the relational model and hence assumes that predicates (fact relations and query results) specify sets of tuples, duplicate tuples in the same predicate are automatically eliminated. This may or may not be true, depending on the Datalog inference engine. However, it is definitely *not* the case in Prolog, so any of the rules in Figure 25.7 that involve duplicate elimination are not correct for Prolog. For example, if we want to specify Prolog rules for the UNION operation with duplicate elimination, we must rewrite them as follows:

    union_one_two(X,Y,Z) :- rel_one(X,Y,Z).

    union_one_two(X,Y,Z) :- rel_two(X,Y,Z), not(rel_one(X,Y,Z)).

However, the rules shown in Figure 25.7 should work for Datalog, if duplicates are automatically eliminated. Similarly, the rules for the PROJECT operation shown in Figure 25.7 should work for Datalog in this case, but they are not correct for Prolog, since duplicates would appear in the latter case.

25.5.3 Evaluation of Nonrecursive Datalog Queries

Implementations of Prolog have been based on the backward chaining approach where ordering of predicates is significant. Since Datalog has been defined as a subset of Prolog, the inference mechanisms for logic programming languages, such as forward chaining or backward chaining, can be used with Datalog. However, if Datalog is to be used in a deductive database system, it is appropriate to define an inference mechanism based on relational database query processing concepts. The inherent strategy involves a bottom-up evaluation, starting with base relations; the order of operations is kept flexible and subject to query optimization. In this section, we discuss an inference mechanism based on relational operations that can be applied to **nonrecursive** Datalog queries. We use the fact and rule base shown in Figures 25.5 and 25.6 to illustrate our discussion.

If a query involves only fact-defined predicates, the inference becomes one of searching among the facts for the query result. For example, a query such as

department(X,research)?

is a selection of all employee names X who work for the `research` department. In relational algebra, it is the query:

$$\pi_{\$1} \left(\sigma_{\$2\,=\,\text{"Research"}} (\text{department}) \right)$$

which can be answered by searching through the fact-defined predicate `department(X,Y)`. The query involves relational SELECT and PROJECT operations on a base relation, and it can be handled by the database query processing and optimization techniques discussed in Chapter 18.

When a query involves rule-defined predicates, the inference mechanism must compute the result based on the rule definitions. If a query is nonrecursive and involves a predicate p that appears as the head of a rule p :- p_1, p_2, ..., p_n, the strategy is first to compute the relations corresponding to p_1, p_2, ..., p_n and then to compute the relation corresponding to p. It is useful to keep track of the dependency among the predicates of a deductive database in a **predicate dependency graph.** Figure 25.8 shows the graph for the fact and rule predicates shown in Figures 25.6 and 25.7. The dependency graph contains a **node** for each predicate. Whenever a predicate A is specified in the body (RHS) of a rule, and the head (LHS) of that rule is the predicate B, we say that B **depends on** A, and we draw a directed edge from A to B. This indicates that, in order to compute the facts for the predicate B (the rule head), we must first compute the facts for all the predicates A in the rule body. If the dependency graph has no cycles, we call the rule set **nonrecursive.** If there is at least one cycle, the rule set is called **recursive.** In Figure 25.8, there is one recursively defined predicate—namely, superior—which has a recursive edge pointing back to itself. In addition, because the predicate subordinate depends on superior, it also requires recursion in computing its result.

A query that includes only nonrecursive predicates is called a **nonrecursive query.** In this section, we discuss only inference mechanisms for nonrecursive queries. In Figure 25.8, any query that does not involve the predicates subordinate or superior is nonrecursive. In the predicate dependency graph, the nodes corresponding to fact-defined

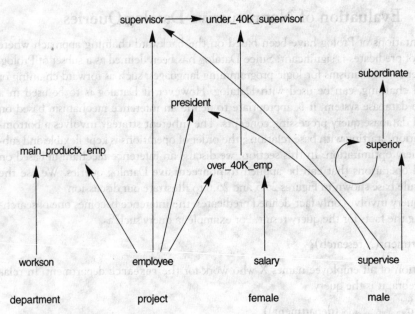

Figure 25.8   Predicate dependency graph for Figures 25.6 and 25.7.

predicates do not have any incoming edges, since all fact-defined predicates have their facts stored in a database relation. The contents of a fact-defined predicate can be computed by directly retrieving the tuples in the corresponding database relation.

The main function of an inference mechanism is to compute the facts that correspond to query predicates. This can be accomplished by generating a **relational expression** involving relational operators as SELECT, PROJECT, JOIN, UNION, and SET DIFFERENCE (with appropriate provision for dealing with safety issues) that, when executed, provides the query result (see Section 7.4.6). The query can then be executed by utilizing the internal query processing and optimization operations of a relational database management system. Whenever the inference mechanism needs to compute the fact set corresponding to a nonrecursive rule-defined predicate p, it first locates all the rules that have p as their head. The idea is to compute the fact set for each such rule and then to apply the UNION operation to the results, since UNION corresponds to a logical OR operation. The dependency graph indicates all predicates q on which each p depends, and since we assume that the predicate is nonrecursive, we can always determine a partial order among such predicates q. Before computing the fact set for p, we first compute the fact sets for all predicates q on which p depends, based on their partial order. For example, if a query involves the predicate `under_40K_supervisor`, we must first compute both supervisor and `over_40K_emp`. Since the latter two depend only on the fact-defined predicates `employee`, `salary`, and `supervise`, they can be computed directly from the stored database relations.

We must also deal with built-in predicates, such as the comparison operators $>$, $<$, and $=$, if they appear in a rule body. In specifying an inference algorithm that computes the fact set of any nonrecursive query, it is common to convert the rules into a canonical form called **rectified rules.** A rule is said to be rectified if all the arguments in the predicate of the rule head are *distinct variables*. If a rule head has constants, or if a variable is repeated twice in the rule head, it can easily be rectified: a constant c is replaced by a variable X, and a predicate equal(X, c) is added to the rule body. Similarly, if a variable Y appears twice in a rule head, one of those occurrences is replaced by another variable Z, and a predicate equal(Y, Z) is added to the rule body.

The evaluation of a nonrecursive query can be expressed as a tree whose leaves are the base relations. What is needed is appropriate application of the relational operations of SELECT, PROJECT, and JOIN, together with set operations of UNION and SET DIFFER-ENCE, until the predicate in the query gets evaluated. An outline of an inference algorithm GET_EXPR(Q) that generates a relational expression for computing the result of a DATALOG query $Q = p(arg_1, arg_2, \ldots, arg_n)$ can informally be stated as follows:

1. Locate all rules S whose head involves the predicate p. If there are no such rules, then p is a fact-defined predicate corresponding to some database relation R_p; in this case, one of the following expressions is returned and the algorithm is terminated (we use the notation $i to refer to the name of the ith attribute of relation R_p);

   a. If all arguments are distinct variables, the relational expression returned is R_p.
   b. If some arguments are constants or if the same variable appears in more than one argument position, the expression returned is

      SELECT<condition>(R_p),

      where the selection <condition> is a conjunctive condition made up of a number of simple conditions connected by AND, and constructed as follows:
      i. if a constant c appears as argument i, include a simple condition ($i = c) in the conjunction.
      ii. If the same variable appears in both argument locations j and k, include a condition ($j = $k) in the conjunction.

   c. For an argument that is not present in any predicate, a unary relation containing values that satisfy all conditions is constructed. Since the rule is assumed to be safe, this unary relation must be finite.

2. At this point, one or more rules S_i, $i = 1, 2, \ldots, n$, $n > 0$ exist with predicate p as their head. For each such rule S_i, generate a relational expression as follows:

   a. Apply selection operations on the predicates in the RHS for each such rule, as discussed in Step 1.
   b. A natural join is constructed among the relations that correspond to the predicates in the body of the rule S_i over the common variables. For arguments that gave rise to the unary relations in Step 1(c), the corresponding relations are brought as members into the natural join. Let the resulting relation from this join be R_S.

c. If any built-in predicate X θ Y was defined over the arguments X and Y, the result of the join is subjected to an additional selection:

$$\text{SELECT}_{X \, \theta \, Y}(R_s),$$

d. Repeat Step 2(b) until no more built-in predicates apply.

3. Take the UNION of the expressions generated in Step 2 (if more than one rule exists with predicate p as its head).

25.5.4   Concepts for Recursive Query Processing in Datalog

Query processing can be separated into two approaches:

- *Pure evaluation approach:* Creating a query evaluation plan that produces an answer to the query.
- *Rule rewriting approach:* Optimizing the plan into a more efficient strategy.

Many approaches have been presented for both recursive and nonrecursive queries. We discussed an approach to nonrecursive query evaluation earlier. Here we first define some terminology for recursive queries, then discuss the naive and seminaive approaches to query evaluation—which generate simple plans—and then present the magic set approach—which is an optimization based on *rule rewriting*.

We have already seen examples involving recursive rules where the same predicate occurs in the head and in the body of a rule. Another example is

ancestor(X,Y) :- ancestor(X,Z), parent(Z,Y)

which states that Y is an ancestor of X if Z is an ancestor of X and Y is a parent of Z. It is in conjunction with the rule

ancestor(X,Y) :- parent (X,Y)

which states that if Y is a parent of X, then Y is an ancestor of X.

A rule is said to be **linearly recursive** if the recursive predicate appears once and only once in the RHS of the rule. For example,

sg(X,Y) :- parent(X,XP), parent(Y,YP), sg(XP,YP)

is a linear rule in which the predicate sg (same-generation cousins) is used only once in RHS. The rule states that X and Y are same-generation cousins if their parents are same-generation cousins. The rule

ancestor(X,Y) :- ancestor(X,Z), parent(Z,Y)

is called **left linearly recursive,** while the rule

ancestor(X,Y) :- parent(X,Z), ancestor(Z,Y),

is called **right linearly recursive**.

Notice that the rule

ancestor(X,Y) :- ancestor(X,Z), ancestor(Z,Y)

is *not* linearly recursive. It is believed that most "real-life" rules can be described as linear recursive rules; algorithms have been defined to execute linear sets of rules efficiently. The preceding definitions become more involved when a set of rules with predicates that occur on both the LHS and the RHS of rules are considered.

A predicate whose relation is stored in the database is called an **extensional database (EDB) predicate,** while a predicate for which the corresponding relation is defined by logical rules is called an **intensional database (IDB) predicate.** Given a Datalog program with relations corresponding to the predicates, the "if" symbol, :-, may be replaced by an equality to form **Datalog equations,** without any loss of meaning. The resulting set of Datalog equations could potentially have many solutions. In a set of relations for the EDB predicates, say R_1, R_2, ..., R_n, a **fixed point** of the Datalog equations is a solution for the relations corresponding to the IDB predicates of those equations.

The fixed point with respect to the given EDB relations, along with those relations, forms a model of the rules from which the Datalog equations were derived. However, it is not true that every model of a set of Datalog rules is a fixed point of the corresponding Datalog equations, because the model may have "too many" facts. It turns out that Datalog programs each have a unique minimal model containing any given EDB relations, and this also corresponds to the unique minimal fixed point, with respect to those EDB relations.

Formally, given a family of solutions $S_i = P_{1(i)},...,P_{m(i)}$, to a given set of equations, the **least fixed point** of a set of equations is obtained by finding the solution whose corresponding relations are the smallest proper subsets for all relations. For example, we say $S_1 \leq S_2$, if relation $P_{k(1)}$ is a subset of relation $P_{k(2)}$ for all k, $1 \leq k \leq m$. Fixpoint theory was first developed in the field of recursion theory as a tool for explaining recursive functions. Since Datalog has an ability to express recursion, fixpoint theory is well suited for describing the semantics of recursive functions.

For example, if we represent a directed graph by the predicate edge(X,Y) such that edge (X,Y) is true if and only if there is an edge from node X to node Y in the graph, the paths in the graph may be expressed by the following rules:

path(X,Y) :- edge(X,Y)

path(X,Y) :- path(X,Z), path (Z,Y)

Notice that there are other ways of defining paths recursively. Let us assume that relations P and A correspond to the predicates path and edge in the preceding rules. The **transitive closure** of relation P contains all possible pairs of nodes that have a path between them, and it corresponds to the least fixed-point solution corresponding to the equations that result from the preceding rules.[6] These rules can be turned into a single equation for the relation P corresponding to the predicate edge.

$$P(X,Y) = A(X,Y) \cup \pi_{X,Y} (P(X,Z) \bowtie P(Z,Y))$$

---

6. For a detailed discussion of fixed points, consult Ullman (1988).

Suppose that the nodes are 3,4,5 and A = {(3,4), (4,5)}. From the first and second rules we can infer that (3,4), (4,5) and (3,5) are in P. We need not look for any other paths, because P = {(3,4),(4,5),(3,5)} is a solution of the above equation:

$$\{(3,4),(4,5),(3,5)\} = \{(3,4),(4,5)\} \cup \pi_{X,Y} (\{(3,4),(4,5),(3,5)\}$$
$$\bowtie \{ (3,4),(4,5),(3.5)\})$$

This solution constitutes a proof theoretic meaning of the rules, as it was derived from the EDB relation A, using just the rules. It is also the minimal model of the rules or the least fixed point of the equation.

For evaluating a set of Datalog rules (equations) that may contain recursive rules, a large number of strategies have been proposed, details of which are beyond our scope. Here we illustrate three important techniques: the naive strategy, the seminaive strategy, and the use of magic sets.

Naive Strategy.   The naive evaluation method is a pure evaluation, bottom-up strategy which computes the least model of a Datalog program. It is an iterative strategy and at each iteration all rules are applied to the set of tuples produced thus far to generate all implicit tuples. This iterative process continues until no more new tuples can be generated.

The naive evaluation process does not take into account query patterns. As a result, a considerable amount of redundant computation is done. We present two versions of the naive method, called Jacobi and Gauss-Seidel solution methods; these methods get their names from well known algorithms for the iterative solution of systems of equations in numerical analysis.

Assume the following system of relational equations, formed by replacing the :- symbol by an equality sign in a Datalog program.

$$R_i = E_i (R_1, R_2, ..., R_n)$$

The Jacobi method proceeds as follows. Initially, the variable relations R_i are set equal to the empty set. Then, the computation $R_i = E_i (R_1, R_2, ..., R_n)$, $i = 1, ..., n$ is iterated until none of the R_i changes between two consecutive iterations (i.e., until the R_i reach a fixpoint).

Algorithm 25.1 Jacobi naive strategy.

```
Input: A system of algebraic equations and an EDB.
Output: The values of the variable relations R₁, R₂, ..., Rₙ.

for i = 1 to n do Rᵢ = ∅;
repeat
     condition = true;
      for i = 1 to n do Sᵢ = Rᵢ;
      for i = 1 to n do
           begin
                  Rᵢ = Eᵢ(S₁, ..., Sₙ);
                  If Rᵢ ≠ Sᵢ then condition = false
           end
until condition;
```

The convergence of the Jacobi method can be slightly improved if, at each step k, in order to compute the new value $R_i(k)$, we substitute in E_i the values of $R_j(k)$ that have just been computed in the same iteration instead of the old values $R_j(k-1)$. This variant of the Jacobi method is called the Gauss-Seidel method, which produces the same result as the Jacobi algorithm. Consider the following example where ancestor(X,Y) means X is ancestor of Y; parent(X,Y) means X is parent of Y.

ancestor(X,Y) :- parent(X,Y).

ancestor(X,Y) :- ancestor(X,Z), parent(Z,Y).

If we define a relation A for the predicate ancestor and P for the parent, the Datalog equation for the above rules can be written in the form:

$$A(X,Y) = \pi_{X,Y} (A(X,Z) \bowtie P(Z,Y)) \cup A(X,Y)$$

Suppose the EDB is given as P = {(bert, alice), (bert, george), (alice, derek), (alice, pat), (derek, frank)}. Let us follow the Jacobi algorithm. The parent tree looks as in Figure 25.9.

Initially, we set A(0) = ∅, enter the *repeat* loop, and set *condition = true*. We then initialize S_1= A = ∅, then compute the first value of A. Since the first join involves an empty relation, we get

$A_{(1)}$ = P = {(bert, alice),(bert, george),(alice, derek),(alice, pat),(derek, frank)}.

$A_{(1)}$ includes parents as ancestors. $A_{(1)} \neq S_1$, thus *condition = false*. We therefore enter the second iteration with S_1 set to $A_{(1)}$. Computing the value of A again, we get,

$A_{(2)}$ = P = {(bert,alice),(bert,george),(alice,derek),(alice,pat),(derek,frank),
(bert,derek), (bert,pat), (alice,frank)}.

It can be seen that $A_{(2)}$ = A(1) ∪ {(bert,derek), (bert,pat), (alice,frank)}. Note that $A_{(2)}$ now includes grandparents as ancestors besides parents. Since $A_{(2)} \neq S_1$, we iterate again, setting S_1 to $A_{(2)}$:

$A_{(3)}$ = P = {(bert,alice),(bert,george),(alice,derek),(alice,pat),(derek,frank),
(bert,derek), (bert,pat), (alice,frank), (bert,frank)}.

Figure 25.9   Parent tree for example facts.

Now, $A_{(3)} = A_{(2)} \cup \{(\text{bert,frank})\}$. $A_{(3)}$ now has great grandparents included among ancestors. Since $A_{(3)}$ is different from S_1, we enter the next iteration, setting $S_1 = A_{(3)}$. We now get,

$$A_{(4)} = P = \{(\text{bert,alice}),(\text{bert,george}),(\text{alice,derek}),(\text{alice,pat}),(\text{derek,frank}),$$
$$(\text{bert,derek}),\ (\text{bert,pat}),\ (\text{alice,frank}),\ (\text{bert,frank})\}.$$

Finally, $A_{(4)} = A_{(3)} = S_1$, the evaluation is finished. Intuitively, from the above parental hierarchy, it is obvious that all ancestors have been computed.

Seminaive Strategy.   Seminaive evaluation is a bottom-up technique designed to eliminate redundancy in the evaluation of tuples at different iterations. This method does not use any information about the structure of the program. There are two possible settings of the seminaive algorithm: the (pure) seminaive and the pseudo rewriting seminaive.

Consider the Jacobi algorithm. Let $R_{i(k)}$ be the temporary value of relation R_i at iteration Step k. The differential of R_i at Step k of the iteration is defined as,

$$D_{i(k)} = R_{i(k)} - R_{i(k-1)}$$

When the whole system is linear, D_i can be substituted for R_i in the Jacobi or Gauss-Seidel algorithms: the result is obtained by the union of the newly obtained term and the old one.

Algorithm 25.2 Seminaive strategy.

```
input: A system of algebraic equations and an EDB.
output: The values of the variable relations R₁, R₂, ..., Rₙ.

for i = 1 to n do Rᵢ = ∅;
for i = 1 to n do Dᵢ = ∅;
    repeat
        for i = 1 to n do Sᵢ = ∅;
        condition = true;
        for i = 1 to n do
            begin
                Dᵢ = Eᵢ[S₁, ..., Sₙ] - Rᵢ;
                Rᵢ = Dᵢ ∪ Rᵢ;
                if Dᵢ ≠ ∅ then condition = false
            end
    until condition
```

The advantage of this method is that, at each iteration step, a differential term D_i is used in each equation instead of the whole R_i. Let us now look at the improvement due to the seminaive evaluation. Consider the EDB to be the same as in the previous example. We have

$$D_{(0)} = \varnothing \ , \ A_{(0)} = \varnothing.$$
$$D_{(1)} = P = \{(\text{bert,alice}),(\text{bert,george}),(\text{alice,derek}),(\text{alice,pat}),$$
$$(\text{derek,frank})\}.$$

Hence,

$$A_{(1)} = D_{(1)} \cup A_{(0)}$$
$$= \{(\text{bert,alice}),(\text{bert,george}),(\text{alice,derek}),(\text{alice,pat}),$$
$$(\text{derek,frank})\}.$$
$$D_{(2)} = \{(\text{bert,alice}),(\text{bert,george}),(\text{alice,derek}),(\text{alice,pat}),$$
$$(\text{derek,frank}), (\text{bert,derek}), (\text{bert,pat}), (\text{alice,frank})\} - A(1)$$
$$= \{(\text{bert,derek}), (\text{bert,pat}), (\text{alice,frank})\}.$$
$$A_{(2)} = D_{(2)} \cup A_{(1)}$$
$$= \{(\text{bert,alice}),(\text{bert,george}),(\text{alice,derek}),(\text{alice,pat}),$$
$$(\text{derek,frank}), (\text{bert,derek}), (\text{bert,pat}), (\text{alice,frank})\}.$$
$$D_{(3)} = \{(\text{bert,frank})\}.$$
$$A_{(3)} = D_{(3)} \cup A_{(2)}$$
$$= \{(\text{bert,frank})\} \cup A_{(2)}$$
$$= \{(\text{bert,alice}),(\text{bert,george}),(\text{alice,derek}),(\text{alice,pat}),$$
$$(\text{derek,frank}), (\text{bert,derek}),(\text{bert,pat}), (\text{alice,frank}),$$
$$(\text{bert,frank})\}.$$

$D_{(4)} = \emptyset$, and hence we have come to the end of our evaluation. Although the computation of the two results is the same, the computation is more efficient in the seminaive evaluation. Only the $D_{(i)}$'s have been involved in the join, whereas in the naive evaluation we had to compute joins for each of the temporary values $A_{(i)}$, which have always had more tuples than $D_{(i)}$.

The Magic Set Rule Rewriting Technique. The problem addressed by the magic sets rule rewriting technique is that frequently a query asks not for the entire relation corresponding to an intentional predicate but for a small subset of this relation. Consider the following program:

```
sg(X,Y) :- flat(X,Y).
sg(X,Y) :- up(X,U), sg(U,V), down(V,Y).
```

Here, sg is a predicate ("same-generation cousin"), and the head of each of the two rules is the atomic formula sg(X, Y). The other predicates found in the rules are flat, up, and down. These are presumably stored extensionally as facts, while the relation for sg is intentional—that is, defined only by the rules. For a query like sg(john, Z)—that is, "who are the same generation cousins of John?"—asked of the predicate, our answer to the query must examine only the part of the database that is *relevant*—namely the part that involves individuals somehow connected to John.

A top-down, or backward-chaining search would start from the query as a goal and use the rules from head to body to create more goals; none of these goals would be irrelevant to the query, although some might cause us to explore paths that happen to "dead-end." On the other hand, a bottom-up or forward-chaining search, working from the bodies of the rules to the heads, would cause us to infer sg facts that would never even be considered in the top-down search. Yet bottom-up evaluation is desirable because it avoids the problems of looping and repeated computation that are inherent in the top-down approach, and allow us to use set-at-a-time operations, such as relational joins.

Magic sets rule rewriting is a technique that allows us to rewrite the rules as a function of the query form only—that is, it considers which arguments of the predicate are bound to constants and which are variable, so that the advantages of top-down and bottom-up methods are combined. The technique focuses on the goal inherent in the top-down evaluation but combines this with the looping freedom, easy termination testing, and efficient evaluation of bottom-up evaluation. Instead of giving the method, of which many variations are known and used in practice, we explain the idea with an example.

Given the previously stated rules and the query sg(john,Z), a typical magic sets transformation of the rules would be

```
sg(X,Y) :-magic-sg(X), flat (X,Y).
sg(X,Y) :-magic-sg(X), up(X,U), sg(U,V), down(V,Y).
magic-sg(U) :-magic-sg(X), up(X,U).
magic-sg(john).
```

Intuitively, we can see that the magic-sg facts correspond to queries or subgoals. The definition of the magic-sg predicate mimics how goals are generated in a top-down evaluation. The set of magic-sg facts is used as a filter in the rules defining sg, to avoid generating facts that are not answers to some subgoal. Thus, a purely bottom-up, forward-chaining evaluation of the rewritten program achieves a restriction of search similar to that achieved by top-down evaluation of the original program. Further details of this technique are beyond our scope.

While the magic sets technique was originally developed to deal with recursive queries, it is applicable to nonrecursive queries as well. Indeed, it has been adapted to deal with SQL queries (which contain features such as grouping, aggregation, arithmetic conditions, and multiset relations that are not present in pure logic queries), and it has been found to be useful for evaluating nonrecursive "nested" SQL queries.

25.5.5 Stratified Negation

A deductive database query language can be enhanced by permitting *negated literals* in the bodies of rules in programs. However, the important property of rules, called the *minimal model*, which we discussed earlier, does not hold. In the presence of negated literals, a program may not have a minimal or least model. For example, the program

```
p(a):- not p(b).
```

has two minimal models: {p(a)} and {p(b)}.

A detailed analysis of the concept of negation is beyond our scope. But for practical purposes, we next discuss **stratified negation,** an important notion used in deductive system implementations.

The meaning of a program with negation is usually given by some "intended" model. The challenge is to develop algorithms for choosing an intended model that does the following:

1. Makes sense to the user of the rules.

2. Allows us to answer queries about the model efficiently.

In particular, it is desirable that the model work well with the magic sets transformation, in the sense that we can modify the rules by some suitable generalization of magic sets, and the resulting rules allow (only) the relevant portion of the selected model to be computed efficiently. (Alternatively, other efficient evaluation techniques must be developed.)

One important class of negation that has been extensively studied is **stratified negation.** A program is **stratified** if there is no recursion through negation. Programs in this class have a very intuitive semantics and can be efficiently evaluated. The example that follows describes a stratified program. Consider the following program P_2:

```
r₁: ancestor(X,Y) :- parent (X,Y).
r₂: ancestor(X,Y) :- parent(X,Z), ancestor(Z,Y).
r₃: nocyc(X,Y):- ancestor(X,Y), not (ancestor(Y,X)).
```

Notice that the third rule has a negative literal in its body. This program is stratified because the definition of the predicate nocyc depends (negatively) on the definition of ancestor, but the definition of ancestor *does not* depend on the definition of nocyc. We are not equipped to give a more formal definition without giving additional notation and definitions. A bottom-up evaluation of P_2 would first compute a fixed point of rules r_1 and r_2 (the rules defining ancestor). Rule r_3 is applied only when all the ancestor facts are known.

A natural extension of stratified programs is the class of locally stratified programs. Intuitively, a program P is *locally stratified* for a given database if, when we substitute constants for variables in all possible ways, the resulting instantiated rules do not have any recursion through negation.

25.6 Deductive Database Systems

The founding event of the deductive database field can be considered to be the Toulouse workshop on "Logic and Databases" organized by Gallaire, Minker, and Nicolas in 1977. The next period of the explosive growth started with the setting up of the MCC (Microelectronics and Computer Technology Corporation), which was a reaction to the Japanese Fifth Generation Project. Several experimental deductive database systems have been developed and a few have been commercially deployed. In this section we briefly review three different implementations of the ideas presented so far: LDL, NAIL!, and CORAL.

25.6.1 The LDL System

The Logic Data Language (LDL) project at Microelectronics and Computer Technology Corporation (MCC) was started in 1984 with two primary objectives:

- To develop a system that extends the relational model yet exploits some of the desirable features of an RDBMS (relational database management system).

- To enhance the functionality of a DBMS so that it works as a deductive DBMS and also supports the development of general-purpose applications.

The resulting system is now a deductive DBMS made available as a product. In this section, we briefly survey the highlights of the technical approach taken by LDL and consider its important features.

Background, Motivation, and Overview. The design of the LDL language may be viewed as a rule-based extension to domain calculus-based languages (see Section 9.4). The LDL system has tried to combine the expressive capability of Prolog with the functionality and facility of a general-purpose DBMS. The main drawback experienced by earlier systems that coupled Prolog with an RDBMS is that Prolog is navigational (tuple-at-a-time) whereas in RDBMSs the user formulates a correct query and leaves the optimization of query execution to the system. The navigational nature of Prolog is manifested in the ordering of rules and goals to achieve an optimal execution and termination. Two options are available:

- Make Prolog more "database-like" by adding navigational database management features. (For an example of navigational query language, see the network model DML in Section C.4 of Appendix C.)
- Modify Prolog into a general-purpose declarative logic language.

The latter option was chosen in LDL, yielding a language that is different from Prolog in its constructs and style of programming in the following ways:

- Rules are compiled in LDL.
- There is a notion of a "schema" of the fact base in LDL at compile time. The fact base is freely updated at run-time. Prolog, on the other hand, treats facts and rules identically, and it subjects facts to interpretation when they are changed.
- LDL does not follow the resolution and unification technique used in Prolog systems that are based on backward chaining.
- The LDL execution model is simpler, based on the operation of matching and the computation of "least fixed points." These operators, in turn, use simple extensions to the relation algebra.

The first LDL implementation, completed in 1987, was based on a language called FAD. A later implementation, completed in 1988, is called SALAD and underwent further changes as it was tested against the "real-life" applications described in Section 25.8. The current prototype is an efficient portable system for UNIX that assumes a single tuple get-next interface between the compiled LDL program and an underlying fact manager.

The LDL Data Model and Language. With the design philosophy of LDL being to combine the declarative style of relational languages with the expressive power of Prolog, constructs in Prolog such as negation, set-of, updates, and cut have been dropped. Instead, the declarative semantics of Horn clauses was extended to support complex terms through the use of function symbols, called *functors* in Prolog.

A particular employee record can therefore be defined as follows:

```
Employee (Name (John Doe), Job(VP),
   Education ({(High school, 1961),
      (College (Fergusson, bs, physics), 1965),
      (College (Michigan, phd, ie), 1976)}))
```

In the preceding record, VP is a simple term, whereas education is a complex term that consists of a term for high school and a nested relation containing the term for college and the year of graduation. LDL thus supports complex objects with an arbitrarily complex structure including lists, set terms, trees, and nested relations. We can think of a compound term as a Prolog structure with the function symbol as the functor.

LDL allows updates in the bodies of rules. For instance, a rule

```
happy (Dept, Raise, Name) <-
    emp (Name, Dept, Sal), Newsal = Sal+Raise
    -emp (Name, Dept, -), +emp(Name,Dept,Newsal).
```

combined with

```
?happy(software, 1000, Name).
```

gives a $1,000 raise to all employees in the software department and returns the names of those happy employees. This query is regarded as an indivisible transaction.

LDL offers an if–then–else construct of clean declarative semantics, for the clear expression and efficient implementation of mutually disjunctive rules. In addition, it offers a nonprocedural "choice" predicate for situations where any answer will do that can be used to obtain a single-answer response, rather than the all-answer solution that represents the default response. In the declarative semantics of LDL, negation has been treated by using stratification and nondeterminism, which is supported through the same construct called "choice."

Even though LDL's semantics is defined in a bottom-up fashion (for example, via stratification), the implementor can use any execution that is faithful to this declarative semantics. In particular, the execution can proceed bottom-up or top-down, or it may be a hybrid execution. These choices enable the compiler/optimizer to be selective in customizing the most appropriate modes of execution for the given program. The LDL compiler and optimizer can select from among several strategies: pipelined or lazy pipelined execution, materialized or lazy materialized execution.

25.6.2 NAIL!

The NAIL! (Not Another Implementation of Logic!) project was started at Stanford University in 1985. The initial goal was to study the optimization of logic by using the database-oriented "all-solutions" model. The aim of the project was to support the optimal execution of Datalog goals over an RDBMS. Assuming that a single workable strategy was inappropriate for all logic programs in general, an extensible architecture was developed, which could be enhanced through progressive additions.

In collaboration with the MCC group, this project was responsible for the idea of magic sets and the first work on regular recursions. In addition, many important contributions to coping with negation and aggregation on logical rules were made by the project, including stratified negation, well-founded negation, and modularly stratified negation. The architecture of NAIL! is illustrated in Figure 25.10.

The preprocessor rewrites the source NAIL! program by isolating "negation" and "set" operators, and by replacing disjunction with several conjunctive rules. After preprocessing, the NAIL! program is represented through its predicates and rules. The

Figure 25.10   NAIL! system architecture.

strategy selection module takes as input the user's goal and produces as output the best execution strategies for solving the user's goal and all the other goals related to it, using the internal language ICODE.

The ICODE statements produced as a result of the strategy selection process are optimized and then executed through an interpreter, which translates ICODE retrieval statements to SQL when needed.

An initial prototype system was built but later abandoned because the purely declarative paradigm was found to be unworkable for many applications. The revised system uses a core language, called GLUE, which is essentially single logical rules, with the power of SQL statements, wrapped in conventional language constructs such as loops, procedures, and modules. The original NAIL! language becomes a view mechanism for GLUE; it permits fully declarative specifications in situations where declarativeness is appropriate.

25.6.3   The CORAL System

The CORAL system, which was developed at the University of Wisconsin at Madison, builds on experience gained from the LDL project. Like LDL, the system provides a declarative language based on Horn clauses with an open architecture. There are many important differences, however, in both the language and its implementation. The CORAL system can be seen as a database programming language that combines important features of SQL and Prolog.

From a language standpoint, CORAL adapts LDL's set-grouping construct to be closer to SQL's GROUP BY construct. For example, consider

```
budget(Dname,sum(<Sal>)) :- dept(Dname,Ename,Sal).
```

This rule computes one budget tuple for each department, and each salary value is added as often as there are people with that salary in the given department. In LDL, the grouping and the sum operation cannot be combined in one step; more importantly, the grouping is defined to produce a *set* of salaries for each department. Therefore, computing the budget is harder in LDL. A related point is that SQL supports a *multiset* semantics for queries when the DISTINCT clause is not specified. CORAL supports such a multiset semantics as well. Thus the following rule can be defined to compute either a set of tuples or a multiset of tuples in CORAL, as occurs in SQL:

```
budget2(Dname,Sal) :- dept(Dname,Ename,Sal)
```

This raises an important point: How can a user specify which semantics (set or multiset) is desired? In SQL, the keyword DISTINCT is used; similarly, an *annotation* is provided in CORAL. In fact, CORAL supports a number of annotations that can be used to choose a desired semantics or to provide optimization hints to the CORAL system. The added complexity of queries in a recursive language makes optimization difficult, and the use of annotations often makes a big difference in the quality of the optimized evaluation plan.

CORAL supports a class of programs with negation and grouping that is strictly larger than the class of stratified programs. The bill-of-materials problem, in which the cost of a composite part is defined as being the sum of the costs of all atomic parts, is an example of a problem that requires this added generality.

CORAL is closer to Prolog than to LDL in supporting nonground tuples; thus, the tuple equal(X,X) can be stored in the database and denotes that every binary tuple in which the first and the second field values are the same is in the relation called equal. From an evaluation standpoint, CORAL's main evaluation techniques are based on bottom-up evaluation, which is very different from Prolog's top-down evaluation. However, CORAL also provides a Prolog-like top-down evaluation mode.

From an implementation perspective, CORAL implements several optimizations to deal with nonground tuples efficiently, in addition to techniques such as magic templates for pushing selections into recursive queries, pushing projections, and special optimizations of different kinds of (left- and right-) linear programs. It also provides an efficient way to compute nonstratified queries. A "shallow-compilation" approach is used, whereby the run-time system interprets the compiled plan. CORAL uses the EXODUS storage manager to provide support for disk-resident relations. It also has a good interface with C++

and is *extensible*, enabling a user to customize the system for special applications by adding new data types or relation implementations. An interesting feature is an *explanation* package that allows a user to examine graphically how a fact is generated; this is useful for debugging as well as for providing explanations.

25.7 Deductive Object-Oriented Databases

The emergence of deductive database concepts is contemporaneous with initial work in Logic Programming. Deductive object-oriented databases (DOODs) came about through the integration of the OO paradigm and logic programming. The observation that OO and deductive database systems generally have complementary strengths and weaknesses gave rise to the integration of the two paradigms.

25.7.1 Overview of DOODs

Since the late 1980s, several DOOD prototypes were developed in universities and research laboratories. VALIDITY, which was developed at Bull, is the first industrial product in the DOOD arena. The LDL and the CORAL systems we reviewed offer some additional object-orientated features—e.g., in CORAL++—and may be considered as DOODs.

The following broad approaches have been adopted in the design of DOOD systems:

- *Language extension:* An existing deductive language model is extended with object-oriented features. For example, Datalog is extended to support identity, inheritance, and other OO features.

- *Language integration:* A deductive language is integrated with an imperative programming language in the context of an object model or type system. The resulting system supports a range of standard programs, while allowing different and complementary programming paradigms to be used for different tasks, or for different parts of the same task. This approach was pioneered by the Glue-Nail system.

- *Language reconstruction:* An object model is reconstructed, creating a new logic language that includes object-oriented features. In this strategy, the goal is to develop an object logic that captures the essentials of the object-oriented paradigm and that can also be used as a deductive programming language in DOODs. The rationale behind this approach is the argument that language extensions fail to combine object-orientation and logic successfully, by losing declarativenesss or by failing to capture all aspects of the object-oriented model.

25.7.2 VALIDITY

VALIDITY combines deductive capabilities with the ability to manipulate complex objects (OIDs, inheritance, methods, etc.). The ability to declaratively specify knowledge as deduction and integration rules brings knowledge independence. Moreover, the logic-based language of deductive databases enables advanced tools, such as those for checking the consistency of a set of rules, to be developed. When compared with systems extending

SQL technology, deductive systems offer more expressive declarative languages and cleaner semantics. VALIDITY provides the following:

1. A DOOD data model and language, called DEL (Datalog Extended Language).

2. An engine working along a client-server model.

3. A set of tools for schema and rule editing, validation, and querying.

The DEL data model provides object-oriented capabilities, similar to those offered by the ODMG data model (see Chapter 12), and includes both declarative and imperative features. The declarative features include deductive and integrity rules, with full recursion, stratified negation, disjunction, grouping, and quantification. The imperative features allow functions and methods to be written. The engine of VALIDITY integrates the traditional functions of a database (persistency, concurrency control, crash recovery, etc.) with the advanced deductive capabilities for deriving information and verifying semantic integrity. The lowest level component of the engine is a fact manager that integrates storage, concurrency control, and recovery functions. The fact manager supports fact identity and complex data items. In addition to locking, the concurrency control protocol integrates read-consistency technology, used in particular when verifying constraints. The higher-level component supports the DEL language and performs optimization, compilation, and execution of statements and queries. The engine also supports an SQL interface permitting SQL queries and updates to be run on VALIDITY data.

VALIDITY also has a deductive wrapper for SQL systems, called DELite. This supports a subset of DEL functionality (no constraints, no recursion, limited object capabilities, etc.) on top of commercial SQL systems.

DEL Data Model. The DEL data model integrates a rich type system with primitives to define persistent and derived data. The DEL type system consists of built-in types, which can be used to implement user-defined and composite types. Composite types are defined using four type constructors: (1) bag, (2) set, (3) list, and (4) tuple.

The basic unit of information in VALIDITY is called a *fact*. Facts are instances of predicates, which are logical constructs characterized by a name and a set of typed attributes. A fact specifies values to the attributes of the predicate of which it is an instance. There are four kinds of predicates and facts in VALIDITY:

1. *Basis facts:* Are persistent units of information stored in the database; they are instances of *basis predicates*, which have attributes and methods and are organized into inheritance hierarchies.

2. *Derived facts:* Are deduced from basis facts stored in the database or other derived facts; they are instances of *derived predicates*.

3. *Computed predicates and facts:* These are similar to derived predicates and facts, but they are computed by means of imperative code instead of derivation. The distance between two points is a typical example.

4. *Built-in predicates and facts:* These are special computed predicates and facts whose associated function is provided by VALIDITY. Comparison operators are an example.

Basis facts have an identity that is analogous to the notion of object identifier in OO databases. Further, external mappings can be defined for a predicate; they enable the retrieval of facts (through their fact-IDs) based on the value of some of their unique attributes. Basis predicates may also have methods in the OO sense—that is, functions can be invoked in the context of a specific fact.

25.8   Applications of Commercial Deductive Database Systems

We discussed two commercial deductive database systems: LDL and VALIDITY. They have been used in a variety of business/industrial applications. We briefly summarize a few of them below.

25.8.1   LDL Applications

The LDL system has been applied to the following application domains:

- *Enterprise modeling:* This domain involves modeling the structure, processes, and constraints within an enterprise. Data related to an enterprise may result in an extended ER model containing hundreds of entities and relationships and thousands of attributes. A number of applications useful to designers of new applications (as well as for management) can be developed based on this "metadatabase," which contains dictionary-like information about the whole enterprise.

- *Hypothesis testing or data dredging:* This domain involves formulating a hypothesis, translating it into an LDL rule set and a query, and then executing the query against given data to test the hypothesis. The process is repeated by reformulating the rules and the query. This has been applied to genome data analysis (see Section 26.7 for more details) in the field of microbiology, where data dredging consists of identifying the DNA sequences from low-level digitized autoradiographs from experiments performed on *E. coli* bacteria.

- *Software reuse:* The bulk of the software for an application is developed in standard procedural code, and a small fraction is rule-based and encoded in LDL. The rules give rise to a knowledge base that contains the following elements:

  A definition of each C module used in the system.

  A set of rules that defines ways in which modules can export/import functions, constraints, and so on.

  The "knowledge base" can be used to make decisions that pertain to the reuse of software subsets. Modules can be recombined to satisfy specific tasks, as long as the relevant rules are satisfied. This is being experimented with in banking software.

25.8.2   VALIDITY Applications

Knowledge independence is a term used by VALIDITY developers to refer to a technical version of business rule independence. From a database standpoint, it is a step beyond data independence that brings about integration of data and rules. The goal is to achieve streamlining of application development (multiple applications share rules managed by the database), application maintenance (changes in definitions and in regulations are more easily done), and ease-of-use (interactions are done through high-level tools enabled by the logic foundation). For instance, it simplifies the task of the application programmer who does not need to include tests in his application to guarantee the soundness of his transactions. VALIDITY claims to be able to express, manage, and apply the business rules governing the interactions among various processes within a company.

VALIDITY is an appropriate tool for applying software engineering principles to application development. It allows the formal specification of an application in the DEL language, which can then be directly compiled. This eliminates the error-prone step that most methodologies based on entity-relationship conceptual designs and relational implementations require between specification and compilation. The following are some application areas of the VALIDITY system:

- *Electronic commerce:* In electronic commerce, complex customer profiles have to be matched against target descriptions. The profiles are built from various data sources. In a current application, demographic data and viewing history compose the viewer's profiles. The matching process is also described by rules, and computed predicates deal with numeric computations. The declarative nature of DEL makes the formulation of the matching algorithm easy.

- *Rules-governed processes:* In a rules-governed process, well-defined rules define the actions to be performed. An application prototype has been developed—its goal being to handle the management of dangerous gases placed in containers—and is coordinated by a large number of frequently changing regulations. The classes of dangerous materials are modeled as DEL classes. The possible locations for the containers are constrained by rules, which reflect the regulations. In the case of an incident, deduction rules identify potential accidents. The main advantage of VALIDITY is the ease with which new regulations are taken into account.

- *Knowledge discovery:* The goal of knowledge discovery is to find new data relationships by analyzing existing data (see Section 26.2). An application prototype developed by the University of Illinois utilizes already existing minority student data that has been enhanced with rules in DEL.

- *Concurrent engineering:* A concurrent engineering application deals with large amounts of centralized data, shared by several participants. An application prototype has been developed in the area of civil engineering. The design data is modeled using the object-orientation power of the DEL language. When an inconsistency is detected, a new rule models the identified problem. Once a solution has been identified, it is turned into a constraint. DEL is able to handle transformation of rules into constraints, and it can also handle any closed formula as an integrity constraint.

25.9 Summary

In this chapter we introduced deductive database systems, a relatively new branch of database management. This field has been influenced by logic programming languages, particularly by Prolog. A subset of Prolog called Datalog, which contains function-free

Horn clauses, is primarily used as the basis of current deductive database work. Concepts of Datalog were introduced here. We discussed the standard backward-chaining inferencing mechanism of Prolog and a forward-chaining bottom-up strategy. The latter has been adapted to evaluate queries dealing with relations (extensional databases), by using standard relational operations together with Datalog. Procedures for evaluating nonrecursive and recursive query processing were discussed and algorithms presented for naive and seminaive evaluation of recursive queries. Negation is particularly difficult to deal with in such deductive databases; a popular concept called *stratified negation* was introduced in this regard.

We surveyed a commercial deductive database system called LDL originally developed at MCC and other experimental systems called CORAL and NAIL!. The latest deductive database implementations are called DOODs. They combine the power of object orientation with deductive capabilities. The most recent entry on the commercial DOOD scene is VALIDITY, which we discussed here briefly. The deductive database area is still in an experimental stage. Its adoption by industry will give a boost to its development. Toward this end, we mentioned practical applications in which LDL and VALIDITY are proving to be very valuable.

Exercises

25.1. Add the following facts to the example database in Figure 25.3:

supervise (ahmad,bob), supervise (franklin,gwen).

First modify the supervisory tree in Figure 25.1(b) to reflect this change. Then modify the diagram in Figure 25.4 showing the top-down evaluation of the query superior(james,Y).

25.2. Consider the following set of facts for the relation parent(X,Y), where Y is the parent of X:

parent(a,aa), parent(a,ab), parent(aa,aaa), parent(aa,aab),
parent(aaa,aaaa), parent(aaa,aaab).

Consider the rules

r_1: ancestor(X,Y) :- parent(X,Y)
r_2: ancestor(X,Y) :- parent(X,Z), ancestor(Z,Y)

which define ancestor Y of X as above.
a. Show how to solve the Datalog query

ancestor(aa,X)?

using the naive strategy. Show your work at each step.
b. Show the same query by computing only the changes in the ancestor relation and using that in rule 2 each time.
[This question is derived from Bancilhon and Ramakrishnan (1986).]

25.3. Consider a deductive database with the following rules:

ancestor(X,Y) :- father(X,Y)
ancestor(X,Y) :- father(X,Z), ancestor(Z,Y)

Notice that "father(X,Y)" means that Y is the father of X; "ancestor(X,Y)" means that Y is the ancestor of X. Consider the fact base

father(Harry,Issac), father(Issac,John), father(John,Kurt).

a. Construct a model theoretic interpretation of the above rules using the given facts.

b. Consider that a database contains the above relations father(X,Y), another relation brother(X,Y), and a third relation birth(X,B), where B is the birth-date of person X. State a rule that computes the first cousins of the following variety: their fathers must be brothers.

c. Show a complete Datalog program with fact-based and rule-based literals that computes the following relation: list of pairs of cousins, where the first person is born after 1960 and the second after 1970. You may use "greater than" as a built-in predicate. (*Note:* Sample facts for brother, birth, and person must also be shown.)

25.4. Consider the following rules:

reachable(X,Y) :- flight(X,Y)
reachable(X,Y) :- flight(X,Z), reachable(Z,Y)

where reachable(X,Y) means that city Y can be reached from city X, and flight(X,Y) means that there is a flight to city Y from city X.

a. Construct fact predicates that describe the following:
   i. Los Angeles, New York, Chicago, Atlanta, Frankfurt, Paris, Singapore, Sydney are cities.
   ii. The following flights exist: LA to NY, NY to Atlanta, Atlanta to Frankfurt, Frankfurt to Atlanta, Frankfurt to Singapore, and Singapore to Sydney. (*Note:* No flight in reverse direction can be automatically assumed.)

b. Is the given data cyclic? If so, in what sense?

c. Construct a model theoretic interpretation (that is, an interpretation similar to the one shown in Figure 25.3) of the above facts and rules.

d. Consider the query

   reachable(Atlanta,Sydney)?

   How will this query be executed using naive and seminaive evaluation? List the series of steps it will go through.

e. Consider the following rule defined predicates:

   round-trip-reachable(X,Y) :- reachable(X,Y), reachable(Y,X)
   duration(X,Y,Z)

   Draw a predicate dependency graph for the above predicates. (*Note:* dura-tion(X,Y,Z) means that you can take a flight from X to Y in Z hours.)

f. Consider the following query: What cities are reachable in 12 hours from Atlanta? Show how to express it in Datalog. Assume built-in predicates like greater-than(X,Y). Can this be converted into a relational algebra state-ment in a straightforward way? Why or why not?

g. Consider the predicate population(X,Y) where Y is the population of city X. Consider the following query: List all possible bindings of the predicate pair (X,Y), where Y is a city that can be reached in two flights from city X, which has over 1 million people. Show this query in Datalog. Draw a corresponding query tree in relational algebraic terms.

25.5. Consider the following rules:

```
sgc(X,Y) :- eq(X,Y).
sgc(X,Y) :- par(X,X1), sgc(X1,Y1), par(Y,Y1).
```

and the EDB, PAR = {(d,g), (e,g), (b,d), (a,d), (a,h), (c,e)}. What is the result of the query

```
sgc(a,Y)?
```

Solve using the naive and seminaive methods.

25.6. The following rules have been given:

```
path(X,Y) :- arc(X,Y).
path(X,Y) :- path(X,Z), path(Z,Y).
```

Suppose that the nodes in a graph are {a,b,c,d} and there are no arcs. Let the set of paths, P = {(a,b),(c,d)}. Show that this model is not a fixed point.

25.7. Consider the frequent flyer Skymiles program database at an airline. It maintains the following relations:

```
99status(X,Y), 98status(X,Y), 98Miles(X,Y).
```

The status data refers to passenger X having a status Y for the year, where Y can be regular, silver, gold, or platinum. Let the requirements for achieving gold status be expressed by:

```
99status(X,'gold') :- 98status(X,'gold') AND 98Miles(X,Y)
    AND Y>45000
99status(X,'gold') :- 98status(X,'platinum') AND 98Miles(X,Y)
    AND Y>40000
99status(X,'gold') :- 98status(X,'regular') AND 98Miles(X,Y)
    AND Y>50000
```

98Miles(X,Y) gives the miles Y flown by passenger X in 1998. Assume that similar rules exist for reaching other statuses.

a. Make up a set of other reasonable rules for achieving platinum status.

b. Is the above programmable in DATALOG? Why or why not?

c. Write a prolog program with the above rules, populate the predicates with sample data, and show how a query like 99status('John Smith',Y) is computed in Prolog.

25.8. Consider a tennis tournament database with predicates rank (X,Y): X holds rank Y, beats (X1,X2): X1 beats X2, and superior (X1,X2): X1 is a superior player to X2. Assume that if a player beats another player he is superior to that player and assume that if a player 1 beats player 2 and player 2 is superior to 3 then 1 is superior to 3. Construct a set of recursive rules using the above predicates. (Note: We shall hypothetically assume that there are no "upsets"— that the above rule is always met.)

a. Construct a set of recursive rules.

b. Populate data for beats relation with 10 players playing 3 matches each.

c. Show a computation of the superior table using this data.

d. Does the superior have a fixpoint? Why or why not? Explain.

For the population of players in the database, assuming John is one of the players, how do you compute "superior (john, X)?" using naive, and seminaive algorithms?

Selected Bibliography

The early developments of the logic and database approach are surveyed by Gallaire et al. (1984). Reiter (1984) provides a reconstruction of relational database theory, while Levesque (1984) provides a discussion of incomplete knowledge in light of logic. Gallaire and Minker (1978) provide an early book on this topic. A detailed treatment of logic and databases appears in Ullman (1989, vol. 2), and there is a related chapter in Volume 1 (1988). Ceri, Gottlob, and Tanca (1990) present a comprehensive yet concise treatment of logic and databases. Das (1992) is a comprehensive book on deductive databases and logic programming. The early history of Datalog is covered in Maier and Warren (1988). Clocksin and Mellish (1994) is an excellent reference on Prolog language.

Aho and Ullman (1979) provide an early algorithm for dealing with recursive queries, using the least fixed-point operator. Bancilhon and Ramakrishnan (1986) give an excellent and detailed description of the approaches to recursive query processing, with detailed examples of the naive and seminaive approaches. Excellent survey articles on deductive databases and recursive query processing include Warren (1992) and Ramakrishnan and Ullman (1993). A complete description of the seminaive approach based on relational algebra is given in Bancilhon (1985). Other approaches to recursive query processing include the recursive query/subquery strategy of Vieille (1986), which is a top-down interpreted strategy, and the Henschen-Naqvi (1984) top-down compiled iterative strategy. Balbin and Rao (1987) discuss an extension of the seminaive differential approach for multiple predicates.

The original paper on magic sets is by Bancilhon et al. (1986). Beeri and Ramakrishnan (1987) extends it. Mumick et al. (1990) show the applicability of magic sets to non-recursive nested SQL queries. Other approaches to optimizing rules without rewriting them appear in Vieille (1986, 1987). Kifer and Lozinskii (1986) propose a different technique. Bry (1990) discusses how the top-down and bottom-up approaches can be reconciled. Whang and Navathe (1992) describe an extended disjunctive normal form technique to deal with recursion in relational algebra expressions for providing an expert system interface over a relational DBMS.

Chang (1981) describes an early system for combining deductive rules with relational databases. The LDL system prototype is described in Chimenti et al. (1990). Krishnamurthy and Naqvi (1989) introduce the "choice" notion in LDL. Zaniolo (1988) discusses the language issues for the LDL system. A language overview of CORAL is provided in Ramakrishnan et al. (1992), and the implementation is described in Ramakrishnan et al. (1993). An extension to support object-oriented features, called CORAL++, is described in Srivastava et al. (1993). Ullman (1985) provides the basis for the NAIL! system, which is described in Morris et al. (1987). Phipps et al. (1991) describe the GLUE-NAIL! deductive database system.

Zaniolo (1990) reviews the theoretical background and the practical importance of deductive databases. Nicolas (1997) gives an excellent history of the developments leading up to DOODs. Falcone et al. (1997) survey the DOOD landscape. References on the VALIDITY system include Friesen et al. (1995), Vieille (1997), and Dietrich et al. (1999).

26 | Data Warehousing And Data Mining

CHAPTER

The increasing processing power and sophistication of analytical tools and techniques have resulted in the development of what are known as data warehouses. These data warehouses provide storage, functionality, and responsiveness to queries beyond the capabilities of transaction-oriented databases. Accompanying this ever-increasing power has come a great demand to improve the data access performance of databases. As we have seen throughout the book, traditional databases balance the requirement of data access with the need to ensure integrity of data. In modern organizations, users of data are often completely removed from the data sources. Many people only need read-access to data, but still need a very rapid access to a larger volume of data than can conveniently be downloaded to the desktop. Often such data comes from multiple databases. Because many of the analyses performed are recurrent and predictable, software vendors and systems support staff have begun to design systems to support these functions. At present there is a great need to provide decision makers from middle management upward with information at the correct level of detail to support decision making. *Data warehousing, on-line analytical processing* (OLAP), and *data mining* provide this functionality. In this chapter we give a broad overview of each of these technologies.

The market for such support has been growing rapidly since the mid-1990s. As managers become increasingly aware of the growing sophistication of analytic capabilities of these data-based systems, they look increasingly for more sophisticated support for their key organizational decisions.

26.1   Data Warehousing

Because data warehouses have been developed in numerous organizations to meet particular needs, there is no single, canonical definition of the term data warehouse.[1] Professional magazine articles and books in the popular press have elaborated on the meaning in a variety of ways. Vendors have capitalized on the popularity of the term to help market a variety of related products, and consultants have provided a large variety of services, all under the data warehousing banner. However, data warehouses are quite distinct from traditional databases in their structure, functioning, performance, and purpose.

26.1.1   Terminology and Definitions

W. H. Inmon[2] characterized a data warehouse as "a subject-oriented, integrated, nonvolatile, time-variant collection of data in support of management's decisions." Data warehouses provide access to data for complex analysis, knowledge discovery, and decision making.

They support high-performance demands on an organization's data and information. Several types of applications—OLAP, DSS, and data mining applications—are supported. **OLAP (on-line analytical processing)** is a term used to describe the analysis of complex data from the data warehouse. In the hands of skilled knowledge workers, OLAP tools use distributed computing capabilities for analyses that require more storage and processing power than can be economically and efficiently located on an individual desktop. DSS **(decision-support systems)** also known as EIS **(executive information systems)** (not to be confused with enterprise integration systems) support an organization's leading decision makers with higher-level data for complex and important decisions. Data mining (which we will discuss in detail in Section 26.2) is used for knowledge discovery, the process of searching data for unanticipated new knowledge.

Traditional databases support **on-line transaction processing** (OLTP), which includes insertions, updates, and deletions, while also supporting information query requirements. Traditional relational databases are optimized to process queries that may touch a small part of the database and transactions that deal with insertions or updates of a few tuples per relation to process. Thus, they cannot be optimized for OLAP, DSS, or data mining. By contrast, data warehouses are designed precisely to support efficient extraction, processing, and presentation for analytic and decision-making purposes. In comparison to traditional databases, data warehouses generally contain very large amounts of data from multiple sources that may include databases from different data models and sometimes files acquired from independent systems and platforms.

---

1. In Chapter 1 we defined database as a collection of related data and a database system as a database and database software together. A data warehouse is also a collection of information as well as a supporting system. However, a clear distinction exists. Traditional databases are transactional (relational, object-oriented, network, or hierarchical). Data warehouses have the distinguishing characteristic that they are mainly intended for decision-support applications. They are optimized for data retrieval, not routine transaction processing.

2. Inmon (1992) has been credited with initially using the term data warehouse.

26.1.2   Characteristics of Data Warehouses

To discuss data warehouses and distinguish them from transactional databases calls for an appropriate data model. The multidimensional data model (explained in more detail below) is a good fit for OLAP and decision-support technologies. In contrast to multidata-bases, which provide access to disjoint and usually heterogeneous databases, a data ware-house is frequently a store of integrated data from multiple sources, processed for storage in a multidimensional model. Unlike most transactional databases, data warehouses typi-cally support time-series and trend analysis, both of which require more historical data than are generally maintained in transactional databases. Compared with transactional databases, data warehouses are nonvolatile. That means that information in the data warehouse changes far less often and may be regarded as non-real-time with periodic updating. In transactional systems, transactions are the unit and are the agent of change to the database; by contrast, data warehouse information is much more coarse grained and is refreshed according to a careful choice of refresh policy, usually incremental. Ware-house updates are handled by the warehouse's acquisition component that provides all required preprocessing.

We can also describe data warehousing more generally as "a collection of decision support technologies, aimed at enabling the knowledge worker (executive, manager, ana-lyst) to make better and faster decisions."[3] Figure 26.1 gives an overview of the concep-tual structure of a data warehouse. It shows the entire data warehousing process. This process includes possible cleaning and reformatting of data before its warehousing. At the back end of the process, OLAP, data mining, and DSS may generate new relevant informa-tion such as rules; this information is shown in the figure going back into the warehouse. The figure also shows that data sources may include files.

Figure 26.1   The overall process of data warehousing.

---

3. Chaudhuri and Dayal (1997) provide an excellent tutorial on the topic, with this as a starting definition.

Data warehouses have the following distinctive characteristics.[4]

- multidimensional conceptual view
- generic dimensionality
- unlimited dimensions and aggregation levels
- unrestricted cross-dimensional operations
- dynamic sparse matrix handling
- client-server architecture
- multi-user support
- accessibility
- transparency
- intuitive data manipulation
- consistent reporting performance
- flexible reporting

Because they encompass large volumes of data, data warehouses are generally an order of magnitude (sometimes two orders of magnitude) larger than the source databases. The sheer volume of data (likely to be in terabytes) is an issue that has been dealt with through enterprise-wide data warehouses, virtual data warehouses, and data marts:

- **Enterprise-wide data warehouses** are huge projects requiring massive investment of time and resources.

- **Virtual data warehouses** provide views of operational databases that are materialized for efficient access.

- **Data marts** generally are targeted to a subset of the organization, such as a department, and are more tightly focused.

26.1.3 Data Modeling for Data Warehouses

Multidimensional models take advantage of inherent relationships in data to populate data in multidimensional matrices called data cubes. (These may be called hypercubes if they have more than three dimensions.) For data that lend themselves to dimensional formatting, query performance in multidimensional matrices can be much better than in the relational data model. Three examples of dimensions in a corporate data warehouse would be the corporation's fiscal periods, products, and regions.

A standard spreadsheet is a two-dimensional matrix. One example would be a spreadsheet of regional sales by product for a particular time period. Products could be shown as rows, with sales revenues for each region comprising the columns. (Figure 26.2 shows this two-dimensional organization.) Adding a time dimension, such as an organization's fiscal quarters, would produce a three-dimensional matrix, which could be represented using a data cube.

---

4. Codd (1993) coined the term OLAP and mentioned these characteristics. We have reordered Codd's original list.

Figure 26.2 Two-dimensional matrix.

In Figure 26.3 there is a three-dimensional data cube that organizes product sales data by fiscal quarters and sales regions. Each cell could contain data for a specific product, specific fiscal quarter, and specific region. By including additional dimensions, a data hypercube could be produced, although more than three dimensions cannot be easily visualized at all or presented graphically. The data can be queried directly in any combination of dimensions, bypassing complex database queries. Tools exist for viewing data

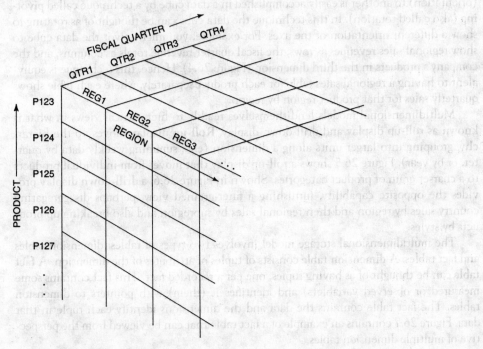

Figure 26.3 A data cube.

Figure 26.4   Pivoted version of the data cube.

according to the user's choice of dimensions. Changing from one dimensional hierarchy (orientation) to another is easily accomplished in a data cube by a technique called **pivoting** (also called rotation). In this technique the data cube can be thought of as rotating to show a different orientation of the axes. For example, you might pivot the data cube to show regional sales revenues as rows, the fiscal quarter revenue totals as columns, and the company's products in the third dimension (Figure 26.4). Hence, this technique is equivalent to having a regional sales table for each product separately, where each table shows quarterly sales for that product region by region.

Multidimensional models lend themselves readily to hierarchical views in what is known as roll-up display and drill-down display. **Roll-up display** moves up the hierarchy, grouping into larger units along a dimension (e.g., summing weekly data by quarter, or by year). Figure 26.5 shows a roll-up display that moves from individual products to a coarser grain of product categories. Shown in Figure 26.6, a **drill-down display** provides the opposite capability, furnishing a finer-grained view, perhaps disaggregating country sales by region and then regional sales by subregion and also breaking up products by styles.

The multidimensional storage model involves two types of tables: dimension tables and fact tables. A **dimension table** consists of tuples of attributes of the dimension. A **fact table** can be thought of as having tuples, one per a recorded fact. This fact contains some measured or observed variable(s) and identifies it (them) with pointers to dimension tables. The fact table contains the data and the dimensions identify each tuple in that data. Figure 26.7 contains an example of a fact table that can be viewed from the perspective of multiple dimension tables.

Figure 26.5   The roll-up operation.

		REGION 1				REGION 2
		SUBREG1	SUBREG2	SUBREG3	SUBREG4	SUBREG1
P123 STYLES	A					
	B					
	C					
	D					
P124 STYLES	A					
	B					
	C					
P125 STYLES	A					
	B					
	C					
	D					

Figure 26.6   The drill-down operation.

Two common multidimensional schemas are the star schema and the snowflake schema. The **star schema** consists of a fact table with a single table for each dimension (Figure 26.7). The **snowflake schema** is a variation on the star schema in which the dimensional tables from a star schema are organized into a hierarchy by normalizing them (Figure 26.8). Some installations are normalizing data warehouses up to the third normal form so that they can access the data warehouse to the finest level of detail. A **fact constellation** is a set of fact tables that share some dimension tables. Figure 26.9 shows a fact constellation with two fact tables, business results and business forecast. These share the dimension table called product. Fact constellations limit the possible queries for the warehouse.

Data warehouse storage also utilizes indexing techniques to support high performance access (see Chapter 6 for a discussion of indexing). A technique called **bitmap indexing** constructs a bit vector for each value in a domain (column) being indexed. It

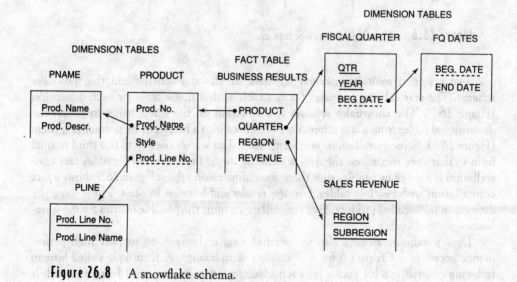

Figure 26.7   A star schema with fact and dimensional tables.

Figure 26.8   A snowflake schema.

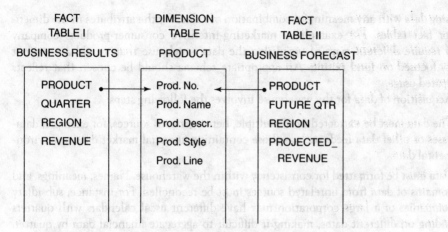

Figure 26.9 A fact constellation.

works very well for domains of low-cardinality. There is a 1 bit placed in the jth position in the vector if the jth row contains the value being indexed. For example, imagine an inventory of 100,000 cars with a bitmap index on car size. If there are four car sizes—economy, compact, midsize, and fullsize—there will be four bit vectors, each containing 100,000 bits (12.5 K) for a total index size of 50K. Bitmap indexing can provide considerable input/output and storage space advantages in low-cardinality domains. With bit vectors a bitmap index can provide dramatic improvements in comparison, aggregation, and join performance. In a star schema, dimensional data can be indexed to tuples in the fact table by **join indexing.** Join indexes are traditional indexes to maintain relationships between primary key and foreign key values. They relate the values of a dimension of a star schema to rows in the fact table. For example, consider a sales fact table that has city and fiscal quarter as dimensions. If there is a join index on city, for each city the join index maintains the tuple IDs of tuples containing that city. Join indexes may involve multiple dimensions.

Data warehouse storage can facilitate access to summary data by taking further advantage of the nonvolatility of data warehouses and a degree of predictability of the analyses that will be performed using them. Two approaches have been used: (1) smaller tables including summary data such as quarterly sales or revenue by product line, and (2) encoding of level (e.g., weekly, quarterly, annual) into existing tables. By comparison, the overhead of creating and maintaining such aggregations would likely be excessive in a volatile, transaction-oriented database.

26.1.4 Building a Data Warehouse

In constructing a data warehouse, builders should take a broad view of the anticipated use of the warehouse. There is no way to anticipate all possible queries or analyses during the design phase. However, the design should specifically support **ad-hoc querying,** that is, accessing data with any meaningful combination of values for the attributes in the dimension or fact tables. For example, a marketing-intensive consumer-products company would require different ways of organizing the data warehouse than would a nonprofit charity focused on fund raising. An appropriate schema should be chosen that reflects anticipated usage.

Acquisition of data for the warehouse involves the following steps:

- The data must be extracted from multiple, heterogeneous sources, for example, databases or other data feeds such as those containing financial market data or environmental data.

- Data must be formatted for consistency within the warehouse. Names, meanings, and domains of data from unrelated sources must be reconciled. For instance, subsidiary companies of a large corporation may have different fiscal calendars with quarters ending on different dates, making it difficult to aggregate financial data by quarter. Various credit cards may report their transactions differently, making it difficult to compute all credit sales. These format inconsistencies must be resolved.

- The data must be cleaned to ensure validity. Data cleaning is an involved and complex process that has been identified as the largest labor-demanding component of data warehouse construction. For input data, cleaning must occur before the data are loaded into the warehouse. There is nothing about cleaning data that is specific to data warehousing and that could not be applied to a host database. However, since input data must be examined and formatted consistently, data warehouse builders should take this opportunity to check for validity and quality. Recognizing erroneous and incomplete data is difficult to automate, and cleaning that requires automatic error correction can be even tougher. Some aspects, such as domain checking, are easily coded into data cleaning routines, but automatic recognition of other data problems can be more challenging. (For example, one might require that City = 'San Francisco' together with State = 'CT' be recognized as an incorrect combination.) After such problems have been taken care of, similar data from different sources must be coordinated for loading into the warehouse. As data managers in the organization discover that their data are being cleaned for input into the warehouse, they will likely want to upgrade their data with the cleaned data. The process of returning cleaned data to the source is called **backflushing** (see Figure 26.1).

- The data must be fitted into the data model of the warehouse. Data from the various sources must be installed in the data model of the warehouse. Data may have to be converted from relational, object-oriented, or legacy databases (network and/or hierarchical) to a multidimensional model.

- The data must be loaded into the warehouse. The sheer volume of data in the warehouse makes loading the data a significant task. Monitoring tools for loads as well as methods to recover from incomplete or incorrect loads are required. With the huge volume of data in the warehouse, incremental updating is usually the only feasible approach. The refresh policy will probably emerge as a compromise that takes into account the answers to the following questions:

- How up-to-date must the data be?

- Can the warehouse go off-line, and for how long?
- What are the data interdependencies?
- What is the storage availability?
- What are the distribution requirements (such as for replication and partitioning)?
- What is the loading time (including cleaning, formatting, copying, transmitting, and overhead such as index rebuilding)?

As we have said, databases must strike a balance between efficiency in transaction processing and supporting query requirements (ad hoc user requests), but a data warehouse is typically optimized for access from a decision maker's needs. Data storage in a data warehouse reflects this specialization and involves the following processes:

- Storing the data according to the data model of the warehouse
- Creating and maintaining required data structures
- Creating and maintaining appropriate access paths
- Providing for time-variant data as new data are added
- Supporting the updating of warehouse data
- Refreshing the data
- Purging data

Although adequate time can be devoted initially to constructing the warehouse, the sheer volume of data in the warehouse generally makes it impossible to simply reload the warehouse in its entirety later on. Alternatives include selective (partial) refreshing of data and separate warehouse versions (requiring double storage capacity for the warehouse!). When the warehouse uses an incremental data refreshing mechanism, data may need to be periodically purged; for example, a warehouse that maintains data on the previous twelve business quarters may periodically purge its data each year.

Data warehouses must also be designed with full consideration of the environment in which they will reside. Important design considerations include the following:

- Usage projections
- The fit of the data model
- Characteristics of available sources
- Design of the metadata component
- Modular component design
- Design for manageability and change
- Considerations of distributed and parallel architecture

We discuss each of these in turn. Warehouse design is initially driven by usage projections; that is, by expectations about who will use the warehouse and in what way. Choice of a data model to support this usage is a key initial decision. Usage projections and the characteristics of the warehouse's data sources are both taken into account. Modular design is a practical necessity to allow the warehouse to evolve with the organization and its information environment. In addition, a well-built data warehouse must be designed for maintainability, enabling the warehouse managers to effectively plan for and manage change while providing optimal support to users.

You may recall the term metadata from Chapter 2; metadata was defined as the description of a database including its schema definition. The **metadata repository** is a key data warehouse component. The metadata repository includes both technical and business metadata. The first, technical metadata, covers details of acquisition processing, storage structures, data descriptions, warehouse operations and maintenance, and access support functionality. The second, business metadata, includes the relevant business rules and organizational details supporting the warehouse.

The architecture of the organization's distributed computing environment is a major determining characteristic for the design of the warehouse. There are two basic distributed architectures: the distributed warehouse and the federated warehouse. For a **distributed warehouse,** all the issues of distributed databases are relevant, for example, replication, partitioning, communications, and consistency concerns. A distributed architecture can provide benefits particularly important to warehouse performance, such as improved load balancing, scalability of performance, and higher availability. A single replicated metadata repository would reside at each distribution site. The idea of the **federated warehouse** is like that of the federated database: a decentralized confederation of autonomous data warehouses, each with its own metadata repository. Given the magnitude of the challenge inherent to data warehouses, it is likely that such federations will consist of smaller-scale components, such as data marts. Large organizations may choose to federate data marts rather than build huge data warehouses.

26.1.5   Typical Functionality of Data Warehouses

Data warehouses exist to facilitate complex, data-intensive, and frequent ad hoc queries. Accordingly, data warehouses must provide far greater and more efficient query support than is demanded of transactional databases. The data warehouse access component supports enhanced spreadsheet functionality, efficient query processing, structured queries, ad hoc queries, data mining, and materialized views. In particular, enhanced spreadsheet functionality includes support for state-of-the-art spreadsheet applications (e.g., MS Excel) as well as for OLAP applications programs. These offer preprogrammed functionalities such as the following:

- Roll-up: Data is summarized with increasing generalization (e.g., weekly to quarterly to annually).
- Drill-down: Increasing levels of detail are revealed (the complement of roll-up).
- Pivot: Cross tabulation (also referred as rotation) is performed.
- Slice and dice: Performing projection operations on the dimensions.
- Sorting: Data is sorted by ordinal value.
- Selection: Data is available by value or range.
- Derived (computed) attributes: Attributes are computed by operations on stored and derived values.

Because data warehouses are free from the restrictions of the transactional environment there is an increased efficiency in query processing. Among the tools and techniques used are: query transformation, index intersection and union, special ROLAP (relational OLAP) and MOLAP (multidimensional OLAP) functions, SQL extensions, advanced join methods, and intelligent scanning (as in piggy-backing multiple queries).

Improved performance has also been attained with parallel processing. Parallel server architectures include symmetric multiprocessor (SMP), cluster, and massively parallel processing (MPP), and combinations of these.

Knowledge workers and decision makers use tools ranging from parametric queries to ad hoc queries to data mining. Thus, the access component of the data warehouse must provide support of structured queries (both parametric and ad hoc). These together make up a managed query environment. Data mining itself uses techniques from statistical analysis and artificial intelligence. Statistical analysis can be performed by advanced spreadsheets, by sophisticated statistical analysis software, or by custom-written programs. Techniques such as lagging, moving averages, and regression analysis are also commonly employed. Artificial intelligence techniques, which may include genetic algorithms and neural networks, are used for classification and are employed to discover knowledge from the data warehouse that may be unexpected or difficult to specify in queries. (We treat data mining in detail in Section 26.2.)

Data Warehousing and Views.   Some people have considered data warehouses to be an extension of database views. Earlier we mentioned materialized views as one way of meeting requirements for improved access to data (see Chapter 8 for a discussion of views). Materialized views have been explored for their performance enhancement. Views, however, provide only a subset of the functions and capabilities of data warehouses. Views and data warehouses are alike in that they both have read-only extracts from databases and subject-orientation. However, data warehouses are different from views in the following ways:

- Data warehouses exist as persistent storage instead of being materialized on demand.
- Data warehouses are not usually relational, but rather multidimensional. Views of a relational database are relational.
- Data warehouses can be indexed to optimize performance. Views cannot be indexed independent from of the underlying databases.
- Data warehouses characteristically provide specific support of functionality; views cannot.
- Data warehouses provide large amounts of integrated and often temporal data, generally more than is contained in one database, whereas views are an extract of a database.

26.1.6   Difficulties of Implementing Data Warehouses

Some significant operational issues arise with data warehousing: construction, administration, and quality control. Project management—the design, construction, and implementation of the warehouse—is an important and challenging consideration that should not be underestimated. The building of an enterprise-wide warehouse in a large organization is a major undertaking, potentially taking years from conceptualization to implementation. Because of the difficulty and amount of lead time required for such an undertaking, the widespread development and deployment of data marts may provide an attractive alternative, especially to those organizations with urgent needs for OLAP, DSS, and/or data mining support.

The administration of a data warehouse is an intensive enterprise, proportional to the size and complexity of the warehouse. An organization that attempts to administer a data warehouse must realistically understand the complex nature of its administration. Although designed for read-access, a data warehouse is no more a static structure than any of its information sources. Source databases can be expected to evolve. The warehouse's schema and acquisition component must be expected to be updated to handle these evolutions.

A significant issue in data warehousing is the quality control of data. Both quality and consistency of data are major concerns. Although the data passes through a cleaning function during acquisition, quality and consistency remain significant issues for the database administrator. Melding data from heterogeneous and disparate sources is a major challenge given differences in naming, domain definitions, identification numbers, and the like. Every time a source database changes, the data warehouse administrator must consider the possible interactions with other elements of the warehouse.

Usage projections should be estimated conservatively prior to construction of the data warehouse and should be revised continually to reflect current requirements. As utilization patterns become clear and change over time, storage and access paths can be tuned to remain optimized for support of the organization's use of its warehouse. This activity should continue throughout the life of the warehouse in order to remain ahead of demand. The warehouse should also be designed to accommodate addition and attrition of data sources without major redesign. Sources and source data will evolve, and the warehouse must accommodate such change. Fitting the available source data into the data model of the warehouse will be a continual challenge, a task that is as much art as science. Because there is continual rapid change in technologies, both the requirements and capabilities of the warehouse will change considerably over time. Additionally, data warehousing technology itself will continue to evolve for some time so that component structures and functionalities will continually be upgraded. This certain change is excellent motivation for having fully modular design of components.

Administration of a data warehouse will require far broader skills than are needed for traditional database administration. A team of highly skilled technical experts with overlapping areas of expertise will likely be needed, rather than a single individual. Like database administration, data warehouse administration is only partly technical; a large part of the responsibility requires working effectively with all the members of the organization with an interest in the data warehouse. However difficult that can be at times for database administrators, it is that much more challenging for data warehouse administrators, as the scope of their responsibilities is considerably broader.

Design of the management function and selection of the management team for a database warehouse are crucial. Managing the data warehouse in a large organization will surely be a major task. Many commercial tools are already available to support management functions. Effective data warehouse management will certainly be a team function, requiring a wide set of technical skills, careful coordination, and effective leadership. Just as we must prepare for the evolution of the warehouse, we must also recognize that the skills of the management team will, of necessity, evolve with it.

26.1.7 Open Issues in Data Warehousing

There has been much marketing hyperbole surrounding the term "data warehouse"; the exaggerated expectations will probably subside, but the concept of integrated data collections to support sophisticated analysis and decision support will undoubtedly endure.

Data warehousing as an active research area is likely to see increased research activity in the near future as warehouses and data marts proliferate. Old problems will receive new emphasis; for example, data cleaning, indexing, partitioning, and views could receive renewed attention.

Academic research into data warehousing technologies will likely focus on automating aspects of the warehouse that currently require significant manual intervention, such as the data acquisition, data quality management, selection and construction of appropriate access paths and structures, self-maintainability, functionality, and performance optimization. Application of active database functionality (see Section 23.1) into the warehouse is likely also to receive considerable attention. Incorporation of domain and business rules appropriately into the warehouse creation and maintenance process may make it more intelligent, relevant, and self-governing.

Commercial software for data warehousing is already available from a number of vendors, focusing principally on management of the data warehouse and OLAP/DSS applications. Other aspects of data warehousing, such as design and data acquisition (especially cleaning), are being addressed primarily by teams of in-house IT managers and consultants.

26.2 Data Mining

Over the last three decades, many organizations have generated a large amount of machine-readable data in the form of files and databases. To process this data, we have the database technology available to us that supports query languages like SQL. The problem with SQL is that it is a structured language that assumes the user is aware of the database schema. SQL supports operations of relational algebra that allow a user to select from tables (rows and columns of data) or join related information from tables based on common fields. In the last section we saw that data warehousing technology affords types of functionality, that of consolidation, aggregation, and summarization of data. It lets us view the same information along multiple dimensions. In this section, we will focus our attention on yet another very popular area of interest known as data mining. As the term connotes, **data mining** refers to the mining or discovery of new information in terms of patterns or rules from vast amounts of data. To be practically useful, data mining must be carried out efficiently on large files and databases. To date, it is *not* well-integrated with database management systems.

We will briefly review the state of the art of this rather extensive field of data mining, which uses techniques from such areas as machine learning, statistics, neural networks, and genetic algorithms. We will highlight the nature of the information that is discovered, the types of problems faced in databases, and potential applications. We also survey the state of the art of a large number of commercial tools available (see Section 26.2.5) and describe a number of research advances that are needed to make this area viable.

26.2.1   An Overview of Data Mining Technology

In reports such as the very popular Gartner Report,[5] data mining has been hailed as one of the top technologies for the near future. In this section we relate data mining to the broader area called knowledge discovery and contrast the two by means of an illustrative example. We also discuss a number of data mining techniques and algorithms in Section 26.2.3.

Data Mining and Data Warehousing.   The goal of a data warehouse is to support decision making with data. Data mining can be used in conjunction with a data warehouse to help with certain types of decisions. Data mining can be applied to operational databases with individual transactions. To make data mining more efficient, the data warehouse should have an aggregated or summarized collection of data. Data mining helps in extracting meaningful new patterns that cannot be found necessarily by merely querying or processing data or metadata in the data warehouse. Data mining applications should therefore be strongly considered early, during the design of a data warehouse. Also, data mining tools should be designed to facilitate their use in conjunction with data warehouses. In fact, for very large databases running into terabytes of data, successful use of database mining applications will depend first on the construction of a data warehouse.

Data Mining as a Part of the Knowledge Discovery Process.   Knowledge Discovery in Databases, frequently abbreviated as KDD, typically encompasses more than data mining. The knowledge discovery process comprises six phases:[6] data selection, data cleansing, enrichment, data transformation or encoding, data mining, and the reporting and display of the discovered information.

As an example, consider a transaction database maintained by a specialty consumer goods retailer. Suppose the client data includes a customer name, zip code, phone number, date of purchase, item·code, price, quantity, and total amount. A variety of new knowledge can be discovered by KDD processing on this client database. During *data selection*, data about specific items or categories of items, or from stores in a specific region or area of the country, may be selected. The *data cleansing* process then may correct invalid zip codes or eliminate records with incorrect phone prefixes. *Enrichment* typically enhances the data with additional sources of information. For example, given the client

---

5. The Gartner Report is one example of the many technology survey publications that corporate managers rely on to make their technology selection decisions.

6. This discussion is largely based on Adriaans and Zantinge (1995).

names and phone numbers, the store may purchase other data about age, income, and credit rating and append them to each record. *Data transformation* and encoding may be done to reduce the amount of data. For instance, item codes may be grouped in terms of product categories into audio, video, supplies, electronic gadgets, camera, accessories, and so on. Zip codes may be aggregated into geographic regions, incomes may be divided into ten ranges, and so on. Earlier, in Figure 26.1, we showed a step called cleaning as a precursor to the data warehouse creation. If data mining is based on an existing warehouse for this retail store chain, we would expect that the cleaning has already been applied. It is only after such preprocessing that *data mining* techniques are used to mine different rules and patterns. For example, the result of mining may be to discover:

- Association rules—e.g., whenever a customer buys video equipment, he or she also buys another electronic gadget.

- Sequential patterns—e.g., suppose a customer buys a camera, and within three months he or she buys photographic supplies, and within six months an accessory item. A customer who buys more than twice in the lean periods may be likely to buy at least once during Christmas period.

- Classification trees—e.g., customers may be classified by frequency of visits, by types of financing used, by amount of purchase, or by affinity for types of items, and some revealing statistics may be generated for such classes.

We can see that many possibilities exist for discovering new knowledge about buying patterns, relating factors such as age, income-group, place of residence, to what and how much the customers purchase. This information can then be utilized to plan additional store locations based on demographics, to run store promotions, to combine items in advertisements, or to plan seasonal marketing strategies. As this retail-store example shows, data mining must be preceded by significant data preparation before it can yield useful information that can directly influence business decisions.

The results of data mining may be reported in a variety of formats, such as listings, graphic outputs, summary tables, or visualizations.

Goals of Data Mining and Knowledge Discovery.   Broadly speaking, the goals of data mining fall into the following classes: prediction, identification, classification, and optimization.

- **Prediction**—Data mining can show how certain attributes within the data will behave in the future. Examples of predictive data mining include the analysis of buying transactions to predict what consumers will buy under certain discounts, how much sales volume a store would generate in a given period, and whether deleting a product line would yield more profits. In such applications, business logic is used coupled with data mining. In a scientific context, certain seismic wave patterns may predict an earthquake with high probability.

- **Identification**—Data patterns can be used to identify the existence of an item, an event, or an activity. For example, intruders trying to break a system may be identified by the programs executed, files accessed, and CPU time per session. In biological applications, existence of a gene may be identified by certain sequences of nucleotide symbols in the DNA sequence. The area known as *authentication* is a form of identification. It ascertains whether a user is indeed a specific user or one from an authorized class; it involves a comparison of parameters or images or signals against a database.

- **Classification**—Data mining can partition the data so that different classes or categories can be identified based on combinations of parameters. For example, customers in a supermarket can be categorized into discount-seeking shoppers, shoppers in a rush, loyal regular shoppers, and infrequent shoppers. This classification may be used in different analyses of customer buying transactions as a post-mining activity. Sometimes classification based on common domain knowledge is used as an input to decompose the mining problem and make it simpler. For instance, health foods, party foods, or school lunch foods are distinct categories in the supermarket business. It makes sense to analyze relationships within and across categories as separate problems. Such categorization may be used to encode the data appropriately before subjecting it to further data mining.

- **Optimization**—One eventual goal of data mining may be to optimize the use of limited resources such as time, space, money, or materials and to maximize output variables such as sales or profits under a given set of constraints. As such, this goal of data mining resembles the objective function used in operations research problems that deals with optimization under constraints.

The term data mining is currently used in a very broad sense. In some situations it includes statistical analysis and constrained optimization as well as machine learning. There is no sharp line separating data mining from these disciplines. It is beyond our scope, therefore, to discuss in detail the entire range of applications that make up this vast body of work.

Types of Knowledge Discovered during Data Mining.   The term "knowledge" is very broadly interpreted as involving some degree of intelligence. Knowledge is often classified as inductive and deductive. We discussed discovery of deductive knowledge in Chapter 25. Data mining addresses inductive knowledge. Knowledge can be represented in many forms: in an unstructured sense, it can be represented by rules, or propositional logic. In a structured form, it may be represented in decision trees, semantic networks, neural networks, or hierarchies of classes or frames. The knowledge discovered during data mining can be described in five ways, as follows.

1. **Association rules**—These rules correlate the presence of a set of items with another range of values for another set of variables. Examples: (1) When a female retail shopper buys a handbag, she is likely to buy shoes. (2) An X-ray image containing characteristics a and b is likely to also exhibit characteristic c.

2. **Classification hierarchies**—The goal is to work from an existing set of events or transactions to create a hierarchy of classes. Examples: (1) A population may be divided into five ranges of credit worthiness based on a history of previous credit transactions. (2) A model may be developed for the factors that determine the desirability of location of a store on a 1–10 scale. (3) Mutual funds may be classified based on performance data using characteristics such as growth, income, and stability.

3. **Sequential patterns**—A sequence of actions or events is sought. Example: If a patient underwent cardiac bypass surgery for blocked arteries and an aneurysm and later developed high blood urea within a year of surgery, he or she is likely to suffer from kidney failure within the next 18 months. Detection of sequential patterns is equivalent to detecting association among events with certain temporal relationships.

4. **Patterns within time series**—Similarities can be detected within positions of the time series. Three examples follow with the stock market price data as a time series: (1) Stocks of a utility company ABC Power and a financial company XYZ Securities show the same pattern during 1998 in terms of closing stock price. (2) Two products show the same selling pattern in summer but a different one in winter. (3) A pattern in solar magnetic wind may be used to predict changes in earth atmospheric conditions.

5. **Categorization and segmentation**—A given population of events or items can be partitioned (segmented) into sets of "similar" elements. Examples: (1) An entire population of treatment data on a disease may be divided into groups based on the similarity of side effects produced. (2) The adult population in the United States may be categorized into five groups from "most likely to buy" to "least likely to buy" a new product. (3) The web accesses made by a collection of users against a set of documents (say, in a digital library) may be analyzed in terms of the keywords of documents to reveal clusters or categories of users.

For most applications, the desired knowledge is a combination of the above types. We expand on each of the above knowledge types in the following subsections.

26.2.2   Association Rules

One of the major technologies in data mining involves the discovery of association rules. The database is regarded as a collection of transactions, each involving a set of items. A common example is that of market-basket data. Here the market basket corresponds to what a consumer buys in a supermarket during one visit. Consider four such transactions in a random sample:

Transaction-id	Time	Items-Brought
101	6:35	milk, bread, juice
792	7:38	milk, juice
1130	8:05	milk, eggs
1735	8:40	bread, cookies, coffee

An **association rule** is of the form

X => Y,

where $X = \{ x_1, x_2, ..., x_n \}$, and $Y = \{ y_1, y_2, ..., y_m \}$ are sets of items, with x_i and y_j being distinct items for all i and all j. This association states that if a customer buys X, he or she is also likely to buy Y. In general, any association rule has the form LHS (left-hand side)

⇒ RHS (right-hand side), where LHS and RHS are sets of items. Association rules should supply both support and confidence.

The **support** for the rule LHS ⇒ RHS is the percentage of transactions that hold all of the items in the union, the set LHS ∪ RHS. If the support is low, it implies that there is no overwhelming evidence that items in LHS ∪ RHS occur together, because the union happens in only a small fraction of transactions. The rule Milk ⇒ Juice has 50% support, while Bread ⇒ Juice has only 25% support. Another term for support is *prevalence* of the rule.

To compute confidence we consider all transactions that include items in LHS. The **confidence** for the association rule LHS ⇒ RHS is the percentage (fraction) of such transactions that also include RHS. Another term for confidence is *strength* of the rule.

For Milk ⇒ Juice, the confidence is 66.7% (meaning that, of three transactions in which milk occurs, two contain juice) and bread ⇒ juice has 50% confidence (meaning that one of two transactions containing bread also contains juice.)

As we can see, support and confidence do not necessarily go hand in hand. The goal of mining association rules, then, is to generate all possible rules that exceed some minimum user-specified support and confidence thresholds. The problem is thus decomposed into two subproblems:

1. Generate all item sets that have a support that exceeds the threshold. These sets of items are called **large itemsets.** Note that large here means large support.

2. For each large item set, all the rules that have a minimum confidence are generated as follows: for a large itemset X and $Y \subset X$, let $Z = X - Y$; then if support (X)/support (Z) ⇒ minimum confidence, the rule $Z \Rightarrow Y$ (i.e., $X - Y \Rightarrow Y$) is a valid rule. [Note: In the previous sentence, $Y \subset X$ reads "Y is a subset of X."]

Generating rules by using all large itemsets and their supports is relatively straightforward. However, discovering all large itemsets together with the value for their support is a major problem if the cardinality of the set of items is very high. A typical supermarket has thousands of items. The number of distinct itemsets is 2^m, where m is the number of items, and counting support for all possible itemsets becomes very computation-intensive.

To reduce the combinatorial search space, algorithms for finding association rules have the following properties:

- A subset of a large itemset must also be large (i.e., each subset of a large itemset exceeds the minimum required support).

- Conversely, an extension of a small itemset is also small (implying that it does not have enough support).

The second property helps in discarding an itemset from further consideration of extension, if it is found to be small.

Basic Algorithms for Finding Association Rules.   The current algorithms that find large itemsets are designed to work as follows:

1. Test the support for itemsets of length 1, called 1-itemsets, by scanning the database. Discard those that do not meet minimum required support.

2. Extend the large 1-itemsets into 2-itemsets by appending one item each time, to generate all candidate itemsets of length two. Test the support for all candidate itemsets by scanning the database and eliminate those 2-itemsets that do not meet the minimum support.

3. Repeat the above steps; at step k, the previously found $(k - 1)$ itemsets are extended into k-itemsets and tested for minimum support.

The process is repeated until no large itemsets can be found. However, the naive version of this algorithm is a combinatorial nightmare. Several algorithms have been proposed to mine the association rules. They vary mainly in terms of how the candidate itemsets are generated, and how the supports for the candidate itemsets are counted.

Some algorithms use such data structures as bitmaps and hashtrees to keep information about itemsets. Several algorithms have been proposed that use multiple scans of the database because the potential number of itemsets, 2^m, can be too large to set up counters during a single scan. We have proposed an algorithm called the **Partition algorithm,**[7] summarized below.

If we are given a database with a small number of potential large itemsets, say, a few thousand, then the support for all of them can be tested in one scan by using a partitioning technique. Partitioning divides the database into nonoverlapping partitions; these are individually considered as separate databases and all large itemsets for that partition are generated in one pass. At the end of pass one, we thus generate a list of large itemsets from each partition. When these lists are merged, they contain some false positives. That is, some of the itemsets that are large in one partition may not qualify in several other partitions and hence may not exceed the minimum support when the original database is considered. Note that there are no false negatives, i.e., no large itemsets will be missed. The union of all large itemsets identified in pass one is input to pass two as the candidate itemsets, and their actual support is measured for the *entire* database. At the end of phase two, all actual large itemsets are identified. Partitions are chosen in such a way that each partition can be accommodated in main memory and a partition is read only once in each phase. The Partition algorithm lends itself to parallel implementation, for efficiency. Further improvements to this algorithm have been suggested.[8]

Association Rules among Hierarchies.   There are certain types of associations that are particularly interesting for a special reason. These associations occur among hierarchies of items. Typically, it is possible to divide items among disjoint hierarchies based on the nature of the domain. For example, foods in a supermarket, items in a department store, or articles in a sports shop can be categorized into classes and subclasses that give rise to hierarchies. Consider Figure 26.10, which shows the taxonomy of items in a supermarket. The figure shows two hierarchies—beverages and desserts, respectively. The entire groups may not produce associations of the form beverages $\Rightarrow$ desserts, or desserts $\Rightarrow$ beverages.

---

7. See Savasere et al. (1995) for details of the algorithm, the data structures used to implement it, and its performance comparisons.

8. See Cheung et al. (1996) and Lin and Dunham (1998).

Figure 26.10 A taxonomy of items in the supermarket.

However, associations of the type Healthy-brand frozen yogurt ⇒ bottled water, or Richcream-brand ice cream ⇒ wine cooler may produce enough confidence and support to be valid association rules of interest.

Therefore, if the application area has a natural classification of the itemsets into hierarchies, discovering associations *within* the hierarchies is of no particular interest. The ones of specific interest are associations *across* hierarchies. They may occur among item groupings at different levels.

Negative Associations.   The problem of discovering a negative association is harder than that of discovering a positive association. A negative association is of the following type: "60% of customers who buy potato chips do not buy bottled water." (Here, the 60% refers to the confidence for the negative association rule.) In a database with 10,000 items, there are 2^{10000} possible combinations of items, a majority of which do not appear even once in the database. If the absence of a certain item combination is taken to mean a negative association, then we potentially have millions and millions of negative association rules with RHSs that are of no interest at all. The problem, then, is to find only *interesting* negative rules. In general, we are interested in cases in which two specific sets of items appear very rarely in the same transaction. This poses two problems:

For a total item inventory of 10,000 items, the probability of any two being bought together is $(1/10,000) * (1/10,000) = 10^{-8}$. If we find the actual support for these two occurring together to be zero, that does not represent a significant departure from expectation and hence is not an interesting (negative) association.

The other problem is more serious. We are looking for item combinations with very low support, and there are millions and millions with low or even zero support. For example, a data set of 10 million transactions has most of the 2.5 billion pairwise combinations of 10,000 items missing. This would generate billions of useless rules.

Therefore, to make negative association rules interesting, we must use prior knowledge about the itemsets. One approach is to use hierarchies. Suppose we use the hierarchies of soft drinks and chips shown in Figure 26.11. A strong positive association has been shown between soft drinks and chips. If we find a large support for the fact that when customers buy Days chips they predominantly buy Topsy and *not* Joke and *not* Wakeup, that would be interesting. This is so because we would normally expect that if there is a strong association between Days and Topsy, there should also be such a strong association between Days and Joke or Days and Wakeup.[9]

In the frozen yogurt and bottled water groupings in Figure 26.10, suppose the Reduce versus Healthy-brand division is 80–20 and the Plain and Clear brands division is 60–40 among respective categories. This would give a joint probability of Reduce frozen yogurt being purchased with Plain bottled water as 48% among the transactions containing a frozen yogurt and a bottled water. If this support, however, is found to be only 20%, that would indicate a significant negative association among Reduce yogurt and Plain bottled water; again, that would be interesting.

The problem of finding negative association is important in the above situations given the domain knowledge in the form of item generalization hierarchies (that is, the beverage given and desserts hierarchies shown in Figure 26.10), the existing positive associations (such as between the frozen yogurt and bottled water groups), and the distribution of items (such as the name brands within related groups). Recent work has been reported by the database group at Georgia Tech in this context (see bibliographic notes). The scope of discovery of negative associations is limited in terms of knowing the item hierarchies and distributions. Exponential growth of negative associations remains a challenge.

Additional Considerations for Association Rules. For very large datasets, one way to improve efficiency is by sampling. If a representative sample can be found that truly represents the properties of the original data, then most of the rules can be found. The problem then reduces to one of devising a proper sampling procedure. This process has the potential danger of discovering some false positives (large itemsets that are not truly large) as

Figure 26.11 Simple hierarchies of soft drinks and chips

---

9. For simplicity we are assuming a uniform distribution of transactions among members of a hierarchy.

well as having false negatives by missing some large itemsets and corresponding association rules.

Mining association rules in real-life databases is further complicated by the following factors.

- The cardinality of itemsets in most situations is extremely large, and the volume of transactions is very high as well. Some operational databases in retailing and communication industries collect tens of millions of transactions per day.

- Transactions show variability in such factors as geographic location and seasons, making sampling difficult.

- Item classifications exist along multiple dimensions. Hence, driving the discovery process with domain knowledge, particularly for negative rules, is extremely difficult.

- Quality of data is variable; significant problems exist with missing, erroneous, conflicting, as well as redundant data in many industries.

Association rules can be generalized for data mining purposes. Although the notion of itemsets was used above to discover association rules, almost any data in the standard relational form with a number of attributes can be used. For example, consider blood-test data with attributes like hemoglobin, red blood cell count, white blood cell count, blood-sugar, urea, age of patient, and so on. Each of the attributes can be divided into ranges, and the presence of an attribute with a value can be considered equivalent to an item. Thus, if the hemoglobin attribute is divided into ranges 0–5, 6–7, 8–9, 10–12, 13–14, and above 14, then we can consider them as items H1, H2, ..., H7. Then a specific hemoglobin value for a patient corresponds to one of these seven items being present. The mutual exclusion among these hemoglobin items can be used to some advantage in the scanning for large itemsets. This way of dividing variable values into ranges allows us to apply the association-rule machinery to any database for mining purposes. The ranges have to be determined from domain knowledge such as the relative importance of each of the hemoglobin values.

26.2.3   Approaches to Other Data Mining Problems

Earlier in this section we presented an overview of the goals of data mining, along with the types of knowledge discovered during data mining, and discussed at length some approaches for discovery of association rules. In the remaining part of this section, we discuss some approaches to other data mining problems and present some techniques associated with them.

Discovery of Sequential Patterns.   The discovery of sequential patterns is based on the concept of a sequence of itemsets. We assume that transactions such as the supermarket-basket transactions we discussed previously are ordered by time of purchase. That ordering yields a sequence of itemsets. For example, {milk, bread, juice}, {bread, eggs}, {cookies, milk, coffee} may be such a **sequence of itemsets** based on three visits of the same customer to the store. The **support** for a sequence S of itemsets is the percentage of the given set U of sequences of which S is a subsequence. In this example, {milk, bread, juice} {bread, eggs} and {bread, eggs} {cookies, milk, coffee} are considered **subsequences.** The problem of identifying sequential patterns, then, is to find all subsequences from the given sets of sequences that have a user-defined minimum support. The sequence $S_1, S_2, S_3, \ldots$ is a **predictor** of the fact that a customer who buys itemset S_1 is likely to buy itemset S_2 and then S_3, and so on. This production is based on the frequency (support) of this sequence in the past. Various algorithms have been investigated for sequence detection.

Discovery of Patterns in Time Series.   Time series are sequences of events; each event may be a given fixed type of a transaction. For example, the closing price of a stock or a fund is an event that occurs every weekday for each stock and fund. The sequence of these values per stock or fund constitutes a time series. For a time series, one may look for a variety of patterns by analyzing sequences and subsequences as we did above. For example, we might find the period during which the stock rose or held steady for n days, or we might find the longest period over which the stock had a fluctuation of no more than 1% over previous closing price, or we might find the quarter during which the stock had the most percentage gain or percentage loss. Time series may be compared by establishing measures of similarity to identify companies whose stocks behave in a similar fashion. Analysis and mining of time series is an extended functionality of temporal data management (see Section 23.2).

Discovery of Classification Rules.   Classification is the process of learning a function that maps (classifies) a given object of interest into one of many possible classes. The classes may be predefined, or may be determined during the task of classification. A simple example is as follows. A bank wishes to classify its loan applicants into those that are loanworthy and those that are not. It may use a simple rule which states that if the current monthly debt obligation (which is a data element for each applicant) exceeds 25% of monthly net income (another data element for the applicant), then the applicant belongs to "not loanworthy" class; otherwise, he or she belongs to the "loanworthy" class.

In general, the classification rules may be more complex, and may be of the following form:

$$(\text{var}_1 \text{ in range}_1) \text{ and } (\text{var}_2 \text{ in range}_2) \text{ and } \ldots (\text{var}_n \text{ in range}_n) \Rightarrow \text{Object O belongs to class } C_1,$$

A similar set of rules would exist for each class.

Variables $\text{var}_1, \ldots, \text{var}_n$ are the attributes of object O and would constitute columns of a relation with one tuple per object. Each tuple of this table would be mapped to a class. It would be possible to write a set of SQL queries that convert the population of the table into the instances of the classes, once these classes are defined. The mining problem is to discover the classes as well as the conditions that define those classes.

The main distinction in forming the above rules in comparison to association rules is that the variables in the above rules take values from a discrete or continuous domain (e.g., number of children, income in dollars) as opposed to the itemsets, which are formed from a predefined set of items in case of association rules. Also, an association rule pertains to a set of transactions (input records), but a classification rule tells us how to map each record into a class.

Regression.   Regression is a special application of the classification rule. If a classification rule is regarded as a function over the variables that maps these variables into a target class variable, the rule is called a **regression rule.** A general application of regression occurs when, instead of mapping a tuple of data from a relation to a specific class, the value of a variable is predicted based on that tuple. For example, consider a relation

LAB_TESTS (patient ID, test 1, test 2, ..., test n)

which contains values that are results from a series of n tests for one patient. The target variable that we wish to predict is P, the probability of survival of the patient. Then the rule for regression takes the form:

(test 1 in range$_1$) and (test 2 in range$_2$) and ... (test n in range$_n$) $\Rightarrow P = x$,
or $x < P < y$

The choice depends on whether we can predict a unique value of P or a range of values for P. If we regard P as a function:

$P = f$ (test 1, test 2, ..., test n)

the function is called a **regression function** to predict P. In general, if the function appears as

$y = f (x_1, x_2, ..., x_n)$,

and f is linear in the domain variables x_i, the process of deriving f from a given set of tuples for $< x_1, x_2, ..., x_n, y >$ is called **linear regression.** Linear regression is a commonly used statistical technique for fitting a set of observations or points in n dimensions with the target variable y.

Regression analysis is a very common tool for analysis of data in many research domains. The discovery of the function to predict the target variable is equivalent to a data mining operation.

Neural Networks.   **Neural network** is a technique derived from artificial intelligence research that uses generalized regression and provides an iterative method to carry it out. Neural networks use the curve-fitting approach to infer a function from a set of samples. This technique provides a "learning approach"; it is driven by a test sample that is used for the initial inference and learning. With this kind of learning method, responses to new inputs may be able to be interpolated from the known samples. This interpolation however, depends on the world model (internal representation of the problem domain) developed by the learning method.

Neural networks can be broadly classified into two categories: supervised and unsupervised networks. Adaptive methods that attempt to reduce the output error are **supervised learning** methods, whereas those that develop internal representations without sample outputs are called **unsupervised learning** methods.

Neural networks self-adapt; that is, they learn from information on a specific problem. They perform well on classification tasks and are therefore useful in data mining. Yet, they are not without problems. Although they learn, they do not provide a good representation of *what* they have learned. Their outputs are highly quantitative and not easy to understand. As another limitation, the internal representations developed by neural networks are not unique. Also, in general, neural networks have trouble modeling time series data. Despite these shortcomings, they are popular and frequently used by several commercial vendors.

Genetic Algorithms. Genetic algorithms (GAs) are a class of randomized search procedures capable of adaptive and robust search over a wide range of search space topologies. Modeled after the adaptive emergence of biological species from evolutionary mechanisms, and introduced by Holland,[10] GAs have been successfully applied in such diverse fields such as image analysis, scheduling, and engineering design.

Genetic algorithms extend the idea from human genetics of the four-letter alphabet (based on the A,C,T,G nucleotides) of the human DNA code. The construction of a genetic algorithm involves devising an alphabet that encodes the solutions to the decision problem in terms of strings of that alphabet. Strings are equivalent to individuals. A fitness function defines which solutions can survive and which cannot. The ways in which solutions can be combined are patterned after the cross-over operation of cutting and combining strings from a father and a mother. An initial population of well-varied population is provided, and a game of evolution is played in which mutations occur among strings. They combine to produce a new generation of individuals; the fittest individuals survive and mutate until a family of successful solutions develops.

The solutions produced by genetic algorithms (GAs) are distinguished from most other search techniques by the following characteristics:

- A GA search uses a set of solutions during each generation rather than a single solution.
- The search in the string-space represents a much larger parallel search in the space of encoded solutions.
- The memory of the search done is represented solely by the set of solutions available for a generation.
- A genetic algorithm is a randomized algorithm since search mechanisms use probabilistic operators.
- While progressing from one generation to next, a GA finds near-optimal balance between knowledge acquisition and exploitation by manipulating encoded solutions.

Genetic algorithms are used for problem solving and clustering problems. Their ability to solve problems in parallel provides a powerful tool for data mining. The drawbacks of GAs include the large overproduction of individual solutions, the random character of the searching process, and the high demand on computer processing. In general, substantial computing power is required to achieve anything of significance with genetic algorithms.

---

10. Holland's seminal work (1975) entitled "Adaptation in Natural and Artificial Systems" introduced the idea of genetic algorithms.

Clustering and Segmentation. Clustering is a data mining technique that is directed toward the goals of identification and classification (see also Section 26.2.1). Clustering tries to identify a finite set of categories or clusters to which each data object (tuple) can be mapped. The categories may be disjoint or overlapping and may sometimes be organized into trees. For example, one might form categories of customers into the form of a tree and then map each customer to one or more of the categories. A closely related problem is that of estimating multivariate probability density functions of all variables that could be attributes in a relation or from different relations.

26.2.4 Applications of Data Mining

Data mining technologies can be applied to a large variety of decision-making contexts in business. In particular, areas of significant payoffs are expected to include the following:

- Marketing—Applications include analysis of consumer behavior based on buying patterns; determination of marketing strategies including advertising, store location, and targeted mailing; segmentation of customers, stores, or products; and design of catalogs, store layouts, and advertising campaigns.

- Finance—Applications include analysis of creditworthiness of clients, segmentation of account receivables, performance analysis of finance investments like stocks, bonds, and mutual funds; evaluation of financing options; and fraud detection.

- Manufacturing—Applications involve optimization of resources like machines, manpower, and materials; optimal design of manufacturing processes, shop-floor layouts, and product design, such as for automobiles based on customer requirements.

- Health Care—Applications include an analysis of effectiveness of certain treatments; optimization of processes within a hospital, relating patient wellness data with doctor qualifications; and analyzing side effects of drugs.

26.2.5 State-of-the-Art of Commercial Data Mining Tools

At the present time, commercial data mining tools use several common techniques to extract knowledge. These include association rules, clustering, neural networks, sequencing, and statistical analysis. We have discussed these earlier. Also used are decision trees, which are a representation of the rules used in classification or clustering, and statistical analyses, which may include regression and many other techniques. Other commercial products use advanced techniques such as genetic algorithms, case-based reasoning, Bayesian networks, nonlinear regression, combinatorial optimization, pattern matching, and fuzzy logic. In this chapter we have already discussed some of these.

Most data mining tools use the ODBC (Open Database Connectivity) interface. ODBC is an industry standard that works with databases; it enables access to data in most of the popular database programs such as Access, dBASE, Informix, Oracle, and SQL Server. Some of these software packages provide interfaces to specific database programs; the most common are Oracle, Access, and SQL Server. Most of the tools work in the Microsoft Windows environment and a few work in the UNIX operating system. The trend is for all products to operate under the Microsoft Windows environment. One tool, Data Surveyor, mentions ODMG compliance; see Chapter 12 where we discuss the ODMG object-oriented standard.

In general, these programs perform sequential processing in a single machine. Many of these products work in the client-server mode. Some products incorporate parallel processing in parallel computer architectures and work as a part of on-line analytical processing (OLAP) tools.

User Interface. Most of the tools run in a graphical user interface (GUI) environment. Some products include sophisticated visualization techniques to view data and rules (e.g., MineSet of SGI), and are even able to manipulate data this way interactively. Text interfaces are rare and are more common in tools available for UNIX, such as IBM's Intelligent Miner.

Application Programming Interface. Usually, the application programming interface (API) is an optional tool. Most products do not permit using their internal functions. However, some of them allow the application programmer to reuse their code. The most common interfaces are C libraries and Dynamic Link Libraries (DLLs). Some tools include proprietary database command languages.

In Table 26.1 we list 10 representative data mining tools. To date there are more than 70 commercial data mining products available worldwide. Non-U.S. products include Data Surveyor from the Netherlands and Polyanalyst from Russia.

Future Directions. Data mining tools are continually evolving, building on ideas from the latest scientific research. Many of these tools incorporate the latest algorithms taken from artificial intelligence (AI), statistics, and optimization.

At present, fast processing is done using modern database techniques—such as distributed processing—in client-server architectures, in parallel databases, and in data warehousing. For the future, the trend is toward developing Internet capabilities more fully. In addition, hybrid approaches will become commonplace, and processing will be done using all resources available. Processing will take advantage of both parallel and distributed computing environments. This shift is especially important because modern databases contain very large amounts of information. Not only are multimedia databases growing, but image storage and retrieval are both slow operations. Also, the cost of secondary storage is decreasing, so massive information storage will be feasible, even for small companies. Thus, data mining programs will have to deal with larger sets of data of more companies.

In the near future it seems that Microsoft Windows NT and UNIX will be the standard platforms, with NT being dominant. Most of data mining software will use the ODBC standard to extract data from business databases; proprietary input formats can be expected to disappear. There is a definite need to include nonstandard data, including images and other multimedia data, as source data for data mining. However, the algorithmic developments for nonstandard data mining have not reached a maturity level sufficient for commercialization.

Table 26.1   Some representative data mining tools

Company	Product	Technique	Platform	Interface*
Acknosoft	Kate	Decision trees, Case-based reasoning	Win NT UNIX	Microsoft Access
Angoss	Knowledge Seeker	Decision trees, Statistics	Win NT	ODBC
Business Objects	Business Miner	Neural nets, Machine learning	Win NT	ODBC
CrossZ	QueryObject	Statistical Analysis Optimization algorithm	Win NT MVS UNIX	ODBC
Data Distilleries	Data Surveyor	Comprehensive, Can mix DM algorithms	UNIX	ODBC ODMG-compliant
IBM	Intelligent Miner	Classification, Association rules, Predictive models	UNIX (AIX)	IBM DB2
Megaputer Intelligence	Polyanalyst	Symbolic knowledge acquisition, Evolutionary programming	Win NT OS/2	ODBC Oracle DB2
NCR	Management Discovery Tool (MDT)	Association rules	Win NT	ODBC
SAS	Enterprise Miner	Decision trees, Association rules, Neural nets, Regression, Clustering	UNIX (Solaris) Win NT Macintosh	ODBC Oracle AS/400
Silicon Graphics	MineSet	Decision trees, Association rules	UNIX (Irix)	Oracle Sybase Informix

*ODBC: Open Data Base Connectivity;
ODMG: Object Data Management Group

26.3 Summary

In this chapter we surveyed two very important branches of database technology that are going to play a significant role over the next decade: data warehousing and data mining.

Data warehousing can be seen as a process that requires a variety of activities to precede it; data mining may be thought as an activity that draws knowledge from an existing data warehouse. We introduced key concepts related to data warehousing and we discussed the special functionality associated with a multidimensional view of data. We also discussed the ways in which data warehouses supply decision makers with information at the correct level of detail, based on an appropriate organization and perspective.

In our discussion we gave an illustrative example of knowledge discovery in databases; this has a wider scope than data mining. For data mining, among the various techniques, we focused on association rules and gave a detailed introduction to their discovery. A variety of other techniques, including the AI-based neural networks and genetic algorithms, were also discussed.

Active research is ongoing in both data warehousing and data mining and we have outlined some of the expected research directions. In the future database technology products market a great deal of activity is expected. We summarized 10 out of 70 available data mining tools available today; future research is expected to extend the number and functionality significantly.

Review Exercises

26.1. What is a data warehouse? How does it differ from a database?

26.2. Define the terms: OLAP (Online Analytical Processing), ROLAP (Relational OLAP), and MOLAP (Multidimensional OLAP), DSS (Decision Support Systems).

26.3. Describe the characteristics of a data warehouse. Divide them into functionality of a warehouse and advantages users derive from it.

26.4. What is the multidimensional data model? How is it used in data warehousing?

26.5. Define these terms: Star Schema, Snowflake Schema, Fact Constellation, Data Marts.

26.6. What types of indexes are built for a warehouse? Illustrate the uses for each with an example.

26.7. Describe the steps of building a warehouse.

26.8. What considerations play a major role in the design of a warehouse?

26.9. Describe the functions a user can perform on a data warehouse and illustrate the results of these functions on a sample multidimensional data warehouse.

26.10. How is the concept of a relational view related to data warehouse and data marts? In what way are they different?

26.11. List the difficulties in implementing a data warehouse.

26.12. List the open issues and research problems in data warehousing.

26.13. What is data mining? How does data mining technology relate to data warehousing technology?

26.14. What are the different phases of the knowledge discovery from databases? Describe a complete application scenario in which new knowledge may be mined from an existing database of transactions.

26.15. What are the goals or tasks that data mining attempts to facilitate?

26.16. What are the five types of knowledge produced from data mining?

26.17. What are association rules as a type of knowledge? Give a definition of support and confidence and use them to define an association rule.

26.18. Describe an association rule among hierarchies with an example.

26.19. What is a negative association rule in the context of the hierarchy of Figure 26.10?

26.20. What are the difficulties of mining association rules from large databases?

26.21. Define a sequential pattern based on sequences of Itemsets.

26.22. Give an example of a pattern in a time series.

26.23. What are classification rules? How is regression related to classification?

26.24. Describe neural networks and genetic algorithms as techniques for data mining. What are the main difficulties in using these techniques?

26.25. Describe clustering and segmentation as data mining techniques.

26.26. What are the main features of data mining tools? Evaluate the features of a data mining tool not mentioned in the list in Table 26.1.

Selected Bibliography

Data warehousing has become a very popular topic and has appeared in many publications in the last few years. Inmon (1992) is credited for giving this term wide acceptance. Codd (1993) popularized the term online analytical processing (OLAP) and defined a set of characteristics for data warehouses to support OLAP. Mattison (1996) is one of the several books on data warehousing that gives a comprehensive analysis of techniques available in data warehouses and the strategies companies should use in deploying them. Bischoff and Alexander (1997) is a compilation of advice from experts. Chaudhuri and Dayal (1997) give an excellent tutorial on the topic, while Widom (1995) points to a number of outstanding research problems.

Literature on data mining comes from several fields, including statistics, mathematical optimization, machine learning, and artificial intelligence. Data mining has only recently become a topic in the database literature. We, therefore, mention only a few database-related works. Chen at al. (1996) give a good summary of the database perspective on data mining. Work at IBM Almaden research has produced a large number of early concepts and algorithms as well as results from some performance studies. Agrawal et al. (1993) report the first major study on association rules. Their a priori algorithm for market basket data in Agrawal and Srikant (1994) is improved by using partitioning in Savasere et al. (1995); Toivonen (1996) proposes sampling as a way to reduce the processing effort. Cheung et al. (1996) extends the partitioning to distributed environments; Lin and Dunham (1998) propose techniques to overcome problems with data skew. Agrawal et al. (1993b) discuss the performance perspective on association rules. Mannila et al. (1994), Park et al. (1995), and Amir et al. (1997) present additional efficient algorithms related to association rules. Srikant (1995) proposes mining generalized rules. Savasere et al. (1998) present the first approach to mining negative associations. Agrawal et al. (1996) describe the Quest system at IBM. Sarawagi et al. (1998) describe an implementation where association rules are integrated with a relational database management system. Piatesky-Shapiro and Frawley (1992) have contributed papers from a wide range of topics related to knowledge discovery.

Adriaans and Zantinge (1996) and Weiss and Indurkhya (1998) are two recent books devoted to the different aspects of data mining and its use in prediction. The idea of genetic algorithms was proposed by Holland (1975); a good survey of genetic algorithms appears in Srinivas and Patnaik (1974). Neural networks have a vast literature; a comprehensive introduction is available in Lippman (1987).

CHAPTER 27

Emerging Database Technologies and Applications

Throughout this book we have discussed a variety of issues related to the modeling, design, and functions of databases as well as to the internal structure and performance issues related to database management systems. In the previous chapter we considered variations of database management technology, such as data warehouses that provide very large databases for decision support.

We now turn our attention in this chapter to two categories of more recent developments in the database field: (1) emerging database technologies, and (2) the major application domains. The first deals with creating new environments and functionality in DBMSs so that a variety of new applications can be supported, including universal access to World Wide Web databases and databases over the Internet; multimedia databases providing additional functionality to support storage and processing of multimedia information; and mobile databases and intermittently connected databases allowing the end user to extract and carry parts of a database while being mobile in the field. Sections 27.1 through 27.3 will briefly introduce and discuss the issues and approaches to solving the specific problems that arise in three different emerging technologies.

We next consider three application domains that have historically relied upon manual processing of file systems, or tailored system solutions. Section 27.4 discusses geographic information systems, which deal with geographic data alone or spatial data combined with non-spatial data, such as census counts. Section 27.5 discusses biological databases, particularly containing genetic data on different organisms, including the human genome data. Section 27.6 discusses digital libraries, large repositories of digital data in multiple media. This is a challenging application of taking the most unstructured, diverse, and unrelated collections of documents and other library items and making them available for efficient retrieval and search within one system. A common characteristic of all these applications is the domain-specific nature of data in each specific application domain. Furthermore, they are all characterized by their "static" nature—a situation where the end user can only retrieve from the database; updating with new information is limited to database domain experts who supervise and analyze the new data being entered.

27.1 Databases on the World Wide Web

The World Wide Web (WWW)—popularly known as "the Web"—originally developed in Switzerland at CERN[1] in early 1990 as a large-scale hypermedia information service system for biological scientists to share information.[2] Today this technology allows universal access to this shared information to anyone having access to the Internet and the Web contains hundreds of millions of Web pages within the reach of millions of users.

In Web technology, a basic client-server architecture underlies all activities. Information is stored on computers designated as Web servers in publicly accessible shared files encoded using **HyperText Markup Language (HTML).** A number of tools enable users to create Web pages formatted with HTML tags, freely mixed with multimedia content—from graphics to audio and even to video. A page has many interspersed **hyperlinks**—literally a link that enables a user to "browse" or move from one page to another across the Internet. This ability has given a tremendous power to end users in searching and navigating related information—often across different continents.

Information on the Web is organized according to a **Uniform Resource Locator (URL)**—something similar to an address that provides the complete pathname of a file. The pathname consists of a string of machine and directory names separated by slashes and ends in a filename. For example, the table of contents of this book is currently at the following URL:

http://www.aw.com/cseng/authors/elmasri/Dbase3e/Dbase3e.html

A URL always begins with a **hypertext transport protocol (http),** which is the protocol used by the **Web browsers,** a program that communicates with the Web server, and vice versa. Web browsers interpret and present HTML documents to users. Popular Web browsers include the Internet Explorer of Microsoft and the Netscape Navigator. A collection of HTML documents and other files accessible via the URL on a Web server is called a **Web site.** In the above URL, "www.awl.com" may be called the Web site of Addison Wesley Publishing.

---

1. CERN stands for the French term "Conseil European pour la Recherche Nucleaire" or the European Council for Nuclear Research.

2. Berners-Lee and his team are credited with this phenomenally successful idea; see Berners-Lee et al. (1992, 1994).

27.1.1   Providing Access to Databases on the World Wide Web

Today's technology has been moving rapidly from static to dynamic Web pages, where content may be in a constant state of flux. The Web server uses a standard interface called the **Common Gateway Interface (CGI)** to act as the **middleware**—the additional software layer between the user interface front-end and the DBMS back-end that facilitates access to heterogeneous databases. The CGI middleware executes external programs or scripts to obtain the dynamic information, and it returns the information to the server in HTML, which is given back to the browser.

As the Web undergoes its latest transformations, it has become necessary to allow users access not only to file systems but to databases and DBMSs to support query processing, report generation, and so forth. The existing approaches may be divided into two categories:

1. *Access using CGI scripts:* The database server can be made to interact with the Web server via CGI. Figure 27.1 shows a schematic for the database access architecture on the Web using CGI scripts, which are written in languages like PERL, Tcl, or C. The main disadvantage of this approach is that for each user request, the Web server must start a new CGI process: each process makes a new connection with the DBMS and the Web server must wait until the results are delivered to it. No efficiency is achieved by any grouping of multiple users' requests; moreover, the developer must

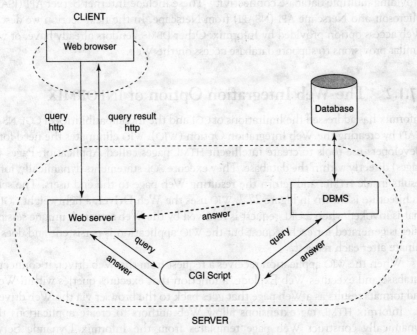

Figure 27.1   Database access on the Web using CGI Scripts.

keep the scripts in the CGI-bin subdirectories only, which opens it to a possible breach of security. The fact that CGI has no language associated with it but requires database developers to learn PERL or Tcl is also a drawback. Manageability of scripts is another problem if the scripts are scattered everywhere.

2. *Access using JDBC:* JDBC is a set of Java classes developed by Sun Microsystems to allow access to relational databases through the execution of SQL statements. It is a way of connecting with databases, without any additional processes for each client request. Note that JDBC is a name trademarked by Sun; it does *not* stand for Java Data Base connectivity as many believe. JDBC has the capabilities to connect to a database, send SQL statements to a database and to retrieve the results of a query using the Java classes Connection, Statement, and ResultSet respectively. With Java's claimed platform independence, an application may run on any Java-capable browser, which loads the Java code from the server and runs it on the client's browser. The Java code is DBMS transparent; the JDBC drivers for individual DBMSs on the server end carry the task of interacting with that DBMS. If the JDBC driver is on the client, the application runs on the client and its requests are communicated to the DBMS directly by the driver. For standard SQL requests, many RDBMSs can be accessed this way. The drawback of using JDBC is the prospect of executing Java through virtual machines with inherent efficiency. The JDBC bridge to Object Database Connectivity (ODBC) remains another way of getting to the RDBMSs.

Besides CGI, other Web server vendors are launching their own middleware products for providing multiple database connectivity. These include Internet Server API (ISAPI) from Microsoft and Netscape API (NSAPI) from Netscape. In the next section we describe the Web access option provided by Informix. Other DBMS vendors already have, or will have similar provisions to support database access on the Web.

27.1.2   The Web Integration Option of INFORMIX

Informix has addressed the limitations of CGI and the incompatibilities of CGI, NSAPI, and ISAPI by creating the Web Integration Option (WIO). WIO eliminates the need for scripts. Developers use tools to create intelligent HTML pages called Application Pages (or App Pages) directly within the database. They execute SQL statements dynamically, format the results inside HTML, and return the resulting Web page to the end users. The schematic architecture is shown in Figure 27.2. WIO uses the **Web Driver,** a lightweight CGI process that is invoked when a URL request is received by the Web server. A unique session identifier is generated for each request but the WIO application is persistent and does *not* terminate after each request.

When the WIO application receives a request from the Web driver, it connects to the database and executes Web Explode, a function that executes queries within Web pages and formats results as a Web page that goes back to the browser via the Web driver.

Informix HTML tag extensions allow Web authors to create applications that can dynamically construct Web page templates from the Informix Dynamic Server and

Figure 27.2 CGI Implementation of the Web integration option in Informix.

present them to the end users. WIO also lets users create their own customized tags to perform specialized tasks. Thus, without resorting to any programming or script development, powerful applications can be designed. Another feature of WIO helps transaction-oriented applications by providing an application programming interface (API) that offers a collection of basic services such as connection and session management that can be incorporated into Web application.

WIO supports applications developed in C, C++, and Java. This flexibility lets developers port existing applications to the Web or develop new applications in these languages. The WIO is integrated with Web server software and utilizes the native security mechanism of the Informix Dynamic Server. The open architecture of WIO allows the use of various Web browsers and servers.

27.1.3 The ORACLE WebServer

ORACLE supports Web access to databases using the components shown in Figure 27.3. The client requests files that are called "static" or "dynamic" files from the Web server. Static files have a fixed content whereas dynamic files may have content that includes results of queries to the database. There is an HTTP demon (a process that runs continuously) called Web Listener running on the server that listens for the requests originating in the clients. A static file (document) is retrieved from the file system of the server and displayed on the Web browser at the client. Request for a dynamic page is passed by the listener to a Web request broker (WRB), which is a multi-threaded dispatcher that adheres

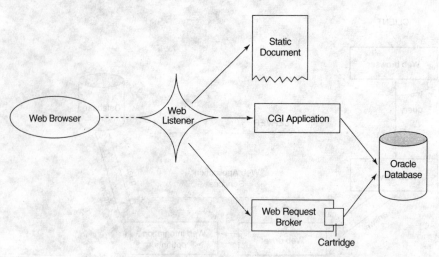

Figure 27.3   Oracle WebServer components.

to cartridges. **Cartridges** are software modules (mentioned earlier in Section 13.2.6) that perform specific functions on specific types of data; they can communicate among themselves. Currently cartridges are provided for PL/SQL, Java, and Live HTML; customized cartridges may be provided as well.

WebServer has been fully integrated with PL/SQL, making it efficient and scalable. The cartridges give it additional flexibility, making it possible to work with other languages and software packages. An advanced secure sockets layer may be used for secure communication over the Internet. The Designer 2000 development tool (see Section 16.1) has a Web generator that enables previous applications developed for LANs to be ported to the Internet and Intranet environments.

27.1.4 Open Problems with Web Databases

The Web is an important factor in planning for enterprise-wide computing environments, both for providing external access to the enterprise's systems and information for customers and suppliers and for marketing and advertising purposes. At the same time, due to security requirements, employees of some organizations are restricted to operate within **intranets**—subnetworks that cannot be accessed freely from the outside world. Among the prominent applications of the intranet and the WWW are databases to support electronic storefronts, parts and product catalogs, directories and schedules, newsstands, and bookstores. **Electronic commerce**—the purchasing of products and services electronically on the Internet—is likely to become a major application supported by such databases.

The future challenges of managing databases on the Web will be many, among them the following:

- Web technology needs to be integrated with the object technology. Currently, the web can be viewed as a distributed object system, with HTML pages functioning as objects identified by the URL.

- HTML functionality is too simple to support complex application requirements. As we saw, the Web Integration Option of Informix adds further tags to HTML. In general, additional facilities will be needed to (1) make Web clients function as application front ends, integrating data from multiple heterogeneous databases; (2) make Web clients present different views of the same data to different users; and (3) make Web clients "intelligent" by providing additional data mining functionality (see Section 26.2).

- Web page content can be made more dynamic by adding more "behavior" to it as an object (see Chapter 11 for a discussion of object modeling). In this respect (1) client and server objects (HTML pages) can be made to interact; (2) Web pages can be treated as collections of programmable objects; and (3) client-side code can access these objects and manipulate them dynamically.

- The support for a large number of clients coupled with reasonable response times for queries against very large (several tens of gigabytes in size) databases will be major challenges for Web databases. They will have to be addressed both by Web servers and by the underlying DBMSs.

Efforts are underway to address the limitations of the current data structuring technology, particularly by the World Wide Web Consortium (W3C). The W3C is designing a Web Object Model. W3C is also proposing an **Extensible Markup Language (XML)** for structured document interchange on the Web. XML defines a subset of SGML **(the Standard Generalized Markup Language),** allowing customization of markup languages with application-specific tags. XML is rapidly gaining ground due to its extensibility in defining new tags. W3C's **Document Object Model (DOM)** defines an object-oriented API for HTML or XML documents presented by a Web client. W3C is also defining metadata modeling standards for describing Internet resources.

The technology to model information using the standards discussed above and to find information on the Web is undergoing a major evolution. Overall, the Web servers have to gain robustness as a reliable technology to handle production-level databases for supporting 24×7 applications—24 hours a day, 7 days a week. Security remains a critical problem for supporting applications involving financial and medical databases. Moreover, transferring from existing database application environments to those on the Web will need adequate support that will enable users to continue their current mode of operation and an expensive infrastructure for handling migration of data among systems without introducing inconsistencies. The traditional database functionality of querying and transaction processing must undergo appropriate modifications to support Web-based applications. One such area is mobile databases, which we focus on in Section 27.3.

27.1.5   Selected Bibliography for World Wide Web Databases

The idea of World Wide Web was proposed by Berners-Lee (1992, 1994) and his group at CERN in Geneva. The Informix Web Integration Option is described in Informix (1998a). Manola (1998) discusses the developments of new standards like XML and the document object model for integration of Web technology with object technology. Mendelzon (1997) describes concepts for query processing on the Web; Gravano and Garcia-Molina (1997) propose the notion of ranking answers to free-form queries on the Web; Atzeni et al. propose a data model named ARANEUS and two languages for querying, building hypertextual views, and deriving data. Fraternali (1999) provides a survey of approaches to supporting data intensive web applications. The area of electronic commerce will draw many benefits from and share many problems with the database development on the Web; a good overview is in Dogac (1998). Several white papers are available on the database vendors' Web sites about their products providing Web access to databases (e.g., www.oracle.com, www.informix.com). The www consortium (W3C) has a Web site where up-to-date information on XML may be found: www.w3.org/XML/; protocols are described at www.w3.org/protocols/. For details on JDBC API specification, consult www.java.sun.com/products/.

27.2   Multimedia Databases

In the years ahead multimedia information systems are expected to dominate our daily lives. Our houses will be wired for bandwidth to handle interactive multimedia applications. Our high-definition TV/computer workstations will have access to a large number of databases, including digital libraries (see Section 27.6) that will distribute vast amounts of multisource multimedia content.

27.2.1   The Nature of Multimedia Data and Applications

In Section 23.3 we discussed the advanced modeling issues related to multimedia data. We also examined the processing of multiple types of data in Chapter 13 in the context of object relational DBMSs (ORDBMSs). DBMSs have been constantly adding to the types of data they support. Today the following types of multimedia data are available in current systems:

- *Text:* May be formatted or unformatted. For ease of parsing structured documents, standards like SGML and variations such as HTML are being used.

- *Graphics:* Examples include drawings and illustrations that are encoded using some descriptive standards (e.g., CGM, PICT, postscript).

- *Images:* Includes drawings, photographs, and so forth, encoded in standard formats such as bitmap, JPEG, and MPEG. Compression is built into JPEG and MPEG. These images are not subdivided into components. Hence querying them by content (e.g., find all images containing circles) is nontrivial.

- *Animations:* Temporal sequences of image or graphic data.
- *Video:* A set of temporally sequenced photographic data for presentation at specified rates—for example, 30 frames per second.
- *Structured audio:* A sequence of audio components comprising note, tone, duration, and so forth.
- *Audio:* Sample data generated from aural recordings in a string of bits in digitized form. Analog recordings are typically converted into digital form before storage.
- *Composite or mixed multimedia data:* A combination of multimedia data types such as audio and video which may be physically mixed to yield a new storage format or logically mixed while retaining original types and formats. Composite data also contains additional control information describing how the information should be rendered.

Nature of Multimedia Applications. Multimedia data may be stored, delivered, and utilized in many different ways. Applications may be categorized based on their data management characteristics as follows:

- *Repository applications:* A large amount of multimedia data as well as metadata is stored for retrieval purposes. A central repository containing multimedia data may be maintained by a DBMS and may be organized into a hierarchy of storage levels—local disks, tertiary disks and tapes, optical disks, and so on. Examples include repositories of satellite images, engineering drawings and designs, space photographs, and radiology scanned pictures.
- *Presentation applications:* A large number of applications involve delivery of multimedia data subject to temporal constraints. Audio and video data are delivered this way; in these applications optimal viewing or listening conditions require the DBMS to deliver data at certain rates offering "quality of service" above a certain threshold. Data is consumed as it is delivered, unlike in repository applications, where it may be processed later (e.g., multimedia electronic mail). Simple multimedia viewing of video data, for example, requires a system to simulate VCR-like functionality. Complex and interactive multimedia presentations involve orchestration directions to control the retrieval order of components in a series or in parallel. Interactive environments must support capabilities such as real-time editing analysis or annotating of video and audio data.
- *Collaborative work using multimedia information:* This is a new category of applications in which engineers may execute a complex design task by merging drawings, fitting subjects to design constraints, and generating new documentation, change notifications, and so forth. Intelligent healthcare networks as well as telemedicine will involve doctors collaborating among themselves, analyzing multimedia patient data and information in real time as it is generated.

All of these application areas present major challenges for the design of multimedia database systems.

27.2.2   Data Management Issues

Multimedia applications dealing with thousands of images, documents, audio and video segments, and free text data depend critically on appropriate modeling of the structure and content of data and then designing appropriate database schemas for storing and retrieving multimedia information. Multimedia information systems are very complex and embrace a large set of issues, including the following:

- *Modeling:* This area has the potential for applying database versus information retrieval techniques to the problem. There are problems of dealing with complex objects (see Chapter 11) made up of a wide range of types of data: numeric, text, graphic (computer-generated image), animated graphic image, audio stream, and video sequence. Documents constitute a specialized area and deserve special consideration.

- *Design:* The conceptual, logical, and physical design of multimedia databases has not been addressed fully, and it remains an area of active research. The design process can be based on the general methodology described in Chapter 16, but the performance and tuning issues at each level are far more complex.

- *Storage:* Storage of multimedia data on standard disklike devices presents problems of representation, compression, mapping to device hierarchies, archiving, and buffering during the input/output operation. Adhering to standards such as JPEG or MPEG is one way most vendors of multimedia products are likely to deal with this issue. In DBMSs, a "BLOB" (Binary Large Object) facility allows untyped bitmaps to be stored and retrieved. Standardized software will be required to deal with synchronization and compression/decompression, and will be coupled with indexing problems, which are still in the research domain.

- *Queries and retrieval:* The "database" way of retrieving information is based on query languages and internal index structures. The "information retrieval" way relies strictly on keywords or predefined index terms. For images, video data, and audio data, this opens up many issues, among them efficient query formulation, query execution, and optimization. The standard optimization techniques we discussed in Chapter 18 need to be modified to work with multimedia data types.

- *Performance:* For multimedia applications involving only documents and text, performance constraints are subjectively determined by the user. For applications involving video playback or audio-video synchronization, physical limitations dominate. For instance, video must be delivered at a steady rate of 60 frames per second. Techniques for query optimization may compute expected response time before evaluating the query. The use of parallel processing of data may alleviate some problems, but such efforts are currently subject to further experimentation.

Such issues have given rise to a variety of open research problems. We look at a few representative problems now.

27.2.3   Open Research Problems

Databases versus Information Retrieval Perspectives.   Modeling data content has not been an issue in database models and systems because the data has a rigid structure and the meaning of a data instance can be inferred from the schema. In contrast, information retrieval (IR) is mainly concerned with modeling the content of text documents (through the use of keywords, phrasal indexes, semantic networks, word frequencies, soundex encoding, and so on) for which structure is generally neglected. By modeling content, the system can determine whether a document is relevant to a query by examining the content-descriptors of the document. Consider, for instance, an insurance company's accident claim report as a multimedia object: it includes images of the accident, structured insurance forms, audio recordings of the parties involved in the accident, the text report of the insurance company's representative, and other information. Which data model should be used to represent multimedia information such as this? How should queries be formulated against this data? Efficient execution thus becomes a complex issue, and the semantic heterogeneity and representational complexity of multimedia information gives rise to many new problems.

Requirements of Multimedia/Hypermedia Data Modeling and Retrieval. To capture the full expressive power of multimedia data modeling, the system should have a general construct that lets the user specify links between any two arbitrary nodes. **Hypermedia links** or hyperlinks have a number of different characteristics:

- Links can be specified with or without associated information, and they may have large descriptions associated with them.
- Links can start from a specific point within a node or from the whole node.
- Links can be directional or nondirectional when they can be traversed in either direction.

The link capability of the data model should take into account all of these variations. When content-based retrieval of multimedia data is needed, the query mechanism should have access to the links and the link-associated information. The system should provide facilities for defining views over all links—private and public. Valuable contextual information can be obtained from the structural information. Automatically generated hypermedia links do not reveal anything new about the two nodes, and in contrast to manually generated hypermedia links, would have different significance. Facilities for creating and utilizing such links, as well as developing and using navigational query languages to utilize the links, are important features of any system permitting effective use of multimedia information. This area is important to interlinked databases on the WWW. (See Section 27.1 for a discussion of WWW databases.)

Indexing of Images. There are two approaches to indexing images: (1) identifying objects automatically through image-processing techniques, and (2) assigning index terms and phrases through manual indexing. An important problem in using image-processing techniques to index pictures relates to scalability. The current state of the art allows the indexing of only simple patterns in images. Complexity increases with the number of recognizable features. Another important problem relates to the complexity of the query. Rules and inference mechanisms, as discussed in Chapter 25, can be used to derive higher-level facts from simple features of images. This allows high-level queries like "find hotel buildings that have open foyers and allow maximum sunshine in the front desk area" in an architectural application.

The information-retrieval approach to image indexing is based on one of three indexing schemes:

1. *Classificatory systems:* Classifies images hierarchically into predetermined categories. In this approach, the indexer and the user should have a good knowledge of the available categories. Finer details of a complex image and relationships among objects in an image cannot be captured.

2. *Keyword-based systems:* Uses an indexing vocabulary similar to that used in the indexing of textual documents. Simple facts represented in the image (like "ice-capped region") and facts derived as a result of high-level interpretation by humans (like permanent ice, recent snowfall, and polar ice) can be captured.

3. *Entity-attribute-relationship systems:* All objects in the picture and the relationships between objects and the attributes of the objects are identified.

In the case of text documents, an indexer can choose the keywords from the pool of words available in the document to be indexed. This is not possible in the case of visual and video data.

Problems in Text Retrieval.   Text retrieval has always been the key feature in business applications and library systems, and although much work has gone into some of the following problems, there remains an ongoing need for improvement, especially regarding the following issues:

- *Phrase indexing:* Substantial improvements can be realized if phrase descriptors (as opposed to single-word index terms) are assigned to documents and used in queries, provided that these descriptors are good indicators of document content and information need.

- *Use of thesaurus:* One reason for the poor recall of current systems is that the vocabulary of the user differs from the vocabulary used to index the documents. One solution is to use a thesaurus to expand the user's query with related terms. The problem then becomes one of finding a thesaurus for the domain of interest.

- *Resolving ambiguity:* One of the reasons for low precision (the ratio of the number of relevant items retrieved to the total number of retrieved items) in text information retrieval systems is that words have multiple meanings. One way to resolve ambiguity is to use an on-line dictionary; another is to compare the contexts in which the two words occur.

In the first three decades of DBMS development—roughly from 1965 to 1995—the primary focus had been on the management of mostly numeric business and industrial data. In the next few decades, nonnumeric textual information will probably dominate database content. As a consequence, a variety of functionalities involving comparison, conceptualization, understanding, indexing, and summarization of documents will be added to DBMSs. We saw the use of the text datablade in Section 13.2.6 for the INFORMIX

DBMS. Multimedia information systems promise to bring about a joining of disciplines that have historically been separate areas: information retrieval and database management.

27.2.4 Multimedia Database Applications

Large-scale applications of multimedia databases can be expected to encompass a large number of disciplines and enhance existing capabilities. Some important applications will be involved:

- *Documents and records management:* A large number of industries and businesses keep very detailed records and a variety of documents. The data may include engineering design and manufacturing data, medical records of patients, publishing material, and insurance claim records.

- *Knowledge dissemination:* The multimedia mode, a very effective means of knowledge dissemination, will encompass a phenomenal growth in electronic books, catalogs, manuals, encyclopedias and repositories of information on many topics.

- *Education and training:* Teaching materials for different audiences—from kindergarten students to equipment operators to professionals—can be designed from multimedia sources. Digital libraries are expected to have a major influence on the way future students and researchers as well as other users will access vast repositories of educational material. (See Section 27.6 on digital libraries.)

- *Marketing, advertising, retailing, entertainment, and travel:* There are virtually no limits to using multimedia information in these applications—from effective sales presentations to virtual tours of cities and art galleries. The film industry has already shown the power of special effects in creating animations and synthetically designed animals, aliens, and special effects. The use of predesigned stored objects in multimedia databases will expand the range of these applications.

- *Real-time control and monitoring:* Coupled with active database technology (see Section 23.1), multimedia presentation of information can be a very effective means for monitoring and controlling complex tasks such as manufacturing operations, nuclear power plants, patients in intensive care units, and transportation systems.

Commercial Systems for Multimedia Information Management.   There are no DBMSs designed for the sole purpose of multimedia data management, and therefore there are none that have the range of functionality required to fully support all of the multimedia information management applications that we discussed above. However, several DBMSs today support multimedia data types; these include Informix Dynamic Server, DB2 Universal database (UDB) of IBM, Oracle 8.0 (see Chapter 10), CA- JASMINE, Sybase, ODB II. All of these DBMSs have support for objects, which is essential for modeling a variety of complex multimedia objects. One major problem with these systems is that the "blades, cartridges, and extenders" for handling multimedia data are designed in a very ad hoc manner. The functionality is provided without much apparent attention to scalability and performance. There are products available that operate either stand-alone or in conjunction with other vendors' systems to allow retrieval of image data by content. They include Virage, Excalibur, and IBM's QBIC. Operations on multimedia need to be standardized. The MPEG-7 and other standards are addressing some of these issues.

27.2.5 Selected Bibliography on Multimedia Databases

Multimedia database management is becoming a very heavily researched area with several industrial projects on the way. Grosky (1994, 1997) provides two excellent tutorials on the topic. Pazandak and Srivastava (1995) provide an evaluation of database systems related to the requirements of multimedia databases. Grosky et al. (1997) contains contributed articles including a survey on content-based indexing and retrieval by Jagadish (1997). Faloutsos et al. (1994) also discuss a system for image querying by content. Li et al. (1998) introduce image modeling in which an image is viewed as a hierarchical structured complex object with both semantics and visual properties. Nwosu et al. (1996) and Subramanian and Jajodia (1997) have written books on the topic. The following WWW references may be consulted for additional information:

CA- JASMINE (Multimedia ODBMS): http://www.cai.com/products/jasmine.htm

ODB II (Multimedia ODBMS): http://www.datamation.com/plugIn/inserts/FOSSI/ODB2/odb2main.html

Excalibur technologies: http://www.excalib.com

Virage, Inc (Content based image retrieval): http://www.virage.com

IBM's QBIC (Query by Image Content) product: http://www.ibm.com

27.3 Mobile Databases

Recent advances in wireless technology have led to **mobile computing**, a new dimension in data communication and processing. The mobile computing environment will provide database applications with useful aspects of wireless technology. The mobile computing platform allows users to establish communication with other users and to manage their work while they are mobile. This feature is especially useful to geographically dispersed organizations. Typical examples might include traffic police, taxi dispatchers, and weather reporting services, as well as financial market reporting and information brokering applications. However, there are a number of hardware as well as software problems that must be resolved before the capabilities of mobile computing can be fully utilized. Some of the software problems—which may involve data management, transaction management, and database recovery—have their origin in distributed database systems. In mobile computing, however, these problems become more difficult to solve, mainly because of the narrow bandwidth of the wireless communication channels, the relatively short active life of the power supply (battery) of mobile units, and the changing locations of required information (sometimes in cache, sometimes in the air, sometimes at the server). In addition, mobile computing has its own unique architectural challenges.

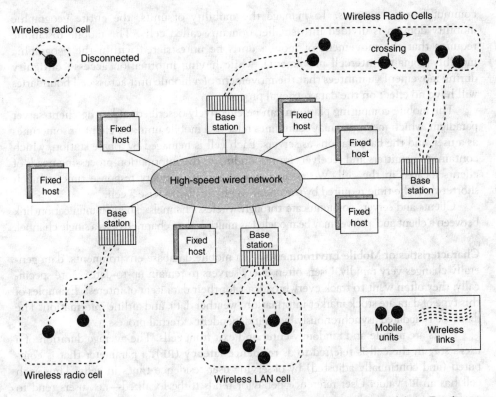

Figure 27.4   A general architecture of a mobile platform. (Adapted from Dunham and Helal (1995).)

27.3.1 Mobile Computing Architecture

The general architecture of a mobile platform is illustrated in Figure 27.4. It is a distributed architecture where a number of computers, generally referred to as **Fixed Hosts (FS)** and **Base Stations (BS),** are interconnected through a high-speed wired network. Fixed hosts are general purpose computers that are not equipped to manage mobile units but can be configured to do so. Base stations are equipped with wireless interfaces and can communicate with mobile units to support data access.

Mobile Units (MU) (or hosts) and base stations communicate through wireless channels having bandwidths significantly lower than those of a wired network. A **downlink channel** is used for sending data from a BS to an MU and an **uplink channel** is used for sending data from an MU to its BS. Recent products for portable wireless have an upper limit of 1 Mbps (megabits per second) for infrared communication, 2 Mbps for radio communication, and 9.14 Kbps (kilobits per second) for cellular telephony. Ethernet, by comparison, provides 10 Mbps fast Ethernet and FDDI provide 100 Mbps and ATM (asynchronous transfer mode) provides 155 Mbps.

Mobile units are battery-powered portable computers that move freely in a **geographic mobility domain,** an area that is restricted by the limited bandwidth of wireless communication channels. To manage the mobility of units, the entire geographic mobility domain is divided into smaller domains called **cells.** The mobile discipline requires that the movement of mobile units be unrestricted within the geographic mobility domain (intercell movement), while having information **access contiguity** during movement guarantees that the movement of a mobile unit across cell boundaries will have no effect on the data retrieval process.

The mobile computing platform can be effectively described under the client-server paradigm, which means we may sometimes refer to a mobile unit as a client or sometimes as a user, and the base stations as servers. Each cell is managed by a base station, which contains transmitters and receivers for responding to the information-processing needs of clients located in the cell. We assume that the average query response time is much shorter than the time required by the client to physically traverse a cell.

Clients and servers communicate through wireless channels. The communication link between a client and a server may be modeled as multiple data channels or as a single channel.

Characteristics of Mobile Environments.   In mobile database environments, data generally changes very rapidly. Users often query servers to remain up-to-date. More specifically, they often want to track every broadcast for their data item of interest. Examples of this type of data are stock market information, weather data, and airline information. The database is updated asynchronously by an independent external process.

Users are mobile and randomly enter and exit from cells. The average duration of a user's stay in the cell is referred to as **residence latency (RL),** a parameter that is computed (and continually adjusted) by observing user residence times in cells. Thus each cell has an RL value. User reference behavior tends to be localized—i.e., users tend to access certain parts of the database very frequently. Servers maintain neither client arrival and departure patterns nor client-specific data request information.

Wireless networks differ from wired networks in many ways. Database users over a wired network remain connected not only to the network but also to a continuous power source. Thus, response time is the key performance metric. In a wireless network, however, both the response time and the active life of the user's power source (battery) are important. While a mobile unit is listening or transmitting on-line, it is considered to be in active mode. For current laptops with CD-ROM drives, estimated battery life in active mode is under 3 hours. In order to conserve energy and extend battery life, clients can slip into a **doze mode,** where they are not actively listening on the channel and they can expend significantly less energy than they do in active mode. Clients can be woken up from the doze mode when the server needs to communicate with the client.

27.3.2   Types of Data in Mobile Applications

Applications that run on mobile hosts have different data requirements. Users either engage in personal communications or office activities, or they simply receive updates on frequently changing information. Mobile applications can be categorized in two ways: (1) vertical applications and (2) horizontal applications.[3] In **vertical applications** users access

---

3. This classification of applications and type of data is proposed by Imielinski and Badrinath (1994).

data within a specific cell, and access is denied to users outside of that cell. For example, users can obtain information on the location of doctors or emergency centers within a cell or parking availability data at an airport cell. In **horizontal applications,** users coop- erate on accomplishing a task, and they can handle data distributed throughout the sys- tem. The horizontal application market is massive; two types of applications most mentioned are mail-enabled applications and information services to mobile users.

Data may be classified into three categories:

1. *Private data:* A single user owns this data and manages it. No other user may access it.

2. *Public data:* This data can be used by anyone who can read it. Only one source updates it. Examples include weather bulletins or stock prices.

3. *Shared data:* This data is accessed both in read and write modes by groups of users. Examples include inventory data for products in a company.

Public data is primarily managed by vertical applications, while shared data is used by horizontal applications, possibly with some replication. Copies of shared data may be stored both in base and mobile stations. This presents a variety of difficult problems in transaction management consistency as well as integrity and scalability of the architecture.

27.3.3 Data Management Issues

From a data management standpoint, mobile computing may be considered a variation of distributed computing. Mobile databases can be distributed under two possible scenarios:

1. The entire database is distributed mainly among the wired components, possibly with full or partial replication. A base station manages its own database with a DBMS-like functionality, with additional functionality for locating mobile units and additional query and transaction management features to meet the require- ments of mobile environments.

2. The database is distributed among wired and wireless components. Data manage- ment responsibility is shared among base stations and mobile units.

Hence, the distributed data management issues we discussed in Chapter 24 can also be applied to mobile databases with the following additional considerations and variations:

1. *Data distribution and replication:* Data is unevenly distributed among the base sta- tions and mobile units. The consistency constraints compound the problem of cache management. Caches attempt to provide the most frequently accessed and updated data to mobile units that process their own transactions and may be dis- connected over long periods.

2. *Transaction models:* Issues of fault tolerance and correctness of transactions are aggravated in the mobile environment. A mobile transaction is executed sequen- tially through several base stations and possibly on multiple data sets depending upon the movement of the mobile unit. Central coordination of transaction exe- cution is lacking, particularly in scenario (2) above. Hence, traditional ACID

properties of transactions (see Chapter 19) may need to be modified and new transaction models must be defined.

3. *Query processing:* Awareness of where the data is located is important and affects the cost/benefit analysis of query processing. The query response needs to be returned to mobile units that may be in transit or may cross cell boundaries yet must receive complete and correct query results.

4. *Recovery and fault tolerance:* The mobile database environment must deal with site, media, transaction, and communication failures. Site failure at an MU is frequently due to limited battery power. If an MU has a voluntary shutdown, it should *not* be treated as a failure. Transaction failures are more frequent during handoff when an MU crosses cells. MU failure causes a network partitioning and affects routing algorithms.

5. *Mobile database design:* The global name resolution problem for handling queries is compounded because of mobility and frequent shutdown. Mobile database design must consider many issues of metadata management—for example, the constant updating of location information.

27.3.4   Intermittently Synchronized Mobile Databases

A different scenario promises to become increasingly commonplace as people conduct their work away from their offices and homes and perform a wide range of activities and functions: all kinds of sales, particularly in pharmaceuticals, consumer goods, and industrial parts; law enforcement; insurance and financial consulting and planning; real estate or property management activities, and so on. In these applications, a server or a group of servers manages the central database and the clients carry laptops or palmtops with a resident DBMS software to do "local" transaction activity for most of the time. The clients connect via a network or a dial-up connection (or possibly even through the Internet) with the server, typically for a short session—say, 30 to 60 minutes. They send their updates to the server, and the server must in turn enter them in its central database, which must maintain up-to-date data and prepare appropriate copies for all clients on the system. Thus, whenever clients connect—through a process known in the industry as synchronization of a client with a server—they receive a batch of updates to be installed on their local database. The primary characteristic of this scenario is that the clients are mostly disconnected; the server is not necessarily able to reach the client. This environment has problems similar to those in distributed and client-server databases, and some from mobile databases, but presents several additional research problems for investigation. We refer to this environment as **Intermittently Synchronized Database Environment (ISDBE),** and the corresponding databases as Intermittently Synchronized Databases (ISDBs).

The following characteristics of ISDB's make them *distinct* from the mobile databases we have discussed thus far:

1. A client connects to server when it wants to receive updates from a server or to send its updates to a server or to process transactions that need nonlocal data. This communication may be *unicast*—one-on-one communication between the

server and the client—or *multicast*—one sender or server may periodically communicate to a set of receivers or update a group of clients.

2. A server cannot connect to a client at will.

3. Issues of wireless versus wired client connections and power conservation are immaterial.

4. A client is free to manage its own data and transactions while it is disconnected. It can also perform its own recovery to some extent.

5. A client has multiple ways of connecting to a server and, in case of many servers, may choose a particular server to connect to based on proximity, communication nodes available, etc.

Because of such differences, there is a need to address a number of problems related to ISDBs that are different from those typically involving mobile database systems. These include server database design for server databases, consistency management among client and server databases transaction and update processing, efficient use of the server bandwidth, and achieving scalability in the ISDB environments.

27.3.5 Selected Bibliography for Mobile Databases

There has been a sudden surge of interest in mobile computing, and research on mobile databases has had a significant growth for the last five to six years. Among books written on this topic, Dhawan (1997) is an excellent source on mobile computing. Wireless networks and their future is discussed in Holtzman and Goodman (1993). Imielinski and Badrinath (1994) provide a good survey of database issues. Dunham and Helal (1995) discuss problems of query processing, data distribution, and transaction management for mobile databases. Foreman and Zahorjan (1994) describe the capabilities and the problems of mobile computing and make a convincing argument in its favor as a viable solution for many information system applications of the future. Pitoura and Samaras (1998) describe all aspects of mobile database problems and solutions. Chintalapati et al. (1997) provide an adaptive location management algorithm while Bertino et al. (1998) discuss approaches to fault tolerance and recovery in mobile databases. The June 1995 issue of *Byte* magazine discusses many aspects of mobile computing. For an initial discussion of the ISDB scalability issues and an approach by aggregation of data and grouping of clients, see Mahajan et al. (1998).

27.4 Geographic Information Systems

Geographic information systems (GIS) are used to collect, model, store, and analyze information describing physical properties of the geographical world. The scope of GIS broadly encompasses two types of data: (1) spatial data, originating from maps, digital images, administrative and political boundaries, roads, transportation networks; physical data such as rivers, soil characteristics, climatic regions, land elevations, and (2) nonspatial data, such as census counts, economic data, and sales or marketing information. GIS is a rapidly developing domain that offers highly innovative approaches to meet some challenging technical demands.

27.4.1 GIS Applications

It is possible to divide GISs into three categories: (1) cartographic applications, (2) digital terrain modeling applications, and (3) geographic objects applications. Figure 27.5 summarizes these categories.

In cartographic and terrain modeling applications, variations in spatial attributes are captured—for example, soil characteristics, crop density, and air quality. In geographic objects applications, objects of interest are identified from a physical domain—for example, power plants, electoral districts, property parcels, product distribution districts, and city landmarks. These objects are related with pertinent application data—which may be, for this specific example, power consumption, voting patterns, property sales volumes, product sales volume, and traffic density.

The first two categories of GIS applications require a field-based representation, whereas the third category requires an object-based one. The cartographic approach involves special functions that can include the overlapping of layers of maps to combine attribute data that will allow, for example, the measuring of distances in three-dimensional space and the reclassification of data on the map. Digital terrain modeling requires a digital representation of parts of earth's surface using land elevations at sample points

Figure 27.5 A possible classification of GIS applications. (Adapted from Adam and Gangopadhyay (1997).)

that are connected to yield a surface model such as a three-dimensional net (connected lines in 3D) showing the surface terrain. It requires functions of interpolation between observed points as well as visualization. In object-based geographic applications, additional spatial functions are needed to deal with data related to roads, physical pipelines, communication cables, power lines, and such. For example, for a given region, comparable maps can be used for comparison at various points of time to show changes in certain data such as locations of roads, cables, buildings, and streams.

27.4.2 Data Management Requirements of GIS

The functional requirements of the GIS applications above translate into the following database requirements.

Data Modeling and Representation.   GIS data can be broadly represented in two formats: (1) vector and (2) raster. Vector data represents geometric objects such as points, lines, and polygons. Thus a lake may be represented as a polygon, a river by a series of line segments. Raster data is characterized as an array of points, where each point represents the value of an attribute for a real-world location. Informally, raster images are n-dimensional arrays where each entry is a unit of the image and represents an attribute. Two-dimensional units are called *pixels*, while three-dimensional units are called *voxels*. Three-dimensional elevation data is stored in a raster-based **digital elevation model (DEM)** format. Another raster format called **triangular irregular network (TIN)** is a topological vector-based approach that models surfaces by connecting sample points as vertices of triangles and has a point density that may vary with the roughness of the terrain. Rectangular grids (or elevation matrices) are two-dimensional array structures. In **digital terrain modeling (DTM),** the model also may be used by substituting the elevation with some attribute of interest such as population density or air temperature. GIS data often includes a temporal structure in addition to a spatial structure. For example, traffic density may be measured every 60 seconds at a set of points.

Data Analysis.   GIS data undergoes various types of analysis. For example, in applications such as soil erosion studies, environmental impact studies, or hydrological runoff simulations, DTM data may undergo various types of **geomorphometric analysis**—measurements such as slope values, *gradients* (the rate of change in altitude), *aspect* (the compass direction of the gradient), *profile convexity* (the rate of change of gradient), *plan convexity* (the convexity of contours and other parameters). When GIS data is used for decision support applications, it may undergo aggregation and expansion operations using data warehousing, as we discussed in Section 26.1.5. In addition, geometric operations (to compute distances, areas, volumes), topological operations (to compute overlaps, intersections, shortest paths), and temporal operations (to compute internal-based or event-based queries) are involved. Analysis involves a number of temporal and spatial operations, which were discussed in Sections 23.2 and 23.3.

Data Integration.   GISs must integrate both vector and raster data from a variety of sources. Sometimes edges and regions are inferred from a raster image to form a vector model, or conversely, raster images such as aerial photographs are used to update vector models. Several coordinate systems such as Universal Transverse Mercator (UTM), latitude/longitude, and local cadastral systems are used to identify locations. Data originating from different coordinate systems requires appropriate transformations. Major public sources of geographic data, including the TIGER files maintained by U.S. Department of Commerce, are used for road maps by many Web-based map drawing tools (e.g., http:// maps.yahoo.com). Often there are high-accuracy, attribute-poor maps that have to be merged with low-accuracy, attribute-rich maps. This is done with a process called "rubberbanding" where the user defines a set of control points in both maps and the transformation of the low accuracy map is accomplished to line up the control points. A major integration issue is to create and maintain attribute information (such as air quality or traffic density) which can be related to and integrated with appropriate geographical information over time as both evolve.

Data Capture.   The first step in developing a spatial database for cartographic modeling is to capture the two-dimensional or three-dimensional geographical information in digital form—a process that is sometimes impeded by source map characteristics such as resolution, type of projection, map scales, cartographic licensing, diversity of measurement techniques, and coordinate system differences. Spatial data can also be captured from remote sensors in satellites such as Landsat, NORA, and Advanced Very High Resolution Radiometer (AVHRR) as well as SPOT HRV (High Resolution Visible Range Instrument), which is free of interpretive bias and very accurate. For digital terrain modeling, data capture methods range from manual to fully automated. Ground surveys are the traditional approach and the most accurate, but they are very time consuming. Other techniques include photogrammetric sampling and digitizing cartographic documents.

27.4.3   Specific GIS Data Operations

GIS applications are conducted through the use of special operators such as the following:

- *Interpolation:* This process derives elevation data for points at which no samples have been taken. It includes computation at single points, computation for a rectangular grid or along a contour, and so forth. Most interpolation methods are based on triangulation that uses the TIN method for interpolating elevations inside the triangle based on those of its vertices.

- *Interpretation:* Digital terrain modeling involves the interpretation of operations on terrain data such as editing, smoothing, reducing details, and enhancing. Additional operations involve patching or zipping the borders of triangles (in TIN data), and merging, which implies combining overlapping models and resolving conflicts among attribute data. Conversions among grid models, contour models, and TIN data are involved in the interpretation of the terrain.

- *Proximity analysis:* Several classes of proximity analysis include computations of "zones of interest" around objects, such as the determination of a buffer around a car on a highway. Shortest path algorithms using 2D or 3D information is an important class of proximity analysis.

- *Raster image processing:* This process can be divided into two categories (1) map algebra, which is used to integrate geographic features on different map layers to produce new maps algebraically; and (2) digital image analysis, which deals with analysis of a digital image for features such as edge detection and object detection. Detecting roads in a satellite image of a city is an example of the latter.

- *Analysis of networks:* Networks occur in GIS in many contexts that must be analyzed and may be subjected to segmentations, overlays, and so on. Network overlay refers to a type of spatial join where a given network—for example, a highway network—is joined with a point database—for example, accident locations—to yield, in this case, a profile of high-accident roadways.

Other Database Functionality. The functionality of a GIS database is also subject to other considerations.

- *Extensibility:* GISs are required to be extensible to accommodate a variety of constantly evolving applications and corresponding data types. If a standard DBMS is used, it must allow a core set of data types with a provision for defining additional types and methods for those types.

- *Data quality control:* As in many other applications, quality of source data is of paramount importance for providing accurate results to queries. This problem is particularly significant in the GIS context because of the variety of data, sources, and measurement techniques involved and the absolute accuracy expected by applications users.

- *Visualization:* A crucial function in GIS is related to visualization—the graphical display of terrain information and the appropriate representation of application attributes to go with it. Major visualization techniques include (1) *contouring* through the use of *isolines*, spatial units of lines or arcs of equal attribute values; (2) *hillshading*, an illumination method used for qualitative relief depiction using varied light intensities for individual facets of the terrain model; and (3) *perspective displays*, three-dimensional images of terrain model facets using perspective projection methods from computer graphics. These techniques impose cartographic data and other three-dimensional objects on terrain data providing animated scene renderings such as those in flight simulations and animated movies.

Such requirements clearly illustrate that standard RDBMSs or ODBMSs do not meet the special needs of GIS. It is therefore necessary to design systems that support the vector and raster representations and the spatial functionality as well as the required DBMS features. A popular GIS called ARC-INFO, which is *not* a DBMS but integrates RDBMS functionality in the INFO part of the system, is briefly discussed in the subsection that follows. More systems are likely to be designed in the future to work with relational or object databases that will contain some of the spatial and most of the nonspatial information.

27.4.4　An Example of a GIS: ARC-INFO

ARC/INFO—a popular GIS launched in 1981 by Environmental System Research Institute (ESRI)—uses the arc node model to store spatial data. A geographic layer—called *coverage* in ARC/INFO—consists of three primitives: (1) nodes (points), (2) arcs (similar to lines), and (3) polygons. The arc is the most important of the three and stores a large amount of topological information. An arc has a start node and an end node (and it therefore has direction too). In addition, the polygons to the left and the right of the arc are also stored along with each arc. As there is no restriction on the shape of the arc, shape points that have no topological information are also stored along with each arc. The database managed by the INFO RDBMS thus consists of three required tables: (1) node attribute table (NAT), (2) arc attribute table (AAT), and (3) polygon attribute table (PAT). Additional information can be stored in separate tables and joined with any of these three tables.

The NAT contains an internal ID for the node, a user-specified ID, the coordinates of the node, and any other information associated with that node (e.g., names of the intersecting roads at the node). The AAT contains an internal ID for the arc, a user-specified ID, the internal ID of the start and end nodes, the internal ID of the polygons to the left and the right, a series of coordinates of shape points (if any), the length of the arc, and any other data associated with the arc (e.g., the name of the road the arc represents). The PAT contains an internal ID for the polygon, a user-specified ID, the area of the polygon, the perimeter of the polygon, and any other associated data (e.g., name of the county the polygon represents).

Typical spatial queries are related to adjacency, containment, and connectivity. The arc node model has enough information to satisfy all three types of queries, but the RDBMS is not ideally suited for this type of querying. A simple example will highlight the number of times a relational database has to be queried to extract adjacency information. Assume that we are trying to determine whether two polygons, A and B, are adjacent to each other. We would have to exhaustively look at the entire AAT to determine whether there is an edge that has A on one side and B on the other. The search cannot be limited to the edges of either polygon as we do not explicitly store all the arcs that make a polygon in the PAT. Storing all the arcs in the PAT would be redundant because all the information is already there in the AAT.

ESRI has released Arc/Storm (Arc Store Manager) which allows multiple users to use the same GIS, handles distributed databases, and integrates with other commercial RDBMSs like ORACLE, INFORMIX, and SYBASE. While it offers many performance and functional advantages over ARC/INFO, it is essentially an RDBMS embedded within a GIS.

27.4.5　Problems and Future Issues in GIS

GIS is an expanding application area of databases, reflecting an explosion in the number of end users using digitized maps, terrain data, space images, weather data, and traffic information support data. As a consequence, an increasing number of problems related to GIS applications have been generated and will need to be solved:

- *New architectures:* GIS applications will need a new client-server architecture that will benefit from existing advances in RDBMS and ODBMS technology. One possible solution is to separate spatial from nonspatial data and to manage the latter entirely by a DBMS. Such a process calls for appropriate modeling and integration as both types of data evolve. Commercial vendors find that it is more viable to keep a small number of independent databases with an automatic posting of updates across them. Appropriate tools for data transfer, change management, and workflow management will be required.

- *Versioning and object life-cycle approach:* Because of constantly evolving geographical features, GISs must maintain elaborate cartographic and terrain data—a management problem that might be eased by incremental updating coupled with update authorization schemes for different levels of users. Under the object life-cycle approach, which covers the activities of creating, destroying, and modifying objects as well as promoting versions into permanent objects, a complete set of methods may be predefined to control these activities for GIS objects.

- *Data standards:* Because of the diversity of representation schemes and models, formalization of data transfer standards is crucial for the success of GIS. The international standardization body (ISO TC211) and the European standards body (CEN TC278) are now in the process of debating relevant issues—among them conversion between vector and raster data for fast query performance.

- *Matching applications and data structures:* Looking again at Figure 27.5, we see that a classification of GIS applications is based on the nature and organization of data. In the future, systems covering a wide range of functions—from market analysis and utilities to car navigation—will need boundary-oriented data and functionality. On the other hand, applications in environmental science, hydrology, and agriculture will require more area-oriented and terrain model data. It is not clear that all this functionality can be supported by a single general-purpose GIS. The specialized needs of GISs will require that general purpose DBMSs must be enhanced with additional data types and functionality before full-fledged GIS applications can be supported.

- *Lack of semantics in data structures:* This is evident especially in maps. Information such as highway and road crossings may be difficult to determine based on the stored data. One way streets are also hard to represent in the present GISs. Transportation CAD systems have incorporated such semantics into GIS.

27.4.6 Selected Bibliography for GIS

There are a number of books written on GIS. Adam and Gangopadhyay (1997) and Laurini and Thompson (1992) focus on GIS database and information management problems. Kemp (1993) gives an overview of GIS issues and data sources. Maguire et al. (1991) have a very good collection of GIS-related papers. Sarasua and O'Neill (1999) concentrate on GIS for transportation systems. The TIGER files for road data in the United States are managed by the U.S. Department of Commerce (1993). Laser-Scan's Web site (http://www.lsl.co.uk/papers) is a good source of information.

Environmental System Research Institute (ESRI) has an excellent library of GIS books for all levels at http://www.esri.com. The GIS terminology is defined at http://www.esri.com/library/glossary/glossary.html.

27.5 Genome Data Management

27.5.1 Biological Sciences and Genetics

The biological sciences encompass an enormous variety of information. Environmental science gives us a view of how species live and interact in a world filled with natural phenomena. Biology and ecology study particular species. Anatomy focuses on the overall structure of an organism, documenting the physical aspects of individual bodies. Traditional medicine and physiology break the organism into systems and tissues and strive to collect information on the workings of these systems and the organism as a whole. Histology and cell biology delve into the tissue and cellular levels and provide knowledge about the inner structure and function of the cell. This wealth of information that has been generated, classified, and stored for centuries has only recently become a major application of database technology.

Genetics has emerged as an ideal field for the application of information technology. In a broad sense, it can be thought of as the construction of models based on information about genes—which can be defined as basic units of heredity—and populations and the seeking out of relationships in that information. The study of genetics can be divided into three branches: (1) Mendelian genetics, (2) molecular genetics, and (3) population genetics. Mendelian genetics is the study of the transmission of traits between generations. Molecular genetics is the study of the chemical structure and function of genes at the molecular level. Population genetics is the study of how genetic information varies across populations of organisms.

Molecular genetics provides a more detailed look at genetic information by allowing researchers to examine the composition, structure, and function of genes. The origins of molecular genetics can be traced to two important discoveries. The first occurred in 1869 when Friedrich Miescher discovered nuclein and its primary component, deoxyribonucleic acid (DNA). In subsequent research DNA and a related compound, ribonucleic acid (RNA), were found to be composed of nucleotides (a sugar, a phosphate, and a base, which combined to form nucleic acid) linked into long polymers via the sugar and phosphate. The second discovery was the demonstration in 1944 by Oswald Avery that DNA was indeed the molecular substance carrying genetic information. Genes were thus shown to be composed of chains of nucleic acids arranged linearly on chromosomes and to serve three primary functions: (1) replicating genetic information between generations, (2) providing blueprints for the creation of polypeptides, and (3) accumulating changes—thereby allowing evolution to occur.

27.5.2 Characteristics of Biological Data

Biological data exhibits many special characteristics that make management of biological information a particularly challenging problem. We will thus begin by summarizing the characteristics related to biological information, and focusing on a multidisciplinary field called **bioinformatics** that has emerged, with graduate degree programs now in place in several universities. Bioinformatics addresses information management of genetic information with special emphasis on DNA sequence analysis. It needs to be broadened into a wider scope to harness all types of biological information—its modeling, storage, retrieval, and management.

Characteristic 1: *Biological data is highly complex when compared with most other domains or applications*. Definitions of such data must thus be able to represent a complex substructure of data as well as relationships and to ensure that no information is lost during biological data modeling. The structure of biological data often provides an additional context for interpretation of the information. Biological information systems must be able to represent any level of complexity in any data schema, relationship, or schema substructure—not just hierarchical, binary, or table data. As an example, MITOMAP is a database documenting the human mitochondrial genome.[4] This single genome is a small, circular piece of DNA encompassing information about 16,569 nucleotide bases; 52 gene loci encoding messenger RNA, ribosomal RNA, and transfer RNA; 1000 known population variants; over 60 known disease associations; and a limited set of knowledge on the complex molecular interactions of the biochemical energy producing pathway of oxidative phosphorylation. As might be expected, its management has encountered a large number of problems; we have been unable to use the traditional RDBMS or ODBMS approches to capture all aspects of the data.

Characteristic 2: *The amount and range of variability in data is high*. Hence, biological systems must be flexible in handling data types and values. With such a wide range of possible data values, placing constraints on data types must be limited since this may exclude unexpected values—e.g., outlier values—that are particularly common in the biological domain. Exclusion of such values results in a loss of information. In addition, frequent exceptions to biological data structures may require a choice of data types to be available for a given piece of data.

Characteristic 3: *Schemas in biological databases change at a rapid pace*. Hence, for improved information flow between generations or releases of databases, schema evolution and data object migration must be supported. The ability to extend the schema, a frequent occurrence in the biological setting, is unsupported in most relational and object database systems. Presently systems such as Genbank rerelease the entire database with new schemas once or twice a year rather than incrementally changing the system as changes become necessary. Such an evolutionary database would provide a timely and orderly mechanism for following changes to individual data entities in biological databases over time. This sort of tracking is important for biological researchers to be able to access and reproduce previous results.

Characteristic 4: *Representations of the same data by different biologists will likely be different (even when using the same system)*. Hence, mechanisms for "aligning" different biological schemas or different versions of schemas should be supported. Given the

---

4. Details of MITOMAP and its information complexity can be seen in Kogelnik et al. (1997, 1998) and at http://www.gen.emory.edu/mitomap.html.

complexity of biological data, there are a multitude of ways of modeling any given entity, with the results often reflecting the particular focus of the scientist. While two individuals may produce different data models if asked to interpret the same entity, these models will likely have numerous points in common. In such situations, it would be useful to biological investigators to be able to run queries across these common points. By linking data elements in a network of schemas, this could be accomplished.

Characteristic 5: *Most users of biological data do not require write access to the database; read-only access is adequate.* Write access is limited to privileged users called *curators*. For example, the database created as part of the MITOMAP project has on average more than 15,000 users per month on the Internet. There are fewer than twenty noncurator generated submissions to MITOMAP every month. In other words, the number of users requiring write access is small. Users generate a wide variety of read-access patterns into the database, but these patterns are not the same as those seen in traditional relational databases. User requested ad hoc searches demand indexing of often unexpected combinations of data instance classes.

Characteristic 6: *Most biologists are not likely to have any knowledge of the internal structure of the database or about schema design.* Biological database interfaces should display information to users in a manner that is applicable to the problem they are trying to address and that reflects the underlying data structure. Biological users usually know which data they require, but they have no technical knowledge of the data structure or how a DBMS represents the data. They rely on technical users to provide them with views into the database. Relational schemas fail to provide cues or any intuitive information to the user regarding the meaning of their schema. Web interfaces in particular often provide preset search interfaces, which may limit access into the database. However, if these interfaces are generated directly from database structures, they are likely to produce a wider possible range of access, although they may not guarantee usability.

Characteristic 7: *The context of data gives added meaning for its use in biological applications.* Hence, context must be maintained and conveyed to the user when appropriate. In addition, it should be possible to integrate as many contexts as possible to maximize the interpretation of a biological data value. Isolated values are of less use in biological systems. For example, the sequence of a DNA strand is not particularly useful without additional information describing its organization, function, and such. A single nucleotide on a DNA strand, for example, seen in context with nondisease causing DNA strands, could be seen as a causative element for sickle cell anemia.

Characteristic 8: *Defining and representing complex queries is extremely important to the biologist.* Hence, biological systems must support complex queries. Without any knowledge of the data structure (see Characteristic 6), average users cannot construct a complex query across data sets on their own. Thus, in order to be truly useful, systems must provide some tools for building these queries. As mentioned previously, many systems provide predefined query templates.

Characteristic 9: *Users of biological information often require access to "old" values of the data—particularly when verifying previously reported results.* Hence, changes to the values of data in the database must be supported through a system of archives. Access to both the most recent version of a data value and its previous version are important in the biological domain. Investigators consistently want to query the most up-to-date data, but they must also be able to reconstruct previous work and reevaluate prior and current information. Consequently, values that are about to be updated in a biological database cannot simply be thrown away.

All of these characteristics clearly point to the fact that today's DBMSs do not fully cater to the requirements of complex biological data. A new direction in database management systems is necessary.[5]

27.5.3 The Human Genome Project and Existing Biological Databases

The term *genome* is defined as the total genetic information that can be obtained about an entity. The **human genome**, for example, generally refers to the complete set of genes required to create a human being—estimated to be between 100,000 and 300,000 genes spread over 23 pairs of chromosomes, with an estimated 3 to 4 billion nucleotides. The goal of the Human Genome Project (HGP) is to obtain the complete sequence—the ordering of the bases—of those nucleotides. At present only 8,000 genes have been identified and less than 10 percent of the human genome has been sequenced. However, the entire sequence is expected to be completed by the year 2002. In isolation, the human DNA sequence is not particularly useful. The sequence can however be combined with other data and used as a powerful tool to help address questions in genetics, biochemistry, medicine, anthropology, and agriculture. In the existing genome databases, the focus has been on "curating" (or collecting with some initial scrutiny and quality check) and classifying information about genome sequence data. In addition to the human genome, numerous organisms such as *E.coli*, *Drosophila*, and *C.elegans* have been investigated. We will briefly discuss some of the existing database systems that are supporting or have grown out of the Human Genome Project.

Genbank. The preeminent DNA sequence database in the world today is Genbank, maintained by the National Center for Biotechnology Information (NCBI) of the National Library of Medicine (NLM). It was established in 1978 as a central repository for DNA sequence data. Since then it has expanded somewhat in scope to include expressed sequence tag data, protein sequence data, three-dimensional protein structure, taxonomy, and links to the biomedical literature (MEDLINE). Its latest release contains over 602,000,000 nucleotide bases of more than 920,000 sequences from over 16,000 species with roughly ten new organisms being added each day. The database size has doubled approximately every eighteen months for five years.

While it is a complex, comprehensive database, the scope of its coverage is focused on human sequences and links to the literature. Other limited data sources (e.g. three-dimensional structure and OMIM, discussed below), have been added recently by

---

5. A database environment called GENOME (Georgia Tech Emory Network Object Management Environment) to address the above issues is prototyped in Kogelnik (1998); see also Kogelnik et al. (1997, 1998).

reformatting the existing OMIM and PDB databases and redesigning the structure of the Genbank system to accommodate these new data sets.

The system is maintained as a combination of flat files, relational databases, and files containing **Abstract Syntax Notation One (ASN.1)**—a syntax for defining data structures developed for the telecommunications industry. Each Genbank entry is assigned a unique identifier by the NCBI. Updates are assigned a new identifier, with the identifier of the original entity remaining unchanged for archival purposes. Older references to an entity thus do not inadvertently indicate a new and possibly inappropriate value. The most current concepts also receive a second set of unique identifiers (UIDs), which mark the most up-to-date form of a concept while allowing older versions to be accessed via their original identifier.

The average user of the database is not able to access the structure of the data directly for querying or other functions, although complete snapshots of the database are available for export in a number of formats, including ASN.1. The query mechanism provided is via the Entrez application (or its World Wide Web version), which allows keyword, sequence, and Genbank UID searching through a static interface.

The Genome Database (GDB).   Created in 1989, the Genome Database (GDB) is a catalog of human gene mapping data, a process that associates a piece of information with a particular location on the human genome. The degree of precision of this location on the map depends upon the source of the data, but it is usually not at the level of individual nucleotide bases. GDB data includes data describing primarily map information (distance and confidence limits), and Polymerase Chain Reaction (PCR) probe data (experimental conditions, PCR primers, and reagents used). More recently efforts have been made to add data on mutations linked to genetic loci, cell lines used in experiments, DNA probe libraries, and some limited polymorphism and population data.

The GDB system is built around SYBASE, a commercial relational DBMS, and its data are modeled using standard Entity-Relationship techniques (see Chapters 3 and 4). The implementors of GDB have noted difficulties in using this model to capture more than simple map and probe data. In order to improve data integrity and to simplify the programming for application writers, GDB distributes a Database Access Toolkit. However, most users use a Web interface to search the ten interlinked data managers. Each manager keeps track of the links (relationships) for one of the ten tables within the GDB system. As with Genbank, users are given only a very high-level view of the data at the time of searching and thus cannot easily make use of any knowledge gleaned from the structure of the GDB tables. Search methods are most useful when users are simply looking for an index into map or probe data. Exploratory ad hoc searching of the database is not encouraged by present interfaces. Integration of the database structures of GDB and OMIM (see below) was never fully established.

On-line Mendelian Inheritance in Man.   On-line Mendelian Inheritance in Man (OMIM) is an electronic compendium of information on the genetic basis of human disease. Begun in hard-copy form by Victor McCusick in 1966 with 1500 entries, it was converted to a full-text electronic form between 1987 and 1989 by the GDB. In 1991 its administration was transferred from Johns Hopkins University to the NCBI, and the entire database was converted to NCBI's Genbank format. Today it contains more than 7000 entries.

OMIM covers material on five disease areas based loosely on organs and systems. Any morphological, biochemical, behavioral, or other properties under study are referred to as **phenotype** of an individual (or a cell). Mendel realized that genes can exist in numerous different forms known as **alleles.** A **genotype** refers to the actual allelic composition of an individual.

The structure of the phenotype and genotype entries contains textual data loosely structured as general descriptions, nomenclature, modes of inheritance, variations, gene structure, mapping, and numerous lesser categories. The full-text entries were converted to an ASN.1 structured format when OMIM was transferred to the NCBI. This greatly improved the ability to link OMIM data to other databases and it also provided a rigorous structure for the data. However, the basic form of the database remained difficult to modify.

EcoCyc. The Encyclopedia of *Escherichia coli* Genes and Metabolism (EcoCyc) is a recent experiment in combining information about the genome and the metabolism of *E. coli* K-12. The database was created in 1996 as a collaboration between Stanford Research Institute and the Marine Biological Laboratory. It catalogs and describes the known genes of *E.coli*, the enzymes encoded by those genes, and the biochemical reactions catalyzed by each enzyme and their organization into metabolic pathways. In so doing, EcoCyc spans the sequence and function domains of genomic information. It contains 1283 compounds with 965 structures as well as lists of bonds and atoms, molecular weights, and empirical formulas. It contains 3038 biochemical reactions described using 269 data classes.

An object-oriented data model was first used to implement the system, with data stored on Ocelot, a frame knowledge representation system. EcoCyc data was arranged in a hierarchy of object classes based on the observations that (1) the properties of a reaction are independent of an enzyme that catalyzes it, and (2) an enzyme has a number of properties that are "logically distinct" from its reactions.

EcoCyc provides two methods of querying: (1) direct (via predefined queries) and (2) indirect (via hypertext navigation). Direct queries are performed using menus and dialogs that can initiate a large but finite set of queries. No navigation of the actual data structures is supported. In addition, no mechanism for evolving the schema is documented.

Table 27.1 summarizes the features of the major genome-related databases, as well as HGMDB and ACEDB databases. Some additional protein databases exist; they contain information about protein structures. Prominent protein databases include SWISS-PROT at the University of Geneva, Protein Data Bank (PDB) at Brookhaven National Laboratory, and Protein Identification Resource (PIR) at National Biomedical Research Foundation.

Over the past ten years, there has been an increasing interest in the applications of databases in biology and medicine. Genbank, GDB, and OMIM have been created as central repositories of certain types of biological data but, while extremely useful, they do not yet cover the complete spectrum of the Human Genome Project data. However, efforts are under way around the world to design new tools and techniques that will alleviate the data management problem for the biological scientists and medical researchers.

Table 27.1   Summary of the Major Genome-Related Databases

Database Name	Major Content	Initial Technology	Current Technology	DB Problem Areas	Primary Data Types
Genbank	DNA/RNA sequence, protein	Text files	Flat-file/ASN.1	Schema browsing, schema evolution, linking to other dbs	Text, numeric, some complex types
OMIM	Disease phenotypes and genotypes, etc.	Index cards/text files	Flat-file/ASN.1	Unstructured, free text entries linking to other dbs	Text
GDB	Genetic map linkage data	Flat file	Relational	Schema expansion/evolution, complex objects, linking to other dbs	Text, numeric
ACEDB	Genetic map linkage data, sequence data (non-human)	OO	OO	Schema expansion/evolution, linking to other dbs	Text, numeric
HGMDB	Sequence and sequence variants	Flat file— application specific	Flat-file— application specific	Schema expansion/evolution, linking to other dbs	Text
EcoCyc	Biochemical reactions and pathways	OO	OO	Locked into class hierarchy, schema evolution	Complex types, text, numeric

27.5.4   Selected Bibliography for Genome Databases

Bioinformatics has become a popular area of research in recent years and many workshops and conferences are being organized around this topic. Robbins (1993) gives a good overview while Frenkel (1991) surveys the human genome project with its special role in bioinformatics at large. Cutticchia et al. (1993), Benson et al. (1996), and Pearson et al. (1994) are references on GDB, Genbank, and OMIM. Wallace (1995) has been a pioneer in the mitochondrial genome research, which deals with a specific part of the human genome; the sequence and organizational details of this area appear in Anderson et al. (1981). Recent work in Kogelnik et al. (1997, 1998) and Kogelnik (1998) addresses the development of a generic solution to the data management problem in biological sciences by developing a prototype solution. The MITOMAP database developed in Kogelnik (1998) can be accessed at http://www.gen.emory.edu/mitomap.html. The biggest protein database SWISS-PROT can be accessed from http://expasy.hcuge.ch/sprot/. The ACEDB database information is available at http://probe.nalusda.gov:8080/acedocs/

27.6 Digital Libraries

Digital libraries are an important and active research area. Conceptually, a digital library is an analog of a traditional library—a large collection of information sources in various media—coupled with the advantages of digital technologies. However, digital libraries differ from their traditional counterparts in significant ways: storage is digital, remote access is quick and easy, and materials are copied from a master version. Furthermore, keeping extra copies on hand is easy and is not hampered by budget and storage restrictions, which are major problems in traditional libraries. Thus, digital technologies overcome many of the physical and economic limitations of traditional libraries.

The introduction to the April 1995 *Communications of the* ACM special issue on digital libraries describes them grandly as the "opportunity . . . to fulfill the age-old dream of every human being: gaining ready access to humanity's store of information." In Chapter 1, we defined a database quite broadly as a "collection of related data." Unlike the related data in a database, a digital library encompasses a multitude of sources, many unrelated. Logically, databases can be components of digital libraries (see Table 27.2).

The Digital Library Initiative (DLI), jointly funded by NSF, DARPA, and NASA, has been a major accelerator of the development of digital libraries. This initiative provided significant funding to six major projects at six universities in its first phase covering a broad spectrum of enabling technologies (as will be discussed below). The Initiative's

Table 27.2 Databases and Digital Libraries: Similarities and Differences

Similarities

- Both collect, organize, store, search, retrieve, process, and provide data.
- Both contain and handle multiple media.
- Both contain and handle heterogeneous data types and complex objects.

Differences

Digital Libraries	Databases
No centralized manager (management by agreed interfaces)	Centralized manager (DBA)
Uncontrolled/less controlled data quality	Controllable data quality

Web pages (see dli.grainger.uiuc.edu/national.htm) define its focus as "to dramatically advance the means to collect, store, and organize information in digital forms, and make it available for searching, retrieval, and processing via communication networks—all in user-friendly ways."

The magnitude of these data collections as well as their diversity and multiple formats provides challenges on a new scale. The future progression of the development of digital libraries is likely to move from the present technology of retrieval via the Internet, through Net searches of indexed information in repositories, to a time of information correlation and analysis by intelligent networks. Techniques for collecting information, storing it, and organizing it to support informational requirements learned in the decades of design and implementation of databases will provide the baseline for development of approaches appropriate for digital libraries. Search, retrieval, and processing of the many forms of digital information will make use of the lessons learned from database operations on those forms of information.

27.6.1 The Digital Libraries Initiative

The University of Illinois at Urbana–Champaign is coordinating national synchronization of the six DLI projects underway at six participating universities. The projects illustrate major aspects of digital library development requirements. The participants and their focuses are as follows:

- *University of California at Berkeley: Environmental Planning and Geographic Information Systems* (see Section 27.4 above for details on GIS). This project will implement a digital library as a collection of distributed information services, emphasizing automated indexing, intelligent retrieval, support by distributed databases, a better client-server retrieval protocol, better data acquisition technology, and a new interaction paradigm.

- *University of California at Santa Barbara: The Alexandria Project.* Spatially referenced map information. This project will develop distributed library services for spatially indexed and graphical information collections (see Section 23.3 on spatial modeling and 27.4 on GIS).

- *Carnegie Mellon University: Informedia Digital Video Library.* Using digital video libraries, this project will focus on full-content search and retrieval.

- *University of Illinois at Urbana-Champaign: Federating Repositories of Scientific Literature.* This project will scale up a digital library for thousands of users and documents.

- *University of Michigan: Intelligent Agents for Information Location.* This project will focus on agent technology, including use of user-interface agents, mediation agents to coordinate searches, and collection agents.

- *Stanford University: Interoperation Mechanisms Among Heterogeneous Services.* This project will develop enabling technologies for an integrated digital library providing uniform access to novel services using networked information collections.

27.6.2   Selected Bibliography on Digital Libraries

The April 1995 issue of *Communications of the* ACM is devoted to digital libraries. In it, Wiederhold (1995) discusses the importance of digital libraries in increasing human productivity in finding new knowledge. The April 1998 issue of *Communications of the* ACM is devoted to giving global scope and unlimited access to digital libraries. Schatz (1995, 1997) provides excellent coverage of information retrieval, search, and analysis as it relates to information on the Internet. The various universities in the Digital Libraries Initiative can be reached through the following URLs:

Digital Libraries Initiative: dli.grainger.uiuc.edu/national.htm

University of Berkeley: elib.cs.berkeley.edu

University of Santa Barbara: alexandria.sdc.ucsb.edu

Carnegie-Mellon University: www.informedia.cs.cmu.edu

University of Illinois Urbana-Champaign: dli.grainger.uiuc.edu/default.htm

University of Michigan: www.si.umich.edu/UMDL

Stanford University: walrus.stanford.edu/diglib

APPENDIX A

Alternative Diagrammatic Notations

Figure A.1 shows a number of different diagrammatic notations for representing ER and EER model concepts. Unfortunately, there is no standard notation: different database design practitioners prefer different notations. Similarly, various CASE (computer-aided software engineering) tools and OOA (object-oriented analysis) methodologies use various notations. Some notations are associated with models that have additional concepts and constraints beyond those of the ER and EER models described in Chapters 3 and 24, while other models have fewer concepts and constraints. The notation we used in Chapter 3 is quite close to the original notation for ER diagrams, which is still widely used. We discuss some alternate notations here.

Figure A.1(a) shows different notations for displaying entity types/classes, attributes, and relationships. In Chapters 3 and 24, we used the symbols marked (i) in Figure A.1(a)—namely, rectangle, oval, and diamond. Notice that symbol (ii) for entity types/classes, symbol (ii) for attributes, and symbol (ii) for relationships are similar, but they are used by different methodologies to represent three different concepts. The straight line symbol (iii) for representing relationships is used by several tools and methodologies.

Figure A.1(b) shows some notations for attaching attributes to entity types. We used notation (i). Notation (ii) uses the third notation (iii) for attributes from Figure A.1(a). The last two notations in Figure A.1(b)—(iii) and (iv)—are popular in OOA methodologies and in some CASE tools. In particular, the last notation displays both the attributes and the methods of a class, separated by a horizontal line.

Figure A.1 Alternative notations. (a) Symbols for entity type/class, attribute, and relationship. (b) Displaying attributes. (c) Displaying cardinality ratios. (d) Various (min, max) notations. (e) Notations for displaying specialization/generalization.

Figure A.1(c) shows various notations for representing the cardinality ratio of binary relationships. We used notation (i) in Chapters 3 and 24. Notation (ii)—known as the *chicken feet* notation—is quite popular. Notation (iv) uses the arrow as a functional reference (from the N to the 1 side) and resembles our notation for foreign keys in the relational model (see Figure 7.7); notation (v)—used in *Bachman diagrams*—uses the arrow in *the reverse direction* (from the 1 to the N side). For a 1:1 relationship, (ii) uses a straight line without any chicken feet; (iii) makes both halves of the diamond white; and (iv) places arrowheads on both sides. For an M:N relationship, (ii) uses chicken feet at both ends of the line; (iii) makes both halves of the diamond black; and (iv) does not display any arrowheads.

Figure A.1(d) shows several variations for displaying (min, max) constraints, which are used to display both cardinality ratio and total/partial participation. Notation (ii) is the alternative notation we used in Figure 3.15 and discussed in Section 3.7.4. Recall that our notation specifies the constraint that each entity must participate in at least min and at most max relationship instances. Hence, for a 1:1 relationship, both max values are 1; and for M:N, both max values are n. A min value greater than 0 (zero) specifies total participation (existence dependency). In methodologies that use the straight line for displaying relationships, it is common to *reverse the positioning* of the (min, max) constraints, as shown in (iii). Another popular technique—which follows the same positioning as (iii)— is to display the *min* as o ("oh" or circle, which stands for zero) or as | (vertical dash, which stands for 1), and to display the max as | (vertical dash, which stands for 1) or as chicken feet (which stands for n), as shown in (iv).

Figure A.1(e) shows some notations for displaying specialization/generalization. We used notation (i) in Chapter 14, where a d in the circle specifies that the subclasses (S1, S2, and S3) are disjoint and an o specifies overlapping subclasses. Notation (ii) uses G (for generalization) to specify disjoint, and Gs to specify overlapping; some notations use the solid arrow, while others use the empty arrow (shown at the side). Notation (iii) uses a triangle pointing toward the superclass, and notation (v) uses a triangle pointing toward the subclasses; it is also possible to use both notations in the same methodology, with (iii) indicating generalization and (v) indicating specialization. Notation (iv) places the boxes representing subclasses within the box representing the superclass. Of the notations based on (vi), some use a single-lined arrow, and others use a double-lined arrow (shown at the side).

The notations shown in Figure A.1 show only some of the diagrammatic symbols that have been used or suggested for displaying database conceptual schemes. Other notations, as well as various combinations of the preceding, have also been used. It would be useful to establish a standard that everyone would adhere to, in order to prevent misunderstandings and reduce confusion.

APPENDIX B | Parameters of Disks

The most important disk parameter is the time required to locate an arbitrary disk block, given its block address, and then to transfer the block between the disk and a main memory buffer. This is the **random access time** for accessing a disk block. There are three time components to consider:

1. **Seek time (s):** This is the time needed to mechanically position the read/write head on the correct track for movable-head disks. (For fixed-head disks, it is the time needed to electronically switch to the appropriate read/write head.) For movable head disks this time varies, depending on the distance between the current track under the read/write head and the track specified in the block address. Usually, the disk manufacturer provides an average seek time in milliseconds. The typical range of average seek time is 10 to 60 msec. This is the main "culprit" for the delay involved in transferring blocks between disk and memory.

2. **Rotational delay (rd):** Once the read/write head is at the correct track, the user must wait for the beginning of the required block to rotate into position under the read/write head. On the average, this takes about the time for half a revolution of the disk, but it actually ranges from immediate access (if the start of the required block is in position under the read/write head right after the seek) to a full disk revolution (if the start of the required block just passed the read/write head after the seek). If the speed of disk rotation is p revolutions per minute (rpm), then the

average rotational delay rd is given by

$$rd = (1/2)*(1/p) \text{ min} = (60*1000)/(2*p) \text{ msec}$$

A typical value for p is 10,000 rpm, which gives a rotational delay of rd = 3 msec. For fixed-head disks, where the seek time is negligible, this component causes the greatest delay in transferring a disk block.

3. **Block transfer time (btt):** Once the read/write head is at the beginning of the required block, some time is needed to transfer the data in the block. This block transfer time depends on the block size, the track size, and the rotational speed. If the **transfer rate** for the disk is tr bytes/msec and the block size is B bytes, then

$$btt = B/tr \text{ msec}$$

If we have a track size of 50 Kbytes and p is 3600 rpm, the transfer rate in bytes/ msec is

$$tr = (50*1000)/(60*1000/3600) = 3000 \text{ bytes/msec}$$

In this case, btt = B/3000 msec, where B is the block size in bytes.

The average time needed to find and transfer a block, given its block address, is estimated by

$$(s + rd + btt) \text{ msec}$$

This holds for either reading or writing a block. The principal method of reducing this time is to transfer several blocks that are stored on one or more tracks of the same cylinder; then the seek time is required only for the first block. To transfer consecutively k *noncontiguous* blocks that are on the *same cylinder,* we need approximately

$$s + (k * (rd + btt)) \text{ msec}$$

In this case, we need two or more buffers in main storage, because we are continuously reading or writing the k blocks, as we discussed in Section 4.3. The transfer time per block is reduced even further when *consecutive blocks* on the same track or cylinder are transferred. This eliminates the rotational delay for all but the first block, so the estimate for transferring k consecutive blocks is

$$s + rd + (k * btt) \text{ msec}$$

A more accurate estimate for transferring consecutive blocks takes into account the interblock gap (see Section 5.2.1), which includes the information that enables the read/ write head to determine which block it is about to read. Usually, the disk manufacturer provides a **bulk transfer rate** (btr) that takes the gap size into account when reading consecutively stored blocks. If the gap size is G bytes, then

$$btr = (B/(B + G)) * tr \text{ bytes/msec}$$

The bulk transfer rate is the rate of transferring *useful bytes* in the data blocks. The disk read/write head must go over all bytes on a track as the disk rotates, including the bytes in the interblock gaps, which store control information but not real data. When the bulk transfer rate is used, the time needed to transfer the useful data in one block out of several consecutive blocks is B/btr. Hence, the estimated time to read k blocks consecutively stored on the same cylinder becomes

s + rd + (k * (B/btr)) msec

Another parameter of disks is the **rewrite time.** This is useful in cases when we read a block from the disk into a main memory buffer, update the buffer, and then write the buffer back to the same disk block on which it was stored. In many cases, the time required to update the buffer in main memory is less than the time required for one disk revolution. If we know that the buffer is ready for rewriting, the system can keep the disk heads on the same track, and during the next disk revolution the updated buffer is rewritten back to the disk block. Hence, the rewrite time T_{rw} is usually estimated to be the time needed for one disk revolution:

$T_{rw} = 2 * rd$ msec

To summarize, here is a list of the parameters we have discussed and the symbols we use for them:

seek time: s msec

rotational delay: rd msec

block transfer time: btt msec

rewrite time: T_{rw} msec

transfer rate: tr bytes/msec

bulk transfer rate: btr bytes/msec

block size: B bytes

interblock gap size: G bytes

APPENDIX C | An Overview of the Network Data Model

This appendix provides an overview of the network data model.[1] The original network model and language were presented in the CODASYL Data Base Task Group's 1971 report; hence it is sometimes called the DBTG model. Revised reports in 1978 and 1981 incorporated more recent concepts. In this appendix, rather than concentrating on the details of a particular CODASYL report, we present the general concepts behind network-type databases and use the term **network model** rather than CODASYL model or DBTG model.

The original CODASYL/DBTG report used COBOL as the host language. Regardless of the host programming language, the basic database manipulation commands of the network model remain the same. Although the network model and the object-oriented data model are both navigational in nature, the data structuring capability of the network model is much more elaborate and allows for explicit insertion/deletion/modification semantic specification. However, it lacks some of the desirable features of the object models that we discussed in Chapter 11, such as inheritance and encapsulation of structure and behavior.

---

1. The complete chapter on the network data model and about the IDMS system from the second edition of this book is available at http://www.awl.com/cseng/titles/0-8053-1755-4. This appendix is an edited excerpt of that chapter.

C.1   Network Data Modeling Concepts

There are two basic data structures in the network model: records and sets.

C.1.1   Records, Record Types, and Data Items

Data is stored in **records;** each record consists of a group of related data values. Records are classified into **record types,** where each record type describes the structure of a group of records that store the same type of information. We give each record type a name, and we also give a name and format (data type) for each **data item** (or attribute) in the record type. Figure C.1 shows a record type STUDENT with data items NAME, SSN, ADDRESS, MAJORDEPT, and BIRTHDATE.

We can declare a virtual data item (or derived attribute) AGE for the record type shown in Figure C.1 and write a procedure to calculate the value of AGE from the value of the actual data item BIRTHDATE in each record.

A typical database application has numerous record types—from a few to a few hundred. To represent relationships between records, the network model provides the modeling construct called *set type,* which we discuss next.

C.1.2   Set Types and Their Basic Properties

A **set type** is a description of a 1:N relationship between two record types. Figure C.2 shows how we represent a set type diagrammatically as an arrow. This type of diagrammatic representation is called a **Bachman diagram.** Each set type definition consists of three basic elements:

- A name for the set type.
- An owner record type.
- A member record type.

STUDENT				
NAME	SSN	ADDRESS	MAJORDEPT	BIRTHDATE

data item name	format
NAME	CHARACTER 30
SSN	CHARACTER 9
ADDRESS	CHARACTER 40
MAJORDEPT	CHARACTER 10
BIRTHDATE	CHARACTER 9

Figure C.1   A record type STUDENT.

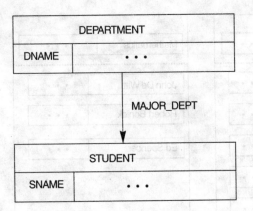

Figure C.2   The set type MAJOR_DEPT.

The set type in Figure C.2 is called MAJOR_DEPT; DEPARTMENT is the **owner** record type, and STUDENT is the **member** record type. This represents the 1:N relationship between academic departments and students majoring in those departments. In the database itself, there will be many **set occurrences** (or **set instances**) corresponding to a set type. Each instance relates one record from the owner record type—a DEPARTMENT record in our example—to the set of records from the member record type related to it— the set of STUDENT records for students who major in that department. Hence, each set occurrence is composed of:

- One owner record from the owner record type.
- A number of related member records (zero or more) from the member record type.

A record from the member record type *cannot exist in more than one set occurrence* of a particular set type. This maintains the constraint that a set type represents a 1:N relationship. In our example a STUDENT record can be related to at most one major DEPARTMENT and hence is a member of at most one set occurrence of the MAJOR_DEPT set type.

A set occurrence can be identified either by the *owner record* or by *any of the member records*. Figure C.3 shows four set occurrences (instances) of the MAJOR_DEPT set type. Notice that each set instance *must* have one owner record but can have any number of member records (**zero** or more). Hence, we usually refer to a set instance by its owner record. The four set instances in Figure C.3 can be referred to as the 'Computer Science', 'Mathematics', 'Physics', and 'Geology' sets. It is customary to use a different representation of a set instance (Figure C.4) where the records of the set instance are shown linked together by pointers, which corresponds to a commonly used technique for implementing sets.

Figure C.3   Four set instances of the set type MAJOR_DEPT.

In the network model, a set instance is *not identical* to the concept of a set in mathematics. There are two principal differences:

- The set instance has one *distinguished element*—the owner record—whereas in a mathematical set there is no such distinction among the elements of a set.

- In the network model, the member records of a set instance are *ordered*, whereas order of elements is immaterial in a mathematical set. Hence, we can refer to the first, second, i[th], and last member records in a set instance. Figure C.4 shows an alternate "linked" representation of an instance of the set MAJOR_DEPT. In Figure C.4 the

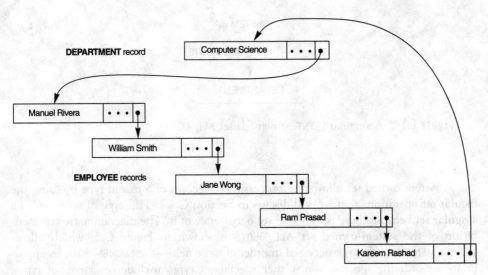

Figure C.4   Alternate representation of a set instance as a linked list.

record of 'Manuel Rivera' is the first STUDENT (member) record in the 'Computer Science' set, and that of 'Kareem Rashad' is the last member record. The set of the network model is sometimes referred to as an **owner-coupled set** or **co-set**, to distinguish it from a mathematical set.

C.1.3   Special Types of Sets

One special type of set in the CODASYL network model is worth mentioning: SYSTEM-owned sets.

System-owned (Singular) Sets.   A **system-owned** set is a set with no owner record type; instead, the system is the owner.[2] We can think of the system as a special "virtual" owner record type with only a single record occurrence. System-owned sets serve two main purposes in the network model:

- They provide *entry points* into the database via the records of the specified member record type. Processing can commence by accessing members of that record type, and then retrieving related records via other sets.

- They can be used to *order* the records of a given record type by using the set ordering specifications. By specifying several system-owned sets on the same record type, a user can access its records in different orders.

---

2. By *system*, we mean the DBMS software.

Figure C.5   A singular (SYSTEM-owned) set ALL_DEPTS.

A system-owned set allows the processing of records of a record type by using the regular set operations that we will discuss in Section C.4.2. This type of set is called a **singular** set because there is only one set occurrence of it. The diagrammatic representation of the system-owned set ALL_DEPTS is shown in Figure C.5, which allows DEPARTMENT records to be accessed in order of some field—say, NAME—with an appropriate set-ordering specification. Other special set types include recursive set types, with the same record serving as an owner and a member, which are mostly disallowed; multimember sets containing multiple record types as members in the same set type are allowed in some systems.

C.1.4   Stored Representations of Set Instances

A set instance is commonly represented as a **ring (circular linked list)** linking the owner record and all member records of the set, as shown in Figure C.4. This is also sometimes called a **circular chain.** The ring representation is symmetric with respect to all records; hence, to distinguish between the owner record and the member records, the DBMS includes a special field, called the **type field,** that has a distinct value (assigned by the DBMS) for each record type. By examining the type field, the system can tell whether the record is the owner of the set instance or is one of the member records. This type field is hidden from the user and is used only by the DBMS.

In addition to the type field, a record type is automatically assigned a **pointer field** by the DBMS for *each set type in which it participates as owner or member.* This pointer can be considered to be *labeled* with the set type name to which it corresponds; hence, the system internally maintains the correspondence between these pointer fields and their set types. A pointer is usually called the **NEXT pointer** in a member record and the **FIRST pointer** in an owner record because these point to the next and first member records, respectively. In our example of Figure C.4, each student record has a NEXT pointer to the next student record within the set occurrence. The NEXT pointer of the *last member record* in a set occurrence points back to the owner record. If a record of the member record type does not participate in any set instance, its NEXT pointer has a special **nil** pointer. If a set occurrence has an owner but no member records, the FIRST pointer points right back to the owner record itself or it can be **nil.**

The preceding representation of sets is one method for implementing set instances. In general, a DBMS can implement sets in various ways. However, the chosen representation must allow the DBMS to do all the following operations:

- Given an owner record, find all member records of the set occurrence.
- Given an owner record, find the first, i[th], or last member record of the set occurrence. If no such record exists, return an exception code.
- Given a member record, find the next (or previous) member record of the set occurrence. If no such record exists, return an exception code.
- Given a member record, find the owner record of the set occurrence.

The circular linked list representation allows the system to do all of the preceding operations with varying degrees of efficiency. In general, a network database schema has many record types and set types, which means that a record type may participate as owner and member in numerous set types. For example, in the network schema that appears later as Figure C.8, the EMPLOYEE record type participates as owner in four set TYPES— MANAGES, IS_ A_SUPERVISOR, E_WORKSON, and DEPENDENTS_OF—and participates as member in two set types—WORKS_FOR and SUPERVISEES. In the circular linked list representation, six additional pointer fields are added to the EMPLOYEE record type. However, no confusion arises, because each pointer is labeled by the system and plays the role of FIRST or NEXT pointer for a *specific set type*.

Other representations of sets allow more efficient implementation of some of the operations on sets noted previously. We briefly mention five of them here:

- *Doubly linked circular list representation:* Besides the NEXT pointer in a member record type, a **PRIOR** pointer points back to the prior member record of the set occurrence. The PRIOR pointer of the first member record can point back to the owner record.
- *Owner pointer representation:* For each set type an additional **OWNER** pointer is included in the member record type that points directly to the owner record of the set.
- *Contiguous member records:* Rather than being linked by pointers, the member records are actually placed in contiguous physical locations, typically following the owner record.
- *Pointer arrays:* An array of pointers is stored with the owner record. The ith element in the array points to the ith member record of the set instance. This is usually implemented in conjunction with the owner pointer.
- *Indexed representation:* A small index is kept with the owner record *for each set occurrence*. An index entry contains the value of a key indexing field and a pointer to the actual member record that has this field value. The index may be implemented as a linked list chained by next and prior pointers (the IDMS system allows this option).

These representations support the network DML operations with varying degrees of efficiency. Ideally, the programmer should not be concerned with how sets are implemented, but only with confirming that they are implemented correctly by the DBMS. However, in practice, the programmer can benefit from the particular implementation of sets, to write more efficient programs. Most systems allow the database designer to choose from among several options for implementing each set type, using a MODE statement to specify the chosen representation.

C.1.5   Using Sets to Represent M:N Relationships

A set type represents a 1:N relationship between two record types. This means that *a record of the member record type can appear in only one set occurrence*. This constraint is automatically enforced by the DBMS in the network model. To represent a 1:1 relationship, the extra 1:1 constraint must be imposed by the application program.

An M:N relationship between two record types cannot be represented by a single set type. For example, consider the WORKS_ON relationship between EMPLOYEEs and PROJECTs. Assume that an employee can be working on several projects simultaneously and that a project typically has several employees working on it. If we try to represent this by a set type, neither the set type in Figure C.6(a) nor that in Figure C.6(b) will represent the relationship correctly. Figure C.6(a) enforces the incorrect constraint that a PROJECT record is related to only one EMPLOYEE record, whereas Figure C.6(b) enforces the incorrect constraint that an EMPLOYEE record is related to only one PROJECT record. Using both set types E_P and P_E simultaneously, as in Figure C.6(c), leads to the problem of enforcing the constraint that P_E and E_P are mutually consistent inverses, plus the problem of dealing with relationship attributes.

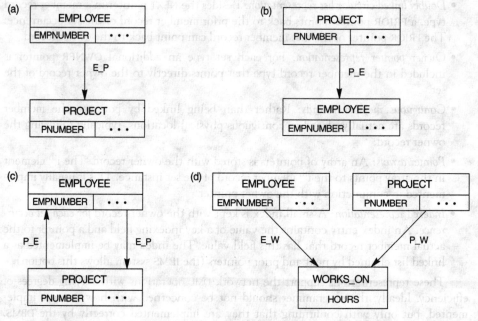

Figure C.6   Representing M:N relationships. (a)–(c) Incorrect representations. (d) Correct representation using a linking record type.

Figure C.6 (*Continued*)   (e) Some instances. (f) Using linked representation.

The correct method for representing an M:N relationship in the network model is to use two set types and an additional record type, as shown in Figure C.6(d). This additional record type—WORKS_ON, in our example—is called a **linking** (or **dummy**) record type. Each record of the WORKS_ON record type must be owned by one EMPLOYEE record through the E_W set and by one PROJECT record through the P_W set and serves to relate these two owner records. This is illustrated conceptually in Figure C.6(e).

Figure C.6(f) shows an example of individual record and set occurrences in the linked list representation corresponding to the schema in Figure C.6(d). Each record of the WORKS_ON record type has two NEXT pointers: the one marked NEXT(E_W) points to the next record in an instance of the E_W set, and the one marked NEXT(P_W) points to the next record in an instance of the P_W set. Each WORKS_ON record relates its two owner records. Each WORKS_ON record also contains the number of hours per week that an employee works on a project. The same occurrences in Figure C.6(f) are shown in Figure C.6(e) by displaying the W records individually, without showing the pointers.

To find all projects that a particular employee works on, we start at the EMPLOYEE record and then trace through all WORKS_ON records owned by that EMPLOYEE, using the FIRST(E_W) and NEXT(E_W) pointers. At each WORKS_ON record in the set occurrence, we find its owner PROJECT record by following the NEXT(P_W) pointers until we find a record of type PROJECT. For example, for the E2 EMPLOYEE record, we follow the FIRST(E_W) pointer in E2 leading to W1, the NEXT(E_W) pointer in W1 leading to W2, and the NEXT(E_W) pointer in W2 leading back to E2. Hence, W1 and W2 are identified as the member records in the set occurrence of E_W owned by E2. By following the NEXT(P_W) pointer in W1, we reach P1 as its owner; and by following the NEXT(P_W) pointer in W2 (and through W3 and W4), we reach P2 as its owner. Notice that the existence of direct OWNER pointers for the P_W set in the WORKS_ON records would have simplified the process of identifying the owner PROJECT record of each WORKS_ON record.

In a similar fashion, we can find all EMPLOYEE records related to a particular PROJECT. In this case the existence of owner pointers for the E_W set would simplify processing. All this pointer tracing is done *automatically by the DBMS*; the programmer has DML commands for directly finding the owner or the next member, as we shall discuss in Section C.4.2.

Notice that we could represent the M:N relationship as in Figure C.6(a) or (b) if we were allowed to duplicate PROJECT (or EMPLOYEE) records. In Figure C.6(a) a PROJECT record would be duplicated as many times as there were employees working on the project. However, duplicating records creates problems in maintaining consistency among the duplicates whenever the database is updated, and it is not recommended in general.

C.2 Constraints in the Network Model

In explaining the network model so far, we have already discussed "structural" constraints that govern how record types and set types are structured. In the present section we discuss "behavioral" constraints that apply to (the behavior of) the members of sets when insertion, deletion, and update operations are performed on sets. Several constraints may be specified on set membership. These are usually divided into two main categories, called insertion options and retention options in CODASYL terminology. These constraints are determined during database design by knowing how a set is required to behave when member records are inserted or when owner or member records are deleted. The constraints are specified to the DBMS when we declare the database structure, using the data definition language (see Section C.3). Not all combinations of the constraints are possible. We first discuss each type of constraint and then give the allowable combinations.

C.2.1 Insertion Options (Constraints) on Sets

The insertion constraints—or options, in CODASYL terminology—on set membership specify what is to happen when we insert a new record in the database that is of a member record type. A record is inserted by using the STORE command (see Section C.4.3). There are two options:

- AUTOMATIC: The new member record is *automatically connected* to an appropriate set occurrence when the record is inserted.[3]
- MANUAL: The new record is not connected to any set occurrence. If desired, the programmer can explicitly (*manually*) connect the record to a set occurrence subsequently by using the CONNECT command.

For example, consider the MAJOR_DEPT set type of Figure C.2. In this situation we can have a STUDENT record that is not related to any department through the MAJOR_DEPT set (if the corresponding student has not declared a major). We should therefore declare the MANUAL insertion option, meaning that when a member STUDENT record is inserted in the database it is not automatically related to a DEPARTMENT record through the MAJOR_DEPT set. The database user may later insert the record "manually" into a set instance when the corresponding student declares a major department. This manual insertion is accomplished by using an update operation called CONNECT, submitted to the database system, as we shall see in Section C.4.4.

The AUTOMATIC option for set insertion is used in situations where we want to insert a member record into a set instance automatically upon storage of that record in the database. We must specify a criterion for *designating the set instance* of which each new record becomes a member. As an example, consider the set type shown in Figure C.7(a), which relates each employee to the set of dependents of that employee. We can declare the EMP_DEPENDENTS set type to be AUTOMATIC, with the condition that a new DEPENDENT record with a particular EMPSSN value is inserted into the set instance owned by the EMPLOYEE record with the same SSN value.

C.2.2 Retention Options (Constraints) on Sets

The retention constraints—or options, in CODASYL terminology—specify whether a record of a member record type can exist in the database on its own or whether it must

---

3. The appropriate set occurrence is determined by a specification that is part of the definition of the set type, the SET OCCURRENCE SELECTION.

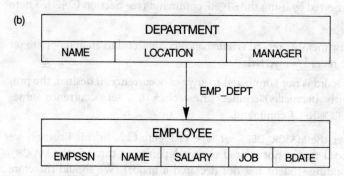

Figure C.7   Different set options. (a) An AUTOMATIC FIXED set. (b) An AUTOMATIC MANDATORY set.

always be related to an owner as a member of some set instance. There are three retention options:

- OPTIONAL: A member record can exist on its own *without being* a member in any occurrence of the set. It can be connected and disconnected to set occurrences at will by means of the CONNECT and DISCONNECT commands of the network DML (see Section C.4.4).

- MANDATORY: A member record *cannot* exist on its own; it must *always* be a member in some set occurrence of the set type. It can be reconnected in a single operation from one set occurrence to another by means of the RECONNECT command of the network DML (see Section C.4.4).

- FIXED: As in MANDATORY, a member record *cannot* exist on its own. Moreover, once it is inserted in a set occurrence, it is *fixed*; it *cannot* be reconnected to another set occurrence.

We now illustrate the differences among these options by examples showing when each option should be used. First, consider the MAJOR_DEPT set type of Figure C.2. To provide for the situation where we may have a STUDENT record that is not related to any department through the MAJOR_DEPT set, we declare the set to be OPTIONAL. In Figure

Table C.1   Set Insertion and Retention Options

	Retention Option		
	OPTIONAL	**MANDATORY**	**FIXED**
MANUAL	Application program is in charge of inserting member record into set occurrence. Can CONNECT, DISCONNECT, RECONNECT	Not very useful.	Not very useful.
AUTOMATIC	DBMS inserts a new member record into a set occurrence automatically. Can CONNECT, DISCONNECT, RECONNECT.	DBMS inserts a new member record into a set occurrence automatically. Can RECONNECT member to a different owner.	DBMS inserts a new member record into a set occurrence automatically. *Cannot* RECONNECT member to a different owner.

C.7(a) EMP_DEPENDENTS is an example of a FIXED set type, because we do not expect a dependent to be moved from one employee to another. In addition, every DEPENDENT record must be related to some EMPLOYEE record at all times. In Figure C.7(b) a MANDA-TORY set EMP_DEPT relates an employee to the department the employee works for. Here, every employee must be assigned to exactly one department at all times; however, an employee can be reassigned from one department to another.

By using an appropriate insertion/retention option, the DBA is able to specify the behavior of a set type as a constraint, which is then *automatically* held good by the system. Table C.1 summarizes the Insertion and Retention options.

C.2.3   Set Ordering Options

The member records in a set instance can be ordered in various ways. Order can be based on an ordering field or controlled by the time sequence of insertion of new member records. The available options for ordering can be summarized as follows:

* *Sorted by an ordering field:* The values of one or more fields from the member record type are used to order the member records within *each set occurrence* in ascending or descending order. The system maintains the order when a new member record is connected to the set instance by automatically inserting the record in its correct position in the order.

* *System default:* A new member record is inserted in an arbitrary position determined by the system.

- *First or last:* A new member record becomes the first or last record in the set occurrence *at the time it is inserted*. Hence, this corresponds to having the member records in a set instance stored in chronological (or reverse chronological) order.

- *Next or prior:* The new member record is inserted after or before the current record of the set occurrence.

The desired options for insertion, retention, and ordering are specified when the set type is declared in the data definition language. Details of declaring record types and set types are discussed in Section C.3 in connection with the network model data definition language (DDL).

C.2.4   Set Selection Options

The following options can be used to select an appropriate set occurrence:

- SET SELECTION IS STRUCTURAL: We can specify set selection by values of two fields that must match—one field from the owner record type, and one from the member record type. This is called a structural constraint in network terminology. Examples are the P_WORKSON and E_WORKSON set type declarations in Figures C.8 and C.9(b).

- SET SELECTION BY APPLICATION: The set occurrence is determined via the application program, which should make the desired set occurrence the "current of set" before the new member record is stored. The new member record is then automatically connected to the current set occurrence.

C.2.5   Data Definition in the Network Model

After designing a network database schema, we must declare all the record types, set types, data item definitions, and schema constraints to the network DBMS. The network DDL is used for this purpose. Network DDL declarations for the record types of the COMPANY schema shown in Figure C.8 are shown in Figure C.9(a). Each record type is given a name by using the **RECORD NAME IS** clause. Figure C.9(b) shows network DDL declarations for the set types of the COMPANY schema shown in Figure C.8. These are more complex than record type declarations, because more options are available. Each set type is given a name by using the **SET NAME IS** clause. The insertion and retention options (constraints), discussed in Section C.2, are specified for each set type by using the **INSERTION IS** and **RETENTION IS** clauses. If the insertion option is AUTOMATIC, we must also specify how the system will select a set occurrence automatically to connect a new member record to that occurrence when the record is first inserted into the database. The **SET SELECTION** clause is used for this purpose.

C.3   Data Manipulation in a Network Database

In this section we discuss how to write programs that manipulate a network database—including such tasks as searching for and retrieving records from the database; inserting, deleting, and modifying records; and connecting and disconnecting records from set

Figure C.8 A network schema diagram for the COMPANY database.

occurrences. A **data manipulation language (DML)** is used for these purposes. The DML associated with the network model consists of record-at-a-time commands that are embedded in a general-purpose programming language called the **host language.** Embedded commands of the DML are also called the **data sublanguage.** In practice, the most commonly used host languages are COBOL[4] and PL/I. In our examples, however, we show program segments in PASCAL notation augmented with network DML commands.

C.3.1 Basic Concepts for Network Database Manipulation

To write programs for manipulating a network database, we first need to discuss some basic concepts related to how data manipulation programs are written. The database system and the host programming language are two separate software systems that are linked together by a common interface and communicate only through this interface. Because

---

4. The CODASYL DML in the DBTG report was originally proposed as a data sublanguage for COBOL.

(a)   SCHEMA NAME IS COMPANY

    RECORD NAME IS EMPLOYEE
        DUPLICATES ARE NOT ALLOWED FOR SSN
        DUPLICATES ARE NOT ALLOWED FOR FNAME, MINIT, LNAME

FNAME	TYPE IS	CHARACTER 15
MINIT	TYPE IS	CHARACTER 1
LNAME	TYPE IS	CHARACTER 15
SSN	TYPE IS	CHARACTER 9
BIRTHDATE	TYPE IS	CHARACTER 9
ADDRESS	TYPE IS	CHARACTER 30
SEX	TYPE IS	CHARACTER 1
SALARY	TYPE IS	CHARACTER 10
DEPTNAME	TYPE IS	CHARACTER 15

    RECORD NAME IS DEPARTMENT
        DUPLICATES ARE NOT ALLOWED FOR NAME
        DUPLICATES ARE NOT ALLOWED FOR NUMBER

NAME	TYPE IS	CHARACTER 15	
NUMBER	TYPE IS	NUMERIC INTEGER	
LOCATIONS	TYPE IS	CHARACTER 15	VECTOR
MGRSTART	TYPE IS	CHARACTER 9	

    RECORD NAME IS PROJECT
        DUPLICATES ARE NOT ALLOWED FOR NAME
        DUPLICATES ARE NOT ALLOWED FOR NUMBER

NAME	TYPE IS	CHARACTER 15
NUMBER	TYPE IS	NUMERIC INTEGER
LOCATION	TYPE IS	CHARACTER 15

    RECORD NAME IS WORKS_ON
        DUPLICATES ARE NOT ALLOWED FOR ESSN, PNUMBER

ESSN	TYPE IS	CHARACTER 9
PNUMBER	TYPE IS	NUMERIC INTEGER
HOURS	TYPE IS	NUMERIC (4,1)

    RECORD NAME IS SUPERVISOR
        DUPLICATES ARE NOT ALLOWED FOR SUPERVISOR_SSN

SUPERVISOR_SSN	TYPE IS	CHARACTER 9

    RECORD NAME IS DEPENDENT
        DUPLICATES ARE NOT ALLOWED FOR EMPSSN, NAME

EMPSSN	TYPE IS	CHARACTER 9
NAME	TYPE IS	CHARACTER 15
SEX	TYPE IS	CHARACTER 1
BIRTHDATE	TYPE IS	CHARACTER 9
RELATIONSHIP	TYPE IS	CHARACTER 10

Figure C.9(a)   Network DDL. (a) Record type declarations.

(b) SET NAME IS ALL_DEPTS
      OWNER IS SYSTEM
         ORDER IS SORTED BY DEFINED KEYS
      MEMBER IS DEPARTMENT
         KEY IS ASCENDING NAME

     SET NAME IS WORKS_FOR
      OWNER IS DEPARTMENT
         ORDER IS SORTED BY DEFINED KEYS
      MEMBER IS EMPLOYEE
         INSERTION IS MANUAL
         RETENTION IS OPTIONAL
         KEY IS ASCENDING LNAME, FNAME, MINIT
         CHECK IS DEPTNAME IN EMPLOYEE = NAME IN DEPARTMENT

     SET NAME IS CONTROLS
      OWNER IS DEPARTMENT
         ORDER IS SORTED BY DEFINED KEYS
      MEMBER IS PROJECT
         INSERTION IS AUTOMATIC
         RETENTION IS MANDATORY
         KEY IS ASCENDING NAME
         SET SELECTION IS BY APPLICATION

     SET NAME IS MANAGES
      OWNER IS EMPLOYEE
         ORDER IS SYSTEM DEFAULT
      MEMBER IS DEPARTMENT
         INSERTION IS AUTOMATIC
         RETENTION IS MANDATORY
         SET SELECTION IS BY APPLICATION

     SET NAME IS P_WORKSON
      OWNER IS PROJECT
         ORDER IS SYSTEM DEFAULT
         DUPLICATES ARE NOT ALLOWED
      MEMBER IS WORKS_ON
         INSERTION IS AUTOMATIC
         RETENTION IS FIXED
         KEY IS ESSN
         SET SELECTION IS STRUCTURAL NUMBER IN PROJECT = PNUMBER IN
         WORKS_ON

     SET NAME IS E_WORKSON
      OWNER IS EMPLOYEE
         ORDER IS SYSTEM DEFAULT
         DUPLICATES ARE NOT ALLOWED
      MEMBER IS WORKS_ON
         INSERTION IS AUTOMATIC
         RETENTION IS FIXED
         KEY IS PNUMBER
         SET SELECTION IS STRUCTURAL SSN IN EMPLOYEE = ESSN IN WORKS_ON

Figure C.9(b) Network DDL. (b) Set type declarations.

```
SET NAME IS SUPERVISEES
    OWNER IS SUPERVISOR
        ORDER IS BY DEFINED KEY
        DUPLICATES ARE NOT ALLOWED
    MEMBER IS EMPLOYEE
        INSERTION IS MANUAL
        RETENTION IS OPTIONAL
        KEY IS LNAME, MINIT, FNAME

SET NAME IS IS_A_SUPERVISOR
    OWNER IS EMPLOYEE
        ORDER IS SYSTEM DEFAULT
        DUPLICATES ARE NOT ALLOWED
    MEMBER IS SUPERVISOR
        INSERTION IS AUTOMATIC
        RETENTION IS MANDATORY
        KEY IS SUPERVISOR_SSN
        SET SELECTION IS BY VALUE OF SSN IN EMPLOYEE
        CHECK IS SUPERVISOR_SSN IN SUPERVISION = SSN IN EMPLOYEE

SET NAME IS DEPENDENTS_OF
    OWNER IS EMPLOYEE
        ORDER IS BY DEFINED KEY
        DUPLICATES ARE NOT ALLOWED
    MEMBER IS DEPENDENT
        INSERTION IS AUTOMATIC
        RETENTION IS FIXED
        KEY IS ASCENDING NAME
        SET SELECTION IS STRUCTURAL SSN IN EMPLOYEE = EMPSSN IN
DEPENDENT
```

Figure C.9(b)   *(Continued)*

DML commands are record-at-a-time, it is necessary to identify specific records of the database as **current records.** The DBMS itself keeps track of a number of current records and set occurrences by means of a mechanism known as **currency indicators.** In addition, the host programming language needs local program variables to hold the records of different record types so that their contents can be manipulated by the host program. The set of these local variables in the program is usually referred to as the **user work area (UWA).** The UWA is a set of program variables, declared in the host program, to communicate the contents of individual records between the DBMS and the host program. For each record type in the database schema, a corresponding program variable with the same format must be declared in the program.

Currency Indicators.   In the network DML, retrievals and updates are handled by moving or **navigating** through the database records; hence, keeping a trace of the search is critical. Currency indicators are a means of keeping track of the most recently accessed records and set occurrences by the DBMS. They play the role of position holders so that we may process new records starting from the ones most recently accessed until we retrieve all the records that contain the information we need. Each currency indicator can be thought of as a record pointer (or record address) that points to a single database record. In a network DBMS, several currency indicators are used:

- *Current of record type:* For each record type, the DBMS keeps track of the most recently accessed record of that record type. If no record has been accessed yet from that record type, the current record is undefined.

- *Current of set type:* For each set type in the schema, the DBMS keeps track of the most recently accessed set occurrence from the set type. The set occurrence is specified by a single record from that set, which is either the owner or one of the member records. Hence, the current of set (or current set) points to a record, even though it is used to keep track of a set occurrence. If the program has not accessed any record from that set type, the current of set is undefined.

- *Current of run unit (CRU):* A run unit is a database access program that is executing (running) on the computer system. For each run unit, the CRU keeps track of the record most recently accessed by the program; this record can be from *any* record type in the database.

Each time a program executes a DML command, the currency indicators for the record types and set types affected by that command are updated by the DBMS.

Status Indicators. Several **status indicators** return an indication of success or failure after each DML command is executed. The program can check the values of these status indicators and take appropriate action—either to continue execution or to transfer to an error-handling routine. We call the main status variable DB_STATUS and assume that it is implicitly declared in the host program. After each DML command, the value of DB_STA-TUS indicates whether the command was successful or whether an error or an exception occurred. The most common exception that occurs is the **END_OF_SET (EOS)** exception.

C.4 Network Data Manipulation Language

The commands for manipulating a network database are called the network **data manipulation language (DML).** These commands are typically embedded in a general-purpose programming language, called the **host programming language.** The DML commands can be grouped into navigation commands, retrieval commands, and update commands. **Navigation commands** are used to set the currency indicators to specific records and set occurrences in the database. **Retrieval commands** retrieve the current record of the run unit (CRU). **Update commands** can be divided into two subgroups—one for updating records, and the other for updating set occurrences. Record update commands are used to store new records, delete unwanted records, and modify field values, whereas set update commands are used to connect or disconnect a member record in a set occurrence or to move a member record from one set occurrence to another. The full set of commands is summarized in Table C.2.

Table C.2   Summary of Network DML Commands

Retrieval

GET	Retrieve the current of run unit (CRU) into the corresponding user work area (UWA) variable.

Navigation

FIND	Reset the currency indicators; always sets the CRU; also sets currency indicators of involved record types and set types. There are many variations of FIND.

Record Update

STORE	Store the new record in the database and make it the CRU.
ERASE	Delete from the database the record that is the CRU.
MODIFY	Modify some fields of the record that is the CRU.

Set Update

CONNECT	Connect a member record (the CRU) to a set instance.
DISCONNECT	Remove a member record (the CRU) from a set instance.
RECONNECT	Move a member record (the CRU) from one set instance to another.

We discuss these DML commands below and illustrate our discussion with examples that use the network schema shown in Figure C.8 and defined by the DDL statements in Figures C.9(a) and (b). The DML commands we present are generally based on the CODA-SYL DBTG proposal. We use PASCAL as the host language in our examples, but in the actual DBMSs in use, COBOL and FORTRAN are predominantly used as host languages. The examples consist of short program segments without any variable declarations. In our programs, we prefix the DML commands with a $-sign to distinguish them from the PASCAL language statements. We write PASCAL language keywords—such as *if*, *then*, *while*, and *for*—in lowercase. In our examples we often need to assign values to fields of the PASCAL UWA variables. We use the PASCAL notation for assignment.

C.4.1   DML Commands for Retrieval and Navigation

The DML command for retrieving a record is the **GET** command. Before the GET command is issued, the program should specify the record it wants to retrieve as the CRU, by using the appropriate navigational **FIND** commands. There are many variations of FIND; we will first discuss the use of FIND in locating record instances of a record type and then discuss the variations for processing set occurrences.

DML Commands for Locating Records of a Record Type.   There are two main variations of the FIND command for locating a record of a certain record type and making that record the CRU and current of record type. Other currency indicators may also be affected, as we shall see. The format of these two commands is as follows, where optional parts of the command are shown in brackets, [...]:

- FIND ANY <record type name> [USING <field list>]
- FIND DUPLICATE <record type name> [USING <field list>]

We now illustrate the use of these commands with examples. To retrieve the EMPLOYEE record for the employee whose name is John Smith and to print out his salary, we can write EX1:

```
EX1: 1    EMPLOYEE.FNAME := 'John'; EMPLOYEE.LNAME := 'Smith';
     2    $FIND ANY EMPLOYEE USING FNAME, LNAME;
     3    if DB_STATUS = 0
     4        then begin
     5            $GET EMPLOYEE;
     6            writeln (EMPLOYEE.SALARY)
     7            end
     8        else writeln ('no record found');
```

The FIND ANY command finds the *first* record in the database of the specified <record type name> such that the field values of the record match the values initialized earlier in the corresponding UWA fields specified in the USING clause of the command. In EX1, lines 1 and 2 are equivalent to saying: "Search for the first EMPLOYEE record that satisfies the condition FNAME = 'John' and LNAME = 'Smith' and make it the current record of the run unit (CRU)." The GET statement is equivalent to saying: "Retrieve the CRU record into the corresponding UWA program variable." The IDMS system combines FIND and GET into a single command, called OBTAIN.

If more than one record satisfies our search and we want to retrieve all of them, we must write a looping construct in the host programming language. For example, to retrieve all EMPLOYEE records for employees who work in the Research department and to print their names, we can write EX2.

```
EX2: EMPLOYEE.DEPTNAME := 'Research';
     $FIND ANY EMPLOYEE USING DEPTNAME;
     while DB_STATUS = 0 do
         begin
         $GET EMPLOYEE;
         writeln (EMPLOYEE.FNAME, EMPLOYEE.LNAME);
         $FIND DUPLICATE EMPLOYEE USING DEPTNAME
         end;
```

The FIND DUPLICATE command finds the *next* (or duplicate) record, starting from the current record, that satisfies the search.

C.4.2 DML Commands for Set Processing

For set processing, we have the following variations of FIND:

- FIND (FIRST | NEXT | PRIOR | LAST | ...) <record type name>
- FIND OWNER WITHIN <set type name>

Once we have established a current set occurrence of a set type, we can use the FIND command to locate various records that participate in the set occurrence. We can locate either the owner record or one of the member records and make that record the CRU. We use FIND OWNER to locate the owner record and one of FIND FIRST, FIND NEXT, FIND LAST, or FIND PRIOR to locate the first, next, last, or prior member record of the set instance, respectively.

Consider the request to print the names of all employees who work full-time—40 hours per week—on the 'ProductX' project; this example is shown as EX3:

```
EX3: PROJECT.NAME := 'ProductX';
     $FIND ANY PROJECT USING NAME;
     if DB_STATUS = 0 then
         begin
         WORKS_ON.HOURS:= '40.0';
         $FIND FIRST WORKS_ON WITHIN P_WORKSON USING HOURS;
         while DB_STATUS = 0 do
             begin
             $GET WORKS_ON;
             $FIND OWNER WITHIN E_WORKSON; $GET EMPLOYEE;
             writeln (EMPLOYEE.FNAME, EMPLOYEE.LNAME),
             $FIND NEXT WORKS_ON WITHIN P_WORKSON USING HOURS
             end
     end;
```

In EX3, the qualification USING HOURS in FIND FIRST and FIND NEXT specifies that only the WORKS_ON records in the current set instance of P_WORKSON whose HOURS field value matches the value in WORKS_ON.HOURS of the UWA, which is set to '40.0' in the program, are found. Notice that the USING clause with FIND NEXT is used to find the *next member record within the same set occurrence;* when we process records of a record type *regardless of the sets they belong to,* we use FIND DUPLICATE rather than FIND NEXT.

We can use numerous embedded loops in the same program segment to process several sets. For example, consider the following query: For each department, print the department's name and its manager's name; and for each employee who works in that department, print the employee's name and the list of project names that the employee works on.

This query requires us to process the system-owned set ALL_DEPTS to retrieve DEPARTMENT records. Using the WORKS_FOR set, the program retrieves the EMPLOYEE records for each DEPARTMENT. Then, for each employee found, the E_WORKSON set is accessed to locate the WORKS_ON records. For each WORKS_ON record located, a "FIND OWNER WITHIN P_WORKSON" locates the appropriate PROJECT.

C.4.3 DML Commands for Updating the Database

The DML commands for updating a network database are summarized in Table C.2. Here, we first discuss the commands for updating records—namely the STORE, ERASE, and MODIFY commands. These are used to insert a new record, delete a record, and modify some fields of a record, respectively. Following this, we illustrate the commands that modify set instances, which are the CONNECT, DISCONNECT, and RECONNECT commands.

The STORE Command. The STORE command is used to insert a new record. Before issuing a STORE, we must first set up the UWA variable of the corresponding record type so that its field values contain the field values of the new record. For example, to insert a new EMPLOYEE record for John F. Smith, we can prepare the data in the UWA variables, then issue

```
$STORE EMPLOYEE;
```

The result of the STORE command is insertion of the current contents of the UWA record of the specified record type into the database. In addition, if the record type is an AUTOMATIC member of a set type, the record is automatically inserted into a set instance.

The ERASE and ERASE ALL Commands. To delete a record from the database, we first make that record the CRU and then issue the ERASE command. For example, to delete the EMPLOYEE record inserted above, we can use EX4:

```
EX4: EMPLOYEE.SSN := '567342793';
     $FIND ANY EMPLOYEE USING SSN;
     if DB_STATUS = 0 then $ERASE EMPLOYEE;
```

The effect of an ERASE command on any member records that are *owned by the record being deleted* is determined by the set retention option. A variation of the ERASE command, **ERASE ALL**, allows the programmer to remove a record and all records owned by it directly or indirectly. This means that *all* member records owned by the record are deleted. In addition, member records owned by any of the deleted records are also deleted, down to any number of repetitions.

The MODIFY Command. The final command for updating records is the MODIFY command, which changes some of the field values of a record.

C.4.4 Commands for Updating Set Instances

We now consider the three set update operations—CONNECT, DISCONNECT, and RECONNECT—which are used to insert and remove member records in set instances. The CONNECT command inserts a member record into a set instance. The member record should be the current of run unit and is connected to the set instance that is the current of set for the set type. For example, to connect the EMPLOYEE record with SSN = '567342793' to the WORKS_FOR set owned by the Research DEPARTMENT record, we can use EX5:

```
EX5: DEPARTMENT.NAME := 'Research';
     $FIND ANY DEPARTMENT USING NAME;
     if DB_STATUS = 0 then
         begin
         EMPLOYEE.SSN := '567342793';
         $FIND ANY EMPLOYEE USING SSN;
         if DB_STATUS = 0 then
             $CONNECT EMPLOYEE TO WORKS_FOR;
         end;
```

Notice that the EMPLOYEE record to be connected should *not be a member* of any set instance of WORKS_FOR before the CONNECT command is issued. We must use the RECONNECT command for the latter case. The CONNECT command can be used only with MANUAL sets or with AUTOMATIC OPTIONAL sets. With other AUTOMATIC sets, the system automatically connects a member record to a set instance, governed by the SET SELECTION option specified, as soon as the record is stored.

The DISCONNECT command is used to remove a member record from a set instance without connecting it to another set instance. Hence, it can be used only with OPTIONAL sets. We make the record to be disconnected the CRU before issuing the DISCONNECT command. For example, to remove the EMPLOYEE record with SSN = '836483873' from the SUPERVISEES set instance of which it is a member, we use EX6:

```
EX6: EMPLOYEE.SSN := '836483873';
     $FIND ANY EMPLOYEE USING SSN;
     if DB_STATUS = 0 then
         $DISCONNECT EMPLOYEE FROM SUPERVISEES;
```

Finally, the RECONNECT command can be used with both OPTIONAL and MANDATORY sets, but not with FIXED sets. The RECONNECT command moves a member record from one set instance to another set instance of the *same* set type. It cannot be used with FIXED sets because a member record cannot be moved from one set instance to another under the FIXED constraint.

Selected Bibliography

Early work on the network data model was done by Charles Bachman during the development of the first commercial DBMS, IDS (Integrated Data Store, Bachman and Williams 1964) at General Electric and later at Honeywell. Bachman also introduced the earliest diagrammatic technique for representing relationships in database schemas, called data structure diagrams (Bachman 1969) or Bachman diagrams. Bachman won the 1973 Turing Award, ACM's highest honor, for his work, and his Turing Award lecture (Bachman 1973) presents the view of the database as a primary resource and the programmer as a "navigator" through the database.

The DBTG of CODASYL was set up to propose DBMS standards. The DBTG 1971 report (DBTG 1971) contains schema and subschema DDLs and a DML for use with COBOL. A revised report (CODASYL 1978) was made in 1978, and another draft revision was made in 1981. The X3H2 committee of ANSI (American National Standards Institute) proposed a standard network language called NDL.

The design of network databases is discussed by Dahl and Bubenko (1982), Whang et al. (1982), Schenk (1974), Gerritsen (1975), and Bubenko et al. (1976). Irani et al. (1979) discuss optimization techniques for designing network schemas from user requirements. Bradley (1978) proposes a high-level query language for the network model. Navathe (1980) discusses structural mapping of network schemas to relational schemas. Mark et al. (1992) discuss an approach to maintaining a network and relational database in a consistent state.

Other popular network model-based systems include VAX-DBMS (of Digital), IMAGE (of Hewlett-Packard), DMS-1100 of UNIVAC, and SUPRA (of Cincom).

APPENDIX D

An Overview of the Hierarchical Data Model

This appendix provides an overview of the hierarchical data model.[1] There are no original documents that describe the hierarchical model, as there are for the relational and network models. The principles behind the hierarchical model are derived from Information Management System (IMS), which is the dominant hierarchical system in use today by a large number of banks, insurance companies, and hospitals as well as several government agencies. Another popular hierarchical DBMS is MRI's System-2000 (which was later sold by SAS Institute).

In this appendix we present the concepts for modeling hierarchical schemas and instances, the concept of a virtual parent-child relationship, which is used to overcome the limitations of pure hierarchies, and the constraints on the hierarchical model. A few examples of data manipulation are included.

---

1. The complete chapter on the hierarchical data model and the IMS system from the second edition of this book is available at the Web site for the book. This appendix is an edited excerpt of that chapter.

941

D.1   Hierarchical Database Structures

D.1.1   Parent-Child Relationships and Hierarchical Schemas

The hierarchical model employs two main data structuring concepts: records and parent-child relationships. A **record** is a collection of **field values** that provide information on an entity or a relationship instance. Records of the same type are grouped into **record types.** A record type is given a name, and its structure is defined by a collection of named **fields** or **data items.** Each field has a certain data type, such as integer, real, or string.

A **parent-child relationship type (PCR type)** is a 1:N relationship between two record types. The record type on the 1-side is called the **parent record type,** and the one on the N-side is called the **child record type** of the PCR type. An **occurrence** (or **instance**) of the PCR type consists of *one record* of the parent record type and a number of records (zero or more) of the child record type.

A **hierarchical database schema** consists of a number of hierarchical schemas. Each **hierarchical schema** (or **hierarchy**) consists of a number of record types and PCR types.

A hierarchical schema is displayed as a **hierarchical diagram,** in which record type names are displayed in rectangular boxes and PCR types are displayed as lines connecting the parent record type to the child record type. Figure D.1 shows a simple hierarchical diagram for a hierarchical schema with three record types and two PCR types. The record types are DEPARTMENT, EMPLOYEE, and PROJECT. Field names can be displayed under each record type name, as shown in Figure D.1. In some diagrams, for brevity, we display only the record type names.

We refer to a PCR type in a hierarchical schema by listing the pair (parent record type, child record type) between parentheses. The two PCR types in Figure D.1 are (DEPARTMENT, EMPLOYEE) and (DEPARTMENT, PROJECT). Notice that PCR types *do not* have a name in the hierarchical model. In Figure D.1 each *occurrence* of the (DEPARTMENT, EMPLOYEE) PCR type relates one department record to the records of the *many* (zero or more) employees who work in that department. An *occurrence* of the (DEPARTMENT, PROJECT) PCR type relates a department record to the records of projects controlled by that department. Figure D.2 shows two PCR occurrences (or instances) for each of these two PCR types.

Figure D.1   A hierarchical schema.

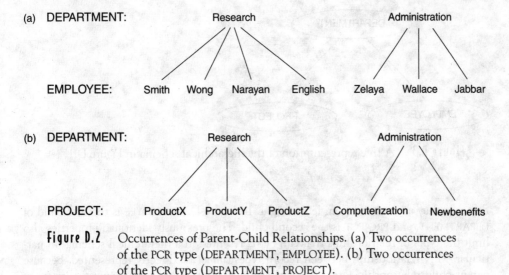

Figure D.2 Occurrences of Parent-Child Relationships. (a) Two occurrences of the PCR type (DEPARTMENT, EMPLOYEE). (b) Two occurrences of the PCR type (DEPARTMENT, PROJECT).

D.1.2 Properties of a Hierarchical Schema

A hierarchical schema of record types and PCR types must have the following properties:

1. One record type, called the **root** of the hierarchical schema, does not participate as a child record type in any PCR type.

2. Every record type except the root participates as a child record type in *exactly one* PCR type.

3. A record type can participate as parent record type in any number (zero or more) of PCR types.

4. A record type that does not participate as parent record type in any PCR type is called a **leaf** of the hierarchical schema.

5. If a record type participates as parent in more than one PCR type, then *its child record types are ordered.* The order is displayed, by convention, from left to right in a hierarchical diagram.

The definition of a hierarchical schema defines a **tree data structure.** In the terminology of tree data structures, a record type corresponds to a **node** of the tree, and a PCR type corresponds to an **edge** (or **arc**) of the tree. We use the terms *node* and *record type,* and *edge* and *PCR type,* interchangeably. The usual convention of displaying a tree is slightly different from that used in hierarchical diagrams, in that each tree edge is shown separately from other edges (Figure D.3). In hierarchical diagrams the convention is that all edges emanating from the same parent node are joined together (as in Figure D.1). We use this latter hierarchical diagram convention.

The preceding properties of a hierarchical schema mean that every node except the root has exactly one parent node. However, a node can have several child nodes, and in

Figure D.3   A tree representation of the hierarchical schema in Figure D.1.

this case they are ordered from left to right. In Figure D.1 EMPLOYEE is the first child of
DEPARTMENT, and PROJECT is the second child. The previously identified properties also
limit the types of relationships that can be represented in a hierarchical schema. In particular, M:N relationships between record types *cannot* be directly represented, because
parent-child relationships are 1:N relationships, and a record type *cannot participate as
child* in two or more distinct parent-child relationships.

   An M:N relationship may be handled in the hierarchical model by allowing duplication of child record instances. For example, consider an M:N relationship between
EMPLOYEE and PROJECT, where a project can have several employees working on it, and
an employee can work on several projects. We can represent the relationship as a
(PROJECT, EMPLOYEE) PCR type. In this case a record describing the same employee can be
duplicated by appearing once under *each* project that the employee works for. Alternatively, we can represent the relationship as an (EMPLOYEE, PROJECT) PCR type, in which
case project records may be duplicated.

EXAMPLE 1: Consider the following instances of the EMPLOYEE:PROJECT relationship:

Project	Employees Working on the Project
A	E1, E3, E5
B	E2, E4, E6
C	E1, E4
D	E2, E3, E4, E5

   If these instances are stored using the hierarchical schema (PROJECT, EMPLOYEE) (with
PROJECT as the parent), there will be four occurrences of the (PROJECT, EMPLOYEE) PCR
type—one for each project. The employee records for E1, E2, E3, and E5 will appear *twice
each* as child records, however, because each of these employees works on two projects.
The employee record for E4 will appear three times—once under each of projects B, C,

and D and may have number of hours that E4 works on each project in the corresponding instance.

To avoid such duplication, a technique is used whereby several hierarchical schemas can be specified in the same hierarchical database schema. Relationships like the preceding PCR type can now be defined across different hierarchical schemas. This technique, called **virtual relationships,** causes a departure from the "strict" hierarchical model. We discuss this technique in Section D.2.

D.1.3 Hierarchical Occurrence Trees

Corresponding to a hierarchical schema, many **hierarchical occurrences,** also called **occurrence trees,** exist in the database. Each one is a **tree structure** whose root is a single record from the root record type. The occurrence tree also contains all the children record occurrences of the root record and continues all the way to records of the leaf record types.

For example, consider the hierarchical diagram shown in Figure D.4, which represents part of the COMPANY database introduced in Chapter 3 and also used in Chapters 7, 8, and 9. Figure D.5 shows one hierarchical occurrence tree of this hierarchical schema. In the occurrence tree, each **node** is a **record occurrence,** and each arc represents a parent-child relationship between two records. In both Figures D.4 and D.5, we use the characters **D, E, P, T, S,** and **W** to represent **type indicators** for the record types DEPARTMENT, EMPLOYEE, PROJECT, DEPENDENT, SUPERVISEE, and WORKER, respectively. A node N and all its descendent nodes form a **subtree** of node N. An **occurrence tree** can be defined as the subtree of a record whose type is of the root record type.

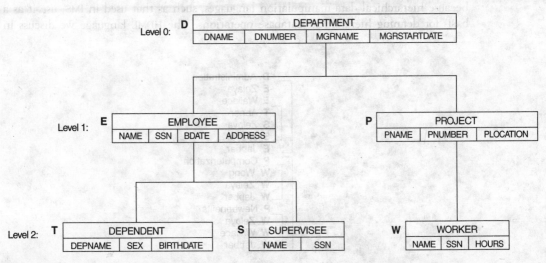

Figure D.4   A hierarchical schema for part of the COMPANY database.

Figure D.5   An occurrence tree of the schema in Figure D.4.

D.1.4   Linearized Form of a Hierarchical Occurrence Tree

A hierarchical occurrence tree can be represented in storage by using any of a variety of data structures. However, a particularly simple storage structure that can be used is the **hierarchical record,** which is a linear ordering of the records in an occurrence tree in the **preorder traversal** of the tree. This order produces a sequence of record occurrences known as the **hierarchical sequence** (or **hierarchical record sequence**) of the occurrence tree; it can be obtained by applying a recursive procedure called the **pre-order traversal,** which visits nodes depth first and in a left-to-right fashion.

The occurrence tree in Figure D.5 gives the hierarchical sequence shown in Figure D.6. The system stores the type indicator with each record so that the record can be distinguished within the hierarchical sequence. The hierarchical sequence is also important because hierarchical data-manipulation languages, such as that used in IMS, use it as a basis for defining hierarchical database operations. The HDML language we discuss in

Figure D.6   Hierarchical sequence for the occurrence tree in Figure D.5.

Section D.3 (which is a simplified version of DL/1 of IMS) is based on the hierarchical sequence. A **hierarchical path** is a sequence of nodes $N_1, N_2, ..., N_i$, where N_1 is the root of a tree and N_j is a child of N_{j-1} for $j = 2, 3, ..., i$. A hierarchical path can be defined either on a hierarchical schema or on an occurrence tree. We can now define a **hierarchical database occurrence** as a sequence of all the occurrence trees that are occurrences of a hierarchical schema. For example, a hierarchical database occurrence of the hierarchical schema shown in Figure D.4 would consist of a number of occurrence trees similar to the one shown in Figure D.5, one for each distinct department.

D.1.5 Virtual Parent-Child Relationships

The hierarchical model has problems when modeling certain types of relationships. These include the following relationships and situations:

1. M:N relationships.

2. The case where a record type participates as child in more than one PCR type.

3. N-ary relationships with more than two participating record types.

Notice that the relationship between EMPLOYEE and EPOINTER in Figure D.7(a) is a 1:N relationship and hence qualifies as a PCR type. Such a relationship is called a **virtual parent-child relationship (VPCR) type**.[2] EMPLOYEE is called the **virtual parent** of EPOINTER; and conversely, EPOINTER is called a **virtual child** of EMPLOYEE. Conceptually, PCR types and VPCR types are similar. The main difference between the two lies in the way they are implemented. A PCR type is usually implemented by using the hierarchical

Figure D.7 Representing M:N relationships using Virtual Parent Child Relationships. (a) EMPLOYEE as virtual parent. (b) PROJECT as virtual parent.

2. The term "virtual" is not used in the IMS system, but it is used here to simplify the distinction between hierarchical relationships within one hierarchy (called Physical in IMS) and across hierarchies (called Logical in IMS).

sequence, whereas a VPCR type is usually implemented by establishing a pointer (a physical one containing an address, or a logical one containing a key) from a virtual child record to its virtual parent record. This mainly affects the efficiency of certain queries.

Figure D.8 shows a hierarchical database schema of the COMPANY database that uses some VPCRs and has no redundancy in its record occurrences. The hierarchical database schema is made up of two hierarchical schemas—one with root DEPARTMENT, and the other with root EMPLOYEE. Four VPCRs, all with virtual parent EMPLOYEE, are included to represent the relationships without redundancy. Notice that IMS *may not allow this* because an implementation constraint in IMS limits a record to being virtual parent of at most one VPCR; to get around this constraint, one can create dummy children record types of EMPLOYEE in Hierarchy 2 so that each VPCR points to a distinct virtual parent record type.

In general, there are many feasible methods of designing a database using the hierarchical model. In many cases, performance considerations are the most important factor in choosing one hierarchical database schema over another. Performance depends

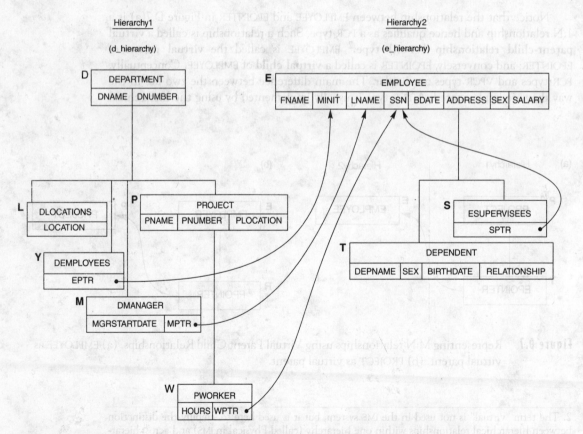

Figure D.8   Using VPCR types to eliminate redundancy in the COMPANY database.

on the implementation options available—for example, whether certain types of pointers are provided by the system and whether certain limits on number of levels are imposed by the DBA.

D.2 Integrity Constraints and Data Definition in the Hierarchical Model

D.2.1 Integrity Constraints in the Hierarchical Model

A number of built-in **inherent constraints** exist in the hierarchical model whenever we specify a hierarchical schema. These include the following constraints:

1. No record occurrences except root records can exist without being related to a parent record occurrence. This has the following implications:

   a. A child record cannot be inserted unless it is linked to a parent record.

   b. A child record may be deleted independently of its parent; however, deletion of a parent record automatically results in deletion of all its child and descendent records.

   c. The above rules do not apply to virtual child records and virtual parent records.

2. If a child record has two or more parent records from the *same* record type, the child record must be duplicated once under each parent record.

3. A child record having two or more parent records of *different* record types can do so only by having at most one real parent, with all the others represented as virtual parents. IMS limits the number of virtual parents to one.

4. In IMS, a record type can be the virtual parent in *only one* VPCR type. That is, the number of virtual children can be only one per record type in IMS.

D.2.2 Data Definition in the Hierarchical Model

In this section we give an example of a hierarchical data definition language (HDDL), which is *not* the language of any specific hierarchical DBMS but is used to illustrate the language concepts for a hierarchical database. The HDDL demonstrates how a hierarchical database schema can be defined. To define a hierarchical database schema, we must define the fields of each record type, the data type of each field, and any key constraints on fields. In addition, we must specify a root record type as such; and for every nonroot record type, we must specify its (real) parent in a PCR type. Any VPCR types must also be specified.

In Figure D.9, either each record type is declared to be of type root or a single (real) parent record type is declared for the record type. The data items of the record are then listed along with their data types. We must specify a virtual parent for data items that are of type *pointer*. Data items declared under the KEY clause are constrained to have unique values for each record. Each KEY clause specifies a separate key; in addition, if a single KEY clause lists more than one field, the combination of these field values must be unique in

```
SCHEMA NAME = COMPANY

HIERARCHIES = HIERARCHY1, HIERARCHY2

RECORD
    NAME = EMPLOYEE
    TYPE = ROOT OF HIERARCHY2
    DATA ITEMS =
        FNAME       CHARACTER 15
        MINIT       CHARACTER 1
        LNAME       CHARACTER 15
        SSN         CHARACTER 9
        BDATE       CHARACTER 9
        ADDRESS     CHARACTER 30
        SEX         CHARACTER 1
        SALARY      CHARACTER 10
    KEY = SSN
    ORDER BY LNAME, FNAME

RECORD
    NAME = DEPARTMENT
    TYPE = ROOT OF HIERARCHY1
    DATA ITEMS =
        DNAME       CHARACTER 15
        DNUMBER     INTEGER
    KEY = DNAME
    KEY = DNUMBER
    ORDER BY DNAME

RECORD
    NAME = DLOCATIONS
    PARENT = DEPARTMENT
    CHILD NUMBER = 1
    DATA ITEMS =
        LOCATION    CHARACTER 15

RECORD
    NAME = DMANAGER
    PARENT = DEPARTMENT
    CHILD NUMBER = 3
    DATA ITEMS =
        MGRSTARTDATE   CHARACTER 9
        MPTR           POINTER WITH VIRTUAL PARENT = EMPLOYEE

RECORD
    NAME = PROJECT
    PARENT = DEPARTMENT
    CHILD NUMBER = 4
    DATA ITEMS =
        PNAME       CHARACTER 15
        PNUMBER     INTEGER
        PLOCATION   CHARACTER 15
    KEY = PNAME
    KEY = PNUMBER
    ORDER BY PNAME

RECORD
    NAME = PWORKER
    PARENT = PROJECT
    CHILD NUMBER = 1
    DATA ITEMS =
        HOURS       CHARACTER 4
        WPTR        POINTER WITH VIRTUAL PARENT = EMPLOYEE
```

Figure D.9   HDDL declarations for the hierarchical schema in Figure D.8.

```
RECORD
    NAME = DEMPLOYEES
    PARENT = DEPARTMENT
    CHILD NUMBER = 2
    DATA ITEMS =
        EPTR          POINTER WITH VIRTUAL PARENT = EMPLOYEE

RECORD
    NAME IS ESUPERVISEES
    PARENT = EMPLOYEE
    CHILD NUMBER = 2
    DATA ITEMS =
        SPTR          POINTER WITH VIRTUAL PARENT = EMPLOYEE

RECORD
    NAME = DEPENDENT
    PARENT = EMPLOYEE
    CHILD NUMBER = 1
    DATA ITEMS =
        DEPNAME       CHARACTER 15
        SEX           CHARACTER 1
        BIRTHDATE     CHARACTER 9
        RELATIONSHIP  CHARACTER 10
    ORDER BY DESC BIRTHDATE
```

Figure D.9   (Continued)

each record. The CHILD NUMBER clause specifies the left-to-right order of a child record type under its (real) parent record type. The ORDER BY clause specifies the order of individual records of the same record type in the hierarchical sequence. For nonroot record types, the ORDER BY clause specifies how the records should be ordered *within each parent record,* by specifying a field called a **sequence key.** For example, PROJECT records controlled by a particular DEPARTMENT have their subtrees ordered alphabetically within the same parent DEPARTMENT record by PNAME, according to Figure D.9.

D.3   Data Manipulation Language for the Hierarchical Model

We now discuss **Hierarchical Data Manipulation Language (HDML),** which is a record-at-a-time language for manipulating hierarchical databases. We have based its structure on IMS's DL/1 language. It is introduced to illustrate the concepts of a hierarchical database manipulation language. The commands of the language must be embedded in a general-purpose programming language called the **host language.**

The HDML is based on the concept of **hierarchical sequence** defined in Section D.1. Following each database command, the last record accessed by the command is called the **current database record.** The DBMS maintains a pointer to the current record. Subsequent database commands *proceed from the current record* and may define a new current record, depending on the type of command.

D.3.1   The GET Command

The HDML command for retrieving a record is the **GET command.** There are many variations of GET; the structure of two of these variations is as follows, with optional parts enclosed in brackets [...]:

- **GET FIRST**[3] <record type name> [WHERE <condition>]
- **GET NEXT** <record type name> [WHERE <condition>]

The simplest variation is the **GET FIRST command,** which always starts searching the database from the *beginning of the hierarchical sequence* until it finds the first record occurrence of <record type name> that satisfies <condition>. This record also becomes the current of database, current of hierarchy, and current of record type and is retrieved into the corresponding program variable. For example, to retrieve the "first" EMPLOYEE record in the hierarchical sequence whose name is John Smith, we write EX1:

```
EX1: $GET FIRST EMPLOYEE WHERE FNAME ='John' AND LNAME='Smith';
```

The DBMS uses the condition following WHERE to search for the first record in order of the hierarchical sequence that satisfies the condition and is of the specified record type. If more than one record in the database satisfies the WHERE condition and we want to retrieve all of them, we must write a looping construct in the host program and use the GET NEXT command. We assume that the GET NEXT starts its search from the *current record of the record type specified in GET NEXT,*[4] and it searches forward in the hierarchical sequence to find another record of the specified type satisfying the WHERE condition. For example, to retrieve records of all EMPLOYEEs whose salary is less than $20,000 and obtain a printout of their names, we can write the program segment shown in EX2:

```
EX2: $GET FIRST EMPLOYEE WHERE SALARY < '20000.00';
     while DB_STATUS = 0 do
         begin
         writeln (P_EMPLOYEE.FNAME, P_EMPLOYEE.LNAME);
         $GET NEXT EMPLOYEE WHERE SALARY < '20000.00'
         end;
```

In EX2, the while loop continues until no more EMPLOYEE records in the database satisfy the WHERE condition; hence, the search goes through to the last record in the database (hierarchical sequence). When no more records are found, DB_STATUS becomes nonzero, with a code indicating "end of database reached," and the while loop terminates.

D.3.2   The GET PATH and GET NEXT WITHIN PARENT Retrieval Commands

So far we have considered retrieving single records by using the GET command. But when we have to locate a record deep in the hierarchy, the retrieval may be based on a series of

---

3. This is similar to the GET UNIQUE (GU) command of IMS.

4. IMS commands generally proceed forward from the *current of database*, rather than from the current of specified record type as HDML commands do.

conditions on records along the entire hierarchical path. To accommodate this, we introduce the GET PATH command:

    GET (FIRST | NEXT) PATH <hierarchical path> [WHERE <condition>]

Here, <hierarchical path> is a list of record types that starts from the root along a path in the hierarchical schema, and <condition> is a Boolean expression specifying conditions on the individual record types along the path. Because several record types may be specified, the field names are prefixed by the record type names in <condition>. For example, consider the following query: "List the lastname and birthdates of all employee-dependent pairs, where both have the first name John." This is shown in EX3:

```
EX3:  $GET FIRST PATH EMPLOYEE, DEPENDENT
      WHERE EMPLOYEE.FNAME='John' AND DEPENDENT.DEPNAME='John';
      while DB_STATUS = 0 do
            begin
            writeln (P_EMPLOYEE.FNAME, P_EMPLOYEE.BDATE,
                     P_DEPENDENT.BIRTHDATE);
            $GET NEXT PATH EMPLOYEE, DEPENDENT
                  WHERE EMPLOYEE.FNAME='John' AND
                  DEPENDENT.DEPNAME='John'
      end;
```

We assume that a GET PATH command retrieves *all records along the specified path* into the user work area variables,[5] and the last record along the path becomes the current database record. In addition, all records along the path become the current records of their respective record types.

Another common type of query is to find all records of a given type that have *the same parent record*. In this case we need the GET NEXT WITHIN PARENT command, which can be used to loop through the child records of a parent record and has the following format:

```
GET NEXT <child record type name>
     WITHIN [VIRTUAL] PARENT [<parent record type name>][6]
     [WHERE <condition>]
```

This command retrieves the next record of the child record type by searching forward from the current of the child record type for the next child record owned by the current parent record. If no more child records are found, DB_STATUS is set to a nonzero value to indicate that "there are no more records of the specified child record type that have the same parent as the current parent record." The <parent record type name> is *optional*, and the default is the immediate (real) parent record type of <child record type name>. For example, to retrieve the names of all projects controlled by the 'Research' department, we can write the program segment shown in EX4:

```
EX4:  $GET FIRST PATH DEPARTMENT, PROJECT
            WHERE DNAME ='Research';
```

---

5. IMS provides the capability of specifying that only *some* of the records along the path are to be retrieved.

6. There is no provision for retrieving all children of a virtual parent in IMS in this way without defining a view of the database.

```
                    (* the above establishes the 'Research' DEPARTMENT record as
                       current parent of type DEPARTMENT, and retrieves the first
                       child PROJECT record under that DEPARTMENT record *)
           while DB_STATUS = 0 do
                begin
                writeln (P_PROJECT.PNAME);
                $GET NEXT PROJECT WITHIN PARENT
                end;
```

D.3.3   HDML Commands for Update

The HDML commands for updating a hierarchical database are shown in Table D.1, along with the retrieval command. The **INSERT** command is used to insert a new record. Before inserting a record of a particular record type, we must first place the field values of the new record in the appropriate user work area program variable.

The INSERT command inserts a record into the database. The newly inserted record also becomes the current record for the database, its hierarchical schema, and its record type. If it is a root record, as in EX8, it creates a new hierarchical occurrence tree with the new record as root. The record is inserted in the hierarchical sequence in the order specified by any ORDER BY fields in the schema definition.

To insert a child record, we should make its parent, or one of its sibling records, the *current record* of the hierarchical schema before issuing the INSERT command. We should also set any virtual parent pointers before inserting the record.

To delete a record from the database, we first make it the current record and then issue the **DELETE** command. The **GET HOLD** is used to make the record the current record, where the HOLD key word indicates to the DBMS that the program will delete or

Table D.1   Summary of HDML Commands

RETRIEVAL	
GET	Retrieve a record into the corresponding program variable and make it the current record. Variations include GET FIRST, GET NEXT, GET NEXT WITHIN PARENT, and GET PATH.

RECORD UPDATE	
INSERT	Store a new record in the database and make it the current record.
DELETE	Delete the current record (and its subtree) from the database.
REPLACE	Modify some fields of the current record.

CURRENCY RETENTION	
GET HOLD	Retrieve a record and hold it as the current record so it can subsequently be deleted or replaced.

update the record just retrieved. For example, to delete all male EMPLOYEEs, we can use EX5, which also lists the deleted employee names <before> deleting their records:

```
EX5:  $GET HOLD FIRST EMPLOYEE WHERE SEX='M';
      while DB_STATUS=0 then
            begin
            writeln (P_EMPLOYEE.LNAME, P_EMPLOYEE.FNAME);
            $DELETE EMPLOYEE;
            $GET HOLD NEXT EMPLOYEE WHERE SEX='M';
            end;
```

D.3.4   IMS—A Hierarchical DBMS

IMS is one of the earliest DBMSs, and it ranks as the dominant system in the commercial market for support of large-scale accounting and inventory systems. IBM manuals refer to the full product as IMS/VS (Virtual Storage), and typically the full product is installed under the MVS operating system. IMS DB/DC is the term used for installations that utilize the product's own subsystems to support the physical database (DB) and to provide data communications (C).

However, other important versions exist that support only the IMS data language—Data Language One (DL/1). Such DL/1-only configurations can be implemented under MVS, but they may also use the DOS/VSE operating system. These systems issue their calls to VSAM files and use IBM's Customer Information Control System (CICS) for data communications. The trade-off is a sacrifice of support features for the sake of simplicity and improved throughput.

A number of versions of IMS have been marketed to work with various IBM operating systems, including (among the recent systems) OS/VS1, OS/VS2, MVS, MVS/XA, and ESA. The system comes with various options. IMS runs under different versions on the IBM 370 and 30XX family of computers. The data definition and manipulation language of IMS is DL/1. Application programs written in COBOL, PL/1, FORTRAN, and BAL (Basic Assembly Language) interface with DL/1.

Selected Bibliography

The first hierarchical DBMS—IMS and its DL/1 language—was developed by IBM and North American Aviation (Rockwell International) in the late 1960s. Few early documents exist that describe IMS. McGee (1977) gives an overview of IMS in an issue of IBM Systems Journal devoted to ims. Bjoerner and Lovengren (1982) formalize some aspects of the IMS data model. Kapp and Leben (1986) is a popular book on IMS programming. IMS is described in a very large collection of IBM manuals.

Recent work has attempted to incorporate hierarchical structures in the relational model (Gyssens et al., 1989; Jagadish, 1989). This includes nested relational models (see Section 13.6).

Selected Bibliography

Abbreviations Used in the Bibliography

ACM: Association for Computing Machinery

AFIPS: American Federation of Information Processing Societies

CACM: Communications of the ACM (journal)

CIKM: Proceedings of the International Conference on Information and Knowledge Management

EDS: Proceedings of the International Conference on Expert Database Systems

ER Conference: Proceedings of the International Conference on Entity-Relationship Approach (now called International Conference on Conceptual Modeling)

ICDE: Proceedings of the IEEE International Conference on Data Engineering

IEEE: Institute of Electrical and Electronics Engineers

IEEE Computer: Computer magazine (journal) of the IEEE CS

IEEE CS: IEEE Computer Society

IFIP: International Federation for Information Processing

JACM: Journal of the ACM

KDD: Knowledge Discovery in Databases

NCC: Proceedings of the National Computer Conference (published by AFIPS)

OOPSLA: Proceedings of the ACM Conference on Object-Oriented Programming Systems, Languages, and Applications

PODS: Proceedings of the ACM Symposium on Principles of Database Systems

SIGMOD: Proceedings of the ACM SIGMOD International Conference on Management of Data

TKDE: IEEE Transactions on Knowledge and Data Engineering (journal)

TOCS: ACM Transactions on Computer Systems (journal)

TODS: ACM Transactions on Database Systems (journal)

TOIS: ACM Transactions on Information Systems (journal)

TOOIS: ACM Transactions on Office Information Systems (journal)

TSE: IEEE Transactions on Software Engineering (journal)

VLDB: Proceedings of the International Conference on Very Large Data Bases (issues after 1981 available from Morgan Kaufmann, Menlo Park, California)

Format for Bibliographic Citations

Book titles are in boldface—for example, **Database Computers**. Conference proceedings names are in italics—for example, ACM *Pacific Conference*. Journal names are in boldface—for example, **TODS** or **Information Systems**. For journal citations, we give the volume number and issue number (within the volume, if any) and date of issue. For example "**TODS,** 3:4, December 1978" refers to the December 1978 issue of ACM *Transactions on Database Systems,* which is Volume 3, Number 4. Articles that appear in books or conference proceedings that are themselves cited in the bibliography are referenced as "in" these references—for example, "in VLDB [1978]" or "in Rustin [1974]." Page numbers (abbreviated "pp.") are provided with pp. at the end of the citation whenever available. For citations with more than four authors, we will give the first author only followed by et al. In the selected bibliography at the end of each chapter, we use et al. if there are more than two authors.

Bibliographic References

Abbott, R., and Garcia-Molina, H. [1989] "Scheduling Real-Time Transactions with Disk Resident Data," in VLDB [1989].

Abiteboul, S., and Kanellakis, P. [1989] "Object Identity as a Query Language Primitive," in SIGMOD [1989].

Abiteboul, S. Hull, R., and Vianu, V. [1995] **Foundations of Databases,** Addison-Wesley, 1995.

Abrial, J. [1974] "Data Semantics," in Klimbie and Koffeman [1974].

Adam, N., and Gongopadhyay, A. [1993] "Integrating Functional and Data Modeling in a Computer Integrated Manufacturing System," in ICDE [1993].

Adriaans, P., and Zantinge, D. [1996] **Data Mining,** Addison-Wesley, 1996.

Afsarmanesh, H., McLeod, D., Knapp, D., and Parker, A. [1985] "An Extensible Object-Oriented Approach to Databases for VLSI/CAD," in VLDB [1985].

Agrawal, D., and ElAbbadi, A. [1990] "Storage Efficient Replicated Databases," **TKDE,** 2:3, September 1990.

Agrawal, R., and Gehani, N. [1989] "ODE: The Language and the Data Model," in SIGMOD [1989].

Agrawal, R., Gehani, N., and Srinivasan, J. [1990] "OdeView: The Graphical Interface to Ode," in SIGMOD [1990].

Agrawal, R., Imielinski, T., and Swami A. [1993] "Mining Association Rules Between Sets of Items in Databases," in SIGMOD [1993].

Agrawal, R., Imielinski, T., and Swami, A. [1993b] "Database Mining: A Performance Perspective," **IEEE TKDE** 5:6, December 1993.

Agrawal, R., Mehta, M., and Shafer, J., and Srikant, R. [1996] "The Quest Data Mining System," in KDD [1996].

Agrawal, R., and Srikant, R. [1994] "Fast Algorithms for Mining Association Rules in Large Databases," in VLDB [1994].

Ahad, R., and Basu, A. [1991] "ESQL: A Query Language for the Relational Model Supporting Image Domains," in ICDE [1991].

Aho, A., Beeri, C., and Ullman, J. [1979] "The Theory of Joins in Relational Databases," **TODS,** 4:3, September 1979.

Aho, A., Sagiv, Y., and Ullman, J. [1979a] "Efficient Optimization of a Class of Relational Expressions," **TODS,** 4:4, December 1979.

Aho, A. and Ullman, J. [1979] "Universality of Data Retrieval Languages," *Proceedings of the POPL Conference,* San Antonio TX, ACM, 1979.

Akl, S. [1983] "Digital Signatures: A Tutorial Survey," **IEEE Computer,** 16:2, February 1983.

Alashqur, A., Su, S., and Lam, H. [1989] "OQL: A Query Language for Manipulating Object-Oriented Databases," in VLDB [1989].

Albano, A., Cardelli, L., and Orsini, R. [1985] "GALILEO: A Strongly Typed Interactive Conceptual Language," **TODS,** 10:2, June 1985.

Allen, F., Loomis, M., and Mannino, M. [1982] "The Integrated Dictionary/Directory System," **ACM Computing Surveys,** 14:2, June 1982.

Alonso, G., Agrawal, D., El Abbadi, A., and Mohan, C. [1997] "Functionalities and Limitations of Current Workflow Management Systems," IEEE **Expert,** 1997.

Amir, A., Feldman, R., and Kashi, R. [1997] "A New and Versatile Method for Association Generation," Information Systems, 22:6, September 1997.

Anderson, S., Bankier, A., Barrell, B., deBruijn, M., Coulson, A., Drouin, J., Eperon, I., Nierlich, D., Rose, B., Sanger, F., Schreier, P., Smith, A., Staden, R., Young, I. [1981] "Sequence and Organization of the Human Mitochondrial Genome." **Nature,** 290:457–465, 1981.

Andrews, T., and Harris, C. [1987] "Combining Language and Database Advances in an Object-Oriented Development Environment," OOPSLA, 1987.

ANSI [1975] American National Standards Institute Study Group on Data Base Management Systems: Interim Report, FDT, 7:2, ACM, 1975.

ANSI [1986] American National Standards Institute: The Database Language SQL, Document ANSI X3.135, 1986.

ANSI [1986a] American National Standards Institute: The Database Language NDL, Document ANSI X3.133, 1986.

ANSI [1989] American National Standards Institute: Information Resource Dictionary Systems, Document ANSI X3.138, 1989.

Anwar, T., Beck, H., and Navathe, S. [1992] "Knowledge Mining by Imprecise Querying: A Classification Based Approach," in ICDE [1992].

Apers, P., Hevner, A., and Yao, S. [1983] "Optimization Algorithms for Distributed Queries," **TSE,** 9:1, January 1983.

Armstrong, W. [1974] "Dependency Structures of Data Base Relationships," *Proceedings of the IFIP Congress,* 1974.

Astrahan, M., et al. [1976] "System R: A Relational Approach to Data Base Management," **TODS,** 1:2, June 1976.

Atkinson, M., and Buneman, P. [1987] "Types and Persistence in Database Programming Languages" in **ACM Computing Surveys,** 19:2, June 1987.

Atluri, V., Jajodia, S., Keefe, T.F., McCollum, C., and Mukkamala, R. [1997] "Multilevel Secure Transaction Processing: Status and Prospects," in **Database Security: Status and Prospects,** Chapman and Hall, 1997, pp. 79–98.

Atzeni, P., and De Antonellis, V. [1993] **Relational Database Theory,** Benjamin/Cummings, 1993.

Atzeni, P., Mecca, G., and Merialdo, P. [1997] "To Weave the Web," in VLDB [1997].

Bachman, C. [1969] "Data Structure Diagrams," **Data Base** (Bulletin of ACM SIGFIDET), 1:2, March 1969.

Bachman, C. [1973] "The Programmer as a Navigator," **CACM,** 16:1, November 1973.

Bachman, C. [1974] "The Data Structure Set Model," in Rustin [1974].

Bachman, C., and Williams, S. [1964] "A General Purpose Programming System for Random Access Memories," *Proceedings of the Fall Joint Computer Conference,* AFIPS, 26, 1964.

Badal, D., and Popek, G. [1979] "Cost and Performance Analysis of Semantic Integrity Validation Methods," in SIGMOD [1979].

Badrinath, B. and Ramamritham, K. [1992] "Semantics-Based Concurrency Control: Beyond Commutativity," **TODS,** 17:1, March 1992.

Baeza-Yates, R., and Larson, P. A. [1989] "Performance of B1-trees with Partial Expansions," **TKDE,** 1:2, June 1989.

Baeza-Yates, R., and Ribero-Neto, B. [1999] Modern Information Retrieval, Addison-Wesley, 1999.

Balbin, I., and Ramamohanrao, K. [1987] "A Generalization of the Different Approach to Recursive Query Evaluation," **Journal of Logic Programming,** 15:4, 1987.

Bancilhon, F., and Buneman, P., eds. [1990] **Advances in Database Programming Languages,** ACM Press, 1990.

Bancilhon, F., Delobel, C., and Kanellakis, P., eds. [1992] **Building an Object-Oriented Database System: The Story of O2,** Morgan Kaufmann, 1992.

Bancilhon, F., Maier, D., Sagiv, Y., and Ullman, J. [1986] "Magic sets and other strange ways to implement logic programs," PODS [1986].

Bancilhon, F., and Ramakrishnan, R. [1986] "An Amateur's Introduction to Recursive Query Processing Strategies, " in SIGMOD [1986].

Banerjee, J., et al. [1987] "Data Model Issues for Object-Oriented Applications," **TOOIS,** 5:1, January 1987.

Banerjee, J., Kim, W., Kim, H., and Korth, H. [1987a] "Semantics and Implementation of Schema Evolution in Object-Oriented Databases," in SIGMOD [1987].

Baroody, A., and DeWitt, D. [1981] "An Object-Oriented Approach to Database System Implementation," TODS, 6:4, December 1981.

Barsalou, T., Siambela, N., Keller, A., and Wiederhold, G. [1991] "Updating Relational Databases Through Object-Based Views," in SIGMOD [1991].

Bassiouni, M. [1988] "Single-Site and Distributed Optimistic Protocols for Concurrency Control," TSE, 14:8, August 1988.

Batini, C., Ceri, S., and Navathe, S. [1992] **Database Design: An Entity-Relationship Approach,** Benjamin/Cummings, 1992.

Batini, C., Lenzerini, M., and Navathe, S. [1987] "A Comparative Analysis of Methodologies for Database Schema Integration," **ACM Computing Surveys,** 18:4, December 1987.

Batory, D., and Buchmann, A. [1984] "Molecular Objects, Abstract Data Types, and Data Models: A Framework," in VLDB [1984].

Batory, D., et al. [1988] "GENESIS: An Extensible Database Management System," TSE, 14:11, November 1988.

Bayer, R., Graham, M., and Seegmuller, G., eds. [1978] **Operating Systems: An Advanced Course,** Springer-Verlag, 1978.

Bayer, R., and McCreight, E. [1972] "Organization and Maintenance of Large Ordered Indexes," **Acta Informatica,** 1:3, February 1972.

Beck, H., Anwar, T., and Navathe, S. [1993] "A Conceptual Clustering Algorithm for Database Schema Design," TKDE, to appear.

Beck, H., Gala, S., and Navathe, S. [1989] "Classification as a Query Processing Technique in the CANDIDE Semantic Data Model," in ICDE [1989].

Beeri, C., Fagin, R., and Howard, J. [1977] "A Complete Axiomatization for Functional and Multivalued Dependencies," in SIGMOD [1977].

Beeri, C., and Ramakrishnan, R. [1987] "On the Power of Magic" in PODS [1987].

Benson, D., Boguski, M., Lipman, D., and Ostell, J., "GenBank," **Nucleic Acids Research,** 24:1, 1996.

Ben-Zvi, J. [1982] "The Time Relational Model," Ph.D. dissertation, University of California, Los Angeles, 1982.

Berg, B. and Roth, J. [1989] **Software for Optical Disk,** Meckler, 1989.

Berners-Lee, T., Caillian, R., Grooff, J., Pollermann, B. [1992] "World-Wide Web: The Information Universe," **Electronic Networking: Research, Applications and Policy,** 1:2, 1992.

Berners-Lee, T., Caillian, R., Lautonen, A., Nielsen, H., and Secret, A. [1994] "The World Wide Web," CACM, 13:2, August 1994.

Bernstein, P. [1976] "Synthesizing Third Normal Form Relations from Functional Dependencies," TODS, 1:4, December 1976.

Bernstein, P., Blaustein, B., and Clarke, E. [1980] "Fast Maintenance of Semantic Integrity Assertions Using Redundant Aggregate Data," in VLDB [1980].

Bernstein, P., and Goodman, N. [1980] "Timestamp-Based Algorithms for Concurrency Control in Distributed Database Systems," in VLDB [1980].

Bernstein, P., and Goodman, N. [1981] "The Power of Natural Semijoins," SIAM **Journal of Computing,** 10:4, December 1981.

Bernstein, P., and Goodman, N. [1981a] "Concurrency Control in Distributed Database Systems," ACM **Computing Surveys,** 13:2, June 1981.

Bernstein, P., and Goodman, N. [1984] "An Algorithm for Concurrency Control and Recovery in Replicated Distributed Databases," TODS, 9:4, December 1984.

Bernstein, P., Hadzilacos, V., and Goodman, N. [1988] **Concurrency Control and Recovery in Database Systems,** Addison-Wesley, 1988.

Bertino, E. [1992] "Data Hiding and Security in Object-Oriented Databases," in ICDE [1992].

Bertino, E., and Kim, W. [1989] "Indexing Techniques for Queries on Nested Objects," TKDE, 1:2, June 1989.

Bertino, E., Negri, M., Pelagatti, G., and Sbattella, L. [1992] "Object-Oriented Query Languages: The Notion and the Issues," TKDE, 4:3, June 1992.

Bertino, E., Pagani, E., and Rossi, G. [1992] "Fault Tolerance and Recovery in Mobile Computing Systems, in Kumar and Han [1992].

Bertino, F., Rabbitti and Gibbs, S. [1988] "Query Processing in a Multimedia Environment," TOIS, 6, 1988.

Bhargava, B., ed. [1987] **Concurrency and Reliability in Distributed Systems,** Van Nostrand-Reinhold, 1987.

Bhargava, B., and Helal, A. [1993] "Efficient Reliability Mechanisms in Distributed Database Systems," CIKM, November 1993.

Bhargava, B., and Reidl, J. [1988] "A Model for Adaptable Systems for Transaction Processing," in ICDE [1988].

Biliris, A. [1992] "The Performance of Three Database Storage Structures for Managing Large Objects," in SIGMOD [1992].

Biller, H. [1979] "On the Equivalence of Data Base Schemas—A Semantic Approach to Data Translation," **Information Systems,** 4:1, 1979.

Bischoff, J., and T. Alexander, eds., **Data Warehouse: Practical Advice from the Experts,** Prentice-Hall, 1997.

Biskup, J., Dayal, U., and Bernstein, P. [1979] "Synthesizing Independent Database Schemas," in SIGMOD[1979].

Bjork, A. [1973] "Recovery Scenario for a DB/DC System," *Proceedings of the* ACM *National Conference,* 1973.

Bjorner, D., and Lovengren, H. [1982] "Formalization of Database Systems and a Formal Definition of IMS," in VLDB [1982].

Blaha, M., Premerlani, W. [1998] **Object-Oriented Modeling and Design for Database Applications,** Prentice-Hall, 1998.

Blakeley, J., Coburn, N., and Larson, P. [1989] "Updated Derived Relations: Detecting Irrelevant and Autonomously Computable Updates," TODS, 14:3, September 1989.

Blakeley, J., and Martin, N. [1990] "Join Index, Materialized View, and Hybrid-Hash Join: A Performance Analysis," in ICDE [1990].

Blasgen, M., and Eswaran, K. [1976] "On the Evaluation of Queries in a Relational Database System," **IBM Systems Journal,** 16:1, January 1976.

Blasgen, M., et al. [1981] "System R: An Architectural Overview," **IBM Systems Journal,** 20:1, January 1981.

Bleier, R., and Vorhaus, A. [1968] "File Organization in the SDC TDMS," *Proceedings of the IFIP Congress.*

Bocca, J. [1986] "EDUCE—A Marriage of Convenience: Prolog and a Relational DBMS," *Proceedings of the Third International Conference on Logic Programming,* Springer-Verlag, 1986.

Bocca, J. [1986a] "On the Evaluation Strategy of EDUCE," in SIGMOD [1986].

Bodorick, P., Riordon, J., and Pyra, J. [1992] "Deciding on Correct Distributed Query Processing," TKDE, 4:3, June 1992.

Booch, G., Rumbaugh, J., and Jacobson, I., **Unified Modeling Language User Guide,** Addison-Wesley, 1999.

Borgida, A., Brachman, R., McGuinness, D., and Resnick, L. [1989] "CLASSIC: A Structural Data Model for Objects," in SIGMOD [1989].

Borkin, S. [1978] "Data Model Equivalence," in VLDB [1978].

Bouzeghoub, M., and Metais, E. [1991] "Semantic Modelling of Object-Oriented Databases," in VLDB [1991].

Boyce, R., Chamberlin, D., King, W., and Hammer, M. [1975] "Specifying Queries as Relational Expressions," CACM, 18:11, November 1975.

Bracchi, G., Paolini, P., and Pelagatti, G. [1976] "Binary Logical Associations in Data Modelling," in Nijssen [1976].

Brachman, R., and Levesque, H. [1984] "What Makes a Knowledge Base Knowledgeable? A View of Databases from the Knowledge Level," in EDS [1984].

Bratbergsengen, K. [1984] "Hashing Methods and Relational Algebra Operators," in VLDB [1984].

Bray, O. [1988] **Computer Integrated Manufacturing—The Data Management Strategy,** Digital Press, 1988.

Breitbart, Y., Silberschatz, A., and Thompson, G. [1990] "Reliable Transaction Management in a Multi-database System," in SIGMOD [1990].

Brodie, M., and Mylopoulos, J., eds. [1985] **On Knowledge Base Management Systems,** Springer-Verlag, 1985.

Brodie, M., Mylopoulos, J., and Schmidt, J., eds. [1984] **On Conceptual Modeling,** Springer-Verlag, 1984.

Brosey, M., and Shneiderman, B. [1978] "Two Experimental Comparisons of Relational and Hierarchical Database Models," **International Journal of Man-Machine Studies,** 1978.

Bry, F. [1990] "Query Evaluation in Recursive Databases: Bottom-up and Top-down Reconciled," TKDE, 2, 1990.

Bukhres, O. [1992] "Performance Comparison of Distributed Deadlock Detection Algorithms," in ICDE [1992].

Buneman, P., and Frankel, R. [1979] "FQL: A Functional Query Language," in SIGMOD [1979].

Burkhard, W. [1976] "Hashing and Trie Algorithms for Partial Match Retrieval," TODS, 1:2, June 1976, pp. 175–87.

Burkhard, W. [1979] "Partial-match Hash Coding: Benefits of Redunancy," TODS, 4:2, June 1979, pp. 228–39.

Bush, V. [1945] "As We May Think," *Atlantic Monthly,* 176:1, January 1945. Reprinted in Kochen, M., ed., **The Growth of Knowledge,** Wiley, 1967.

Byte [1995] Special Issue on Mobile Computing, June 1995.

CACM [1995] Special issue of the **Communications of the ACM,** on Digital Libraries, 38:5, May 1995.

CACM [1998] Special issue of the **Communications of the ACM** on Digital Libraries: Global Scope and Unlimited Access, 41:4, April 1998.

Cammarata, S., Ramachandra, P., and Shane, D. [1989] "Extending a Relational Database with Deferred Referential Integrity Checking and Intelligent Joins," in SIGMOD [1989].

Campbell, D., Embley, D., and Czejdo, B. [1985] "A Relationally Complete Query Language for the Entity-Relationship Model," in ER Conference [1985].

Cardenas, A. [1985] **Data Base Management Systems,** 2nd ed., Allyn and Bacon, 1985.

Carey, M., et al. [1986] "The Architecture of the EXODUS Extensible DBMS," in Dittrich and Dayal [1986].

Carey, M., DeWitt, D., Richardson, J. and Shekita, E. [1986a] "Object and File Management in the EXODUS Extensible Database System," in VLDB [1986].

Carey, M., DeWitt, D., and Vandenberg, S. [1988] "A Data Model and Query Language for Exodus," in SIGMOD [1988].

Carey, M., Franklin, M., Livny, M., and Shekita, E. [1991] "Data Caching Tradeoffs in Client-Server DBMS Architectures," in SIGMOD [1991].

Carlis, J. [1986] "HAS, a Relational Algebra Operator or Divide Is Not Enough to Conquer," in ICDE [1986].

Carlis, J., and March, S. [1984] "A Descriptive Model of Physical Database Design Problems and Solutions," in ICDE [1984].

Carroll, J. M., [1995] **Scenario Based Design: Envisioning Work and Technology in System Development,** Wiley, 1995.

Casanova, M., Fagin, R., and Papadimitriou, C. [1981] "Inclusion Dependencies and Their Interaction with Functional Dependencies," in PODS [1981].

Casanova, M., Furtado, A., and Tuchermann, L. [1991] "A Software Tool for Modular Database Design," TODS, 16:2, June 1991.

Casanova, M., Tuchermann, L., Furtado, A., and Braga, A. [1989] "Optimization of Relational Schemas Containing Inclusion Dependencies," in VLDB [1989].

Casanova, M., and Vidal, V. [1982] "Toward a Sound View Integration Method," in PODS [1982].

Cattell, R., and Skeen, J. [1992] "Object Operations Benchmark," TODS, 17:1, March 1992.

Castano, S., DeAntonellio, V., Fugini, M.G., and Pernici, B. [1998] "Conceptual Schema Analysis: Techniques and Applications," TODS, 23:3, September 1998, pp. 286–332.

Catarci, T., Costabile, M. F., Santucci, G., and Tarantino, L., eds. [1998] *Proceedings of the Fourth International Workshop on Advanced Visual Interfaces,* ACM Press, 1998.

Catarci, T., Costabile, M. F., Levialdi, S., and Batini, C. [1997] "Visual Query Systems for Databases: A Survey," **Journal of Visual Languages and Computing,** 8:2, June 1997, pp. 215–60.

Cattell, R., ed. [1993] **The Object Database Standard: ODMG-93, Release 1.2,** Morgan Kaufmann, 1993.

Cattell, R., ed. [1997] **The Object Database Standard: ODMG, Release 2.0,** Morgan Kaufmann, 1997.

Ceri, S., and Fraternali, P. [1997] **Designing Database Applications with Objects and Rules: The IDEA Methodology,** Addison-Wesley, 1997.

Ceri, S., Gottlob, G., Tanca, L. [1990], **Logic Programming and Databases,** Springer-Verlag, 1990.

Ceri, S., Navathe, S., and Wiederhold, G. [1983] "Distribution Design of Logical Database Schemas," TSE, 9:4, July 1983.

Ceri, S., Negri, M., and Pelagatti, G. [1982] "Horizontal Data Partitioning in Database Design," in SIG-MOD [1982].

Ceri, S., and Owicki, S. [1983] "On the Use of Optimistic Methods for Concurrency Control in Distributed Databases," *Proceedings of the Sixth Berkeley Workshop on Distributed Data Management and Computer Networks*, February 1983.

Ceri, S., and Pelagatti, G. [1984] "Correctness of Query Execution Strategies in Distributed Databases," TODS, 8:4, December 1984.

Ceri, S., and Pelagatti, G. [1984a] **Distributed Databases: Principles and Systems,** McGraw-Hill, 1984.

Ceri, S., and Tanca, L. [1987] "Optimization of Systems of Algebraic Equations for Evaluating Datalog Queries," in VLDB [1987].

Cesarini, F., and Soda, G. [1991] "A Dynamic Hash Method with Signature," TODS, 16:2, June 1991.

Chakravarthy, S. [1990] "Active Database Management Systems: Requirements, State-of-the-Art, and an Evaluation," in ER Conference [1990].

Chakravarthy, S. [1991] "Divide and Conquer: A Basis for Augmenting a Conventional Query Optimizer with Multiple Query Processing Capabilities," in ICDE [1991].

Chakravarthy, S., Anwar, E., Maugis, L., and Mishra, D. [1994] Design of Sentinel: An Object-oriented DBMS with Event-based Rules, **Information and Software Technology,** 36:9, 1994.

Chakravarthy, S., et al. [1989] "HiPAC: A Research Project in Active, Time Constrained Database Management," Final Technical Report, XAIT-89-02, Xerox Advanced Information Technology, August 1989.

Chakravarthy, S., Karlapalem, K., Navathe, S., and Tanaka, A. [1993] "Database Supported Co-operative Problem Solving," in **International Journal of Intelligent Co-operative Information Systems,** 2:3, September 1993.

Chakravarthy, U., Grant, J., and Minker, J. [1990] "Logic-Based Approach to Semantic Query Optimization," TODS, 15:2, June 1990.

Chalmers, M., and Chitson, P. [1992] "Bead: Explorations in Information Visualization," *Proceedings of the ACM SIGIR International Conference*, June 1992.

Chamberlin, D., and Boyce, R. [1974] "SEQUEL: A Structured English Query Language," in SIGMOD [1984].

Chamberlin, D., et al. [1976] "SEQUEL 2: A Unified Approach to Data Definition, Manipulation, and Control," **IBM Journal of Research and Development,** 20:6, November 1976.

Chamberlin, D., et al. [1981] "A History and Evaluation of System R," CACM, 24:10, October 1981.

Chan, C., Ooi, B., and Lu, H. [1992] "Extensible Buffer Management of Indexes," in VLDB [1992].

Chandy, K., Browne, J., Dissley, C., and Uhrig, W. [1975] "Analytical Models for Rollback and Recovery Strategies in Database Systems," TSE, 1:1, March 1975.

Chang, C. [1981] "On the Evaluation of Queries Containing Derived Relations in a Relational Database" in Gallaire et al. [1981].

Chang, C., and Walker, A. [1984] "PROSQL: A Prolog Programming Interface with SQL/DS," in EDS [1984].

Chang, E., and Katz, R. [1989] "Exploiting Inheritance and Structure Semantics for Effective Clustering and Buffering in Object-Oriented Databases," in SIGMOD [1989].

Chang, N., and Fu, K. [1981] "Picture Query Languages for Pictorial Databases," IEEE **Computer,** 14:11, November 1981.

Chang, P., and Myre, W. [1988] "OS/2 EE Database Manager: Overview and Technical Highlights," IBM **Systems Journal,** 27:2, 1988.

Chang, S., Lin, B., and Walser, R. [1979] "Generalized Zooming Techniques for Pictorial Database Systems," NCC, AFIPS, 48, 1979.

Chen, M., and Yu, P. [1991] "Determining Beneficial Semijoins for a Join Sequence in Distributed Query Processing," in ICDE [1991].

Chatzoglu, P. D., and McCaulay, L. A. [1997] "Requirements Capture and Analysis: A Survey of Current Practice," **Requirements Engineering,** 1997, pp. 75–88.

Chaudhuri, S., and Dayal, U. [1997] "An Overview of Data Warehousing and OLAP Technology," **SIG-MOD Record,** Vol. 26, No. 1, March 1997.

Chen, M., Han, J., Yu, P.S., [1996] " Data Mining: An Overview from a Database Perspective," IEEE TKDE, 8:6, December 1996.

Chen, P. [1976] "The Entity Relationship Mode—Toward a Unified View of Data," TODS, 1:1, March 1976.

Chen, P., Lee E., Gibson G., Katz, R., and Patterson, D. [1994] RAID High Performance, Reliable Secondary Storage, ACM **Computing Surveys,** 26:2, 1994.

Chen, P., and Patterson, D. [1990]. "Maximizing performance in a striped disk array," in *Proceedings of Symposium on Computer Architecture*, IEEE, New York, 1990.

Chen, Q., and Kambayashi, Y. [1991] "Nested Relation Based Database Knowledge Representation," in SIGMOD [1991].

Cheng, J. [1991] "Effective Clustering of Complex Objects in Object-Oriented Databases," in SIGMOD [1991].

Cheung, D., Han, J., Ng, V., Fu, A.W., and Fu, A.Y., "A Fast and Distributed Algorithm for Mining Association Rules," in *Proceedings of International Conference on Parallel and Distributed Information Systems*, PDIS [1996].

Childs, D. [1968] "Feasibility of a Set Theoretical Data Structure—A General Structure Based on a Reconstituted Definition of Relation," *Proceedings of the IFIP Congress*, 1968.

Chimenti, D., et al. [1987] "An Overview of the LDL System," MCC Technical Report #ACA-ST-370-87, Austin, TX, November 1987.

Chimenti, D., et al. [1990] "The LDL System Prototype," TKDE, 2:1, March 1990.

Chin, F. [1978] "Security in Statistical Databases for Queries with Small Counts," TODS, 3:1, March 1978.

Chin, F., and Ozsoyoglu, G. [1981] "Statistical Database Design," TODS, 6:1, March 1981.

Chintalapati, R. Kumar, V. and Datta, A. [1997] "An Adaptive Location Management Algorithm for Mobile Computing," *Proceedings of 22nd Annual Conference on Local Computer Networks (LCN '97)*, Minneapolis, 1997.

Chou, H., and Kim, W. [1986] "A Unifying Framework for Version Control in a CAD Environment," in VLDB [1986].

Christodoulakis, S., et al. [1984] "Development of a Multimedia Information System for an Office Environment," in VLDB [1984].

Christodoulakis, S., and Faloutsos, C. [1986] "Design and Performance Considerations for an Optical Disk-Based Multimedia Object Server," IEEE **Computer,** 19:12, December 1986.

Chu, W., and Hurley, P. [1982] "Optimal Query Processing for Distributed Database Systems," IEEE **Transactions on Computers,** 31:9, September 1982.

Ciborra, C., Migliarese, P., and Romano, P. [1984] "A Methodological Inquiry of Organizational Noise in Socio Technical Systems," **Human Relations,** 37:8, 1984.

Claybrook, B. [1983] **File Management Techniques,** Wiley, 1983.

Claybrook, B. [1992] OLTP: **OnLine Transaction Processing Systems,** Wiley, 1992.

Clifford, J., and Tansel, A. [1985] "On an Algebra for Historical Relational Databases: Two Views," in SIGMOD [1985].

Clocksin, W. F., and Mellish, C. S. [1984] **Programming in Prolog,** 2nd ed., Springer-Verlag, 1984.

CODASYL [1978] Data Description Language Journal of Development, Canadian Government Publishing Centre, 1978.

Codd, E. [1970] "A Relational Model for Large Shared Data Banks," CACM, 13:6, June 1970.

Codd, E. [1971] "A Data Base Sublanguage Founded on the Relational Calculus," *Proceedings of the ACM SIGFIDET Workshop on Data Description, Access, and Control,* November 1971.

Codd, E. [1972] "Relational Completeness of Data Base Sublanguages," in Rustin [1972].

Codd, E. [1972a] "Further Normalization of the Data Base Relational Model," in Rustin [1972].

Codd, E. [1974] "Recent Investigations in Relational Database Systems," *Proceedings of the IFIP Congress,* 1974.

Codd, E. [1978] "How About Recently? (English Dialog with Relational Data Bases Using Rendezvous Version 1)," in Shneiderman [1978].

Codd, E. [1979] "Extending the Database Relational Model to Capture More Meaning," TODS, 4:4, December 1979.

Codd, E. [1982] "Relational Database: A Practical Foundation for Productivity," CACM, 25:2, December 1982.

Codd, E. [1985] "Is Your DBMS Really Relational?" and "Does Your DBMS Run By the Rules?," COMPUTER WORLD, October 14 and October 21, 1985.

Codd, E. [1986] "An Evaluation Scheme for Database Management Systems That Are Claimed to Be Relational," in ICDE [1986].

Codd, E. [1990] Relational Model for Data Management-Version 2, Addison-Wesley, 1990.

Codd, E. F., Codd, S. B., and Salley, C. T. [1993] "Providing OLAP (On-Line Analytical Processing) to User Analyst: An IT Mandate," a white paper at http://www.arborsoft.com/OLAP.html, 1993.

Comer, D. [1979] "The Ubiquitous B-tree," ACM Computing Surveys, 11:2, June 1979.

Comer, D. [1997] Computer Networks and Internets, Prentice-Hall, 1997.

Cornelio, A. and Navathe, S. [1993] "Applying Active Database Models for Simulation," in Proceedings of 1993 Winter Simulation Conference, IEEE, Los Angeles, December 1993.

Cosmadakis, S., Kanellakis, P. C., and Vardi, M. [1990] "Polynomial-time Implication Problems for Unary Inclusion Dependencies," JACM, 37:1, 1990, pp. 15–46.

Cruz, I. [1992] "Doodle: A Visual Language for Object-Oriented Databases," in SIGMOD [1992].

Curtice, R. [1981] "Data Dictionaries: An Assessment of Current Practice and Problems," in VLDB [1981].

Cuticchia, A., Fasman, K., Kingsbury, D., Robbins, R., and Pearson, P. [1993] "The GDB Human Genome Database Anno 1993." Nucleic Acids Research, 21:13, 1993.

Czejdo, B., Elmasri, R., Rusinkiewicz, M., and Embley, D. [1987] "An Algebraic Language for Graphical Query Formulation Using an Extended Entity-Relationship Model," Proceedings of the ACM Computer Science Conference, 1987.

Dahl, R., and Bubenko, J. [1982] "IDBD: An Interactive Design Tool for CODASYL DBTG Type Databases," in VLDB [1982].

Dahl, V. [1984] "Logic Programming for Constructive Database Systems," in EDS [1984].

Das, S. [1992] Deductive Databases and Logic Programming, Addison-Wesley, 1992.

Date, C. [1983] An Introduction to Database Systems, Vol. 2, Addison-Wesley, 1983.

Date, C. [1983a] "The Outer Join," Proceedings of the Second International Conference on Databases (ICOD-2), 1983.

Date, C. [1984] "A Critique of the SQL Database Language," ACM SIGMOD Record, 14:3, November 1984.

Date, C. [1995] An Introduction Database Systems, 6th ed., Addison-Wesley, 1995.

Date, C. J., and Darwen, H. [1993] A Guide to the SQL Standard, 3rd ed., Addison-Wesley.

Date, C., and White, C. [1989] A Guide to DB2, 3rd ed., Addison-Wesley, 1989.

Date, C., and White, C. [1988a] A Guide to SQL/DS, Addison-Wesley, 1988.

Davies, C. [1973] "Recovery Semantics for a DB/DC System," Proceedings of the ACM National Conference, 1973.

Dayal, U., and Bernstein, P. [1978] "On the Updatability of Relational Views," in VLDB [1978].

Dayal, U., Hsu, M., and Ladin, R. [1991] "A Transaction Model for Long-Running Activities," in VLDB [1991].

Dayal, U., et al. [1987] "PROBE Final Report," Technical Report CCA-87-02, Computer Corporation of America, December 1987.

DBTG [1971] Report of the CODASYL Data Base Task Group, ACM, April 1971.

Delcambre, L., Lim, B., and Urban, S. [1991] "Object-Centered Constraints," in ICDE [1991].

DeMarco, T. [1979] Structured Analysis and System Specification, Prentice-Hall, 1979.

DeMichiel, L. [1989] "Performing Operations Over Mismatched Domains," in ICDE [1989].

Denning, D. [1980] "Secure Statistical Databases with Random Sample Queries," TODS, 5:3, September 1980.

Denning, D., and Denning, P. [1979] "Data Security," ACM Computing Surveys, 11:3, September 1979.

Deshpande, A. [1989] "An Implementation for Nested Relational Databases," Technical Report, Ph.D. dissertation, Indiana University, 1989.

Devor, C., and Weeldreyer, J. [1980] "DDTS: A Testbed for Distributed Database Research," *Proceedings of the* ACM *Pacific Conference*, 1980.

Dewire, D. [1993] **Client Server Computing,** McGraw-Hill, 1993.

DeWitt, D., et al. [1984] "Implementation Techniques for Main Memory Databases," in SIGMOD [1984].

DeWitt, D., et al. [1990] "The Gamma Database Machine Project," **TKDE,** 2:1, March 1990.

DeWitt, D., Futtersack, P., Maier, D., and Velez, F. [1990] "A Study of Three Alternative Workstation Server Architectures for Object-Oriented Database Systems," in VLDB [1990].

Dhawan, C. [1997] **Mobile Computing,** McGraw-Hill, 1997.

Dietrich, S., Friesen, O., W. Calliss [1998] On Deductive and Object Oriented Databases: The VALID-ITY Experience," Technical Report, Arizona State University, 1999.

Diffie, W., and Hellman, M. [1979] "Privacy and Authentication," **Proceedings of the** IEEE, 67:3, March 1979.

Dipert, B., and Levy M. [1993] **Designing with Flash Memory,** Annabooks 1993.

Dittrich, K. [1986] "Object-Oriented Database Systems: The Notion and the Issues," in Dittrich and Dayal [1986].

Dittrich, K., and Dayal, U., eds. [1986] *Proceedings of the International Workshop on Object-Oriented Database Systems,* IEEE CS, Pacific Grove, CA, September 1986.

Dittrich, K., Kotz, A., and Mulle, J. [1986] "An Event/Trigger Mechanism to Enforce Complex Consistency Constraints in Design Databases," in SIGMOD Record, 15:3, 1986.

Dodd, G. [1969] "APL—A Language for Associative Data Handling in PL/I," *Proceedings of the Fall Joint Computer Conference,* AFIPS, 29, 1969.

Dodd, G. [1969] "Elements of Data Management Systems," ACM **Computing Surveys,** 1:2, June 1969.

Dogac, A., Ozsu, M. T., Bilins, A., Sellis, T., eds. [1994] **Advances in Object-oriented Databases Systems,** Springer-Verlag, 1994.

Dogac, A., [1998] Special Section on Electronic Commerce, ACM **Sigmod Record** 27:4, December 1998.

Dos Santos, C., Neuhold, E., and Furtado, A. [1979] "A Data Type Approach to the Entity-Relationship Model," in ER Conference [1979].

Du, D., and Tong, S. [1991] "Multilevel Extendible Hashing: A File Structure for Very Large Databases," **TKDE,** 3:3, September 1991.

Du, H., and Ghanta, S. [1987] "A Framework for Efficient IC/VLSI CAD Databases," in ICDE [1987].

Dumas, P., et al. [1982] "MOBILE-Burotique: Prospects for the Future," in Naffah [1982].

Dumpala, S., and Arora, S. [1983] "Schema Translation Using the Entity-Relationship Approach," in ER Conference [1983].

Dunham, M., and Helal, A. [1995] "Mobile Computing and Databases: Anything New?" SIGMOD **Record,** 24:4, December 1995.

Dwyer, S., et al. [1982] "A Diagnostic Digital Imaging System," *Proceedings of the* IEEE CS *Conference on Pattern Recognition and Image Processing,* June 1982.

Eastman, C. [1987] "Database Facilities for Engineering Design," **Proceedings of the** IEEE, 69:10, October 1981.

EDS [1984] **Expert Database Systems,** Kerschberg, L., ed. (*Proceedings of the First International Workshop on Expert Database Systems,* Kiawah Island, SC, October 1984), Benjamin/Cummings, 1986.

EDS [1986] **Expert Database Systems,** Kerschberg, L., ed. (*Proceedings of the First International Conference on Expert Database Systems,* Charleston, SC, April 1986), Benjamin/Cummings, 1987.

EDS [1988] **Expert Database Systems,** Kerschberg, L., ed. (*Proceedings of the Second International Conference on Expert Database Systems,* Tysons Corner, VA, April 1988), Benjamin/Cummings (forthcoming).

Eick, C. [1991] "A Methodology for the Design and Transformation of Conceptual Schemas," in VLDB [1991].

ElAbbadi, A., and Toueg, S. [1988] "The Group Paradigm for Concurrency Control," in SIGMOD [1988].

ElAbbadi, A., and Toueg, S. [1989] "Maintaining Availability in Partitioned Replicated Databases," **TODS,** 14:2, June 1989.

Ellis, C., and Nutt, G. [1980] "Office Information Systems and Computer Science," ACM **Computing Surveys,** 12:1, March 1980.

Elmagarmid A. K., ed. [1992] **Database Transaction Models for Advanced Applications,** Morgan Kaufmann, 1992.

Elmagarmid, A., Leu, Y., Litwin, W., and Rusinkiewicz, M. [1990] "A Multidatabase Transaction Model for Interbase," in VLDB [1990].

Elmasri, R., James, S., and Kouramajian, V. [1993] "Automatic Class and Method Generation for Object-Oriented Databases," *Proceedings of the Third International Conference on Deductive and Object-Oriented Databases (DOOD-93)*, Phoenix, AZ, December 1993.

Elmasri, R., Kouramajian, V., and Fernando, S. [1993] "Temporal Database Modeling: An Object-Oriented Approach," CIKM, November 1993.

Elmasri, R., and Larson, J. [1985] "A Graphical Query Facility for ER Databases," in ER Conference [1985].

Elmasri, R., Larson, J., and Navathe, S. [1986] "Schema Integration Algorithms for Federated Databases and Logical Database Design," Honeywell CSDD, Technical Report CSC-86-9: 8212, January 1986.

Elmasri, R., Srinivas, P., and Thomas, G. [1987] "Fragmentation and Query Decomposition in the ECR Model," in ICDE [1987].

Elmasri, R., Weeldreyer, J., and Hevner, A. [1985] "The Category Concept: An Extension to the Entity-Relationship Model," **International Journal on Data and Knowledge Engineering**, 1:1, May 1985.

Elmasri, R., and Wiederhold, G. [1979] "Data Model Integration Using the Structural Model," in SIGMOD [1979].

Elmasri, R., and Wiederhold, G. [1980] "Structural Properties of Relationships and Their Representation," NCC, AFIPS, 49, 1980.

Elmasri, R., and Wiederhold, G. [1981] "GORDAS: A Formal, High-Level Query Language for the Entity-Relationship Model," in ER Conference [1981].

Elmasri, R., and Wuu, G. [1990] "A Temporal Model and Query Language for ER Databases," in ICDE [1990], in VLDB [1990].

Elmasri, R., and Wuu, G. [1990a] "The Time Index: An Access Structure for Temporal Data," in VLDB [1990].

Engelbart, D., and English, W. [1968] "A Research Center for Augmenting Human Intellect," *Proceedings of the Fall Joint Computer Conference*, AFIPS, December 1968.

Epstein, R., Stonebraker, M., and Wong, E. [1978] "Distributed Query Processing in a Relational Database System," in SIGMOD [1978].

ER Conference [1979] **Entity-Relationship Approach to Systems Analysis and Design,** Chen, P., ed. (*Proceedings of the First International Conference on Entity-Relationship Approach*, Los Angeles, December 1979), North-Holland, 1980.

ER Conference [1981] **Entity-Relationship Approach to Information Modeling and Analysis,** Chen, P., eds. (*Proceedings of the Second International Conference on Entity-Relationship Approach*, Washington, October 1981), Elsevier Science, 1981.

ER Conference [1983] **Entity-Relationship Approach to Software Engineering,** Davis, C., Jajodia, S., Ng, P., and Yeh, R., eds. (*Proceedings of the Third International Conference on Entity-Relationship Approach*, Anaheim, CA, October 1983), North-Holland, 1983.

ER Conference [1985] *Proceedings of the Fourth International Conference on Entity-Relationship Approach*, Liu, J., ed., Chicago, October 1985, IEEE CS.

ER Conference [1986] *Proceedings of the Fifth International Conference on Entity-Relationship Approach*, Spaccapietra, S., ed., Dijon, France, November 1986, Express-Tirages.

ER Conference [1987] *Proceedings of the Sixth International Conference on Entity-Relationship Approach*, March, S., ed., New York, November 1987.

ER Conference [1988] *Proceedings of the Seventh International Conference on Entity-Relationship Approach*, Batini, C., ed., Rome, November 1988.

ER Conference [1989] *Proceedings of the Eighth International Conference on Entity-Relationship Approach*, Lochovsky, F., ed., Toronto, October 1989.

ER Conference [1990] *Proceedings of the Ninth International Conference on Entity-Relationship Approach*, Kangassalo, H., ed., Lausanne, Switzerland, September 1990.

ER Conference [1991] *Proceedings of the Tenth International Conference on Entity-Relationship Approach*, Teorey, T., ed., San Mateo, CA, October 1991.

ER Conference [1992] *Proceedings of the Eleventh International Conference on Entity-Relationship Approach*, Pernul, G., and Tjoa, A., eds., Karlsruhe, Germany, October 1992.

ER Conference [1993] *Proceedings of the Twelfth International Conference on Entity-Relationship Approach*, Elmasri, R., and Kouramajian, V., eds., Arlington, TX, December 1993.

ER Conference [1994] *Proceedings of the Thirteenth International Conference on Entity-Relationship Approach*, Loucopoulos, P., and Theodoulidis, B., eds., Manchester, England, December 1994.

ER Conference [1995] *Proceedings of the Fourteenth International Conference on ER-OO Modeling*, Papazouglou, M., and Tari, Z., eds., Brisbane, Australia, December 1995.

ER Conference [1996] *Proceedings of the Fifteenth International Conference on Conceptual Modeling*, Thalheim, B., ed., Cottbus, Germany, October 1996.

ER Conference [1997] *Proceedings of the Sixteenth International Conference on Conceptual Modeling*, Embley, D., ed., Los Angeles, October 1997.

ER Conference [1998] *Proceedings of the Seventeenth International Conference on Conceptual Modeling*, Ling, T.-K., ed., Singapore, November 1998.

Eswaran, K., and Chamberlin, D. [1975] "Functional Specifications of a Subsystem for Database Integrity," in VLDB [1975].

Eswaran, K., Gray, J., Lorie, R., and Traiger, I. [1976] "The Notions of Consistency and Predicate Locks in a Data Base System," CACM, 19:11, November 1976.

Everett, G., Dissly, C., and Hardgrave, W. [1971] *RFMS User Manual*, TRM-16, Computing Center, University of Texas at Austin, 1981.

Fagin, R. [1977] "Multivalued Dependencies and a New Normal Form for Relational Databases," TODS, 2:3, September 1977.

Fagin, R. [1979] "Normal Forms and Relational Database Operators," in SIGMOD [1979].

Fagin, R. [1981] "A Normal Form for Relational Databases That Is Based on Domains and Keys," TODS, 6:3, September 1981.

Fagin, R., Nievergelt, J., Pippenger, N., and Strong, H. [1979] "Extendible Hashing—A Fast Access Method for Dynamic Files," TODS, 4:3, September 1979.

Falcone, S., and Paton, N. [1997]. "Deductive Object-Oriented Database Systems: A Survey," *Proceedings of the 3rd International Workshop Rules in Database Systems (RIDS'97)*, Skovde, Sweden, June 1997.

Faloutsos, C. [1996] **Searching Multimedia Databases by Content,** Kluwer, 1996.

Faloutsos, G., and Jagadish, H. [1992] "On B-Tree Indices for Skewed Distributions," in VLDB [1992].

Faloutsos, C., Barber, R., Flickner, M., Hafner, J., Niblack, W., Perkovic, D., and Equitz, W. [1994] Efficient and effective querying by image content," in **Journal of Intelligent Information Systems,** 3:4, 1994.

Farag, W., and Teorey, T. [1993] "FunBase: A Function-based Information Management System," CIKM, November 1993.

Fernandez, E., Summers, R., and Wood, C. [1981] **Database Security and Integrity,** Addison-Wesley, 1981.

Ferrier, A., and Stangret, C. [1982] "Heterogeneity in the Distributed Database Management System SIRIUS-DELTA," in VLDB [1982].

Fishman, D., et al. [1986] "IRIS: An Object-Oriented DBMS," **TOOIS,** 4:2, April 1986.

Folk, M. J., Zoellick, B., and Riccardi, G. [1998] **File Structures: An Object Oriented Approach with C++,** 3rd ed., Addison-Wesley, 1998.

Ford, D., Blakeley, J., and Bannon, T. [1993] "Open OODB: A Modular Object-Oriented DBMS," in SIGMOD [1993].

Ford, D., and Christodoulakis, S. [1991] "Optimizing Random Retrievals from CLV Format Optical Disks," in VLDB [1991].

Foreman, G., and Zahorjan, J. [1994] "The Challenges of Mobile Computing" IEEE **Computer,** April 1994.

Fowler, M., and Scott, K. [1997] **UML distilled,** Addison-Wesley, 1997.

Franaszek, P., Robinson, J., and Thomasian, A. [1992] "Concurrency Control for High Contention Environments," TODS, 17:2, June 1992.

Franklin, F., et al. [1992] "Crash Recovery in Client-Server EXODUS," in SIGMOD [1992].

Fraternali, P. [1999] Tools and Approaches for Data Intensive Web Applications: A Survey, ACM *Computing Surveys*, 31:3, September 1999.

Frenkel, K. [1991] "The Human Genome Project and Informatics," CACM, November 1991.

Friesen, O., Gauthier-Villars, G., Lefelorre, A., and Vieille, L., "Applications of Deductive Object-Oriented Databases Using DEL," in Ramakrishnan (1995).

Furtado, A. [1978] "Formal Aspects of the Relational Model," **Information Systems,** 3:2, 1978.

Gadia, S. [1988] "A Homogeneous Relational Model and Query Language for Temporal Databases," TODS, 13:4, December 1988.

Gait, J. [1988] "The Optical File Cabinet: A Random-Access File System for Write-Once Optical Disks," IEEE Computer, 21:6, June 1988.

Gallaire, H., and Minker, J., eds. [1978] Logic and Databases, Plenum Press, 1978.

Gallaire, H., Minker, J., and Nicolas, J. [1984] "Logic and Databases: A Deductive Approach," ACM Computing Surveys, 16:2, June 1984.

Gallaire, H., Minker, J., and Nicolas, J., eds. [1981], Advances in Database Theory, vol. 1, Plenum Press, 1981.

Gamal-Eldin, M., Thomas, G., and Elmasri, R. [1988] "Integrating Relational Databases with Support for Updates," Proceedings of the International Symposium on Databases in Parallel and Distributed Systems, IEEE CS, December 1988.

Gane, C., and Sarson, T. [1977] Structured Systems Analysis: Tools and Techniques, Improved Systems Technologies, 1977.

Gangopadhyay, A., and Adam, N. [1997]. Database Issues in Geographic Information Systems, Kluwer Academic Publishers, 1997.

Garcia-Molina, H. [1982] "Elections in Distributed Computing Systems," IEEE Transactions on Computers, 31:1, January 1982.

Garcia-Molina, H. [1983] "Using Semantic Knowledge for Transaction Processing in a Distributed Database," TODS, 8:2, June 1983.

Gehani, N., Jagdish, H., and Shmueli, O. [1992] "Composite Event Specification in Active Databases: Model and Implementation," in VLDB [1992].

Georgakopoulos, D., Rusinkiewicz, M., and Sheth, A. [1991] "On Serializability of Multidatabase Transactions Through Forced Local Conflicts," in ICDE [1991].

Gerritsen, R. [1975] "A Preliminary System for the Design of DBTG Data Structures," CACM, 18:10, October 1975.

Ghosh, S. [1984] "An Application of Statistical Databases in Manufacturing Testing," in ICDE [1984].

Ghosh, S. [1986] "Statistical Data Reduction for Manufacturing Testing," in ICDE [1986].

Gifford, D. [1979] "Weighted Voting for Replicated Data," Proceedings of the Seventh ACM Symposium on Operating Systems Principles, 1979.

Gladney, H. [1989] "Data Replicas in Distributed Information Services," TODS, 14:1, March 1989.

Gogolla, M., and Hohenstein, U. [1991] "Towards a Semantic View of an Extended Entity-Relationship Model," TODS, 16:3, September 1991.

Goldberg, A., and Robson, D. [1983] Smalltalk-80: The Language and Its Implementation, Addison-Wesley, 1983.

Goldfine, A., and Konig, P. [1988] A Technical Overview of the Information Resource Dictionary System (IRDS), 2nd ed., NBS IR 88-3700, National Bureau of Standards.

Gotlieb, L. [1975] "Computing Joins of Relations," in SIGMOD [1975].

Graefe, G. [1993] "Query Evaluation Techniques for Large Databases," ACM Computing Surveys, 25:2, June 1993.

Graefe, G., and DeWitt, D. [1987] "The EXODUS Optimizer Generator," in SIGMOD [1987].

Gravano, L., and Garcia-Molina, H. [1997] "Merging Ranks from Heterogeneous Sources," in VLDB [1997].

Gray, J. [1978] "Notes on Data Base Operating Systems," in Bayer, Graham, and Seegmuller [1978].

Gray, J. [1981] "The Transaction Concept: Virtues and Limitations," in VLDB [1981].

Gray, J., Lorie, R., and Putzulo, G. [1975] "Granularity of Locks and Degrees of Consistency in a Shared Data Base," in Nijssen [1975].

Gray, J., McJones, P., and Blasgen, M. [1981] "The Recovery Manager of the System R Database Manager," ACM Computing Surveys, 13:2, June 1981.

Gray, J., and Reuter, A. [1993] Transaction Processing: Concepts and Techniques, Morgan Kaufmann, 1993.

Griffiths, P., and Wade, B. [1976] "An Authorization Mechanism for a Relational Database System," TODS, 1:3, September 1976.

Grochowski, E., and Hoyt, R. F. [1996] "Future Trends in Hard Disk Drives," IEEE Transactions on Magnetics, 32:3, May 1996.

Grosky, W. [1994] "Multimedia Information Systems," in IEEE Multimedia, 1:1, Spring 1994.

Grosky, W. [1997] "Managing Multimedia Information in Database Systems," in CACM, 40:12, December 1997.

Grosky, W., Jain, R., and Mehrotra, R., eds. [1997], **The Handbook of Multimedia Information Management,** Prentice-Hall PTR, 1997.

Guttman, A. [1984] "R-Trees: A Dynamic Index Structure for Spatial Searching," in SIGMOD [1984].

Gwayer, M. [1996] **Oracle Designer/2000 Web Server Generator Technical Overview** (version 1.3.2), Technical Report, Oracle Corporation, September 1996.

Halsaal, F. [1996] **Data Communications, Computer Networks and Open Systems,** 4th ed., Addison-Wesley, 1996.

Haas, P., Naughton, J., Seshadri, S. and Stokes, L. [1995] Sampling-based Estimation of the Number of Distinct Values of an Attribute," in VLDB [1995].

Haas, P., and Swami, A.[1995] "Sampling-based Selectivity Estimation for Joins Using Augmented Frequent Value Statistics," in ICDE [1995].

Hachem, N. and Berra, P. [1992] "New Order Preserving Access Methods for Very Large Files Derived from Linear Hashing," TKDE, 4:1, February 1992.

Hadzilacos, V. [1983] "An Operational Model for Database System Reliability," in *Proceedings of SIGACT-SIGMOD Conference,* March 1983.

Hadzilacos, V. [1986] "A Theory of Reliability in Database Systems," 1986.

Haerder, T., and Rothermel, K. [1987] "Concepts for Transaction Recovery in Nested Transactions," in SIGMOD [1987].

Haerder, T., and Reuter, A. [1983] "Principles of Transaction Oriented Database Recovery—A Taxonomy," ACM **Computing Surveys,** 15:4, September 1983, pp. 287–318.

Hall, P. [1976] "Optimization of a Single Relational Expression in a Relational Data Base System," IBM **Journal of Research and Development,** 20:3, May 1976.

Hamilton, G., Catteli, R., and Fisher, M. [1997] JDBC **Database Access with Java–A Tutorial and Annotated Reference,** Addison Wesley, 1997.

Hammer, M., and McLeod, D. [1975] "Semantic Integrity in a Relational Data Base System," in VLDB [1975].

Hammer, M., and McLeod, D. [1981] "Database Description with SDM: A Semantic Data Model," TODS, 6:3, September 1981.

Hammer, M., and Sarin, S. [1978] "Efficient Monitoring of Database Assertions," in SIGMOD [1978].

Hanson, E. [1992] "Rule Condition Testing and Action Execution in Ariel," in SIGMOD [1992].

Hardgrave, W. [1984] "BOLT: A Retrieval Language for Tree-Structured Database Systems," in TOU [1984].

Hardgrave, W. [1980] "Ambiguity in Processing Boolean Queries on TDMS Tree Structures: A Study of Four Different Philosophies," TSE, 6:4, July 1980.

Harrington, J. [1987] **Relational Database Management for Microcomputer: Design and Implementation,** Holt, Rinehart, and Winston, 1987.

Harris, L. [1978] "The ROBOT System: Natural Language Processing Applied to Data Base Query," *Proceedings of the* ACM *National Conference,* December 1978.

Haskin, R., and Lorie, R. [1982] "On Extending the Functions of a Relational Database System," in SIGMOD [1982].

Hasse, C., and Weikum, G. [1991] "A Performance Evaluation of Multi-Level Transaction Management," in VLDB [1991].

Hayes-Roth, F., Waterman, D., and Lenat, D., eds. [1983] **Building Expert Systems,** Addison-Wesley, 1983.

Hayne, S., and Ram, S. [1990] "Multi-User View Integration System: An Expert System for View Integration," in ICDE [1990].

Heiler, S., and Zdonick, S. [1990] "Object Views: Extending the Vision," in ICDE [1990].

Heiler, S., Hardhvalal, S., Zdonik, S., Blaustein, B., and Rosenthal, A. [1992] "A Flexible Framework for Transaction Management in Engineering Environment," in Elmagarmid [1992].

Helal, A., Hu, T., Elmasri, R., and Mukherjee, S. [1993] "Adaptive Transaction Scheduling," CIKM, November 1993.

Held, G., and Stonebraker, M. [1978] "B-Trees Reexamined," CACM, 21:2, February 1978.

Henschen, L., and Naqvi S. [1984], "On Compiling Queries in Recursive First-Order Databases," JACM, 31:1, January 1984.

Hernandez, H., and Chan., E. [1991] "Constraint-Time-Maintainable BCNF Database Schemes," TODS, 16:4, December 1991.

Herot, C. [1980] "Spatial Management of Data," TODS, 5:4, December 1980.

Hevner, A., and Yao, S. [1979] "Query Processing in Distributed Database Systems," TSE, 5:3, May 1979.

Hoffer, J. [1982] "An Empirical Investigation with Individual Differences in Database Models," *Proceedings of the Third International Information Systems Conference*, December 1982.

Holland, J. [1975] **Adaptation in Natural and Artificial Systems,** University of Michigan Press, 1975.

Holsapple, C., and Whinston, A., eds. [1987] **Decisions Support Systems Theory and Application,** Springer-Verlag, 1987.

Holtzman J. M., and Goodman D. J., eds. [1993] **Wireless Communications: Future Directions,** Kluwer, 1993.

Hsiao, D., and Kamel, M. [1989] "Heterogeneous Databases: Proliferation, Issues, and Solutions," TKDE, 1:1, March 1989.

Hsu, A., and Imielinsky, T. [1985] "Integrity Checking for Multiple Updates," in SIGMOD [1985].

Hull, R., and King, R. [1987] "Semantic Database Modeling: Survey, Applications, and Research Issues," **ACM Computing Surveys,** 19:3, September 1987.

IBM [1978] QBE Terminal Users Guide, Form Number SH20-2078-0.

IBM [1992] Systems Application Architecture Common Programming Interface Database Level 2 Reference, Document Number SC26-4798-01.

ICDE [1984] *Proceedings of the IEEE CS International Conference on Data Engineering*, Shuey, R., ed., Los Angeles, CA, April 1984.

ICDE [1986] *Proceedings of the IEEE CS International Conference on Data Engineering*, Wiederhold, G., ed., Los Angeles, February 1986.

ICDE [1987] *Proceedings of the IEEE CS International Conference on Data Engineering*, Wah, B., ed., Los Angeles, February 1987.

ICDE [1988] *Proceedings of the IEEE CS International Conference on Data Engineering*, Carlis, J., ed., Los Angeles, February 1988.

ICDE [1989] *Proceedings of the IEEE CS International Conference on Data Engineering*, Shuey, R., ed., Los Angeles, February 1989.

ICDE [1990] *Proceedings of the IEEE CS International Conference on Data Engineering*, Liu, M., ed., Los Angeles, February 1990.

ICDE [1991] *Proceedings of the IEEE CS International Conference on Data Engineering*, Cercone, N.; and Tsuchiya, M., eds., Kobe, Japan, April 1991.

ICDE [1992] *Proceedings of the IEEE CS International Conference on Data Engineering*, Golshani, F., ed., Phoenix, AZ, February 1992.

ICDE [1993] *Proceedings of the IEEE CS International Conference on Data Engineering*, Elmagarmid, A., and Neuhold, E., eds., Vienna, Austria, April 1993.

ICDE [1994] *Proceedings of the IEEE CS International Conference on Data Engineering*.

ICDE [1995] *Proceedings of the IEEE CS International Conference on Data Engineering*, Yu, P. S., and Chen, A. L. A., eds., Taipei, Taiwan, 1995.

ICDE [1996] *Proceedings of the IEEE CS International Conference on Data Engineering*, Su, S. Y. W., ed., New Orleans, 1996.

ICDE [1997] *Proceedings of the IEEE CS International Conference on Data Engineering*, Gray, A., and Larson, P. A., eds., Birmingham, England, 1997.

ICDE [1998] *Proceedings of the IEEE CS International Conference on Data Engineering*, Orlando, FL, 1998.

ICDE [1999] *Proceedings of the IEEE CS International Conference on Data Engineering*, Sydney, Australia, 1999.

IGES [1983] International Graphics Exchange Specification Version 2, National Bureau of Standards, U.S. Department of Commerce, January 1983.

Imielinski, T., and Badrinath, B. [1994] "Mobile Wireless Computing: Challenges in Data Management," CACM, 37:10, October 1994.

Imielinski, T., and Lipski, W. [1981] "On Representing Incomplete Information in a Relational Database," in VLDB [1981].

Informix [1998] "Web Integration Option for Informix Dynamic Server," available at http://www.informix.com.

Inmon, W. H. [1992] **Building the Data Warehouse,** Wiley, 1992.

Ioannidis, Y., and Kang, Y. [1990] "Randomized Algorithms for Optimizing Large Join Queries," in SIGMOD [1990].

Ioannidis, Y., and Kang, Y. [1991] "Left-Deep vs. Bushy Trees: An Analysis of Strategy Spaces and Its Implications for Query Optimization," in SIGMOD [1991].

Ioannidis, Y., and Wong, E. [1988] "Transforming Non-Linear Recursion to Linear Recursion," in EDS [1988].

Iossophidis, J. [1979] "A Translator to Convert the DDL of ERM to the DDL of System 2000," in ER Conference [1979].

Irani, K., Purkayastha, S., and Teorey, T. [1979] "A Designer for DBMS-Processable Logical Database Structures," in VLDB [1979].

Jacobson, I., Christerson, M., Jonsson, P., Overgaard, G. [1992] **Object Oriented Software Engineering: A Use Case Driven Approach,** Addison-Wesley, 1992.

Jagadish, H. [1989] "Incorporating Hierarchy in a Relational Model of Data," in SIGMOD [1989].

Jagadish, H. [1997] "Content-based Indexing and Retrieval," in Grosky et al. [1997].

Jajodia, S., and Kogan, B. [1990] "Integrating an Object-oriented Data Model with Multilevel Security," *IEEE Symposium on Security and Privacy,* May 1990, pp. 76–85.

Jajodia, S., and Mutchler, D. [1990] "Dynamic Voting Algorithms for Maintaining the Consistency of a Replicated Database," **TODS,** 15:2, June, 1990.

Jajodia, S., Ng, P., and Springsteel, F. [1983] "The Problem of Equivalence for Entity-Relationship Diagrams," **TSE,** 9:5, September, 1983.

Jajodia, S., and Sandhu, R. [1991] "Toward a Multilevel Secure Relational Data Model," in SIGMOD [1991].

Jardine, D., ed. [1977] **The ANSI/SPARC DBMS Model,** North-Holland, 1977.

Jarke, M., and Koch, J. [1984] "Query Optimization in Database Systems," **ACM Computing Surveys,** 16:2, June 1984.

Jensen, C., and Snodgrass, R. [1992] "Temporal Specialization," in ICDE [1992].

Jensen, C., et al. [1994] "A Glossary of Temporal Database Concepts," **ACM SIGMOD Record,** 23:1, March 1994.

Johnson, T., and Shasha, D. [1993] "The Performance of Current B-Tree Algorithms," **TODS,** 18:1, March 1993.

Kaefer, W., and Schoening, H. [1992] "Realizing a Temporal Complex-Object Data Model," in SIGMOD [1992].

Kamel, I., and Faloutsos, C. [1993] "On Packing R-trees," *CIKM,* November 1993.

Kamel, N., and King, R. [1985] "A Model of Data Distribution Based on Texture Analysis," in SIGMOD [1985].

Kapp, D., and Leben, J. [1978] **IMS Programming Techniques,** Van Nostrand-Reinhold, 1978.

Kappel, G., and Schrefl, M. [1991] "Object/Behavior Diagrams," in ICDE [1991].

Karlapalem, K., Navathe, S. B., and Ammar, M. [1996] "Optimal Redesign Policies to Support Dynamic Processing of Applications on a Distributed Relational Database System," **Information Systems,** 21:4, 1996, pp. 353–67.

Katz, R. [1985] **Information Management for Engineering Design: Surveys in Computer Science,** Springer-Verlag, 1985.

Katz, R., and Wong, E. [1982] "Decompiling CODASYL DML into Relational Queries," **TODS,** 7:1, March 1982.

KDD [1996] *Proceedings of the Second International Conference on Knowledge Discovery in Databases and Data Mining,* Portland, Oregon, August 1996.

Kedem, Z., and Silberschatz, A. [1980] "Non-Two Phase Locking Protocols with Shared and Exclusive Locks," in VLDB [1980].

Keller, A. [1982] "Updates to Relational Database Through Views Involving Joins," in Scheuermann [1982].

Kemp, K. [1993]. "Spatial Databases: Sources and Issues," in **Environmental Modeling with GIS,** Oxford University Press, New York, 1993.

Kemper, A., Lockemann, P., and Wallrath, M. [1987] "An Object-Oriented Database System for Engineering Applications," in SIGMOD [1987].

Kemper, A., Moerkotte, G., and Steinbrunn, M. [1992] "Optimizing Boolean Expressions in Object Bases," in VLDB [1992].

Kemper, A., and Wallrath, M. [1987] "An Analysis of Geometric Modeling in Database Systems," ACM Computing Surveys, 19:1, March 1987.

Kent, W. [1978] Data and Reality, North-Holland, 1978.

Kent, W. [1979] "Limitations of Record-Based Information Models," TODS, 4:1, March 1979.

Kent, W. [1991] "Object-Oriented Database Programming Languages," in VLDB [1991].

Kerschberg, L., Ting, P., and Yao, S. [1982] "Query Optimization in Star Computer Networks," TODS, 7:4, December 1982.

Ketabchi, M. A., Mathur, S., Risch, T., and Chen, J. [1990] "Comparative Analysis of RDBMS and OODBMS: A Case Study," IEEE International Conference on Manufacturing, 1990.

Khoshafian, S. and Baker A., [1996] Multimedia and Imaging Databases, Morgan Kaufmann, 1996.

Khoshafian, S., Chan, A., Wong, A., and Wong, H. K. T. [1992] Developing Client Server Applications, Morgan Kaufmann, 1992.

Kifer, M., and Lozinskii, E. [1986] "A Framework for an Efficient Implementation of Deductive Databases," Proceedings of the Sixth Advanced Database Symposium, Tokyo, August 1986.

Kim, P. [1996] "A Taxonomy on the Architecture of Database Gateways for the Web," Working Paper TR-96-U-10, Chungnam National University, Taejon, Korea (available from http://grigg.chungnam.ac.kr/projects/UniWeb).

Kim, W. [1982] "On Optimizing an SQL-like Nested Query," TODS, 3:3, September 1982.

Kim, W. [1989] "A Model of Queries for Object-Oriented Databases," in VLDB [1989].

Kim, W. [1990] "Object-Oriented Databases: Definition and Research Directions," TKDE, 2:3, September 1990.

Kim W. [1995] Modern Database Systems: The Object Model, Interoperability, and Beyond, ACM Press, Addison-Wesley, 1995.

Kim, W., Reiner, D., and Batory, D., eds. [1985] Query Processing in Database Systems, Springer-Verlag, 1985.

Kim, W. et al. [1987] "Features of the ORION Object-Oriented Database System," Microelectronics and Computer Technology Corporation, Technical Report ACA-ST-308-87, September 1987.

Kimball, R. [1996] The Data Warehouse Toolkit, Wiley, Inc. 1996.

King, J. [1981] "QUIST: A System for Semantic Query Optimization in Relational Databases," in VLDB [1981].

Kitsuregawa, M., Nakayama, M., and Takagi, M. [1989] "The Effect of Bucket Size Tuning in the Dynamic Hybrid GRACE Hash Join Method," in VLDB [1989].

Klimbie, J., and Koffeman, K., eds. [1974] Data Base Management, North-Holland, 1974.

Klug, A. [1982] "Equivalence of Relational Algebra and Relational Calculus Query Languages Having Aggregate Functions," JACM, 29:3, July 1982.

Knuth, D. [1973] The Art of Computer Programming, Vol. 3: Sorting and Searching, Addison-Wesley, 1973.

Kogelnik, A. [1998] "Biological Information Management with Application to Human Genome Data," Ph.D. dissertation, Georgia Institute of Technology and Emory University, 1998.

Kogelnik, A., Lott, M., Brown, M., Navathe, S., Wallace, D. [1998] "MITOMAP: A human mitochondrial genome database—1998 update." Nucleic Acids Research, 26:1, January 1998.

Kogelnik, A., Navathe, S., Wallace, D. [1997] "GENOME: A system for managing Human Genome Project Data." Proceedings of Genome Informatics '97, Eighth Workshop on Genome Informatics, Tokyo, Japan, Sponsor: Human Genome Center, University of Tokyo, December 1997.

Kohler, W. [1981] "A Survey of Techniques for Synchronization and Recovery in Decentralized Computer Systems," ACM Computing Surveys, 13:2, June 1981.

Konsynski, B., Bracker, L., and Bracker, W. [1982] "A Model for Specification of Office Communications," IEEE Transactions on Communications, 30:1, January 1982.

Korfhage, R. [1991] "To See, or Not to See: Is that the Query?" in Proceedings of the ACM SIGIR International Conference, June 1991.

Korth, H. [1983] "Locking Primitives in a Database System," JACM, 30:1, January 1983.

Korth, H., Levy, E., and Silberschatz, A. [1990] "A Formal Approach to Recovery by Compensating Transactions," in VLDB [1990].

Kotz, A., Dittrich, K., Mulle, J. [1988] "Supporting Semantic Rules by a Generalized Event/Trigger Mechanism," in VLDB [1988].

Krishnamurthy, R., Litwin, W., and Kent, W. [1991] "Language Features for Interoperability of Databases with Semantic Discrepancies," in SIGMOD [1991].

Krishnamurthy, R., and Naqvi, S., [1988] "Database Updates in Logic Programming, Rev. 1," MCC Technical Report #ACA-ST-010-88, Rev. 1, September 1988.

Krishnamurthy, R., and Naqvi, S. [1989] "Non-Deterministic Choice in Datalog," *Proceeedings of the 3rd International Conference on Data and Knowledge Bases*, Jerusalem, June 1989.

Krovetz, R., and Croft B. [1992] "Lexical Ambiguity and Information Retrieval" in TOIS, 10, April 1992.

Kulkarni K., Carey, M., DeMichiel, L., Mattos, N., Hong, W., and Ubell M., "Introducing Reference Types and Cleaning Up SQL3's Object Model," *ISO WG3 Report X3H2-95-456*, November 1995.

Kumar, A. [1991] "Performance Measurement of Some Main Memory Recovery Algorithms," in ICDE [1991].

Kumar, A., and Segev, A. [1993] "Cost and Availability Tradeoffs in Replicated Concurrency Control," TODS, 18:1, March 1993.

Kumar, A., and Stonebraker, M. [1987] "Semantics Based Transaction Management Techniques for Replicated Data," in SIGMOD [1987].

Kumar, V., and Han, M., eds. [1992] **Recovery Mechanisms in Database Systems,** Prentice-Hall, 1992.

Kumar, V., and Hsu, M. [1998] **Recovery Mechanisms in Database Systems,** Prentice-Hall (PTR), 1998.

Kumar, V., and Song, H. S. [1998] Database Recovery, Kluwer Academic, 1998.

Kung, H., and Robinson, J. [1981] "Optimistic Concurrency Control," TODS, 6:2, June 1981.

Lacroix, M., and Pirotte, A. [1977] "Domain-Oriented Relational Languages," in VLDB [1977].

Lacroix, M., and Pirotte, A. [1977a] "ILL: An English Structured Query Language for Relational Data Bases," in Nijssen [1977].

Lamport, L. [1978] "Time, Clocks, and the Ordering of Events in a Distributed System," CACM, 21:7, July 1978.

Langerak, R. [1990] "View Updates in Relational Databases with an Independent Scheme," TODS, 15:1, March 1990.

Lanka, S., and Mays, E. [1991] "Fully Persistent B1-Trees," in SIGMOD [1991].

Larson, J. [1983] "Bridging the Gap Between Network and Relational Database Management Systems," IEEE Computer, 16:9, September 1983.

Larson, J., Navathe, S., and Elmasri, R. [1989] "Attribute Equivalence and its Use in Schema Integration," TSE, 15:2, April 1989.

Larson, P. [1978] "Dynamic Hashing," BIT, 18, 1978.

Larson, P. [1981] "Analysis of Index-Sequential Files with Overflow Chaining," TODS, 6:4, December 1981.

Laurini, R., and Thompson, D. [1992] **Fundamentals of Spatial Information Systems,** Academic Press, 1992.

Lehman, P., and Yao, S. [1981] "Efficient Locking for Concurrent Operations on B-Trees," TODS, 6:4, December 1981.

Lee, J., Elmasri, R., and Won, J. [1998] " An Integrated Temporal Data Model Incorporating Time Series Concepts," Data and Knowledge Engineering, 24, 1998, pp. 257–276.

Lehman, T., and Lindsay, B. [1989] "The Starburst Long Field Manager," in VLDB [1989].

Leiss, E. [1982] "Randomizing: A Practical Method for Protecting Statistical Databases Against Compromise," in VLDB [1982].

Leiss, E. [1982a] **Principles of Data Security,** Plenum Press, 1982.

Lenzerini, M., and Santucci, C. [1983] "Cardinality Constraints in the Entity Relationship Model," in ER Conference [1983].

Leung, C., Hibler, B., and Mwara, N. [1992] "Picture Retrieval by Content Description," in **Journal of Information Science,** 1992, pp. 111–19.

Levesque, H. [1984] " The Logic of Incomplete Knowledge Bases," in Brodie et al., ch. 7 [1984].

Li, W., Seluk Candan, K., Hirata, K., and Hara, Y. [1998] Hierarchical Image Modeling for Object-based Media Retrieval in DKE, 27:2, September 1998, pp. 139–76.

Lien, E., and Weinberger, P. [1978] "Consistency, Concurrency, and Crash Recovery," in SIGMOD [1978].

Lieuwen, L., and DeWitt, D. [1992] "A Transformation-Based Approach to Optimizing Loops in Database Programming Languages," in SIGMOD [1992].

Lilien, L., and Bhargava, B. [1985] "Database Integrity Block Construct: Concepts and Design Issues," TSE, 11:9, September 1985.

Lin, J., and Dunham, M. H. [1998] "Mining Association Rules," in ICDE [1998].

Lindsay, B., et al. [1984] "Computation and Communication in R*: A Distributed Database Manager," TOCS, 2:1, January 1984.

Lippman R. [1987] "An Introduction to Computing with Neural Nets," IEEE ASSP Magazine, April 1987.

Lipski, W. [1979] "On Semantic Issues Connected with Incomplete Information," TODS, 4:3, September 1979.

Lipton, R., Naughton, J., and Schneider, D. [1990] "Practical Selectivity Estimation through Adaptive Sampling," in SIGMOD [1990].

Liskov, B., and Zilles, S. [1975] "Specification Techniques for Data Abstractions," TSE, 1:1, March 1975.

Litwin, W. [1980] "Linear Hashing: A New Tool for File and Table Addressing," in VLDB [1980].

Liu, K., and Sunderraman, R. [1988] "On Representing Indefinite and Maybe Information in Relational Databases," in ICDE [1988].

Liu, L., and Meersman, R. [1992] "Activity Model: A Declarative Approach for Capturing Communication Behavior in Object-Oriented Databases," in VLDB [1992].

Livadas, P. [1989] **File Structures: Theory and Practice,** Prentice-Hall, 1989.

Lockemann, P., and Knutsen, W. [1968] "Recovery of Disk Contents After System Failure," CACM, 11:8, August 1968.

Lorie, R. [1977] "Physical Integrity in a Large Segmented Database," TODS, 2:1, March 1977.

Lorie, R., and Plouffe, W. [1983] "Complex Objects and Their Use in Design Transactions," in SIGMOD [1983].

Lozinskii, E. [1986] "A Problem-Oriented Inferential Database System," TODS, 11:3, September 1986.

Lu, H., Mikkilineni, K., and Richardson, J. [1987] "Design and Evaluation of Algorithms to Compute the Transitive Closure of a Database Relation," in ICDE [1987].

Lubars, M., Potts, C., and Richter, C. [1993] " A Review of the State of Practice in Requirements Modeling," *IEEE International Symposium on Requirements Engineering,* San Diego, CA, 1993.

Lucyk, B. [1993] **Advanced Topics in DB2,** Addison-Wesley, 1993.

Maguire, D., Goodchild, M. and Rhind D., eds. [1997] **Geographical Information Systems: Principles and Applications.** vols. 1 and 2, Longman Scientific and Technical, New York.

Mahajan, S., Donahoo. M. J., Navathe, S. B., Ammar, M., Malik, S. [1998] "Grouping Techniques for Update Propagation in Intermittently Connected Databases," in ICDE [1998].

Maier, D. [1983] **The Theory of Relational Databases,** Computer Science Press, 1983.

Maier, D., Stein, J., Otis, A., and Purdy, A. [1986] "Development of an Object-Oriented DBMS," OOPSLA, 1986.

Malley, C. and Zdonick, S. [1986] "A Knowledge-Based Approach to Query Optimization," in EDS [1986].

Maier, D., and Warren, D. S. [1988] **Computing with Logic,** Benjamin Cummings, 1988.

Mannila, H., Toivonen, H., and Verkamo A. [1994] "Efficient Algorithms for Discovering Association Rules," in *KDD-94, AAAI Workshop on Knowledge Discovery in Databases,* Seattle, 1994.

Manola. F. [1998] "Towards a Richer Web Object Model," in **SIGMOD Record,** 27:1, March 1998.

March, S., and Severance, D. [1977] "The Determination of Efficient Record Segmentations and Blocking Factors for Shared Files," TODS, 2:3, September 1977.

Mark, L., Roussopoulos, N., Newsome, T., and Laohapipattana, P. [1992] "Incrementally Maintained Network to Relational Mappings," **Software Practice & Experience,** 22:12, December 1992.

Markowitz, V., and Raz, Y. [1983] "ERROL: An Entity-Relationship, Role Oriented, Query Language," in ER Conference [1983].

Martin, J., Chapman, K., and Leben, J. [1989] **DB2-Concepts, Design, and Programming,** Prentice-Hall, 1989.

Martin, J., and Odell, J. [1992] **Object Oriented Analysis and Design,** Prentice Hall, 1992.

Maryanski, F. [1980] "Backend Database Machines," ACM **Computing Surveys,** 12:1, March 1980.

Masunaga, Y. [1987] "Multimedia Databases: A Formal Framework," *Proceedings of the IEEE Office Automation Symposium*, April 1987.

Mattison, R., **Data Warehousing: Strategies, Technologies, and Techniques,** McGraw-Hill, 1996.

McFadden, F. and Hoffer, J. [1988] **Database Management,** 2nd ed., Benjamin/Cummings, 1988.

McFadden, F. R., and Hoffer, J. A. [1994] **Modern Database Management,** 4th ed., Benjamin Cummings, 1994.

McGee, W. [1977] "The Information Management System IMS/VS, Part I: General Structure and Operation," **IBM Systems Journal,** 16:2, June 1977.

McLeish, M. [1989] "Further Results on the Security of Partitioned Dynamic Statistical Databases," TODS, 14:1, March 1989.

McLeod, D., and Heimbigner, D. [1985] "A Federated Architecture for Information Systems," **TOOIS,** 3:3, July 1985.

Mehrotra, S., et al. [1992] "The Concurrency Control Problem in Multidatabases: Characteristics and Solutions," in SIGMOD [1992].

Melton, J., Bauer, J., and Kulkarni, K. [1991] "Object ADTs (with improvements for value ADTs)," *ISO WG3 Report X3H2-91-083*, April 1991.

Melton, J., and Mattos, N. [1996] *An Overview of SQL3—The Emerging New Generation of the SQL Standard*, Tutorial No. T5, VLDB, Bombay, September 1996.

Melton, J., and Simon, A. R. [1993] **Understanding the New SQL: A Complete Guide,** Morgan Kaufmann.

Menasce, D., Popek, G., and Muntz, R. [1980] "A Locking Protocol for Resource Coordination in Distributed Databases," TODS, 5:2, June 1980.

Mendelzon, A., and Maier, D. [1979] "Generalized Mutual Dependencies and the Decomposition of Database Relations," in VLDB [1979].

Mendelzon, A., Mihaila, G., Milo, T. [1997] "Querying the World Wide Web," **Journal of Digital Libraries,** 1:1, April 1997.

Metais, E., Kedad, Z., Comyn-Wattiau, C., Bouzeghoub, M., "Using Linguistic Knowledge in View Integration: Toward a Third Generation of Tools," in DKE 23:1, June 1977.

Mikkilineni, K., and Su, S. [1988] "An Evaluation of Relational Join Algorithms in a Pipelined Query Processing Environment," TSE, 14:6, June 1988.

Miller, N. [1987] **File Structures Using PASCAL,** Benjamin Cummings, 1987.

Minoura, T., and Wiederhold, G. [1981] "Resilient Extended True-Copy Token Scheme for a Distributed Database," TSE, 8:3, May 1981.

Missikoff, M., and Wiederhold, G. [1984] "Toward a Unified Approach for Expert and Database Systems," in EDS [1984].

Mitschang, B. [1989] "Extending the Relational Algebra to Capture Complex Objects," in VLDB [1989].

Mohan, C. [1993] "IBM's Relational Database Products: Features and Technologies," in SIGMOD [1993].

Mohan, C., Haderle, D., Lindsay, B., Pirahesh, H. and Schwarz, P. [1992] "ARIES: A Transaction Recovery Method Supporting Fine-Granularity Locking and Partial Rollbacks using Write-Ahead Logging," TODS, 17:1, March 1992.

Mohan, C., and Levine, F. [1992] "ARIEL/IM: An Efficient and High-Concurrency Index Management Method Using Write-Ahead Logging," in SIGMOD [1992].

Mohan, C., and Narang, I. [1992]. "Algorithms for Creating Indexes for Very Large Tables without Quiescing Updates," in SIGMOD [1992].

Mohan, C. et al. [1992] "ARIEL: A Transaction Recovery Method Supporting Fine-Granularity Locking and Partial Rollbacks Using Write-Ahead Logging," TODS, 17:1, March 1992.

Morris, K., Ullman, J., and VanGelden, A. [1986] "Design Overview of the NAIL! System," *Proceedings of the Third International Conference on Logic Programming*, Springer-Verlag, 1986.

Morris, K., et al. [1987] "YAWN! (Yet Another Window on NAIL!), in ICDE [1987].

Morris, R. [1968] "Scatter Storage Techniques," CACM, 11:1, January 1968.

Morsi, M., Navathe, S., and Kim, H. [1992] "An Extensible Object-Oriented Database Testbed," in ICDE [1992].

Moss, J. [1982] "Nested Transactions and Reliable Distributed Computing," *Proceedings of the Symposium on Reliability in Distributed Software and Database Systems*, IEEE CS, July 1982.

Motro, A. [1987] "Superviews: Virtual Integration of Multiple Databases," TSE, 13:7, July 1987.

Mukkamala, R. [1989] "Measuring the Effect of Data Distribution and Replication Models on Performance Evaluation of Distributed Systems," in ICDE [1989].

Mumick, I., Finkelstein, S., Pirahesh, H., and Ramakrishnan, R. [1990] "Magic Is Relevant," in SIGMOD [1990].

Mumick, I., Pirahesh, H., and Ramakrishnan, R. [1990] "The Magic of Duplicates and Aggregates," in VLDB [1990].

Muralikrishna, M. [1992] "Improved Unnesting Algorithms for Join and Aggregate SQL Queries," in VLDB [1992].

Muralikrishna, M., and DeWitt, D. [1988] "Equi-depth Histograms for Estimating Selectivity Factors for Multi-dimensional Queries," in SIGMOD [1988].

Mylopolous, J., Bernstein, P., and Wong, H. [1980] "A Language Facility for Designing Database-Intensive Applications," TODS, 5:2, June 1980.

Naish, L., and Thom, J. [1983] "The MU-PROLOG Deductive Database," Technical Report 83/10, Department of Computer Science, University of Melbourne, 1983.

Navathe, S. [1980] "An Intuitive View to Normalize Network-Structured Data," in VLDB [1980].

Navathe, S., and Ahmed, R. [1989] "A Temporal Relational Model and Query Language," **Information Sciences,** 47:2, March 1989, pp. 147–75.

Navathe, S., Ceri, S., Wiederhold, G., and Dou, J. [1984] "Vertical Partitioning Algorithms for Database Design," **TODS,** 9:4, December 1984.

Navathe, S., Elmasri, R., and Larson, J. [1986] "Integrating User Views in Database Design," IEEE **Computer,** 19:1, January 1986.

Navathe, S., and Gadgil, S. [1982] "A Methodology for View Integration in Logical Database Design," in VLDB [1982].

Navathe, S. B. Karlapalem, K., and Ra, M.Y. [1996] "A Mixed Fragmentation Methodology for the Initial Distributed Database Design," **Journal of Computers and Software Engineering,** 3:4, 1996.

Navathe, S., and Kerschberg, L. [1986] "Role of Data Dictionaries in Database Design," **Information and Management,** 10:1, January 1986.

Navathe, S., and Pillalamarri, M. [1988] "Toward Making the ER Approach Object-Oriented," in ER Conference [1988].

Navathe, S., Sashidhar, T., and Elmasri, R. [1984a] "Relationship Merging in Schema Integration," in VLDB [1984].

Navathe, S., and Savasere, A. [1996] "A Practical Schema Integration Facility using an Object Oriented Approach," in **Multidatabase Systems** (A. Elmagarmid and O. Bukhres, eds.), Prentice-Hall, 1996.

Navathe, S. B., Savasere, A., Anwar, T. M., Beck, H., and Gala, S. [1994] "Object Modeling Using Classification in CANDIDE and Its Application," in Dogac et al. [1994].

Navathe, S., and Schkolnick, M. [1978] "View Representation in Logical Database Design," in SIGMOD [1978].

Negri, M., Pelagatti, S., and Sbatella, L. [1991] "Formal Semantics of SQL Queries," **TODS,** 16:3, September 1991.

Ng, P. [1981] "Further Analysis of the Entity-Relationship Approach to Database Design," **TSE,** 7:1, January 1981.

Nicolas, J. [1978] "Mutual Dependencies and Some Results on Undecomposable Relations," in VLDB [1978].

Nicolas, J. [1997] "Deductive Object-oriented Databases, Technology, Products, and Applications: Where Are We?" *Proceedings of the Symposium on Digital Media Information Base (DMIB'97)*, Nara, Japan, November 1997.

Nicolas, J., Phipps, G., Derr, M., and Ross, K. [1991] "Glue-NAIL!: A Deductive Database System," in SIGMOD [1991].

Nievergelt, J. [1974] "Binary Search Trees and File Organization," ACM **Computing Surveys,** 6:3, September 1974.

Nievergelt, J., Hinterberger, H., and Seveik, K. [1984]. "The Grid File: An Adaptable Symmetric Multikey File Structure," TODS, 9:1, March 1984, pp. 38–71.

Nijssen, G., ed. [1976] **Modelling in Data Base Management Systems,** North-Holland, 1976.

Nijssen, G., ed. [1977] **Architecture and Models in Data Base Management Systems,** North-Holland, 1977.

Nwosu, K., Berra, P., Thuraisingham, B., eds. [1996], **Design and Implementation of Multimedia Database Management Systems,** Kluwer Academic, 1996.

Obermarck, R. [1982] "Distributed Deadlock Detection Algorithms," TODS, 7:2, June 1982.

Oh, Y-C., [1999] "Secure Database Modeling and Design," Ph.D. dissertation, College of Computing, Georgia Institute of Technology, March 1999.

Ohsuga, S. [1982] "Knowledge Based Systems as a New Interactive Computer System of the Next Generation," in **Computer Science and Technologies,** North-Holland, 1982.

Olle, T. [1978] **The CODASYL Approach to Data Base Management,** Wiley, 1978.

Olle, T., Sol, H., and Verrijn-Stuart, A., eds. [1982] **Information System Design Methodology,** North-Holland, 1982.

Omiecinski, E., and Scheuermann, P. [1990] "A Parallel Algorithm for Record Clustering," TODS, 15:4, December 1990.

O'Neill, P. [1994] **Database: Principles, Programming, Performance,** Morgan Kaufmann, 1994.

Oracle [1992a] RDBMS **Database Administrator's Guide,** ORACLE, 1992.

Oracle [1992 b] **Performance Tuning Guide,** Version 7.0, ORACLE, 1992.

Oracle [1997a] **Oracle 8 Server Concepts,** vols. 1 and 2, Release 8-0, Oracle Corporation, 1997.

Oracle [1997b] **Oracle 8 Server Distributed Database Systems,** Release 8.0, 1997.

Oracle [1997c] PL/SQL **User's Guide and Reference,** Release 8.0, 1997.

Oracle [1997d] **Oracle 8 Server SQL Reference,** Release 8.0, 1997.

Oracle [1997e] **Oracle 8 Parallel Server, Concepts and Administration,** Release 8.0, 1997.

Oracle [1997f] **Oracle 8 Server Spatial Cartridge, User's Guide and Reference,** Release 8.0.3, 1997.

Osborn, S. [1977] **Normal Forms for Relational Databases,** Ph.D. dissertation, University of Waterloo, 1977.

Osborn, S. [1979] "Towards a Universal Relation Interface," in VLDB [1979].

Osborn, S. [1989] "The Role of Polymorphism in Schema Evolution in an Object-Oriented Database," TKDE, 1:3, September 1989.

Ozsoyoglu, G., Ozsoyoglu, Z., and Matos, V. [1985] "Extending Relational Algebra and Relational Calculus with Set Valued Attributes and Aggregate Functions," TODS, 12:4, December 1987.

Ozsoyoglu, Z., and Yuan, L. [1987] "A New Normal Form for Nested Relations," TODS, 12:1, March 1987.

Ozsu, M. T., and Valduriez, P. [1999] **Principles of Distributed Database Systems,** 2nd ed., Prentice-Hall, 1999.

Papadimitriou, C. [1979] "The Serializability of Concurrent Database Updates," JACM, 26:4, October 1979.

Papadimitriou, C. [1986] **The Theory of Database Concurrency Control,** Computer Science Press, 1986.

Papadimitriou, C., and Kanellakis, P. [1979] "On Concurrency Control by Multiple Versions," TODS, 9:1, March 1974.

Papazoglou, M., and Valder, W. [1989] **Relational Database Management: A Systems Programming Approach,** Prentice-Hall, 1989.

Paredaens, J., and Van Gucht, D. [1992] "Converting Nested Algebra Expressions into Flat Algebra Expressions," TODS, 17:1, March 1992.

Parent, C., and Spaccapietra, S. [1985] "An Algebra for a General Entity-Relationship Model," TSE, 11:7, July 1985.

Paris, J. [1986] "Voting with Witnesses: A Consistency Scheme for Replicated Files," in ICDE [1986].

Park, J., Chen, M., and Yu, P. [1995] "An Effective Hash Based Algorithm for Mining Association Rules," in SIGMOD [1995].

Paton, A. W., ed. [1999] **Active Rules in Database Systems,** Springer Verlag, 1999.

Paton, N. W., and Diaz, O. [1999] Survey of Active Database Systems, ACM **Computing Surveys,** to appear.

Patterson, D., Gibson, G., and Katz, R. [1988]. "A Case for Redundant Arrays of Inexpensive Disks (RAID)," in SIGMOD [1988].

Paul, H., et al. [1987] "Architecture and Implementation of the Darmstadt Database Kernel System," in SIGMOD [1987].

Pazandak, P., and Srivastava, J., "Evaluating Object DBMSs for Multimedia," IEEE **Multimedia,** 4:3, pp. 34–49.

PDES [1991] "A High-Lead Architecture for Implementing a PDES/STEP Data Sharing Environment." Publication Number PT 1017.03.00, PDES Inc., May 1991.

Pearson, P., Francomano, C., Foster, P., Bocchini, C., Li, P., and McKusick, V. [1994] *The Status of Online Mendelian inheritance in Man (OMIM) Medio 1994* **Nucleic Acids Research** 22:17, 1994.

Peckham, J., and Maryanski, F. [1988] "Semantic Data Models," ACM **Computing Surveys,** 20:3, September 1988, pp. 153–89.

Phipps, G., Derr, M., Ross, K. [1991] "Glue-NAIL!: A Deductive Database System," in SIGMOD [1991].

Piatesky-Shapiro, G., and Frauley, W., eds. [1991] **Knowledge Discovery in Databases,** AAAI Press/MIT Press, 1991.

Pistor P., and Anderson, F. [1986] "Designing a Generalized NF^2 Model with an SQL-type Language Interface," in VLDB [1986], pp. 278–85.

Pitoura, E., Bukhres, O., and Elmagarmid, A. [1995] "Object Orientation in Multidatabase Systems," ACM **Computing Surveys,** 27:2, June 1995.

Pitoura, E., and Samaras, G. [1998] **Data Management for Mobile Computing,** Kluwer, 1998.

Poosala, V., Ioannidis, Y., Haas, P., and Shekita, E. [1996] "Improved Histograms for Selectivity Estimation of Range Predicates," in SIGMOD [1996].

Potter, B., Sinclair, J., Till, D. [1991] **An Introduction to Formal Specification and Z,** Prentice-Hall, 1991.

Rabitti, F., Bertino, E., Kim, W., and Woelk, D. [1991] "A Model of Authorization for Next-Generation Database Systems," TODS, 16:1, March 1991.

Ramakrishnan, R., ed. [1995] **Applications of Logic Databases,** Kluwer Academic, 1995.

Ramakrishnan, R. [1997] **Database Management Systems,** McGraw-Hill, 1997.

Ramakrishnan, R., Srivastava, D. and Sudarshan, S. [1992] "{CORAL}: {C}ontrol, {R}elations and {L}ogic," in VLDB [1992].

Ramakrishnan, R., Srivastava, D., Sudarshan, S. and Sheshadri, P. [1993] "Implementation of the {CORAL} deductive database system," in SIGMOD [1993].

Ramakrishnan, R., and Ullman, J. [1995] "Survey of Research in Deductive Database Systems," **Journal Of Logic Programming,** 23:2, 1995, pp. 125–49.

Ramamoorthy, C., and Wah, B. [1979] "The Placement of Relations on a Distributed Relational Database," *Proceedings of the First International Conference on Distributed Computing Systems,* IEEE CS, 1979.

Ramesh, V., and Ram, S. [1997] "Integrity Constraint Integration in Heterogeneous Databases an Enhanced Methodology for Schema Integration," **Information Systems,** 22:8, December 1997, pp. 423–46.

Reed, D. [1983] "Implementing Atomic Actions on Decentralized Data," TOCS, 1:1, February 1983.

Reisner, P. [1977] "Use of Psychological Experimentation as an Aid to Development of a Query Language," TSE, 3:3, May 1977.

Reisner, P. [1981] "Human Factors Studies of Database Query Languages: A Survey and Assessment," ACM **Computing Surveys,** 13:1, March 1981.

Reiter, R. [1984] "Towards a Logical Reconstruction of Relational Database Theory," in Brodie et al., ch. 8. [1984].

Ries, D., and Stonebraker, M. [1977] "Effects of Locking Granularity in a Database Management System," TODS, 2:3, September 1977.

Rissanen, J. [1977] "Independent Components of Relations," TODS, 2:4, December 1977.

Robbins, R. [1993] "Genome Informatics: Requirements and Challenges," *Proceedings of the Second International Conference on Bioinformatics, Supercomputing and Complex Genome Analysis,* World Scientific Publishing, 1993.

Roth, M., and Korth, H. [1987] "The Design of Non-1NF Relational Databases into Nested Normal Form," in SIGMOD [1987].

Roth, M. A., Korth, H. F., and Silberschatz, A. [1988] Extended Algebra and Calculus for non-1NF relational Databases," TODS, 13:4, 1988, pp. 389–417.

Rothnie, J., et al. [1980] "Introduction to a System for Distributed Databases (SDD-1)," TODS, 5:1, March 1980.

Roussopoulos, N. [1991] "An Incremental Access Method for View-Cache: Concept, Algorithms, and Cost Analysis," TODS, 16:3, September 1991.

Rozen, S., and Shasha, D. [1991] "A Framework for Automating Physical Database Design," in VLDB [1991].

Rudensteiner, E. [1992] "Multiview: A Methodology for Supporting Multiple Views in Object-Oriented Databases," in VLDB [1992].

Ruemmler, C., and Wilkes, J. [1994] "An Introduction to Disk Drive Modeling," IEEE Computer, 27:3, March 1994, pp. 17–27.

Rumbaugh, J., Blaha, M., Premerlani, W., Eddy, F., and Lorensen, W. [1991] **Object Oriented Modelng and Design,** Prentice-Hall, 1991.

Rusinkiewicz, M., et al. [1988] "OMNIBASE—A Loosely Coupled: Design and Implementation of a Multi-database System," IEEE **Distributed Processing Newsletter,** 10:2, November 1988.

Rustin, R., ed. [1972] **Data Base Systems,** Prentice-Hall, 1972.

Rustin, R., ed. [1974] *Proceedings of the BJNAV2.*

Sacca, D., and Zaniolo, C. [1987] "Implementation of Recursive Queries for a Data Language Based on Pure Horn Clauses," *Proceedings of the Fourth International Conference on Logic Programming,* MIT Press, 1986.

Sadri, F., and Ullman, J. [1982] "Template Dependencies: A Large Class of Dependencies in Relational Databases and Its Complete Axiomatization," **JACM,** 29:2, April 1982.

Sagiv, Y., and Yannakakis, M. [1981] "Equivalence among Relational Expressions with the Union and Difference Operators," **JACM,** 27:4, November 1981.

Sakai, H. [1980] "Entity-Relationship Approach to Conceptual Schema Design," in SIGMOD [1980].

Salzberg, B. [1988] **File Structures: An Analytic Approach,** Prentice-Hall, 1988.

Salzberg, B., et al. [1990] "FastSort: A Distributed Single-Input Single-Output External Sort," in SIGMOD [1990].

Salton, G., and Buckley, C. [1991] "Global Text Matching for Information Retrieval" in **Science,** 253, August 1991.

Samet, H. [1990] **The Design and Analysis of Spatial Data Structures,** Addison-Wesley, 1990.

Samet, H. [1990a] **Applications of Spatial Data Structures: Computer Graphics, Image Processing and GIS,** Addison-Wesley, 1990.

Sammut, C., and Sammut, R. [1983] "The Implementation of UNSW-PROLOG," **The Australian Computer Journal,** May 1983.

Sarasua, W., and O'Neill, W. [1999]. GIS in Transportation, in Taylor and Francis [1999].

Sarawagi, S., Thomas, S., Agrawal, R. [1998] "Integrating Association Rules Mining with Relational Database systems: Alternatives and Implications," in SIGGMOD [1998].

Savasere, A., Omiecinski, E., and Navathe, S. [1995] "An Efficient Algorithm for Mining Association Rules," in VLDB [1995].

Savasere, A., Omiecinski, E., and Navathe, S. [1998] "Mining for Strong Negative Association in a Large Database of Customer Transactions," in ICDE [1998].

Schatz, B. [1995] "Information Analysis in the Net: The Interspace of the Twenty-First Century," *Keynote Plenary Lecture at American Society for Information Science (ASIS) Annual Meeting,* Chicago, October 11, 1995.

Schatz, B. [1997] "Information Retrieval in Digital Libraries: Bringing Search to the Net," **Science,** vol. 275, 17 January 1997.

Schek, H. J., and Scholl. M. H. [1986] "The Relational Model with Relation-valued Attributes," **Information Systems,** 11:2, 1986.

Schek, H. J., Paul, H. B., Scholl, M. H., and Weikum, G. [1990] "The DASDBS Project: Objects, Experiences, and Future Projects," IEEE TKDE, 2:1, 1990.

Scheuermann, P., Schiffner, G., and Weber, H. [1979] "Abstraction Capabilities and Invariant Properties Modeling within the Entity-Relationship Approach," in ER Conference [1979].

Schlimmer, J., Mitchell, T., McDermott, J. [1991] "Justification Based Refinement of Expert Knowledge" in Piatesky-Shapiro and Frawley [1991].

Schmidt, J., and Swenson, J. [1975] "On the Semantics of the Relational Model," in SIGMOD [1975].

Sciore, E. [1982] "A Complete Axiomatization for Full Join Dependencies," **JACM,** 29:2, April 1982.

Selinger, P., et al. [1979] "Access Path Selection in a Relational Database Management System," in SIGMOD [1979].

Senko, M. [1975] "Specification of Stored Data Structures and Desired Output in DIAM II with FORAL," in VLDB [1975].

Senko, M. [1980] "A Query Maintenance Language for the Data Independent Accessing Model II," **Information Systems,** 5:4, 1980.

Shapiro, L. [1986] "Join Processing in Database Systems with Large Main Memories," TODS, 11:3, 1986.

Shasha, D. [1992] **Database Tuning: A Principled Approach,** Prentice-Hall, 1992.

Shasha, D., and Goodman, N.[1988] "Concurrent Search Structure Algorithms," TODS, 13:1, March 1988.

Shekita, E., and Carey, M. [1989] "Performance Enhancement Through Replication in an Object-Oriented DBMS," in SIGMOD [1989].

Shenoy, S., and Ozsoyoglu, Z. [1989] "Design and Implementation of a Semantic Query Optimizer," **TKDE,** 1:3, September 1989.

Sheth, A., Gala, S., Navathe, S. [1993]" On Automatic Reasoning for Schema Integration," in **International Journal of Intelligent Co-operative Information Systems,** 2:1, March 1993.

Sheth, A. P., and Larson, J. A. [1990] "Federated Database Systems for Managing Distributed, Heterogeneous, and Autonomous Databases," **ACM Computing Surveys,** 22:3, September 1990, pp. 183–236.

Sheth, A., Larson, J., Cornelio, A., and Navathe, S. [1988] "A Tool for Integrating Conceptual Schemas and User Views," in ICDE [1988].

Shipman, D. [1981] "The Functional Data Model and the Data Language DAPLEX," TODS, 6:1, March 1981.

Shlaer, S., Mellor, S. [1988] **Object-Oriented System Analysis: Modeling the World in Data,** Yourdon Press, 1988.

Shneiderman, B., ed. [1978] **Databases: Improving Usability and Responsiveness,** Academic Press, 1978.

Sibley, E., and Kerschberg, L. [1977] "Data Architecture and Data Model Considerations," NCC, AFIPS, 46, 1977.

Siegel, M., and Madnick, S. [1991] "A Metadata Approach to Resolving Semantic Conflicts," in VLDB [1991].

Siegel, M., Sciore, E., and Salveter, S. [1992] "A Method for Automatic Rule Derivation to Support Semantic Query Optimization," TODS, 17:4, December 1992.

SIGMOD [1974] *Proceedings of the ACM SIGMOD-SIGFIDET Conference on Data Description, Access, and Control,* Rustin, R., ed., May 1974.

SIGMOD [1975] *Proceedings of the 1975 ACM SIGMOD International Conference on Management of Data,* King, F., ed., San Jose, CA, May 1975.

SIGMOD [1976] *Proceedings of the 1976 ACM SIGMOD International Conference on Management of Data,* Rothnie, J., ed., Washington, June 1976.

SIGMOD [1977] *Proceedings of the 1977 ACM SIGMOD Internaitonal Conference on Management of Data,* Smith, D., ed., Toronto, August 1977.

SIGMOD [1978] *Proceedings of the 1978 ACM SIGMOD International Conference on Management of Data,* Lowenthal, E. and Dale, N., eds., Austin, TX, May/June 1978.

SIGMOD [1979] *Proceedings of the 1979 ACM SIGMOD International Conference on Management of Data,* Bernstein, P., ed., Boston, MA, May/June 1979.

SIGMOD [1980] *Proceedings of the 1980 ACM SIGMOD International Conference on Management of Data,* Chen, P. and Sprowls, R., eds., Santa Monica, CA, May 1980.

SIGMOD [1981] *Proceedings of the 1981 ACM SIGMOD International Conference on Management of Data,* Lien, Y., ed., Ann Arbor, MI, April/May 1981.

SIGMOD [1982] *Proceedings of the 1982 ACM SIGMOD International Conference on Management of Data,* Schkolnick, M., ed., Orlando, FL, June 1982.

SIGMOD [1983] *Proceedings of the 1983 ACM SIGMOD International Conference on Management of Data,* DeWitt, D. and Gardarin, G., eds., San Jose, CA, May 1983.

SIGMOD [1984] *Proceedings of the 1984 ACM SIGMOD Internaitonal Conference on Management of Data,* Yormark, E., ed., Boston, MA, June 1984.

SIGMOD [1985] *Proceedings of the 1985 ACM SIGMOD International Conference on Management of Data,* Navathe, S., ed., Austin, TX, May 1985.

SIGMOD [1986] *Proceedings of the 1986 ACM SIGMOD Internaitonal Conference on Management of Data,* Zaniolo, C., ed., Washington, May 1986.

SIGMOD [1987] *Proceedings of the 1987* ACM SIGMOD *International Conference on Management of Data*, Dayal, U. and Traiger, I., eds., San Francisco, CA, May 1987.

SIGMOD [1988] *Proceedings of the 1988* ACM SIGMOD *International Conference on Management of Data*, Boral, H., and Larson, P., eds., Chicago, June 1988.

SIGMOD [1989] *Proceedings of the 1989* ACM SIGMOD *International Conference on Management of Data*, Clifford, J., Lindsay, B., and Maier, D., eds., Portland, OR, June 1989.

SIGMOD [1990] *Proceedings of the 1990* ACM SIGMOD *International Conference on Management of Data*, Garcia-Molina, H., and Jagadish, H., eds., Atlantic City, NJ, June 1990.

SIGMOD [1991] *Proceedings of the 1991* ACM SIGMOD *International Conference on Management of Data*, Clifford, J. and King, R., eds., Denver, CO, June 1991.

SIGMOD [1992] *Proceedings of the 1992* ACM SIGMOD *International Conference on Management of Data*, Stonebraker, M., ed., San Diego, CA, June 1992.

SIGMOD [1993] *Proceedings of the 1993* ACM SIGMOD *International "Conference on Management of Data*, Buneman, P. and Jajodia, S., eds., Washington, June 1993.

SIGMOD [1994] *Proceedings of 1994* ACM SIGMOD *International Conference on Management of Data*, Snodgrass, R. T., and Winslett, M., eds., Minneapolis, MN, June 1994.

SIGMOD [1995] *Proceedings of 1995* ACM SIGMOD *International Conference on Management of Data*, Carey, M., and Schneider, D. A., eds., Minneapolis, MN, June 1995.

SIGMOD [1996] *Proceedings of 1996* ACM SIGMOD *International Conference on Management of Data*, Jagadish, H. V., and Mumick, I. P., eds., Montreal, June 1996.

SIGMOD [1997] *Proceedings of 1997* ACM SIGMOD *International Conference on Management of Data*, Peckham, J., ed., Tucson, AZ, May 1997.

SIGMOD [1998] *Proceedings of 1998* ACM SIGMOD *International Conference on Management of Data*, Haas, L., and Tiwary, A., eds., Seattle, WA. June 1998.

SIGMOD [1999] *Proceedings of 1999* ACM SIGMOD *International Conference on Management of Data*, Faloutsos, C., ed., Philadelphia, PA, May 1999.

Silberschatz, A., Stonebraker, M., and Ullman, J. [1990] "Database Systems: Achievements and Opportunities," in **ACM SIGMOD Record,** 19:4, December 1990.

Silberschatz, A., Korth, H., and Sudarshan, S. [1998] Database System Concepts, 3rd ed., McGraw-Hill, 1998.

Smith, G. [1990] "The Semantic Data Model for Security: Representing the Security Semantics of an Application," in ICDE [1990].

Smith, J., and Chang, P. [1975] "Optimizing the Performance of a Relational Algebra Interface," **CACM,** 18:10, October 1975.

Smith, J., and Smith, D. [1977] "Database Abstractions: Aggregation and Generalization," **TODS,** 2:2, June 1977.

Smith, J., et al. [1981] "MULTIBASE: Integrating Distributed Heterogeneous Database Systems," NCC, AFIPS, 50, 1981.

Smith, K., and Winslett, M. [1992] "Entity Modeling in the MLS Relational Model," in VLDB [1992].

Smith, P., and Barnes, G. [1987] **Files and Databases: An Introduction,** Addison-Wesley, 1987.

Snodgrass, R. [1987] "The Temporal Query Language TQuel," **TODS,** 12:2, June 1987.

Snodgrass, R., ed. [1995] **The TSQL2 Temporal Query Language,** Kluwer, 1995.

Snodgrass, R., and Ahn, I. [1985]."A Taxonomy of Time in Databases," in SIGMOD [1985].

Soutou, G. [1998] "Analysis of Constraints for N-ary Relationships," in ER98.

Spaccapietra, S., and Jain, R., eds. [1995] *Proceedings of the Visual Database Workshop*, Lausanne, Switzerland, October 1995.

Spooner D., Michael, A., and Donald, B. [1986] "Modeling CAD Data with Data Abstraction and Object Oriented Technique," in ICDE [1986].

Srikant, R., and Agrawal, R. [1995] "Mining Generalized Association Rules," in VLDB [1995].

Srinivas, M., and Patnaik, L. [1994] "Genetic Algorithms: A Survey," **IEEE Computer,** June 1994.

Srinivasan, V., and Carey, M. [1991] "Performance of B-Tree Concurrency Control Algorithms," in SIGMOD [1991].

Srivastava, D., Ramakrishnan, R., Sudarshan, S., and Sheshadri, P. [1993] "Coral++: Adding Object-orientation to a Logic Database Language," in VLDB [1993].

Stachour, P., and Thuraisingham, B. [1990] "The Design and Implementation of INGRES," TKDE, 2:2, June 1990.

Stallings, W. [1997] Data and Computer Communications, 5th ed., Prentice-Hall, 1997.

Stonebraker, M. [1975] "Implementation of Integrity Constraints and Views by Query Modification," in SIGMOD [1975].

Stonebraker, M. [1993] "The Miro DBMS" in SIGMOD [1993].

Stonebraker, M., ed. [1994] **Readings in Database Systems,** 2nd ed., Morgan Kaufmann, 1994.

Stonebraker, M., Hanson, E., and Hong, C. [1987] "The Design of the POSTGRES Rules System," in ICDE [1987].

Stonebraker, M., with Moore, D. [1996], **Object-Relational DBMSs: The Next Great Wave,** Morgan Kaufman, 1996.

Stonebraker, M., and Rowe, L. [1986] "The Design of POSTGRES," in SIGMOD [1986].

Stonebraker, M., Wong, E., Kreps, P., and Held, G. [1976] "The Design and Implementation of INGRES," TODS, 1:3, September 1976.

Su, S. [1985] "A Semantic Association Model for Corporate and Scientific-Statistical Databases," **Information Science,** 29, 1985.

Su, S. [1988] **Database Computers,** McGraw-Hill, 1988.

Su, S., Krishnamurthy, V., and Lam, H. [1988] "An Object-Oriented Semantic Association Model (OSAM*)," in **AI in Industrial Engineering and Manufacturing: Theoretical Issues and Applications,** American Institute of Industrial Engineers, 1988.

Subrahmanian, V. [1998] **Principles of Multimedia Databases Systems,** Morgan Kaufmann, 1998.

Subramanian V. S., and Jajodia, S., eds. [1996] **Multimedia Database Systems: Issues and Research Directions,** Springer Verlag. 1996.

Sunderraman, R. [1999] ORACLE **Programming: A Primer,** Addison Wesley Longman, 1999.

Swami, A., and Gupta, A. [1989] "Optimization of Large Join Queries: Combining Heuristics and Combinatorial Techniques," in SIGMOD [1989].

Tanenbaum, A. [1996] **Computer Networks,** Prentice Hall PTR, 1996.

Tansel, A., et al., eds. [1993] **Temporal Databases: Theory, Design, and Implementation,** Benjamin Cummings, 1993.

Teorey, T. [1994] **Database Modeling and Design: The Fundamental Principles,** 2nd ed., Morgan Kaufmann, 1994.

Teorey, T., Yang, D., and Fry, J. [1986] "A Logical Design Methodology for Relational Databases Using the Extended Entity-Relationship Model," ACM **Computing Surveys,** 18:2, June 1986.

Thomas, J., and Gould, J. [1975] "A Psychological Study of Query by Example," NCC AFIPS, 44, 1975.

Thomas, R. [1979] "A Majority Consensus Approach to Concurrency Control for Multiple Copy Data Bases," TODS, 4:2, June 1979.

Thomasian, A. [1991] "Performance Limits of Two-Phase Locking," in ICDE [1991].

Todd, S. [1976] "The Peterlee Relational Test Vehicle—A System Overview," IBM **Systems Journal,** 15:4, December 1976.

Toivonen, H., "Sampling Large Databases for Association Rules," in VLDB [1996].

Tou, J., ed. [1984] **Information Systems** COINS-IV, Plenum Press, 1984.

Tsangaris, M., and Naughton, J. [1992] "On the Performance of Object Clustering Techniques," in SIGMOD [1992].

Tsichritzis, D. [1982] "Forms Management," CACM, 25:7, July 1982.

Tsichritzis, D., and Klug, A., eds. [1978] **The** ANSI/X3/SPARC DBMS **Framework,** AFIPS Press, 1978.

Tsichritzis, D., and Lochovsky, F. [1976] "Hierarchical Data-base Management: A Survey," ACM **Computing Surveys,** 8:1, March 1976.

Tsichritzis, D., and Lochovsky, F. [1982] **Data Models,** Prentice-Hall, 1982.

Tsotras, V., and Gopinath, B. [1992] "Optimal Versioning of Object Classes," in ICDE [1992].

Tsou, D. M., and Fischer, P. C. [1982] "Decomposition of a Relation Scheme into Boyce Codd Normal Form," SIGACT News, 14:3, 1982, pp. 23–29.

Ullman, J. [1982] **Principles of Database Systems,** 2nd ed., Computer Science Press, 1982.

Ullman, J. [1985] "Implementation of Logical Query Languages for Databases," TODS, 10:3, September 1985.

Ullman, J. [1988] **Principles of Database and Knowledge-Base Systems,** vol. 1, Computer Science Press, 1988.

Ullman, J. [1989] **Principles of Database and Knowledge-Base Systems,** vol. 2, Computer Science Press, 1989.

Ullman, J. D. and Widom, J. [1997] **A First Course in Database Systems,** Prentice-Hall, 1997.

U.S. Congress [1988] "Office of Technology Report, Appendix D: Databases, Repositories, and Informatics," in **Mapping Our Genes: Genome Projects: How Big, How Fast?** John Hopkins University Press, 1988.

U.S. Department of Commerce [1993]. **TIGER/Line Files,** Bureau of Census, Washington, 1993.

Valduriez, P., and Gardarin, G. [1989] **Analysis and Comparison of Relational Database Systems,** Addison-Wesley, 1989.

Vassiliou, Y. [1980] "Functional Dependencies and Incomplete Information," in VLDB [1980].

Verheijen, G., and VanBekkum, J. [1982] "NIAM: An Information Analysis Method," in Olle et al. [1982].

Verhofstadt, J. [1978] "Recovery Techniques for Database Systems," ACM **Computing Surveys,** 10:2, June 1978.

Vielle, L. [1986] "Recursive Axioms in Deductive Databases: The Query-Subquery Approach," in EDS [1986].

Vielle, L. [1987] "Database Complete Proof Production Based on SLD-resolution," in *Proceedings of the Fourth International Conference on Logic Programming,* 1987.

Vielle, L. [1988] "From QSQ Towards QoSaQ: Global Optimization of Recursive Queries," in EDS [1988].

Vieille, L. [1998] "VALIDITY: Knowledge Independence for Electronic Mediation," invited paper, in *Practical Applications of Prolog/Practical Applications of Constraint Technology (PAP/PACT '98),* London, March 1998, available from lvieille@computer.org.

Vin, H., Zellweger, P., Swinehart, D., and Venkat Rangan, P. [1991] "Multimedia Conferencing in the Etherphone Environment," IEEE **Computer,** Special Issue on Multimedia Information Systems, 24:10, October 1991.

VLDB [1975] *Proceedings of the First International Conference on Very Large Data Bases,* Kerr, D., ed., Framingham, MA, September 1975.

VLDB [1976] **Systems for Large Databases,** Lockemann, P. and Neuhold, E., eds., in *Proceedings of the Second International Conference on Very Large Data Bases,* Brussels, Belgium, July 1976, North-Holland, 1976.

VLDB [1977] *Proceedings of the Third International Conference on Very Large Data Bases,* Merten, A., ed., Tokyo, Japan, October 1977.

VLDB [1978] *Proceedings of the Fourth International Conference on Very Large Data Bases,* Bubenko, J., and Yao, S., eds., West Berlin, Germany, September 1978.

VLDB [1979] *Proceedings of the Fifth International Conference on Very Large Data Bases,* Furtado, A., and Morgan, H., eds., Rio de Janeiro, Brazil, October 1979.

VLDB [1980] *Proceedings of the Sixth International Conference on Very Large Data Bases,* Lochovsky, F., and Taylor, R., eds., Montreal, Canada, October 1980.

VLDB [1981] *Proceedings of the Seventh International Conference on Very Large Data Bases,* Zaniolo, C., and Delobel, C., eds., Cannes, France, September 1981.

VLDB [1982] *Proceedings of the Eighth International Conference on Very Large Data Bases,* McLeod, D., and Villasenor, Y., eds., Mexico City, September 1982.

VLDB [1983] *Proceedings of the Ninth International Conference on Very Large Data Bases,* Schkolnick, M., and Thanos, C., eds., Florence, Italy, October/November 1983.

VLDB [1984] *Proceedings of the Tenth International Conference on Very Large Data Bases,* Dayal, U., Schlageter, G., and Seng, L., eds., Singapore, August 1984.

VLDB [1985] *Proceedings of the Eleventh International Conference on Very Large Data Bases,* Pirotte, A., and Vassiliou, Y., eds., Stockholm, Sweden, August 1985.

VLDB [1986] *Proceedings of the Twelfth International Conference on Very Large Data Bases,* Chu, W., Gardarin, G., and Ohsuga, S., eds., Kyoto, Japan, August 1986.

VLDB [1987] *Proceedings of the Thirteenth International Conference on Very Large Data Bases,* Stocker, P., Kent, W., and Hammersley, P., eds., Brighton, England, September 1987.

VLDB [1988] *Proceedings of the Fourteenth International Conference on Very Large Data Bases,* Bancilhon, F., and DeWitt, D., eds., Los Angeles, August/September 1988.

VLDB [1989] *Proceedings of the Fifteenth International Conference on Very Large Data Bases*, Apers, P., and Wiederhold, G., eds., Amsterdam, August 1989.

VLDB [1990] *Proceedings of the Sixteenth International Conference on Very Large Data Bases*, McLeod, D., Sacks-Davis, R., and Schek, H., eds., Brisbane, Australia, August 1990.

VLDB [1991] *Proceedings of the Seventeenth International Conference on Very Large Data Bases*, Lohman, G., Sernadas, A., and Camps, R., eds., Barcelona, Catalonia, Spain, September 1991.

VLDB [1992] *Proceedings of the Eighteenth International Conference on Very Large Data Bases*, Yuan, L., ed., Vancouver, Canada, August 1992.

VLDB [1993] *Proceedings of the Nineteenth International Conference on Very Large Data Bases*, Agrawal, R., Baker, S., and Bell, D.A., eds., Dublin, Ireland, August 1993.

VLDB [1994] *Proceedings of the 20th International Conference on Very Large Data Bases*, Bocca, J., Jarke, M., and Zaniolo, C., eds., Santiago, Chile, September 1994. .

VLDB [1995] *Proceedings of the 21st International Conference on Very Large Data Bases*, Dayal, U., Gray, P.M.D., and Nishio, S., eds., Zurich, Switzerland, September 1995.

VLDB [1996] *Proceedings of the 22nd International Conference on Very Large Data Bases*, Vijayaraman, T. M., Buchman, A. P., Mohan, C., and Sarda, N. L., eds., Bombay, India, September 1996.

VLDB [1997] *Proceedings of the 23rd International Conference on Very Large Data Bases*, Jarke, M., Carey, M. J., Dittrich, K. R., Lochovsky, F. H., and Loucopoulos, P.(editors), Zurich, Switzerland, September 1997.

VLDB [1998] *Proceedings of the 24th International Conference on Very Large Data Bases*, Gupta, A., Shmueli, O., and Widom, J., eds., New York, September 1998.

VLDB [1999] *Proceedings of the 25th International Conference on Very Large Data Bases*, Zdonik, S. B., Valduriez, P., and Orlowska, M., eds., Edinburgh, Scotland, September 1999.

Vorhaus, A., and Mills, R. [1967] "The Time-Shared Data Management System: A New Approach to Data Management," System Development Corporation, Report SP-2634, 1967.

Wallace, D. [1995] "1994 William Allan Award Address: Mitochondrial DNA Variation in Human Evolution, Degenerative Disease, and Aging." **American Journal of Human Genetics,** 57:201–223, 1995.

Walton, C., Dale, A., and Jenevein, R. [1991] "A Taxonomy and Performance Model of Data Skew Effects in Parallel Joins," in VLDB [1991].

Wang, K. [1990] "Polynomial Time Designs Toward Both BCNF and Efficient Data Manipulation," in SIGMOD [1990].

Wang, Y., and Madnick, S. [1989] "The Inter-Database Instance Identity Problem in Integrating Autonomous Systems," in ICDE [1989].

Wang, Y. and Rowe, L. [1991] "Cache Consistency and Concurrency Control in a Client/Server DBMS Architecture," in SIGMOD [1991].

Warren, D. [1992] "Memoing for Logic Programs," CACM, 35:3, ACM, March 1992.

Weddell, G. [1992] "Reasoning About Functional Dependencies Generalized for Semantic Data Models," TODS, 17:1, March 1992.

Weikum, G. [1991] "Principles and Realization Strategies of Multilevel Transaction Management," TODS, 16:1, March 1991.

Weiss, S. and Indurkhya, N. [1998] **Predictive Data Mining: A Practical Guide,** Morgan Kaufmann, 1998.

Whang, K. [1985] "Query Optimization in Office By Example," IBM Research Report RC 11571, December 1985.

Whang, K., Malhotra, A., Sockut, G., and Burns, L. [1990] "Supporting Universal Quantification in a Two-Dimensional Database Query Language," in ICDE [1990].

Whang, K., and Navathe, S. [1987] "An Extended Disjunctive Normal Form Approach for Processing Recursive Logic Queries in Loosely Coupled Environments," in VLDB [1987].

Whang, K., and Navathe, S. [1992] "Integrating Expert Systems with Database Management Systems— an Extended Disjunctive Normal Form Approach," **Information Sciences,** 64, March 1992.

Whang, K., Wiederhold, G., and Sagalowicz, D. [1982] "Physical Design of Network Model Databases Using the Property of Separability," in VLDB [1982].

Widom, J., "Research Problems in Data Warehousing," CIKM, November 1995.

Widom, J., and Ceri, S. [1996] **Active Database Systems,** Morgan Kaufmann, 1996.

Widom, J., and Finkelstein, S. [1990] "Set Oriented Production Rules in Relational Database Systems" in SIGMOD [1990].

Wiederhold, G. [1983] **Database Design,** 2nd ed., McGraw-Hill, 1983.

Wiederhold, G. [1984] "Knowledge and Database Management," IEEE **Software,** January 1984.

Wiederhold, G. [1995] "Digital Libraries, Value, and Productivity," CACM, April 1995.

Wiederhold, G., Beetem, A., and Short, G. [1982] "A Database Approach to Communication in VLSI Design," IEEE **Transactions on Computer-Aided Design of Integrated Circuits and Systems,** 1:2, April 1982.

Wiederhold, G., and Elmasri, R. [1979] "The Structural Model for Database Design," in ER Conference [1979].

Wilkinson, K., Lyngbaek, P., and Hasan, W. [1990] "The IRIS Architecture and Implementation," TKDE, 2:1, March 1990.

Willshire, M. [1991] "How Spacey Can They Get? Space Overhead for Storage and Indexing with Object-Oriented Databases," in ICDE [1991].

Wilson, B., and Navathe, S. [1986] "An Analytical Framework for Limited Redesign of Distributed Databases," *Proceedings of the Sixth Advanced Database Symposium*, Tokyo, August 1986.

Wiorkowski, G., and Kull, D. [1992] **DB2-Design and Development Guide,** 3rd ed., Addison-Wesley, 1992.

Wirth, N. [197] **Algorithms + Data Structures = Programs,** Prentice-Hall, 1972.

Wood, J., and Silver, D. [1989] **J Joint Application Design: How to Design Quality Systems in 40% Less Time,** Wiley, 1989.

Wong, E. [1983] "Dynamic Rematerialization-Processing Distributed Queries Using Redundant Data," TSE, 9:3, May 1983.

Wong, E., and Youssefi, K. [1976] "Decomposition—A Strategy for Query Processing," TODS, 1:3, September 1976.

Wong, H. [1984] "Micro and Macro Statistical/Scientific Database Management," in ICDE [1984].

Wu, X., and Ichikawa, T. [1992] "KDA: A Knowledge-based Database Assistant with a Query Guiding Facility," TKDE 4:5, October 1992.

Yannakakis, Y. [1984] "Serializability by Locking," JACM, 31:2, 1984.

Yao, S. [1979] "Optimization of Query Evaluation Algorithms," TODS, 4:2, June 1979.

Yao, S., ed. [1985] **Principles of Database Design,** vol. 1: **Logical Organizations,** Prentice-Hall, 1985.

Youssefi, K., and Wong, E. [1979] "Query Processing in a Relational Database Management System," in VLDB [1979].

Zadeh, L. [1983] "The Role of Fuzzy Logic in the Management of Uncertainty in Expert Systems," **Fuzzy Sets and Systems,** 11, North-Holland, 1983.

Zaniolo, C. [1976] "Analysis and Design of Relational Schemata for Database Systems," Ph.D. dissertation, University of California, Los Angeles, 1976.

Zaniolo, C. [1988] "Design and Implementation of a Logic Based Language for Data Intensive Applications," MCC Technical Report #ACA-ST-199-88, June 1988.

Zaniolo, C., et al. [1986] "Object-Oriented Database Systems and Knowledge Systems," in EDS [1984].

Zaniolo, C., et al. [1997] **Advanced Database Systems,** Morgan Kaufmann, 1997.

Zave, P. [1997] "Classification of Research Efforts in Requirements Engineering," ACM **Computing Surveys,** 29:4, December 1997.

Zicari, R. [1991] "A Framework for Schema Updates in an Object-Oriented Database System," in ICDE [1991].

Zloof, M. [1975] "Query by Example," NCC, AFIPS, 44, 1975.

Zloof, M. [1982] "Office By Example: A Business Language That Unifies Data, Word Processing, and Electronic Mail," IBM **Systems Journal,** 21:3, 1982.

Zobel, J., Moffat, A., and Sacks-Davis, R. [1992] "An Efficient Indexing Technique for Full-Text Database Systems," in VLDB [1992].

Zook, W., et al. [1977] INGRES **Reference Manual,** Department of EECS, University of California at Berkeley, 1977.

Zvieli, A. [1986] "A Fuzzy Relational Calculus," in EDS [1986].

Index